The Bill of Rights and American Legal History

A 20-volume
series reproducing over
300 key articles which explore
the 200-year history
of the rights of
American
citizens

EDITED WITH INTRODUCTIONS BY
Paul L. Murphy
University of Minnesota

A Garland Series

Books in the Series

I. The Historic Background of the Bill of Rights

II. Pre-1960 Developments in the Bill of Rights Area
— 2 Volumes —

III. Free Speech
— 4 Volumes —

IV. Free Press
— 3 Volumes —

V. Rights of Assembly, Petition, Arms and Just Compensation

VI. Religious Freedom: Separation and Free Exercise
— 2 Volumes —

VII. The Right to Privacy and the Ninth Amendment
— 2 Volumes —

VIII. Criminal Procedure
— 4 Volumes —

IX. The Bill of Rights and the States

Pre-1960 Developments in the Bill of Rights Area

IN TWO VOLUMES

VOLUME II

EDITED WITH AN INTRODUCTION BY
Paul L. Murphy

GARLAND PUBLISHING, INC.
New York & London
1990

Library of Congress Cataloging-in-Publication Data

The Bill of Rights and American legal history /
edited with introductions by Paul L. Murphy.
p. cm.
ISBN 0-8240-5859-3 (v. 2, alk. paper)
1. Civil rights—United States—History. 2. United States—Constitutional law—Amendments—1st–10th—History. I. Murphy, Paul L., 1923– .
Kf47.49.A2B55 1990
342.73.'085'09—dc20
[347.3028509] 89-25876

Printed on acid-free, 250-year-life paper.

Manufactured in the United States of America

CONTENTS

Volume One

Introduction

1. Ackerman, Bruce A. "Beyond *Carolene Products*," *Harvard Law Review* 98 (1985), 713–746. 1

2. Arons, Stephen. "The Separation of School and State: *Pierce* Reconsidered," *Harvard Educational Review* 46 (1976), 76–104. 36

3. Black, Hugo L. "The Bill of Rights," *New York University Law Review* 35 (1960), 865–881. 65

4. Blanchard, Margaret A. "Filling in the Void: Speech and Press in State Courts Prior to *Gitlow*," in Chamberlain, Bill and Charlene J. Brown, eds., *The First Amendment Reconsidered* (New York: Longmans, 1982), 14–59, 194–204. 82

5. Bogen, David S. "The Supreme Court's Interpretation of the Guarantee of Freedom of Speech," *Maryland Law Review* 35 (1976), 555–616. 139

6. Boudin, Louis B. "'Seditious Doctrines' and the 'Clear and Present Danger' Rule," *Virginia Law Review* 38 (1952), 143–186, 315–356. 201

7. Brennan, William J, Jr. "The Supreme Court and the Meiklejohn Interpretation of the First Amendment," *Harvard Law Review* 1 (1965), 1–120. 287

8. Cahn, Edmond. "Justice Black and First Amendment 'Absolutes': A Public Interview," *New York University Law Review* 37 (1962),549–563. 307

9. Cover, Robert M. "The Left, the Right and the First Amendment: 1918–1928," *Maryland Law Review* 40 (1981), 349–388. 323

10. Fellman, David. "The Constitutional Right to Counsel in Federal Courts," *Nebraska Law Review* 30 (1951), 559–599. 363

11. Foster, George, Jr. "The 1931 Personal Liberties Cases," *New York University Law Quarterly Review* 9 (1931), 64–81. 404

12. Frankfurter, Felix. "Memorandum on 'Incorporation' of the Bill of Rights Into the Due Process Clause of the Fourteenth Amendment," *Harvard Law Review* 78 (1965), 746–783. 422

13. Garrison, Lloyd K. "Some Observations on the Loyalty–Security Program," *University of Chicago Law Review* 23 (1955), 1–11. 461

14. Green, John Raeburn. "The Bill of Rights, the Fourteenth Amendment and the Supreme Court," *Michigan Law Review* 46 (1948), 869–910. 473

15. Green, John Raeburn. "The Supreme Court, the Bill of Rights and the States," *University of Pennsylvania Law Review* 97 (1949), 608–640. 516

16. Henkin, Louis. "'Selective Incorporation' In the Fourteenth Amendment," *Yale Law Journal* 73 (1963), 74–88. 550

17. Holtzoff, Alexander. "The Right of Counsel Under the Sixth Amendment," *New York University Law Quarterly Review* 20 (1944), 1–22. 565

18. Kaczorowski, Robert J. "Searching for the Intent of the Framers of the Fourteenth Amendment," *Connecticut Law Review* 5 (1973), 368–398. 588

19. Kalven, Harry Jr. "Professor Ernst Freund and *Debs v. United States*," *University of Chicago Law Review* 40 (1973), 235–242. 619

20. Lacy, Alex B Jr. "The Bill of Rights and the Fourteenth Amendment: The Evolution of the Absorption Doctrine," *Washington and Lee Law Review* 23 (1966), 37–65. 627

21. Lange, David. "The Speech and Press Clauses," *U.C.L.A. Law Review* 23 (1975), 77-123. 657

VOLUME TWO

22. Levinson, Sanford. "Judicial Review and the Problem of the Comprehensible Constitution," *Texas Law Review* 59 (1981), 395–420. 1

23. Levy, Leonard W. "On the Origins of the Free Press Clause," *U.C.L.A. Law Review* 32 (1984), 177–218. 27

24. McKay, Robert B. "The Preference For Freedom," *New York University Law Review* 34 (1959), 1182–1227. 70

25. Mendelson, Wallace. "Clear and Present Danger—From Schenck to Dennis," *Columbia Law Review* 52 (1952), 313–333. 117

26. Mollan, Robert. "Smith Act Prosecutions: The Effect of the *Dennis* and *Yates* Decisions," *University of Pittsburgh Law Review* 26 (1965), 705–748. 139

27. Monaghan, Henry Paul. "Of 'Liberty' and 'Property'," *Cornell Law Review* 62 (1977), 405–444 183

28. Murphy, Walter F. "Deeds Under A Doctrine: Civil Liberties in the 1963 Term" *American Political Science Review* 59 (1965), 64–79. 224

29. Nimmer, Melville B. "Is Freedom of the Press a Redundancy: What Does It Add to Freedom of Speech?" *Hastings Law Journal* 26 (1975), 639–658. 241

30. O'Brien, Kenneth B, Jr. "Education, Americanization and the Supreme Court : The 1920's," *American Quarterly* 13 (1961), 161–171. 261

31. Pfeffer, Leo. "Court, Constitution and Prayer," *Rutgers Law Review* 16 (1962), 735–752. 273

32. Plumb, William T, Jr. "Illegal Enforcement of the Law," *Cornell Law Review* 24 (1939), 337–393. 291

33. Powell, Lewis F., Jr. "*Carolene Products* Revisited," *Columbia Law Review* 82 (1982), 1087–1092. 349

34. Prosser, William L. "Privacy," *California Law Review* 48 (1960), 383–423. 355

35. Prude, Jonathan. "Portrait of a Civil Libertarian: The Faith and Fear of Zechariah Chafee, Jr." *Journal of American History* 60 (1973), 633–656. 397

36. Raggi, Reena. "An Independent Right to Freedom of Association," *Harvard Civil Rights—Civil Liberties Law Review* 12 (1977), 1–30. 421

37. Robinson, Glen O. "The FCC and the First Amendment: Observations on 40 Years of Radio and Television Regulation," *Minnesota Law Review* 52 (1967), 67–163. 451

38. Rogat, Yosal and James M. O'Fallon. "Mr. Justice Holmes: A Dissenting Opinion—The Speech Cases," *Stanford Law Review* 36 (1984), 1349–1406. 549

39. Note: "The Right to Privacy in Nineteenth Century America." *Harvard Law Review* 94 (1981), 1892–1910. 608

40. Shulman, Harry. "The Supreme Court's Attitude Toward Liberty of Contract and Freedom of Speech," *Yale Law Journal* 41 (1931), 262–271. 628

41. Solter, Myron W. "Freedom of Association—A New and Fundamental Civil Right," *George Washington Law Review* 27 (1959), 653–672. 639

42. Tribe, Lawrence H. "The Puzzling Persistence of Process-Based Constitutional Theories," *Yale Law Journal* 89 (1980), 1063–1080. 659

43. Van Alstyne, William W. "The Recrudescence of Property Rights as the Foremost Principle of Civil Liberties: The First Decade of the Burger Court," *Law and Contemporary Problems* 43 (Summer 1980), 66–82. 678

44. Walker, Frank H. Jr. "Constitutional Law—Was It Intended that the Fourteenth Amendment Incorporate the Bill of Rights?," *North Carolina Law Review* 42 (1964), 925–936. 695

45. Warren, Charles. "The New 'Liberty' Under the Fourteenth Amendment," *Harvard Law Review* 39 (1926), 431–465. 707

Judicial Review and the Problem of the Comprehensible Constitution

JUDICIAL REVIEW AND THE NATIONAL POLITICAL PROCESS. By Jesse H. Choper.† Chicago: University of Chicago Press, 1980. Pp. xviii, 494. $28.50.

DEMOCRACY AND DISTRUST: A THEORY OF JUDICIAL REVIEW. By John Hart Ely.‡ Cambridge: Harvard University Press, 1980. Pp. viii, 268. $15.00.

Reviewed by Sanford Levinson*

I. Introduction

The first thing one should note about these two important books[1] is their titles: both are books about judicial review, not analyses of the Constitution that inevitably happen to touch on the role of the courts. In effect, the books stand the initial treatment of judicial review—*Marbury v. Madison*[2]—on its head. Chief Justice Marshall's argument in *Marbury* cannot be understood apart from his emphasis on the importance of a written Constitution. He noted generally that in America "written constitutions have been viewed with so much rever-

† Professor of Law, University of California at Berkeley.

‡ Professor of Law, Harvard University.

* Professor of Law, The University of Texas. A.B. 1962, Duke University; Ph.D. 1969, Harvard University; J.D. 1973, Stanford University. Some of the themes suggested in this Review about the notion of constitutional comprehensibility will be elaborated in Levinson, *Law as Literature* (to be published in the *Texas Law Review*). This forthcoming essay will examine the implications of contemporary literary theory for those who would be "guided" by the text of the Constitution, whether by its "plain words" or its purported "structure." This Review was substantially completed before publication of the superb symposium in 42 OHIO ST. L.J. (1981). A number of articles in that issue relate to the concerns of this Review; in the best of all possible worlds, which this is not, I would have been able to take serious account of them.

For help on this Review, I am indebted to Mark Yudof and James E. Fleming. Fleming helped me to understand better Professor Ely's approach toward constitutional analysis. His forthcoming Ph.D. dissertation at Princeton University, "Toward the Ultimate Interpretivism of Constitutional Democracy," promises to be a major contribution toward the assessment and, one prays, the synthesis of many competing paradigms of constitutional interpretation. I should also note the contribution of several discussions with Douglas Gordon, Class of 1980, The University of Texas School of Law.

1. J. CHOPER, JUDICIAL REVIEW AND THE NATIONAL POLITICAL PROCESS (1980) [hereinafter cited as J. CHOPER]; J. ELY, DEMOCRACY AND DISTRUST: A THEORY OF JUDICIAL REVIEW (1980) [hereinafter cited as J. ELY].

2. 5 U.S. (1 Cranch) 137 (1803).

ence,"[3] and he labeled a "written constitution" as "the greatest improvement on political institutions"[4] made by the citizenry of the new United States.

The charm of a written Constitution is the possibility of its providing "a set of objectively knowable principles setting limits on the power of all governmental organs, not excluding the Court, regardless of political pressure on particular issues."[5] Indeed, this was the basis of Marshall's argument in *Marbury*: "Certainly all those who have framed written constitutions contemplate them as forming the fundamental and paramount law of the nation, and consequently the theory of every such government must be, that an act of the legislature, repugnant to the constitution is void."[6]

It is, however, precisely the "knowability" of our written Constitution that is no longer a secure part of our contemporary intellectual climate, and it appears increasingly implausible to view judicial decisions as the simple transmission of messages garnered from the Constitution itself. Consider the following comment by Professor Brest:

> In sum, if you consider the evolution of doctrines in just about any extensively-adjudicated area of constitutional law—whether "under" the commerce, free speech, due process, or equal protection clauses—explicit reliance on originalist sources has played a very small role compared to the elaboration of the Court's own precedents. It is rather like having a remote ancestor who came over on the Mayflower.[7]

Brest's image brilliantly captures the sense of a distant Constitution. The Constitution may "exist" more surely than most contemporary intellectuals believe that God exists,[8] but its ability to serve as a source of

3. *Id.* at 178.

4. *Id.*

5. L. LUSKY, BY WHAT RIGHT? 356 (1975). Professor Lusky does not endorse a purely textual approach to constitutional interpretation; indeed, the major point of his book is the development of a theory of implied judicial power that justifies at least some judicial intervention even in the absence of explicit textual warrant. His book is well worth reading, especially given his status as one of the de facto authors (as Justice Stone's law clerk) of footnote four of United States v. Carolene Products Co., 304 U.S. 144, 152 n.4 (1938), to which much of Professor Ely's book is indebted.

6. 5 U.S. (1 Cranch) at 177.

7. Brest, *The Misconceived Quest for the Original Understanding*, 60 B.U.L. REV. 204, 234 (1980). By "originalism," Brest means an attempt to ground constitutional adjudication on what can be found "in" the document—assuming that the Constitution *is* a document rather than a set of institutional practices. This is not synonymous with "textualism," insofar as that approach often emphasizes guidance by the unadorned "plain meaning" of constitutional language, whereas other originalists look to shared understandings of 1787 language or to specific intentions of "the Framers." Brest attacks all such approaches to original understanding. *See also* Wofford, *The Blinding Light: The Uses of History in Constitutional Interpretation*, 31 U. CHI. L. REV. 502 (1964).

8. I have discussed the analogy between religious and constitutional faith in Levinson, *"The Constitution" in American Civil Religion*, 1979 SUP. CT. REV. 123 (1980). Justice Black certainly

meaningful guidance is equally dubious.

Although the source of discontent about the knowability of constitutional command goes back at least as far as the "legal realists" of the 1920s and 1930s,[9] one might profitably focus on the work of Professor Charles Black of the Yale Law School. His seminal book, *Structure and Relationship in Constitutional Law*,[10] has good claim to being the single most influential essay on this generation of constitutional theorists. A source of its influence, one suspects, is its rejection of radical legal realism—that is, the dismissal of the very notion of a meaningful Constitution[11]—even as it embraces some of the realists' skepticism regarding an easily read Constitution.

Black joins many realists in dismissing "the method of *purported* explication or exegesis of the particular textual passage."[12] He views this "method" as substituting "Humpty-Dumpty textual manipulation" for candid "political inference which not only underlies the textual manipulation but is, in a well constructed opinion, usually invoked to support the interpretation of the cryptic text."[13]

According to Black, if the text itself is no longer genuinely readable, or is merely the source of instrumental manipulation rather than of plausible "exegesis," then we must learn to find constitutional meaning between the lines—in the very structure of the Constitution. Although this view overthrows the textual emphasis of *Marbury*, Marshall conveniently provided the necessary alternative in *McCulloch v. Maryland*:[14] "There is no express provision for the case, but the claim has been sustained on a principle which so entirely pervades the constitution, is so intermixed with the materials which compose it, so interwoven with its web, so blended with its texture, as to be incapable of being separated

did retain belief in Marshall's argument: "It is of paramount importance to me that our country has a written constitution." H. BLACK, A CONSTITUTIONAL FAITH 3 (1969). But Black has had no true successor on the Court, nor is the legal academy filled with persons who think that clearer methods of reading will provide answers to important constitutional disputes.

9. For two good historical treatments of the realist movement, see E. PURCELL, THE CRISIS OF DEMOCRATIC THEORY: SCIENTIFIC NATURALISM AND THE PROBLEM OF VALUE (1973) and W. RUMBLE, AMERICAN LEGAL REALISM: SKEPTICISM, REFORM, AND THE JUDICIAL PROCESS (1968).

10. C. BLACK, STRUCTURE AND RELATIONSHIP IN CONSTITUTIONAL LAW (1969).

11. Probably the most extreme adherent of such "realism" was Fred Rodell of the Yale Law School. "And it is worth repeating, and remembering, that the alleged logic of Constitutional Law is equally amorphous, equally unconvincing, equally silly whether the decisions the Court is handing down are 'good' or 'bad,' 'progressive' or 'reactionary,' 'liberal' or 'illiberal.' . . . No matter in which direction the legal wand is waved, the hocus-pocus remains the same." F. RODELL, WOE UNTO YOU, LAWYERS! 64-65 (1980). Rodell's book was originally published in 1939.

12. *See* C. BLACK, *supra* note 10, at 7 (emphasis added).

13. *Id.* at 29.

14. 17 U.S. (4 Wheat.) 316 (1819).

from it, without rending it into shreds."[15]

Note that "texturalism," like more orthodox "textualism," is oriented, in some strong sense, to the document known as the United States Constitution. Black is antirealist because he views the essential meaning of the Constitution as genuinely comprehensible, even as he sounds like the realists in disdaining conventional emphasis on textual words and phrases. Black's structuralism thus fits into what Professor John Hart Ely calls "interpretivism"—the view that "judges deciding constitutional issues should confine themselves to enforcing norms that are stated or clearly implicit in the written Constitution."[16] Structuralism remains within "the four corners of the document,"[17] even though it emphasizes the angle or shape of the corner rather than the words themselves.

Both structuralism and orthodox textualism are sharply distinct from noninterpretivism—the judicial enforcement of norms that cannot be discovered within the four corners of the document.[18] Incidentally, a court's refusal to enforce norms that are discoverable within the Constitution—a possibility raised by Professor Choper in the volume here reviewed[19]—would be equally noninterpretivist. As noninterpretivists admit, recognition of an "unwritten Constitution" complements the reliance on a "written constitution."[20] And an unwritten Constitution raises the most profound problems for traditional constitutional theory, even as modified by the structural approach of Professor Black.

Yet the shift from written text to "texture" as the basis for judicial review creates its own disquiet, even for those who agree that the text does not provide the kind of scaffolding for judicial power that Marshall claimed in *Marbury*. Professor Blasi, reviewing Black's argument just after its publication, noted the possibility that "structural reasoning [will] likewise, and to the same extent, fall prey to 'Humpty-Dumpty manipulation.' "[21]

15. *Id.* at 426.
16. J. ELY 1.
17. *Id.*
18. *Id.*
19. J. CHOPER 409.
20. *See* Grey, *Do We Have an Unwritten Constitution?*, 27 STAN. L. REV. 703 (1975); Richards, *Sexual Autonomy and the Constitutional Right to Privacy: A Case Study in Human Rights and the Unwritten Constitution*, 30 HAST. L.J. 957 (1979). Mention should also be made of the as yet unpublished manuscript by Professor Michael Perry of Ohio State University, THE CONSTITUTION, THE COURTS, AND HUMAN RIGHTS: AN INQUIRY INTO THE LEGITIMACY OF CONSTITUTIONAL POLICYMAKING BY THE JUDICIARY (forthcoming), which is certainly the most extensive attempt to defend "noninterpretivism" in light of the specific challenges posed by Ely and others.
21. Blasi, *Creativity and Legitimacy in Constitutional Law*, 80 YALE L.J. 176, 189 (1970). *See also* C. BLACK, DECISION ACCORDING TO LAW 20 (1981).

As if to corroborate Blasi's fears Justice Rehnquist's opinion in *National League of Cites v. Usery*[22] is probably the most brilliant and audacious example in recent years of the Supreme Court's structural reasoning/manipulation. *National League of Cities* prevented Congress from extending the benefits (such as they are) of minimum wage laws to state employees. Although Justice Rehnquist found that the tenth amendment prohibited the imposition of federal minimum wage standards upon state employees, [23] he made clear that the amendment is relevant only insofar as it is "an express declaration"[24] of a preexisting limitation on national power. It is our "federal system of government," not the text, that "imposes definite limits upon the authority of Congress to regulate the activities of the States as States by means of the commerce power."[25]

Justice Rehnquist's opinion provoked one of the angriest dissents in years from Justice Brennan, joined by Justices White and Marshall. At the very least, one cannot say that structural analysis carries with it the kind of "knowability" that persuades those dubious of its answers. Although no evidence exists that Black was specifically influenced by the structuralist movement in linguistics and anthropology, identified with such theorists as Saussure[26] and Levi-Strauss,[27] the movement has been notoriously plagued by the problem of validity in interpretations.

> There is no telling whether any really informed and intelligent observer ever quite fully believed that the courts did or can or ought to decide all cases and all questions as an act of obedience to clearly ascertainable commands of law, without there entering anything like the judges' "will." The important thing now is that the most fundamental work of our century on the nature and functioning of law has demonstrated, to the satisfaction of virtually every competent student, that this picture is illusory. The point is not that, although definite "law," susceptible of being definitely obeyed, is *there*, it is very hard to discover, so that judges make many mistakes; it is rather that the very nature of the material we call "law," of the material we look to when we look for "law," and of the methods we use in this search for right "law," are such that they very often make it not merely *possible* but *inevitable* that the beliefs and even the feelings of the judge go into the making of judgment. This is true because the whole body of "law," separate from those beliefs and feelings—even if fully known and handled with the highest expertness—very often does not suffice to lead the mind, by scientific or logical manipulations, to an unequivocally established right result, and must in the nature of things fail to do this.

Id. (citation omitted) (emphasis in original). There is a clear tension in Professor Black's work between the "realism" revealed above (and its concomitant invitation to instrumental manipulation) and his eloquent insistence that the Constitution genuinely contains certain core values. *See* C. BLACK, *supra*, *passim*. One wonders what Professor Blasi will have to say about Professor Black's latest work.

22. 426 U.S. 833 (1976).

23. *Id*. at 842.

24. *Id*. at 843.

25. *Id*. at 842.

26. *See* J. CULLER, SAUSSURE (1976); J. CULLER, STRUCTURALIST POETICS 5-16 (1975).

27. *See* J. CULLER, STRUCTURALIST POETICS 40-54 (1975); E. LEACH, CLAUDE LEVI-STRAUSS (1976).

Moreover, what links structuralism and traditional legalism is the attempt to escape the role of contingency, replacing the "rule of (wo)men" with the abstract "rule of law." As Judith Shklar points out in her valuable study *Legalism*,[28] the legitimacy of traditional legal analysis depends on its assertion that the body of rules "out there" in the world can be known or, in traditional language, discovered. The realists' emphasis on the crucial role of individuals who happen to be judges threatens the ideology of legalism as much as the focus on individual idiosyncracy challenges the conceptual foundations of structuralism.

One might think, then, that the central task facing constitutional theorists is to develop a theory of constitutional meaning, because the alternative is to recognize how opaque the Constitution has become—an ancient ancestor, perhaps venerable but not really understandable. Or, if opacity is not a satisfying image, one might refer to the Constitution as the equivalent of a thematic apperception test in psychology—an ambiguous stimulus whose "story" *we* complete by projecting onto it our own fears and fantasies, myths and hopes. In either case, one has given up the illusion that the Constitution "speaks" for itself.

If the Constitution "speaks," judges ultimately are only the "messengers" bringing constitutional truth to the public at large. A silent or opaque Constitution, on the other hand, requires the use of different metaphors to describe the role of constitutional interpreters. It is no secret that one contributing factor to the publication of such books as those under review is the continuing public and scholarly controversy about the propriety of certain judicial decisions, probably the most important of which is *Roe v. Wade*.[29] Arguably, *Roe* has had more impact on American politics than any other decision since *Dred Scott v. Sandford*,[30] perhaps with equally lamentable results. Partly because of *Roe*, the foundations of our legal order interest a far wider constituency than simply those legal academics who have chosen it as their life's study.

Both of the books under review offer interestingly different, though less than satisfactory, approaches to the problem of constitutional meaning. Professor John Hart Ely proffers a quite specific notion of the Constitution. He thus takes the problem of meaning far more seriously than does Professor Choper, who dispenses with it in favor of an almost purely functional analysis of the desirable role of the

28. J. Shklar, Legalism (1964).
29. 410 U.S. 113 (1973).
30. 60 U.S. (19 How.) 393 (1857).

Supreme Court within the American political structure. But the central question for both Ely and Choper is the role of the Supreme Court in checking the decisions made by the overtly political branches[31] of government.

There is one all-important difference between the Ely and Choper volumes. Ely, though critical of much judicial intervention, is primarily interested in sketching out the proper circumstances for continued activism. Choper, though indicating his support for certain judicial intervention, devotes the overwhelming bulk of his book, which is almost twice as long as Ely's, to a call for complete judicial withdrawal from specific areas of constitutional interpretation.

I shall discuss each book separately, beginning with Choper's, though the end of this Review considers further the contemporary crisis regarding the notion of a comprehensible Constitution.

II. Choper

Professor Choper's argument can be summarized by referring to what he terms his four "Proposals."

1. The Federalism Proposal: The Supreme Court and all other judicial bodies should withdraw from adjudicating any question turning solely on "the scope of national power vis-a-vis the states."[32] "It should be emphasized," says Choper, that this proposal does not speak "to the substantive question of whether, in any given instance, the national government has overreached its delegated authority. Rather, the Federalism Proposal is addressed solely to the question of which branch of government should decide this constitutional issue."[33] The answer to this latter question is Congress, limited only by the President's veto power.

31. The phrase "overtly political" is not without its problems. Perhaps betraying my background as a political scientist, I would be happy to defend the proposition that the Court is an overtly political branch. *See, e.g.*, M. SHAPIRO, LAW AND POLITICS IN THE SUPREME COURT (1964). Nonetheless, the conventions of American political discourse reserve the term "political branch" for those institutions inhabited by people elected overtly on the basis of political policy preferences. Increasingly, of course, one of the political policy preferences discussed, especially at the presidential level, is the character of judicial appointments (and values held by appointees) likely to be made by the respective candidate. I probably find this less offensive than do many readers of this law review. *See* Levinson, *U.S. Judges: The Case for Politics*, in COURTS, JUDGES, AND POLITICS: AN INTRODUCTION TO THE JUDICIAL PROCESS 139 (3d ed. W. Murphy & H. Pritchett 1979). For a discussion of the profession's response to the 1980 Republican Party platform promise to work for the appointment of judges who respect traditional family values and the sanctity of innocent human life, see *GOP Blasted on Judges' Plank*, NAT'L L.J., July 28, 1980, at 3, col. 1.

32. J. CHOPER 193.

33. *Id.* at 175-76.

2. The Separation Proposal: "The federal judiciary should not decide constitutional questions concerning the respective powers of Congress and the President vis-a-vis one another." Conflicts concerning these matters "should be held to be nonjusticiable, their final resolution to be remitted to the interplay of the national political process."[34]

3. The Individual Rights Proposal: "Since, almost by definition, the processes of democracy bode ill for the security of personal rights and, as experience shows, such liberties are not infrequently endangered by popular majorities, the task of custodianship should be assigned to a governing body that is insulated from political responsibility and unbeholden to self-absorbed and excited majoritarianism."[35] That body, to no one's surprise, is the judiciary.

4. The Judicial Proposal: "[T]he Supreme Court should pass final constitutional judgment on questions concerning the permissible reach and circumscription of 'the judicial power.' "[36]

As I already have noted, Choper devotes most of this book to defending the first two proposals, though his recurrent mention of the third assures us that his is by no means a traditional "judicial restraint" argument in the Frankfurterian mode. Choper immersed himself in a vast amount of political science literature; he devotes much space to effectively summarizing that literature, particularly as it relates to his first two proposals. For example, he argues that it is little short of preposterous to believe that states need any protection from the Supreme Court beyond the manifold protections contained in the very fabric of American politics.[37] Choper would inter *National League of Cities v. Usery*[38] not because Justice Rehnquist's opinion was "wrong," but because the Court simply should get out, once and for all, of the business of deciding federalism cases.

The basis of Choper's argument, though, is a bit odd. It is one thing to say that the Court should not intervene because the states are well enough protected anyway. He does say this, and I agree with him wholeheartedly. But he goes on to make a quite different argument as well, which is that the Court should withdraw its jurisdiction from federalism issues in order to preserve its scarce power for use when it is really necessary—to preserve individual rights.[39] This argument, remi-

34. *Id.* at 263.
35. *Id.* at 68.
36. *Id.* at 382.
37. *Id.* at 176-90.
38. 426 U.S. 833 (1976).
39. J. CHOPER 169-70.

niscent of Robert McCloskey's earlier exercises in *realpolitical* analysis of the Court's role,[40] rises or falls on its political cogency, and I confess myself almost wholly unconvinced.

Despite law professors' excitement over or fury at *National League of Cities*, it is impossible for me to believe that any average person in the street today cares about the current doctrine of American federalism. To be sure, this was once a vitally important topic; indeed, the country fought a civil war over the issue.[41] But if ever one is locking the barn after the demise of the horse, Choper does so with his federalism proposal. It seems unlikely that anyone furious about the contemporary Court—and I unscientifically suspect that ninety-eight percent of the fury results from cases that courts would continue to decide under Choper's Individual Rights Proposal—would find reassurance upon being reminded that the Court is not deciding abstruse cases dealing with federalism or separation of powers.

Choper's faith that the public will sit still for an activist court in regard to individual rights is a bit politically naive. The great "individual rights courts" of the early 1940s and 1960s might well be described as accidents. Neither President Roosevelt nor President Eisenhower had more than the slightest interest, if that, in the protection of individual liberties in which "their Justices" engaged. As Presidents and the public (including Senators elected by the public) become more sophisticated about what courts can and are willing to do, appointees with the commitments of a William O. Douglas or William J. Brennan seem unlikely. Martin Shapiro, the extremely able political scientist who has emphasized the Court's special relationship to constituencies that otherwise could not protect themselves effectively in the legislative or executive branch,[42] never explained why politicians who would not give the time of day to certain groups lobbying for protective legislation would nonetheless appoint judges who would see their central role as protecting these same groups.

American politicians may be venal, but they are rarely stupid. Yet the sophisticated functionalism espoused by Shapiro and Choper depends for its operational success on an ultimately glazed public incapable of figuring out that they are receiving something quite trivial (withdrawal from cases involving federalism and separation of powers)

40. *See* R. McCloskey, The Modern Supreme Court (1970); R. McCloskey, The American Supreme Court (1960).

41. For a fascinating and important study of the legal and political implications of federalism on the coming of the Civil War, see P. Finkelman, An Imperfect Union: Slavery, Federalism, and Comity (1981).

42. *See* M. Shapiro, Freedom of Speech and the Supreme Court (1966).

in return for judicial *carte blanche* in protecting unpopular individuals—such as Communists, criminals, and Iranian students—from various depredations that the public visits upon them. I wish Choper all the success in the world; his values are roughly my values, and I would love to see a national consensus develop around his proposals. But I am not optimistic. Moreover, such a consensus would make less necessary the judicial role that he espouses, for political leaders then would know that their constituents will judge them in part on how well they protect individual rights.

Choper's method of argument is wholly political-functional, having quite literally nothing to do with the traditional constitutional discourse found in law schools or judicial opinions.[43] Although this fact bothers me less than it probably will many other lawyer-readers (I only wish that his political argument made more sense), at least one implication of his method is worth addressing.

I return to Choper's concession, quoted above, that it remains a theoretically conceivable "substantive question of whether, in any given instance, the national government has overreached its delegated authority."[44] What can this mean? One approach to answering this question is that provided by Paul Brest.[45] A conscientious member of Congress would be obliged to believe that federalism means something and, therefore, that she could not cast her vote on certain issues without first considering the implications of federalism for the constitutionality of the proposed legislation. After all, she has taken an oath to support, protect, and defend the Constitution, and her responsibilities are no less awesome than those of John Marshall, who parlayed the written Constitution plus the oath of office into full-scale judicial review.

Consider therefore the "Energy Conservation Act of 1984." Because locating state capitals in cities other than the largest city within a state wastes a lot of energy and disrupts the flow of commerce, Congress exercises its constitutional authority to encourage a more efficient flow of commerce and mandates that state capitals be moved to cities fitting a designated profile—for example, to cities scoring highest on some combination of size, access to major financial institutions, and airport facilities. The capital of Texas would become Dallas or Houston; of California, Los Angeles; of Oregon, Portland.

43. This point is a description, not a criticism. *See* Tushnet, *Truth, Justice, and the American Way: An Interpretation of Public Law Scholarship in the Seventies*, 57 TEXAS L. REV. 1307 (1979).

44. J. CHOPER 175-76.

45. Brest, *The Conscientious Legislator's Guide to Constitutional Interpretation*, 27 STAN. L. REV. 585 (1975).

I do not defend the merits of the bill outlined above, but I am curious about what the Constitution might "say." Justice Rehnquist emphasized in *National League of Cities* that the Constitution protects a state's right to locate its capital wherever it pleases.[46] (Presumably the right to select a state flag, bird, song, and motto is equally protected.) I confess my skepticism on this point—after all, the Constitution does not explicitly grant any such right—and I might advise my conscientious senator or representative that the Constitution does not prevent such a law. Two answers can handle the objection that judicial precedents indicate otherwise. First, courts have been known to make mistakes and overrule previous decisions when faced with congressional statutes that obviously exceed "bounds" established by precedent.[47] Second, Choper's theory, under which the conscientious legislator is operating, has no "savings clause" for cases decided before the self-willed withdrawal from federalism conflicts. If the Court has no business intervening now, it never did, so the legislator can ignore the precedents. In any case, the Energy Conservation Act passes.

Under Choper's proposal, the Court would decline all jurisdiction, saying modestly that this is an issue for the political branches to resolve. Note that the Court does not simply respond that reasonable people can disagree about the question and that courts should not intervene in the absence of a clear legislative mistake.[48] Nor does the Court argue that the writtten Constitution textually assigns interpretations concerning the limits of federalism to Congress.[49] Instead, the Court is reduced to saying one of two things:

(1) "It is no longer possible to tell what federalism means; the word is no longer a meaningful part of our language. To the extent that the Constitution seems to refer to states, we can only sadly confess we don't understand what it means. 'Whereof one cannot speak, thereof one must be silent.' "[50]

(2) "We agree that Congress could not plausibly think that the Constitution authorizes the Energy Conservation Act, but we're not go-

46. 426 U.S. at 845.

47. *See, e.g.,* United States v. Darby, 312 U.S. 100 (1941) (overruling Hammer v. Dagenhart, 247 U.S. 251 (1918)). Although "[j]udicial exegesis is unavoidable . . . the ultimate touchstone of constitutionality is the Constitution itself and not what we have said about it." Graves v. New York, 306 U.S. 466, 491-92 (1939) (Frankfurter, J., concurring) (overruling Collector v. Day, 78 U.S. (11 Wall.) 113 (1871)).

48. *See* Thayer, *The Origin and Scope of the American Doctrine of Constitutional Law*, 7 HARV. L. REV. 129 (1893).

49. *See, e.g.,* Powell v. McCormack, 395 U.S. 486, 521 (1969).

50. L. WITTGENSTEIN, TRACTATUS LOGICO-PHILOSOPHICUS 6.54 (1921).

ing to help you out by declaring the Act unconstitutional. Your only remedy is to sear their consciences and then vote the rascals out."

"But why?" the plaintive state attorneys-general ask. "Because," the Court replies, "we wish to save our political clout for the important issues of individual rights."

That I am not particularly offended by this scenario may only evidence my inability to take very seriously traditional constitutional argumentation. But I suspect that Choper's understanding of the relationship between the Court and the Constitution is alien to both traditional constitutional theorists and ordinary citizens. Choper may think he is making only a set of modest proposals, but full acceptance of his extraordinarily provocative arguments would trigger nothing less than a revolutionary reordering of the way we conceptualize our political-constitutional world.[51]

"[T]o imagine a language means to imagine a form of life," Wittgenstein noted.[52] And a Constitution is just that—an imagination of a form of life that takes language with the utmost seriousness. Choper's imaginings call forth, in ways that he apparently does not begin to recognize, the most basic questions about the peculiar American fixation on written constitutions.

One should consider carefully Choper's proposals, upon which this Review has just touched. (And I hope the University of Chicago Press will bring out a paperback version allowing people to read the book without paying $28.50 or violating the laws of copyright.) Even traditional analysts will benefit from some of his arguments. Choper demonstrates, for example, that the problem of "state action" is nothing more than federalism in another guise,[53] since the sole issue in part of that hoary set of cases is whether the national government can do what the state government clearly can do. The *Civil Rights Cases*[54] would thus get the burial they have deserved from the instant of their unfortunate creation, since no issue of individual rights is genuinely present from the perspective of those raising the state action defense against the federal law. Even if one rejects Choper's injunction that the Court

51. For the influential notion of paradigms and paradigm changes, see T. KUHN, THE ESSENTIAL TENSION: SELECTED STUDIES IN SCIENTIFIC TRADITION AND CHANGE (1977), and T. KUHN, THE STRUCTURE OF SCIENTIFIC REVOLUTIONS (2d ed. 1970). It is increasingly clear that contemporary constitutional theory is without the guiding paradigm that makes a "normal science," including the "science of law"—that is, thinking like a lawyer—possible. Choper and Ely merely represent the latest contestants in an ever-longer list of those who seek to make sense out of the anomalies of constitutional law.

52. L. WITTGENSTEIN, PHILOSOPHICAL INVESTIGATIONS 83 (3d ed. 1958).

53. J. CHOPER 198-200.

54. 109 U.S. 3 (1883).

withdraw entirely from federalism questions, one might endorse *in toto* the analytical symbiosis between state action and federalism. I have ignored entirely, moreover, Choper's extremely interesting and supple arguments in defense of his "Separation Proposal."[55]

Choper's book contains scattered hints that the book is simply the first volume of a more sustained reinterpretation of American constitutional theory.[56] If so, one hopes especially that subsequent volumes will address the interpretive issues that Choper so artfully avoids.

III. Ely

Choper's view of the Constitution as basically opaque must be inferred from the general structure of his argument. Ely addresses the problem much more directly, although his argument is suitably complex. He recognizes "The Allure of Interpretivism"[57]—firm guidance and restriction by the written text—but he immediately demonstrates all too successfully "The Impossibility of a Clause-Bound Interpretivism."[58] Yet his argument has a twist that enables him to refer to himself as engaging in "ultimate interpretivism."[59] Ely notes that interpretivists have figured out no coherent way to handle those written parts of the Constitution, particularly the ninth amendment[60] and the privileges and immunities clause of the fourteenth amendment,[61] that seemingly direct the reader beyond themselves. His taking seriously these parts of the written Constitution leads to the possibility of "ultimate interpretivism."

However, Ely hastens to add that these clauses do not invite courts to read additional substantive rights into the Constitution. Judicial intervention, he argues, denies the essentially representative-democratic premises upon which he thinks this country is founded.[62] Indeed, he is particularly effective in castigating the various theories, whether allegedly based on text or on the "unwritten Constitution," that supposedly justify intervention in the name of generalized "fundamental values."[63]

55. J. CHOPER 315-79.

56. *See, e.g., id.* at 77, 79.

57. This is the title of Ely's first chapter. J. ELY 1-9.

58. This is the title of Ely's second chapter. *Id.* at 11-41.

59. *Id.* at 88.

60. "The enumeration in the Constitution, of certain rights, shall not be construed to deny or disparage others retained by the people." U.S. CONST. amend. IX.

61. "No State shall make or enforce any law which shall abridge the privileges or immunities of citizens of the United States . . . ." *Id.* amend. XIV, § 1. Like Professor Lusky, Ely views as ripe for overruling the evisceration of the clause in the Slaughterhouse Cases, 83 U.S. (16 Wall.) 36 (1873). *See* J. ELY 22-30; L. LUSKY, *supra* note 5, at 183-202.

62. J. ELY 40-41.

63. *Id.* at 43-72.

He especially criticizes the use of such values to overturn substantive policies enacted by state or federal legislatures.[64] He does not advise ignoring the so-called "open-ended" provisions of the Constitution, but instead argues that they are best read as directed only at the procedures of democratic governance.[65] He describes his approach as one that "bounds judicial review under the Constitution's open-ended provisions by insisting that it can appropriately concern itself *only* with questions of participation, and not with the substantive merits of the political choice under attack."[66] He thus stands at the furthest distance from his Harvard colleague Laurence Tribe, whose monumental treatise *American Constitutional Law*[67] is in part a program for continued judicial imposition of preferred substantive values in the face of majoritarian indifference or hostility. Ely's Constitution does not, under any interpretation he finds plausible, grant judges power to set aside majoritarian policies in the name of substantive values extrinsic to majoritarian democracy itself. The Constitution does outline a set of procedures that a state must go through before legitimately exercising its power against a recalcitrant citizen, but he sees no genuine substantive constraints upon the state, once it follows those procedures. As one might imagine, Ely's particular *bête noire* is *Roe v. Wade*,[68] in which the Court impregnated the Constitution with the substantive right of abortion.[69]

Ely, however, is scarcely eager to return to the impotent judiciary championed by Felix Frankfurter, a judiciary whose task, in Judith Shklar's words, was "not to restrain Congress, but only to legitimize its acts by providing rationalizations which allow them to be fitted into the Constitution."[70] The judiciary, in Ely's view, retains a central role in making sure that the procedures operate effectively.[71] As Ely freely

64. *Id.* at 43.

65. *Id.*

66. *Id.* at 181 (emphasis added).

67. L. TRIBE, AMERICAN CONSTITUTIONAL LAW (1978). *See also* Monaghan, *The Constitution Goes to Harvard*, 13 HARV. C.R.-C.L. L. REV. 117 (1978). Tribe's own views of Ely's endeavor can be found in Tribe, *The Puzzling Persistence of Process-Based Constitutional Theories*, 89 YALE L.J. 1063 (1980). Tribe's article follows Mark Tushnet's essay-review of Ely, Tushnet, *Darkness on the Edge of Town: The Contributions of John Hart Ely to Constitutional Theory*, 89 YALE L.J. 1037 (1980). Ely's book is probably the most widely reviewed book in constitutional theory since A. BICKEL, THE LEAST DANGEROUS BRANCH (1962).

68. 410 U.S. 113 (1973).

69. Professor Lusky shares Ely's view of *Roe*. *See* L. LUSKY, *supra* note 5, at 14-20. For Tribe's quite different reaction, see L. TRIBE, *supra* note 67, at 924-33 (replacing an earlier defense, *see* Tribe, *The Supreme Court, 1972 Term—Foreword: Toward a Model of Roles in the Due Process of Life and Law*, 87 HARV. L. REV. 1 (1973)).

70. J. SHKLAR, *supra* note 28, at 216.

71. J. ELY 74.

admits,[72] he is adumbrating the implications of footnote four of *United States v. Carolene Products Co.*,[73] particularly the footnote's second and third paragraphs.[74]

The courts' central role of monitoring the actual processes of representative democracy generates two basic inquiries. The first scrutinizes constraints blocking effective participation in the political process. This, of course, is the basic rationale for vigorously enforcing the first amendment to ensure a variegated presentation of ideas, issues, and candidates to the public. But this emphasis on a formally unblocked political process is not enough to ensure what Ely labels "representation reinforcement."[75] A second inquiry is also necessary: does legislation cut against certain groups whose position in American society is such that one can legitimately suspect that their interests are systematically undervalued through prejudice and hostility?

Ely borrows from Professor Dworkin the notion that all participants in the American polity are entitled to equal concern and respect.[76] When it has reason to believe that equal concern and respect are absent, the Court should step in, not necessarily to invalidate legislation, but to make sure that the legislative rationale is especially strong.[77] When legislation implicates no such groups—what lawyers have been trained to call "suspect classifications"—Ely requires almost no scrutiny.[78] He takes great pains to attack the general brief for rationality review, by which courts assess the nexus between supposed ends and legislative means, that Gerald Gunther[79] among others has articulated.[80]

In a helpful distinction suggested by James Fleming,[81] one might regard Ely's first inquiry, and the second paragraph of the *Carolene*

72. *Id.* at 75-77.

73. 304 U.S. 144, 152 n.4 (1938).

74. Professor Lusky, one of the authors of that footnote, *see* A. MASON, HARLAN FISKE STONE 513 (1956), points out that paragraph one, referring to those "specific" portions of the Constitution, was added at the behest of Chief Justice Hughes. L. LUSKY, *supra* note 5, at 110-11. This bow to pure textualism makes little analytical sense when placed next to the pure functionalism of paragraphs two and three, which are based respectively on impediments to democratic process and prejudice against discrete and insular minorities. As one might expect given Ely's views about textualism, *his* footnote four, like that of most of its latter-day adherents (including myself) simply ignores the first paragraph.

75. *See* J. ELY 73-134.

76. *Id.* at 82 (citing R. DWORKIN, TAKING RIGHTS SERIOUSLY 180 (1977)).

77. *Id.* at 101-04.

78. *Id.*

79. Gunther, *The Supreme Court, 1971 Term—Foreword: In Search of Evolving Doctrine on a Changing Court: A Model for a Newer Equal Protection*, 86 HARV. L. REV. 1 (1972).

80. *See* J. ELY 125-31.

81. Personal communication.

Products footnote, as directed at the *actual* representation allowed plaintiffs claiming blockage from the use of tactics such as suppression of speech, inordinately high election filing fees, or needlessly complicated requirements for access to ballots. Such blockage harms not only minority dissenters, but also, at least in theory, the majority itself, which presumably might benefit from exposure to the blocked plaintiff. The second inquiry addresses the *virtual* representation of minorities within the political system: do nonminority representatives demonstrate enough concern and respect for the outvoted minority to justify viewing legislation as something more than the ruthless ganging up of those with power against those without? As Professor Baker recently has shown,[82] this second inquiry raises the most complicated problems for democratic political theory because it challenges the particular kinds of preferences that a majoritarian system can legitimately take into account on other than purely substantive grounds. Nonetheless, how one can escape the questions that Ely raises is hard to see.

It should be emphasized that Ely, unlike Choper, purports to find guidance in a specific notion of the initial Constitution. "[M]y claim is only that the original Constitution was principally, indeed I would say overwhelmingly, dedicated to concerns of process and structure and not the identification and preservation of specific substantive values."[83] This is obviously a controversial reading of the initial Constitution.[84] Yet Ely does not seriously purport to be writing constitutional history, and I do not consider here the accuracy of his claim. Any complete assessment of his arguments must analyze the plausibility of his assertion concerning the intentions of the Constitution's framers and ra-

82. Baker, *Neutrality, Process, and Rationality: Flawed Interpretations of Equal Protection*, 58 TEXAS L. REV. 1029, 1044-48 (1980).

83. J. ELY 92.

84. For some effective ripostes, see Tribe, *supra* note 67. Moreover, as Charles Fried has noted in regard to some claims of the economics-rights theorists of law, themselves highly process oriented, one cannot make sense of the right to engage meaningfully in a process like contract (or political representation) without having a wholly nonprocess-based substantive theory of human personality that gives the process its integrity. *See* C. FRIED, RIGHT AND WRONG 81-107 (1978).

Although I share Ely's doubts about the ability of courts and judges to engage in the articulation of substantive rights endorsed by Tribe, Tribe has the better of the argument over whether one can so completely divorce an understanding of process from that of the character of the individuals engaging in it. Whether the judiciary should be so substance oriented is a completely different question than whether law and legal discussion should be concerned with substance. It would be a tragedy if the moral of Ely's book was wrongly taken to be that discussions of substantive rights or conceptions of the human *persona* are senseless. Indeed, if Ely has much to say to judges, he has almost nothing to say to legislators; if Tribe perhaps is mistaken in his message to judges, it is absolutely crucial that legislators read him so they can do *their* jobs effectively. We should learn to talk about the Constitution more and about judicial review less, or at least put judicial review back in its place as only one aspect of constitutional theory, not the major focus. To this extent, both Choper and Ely disserve the future development of constitutional theory.

tifiers. But the nature of the "historical" Constitution does not necessarily decide what we wish "our" Constitution to mean,[85] and the heart of Ely's enterprise is this latter question.

Ely's argument against a judicial mandate to declare fundamental rights or values as sanctuaries against legislative intervention rests on a simple but, I think, accurate point: If rights or values are truly "fundamental," integral to our collective self-definition as as social order, then there is no reason to believe that legislatures will prove incompetent or unwilling to enforce them.[86] Almost by definition, a fundamental value should be of interest to every member of the polity; there is no need for, or legitimacy in, judicial declarations that majoritarian institutions cannot figure out what is fundamental about our society.[87] But the legitimacy of legislative decisions depends on the integrity of the underlying political process and on particular care that specific minorities are not singled out for unjustified discrimination. I turn now to some specific problems with Ely's theory, especially insofar as he summarizes its thrust as "representation reinforcement."

The initial judicial inquiry suggested by Ely, which examines the formal nature of the political process, has at least two problems. One is pragmatic; the other is more theoretical. Concerning the former, note that representation reinforcement offers a thoroughly adequate defense of free speech and press decisions dealing with *political* topics. One can hardly respect majoritarian decisions unless they are the product of potential exposure to all competing points of view. This is nothing more than the now hoary free market of ideas theory of political speech.[88] But representation reinforcement offers little, if any, protection to modes of nonpolitical expression, which range from so-called commercial speech to pornography.[89]

85. *See* Cover, Book Review, THE NEW REPUBLIC, Jan. 14, 1978, at 26-28; and the letter in response by Raoul Berger, THE NEW REPUBLIC, Feb. 11, 1978, p. 7.

86. J. ELY 67.

87. The particular target of Ely's criticism is Alexander Bickel, particularly in regard to arguments made in *The Least Dangerous Branch*, *see* A. BICKEL, *supra* note 67. Owen Fiss more recently has defended the judiciary's basic role as articulator of collective norms. Fiss, *The Supreme Court, 1979 Term—Foreword: The Forms of Justice*, 93 HARV. L. REV. 1 (1979).

88. For Ely's exposition of his own ideas on this point, see J. ELY 105-16.

89. Professor Ely's sole discussion of this point is the following:

> We can attribute other functions [beyond protection of the integrity of the political process] to freedom of expression, and some of them must have played a role, but the exercise has the smell of the lamp about it: the view that free expression per se, without regard to what it means to the process of government, is our preeminent right has a highly elitist cast. Positive law has its claims, and I am not suggesting that such other purposes as are plausibly attributable to the language should not be attributed: the amendment's language is not limited to political speech and it should not be so limited by construction (even assuming someone could come up with a determinate definition of "political").

Id. at 94 (footnote omitted). This conclusion is sheer assertion, for Ely offers no guidance to the

It may be a sign of my own inconsistency, rather than Ely's, that I accept his view as to the illegitimacy of *Roe* yet wish to protect nonpolitical speech and expression. However, he does not devote adequate attention to how much his argument would curtail the contemporary protection given to such expression. For example, Professor Bork, who has proferred a somewhat similar political process view of the first amendment, clearly would give no protection to nonpolitical speech, at least as a matter of constitutional right.[90] That Ely takes us where we might not want to go is not necessarily fatal to his argument. But he should have confronted more directly the tension between his overarching view of the Constitution as only procedural and the substantive limitations on regulation of speech and conduct that the Supreme Court has read into the Constitution over the past several decades.[91]

Ely's notion of representation reinforcement as an adequately neutral guide to the judiciary contains theoretical, as well as pragmatic, problems. Professor Tushnet emphasizes one of these problems.[92] Ely generally defends all the Court's access-to-ballot decisions, from *Baker v. Carr*[93] to *Kramer v. Union Free School District*,[94] on what he claims are almost self-evident grounds: "[U]nblocking stoppages in the democratic process is what judicial review ought preeminently to be about, and denial of the vote seems the quintessential stoppage."[95] But Tushnet, borrowing from Justice Stewart's dissent in *Kramer*,[96] has a devastating riposte.[97] Kramer, who could not vote in the local school board election since he was not a property owner, a renter of a taxed apartment, or a parent of a schoolchild, could vote for representatives

"positive law" of the first amendment beyond process-protection. Moreover, the problem of deciding what can be plausibly attributed to the language of the amendment itself raises complex difficulties of interpretation that Ely hardly addresses. *See generally* P. BREST, PROCESSES OF CONSTITUTIONAL DECISIONMAKING (1975); Levinson, *supra* note *.

90. *See* Bork, *Neutral Principles and Some First Amendment Problems*, 47 IND. L.J. 1 (1971).

91. Indeed, Professor Perry emphasizes the extent to which most contemporary decisions protecting freedom of expression can be analyzed only in terms of the judiciary's going well beyond anything "in" the text and adopting instead civil liberties theories that have no textual basis. M. PERRY, *supra* note 20; Perry, *Interpretivism, Freedom of Expression, and Equal Protection*, 42 OHIO ST. L.J. 241 (1981). Perry hardly opposes this; instead, he makes his point as a means of demonstrating to "interpretivists" (including those of Ely's type) how much of contemporary constitutional doctrine we would sacrifice if we genuinely wished to remain guided only by the Constitution. Paul Brest presumably would agree. *See* text accompanying note 7 *supra*.

92. Tushnet, *supra* note 67, at 1045-48.

93. 369 U.S. 186 (1962).

94. 395 U.S. 621 (1969).

95. J. ELY 117. One might add to "denial of the vote" any diminution of one's voting power, such as assigning farmers a stronger vote than city dwellers. *See* Baker v. Carr, 369 U.S. at 234-37.

96. 395 U.S. at 639 (Stewart, J., dissenting).

97. Tushnet, *supra* note 67, at 1049-51.

to the New York State Legislature, which had authorized the discrimination in question. Why wasn't *that* right to vote sufficient? Why could the Supreme Court reinforce Kramer's representation in that specific election? Ely refers to "unjustified discriminations in the distribution of the franchise,"[98] but unless he believes that the Constitution mandates the right to vote in any election, he does not make clear how an unjustified distribution of the franchise differs from any other legislative distribution, such as subsidizing wheat and not cotton. Although he rejects, without adequate argumentation, Paul Brest's suggestion that the Constitution grants no substantive right to vote at all,[99] Ely does not even begin to defend the much broader argument suggested in the previous sentence.[100]

Let me retreat once more to the favorite approach of law professors—a hypothetical case designed to expose difficulties in an argument. A disadvantage with living in New Jersey, one of my several former domiciles, is that a citizen may vote, in elections concerning the executive branch of New Jersey Government, only for the Governor. One gets no vote for the judiciary, whose members are nominated by the (elected) Governor and confirmed by the (elected) senate. Compare New Jersey with several other states.

In Texas I may vote for a whole array of executive officials, such as the Attorney General and the Comptroller, as well as members of important regulatory bodies like the Texas Railroad Commission, which controls basic energy pricing in Texas. And my duties as a voting citizen do not end there: I get to vote for local constables, justices of the peace, and members of the Texas Supreme Court and the Texas Court of Criminal Appeals. California and North Carolina are fairly similar, although California does not formally elect the judiciary. Instead, the voters have the option of booting out judges they do not like. Massachusetts gave me no opportunity to vote for judges, but the ballot contained an otherwise dazzling panoply of offices, including sheriff. New Jersey, though, reduced me to an almost abject poverty of voting possibilities. Was that fair? Or, even more to the point, was that constitutional? Does New Jersey *really* have a republican form of govern-

98. J. Ely 119.

99. J. Ely 116-17, 234 n.30 (citing Brest, *supra* note 45, at 595).

100. *But see* J. Ely 118 n.* ("[W]hatever additional content Article IV's Republican Form of Government Clause may have, at a bare minimum it means that *states must hold popular elections*. . . . One of the things we mean by labeling something a right is that it shall not be denied, or granted in only watered-down form, to some subset of persons unless there is a good reason for doing so.") (emphasis added) (citation omitted). Clearly, a strong difference exists between the claim asserted in the first quoted sentence and the much milder suggestion that, once the state has decided to have a popular election, it must distribute the franchise equally.

ment?[101]

As a political scientist I can point out that forcing me to aggregate my complex policy preferences into one all-or-nothing vote for Governor deprives me of all sorts of opportunities for meaningful representation. Although one often votes for a candidate only because one is willing to overlook the candidate's position on some issues in favor of those positions that one likes, this scarcely counts as a full measure of representation, especially when measured against the triumph of representative democracy that is Texas! So why does representation reinforcement not permit (nay, require) the judiciary to declare New Jersey's way of doing things unconstitutional? If Kramer's rather trivial interests are worthy of protection, why aren't my substantially greater ones protected?[102]

That any well-trained lawyer in 1981 would regard my suit as frivolous is beside the point, for books such as those under review are eloquent testimony to the emptiness of the Supreme Court's claim to being the ultimate interpreter of the Constitution[103] in any other than a posi-

101. *See id.*

102. The debate over the cogency of *Kramer* continues within the Court. Justice Stewart, writing for the majority in Ball v. James, 101 S. Ct. 1811 (1981), upholding a property-weighted voting scheme for an Arizona water district, included a footnote pointing out that "appellees, of course, are qualified voters in Arizona and so remain equal participants in the election of the state legislators who created and have the power to change the District." *Id* at 1821 n.20. Justice Powell, concurring, also noted that *Kramer*, though formally unaffected by *Ball*, "has been questioned." *Id.* at 1822 n.2.

The four dissenters, in an opinion by Justice White, pick up the challenge in a footnote of their own:

> It is suggested by the Court in footnote 20 . . . and by Justice Powell in his concurring opinion that since the nonvoters living in the district may, of course, vote in the state legislature elections, their interests are sufficiently represented since the state legislature maintains ultimate control over the operation and authority of the District. This suggestion lacks merit and has been specifically rejected in past decisions of this Court. . . . In most situations involving a state agency or even a city, the state legislature and ultimately the people could exercise control since any municipal corporation is a creature of the State. *The Fourteenth Amendment requires a far more direct sense of democratic participation in elective schemes which is not satisfied by the indirect and imprecise voter control* suggested by the Court and by Justice Powell.

Id. at 1829 n.11 (citation omitted) (emphasis added). This response contains the same ambiguity as Ely's argument. "Democratic participation in elective schemes" may simply mean that the vote must be available to everyone whenever it is available to anyone. This still allows the vote to be available to no one should the legislature decide against elections at all in regard to given officials.

But the quoted language can be read far more radically as a requirement of "democratic participation" per se. Such a requirement might call into question the legitimacy of legislative decisions establishing appointment rather than election as the process of office selection—if not, as suggested in the text, the legitimacy of various state constitutions insufficiently committed to participatory democracy. If the Constitution requires a "direct sense of democratic participation," why is there enjoyment of this right only when a state has established "elective schemes"? Why are the "schemes" themselves not a constitutional requirement?

103. *See, e.g.,* United States v. Nixon, 418 U.S. 683, 704 (1974); Powell v. McCormack, 395 U.S. 486, 521 (1969); Cooper v. Aaron, 358 U.S. 1, 18 (1958). *See also* Levinson, *supra* note 8, at 137-48.

tivist sense. Both books argue eloquently and at length that the Court's view of the Constitution has been seriously mistaken. Most relevant in the context of this Review, however, is Ely's likely response to my hypothetical suit, because how *he* could regard it as frivolous is not clear, unless he significantly modified his zeal for representation reinforcement as the Supreme Court's master key to reading the Constitution correctly.

Ely is a great friend of "the right to vote in state elections [as] a rather special constitutional prerogative,"[104] and whether my having a chance to vote only for the Governor and a local state representative fulfills that prerogative is questionable, especially given Ely's endorsement of the majority decision in *Kramer*. One answer to my suit is simply to say that the citizenry has no right to vote for any particular office; that is a question for constitutional framers. Once selection of an office is thrown open to the voters, everyone must have an equal vote. Even this answer has problems since everyone does not have the right to vote—witness children, felons, and non-citizens. Moreover, this answer causes us to drift into a discussion of equality, not of representation reinforcement. Equality is a good thing, and it amply justifies *Reynolds v. Sims*[105] and *Harper v. Virginia Board of Elections*.[106] But this is not the framework that Ely adopts, and his interesting and provocative emphasis on representation reinforcement is disconcertingly sketchy, given the weight he places on it.

Ely's unwillingness to confront *Buckley v. Valeo*,[107] which he mentions only in a footnote,[108] is especially disappointing. I regard *Buckley* as perhaps the worst decision—considering both attempts at rationales and results—in the past forty years. It seems especially egregious as a violation of any notion of representation reinforcement, since it limits participation in political campaigns through campaign contributions and, much more seriously, protects the Democratic and Republican parties from significant marketplace competition by upholding the massive public subsidies to those parties (and, at least pre-election, to those parties alone). One might think that Professor Ely would object to *Buckley* as much as to *Roe*, about which he has written with justified passion.[109] Could he possibly think that *Buckley* was correctly de-

104. J. Ely 118 n.*.
105. 377 U.S. 533 (1964).
106. 383 U.S. 663 (1966).
107. 424 U.S. 1 (1976).
108. J. Ely 234 n.27.
109. *See* Ely, *The Wages of Crying Wolf: A Comment on* Roe v. Wade, 82 Yale L.J. 920 (1973).

cided?

The question is not as simple as my remarks might suggest. As Dean Wellington recently argued, there is a theory of representation reinforcement (although he does not use this term) that could justify the federal statutes considered in *Buckley*.[110] Indeed, marketplace of ideas buffs would recognize traditional state interventions in the economic marketplace as an embodiment of the same theory: when monopolists (large contributors) threaten the maintenance of a truly competitive marketplace, the state can legitimately intervene by passing antitrust laws (laws regulating campaign finances). One might still reject this theory, either by criticizing its empirical foundation or by grounding freedom of expression in some theory other than the free marketplace of ideas.[111] But one must recognize the centrality of the issues presented by *Buckley* to the debate over the contemporary meaning of the first amendment and the realities of modern representative government. Ely's failure to confront *Buckley* adequately adds to my suspicion that representation reinforcement, when all is said and done, reduces simply to a somewhat fancy phrase trotted out to explain the access-to-ballot cases.

At the very least, representation reinforcement scarcely serves as a means of assigning to courts a clearly delimited area within which intervention is permissible while differentiating those areas in which the results reached by ordinary political processes should control. Read expansively, it licenses a form of judicial intervention that makes the access-to-ballot cases look like a tea party. Read restrictively, it justifies some decisions of the 1960s while removing theoretical support from more general protection of freedom of expression.

I have little to say regarding Professor Ely's second major theoretical discussion—the role of the judiciary in safeguarding the integrity of the political process by paying special attention to the results reached when certain groups seem to be the legislative losers. I find his arguments convincing, both as an explanation of the decided cases and as a guide for further discussion. He recognizes all the problems involved in identifying the "suspect classes" whose treatment should trigger "strict scrutiny."[112] He realizes full well that he has not yet provided

110. Wellington, *On Freedom of Expression*, 88 YALE L.J. 1105, 1126-42 (1979).

111. *See* P. BREST & S. LEVINSON, PROCESSES OF CONSTITUTIONAL DECISIONMAKING 197-203 (Supp. 1980).

112. J. ELY 145-70. As a result of reading Brest, *The Substance of Process*, 42 OHIO ST. L.J. 131 (1981), I would modify my statement that Ely recognizes "all" the problems, since Brest persuasively argues that there is no way of deciding what groups are entitled to suspect status without some substantive theory of politics. *See also* Alexander, *Modern Equal Protection Theories: A*

completely satisfying answers to all the conundrums that can be raised about such identification. His attempt to divide the political world into "we's" and "they's," so that legislation seemingly directed against "them" will be scrutinized more carefully than legislation that burdens "us," is a decent first approximation, especially in regard to issues such as the constitutionality of affirmative action.[113]

Although there are certain overlaps between Choper and Ely, Ely scarcely sympathizes with Choper's general program of the courts as guardians of individual rights, unless such rights can be put within the representation-reinforcing mode or the special procedural rights of criminal defendants. Although Choper does not say for sure, he may wish to defend *Roe* as a protection of individual rights; Ely obviously rejects *in toto* any special judicial role to protect that kind of individual right, however much he would support legislation to that end. On the other hand, it is hard to imagine that Choper would reject any of Ely's affirmative program, though he presumably would not think it sufficient.

IV. Conclusion

Fewer and fewer books or articles seem genuinely to believe that we can any longer speak meaningfully of the 1787 Constitution, even as amended, except in the context of Brest's "remote ancestor" metaphor.[114] Choper makes several attempts to show that his views are "consistent" with the Founders' vision,[115] but he clearly is not animated by any special concern to follow that vision. Ely, too, while tipping his hat to the Founders,[116] speaks to us directly as citizens facing the tasks of maintaining a common life in 1981 rather than as members of a political family seeking only to follow the terms of great-grandfather's will.

One can call this "living" constitutionalism, but, as Raoul Berger

Metatheoretical Taxonomy and Critique*, 42 OHIO ST. L.J. 3 (1981); Baker, *supra* note 82. Parker, *The Past of Constitutional Theory—and Its Future*, 42 OHIO ST. L.J. 223 (1981), contains some telling criticisms of the specific vision of American politics that underlies both Choper's and Ely's arguments and thus limits their capacity to be sufficiently aware of the actualities of representation and participation in contemporary American society.

113. *Id.* at 170-72. Affirmative action, according to Ely, is constitutional because the white majority bears the cost of such programs. Because there is no reason to believe that whites have any difficulty in exercising their will within the ordinary political process, they have no claim to special judicial scrutiny.

114. *See* text accompanying note 11 *supra*. *See also* Saphire, *The Search for Legitimacy in Constitutional Theory: What Price Purity?*, 42 OHIO ST. L.J. 336 (1981).

115. J. CHOPER 62, 241, 244, 385.

116. J. ELY 39.

has pointed out over and over again,[117] the very point of constitutionalism, from the perspective of the Framers, was to fetter the future. "In questions of power," Thomas Jefferson wrote in the Kentucky Resolutions of 1798, "let no more be heard of confidence in man, but bind him down from mischief by the chains of the constitution."[118] Had the Framers been great optimists about the caliber of their descendants, they scarcely would have felt it necessary to frame a very complex Constitution or, especially, to make formal amendment so ludicrously difficult. To draw on Brest's metaphor once more, one might note that most adults who came over on the Mayflower were still sufficiently imbued with traditional values of patriarchy to believe that they (particularly the fathers) would "govern" their children in the accustomed manner.[119] In this, as in so many other aspects, settlement in America was a great human tragedy instead of a triumph, as Perry Miller has pointed out so stunningly.[120] The Founding Fathers also had great hopes that their control would reach into the future and prevent the almost inevitable corruption of their wastrel sons. Thus, they gave us the Constitution and bequeathed to us the tensions of attempting to take it altogether seriously as a source of continuing guidance for our lives.

"How blind they are," said Hegel, "who may hope that institutions, constitutions, laws which no longer correspond to human manners, needs, and opinions, from which the spirit has flown, can subsist any longer; or that forms in which intellect and feeling now take no interest are powerful enough to be any longer the bond of a nation!"[121] From one perspective, of course, the very books under review testify to the continuing presence of "intellect and feeling" about our 1787 Constitution. But I wish to emphasize the other side of the message revealed by scrutiny of the books' arguments: the books' relative inability to view the Constitution as other than opaque to the modern reader. And a major reason for the opacity is precisely that our contemporary "manners, needs, and opinions" are so radically different from those of two centuries ago.[122] As Hegel implied, the crisis about the meaning of constitutional fidelity is not a professional argument

117. *E.g.*, Berger, *supra* note 85, at 7.

118. *Id.*

119. *See* P. MILLER, ERRAND INTO THE WILDERNESS (1956).

120. *Id.*

121. HEGEL'S POLITICAL WRITINGS 244 (T. Knox trans. 1964).

122. This is not a new theme of mine. *See, e.g.*, *A.A.L.S. Law and Religion Panel: Law as Our Civil Religion*, 31 MERCER L. REV. 477 (1980); Levinson, *The Specious Morality of the Law*, HARPER'S May 1977, at 35; Levinson, Book Review, 57 TEXAS L. REV. 847 (1979).

restricted to lawyers, but an integral part of the cultural crisis of our times.

The very brilliance of the books under review—not to mention Professor Tribe's[123] and other books and articles not singled out here for extensive comment—is thus as much a cause for alarm as for pleasure. Everyone seems more successful at demolishing existing approaches to the interplay between court and Constitution, especially as revealed in opinions of the Supreme Court, than at putting forth a new understanding around which our discourse might cohere. Only modernist intellectuals confuse the brilliance of intellectual fireworks, and concomitant "deconstruction," with the preconditions of political order, whether defined in terms of stability or justice.

"Teachers" of constitutional theory have more and more fascinating books to assign their students, all in the name of learning to "think like a (professional) lawyer." But one wonders what the students will make of the mutually exclusive visions of the Constitution and of the judiciary contained in those books. One also wonders what beyond possession of a law degree denotes "professionalism," particularly in regard to the subject of constitutional law.

Ultimately, one must recognize the extent to which discussions of constitutional theory implicate the very notion of our identity as Americans and, more particularly, our relationship to our national past. In a fundamental sense, no nation is so obsessed with the symbols of its political past as is the United States, just as perhaps no nation has as much trouble resolving the tensions between its zeal for modernity and its profession of consistency with a heritage rooted in the dim past. Part of that heritage is the Constitution of the United States; it is incumbent upon us to decide whether that heritage can structure our own lives.

* * * *

> On the last night, with my trunk packed and my car sold to the grocer, I went over and looked at that huge incoherent failure of a house once more. On the white steps an obscene word, scrawled by some boy with a piece of brick, stood out clearly in the moonlight, and I erased it, drawing my shoe raspingly along the stone. Then I wandered down to the beach and sprawled out on the sand.
>
> Most of the big shore places were closed now and there were hardly any lights except the shadowy, moving glow of a ferryboat across the Sound. And as the moon rose higher the inessential

123. L. TRIBE, *supra* note 67.

houses began to melt away until gradually I became aware of the old island here that flowered once for Dutch sailors' eyes—a fresh, green breast of the new world. Its vanished trees, the trees that had made way for Gatsby's house, had once pandered in whispers to the last and greatest of all human dreams; for a transitory enchanted moment man must have held his breath in the presence of this continent, compelled into an aesthetic contemplation he neither understood nor desired, face to face for the last time in history with something commensurate to his capacity for wonder.

And as I sat there brooding on the old, unknown world, I thought of Gatsby's wonder when he first picked out the green light at the end of Daisy's dock. He had come a long way to this blue lawn, and his dream must have seemed so close that he could hardly fail to grasp it. He did not know that it was already behind him, somewhere back in that vast obscurity beyond the city, where the dark fields of the republic rolled on under the night.

Gatsby believed in the green light, the orgiastic future that year by year recedes before us. It eluded us then, but that's no matter—tomorrow we will run faster, stretch out our arms farther. . . . And one fine morning—

And so we beat on, boats against the current, borne back ceaselessly into the past.[124]

124. F. FITZGERALD, THE GREAT GATSBY 181-82 (1953).

ARTICLES

ON THE ORIGINS OF THE FREE PRESS CLAUSE

Leonard W. Levy*

TABLE OF CONTENTS

I. INTRODUCTION 178
II. ANDERSON'S VIEWS 181
A. *Whether the Law of Seditious Libel Was Impotent* 182
1. Seditious Libel in England 182
2. Seditious Libel In America 185
a. *Whiting* 187
b. *Freeman* 187
c. *Oswald* 188
d. *The Pennsylvania Constitution* 191
B. *Whether Parliamentary Privilege Had Become Ineffective* 192
C. *Whether Principled Opposition Existed to the Law of Seditious Libel* 194
1. The Massachusetts Radicals 195
2. The Quebec Declaration 196
3. Oswald's Case 197
4. Cato 198
5. Cushing and Adams 199
6. Madison 200
D. *What the Framers Meant by "Freedom of the Press"* 202
E. *What the Framers Meant by "Congress Shall Make No Law"* 206

* Andrew W. Mellon All Claremont Professor of Humanities and Chairman, Graduate Faculty of History, Claremont Graduate School.

F. *Whether the Framers Believed in a Federal Common Law of Crimes* 208
III. ANDERSON'S METHODOLOGY 211
A. *Anderson's Critique of the "Levy Thesis"* 212
B. *Anderson's Use of Historical Evidence*............. 214
IV. NEW DIRECTIONS 218

I. INTRODUCTION

In 1806 the United States commenced common law prosecutions of six Connecticut citizens for seditious libel against President Thomas Jefferson.[1] According to the indictments, two of the defendants had committed the crime in the course of preaching sermons and the others in newspaper print. The infamous Sedition Act of 1798 having expired, and Federalist party control of Connecticut stymieing state punishment, the government prosecuted the cases in the belief that the federal courts possessed jurisdiction over the common law crime of seditious libel.[2] Eventually, political considerations also forced Jefferson's administration to reverse itself on the issue of a federal common law of crimes and to drop the prosecutions except for those against Barzillai Hudson and George Goodwin, the editors of a Federalist newspaper in Hartford. Prior to trial, their case was appealed to the Supreme Court for a decision on the question of whether the federal courts possessed jurisdiction over nonstatutory criminal offenses. Somehow a decision was deferred until Republican appointees dominated the Supreme Court, which finally ruled in 1812 against the existence of a federal common law of crimes.[3] The case was decided without argument by counsel and without reasoned consideration by a divided Court which did not note the fact of division.[4] It was decided against several circuit court precedents established by members of the Supreme Court who had been important Framers of the Constitution or

1. L. LEVY, JEFFERSON AND CIVIL LIBERTIES 61–66 (1963).

2. J. SMITH, FREEDOM'S FETTERS 188–220 (1956) discusses federal common law prosecutions for seditious libel prior to the Sedition Act of 1798. None of the prosecutions reached the trial stage.

3. United States v. Hudson and Goodwin, 11 U.S. (7 Cranch) 32, 34 (1812).

4. That the Court divided is known from Justice Story's dissent in a circuit decision of the next year, United States v. Coolidge, 1 Gallison 488, 494–95 (1st Cir. 1813), and from the later statement of Justice Johnson in United States v. Coolidge, 14 U.S. (1 Wheat.) 415, 416 (1816). 2 W. CROSSKEY, POLITICS AND THE CONSTITUTION 782 (1953) stated that Chief Justice Marshall and Justice Washington dissented without noting that fact for the record. Crosskey offered no proof; however, one may surmise those justices' views tentatively from their being Federalists of the founding generation who believed in the existence of a federal common law of crimes and from Marshall's approving depiction of the 1793 prosecution of Gideon Henfield in 5 J. MARSHALL, THE LIFE OF WASHINGTON 40–42 (Citizens' Guild ed. 1926).

closely associated with the Framers.[5] Although the bizarre prosecutions of 1806 came to nothing, they did not bespeak a broad Jeffersonian conception of the scope of political opinions or a fixed belief that the first amendment conflicted with the law of seditious libel.

In 1806 Thomas Paine, the foremost pamphleteer in the English language, a friend of the radicals in England and France as well as those in America, and a condemned seditionist, published an essay on "Liberty of the Press" in a New York newspaper.[6] He began by criticizing the "licentiousness" of Federalist editors and noted that nothing was more common than "the continual cry of the *Liberty of the Press*."[7] Undertaking to define the term because it was being used "without being understood,"[8] Paine drew from English history a Blackstonian conclusion[9] that the abolition of previous censorship had made the press only as free as speech had always been. He ended:

> A man does not ask liberty beforehand to say something he has a mind to say, but he becomes answerable afterwards for the atrocities he may utter.
>
> In like manner, if a man makes the press utter atrocious things he becomes as answerable for them as if he had uttered them by word of mouth. Mr. Jefferson has said in his inaugural speech, that '*error of opinion might be tolerated, when reason was left free to combat it*.' This is sound philosophy in cases of error. But there is a difference between error and licentiousness.
>
> Some lawyers in defending their clients . . . have often given their opinion of what they defined the liberty of the press to be. One said it was this, another said it was that, and so on, according to the case they were pleading. Now these men ought to have known that the term *liberty of the press* arose from a FACT, the abolition of the office of Imprimateur [*sic*], and that opinion has nothing to do with the case. The term refers to the fact of printing *free from prior restraint*, and not at all to the

5. Among the Supreme Court justices who accepted jurisdiction of common law crimes while on circuit duty were John Jay, James Wilson, Oliver Ellsworth, William Paterson, James Iredell, and Samuel Chase. In United States v. Worrall, 2 U.S. (2 Dall.) 384, 391 (1798), Chase rejected the existence of a federal common law of crimes, but in United States v. Sylvester (1799), an unreported case in manuscript, FINAL RECORD OF THE UNITED STATES CIRCUIT COURTS OF MASSACHUSETTS, 1790–1799, at 303, 305 (1800), Chase changed his mind when presiding over a common law prosecution for counterfeiting which ended in a conviction. For further cases, see LEVY, *supra* note 1, at 201 n.72; for an excellent discussion of the subject, see Presser, *A Tale of Two Judges*, 73 NW. U.L. REV. 26, 46–72 (1978).

6. The American Citizen (N.Y.), Oct. 20, 1806, *reprinted in* 10 THE LIFE AND WORKS OF THOMAS PAINE 287 (W. Van der Weyde ed. 1925) [hereinafter cited as PAINE].

7. *Id.* at 288.

8. *Id.*

9. For Sir William Blackstone's views on freedom of the press, see *infra* note 30 and accompanying text.

> matter printed, whether good or bad. The public at large—or in case of prosecution, a jury of the country—will be judges of the matter.[10]

Paine's views in this respect represented those of the Framers of the Constitution and the first amendment.[11]

The Framers had a genius for studied imprecision. They deliberately phrased the Constitution in generalized terms and without a lexicographical guide; they outlined an instrument that would serve future generations. Like Martin Chuzzlewit's grandnephew who had no more than "the first idea and sketchy notions of a face,"[12] the Constitution, including the Bill of Rights, purposely was made to embody first ideas and sketchy notions. Men trained in the common law, such as the Framers, avoided detailed codes, which become obsolete with a change in the particular circumstances for which they were adopted, and instead tended to formulate expansive and comprehensive principles. The principles—not the Framers' understanding and applications of them—were meant to endure.

The first amendment's injunction, that there shall be no law abridging the freedom of speech or press, was boldly stated if narrowly understood. The bold statement, not the narrow understanding, was written into the fundamental law.[13] There is no evidence to warrant the belief, nor is there valid cause or need to believe, that the Framers possessed the ultimate wisdom and best insights on the meaning of freedom of expression. But what the first amendment said is far more important than what its Framers meant. It is enough that they gave constitutional recognition to the principle of freedom of speech and press in unqualified and undefined terms.

But it is not enough for David A. Anderson.[14] He craves the comfort of knowing that a patriotic lineage, the fatherhood of the Framers, buttresses his civic convictions about the Constitution. Although the Framers' wisdom may well have passed out-of-date, Anderson needs the past's original intentions to anchor present preferences. He finds "solace," he tells us,[15] in knowing that

---

10. 10 PAINE, *supra* note 6, at 289–90 (emphasis in original).

11. A major theme of L. LEVY, LEGACY OF SUPPRESSION (1960) is that freedom of the press during the period of the framing (1787–1791) meant exemption from prior restraint but responsibility, under the criminal law, for abuse of the liberty to publish whatever one pleased.

12. C. DICKENS, MARTIN CHUZZLEWIT 76 (National Library ed. 1930).

13. The Framers addressed the future, not the past. Their insistence that they were merely expressing a common understanding reflected an Anglo-American habit of going forward while facing backwards: Rights that should exist are established on the fictitious pretense that they have ever existed, and arguments are concocted to give the fiction the appearance of both reality and legality.

14. Anderson, *The Origin of the Press Clause*, 30 UCLA L. REV. 455 (1983).

15. *Id.* at 496.

whatever those original intentions may have been, the Supreme Court will not at this late date exempt states and federal courts from the first amendment. He is alarmed, however, by the thought that those intentions are "not irrelevant" with respect to future cases on the free press clause.[16] "If Levy's interpretation is correct, then history provides no support whatsoever for the rights now being asserted in the name of freedom of the press . . . ."[17] And, he adds, if my interpretation is correct, the Supreme Court has misread history or has given it short shrift in various opinions of which he approves.[18] Accordingly, Anderson succumbs to the impulse to recreate the past. He must make it coincide with our rhetorical traditions of freedom and yield a message that will edify the judicial mind. Thus, some touching up here and there on behalf of a good cause seems in order. This Article examines Anderson's contentions and the methodology he uses to conform the origins of the free press clause to his views.

II. Anderson's Views

Anderson's rewriting of the past is based upon his view that the law of seditious libel was invalid by the time of the American Revolution. He writes that the doctrine had become "impotent,"[19] and that there was "principled opposition" to seditious libel on the part of the public.[20] He states that the power of the legislature to punish for breach of parliamentary privilege had become ineffective by the time of the Revolution.[21] While admitting that what the Framers meant by "freedom of the press" is uncertain,[22] he argues that full protection of the press was intended,[23] that the "Congress shall not" formulation of the first amendment was to have "no significance whatsoever,"[24] and that the Framers did not believe in a federal common law of crimes.[25] Each of these contentions will be

---

16. *Id.*

17. *Id.*

18. *Id.* at 506 n.288. Apparently, I would have been to blame if the Court had decided those cases according to my "reading" of history, but I get no credit when it produces "good" results. When Anderson quotes from New York Times Co. v. Sullivan, 376 U.S. 254, 276 (1964), *see* Anderson, *supra* note 14, at 521 n.372, ellipsis marks appear where the Court cited *Legacy of Suppression* as authority for the proposition that the verdict of history proves the unconstitutionality of the Sedition Act of 1798. Personally, I do not believe that historians influence appellate judges, who use scholarship as a garnish to provide the appearance of objectivity and respectability.

19. Anderson, *supra* note 14, at 510; *see infra* notes 26–75 and accompanying text.

20. Anderson, *supra* note 14, at 512; *see infra* notes 92–134 and accompanying text.

21. Anderson, *supra* note 14, at 513–14; *see infra* notes 76–91 and accompanying text.

22. Anderson, *supra* note 14, at 486–87.

23. *Id.* at 488; *see infra* notes 135–47 and accompanying text.

24. Anderson, *supra* note 14, at 501; *see infra* notes 148–57 and accompanying text.

25. Anderson, *supra* note 14, at 503; *see infra* notes 158–72 and accompanying text.

examined below.

A. *Whether the Law of Seditious Libel Was Impotent*

Anderson believes that as a result of popular opposition, the law of seditious libel had become "impotent" by the time of the American Revolution.[26] He states this under the section headed "The Meaning of Freedom of the Press in 1789," therefore implying that because the law of seditious libel had lost its teeth, freedom of the press could not entail a criminal responsibility for publications of a seditious character, at least not for criticism of government. "If," asks Anderson, "the Framers expected the press to operate as an effective check on government, how could they have tolerated the law of seditious libel, which made criticism of government a crime?"[27] Anderson's mistake is in thinking that criticism of the government was a crime.[28] It was not—not even in England, where, presumably, Anderson would concede that the law of seditious libel had not become impotent.

1. Seditious Libel in England

The common law did not stigmatize or condemn criticism of the government as criminal. The inherent vagueness of the crime of seditious libel made satisfactory definition of it difficult. The definition of the crime could take into account the malicious or criminal intent of the accused, or the bad tendency or falsity of his remarks. Seditious libel always had been an accordionlike concept, expandable or contractable at the whim of judges.

Judged by actual prosecutions, the crime consisted of defaming, condemning, or ridiculing the government—its form, constitution, officers, laws, conduct, or policies—to the jeopardy of the public peace. In effect, any malicious criticism which could be construed as having the tendency to lower the government in the public's esteem, to hold it up to contempt or hatred, or to disturb the peace was seditious libel and exposed the speaker or writer to criminal prosecution. Words damaging to the government that tended, however remotely, to cause a breach of the peace, constituted seditious libel according to the courts. But such reasoning explained nothing because *every* crime theoretically breached the king's peace. Thus, criticism of the government that went too far, not the tendency of the words to breach the peace, distinguished the crime of seditious libel, although loose judicial language sometimes suggested otherwise. Loose language invariably characterized the

26. Anderson, *supra* note 14, at 510.
27. *Id.* at 493.
28. *Id.* at 509, 514.

crime, because the government always alleged that the defendant spoke or wrote wickedly, falsely, scandalously, scurrilously, and seditiously, or some combination thereof. Theoretically, one might say or print what he pleased, but he was responsible to the common law for malicious utterances that tended towards contempt, ridicule, hatred, scorn, or disrepute of other persons, religion, government, or morality.

Blackstone, the oracle of the common law to the American Framers, summarized the law of crown libels in 1769:

> [W]here blasphemous, immoral, treasonable, schismatical, seditious, or scandalous libels are punished by the English law . . . the *liberty of the press*, properly understood, is by no means infringed or violated. The liberty of the press is indeed essential to the nature of a free state; but this consists in laying no *previous* restraints upon publications, and not in freedom from censure for criminal matter when published. Every freeman has an undoubted right to lay what sentiments he pleases before the public; to forbid this is to destroy the freedom of the press; but if he publishes what is improper, mischievous, or illegal, he must take the consequences of his own temerity. . . . But to punish (as the law does at present) any dangerous or offensive writings, which, when published, shall on a fair and impartial trial[29] be adjudged of a pernicious tendency, is necessary for the preservation of peace and good order, of government and religion, the only solid foundations of civil liberty. Thus the will of individuals is still left free; the abuse only of that free will is the object of legal punishment. Neither is any restraint hereby laid upon freedom of thought or inquiry: liberty of private sentiment is still left; the disseminating or making public of bad sentiments, destructive of the ends of society, is the crime which society corrects.[30]

Thus, men trained in the common law believed that the press most effectively could discharge its function as a check on government if it did not indulge in malicious offensiveness which discredited it.

Some harmless animadversions did result in prosecutions, but the law's potential suppressiveness notwithstanding, the English press hardly could have been freer in practice than it was. Newspapers and tracts spewed forth vitriolic aspersions on public men and measures and commented unrestrainedly on all sorts of matters of public concern. Without a constitutional guarantee of freedom of

29. Blackstone's endorsement of a "fair and impartial" trial was meaningless to the libertarians of the time, because he explicitly repudiated one of their two major gauges of fairness, the right of the defendant to prove the truth of his alleged libel. Moreover, Blackstone ignored the other libertarian gauge of fairness at a time when it was the principal issue of contention: the right of the jury rather than of the judge to decide the criminality of the alleged libel. For a discussion of that issue, see LEVY, *supra* note 11, at 151–63.

30. 4 W. BLACKSTONE, COMMENTARIES *151–52 (1769), *reprinted in* L. LEVY, FREEDOM OF THE PRESS FROM ZENGER TO JEFFERSON 104–05 (1966) (emphasis in original).

the press and despite occasional prosecutions that were meant to be exemplary, the English press fearlessly and vigorously criticized as it pleased. English libertarian theory stayed far ahead of its American counterpart throughout the eighteenth century, and not until the 1760's did the press in America become as free as the press had been in England since the end of the licensing system in 1694. The fact that seditious libel was a crime did not make criticism of the government illegal or even risky.

Partisanship and polemics so characterized the English press that as early as 1712 a writer, possibly Joseph Addison, signing himself as "Tory Author" and taking for granted the right to criticize the government, sought to define the bounds of that right. He approvingly quoted an unnamed Whig who said, "There never was a good Government that stood in fear of Freedom of Speech, which is the natural Liberty of Mankind; nor was ever any Administration afraid of Satyr [satire] but such as deserv'd it."[31] Private persons should have the right to criticize the government, but there must be reasonable restraints. Freedom of speech, as well as of press, should be confined to the limits set by truthfulness, good taste, due submission, and innocency of malice. Tory Author favored "Legal Liberty," the right to speak, write, or print "whatever is not against Law." He stated:

> I believe all we mean by Restraining the Press, is to hinder the Printing of any Seditious, Schismatical, Heretical or Antimonarchical Pamphlets. We do not intend to destroy Printing itself or to abridge any one Set of Men of the Liberties of *Englishmen*; That is, of Writing and Printing what the Law allows; what may be consistent with our Loyalty to the Q—n, and our Love to the Publick Peace; what is not against Morals or Good Manners. And surely there may be a Restraint put upon such Things without striking at the Press itself.[32]

Thus, Tory Author believed that freedom of expression had a broad scope and a high value when kept under the reasonable restraints of the common law, without which true liberty would degenerate to licentiousness.

The right to criticize the government was an eighteenth-century cliche and not seriously disputed. At the close of the century, James Madison noted that in England, where the common law threatened those who used the press in a manner offensive to the government, punishment was "occasional," yet everyone knew that "the freedom exercised by the press, and protected by public opinion far exceeds the limits prescribed by the ordinary rules of law." The English press, Madison declared, criticized the government

31. THOUGHTS OF A TORY AUTHOR 13 (London 1712).

32. *Id.* at 1–2 (emphasis in original).

"with peculiar freedom."[33]

2. Seditious Libel In America

Had the common law of seditious libel become impotent in America by the time of the Revolution? In the period between the Declaration of Independence and the ratification of the first amendment (1776–1791), America had its first opportunity to develop a legal system and a society in which all men were free to express their opinions, however unpopular, on any subject, short of direct and immediate incitement to crime. But no American state took the opportunity to abandon or seriously to limit the oppressive common law of seditious libel.

On the contrary, ten of the thirteen original states, all but Rhode Island, Connecticut, and South Carolina, expressly adopted the common law system after separating from England. Virginia, for example, did so by statute in 1776: "[T]he common law of England . . . shall be the rule of decision, and shall be considered as in full force, until the same shall be altered by the legislative power of this colony."[34] Six states did so by their constitutions. New Jersey, for example, provided in its constitution of 1776 that "the common law of England, as well as so much of the statute law, as have been heretofore practiced in this Colony, shall remain in force, until they shall be altered by a future law . . . ."[35] No state statute abolished or altered the common law of criminal defamation in general, or seditious libel in particular, and no state court ruled that the free press clause of its state constitution rendered void the prosecution of a libel. Every state with a free press clause in its constitution provided that England's common law before the Revolution was to operate unless inconsistent with or repugnant to some other constitutional or statutory provision.[36] In New York and the three other states which did not protect freedom of the press, there is no basis for implying that the idea that a republican form of government may be criminally libeled by the opinions of its citizens was to be

33. 4 J. MADISON, LETTERS AND WRITINGS 544 (1865) (Richmond 1850).

34. 9 THE STATUTES AT LARGE; BEING A COLLECTION OF ALL THE LAWS OF VIRGINIA FROM THE FIRST SESSION OF THE LEGISLATURE, IN THE YEAR 1619 127 (W. Hening ed. 1823).

35. N.J. CONST. of 1776, art. XXII, *reprinted in* 5 THE FEDERAL AND STATE CONSTITUTIONS, COLONIAL CHARTERS, AND OTHER ORGANIC LAWS 2598 (F. Thorpe ed. 1909) [hereinafter cited as Thorpe]. For the constitutional provisions of the other five states, see DEL. CONST. of 1776, *reprinted in* 1 Thorpe, at 567; MD. CONST. of 1776, art. III, *reprinted in* 3 Thorpe, at 1686–87; N.Y. CONST. of 1777, art. XXXV, *reprinted in* 5 Thorpe, at 2635; MASS. CONST. of 1780, art. VI, *reprinted in* 3 Thorpe, at 1910; N.H. CONST. of 1784, *reprinted in* 4 Thorpe, at 2469.

36. Hall, *The Common Law: An Account of Its Reception in the United States*, 4 VAND. L. REV. 791, 797–800 (1951) and 1 R. POWELL, THE LAW OF REAL PROPERTY §§ 48–63 (1981) survey the reception state by state.

discarded.[37] As for the nine states that constitutionally protected freedom of the press, one may argue that the law of criminal utterances was inconsistent with or repugnant to a free press guarantee; but such an argument must be based on inferences from later libertarian premises and would lack the support of evidence from the 1776–1791 period. The evidence supports the opposing view, as in the two Carolinas, whose constitutions banned seditious utterances.[38]

Anderson professes reluctance to "believe that the press clauses that were included in nine state constitutions were intended to do nothing more than preserve the English common law."[39] He assumes a far greater degree of rationality and purposefulness in the writing of the press clause than actually existed.[40] He also assumes that a free press clause made a significant difference, although the presses in states without free press clauses functioned as freely as those in states with such clauses—and in England, the home of Blackstone and Mansfield, the press behaved as if the common law did not exist and was as free in practice as its American counterparts. If to repudiate the Blackstone–Mansfield view of the common law's restrictions on political expression was a revolutionary objective, the Americans of the revolutionary period strangely did

37. The lack of protection given to freedom of the press in New York is interesting because New York had been the home of Zenger's case forty years earlier. John Peter Zenger was prosecuted for seditious libel in 1735 by New York as a result of his aspersions on Governor William Cosby in the *New York Weekly Journal*, which Zenger printed. At his trial Zenger's counsel, Andrew Hamilton, offered to prove that the words charged as libelous were true and argued that truth should be a defense against a charge of libel. He further argued that the jury should render a general verdict of guilty or not guilty—deciding whether the words were libelous as a matter of law—rather than render a special verdict on the factual issue of whether the defendant printed the words charged and leave to the court the question of whether the words constituted libel as a matter of law. The jury, ignoring the court's instructions, acquitted Zenger. *See generally* J. ALEXANDER, A BRIEF NARRATIVE OF THE CASE AND TRIAL OF JOHN PETER ZENGER (Katz ed. 1972). In effect, New York repudiated the principles of the Zenger defense when the state constitution of 1777 expressly adopted the common law as of the date of the outbreak of the war with England. *See* N.Y. CONST. of 1777, art. XXXV, *reprinted in* 5 Thorpe, *supra* note 35, at 2635–36.

38. N.C. CONST. of 1776, art. XXXIV, *reprinted in* 5 Thorpe, *supra* note 35, at 2793; S.C. CONST. of 1778, art. XXXVIII, *reprinted in* 6 Thorpe, *supra* note 35, at 3257.

39. Anderson, *supra* note 14, at 534.

40. Americans executed the task of writing their revolutionary constitutions and declarations of rights in a seemingly haphazard fashion. Inexplicably, of the eleven original states that framed constitutions (Rhode Island and Connecticut simply retained their charters with references to Britain deleted), two passed over freedom of the press; four ignored the right of a defendant to be represented by counsel in a criminal case; six failed to protect the right against unreasonable searches and seizures; six omitted a provision against compulsory self-incrimination; incredibly, six neglected the right to the writ of habeas corpus; six, again, took no notice of a right to indictment by grand jury; and eight made no provision against bills of attainder. *See also* Dumbauld, *State Precedents for the Bill of Rights*, 7 J. PUB. L. 323 (1958), especially Appendix A, "Table of Topics in State Bills of Rights," at 343–44.

not say so. No state asserted in any way that the law of seditious libel was incompatible with a constitutional guarantee of freedom of the press or with a republican form of government.

a. *Whiting*. If the law of seditious libel had become impotent or if a free press clause in a state constitution superseded the common law of libels, how do we explain the conviction of Dr. William Whiting? In 1787 a jury convicted him before the Supreme Judicial Court of Massachusetts sitting in Great Barrington, the scene of Whiting's crime. No ordinary libeler, Whiting was Chief Justice of the Court of Common Pleas of Berkshire County. In 1786, shortly before the fall term of his court, he had written an article, signed "Gracchus," censuring the government for unjust laws and recommending that a virtuous people who lacked redress of grievances should "disturb the government."[41] Whiting did not publish the article but read it to insurgents who supported Shays' rebellion. Whiting was dismissed from his judicial post, convicted of writing a seditious libel, and received a sentence of imprisonment for seven months, a one hundred pound fine, and sureties for good behavior for five years. Governor James Bowdoin and his Council denied a petition for a pardon but remitted the prison sentence. No one claimed that the free press clause of the state constitution stood in the way of a prosecution for seditious libel.[42]

b. *Freeman*. In 1791 Edmund Freeman, a newspaper editor, for having grossly libeled the private life of a member of the Massachusetts legislature, was criminally prosecuted on the theory that his words tended to breach the public peace of the Commonwealth. The prosecutor, Attorney-General James Sullivan, later the Jeffersonian governor of the state, maintained that the constitutional guarantee of a free press meant only the absence of a licensing act. He quoted Blackstone at interminable length to prove the point and urged that licentiousness must be distinguished from liberty. The defendant's attorneys did not disagree but denied that Freeman had licentiously breached the peace and sought to prove the accuracy of his publication.[43]

Three judges of the state's high court presided at the trial.

---

41. Riley, *Dr. William Whiting and Shays' Rebellion*, 66 PROC. AM. ANTIQUARIAN SOC. 119, 124 (1956).

42. *See generally id.* For Whiting's essay and letters, see *id.* at 131–66. Anderson, *supra* note 14, at 513 n.324, refers to a statement by Congressman John Nicholas, Feb. 25, 1799, which asserted that the law of libels was "a dead letter" because of the state free press clauses and that he knew of "no use of the law to punish seditious libels." Nicholas was wrong, as is shown by the Whiting case, and the Oswald and Keteltas cases described below. *See infra* notes 47–69, 76–83 and accompanying text.

43. The case is reported in the Boston *Independent Chronicle*. The indictment, the allegedly libelous publication, and Sullivan's introductory address are reprinted in Independent Chronicle (Boston), Feb. 24, 1791. The arguments of defense counsel appear at *id.*, Mar. 3, 1791, and Mar. 10, 1791.

Chief Justice Francis Dana charged the jury in full accordance with prosecutor Sullivan's argument on the definition of liberty of the press, although Dana informed the jury that he sympathized with the defense of truth even as he noted that he reserved a ruling on the question.[44] The jury's verdict was not guilty, but as the historian of *The Development of Freedom of the Press in Massachusetts* concluded:

> [A] judicial construction of liberty of the press in the state had been announced, differing in no wise from the opinions of Chief Justice Hutchinson in 1768 or of the Superior Court of Judicature in 1724. In effect it was affirmed that the constitutional provision of 1780 was merely declaratory of the law as it had existed for nearly sixty years, with an added prohibition of any possible reestablishment of censorship.[45]

Eight years later, in 1799, Massachusetts convicted an editor of the Boston *Independent Chronicle* for seditious libel.[46]

c. *Oswald.* Politics, not a free press clause, saved Eleazar Oswald of the Philadelphia *Independent Gazetteer* when he challenged the Pennsylvania Supreme Court in 1782.[47] Oswald's newspaper spoke for the state's party that backed the nationalist cause in Congress and sought modification of the state's majoritarian constitution of 1776. The party's leadership, which included James Wilson, John Dickinson, and Robert Morris, contributed to the *Independent Gazetteer* under pen names, but "the public generally knew who the authors were."[48] Nothing in Oswald's credo for a free press prepared readers for his slashing journalism.[49] In his first issue, in which he attempted a "just Definition of the Liberty of the Press," he sounded respectful of the law. "Some contend for an unbounded liberty," he wrote, but not he. An unbounded liberty would turn the freedom of the press "to the worst Purposes, and occasion much more Evil than Good." He did, however, support everyone's right to communicate his sentiments "if delivered with Decency, and under reasonable Regulations."[50]

---

44. Sullivan's closing argument is at *id.*, Mar. 17, 1791, and Dana's charge is at *id.*, Mar. 24, 1791. The trial testimony was not reproduced.

45. C. DUNIWAY, THE DEVELOPMENT OF FREEDOM OF THE PRESS IN MASSACHUSETTS 143 (1906).

46. LEVY, *supra* note 11, at 209–12 (case of T. Adams and A. Adams).

47. *See generally* Teeter, *The Printer and the Chief Justice: Seditious Libel in 1782–83*, 45 JOURNALISM Q. 235 (1968).

48. R. BRUNHOUSE, THE COUNTER-REVOLUTION IN PENNSYLVANIA, 1776–1790, at 5 (1942).

49. On Oswald, see J. WHEELER, THE MARYLAND PRESS, 1777–1790, at 19–36 (1938).

50. Independent Gazetteer (Philadelphia), Apr. 23, 1782. That was the conventional way of acknowledging the common law's restraints. In Teeter, *Decent Animadversions: Notes Toward a History of Free Press Theory*, *reprinted in* NEWSLETTERS TO NEWSPAPERS 237–45 (D. Bond & W. McLeod eds. 1977), Teeter omitted Oswald's

Less than six months after Oswald's first issue, the sheriff arrested him on a warrant from Chief Justice Thomas McKean of the state supreme court. When Oswald accused the court of bias and severity, McKean charged him with having published a "seditious, scandalous, and infamous LIBEL" on the court's administration of justice.[51] Released on bail, Oswald showed his contempt by reprinting the offensive article, by lampooning Judge George Bryan as "that excrescence,"[52] and by damning McKean as another bloody Jefferies.[53] The court rearrested him and raised his bail to one thousand pounds. Oswald wrote to a friend that the chief justice of Pennsylvania had attacked the freedom of the press and that he, Oswald, was "to have a public Trial . . . as a *Libeller*. The infamous English doctrine of Libels being introduced by the more infamous Judges and Lawyers, in an American court."[54] Because Oswald must have heard of precedents such as Zenger's case or McDougall's,[55] his meaning seems unfathomable, but one or two of his contributors repudiated the very concept of seditious libel.[56] So heroic and unprecedented an accomplishment makes Oswald's case memorable.

McKean could order Oswald's arrest but could not try him without an indictment by a grand jury. Although he tried twice, he could not wrest an indictment from that body.[57] Oswald believed that the grand jury thereby rejected "the Doctrine of Libels," but as Judge George Bryan said, writing as "Adrian," witnesses before the grand jury testified that the printer had been misinformed and the grand jury inferred that his mistake involved no guilt. Bryan, the probable author of Pennsylvania's free press clause, believed that

---

rejection of an "unbounded Liberty," leaving the misleading impression that Oswald supported it.

51. Independent Gazetteer, Oct. 15, 1782.

52. *Id.*; see *id.*, Jan. 11, 1783, for Oswald's later account.

53. *See* Teeter, *supra* note 47, at 238.

54. Letter from Oswald to General John Lamb (Nov. 26, 1782) (*quoted in* Teeter, *supra* note 47, at 239). Teeter thought that Oswald's remark showed "disgust with seditious libel" and that "Wilkes" in Independent Gazetteer, Oct. 19, 1782, showed the same disgust. Teeter, *supra* note 47, at 239. Oswald did not use the term or anything like it, nor did "Wilkes," who merely believed that the state constitution vested a right to comment on public proceedings, including the conduct of courts.

55. On *McDougall's Case*, see *infra* notes 85–86 and accompanying text.

56. "Junius Wilkes" in Independent Gazetteer, Nov. 9, 1782; "Candid," in *id.*, Dec. 14, 1782. Teeter, *supra* note 47, at 240 purported to describe "Candid's" views but confused him with "Koster." "Impartial" in Freeman's Journal (Philadelphia), Jan. 1, 1783, mentions Pennsylvania criminal libel prosecutions contradicting Oswald's remark that the doctrine of libels was being introduced in his case.

57. *See* Independent Gazetteer, Dec. 31, 1782; Jan. 1, 1783; Jan. 11, 1783; Jan. 18, 1783; see also EXTRACTS FROM THE DIARY OF JACOB HILTZHEIMER, 1765–1798, at 52–54 (J. Parsons ed. 1893) for remarks by a member of the grand jury; Pennsylvania Gazette (Philadelphia), Jan. 8, 1783, for the grand jury's apologia.

Oswald had seditiously libeled the court.[58] McKean and the grand jury went public with their dispute, dealing mainly with the question of whether the grand jury could interview witnesses not previously approved by the court. It is of interest that Oswald, his lawyer, and the foreman of the grand jury were seen conversing privately in a tavern. Moreover, among the witnesses whom the grand jury interviewed without McKean's approval were major political figures including James Wilson, the lawyer for one of the defendants to whom Oswald had extended his sympathy when he slammed the court for its bias and severity.[59] Oswald's party thus outmaneuvered the court in influencing the grand jury.

The Oswald case shows the Pennsylvania Supreme Court's belief that the constitutional guarantee of a free press was compatible with the doctrine of seditious libel, although two writers and probably others disagreed. The emergence of a sweeping libertarian opinion in Pennsylvania was especially significant and precocious, but infertile. No one anywhere in the nation repeated the thought until the Sedition Act controversy.

Within six years McKean convicted Oswald in *Respublica v. Oswald*.[60] A grand jury more compliant than that of 1782 indicted the editor for a criminal libel. Oswald defended himself in his *Independent Gazetteer*. Alluding to "prejudices . . . against me on the bench,"[61] he appealed to his jury for a fair trial. More out of hope than accuracy, he added, "The doctrine of libels being a doctrine incompatible with law and liberty, and at once destructive of the privileges of a free country in the communication of our thoughts, has not hitherto gained any footing in *Pennsylvania*."[62] He supposed that his fellow citizens would not allow the freedom of the press to be violated "upon any refined pretence . . . which oppressive ingenuity or courtly study can invent."[63]

McKean ordered Oswald's arrest, promptly tried him without a jury, and convicted him for his seditious contempt of the court. The chief justice ruled that "there is nothing in the constitution of this state, respecting the liberty of the press, that has not been authorized by the constitution of that kingdom [England] for near a

58. Freeman's Journal, Jan. 15, 1783, and Jan. 29, 1783 (Bryan as "Adrian").

59. Pennsylvania Gazette, Jan. 29, 1783, for McKean writing as "Jurisperitus." "Aristides," *id.*, Jan. 22, 1783, like Oswald, Independent Gazetteer, Jan. 11, 1783, believed that the grand jury rejected the doctrine of libels. Teeter, *supra* note 47, at 242, makes Aristides reject the law of seditious libel, which Aristides indirectly had mentioned as "the doctrine of criminal libels," while mistakenly observing in passing that Pennsylvania's courts had not received that doctrine.

60. 1 U.S. (1 Dall.) 319 (Pa. 1788).

61. 1 U.S. (1 Dall.) at 320 (quoting Independent Gazetteer, July 1, 1788).

62. *Id.*

63. *Id.*

century past."[64] He also observed that although every man might publish his opinions, the peace and dignity of society required an inquiry into a writer's motives so as to distinguish between publications "which are meant for use and reformation, and with an eye solely to the public good, and those which are intended merely to delude and defame. To the latter description, it is impossible that any good government should afford protection and impunity."[65] Oswald's crime, McKean believed, consisted of his willful attempt to prejudice his jury and corrupt the administration of justice.[66] Oswald received a sentence of one month in prison and a ten pound fine.

Oswald then requested the Pennsylvania Assembly to prefer impeachment charges against McKean and his associates for procedural irregularities and for violating the liberty of the press. William Lewis, who had prosecuted Oswald, defended the judges before the Assembly in a speech endorsing Blackstone's definition of a free press. Lewis concluded that the "dawn of true freedom" had arisen in England with the expiration of the licensing system.[67] Oswald received considerable support for his accusation of procedural irregularities, but no one endorsed his repudiation of the law of criminal libels, although William Findley noted that every person had a right to state his opinion on "public proceedings," and he warned of the danger of allowing judges to punish contempts against themselves. The Assembly resolved that Oswald's charges were groundless.[68] In 1797 McKean, the Jeffersonian chief justice, again ruled that the state's free press clause was merely declaratory of the common law.[69]

d. *The Pennsylvania Constitution.* Pennsylvania adopted a new state constitution in 1790, shortly after it ratified the first amendment.[70] James Wilson drafted the new constitution, the speech and press clause of which explicitly made citizens criminally liable for abuse of that freedom. The new clause, preceding Fox's Libel Act[71] by two years, allowed the jury to decide whether the

---

64. 1 U.S. (1 Dall.) at 322.

65. *Id.* at 325.

66. *Id.* at 326.

67. *Id.* at 331 n.*.

68. The record of the impeachment proceedings appears *id.* at 330–37 n.*. The *Independent Gazetteer* published many articles on Oswald's behalf but not on the free press or criminal libel issue. No Junius Wilkes came forward, as in 1782. The focus in 1788 fell on the procedural irregularities: With no grand jury indictment or jury trial, Oswald was convicted by a judge who had a stake in the outcome of the case.

69. Trial of William Cobbett, *reprinted in* STATE TRIALS OF THE UNITED STATES DURING THE ADMINISTRATIONS OF WASHINGTON AND ADAMS 324–32 (F. Wharton ed. 1849) [hereinafter cited as Wharton].

70. PA. CONST. of 1790, *reprinted in* 5 Thorpe, *supra* note 35, at 3092–103.

71. 32 Geo. 3, ch. 60 (1792).

accused's statement was libelous as a matter of law; it also preceded Lord Campbell's Act of 1843[72] by making truth a defense in a prosecution for criminal libel.[73] Pennsylvania's constitution of 1790 was the first to embody these Zengerian reforms, which unquestionably liberalized the law of libel.

Anderson distorts the 1790 free press clause with a mistaken remark that the state constitution of 1790 was " 'exceedingly reactionary.' "[74] He does not understand that James Alexander, Cato, Father of Candor, and other libertarians whom he approvingly quotes advocated the very reforms that the free press clause of 1790 guaranteed. Anderson later observes that the Federalists of 1789, who framed the first amendment, "were a very different group" from the Federalists of 1798, who adopted the Sedition Act.[75] But the Pennsylvania Federalists of 1790—Wilson, Dickinson, Morris, and company—were among the Framers of the Constitution, who were the Federalists of 1789.

B. *Whether Parliamentary Privilege Had Become Ineffective*

The power of the legislature to punish for breach of parliamentary privilege had not become ineffective by the time of the Revolution, contrary to Anderson.[76] It remained a vital power, usable when the occasion warranted, as the Keteltas case demonstrated. In 1796 William Keteltas published blistering criticisms of the New York Assembly in the newspapers. The Assembly, smarting from his censure, which it took to be seditious, summoned him to appear before its bar. Keteltas admitted authorship of the offensive arti-

---

72. 6 & 7 Vict., ch. 96 (1843).

73. 2 J. STEPHEN, A HISTORY OF THE CRIMINAL LAW OF ENGLAND 343–84 (1883). Previously, the law of criminal libel allowed the jury to decide only whether the accused had in fact made the statement alleged, leaving to the judge the right to decide as a matter of law whether the statement was libelous. Furthermore, truth was not a defense because the greater the truth, the greater the provocation and therefore the greater the libel.

74. Anderson, *supra* note 14, at 490 n.211 (quoting J. SELSAM, THE PENNSYLVANIA CONSTITUTION OF 1776, at 259 (1971)).

75. *Id.* at 518. The Sedition Act of 1798 also recognized truth as a defense and the power of the jury to return a general verdict. Until 1798 libertarians relied completely on the Zenger defense, which did not repudiate the crime of seditious libel.

76. *Id.* at 513–14, relying on Teeter, A Legacy of Suppression: Philadelphia Newspapers and Congress During the War for Independence, 1775–1783 (unpublished dissertation, University of Wisconsin, 1966) [hereinafter cited as Teeter, Legacy of Suppression], shows that the Philadelphia newspapers freely attacked the Continental Congress and public measures and officials of Pennsylvania. Anderson fails to add Teeter's explanation of the reason that newspapers enjoyed a practical "immunity" from prosecution. The Continental Congress had no power to punish its critics, and, as for attacks on government in state politics, "Powerful men or men with powerful friends wrote for the newspapers. Political power helped to shield the printers from punishment." Teeter, *Press Freedom and the Public Printing: Pennsylvania, 1775–83*, 45 JOURNALISM Q. 445, 448–49 (1968); *see also id.* at 449 n.28 (Congress).

cles. The Assembly promptly and without debate found him guilty of a breach of parliamentary privilege. When Keteltas refused to humble himself by admitting his wrong and asking pardon, the Assembly immediately ordered him jailed.[77]

The case presented a perfect opportunity for a libertarian argument in defense of Keteltas. Representative John Bird, a Republican member of the Assembly, raised the issue in the right terms: "[S]hall we attempt to prevent citizens from *thinking*, from giving their *opinion* on the acts of the legislature? *Shall we stop the freedom of the press?*"[78] Bird spoke in vain; his questions were ignored. Although Keteltas became a popular hero among the Jeffersonian faithful in New York, and his case became a *cause celebre*, freedom of the press and the right of a citizen to criticize the government played no part in the extensive arguments on Keteltas' behalf. Not even Keteltas himself, an experienced politician and lawyer, spoke to the issue, although while in prison he published five articles protesting the "unconstitutional, tyrannical, and illegal" proceedings of the Assembly.[79] He based his defense on the narrow argument that he had not breached any of the privileges of the house and that the house could not lawfully deprive any citizen of his liberty without benefit of grand jury proceedings and trial by jury.

An anonymous supporter of Keteltas signing himself "Camillus Junius," possibly Brockholst Livingston, acknowledged that verbal insults to the house "ought not to pass unpunished."[80] The proper remedy, he said, was a jury trial that protected the rights of the accused:

> The Courts of criminal jurisdiction are open to prosecutions, which the Attorney General may commence by information or indictment. A libel tending to asperse or vilify the house of Assembly or any of its members, may be as severely punished in the Supreme Court, as a libel against government. This, then, . . . is the remedy they should appeal to . . . .[81]

Keteltas, freed on a writ of habeas corpus as soon as the legislature ended its session, brought an unsuccessful suit for false imprisonment against the speaker of the house. The Assembly supported its speaker by a vote of 88 to 1, and the court ruled

77. For the best discussion of the Keteltas case, see A. YOUNG, THE DEMOCRATIC REPUBLICANS OF NEW YORK 480–93 (1967). *See also* JOURNAL OF THE VOTES AND PROCEEDINGS OF THE GENERAL ASSEMBLY OF NEW YORK, 19th Sess. (March 8, 1796); Greenleaf's New York Journal and Patriotic Register (N.Y.), Mar. 11, 1796 [hereinafter cited as New York Journal].

78. New York Journal, Mar. 11, 1796 (emphasis in original).

79. The Argus, or Greenleaf's New Daily Advertiser (N.Y.), Apr. 4, 1796; Apr. 5, 1796; Apr. 7, 1796; Apr. 8, 1796; Apr. 12, 1796 [hereinafter cited as The Argus].

80. The Argus, Mar. 15, 1796, *reprinted in* LEVY, *supra* note 30, at 165.

81. *Id.*

against Keteltas.[82] Four years later the Senate of the United States found that a printer's allegedly seditious publication constituted a "high breach of privileges."[83]

Anderson confuses the facts about parliamentary privilege cases, which he knows about only from *Legacy of Suppression*. The Massachusetts House did not release Daniel Fowle because public opinion opposed the legislative power to imprison for seditiousness; it released him because public opinion, according to Fowle, demanded merciful consideration for his sick wife. More important, Fowle never referred to liberty of the press or to any aspect of free discussion.[84] Likewise, Anderson wholly misreads the Alexander McDougall case of New York, 1770–1771, a case that strongly illustrated the power of the legislature to do as it pleased with citizens who published offensive remarks.[85] George Clinton, one of McDougall's few supporters in the legislature, remarked that the legislature could throw him out the window if it pleased.[86] Although public opinion probably supported McDougall, Anderson alleges that it did so because it opposed the legislative power to punish for seditious contempts. There is no basis for that allegation.[87] The cases of Pride in Virginia,[88] Husband in North Carolina,[89] Powell in South Carolina,[90] McDougall in New York, and Rome in Rhode Island[91] prove that the power to punish for breach of parliamentary privilege was still effective on the eve of the Revolution.

C. *Whether Principled Opposition Existed to the Law of Seditious Libel*

Political resistance to royal authority underlay the public opposition in Massachusetts to indictments of patriot writers. Ander-

82. The Time Piece (N.Y.), Dec. 22, 1797.

83. SMITH, *supra* note 2, at 294 (case of William Duane).

84. LEVY, *supra* note 11, at 39–41. *Cf.* Anderson, *supra* note 14, at 511–12.

85. *See* LEVY, *supra* note 11, at 78–85.

86. NEW YORK GENERAL ASSEMBLY, JOURNAL OF VOTES AND PROCEEDINGS OF THE GENERAL ASSEMBLY OF THE COLONY OF NEW YORK, 1769–1771, at 8 (Albany 1820).

87. *See* LEVY, *supra* note 11, at 78–83.

88. JOURNALS OF THE HOUSE OF BURGESSES OF VIRGINIA, 1766–1769, at 91, 97, 98–99, 100, 110, 120–21, 125 (J. Kennedy ed. 1906).

89. *See* LEVY, *supra* note 11, at 75–76. Anderson, *supra* note 14, at 511, reports only that grand juries would not indict Husband, but not that the House expelled him from membership and held him in jail.

90. *See* LEVY, *supra* note 11, at 76–78. Anderson, *supra* note 14, at 511 n.318, reports that the Assembly challenged the Council's authority to punish for breach of parliamentary privilege but not that the Assembly used Powell's case to advance its own in an intramural struggle with the Council. Each house protested against the other. The Assembly denied that the Council was a parliamentary body thus to augment its own powers, not to protect freedom of the press.

91. *See* L. LEVY, ORIGINS OF THE FIFTH AMENDMENT 413 (1968).

son, however, sees "principled opposition to seditious libel" on the part of the public, which, he alleges, was "hostile to the use of seditious libel by its own elected representatives in the Assembly."[92] Such an assertion cannot be taken seriously.

If a grand jury refused to indict, Anderson sees principled opposition to the law of seditious libel, not an insufficiency of evidence, or popular support for a local factional leader, or a grand jury intimidated by patriot mobs. If a trial jury refused to convict, Anderson sees principled hostility to the law of seditious libel, not a reasonable doubt of guilt or a belief that truth should be a defense to a charge of libel. If a legislature jailed a seditious libeler, Anderson sees his release, when the legislature is no longer in session and without further authority to hold the libeler in prison, as principled opposition and a victory for public opinion.[93]

Anderson, who is supposedly proving that by the time of the Revolution public opinion had rendered the legislative power to imprison for seditious insults ineffective, hedges his bets by concluding that anything that happened before 1776 does not really count (unless he wants to use it).[94] It does not count, we belatedly learn, because state constitutional provisions protecting freedom of the press did not yet exist. But the evidence before 1776 must count because the significant issue is what the concept of freedom of the press meant to Americans. In the absence of evidence to the contrary, the conceptual meaning of freedom of the press did not change in 1776 from its earlier meaning at the time of Fowle's case in 1754 or McDougall's in 1770–1771. If the pre-1776 evidence is not relevant, Anderson should not produce the testimony of the colonial period from *Cato's Letters*, Zenger's defense, James Alexander, Father of Candor, and the Quebec declaration.[95]

1. The Massachusetts Radicals

As for the supposed opposition to the doctrine of seditious libel by the Massachusetts radicals during the controversy with England, one of their leaders, John Adams, defiantly urged in the columns of the *Boston Gazette* in 1765 that its editors should fearlessly publish "with the utmost freedom, whatever can be warranted by the laws of your country"[96]—no rejection of the doctrine of seditious libel. The same newspaper, the mouthpiece of the radicals, told its readers in 1767, "Political liberty consists in a freedom of speech and

92. Anderson, *supra* note 14, at 512.

93. *Id.* at 510–13.

94. *See id.* at 512–13.

95. *Id.* at 463–64, 488–89, 491–92, 509–12, 523–28.

96. Boston Gazette (Boston), August 1765, *reprinted in* 3 THE WORKS OF JOHN ADAMS 447–64 (C.F. Adams 2d ed. 1865) (1st ed. Boston 1850) [hereinafter cited as ADAMS].

action, so far as the laws of a community will permit, and no farther: all beyond is criminal, and tends to the destruction of Liberty itself."[97] Joseph Warren and Samuel Adams toasted a grand jury for vindicating the freedom of the press—not because the jury rejected the doctrine of seditious libel, but because it rejected "the absurd doctrine, *the more true, the more libellous*."[98] In his *Novanglus* letters, John Adams in 1774 censured "the scandalous license of the tory presses,"[99] and though he differed with Governor Thomas Hutchinson on what words constituted abuse of the press, he and Hutchinson agreed on the fundamental principle that abuse of the press, as each understood it, existed apart from true liberty of the press.[100] By early 1776 Adams proposed that making adherence to the independence movement the legal test of loyalty would have the beneficial result of stopping "unfriendly" newspapers, and then "[t]he presses will produce no more seditious or traitorous speculations. Slanders upon public men and measures will be lessened."[101] Adams did not disagree with Blackstone about the criminality of seditious libel, but only as to the particular words that constituted the crime. Twenty-two years later President Adams acted consistently when he signed the Sedition Act and urged prosecutions under it.

2. The Quebec Declaration

The Quebec declaration of the Continental Congress in 1774 made a strong statement about the functions of a free press, as Anderson points out three times,[102] but he neglects to inform readers that the Quebec declaration endorsed only the diffusion of "liberal" sentiments on the administration of government. The Committee of Inspection for Newport, Rhode Island, which included the censorship and intimidation of printers among its duties, demonstrated the American understanding of the Quebec declaration by invoking it as justification for boycotting printers who diffused illiberal or "wrong sentiments respecting the measures now carrying on for the recovery and establishment of our rights."[103] In 1776 Congress

97. Boston Gazette, March 9, 1767, *reprinted in* LEVY, *supra* note 30, at 95.

98. J. QUINCY, REPORTS OF CASES ARGUED AND ADJUDGED IN THE SUPERIOR COURT OF JUDICATURE OF THE PROVINCE OF MASSACHUSETTS BAY, BETWEEN 1761 AND 1772, at 278 (reissued 1969) (1st ed. Boston 1865) [hereinafter cited as REPORTS OF CASES] (emphasis in original).

99. 4 ADAMS, *supra* note 96, at 32.

100. For Hutchinson's views, which were like Blackstone's, see REPORTS OF CASES, *supra* note 98, at 244–45, 263, *discussed in* LEVY, *supra* note 11, at 67–70.

101. Letter to J. Winthrop, June 23, 1776, *reprinted in* 9 ADAMS, *supra* note 96, at 409.

102. Anderson, *supra* note 14, at 463–64, 490–91, 523–24.

103. LEVY, *supra* note 11, at 177 (quoting 2 AMERICAN ARCHIVES CONSISTING OF A COLLECTION OF AUTHENTIC RECORDS 12–13 (P. Force ed. 4th ser. 1839)).

urged that the states enact legislation to prevent people from being "deceived and drawn into erroneous opinion."[104] The Quebec declaration at its time was propaganda, and Anderson himself uses it as propaganda.

3. Oswald's Case

When I wrote *Legacy of Suppression* I discovered not a single instance of anyone prior to the ratification of the first amendment advocating that the law of seditious libel conflicted with free government or with political liberty. *Legacy of Suppression* produced a generation of critics, but only one, Dwight L. Teeter, discovered that such libertarian advocacy existed before 1791. When Oswald's case agitated Pennsylvania in 1782, according to Teeter, several newspaper articles, all signed with pen names, showed that their authors rejected the law of seditious libel.[105] Teeter broke new ground, although he made mistakes and exaggerated the extent of his discovery. Only two writers, one signing himself "Junius Wilkes" and the other "Candid," took the position ascribed to them by Teeter.[106] Chief Justice McKean, not "Junius Wilkes" or "Candid," authoritatively described the law of Pennsylvania on the meaning of freedom of the press in 1782. McKean did so again in Blackstonian terms in 1788, on the occasion of the second Oswald case,[107] and still again in 1799, when Pennsylvania prosecuted William Cobbett.[108] When McKean imprisoned Oswald in 1788 for his seditious contempt, and the printer again declared that the chief justice had violated his freedom of the press, the Philadelphia newspapers printed no articles supporting Oswald on that point. The pseudononymous views of "Junius Wilkes" and "Candid" had

104. LEVY, *supra* note 11, at 181 (quoting 4 JOURNALS OF THE CONTINENTAL CONGRESS 18 (W. Ford ed. 1906)).

105. Teeter, *supra* note 47, at 239–41.

106. *See supra* notes 54–57 for some of Teeter's errors. He attributed to "Koster" the views of "Candid," a genuine radical. "Koster," "Aristides," and "Wilkes" did not repudiate the doctrine of seditious libel. Nor did Francis Bailey, the editor of Philadelphia's *Freeman's Journal*. Teeter mistakenly believed that the principles of the Zenger defense—truth as a defense to the charge of libel and the right of the jury to decide the criminality of the words—repudiated the doctrine of seditious libel. He also believed that the free press clause of the Pennsylvania Constitution of 1776 was incompatible with Blackstonianism, and therefore alleged that Bailey contradicted himself because he invoked the free press clause's protection of an unrestrained press yet endorsed the law of seditious libel. *See* Teeter, *supra* note 50, at 241. Bailey had no quarrel with that law, as shown by his credo in Freeman's Journal, June 13, 1782. Anderson, relying on Teeter for far more than Teeter proves, cautiously says that Bailey did not repudiate the law of seditious libel "altogether." Anderson, *supra* note 14, at 527. Bailey did not repudiate it at all. Without the support of Teeter, or, rather, supported only by "Junius Wilkes" and "Candid," whom Anderson did not read except in Teeter, a substantial section of Anderson's argument dies.

107. *See supra* text accompanying notes 60–69.

108. Trial of Cobbett, *reprinted in* Wharton, *supra* note 69, at 323.

fallen on barren ground. Not later referred to or repeated in substance or in name, they were as dead as yesterday's newspaper; they surely did not represent a significant sector of public opinion.

4. Cato

Anderson also declares that *Cato's Letters*, the influential essays that originally appeared in the *London Journal* in 1720, "objected to seditious libel."[109] Anderson mistakenly believes that because Cato advocated truth as a defense and a rule providing that any ambiguity in a publication should be construed as revealing an innocent intent, Cato "repudiated the existing common law of seditious libel."[110] But elsewhere in his article Anderson accurately recognizes that truth as a defense scarcely modified Blackstonian principles.[111] The Sedition Act of 1798 required a showing of malicious intent and allowed the defense of truth, yet was Blackstonian at its core. Zengerian principles and the law of seditious libel harmonized.

Moreover, for all his criticisms of the enforcement of that law, Cato declared that he did not wish to be misunderstood as arguing for the uncontrolled liberty of men to calumniate each other or the government. As to "Libels against Government, like all others, they are always base and unlawful,"[112] especially when untrue, and should be punished as an abuse of liberty so long as England's "very good Laws" were "prudently and honestly executed, which I really believe they have for the most part been since the Revolution."[113] In a related essay, Cato reinforced the thought, saying, "I do agree, when the natural and genuine Meaning and Purport of Words and Expressions in libellous Writings carry a criminal Intention, that the Writer ought not to escape Punishment by Subterfuge or Evasion . . . ."[114] Cato did not condemn the doctrine of seditious libel, did not call it a Star Chamber doctrine, which it was, and did not advocate an overt acts test or immunity for political opinions.[115]

109. That is, to the *law* of seditious libel. Anderson, *supra* note 14, at 526. "Cato" was John Trenchard and Thomas (not William) Gordon, joint authors of CATO'S LETTERS: OR, ESSAYS ON LIBERTY, CIVIL AND RELIGIOUS (6th ed. 1755) [hereinafter cited as CATO'S LETTERS].

110. Anderson, *supra* note 14, at 526.

111. *Id.* at 528–29 n.414.

112. 1 CATO'S LETTERS, *supra* note 109, at 250 ("Reflections upon Libelling").

113. 3 *id.* at 299 ("Discourse upon Libels").

114. *Id.* at 302–03 ("Second Discourse upon Libels").

115. Anderson mauls my treatment of Cato, which he finds "perplexing." Anderson, *supra* note 14, at 525 n.395. I myself was perplexed by his presentation of it until I compared what he says I said with what I actually said, and discovered that his presentation was inaccurate. Anderson says, "Levy implies that Cato approved of libel prosecutions under some circumstances, yet he recognizes that Cato's approval of good libel laws 'prudently and honestly executed' was merely a 'genuflection toward the law—keeping Cato on the safe side.' " *Id.* This is what I said: "But it was abundantly clear,

5. Cushing and Adams

Anderson also contends that the opinion of Chief Justice William Cushing of Massachusetts, expressed in a letter to John Adams in 1789, suggests "that the American view of freedom of the press was not Blackstone's."[116] That is false. Anderson quotes Cushing as saying that the free press clause of the Massachusetts Constitution "must exclude *subsequent* restraints, as much as *previous restraints*,"[117] a quotation that is out of context and deceiving. If Anderson read the entire Cushing-Adams correspondence, which I made available in two books,[118] and if he read five pages of my commentary on that text, he knows that Cushing meant to exclude from subsequent punishment only defendants who could prove the truth of their alleged libels. Cushing also said, "When the press is made the vehicle of falsehood and scandal, let the authors be punished with becoming rigour."[119] In connection with the Cushing–Adams correspondence, Anderson concedes that truth as a defense constituted "only a minor (and generally ineffectual) modification of Blackstonian principles."[120] That concession contradicts his view that Cushing repudiated subsequent restraint or represented a dissenting tradition that repudiated Blackstonianism.

Although he knows that Adams and Cushing both supported the Sedition Act of 1798, Anderson adds that both nevertheless recognized the inadequacy of Blackstonianism. Apparently, a point requires emphasis: The Sedition Act embodied Zengerian reforms, and in that sense, it was the epitome of everything eighteenth-century libertarians had fought for. They had advocated that a defendant charged with seditious libel should have the opportunity of

---

notwithstanding this genuflection toward the law—keeping Cato on the safe side—that he thought the law of criminal libel was neither good nor prudently executed, indeed that it was quite dangerous to public liberty and good government." LEVY, *supra* note 11, at 119. Also, Anderson concludes, "Levy dismisses Cato as a 'flashing star . . . .' " Anderson, *supra* note 14, at 527. I hardly think that I *dismiss* Cato, whose work I feature as the leading libertarian statement on freedom of the press in the eighteenth century on either side of the Atlantic, until the Sedition Act forced Americans to repudiate the law of seditious libel. *Legacy* is devoted to Cato. *See* LEVY, *supra* note 11, at 115–21. LEVY, *supra* note 30, at 10–24, reprints Cato on freedom of the press and libel law as presented to Americans by Zenger's press. The copy of *Cato's Letters* used by Anderson and wrongly dated 1791 rather than 1971—the first reprint of the work since 1755—was produced under my general editorship. Cato is a favorite of mine, and my saying that he was far ahead of his time is no dismissal. It was I who said Cato was "adored, quoted, and plagiarized" in America. LEVY, *supra* note 30, at xxvi. This is important because Anderson says I disparage Cato's importance in America and dismiss him because he was English. On the overt acts test, see *infra* note 206.

116. Anderson, *supra* note 14, at 528.

117. *Id.* (quoting letter from William Cushing to John Adams (Feb. 18, 1789), *reprinted in* LEVY, *supra* note 30, at 150 (emphasis Cushing's)).

118. LEVY, *supra* note 11, at 193–96; LEVY, *supra* note 30, at 147–53.

119. LEVY, *supra* note 11, at 194–95.

120. Anderson, *supra* note 14, at 529 n.414.

proving the truth of his statements and that if the jury believed him, he should be acquitted. The Sedition Act guaranteed truth as a defense and the jury's power to return a general verdict. The statute also accepted the crux of the Blackstonian concept of criminal responsibility for publishing seditious libel. Thus, the acceptance of Zenger meant the acceptance of Blackstone. The Zenger defense had not rejected the crime of seditious libel.

The frail protection offered to freedom of the press by the Cushing–Adams proposals of 1789 manifested itself when only one Sedition Act jury returned a verdict of acquittal.[121] The Sedition Act juries, like Cushing and Adams, shared a belief in the predominant doctrine that opinions can criminally assault government. To be sure, those opinions had to be malicious and false, but the law of seditious libel, even modified, implied an extremely narrow concept of freedom of the press.

A final observation must be made about the Cushing–Adams correspondence: It is not a dependable revelation of the intention underlying constitutional guarantees of freedom of the press or speech. Cushing and Adams were proposing, not disposing. They were not representing the constitutional law of Massachusetts as of 1789 or for many years thereafter.[122] As Cushing's bewilderment about the meaning of the state's free press clause[123] showed and as his comment that the questions he raised had never been decided[124] also showed, he clearly did not expose the general understanding of that clause's meaning in the minds of the 1780 convention that framed it. Cushing had been at that convention; Adams actually had written the first draft. Adams agreed in 1789 that it "would be" better to construe the clause as Cushing suggested, namely that "truth of fact" should be a defense to a charge of criminal libel. The two were discussing an "innovation," the word Adams used, exactly as Madison had, to describe the defense of truth.[125]

6. Madison

Madison is Anderson's last and "most important dissenter" on his list of those who supposedly repudiated the concept of seditious libel.[126] Indeed Madison did, as I explained at length in *Legacy of Suppression*, but he did not do so until 1799, after the Sedition Act had radicalized his thinking and produced a new libertarian system

121. SMITH, *supra* note 2, at 185.

122. *See* LEVY, *supra* note 11, at 212 n.72. Commonwealth v. Blanding, 20 Mass. (3 Pick.) 304, 313 (1825), still interpreted freedom of the press in Blackstonian terms.

123. *See* LEVY, *supra* note 11, at 193–95.

124. LEVY, *supra* note 30, at 149.

125. *See infra* text accompanying note 144.

126. Anderson, *supra* note 14, at 529.

of thought.[127] Madison's views of 1799 were ad hoc in nature, not reflections of a position that he had held in 1789. If his statements in his great *Virginia Report* of 1799–1800 can be admitted as evidence of prior belief, so can the later beliefs of other Framers and their allies, such as John Adams, William Cushing, Samuel Chase, Oliver Ellsworth, James Iredell, Alexander Hamilton, John Marshall, William Paterson, and many others who believed not only in a Blackstonian understanding of the freedom of the press but even in the constitutionality of the Sedition Act of 1798.

Anderson's treatment of Madison's views might not warrant further consideration because at one point he completely agrees with me: "[I]t is true that he [Madison] never articulated a 'libertarian' theory of freedom of the press until the Sedition Act controversy."[128] But Anderson also states that Madison asserted in his 1799–1800 *Report* "not only that the press clause superseded the common law, but that it was so understood in the First Congress."[129] Anderson then adds that if my view is to be accepted, "We must believe that Madison in 1799 misrepresented (or misunderstood) his own views of ten years earlier,"[130] and in a footnote says, "Levy never explains why Madison, in 1799, would misstate his own views of 1789."[131] I have never explained because Madison did not misstate or misrepresent his earlier views. Anderson misunderstands him. Anderson's authority for Madison's earlier views, which are supposed to be similar to his views of 1799, is my abridgment of Madison's *Virginia Report*. Anderson does not quote from the *Report* to prove his point, because he cannot prove it. Madison wrote as follows:

> To these observations, one fact will be added, which demonstrates that the common law cannot be admitted as the *universal* expositor of American terms, which may be the same with those contained in that law. The freedom of conscience, and of religion, are found in the same instruments which assert the freedom of the press. It will never be admitted, that the meaning of the former, in the common law of England, is to limit their meaning in the United States.[132]

I do not read that passage to be a declaration that the First Congress understood the press clause to supersede the common law. On the contrary, Madison is saying that the religious liberty clause should not be construed in common law terms. Neither in the pas-

127. LEVY, *supra* note 11, at 273–82.

128. Anderson, *supra* note 14, at 531.

129. *Id.*

130. *Id.* at 535.

131. *Id.* at 535 n.446.

132. J. MADISON, VIRGINIA REPORT OF 1799–1800, *reprinted in* LEVY, *supra* note 30, at 216–17.

sage quoted nor in any other does Madison refer to the understanding of the free press clause by the First Congress. Earlier in the *Report*, when Madison discusses the common law meaning of freedom of the press, he does not even imply that the First Congress had a different understanding, because nowhere in the *Report* does he mention what the First Congress understood the free press clause or the concept of freedom of the press to mean. In addition to misreading Madison's *Report*, Anderson uncritically accepts Vincent Blasi's assertion that in 1789, when recommending the proposition that became the first amendment, Madison had outlined his theory of liberty upon which his later *Report* was based.[133] But Madison's great speech introducing the proposals that became the Bill of Rights did not in any way bear out the contention that his views of 1799 on the free press clause were like those of 1789. All of Blasi's quotations and paraphrases from Madison come from the *Report* of 1799–1800.[134] Blasi produces no proof of his assertion by comparing what Madison said in 1789 with what he said ten years later. Until that proof is produced, Blasi and Anderson will convince only those who assume the infallibility of their words. Madison did not even discuss or explain his free press proposal in 1789. The issue is not whether in 1789 Madison believed that Congress had no power to legislate on the press; it is, rather, the meaning of the concept of freedom of the press, of seditious libel, and of the continuing validity of the common law—Madison addressed none of these in 1789.

D. *What the Framers Meant by "Freedom of the Press"*

I have taken the view that the Framers must have understood the concept of the freedom of the press in the conventional Blackstonian sense, because any novel understanding would have required some explanation.[135] Neither the legislative history[136] nor

---

133. Blasi states:

> In attempting to assess the original understanding of the First Amendment, it is important that Madison articulated as early as 1789 the theory of liberty on which he based his Virginia Report of 1799–1800. This fact casts some doubt on the thesis advanced by Professor Levy that a libertarian theory of freedom of speech was not accepted at the time the First Amendment was adopted and only emerged 10 years later as a result of the political jockeying over the Alien and Sedition Acts of 1798.

Blasi, *The Checking Value in First Amendment Theory*, AM. B. FOUND. RESEARCH J. 521, 535–36 n.60 (1977).

134. *Id.* at nn.58–66 and accompanying text constitutes the questionable material. Although none of Blasi's Madison sources is from 1789, the reader cannot know that fact from Blasi's footnotes, which do not identify the document from which Blasi is quoting. Anderson, *supra* note 14, at 510 n.308, attributes a statement by Madison to 1789, but the source which Anderson cites in that note clearly shows that the date was 1800.

135. *See* LEVY, *supra* note 11, at 225.

the debate on the ratification of the Constitution revealed a novel understanding of freedom of the press, a fact that Anderson does not contest. However, he states that my reasoning is "dubious" because the "Bill of Rights contained numerous provisions that had no established common law meanings—the establishment clause, the free exercise clause, and the due process clause, to name the most obvious. Yet there is no record of any debate about the meaning of these either."[137] What seems obvious is that Anderson is confused. The term "due process of law" had an established common law meaning that derived from English history going back to

136. Anderson relies heavily on the legislative history of the first amendment's free press clause. A quarter of his article describes that legislative history, which he alleges casts doubt on "the Levy interpretation." Anderson, *supra* note 14, at 494. He also declares that the legislative history has been ignored because it is inconsistent with the conclusions of my work. *Id.* at 534. That is an equally unsupportable judgment. The legislative history of the clause is consistent with my interpretation; if the two had conflicted, someone during the past quarter of a century eagerly would have exposed the conflict. We now have only Anderson's ipse dixit that the conflict exists, not proof that it does.

I did not ignore the legislative history, nor did my predecessors. Francis N. Thorpe and David Matteson had reviewed it when tracing the framing of the Bill of Rights, and Milton Konvitz had focused on the framing of the first amendment. 2 F. THORPE, THE CONSTITUTIONAL HISTORY OF THE UNITED STATES 199–263 (1901); Matteson, *The Organization of the Government under the Constitution*, in S. BLOOM, HISTORY OF THE FORMATION OF THE UNION UNDER THE CONSTITUTION 294–328 (1943); M. KONVITZ, FUNDAMENTAL LIBERTIES OF A FREE PEOPLE 345–61 (1957). Anderson used no sources that I and the others had not used; he has not discovered anything. In fact he has grossly inflated the importance of the legislative history of the free press clause. Having reviewed it for 22 pages—more fully, to be sure, than anyone previously—he concludes, "The legislative history of the press clause is, of course, inconclusive . . . because the Framers simply did not articulate what they meant by 'freedom of the press,'" and "there is no record whatever of the meanings ascribed to the amendment by the ratifying legislatures." Anderson, *supra* note 14, at 486. Therefore, any doubt cast on my view is based on Anderson's presuppositions, not on the legislative history. On one matter concerning the legislative history I concede a point to Anderson. When the free press clause was before the Senate, a motion was made and defeated to protect freedom of the press "in as ample a manner as hath at any time been secured by the common law." In *Legacy* I remarked that we do not know whether the Senate defeated that motion "on the ground that it was too narrow, too broad, or simply unnecessary." LEVY, *supra* note 11, at 224. Anderson argues that it could not have been too broad. I agree, but not for his reason, that there were broader views "in the air." Anderson, *supra* note 14, at 500. I have breathed the air deeply and detect only the aroma of "Junius Wilkes" and "Candid." *See supra* notes 56, 108–09. We do not know why the proposer of the motion in the Senate said "in as ample a manner as hath at any time been secured by the common law" instead of "as secured by the common law." He may have had Zengerian principles in mind. He may have identified the common law, as so many Americans did, with a system of law that protected personal liberties and restrained government. His motion need not be read in narrow Blackstonian terms, which is why I guessed that the Senate could have defeated it because it was too broad; but the chances are greater that the motion was defeated because the Senate believed that it was too narrow or unnecessary.

137. Anderson, *supra* note 14, at 486 n.192.

1354.[138] The unique American experience with establishments of religion and religious liberty had produced a general understanding of the meaning of establishments and free exercise. America never had an establishment of religion in the European sense of a national church or a formal union between a nation state and a single church, with that church alone enjoying financial support and special privileges denied to all other churches.[139] By 1789 America understood the term "establishment of religion" to mean government aid to religion, whether on an impartial or preferential basis.[140]

Experience also supplied a widespread understanding of the meaning of the free exercise clause, namely that people could believe what they wanted about religion and that, within reason, the state ought not to command what conscience prohibits nor prohibit what conscience commands. The term "free exercise" of religion had an American history going back to the Maryland Toleration Act of 1649.[141] Given the American experience with religious liberty and establishments of religion, no one could have believed that the first amendment incorporated the common law meaning or any meaning other than that dictated by experience.

By contrast, the free press clause, like the due process clause, had only an established common law meaning: freedom to speak, write, and publish as one pleased, subject to subsequent punishment for being too offensive. If the first amendment's free press clause comprehended another meaning, what could it have been? Two other meanings were possible, one deriving from the Zenger case and the other from a repudiation of seditious libel's core concept that government can be criminally assaulted by words alone.

The compatibility of the Zenger defense and the common law

138. *See* R. MOTT, DUE PROCESS OF LAW 1–24 (1926); *see generally* Jurow, *Untimely Thoughts: A Reconsideration of the Origins of the Due Process of Law*, 19 AM. J. LEGAL HIST. 265 (1975).

139. In the five southern colonies the Church of England had been legally established, but no state church existed in the other colonies. Five (Rhode Island, Pennsylvania, Delaware, New Jersey, and New York) never had any kind of establishment, and the remaining three (Massachusetts, Connecticut, and New Hampshire) had uniquely American dual establishments by the 1730's. After the Revolution the only establishments of religion in the United States were multiple establishments, which were unknown to England or Europe: the public support of several different churches or of all with preference to none. Six states (Massachusetts, Connecticut, New Hampshire, Maryland, South Carolina, and Georgia) allowed multiple establishments, and no establishment existed in the other seven states.

140. *See generally* L. LEVY, *No Establishment of Religion: The Original Understanding*, in JUDGMENTS: ESSAYS ON AMERICAN CONSTITUTIONAL HISTORY 169 (1972).

141. *See generally* S. COBB, THE RISE OF RELIGIOUS LIBERTY IN AMERICA (1902). On the Maryland Toleration Act, see DOCUMENTS IN AMERICAN HISTORY 31–32 (H. Commager ed. 1949).

is clear from the Pennsylvania press clause of 1790. Notwithstanding its recognition of truth as a defense to a charge of libel and its recognition of the power of a jury to decide the criminality of a publication, Anderson properly interprets the Pennsylvania clause as Blackstonian because it stipulated the responsibility of anyone abusing the liberty of the press.[142] Thus, even if the principles of the Zenger defense had received widespread acceptance at the time of the framing of the first amendment, the free press clause still incorporated a Blackstonian meaning. In 1789, however, those principles of 1735 were still controversial and were not yet established.

In 1788, for example, when urging Madison to add a bill of rights to the proposed Constitution, Jefferson stated, "A declaration that the federal government will never restrain the presses from printing any thing they please, will not take away the liability of the printers for false facts printed."[143] The phrasing shows Jefferson's belief that a free press guarantee did not foreclose subsequent punishment for abuse of the press; Jefferson accepted the crux of Blackstone on criminal libels. Madison, who construed Jefferson's recommendation in its most favorable light, observed in reply, "The Exemption of the press from liability in every case for *true facts* is also an innovation and as such ought to be well considered."[144] The remark shows that after half of a century the principle of the Zenger defense was still an "innovation." On consideration, Madison did not add the truth-as-a-defense principle to the amendment that he proposed to Congress. Jefferson thought that Madison's free press proposal was too broad and urged its alteration to exclude freedom to publish "false facts . . . affecting the peace of the confederacy with foreign nations."[145] In a political dispute such as that triggered by Jay's Treaty, Jefferson's proposal, if adopted, could have had suppressive effects.

As for the repudiation of the law of seditious libel, an intention to supersede the doctrine does not emerge from the legislative history of the free press clause. Furthermore, at a time when truth as a defense, a mere modification of the common law, was still an innovation, the constitutional guarantee of freedom of the press hardly could have meant that the common law on seditious libel had been superseded, as Anderson contends. A free press clause without the law of seditious libel would have emancipated all political opinions. If Madison had been bent on revolutionizing the common law of

142. Anderson, *supra* note 14, at 488, 490 n.211.

143. Letter to Madison, July 31, 1788, *reprinted in* 13 PAPERS OF THOMAS JEFFERSON 442 (J. Boyd ed. 1950).

144. 6 *id.* at 316 (remarks on Jefferson's draft of a constitution for Virginia, *ca.* Oct. 15, 1788) (emphasis in original).

145. 15 *id.* at 367 (to Madison, Aug. 28, 1789).

seditious libel, he hardly would have written privately that he was engaged in "the nauseous project of amendments" whose main objective was "to kill the opposition every where,"[146] and he would not have told the House that "if we confine ourselves to an enumeration of simple acknowledged principles, the ratification will meet with but little difficulty. Amendments of a doubtful nature will have a tendency to prejudice the whole system . . . ."[147]

E. *What the Framers Meant by "Congress Shall Make No Law"*

In 1789 when Madison proposed a free press clause to Congress, he neglected to use language recommended by the Virginia ratifying convention that the freedom of the press "cannot be cancelled, abridged, restrained, or modified, by any authority of the United States."[148] Compared to the formulation of the finished amendment, "Congress shall make no law," Virginia's more comprehensive version would have applied to the President and federal judiciary, making impossible a federal common law of seditious libel or other abridgments by the executive or the courts. But Anderson diminishes the importance of the Virginia phrase "by any authority of the United States" and adds that the final specification of Congress was meaningless.[149]

Anderson rightly observes that Madison proposed a free press clause similar to the one urged by the Virginia ratifying convention in its recommended bill of rights. The phrase "by any authority of the United States," Anderson writes, "appeared only in the 'form of ratification' by which the convention officially assented to the original Constitution," and that "form of ratification" was drafted by a committee different from that which drafted the proposed bill of rights.[150] However, Madison was a member of both committees, and, even had he not been, the preface to the form of ratification scarcely can be dismissed. The Virginia convention surely attached considerable importance to its formal ratification statement that any power not granted to the United States could not be exercised by any authority of the United States, and that the two rights that Madison later called the "choicest"[151]—the liberty of conscience and freedom of the press—could not be abridged by any authority

146. Letter to R. Peters, Aug. 19, 1789, *reprinted in* 12 THE PAPERS OF JAMES MADISON 346–47 (R. Rutland ed. 1979) [hereinafter cited as PAPERS OF MADISON].

147. *Id.* at 340 (Aug. 15, 1789).

148. 3 J. ELLIOT, THE DEBATES IN THE SEVERAL STATE CONVENTIONS ON THE ADOPTION OF THE FEDERAL CONSTITUTION 656 (2d ed. Philadelphia 1901) (1st ed. Philadelphia 1836) [hereinafter cited as ELLIOT, DEBATES].

149. Anderson, *supra* note 14, at 501, 502–03.

150. *Id.* at 502.

151. Speech of June 8, 1789, in Congress, *reprinted in* 12 PAPERS OF MADISON, *supra* note 146, at 203.

of the United States. Anderson clearly goes too far when he declares that the reference to Congress in the final draft of the first amendment "had no significance whatsoever," meaning that the Framers understood "Congress" as equivalent to the federal government.[152] That interpretation is unlikely. By deliberately specifying Congress, the Framers must have meant not to specify the United States. They had constructed a government of three branches and knew the difference between the government of the United States and its legislative branch. Anderson also is capable of appreciating clear language when he wants to—he observes, for example, that if Congress had meant the free press clause to have a common law meaning, it could have specifically said so, as it did in the seventh amendment.[153] By the same logic Congress could have said "the federal government" if that is what it meant. In any case the first amendment's language must take precedence over its Framers' possible misunderstanding of that language. We should not be too hasty to conclude that the Framers did not mean what they said or that they said one thing and meant something very different.

Anderson concludes his point with an extraordinary concession—that even if the specification of Congress "was purposeful, its apparent purpose would have been merely to make clear that the amendment imposed no limitation on the states."[154] On the contrary, that purpose would have been equally fulfilled if the amendment had specified the government of the United States or any authority of the United States. The specification of Congress, rather, made clear that Congress had no power to abridge the freedom of the press, thereby satisfying the public demand for that restriction on the powers of Congress. Specifying Congress "to make clear that the amendment imposed no limitation on the states" seems to be an indirect way to reserve power to the states. I agree, however, that a primary purpose of the first amendment was to reserve to the states an exclusive authority to *legislate* in the field of speech and press. Anderson calls that remark of mine "Levy's states' rights argument"[155] and exposes it to some scorn.[156] Yet he makes the same point: The amendment specified Congress "merely

152. Anderson, *supra* note 14, at 501.

153. *Id.* at 499. What the Framers of the seventh amendment meant by their explicit reference to the common law is not clear. We do not know whether they intended the common law of England, as Justice Story asserted in United States v. Wonson, 28 F. Cas. 745 (C.C.D. Mass. 1812) (No. 16,750), or the common law of the individual states in which cases were to be tried by federal courts. Whatever was meant, the reference to common law was intended to appease public opinion, which demanded a guarantee of jury trial in civil as well as in criminal cases. *See* Wolfram, *The Constitutional History of the Seventh Amendment*, 57 MINN. L. REV. 639, 653–730 (1973).

154. Anderson, *supra* note 14, at 501.

155. *Id.* at 508.

156. For example, he says that the argument requires that the amendment be read as

to make clear that the amendment imposed no limitation on the states."[157]

F. *Whether the Framers Believed in a Federal Common Law of Crimes*

James Wilson of Pennsylvania, who was second only to Madison in influencing the shape of the Constitution and second to none as a master of law, had opinions on freedom of the press that Anderson finds unpalatable. He therefore degrades Wilson's significance. After quoting a few lines from Wilson, beginning with the word "if," Anderson explains that Wilson was speaking hypothetically about a procedure that would be employed in the event that Congress passed a sedition act. Anderson claims that the statement he quotes from Wilson indicates nothing about a federal common law of crimes, contrary to my contention.[158]

But Wilson was not speaking hypothetically, no more than any Framer did in Philadelphia in 1787 or during the ratification controversy, when explaining how he expected the new national gov-

---

"Congress shall make no law abridging *the power of the states to abridge* the freedom of speech, or of the press." *Id.* at 507 (emphasis Anderson's).

157. *Id.* at 501.

158. *Id.* at 504. Anderson adds that I emphasized Wilson's statement because he was an influential Framer and "the only one to express himself on the meaning of freedom of the press." *Id.* at 504 n.285. Anderson then doubts that Wilson was a spokesman for those who framed the first amendment because he was not a member of the First Congress, which adopted it. But I did not connect Wilson in any way with the framing of the first amendment. I counted him as a major witness on the meaning of the concept of a free press, but I did not assert that he was the only Framer who explained the meaning of the term "freedom of the press," because he was not. Hugh Williamson of North Carolina, another signer of the Constitution, declared in a 1788 essay that when the licensing system expired in England, "the press became perfectly free." REMARKS ON THE NEW PLAN OF GOVERNMENT (1788), *reprinted in* ESSAYS ON THE CONSTITUTION 394–408 (P. Ford ed. 1892). George Nicholas of Virginia and James Iredell of North Carolina, close associates of the Framers, similarly construed freedom of the press to mean no prior restraints. *See* 3 ELLIOT, DEBATES, *supra* note 148, at 247 (2d ed. rev. 1941); ANSWERS TO MR. MASON'S OBJECTIONS TO THE NEW CONSTITUTION (1788), *reprinted in* PAMPHLETS ON THE CONSTITUTION 333–70 (P. Ford ed. 1888) [hereinafter cited as PAMPHLETS]. Anti-Federalists, contrary to Anderson, *supra* note 14, at 497, did not have more expansive views than the Framers or the Federalists in the First Congress who backed the first amendment. Melancthon Smith of New York and Richard Henry Lee of Virginia believed that England had a free press because the licensing system no longer existed. *See* AN ADDRESS TO THE PEOPLE OF THE STATE OF NEW YORK (1788), *reprinted in* PAMPHLETS, *supra*, at 87–115; OBSERVATIONS . . . IN A NUMBER OF LETTERS FROM THE FEDERAL FARMER, Letter IV (1787), *reprinted in* 2 THE COMPLETE ANTI-FEDERALIST 245–51 (H. Storing ed. 1981) [hereinafter cited as ANTI-FEDERALIST]. Lee's praise of England, which equated no prior restraints with freedom of the press, appeared in the most widely circulated of all Anti-Federalist tracts, *Letters from the Federal Farmer*. Anti-Federalists sought to sabotage or defeat the Bill of Rights after Madison urged it in the First Congress. *See* LEVY, *supra* note 11, at 226–33.

ernment would operate.[159] Wilson was answering anti-ratificationist critics who had denounced his widely reported Statehouse Yard speech for ratification and against the need for a bill of rights.[160] That speech had provoked many Anti-Federalist replies. "A Democratic Federalist" answered that the federal courts probably would prosecute those who libeled the United States. If the judicial power of the United States extended "to ALL CASES, in *law* and *equity*, arising under this [C]onstitution," then, the writer argued, "the tribunal of the United States may claim a right to the cognizance of all offenses against the *general government*, and *libels* will not probably be excluded."[161] The Zenger case, he recalled, proved that men in high power disliked liberty of the press.[162]

A pamphlet by "A Federalist Republican" also answered Wilson. Without speaking to the issue of libel prosecutions, the writer contended that the press faced real danger from Congress' delegated power to tax; stamp duties could "as effectually abolish the freedom of the press as any express declaration."[163] Another Pennsylvania Anti-Federalist, probably William Findley, warned in an essay for Oswald's newspaper:

> The Liberty of the Press is not secured, and the powers of Congress are fully adequate to its destruction, as they are to have the trial of *libels*, or *pretended libels* against the United States, and may by a cursed abominable Stamp Act (as the *Bowdoin Administration* has done in Massachusetts) preclude you effectually from all means of information. Mr. W[ilson] has given you no answer to these arguments.[164]

At the Pennsylvania ratifying convention, John Smilie, who like William Findley was an Anti-Federalist leader, advocated that a bill of rights be appended to the Constitution. "Suppose," declared Smilie, "Congress to pass an act for the punishment of libels and restrain the liberty of the press, for they are warranted to do this. What security would a printer have, tried in one of their courts?"[165] On the next day, December 1, 1787, Robert Whitehall, another Anti-Federalist leader, declared that Congress could "destroy the

159. Even if Wilson were speaking hypothetically, he could no more be dismissed for that reason than could the essays by Hamilton, Madison, and Jay in *The Federalist*. But, rather than speaking hypothetically, Wilson was discussing a procedure that would be followed if Congress exercised a power that he insisted it did not have.

160. 2 THE DOCUMENTARY HISTORY OF THE RATIFICATION OF THE CONSTITUTION 167 (M. Jensen ed. 1976) [hereinafter cited as DOCUMENTARY HISTORY].

161. Pennsylvania Herald (Philadelphia), Oct. 17, 1787, *reprinted in* 2 DOCUMENTARY HISTORY, *supra* note 160, at 193–98 (emphasis in original).

162. *Id.*

163. A REVIEW OF THE CONSTITUTION . . . BY A FEDERAL REPUBLICAN (1787), *reprinted in* 3 ANTI-FEDERALIST, *supra* note 158, at 81.

164. Independent Gazetteer, Nov. 6, 1787, *reprinted in* 3 ANTI-FEDERALIST, *supra* note 158, at 93 (emphasis in original).

165. 2 DOCUMENTARY HISTORY, *supra* note 160, at 441.

liberty of the press." Under the copyright clause, he observed, Congress could secure to authors "the right of their writings. Under this, they may license the press, *no doubt;* and under licensing the press, they may suppress it."[166] Once again Smilie added that "Congress have a power to restrain libels."[167]

James Wilson's speech of December 1 at the ratifying convention directly answered his critics. After reasserting that the new government had "no power whatsoever" concerning the press and that "no law in pursuance of the Constitution can possibly be enacted to destroy that liberty," he declared:

> I presume it was not in the view of the honorable gentleman to say that there is no such thing as a libel or that the writers of such ought not to be punished. The idea of the liberty of the press is not carried so far as this is any country—*what is meant by liberty of the press, is that there should be no antecedent restraint upon it;* but that every author is responsible when he attacks the security or welfare of the government or the safety, character, and property of the individual. With regard to attacks upon the public, the mode of proceeding is by a prosecution . . . . Now, sir, if this libel is to be tried, it must be tried where the offense was committed; for under this Constitution, as declared in the second section of the third Article, the trial must be held in the state; therefore on this occasion it must be tried where it was published, if the indictment is for publishing; and it must be tried likewise by a jury of that state.[168]

If Congress had no power to legislate on the press and yet a libel against the United States was punishable in a federal court in the state where the publication was made, Wilson assumed the existence of a federal common law of crimes; he assumed, that is, that the federal courts possessed jurisdiction over nonstatutory crimes against the United States. His point was that although libels were subject to federal prosecution, the defendant would not be worse off than a defendant prosecuted in a state court for libeling the state. Wilson went further by contending that the federal defendant would be no worse off even if "the general government . . . had the power to make laws on this subject," which he denied. No Anti-Federalist disagreed with Wilson on the key point, however. They did not accept Wilson's contention that Congress lacked power to abridge the press, but they did not contest his claim that the federal courts could prosecute libels against the United States—and no one

166. 2 *id.* at 454. Whitehall professed to believe that the fear of prior restraint as well as of subsequent punishment was still real. He advocated a free press clause to prevent censorship in advance of publication. Blackstone too had defined freedom of the press as the absence of prior restraints.

167. *Id.*

168. *Id.* at 455 (emphasis added).

said that a free press guarantee would operate to prevent such prosecutions.

At his first opportunity, Justice Wilson, on circuit duty, presided over the trial of a person charged with commission of a non-statutory crime. All members of the Supreme Court during its first decade believed in the existence of a federal common law of crimes.[169] In Henfield's case, members of Washington's cabinet, including Hamilton and Jefferson, supported the prosecution and John Marshall later noted with regret that a jury acquitted Henfield after he had been indicted, in part, "at common law, for disturbing the peace of the United States."[170]

Anderson's treatment of the matter of a federal common law of crimes is odd. He concedes the facts but adds that because the Supreme Court repudiated a federal common law of crimes "at its earliest opportunity, early judicial assumptions to the contrary cannot be considered authoritative on the issue of the Framers' intent."[171] However, the Supreme Court's decision of 1812 is worthless as a revelation of the Framers' intent, especially since the Court decided the case without arguments and without reasoned judgment, and the Justices were divided. Chief Justice John Marshall and Justices Story and Washington were the probable dissenters, although we know for certain only that Story dissented.[172] Moreover, those "early judicial assumptions" were held by important Framers including James Wilson, William Paterson, Oliver Ellsworth, and close associates such as John Jay and James Iredell, all of whom spoke more authoritatively about the Framers' intent than did the majority Justices in 1812.

III. ANDERSON'S METHODOLOGY

Having discussed Anderson's views concerning the free press clause,[173] this Article now will examine the methodology by which Anderson reaches his conclusions. This methodology includes his general critique of "the Levy thesis"[174] and his use of historical evidence.[175]

---

169. Trial of Gideon Henfield (1793), *reprinted in* Wharton, *supra* note 69, at 49–89; *see also supra* note 5. Justice Samuel Chase initially disagreed but changed his mind. *See supra* note 5.

170. 5 J. MARSHALL, *supra* note 4, at 41.

171. Anderson, *supra* note 14, at 503.

172. *See supra* note 4.

173. *See supra* notes 19–172 and accompanying text.

174. Anderson, *supra* note 14, at 494–509; *see infra* notes 176–202 and accompanying text.

175. *See infra* notes 203–10 and accompanying text.

A. *Anderson's Critique of the "Levy Thesis"*

As I read Anderson, a significant part of his article consists either of criticizing propositions that I have advanced and later accepting them despite the criticisms, or of exploding propositions that he attributes to me but which I did not make. An example of the first device, discussed above,[176] is his acceptance of the first amendment as a states' rights amendment—that is, one reserving to the states a power to legislate on the subject of the press. Another example is Anderson's treatment of my statement that to the Federalists, "the national government, *even in the absence of the First Amendment*, could not make speech or press a legitimate subject of restrictive legislation. The amendment itself was superfluous."[177] Anderson has fun with that statement as he asserts that "Levy concedes that his reading makes the press clause meaningless . . . ."[178] I concede nothing of the kind. Anderson himself twice quotes a statement by me concerning one purpose of the amendment that makes it considerably more than meaningless: The amendment "was intended to prohibit any Congressional regulation of the press, whether by means of a licensing act, a tax act, or a sedition act."[179] Anderson notes another purpose that I ascribed to the amendment: "[t]o quiet public apprehension [by offering] an added security that Congress would be limited to the exercise of its delegated powers."[180] Anderson calls that a "sop." Yet Madison thought that sop indispensable to persuade a hesitant public to support the new government with confidence that it would respect its limitations.[181] Still another purpose of the amendment is reiterated by Anderson throughout his article—the one he calls the "structural role of press freedom" as a bulwark of liberty or a check on government.[182] Anderson's many proofs that that was a purpose of the amendment, or, at least, a meaning of freedom of the press, all derive directly from *Legacy of Suppression*. To be sure, he cites primary sources such as *Cato's Letters*, Congress' Quebec declaration, and Virginia's Declaration of Rights, but all that material appears in *Legacy*.[183] Anderson does not quote properly another appropriate source, Blackstone. As readers will note from my quotation from Black-

---

176. *See supra* notes 154–57 and accompanying text.

177. Anderson, *supra* note 14, at 505–06 (quoting LEVY, *supra* note 30, at lvii (emphasis in original)).

178. Anderson, *supra* note 14, at 505.

179. *Id.* at 496, 498–99 (quoting LEVY, *supra* note 30, at lvi).

180. Anderson, *supra* note 14, at 506 (quoting LEVY, *supra* note 30, at lvii).

181. *See* 12 PAPERS OF MADISON, *supra* note 146, at 347 (Madison to Peters, Aug. 19, 1789) and Madison's great speech to Congress on June 8, 1789, recommending the amendments that became the Bill of Rights. In the speech he made the point at least seven times. *See id.* at 197–209.

182. Anderson, *supra* note 14, at 488–94.

183. *See, e.g.*, LEVY, *supra* note 11, at 15–20, 176–77.

stone above,[184] he also supported the structural role of press freedom. Interestingly, Anderson's version of Blackstone is as follows: "The liberty of the press . . . consists in laying no previous restraints upon publications, and not in freedom from censure for criminal matter when published."[185] Anderson's ellipsis marks delete these words from Blackstone: "The liberty of the press is indeed essential to the nature of a free state . . ."—the crux of the structural role of press freedom. It was Blackstonian as well as Catonian. Yet when the same point suits Anderson's purpose he adopts it: "The one point upon which the Framers did make their intention clear was that Congress had no legitimate power to pass *any* law respecting the press."[186] That concession contradicts several pages of Anderson's criticism of my work.[187]

A proposition that Anderson attributes to me and then lambasts is that the first amendment was the source of reserved state power over the press.[188] Anderson correctly says that the Framers inferred the power "from the limited nature of the federal government's power over the press."[189] I said this in *Legacy of Suppression*.[190] But Anderson declares, "Without the states' rights purpose, the Levy interpretation ascribes to the press clause no legal effect at all."[191] Elsewhere, however, he accurately remarks that I regard the clause primarily as an added limitation on the powers of Congress, preventing it from enacting a sedition act.[192] That limitation gives the clause some legal effect.

Anderson also states that I fail to see the free press clause as a general guarantee of freedom of the press.[193] I do indeed fail to see that. The amendment is a general denial to Congress of a power to legislate. It is not a positive recognition of a right held by all to freedom of the press. The Bill of Rights is a bill of restraints upon government. The theory underlying the Bill of Rights—indeed, the Constitution—is that the people reserve all rights not ceded to government. The theory is not that the Constitution must affirmatively recognize a right before it can be said to exist. We have become too accustomed to the assumption that the only rights we have are those that the government has been expressly denied the power to

184. *See supra* note 30 and accompanying text.

185. Anderson, *supra* note 14, at 495 n.244.

186. Anderson, *supra* note 14, at 522; see also *id.* at 536 for another statement of the same point: The Framers "had denied that the federal government had any power to control the press, even in the absence of a first amendment."

187. *Id.* at 500–06.

188. *Id.* at 507.

189. *Id.*

190. LEVY, *supra* note 11, at 225–26.

191. Anderson, *supra* note 14, at 508.

192. *Id.* at 496, 499.

193. *Id.* at 496.

violate. In our constitutional system of government, we are free because the government is not; the government is not free because of the limitations imposed upon it by the Constitution, including the Bill of Rights. We are free not because the Constitution enumerates rights positively, but because it limits government and protects some rights negatively.

When Anderson dissects the "Levy thesis," he finds that it consists of three tenets. The first is that, to the Framers, freedom of the press meant "nothing more than freedom from prior restraint."[194] The fatuousness of that proposition is mine, not Anderson's. Freedom of the press at the time of the first amendment's framing meant no prior restraints, but that is hardly all that it meant. My mistake appeared not in *Legacy of Suppression* but in my introduction to a collection of primary sources on the first amendment, where I declared that freedom of the press meant "merely" no prior restraints.[195] One word, "merely," provides Anderson with a target that he justifiably strikes at again and again. What he calls my second tenet is that the Framers meant Congress to be wholly powerless over the press.[196] As I noted earlier,[197] Anderson himself embraces that proposition quite explicitly.[198] The third tenet, Anderson states, is that "the real purpose of the press clause was to reserve to the states exclusive power to regulate the press."[199] My word was "primary"[200] rather than "real," and I did not say that the first amendment was "the source" of the reservation of state power,[201] but no matter; Anderson should have criticized the statement because the amendment has many purposes, only one of which was to reserve regulatory power to the states. Despite his criticism, however, he finally embraces that proposition also, as noted earlier,[202] when he stated that the apparent purpose of the specification of Congress was "to make clear that the amendment imposed no limitation on the states."

B. *Anderson's Use of Historical Evidence*

Apart from Anderson's misrepresentation of my work, his use of historical evidence is irresponsible and a major weakness of his

---

194. *Id.* at 498.

195. LEVY, *supra* note 30, at lv. Anderson, *supra* note 14, at 498 n.253, says that he relied primarily on the 1966 introduction to my anthology "as the most mature statement of Levy's position," but the introduction was merely an abridged version of *Legacy* with qualifications and subtleties as well as supporting evidence eliminated.

196. Anderson, *supra* note 14, at 498–99.

197. *See supra* notes 177–87 and accompanying text.

198. Anderson, *supra* note 14, at 522.

199. *Id.* at 499.

200. LEVY, *supra* note 30, at lix.

201. *See id.*

202. *See supra* notes 154–57 and accompanying text.

article. Even when he sounds plausible and cites appropriate authorities, he misleads; the reader, unless familiar with those authorities, cannot know that they do not sustain Anderson's interpretation or that he misstates the facts.

I have chosen for illustration the following paragraph from Anderson's section "Interpreting the Legislative History," because he thinks that section is important, because he presents the paragraph as the most important of his conclusions about the legislative history of the first amendment, and because he is frankly interpretative. He writes:

> Fourth (and most important), freedom of the press was viewed not merely as a desirable civil liberty, but as a matter integral to the structure of the new government. The press clause was the product of revolutionary ferment. There were no guarantees of press freedom in colonial charters and little agitation to add them. The demand for legal protection of the press was contemporaneous with the demand for independence and self-government. The rhetoric often came from the pens of Englishmen, such as John Wilkes, "Cato," and "Father of Candor," but the realities that made the rhetoric relevant were the confrontations of American printers like John Peter Zenger and Eleazer Oswald with royal governors and other local representatives of the crown.[203]

Very little in that paragraph conforms with historical fact. The quoted paragraph has five sentences; the five paragraphs in the following discussion correspond to those sentences.

First: From Cato to Blackstone, the view of the press as integral to liberty was English. Freedom of the press, therefore, was as integral to government in England as in America; nothing was unique or special about the structural role of the press to "the new government." Except for advocating truth as a defense, English libertarians before 1763 recommended no substantive change in the common law of seditious libel. Accordingly, the structural role of the press harmonized with the common law.

Second: Although the press clause, like every clause, first appeared in American constitutions that were written during the American Revolution, freedom of the press was not a product of revolutionary ferment any more than was freedom of religion or trial by jury. The British did not attack the colonists' freedom of the press, and the colonists did not list British violations of freedom of the press in any of their numerous documents of protest. The revolutionary controversy did produce some rights—for example, the American concept of unreasonable searches and seizures was in part a product of revolutionary ferment against the British use of writs of assistance. But the American press could not have been

203. Anderson, *supra* note 14, at 488–89.

freer than it was in fact from the Stamp Act controversy to the battle of Lexington.

Third: So what? Colonial charters contained no guarantees of a score of rights, and there was no agitation, not a "little" agitation, to add them. Charters could not be added to. Anderson does not understand the nature and function of those charters.

Fourth: No demand at all existed for the legal protection of the press, and Anderson cites none. The first free press clause, in the Virginia Declaration of Rights, was the product of George Mason, the great planter and amateur political theorist, who composed alone and without being confronted by demands. Mason wrote on the premise that separation from England had thrust Virginians back into a state of nature from which they might emerge by entering into a new social compact, reserving to the people their fundamental rights. Political theory, not demands for legal protection of the press, produced the first press clause. Furthermore, the demand for independence had nothing to do with a demand for a press clause. Rather, independence was the occasion of the first written constitutions, nine of which included press clauses. The second press clause appeared in Pennsylvania's Constitution of 1776, the only constitution that also guaranteed freedom of speech. The convention that adopted that clause on freedom of speech and press, according to Dwight A. Teeter, also passed a sedition law punishing verbal opposition to the war and providing that two justices of the peace might imprison for the war's duration anyone whom they found to be "dangerous."[204] The other states tended to copy or improvise from the Virginia or Pennsylvania press clauses and acted out of imitativeness and a conscious carrying out of the social contract theory, rather than out of responsiveness to demands for a press clause.

Fifth: John Wilkes supplied no rhetoric for freedom of the press; he held orthodox opinions on the subject. In all of his work, nothing suggests disagreement with the common law of seditious libel. He declared that the expression of opinion should not give any public offense to any establishment or individual. "The crime," he declared, "commences from thence, and the magistrate has a right to interpose or even to punish outrageous and indecent attacks on what any community has decreed to be sacred; not only the rules of good breeding, but the laws of society are then infringed."[205] Father of Candor suggested wider bounds for freedom of the press, but unlike Cato he was not admired or quoted in America. No American of the 1776–1791 period emulated Father of Candor in rejecting

204. Teeter, Legacy of Suppression, *supra* note 76, at 79–80.

205. J. WILKES, ENGLISH LIBERTY 132 (London 1769), *quoted in* LEVY, *supra* note 11, at 147–48.

the bad tendency test of political opinions and applying in its place the overt acts test.[206] On the other hand, Father of Candor also regarded wilfully false opinions against a just administration as seditious. The defense of the press upon which he most relied derived from the Zenger case.[207] Zenger himself, whom Anderson invokes in mythic opposition to royal tyranny, representated a popular cause. No grand jury would indict him. He had the support of the popular assembly. Had he attacked the assembly, he would have been a forgotten victim of the legislature's power to punish critics for breach of parliamentary privilege. Anderson uses Zenger's name to rely on conventional images rather than historical facts. He ignores that the royal judges posed no real threat to the colonial press, a point he himself makes elsewhere,[208] and neglects to notice that in *Legacy* I said, "The notoriety of the Zenger trial derives in part because it was so isolated a phenomenon."[209] I also demonstrated that, in New York in particular, the popular assemblies kept printers submissive.[210] Moreover, the Zenger case stands for the proposition that the jury should decide the criminality of an utterance and that truth should be a defense to a charge of criminal libel. Those propositions were not clarion calls of the American Revolution, were still "innovative" to Madison in 1788 and to John Adams in 1789, and were not accepted in American law until 1790 by the "reactionary" Pennsylvania Constitution and the Sedition Act of 1798. As for Eleazer Oswald, he never had a confrontation with a royal governor or his representatives. Oswald's nemesis was a revo-

206. The overt acts test is a test to determine the permissible scope of freedom of expression. According to that test, opinions should be immune from criminal punishment, and only illegal conduct or criminal acts should be penalized. The test originated in the seventeenth century in suggestive remarks by Roger Williams, William Walwyn, and Baruch Spinoza, primarily to promote the cause of religious liberty. To the same end, the Reverend Philip Furneaux developed the test fully in the next century and Thomas Jefferson adopted it. *See* LEVY, *supra* note 11, at 90–91, 95, 154–57, 166–68, 188–89. Such libertarians advocated the test as an alternative to the prevailing bad tendency test, according to which the expression of an opinion was punishable if it tended to stir animosity to the established religion of a state or to the government, its officers, or measures. Thus, the preamble to Jefferson's Virginia Statute of Religious Freedom declared that allowing the civil magistrate to restrain the profession of opinions "on the supposition of their ill tendency . . . at once destroys all religious liberty." The government's rightful purposes, Jefferson continued, were served if its officers did not interfere until "principles break out into overt acts against peace and good order." 2 PAPERS OF THOMAS JEFFERSON, *supra* note 143, at 546. The overt acts test, therefore, sharply distinguished words from deeds, and, in Furneaux's words, was based on the proposition that the "penal laws should be directed against *overt acts only* . . . and not against *principles*, or the *tendency* of principles." P. FURNEAUX, *Letters to . . . Blackstone*, in THE PALLADIUM OF CONSCIENCE 34 (Letter III) (facsimile ed. 1974) (1st ed. Philadelphia 1773) (emphasis in original).

207. *See* LEVY, *supra* note 11, at 149–54.

208. Anderson, *supra* note 14, at 510.

209. LEVY, *supra* note 11, at 19.

210. *Id.* at 44–49, 78–85.

lutionary leader and signer of the Declaration of Independence, Thomas McKean.

V. New Directions

Legacy of Suppression is far more reliable than the introduction to the anthology upon which Anderson directed most of his ammunition, but not even the original book is acceptable to me now. That book bears a title, and a thesis implied by that title, that I no longer accept as valid. The forthcoming *Emergence of a Free Press*, a revision and substantial expansion of the original, more accurately expresses my view of the additional evidence that I have sifted. Anderson concludes his article by suggesting that the Framers understood both the relationship of a free press to free government and the need for protecting the press's freedom.[211] That proposition is timid and tautological. Anyone who has read American newspapers from 1776 to 1791, when the first press clauses in the state constitutions and the first amendment were framed, would realize that the American press, like the British, was astonishingly scurrilous. Politically, it was beyond the capacity of the law of criminal libels to control. I would conclude that by the time of the framing of the first amendment, those who wrote it, being practical politicians, must have intended to protect the press with which they were familiar. They could not have done otherwise.

211. Anderson, *supra* note 14, at 537.

THE PREFERENCE FOR FREEDOM

ROBERT B. McKAY

VAST erudition and enormous scholarly research have been devoted to determining whether the first amendment to the United States Constitution stands somehow apart from, and above, other provisions of the Constitution, even other provisions of the Bill of Rights. Were it not for the subtle legalisms said to be involved in the controversy and the impressive credentials of the disputants, including members of the United States Supreme Court, one might well have thought that to ask the question was to command the only answer which a free society can give, an answer which Justice Cardozo articulated with eloquent simplicity. Freedom of speech and thought, he said, is "the matrix, the indispensable condition, of nearly every other form of freedom."[1]

It will be the first aim of this article to show that the answer really should be that easy, that it has always been so, and that there now remains no room for doubt that it is so. Nonetheless, disagreement, or at least misunderstanding, continues as to whether the first amendment should hold a "preferred position" within the hierarchy of constitutional values. This controversy, like so many others, depends for its existence upon misapprehension by the parties of the opposing contentions. The supporters of the so-called preferred position theory have erroneously believed that the opposing argument altogether denies special significance to the first amendment, whereas in fact all concede that there is a quality of "firstness" about the first amendment that is more than numerical.[2] Similarly, those who profess to reject the preferred position doctrine fail to comprehend properly the limits to the claims of its advocates. The difficulty is the familiar one of assuring a mistaken answer by asking the wrong question. The proper question involves an inquiry into the degree of preference which should be accorded the first amendment and an evaluation of the various techniques and procedures which may be appropriate in assuring that its preeminent position is preserved.

It will be the second aim of this article to examine the varieties of preference, with a view to giving them contextual significance in relation to freedom of expression. It is hoped in this way to redirect attention where it belongs, to the proper means for the protection from abridgment of those vital freedoms and to their affirmative extension.

Robert B. McKay is Professor of Law at New York University School of Law and a Member of the District of Columbia and Kansas Bars.

[1] Palko v. Connecticut, 302 U.S. 319, 327 (1937).

[2] See Cahn, The Firstness of the First Amendment, 65 Yale L.J. 464 (1956).

Emphasis will be upon freedom of expression, giving only incidental consideration to other first amendment freedoms. In so doing there is, of course, no intention to suggest a preference within the first amendment as to freedom of thought and speech over freedom of the press, free assembly, the right of petition, or the rights of conscience—freedom of religion and the prohibition against the establishment of religion.

I

The Myth and the Reality

A. *Confusion Compounded*

Much of the confusion over the priority to be accorded freedom of speech and thought might have been avoided if the expressive phrase "preferred position" had at its first use been given the natural meaning which the words suggest and which they are now more commonly understood to comprehend. Unfortunately, however, when Chief Justice Stone first noted that the Constitution accorded freedom of speech a "preferred position,"[3] the sweep of his statement was generally ignored; and attention was centered instead on the "embattled footnote" in his earlier opinion in *United States v. Carolene Products Co.*[4] This footnote, while important, merely raised a query as to the propriety of applying the presumption of constitutionality to statutes impinging on specific constitutional prohibitions, such as those in the Bill of Rights. However, the narrowing of the presumption of constitutionality in relation to statutes repressive of free speech is but a single fragment of the larger concept which may properly be labeled preferred position. Unfortunately, this restricted interpretation of the term resulted in misdirection of emphasis and argument where there should have been agreement.

A second factor obscuring the vital principle suggested by these two words is the regrettable fact that the "clear and present danger" test, in reality simply another device for registering preference, has often been misconceived as the exclusive means for restraining first amendment abridgments. Unfortunately, the danger test has proved insufficient to protect liberty where the pressures on freedom were strongest. This may in part be explained by the ambiguity implicit in the test itself and in part by the improper balancing of the opposing

---

3 Jones v. Opelika, 316 U.S. 584, 608 (1942) (dissenting opinion). The dissenting opinion was adopted on rehearing, 319 U.S. 103 (1943) (per curiam).

4 304 U.S. 144, 152 n.4 (1938). The footnote was described as "embattled" in Mason, The Core of Free Government, 1938-40: Mr. Justice Stone and "Preferred Freedoms," 65 Yale L.J. 597, 600 (1956).

interests upon which speech restrictions have been based. These matters are discussed below.[5]

Whatever may have been the reason, the fact remains that much of the argument has been at the fringes rather than at the core. The central, the inescapable proposition to which this study is directed is the notion that the freedom of expression is so vital in its relationship to the objectives of the Constitution that inevitably it must stand in a preferred position. In looking toward the fulfillment of that objective, there are a variety of devices, to be employed separately or in combination, which enable the courts to express the constitutionally mandated preference for freedom of speech and thought. Among these are the clear and present danger test; narrowing of the presumption of constitutionality; strict construction of statutes to avoid limitation of first amendment freedoms; the prohibitions against prior restraint and subsequent punishment; relaxation of the requirement of standing to sue where first amendment issues are involved; and generally higher standards of procedural due process where these freedoms are in jeopardy. Not one, but the sum total of these—and more—make up the preferred position concept. They embody the principled response of a judiciary alert to its highest duty—that of preserving and fostering the republic in the only way it can be made to survive—through assiduous striving after the "blessings of liberty."[6]

B. *Behind the Beginning*

It is often suggested that the preferred position originated in 1938 in Justice Stone's now-celebrated footnote in the *Carolene* case.[7] Except for the frequency of reiteration of this misconception, refutation would scarcely be necessary. Now, however, a word may be appropriate. In the first place, he did not use the words preferred position in that footnote, but spoke only of the narrowing of the presumption of constitutionality as to statutes impinging on rights protected by the Bill of Rights. When, four years later, Chief Justice Stone first spoke of the preferred position, there is no indication that he intended anything but the widest scope for the phrase. Certainly he did not tie the words to the earlier footnote in the *Carolene* case by

---

[5] See The Past and Future of Clear and Present, pages 1203-12 infra.

[6] See Chafee, The Blessings of Liberty (1956), for a meaningful exposition.

[7] United States v. Carolene Prods. Co., 304 U.S. 144, 152 n.4 (1938). The first paragraph of that note is as follows: "There may be narrower scope for operation of the presumption of constitutionality when legislation appears on its face to be within a specific prohibition of the Constitution, such as those of the first ten Amendments, which are deemed equally specific when held to be embraced within the Fourteenth."

citation of that case or even by reference to presumptions of constitutionality of legislation. Rather, he spoke in sweeping terms:

> The First Amendment is not confined to safeguarding freedom of speech and freedom of religion against discriminatory attempts to wipe them out. On the contrary, the Constitution, by virtue of the First and Fourteenth Amendments, has put those freedoms in a preferred position.[8]

In short, Chief Justice Stone should be credited with the expression, but he of course did not claim authorship of the idea that lies behind that neatly capsulized reminder of the proper significance of the first amendment freedoms.

Where, then, are the proper beginnings? The American origins arise out of the discussion and correspondence, principally between Jefferson and Madison, that led to the proposing and adoption of the first amendment. Behind that decision to have an explicit prohibition upon governmental interference with speech and thought was the consciousness of centuries of less than freedom in England and the Colonies. Justice Black has stated forcefully this awareness:

> No purpose in ratifying the Bill of Rights was clearer than that of securing for the people of the United States much greater freedom of religion, expression, assembly, and petition than the people of Great Britain had ever enjoyed.[9]

That these considerations were indeed uppermost in the mind of Madison, the proposer of the first amendment, has been fully documented by Professor Cahn.[10] It is especially significant to observe that Madison demonstrated a willingness to grade the rights within the Bill of Rights, and that in his judgment "the freedoms embodied in the First Amendment must always secure paramountcy."[11] Thus, it is clear that the two concepts which are central to the preferred position theory—primacy of the rights of mind and conscience, and the need for choice even within the Bill of Rights—can both be traced unmistakably to the period before 1791 when the first amendment was ratified.

It is curious that the first amendment received very little specific analysis from the Supreme Court for more than 120 years. Not that there were no governmental acts restrictive of freedom.[12] The Alien

---

8 Jones v. Opelika, 316 U.S. 584, 608 (1942) (dissenting opinion).

9 Bridges v. California, 314 U.S. 252, 265 (1941).

10 Cahn, The Firstness of the First Amendment, 65 Yale L.J. 464 (1956).

11 Id. at 473.

12 Professor Chafee has observed: "There was hot discussion at long intervals—over the Sedition Act of 1798 and the exclusion of Abolitionist pamphlets from the mails and the treatment of Copperheads—and legal treatises did some speculating, but nobody knew what the First Amendment did or did not protect. Such knowledge could

and Sedition Acts of 1798,[13] briefly enforced until 1800, could well have been challenged under the first amendment.[14] But no cases came to the Supreme Court, and the possible crisis was forestalled with the failure of congressional reenactment and Jefferson's inauguration in 1801.

Similarly, the Civil War was not without its speech-repressive features; but again no cases actually reached the Supreme Court that required decision on first amendment grounds. However, in two cases which arose during the course of that war, but which were not decided until 1866, rights which we might now think of as coming within the protection of the first amendment were upheld on the basis of other constitutional principles. *Ex parte Garland*[15] involved a wartime act of Congress which excluded from practice in United States courts any attorney who did not take an oath affirming, among other things, that he had never voluntarily given aid or counsel to persons engaged in armed hostility to the United States. *Cummings v. Missouri*,[16] decided the same day, involved an even more extensive oath required of state government officials, corporation officers, teachers, and ministers, which was "directed not merely against overt and visible acts of hostility to the government, but was intended to reach words, desires, and sympathies, also."[17] In that case the defendant was a Roman Catholic priest who had been convicted of the crime of teaching and preaching without having taken the oath.

In both cases the Court held the oath requirements violative of the constitutional prohibitions, applicable against the federal and state governments, which forbid bills of attainder and laws with criminal sanctions having an ex post facto effect. Neither case was decided on grounds of freedom of speech or religion.[18] However, it is worthy of note that the Court regarded these oath requirements with special disfavor because they involved "deprivation or suspension of political or civil rights."[19] It seems fair to say that if the *Cummings* case, for example, were to come before the Court today, the test oath could, and

---

come only from court decisions and there was little occasion for these until the day when the United States declared war against Germany for the first time." The Blessings of Liberty 64 (1956).

13 Act of June 25, 1798, 1 Stat. 570; Act of July 14, 1798, 1 Stat. 596.

14 See Chafee, Free Speech in the United States 27-28 (1941).

15 71 U.S. (4 Wall.) 333 (1867).

16 71 U.S. (4 Wall.) 277 (1867).

17 Id. at 318.

18 Of course the state case could not have been decided on such grounds, arising as it did before the adoption of the fourteenth amendment.

19 71 U.S. (4 Wall.) at 322.

possibly would,[20] be held violative of both the freedom of speech and freedom of religion clauses of the first amendment as incorporated into the fourteenth amendment prohibitions against the states.[21]

The fact that these cases turned on issues other than freedom of mind and conscience is representative of the scanty history of the first amendment before the period immediately following World War I. It is curious but true that until the celebrated decision in *Schenck v. United States*[22] the first amendment received no genuine analysis from the Supreme Court.[23]

C. *A Rehearsal of the Obvious*

Some important ideas, upon even the most casual reflection, so commend themselves to the mind that, once the question has been raised, there can be no doubt of the answer. Such an idea is the proposition that the freedoms of speech and thought are primary values in a free society. Indeed, the firstness of freedom of speech and thought in the free society is sufficiently important to call for frequent restatement even of the obvious. That is the purpose of the reflections which follow.

The Why of Firstness.—It is of course no accident that the freedoms of mind and conscience were accorded primacy of position in the Bill of Rights. Of all the lists of guarantees proposed for inclusion in the Bill of Rights, what we now call the first amendment freedoms were the most commonly reiterated demands.[24] The reason is clear. The absence of these very protections against the British Government was a principal motivating factor leading to the breach between Colonies and Crown.[25] Indeed, the real truth is that the preference for freedom goes back much farther. If this freedom of mind and con-

---

20 Cf. Speiser v. Randall, 357 U.S. 513 (1958); Wieman v. Updegraff, 344 U.S. 183, 192, 194 (1952) (concurring opinions).

21 But compare In re Summers, 325 U.S. 561 (1945), where the Court permitted the State of Illinois to deny membership in its bar to an otherwise qualified applicant who, as a conscientious objector unwilling to serve in the state militia in wartime, was unable to take the required oath to support the state constitution. See also Garner v. Board of Pub. Works, 341 U.S. 716 (1951).

22 249 U.S. 47 (1919).

23 See, e.g., Toledo Newspaper Co. v. United States, 247 U.S. 402, 419 (1918); Fox v. Washington, 236 U.S. 273 (1915); Gompers v. Bucks Stove & Range Co., 221 U.S. 418, 439 (1911); Patterson v. Colorado ex rel. Attorney General, 205 U.S. 454, 462 (1907); Davis v. Massachusetts, 167 U.S. 43 (1897); Robertson v. Baldwin, 165 U.S. 275, 281 (1897). This may be explained in part by the fact that it was not until 1925 that the fourteenth amendment was held to include as prohibitions against the states the provisions of any part of the first amendment in Gitlow v. New York, 268 U.S. 652 (1925).

24 Dumbauld, The Bill of Rights 160 (1957).

25 See Bridges v. California, 314 U.S. 252, 265 (1941).

science can be traced only indefinitely to Magna Carta, surely the trail becomes much clearer with the Petition of Right in 1628 and the Bill of Rights in 1689.[26] What was in the seventeenth century only a path for the few had become by 1791 a highway for the many; and it led unmistakably toward the formulation of the first amendment.

That the primacy of position signified also a primacy in importance is a matter of ready understanding to every person familiar with the works of Jefferson and Madison, who were most articulate in the formulation of the Bill of Rights. The correspondence between these two shows definitely that they supported a grading of rights which would favor those enumerated in the first amendment.[27]

Indeed, could it have been otherwise? To the extent that a democracy is to flourish, or even to survive, a meaningful exercise of the franchise must be assured. It makes no difference whether the number of qualified electors be small, as was then the case, or nearly universal among adults, as is today true; intelligent decisions can emanate only from an informed electorate.[28] It is not too strong to say that without freedom of speech and thought, all other provisions in the Constitution would lack foundation and might well not survive. On the other hand, if all were to be removed save these freedoms, a free society could be reconstructed out of the minds of men free to profit from an interchange of ideas.

Finally, in addition to the reasons already recognized for according special emphasis to the first amendment, there is the uncompromising inflexibility of the text of the amendment itself: "Congress shall make no law . . . abridging the freedom of speech or of the press; or the right of the people peaceably to assemble, and to petition the Government for a redress of grievances." With this categorical language may be contrasted the less rigid language of other important substantive provisions in the Bill of Rights, such as the fourth amendment's guaranty of freedom from "unreasonable" searches and seizures and the assurance that warrants may be issued only for "probable cause"; the fifth amendment's protection against the deprivation of life, liberty, or property without "due process of law" and against the taking of private property for public use without "just" compensation;

---

[26] For a valuable discussion and texts of these and other relevant documents, see Sources of Our Liberties (Perry ed. 1959).

[27] See Cahn, supra note 2.

[28] As Justice Brandeis observed: "The right of a citizen of the United States to take part, for his own or the country's benefit, in the making of federal law and in the conduct of the Government, necessarily includes the right to speak or write about them. . . . Full and free exercise of this right by the citizen is ordinarily also his duty; for its exercise is more important to the Nation than it is to himself." Gilbert v. Minnesota, 254 U.S. 325, 337-38 (1920) (dissenting opinion).

and the requirement of the eighth amendment that bail shall not be "excessive" and punishments may not be "cruel and unusual." The fact that some other provisions are couched in terms of absolute command or prohibition does not detract from the argument. The only other important provisions in the Bill of Rights—those parts of the fifth amendment not already mentioned, plus the sixth and seventh amendments—deal exclusively with specific procedural rights for which it is proper to prescribe a definite rule.

Moreover, it makes no difference to this argument that the first amendment has never in fact been regarded as imposing an absolute prohibition upon governmental action that in any way restricts speech.[29] It is apparent that not every limitation is an abridgment. As Justice Holmes said, "the First Amendment, while prohibiting legislation against free speech as such cannot have been, and obviously was not, intended to give immunity for every possible use of language."[30] This is not to solve the difficulty, but only to concede that there are choices to be made, lines to be drawn, all matters of degree. Such policy decisions are necessarily committed to the courts, bodies peculiarly well equipped to perform this most difficult of all legal functions. In fact, there is no other way.

The Practice of Firstness.—All Justices who have sat on the United States Supreme Court since 1919, and who have had occasion to express themselves on the first amendment, have accorded a special significance to its command. The fact to be particularly noted is that this preference for the first or grading, as it has been called, has not been indulged in exclusively by the past and present libertarians on the Court. Even when the Court held that a claimed right did not come within first amendment protection, it has been the not-infrequent custom to preface the denial with a reminder of the special favoritism with which the first amendment should be regarded. Lest this seem anomalous it should be remembered that the right is not absolute, and in many instances the questions for decision are close and difficult. A sample of some of the opinions over the intervening years demonstrates the uniform acknowledgment that the first amendment does stand apart—and above. For convenience of reference a number of repre-

29 Even those who profess to read an absolute prohibition into the first amendment find occasion for some deviation from that strict standard when confronted with actual cases. See the discussion of Mr. Meiklejohn's position at pages 1194-95 infra.

30 Frohwerk v. United States, 249 U.S. 204, 206 (1919). See also Chief Justice Hughes: "These [first amendment] rights may be abused by using speech or press or assembly in order to incite to violence and crime. The people through their legislatures may protect themselves against that abuse. But the legislative intervention can find constitutional justification only by dealing with the abuse. The rights themselves must not be curtailed." De Jonge v. Oregon, 299 U.S. 353, 364-65 (1937).

sentative statements are brought together in an appendix at pages 1223-27. At this point it is necessary only to note that every member of the Court since 1919 has concurred in one or many of the collected expressions of preference for the first amendment. The issue, if issue there ever was, would no longer seem to be an open one. The first amendment *does* stand in a preferred position.

One Justice, and apparently only one, has taken some pains to deny that the first amendment is to be preferred; but one can find even in his opinions considerable indication of the favored place conferred upon the freedoms of speech and thought. The reference of course is to Justice Frankfurter who has at least four times denied that he accords to the first amendment a preferred position.[31]

There is an aura of unreality about the debate over whether the first amendment has or should have a preferred position. Had the validity of the preferred position doctrine not been contested by so able a scholar and judge as Justice Frankfurter, it would seem the purest show of pedantry to review the origins and standing of the concept. Perhaps the difficulty has arisen from the fact that the preferred position concept does no more than state a mood; its admonitory quality recalls to mind the simple but majestic fact that here is a society in which the important freedoms count for something. Even if other values, almost equally precious, must on occasion be sacrificed, the price is not too great to preserve unblemished the safeguards of liberty.

The difficulty in this unreal dispute between disputants who do not disagree, then, has perhaps been a failure to accept the full constitutional implications of the preference for freedom. To attempt to reduce the core principle of democracy to a formula, however malleable, is to sacrifice its essential worth. To fragmentize the grand design of the idea of freedom is inevitably to reduce the sum of the parts to something less than the whole. But the question has been raised, and it is therefore important to accept and answer the challenge.

It has already been shown that the first amendment has been accorded a preferred position in this larger sense at least since 1791.[32] Thus, it is clearly inaccurate to speak of the preferred position concept as having been derived from Justice Stone's magnificently ambiguous footnote in the *Carolene* case. It is equally incorrect to credit the inception of the concept, as does Justice Frankfurter, to *Herndon v.*

[31] Ullmann v. United States, 350 U.S. 422, 428 (1956); Dennis v. United States, 341 U.S. 494, 526-27 (1951) (concurring opinion); Kovacs v. Cooper, 336 U.S. 77, 90-96 (1949) (concurring opinion); West Virginia State Bd. of Educ. v. Barnette, 319 U.S. 624, 648-49 (1943) (dissenting opinion).

[32] See text accompanying notes 9-14 supra.

Lowry.[33] If one is reluctant to trace origins before 1791, or even back to that year as a starting point, it appears essential to recognize at least that the original formulation of the clear and present danger test by Justice Holmes in *Schenck v. United States*[34] was a recognition that when first amendment values are involved, the otherwise permissible prohibitions which government might impose are to be examined in a different context and measured by a more critical standard. This, then, is the essence of the preferred position—the exercise of judgment to protect first amendment freedoms in a variety of ways.

It remains, then, only to note why it is that Justice Frankfurter dissents from what seems otherwise to be harmonious agreement. Four observations come to mind.

First. Justice Frankfurter has objected several times to the expression preferred position, which he regards as a "mischievous phrase."[35] His principal argument appears in a concurring opinion in *Kovacs v. Cooper,*[36] where it becomes clear that whatever his difference with the majority may be in terms of semantics, it scarcely amounts to a difference in substance. The ostensible disagreement is with "the thought, which it may subtly imply, that any law touching communication is infected with presumptive invalidity."[37] There are two difficulties with this argument. In the first place, neither the cases he cites nor the somewhat more extended list included in the appendix to this study justify his conclusion that the doctrine has ever been so regarded. Rather, as Justice Stone remarked in the *Carolene* footnote, "there may be narrower scope for the presumption of constitutionality when legislation appears on its face to be within a specific prohibition of the Constitution, such as those of the first ten amendments . . . ."[38] That is, legislation claimed to impinge on rights of free speech and thought should be inspected more critically by the judiciary than where exclusively economic rights are at issue. But this is emphatically not to say that those who agree that the first amendment is to be preferred start with a presumption that controlling legislation is unconstitutional where it touches free speech. Thus, Justice Reed, writing for the majority in *Kovacs v. Cooper,* said that "the preferred position of freedom of speech in a society that cherishes liberty for all does not

---

33 301 U.S. 242, 258 (1937). See the concurring opinion of Justice Frankfurter in Kovacs v. Cooper, 336 U.S. 77, 90 (1949).

34 249 U.S. 47, 52 (1919).

35 Kovacs v. Cooper, 336 U.S. 77, 90 (1949) (concurring opinion).

36 Id. at 89-97.

37 Id. at 90. See also id. at 94-95.

38 United States v. Carolene Prods. Co., 304 U.S. 144, 152 n.4 (1938).

require legislators to be insensible to claims by citizens to comfort and convenience."[39]

The second and more important difficulty with his argument is that it too narrowly conceives the concept of preferred position. The whole question as to the presumption of constitutionality of legislation is simply a part—and not the most important part—of what should properly be regarded as the reach of the preferred position. That concept represents a whole manner of approaching freedom of speech and thought. To miss this is to miss the point altogether.

Second. If Justice Frankfurter intends to reject the primacy of the first amendment he stands alone. But that does not seem to be a correct statement of his position. For he has made in *Kovacs v. Cooper* a statement of credo which is one of the most eloquent testimonials to the vitality of the preferred position concept:

> [W]ithout freedom of expression, thought becomes checked and atrophied. Therefore, in considering what interests are so fundamental as to be enshrined in the Due Process Clause, those liberties of the individual which history has attested as the indispensable conditions of an open as against a closed society come to this Court with a momentum for respect lacking when appeal is made to liberties which derive merely from shifting economic arrangements.[40]

Justice Rutledge, in reference to these words, drily remarked that:

> I think my brother FRANKFURTER demonstrates the conclusion opposite to that which he draws, namely, that the First Amendment guaranties of the freedoms of speech, press, assembly, and religion occupy preferred position not only in the Bill of Rights but also in the repeated decision of this Court.[41]

Third. As long as he has been on the Court, Justice Frankfurter has insisted on the grading of rights. He clearly differentiates among the provisions of the Bill of Rights, believing that not all its guarantees are "of the very essence of a scheme of ordered liberty,"[42] and that those which do not so measure up are not deserving of incorporation into the fourteenth amendment as limitations upon the states. As

[39] 336 U.S. at 88. See also Ullmann v. United States, 350 U.S. 422, 439-40 (1956); Poulos v. New Hampshire, 345 U.S. 395, 405 (1953); Jones v. Opelika, 316 U.S. 584, 594-96 (1942).

[40] 336 U.S. at 95 (concurring opinion). See also Dennis v. United States, 341 U.S. 494, 548-50 (1951) (concurring opinion); Marsh v. Alabama, 326 U.S. 501, 510-11 (1946) (concurring opinion).

[41] 336 U.S. at 106 (dissenting opinion).

[42] The phrase is from Palko v. Connecticut, 302 U.S. 319, 325 (1937), a decision before Justice Frankfurter was a member of the Court. But he has expressed enthusiastic acceptance of the phrase in Adamson v. California, 332 U.S. 46, 65 (1947) (concurring opinion), and elsewhere.

already indicated, he agrees that the first amendment comes within the charmed circle, but he would exclude others. Is not this an expression of preference?[43]

Fourth. Not only has Justice Frankfurter thus demonstrated his willingness to grade rights on the basis of considerations not explicitly stated in the Constitution—and thus his willingness to have the Court sit in judgment over legislative findings based on various and unspecified judicial criteria—but he has also proved willing to grade rights even *within* the first amendment. His preference for freedom of religion is unmistakable.[44] What, then, remains of his reluctance to use the term preferred position? Is it simply a refusal to concede that he does not defer to legislative findings in these cases as in others, or does it conceal the application of idiosyncratic standards not ascertainable in advance? Answers to these questions will be sought in the following section.

D. *A Question of Degree: Herein of Balancing*

Another important aspect of the application of the constitutional guarantees of freedom of speech and thought, and one that is equally enmeshed in misapprehensions on the bench and off, is the question of balancing. There are at least two pertinent questions. First, is it permissible, or is it not, to weigh the constitutional interest in free speech ("Congress shall make no law . . . .") against another societal interest so important as the national security or so relatively unimportant as the interest in maintaining clean streets in a municipality? Second, if such balancing is permissible, what are the weights to be used, and in whose scales is the weighing to be done?

A categorical answer to the first question is possible. Just as all members of the Court hold freedom of speech and thought in a preferred position, so they are all accustomed to balancing opposing interests. Indeed, the acceptance of the preferred concept implies a balancing of the preferred freedom at issue against any other interest

---

43 Or possibly a disregard for those provisions not favored, as Professor Cahn points out in Fact-Skepticism and Fundamental Law, 33 N.Y.U.L. Rev. 1, 13-16 (1958). In the present context it makes no difference which, so long as there is a grading of rights, which is clearly manifested. See also Marsh v. Alabama, 326 U.S. 501, 511 (1946), where Justice Frankfurter, concurring, said: "Where the First Amendment applies, it is a denial of all governmental power in our Federal system."

44 See, e.g., Zorach v. Clauson, 343 U.S. 306, 320 (1952) (dissenting opinion); Saia v. New York, 334 U.S. 558, 564-65 (1948) (dissenting opinion); Illinois ex rel. McCollum v. Board of Educ., 333 U.S. 203, 212 (1948) (concurring opinion); Everson v. Board of Educ., 330 U.S. 1, 18, 28 (1947) (dissenting opinions of Jackson and Rutledge, JJ., joined by Frankfurter, J.). But cf. West Virginia State Bd. of Educ. v. Barnette, 319 U.S. 624, 646 (1943) (dissenting opinion).

which stands in opposing counterbalance. Even so, there has been some doubt as to the propriety of balancing, a doubt encouraged by the imperatively negative command of the first amendment. Voices both on the Court and apart from it are sometimes heard insisting upon an absolutist view of the first amendment which would impliedly deny to Congress as well as to state and local legislative bodies all authority to enact legislation that even relates to speech. As will be seen, however, the argument proves too much. All adherents of the absolutist view must in the last analysis fix some limit beyond which speech is not protected against regulation. After all, the amendment only forbids "abridging the freedom of speech." So what seems at first glance to be an absolute prohibition is seen on investigation to permit an inquiry into at least two subsidiary questions: (1) when does speech lose its protection because it is not speech but "verbal acts"?[45] And, (2) where should the line be drawn between "abridging," which is flatly forbidden, and reasonable regulation, which may in some circumstances be permissible?

To ask the questions is not to suggest that there are any easy answers. There are not. And this is the whole sense of the preferred position as a recognition of the respect to be accorded the enumerated freedoms. The moment the necessity for drawing lines is conceded, as inevitably it must be, the argument comes into focus; and the issues admit of definition. Who should draw the lines and by what standards? Here at last are the real issues, and they are difficult ones on which reasonable men may differ. In this context it becomes relevant to reexamine the clear and present danger test; to determine whether legislative acts may be assisted by a presumption of constitutionality; to reflect upon the higher procedural standards required for limitation of free speech; and all the other aspects of the preferred position. These will be discussed in part II below, but first it is appropriate to deal with the so-called absolutist views.

Most prominent among the non-Court spokesmen for the absolutist position is Alexander Meiklejohn whose position is stated most fully in *Free Speech and Its Relation to Self-Government*.[46] Initially he concedes that "the legislature has both the right and the duty to prohibit certain forms of speech,"[47] including libel and slander. Because "words which incite men to crime are themselves criminal and must be dealt with as such,"[48] punishment is also possible for sedition

45 Gompers v. Bucks Stove & Range Co., 221 U.S. 418, 439 (1911).

46 Published in 1948. See also Meiklejohn, What Does The First Amendment Mean?, 20 U. Chi. L. Rev. 461 (1953).

47 Meiklejohn, Free Speech and Its Relation to Self-Government 18 (1948).

48 Ibid.

and treason. Legislative action in these areas may be an abridging of speech, but not an abridging of the *freedom* of speech; and only the latter is forbidden. He recognizes also the permissibility of reasonable regulation of the time and place of speaking.[49] Essentially his insistence is that speech necessary to reach an informed decision on matters political, economic, or social shall be available.

> What is essential is not that everyone shall speak, but that everything worth saying shall be said[50] . . . [and] conflicting views may be expressed, must be expressed, not because they are valid, but because they are relevant.[51]

Reduced to these essential premises, there is nothing so very startling about either theme or conclusions.[52]

The only members of the present Supreme Court who might be said to have expressed absolutist views are Justices Black and Douglas. Thus, Justice Black, dissenting in *Carlson v. Landon,* stated:

> My belief is that we must have freedom of speech, press and religion for all or we may eventually have it for none. I further believe that the First Amendment grants an absolute right to believe in any governmental system, discuss all governmental affairs, and argue for desired changes in the existing order.[53]

Similarly, Justice Douglas, in *Beauharnais v. Illinois,* stated:

> The First Amendment is couched in absolute terms—freedom of speech shall not be abridged. Speech has therefore a preferred position as contrasted to some other civil rights. For example, privacy, equally sacred to some, is protected by the Fourth Amendment only against unreasonable searches and seizures. There is room for regulation of the ways and means of invading privacy. No such leeway is granted the invasion of the right of free speech guaranteed by the First Amendment.[54]

---

49 Id. at 24-27.

50 Id. at 25.

51 Id. at 27.

52 It is surprising, however, to find, at the conclusion of the lectures that form Mr. Meiklejohn's book, he appears to concede the possible necessity and propriety, in the light of atomic and biological discoveries, to "abridge the private desire of the scholar—or of those who subsidize him—to study whatever he may please." Id. at 100. Does he not give away more than he preserves?

His general thesis is based additionally upon an argument that certain private rights of speech are given only the reasonable protection afforded by the due process clause (for example, the merchant advertising his wares or the paid lobbyist speaking for his client), while the public rights of speech have the full protection of the first amendment. The only difficulty with this, as the late Professor Chafee pointed out, is the fact that there is no historical or logical basis for this dichotomy of speech interests. See Chafee, Book Review, 62 Harv. L. Rev. 891 (1949).

53 342 U.S. 524, 555 (1952) (dissenting opinion). See also Beauharnais v. Illinois, 343 U.S. 250, 274-75 (1952) (dissenting opinion); Adler v. Board of Educ., 342 U.S. 485, 496-97 (1952) (dissenting opinion).

54 343 U.S. 250, 285 (1952) (dissenting opinion).

It will be noted, however, that neither of the foregoing statements categorically forbids legislation which touches upon speech. The standard of judgment in every case depends upon the drawing of a line between action and speech. As Justice Douglas observed in *Speiser v. Randall,* "Advocacy which is in no way brigaded with action should always be protected by the first amendment. That protection should extend even to the ideas we despise."[55] Similarly, Justice Black, in *Martin v. City of Struthers,* before holding invalid a municipal ordinance forbidding any person to knock on doors, ring bells, or otherwise summon occupants to the door for the purpose of distributing handbills, framed the issue as follows:

> We are faced in the instant case with the necessity of weighing the conflicting interests of the appellant in the civil rights she claims as well as the right of the individual householder to determine whether he is willing to receive her message, against the interest of the community which by this ordinance offers to protect the interests of all of its citizens, whether particular citizens want that protection or not.[56]

The same theme, emphasizing the necessity of balancing, appears in a number of other cases holding invalid various kinds of governmental action;[57] and, of course, statements to the same effect are emphasized even more strongly in opinions denying the claimed right.[58]

There is, then, substantial ground for believing that the concept of balancing, and not any absolutistic view, is accepted by all members of the Court in free speech cases.[59] The division within the Court relates exclusively to the techniques of balancing, that is, how the opposing interests shall be arrayed against each other. Here, again,

55 357 U.S. 513, 536-37 (1958) (concurring opinion). Justice Douglas made his position unmistakably clear in his dissent in Dennis v. United States, 341 U.S. 494, 581 (1951), where he said: "The freedom to speak is not absolute; the teaching of methods of terror and other seditious conduct should be beyond the pale along with obscenity and immorality."

56 319 U.S. 141, 143 (1943).

57 E.g., Thomas v. Collins, 323 U.S. 516, 530 (1945); Thornhill v. Alabama, 310 U.S. 88, 95 (1940). Cf. Watkins v. United States, 354 U.S. 178, 198-99 (1957).

58 E.g., Barenblatt v. United States, 360 U.S. 109, 126-27 (1959); Beauharnais v. Illinois, 343 U.S. 250 (1952); Adler v. Board of Educ., 342 U.S. 485, 493 (1952); Dennis v. United States, 341 U.S. 494, 508-11 (1951); Feiner v. New York, 340 U.S. 315 (1951); American Communications Ass'n v. Douds, 339 U.S. 382, 397 (1950). Cf. Barr v. Matteo, 360 U.S. 564, 570-71 (1959). And of course all the clear and present danger cases not cited above are in reality balancing cases.

59 But cf. Chief Justice Warren's dictum in Sweezy v. New Hampshire, 354 U.S. 234, 251 (1957), where the Court held that the state had violated due process rights of a witness in a state legislative investigation that impinged on academic freedoms. "We do not now conceive of any circumstances wherein a state interest would justify infringement of rights in these fields. But we do not need to reach such fundamental questions of state power to decide this case." See also Justice Black's dissent in Barenblatt v. United States, 360 U.S. 109, 134 (1959), which is discussed below.

the idea that the first amendment is to be preferred is a significant element in the weighing process. One who believes strongly, not only in the formalism of preference but as well in the underlying substance of that position, necessarily arranges his balances differently than one who reluctantly acknowledges the preferred position. The point is best illustrated in the cases; and again the matter is brought into clearest perspective by contrasting the views of Justice Frankfurter on the one hand with those of others (particularly Justice Black) who hold sharply different views.

Balancing and the Judicial Function.—Nearly all cases which go to the United States Supreme Court for final decision involve complex and troublesome issues whose solution requires sufficiently high legal attainments to warrant calling the resulting process the art of judging.[60] Infinitely the most difficult are those cases which call for constitutional judgment. The commands and the prohibitions of the Constitution are seldom categorical or precise. The magnificent indefiniteness of the constitutional text has proved at once the genius of the instrument and a source of constant despair to those faced with the necessity of decision. How can one know a priori what is a too-great interference with the free movement of commerce "among the States"; who can be sure when a search and seizure is "unreasonable"; and what test for "due process" can be devised that does not arise in the viscera?

Fortunately, in dealing with first amendment questions the constitutional uncertainties are reduced, as compared to the semantic jungle of due process and the shadowy limbo of interstate commerce. There is initially the emphatic command that "Congress shall make no law . . . ." Even though it be recognized that the prohibition is not absolute, separation of the permissible from the forbidden takes meaning from the common sense mandate of the preferred position.

In any event, there is no escape from the necessity of decision. Even a ruling that the Court must accept any legislative judgment for which there is a "rational basis,"[61] regardless of the strain it imposes on constitutional text, is at least negatively also a decision. During one long period, for example, the judicial thumb weighed heavily on the substantive due process scale that read "freedom of contract."[62] But this is no longer the fashion, and no member of the present Court regrets the passing of that interlude. Now it is said that Congress and the states may experiment in matters of social and economic policy,

60 See, e.g., Cardozo, The Growth of the Law 56 (1924).

61 West Virginia State Bd. of Educ. v. Barnette, 319 U.S. 624, 639 (1943); United States v. Carolene Prods. Co., 304 U.S. 144, 152 (1938).

62 The limits may be marked roughly between Lochner v. New York, 198 U.S. 45 (1905) and Nebbia v. New York, 291 U.S. 502 (1934).

almost entirely free from judicial interference on the old ground of taking property without due process.

By way of contrast, the present is a period in which liberty of the person emerges as the central value. As already pointed out, all members of the Court agree that certain manifestations of that liberty—freedom of speech and thought—are values which merit special emphasis. But some are troubled that a distinction should thus be drawn between deference to the legislative judgment in matters economic and in matters of liberty. Why, and in what circumstances, should nine men substitute their collective constitutional judgment for the legislative determination which says in effect, "This is needed for the proper functioning of government"?

The answer to this inquiry would seem to be that the Court is required to judge, and there is no easy escape for individual Justices from the necessity of decision. As to the difference in emphasis between review of economic issues and review where fundamental liberties are involved, the answer once again inheres in the doctrine of the preferred position and the reasons already stated for that preference. In addition, in the context of deference to legislative action, there are further reasons for giving special scrutiny to alleged abridgments of freedom of speech and thought. The legislative process is in general well-suited to an examination of competing values in connection with social and economic programs, where the essential balancing can take place within the legislature. But the situation is different when the opposing values are free speech and the danger of violent acts, or where the balance is between freedom of the press and censorship. In these instances there is little balancing in the legislature. As Professor Chafee expressed the difficulties,

> [F]ree speech gets little attention and the dangers are everything. . . . So the indispensable balancing will have to be done by the courts or not at all. If judges cannot or will not review suppressions, then legislators and officials are left free to penalize speech and even thoughts as much as they may desire, and they desire a great deal.[63]

While these problems of balancing are necessarily involved in the decisions of all members of the Court, Justice Frankfurter has more consistently than the others sought to disclose the premises that for him have been compelling; but in examining the record of his more than twenty years on the Court it is not always easy to unravel and fit together the various themes. Thus, he has repeatedly called for judicial assessment of competing interests in cases involving due process,[64]

[63] Chafee, The Blessings of Liberty 85 (1956).

[64] E.g., Rochin v. California, 342 U.S. 165, 170-72 (1952); Adamson v. California,

unreasonable search and seizure,[65] and, to some extent, the commerce clause.[66] However, in cases involving the first amendment, at least until recent years, he has shown a curious, almost subservient, deference to the legislative judgment, whether it be act of Congress, state legislative act, or municipal ordinance.[67]

A characteristic expression is the following from his concurrence in *Dennis v. United States:*

> The demands of free speech in a democratic society as well as the interest in national security are better served by candid and informed weighing of the competing interests, within the confines of the judicial process, than by announcing dogmas too inflexible for the non-Euclidian problems to be solved.
>
> But how are competing interests to be assessed? Since they are not subject to quantitative ascertainment, who is to make adjustment?—who is to balance the relevant factors and ascertain which interest is in the circumstance to prevail? Full responsibility for the choice cannot be given to the courts. Courts are not representative bodies. They are not designed to be a good reflex of a democratic society. Their judgment is best informed, and therefore most dependable, within narrow limits . . . .
>
> Primary responsibility for adjusting the interests which compete in the situation before us of necessity belongs to the Congress . . . . We are to set aside the judgment of those whose duty it is to legislate only if there is no reasonable basis for it.[68]

This statement is, of course, consistent with Justice Frankfurter's view that the first amendment should not be described as preferred, despite his recognition that it comes to the Court "with a momentum for respect lacking when appeal is made" to economic liberties.[69] If we were to judge his views exclusively by the *Dennis* opinion above quoted, it would be necessary to say that Justice Frankfurter would

332 U.S. 46, 59 (1948) (concurring opinion). See, generally, Pollak, Mr. Justice Frankfurter: Judgment and the Fourteenth Amendment, 67 Yale L.J. 304 (1957).

65 E.g., On Lee v. United States, 343 U.S. 747, 758 (1952) (dissenting opinion); Schwartz v. Texas, 344 U.S. 199, 204 (1952) (concurring opinion); Wolf v. Colorado, 338 U.S. 25 (1949). See, generally, Handler, The Fourth Amendment and Mr. Justice Frankfurter, 8 Syracuse L. Rev. 166 (1957).

66 E.g., Capitol Greyhound Lines v. Brice, 339 U.S. 542, 548 (1950) (dissenting opinion); Southern Pac. Co. v. Arizona ex rel. Sullivan, 325 U.S. 761 (1945) (opinion of Stone, C.J.); Carter v. Virginia, 321 U.S. 131, 139 (1944) (concurring opinion). See, generally, Brown, The Open Economy: Justice Frankfurter and the Position of the Judiciary, 67 Yale L.J. 219 (1957).

67 E.g., Staub v. City of Baxley, 355 U.S. 313, 325 (1958) (dissenting opinion); Ullmann v. United States, 350 U.S. 422 (1956); Beauharnais v. Illinois, 343 U.S. 250 (1952); Dennis v. United States, 341 U.S. 494, 517 (1951) (concurring opinion); Niemotko v. Maryland, 340 U.S. 268, 273 (1951) [concurring opinion applying also to Feiner v. New York, 340 U.S. 315 (1951), and Kunz v. New York, 340 U.S. 290 (1951)]; Kovacs v. Cooper, 336 U.S. 77, 89 (1949) (concurring opinion).

68 341 U.S. 494, 524-25 (1951).

69 Kovacs v. Cooper, 336 U.S. 77, 95 (1949) (concurring opinion).

place the first amendment in a *subordinate* position. There is now, however, persuasive evidence that he has moved to a more generous interpretation of the importance of free speech, at least where the intrusion is by a state upon academic freedom. In upholding a refusal to answer nonrelevant questions, Justice Frankfurter said in *Sweezy v. New Hampshire:*

> To be sure, this is a conclusion based on a judicial judgment in balancing two contending principles—the right of a citizen to political privacy, as protected by the Fourteenth Amendment, and the right of the State to self-protection. And *striking the balance implies the task of judgment. This is the inescapable judicial task in giving substantive content, legally enforced, to the Due Process Clause, and it is a task ultimately committed to this Court* . . . . Such a judgment must be arrived at in a spirit of humility when it counters the judgment of the State's highest court. *But, in the end, judgment cannot be escaped—the judgment of this Court.* (Emphasis added.)[70]

On the face of it, the more recent opinion just quoted suggests an abrupt change from the opinion expressed six years earlier. In only two ways might the two be reconciled, but neither seems supportable. It might be suggested that Justice Frankfurter ranks freedom of academic speech above freedom of political speech, but for one who denies the validity of grading this would seem unlikely. Alternatively, the argument could be made that he finds in the fourteenth amendment a more severe limitation on state legislatures than in the first amendment as a limitation on Congress; but it would seem impossible to draw from the generality of due process a more stringent prohibition than from the command that "Congress shall make no law . . . ."[71] In short, Justice Frankfurter may now have come around to the position that other members of the Court seem to have accepted all along, namely, that the weighing of competing considerations is the very essence of the judicial function in matters of speech as well as in matters of economics or procedural due process. Indeed, as should by now be clear, it is the thesis of this study that the judicial obligation of decision is particularly acute when the first amendment is involved. This, too, Justice Frankfurter seems to acknowledge in his opinion in *Sweezy*.

Balancing and the Choice of Scales.—Since the remainder of this study will be concerned with various devices by which the Court has balanced the interests in first amendment cases, it may be well at this

70 Sweezy v. New Hampshire, 354 U.S. 234, 266-67 (1957) (concurring opinion).

71 For discussion of an opposite conclusion, namely, that the prohibitions of the first amendment are more nearly absolute as limitations upon the federal government than as limitations upon the state governments through the fourteenth amendment, see Rogge, "Congress Shall Make No Law . . . ," 56 Mich. L. Rev. 331 (1958); Rogge, State Power Over Sedition, Obscenity and Picketing, 34 N.Y.U.L. Rev. 817 (1959).

point to make some preliminary observations about the right and the wrong way to balance. Manifestly, if the interests on one side are heavily weighted, and a negligible interest is balanced against it, the result is foreclosed before the question is even posed. So the choice of scales and of values becomes the significant inquiry. Dean Roscoe Pound has made this point effectively.

> When it comes to weighing or valuing claims or demands with respect to other claims or demands, we must be careful to compare them on the same plane. If we put one as an individual interest and the other as a social interest we may decide the question in advance in our way of putting it.[72]

In this area Justice Black has been the most articulate member of the Court in cautioning against mistaking the opposing interests. Thus, in *Marsh v. Alabama*[73] the Court held that the first amendment forbids a state to impose criminal punishment on a person for distributing religious literature on the public sidewalk of a company-owned town contrary to company regulations. The dissent would have reached a different result by balancing the interest of the property owner against that of the distributor of religious literature, described simply as a trespasser.[74] So to describe the interests of course predetermines the desired result. In rejecting such a distortion Justice Black said:

> When we balance the Constitutional rights of owners of property against those of the people to enjoy freedom of press and religion, as we must here, we remain mindful of the fact that the latter occupy a preferred position. . . . In our view the circumstance that the property rights to the premises where the deprivation of liberty, here involved, took place, were held by others than the public, is not sufficient to justify the State's permitting a corporation to govern a community of citizens so as to restrict their fundamental liberties and the enforcement of such restraint by the application of a state statute.[75]

The proper alignment of interests, then, required a balancing of the right of the company—a municipality in every real sense—to regulate the use of its property against "the preservation of a free society," as here manifested by "the right of each individual citizen to receive such literature as he himself might desire."[76] It was not owner against trespasser, as the dissenters would have had it, but owner against a significant aspect of the free society.[77]

---

[72] Pound, A Survey of Social Interests, 57 Harv. L. Rev. 1, 2 (1943); also as a chapter in Vanderbilt, Studying Law 439, 440 (2d ed. 1955).

[73] 326 U.S. 501 (1946). Cf. Tucker v. Texas, 326 U.S. 517 (1946).

[74] 326 U.S. at 516.

[75] Id. at 509.

[76] Id. at 505.

[77] See also the discussion of this point in Cahn, The Firstness of the First Amendment, 65 Yale L.J. 464, 478-81 (1956).

Justice Black subsequently made more specific his views on the appropriate uses for balancing in *Barenblatt v. United States:*

> [C]ases suggesting that a law which primarily regulates conduct but which might also indirectly affect speech can be upheld if the effect on speech is minor in relation to the need for control of the conduct. . . . But even such laws governing conduct, we emphasized, must be tested, though only by a balancing process, if they indirectly affect ideas. On one side of the balance, we pointed out, is the interest of the United States in seeing that its fundamental law protecting freedom of communication is not abridged; on the other the obvious interest of the State to regulate conduct within its boundaries.[78]

But where the impact of governmental regulation had more than an indirect effect on speech, Black said, "I do not agree that laws directly abridging First Amendment freedoms can be justified by a congressional or judicial balancing test."[79]

It now becomes clear that the two opposing interests are *both* governmental—one an effectuation of the immediate legislative purpose, the other preservation of the free society as mandated in the Constitution. It is small wonder that as these values are properly sorted out, the societal interest in the democratic process should be preferred.

The *Barenblatt* case, quoted from above, involved a prosecution for contempt of Congress for petitioner's refusal to answer questions about past or present membership in the Communist Party, as put to him by the House Un-American Activities Committee. Justice Harlan, for the majority, said that the result depended on "a balancing by the courts of the competing private and public interests at stake in the particular circumstances shown."[80] He thus weighted the scales falsely in describing as "private" what was really the public interest in the free society. Then he described the governmental interest in this investigation (and thus in the answers to these questions) as "the right of self-preservation" in light of "the long and widely held view that the tenets of the Communist Party include the ultimate overthrow of the Government of the United States by force and violence."[81] Against this formidable array Justice Harlan saw only the petitioner's interest in remaining silent. But this misconceived the issue. As Justice Black commented on this balance:

> [I]t completely leaves out the real interest in Barenblatt's silence, the interest of the people as a whole in being able to join organizations, advocate causes and make political "mistakes" without later being

78 360 U.S. 109, 141 (1959) (dissenting opinion).
79 Ibid.
80 Id. at 126.
81 Id. at 128.

> subjected to governmental penalties for having dared to think for themselves. It is this right, the right to err politically, which keeps us strong as a Nation. For no number of laws against communism can have as much effect as the personal conviction which comes from having heard its arguments and rejected them, or from having once accepted its tenets and later recognized their worthlessness.[82]

The balancing concept is useful within its proper limits, but is distorted into meaninglessness when applied as it was in the *Barenblatt* case.[83] The balancing concept should be restored to the meaning Justice Roberts gave it a number of years ago in *Schneider v. State:*

> [T]he courts should be astute to examine the effect of the challenged legislation. Mere legislative preferences or beliefs . . . may well support regulation directed at other personal activities, but be insufficient to justify such as diminishes the exercise of rights so vital to the maintenance of democratic institutions.[84]

II

The Variety of Preferences

A. *The Past and Future of Clear and Present*

The literature concerning the clear and present danger test, in judicial decisions and in scholarly comment, is voluminous.[85] Despite the completeness of the scrutiny and the minuteness of the dissection of the component parts, nearly all of this vast erudition has failed to emphasize sufficiently one central point without which the test loses its principal significance in relation to the first amendment. The misconception is an apparent assumption that the clear and present danger test has been *the* device for screening out impermissible abridgments of the first amendment freedoms. The truth is, however, that the clear and present danger formula is simply one device among many for making the necessary constitutional choices; and there is considerable reason for believing that it has been one of the least successful. Other

---

82 Id. at 144.

83 See also the discussion at page 1209 infra of the similar distortion of balancing in the application of the clear and present danger test in, for example, Dennis v. United States, 341 U.S. 494 (1951).

84 308 U.S. 147, 161 (1939).

85 Chafee, Free Speech in the United States (2d ed. 1948); Meiklejohn, Free Speech and Its Relation to Self-Government (1948); Antieau, The Rule of Clear and Present Danger—Its Origin and Application, 13 U. Det. L.J. 198 (1950); Antieau, The Rule of Clear and Present Danger: Scope of Its Applicability, 48 Mich. L. Rev. 811 (1950); Antieau, "Clear and Present Danger"—Its Meaning and Significance, 25 Notre Dame Law. 603 (1950); Boudin, "Seditious Doctrines" and the "Clear and Present Danger" Rule, 38 Va. L. Rev. 143 (1952); Green, Liberty Under the Fourteenth Amendment, 27 Wash. U.L.Q. 497 (1942); Mendelson, Clear and Present Danger—From Schenck to Dennis, 52 Colum. L. Rev. 313 (1952); Notes, 28 Calif. L. Rev. 733 (1940); 47 Colum. L. Rev. 595 (1947); 57 Yale L.J. 806 (1948).

legal principles and theories which have done service in the same cause—that is, promotion of the generally accepted concept of the preferred position—include the narrowing of the presumption of constitutionality of legislation in first amendment cases; strict construction of statutes to avoid limitation of speech or thought; increased flexibility in permitting standing to sue; and insistence upon more exacting standards of procedural due process where freedom of speech is in any way regulated. Clearly these are all manifestations of the preferred position, each serving in particular circumstances the larger cause of preserving the open society. It is proper to begin the discussion of these devices with the clear and present danger test because it has had the most attention and caused the most difficulty.

That the clear and present danger test is not the sole—or by any means the most reliable—champion of first amendment causes is apparent from its fluctuating history. The test originated in a case in 1919 which upheld a conviction against the claimed right of free speech;[86] but it quickly lost majority support when Justices Holmes and Brandeis sought to apply it to disapprove, rather than to endorse, government action.[87] Indeed, the clear and present danger test did not really become majority doctrine until 1937,[88] and at best it was used in only a meager handful of cases to upset government action that could probably have been set aside on other grounds equally well. By 1951, in *Dennis v. United States*[89] the doctrine was drastically altered into a "probable" danger test and the Court has not employed the danger test, either as originally conceived or as modified in *Dennis,* in any subsequent case through the October 1958 Term ending in June 1959. Accordingly, it might well not seem very worthwhile to examine the danger test again save for the fact that the Court called for reargument in the October 1959 Term on the applicability of the test to the Communist "membership" case, *Scales v. United States.*[90] In the order for reargument the Court listed five questions to which counsel were requested to address themselves. Only one of the questions makes specific reference to the clear and present danger test, but all are closely related to it:

(1) Is the Membership Clause of the Smith Act, 18 U.S.C. § 2385,

---

86 Schenck v. United States, 249 U.S. 47 (1919) (Holmes, J.).

87 Pierce v. United States, 252 U.S. 239 (1920); Schaefer v. United States, 251 U.S. 466 (1920); Abrams v. United States, 250 U.S. 616 (1919).

88 Herndon v. Lowry, 301 U.S. 242 (1937).

89 341 U.S. 494 (1951).

90 260 F.2d 21 (4th Cir.), cert. granted, 358 U.S. 917 (1958), reargument ordered, 360 U.S. 924 (1959). For the considerable earlier history of the case, see Justice Clark's memorandum in opposition to the reargument order. Id. at 925. See also United States v. Noto, 262 F.2d 501 (2d Cir. 1958), cert. granted, 28 U.S.L. Week 3109 (Oct. 12, 1959).

valid under the Constitution of the United States if it be interpreted to permit a conviction based only on proof that the accused was a member of a society, group or assembly of persons described in the Act knowing the purposes thereof?

(2) If not, is the Membership Clause constitutionally valid if interpreted as also requiring proof that the membership was accompanied by a specific intent of the accused to accomplish those purposes as speedily as circumstances would permit? Does the Smith Act permissibly bear such an interpretation?

(3) If the Membership Clause would not be constitutionally valid as interpreted under (1) or (2), would the clause be constitutionally valid if interpreted as requiring as an element of the crime proof that the accused was an "active" member? Does the Smith Act permissibly bear such an interpretation? If not, and if the clause be valid without such element, does a constitutional application of the Membership Clause depend upon any such requirement, and if so was such a requirement properly applied by the courts in this case?

(4) Whether the "clear and present danger" doctrine, as interpreted by counsel, has application to the Membership Clause, either with respect to the accused or with respect to the "society, group, or assembly of persons" described in the statute. If applicable, whether such doctrine was or can now be, properly applied in this case.

(5) Is § 4(f) of the Internal Security Act, 50 USCA 780, a bar to the present prosecution? Counsel are requested to discuss the relevance of the registration provisions of that Act to this question.

The request for argument on the applicability of the danger test may be explained in either of two ways: (1) recognizing the uncertainties in the present status of the test, the Court may contemplate another attempt at a working definition; or (2) the Court may regard this as a proper occasion for the outright abandonment of a doctrine which, while possibly once valuable, no longer can serve any useful function. The following remarks will be addressed to the proposition that, if ever the danger test was valid and meaningful, it no longer can be so regarded. Because it was the first formula which offered, even gropingly, a haven for the preferred freedoms of the first amendment, the idea deserves respect. But the performance, as briefly reviewed below, proves the hope of shelter to have been false and demonstrates the propriety of a definitive rejection of the theory. The historical aspects of the subject naturally divide themselves into three periods: 1919-1937; 1937-1951; and the period from 1951 to the present.

Concurrence and Dissent: 1919-1937.—Although the danger test was originally stated in a majority opinion by Justice Holmes for a unanimous Court,[91] he conceded that the conviction in that case could have been upheld on the basis of an earlier decision,[92] without reference

[91] Schenck v. United States, 249 U.S. 47 (1919).
[92] Goldman v. United States, 245 U.S. 474, 477 (1918).

to the test at all. "But as the right to free speech was not referred to specially, we have thought fit to add a few words."[93] The "few words" added introduced the clear and present danger test: "The question in every case is whether the words used are used in such circumstances and are of such a nature as to create a clear and present danger that they will bring about the substantive danger that Congress has a right to prevent."[94] And he added, significantly, as the next sentence, "It is a question of proximity and degree."[95]

Precisely what Justice Holmes meant by these cryptic words, and how he would have decided cases arising after his death (when, for the first time, the doctrine moved into majority status in cases allowing for disagreement), no one can know for certain. And there is no intention now either to review in detail the argument on this score, or to add new second guesses. One thing, however, seems reasonably certain. As Professor Freund points out:

> The test is pretty clearly drawn from the criminal law, and in particular from Holmes's analysis of the criminal law as scholar and state court judge; for the criminal law is necessarily concerned with the line at which innocent preparation ends and a guilty conspiracy attempt begins.[96]

The significance of this origin of the doctrine lies in the fact that it was apparently intended as a means of drawing the line between speech and action, but so framed as to assure that speech would be as free as possible, in short, that speech should be preferred.

If this was the proper meaning, Holmes' colleagues, with the exception of Justice Brandeis, either failed to grasp this fairly simple point or, perhaps more likely, simply rejected the test. In any event, the majority opinions in cases decided during the balance of the tenure of Holmes and Brandeis on the Court did not again refer to the danger test[97] except, in *Gitlow v. New York*,[98] where the Court held the danger test inapplicable and applied a "dangerous tendency" test in support of a conviction for violation of New York's criminal syndicalism

93 Schenck v. United States, 249 U.S. 47, 52 (1919).

94 Ibid.

95 Ibid.

96 Freund, On Understanding the Supreme Court 25 (1949). Relevant earlier opinions of Justice Holmes include the following: Graves v. Johnson, 179 Mass. 53, 60 N.E. 383 (1901); Commonwealth v. Peaslee, 177 Mass. 267, 272 (1901). Cf. Hyde v. United States, 225 U.S. 347, 387-88 (1912) (dissenting opinion); Swift & Co. v. United States, 196 U.S. 375, 396 (1905).

97 Even Justice Holmes wrote majority opinions in two cases upholding convictions of wartime offenses without mentioning the danger test, although it might have been applied in both. Debs v. United States, 249 U.S. 211 (1919); Frohwerk v. United States, 249 U.S. 204 (1919).

98 268 U.S. 652 (1925).

statute. The 1920's, then, were the years of the great dissents[99] and the striking concurrence[100] upon which the later acceptance of the danger test was based. Particularly eloquent was Justice Brandeis in demonstrating the necessary relationship between free speech and the adequate functioning of the democratic process. "It is," he said, "the function of speech to free men from the bondage of irrational fears."[101] And again:

> Those who won our independence by revolution were not cowards. They did not fear political change. They did not exalt order at the cost of liberty. To courageous, self-reliant men, with confidence in the power of free and fearless reasoning applied through the processes of popular government, no danger flowing from speech can be deemed clear and present, unless the incidence of the evil apprehended is so imminent that it may befall before there is opportunity for full discussion. If there be time to expose through discussion the falsehoods and fallacies, to avert the evil by the processes of education, the remedy to be applied is more speech, not enforced silence.[102]

But these ideas, however persuasive as rhetoric, were slow to shape decisions. In its first eighteen years the clear and present danger test amounted only to this: one majority opinion (upholding the conviction claimed to abridge the freedom of speech), one concurrence, and five dissents.

The Clear and Present Danger Test Accepted: 1937-1951.—Only during the fourteen years from 1937 to 1951 can it be said that the danger test had any real impact, and even then its limited success was dependent as often as not on the barest majority made up of differing members of the Court who agreed to the use of the test, one may suspect, for varied reasons. The negative record is more substantial. Although first amendment rights were upheld in a substantial number of cases in the 1930's and early 1940's in which the danger test might have been applied, it was relied on specifically to uphold the claimed right in only nine cases.[103] By a parity of reasoning, but employing

---

99 Gitlow v. New York, 268 U.S. 652, 672 (1925); Gilbert v. Minnesota, 254 U.S. 325, 334 (1920); Pierce v. United States, 252 U.S. 239, 253 (1920); Schaefer v. United States, 251 U.S. 466, 482 (1920); Abrams v. United States, 250 U.S. 616, 624 (1919).

100 Whitney v. California, 274 U.S. 357, 372 (1927).

101 Id. at 376.

102 Id. at 377.

103 Craig v. Harney, 331 U.S. 367, 373 (1947); Pennekamp v. Florida, 328 U.S. 331, 335 (1946); Thomas v. Collins, 323 U.S. 516, 530 (1945); West Virginia State Bd. of Educ. v. Barnette, 319 U.S. 624, 633-34 (1943); Taylor v. Mississippi, 319 U.S. 583, 588-90 (1943); Bridges v. California, 314 U.S. 252, 263 (1941); Carlson v. California, 310 U.S. 106, 113 (1940); Thornhill v. Alabama, 310 U.S. 88, 104-05 (1940); Herndon v. Lowry, 301 U.S. 242, 260 (1937). See also Terminiello v. Chicago, 337 U.S. 1, 4-5 (1949); Cantwell v. Connecticut, 310 U.S. 296, 308-11 (1940), where the reference to the danger test appears to be dictum.

different words, the test may have figured in three additional cases.[104] There is little, if any, indication that any of these cases would have been decided differently if the clear and present danger formula had not been used.

There have never been more than four consistent supporters of the formula sitting as members of the Court at any one time.[105] Even that number has since been further reduced to the point where now perhaps no real support for the doctrine can be found on the Supreme Court.[106]

In 1950 began the falling away that culminated in the overthrow of the original formulation a year later in *Dennis*. The significant 1950 decisions were *American Communications Ass'n v. Douds*[107] and *Feiner v. New York*.[108] In the *Douds* case the issue was the constitutionality of the non-Communist affidavit required of union officers as a condition of the union's securing benefits under the National Labor Relations Act. Although the clear and present danger test was not rejected out of hand, and despite the conceded fact that the oath requirement "undeniably discouraged the lawful exercise of political freedoms,"[109] the Court held the test inapplicable in such a way as to deprive the test of real meaning. In the same year, in *Feiner*, for the first time since 1919, the Court used the clear and present danger test to balance the opposing interests and *deny* the claimed first amendment right.[110] The danger of disorder that might result as a reaction to petitioner's speaking was found to be a sufficiently clear and present danger to justify police action, not to discipline the crowd, but to stop the speaker and convict *him* of an incitement of breach of the peace.

The special application of the clear and present danger test in determining the permissible limits of comment on pending judicial proceedings is discussed in Note, Free Speech; Fair Trial—Rights in Collision, 34 N.Y.U.L. Rev. 1278 (1959). The cases involved are Craig v. Harney, supra, Pennekamp v. Florida, supra, and Bridges v. California, supra.

104 Hartzel v. United States, 322 U.S. 680, 686-87 (1944) (dictum); Bakery Drivers v. Wohl, 315 U.S. 769, 775 (1942); AFL v. Swing, 312 U.S. 321, 325 (1941). There are, to be sure, other cases in which it might be argued, in view of discussion of "imminence" of danger and the like, that the danger test was in fact being applied. Justice Douglas has a comprehensive listing of such cases in the appendix to his opinion in Dennis v. United States, 341 U.S. 494, 591-92 (1951). But the fact is that, apart from the twelve cases noted in this note and note 103 supra, the other decisions favorable to first amendment rights during this period relied primarily on other methods of expressing the preferred position. See the discussion in §§ B through F, infra pp. 1212-22.

105 Mendelson, Clear and Present Danger—From Schenck to Dennis, 52 Colum. L. Rev. 313, 320 (1952).

106 See text at notes 113-25 infra.

107 339 U.S. 382 (1950). See also Osman v. Douds, 339 U.S. 846 (1950).

108 340 U.S. 315 (1950).

109 339 U.S. at 393.

110 Cf. Giboney v. Empire Storage & Ice Co., 336 U.S. 490, 502-03 (1949), where picketing was enjoined because its purpose was to compel violation of valid state law.

Thereafter, it was but a step to the jettisoning of the test in *Dennis* by a recasting of the elements to be taken into account. Adopting the test suggested by Judge Learned Hand in the court below, Chief Justice Vinson announced the new formulation as follows: "In each case . . . [courts] must ask whether the gravity of the 'evil,' discounted by its improbability, justifies such invasion of free speech as is necessary to avoid the danger."[111] Whatever may have been Judge Hand's inspiration for this rephrasing,[112] two things at least seem clear: (1) affirmance of the conviction would not have been likely under the original phraseology as construed in the intervening cases; and (2) in referring to "the gravity of the 'evil' discounted by its improbability" as the test of remoteness to justify an "invasion of free speech," one may speculate that the test has become simply one of "probability"—a balancing test that is devoid of any preference for the first amendment. When the opposing interests are described as the state's interest in survival against the right of a few men to speak freely, the result is a drastic shift in the center of "gravity" that predetermines the outcome. The effect is to deny the preferred position which freedom of speech has historically held and which should not now be casually relinquished.

The Demise of Clear and Present Danger: 1951-1959.—Whatever the proper meaning of the rephrased test, the reformulation in *Dennis,* whether so intended or not, had the effect of killing the clear and present danger rule. Neither in its original form nor as recast has the doctrine since been used as the basis for decision in a majority opinion.[113] If it seems surprising that nothing was heard of the clear and present danger test between 1951 and 1959, the first step toward comprehension can be found in the opinion of Chief Justice Vinson, who substituted for the old test the new and less exacting formula.

[111] Dennis v. United States, 341 U.S. 494, 510 (1951), quoting from the lower court opinion at 183 F.2d 201, 212 (2d Cir. 1950).

[112] This may be a nearly precise lifting of the language of an early opinion of Justice Holmes when Chief Justice of the Supreme Judicial Court of Massachusetts. There, in a case involving the sufficiency of an intent to violate state law as a basis for avoidance of a contract obligation, Holmes drew an analogy from criminal attempts, where "the line of proximity will vary somewhat according to the gravity of the evil apprehended." Graves v. Johnson, 179 Mass. 53, 58, 60 N.E. 383 (1901). Or Judge Hand may have had in mind § 283(c) of the Restatement of Torts, as quoted in his recent volume, Bill of Rights 25 (1958): "The proper question to put to oneself in such cases [reasonable care] is 'whether the magnitude of the risk outweighs the value which the law attaches to the conduct which involves it.' "

[113] The test was rejected as irrelevant in Beauharnais v. Illinois, 343 U.S. 250, 266 (1952) ("libelous utterances not being within the area of constitutionally protected speech") and Roth v. United States, 354 U.S. 476, 486-87 (1957) ("obscenity is not protected speech").

Joining his opinion were Justices Reed, Burton, and Minton, who may thus also be deemed no friends of clear and present danger. Justice Frankfurter, concurring in the result, suggested no regret at the relinquishment of the formula "expressed by those attractive but imprecise words."[114] But neither did he give any sign of enthusiasm for the reformulation, for he said the defendants' argument "cannot be met by reinterpreting the Court's frequent use of 'clear' and 'present' to mean an entertainable 'probability.'"[115] Ultimately, however, the Frankfurter position may not be too different from the Vinson conclusion; for both would permit a weighing of national security against freedom of speech for the individual defendants.[116] In Justice Frankfurter's scales the result is also not difficult to predict, because "not every type of speech occupies the same position on the scale of values."[117] And the kind of speech indulged in by the defendants "ranks low."[118]

Justice Jackson, too, disavowed the clear and present danger test in cases involving charges as serious as those in *Dennis*. He proposed its limitation

> . . . for application as a rule of reason in the kind of case for which it was devised. When the issue is criminality of a hot-headed speech on a street corner, or circulation of a few incendiary pamphlets, or parading by some zealots behind a red flag, or refusal of a handful of school children to salute our flag, it is not beyond the capacity of the judicial process to gather, comprehend, and weigh the necessary materials for decision whether it is a clear and present danger of substantive evil or a harmless letting off of steam.[119]

Justice Black, dissenting, noted that application of the clear and present danger test in its pre-*Dennis* meaning would require reversal; but his own reasons for urging reversal were different: "No matter how . . . [the indictment] is worded, this is a virulent form of prior censorship of speech and press, which I believe the First Amendment

---

114 341 U.S. 494, 527 (1951).

115 Ibid.

116 "A survey of the relevant decisions indicates that the results which we have reached are on the whole those that would ensue from careful weighing of conflicting interests." Id. at 542 (concurring opinion of Frankfurter, J.). To the same effect Justice Frankfurter quotes from Professor Freund's study, On Understanding the Supreme Court 27 (1949); "'No matter how rapidly we utter the phrase "clear and present danger," or how closely we hyphenate the words, they are not a substitute for the weighing of values.'" 341 U.S. at 542-43.

117 341 U.S. at 544.

118 Id. at 545.

119 Id. at 568 (concurring opinion).

forbids. I would hold § 3 of the Smith Act authorizing this prior restraint unconstitutional on its face and as applied."[120]

Of all the members of the Court who participated in the decision,[121] only Justice Douglas had an affirmatively good word to say for the clear and present danger formula; but even his basic reason for urging reversal was that this was an abridgment of the freedom of speech which, according to the proof, was not accompanied by any action.[122] Quite clearly, to the extent that Douglas suggested acceptance of the danger test, it was only as an intermediate point on the way to some assurance of still greater protection for speech not "brigaded with action" (as he was to describe the difference in a later case).[123] Out of Court he has recognized the confusion and inadequacies of the danger test as it has been applied. " 'Clear and present danger,' " he has written, "has become merely a convenient excuse for suppression."[124]

In light of the opinions in the *Dennis* case, at that time one would scarcely have expected to see the clear and present danger test employed again. The majority clearly rejected it, and not even the dissenters were persuaded that the test offered the proper long-range solution. Indeed, there has been no revival of the danger test on behalf of the majority of the Court until the request for argument on this issue in the *Scales* case. Nor does it appear likely that readoption is in prospect.[125]

---

120 Id. at 579. Justice Black also employed clear and present danger language in Bridges v. California, 314 U.S. 252, 262-63 (1941), in reversing a contempt conviction for an out-of-court publication concerning a pending case. But he made it clear here, too, that this was only an intermediate rather than an ultimate test of first amendment rights. The clear and present danger cases, he said, "do no more than recognize a minimum compulsion of the Bill of Rights." Id. at 263. It would seem that Justice Black does not consider the danger test indispensable to the protection of freedom of expression.

121 Justice Clark did not participate. He has shown his approval of the majority opinion in Dennis, however, in Yates v. United States, 354 U.S. 298, 344-45 (1957) (dissenting opinion).

122 341 U.S. at 581-92 (dissenting opinion).

123 Speiser v. Randall, 357 U.S. 513, 536 (1958) (concurring opinion).

124 Douglas, The Right of the People 54 (1958). See also generally id. at 17-66.

125 The membership clause of the Smith Act reads as follows: "Whoever . . . becomes or is a member of, or affiliates with, any [society, group, or assembly of persons who teach, advocate, or encourage the overthrow of government by force or violence], knowing the purposes thereof" shall be subjected to fine or imprisonment or both. 18 U.S.C. § 2385 (1958).

Petitioner Scales was indicted for having been a member of the Communist Party, knowing that the Party was and is a society of persons who allegedly teach and advocate the overthrow of the Government of the United States as speedily as circumstances would permit. To sustain the conviction and uphold the constitutionality of the statute, the Government found it necessary to supplement the scanty text of the statute with the following arguments: (1) Although the membership clause does not state ex-

When *Dennis* was decided, it must have seemed possible that the new test would appear in subsequent decisions. But to date it, too, has not been mentioned. Indeed, the only other Smith Act case prior to *Scales* which might have raised these issues, *Yates v. United States*,[126] was decided on the basis of statutory construction.[127] One may now venture the prediction that the probable danger test is gone beyond resurrection along with its parent, the clear and present danger test.

The abandonment of these attempts to balance the scales of interests, well-intentioned though they may have been, will be little lamented. Neither the original formulation of the danger test nor its tortured remnant after *Dennis* ever offered a handle of meaning for the grasp of judge or scholar. Surely a test whose history shows how little assistance it has been to members of the Supreme Court has failed pragmatically. For the preferred position to assume its proper role, it is necessary that the danger test be rejected. As Judge Hand said in reference to the Holmes creation, "I cannot help thinking that for once Homer nodded."[128]

B. *Legislation and the Presumption of Constitutionality*

On the assumption that the clear and present danger test and its successor, the probable danger test, have both been abandoned, the way is now clear for an examination of the various proper ways for

pressly the requirement of personal intent, as do other clauses of the Smith Act, that deficiency can be corrected by implication. Brief for the United States, pp. 46-56, Scales v. United States, No. 488, Oct. Term 1958. The difficulty is that unless such specific intent can be incorporated into the statute as an element of the offense, along with membership and knowledge of the purposes of the Communist Party, the statute may be constitutionally defective. See question 2 on which the Court requested reargument, as noted in text accompanying note 90 supra. (2) Once membership, knowledge, and specific intent have been proved, the Government seems to concede that there might still be constitutional difficulty in convicting for mere passive membership in the Communist Party. Accordingly, the Government has suggested that where active membership (whatever that may mean) can be proved, the clear and present danger test may be applied as a question of law to determine whether the particular conviction can stand. Brief for the United States, id. at pp. 64-68. Petitioner objects to adding by implication this further element not found in statute or indictment and of course reads the clear and present danger test as a means of reversing conviction rather than, as the Government does, a means to assure upholding the conviction. Petitioner's Supplemental Brief on Reargument, pp. 11-27, Scales v. United States, No. 8, Oct. Term 1959.

Apart from the serious questions of statutory interpretation which are presented in the case, application of the danger test scarcely seems meaningful when it cannot be discussed on any intelligible common ground.

126 354 U.S. 298 (1957).

127 Justice Harlan emphasized that the statutory construction was aided by the assumption that Congress would not choose "to disregard a constitutional danger zone so clearly marked." Id. at 319.

128 Hand, The Bill of Rights 59 (1958).

recognition of the preferred position accorded freedom of speech and thought. There is a difference between the presumption of constitutionality that is accorded legislation regulating economic and social matters and the absence of any such presumption where legislation touches upon first amendment rights. Since at least 1938 it has been a truism of constitutional law that the Court will reject economic and social legislation only if there is no "rational basis" for the law.[129]

The rule is different where legislation impinges on freedom of mind or conscience. In such instances to say that there is no presumption of constitutionality is simply to recognize in one way the preferred position of these freedoms. This is not to say, however, as Justice Frankfurter has feared, that there is a presumption that such legislation is unconstitutional. It is rather no more than a way of signaling the special importance to society of these rights and noting that they may not be regulated by showing a mere "rational basis" for legislation. The alarm occasioned in some quarters by this elementary caution has been misdirected. In fact, the Supreme Court has yet to hold unconstitutional any act of Congress for violation of the first amendment. Even in those few cases where state legislation has been held to violate the first amendment, as incorporated into the fourteenth, the narrowing of the presumption of constitutionality seems to have played little part. The laws invalidated were for the most part so clearly infringements of liberty that even a presumption of constitutionality could not have saved them.[130] One might almost wonder whether the principle has been applied with sufficient vigor or whether it has proved too innocuous to overcome the insistent demands that legislation be supported. Probably the answer is that neither Chief Justice Stone, in first expressing the idea, nor those who have since approved the suggestion, had any idea that this was more than a starting point. It seems to amount only to this: when a legislative act comes before a court for constitutional review, if it appears to abridge, regulate, or even touch upon first amendment freedoms, the high regard in which they are necessarily held dictates a special scrutiny. To aid in this scrutiny other doctrinal aids are available, to which we now turn.

---

129 United States v. Carolene Prods. Co., 304 U.S. 144, 152 (1938).

130 For example, a number of state statutes and local ordinances have been held invalid on their face for manifest violation of the freedom of expression. See Staub v. City of Baxley, 355 U.S. 313 (1958); Kunz v. New York, 340 U.S. 290 (1951); Largent v. Texas, 318 U.S. 418 (1943); Cantwell v. Connecticut, 310 U.S. 296 (1940); Thornhill v. Alabama, 310 U.S. 88 (1940); Schneider v. State, 308 U.S. 147, 163-64 (1939); Hague v. CIO, 307 U.S. 496 (1939); Lovell v. City of Griffin, 303 U.S. 444 (1938).

The doctrine, of course, is not limited to first amendment cases, but may be employed equally in any instances in which questions of statutory construction come up in the context of constitutional issues.

C. *Legislation and Strict Construction*

A logical corollary of the proposition that legislation impinging on first amendment rights will be given careful scrutiny, is the well-established rule of strict construction. The idea is that where there are two possible constructions of a legislative act or regulation, one of which would be constitutionally valid and the other either invalid or doubtful, that construction will be chosen which allows the courts to uphold the statute.[131] Probably the most significant application of this doctrine in constitutional cases has been in connection with first amendment issues.

The unquestioned acceptance of this doctrine is further proof that there is no presumption of unconstitutionality in first amendment cases. If there were, the construction of the statute which would deny constitutionality would be the one chosen—an unthinkable result. Obviously, the intent of the strict construction rule is to preserve legislation and, at the same time, to protect the preferred rights of the first amendment. The doctrine has had a number of interesting applications, three of which may be recounted here.

The problem of protecting freedom of speech, thought, and association in connection with congressional investigations, without at the same time limiting unduly the reach of congressional power, has found an accommodation, albeit somewhat uneasy, in the principle of strict construction. The cases of *United States v. Rumely*[132] and *Watkins v. United States*[133] offer interesting similarities and contrasts. One involved a reluctant witness of rightist ideology and the other one of leftist persuasion; both witnesses were charged with contempt of Congress for refusal to answer questions. The principle of strict construction was applied in both cases to free the defendants. In *Rumely,* in what was possibly a strained construction, the Court held that the resolution defining the committee's powers had not conferred upon it

[131] As Chief Justice Hughes observed, "if a serious doubt of constitutionality is raised, it is a cardinal principle that this Court will first ascertain whether a construction of the statute is fairly possible by which the question may be avoided." Crowell v. Benson, 285 U.S. 22, 62 (1932). See also Greene v. McElroy, 360 U.S. 474 (1959); Scull v. Virginia ex rel. Comm. on Law Reform & Racial Activities, 359 U.S. 344 (1959); Peters v. Hobby, 349 U.S. 331 (1955); United States v. CIO, 335 U.S. 106 (1948); Ex parte Endo, 323 U.S. 283, 299-302 (1944). And a corollary of the same principle is applied in the construction of criminal statutes. See Yates v. United States, 354 U.S. 298, 304-05 (1957), quoting from United States v. Wiltberger, 18 U.S. (5 Wheat.) 76, 95-96 (1820). See also United States v. Petrillo, 332 U.S. 1 (1947); Screws v. United States, 325 U.S. 91 (1945).

[132] 345 U.S. 41 (1953). Cf. United States v. Harriss, 347 U.S. 612 (1954).

[133] 354 U.S. 178 (1957). Cf. Sweezy v. New Hampshire, 354 U.S. 234 (1957). But cf. Barenblatt v. United States, 360 U.S. 109 (1959); Uphaus v. Wyman, 360 U.S. 72 (1959).

authority to investigate attempts to influence public opinion. And in *Watkins* the Court held that petitioner was justified in refusing to answer because it had not been made clear to him that the questions addressed to him were pertinent to the question under inquiry.

Where the issue was the permissibility of State Department denial of passports to members and supporters of the Communist Party, the Court denied the Department's claim on the ground of lack of congressional authorization. As Justice Douglas observed in *Kent v. Dulles:*

> Since we start with an exercise by an American citizen of an activity included in constitutional protection [the right of travel as related to beliefs and associations], we will not readily infer that Congress gave the Secretary of State unbridled discretion to grant or withhold it.[134]

Yates v. United States[135] is a third illustration of the principle of strict construction as an expression of the preferred position. In that case fourteen leaders of the Communist Party in California had been convicted of conspiring (1) to advocate and teach the duty and necessity of overthrowing the Government of the United States by force and violence, and (2) to organize the Communist Party of the United States as a society advocating such overthrow. Applying the rule of strict construction applicable to criminal statutes generally, the word "organize" was held applicable only to acts entering into the creation of a new organization, so that prosecution under that count was barred by the statute of limitations. Moreover, on the advocacy count the Court found that the charge to the jury had failed to distinguish properly between "advocacy of abstract doctrine and advocacy directed at promoting unlawful action."[136] The effect was to free some of the defendants and remand the balance for retrial. In so construing the statute, the Court noted that it was avoiding "a constitutional danger zone."[137] Moreover, of course, this construction made it possible to avoid dealing again with the troublesome problems of *Dennis.*

D. *Prior Restraint*

As one aspect of the larger concept of the preferred position, the doctrine of prior restraint[138] has appeared in Supreme Court decisions

134 357 U.S. 116, 129 (1958). See also Dayton v. Dulles, 357 U.S. 144 (1958).

135 354 U.S. 298 (1957).

136 Id. at 318.

137 Id. at 319.

138 For an excellent account, see Emerson, The Doctrine of Prior Restraint, 20 Law & Contemp. Prob. 648 (1955).

only relatively recently; but there seems no doubt that it has secure status as a constitutional principle.[139]

Prohibitions against prior restraint, although always assumed to be within the intendment of the first amendment prohibitions, did not become the basis for a Supreme Court decision until 1931 in *Near v. Minnesota*.[140] In striking down a Minnesota statute which allowed the enjoining of publication of periodicals found to be "malicious, scandalous, and infamous," Chief Justice Hughes stated that freedom of the press in the first amendment "has meant, principally although not exclusively, immunity from previous restraints or censorship."[141]

Since that time the prior restraint doctrine has proved one of the most useful instruments for securing judicial protection of first amendment rights. Thus, the doctrine has been invoked to prevent restriction on publication;[142] to permit freedom within reasonable limits to distribute pamphlets and circulars in public places[143] and in private homes;[144] to assure the right of assembly in public places;[145] to forbid arbitrary refusals to license the use of sound trucks;[146] to prevent cen-

---

139 The related doctrine of freedom from subsequent punishment has also played a part, but a subordinate one. It was suggested as early as 1919 in Schenck v. United States, 249 U.S. 47, 51-52, that the first amendment prohibition could protect against subsequent punishment as well as against prior restraint. See also Near v. Minnesota, 283 U.S. 697, 714-15 (1931) (dictum). It is clear that the threat of subsequent punishment may be as effective a deterrent to speech as advance censorship. However, it is also clear that subsequent punishment must sometimes be permitted where prior restraint would not, as in defamation and perhaps obscenity. See, e.g., Roth v. United States, 354 U.S. 476 (1957). Cf. Kingsley Books, Inc. v. Brown, 354 U.S. 436 (1957). These matters raise extraneous considerations too complex for discussion here. See Freund, The Supreme Court and Civil Liberties, 4 Vand. L. Rev. 533, 537-45 (1951).

140 283 U.S. 697 (1931).

141 Id. at 716.

142 Butler v. Michigan, 352 U.S. 380 (1957); Grosjean v. American Press Co., 297 U.S. 233 (1936). Cf. Sunshine Book Co. v. Summerfield, 355 U.S. 372 (1958) (per curiam), reversing 249 F.2d 114 (D.C. Cir. 1957), affirming 128 F. Supp. 564 (D.D.C. 1955); One, Inc. v. Olesen, 355 U.S. 371 (1958) (per curiam), reversing 241 F.2d 772 (9th Cir. 1957).

143 Cantwell v. Connecticut, 310 U.S. 296 (1940); Schneider v. State, 308 U.S. 147 (1939); Lovell v. City of Griffin, 303 U.S. 444 (1938).

144 Follett v. Town of McCormick, 321 U.S. 573 (1944); Martin v. City of Struthers, 319 U.S. 141 (1943); Murdock v. Pennsylvania, 319 U.S. 105 (1943); Jones v. Opelika, 319 U.S. 103 (1943) (per curiam). In Breard v. Alexandria, 341 U.S. 622 (1951), the Court refused to extend immunity to commercial solicitation. Cf. City of Corona v. Corona Daily Independent, 115 Cal. App. 2d 382, 252 P.2d 56, cert. denied, 346 U.S. 833 (1953).

145 Kunz v. New York, 340 U.S. 290 (1951); Niemotko v. Maryland, 340 U.S. 268 (1951); Thomas v. Collins, 323 U.S. 516 (1945); Hague v. CIO, 307 U.S. 496 (1939). But cf. Poulos v. New Hampshire, 345 U.S. 395 (1953); Cox v. New Hampshire, 312 U.S. 569 (1941).

146 Saia v. New York, 334 U.S. 558 (1948). But cf. Kovacs v. Cooper, 336 U.S. 77 (1949).

sorship of motion pictures;[147] and in a variety of other cases.[148]

E. *Standing to Sue and the First Amendment*

A major difficulty in securing review of constitutional issues has been the requirement that such an issue can be raised only by a person who has standing to sue, that is, by one who has suffered direct and personal injury as a result of the alleged unconstitutional action.[149] To an extent not altogether clear, the standing requirement has a constitutional basis in the "case or controversy" requirement of article III;[150] but to some extent also it is a rule of the Court.[151] The doctrine has served on a number of occasions to prevent the adjudication of claimed deprivation of political rights, particularly in connection with legislative apportionment,[152] a problem closely related to first amendment issues. In other cases in which the first amendment issue was the primary right sought to be adjudicated, the standing requirement has also been held sufficient to foreclose discussion of the constitutional issue.[153]

In recent years the most serious difficulty presented by the standing requirement so far as the raising of first amendment issues is concerned has been the rule that the interest of one person or group could not be raised by another person or group.[154] But the doctrine has never been inflexible, and the easing of the requirement has often been facilitated where the substantive issue raised was a claimed invasion of first amendment rights.[155] The most significant case advancing the preferred position of the first amendment by the easing of the for-

147 Kingsley Int'l Pictures Corp. v. Regents of Univ. of New York, 360 U.S. 684 (1959); Times Film Corp. v. City of Chicago, 355 U.S. 35 (1957) (per curiam), reversing 244 F.2d 432 (7th Cir. 1957), affirming 139 F. Supp. 837 (N.D. Ill. 1956); Holmby Prods., Inc. v. Vaughn, 350 U.S. 870 (1955) (per curiam); Superior Films, Inc. v. Department of Educ., 346 U.S. 587 (1954); Gelling v. Texas, 343 U.S. 960 (1952) (per curiam); Joseph Burstyn, Inc. v. Wilson, 343 U.S. 495 (1952).

148 Staub v. City of Baxley, 355 U.S. 313 (1958); Hannegan v. Esquire, Inc., 327 U.S. 146 (1946); Thornhill v. Alabama, 310 U.S. 88 (1940). See also Dennis v. United States, 341 U.S. 494, 579 (1951) (Black, J., dissenting).

149 See Massachusetts v. Mellon, 262 U.S. 447 (1923).

150 See Muskrat v. United States, 219 U.S. 346 (1911).

151 See Ashwander v. TVA, 297 U.S. 288, 347-48 (1936) (Brandeis, J., concurring); Note, The Supreme Court and Standing to Sue, 34 N.Y.U.L. Rev. 141-42 (1959).

152 South v. Peters, 339 U.S. 276 (1950); MacDougall v. Green, 335 U.S. 281 (1948); Cook v. Fortson, 329 U.S. 675 (1946) (per curiam); Colegrove v. Green, 328 U.S. 549 (1946). See also Lewis, Legislative Apportionment and the Federal Courts, 71 Harv. L. Rev. 1057 (1958).

153 UPW v. Mitchell, 330 U.S. 75 (1947). See also Doremus v. Board of Educ., 342 U.S. 429, 433-34 (1952).

154 See Tileston v. Ullman, 318 U.S. 44 (1943).

155 See Pierce v. Society of Sisters, 268 U.S. 510 (1925). Cf. Barrows v. Jackson, 346 U.S. 249 (1953); Truax v. Raich, 239 U.S. 33 (1915).

malistic standing requirements is *NAACP v. Alabama ex rel. Patterson*.[156] In that case the Court allowed the National Association for the Advancement of Colored People, a membership corporation, to assert on behalf of its members the claim that a compelled disclosure to the state of members' names would invade their constitutional right of free association. Justice Harlan said:

> If petitioner's rank and file members are constitutionally entitled to withhold their connection with the Association despite the production order, it is manifest that this right is properly assertable by the Association. To require that it be claimed by the members themselves would result in nullification of the right at the very moment of its assertion.[157]

This is the preferred position at its best, clearing away procedural barriers to the adjudication of claimed abridgments of the freedom of speech, thought, or, as in this case, freedom of association.[158]

F. *Procedural Due Process and the First Amendment*

Sometimes the best known, the most obvious principles prove also to be the ones most readily overlooked. Thus, in concentrating on substantive rights, such as freedom of expression, it is a common mistake to disregard the procedural connotations, which are necessary to understand both derivation and contemporary setting. It is easy to forget the importance of Sir Henry Maine's reminder that liberty is secreted "in the interstices of procedure."[159] In matters of freedom the procedural aspects of the struggle have been particularly significant. Thus, Justice Douglas has remarked that "it is not without significance that most of the provisions of the Bill of Rights are procedural."[160] In similar vein Justice Brandeis wrote that "in the development of our liberty insistence upon procedural regularity has been a large factor."[161] Gradually these generalized verities have been given content to demonstrate their particular relevance where the right claimed to have been involved was a freedom protected by the first amendment. Thus, in 1936 Justice Brandeis recognized the necessity for higher standards of procedural due process when "liberty of person and other constitu-

---

156 357 U.S. 449 (1958). Cf. Staub v. City of Baxley, 355 U.S. 313, 319-20 (1958).

157 Id. at 459.

158 Cf. Joint Anti-Fascist Refugee Comm. v. McGrath, 341 U.S. 123 (1951).

159 Maine, Early Law and Custom 389 (1883).

160 Joint Anti-Fascist Refugee Comm. v. McGrath, 341 U.S. 123, 179 (1951) (concurring opinion).

161 Burdeau v. McDowell, 256 U.S. 465, 477 (1921) (dissenting opinion). See also Shaughnessy v. United States ex rel. Mezei, 345 U.S. 206, 224-25 (1953) (dissenting opinion); Malinski v. New York, 324 U.S. 401, 414 (1945) (concurring opinion).

tional rights" are in question.[162] Here, then, is the preferred position in procedural garb. The proposition has since become more specific and in recent years it has gained new dimension and further stature. Although subject to infinite variation in application, the proposition in simplest form is that where first amendment rights are threatened with limitation in any degree, the most exacting measure of procedural due process will be prescribed to ensure their maximum protection. Some of the most important variations are discussed below.

The Rule Against Vagueness.—The doctrine of unconstitutional uncertainty, or the rule against vagueness, has been called "inherently perplexing."[163] The task of reconciling the apparently conflicting lines of cases becomes less puzzling, however, when the concept of the preferred position is employed as a rationalizing factor. It is true, to be sure, that the prohibition against vagueness originated in the command of the sixth amendment that the accused "shall be informed of the nature and cause of the accusation," coupled with the due process requirement of the fifth amendment. The two, read together,[164] amount to a requirement that criminal statutes fix ascertainable standards of guilt. Nevertheless, this procedural requirement carries with it a substantive command as well that adds a note of imperativeness when applied to statutes, whether criminal or civil, which may impinge upon first amendment freedoms. Indeed, there is a substantial difference in judicial emphasis between void-for-vagueness cases not involving first amendment intrusions and those in which first amendment rights are the ultimate values to be protected.[165] An illustrative case is *Winters v. New York*,[166] which involved the conviction of a book-dealer for violation of a criminal statute which forbade distribution of a magazine principally made up of news or stories of criminal deeds of bloodshed or lust so massed as to become vehicles for inciting violent and depraved crimes against the person. In holding the statute void for vagueness, Justice Reed said:

> It is settled that a statute so vague and indefinite, in form and as interpreted, as to permit within the scope of its language, the punishment of incidents fairly within the protection of the guarantee of free speech is void, on its face, as contrary to the Fourteenth Amendment.[167]

---

162 St. Joseph Stock Yards Co. v. United States, 298 U.S. 38, 77 (1936) (concurring opinion).

163 Collings, Unconstitutional Uncertainty—An Appraisal, 40 Cornell L.Q. 195 (1955).

164 United States v. L. Cohen Grocery Co., 255 U.S. 81 (1921).

165 Collings, supra note 163, at 212-14.

166 333 U.S. 507 (1948).

167 Ibid. See Stromberg v. California, 283 U.S. 359, 369 (1931) (statute punishing display of flags as a symbol of opposition to organized government, as construed by

A special aspect of the problem of vagueness is the overbroad statute which might be found unconstitutional on its face, rather than condemned only insofar as applied to litigants before the court. The 1958 decision in *Staub v. City of Baxley*[168] is representative. In that case a city ordinance made it an offense to "solicit" citizens of the city for membership in any organization requiring payment of dues, without first having received a permit from the mayor and council. Because the permit could be granted or withheld in the uncontrolled discretion of mayor and council, the Court held the ordinance invalid on its face as a prior restraint upon the free exercise of free speech. This case is only the most recent of a number of cases which have thus emphasized the special importance of assuring freedom of communication by striking down statutes or ordinances which on their face showed abridgment of first amendment freedoms.[169]

Insufficiency of Evidence of Intent.—In his dissent in *Abrams v. United States,*[170] Justice Holmes argued that when a criminal statute, no matter how valid, restricts in any way the freedom to speak or write, "this statute must be taken to use its words in a strict and accurate sense."[171] This statement, little more than a dictum, was picked up twenty-five years later and made majority doctrine in *Hartzel v. United States.*[172] In that case petitioner had been convicted of a violation of the Espionage Act of 1917 upon an indictment charging his wilful attempt in wartime to cause disloyalty in the armed forces and his wilful obstruction of recruiting. The validity of the statute was not denied; and the acts charged were conceded to be sufficient for conviction but for the failure of sufficient proof of intent. Of course, it is familiar doctrine that criminal intent may not be presumed, but must be proved as a fact.[173] But in this case, the impingement on first amendment rights was thought to require something more in the way of proof of intent. Justice Murphy said that "such legislation, being penal in nature and restricting the right to speak and write freely, must be construed narrowly and 'must be taken to use its words in a

state court, held unconstitutionally indefinite). See also Herndon v. Lowry, 301 U.S. 242, 258 (1937).

168 355 U.S. 313 (1958).

169 Kunz v. New York, 340 U.S. 290, 293 (1951); Niemotko v. Maryland, 340 U.S. 268, 271 (1951); Jones v. Opelika, 319 U.S. 103 (1943), adopting per curiam on rehearing the dissenting opinion in 316 U.S. 584, 600-02 (1942); Largent v. Texas, 318 U.S. 418, 422 (1943); Cantwell v. Connecticut; 310 U.S. 296 (1940); Thornhill v. Alabama, 310 U.S. 88 (1940); Schneider v. Town of Irvington, 308 U.S. 147, 163-64 (1939); Hague v. CIO, 307 U.S. 496, 516 (1939); Lovell v. City of Griffin, 303 U.S. 444, 452 (1938).

170 250 U.S. 616, 624 (1919).

171 Id. at 627.

172 322 U.S. 680 (1944).

173 See, e.g., Morissette v. United States, 342 U.S. 246, 273-76 (1952).

strict and accurate sense.' "[174] While it is doubtful that the principle of this case goes much beyond the ordinary requirement, even in non-speech cases, that intent must be sufficiently proved, it is at least evidence of another aspect of first amendment preference.

Burden of Proof.—In 1958 a distinctively new variation of the preferred position was imaginatively supplied by Justice Brennan in *Speiser v. Randall.*[175] That case involved a provision in the California Constitution which conditioned the grant of certain exemptions from property tax upon the taking of oaths that the applicants for exemption did not advocate the overthrow of government by force, violence, or other unlawful means, and did not advocate the support of a foreign government against the United States in the event of hostilities. As to the substance of this unusual oath the Court assumed without deciding that California was entitled to "deny tax exemptions to persons who engage in the proscribed speech for which they might be fined or imprisoned."[176] However, taking of the oath was not conclusive as to eligibility for exemption, so that where the assessor doubted qualification in any respect, the burden of proving eligibility was left on the taxpayer. This is not an unusual scheme for the allocation of burden of proof in ordinary tax matters, and the Court did not dispute the right of the state in usual tax matters to require the taxpayer to prove his claim of exemption. But it is at this point that the preferred position of the first amendment made a difference.

> Where the transcendent value of speech is involved, due process certainly requires in the circumstances of this case that the State bear the burden of persuasion to show that the appellants engaged in criminal speech.[177]

The reason for this shift was the following:

> The vice of the present procedure is that, where particular speech falls close to the line separating the lawful and the unlawful, the possibility of mistaken factfinding—inherent in all litigation—will create the danger that the legitimate utterance will be penalized. The man who knows that he must bring forth proof and persuade another of the lawfulness of his conduct necessarily must steer far wider of the unlawful zone than if the State must bear these burdens. . . . How can a claimant whose declaration is rejected possibly sustain the burden of proving the negative of these complex factual elements? In practical operation, therefore, this procedural device must necessarily produce a result which the State could not command directly. It can only result in a deterrence of speech which the Constitution makes free.[178]

174 322 U.S. at 686 (quoting Justice Holmes). See note 170 supra.
175 357 U.S. 513 (1958).
176 Id. at 520.
177 Id. at 526.
178 Ibid. See also Kingsley Books, Inc. v. Brown, 354 U.S. 436, 441-42 (1957);

This is creative jurisprudence at its best. Previously it has frequently been observed that higher standards of procedural due process are required in criminal cases involving possible infringement of freedom of speech and thought. But here, apparently for the first time in a civil case, the new and logical step of shifting the burden of proof was taken to apply the preferred position principle to a situation in which the claim of common sense demanded further advance.[179]

III

Conclusion

The preferred position, whether known by that or some other name, is a fact of American constitutional law. The significance is plain but meaningful: The freedoms of the first amendment, particularly the freedoms of speech and thought, are so vital to the tradition of the free society that their primacy must be recognized in sufficiently varied ways to accommodate to the various contexts in which these crucial rights may be challenged.

The clear and present danger test and its later variant, the probable danger test, have been here disapproved. Although the danger test represented the first groping attempt to express the proper relationship between society's interest in free speech and those other interests which also must be promoted and safeguarded, now, however, under the burden of confused and conflicting interpretations, that test should be rejected because it no longer permits the proper selection or balancing of the relevant interests.

There remains a substantial variety of techniques by which the preferred position may be applied in appropriate cases. It is a happy fact that the preferred position is sufficiently flexible to be capable of growth and invention as new challenges arise. Encouragement is found also in the fact of judicial alertness to defend these preferred rights and to offer creative solutions for future needs. In this lies the past history of the preferred position and its future promise. There is a preference for freedom.

Near v. Minnesota, 283 U.S. 697 (1931). Cf. Staub v. City of Baxley, 355 U.S. 313 (1958); Cantwell v. Connecticut, 310 U.S. 296, 305 (1940).

[179] Cf. Bridges v. Wixon, 326 U.S. 135 (1945); Schneiderman v. United States, 320 U.S. 118, 124-25 (1943). Although burden of proof questions as such were not involved in these two cases, the central problem in each was the sufficiency of proof to satisfy a statute authorizing denaturalization or deportation. Because political freedoms were involved in both, the Court imposed on the Government the strictest standards of proof.

APPENDIX

Preferred Position of the First Amendment

Holmes: Persecution for the expression of opinions seems to me perfectly logical. If you have no doubt of your premises or your power and want a certain result with all your heart you naturally express your wishes in law and sweep away all opposition. To allow opposition by speech seems to indicate that you think the speech impotent, as when a man says that he has squared the circle, or that you do not care whole-heartedly for the result, or that you doubt either your power or your premises. But when men have realized that time has upset many fighting faiths, they may come to believe even more than they believe the very foundations of their own conduct that the ultimate good desired is better reached by free trade in ideas—that the best test of truth is the power of the thought to get itself accepted in the competition of the market, and that truth is the only ground upon which their wishes safely can be carried out. That at any rate is the theory of our Constitution. *Abrams v. United States,* 250 U.S. 616, 630 (1919) (dissenting opinion).

Brandeis: Those who won our independence believed that the final end of the State was to make men free to develop their faculties; and that in its government the deliberative forces should prevail over the arbitrary. They valued liberty both as an end and as a means. They believed liberty to be the secret of happiness and courage to be the secret of liberty. They believed that freedom to think as you will and to speak as you think are means indispensable to the discovery and spread of political truth; that without free speech and assembly discussion would be futile; that with them, discussion affords ordinarily adequate protection against the dissemination of noxious doctrine; that the greatest menace to freedom is an inert people; that public discussion is a political duty; and that this should be a fundamental principle of the American government. *Whitney v. California,* 274 U.S. 357, 375 (1927) (concurring opinion).

Holmes: . . . [I]f there is any principle of the Constitution that more imperatively calls for attachment than any other it is the principle of free thought—not free thought for those who agree with us but freedom for the thought that we hate. *United States v. Schwimmer,* 279 U.S. 644, 654-55 (1929) (dissenting opinion).

Hughes: The maintenance of the opportunity for free political discussion to the end that government may be responsive to the will of the people and that changes may be obtained by lawful means, an opportunity essential to the security of the Republic, is a fundamental principle of our constitutional system. *Stromberg v. California,* 283 U.S. 359, 369 (1931).

Roberts: The power of a state to abridge freedom of speech and of assembly is the exception rather than the rule and the penalizing even of utterances of a defined character must find its justification in a reasonable apprehension of danger to organized government. *Herndon v. Lowry,* 301 U.S. 242, 258 (1937).

Cardozo: Of . . . [the freedom of thought and speech] one may say that it is the matrix, the indispensable condition, of nearly every other form of freedom. With rare aberrations a pervasive recognition of that truth can be traced in our history, political and legal. So it has come about that the domain of liberty, withdrawn by the Fourteenth Amendment from encroachment by the states, has been enlarged by latter-day judgments to include liberty of the mind as well as liberty of action. The extension became, indeed, a logical imperative when once it was recognized, as long ago it was, that liberty is something more than exemption from physical restraint, and that even in the field of substantive rights and duties the legislative judgment, if oppressive and arbitrary, may be overridden by the courts. *Palko v. Connecticut,* 302 U.S. 319, 327 (1937).

Hughes: Freedom of speech and freedom of the press . . . are among the fundamental personal rights and liberties which are protected by the Fourteenth Amendment from invasion by state action. *Lovell v. City of Griffin,* 303 U.S. 444, 450 (1938).

Stone: There may be narrower scope for operation of the presumption of constitutionality when legislation appears on its face to be within a specific prohibition of the Constitution, such as those of the first ten amendments, which are deemed equally specific when held to be embraced within the fourteenth. *United States v. Carolene Prods. Co.,* 304 U.S. 144, 152 n.4 (1938).

Roberts: This court has characterized the freedom of speech and that of the press as fundamental personal rights and liberties. The phrase is not an empty one and was not lightly used. It reflects the belief of the framers of the Constitution that exercise of the rights lies at the foundation of free government by free men. It stresses, as do many opinions of this court, the importance of preventing the restriction of enjoyment of these liberties.

In every case, therefore, where legislative abridgment of the rights is asserted, the courts should be astute to examine the effect of the challenged legislation. Mere legislative preferences or beliefs respecting matters of public convenience may well support regulation directed at other personal activities, but be insufficient to justify such as diminishes the exercise of rights so vital to the maintenance of democratic institutions. *Schneider v. State,* 308 U.S. 147, 161 (1939).

Black: For the First Amendment does not speak equivocally. It prohibits any law "abridging the freedom of speech, or of the press." It must be taken as a command of the broadest scope that explicit language, read in the context of a liberty-loving society, will allow. *Bridges v. California,* 314 U.S. 252, 263 (1941).

Stone: The First Amendment is not confined to safeguarding freedom of speech and freedom of religion against discriminatory attempts to wipe them out. On the contrary, the Constitution, by virtue of the First and the Fourteenth Amendments, has put those freedoms in a preferred position. *Jones v. Opelika,* 316 U.S. 584, 608 (1942) [dissenting opinion, adopted on rehearing, 319 U.S. 103 (1943)].

Douglas: The fact that the ordinance is "nondiscriminatory" is immaterial. The protection afforded by the First Amendment is not so restricted. A license tax certainly does not acquire constitutional validity because it classifies the privileges protected by the First Amendment along with the wares and merchandise of hucksters and peddlers and treats them all alike. Such equality in treatment does not save the ordinance. Freedom of press, freedom of speech, freedom of religion are in a preferred position. *Murdock v. Pennsylvania,* 319 U.S. 105, 115 (1943).

Black: The right of freedom of speech and press has broad scope. The authors of the First Amendment knew that novel and unconventional ideas might disturb the complacent, but they chose to encourage a freedom which they believed essential if vigorous enlightenment was ever to triumph over slothful ignorance. *Martin v. City of Struthers,* 319 U.S. 141, 143 (1943).

Jackson: The right of a State to regulate, for example, a public utility may well include, so far as the due process test is concerned, power to impose all of the restrictions which a legislature may have a "rational basis" for adopting. But freedoms of speech and of press, of assembly, and of worship may not be infringed on such slender grounds. *West Virginia State Bd. of Educ. v. Barnette,* 319 U.S. 624, 639 (1943).

Rutledge: . . . [I]t may be doubted that any of the great liberties insured by the First Article can be given higher place than the others. All have preferred position in our basic scheme. . . . All are interwoven there together. Differences there are, in them and in the modes appropriate for their exercise. But they have unity in the charter's prime place because they have unity in their human sources and functionings. Heart and mind are not identical. Intuitive faith and reasoned judgment are not the same. Spirit is not always thought. But in the everyday business of living, secular or otherwise, these variant aspects of personality find inseparable expression in a thousand ways. They cannot be altogether parted in law more than in life. *Prince v. Massachusetts,* 321 U.S. 158, 164-65 (1944).

Rutledge: The case confronts us again with the duty our system places on this Court to say where the individual's freedom ends and the State's power begins. Choice on that border, now as always delicate, is perhaps more so where the usual presumption supporting legislation is balanced by the preferred place given in our scheme to the great, the indispensable democratic freedoms secured by the First Amendment. . . . That priority gives these liberties a sanctity and a sanction not permitting dubious intrusions. And it is the character of the right, not of the limitation, which determines what standard governs the choice. *Thomas v. Collins,* 323 U.S. 516, 529-30 (1945).

Black: When we balance the Constitutional rights of owners of property against those of the people to enjoy freedom of press and religion, as we must here, we remain mindful of the fact that the latter occupy a preferred position. *Marsh v. Alabama,* 326 U.S. 501, 509 (1946).

Frankfurter: Where the First Amendment applies, it is a denial of all governmental power in our Federal system. *Marsh v. Alabama,* 326 U.S. 501, 511 (1946) (concurring opinion).

Douglas: Courts must balance the various community interests in passing on the constitutionality of local regulations of the character involved here. But in that process they should be mindful to keep the freedoms of the First Amendment in a preferred position. *Saia v. New York,* 334 U.S. 558, 562 (1948).

Frankfurter: . . . [W]ithout freedom of expression, thought becomes checked and atrophied. Therefore, in considering what interests are so fundamental as to be enshrined in the Due Process Clause, those liberties of the individual which history has attested as the indispensable conditions of an open as against a closed society come to this Court with a momentum for respect lacking when appeal is made to liberties which derive merely from shifting economic arrangements. *Kovacs v. Cooper,* 336 U.S. 77, 95 (1949) (concurring opinion).

Reed: So important to a constitutional democracy is the right of discussion that any challenge to legislative abridgment of those privileges of a free people calls for careful judicial appraisal. *Beauharnais v. Illinois,* 343 U.S. 250, 279 (1952) (dissenting opinion).

Black: It seems self-evident that all speech criticizing government rulers and challenging current beliefs may be dangerous to the status quo. With full knowledge of this danger the Framers rested our First Amendment on the premise that the slightest suppression of thought, speech, press, or public assembly is still more dangerous. This means that individuals are guaranteed an undiluted and unequivocal right to express themselves on questions of current public interest. . . . In my view this uncompromising interpretation of the Bill of Rights is the one that must prevail if its freedoms are to be saved. *Wieman v. Updegraff,* 344 U.S. 183, 194 (1952) (concurring opinion).

Douglas: But when a legislature undertakes to proscribe the exercise of a citizen's constitutional right to free speech, it acts lawlessly; and the citizen can take matters in his own hands and proceed on the basis that such a law is no law at all . . . .

The reason is the preferred position granted freedom of speech, freedom of press, freedom of assembly, and freedom of religion by the First Amendment. *Poulos v. New Hampshire,* 345 U.S. 395, 423 (1953) (dissenting opinion).

Douglas: . . . [The cited cases] are illustrative of the preferred position granted speech and the press by the First Amendment. The command that "Congress shall make no law . . . abridging the freedom of speech, or of the press" has behind it a long history. It expresses the confidence that the safety of society depends on the tolerance of government for hostile as well as friendly criticism, that in a community where men's minds are free, there must be room for the unorthodox as well as the orthodox views. *United States v. Rumely,* 345 U.S. 41, 56-57 (1953) (concurring opinion).

Whittaker: It is undeniable that the ordinance authorized the Mayor and Council of the City of Baxley to grant "or refuse to grant" the required permit in their uncontrolled discretion. It thus makes enjoyment of speech contingent upon the will of the Mayor and Council of the City, although that fundamental right is made free from congressional abridgment by the First Amendment and is protected by the Fourteenth from invasion by state action. For these reasons, the ordinance, on its face, imposes an unconstitutional prior restraint upon the enjoyment of First Amendment freedoms and lays "a forbidden burden upon the exercise of liberty protected by the Constitution." *Staub v. City of Baxley,* 355 U.S. 313, 325 (1958).

Harlan: Effective advocacy of both public and private points of view, particularly of controversial ones, is undeniably enhanced by group association, as this Court has more than once recognized by remarking upon the close nexus between the freedoms of speech and assembly. . . . It is beyond debate that freedom to engage in association for the advancement of beliefs and ideas is an inseparable aspect of the "liberty" assured by the Due Process Clause of the Fourteenth Amendment, which embraces freedom of speech. . . . Of course, it is immaterial whether the beliefs sought to be advanced by association pertain to political, economic, religious or cultural matters, and state action which may have the effect of curtailing the freedom to associate is subject to the closest scrutiny.

. . . In the domain of these indispensable liberties, whether of speech, press, or association, the decisions of this Court recognize that abridgment of such rights, even though unintended, may inevitably follow from varied forms of governmental action. *NAACP v. Alabama ex rel. Patterson,* 357 U.S. 449, 460-61 (1958).

Brennan: When the State undertakes to restrain unlawful advocacy it must provide procedures which are adequate to safeguard against infringement of constitutionally protected rights—rights which we value most highly and which are essential to the workings of a free society. Moreover, since only considerations of the greatest urgency can justify restrictions on speech, and since the validity of a restraint on speech in each case depends on careful analysis of the particular circumstances, . . . the procedures by which the facts of the case are adjudicated are of special importance and the validity of the restraint may turn on the safeguards which they afford. *Speiser v. Randall,* 357 U.S. 513, 521 (1958).

Brennan: . . . [I]t must be admitted that maintenance of the separation of powers in the States is not, in and of itself, a concern of the Federal Constitution. . . . But for an investigation in the field of the constitutionally protected freedoms of speech and assemblage to be upheld by the broad standards of relevance permissible in a legislative inquiry, some relevance to a valid legislative purpose must be shown. . . . The bare fact that the Legislature has authorized the inquiry does not mean that the inquiry is for a valid legislative end when viewed in the light of the federal constitutional test we must apply. Nor, while it is entitled to weight, is the determination by a state court that the inquiry relates to a valid legislative end conclusive. *Uphaus v. Wyman,* 360 U.S. 72, 100-01 (1959) (dissenting opinion).

Stewart: . . . [The Constitution's] guarantee is not confined to the expression of ideas that are conventional or shared by a majority. It protects advocacy of the opinion that adultery may sometimes be proper, no less than advocacy of socialism or the single tax. And in the realm of ideas it protects expression which is eloquent no less than that which is unconvincing. *Kingsley Int'l Pictures Corp. v. Regents of Univ. of N.Y.,* 360 U.S. 684, 689 (1959).

COLUMBIA LAW REVIEW

Vol. 52 MARCH, 1952 No. 3

CLEAR AND PRESENT DANGER—FROM SCHENCK TO DENNIS

WALLACE MENDELSON

Some legal doctrines are more important as manifestations of attitude than as guides to decision in specific cases. Not long ago "liberty of contract" was little more than a shorthand symbol for Spencerian sociology. More happily, in recent years "clear and present danger" has embodied a deeply democratic instinct favoring the free expression of ideas. But like "economic due process," it has been more significant as a pervasive atmospheric pressure, than as a reliable standard for the decision of a specific case or as a rationale for a line of cases.[1] The policy decision implicit in the choice of one legal doctrine over another often explains more than does the chosen doctrine itself.

The influence of danger doctrine can hardly be overrated; indeed, it has become one of our democratic traditions. But we are not without evidence that protection for civil liberties is least available when needed most. It may be that the apparent softening at present of judicial concern for free utterance—like the demise of "economic due process"—indicates that doctrines which are long on atmosphere and short on concrete standards find themselves at a disadvantage in time of crisis. Yet even in less troubled times danger doctrine has not been a reliable guide. The step from general ideal to specific application is always difficult. And, since the departure of Mr. Justice Holmes, "clear and present danger" has suggested all things to all justices.

Notwithstanding its admitted influence as an ideal, analysis of free expression opinions suggests that, as a judicial instrument, the danger test has never had more than four enthusiasts on the Supreme Court at any one time. Given a lack of doctrinal agreement among the remaining justices and the economy of effort which the pressure of Supreme Court business imposes, a vigorous minority of four will often find a fifth to endorse its language—

1. See Latham, *The Theory of the Judicial Concept of Freedom of Speech*, 12 J. Pol. Econ. 637 (1950).

especially, though perhaps not exclusively, if the fifth is not averse to the conclusion reached:

> The considerations that move a judge to yield concurrence in an opinion reaching an approved result through uncongenial doctrine are among the most teasing mysteries. . . . Long-term strategy or immediate fatigue, hopelessness of opposition or deprecation of the importance of the pronouncement, bonhommie of common labors or avoidance of undue division [all may be involved].[2]

But harmony so achieved is highly volatile for, as Mr. Justice Frankfurter has noted, "different nuances in phrasing the same conclusion lead to different emphasis and thereby eventually may lead to different conclusions in slightly different situations."[3]

To test the more important of these hypotheses and to uncover the hard core of meaning behind Mr. Justice Holmes' danger rhetoric is the object of what follows—for it may be that by returning to his position we can combine the power of an ideal with the stability that is implicit in a rule of law.

I. 1919 TO 1930

The danger rule was born in *Schenck v. United States*,[4] in March, 1919. By urging resistance to the draft Schenck had run afoul of the Espionage Act of 1917; he defended on free speech grounds. Mr. Justice Holmes, for a unanimous Court, observed:

> the character of every act depends upon the circumstances in which it was done. . . . The most stringent protection of free speech would not protect a man in falsely shouting fire in a theatre, and causing a panic. It does not even protect a man from an injunction against uttering words that may have all the effect of force. . . . The question in every case is whether the words used are used in such circumstances and are of such a nature as to create a clear and present danger that they will bring about the substantive evils that Congress has a right to prevent. It is a question of proximity and degree.[5]

The test was found to have been met and the conviction accordingly sustained.

The *Schenck* decision was cited by the Court as controlling in six subsequent cases during 1919 and 1920,[6] but the danger test was not mentioned

2. FRANKFURTER, THE COMMERCE CLAUSE 56 (1937).
3. American Communications Ass'n, CIO v. Douds, 339 U.S. 382, 418 (1950) (concurring in part and dissenting in part).
4. 249 U.S. 47 (1919).
5. *Id.* at 52.
6. Gilbert v. Minnesota, 254 U.S. 325 (1920); Pierce v. United States, 252 U.S. 239 (1920); Schaefer v. United States, 251 U.S. 468 (1920); Abrams v. United States, 250 U.S. 616 (1919); Debs v. United States, 249 U.S. 211 (1919); Frowerk v. United States, 249 U.S. 204 (1919).

nor was the evidence analyzed in danger terms. A conviction was sustained in each instance. Throughout the next ten years the rule was mentioned in only one majority opinion and then it was merely distinguished to permit upholding a conviction.[7] Justices Holmes and Brandeis alone kept "clear and present danger" alive in a series of six concurring or dissenting opinions.[8] This is the full history of the rule down to 1930.[9] For all but two justices it seems to have been nothing more than a device enabling the Court to send men to jail. Nevertheless, because of the brilliance with which they wrote, Justices Holmes and Brandeis left a deep mark upon the law of free expression.

In origin "clear and present danger" was a rule of evidence designed to keep the application of espionage and criminal syndicalism statutes within constitutional bounds. Drawing upon the common law of incitement to crime, Mr. Justice Holmes used the danger test to determine where discussion ends and incitement or attempt begins.[10] The core of his position was that the First Amendment protects only utterance that seeks acceptance via the democratic processes of discussion and agreement. "Words that may have all the effect of force"[11]—that is, utterance calculated to achieve its goal by circumventing the democratic processes—are not so protected. Falsely shouting fire in a crowded theater does not invite debate; it incites panic in which force and injury are inevitable. But how is the line to be drawn between discussion and incitement on the border where, as Mr. Justice Cardozo observed, "thought merges into action"?[12] The common law of incitement to crime suggested an answer. The danger test, as Justices Holmes and Brandeis used it, assumes that the normal cure for allegedly harmful talk is time and debate. Repression is permissible only if

> the evil apprehended is so imminent that it may befall before there is opportunity for full discussion. If there be time to expose through discussion the falsehood and fallacies, to avert the evil by the process of education the remedy to be applied is more speech, not enforced silence.[13]

---

7. Gitlow v. New York, 268 U.S. 652 (1925).

8. *See* Whitney v. California, 274 U.S. 357, 372 (1927); Gitlow v. New York, 268 U.S. 652, 672 (1925); Gilbert v. Minnesota, 254 U.S. 325, 334 (1920); Pierce v. United States, 252 U.S. 239, 253 (1920); Schaefer v. United States, 251 U.S. 468, 482 (1920); Abrams v. United States, 250 U.S. 616, 624 (1919).

9. Fiske v. Kansas, 274 U.S. 380 (1927), which turned on the inadequacy of the charge and the evidence, is the only case during this period in which a First Amendment claim was sustained. The other civil liberties cases are: New York *ex rel.* Bryant v. Zimmerman, 278 U.S. 63 (1928); Burns v. United States, 274 U.S. 328 (1927); United States *ex rel.* Milwaukee Social Democratic Pub. Co. v. Burleson, 255 U.S. 407 (1921).

10. See CHAFEE, FREE SPEECH IN THE UNITED STATES 82 (1942).

11. Schenck v. United States, 249 U.S. 47, 52 (1919).

In Masses Publishing Co. v. Patten, 244 Fed. 535, 540 (S.D.N.Y. 1917), Judge Learned Hand noted a distinction between words used as "keys of persuasion" and as "triggers of action."

12. Cardozo, *Mr. Justice Holmes*, 44 HARV. L. REV. 682, 688 (1931).

13. Whitney v. California, 274 U.S. 357, 377 (1927) (concurring opinion).

Mr. Justice Holmes, however, did not suppose that a context of force constitutes the sole ground for cutting off or punishing discourse. There are other abuses of democratic freedoms—abuses that cannot be measured in terms of danger that goals will be reached without running the gauntlet of community discussion. When Nebraska's legislature sought to foster cultural unity by forbidding grade school teachers to teach in foreign languages, the Court balked.[14] Mr Justice Holmes, dissenting, did not attempt to weigh the conflicting interests in danger terms as did some of his successors in the comparable flag salute litigation.[15] Of course there is no threat of bypassing democratic processes in either situation. That the danger test reveals none is just as meaningless as the failure of a barometer to record the imminence of an avalanche.

The Constitution does not protect the utterance of "force words"; neither does it prohibit majorities from being "foolish." It requires only that dissenters be free to exploit such "foolishness" in argument. Prohibiting a teacher's "free speech" in German represses no ideas, blocks no one's participation in democratic politics, and forecloses no efforts to change the public mind. In short, the purpose of the First Amendment is not violated. On the Massachusetts bench Mr. Justice Holmes upheld state efforts to forbid certain political activities by policemen[16] and to outlaw speech-making on Boston Commons.[17] Democratic processes are not materially impeded, nor are reasonable men necessarily offended, when policemen are deterred from mixing politics and law enforcement or a park is set aside as a haven for repose free from political and religious polemics. The most that a court may ask in such circumstances is whether there are reasonable opportunities for adequate public discussion elsewhere or by other means.

All the evidence indicates that Mr. Justice Holmes distinguished between restrictions on the mind and regulation of modes of expression. Only when a government's thrust was against an idea itself did he use the danger test, his purpose being to give all ideas complete freedom to seek acceptance in the democratic forum. But when the public animus was not calculated to suppress ideas, but merely to regulate the time, place, or manner of expressing them, Mr. Justice Holmes' guide was the less stringent reasonable basis rule.[18] "Congress [like the states] certainly cannot forbid

---

14. *See* Meyer v. Nebraska, 262 U.S. 390, 412 (1923).
15. West Virginia State Board of Education v. Barnette, 319 U.S. 624 (1943). See Chafee, *op. cit. supra* note 10, at 321.
16. McAuliffe v. New Bedford, 155 Mass. 216, 29 N.E. 517 (1891), *cf.* Kovacs v. Cooper, 336 U.S. 77 (1949); Saia v. New York, 334 U.S. 558 (1948).
17. Commonwealth v. Davis, 162 Mass. 510, 39 N.E. 113 (1895).
18. Mr. Justice Holmes' vote in Pierce v. Society of Sisters, 268 U.S. 510 (1925), may be explained on the ground that he saw in the Ku Klux Klan-inspired restriction there at issue far more than a mere time, place, or manner regulation.

all effort to change the mind of the [community];"[19] democracy requires substantial opportunity for full discussion of all ideas. But it does not require that everyone be free to say anything he wants anywhere, anytime, and at any place. The great contribution of Mr. Justice Holmes was that he looked through the deceptively simple language of the First Amendment to its plain purpose—the safeguarding of society's thinking processes.

II. 1930 to 1940

The chief justiceship of Mr. Hughes clearly marks a new dispensation. The decade of the thirties far surpasses all prior decades in the number of Supreme Court decisions vindicating civil liberties. The danger rule, however, was mentioned only twice—once as an oblique underpinning for the Court's position[20] and once in a dissent by Mr. Justice Cardozo.[21] Despite his position of leadership in the struggle to protect civil liberties, neither as associate nor as chief justice did Mr. Hughes ever write an opinion in which the danger test was used. Blackstone's old doctrine of "prior restraint" as the essence of forbidden censorship served in several cases;[22] the others were handled largely *ad hoc* with no discernible thread of doctrinal continuity.[23]

III. The Early Roosevelt Court—1940 to May, 1943

Mr. Justice Murphy's first civil liberties opinion, delivered in 1940, marks the beginning of another cycle. *Thornhill v. Alabama*[24] concerned the validity of a conviction under a general statutory prohibition against picketing. Building on a famous remark of Mr. Justice Brandeis,[25] and speaking for all but Mr. Justice McReynolds, Mr. Justice Murphy observed:

> In the circumstances of our times the dissemination of information concerning the facts of a labor dispute must be regarded as within that area of free discussion that is guaranteed by the Constitution. . . . Free discussion concerning the conditions in indus-

---

19. Abrams v. United States, 250 U.S. 616, 628 (1919) (dissenting opinion).
20. Herndon v. Lowry, 301 U.S. 242 (1937).
21. Herndon v. Georgia, 295 U.S. 441, 448 (1935).
22. Schneider v. Irvington, 308 U.S. 147 (1939); Lovell v. City of Griffin, 303 U.S. 444 (1938); Near v. Minnesota, 283 U.S. 697 (1931); *cf.* Hague v. CIO, 307 U.S. 496 (1939); see 1 Bl. Comm. *151.
23. Associated Press v. NLRB, 301 U.S. 103 (1937); DeJonge v. Oregon, 299 U.S. 353 (1937); Hamilton v. University of California, 293 U.S. 245 (1934); Stromberg v. California, 283 U.S. 359 (1931); Grosjean v. American Press Co., 297 U.S. 233 (1926).
24. 310 U.S. 88 (1940).
25. The dictum quoted is: "Members of a union might, without special statutory authorization by a State, make known the facts of a labor dispute, for freedom of the press is guaranteed by the Federal Constitution." *Id.* at 103. Mr. Justice Murphy failed, however, to quote Mr. Justice Brandeis' next sentence, which is: "The State may, in the exercise of its police power, regulate the *methods and means* of publicity as well as the use of public streets." Senn v. Tile Layers Protective Union, 301 U.S. 468, 478 (1937) (emphasis added).

> try and the causes of labor disputes appears to us indispensable to the effective and intelligent use of the processes of popular government to shape the destiny of modern industrial society.[26]

Granting that discussion of the subject matter involved, "the facts of a labor dispute," is constitutionally protected, what of picketing as a mode of expression? Mr. Justice Murphy cited a group of "police power" (reasonable basis) decisions[27] in support of the proposition that

> the rights of employers and employees to conduct their economic affairs and to compete with others for a fair share in the products of industry are subject to modification or qualification in the interests of the society in which they exist. . . . This is but an instance of the power of the state to set the limits of permissible contest open to industrial combatants.[28]

Thus, following Mr. Justice Holmes, the Court drew a distinction between the form and the content of expression and, as indicated by the line of decisions cited, took the position that the validity of restraints on form should be tested by the reasonable basis rule.

But, continued Mr. Justice Murphy:

> It does not follow that the State in dealing with the evils arising from industrial disputes may impair the *effective* exercise of the right to discuss freely industrial relations which are matters of public concern. A contrary conclusion could be used to support abridgment of freedom of speech and of the press concerning almost every matter of importance to society.[29]

The key word is "effective" which bridges the distinction between form and content. For if the effective way of expressing "the facts of a labor dispute" —that is, peaceful picketing—is prohibited, the prohibition becomes in fact a substantive restraint.[30] In that event the danger test is relevant.[31]

In a word, the *Thornhill* case brought both aspects of the Holmesian approach back into the law, for it recognized as constitutionally significant the difference between censorship and reasonable time, place, or manner regulations. Indeed, *Thornhill* went a step farther and made explicit what Mr. Justice Holmes had only implied, namely, that a regulation of the manner of expression may in some circumstances be a serious impediment to ideas themselves.

---

26. Thornhill v. Alabama, 310 U.S. 88, 102 (1940).
27. *Id.* at 103. The cases cited begin with Holden v. Hardy, 169 U.S. 366 (1898), and include Nebbia v. New York, 291 U.S. 502 (1934), and West Coast Hotel Co. v. Parrish, 300 U.S. 379 (1937).
28. Thornhill v. Alabama, 310 U.S. 88, 103 (1940).
29. *Id.* at 104 (emphasis added).
30. *Cf.* Bakery & Pastry Drivers v. Wohl, 315 U.S. 769, 775 (1942). There the Court expressly recognized that an unusual form of picketing was justified by the unavailability of any other practical method for petitioners to make their case known to the public.
31. See Thornhill v. Alabama, 310 U.S. 88, 104 (1940).

Four more decisions during this period followed *Thornhill* in striking down general restraints on peaceful picketing.[32] Two others, following the implication of *Thornhill*, approved restricted limitations upon picketing on reasonable basis grounds.[33] Finally, in *Cox v. New Hampshire*[34] and *Minersville School District v. Gobitis*,[35] the early Roosevelt Court upheld a "license" requiriment for parades and a compulsory public school flag salute, both of which had been attacked by Jehovah's Witnesses on First Amendment grounds. In each instance the Court treated the restraint involved as a reasonable time, place, or manner regulation which did not hinder substantially either freedom of religion or democratic political processes.[36]

The early Roosevelt Court did not, however, always follow Mr. Justice Holmes' path. In *Cantwell v. Connecticut*,[37] decided unanimously less than a month after *Thornhill*, a statutory requirement of advance discretionary approval for religious canvassing was invalidated on prior restraint grounds. The same result might have been reached via Mr. Justices Holmes' approach. Presumably historical tradition and the recent glory of *Near v. Minnesota*[38] explain this Court's retention of "prior restraint" in the limited factual context where it is applicable.[39] But its implication that expression may be penalized on a *post hoc* basis makes it a hopeless anachronism. Apparently "clear and present danger" was revived to supplement Blackstone in *Thornhill* and other subsequent punishment cases. In the preceding decade, under the leadership of Chief Justice Hughes, the Court had relied largely upon *ad hoc* tactics when the facts of a case could not be brought within the narrow limits of the prior restraint rule.

While the year 1940 marks at least a partial fruition of Mr. Justice Holmes' efforts in the area of civil liberties, it also marks the beginning of an entirely different cycle. In that year Mr. Justice Stone, writing his first civil liberties opinion, dissented alone in the first flag salute case.[40] By 1941 Justices Black and Douglas were in dissent;[41] by 1942 Mr. Justice Murphy had joined them.[42] The common element in all these dissents is disenchantment with the reasonable basis approach in civil liberties cases. Finally, in

---

32. Bakery & Pastry Drivers v. Wohl, 314 U.S. 769 (1942); Hotel & Restaurant Employees v. Wisconsin Employment Relations Bd., 315 U.S. 437 (1942); AFL v. Swing, 312 U.S. 321 (1941); Carlson v. California, 310 U.S. 106 (1940).
33. Carpenters & Joiners Union v. Ritters Cafe, 315 U.S. 722 (1942); Milkwagon Drivers v. Meadowmoor Dairies, 312 U.S. 287 (1941).
34. 312 U.S. 569 (1941).
35. 310 U.S. 586 (1940).
36. *See id.* at 593, 594, 599.
37. 310 U.S. 296 (1940).
38. 283 U.S. 697 (1930).
39. See Largent v. Texas, 318 U.S. 418 (1943); Jamison v. Texas, 318 U.S. 412 (1943).
40. Minersville School District v. Gobitis, 310 U.S. 586, 601 (1940).
41. Milkwagon Drivers v. Meadowmoor Dairies, 312 U.S. 287, 299 (1941).
42. Carpenters & Joiners Union v. Ritters Cafe, 315 U.S. 722, 729 (1942).

Jones v. Opelika,[43] Justices Black, Douglas, and Murphy not only joined in a dissent by Chief Justice Stone, but wrote a separate opinion to announce "gratuitously" that they now conceived themselves to have been in error in the first flag salute case, the leading modern exposition of the reasonable basis rule. By the spring of 1943, when Mr. Justice Byrnes resigned from the bench, four of its members were unmistakably out of sympathy with the reasonable basis aspect of the Holmesian approach—the aspect which so often seemed to justify imposition of governmental restraints on expression. Conversely, Justices Frankfurter and Roberts, as well as Chief Justice Stone on occasion, had shown signs of sharp displeasure with the manner in which the others had, as they thought, improperly used danger rhetoric to achieve results that Mr. Justice Holmes could not have contemplated.[44] Chief Justice Stone was to be found sometimes in one camp and sometimes in the other; he seemed satisfied with neither the danger nor the reasonable basis test in civil liberties cases.

IV. The Mature Roosevelt Court—May, 1943 to July, 1949

The tenure of Mr. Justice Rutledge marks the era *par excellence* of civil liberties—some would say civil anarchy—in American jurisprudence. An increasingly libertarian attitude on the part of Justices Black, Douglas, and Murphy had been indicated during the formative period of the Roosevelt Court. To that bloc was now added another. Since four votes are decisive in the disposition of writs of certiorari, it is not surprising to find more decisions involving First Amendment freedoms during this period than in the entire previous history of the Supreme Court. If "clear and present danger" was ever "the law," it was while the four libertarians, Justices Black, Douglas, Murphy, and Rutledge, were together on the bench.

During these six years forty-one expression decisions were handed down.[45] Seven may be dismissed at the outset as involving only specious

---

43. 316 U.S. 584 (1942).
This case, like Chaplinsky v. New Hampshire, 315 U.S. 568 (1942), and Valentine v. Christensen, 316 U.S. 52 (1942), went on the ground that commercial activities and offensive language are not protected by the First Amendment.

44. *See* Bridges v. California, 314 U.S. 252, 279 (1941) (dissenting opinion).
Hartzel v. United States, 322 U.S. 680 (1944), indicates that neither Chief Justice Stone nor Justices Black, Murphy, Roberts, and Rutledge would have joined in Mr. Justice Holmes' opinion in the *Schenck* case.

45. Terminiello v. Chicago, 337 U.S. 1 (1949); Giboney v. Empire Storage & Ice Co., 336 U.S. 490 (1949); Fisher v. Pace, 336 U.S. 155 (1949); Railway Express Co. v. New York, 336 U.S. 106 (1949); Kovacs v. Cooper, 336 U.S. 77 (1949); Doubleday & Co. v. New York, 335 U.S. 848 (1948); AFL v. American Sash & Door Co., 335 U.S. 538 (1949); Lincoln Federal Labor Union v. Northwestern Iron Co., 335 U.S. 525 (1949); United States v. CIO, 335 U.S. 106 (1948); Saia v. New York, 334 U.S. 558 (1948); United States v. Paramount Pictures, 334 U.S. 131 (1948); Winters v. New York, 333 U.S. 507 (1948); Donaldson v. Read Magazine, 333 U.S. 178 (1948); Musser v. Utah, 333 U.S. 95 (1948); United States v.

claims:[46] for example, a group of newspaper publishers sought exemption from the Sherman Antitrust and Fair Labor Standards Acts on free press grounds.[47] Without dissent, the Court refused to treat such claims seriously. Another five were disposed of without reaching a First Amendment question.[48] Three of these cases involved acts of Congress;[49] there freedom of expression was sustained either by a strained interpretion of the statutes[50] or by finding insufficient evidence.[51] The result, of course, reflects the Roosevelt Court's reluctance to invalidate national legislation. Indeed since the judicial revolution of 1937 no act of Congress has been invalidated on First Amendment grounds—demonstrating that sometimes one may eat one's cake and have it too.

That the substitution of Mr. Justice Rutledge for Mr. Justice Byrnes would bring changes in the law was made clear on May 3, 1943, when the *Opelika* decision was reversed on rehearing[52] and two other important cases were decided.[53] The four dissenters in the original *Opelika* case had gained an ally—at least when decision could be based on what were essentially prior restraint considerations. In the following month the Court did an about-face on the flag salute issue.[54] Simultaneously it abandoned Mr.

Petrillo, 332 U.S. 1 (1947); Craig v. Harney, 331 U.S. 367 (1947); Oklahoma v. United States Civil Service Comm'n, 330 U.S. 127 (1947); United Public Workers v. Mitchell, 330 U.S. 75 (1947); Pennekamp v. Florida, 328 U.S. 331 (1946); Oklahoma Press Pub. Co. v. Walling, 327 U.S. 186 (1946); Mabee v. White Plains Pub. Co., 327 U.S. 178 (1946); Tucker v. Texas, 326 U.S. 517 (1946); Marsh v. Alabama, 326 U.S. 501 (1946); May Dep't Stores v. NLRB, 326 U.S. 376 (1945); Associated Press v. United States, 326 U.S. 1 (1945); *In re* Summers, 325 U.S. 561 (1945); Thomas v. Collins, 323 U.S. 516 (1945); Keegan v. United States, 325 U.S. 478 (1945); Hartzel v. United States, 322 U.S. 680 (1944); United States v. Ballard, 322 U.S. 78 (1944); Follett v. Town of McCormick, 321 U.S. 573 (1944); Prince v. Massachusetts, 321 U.S. 158 (1944); Cafeteria Employees Union v. Angelos, 320 U.S. 293 (1943); West Virginia State Board of Education v. Barnette, 319 U.S. 624 (1943); Taylor v. Mississippi, 319 U.S. 583 (1943); NLRB v. Virginia Electric & Power Co., 319 U.S. 533 (1943); National Broadcasting Co. v. United States, 319 U.S. 190 (1943); Douglas v. City of Jeanette, 319 U.S. 157 (1943); Martin v. Struthers, 319 U.S. 141 (1943); Murdock v. Pennsylvania, 319 U.S. 105 (1943); Jones v. Opelika, 319 U.S. 103 (1943).

Danger language was used in two non-expression cases: Korematsu v. United States, 323 U.S. 214 (1944); Bridges v. Wixon, 326 U.S. 135 (1945).

46. AFL v. American Sash & Door Co., 335 U.S. 538 (1949); Lincoln Federal Labor Union v. Northwestern Iron & Metal Co., 335 U.S. 525 (1949); United States v. Paramount Pictures, 334 U.S. 131 (1948); Oklahoma Press Pub. Co. v. Walling, 327 U.S. 186 (1946); Mabee v. White Plains Pub. Co., 327 U.S. 178 (1946); Associated Press v. United States, 326 U.S. 1 (1945); National Broadcasting Co. v. United States, 319 U.S. 190 (1943).

47. Associated Press v. United States, *supra* note 46.

48. United States v. CIO, 335 U.S. 106 (1948); Winters v. New York, 333 U.S. 507 (1948); Musser v. Utah, 333 U.S. 1 (1948); Keegan v. United States, 325 U.S. 478 (1945); Hartzel v. United States, 322 U.S. 680 (1944). *Cf.* United States v. Petrillo, 332 U.S. 1 (1947); Douglas v. City of Jeanette, 319 U.S. 157 (1943).

49. United States v. CIO, Keegan v. United States, Hartzel v. United States, *supra* note 48.

50. United States v. CIO, *supra* note 48.

51. Keegan v. United States, Hartzel v. United States, *supra* note 48.

52. Jones v. Opelika, 319 U.S. 103 (1943).

53. Martin v. Struthers, 319 U.S. 141 (1943); Murdock v. Pennsylvania, 319 U.S. 105 (1943).

54. West Virginia State Board of Education v. Barnette, 319 U.S. 624 (1943), *overruling* Minersville School District v. Gobitis, 310 U.S. 586 (1940).

Justice Holmes' distinction between suppression of ideas and mere regulation of the time, place, or manner of expressing them. "Reasonable basis" was discarded in First Amendment cases and "clear and present danger" expanded to fill the resulting vacuum. A test originally intended to detect the point at which discussion ripens into illegal conduct became the criterion for permissible grade school curricula:

> here the power of compulsion is invoked without any allegation that remaining passive during a flag salute ritual creates a clear and present danger. . . . The right of a state to regulate, for example, a public utility, may well include, so far as the due process test is concerned, power to impose all of the restrictions which a legislature may have a "rational basis" for adopting. But freedoms of speech and of press, of assembly and of worship may not be infringed on such slender grounds. They are susceptible of restriction only to prevent grave and immediate danger to interests which the state may lawfully protect.[55]

Of course a test designed to deal with serious criminality would be insensitive to the conduct of moppets in their school rooms. To make "clear and present danger" the sole test in First Amendment cases is to imply that incitement to crime is the only abuse of free expression.[56]

Cut loose from its anchor in the distinction between discussion and incitement, the danger rule lost its intrinsic meaning. No longer a guide to decision, it became a cloak for "vague but fervent transcendentalism." During the remainder of the Rutledge era only two cases presented problems of incitement and censorship,[57] though danger talk occurs in at least fifteen of the opinions.[58] But having "reinterpreted" the rule and thereby stretched it far beyond its original meaning, the Court failed, as we shall see, to use it in all cases logically within its new ambit. To have done so would often have led to results apparently too unreasonable even for the libertarians.

A. *Opinions in which the Danger Rule Was Mentioned*

During the period from 1943 to 1949 danger language was used in fifteen opinions in thirteen cases.[59] Twelve of these were written by either

55. West Virginia State Board of Education v. Barnette, 319 U.S. 624, 633, 639 (1943).
56. See *id.* at 654, 655, 663 (Justice Frankfurter dissenting).
57. Musser v. Utah, 333 U.S. 95 (1948); Taylor v. Mississippi, 319 U.S. 583 (1943).
58. See cases cited notes 59-61, 65-69, *infra.*
59. See note 58 *supra.*

The following cases or opinions are not included for the reasons indicated: Giboney v. Empire Storage & Ice Co., 336 U.S. 490 (1949) (a single danger phrase used); Hartzel v. United States, 322 U.S. 680 (1944) (danger rule mentioned with approval but not used to decide case); Schneiderman v. United States, 320 U.S. 118 (1943) (same); Cafeteria Employees Union v. Angelos, 320 U.S. 293 (1943) (a clear and present danger case cited); Terminiello v. Chicago, 337 U.S. 1, 13 (1949) (dissenting opinion; danger test mentioned to show majority wrong even by its own standard); Craig v. Harney, 331 U.S. 367, 384 (1947) (same).

Justices Black, Douglas, Murphy, or Rutledge; the remaining three by Justices Roberts, Reed, and Jackson, none of whom can be called a clear and present danger enthusiast. Mr. Justice Roberts and Mr. Justice Reed, each in turn, resorted to danger language on an occasion when the result was obvious enough to get unanimous approval. In one case a newspaper's citation for contempt was challenged, the crux of the decision being that publication had occurred too late to be contumacious.[60] The other case put in issue a dragnet statute which, as construed by the state court, made it a crime "to communicate views and opinions respecting governmental policies, and prophesies concerning the future of our own and other nations."[61]

While Mr. Justice Jackson, speaking for the Court, used danger language in the second flag salute case,[62] it is difficult to imagine a mind less congenial to the new approach than his. Apparently Mr. Justice Jackson was chosen to write the opinion as a compromise between the libertarians' danger views and Chief Justice Stone's *Gobitis* position. Not unnaturally he threw a few bones in both directions, but his own rule for drawing the line between liberty and authority is mentioned first[63]—a rule which he has been at pains to express on other occasions[64] and which is quite unlike the danger test.

In addition to the two already-mentioned unanimous opinions, there are four divided opinions of the Court employing danger language. In all four, Justices Black, Douglas, Murphy, and Rutledge supported it. But who would supply the other vote to make a majority was difficult to predict; only Mr. Justice Reed voted with them as often as twice. In the second flag salute case the libertarian quartet had the support of Justices Stone and Jackson; in *Thomas v. Collins*[65] they could not get a fifth to join in their language, though Mr. Justice Jackson joined in their result; in *Craig v. Harney*[66] the fifth and sixth votes came from Justices Burton and Reed; in the *Terminiello* case[67] Mr. Justice Reed made a fifth. These cases involved respectively a compulsory flag salute in public schools, a statutory requirement of advance registration for union organizers, another newspaper contempt citation, and a "lunatic fringe" hate speech which caused some public disturbance.

---

60. Pennekamp v. Florida, 328 U.S. 331 (1946).
61. Taylor v. Mississippi, 319 U.S. 583, 589 (1943).
62. West Virginia State Board of Education v. Barnette, 319 U.S. 624 (1943).
63. *Id.* at 630.
64. See American Communications Ass'n, CIO v. Douds, 339 U.S. 382, 443 (1950); Douglas v. City of Jeanette, 319 U.S. 157, 180 (1943).
65. 323 U.S. 516 (1945).
66. 331 U.S. 367 (1947).
67. Terminiello v. Chicago, 337 U.S. 1 (1949).

Finally, each of the three concurring[68] and five dissenting[69] opinions (in seven cases) that employ danger language was written and supported only by one or more of the libertarians. Since the latter were themselves divided in all the cases in which the danger test was referred to in dissent, it is not surprising that "conservative" views prevailed. These cases passed on the Hatch Act prohibition on the political activities of certain federal and state employees,[70] a conviction for advocacy of plural marriage,[71] the application of a child labor law to religious activities,[72] and the war-time exclusion from the West Coast of persons of Japanese ancestry.[73]

Of the three cases in which the danger test is found in concurring opinions, one is the second flag salute case where Justices Black and Douglas, joining fully in the Court's views, added a few words merely to explain their shift in position since the earlier flag litigation. But in *Bridges v. Wixon*[74] only Mr. Justice Murphy ventured to assert that the national power to deport aliens is limited by the danger test.[75] A majority, including Justices Black, Douglas, and Rutledge, were satisfied to reach the same result by means of statutory construction. On the other hand, in *United States v. CIO*[76] where the constitutional possibilities were not so far-fetched, all the libertarians were willing to strike down a part of the Taft-Hartley Act on danger grounds[77]—a result which the majority again reached via statutory construction.

The striking thing about these fifteen opinions is that all were written in support of First Amendment claims. Thus, just as in the early Roosevelt period, "clear and present danger" was a one-way ticket. When First Amendment arguments were rejected, other linguistic formulae were used.

B. *Cases Sustaining First Amendment Claims Without Resort to the Danger Rule*

Seven cases sustained First Amendment claims without mention of "clear and present danger." All turned more or less clearly on prior restraint grounds. Six are the well known proselytizing cases in which Jehovah's Witnesses ran afoul of tax or license impediments, or outright prohibitions,

68. United States v. CIO, 335 U.S. 106, 129 (1948); Bridges v. Wixon, 326 U.S. 135, 157 (1945); West Virginia State Board of Education v. Barnette, 319 U.S. 624, 644 (1943).
69. Musser v. Utah, 333 U.S. 95, 98 (1948); United Public Workers v. Mitchell, 330 U.S. 75, 105, 115 (1947); Korematsu v. United States, 323 U.S. 214, 233 (1944) (a case not involving the First Amendment); Prince v. Massachusetts, 321 U.S. 158, 171 (1944).
70. United Public Workers v. Mitchell, *supra* note 69.
71. Musser v. Utah, *supra* note 69.
72. Prince v. Massachusetts, *supra* note 69.
73. Korematsu v. United States, *supra* note 69.
74. 326 U.S. 135 (1945).
75. *Id.* at 157.
76. 335 U.S. 106 (1948).
77. *Id.* at 129.

on their door-to-door activities.[78] The seventh was a challenge to the constitutionality of an ordinance requiring that permission be obtained before using a sound truck.[79] In each, the Court's opinion was written by one of the libertarians, and supported by all the others participating. At first Chief Justice Stone supplied the deciding vote. By the time he felt the libertarians had gone too far, Mr. Justice Frankfurter had joined them because he thought the precedent of the earlier decisions binding. Unlike the Chief Justice, he could not distinguish them.[80] Mr. Justice Reed went over one case earlier than his brother Frankfurter and for similar reasons,[81] but along with the Chief Justice he was able to distinguish the last two proselytizing cases. In the *Saia* sound truck case a new chief justice furnished the vote necessary to make a majority.

Obviously these cases were decided by the barest margin; Chief Justice Stone cast the decisive vote in the first instance and thus established the precedent later deemed controlling by other justices. This may be the clue to the use of the prior restraint approach in these decisions. Having no more patience with subsequent punishment than with prior restraints on expression, Justices Black, Douglas, Murphy, and Rutledge doubtless would have preferred to frame these decisions in terms of "clear and present danger." Indeed they did exactly that in another advance permission case[82] in which a separate concurring opinion by Mr. Justice Jackson relieved them of the necessity to compromise on methodology. But in *Jones v. Opelika*, the first of the Jehovah's Witnesses' proselytizing cases, the price of Chief Justice Stone's crucial vote presumably was abandonment of that approach. In his long judicial career Mr. Justice Stone did not once write an opinion using danger language; as a matter of fact, during the twenties he voted with the majority in a decision from which Justices Holmes and Brandeis dissented on clear and present danger grounds.[83] Chief Justice Stone joined in only two opinions using danger language—one in a unanimously-decided case,[84] the other in the second flag salute case.[85] But his real views on saluting the flag are to be found in his lone dissent in the *Gobitis* case.[86]

---

78. Tucker v. Texas, 326 U.S. 517 (1946); Marsh v. Alabama, 326 U.S. 501 (1946); Follett v. Town of McCormick, 321 U.S. 573 (1944); Martin v. Struthers, 319 U.S. 141 (1943); Murdock v. Pennsylvania, 319 U.S. 105 (1943); Jones v. Opelika, 319 U.S. 103 (1943). *Cf.* United States v. Ballard, 322 U.S. 78 (1944).

79. Saia v. New York, 334 U.S. 558 (1948). This is the only case during this period which explicitly follows the prior restraint doctrine.

80. Tucker v. Texas, 326 U.S. 517 (1946); Marsh v. Alabama, 326 U.S. 501 (1946).

81. *See* Follett v. Town of McCormick, 321 U.S. 573, 578 (1944).

82. Thomas v. Collins, 323 U.S. 516 (1945).

83. Gitlow v. New York, 268 U.S. 652 (1925). *Cf.* Whitney v. California, 274 U.S. 357 (1927). According to Professor Alpheus Mason, Mr. Justice Stone did not participate in the *Gitlow* decision, the official report notwithstanding.

84. Pennekamp v. Florida, 328 U.S. 331 (1946).

85. West Virginia State Board of Education v. Barnette, 319 U.S. 624 (1943). *Cf.* Herndon v. Georgia, 295 U.S. 441, 451 (1935).

86. Minersville School District v. Gobitis, 310 U.S. 586, 601 (1940).

Vote "purchasing" is only one possible explanation for the choice of "prior restraint" rather than "clear and present danger" as the rationale for these decisions. Perhaps the latter was abandoned because in its new non-Holmesian version it would have led to results the libertarians did not like—for *a priori* much of the proselytizing would seem to have occurred "in such circumstances . . . as to create a clear and present danger that . . . [it would] bring about the substantive evils [for example, violation of privacy of the home] that [state legislatures have] . . . a right to prevent."[87] The same is true in regard to the sound truck case. Just as "reasonableness" had been used by the early Roosevelt Court in *Cox v. New Hampshire* to avoid the prior restraint rule, so the latter may have been used here to avoid the unwelcome implications of "clear and present danger." To complete the circle, moreover, not all previous impediments to free expression were disposed of via the prior restraint rule; the danger test did the job in *Thomas v. Collins*.

C. *Cases in Which the Danger Rule Was Ignored and First Amendment Claims Denied Protection*

In six of the remaining nine expression cases during this period, First Amendment claims were rejected more or less clearly on reasonable basis grounds. At issue in five of these cases were: the Hatch Act's prohibition,[88] a "test-oath" used to preclude a pacifist from practicing law,[89] a contempt citation of a lawyer whose talk had offended a trial judge,[90] and another sound truck regulation.[91] Significantly, in each case the majority opinion was written by Mr. Justice Reed. Every vote of Justices Black, Douglas, Murphy, and Rutledge was cast in dissent. The loss of the vote of the chief justice,[92] and the inability to attract a replacement, lost the day for the libertarians. In dissent, where it was no longer necessary to appease a fifth colleague, they were free to indulge in clear and present danger language.[93]

---

87. Schenck v. United States, 249 U.S. 47, 52 (1918).

88. Oklahoma v. United States Civil Service Comm'n, 330 U.S. 127 (1947); United Public Workers v. Mitchell, 330 U.S. 75 (1947).

89. *In re* Summers, 325 U.S. 561 (1945).

90. Fisher v. Pace, 336 U.S. 155 (1949).

91. Kovacs v. Cooper, 336 U.S. 77 (1949). *Cf.* Railway Express Co. v. New York, 336 U.S. 106 (1949) (commercial advertising not within First Amendment); Donaldson v. Read Magazine, 333 U.S. 178 (1948) (use of the mails not within First Amendment).

Doubleday & Co. v. New York, 335 U.S. 848 (1949), upheld censorship of a collection of short stories, but is not included in the list of nine cases discussed in the text because it was decided per curiam by an evenly divided bench, Mr. Justice Frankfurter not participating.

92. In his last years on the bench, Chief Justice Stone often disagreed with the libertarian quartet. Nevertheless, upon him probably rested their chief hope of gaining a majority. His replacement in the spring of 1946 by Chief Justice Vinson made the prospect of obtaining the necessary vote less likely.

93. The dissents in Fisher v. Pace, 336 U.S. 155 (1949), are *ad hoc*, relying on the par-

On their facts four of these cases differ so greatly from the cases previously discussed in which First Amendment claims were sustained in terms of prior restraint doctrine that the significance of the Chief Justice's vote is obscured. But the *Kovacs* sound truck case removes the obscurity. There Mr. Justice Reed, speaking also for Chief Justice Vinson and Mr. Justice Burton, made a brave show of distinguishing the *Saia* case in the course of sustaining the regulation, but at least four justices in concurrence or dissent recognized that it had been abandoned.[94]

Prince v. Massachusetts[95] is the remaining and most fascinating of this group of six cases. It presented a typical Jehovah's Witness proselytizing problem, except that here the proselytors were children who had violated a child labor law. Of course, the four "conservatives" voted to uphold the conviction, just as they had in the earlier proselytizing cases. But in the *Prince* case they were joined not only by Chief Justice Stone, but by Justices Black, Douglas, and Rutledge as well. Indeed, Mr. Justice Rutledge, undismayed, wrote the opinion for the Court, distinguishing the previous decisions on the ground that the proselytors in *Prince* were children—without commenting on the childhood of those who had previously refused to salute the flag.[96] This was too much for Mr. Justice Murphy, who dissented in clear and present danger terms.[97] In a concurring opinion, Justices Frankfurter, Jackson, and Roberts did not fail to note that the activity at issue was exactly what the libertarians a few months earlier had held to "occupy the same high estate" as worship in a church.[98] One can only speculate as to whether Justices Black, Douglas, and Rutledge withheld dissent in exchange for the privilege of writing for the Court. By doing so Mr. Justice Rutledge at least had an opportunity to save the earlier proselytizing cases from the subsequent fate of the *Saia* sound truck decision.

Three labor relations cases[99] complete this group of nine. "Clear and present danger" was ignored; the decisions turned on the proposition that freedom of speech may not be used to shield illegal conduct. Yet, oddly enough, this is the exact situation for which Mr. Justice Holmes designed the present danger test: namely, to determine when utterance ceases to be mere discussion and becomes a "trigger of action." Certainly some picket

ticular facts involved. Those in Kovacs v. Cooper, 336 U.S. 77 (1949), are based largely on the first sound truck case, Saia v. New York, 334 U.S. 558 (1948). Dissenting opinions in the remaining cases employ danger language or citations.

94. *See* Kovacs v. Cooper, 336 U.S. 77, 97 (1949).

95. 321 U.S. 158 (1944).

96. See West Virginia State Board of Education v. Barnette, 319 U.S. 624 (1943); Minersville School District v. Gobitis, 310 U.S. 586 (1940).

97. Prince v. Massachusetts, 321 U.S. 158, 171 (1944).

98. *Id.* at 176.

99. Giboney v. Empire Storage & Ice Co., 336 U.S. 490 (1949) [see note 59 *supra*]; May Dep't Stores v. NLRB, 326 U.S. 376 (1945); Virginia Electric & Power Co. v. NLRB, 319 U.S. 533 (1943); NLRB v. Virginia Electric & Power Co., 314 U.S. 469 (1941).

lines and some employer's speeches to workmen are calculated not to enlighten but to compel immediate, unreasoned action.

V. The Truman Court

The substitution of Justices Minton and Clark for Justices Rutledge and Murphy seems to introduce another epoch in civil liberties litigation. In the six relevant decisions during its 1949 Term, the Court rejected all claims based on freedom of expression. Three cases,[100] following the implications of *Thornhill* and *Giboney*, sustained limited restrictions on picketing. So thoroughly was reasonableness emphasized that Mr. Justice Black found it necessary to disassociate himself from the Court's language in two instances[101] and to dissent in the third.[102] Mr. Justice Douglas did not participate in these cases nor in another in which the Court unanimously upheld a conviction under a state statute which had been construed to prohibit persons acting in concert from assembling to prevent others by force or violence from engaging in lawful occupations.[103] Danger language was used in none of the opinions in these cases.

But in the two Taft-Hartley non-communist oath cases[104] the danger test got a "new" twist. Speaking for the Court, Chief Justice Vinson observed that Congress clearly has the power to attempt to prevent political strikes and other direct burdens upon interstate commerce. "But the more difficult problem here arises because, in drawing lines on the basis of beliefs and political affiliations . . . Congress has undeniably discouraged the lawful exercise of political freedoms as well."[105] Such a problem

> is not the same one that Justices Holmes and Brandeis found convenient to consider in terms of clear and present danger. The Government's interest here is not in preventing the dissemination of Communist doctrine or the holding of particular beliefs . . . [The legislation] is designed to protect the public not against what Communists . . . advocate or believe, but what Congress has concluded they have done and are likely to do again [*i.e.*, disrupt interstate commerce by political strikes].[106]

Having found the danger approach inapplicable when the regulation of conduct "results in an indirect, conditional, partial abridgment of speech,"

100. Building Service Employees v. Gazzam, 339 U.S. 532 (1950); International Brotherhood of Teamsters v. Hanke, 339 U.S. 470 (1950); Hughes v. Superior Court, 339 U.S. 460 (1950).

101. Building Service Employees v. Gazzam; Hughes v. Superior Court, *supra* n. 100.

102. International Brotherhood of Teamsters v. Hanke, *supra* n. 100.

103. Cole v. Arkansas, 338 U.S. 345 (1949).

104. American Communications Ass'n, CIO v. Douds, 339 U.S. 382 (1950); Osman v. Douds, 339 U.S. 846 (1950). A "non-communist oath" was required of the officers of a labor union as a condition precedent to the enjoyment by their union of the benefits of the Taft-Hartley Act.

105. American Communications Ass'n, CIO v. Douds, 339 U.S. 382, 392 (1950).

106. *Id.* at 396.

the Chief Justice proceeded to uphold the oath requirement on reasonable basis grounds.[107]

On the record before it, the Court undoubtedly was justified in finding that Congress had sought only to control political strikes and not to censor political views. In that event Mr. Justice Holmes, too, presumably would have used the reasonable basis rule to uphold the statute—provided he were also satisfied that, regardless of purpose, such a regulation of conduct did not in effect constitute a censorship of ideas. Chief Justice Vinson's rather cavalier treatment of the latter point weakens the Court's position in the Taft-Hartley oath cases. Nevertheless, these two decisions constitute a somewhat inarticulate return to the Holmesian distinction between regulation and censorship. Of course, the two remaining libertarians dissented[108]—not to mention the partial dissents of Justices Jackson and Frankfurter (with whom Mr. Justice Holmes doubtless would have agreed) on the part of the oath concerning beliefs. None of the dissenters used danger language, however, and there is a hint in the opinions of Justices Black and Douglas that they may be abandoning the danger approach altogether in favor of one which would protect all utterance not connected with overt criminal action.[109]

During its 1950 Term the Court disposed of *Niemotko v. Maryland*[110] and *Kunz v. New York*[111] on prior restraint grounds. Both involved advance permit requirements for the use of public parks or streets by religious proselytizers. Mr. Justice Jackson, dissenting in the *Kunz* case, found it "peculiar that today's opinion makes no reference to the 'clear and present danger' test."[112] He argued that if it had been adopted the decision would have been otherwise, for "the approach will determine the result."[113] In short, as already intimated, Holmes and Blackstone are not logically complementary. The choice of one instead of the other in a particular case involves a *tour de force.*[114]

In *Feiner v. New York*[115] the Chief Justice, speaking for the Court, used "clear and present danger" for the first time since 1920 to justify punishment for speech-making which the Court and some members of the audience

107. *Id.* at 399 *et seq.*

108. *Id.* at 445 (Justice Black dissenting). Mr. Justice Douglas participated only in the second decision, but his position there clearly covers both cases. *See* Osman v. Douds, 339 U.S. 846, 848 (1950).

109. *See* American Communications Ass'n, CIO v. Douds, 339 U.S. 382, 452 (1950); Osman v. Douds, 339 U.S. 846, 848 (1950).

110. 340 U.S. 268 (1951).

111. 340 U.S. 290 (1951).

112. *Id.* at 300.

113. *Id.* at 301.

114. *See* Cantwell v. Connecticut, 310 U.S. 296, 308 (1940). The Court there recognizes that a clear and present danger would justify a prior restraint.

115. 340 U.S. 315 (1951).

found overstimulating. Justices Black and Douglas dissented on *ad hoc* gounds, indicating a somewhat dimmed enthusiasm for the danger test when used to send a man to jail.

In *Breard v. Alexandria*[116] the Court upheld a conviction under a municipal ordinance which restricted door-to-door solicitation for the sale of merchandise. The merchandise in question was magazine subscriptions. Again Justices Black and Douglas dissented. For them the Court's reasonableness approach could not be reconciled with *Opelika*, *Murdock*, and *Struthers*,[117] the three crucial cases of early 1943 which, thanks to the vote of Mr. Justice Rutledge, had introduced the libertarian phase of the Roosevelt Court. Once more there was no reference to the danger test. The same can be said of *Garner v. Board of Public Works*,[118] which upheld a non-communist oath requirement for municipal employees—Justices Black and Douglas dissenting altogether and Justices Burton and Frankfurter in part.

Finally, in *Dennis v. United States*[119] Chief Justice Vinson, for the Court, sustained the conviction of eleven Communist Party leaders for conspiring to teach and advocate the violent overthrow of the government. Following the dicta and implications of the non-communist oath cases, the plurality opinion held that because here Congress had put a "direct restriction upon speech"[120] the clear and present danger rule was applicable. But the Chief Justice found it necessary to adopt Judge Learned Hand's "reinterpretation" to the effect that

> In each case . . . [courts] must ask whether the gravity of the "evil," discounted by its improbability, justifies such invasion of free speech as is necessary to avoid the danger.[121]

As Judge Hand explained below, "improbability" was substituted for "remoteness" because "that must be the right interpretation. Given the same probability, it would be wholly irrational to condone future evils which we should prevent if they were immediate. . . ."[122]

The remoteness element, however, is the heart of the danger test; it was Mr. Justice Holmes' answer to the "bad tendency" attitude of most of his colleagues. The question is, did the Communist leaders conspire to "teach and advocate" under conditions allowing free play for the democratic corrective of counter-discussion? An overwhelming preponderance of evidence indicates that they did not. They sought to bypass the democratic processes,

116. 341 U.S. 622 (1951).
117. See p. 321 *supra*. Chief Justice Vinson dissented in the principal case on commerce clause grounds.
118. 341 U.S. 716 (1951).
119. 341 U.S. 494 (1951).
120. *Id.* at 508.
121. *Id.* at 510.
122. Dennis v. United States, 183 F.2d 201, 212 (2d Cir. 1950).

not to use them. They tried to attain their ends "without advocacy or persuasion that seeks acceptance in the competition of the market."[123] Taking into account their widespread and highly organized activities, largely *sub rosa*, this constituted the danger. In short, democracy and free speech provide a testing ground for ideas, but not for conspiracies. The law would be "a ass" not to notice the distinction. What Judge Hand really did was to hold that in the circumstances, application of the clear and present danger test would be "irrational." That he did so by means of "reinterpretation" is what may be expected when a great, creative lower court judge is caught between the demands of good sense in the case before him and the pressure of the unwieldy danger-language precedents of the Supreme Court—to say nothing of the position of the trial judge. The difference between "clear and probable danger" and "reasonable basis" certainly is not obvious. It may be that the former will be reserved for use in cases involving restraints upon conspiratorial, underground "discussion."

In any event, the probable danger rule was accepted by only four members of the Supreme Court. Mr. Justice Clark did not participate in the decision. Justices Frankfurter and Jackson, though they concurred in the result, took pains to disassociate themselves from the "reinterpretation." Justices Black and Douglas dissented. Again there is an indication that Mr. Justice Black has more to say on the subject: "At least as to speech in the realm of public matters, I believe that the 'clear and present danger' test does not mark the furthermost constitutional boundaries of protected expression" but does "no more than recognize a minimum compulsion of the Bill of Rights."[124] Thus while the Court's apparent return to Mr. Justice Holmes in the non-communist oath cases had the support of six out of eight participating justices, "reinterpretation" of the master had the support of but four out of eight participants. In only one other case, *Feiner v. New York*, has the Truman Court, or any of its members, used danger language, and there four justices thought it improperly applied. It may be that now, as in Mr. Justice Holmes' day, the danger approach is to be a one-way road leading only to jail.

VI. Conclusion

If by law we mean a reasonably accurate prediction as to how a court will dispose of a given controversy, the clear and present danger test has never been law. Mr. Justice Holmes himself suggested that he was chosen to write for the Court in the *Schenck* case in part because he would "go further probably than the majority in favor of" free speech.[125] Apparently

---

123. Dennis v. United States, 341 U.S. 494, 502 (1951).
124. Dennis v. United States, 341 U.S. 494, 580 (1951).
125. 2 Howe, Holmes-Pollock Letters 7 (1941). See Chafee, *op. cit. supra* note 10, at 86.

Mr. Justice Holmes' associates were willing to use his heroic liberal reputation to sugarcoat an unpleasant decision. In all other First Amendment cases decided while Mr. Justice Holmes was on the bench, the danger rule found expression only in dissenting or concurring opinions joined in by at most two judges. Thereafter until 1940 it was mentioned, and then obliquely, only twice, notwithstanding the flood of expression cases during the tenure of Chief Justice Hughes.

Early in the forties Mr. Justice Holmes' dual approach of "clear and present danger" and "reasonable basis" was revived by a virtually unanimous Court. Almost immediately, however, a vigorous quartet of libertarians purported to reject "reasonable basis" and put all expression eggs in the danger basket. But lacking reliable accompaniment, they could never depend on getting their truncated approach into a majority opinion. Get it in they sometimes did, but voting records suggest that this was accomplished only by the kind of horse trading "Court opinions" encourage and not because of general acceptance of the new view as a rule of law. Often Justices Black, Douglas, Murphy, and Rutledge were out-traded and found themselves either dissenting or supporting prior restraint language, as though for them prior restraint was worse than subsequent punishment of expression.

But while the "liberal" quartet loved freedom well, even they sometimes found it abused. In such cases they rather pointedly refused to blemish "clear and present danger" by finding its test to have been met. Other linguistic formulae were employed for the dirty work. "Reasonable basis," having been ruled out of court, was on occasion surreptitiously readmitted. If the associates of Justices Holmes and Brandeis used the danger doctrine only to send men to jail, its ardent supporters in the 1940's used it only to get them out. Chief Justice Stone's early inclination to vote "liberal" coupled with his distaste for the libertarians' doctrinaire approach accounts for a large part of the judicial maneuvering during the period in which he presided. The picture is further complicated by the tendency of the Roosevelt Court to avoid questioning the constitutionality of national legislation.

With the death of Justices Rutledge and Murphy and the emergence of the Truman Court, the libertarians' conception of the danger rule was clearly dead. Recent opinions seem to trace at least some of the steps back to Holmes—or perhaps merely back to *Gitlow*. But as before, the Court is too obviously divided to warrant prediction. At any rate, decisions since the demise of two of the four libertarians have been quite different—as Terminiello might attest upon contemplation of Feiner's fate. Meanwhile Justices Black and Douglas, finding their favorite rule now turned against them when it is used at all, show signs of looking elsewhere for a suitable vehicle for their ideas.

All this suggests that except in the hands of Justices Holmes and Brandeis "clear and present danger" has been something less than a guide to decision. Nevertheless it reflects a great ideal, tarnished somewhat in its service as a mask to cover disagreements and perplexities on the bench.[126]

---

126. *See* Kunz v. New York, 340 U.S. 290, 299 (1951).

SMITH ACT PROSECUTIONS: THE EFFECT OF THE *DENNIS* AND *YATES* DECISIONS

*Robert Mollan**

*Prosecutions of Communist Party leaders under the Smith Act have been criticized both from liberal and conservative viewpoints. In an effort to bring clarity of understanding into a somewhat confused area of law, Mr. Mollan, in this article, examines the history of prosecutions under the "advocacy," "organizational," and "membership" clauses of the Smith Act. Emphasis is laid on the time period between the two significant United States Supreme Court decisions—*Dennis *and* Yates*. The author concludes by asserting that there are two possible judicial interpretations of the* Yates *decision; which interpretation will prevail only will be decided in future case applications of the Smith Act.*

I. Introduction

THE possible threat to the internal security of the United States posed by groups and individuals variously labelled as "subversive" was a matter of extreme concern in the 1950's. During this period there was intense fear that subversive activities posed an imminent, massive threat to the security of the United States. Conversely, many were concerned that the reactions by the anti-subversives to this threat endangered traditional American liberties more than the subversives themselves. This article discusses certain aspects of one of the many governmental programs intended to counteract the threat of subversive activities—the prosecution of Communist Party leaders under various provisions of the Smith Act.[1] Concentration is placed on the events following the Supreme Court's decision in *Dennis*

* Acting Assistant Professor of Political Science, The University of Kansas, Lawrence, Kansas.

1. 62 Stat. 808 (1948), as amended, 18 U.S.C.A. § 2385 (Supp. 1964). The Act provides:

> Whoever knowingly or willfully advocates, abets, advises, or teaches the duty, necessity, desirability, or propriety of overthrowing or destroying the government of the United States or the government of any State, Territory, District or Possession thereof, or the government of any political subdivision therein, by force or violence, or by the assassination of any officer of any such government; or
>
> Whoever, with intent to cause the overthrow or destruction of any such government, prints, publishes, edits, issues, circulates, sells, distributes, or publicly displays any written or printed matter advocating, advising, or teaching the duty, necessity, desirability, or propriety of overthrowing or destroying any government in the United States by force or violence, or attempts to do so; or
>
> Whoever organizes or helps or attempts to organize any society, group or assembly of persons who teach, advocate, or encourage the overthrow or destruction of any such government by force or violence; or becomes or is a member of, or affiliates with, any such society, group, or assembly of persons, knowing the purposes thereof . . . [Shall be punished as specified.]

The Smith Act at one time prohibited conspiracy of two or more persons to commit any offense named therein, but this was later omitted because it was covered by the general conspiracy provision, 69 Stat. 701 (1948), 18 U.S.C.A. § 371 (1950).

v. United States,[2] the first such case in which conviction was upheld.

The prosecuting of Communist Party leaders under the Smith Act carried on by the Department of Justice during the Truman and Eisenhower administrations necessitated the handling of protracted litigation. The trials themselves were often long, drawn-out affairs, and the resulting collateral and appellate litigation was equally extensive. Many appeals were taken as to procedural matters; constitutional challenges were made in every district court; these were carried to the courts of appeal and often to the Supreme Court.

The Smith Act[3] was passed shortly before World War II, and apparently was aimed primarily at the activities of Nazi and Fascist-oriented groups then existing in this country.[4] Still, it did contain provisions which broadened its applicability to include Communist groups. Only two prosecutions under the act occurred during the war, one involving leftist labor leaders in Minnesota,[5] and one involving alleged pro-Nazis.[6] After the war, however, the Government did make active use of the Smith Act in pursuing vigorously a large number of prosecutions, but only after the act's constitutionality had been upheld in *Dennis v. United States*.[7] The Supreme Court, however, subsequently revised its position on certain crucial constitutional and statutory points in the case of *Yates v. United States*,[8] which had a drastic effect upon the prosecutions then being appealed.

While the Smith Act operates upon activities one step removed from the actual performance of any act, there are other statutes which prohibit the performance of the substantive evils themselves. Conspiracy to "overthrow, put down, or destroy by force, the Government of the United States . . . or to oppose by force the authority thereof, or by force to prevent, hinder or delay the execution of any law of the United States," has been a statutory offense since 1861.[9] Conspiracy to commit any offense against the Government by overt acts was outlawed in 1867.[10] Actual force or violence was not required.

2. 341 U.S. 494 (1951).

3. Smith Act of June 28, 1940, ch. 439, tit. 1, §§ 2, 3, 5, 54 Stat. 670, 671.

4. CHASE, SECURITY AND LIBERTY: THE PROBLEMS OF NATIVE COMMUNISTS, 1947-1955 25 (1955).

5. Sections 1 and 2 were invoked in 1941 in a successful prosecution of eighteen members of the Socialist Workers Party. Dunne v. United States, 138 F.2d 137 (8th Cir.), *cert. denied*, 320 U.S. 790 (1943).

6. In 1942, Section 2 was invoked against twenty-eight alleged pro-Nazis. The judge died before the completion of the trial, and no retrial was begun, so the case was dismissed for failure to prosecute. United States v. McWilliams, 163 F.2d 695 (D.C. Cir. 1947).

7. 341 U.S. 494 (1951).

8. 354 U.S. 298 (1957).

9. Act to define and punish certain conspiracies, July 31, 1861, 12 Stat. 284.

10. Act of March 2, 1867, § 30, 14 Stat. 484. See 62 Stat. 808 (1948), 18 U.S.C.A. § 2383 (1951):

Many libertarians would argue that Smith Act prosecutions are completely unnecessary; any conspiracy which goes beyond the initial stage of mere advocacy and discussion and reaches the definite stage of planning to commit overt acts could be stopped quickly by the application of the other internal security statutes. They would argue further that any Smith Act prosecution violates an essential principle of democracy because it penalizes the mere expression of opinions, which is protected against governmental interference by the first amendment. They would counsel governmental restraint until a conspiracy has passed out of the realm of belief, expression, or sympathetic association, and has progressed to the stage of actual preparation to commit illegal acts of a more substantive and directly harmful nature.

Those people who believe that the Smith Act, as applied to Communist Party leaders, does not invade first amendment rights argue that this act strikes at what is, after all, a conspiracy to commit or to bring about the commission of illegal acts. They assert that such prosecutions strike at the initial stages of a conspiracy while it is still at the point of advocacy and discussion. Although the eventual commission of illegal acts might be far in the future, all of these activities are of such a closely related whole that to strike at such activities at any stage is justified by the necessity of preventing the final, desired outcome.

II. The *Dennis* Decision

The latter view was adopted by the Supreme Court in upholding the constitutionality of the Smith Act in *Dennis v. United States.*[11] The Court felt that the "clear and present danger"[12] doctrine applied to even the earliest phases of such a conspiracy.

> Whoever incites, sets on foot, assists, or engages in any rebellion or insurrection against the authority of the United States or the laws thereof, or gives aid or comfort thereto, shall be fined not more than $10,000 or imprisoned not more than ten years, or both . . . .

Also see, 62 Stat. 808 (1948), as amended, 18 U.S.C.A. § 2484 (1951):

> If two or more persons in any State or Territory, or in any place subject to the jurisdiction of the United States, conspire to overthrow, put down, or to destroy by force the Government of the United States, or to levy war against them, or to oppose by force the authority thereof, or by force to prevent, hinder or delay the execution of any law of the United States, or by force to seize, take, or possess any property of the United States contrary to the authority thereof, they shall each be fined not more than $20,000 or imprisoned not more than twenty years, or both.

11. 341 U.S. 494 (1951).

12. The doctrine was first announced by Mr. Justice Holmes in Schenck v. United States, 249 U.S. 47 (1919). In essence, it permits proscription of speech where "the words used are used in such circumstances and are of such a nature as to create a clear and present danger that they will bring about the substantive evils that Congress has a right to prevent." *Id.* at 52.

> Obviously, the words cannot mean that before the Government may act, it must wait until the *putsch* is about to be executed, the plans have been laid and the signal is awaited. If Government is aware that a group aiming at its overthrow is attempting to indoctrinate its members and to commit them to a course whereby they will strike when the leaders feel the circumstances permit, action by the Government is required.[13]
>
> * * *
>
> The mere fact that from the period 1945 to 1948 petitioners' activities did not result in an attempt to overthrow the Government by force and violence is of course no answer to the fact that there was a group that was ready to make the attempt . . . and this analysis disposes of the contention that a conspiracy to advocate, as distinguished from the advocacy itself, cannot be constitutionally restrained, because it comprises only the preparation. It is the existence of the conspiracy which creates the danger. . . . If the ingredients of the reaction are present, we cannot bind the Government to wait until the catalyst is added.[14]

Although stating that it was following the "clear and present danger" test in regard to this conspiracy, the Court quoted with approval the balancing test employed by Chief Judge Learned Hand in the court below: "In each case [courts] must ask whether the gravity of the 'evil,' discounted by its improbability, justifies such invasion of free speech as is necessary to avoid the danger."[15] This seemed to mean that even if the danger was remote, an extremely serious or unpleasant evil would be a ground for upholding a conviction. This test, then, would not focus upon the possible effectuation of the substantive evil which might flow from the expression of the idea, but rather upon the nature of the evil itself. In this the Court appeared to be turning away from the essence of the "clear and present danger" doctrine—the possibility of an actual occurrence of a substantive evil as the result of advocacy—and turning instead toward a consideration of the characteristics of the substantive evil.

III. Prosecutions Following *Dennis*

As a practical result of the *Dennis* decision, the Department of Justice during the Truman administration, which had withheld instituting any further prosecutions until the Court had ruled on the constitutionality of the Smith Act, immediately began a series of

13. 341 U.S. at 509.
14. *Id.* at 510-11. Justice Robert Jackson's concurring opinion is explicit in invoking the law of conspiracy. *Id.* at 561-79.
15. *Id.* at 510, quoting from United States v. Dennis, 183 F.2d 201, 212 (2d Cir. 1950).

prosecutions of secondary Communist Party leaders in various parts of the country. These prosecutions were similar to those of the *Dennis* group in that they involved the same sections of the Smith Act proscribing conspiracy to advocate the violent or forceful overthrow and destruction of the Government, and conspiracy to organize a group to so advocate.[16] The arrest and indictment of these groups of defendants (which will be referred to as groups two through seven) took place in the summer of 1951.[17] A year after this wave of arrests, in September 1952, more groups (eight through ten) were arrested and indicted.[18] The Justice Department arrested and indicted an eleventh

16. See quoted material, *supra* note 1.

17. The second group was arrested in New York and included the following: Marion Bachrach, Alexander Bittelman, George B. Charney, Fred Fine, E. G. Flynne, Betty Gannet, James E. Jackson, V. J. Jerome, Arnold S. Johnson, Claudia Jones, Albert Lannon, William Norman Marron, Jacob Mindel, P. Perry, Sidney Steinberg, Alexander Trachtenberg, Louis Weinstock, and William Weinstone. See N.Y. Times, June 21, 1951, p. 1, col. 7; p. 16, col. 7, and N.Y. Times, April 25, 1952, p. 8, col. 3. They were convicted on January 21, 1953. See N.Y. Times, Jan. 22, 1953, p. 1, col. 1; p. 5, col. 3.

The third group was arrested in California and included the following: Oleta O'Connor Yates, Henry Steinberg, Loretta Starvus Stack, William Schneiderman, Al Richmond, Albert Jason Lima, Carl Rude Lambert, Rose Chernin Kusnitz, Ernest Otto Fox, Dorothy Healey Connelly, and Philip M. Connelly. See N.Y. Times, July 27, 1951, p. 1, col. 1; N.Y. Times, July 29, 1951, § 1, p. 54, col. 1; N.Y. Times, Aug. 1, 1951, p. 7, col. 1. They were convicted on August 5, 1952. See N.Y. Times, Aug. 6, 1952, p. 1, col. 2.

The fourth group was arrested in New York, Baltimore, Maryland, and Cleveland, Ohio, and included the following: Philip Frankfeld, Regina Frankfeld, George Meyers, Leroy Wood, Dorothy Rose Blumberg, and Maurice Braverman. See N.Y. Times, Aug. 8, 1951, p. 1, col. 7; p. 5, col. 1; N.Y. Times, Aug. 15, 1951, p. 5, col. 2. They were convicted on April 1, 1952, in Baltimore. See N.Y. Times, March 11, 1952, p. 10, col. 2; N.Y. Times, April 2, 1952, p. 10, col. 3.

The fifth group was arrested in Pennsylvania and included the following: Steve Nelson (Stephen Mesarosh), Benjamin Careathers, J. Dolsen, Irving Weissman, and William Albertson. See N.Y. Times, Aug. 18, 1951, p. 1, col. 2; N.Y. Times, Aug. 24, 1951, p. 8, col. 2. They were convicted in Pittsburgh on August 20, 1953. See N.Y. Times, Aug. 21, 1953, p. 7, col. 2.

A sixth group was arrested in Hawaii, and included the following: Jack Hall, John Reinecke, Charles Fujimoto, Eileen Fujimoto, Dwight Freeman, Koji Ariyoshi, and Jack Kimoto. See N.Y. Times, Aug. 29, 1951, p. 1, col. 6; N.Y. Times, Aug. 30, 1951, p. 12, col. 3. This group was convicted on June 19, 1953. See N.Y. Times, June 20, 1953, p. 1, col. 7.

A seventh group was arrested in Los Angeles, California, and included the following: F. Carlson, F. E. Spector, and Ben Dobbs. See N.Y. Times, Sept. 1, 1951, p. 5, col. 1. Their cases were placed with those of the third group (the California or Yates group) for trial. See N.Y. Times, Feb. 2, 1952, p. 5, col. 5.

18. The eighth group was arrested in Detroit, Michigan, and included the following: Helen Winter, Saul Wellman, Nathan Kaplan, William Allan, Philip Schatz, and Thomas Dennis, Jr. See N.Y. Times, Sept. 18, 1952, p. 1, col. 2; p. 14, col. 5; N.Y. Times, Sept. 23, 1952, p. 9, col. 1. They were convicted on February 16, 1954. See N.Y. Times, Oct. 27, 1953, p. 20, col. 7; N.Y. Times, Feb. 17, 1954, p. 19, col. 3.

A ninth group was arrested in Seattle, Washington, and included the following: Henry Huff, William Pennock, Karly Larsen, Terry Pettus, Barbara Hartle, John Daschback, and Paul M. Bowen. See N.Y. Times, Sept. 18, 1952, p. 1, col. 2; p. 14, col. 5; N.Y. Times, Sept. 25, 1952, p. 10, col 4. The jury acquitted one defendant and convicted the other five on October 10, 1953. See N.Y. Times, April 16, 1953, p. 4, col. 7; N.Y. Times, Oct. 11, 1953, § 1, p. 53, col. 1.

group in the summer of 1953, and by 1956, groups twelve through sixteen had been arrested and indicted.[19]

A. *Prosecutions under the "Advocacy" and "Organizational" Clauses*

After the Supreme Court had upheld the first conviction of Communist Party leaders in *Dennis* a large number of subsequent convictions were obtained. The appeals from these convictions contained the same argument as presented in *Dennis*, namely that conviction for such conspiracies infringed upon first amendment rights. Thus the federal appellate courts were faced with the problem of interpreting *Dennis* and properly applying it.

The lower federal courts, in applying *Dennis*, evolved a bewilder-

---

A tenth group was arrested in St. Louis, Missouri, and included the following: Mr. and Mrs. J. F. Forest, Marcus Murphy, William Sentner, and Robert Manewitz. See N.Y. Times, Sept. 18, 1952, p. 1, col. 4, and N.Y. Times, Sept. 25, 1952, p. 10, col. 4. They were convicted on May 28, 1954. See N.Y. Times, May 29, 1954, p. 9, col. 5.

19. An eleventh group was arrested in Philadelphia, Pennsylvania and Weymouth, New Jersey, late in July of 1953, and included the following: J. Kuzma, Sam Gobenloff, David Dubensky, T. Nabried, Robert Klonsky, Walter Lowenfels, S. Labowitz, Benjamin Weiss, and Irvin Cats. See N.Y. Times, July 30, 1953, p. 24, col. 4; N.Y. Times, Aug. 4, 1953, p. 11, col. 3, and N.Y. Times, Aug. 18, 1953, p. 10, col. 3. They were convicted in Philadelphia on August 13, 1954. See N.Y. Times, April 9, 1954, p. 8, col. 7, and N.Y. Times, Aug. 14, 1954, p. 5, col. 1.

A twelfth group was arrested on October 6, 1953, and included the following: Joseph Brandt, Lucille Bethencourt, Frank Hashmall, Robert A. Campbell, David Katz, Frieda Zucker Katz, Elvador C. Greenfield, and Joseph Michael Dougher. See N.Y. Times, Oct. 7, 1953, p. 20, col. 3.

A thirteenth group was arrested in Pittsburgh, Pennsylvania, on November 4, 1953, and included the following: George Watt, Martin Chancey, and Anthony Krchmarek. See N.Y. Times, Nov. 5, 1953, p. 36, col. 6. They were returned to Cleveland, Ohio, and were tried together with members of the twelfth group. See N.Y. Times, Nov. 14, 1953, p. 12, col. 5. On February 10, 1956, the trial judge directed a verdict of acquittal for David Katz, and the jury acquitted Campbell, Greenfield and Dougher while convicting the remaining six. See N.Y. Times, Feb. 11, 1956, p. 3, col. 4.

A fourteenth group was arrested in New Haven and Hartford, Connecticut on May 29, 1954, and was later indicted in New Haven. It included the following: Simon Silverman, Robert Ekins, Jacob Goldring, Alfred Marder, Joseph Diman, Sidney Sussman Resnick, James Tate, and Martha Stone Asher. See N.Y. Times, May 30, 1954, § 1, p. 1, col. 1; N.Y. Times, June 5, 1954, p. 10, col. 3, and N.Y. Times, March 5, 1955, p. 7, col. 2. The name of Martha Stone Asher was added to the group when it was re-indicted. On March 29, 1956, the jury acquitted Alfred Marder, failed to reach agreement regarding Sidney Sussman Resnick, and convicted the other six. See N.Y. Times, March 30, 1956, p. 4, col. 2.

A fifteenth group was arrested in Denver, Colorado, and in Los Angeles, California, early in August of 1954, and indicted in Denver. See N.Y. Times, Aug. 2, 1954, p. 18, col. 3; N.Y. Times, Aug. 3, 1954, p. 8, col. 5, and N.Y. Times, Aug. 10, 1954, p. 14, col. 8. It included the following: Arthur Bary, Anna Bary, Pat Blau, Lewis M. Johnson, Harold Zepelin, Joseph William Scherrer, and Maia Scherrer. They were convicted on May 27, 1955. See N.Y. Times, May 27, 1955, p. 46, col. 2.

A sixteenth group was arrested in Boston, Massachusetts, on May 29, 1956 and included the following: Otis Hood, Sidney Lipshires, Ann Timpson, Daniel Schirmer, Michael Russo, Edward Strong, and Geoffrey White. See N.Y. Times, May 30, 1956, p. 8, col. 5. This group was never tried, for reasons that are discussed on p. 732, *infra*.

ing variety of interpretations. Significantly, in the period between the *Dennis* ruling and the Supreme Court's reconsideration of the whole problem in *Yates v. United States*,[20] the lower courts refused to acknowledge the validity of the first amendment objections. Although they avowedly followed the guidelines laid down in *Dennis*, their interpretations showed little resemblance to *Dennis*. The only apparent point of similarity between the various courts' interpretations and the actual *Dennis* case was the conclusion that neither the first amendment nor the guidelines set forth in *Dennis* were barriers to sustaining the particular convictions appealed.

An example of this dissimilarity is found in *Frankfeld v. United States*,[21] the appeal of the fourth group, who had been arrested and indicted in 1951 soon after *Dennis*, and convicted in 1952 of conspiracy to "advocate" and to "organize." The Fourth Circuit Court of Appeals, in *Frankfeld*, upheld the conviction as a criminal conspiracy; no issue concerning freedom of speech or of the right to organize freely for political purposes was even considered to have been presented. In this regard the court said that "the danger of such conspiracies is ever 'clear and present.'"[22] Thus, no factual showing of a clear and present danger had to be made; simple conspiracy to commit a crime might be punished, whether or not there was evidence that the crime in fact would have been committed.

After considering the evidence the court concluded (1) that the Party was actively teaching and advocating the overthrow and destruction of the Government by force and violence as soon as circumstances would permit; and (2) that it was training a hard core membership in the methods of revolution, for the time when a favorable opportunity should arise. These activities included the conducting of schools in which Party members "were instructed in the techniques to be followed in overturning existing governments and in seizing and holding power."[23] Such evidence, the court felt, showed much more than the planning or conspiring to express ideas, and indicated that steps were being taken which clearly were related to the commission of illegal acts of violence. It is interesting to note, however, that this conviction was brought under the Smith Act. That is, the prosecutions were for the advocacy and for the organization of a political group, rather than for a conspiracy to commit the acts of violence which

20. 354 U.S. 298 (1957).
21. 198 F.2d 679 (4th Cir. 1952).
22. *Id.* at 682.
23. *Id.* at 685.

would be involved in an actual attempt to overthrow and destroy the Government.[24] The defendants were not viewed as directly preparing to commit overt acts, but rather as teaching and advocating ideas that conceivably could lead to the commission of overt acts. As the court said, it was a criminal conspiracy involving advocacy—not a conspiracy to advocate.

The defendants appealed to the Supreme Court, which denied certiorari and a subsequent motion for rehearing.[25] The conviction was not to be affected by the subsequent *Yates* decision.

United States v. Flynn[26] was another of the early convictions (second group) sustained by a circuit court, which the Supreme Court refused to review. In *Flynn* the second circuit affirmed on the basis that a clear and present danger existed. The test as framed by the circuit court, however, could be described more accurately as the doctrine of "clear and possible danger." The defense argued that the evidence did not support the conclusion that a clear and present danger existed. It reasoned that a clear and present danger involved the questions of (1) what circumstances did the defendants and their alleged co-conspirators contemplate or teach as those in which an attempt at overthrow might be made, and (2) what probability was there at the time of the indictment that such circumstances would indeed occur?

The court rejected this approach to the question and stated:

> "Clear and present danger" does not mean . . . that the Trial Court must find that the alleged conspirators have agreed upon a precise set of circumstances under which they will attempt to strike down the Government, and, further, the existence or likely existence of those particular circumstances.[27]

The court reasoned that the defense's argument could be rejected on the basis that the defendants themselves did not clearly foresee when they would strike. It then announced its understanding of the clear and present danger doctrine, which was "no more than that the setting in which the defendants have conspired is such as to lead reasonably to the conclusion that their teachings *may* result in an attempt at overthrow."[28] Thus "clear and present danger" meant that,

24. See note 10 *supra*, and accompanying text.

25 *Cert. denied*, 344 U.S. 922 (1953), *rehearing denied*, 345 U.S. 913 (1954). In the interim period between the court of appeals ruling and the refusal of the Supreme Court to review, a motion for a new trial on the basis of newly discovered evidence was denied. See United States v. Frankfield, 111 F. Supp. 919 (D. Md. 1953), *aff'd sub nom.* Meyers v. United States, 207 F.2d 413 (4th Cir. 1953).

26. 216 F.2d 354 (2d Cir. 1954), *cert. denied*, 348 U.S. 909 (1955).

27. *Id.* at 366.

28. *Ibid.* (Emphasis added.)

if harm might conceivably result from the advocacy, the advocacy was illegal.

After the Supreme Court denied certiorari and a subsequent petition for rehearing,[29] this group moved, in federal district court, to set aside the verdict of guilty because of false testimony by prosecution witness Harvey Matusow. The court held that there was sufficient independent evidence, apart from the false testimony, to sustain the conviction of all but two of the defendants[30] for whom a new trial was ordered. They subsequently were retried along with several new defendants.[31]

In *Flynn* the court of appeals at least ostensibly applied the "clear and present danger" doctrine in a Smith Act prosecution. But the doctrine was ignored by the District Court for the Southern District of California, trying the third group of defendants.[32] The district court's attention was focused on the subjective question of the defendants' intent rather than upon outwardly observable circumstances. The defendants had been convicted of conspiracy to "advocate" and to "organize"; the court found that:

> Each of the defendants actively and understandingly supported the aims and objectives of the Communist Party, including that of teaching and advocating the necessity and duty of overthrowing and destroying the Government of the United States by force and violence, and helped to promote the organizational growth and the functioning of the Communist Party; all with the *intent* of causing or bringing about the forcible and violent overthrow and destruction of the Government as speedily as circumstances would permit.[33]

This emphasis upon the subjective state of mind of the defendants is unmistakable in the court's discussion of *Dennis*. It said that the

29. *Cert. denied*, 348 U.S. 909 (1955), *rehearing denied*, 348 U.S. 956 (1955).

30. United States v. Flynn, 130 F. Supp. 412 (S.D.N.Y. 1955), *motion for reargument denied*, 131 F. Supp. 742 (S.D.N.Y. 1955).

31. The two were Alexander Trachtenberg and George Blake Charney. They were tried again, beginning on April 30, 1956 (N.Y. Times, May 1, 1956, p. 11, col. 2) along with Marion Bachrach (who had been originally indicted with the second group but who had won a trial severance because of illness, but who now was ruled able to stand trial); Sidney Stein (who was captured in the Sierra Nevada mountain hideout and who had been originally indicted with the second group); Fred Fine (who had been originally indicted with the second group, but who had disappeared at that time, and now voluntarily surrendered); William Norman Marron (the same as Fred Fine); and James E. Jackson, Jr. (the same as Fred Fine). Mrs. Bachrach was given a directed verdict of acquittal by the trial judge. N.Y. Times, June 19, 1956, p. 14, col. 3. The others were convicted. N.Y. Times, Aug. 1, 1956, p. 1, col. 3; p. 52, col. 3.

32. United States v. Schneiderman, 106 F. Supp. 906 (S.D. Cal. 1952).

33. *Id.* at 922. (Emphasis added.)

"clear" danger envisioned by the Smith Act was in "proscribed advocacy or teaching with *intent* to bring about ultimately the overthrow of the Government,"[34] and that the "present danger consists in the specific *intent* of teacher or advocate to accomplish the objective of forcible overthrow [of the Government] as speedily as possible."[35]

The district court's identification of "clear and present danger" with inner states of consciousness was followed by the Ninth Circuit Court of Appeals.[36] Although it was stated that advocacy and teaching, which are normally "lawful and protected" by "constitutional guarantees," were involved in this conspiracy, the fact that the advocacy was intended to cause the destruction and overthrow of the Government made the whole matter a criminal conspiracy. The advocacy was meant to effect an unlawful purpose, thus its whole character was changed due to the question of motivation.

The *Yates* conviction was reversed by the Supreme Court in 1957, creating a judicial revolution in Smith Act decisions.[37] Other early convictions sustained by the courts of appeal prior to *Yates* were later to be reversed on the authority of that decision.

The same element of intent seemed to be central to the third circuit's decision[38] involving the appeal of five Pennsylvania communists (the fifth group) who, in 1953, had been convicted of conspiracy to teach and advocate the overthrow and destruction of the Government of the United States, with the intent of causing this overthrow as speedily as circumstances would permit.[39]

The third circuit gave substantial weight to evidence that the defendants were in agreement as to their intent to teach the violent overthrow of the Government. It was stated that both the pamphlets and books which they distributed and the classroom instruction which they gave included violent overthrow as a part of the recommended proletarian revolution. Furthermore, the defendants' roles as active Party leaders were taken as indications of their personal knowledge of the Party's general intent to bring about this result. Finally, several of them had been quoted as saying that violence would be necessary for the success of the Party; another had spoken of the use of sabotage at the proper time.

---

34. *Id.* at 923. (Emphasis added.)
35. *Ibid.* (Emphasis added.)
36. Yates v. United States, 225 F.2d 146 (9th Cir. 1955).
37. 354 U.S. 298 (1957); see textual discussion under part IV, The *Yates* Decision, p. 725 *infra*.
38. United States v. Mesarosh, 223 F.2d 449 (3d Cir. 1955).
39. The district court entered a judgment of conviction. United States v. Mesarosh, 116 F. Supp. 345 (W.D. Pa. 1953).

The third circuit considered these indications of intent sufficient to establish a "clear and present danger," which was in turn sufficient to affirm the convictions. The court quoted with approval the trial judge's charge to the jury, stating at one point that if the Communist Party advocated overthrow of the Government to accomplish revolutionary change, with the intent to accomplish such change as speedily as circumstances would permit, then "that situation constitutes a clear and present danger. . . . The existence of such a highly organized conspiracy, with rigidly disciplined members subject to call when the leaders feel that the time has become opportune for action . . . constitutes a clear and present danger."[40] Thus the convictions were upheld upon much the same considerations as had been decisive to the ninth circuit in the *Yates* case[41]—the defendants' subjective states of mind.

Two judges dissented in this case, arguing that punishable speech and advocacy ought to incite directly or bring the possibility of violent action into direct proximity to satisfy the clear and present danger test. These judges did not find any such evidence on the record in this case.[42]

An appeal was carried to the Supreme Court, which granted certiorari on December 12, 1955.[43] Subsequently, it became apparent that the trial testimony of a Government witness, Joseph Mazzei, a former FBI undercover informant, might have been perjured. The Government took the initiative in pointing this out; the Solicitor General asked the Supreme Court to remand the case to the district court for an examination of the credibility of Mazzei's testimony.[44]

Attorneys for the defendants asked the Supreme Court to reject this request, asking instead for a new trial.[45] The Supreme Court granted the defendants' request, ruling that the disclosures of the Solicitor General regarding Mazzei's untruthful testimony in other

---

40. 223 F.2d at 456-57.

41. Yates v. United States, 225 F.2d 146 (9th Cir. 1955).

42. The dissenters suggested that if the Communist Party's

> present tactic is a waiting game, characterized by the teaching of revolutionary theory while incitation to action is left for the indefinite future, the First Amendment prevents the Government from proscribing their teaching. Our lawful recourse during such a period lies in the field of education and demonstration, which will increase devotion to our democratic institutions and thus frustrate Communist preachments. There is some risk in such a course. But the adoption of the First Amendment has committed us to it. 223 F.2d at 464.

43. Mesarosh v. United States, 350 U.S. 922 (1955).

44. N.Y. Times, Sept. 29, 1956, p. 7, col. 5. The Government stated that it still believed his testimony in this trial to be true. "It is still the position of the Government that the testimony given by Mazzei at the trial was entirely truthful and credible." But Mazzei had testified before other tribunals and made statements which the Government now had "serious reason" to doubt.

45. N.Y. Times, Oct. 3, 1956, p. 33, col. 1.

proceedings had wholly discredited his testimony in the present case, and, further, that this testimony had tainted the whole case.[46]

The case of *Wellman v. United States*[47] was the last of the convictions for conspiracy to advocate and organize to be affirmed by a court of appeals prior to the Supreme Court's decision in *Yates*. The sixth circuit, citing *Dennis* as controlling, held that, to sustain a conviction over first amendment objections, the prosecution must show the presence of a "clear and present danger" of a substantive, serious evil that Congress has a right to prevent. The language of the balancing test of the "gravity of the evil, discounted by its improbability" was also repeated. In examining the evidence in this case, the circuit court interpreted *Dennis* to mean that "under the First Amendment the mere teaching and advocacy of the forbidden doctrines does not by itself constitute the crime, but that to be punishable the teaching and advocacy must be 'by language reasonably and ordinarily calculated to incite persons to such action.'"[48] The court then concluded that the evidence "strongly [supported] . . . the reasonable conclusion that the Party was not conducting 'a seminar in political theory,' but that the principles of Marxism-Leninism were being taught as a guide to action which was expected to follow at a later propitious time."[49] Thus the grounds for affirming the conviction did involve the connection of advocacy with possible resultant unlawful acts, a connection not made so clearly in some of the other cases (for example, those of the third or the fifth group).[50]

B. *Prosecutions under the "Membership" Clause*

In addition to the action directed against the Communist Party leaders originally charged with conspiracy to "advocate" and "organize," the Department of Justice during the Eisenhower administration also launched a series of prosecutions against several of these same Party leaders individually for violation of the so-called "membership" clause of the Smith Act.

1. *The Clause*

The "membership" clause of the Smith Act makes unlawful the willful and knowing membership in any group or organization which

46. Mesarosh v. United States, 352 U.S. 1 (1956).
47. 227 F.2d 757 (6th Cir. 1955).
48. *Id.* at 773.
49. *Ibid.*
50. See note 17 *supra*, for members of the third and fifth groups.

teaches or advocates the duty, necessity, propriety, or desirability of overthrowing and destroying the Government of the United States by force or violence.[51] Although it was directed against mere membership in the Communist Party, as applied by the Government and interpreted by the federal courts, its coverage extends only to active membership by one aware of the character of the Communist Party and of its aims. Thus it does not apply to casual or innocent membership, unaccompanied by any evidence of awareness of, and acceptance of, the purpose of the Party.

This interpretation of the membership provision was in part made necessary by certain language in the Internal Security Act of 1950, which specified that membership in the Communist Party was not per se a violation of any criminal statute of the United States.[52] Federal prosecutors understood this to mean that mere casual membership was no longer prohibited by the Smith Act, but that membership accompanied by something more was still illegal. This "something more" was taken to be active membership in the Party, evidenced by such facts as the holding of office or of positions of leadership, or the participation as an instructor in Party schools. Federal prosecutions were aimed at such individuals. The federal courts also began to hold that the "per se" provision required proof of something more than mere membership to support a valid conviction. They found that the evidence submitted by federal prosecutors was satisfactory in this regard.

2. *The Prosecutions*

During the years 1952 to 1960, the national Communist Party leaders named in the *Dennis* indictment began to be released from imprisonment upon completion of their sentences under the initial conviction. As they were released, many were immediately re-arrested

51. 62 Stat. 808 (1948), as amended, 18 U.S.C.A. § 2385 (Supp. 1964). The Act in pertinent part provides:

> Whoever organizes or helps or attempts to organize any society, group, or assembly of persons who teach, advocate, or encourage the overthrow or destruction of any such government by force or violence; *or becomes or is a member of, or affiliates with, any such society, group, or assembly of persons, knowing the purposes thereof*—[Shall be punished as specified.] (Emphasis added.)

52. Internal Security Act of 1950 § 4(f), 64 Stat. 991, ch. 1024, tit. 1 § 4, 50 U.S.C.A. § 783(f) (1951):

> Neither the holding of office nor membership in any Communist organization by any person shall constitute per se a violation of subsection (a) or subsection (c) of this section or of any other criminal statute. The fact of the registration of any person under section 789 or section 788 of this title as an officer or member of any Communist organization shall not be received in evidence against such person in any prosecution for any alleged violation of subsection (a) or subsection (c) of this section or for any alleged violation of any other criminal statute.

and re-indicted under the "membership" clause, and then released on bail.[53]

The Government had retained the right to institute legal proceedings against these persons under the original indictment which had not only charged (1) conspiracy to organize as the Communist Party to teach and advocate the overthrow and destruction of the Government of the United States by force and violence, and (2) conspiracy to knowingly and willfully teach the overthrow and destruction of the Government of the United States by force and violence upon which the previous convictions had been obtained, but also (3) actual membership in such an organization (the Communist Party).

Irving Potash, the first of the eleven to complete his sentence, was indicted in December of 1954 on the "membership" charge.[54] However, he was not to be tried under this indictment, but eventually was sent to Poland (not to his native Russia). He agreed to leave the United States, in return for the Government's motion to remove his pending trial from the court calendar.[55]

Others of the *Dennis* group who were subsequently released from prison also faced trials for "membership" in the Communist Party. Eugene Dennis, John Gates, Carl Winter, Benjamin Davis, John Williamson and Jacob Stackel were released from prison on March 1, 1955, and all but Benjamin Davis were immediately arrested on the "membership" charge and freed on bail.[56] Davis first had to serve a brief sentence for contempt of court, imposed upon him while testifying at the trial of other Communist Party leaders in Pittsburgh, Pennsylvania.[57] Williamson filed a petition in federal district court requesting permission to return to Great Britain, which he did after the Govern-

53. For example, William Z. Foster, although indicted with the *Dennis* group, had been granted a separate trial because of a heart condition when the original eleven were tried. N.Y. Times, May 3, 1954, p. 12, col. 1. In 1953, the government moved to bring him to trial, but a court-appointed physician reported that he was still unable to stand trial. In May of 1954 the government again tried to bring him to trial, with a similar result. N.Y. Times, May 3, 1954, p. 12, col. 1; N.Y. Times, May 6, 1954, p. 17, col. 1. Then on March 14, 1956, the government for a third time, moved to bring him to trial on the original 1948 indictment, although the United States Attorney said that he might be tried on the "membership" count of the indictment, rather than the "conspiracy" count. N.Y. Times, March 15, 1956, p. 14, col. 1. But on April 25, 1956, a federal judge ruled that Foster's health was still such that the rigors of the trial might cause his death. N.Y. Times, April 26, 1956, p. 12, col. 4. Later, Foster took the initiative himself. In a federal district court he moved to have dismissed the two 1948 indictments. His motion was denied. N.Y. Times, June 25, 1959, p. 2, col. 4; N.Y. Times, July 9, 1959, p. 20, col. 6.

54. N.Y. Times, Dec. 10, 1954, p. 10, col. 6; N.Y. Times, Dec. 16, 1954, p. 29, col. 3.

55. N.Y. Times, Feb. 27, 1955, p. 34, col. 3; N.Y. Times, March 2, 1955, p. 1, col. 7; p. 10, col. 3. N.Y. Times, March 5, 1955, p. 6, col. 4.

56. N.Y. Times, Feb. 27, 1955, p. 34, col. 3.

57. N.Y. Times, March 2, 1955, p. 1, col. 7; p. 10, col. 3.

ment indicated that it would not oppose the petition.[58] Stackel also was deported rather than tried on the indictment.

Gus Hall, who originally had failed to surrender to begin serving his sentence, but who was apprehended later,[59] was released from prison on March 30, 1957.[60] Upon his release, he was placed under 5,000 dollars bail on the "membership" clause section of the original indictment.[61]

All of those who completed their prison terms during the years 1952 to 1960 thus faced subsequent Government prosecutions under the "membership" provision of the indictments.[62] Those who were

58. N.Y. Times, April 28, 1955, p. 15, col. 1; N.Y. Times, May 5, 1955, p. 17, col. 3. Voluntary departure necessitated court permission because he was under deportation orders and free on bail on the membership indictment.

59. N.Y. Times, Aug. 28, 1953, p. 1, col. 5.

60. N.Y. Times, March 31, 1957, § 1, p. 72, col. 6.

61. N.Y. Times, April 16, 1957, p. 8, col. 3.

62. Other litigation of a quite different nature arose during the Eisenhower Administration in regard to this first group of Communist Party leaders. After the Supreme Court upheld their convictions in 1951, Gus Hall, Robert Thompson, Gilbert Green, and Henry Winston failed to surrender to begin serving their sentences. Hall was arrested in Mexico in 1952 and returned to the United States. N.Y. Times, Aug. 28, 1953, p. 1, col. 5. Thompson was apprehended on August 27, 1953, with Carl Edwin Rasi and Samuel Coleman (two Party officials), a Mrs. Shirley Keith Kremen and Sidney Steinberg (who had evaded arrest since June 1951, when he had been indicted for conspiracy under the Smith Act as one of the second group of Communist Party leaders). N.Y. Times, Aug. 28, 1953, p. 1, col. 5. Both Hall and Thompson were found guilty of contempt of court for failing to surrender. N.Y. Times, Sept. 10, 1953, p. 4, col. 5. See United States v. Thompson, 117 F. Supp. 685 (S.D.N.Y. 1953), *aff'd*, 214 F.2d 545 (2d Cir.), *cert. denied*, 348 U.S. 841 (1954); United States v. Hall, 101 F. Supp. 666 (S.D.N.Y. 1951), *aff'd*, 198 F.2d 726 (2d Cir. 1952), *cert. denied*, 345 U.S. 905 (1953). The government also moved quickly against those arrested with Thompson, trying them on charges of harboring a fugitive. N.Y. Times, Aug. 29, 1953, p. 7, col. 6; N.Y. Times, Sept. 17, 1953, p. 19, col. 3. Their names were: Carl Edwin Rasi, Samuel Coleman, Shirley Keith Kremen, Janet Conroy (Pat Blau), and Sidney Steinberg. They were found guilty by a jury on April 26, 1954, (N.Y. Times, April 27, 1954, p. 15, col. 1), and their conviction was later upheld on appeal by a two to one vote. Kremen v. United States, 231 F.2d 155 (9th Cir. 1956). The Supreme Court reversed and remanded for a new trial on the ground that some of the evidence used at the trial had been obtained by an unlawful seizure. Kremen v. United States, 353 U.S. 346 (1957).

The two remaining fugitives, Gilbert Green and Henry Winston, announced in separate letters to newspapers in 1956 that each was planning to surrender to the federal authorities to begin serving his sentence. N.Y. Times, Feb. 25, 1956, p. 11, col. 4; N.Y. Times, March 2, 1956, p. 7, col. 1. Each did voluntarily surrender a few days later, (N.Y. Times, Feb. 28, 1956, p. 15, col. 1; N.Y. Times, March 6, 1956, p. 18, col. 3), and the United States Attorney moved immediately to have each cited for contempt of court. *Ibid.* Each was convicted of criminal contempt of court and sentenced to an additional three years imprisonment. United States v. Green, 140 F. Supp. 117 (S.D.N.Y. 1956), *aff'd*, 241 F.2d 631 (2d Cir. 1957); see N.Y. Times, March 27, 1956, p. 22, col. 3. On appeal, a sharply divided Supreme Court held that a jury trial was not necessary for the imposition of punishments for criminal contempts of court and that the three-year sentences did not constitute an abuse of judicial discretion. Green v. United States, 356 U.S. 165 (1958). This decision closed the matter of summary punishment for criminal contempt of court, it seemed, but Robert Thompson, whose case had been decided earlier, was still free on bail awaiting the decision of the Supreme Court in the case of Green and Winston. When that decision was rendered, he again appealed his conviction to a court of appeals, asking for a re-examination of the

born abroad were allowed to leave the United States voluntarily or else were deported. Those who remained, however, were never tried. The Government had decided to wait until after the determination of several prosecutions under the "membership" clause then in progress.[63] Final judicial disposition of these original prosecutions did not take place until 1961.[64]

3. *The "Membership" Clause Appeals*

The first two convictions for "membership," *Scales v. United States*[65] and *United States v. Lightfoot*,[66] were appealed and affirmed, before the Supreme Court rendered its crucial decision in *Yates*. These were decided after *Dennis*, during the period when federal courts of appeals, without exception, were affirming convictions of Communist Party leaders tried under the "advocate" and "organize" sections of the Smith Act. Even though *Dennis* was not directly involved in the "membership" prosecutions, the actions of the courts of appeals in upholding

---

record in the light of the opinions, including the dissents, in the Green and Winston case. But the court of appeals simply affirmed both the conviction and the sentence, United States v. Thompson, 261 F.2d 809 (2d Cir. 1958), *cert. denied*, 359 U.S. 967 (1959).

63. N.Y. Times, March 2, 1955, p. 1, col. 7.

64. Dr. Emmanuel Blumberg was apparently the first individual to be arrested under a "membership" charge alone. He was arrested in New York on September 30, 1954 (N.Y. Times, Oct. 1, 1954, p. 15, col. 5), was indicted a few days later in Philadelphia (N.Y. Times, Oct. 7, 1954, p. 11, col. 1), and was convicted by a jury on March 7, 1956 (N.Y. Times, March 8, 1956, p. 21, col. 3). "On June 29, 1962, the district court granted a new trial on *Jencks* grounds but denied a motion for acquittal." The government had not moved for a new trial as of October 23, 1962. See Jencks v. United States, 353 U.S. 657 (1957). Also see personal letter from Anthony Lewis, of the New York Times Washington Bureau, in the possession of the author.

Junius Irving Scales was arrested soon after in Memphis, Tennessee. He went on trial in the spring of 1955 in Greensboro, North Carolina and was found guilty by a jury on April 21, 1955. N.Y. Times, April 22, 1955, p. 4, col. 6.

At about the same time Claude Mack Lightfoot was arrested in Chicago. N.Y. Times, June 28, 1954, p. 13, col. 2. He was found guilty of illegal "membership" by a jury late in January 1955, N.Y. Times, Jan. 26, 1955, p. 18, col. 2; N.Y. Times, Jan. 27, 1955, p. 1, col. 2.

In Buffalo, New York, on August 31, 1955, John Francis Noto was arrested on a membership charge (N.Y. Times, Sept. 1, 1955, p. 3, col. 6), and was convicted by a jury on April 12, 1956. N.Y. Times, April 13, 1956, p. 12, col. 4.

Max Morris Weiss was arrested in New York on September 19, 1955. He was then under indictment in Chicago on a "membership" charge. N.Y. Times, Sept. 20, 1955, p. 19, col. 2. "The Weiss indictment is still outstanding, and no one knows when if ever it will be tried." (Personal letter from Lewis, *supra*.) On March 28, 1956, Emanuel Blum was arrested in Chicago on a similar charge. N.Y. Times, March, 28, 1956, p. 5, col. 5. "Emanuel Blum's indictment was dismissed on the Government's motions on November 27, 1957, again on *Yates* evidentiary grounds." (Personal letter from Lewis, *supra*.)

"John C. Hellman of Montana was convicted May 27, 1958, but on December 29, 1961, the 9th Circuit reversed on evidentiary ground . . . ." *Ibid*. "Michael Russo was also indicted for membership, but this was dismissed on *Yates*, October 4, 1962." *Ibid*.

65. Scales v. United States, 227 F.2d 581 (4th Cir. 1955).

66. United States v. Lightfoot, 228 F.2d 861 (7th Cir. 1956).

the two "membership" convictions were not surprising, as they were consistent in spirit with the broad construction given *Dennis* in the "advocate and organize" convictions.

In neither *Scales* nor *Lightfoot* did the court have any great difficulty in holding the "membership" clause constitutional. In each case the jury's finding that the Communist Party did teach and advocate the violent overthrow of the Government was approved, as well as additional findings that each defendant, while a member had knowledge of this advocacy, and intended to bring about that which was advocated, "as speedily as circumstances would permit."

In *Scales*, the fourth circuit court denied that "guilt by association" was involved, because more than mere association had been proved. That "more" was the Party advocacy and the individual's knowledge and intent. Thus, to the court, the content of the advocacy, plus the subjective state of consciousness of the defendant, were sufficient to lift this whole matter out of the realm of simple association.

But the court used more positive grounds for rejecting the defendants' challenge to the validity of the "membership" clause; it held that the whole question was basically one of criminal conspiracy, and that this was decisive.

> The membership clause of the statute is, of course, nothing more nor less than a statute denouncing and making criminal a conspiracy to overthrow the government by force and violence. It is elementary that a conspiracy is a partnership in criminal purposes and that all are guilty who join it with knowledge of such purposes; and all that the statute does is apply this fundamental concept of conspiracy to an organization having for its purpose the forcible overthrow of the government.[67]

The court also quoted with approval the *Dennis* language regarding action at the earliest phases of the activities of such an organization, rather than waiting "'until the putsch is about to be executed, the plans have been laid, and the signal is awaited.'"[68]

Finally, it was stated directly that the "clear and present danger" doctrine had no applicability to prosecutions under the "membership" clause. The court did not find that freedom of expression or freedom of association were directly involved here—but only criminal conspiracy.

> The "clear and present danger" rule has no application to the statute, since what the statute denounces is a conspiracy to over-

67. 227 F.2d at 587.
68. *Id.* at 588, quoting from *Dennis*, 341 U.S. at 509.

> throw the government by violence; and Congress may unquestionably forbid incitement to crime and organization for that purpose and may make such organization criminal, irrespective of the immediacy of the danger resulting from such organization.[69]

The holding in *Lightfoot* was similar to that in *Scales*. The court did not rely upon the existence of a "clear and present danger" in affirming the conviction. Instead, the seventh circuit held that "substantial evidence" supported the charges that (1) the Communist Party advocated overthrow of the Government by force "as speedily as circumstances would permit"; (2) the defendant had knowledge of the Communist Party's engagement in such advocacy; and (3) he personally had the specific intent to bring about such overthrow.

In the *Lightfoot* appeal the court did not engage in a review of the several factors considered in *Scales*, but concentrated instead on two related issues, Lightfoot's knowledge of Party advocacy, and his intent to accomplish the aim advocated. Thus the court was concerned almost entirely with the defendant's subjective understandings. He was found to have awareness or knowledge because he had taught courses about the Communist classics and had written articles about them. A number of other factors were taken to indicate that intent: (1) the inference which could be drawn from his dedicated and zealous service to the Party; (2) the presumption that members of the Party have the unlawful states of consciousness, which arises because of the Party's monolithic organization and rigid, centralized discipline. The court gave little consideration to the character and context of the Party advocacy; the opinion clearly indicates that the defendant's offense was based on subjective factors—having knowledge of advocacy and approving the sentiments advocated.

In neither case did the court have doubts about the "per se" provision of the Internal Security Act of 1950.[70] Although membership per se was not to be construed as a violation of the Smith Act, both courts felt that the evidence demonstrated something beyond the mere fact of membership alone. That is, the evidence proved that each defendant had knowingly and willfully been a member of the Communist Party with specific awareness of its aims and character and with specific intent to achieve these aims. In each case, the court believed that much more than mere casual or unwitting membership had been proved.

---

69. 227 F.2d at 588.
70. 64 Stat. 987, 50 U.S.C.A. §§ 781-826 (1951).

Both the defendants raised the issue which the Supreme Court was to rule on later in *Jencks v. United States*,[71] by asking that the FBI produce for examination by the defense the original reports made to the FBI by prosecution witnesses. Both courts denied the request.

Both defendants appealed to the Supreme Court, which granted certiorari.[72] After a year and one-half, the Supreme Court reversed the convictions in a per curiam opinion, saying: "Upon consideration of the entire record and the confession of error by the Solicitor General, the judgment is . . . reversed."[73] The Justice Department itself recognized that reversals and new trials were in order, for on September 24, 1957, Solicitor General J. Lee Rankin filed a memorandum with the Court, admitting that both convictions "must be reversed for further proceedings in the light of the *Jencks* decision."[74] The Justice Department stated, however, that it would re-try the defendants under the *Jencks* rule.[75]

C. *Conclusions Regarding Decisions Under Dennis*

Although the diversity of interpretation of the several courts of appeals in these cases is interesting, several other factors are of equal importance. Of inescapable significance is the fact that all the Smith Act convictions appealed during the period between the Supreme Court decisions in *Dennis* and *Yates* were affirmed at the intermediate appellate level. In none of these cases did the appellate courts have much difficulty in reaching their decisions, however much their reasoning might have differed from each other, or from *Dennis*. Furthermore, in none of these cases did the Supreme Court, prior to *Yates*, seriously question the results reached by the lower courts as to first amendment claims.

It is true that in one case, that involving the fifth group, the Supreme Court vacated the convictions and remanded for a new trial.[76] The grounds for reversal, however, were evidentiary not sub-

71. 353 U.S. 657 (1956).

72. Scales v. United States, 350 U.S. 992 (1956); Lightfoot v. United States, 350 U.S. 992 (1956).

73. Scales v. United States, 355 U.S. 1 (1957); Lightfoot v. United States, 355 U.S. 2 (1957).

74. N.Y. Times, Sept. 25, 1957, p. 31, col. 8; N.Y. Times, Oct. 16, 1957, p. 28, col. 6.

75. Under the *Jencks* rule, if the Government has introduced at the trial information which may be material to the accused's defense, it may not, by invoking the governmental privilege for the protection of vital national interests, refuse to produce such information for examination. Such refusal can result in the reversal of the accused's conviction. See Jencks v. United States, 353 U.S. at 669-72. Also see United States v. Reynolds, 345 U.S. 1 (1953).

76. Mesarosh v. United States, 352 U.S. 1 (1956).

stantive. In another case,[77] a district court reversed the convictions of two members of a larger group, the second, and ordered those two defendants re-tried. But these convictions also were overturned on evidentiary grounds. In the two "membership" clause cases,[78] the Supreme Court reversed the conviction on *Jencks* grounds.

In two cases,[79] involving the second and fourth groups, the Supreme Court refused to grant certiorari; another, involving the fifth group, was remanded for a new trial for evidentiary reasons. *Yates* was the first case in which the Supreme Court seriously reconsidered the first amendment questions it had decided in *Dennis*. The eighth or last of the group convictions upheld by a court of appeals was not decided by the Supreme Court until June 24, 1957,[80] a few days after its *Yates* ruling, on June 17.

It is significant that the Supreme Court chose *Yates* as the occasion for reconsidering the constitutional problem presented by Smith Act prosecutions. The lower court decisions in *Yates* represented the broadest interpretation of the *Dennis* doctrine in any of the group cases decided during this period. Earlier, in 1953, the Supreme Court had refused to review the fourth group case, where the fourth circuit court had identified the activities of the defendants as a criminal conspiracy.[81] In the second group case, in 1955, the Supreme Court refused to review the decision of the second circuit court,[82] which had held that the activities of the defendants constituted a "clear and possible danger," although the appellate court itself relied upon the language of "clear and present danger." In both of these cases, the lower court decision noted the possibility of illegal overt acts as the result of advocacy.

In *Yates*, and the fifth group case, however, the lower courts stressed other factors in affirming the convictions. In each decision intent was the crucial element. Intent as viewed by the courts relates to the subjective state of consciousness of an individual, and not to external, observable facts pertinent to a judgment as to whether a certain state of affairs will likely result from advocacy.

---

77. United States v. Flynn, 130 F. Supp. 412 (S.D.N.Y. 1955).

78. Scales v. United States, 355 U.S. 1 (1957); Lightfoot v. United States, 355 U.S. 2 (1957).

79. Flynn v. United States, 348 U.S. 909 (1955); Frankfeld v. United States, 344 U.S. 922 (1953).

80. Wellman v. United States, 354 U.S. 937 (1957).

81. Frankfeld v. United States, 198 F.2d 679 (4th Cir. 1952), *cert. denied*, 344 U.S. 992 (1953), *rehearing denied*, 345 U.S. 913 (1954).

82. United States v. Flynn, 216 F.2d 354 (2d Cir. 1954), *cert. denied*, 348 U.S. 909, *rehearing denied*, 348 U.S. 956 (1955).

IV. The *Yates* Decision

Of all the above cases, only *Yates v. United States*[83] was decided on first amendment grounds. There the Supreme Court was confronted with a case in which a lower court had given wider latitude to the power to prohibit advocacy than in any other case. This is striking in view of the fact that, at the same time, the Supreme Court accepted for review the last of the court of appeals' pre-*Yates* group cases. In this case, that of the eighth group, the court of appeals had attempted to apply conscientiously the *Dennis* doctrine. But *Yates* was chosen by the Supreme Court as the occasion to re-examine its holding in *Dennis*, and it was the language of *Yates* that was subsequently used by all of the federal courts to deal with the remaining appeals from Smith Act convictions.

The Supreme Court granted certiorari[84] on October 17, 1955, seven months after the conviction was affirmed by the ninth circuit.[85] The decision, which was not announced until the last day of the 1956 term, dealt with two provisions of the Smith Act making unlawful: (1) conspiracies to organize the Communist Party of the United States to advocate the duty and necessity of overthrow of the Government of the United States by force and violence, and (2) conspiracies to advocate such ideas. The Court nullified the "organize" provision insofar as the Communist Party was concerned. The term "organize," said the Court, did not mean "a continuing process which goes on throughout the life of an organization,"[86] as contended by the Government, nor did it include such things as "the recruiting of new members and the forming of new units, and the regrouping or expansion of existing clubs, classes and other units of any society, party, group or other organization."[87] Rather, to "organize" the Communist Party meant to establish it initially as a group. The most recent reconstitution of this group had occurred in 1945.

> We conclude, therefore, that since the Communist Party came into being in 1945, and the indictment was not returned until 1951, the three year statute of limitations had run on the "organizing" charge, and required the withdrawal of that part of the indictment from the jury's consideration.[88]

83. 354 U.S. 298 (1957).
84. Yates v. United States, 350 U.S. 860 (1955).
85. Yates v. United States, 225 F.2d 146 (9th Cir. 1955).
86. 354 U.S. at 304.
87. *Ibid.*
88. *Id.* at 312.

This meant that only the "advocacy" and "membership" sections of the Smith Act would henceforth be applicable to the Communist Party of the United States, unless it witlessly should attempt to reorganize or to reconstitute itself at some future time.

The Court purported to follow the basic orientation of *Dennis* in regard to the "advocacy" provision, but it is apparent that the *Yates* decision faced in a new direction. The basic question regarding the validity of Smith Act prosecutions was stated in different terms than in *Dennis:*

> We are thus faced with the question whether the Smith Act prohibits advocacy and teaching of forcible overthrow as an abstract principle, divorced from any effort to instigate action to that end, so long as such advocacy, or teaching is engaged in with evil intent. We hold that it does not.[89]

The Court went on to indicate in much the same language the way in which such questions were to be decided. This was through use of "the distinction between advocacy of abstract doctrine and advocacy directed at promoting unlawful action . . . ."[90]

The Court's new stance was quite a contrast to *Dennis.* There the question was taken to be "whether the gravity of the 'evil' discounted by its improbability, justifies such invasion of free speech as is necessary to avoid the danger."[91] In *Yates* there was no attempt to use such a balancing test. Nor did the Court focus its attention upon any danger which might conceivably arise from advocacy or teaching. Instead it devoted its attention to the actual character of the advocacy. If the advocacy seemed to be related to the commission of overt acts, that is, if it seemed to take the form of incitement to action, then it was proscribed. If such character could not be attributed to it, then it was abstract doctrine—the discussion of theoretical principles in a context other than one which would lead to the commission of overt acts—and, thus, protected.

This test is not the same as that in *Dennis;* it focuses attention only on the form of the advocacy or teaching. Nor is this test the same as the "clear and present danger" test, although implicit in it is a similar concern with actions which may result from teaching or advocacy.

One of the most striking differences between the language of *Yates* and that of *Dennis* is the apparent refusal in *Yates* to consider the long

89. *Id.* at 318.
90. *Ibid.*
91. Dennis v. United States, 341 U.S. 494, 509 (1951).

range effects of the advocacy. The concept of incitement strongly suggests emphasis on the immediate, and disregard of the long range effects as too remote to be relevant. The district court in the *Yates* trial did not seem to comprehend the concept in this manner. As explained by the Supreme Court:

> In failing to distinguish between advocacy of forcible overthrow as an abstract doctrine and advocacy of action to that end, the District Court appears to have been led astray by the holding in *Dennis* that advocacy of violent action to be taken at some future time was enough. It seems to have considered that, since "inciting" speech is usually thought of as something calculated to induce immediate action, and since *Dennis* held advocacy of action for future overthrow sufficient, this meant that advocacy, irrespective of its tendency to generate action, is punishable, provided only that it is uttered with a specific intent to accomplish overthrow. In other words, the District Court apparently thought that *Dennis* obliterated the traditional dividing line between advocacy of abstract doctrine and advocacy of action.[92]

In *Yates*, the Supreme Court did feel that the long range effects of advocacy could include the character of incitement. This aspect was in accord with the basic orientation of *Dennis*, and would permit the punishment of a wider range of advocacy than that which was merely incitement to the commission of illegal acts in the immediate future. In other words, under *Yates*, the long range psychological effect of the language used in subjectively preparing listeners to be ready to heed a "call to action" at some indefinite future time could be the basis of a violation.

> [As Chief Justice Vinson said] the Government need not hold its hand until the *putsch* is about to be executed, the plans have been laid and the signal is awaited. If Government is aware that a group aiming at its overthrow is attempting to indoctrinate its members and to commit them to a course whereby they will strike when the leaders feel the circumstances permit, action by the Government is required. . . . This is quite a different thing from the view of the District Court here that mere doctrinal justification of forcible overthrow, if engaged in with the intent to accomplish overthrow, is punishable *per se* under the Smith Act. That sort of advocacy, even though uttered with the hope that it may ultimately lead to violent revolution, is too remote from concrete action to be regarded as the kind of indoctrination preparatory to action which was condemned in *Dennis*.[93]

92. 354 U.S. at 320.
93. *Id.* at 321-22.

The *Yates* test took into account real differences in the character and context of the advocacy. Five of the defendants were ordered acquitted; the evidence did not indicate that they had engaged in advocacy amounting to incitement. These were the first convictions under the Smith Act to be reversed on an appeal concerning the nature of the advocacy. As to the other nine defendants, the Court remanded, feeling that, while there was a real possibility that they had engaged in advocacy amounting to incitement, further evidence on this point would have to be taken.

In regard to these defendants the Court was most explicit in suggesting that the long range effects of advocacy could give it the character of incitement. The Court discussed the possible alternatives that additional evidence might show:

> There occurred what might be considered to be systematic teaching and advocacy of illegal action which is condemned by the statute. It might be found that one of the purposes of such classes was to develop in the members of the group a readiness to engage at the crucial time, perhaps during war or during attack upon the United States from without, in such activities as sabotage and street fighting, in order to divert and diffuse the resistance of the authorities and if possible to seize local vantage points.[94]
>
> * * *
>
> [I]t might be found that individuals considered to be particularly trustworthy were taken into an "underground" apparatus and there instructed in tasks which would be useful when the time for violent action arrived. . . . It might be found, under all the circumstances, that the purpose of this teaching was to prepare the members of the underground apparatus to engage in, to facilitate, and to cooperate with violent action directed against government when the time was ripe.[95]

At first glance, this aspect of the Court's holding did not appear to be the most important part of the decision, yet it was relied upon in affirming later prosecutions.[96]

---

94. *Id.* at 331.

95. *Id.* at 332.

96. The Supreme Court also ruled that the Smith Act proscription on organizing a political group to advocate or teach the overthrow of the Government by force or violence applied only to the initial act of creating a group, and not to acts subsequent thereto. Thus the statute of limitations barred prosecutions based on the organize clause, for the initial organization took place several years previously, in 1946. The import of this holding was that all Smith Act convictions would have to be for advocacy alone, and that evidence regarding organizing the Communist Party would not be relevant.

V. The Effects of *Yates*

The Supreme Court's decision in *Yates* has been widely discussed. Much attention has been given to the possibility that the decision would cripple the Government's efforts to control the real and dangerous domestic menace presented by the Communist Party. Most of the commentary on this aspect has consisted of bitter criticism of the Court's ruling as unduly restrictive of legitimate governmental activity in trying to preserve its own existence. The introduction of several bills in Congress during this period to nullify *Yates* by amending the "advocate" and "organize" provisions of the Smith Act is weighty evidence of congressional concern with subversive activities.

Other criticism expressed concern over the degree to which the decision limited the protection given first amendment rights. There was a feeling that *Yates,* in giving less than absolute protection to these rights, in reality might have harmful effects. This criticism suggested that although *Yates* might appear on the surface to extend greater protection to freedom of expression than *Dennis,* in the long run it might be used to justify serious restrictions on this right in a variety of instances. Thus, there were two opposing criticisms of *Yates,* one stressing possible damage to national security, and the other stressing possible resultant damage to the unhindered exercise of first amendment rights.

At the same time there was a great deal of commentary upon the other potential effects of *Yates.* Government attorneys were concerned with the effect which it would have upon the other Smith Act cases still pending. Legal scholars were concerned with the degree to which it had modified or overruled *Dennis.* They also were concerned with the meaning of *Yates* in the context of first amendment rights and with its effects on the "clear and present danger" doctrine. The "clear and present danger" doctrine had been subjected to a great deal of reinterpretation since first enunciated by Mr. Justice Holmes.[97] It had often been ignored. The phrase was not invoked by the court in *Yates,* yet the question remained whether *Yates* was consistent with this doctrine.

In light of this widespread and varied concern over *Yates,* the practical consequences of the decision are of considerable interest. Indeed these consequences shed considerable light on its real meaning and importance. Perhaps they do not indicate the ultimate position which

97. Schenck v. United States, 249 U.S. 47 (1919).

will be given to *Yates* in the overall constitutional interpretation, yet the actual effects of the decision on similar Smith Act prosecutions during the same period are of great help in explaining the case's significance. By examination of these applications of *Yates* by both lower federal courts and the Supreme Court, it is possible to gain some insight into the potential application of the *Yates* rule in the future.

Two members of the first (*Dennis*) group also took an appeal to the Supreme Court. Many were then being released from imprisonment upon completion of their sentences. Two others, who were still serving their sentences after having failed to report with their codefendants,[98] sought a review of their convictions on the basis of *Yates*, which the Supreme Court denied.[99] This meant that all the members of the first group served their full sentences. It also meant that none of the cases which had been finally disposed of before *Yates* were altered by that decision; it affected only appeals pending at the time of its decision.

However, *Yates* had an effect on the pending Smith Act cases which was immediate and decisive. In all but one of these cases the result was the dropping of the charges against the defendants. Legal action ended in one of three ways: (1) reversal of the convictions by the court of appeals, (2) dismissal of the charges by the district court, or (3) motion by the Justice Department for dismissal of the indictments.

A. *Reversal of Convictions and Dismissal of Indictments by Courts of Appeals*

The first of the cases disposed of in this way, in point of time, was the case of the fourteenth group, decided on September 11, 1957.[100] The second circuit ordered the district court to enter judgments of acquittal for all of the defendants, finding that the evidence presented was insufficient under *Yates* to sustain the convictions. Up to this time a final disposition of convictions adversely to the Government had been made by the Supreme Court only as to five of the members of the *Yates* group itself.

A short time after the second circuit's decision a somewhat similar result was announced by the third circuit in disposing of the appeal of

98. See note 62 *supra*.

99. Dennis v. United States, 355 U.S. 936 (1958). The Court upheld, 5-4, the validity of the three year prison sentences imposed on these two for criminal contempt of court for their failure to report to begin serving their prison sentences.

100. United States v. Silverman, 248 F.2d 671 (2d Cir. 1957), *cert. denied*, 355 U.S. 942 (1958).

the eleventh group. Here the Government set a pattern which it was to follow in a number of later cases; it admitted that no new case could be built against two of the defendants in view of the Supreme Court's decision in *Yates*. The court added to this its own judgment that there was no new convincing evidence against two other defendants, and directed that judgments of acquittal be entered in favor of all four.[101] The court was less certain about the evidence against the remaining five defendants, and accordingly, ordered that they be retried.[102]

Early in 1958 the ninth circuit considered two cases together, those of the sixth and ninth groups, and ordered a directed verdict of acquittal for each member of each group.[103] This result was required by *Yates* according to the circuit court.

In a case involving two members of the second group, the defendants had been granted a new trial in 1955 because a major witness for the prosecution had given perjured testimony against them. They were retried with several new defendants and found guilty by a jury on June 31, 1956.[104] On appeal from this second conviction the second circuit applied the *Yates* doctrine and concluded that the convictions should be reversed and remanded, with instructions to dismiss the indictment.[105]

B. *Dismissal of Indictments by District Courts*

Although in many cases, the courts of appeals themselves made final dispositions of Smith Act prosecutions, others were remanded for new trials under the *Yates* standard. In the latter instance the appellate courts refused to say whether or not the evidence already presented met the new requirements. In some of these cases the district courts dismissed the indictments, finding insufficient evidence to warrant a conviction.

Convictions of the eighth group were reversed and remanded by the Supreme Court a few days after *Yates*.[106] The defendants had been convicted of conspiracy (1) to advocate the overthrow of the government by force or violence and (2) to organize the Communist Party as a group to carry on such advocacy. On remand the sixth circuit, following the interpretation given to the word "organize" in *Yates*, held that the charge relating to organizing was barred by the statute of limita-

101. United States v. Kuzma, 249 F.2d 619 (3d Cir. 1957).
102. *Ibid.*
103. Fujimoto v. United States, 251 F.2d 342 (9th Cir. 1958); Huff v. United States, 251 F.2d 342 (9th Cir. 1958).
104. N.Y. Times, Aug. 1, 1956, p. 1, col. 3.
105. United States v. Jackson, 257 F.2d 830 (2d Cir. 1958).
106. Wellman v. United States, 354 U.S. 931 (1957).

tions.[107] The circuit court, however, did order a new trial on the advocacy charge, holding that the evidence on the advocacy conviction would not be "palpably insufficient," and refusing to indulge in a rigorous review of this evidence. On retrial, the district court judge dismissed the indictments for lack of evidence which would satisfy the *Yates* requirements.

A similar result obtained in the case of the eleventh group. Their appeal had been decided by the third circuit in 1957. Because of admissions by the Government, and other independent determinations by this court, the case against four of these defendants was dropped.[108] However, as to the remaining five defendants the court found the evidence less clear and ordered a new trial.[109] In the district court, the case was dismissed for lack of additional evidence.

C. *Motions by the Government for Dismissal of Indictments*

In several cases returned to the district courts, indictments were dismissed upon motions by the Government. The most notable of these arose out of the *Yates* case itself. Although the Supreme Court ordered the acquittal of five of the defendants, nine others were ordered given a new trial. The new trial was never held. The Government requested the district court to dismiss the indictments, explaining in a letter that: "'The comprehensive review conducted by departmental attorneys assigned to the preparation and retrial of this case establishes that we cannot satisfy the evidentiary requirements laid down by the Supreme Court in its opinion reversing the conviction in this matter.'"[110]

Thus all members of the *Yates* group, at some stage in the legal process, were set free, because the Government, either by its own admission, or in the view of the Supreme Court, could not produce evidence that any member had conspired to "advocate" in the sense of "incitement to action" required by *Yates*.

A similar reaction produced dismissal in the case involving the sixteenth group.[111] In the fall of 1957 the Government moved for dismissal of the indictment as to all seven defendants, on the ground that it lacked sufficient evidence under the *Yates* requirement of "incitement to action."

A third such result occurred in the case of the tenth group.[112] Shortly

107. Wellman v. United States, 253 F.2d 601 (6th Cir. 1958).
108. See pp. 730-31 *supra*.
109. Kuzma v. United States, 249 F.2d 619 (3d Cir. 1957).
110. N.Y. Times, Dec. 3, 1957, p. 71, col. 4.
111. United States v. Russo, 155 F. Supp. 251 (D. Mass. 1957).
112. Sentner v. United States, 253 F.2d 310 (8th Cir. 1958); N.Y. Times, April 5, 1958, p. 2, col. 7; N.Y. Times, June 29, 1957, p. 17, col. 2.

after the *Yates* decision, the eighth circuit ordered their appeals sent down for reargument and reconsideration in light of *Yates*. The court eventually ordered a new trial, explaining that it did not want to attempt to predict, in advance, whether the Government could produce the character of evidence now required. Eventually the Government decided not to retry the case in view of the restrictions of the *Yates* decision.[113] The district court dismissed the indictments.

Other groups of Communist Party leaders, the twelfth and thirteenth, had been convicted of conspiracy to "advocate" and to "organize" in 1956. The sixth circuit held, in 1958, that they were entitled to a new trial, because the jury had considered the evidence in regard to "organizing" the Communist Party in reaching its verdict.[114] The new trial was granted on the issue of "advocacy" alone. The court refused to arrive at any conclusion in advance as to whether the Government could produce sufficient evidence for a conviction at the new trial. The trial was never held. The United States Attorney stated that "we can't meet the requirements set down by the Supreme Court,"[115] and the indictments were dismissed.

Thus in four group cases, including the *Yates* group, the indictments were dismissed after the courts of appeals had remanded the cases for new trials at the Government's request. The Government admitted that it could not produce the kind of evidence now required.

The fifth group case also came to the same conclusion. The Supreme Court had reversed the conviction and remanded the case for retrial prior to *Yates* because of doubt as to the credibility of one of the prosecution witnesses.[116] Shortly after *Yates* the Government obtained court permission to drop the indictment. The United States Attorney said: "A careful re-examination of this case in the light of recent Supreme Court decisions has led us to conclude that we cannot successfully retry these defendants on the basis of evidence presently available to the government."[117]

This might have seemed to be a clear admission of the same inability to produce appropriate evidence as was seen in the other requests for dismissal. However, here there were indications that some of the previously presented evidence was no longer available: Two of the original trial witnesses had died and several other witnesses were no longer available for other reasons.[118] Thus, this case is not a clear

113. N.Y. Times, Oct. 11, 1958, p. 11, col. 6.
114. Brandt v. United States, 256 F.2d 79 (6th Cir. 1958).
115. N.Y. Times, Aug. 20, 1959, p. 10, col. 3.
116. See pp. 715-16 *supra*.
117. N.Y. Times, Sept. 14, 1957, p. 38, col. 5.
118. *Ibid.*

example of *Yates'* impact. Even though the practical effect was similar, the result might have been reached without *Yates*.

The above discussion clearly indicates the profound effect which *Yates* had on the outstanding Smith Act prosecutions under the "advocate" and "organize" clauses. It brought an end to these prosecutions in a variety of ways. This effect is all the more remarkable because the Government itself announced that it did not have evidence of the type made necessary by *Yates*.

In only one case did the Government feel that it had the requisite evidence. This was the case of the fifteenth group, originally convicted in 1955.[119] Shortly after *Yates*, the tenth circuit reversed the convictions because the jury had been permitted to consider evidence on the "organize" charge in reaching its verdict as to both the "advocate" and "organize" charges. Since *Yates* in effect had nullified the "organize" provision of the Smith Act as applied to the Communist Party, a verdict based in whole or in part on evidence relating to this charge could not stand. The court, therefore, reversed the convictions and remanded the case for a new trial in which only evidence regarding the charge of conspiracy to advocate would be considered.[120]

Some time later this new trial did take place, and the defendants were again convicted, this time of only conspiracy to "advocate."[121] However, these new convictions were reversed and remanded on Jencks Act[122] grounds, on May 31, 1961, by the tenth circuit.[123] The circuit court found that trial procedures had not been consistent with the requirements of the act, because the Government had failed to deliver all relevant "statements" in its possession to the trial judge for examination.

Of all of the cases involving groups of Communist Party leaders, in only one, involving six individual defendants, was the Government, to its own satisfaction or to that of the courts, able to present evidence of the type required by *Yates*; and, as indicated above, only one of the "membership" clause convictions was able to stand after *Yates*. Several conclusions may be drawn as to the meaning of *Yates*. It did prove to be a major block to prosecution of Communist Party leaders under the "advocacy" clause of the Smith Act, and an absolute bar to use of the "organize" clause. The Government, with the excep-

119. N.Y. Times, May 27, 1955, p. 46, col. 2; N.Y. Times, June 24, 1955, p. 22, col. 2.
120. Bary v. United States, 248 F.2d 201 (10th Cir. 1957).
121. N.Y. Times, March 12, 1959, p. 59, col. 8.
122. Jencks Act of 1957, 71 Stat. 595 (1957), 18 U.S.C.A. § 3500 (Supp. 1964). See note 75, *supra*.
123. Bary v. United States, 292 F.2d 53 (10th Cir. 1961).

tions just mentioned, was unable to furnish convincing evidence of planning or preparation to incite to action, rather than merely of discussing or advocating ideas in a less urgent way, divorced from any "call to action." This may have been because the Communist Party was skillful in preventing discovery of such planning, preparation, or conspiracy. But the extent to which the FBI had infiltrated the Party makes this an unlikely hypothesis. Many of the Government's witnesses were informers who had succeeded in assuming positions of trust and leadership within the Party. That the real aims of the Party would be so completely concealed from all of these informers as to make evidence of such aims or intentions impossible to obtain seems at best a remote possibility.

Viewed in this light, it may be suggested that the decision in *Yates* mainly served to bar legal action against Communist leaders about whom there was little real evidence of activity presenting any immediately observable threat to the security of the United States. In this regard it is well to keep in mind that these individuals were being tried not for overt acts threatening the United States (which are prohibited by other statutes), nor for conspiracy to commit such overt acts (which are prohibited by other statutes), nor for actual advocacy in the form of incitement to illegal action. Thus, despite its effect of barring all but one of the group convictions under the "advocacy" section, and one "membership" prosecution,[124] *Yates* should not be assailed as opening a wide breach in the internal security of the United States. Moreover, its doctrine should not necessarily be branded as anti-libertarian; for example, *Yates* resulted in widespread reversals of convictions where there was no clear evidence of advocacy related to the commission of overt acts.[125]

Perhaps the meaning of *Yates* can be ascertained more clearly by examining its application by the circuit courts in the group cases. There was, it is true, wide variation in the circuit courts' understanding of *Yates*. And there was some evidence of personal dissatisfaction with the decision, although most courts applied the new doctrine without extraneous comment. The most extreme example of judicial reaction was the opinion of Judge Chambers of the ninth

124. See p. 734 *supra*.

125. It may be argued that *all* advocacy ought to be constitutionally protected, regardless of any relationship which it may have to the commission of illegal acts. However, in the U.S., there has been rather widespread agreement that advocacy which causes illegal behavior as an immediate result is not deserving of constitutional protection. This agreement has been present at least since Holmes' enunciation of the clear and present danger doctrine.

circuit regarding the sixth and ninth groups.[126] In ordering the convictions reversed, and the indictments dismissed, Judge Chambers wrote:

> One may as well recognize that the *Yates* decision leaves the Smith Act, as to any further prosecution under it, a virtual shambles—unless the American Communist Party should witlessly set out to reconstitute itself again with a new "organization."
>
> Government attorneys, reeling from the blow of *Yates*, have striven gallantly and arduously to try to secure here an order for a new trial as to all defendants, admitting, as they must, that not less than a new trial here was required by that decision.[127]

Further evidence of judicial displeasure with *Yates* was expressed in the eighth group of cases. The original convictions had been reversed and the case remanded for a new trial.[128] The trial judge, finding insufficient new evidence, and dismissing the indictments, said at the time that he disagreed with the Supreme Court decision.[129]

There was far less variation in lower court applications of *Yates* than there had been previously in the application of *Dennis*. Some variation did occur, however, as became apparent when various courts of appeals began restating the language of *Yates*. Circuit Judge Stewart noted this in *Brandt v. United States*,[130] pointing out that in the appellate courts "widely divergent views had developed as to the true import of Yates."[131] He then offered his own view that to sustain a conviction under *Yates*, "the evidence must show not that the appellants conspired to advocate forcible government overthrow as an abstract idea, but to incite action to that end."[132]

There were two other particularly notable examples of variation in the application of *Yates*. One, a singularly libertarian interpretation, gave wide latitude to freedom of expression. The third circuit, considering the case of the eleventh group, ordered the outright acquittal of four defendants and remanded the case of the remaining five for a new trial.[133] The court outlined the need for evidence of rather specific advocacy as the only type that could be punished under *Yates*.

---

126. Fujimoto v. United States, 251 F.2d 342 (9th Cir. 1958); Huff v. United States, 251 F.2d 342 (9th Cir. 1958).

127. *Ibid.* The other two judges concurred but objected to the language referring "to the effect of the Yates decision upon further prosecutions under the Smith Act. In our view, this statement is unnecessary to the decision." *Ibid.*

128. Wellman v. United States, 354 U.S. 931 (1957).

129. N.Y. Times, Sept. 17, 1958, p. 10, col. 1.

130. 256 F.2d 79 (6th Cir. 1958).

131. *Id.* at 82.

132. *Ibid.*

133. United States v. Kuzma, 249 F.2d 619 (3d Cir. 1957).

Its prescription for the evidence required was far stricter than that laid down by any court under *Dennis,* or by any other court under *Yates.* The third circuit used language similar to the Supreme Court in saying that there must be planning or preparation for " 'advocacy and teaching of concrete action for the forcible overthrow of the government.' "[134] " 'Those to whom the advocacy is addressed must be urged to *do* something.' "[135] And, the court said that not even " 'an agreement to advocate forcible overthrow itself [is] an unlawful conspiracy if it does not call for advocacy of action.' "[136] But the court went on to say that the Government must prove a "conspiracy to teach people to take concrete action toward the violent overthrow of the existing government as soon as possible."[137]

This language seems to suggest that the important evidentiary question should be whether persons were being instructed in techniques or methods of action, *i.e.,* whether an actual conspiracy to commit overt acts was evident. At the very least, this language would require evidence that actual concrete actions were advocated or advised, and it would require evidence that this action be advised in the near future, rather than at some vague, indefinite, or unknown time in the distant future. This behavior, moreover, had to be directed at the forcible overthrow of the government.

In contrast to this strict interpretation of *Yates,* the tenth circuit reached a far more permissive view of the evidence necessary for a conviction in the case of the fifteenth group.[138] Significantly, this was the one group case in which the Government did elect to retry the defendants, and, in fact, did obtain a new conviction. The circuit court, in remanding the case, laid down an evidentiary standard which emphasized the subjective element of intent. This standard made punishable the advocacy of any preliminary step which might be related to future acts of force or violence. The court's treatment of the time element was similar to the decisions under *Dennis,* making punishable any preliminary advocacy of action to be accomplished at some point in time, although far removed from the present. The element emphasized by the court was the subjective readiness of a group, as the result of present advocacy, to engage in action at some unspecified time in the distant future. This element had been included in the Supreme Court's *Yates'* decision, but had not been seized upon by courts of

134. *Id.* at 621, quoting from *Yates,* 354 U.S. 298, 320 (1957).
135. *Ibid.,* quoting from 354 U.S. at 325.
136. *Ibid.,* quoting from 354 U.S. at 323.
137. *Id.* at 621-22.
138. Bary v. United States, 248 F.2d 201 (10th Cir. 1957).

appeal in other group cases. This emphasis may be seen in the tenth circuit's statement regarding advocacy.

> It is now the definitely charted rule that mere advocacy in the abstract that the Government should be overthrown and destroyed, if unrelated to any effort to incite or instigate action to that end by force and violence, falls within the range of free speech protected by the First Amendment. But at the same time there is no area for doubt that as a reasonable concomitant of the right of the Government to protect itself against overthrow or destruction by force or violence from within, Congress may enact legislation making penal declarations, statements, utterances, or teachings in the nature of incitement to action *intended* to produce the forbidden result of overthrow or destruction by force and violence. . . . It is enough if the incitement is directed with *intended* precision to the taking of steps or the doing of things in preliminary preparation for the employment of force and violence in an effort to effectuate the overthrow or destruction of the Government when the propitious moment is at hand.[139]

The court indulged in an extensive survey of the facts surrounding the defendants' advocacy, and concluded that the defendants believed that violence was a part of the program of the Communist Party.[140] Many of the defendants' quoted statements seem to be merely descriptive, or suggestive, or even predictive, but certainly not incitement to any immediate action, or incitement to any action in the foreseeable future. Some of these statements may have been of the kind that would prepare listeners emotionally to be ready and willing to act at some time in the distant future. But the court concluded that this was incitement. This was the same view of incitement to action as was found in the *Scales* "membership" appeal (the only other instance in which a conviction was sustained).[141]

> The evidence did not merely disclose advocacy, utterances, or teachings in the abstract—unrelated to or divorced from incitement to action. . . . Neither did it merely disclose discussion or exposition of violent overthrow as an abstract theory. Considered in its totality, the evidence disclosed as to each of the appellants incitement and advocacy of action in an effort to overthrow the Government by force and violence as speedily as circumstances would permit, within the intent and meaning of the Smith Act . . . .[142]

139. *Id.* at 207. (Emphasis added.)
140. *Id.* at 210-13.
141. Scales v. United States, 227 F.2d 581 (4th Cir. 1955).
142. 248 F.2d at 213.

These decisions display the polarized variations on the interpretive theme of *Yates.*

On other occasions for interpretation, a much more uniform result was reached, involving mostly a repetition or paraphrasing of the Supreme Court's language. The first of these instances involved the convictions of the fourteenth group.[143] The second circuit, in reversing the convictions, stated that *Yates* required "proof of a plan to use language reasonably calculated to incite the audience to use violence against the Government of the United States, either immediately or in the future."[144] Here the defendants had been prosecuted for actual advocacy which already had taken place, but the court found no examples of real incitement to action.

> We resolve all issues of credibility in favor of the prosecution and draw all inferences in its favor. Even so, the single, most remarkable fact in the record is that there is no example of revolutionary advocacy of either the legal or illegal sort during the period covered by the indictment.[145]
>
> Here on the critical issue of whether these defendants or the Party engaged in criminal speech during the three years prior to the indictment, there is no direct evidence of a single example of such advocacy. . . . We would mock both fair trial and free speech as meaningful constitutional guarantees were we to ignore the deficiencies of this record.[146]

The sixth circuit,[147] on remand of the eighth group's case from the Supreme Court, further remanded the case to the district court for a new trial, indicating that the evidence introduced at the new trial must be evaluated in the light of *Yates.* As to its own view of *Yates,* the sixth circuit simply recited similar language to that found in *Yates,* to the effect that, for conviction, it must be proved that " 'those to whom the advocacy is addressed must be urged to do something, now or in the future, rather than merely to believe in something . . . .' "[148]

Another instance of this kind of interpretation occurred in the case of two members of the second group who had been retried along with four new defendants.[149] The second circuit, reversing the several convictions, suggested, as its understanding of *Yates,* that the

143. United States v. Silverman, 248 F.2d 671 (2d Cir. 1957).
144. *Id.* at 676.
145. *Id.* at 677.
146. *Id.* at 686.
147. Wellman v. United States, 253 F.2d 601 (6th Cir. 1958).
148. *Id.* at 605.
149. United States v. Jackson, 257 F.2d 830 (2d Cir. 1958).

> Smith Act requires more than the teaching or advocacy of an abstract doctrine that the government should be overthrown by force and violence. . . . [I]t must be clear in some fashion that the teaching and advocacy was directed to some sort of action, not merely to the belief in some abstract doctrine. In distinguishing this extremely narrow difference between the advocacy or teaching which constitutes a violation and that which does not, the Supreme Court said: "The essential distinction is that those to whom the advocacy is addressed must be urged to *do* something, now or in the future, rather than merely *believe* in something." Summed up, the court held that the Smith Act does not denounce advocacy or teaching in the sense of abstractly preaching the propriety and desirability of the forcible overthrow of the government, but reaches only an advocacy or teaching of *action* to accomplish such overthrow by force and violence.[150]

Here the court plainly pointed out that the subjective states of consciousness generated by advocacy were not the deciding factor in judging whether such advocacy could be proscribed. Rather, the form of advocacy was controlling, and only advocacy in the form of incitement to action was subject to penalty. Under this interpretation, language which only prepared listeners emotionally, to be ready to engage in action at a later time, was not subject to penalty. Language which only prompted listeners to take preliminary steps toward action at a much further removed date was also protected.

VI. "MEMBERSHIP" CLAUSE PROSECUTIONS AFTER *Yates*

Yates also had an effect upon "membership" clause prosecutions, which were at an incomplete stage when it was decided. However, the effect here was neither as immediate nor as marked as in the other Smith Act prosecutions. Indeed, the diversity of federal court interpretation of *Yates* in "membership" cases left the whole matter in an ambiguous state. Some convictions were affirmed, others reversed, and some trials never were held. The courts disagreed over whether *Yates* was applicable in this area, and, if it was, what its proper application should be.

In several "membership" cases the defendants never were brought to trial. Dr. Albert Emanuel Blumberg was granted a new trial on Jencks Act grounds on June 29, 1962, but no new trial has been held;[151] nor was Max Morris Weiss ever tried; Dr. Blumberg's indictment was dismissed on a Government motion on *Yates* evidentiary grounds;[152]

---

150. *Id.* at 831. (Citation omitted.) (Emphasis on *action* added.)
151. See letter from Anthony Lewis, *supra* note 64.
152. *Ibid.*

the indictment against Michael Russo also was dismissed on *Yates* grounds.[153]

Other cases applied *Yates* with far less uniformity. John C. Hellman was tried and convicted, but his conviction was reversed on appeal on evidentiary grounds[154] on December 29, 1961, after the final Supreme Court disposition of the *Scales* case. The court followed *Scales* in saying that proof of the defendant's intent to accomplish the overthrow of the Government by force as soon as circumstances would permit was necessary to sustain a conviction. The evidence was found to be insufficient to establish such intent conclusively. *Yates* was not mentioned in the opinion.

During the period following *Yates*, the Justice Department instituted the retrial of Junius Irving Scales, under the evidentiary rules of the Jencks Act. The jury found Scales guilty.[155] Claude Mack Lightfoot was not retried although at the time of the reversal of their original convictions the Government had indicated that it would retry both Scales and Lightfoot.[156] The Government decided to wait until determination of the appeals of Scales and John Francis Noto,[157] another outstanding appeal in a "membership" clause conviction. These appeals were affirmed by the circuit courts in 1958,[158] a year and one half after the *Yates* decision.

In upholding Scales' second conviction the fourth circuit noted the applicability of *Yates*, quoting at length from that opinion.[159] The court did consider the actual evidence against Scales, which had indicated that forcible overthrow was clearly a key part of the program presented by the Party organization to its members. But this advocacy of forceful overthrow hardly could be said to be concrete planning to commit specific acts at any foreseeable time in the future. The evidence against Scales indicated that he taught much the same ideas concerning the necessity of eventual revolution by force. Considered in light of *Yates*, the question raised by this evidence was whether this was abstract discussion, divorced from a call to action, or advocacy in the realm of incitement? The court's conclusion from this evidence was that:

153. *Ibid.*
154. Hellman v. United States, 298 F.2d 810 (9th Cir. 1961).
155. N.Y. Times, Feb. 22, 1958, p. 6, col. 5.
156. See p. 723 *supra*.
157. As of October 23, 1962, the case is still pending, and the government will not say when, or whether, the case will go to trial. See letter from Anthony Lewis, *supra* note 64.
158. Scales v. United States, 260 F.2d 21 (4th Cir. 1958); United States v. Noto, 262 F.2d 501 (2d Cir. 1958).
159. 260 F.2d at 25.

> [T]he evidence in regard to the activities of the Communist Party and of Scales constituted proof of advocacy of concrete action, as distinguished from the promulgation of a theory, which created a clear and present danger of substantive evil beyond the protections of the First Amendment and within the right and power of Congress to prohibit. In our opinion, this conclusion is in accord with the approval given in Yates . . . to the essence of the Dennis holding . . . .[160]

Not only did the court stress advocacy of action, rather than incitement to action, as being decisive, but it also referred back to the *Dennis* idea that any prior stage in a seditious conspiracy, no matter how far removed from the eventual commission of acts, could be punished. It asserted that although the *Yates* test "did not justify the conclusion that the defendants' advocacy was directed at, or created any danger of, immediate overthrow, it did establish that the advocacy was aimed at building up a seditious group and maintaining it in readiness for action at a propitious time."[161] The court concluded that a clear and present danger existed simply because of the nature of the organization involved.

> It is too clear for argument that membership in an organization with knowledge of its purposes and an intent to make them effective is a joint rather than an individual undertaking which gathers its strength from an association or group of individuals inspired by a common purpose. The activities of such a group constitute a clear and present danger to the state and he who joins with open eyes becomes a party to all that he sees.[162]

The court meant that advocacy was an initial step in a process by which a group of persons was prepared psychologically for a possible response to incitement to action at a time in the unforeseeable future.

This interpretation of the *Yates* decision closely approximated *Dennis*, and was relied upon in every instance after *Yates* where a conviction was affirmed. Little attention was given to the immediate effects of the advocacy. In fact, the advocacy need not even have the character usually attributed to incitement—which would normally entail a stimulus to action immediately, or at least at some related time. General statements, not calling for the commission of overt acts at any foreseeable time, could be characterized as "incitement" under this view of *Yates*.

160. *Id.* at 37.
161. *Ibid.*, quoting from 354 U.S. 298, 321.
162. *Id.* at 26.

The court also held that this "membership" prosecution contravened neither first nor fifth amendment rights, neither by abridging freedom of speech nor by imputing guilt from mere association, unaccompanied by unlawful conduct.[163] The court found that the Communist Party advocated the forcible overthrow of the Government, and that the defendant had knowledge or awareness of this fact when he was a member. Thus the court's holding seems to imply that, if a defendant was informed that the group to which he belonged carried on certain proscribed illegal advocacy, the first amendment no longer barred prosecution.

In the *Noto* case the second circuit noted with approval the trial judge's finding of a "clear and present danger."[164] In upholding the conviction, the court stressed several facts apparently as being decisive. The court held that the Communist Party did in fact teach and advocate the forcible overthrow and destruction of the Government as speedily as circumstances would permit; that the defendant had knowledge of this advocacy; and that the defendant intended to achieve this purpose. Thus the elements of personal awareness and intent, coupled with advocacy by an organization of which the person was a member, seemed to be sufficient to establish the existence of a "clear and present danger." No reference was made to external facts relevant to the concrete situation in which the advocacy took place.

The court ignored *Yates,* and the "incitement" test. It felt that the facts were such that *Yates* did not even apply.

> This case does not confront the court with the prosecution of a leader, organizer, or teacher of the Communist Party charged during the indictment period with advocating and teaching the duty and necessity of overthrowing the Government by force and violence or of organizing a society to so advocate. Consequently the incitement of action test enunciated in Yates . . . is inapplicable.[165]

Thus, although in striking contrast to the results in the advocacy cases, both of these "membership" convictions were upheld, in one *Yates* was not construed in the typical fashion, and in the other it was denied relevance. In each, it remained for the Supreme Court to make clear the proper application of *Yates.*

The courts of appeals found no difficulty in upholding the applicability of the "membership" clause against the contention that the

163. *Id.* at 24-26.
164. 262 F.2d at 509.
165. *Ibid.*

"per se" provision of the Internal Security Act of 1950 rendered it unusable.[166] As in the *Lightfoot* and the first *Scales* appeals, the courts held that the evidence supported the finding that each defendant was more than a mere member, *i.e.*, that each defendant also knew that the Communist Party was engaged in illegal advocacy and that each intended that the aim of this advocacy be achieved. Furthermore, each of these defendants also had played an active and leading role in Party affairs, as teacher, officer, paid employee, and the like. Thus, they could not claim that they were not directly involved.[167]

These two cases were taken to the Supreme Court, which granted certiorari.[168] The Court had some serious doubts as to the constitutionality of the "membership" clause, and as to the statutory validity of these convictions. Counsel were requested to address themselves to several specific questions, which indicated the possible presence in the case of serious problems of constitutional and statutory interpretation.

The Court asked the attorneys to address themselves to the question of whether the "membership" clause was constitutionally valid, if interpreted so as to permit a conviction based only on proof that the accused person was a member of a group which advocated the forcible overthrow of the Government, when the accused person knew that the group engaged in such advocacy.

If the clause was not constitutional under this interpretation, was it constitutional if interpreted so as to require proof of membership accompanied by specific intent of the accused to accomplish these purposes as speedily as circumstances would permit?

If the membership clause would not be constitutional under either of these interpretations, would it be constitutionally valid if inter-

---

166. See p. 722 *supra*.

167. The Jencks issue was also raised again in the Scales appeal. Following the Jencks decision by the Supreme Court, Congress passed the so-called Jencks Act, 18 U.S.C. 3500, which provided for procedures not strictly in accordance with the language of the Supreme Court's decision. Instead of allowing the entire collection of F.B.I. reports by prosecution witnesses to be examined by the defense, the Jencks Act allowed the trial judge to make the initial examination of the F.B.I. reports, so that he could turn over to the defense only those portions which were relevant to the trial testimony of the prosecution witnesses. This procedure was used in the second Scales trial, and in the appeal it was argued that this violated the requirements set forth by the Supreme Court. The Court of Appeals ruled against this contention. "In any event, it is our opinion that this statutory provision, whether it be regarded as an addition to or a change in the Jencks procedure does not amount to a denial of the due process required by the Fifth Amendment, but is merely a procedural regulation which preserves certain substantial rights of the accused and at the same time protects the Government files from the danger of unnecessary disclosure of its sources of information." 260 F.2d at 43.

168. Scales v. United States, 358 U.S. 917 (1958); Noto v. United States, 361 U.S. 813 (1959).

preted so as to require, as an element of the crime, proof that the accused person was an active member of the organization? Could the "membership" clause permissibly bear such an interpretation? If not, and if it was constitutional without proof of active membership, would a constitutional application of the clause depend upon any such requirement? If so, was such a requirement properly applied by the courts in this case?

Would the "clear and present danger doctrine" have application to the "membership" clause either with respect to the accused or with respect to the group of persons of which he was a member? If so applicable, could such doctrine be properly applied in this case?

Finally, was Section 4(f) of the Internal Security Act of 1950[169] a bar to the present prosecution? Were the registration provisions of that Act relevant to this question?

These questions clearly indicate the seriousness with which the Supreme Court reviewed the constitutional questions involved in prosecutions under the "membership" clause. The Court did not render a final decision in these cases until two years later, at the end of the 1961 term.

The Supreme Court's decision in the *Scales*[170] and *Noto*[171] cases showed plainly that substantial agreement had not been reached. Two justices felt that the "per se" provision rendered the "membership" clause inoperative.[172] On first amendment grounds, two other justices objected to the whole idea of "membership" prosecutions.[173] The five man majority agreed, after a lengthy review of the legislative history, that the "membership" clause was not nullified by the "per se" provision. They also agreed that in light of the "per se" provision something more than mere membership had to be proved. Some evidence of active rather than passive or merely nominal membership had to be shown, including knowledge of the Party's advocacy, and the specific intent to bring about violent overthrow of the Government as speedily as circumstances would permit.

The decision affirming Scales' conviction included a prolonged attempt to assess the evidence in accordance with the *Yates* test. Much

169. 64 Stat. 991, c. 1024, tit. I § 4 (1950), 50 U.S.C.A. § 783(f) (1951).

170. Scales v. United States, 367 U.S. 203 (1961).

171. Noto v. United States, 367 U.S. 290 (1961).

172. 367 U.S. at 278 (Mr. Justice Brennan with whom the Chief Justice and Mr. Justice Douglas join dissenting); *id.* at 300 (Mr. Justice Brennan and the Chief Justice in favor of dismissal based on the former's dissent in *Scales*).

173. 367 U.S. at 259 (Mr. Justice Black dissenting); *id.* at 262 (Mr. Justice Douglas dissenting); 367 U.S. at 300 (Mr. Justice Black concurring); *id.* at 302 (Mr. Justice Douglas concurring).

of this evidence indicated that the eventual use of force and violence was an essential part of the Party program. Included were several statements by the defendant, in various contexts, that forcible revolution was the only way in which the Party could expect to achieve its goals, and that attempts at peaceful change were to be disregarded as useless.

The problem for the Court was to decide whether this was indeed "'advocacy of action' to accomplish overthrow either immediately or as soon as circumstances proved propitious, and uttered in terms reasonably calculated to 'incite' to such action."[174] In considering this point the Court explicitly stated that "the evidentiary question here is controlled in large part by *Yates*."[175]

The majority's examination of the evidence led it to the conclusion that the advocacy was illegal. This was the only appeal since *Yates* in which the evidence was found to be sufficient to satisfy *Yates* requirements. In reaching this conclusion the Supreme Court relied on concepts ignored by most of the lower courts. Crucial to the Court's decision was the conclusion that the Community Party was a group preparing itself for action in the far distant, unforeseeable future, rather than at any immediate or foreseeable future. Indeed, none of the evidence presented indicated the possibility of action in the present or near future; readiness for action at some remote time was the only sense in which the advocacy could be related to acts.

> We conclude that this evidence sufficed to make a case for the jury on the issue of illegal Party advocacy. *Dennis* and *Yates* have definitely laid at rest any doubt that present advocacy of *future* action for violent overthrow satisfies statutory and constitutional requirements equally with advocacy of *immediate* action to that end. . . . Hence this record cannot be considered deficient because it contains no evidence of advocacy for immediate overthrow. Since the evidence amply showed that Party leaders were continuously preaching during the indictment period inevitability of eventual forceful overthrow, the first and basic question is a narrow one: whether the jury could permissibly infer that such preaching, in whole or in part, 'was aimed at building up a seditious group and maintaining it in readiness for action at a propitious time . . . the kind of indoctrination preparatory to action which was condemned in *Dennis*.'[176]

None of the four dissenters disagreed with the majority's application of the *Yates* requirements. Justices Black and Douglas argued

174. 367 U.S. at 230.
175. *Id.* at 232.
176. *Id.* at 251-52.

for full constitutional protection of freedom of expression and association, while Justice Brennan and Chief Justice Warren argued that the "per se" provision of the Internal Security Act of 1950 meant that Communist Party membership was no longer criminal. The majority did not feel that the form of the advocacy was controlling, but instead looked to the possible long range effect of the advocacy in preparing the hearers to be ready to heed a "call to action" at some unforseeable time in the indefinite future. This interpretation allowed wider latitude for prosecution that had *Yates*, but did not result automatically in the affirmance of every conviction.

In the *Noto* case, decided the same day as *Scales*, the conviction was reversed on the ground that the evidence did not provide a sufficient basis for the conclusion that the defendant had engaged in "advocacy of action." Since the evidence was not of the requisite kind, no elaborate discussion of types of incitement to action was necessary. There was lacking any indication of long, continued and consistent teaching by Noto or his Party group that violence was the necessary, inevitable, and single means by which Party objectives could be obtained. This indicated to the Court that Noto's activities constituted merely the teaching of abstract doctrine:

> The kind of evidence which we found in *Scales* sufficient to support the jury's verdict of present illegal Party advocacy is lacking here in any adequately substantial degree. It need hardly be said that it is upon the particular evidence in a particular record that a particular defendant must be judged, and not upon the evidence in some other record or upon what may be supposed to be the tenets of the Communist Party.[177]

VII. Conclusion

Considering all of the foregoing regarding the language of the Supreme Court in *Yates*, and the various reactions by the Supreme Court itself, the courts of appeals, the district courts, and the Government, several conclusions can be drawn as to the meaning of *Yates* in the context of legal action against the expression of ideas.

Two different interpretations developed. The one most frequently employed to bar convictions was based on only part of the *Yates* language. This view regarded the protection extended to advocacy in the realm of abstract doctrine as applicable to expressions of the duty and necessity of overthrow and destruction of the government by illegal means. Statements in the nature of "oughts" were not

177. 367 U.S. at 299.

punishable merely because they might have a tendency to prepare others emotionally or intellectually for illegal action at some distant future time. The emphasis on the mental readiness of persons to act, characteristic of the decision in *Dennis* and those which followed it, was no longer pertinent. Irrelevant also was the intent which motivated the advocacy of certain ideas, including intent to produce harmful effects. Expression motivated by the most harmful desires might take the form of abstract doctrine, and, if so, be protected. Tenuous connections between speech and subsequent actions were to be disregarded as irrelevant.

Punishable expression had to have a form which was quite obviously an incitement to the commission of overt illegal acts by the listeners. Thus, an examination of the character and context of the advocacy had to be made, and a determination of whether it was of such a type as to constitute a call to illicit behavior at some time in the forseeable future. Seen in this aspect, *Yates* can be said to have made immaterial many of the concerns manifested by courts at a prior time, and to have severely reduced the type of speech proscribed by the Smith Act. In effect, *Yates* did encourage courts and the Government to engage in rigorous scrutiny of the evidence before deciding whether real incitement, or conspiracy aimed at incitement, had taken place. In all but one group case,[178] and one "membership" case,[179] the conclusion was that it had not.

In those two exceptional cases, the Court construed a continued expression of commitment to violent overthrow as a form of incitement, and, therefore, proscribed. Thus, it was still possible to convict for advocacy containing no semblance of a "call to action" in the foreseeable future. Expressions in the form of statements of belief, or of passionate desire, or of fervent expectation might be construed to be related to the creation of attitudes in an audience which would render it susceptible to an incitement to action at some time in the indefinite future.

It appears to the author that the *Yates* decision suggested two separate bases for judgment, leading to strikingly different results in application. In one, the essential factor was the form of the advocacy. In the other, it was the possible effect of the advocacy, *i.e.*, possible psychological changes in an audience which might not be apparent at any definite moment in time or through any specific kind of evidence. Subsequent applications of *Yates* could develop in either of these directions.

178. See p. 734 *supra*.
179. *Ibid.*

OF "LIBERTY" AND "PROPERTY"*

Henry Paul Monaghan†

After a century of experience, we are now thoroughly accustomed to viewing the fourteenth amendment as imposing upon the experimentation otherwise permitted in our fifty separate "laboratories" limitations that do not materially differ from those fastened upon the national government by the bill of rights.[1] The history of this evolution is far too well known to justify rehearsing here even in the barest outline.[2] But it bears noting that few, if any, observers believe that the language of the amendment has played a significant role in this historical evolution. Here, as elsewhere, "[b]ehind the words . . . are postulates which limit and control."[3]

The governing postulates, to be sure, have shifted over time, ranging from conceptions of vested rights and laissez-faire economics to more recent concerns for representative democracy, equality, and individual dignity. But postulates, not textual analysis, have been the impelling force behind the various theories used to justify application of most of the specific guarantees of the bill of rights to the states as part of the "liberty" secured by the due process clause.[4] Similarly, postulates, not language, have been at the root of the apparently unending controversy over the extent to which the Supreme Court may properly invoke the amendment to constitutionalize values not readily inferable from the constitutional text, structure, or history.[5]

Whatever the governing set of ideological postulates, they have rendered largely unimportant, except as a forensic matter, any

---

* This Article was prepared in connection with a lecture delivered by the author on October 27, 1976, for the Frank Irvine Lecture Series at the Cornell Law School.

† Professor of Law, Boston University School of Law. B.A. 1955, University of Massachusetts; LL.B. 1958, Yale University; LL.M. 1960, Harvard University.

[1] Compare this view with the initial view of the amendment announced in the Slaughter-House Cases, 83 U.S. (16 Wall.) 36 (1873).

[2] The standard treatment remains E. CORWIN, LIBERTY AGAINST GOVERNMENT (1948).

[3] Monaco v. Mississippi, 292 U.S. 313, 322 (1934).

[4] *See, e.g.*, Dixon, *The "New" Substantive Due Process*, 1976 B.Y.U. L. REV. 43, 64-69 (1976). *See generally* G. GUNTHER, CASES AND MATERIALS ON CONSTITUTIONAL LAW 506-47 (9th ed. 1975). Ludwig v. Massachusetts, 96 S. Ct. 2781 (1976), potentially the most recent round in the continuing controversy, carefully skirts the basic issues. *Id.* at 2787.

[5] Monaghan, *The Supreme Court, 1974 Term—Foreword: Constitutional Common Law*, 89 HARV. L. REV. 1, 44-45 (1975).

distinction between equal protection and substantive due process.[6] To be sure, the greater appeal of equal protection in terms of current constitutional and political theory is apparent. But for all practical purposes, the equal protection clause forbids few discriminations that are not similarly forbidden by the due process clause of the fifth amendment.[7] That fact will become increasingly clear as the noxious odor long surrounding the concept of substantive due process steadily dissipates.[8] In reality, then, the history of the fourteenth amendment has always been the history of the due process clause—so far, that is, as it can be viewed as the history of any textual provision.

For decades the crucial fourteenth amendment battles have been fought over the substantive validity of action taken by the states. This has occasioned considerable controversy both within and without the Court over whether some individual interests might weigh more heavily than others for constitutional purposes.[9] But these well-publicized disputes have concealed at least one important area of agreement. Save for Mr. Justice Harlan's singular insistence that voting in state elections is an interest not encompassed by the first section of the fourteenth amendment,[10] there seems to have been an overriding consensus that every individual "interest" worth talking about is encompassed within the "liberty"

[6] L. HAND, THE BILL OF RIGHTS 56 (1958). *But see* Linde, *Judges, Critics, and the Realist Tradition*, 82 YALE L.J. 227, 233-35 (1972) (arguing that, for advocates of judicial "realism," "beneficial" results might follow from treating the two clauses as not identical). *See also* A. COX, THE ROLE OF THE SUPREME COURT IN AMERICAN GOVERNMENT 70 (1976).

[7] *E.g.*, Hampton v. Mow Sun Wong, 426 U.S. 88, 103-04 (1976); Examining Bd. v. Flores De Otero, 426 U.S. 572, 599-601 (1976); Mathews v. De Castro, 97 S. Ct. 431, 432 n.1 (1976). Mr. Justice Jackson's widely admired concurrence in Railway Express v. New York, 336 U.S. 106, 111-12 (1949), asserting that due process permanently disables a state from enacting legislation while equal protection requires only that the legislation be generalized is plainly wrong. Due process is often concerned only with the discrimination created by federal statutes. Hampton v. Mow Sun Wong, *supra*. *See also* United States Dep't of Agriculture v. Moreno, 413 U.S. 528, 533 (1973). Equal protection analysis is concerned with assessing the validity of certain governmental ends. *See, e.g.*, Shapiro v. Thompson, 394 U.S. 618 (1969). The equal protection clause is also quite capable of raising essentially procedural due process issues. *See, e.g.*, Stanley v. Illinois, 405 U.S. 645, 658 (1972).

[8] Roe v. Wade, 410 U.S. 113 (1973), is the most dramatic illustration of the reemergence of substantive due process. Substantive due process has always had academic admirers who spend considerable time and inventiveness in efforts to justify and limit the concept. *See generally* Grey, *Do We Have An Unwritten Constitution?*, 27 STAN. L. REV. 703 (1975); Perry, *Abortion, The Public Morals, and the Police Power: The Ethical Function of Substantive Due Process*, 23 U.C.L.A. L. REV. 689 (1976); Tushnet, *The Newer Property: Suggestions For The Revival of Substantive Due Process*, 1975 SUP. CT. REV. 261. *But see* Dixon, *supra* note 4.

[9] *See, e.g.*, Massachusetts Bd. of Retirement v. Murgia, 96 S. Ct. 2562, 2569-90 (1976) (dissenting opinion, Marshall, J.).

[10] Oregon v. Mitchell, 400 U.S. 112, 152-219 (1970) (dissenting in part, Harlan, J.).

and "property" secured by the due process clause and thus entitled to some constitutional protection, if only that of the "baseline requirement of 'rationality.' "[11] The "right-privilege" distinction, the last barrier to such a consensus, has completely fallen.[12] That doctrine had been invoked to justify a denial of due process scrutiny of some types of governmental conduct in the public sector; for example, since there was no independent "right" to welfare payments, their denial, standing alone, did not implicate any constitutional value. So ran the argument, at least. But the logic of this argument was flawed. Whether they constituted "rights" or not in some technical sense, the "entitlement" interests created by statutory law could still amount to "liberty" or "property" in the constitutional sense.[13] The "right-privilege" doctrine's lack of solid theoretical underpinning resulted in its erratic enforcement and, ultimately, its demise.[14]

Most importantly, the criterion for determining whether an interest deserved due process clause protection involved a simple pragmatic assessment of its "importance" to the individual. *Bell v. Burson*,[15] decided in 1971, represented the high-water mark of this approach. In sustaining a procedural due process objection to a state automobile license suspension statute, the Court hurried over the threshold question of whether the clause was applicable at all. The Court simply observed that a license "may become essential in the pursuit of a livelihood,"[16] and then said that its suspension "thus involves state action that adjudicates important interests of the licensees."[17]

Bell wholly eschewed a tight, textually-oriented examination of the interests secured by the due process clause. The Court could have said that the license was sufficient to qualify as "property," or that a suspension of an individual's freedom to drive was a restriction on his "liberty." The Court said neither; the importance of the

---

[11] Ely, *The Wages of Crying Wolf: A Comment on Roe v. Wade*, 82 YALE L.J. 920, 928 (1973).

[12] *See, e.g.*, Elrod v. Burns, 96 S. Ct. 2673, 2684 n.15 (1976) (plurality opinion); Perry v. Sindermann, 408 U.S. 593, 596-98 (1972).

[13] As Justice Holmes once trenchantly noted: "Such words as 'right' are a constant solicitation to fallacy." Jackman v. Rosenbaum Co., 260 U.S. 22, 31 (1922).

[14] For an analysis of the erratic reach of the doctrine—which was applied even to bar claims made with respect to specific constitutional rights such as freedom of speech—before its total collapse, see Van Alstyne, *The Demise of the Right-Privilege Distinction In Constitutional Law*, 81 HARV. L. REV. 1439 (1968). *See also* Van Alstyne, *Cracks in the New Property*, 62 CORNELL L. REV. 445 (1977).

[15] 402 U.S. 535 (1971).

[16] *Id.* at 539.

[17] *Id.* There were no dissents, but three justices silently concurred only in the result. *Id.* at 543.

interest alone sufficed, and "importance" was determined as a matter of federal, not state, law. Whatever else may be said of *Bell*, it fitted comfortably with current standing doctrine in its recognition that "injury in fact" normally constituted a constitutionally sufficient predicate for the invocation of federal judicial power.[18] And it is fair to say that when *Bell* was decided there were few lawyers, on or off the bench, who had serious problems with its pragmatic approach to deciding what individual interests implicated the due process clause.

But in fact *Bell*'s latitudinarian approach to "liberty" and "property" was soon eroded. New postulates that limit and control pressed for recognition, and they now find at least partial expression in a more restrictive conception of what constitutes constitutional "liberty" and "property." Those postulates are clear enough. Rightly or wrongly, a majority of the present Court is struggling to place limits on the level of federal superintendence of the operations of state and local government, a struggle which has occurred largely in the context of "section 1983" actions.[19] That statute creates a federal right of action for state conduct which deprives a person of "*any* rights, privileges, or immunities secured by the Constitution."[20] Under its aegis, aggressive and inventive lawyers have brought a staggering range of complaints to the courts. From their perspective, they are simply attempting to "constitutionalize" the realm of state and local government. But, quite plainly, a majority of the Court rejects this approach and seems determined to prevent the escalation of every grievance against state and local government into a constitutional claim.[21]

Read literally, section 1983 incorporates every "liberty" or "property" interest protected by the fourteenth amendment. Accordingly, statutory explication necessarily becomes constitutional exegesis as well. With increasing frequency, the Court has concluded that neither "liberty" nor "property" has been threatened by state action and hence no section 1983 claim has been stated. *Morrissey v. Brewer*,[22] a due process challenge to parole revocation procedures decided in the term following *Bell*, laid the groundwork. In passing upon the constitutional challenge, the Court did mention the importance of the individual interest, but it stressed

[18] Simon v. Eastern Ky. Welfare Rights Org., 426 U.S. 26, 37-39 (1976).

[19] 42 U.S.C. § 1983 (1970).

[20] *Id.* (emphasis added).

[21] *E.g.*, Meachum v. Fano, 96 S. Ct. 2532, 2540 (1976); Bishop v. Wood, 426 U.S. 341, 349-50 (1976); Paul v. Davis, 424 U.S. 693, *rehearing denied*, 425 U.S. 985 (1976).

[22] 408 U.S. 471 (1972).

that "[t]he question is not merely the 'weight' of the individual's interest, but whether the nature of the interest is one within . . . the 'liberty or property' language"[23] of the due process clause. This language was repeated later in the term in *Board of Regents v. Roth*,[24] where, for the first time, a divided Court rejected a procedural due process claim because it implicated neither "liberty" nor "property." The "range of interests protected by procedural due process,"[25] said the Court, is "broad indeed,"[26] but "not infinite."[27]

The analytical shift worked by *Roth* is significant. Prior to *Roth*, Supreme Court definitions of "liberty" and "property" had amounted to taking the words "life, liberty or property" as a unitary concept embracing all interests valued by sensible men. After *Roth*, however, each word of the clause must be examined separately; so examined, we find that they do not embrace the full range of state conduct having serious impact upon individual interests. For *Roth*'s emphasis on the need for careful analysis of the "*nature* of the interest at stake"[28] has not proved to be an isolated phenomenon. Indeed, in the last term, this concern reached almost epidemic proportions. Several decisions expressed doubt as to whether the challenged state conduct interfered with "liberty" or "property,"[29] and the lack of a protectible interest proved decisive in three important cases. In *Paul v. Davis*,[30] a sharply divided Court held that state defamation of a private individual "standing alone and apart from any other governmental action"[31] did not implicate any "liberty" protected by the due process clause. The five-man majority argued that "reputation alone, apart from some more tangible interests" lay outside the range of liberties protected by

---

[23] *Id.* at 481.

[24] 408 U.S. 564, 570-71 (1971). In *Roth* "[w]e . . . held that the determining factor is the nature of the interest involved rather than its weight." Meachum v. Fano, 96 S. Ct. 2532, 2538 (1976).

[25] 408 U.S. at 570.

[26] *Id.* at 572.

[27] *Id.* at 570. The Court specifically rejected the view that the collateral consequences, in terms of reduced job mobility, of the decision not to rehire were enough to implicate due process. *Id.* at 574 n.13.

[28] *Id.* at 571 (emphasis in original).

[29] In Kelley v. Johnson, 425 U.S. 238, 244 (1976), for example, the Court was only willing to assume arguendo that liberty was implicated by hair-length regulation as a condition of police employment. *See also* City of Eastlake v. Forest City Enterprises, 426 U.S. 668, 680-81 (1976) (dissenting opinion, Stevens, J.); Tennessee v. Dunlap, 426 U.S. 312, 316 n.3 (1976).

[30] 424 U.S. 693, *rehearing denied*, 425 U.S. 985 (1976).

[31] 424 U.S. at 694.

the fourteenth amendment.[32] This decision would have created no great surprise in 1876; one hundred years later, however, it can be expected to generate considerable negative response.[33] *Paul* was followed by *Meachum v. Fano*,[34] where, in a six to three decision, the Court held that a state prisoner attacking the procedures surrounding his transfer from a less restrictive to a more restrictive prison asserted no "liberty" interest.[35] Sandwiched between those cases came the five to four decision in *Bishop v. Wood*,[36] which denied that any "property" interest was implicated in the termination of the employment of a nonprobationary public employee.

The analytical framework of these decisions represents an important and acknowledged break with traditions developed over the last half century which appeared to be firmly embedded in our constitutional order. These decisions, therefore, demand a new assessment of the nature of the interests secured by the due process clause. We must disinter long buried history, and examine anew the criteria for giving meaning to the "blind concepts" of "liberty" and "property."[37]

---

[32] *Id.* at 701.

[33] *See, e.g.*, Shapiro, *Mr. Justice Rehnquist: A Preliminary View*, 90 HARV. L. REV. 293, 322-38 (1976); *The Supreme Court, 1975 Term*, 90 HARV. L. REV. 58, 86-104 (1976).

[34] 96 S. Ct. 2532 (1976).

[35] *Id.* at 2538.

[36] 426 U.S. 341 (1976). The Court also rejected a "liberty" claim on the authority of *Roth*. *Id.* at 348.

[37] Fried, *Two Concepts of Interests: Some Reflections On The Supreme Court's Balancing Test*, 76 HARV. L. REV. 755 (1963).

In focusing upon "liberty" and "property," I do not minimize the future importance of giving some content to the word "life." But that is a subject requiring separate treatment. I offer a few preliminary comments here. We are at the beginning of an attempt to form a new public consensus—or rather, a new public philosophy—on the meaning of life and death, a problem forced upon us by developments in modern technology. *See* Steele & Hill, *A Legislative Proposal for a Legal Right to Die*, 12 CRIM. L. BULL. 140 (1976). This development necessarily implicates the guarantee of "life" contained in the due process clause.

The common-law definition of "life" was entirely in accord with the existing medical technology: life ended with failure of heart and breath. The adequacy of this definition raised some questions, particularly in the context of euthanasia. But the necessity for a coherent definition of life has, in our time, become vastly more acute because modern science has invented "life"-prolonging medical devices. A body can be kept "alive"—heart beating, breathing secure—long after cognitive functions have been wholly and irreversibly destroyed. Several states have responded to this phenomenon by redefining death in terms of brain activity. Does the use of the new criterion to justify withdrawal of life-supporting devices deprive a person of "life" within the meaning of the due process clause? It is difficult for me to believe that state law definitions of life should have any role in giving content to that word for purposes of the due process clause. The mind, to say nothing of the spirit, boggles at the notion that a person may, for constitutional purposes, be "alive" in one state but "dead" when moved across a state line. If life-sustaining support can validly be withdrawn from a patient, it is not because that person is not "alive" within the meaning

I

LIBERTY

A. *Historical Origins*

The importance of the due process clause as a restriction on state conduct has rested in large measure upon a spacious conception of the word "liberty." Prior to the Civil War, as Judge Hough noted in his 1918 Irvine Lecture on this subject, there was little evidence that due process "liberty" meant anything more than freedom from personal restraint.[38] This was certainly the common-law understanding of the term. For Blackstone, "liberty"—"the power of locomotion . . . without imprisonment or restraint, unless by due course of law"[39]—was only one of the three "abso-

---

of the fourteenth amendment but because, in the circumstances, the withdrawal is not a deprivation of due process. And this is not the only, indeed, perhaps not even the most important, context in which the issue arises. For some of these devices, such as kidney machines, are scarce resources, and the demand may exceed the supply. To what extent, and under what criteria, are such machines to be used on persons in the condition of Karen Ann Quinlan? *See* Note, *Due Process in the Allocation of Scarce Lifesaving Medical Resources*, 84 YALE L.J. 1734 (1975).

We may yet come to recognize that a grey area exists, where some persons, while not totally dead, are not fully alive either, and that their interests may, in some circumstances, be subordinated to the interests of those whose consciousness is not irreversibly destroyed. This is a frightening thought, one with profound moral and legal implications. But it is a thought, I fear, which we will be unable to avoid as the "new biology" develops ever more elaborate life-sustaining devices. The Court will, in any event, be forced to provide some content for the word "life," something it (unsuccessfully) sought to avoid in the abortion cases. Epstein, *Substantive Due Process By Any Other Name*, 1973 SUP. CT. REV. 159, 167-81. My own view is that whatever the ultimate substantive and procedural resolutions, "life" in the due process clause encompasses the common-law definition. That is clearly the historical understanding, since there could be no other. But I recognize that the Court has forsaken history in other situations where it seemed controlling.

[38] Hough, *Due Process of Law—To-Day*, 32 HARV. L. REV. 218, 222-23 (1918). Generally, this concern with freedom from personal restraint did not include an assessment of the validity of the substantive reasons for the restraint, only the adequacy of the procedure. For an excellent discussion, see Shattuck, *The True Meaning of the Term "Liberty" in Those Clauses In The Federal and State Constitutions Which Protect "Life, Liberty, and Property,"* 4 HARV. L. REV. 365 (1891). This is not to overlook the fact that, at least until 1830, many judges appealed to extra-constitutional theories such as natural law to question the substantive validity of governmental action. Justice Chase's opinion in Calder v. Bull, 3 U.S. (3 Dall.) 386 (1798), is the most famous example. *See also* Terrett v. Taylor, 13 U.S. (9 Cranch) 43 (1815); Fletcher v. Peck, 10 U.S. (6 Cranch) 87 (1810). Although there is some disagreement (*see* Strong, *The Economic Philosophy of Lochner: Emergence, Embrasure and Emasculation*, 15 ARIZ. L. REV. 419-20 (1973)), this mode of thinking does not seem to have been tied to the due process clause, but to general reasoning about the nature of society and government. In any event, from about 1830-1860, this mode of reasoning fell into discard. *See* E. CORWIN, *supra* note 2, at 58-115.

[39] 1 W. BLACKSTONE, COMMENTARIES ON THE LAW OF ENGLAND: OF THE RIGHTS OF PERSONS *134.

lute rights of every Englishman."[40] The others were the right of property and the right of personal security,[41] the latter term, incidentally, including "reputation."[42] The Blackstonian conception of liberty is both purely negative—*i.e.*, freedom from governmental interference—and limited. It is not the equivalent of an all encompassing "right to be let alone";[43] it is a right to be let alone *only* with respect to one's bodily movement.[44] It is the kind of interest, roughly speaking, that common-law courts protected in habeas corpus and false imprisonment actions.

Following the Civil War, the bar, always, as de Tocqueville said, "eminently conservative and anti-democratic,"[45] and enchanted with notions of natural law and Herbert Spenser's Social Darwinian restrictions on state legislation, sought some textual vehicle for imposing limits upon the rapidly increasing state legislation that, in its view, interfered with the "right of property." The bar increasingly seized upon the due process clause, a text appearing in both the federal and state constitutions, and urged that it "might be construed so as to include within [its] scope all civil rights pertaining to the individual."[46] "Liberty," in particular, "seemed an especially convenient vehicle into which to pack all kinds of rights."[47]

The bar triumphed, first in the state courts, then in dissenting opinions in the Supreme Court, and finally in the full Court.[48] *Allgeyer v. Louisiana*[49] explicitly repudiated the proposition that "liberty" embraced "only the right of the citizen to be free from the

---

[40] *Id.* at *128.

[41] *Id.* at *129.

[42] *Id.* at *134. The common law did not conceive of "reputation" as a property interest.

[43] Olmstead v. United States, 277 U.S. 438, 478 (1928) (dissenting opinion, Brandeis, J.).

[44] "Next to personal security, the law of England regards, asserts, and preserves the personal liberty of individuals. This personal liberty consists in the power of locomotion, of changing situation, or removing one's person to whatsoever place one's own inclination may direct; without imprisonment or restraint, unless by due course of law." W. BLACKSTONE, *supra* note 39, at *134.

[45] A. DE TOCQUEVILLE, DEMOCRACY IN AMERICA 285 (Bradley ed. 1953). For an argument that the bar is not much better today, see J. AUERBACH, UNEQUAL JUSTICE: LAWYERS AND SOCIAL CHANGE IN MODERN AMERICA (1976).

[46] Warren, *The New "Liberty" Under The Fourteenth Amendment*, 39 HARV. L. REV. 431, 439 (1926). Invocation of the general language of the due process clause simply gave textual articulation to a practice that, at one time, was more frankly extraconstitutional.

[47] *Id. See also* note 38 and accompanying text *supra*.

[48] On the influential role of the bar, see B. TWISS, LAWYERS AND THE CONSTITUTION 18-173 (1942).

[49] 165 U.S. 578 (1897).

mere physical restraint of his person."[50] The Court began in earnest the famous "gradual process of judicial inclusion and exclusion,"[51] but it was an entirely one-way process. Decision after decision sustained a broad, inclusive conception of the word "liberty."[52] In 1916, in *Butler v. Perry*,[53] Mr. Justice McReynolds said that fourteenth amendment "liberty" "was intended to preserve and protect fundamental rights long recognized under the common law system."[54] *Meyer v. Nebraska*,[55] decided in 1923, summarized the development. Once again speaking through Justice McReynolds, the Court stated that "liberty"

> denotes not merely freedom from bodily restraint but also the right of the individual to contract, to engage in any of the common occupations of life, to acquire useful knowledge, to marry, establish a home and bring up children, to worship God according to the dictates of his own conscience, and generally *to enjoy those privileges long recognized at common law as essential to the orderly pursuit of happiness by free men*.[56]

This definition assumes that the due process clause itself creates rights; freedom of contract, for example, becomes a right of constitutional, rather than state law, origin. And although this approach does not, as a matter of logic, exclude the possibility of still additional liberties being created by state law, the broad sweep of the liberties created by the due process clause itself left that possibility a dormant one.[57]

Accordingly, for nearly a half century, controversy has focused upon the adequacy of the justification offered by the state for interference with admitted constitutionally created liberties, and not on the threshold issue of whether any "liberties" were threatened by the state action. For example, none of *Roe v. Wade*'s[58] vigorous critics had any doubt that a woman's freedom to choose an abortion at least *implicates* a constitutional liberty. "Of course" it does, writes Professor Ely, as does "anyone's freedom to do what he

---

[50] *Id.* at 589.

[51] Davidson v. New Orleans, 96 U.S. 97, 104 (1878).

[52] The history is well told in Warren, *supra* note 46, at 454-64.

[53] 240 U.S. 328 (1916).

[54] *Id.* at 333.

[55] 262 U.S. 390 (1923).

[56] *Id.* at 399 (emphasis added).

[57] As we shall see, the expanded definition of "liberty" swallowed up "property" and made inevitable the application of the specifics of most of the bill of rights to the states. *See* text accompanying notes 187-201 *infra*.

[58] 410 U.S. 113 (1973).

wants."[59] So viewed, the "liberty" of the due process clause had been transformed over time from a specific freedom from interference with locomotion to a general right of private autonomy. In that process the language and theory of the opinions seemed to absorb at the very least all the Blackstonian rights of personal security, including reputation.[60] Those rights, protected by the common law from private interference, were transformed into liberties protected from governmental interference—unless the government adequately justified its actions, a question going to the merits and not to a threshold inquiry into the applicability of the due process clause.[61] In so summarizing the cases I do not wish to fall into what, for these purposes, is an irrelevant semantic argument over whether this "liberty" is a wholly negative conception—a right to be let alone.[62] But I think that such a conception is generally accurate. For, in the main at least, this conception did not embrace affirmative claims for governmental money, property, or employment.[63]

B. *A Note on Language*

The ascription of a content to "liberty" beyond that of simple freedom from physical restraint was a necessary predicate for the concept of due process as a restraint upon the substance of legislation. That result is, I recognize, far too thoroughly embedded in our constitutional jurisprudence to be now called into question. But for me, giving a substantive content to "liberty" raises most acutely the question of whether the language of the Constitution has much to do with constitutional law. One has the impression that many political scientists and some lawyers do not think so. Leonard Levy puts this thesis sharply: "Justices who look to the

[59] Ely, *supra* note 11, at 935. For a philosophical discussion of the idea, and references to sources, see J. RAWLS, A THEORY OF JUSTICE § 32 (1971). Undoubtedly because of myopic vision, I do not see that discussion at the level of philosophy is of much relevance here.

[60] The decisions in this regard had absorbed the protection granted citizens by the Massachusetts Body of Liberties of 1641, which provided that "no mans honour or good name shall be stayned" by government. SOURCES OF OUR LIBERTIES 148 (R. Perry ed. 1959).

[61] *See* Monaghan, *Constitutional Adjudication: The Who and When*, 82 YALE L.J. 1363, 1366 n.18 (1973).

[62] *See* I. BERLIN, FOUR ESSAYS ON LIBERTY xxxvii-lxii, 122-72 (1969). *See also* L. HAND, THE SPIRIT OF LIBERTY 144-54 (3d ed. 1960).

[63] One must be careful not to overplay a negative-positive distinction. For example, restrictions on government employment are now assumed at least to implicate some "liberty" interest even though, on the state level, they were generally analyzed in equal protection terms. *Compare* Powell, *The Right to Work for the State*, 16 COLUM. L. REV. 99 (1916), *with* cases cited in note 7 *supra*.

Constitution for more than a puzzling, if majestic, phrase might just as well turn to the comic strips for all the guidance they will find on how to decide most of the great cases that involve national public policy . . . ."[64] But most lawyers are far from comfortable with this conception, since, in the end, it denies any distinction between law and politics.[65] The absence of such a distinction, in turn, raises grave questions as to the legitimacy of judicial review in a democracy.[66]

Any serious effort to mark some boundary between law and politics must take into account the constitutional text. A textual exegesis at least confines judgment—the judicial construction must be capable of being related to the text and to the structure it creates.[67] This, of course, still leaves a wide margin for judicial activity. At the minimum it permits application of the Constitution to new situations involving "the sorts of evils the framers meant to combat and . . . their twentieth century counterparts."[68] But even this premise does not justify giving a *substantive* content to "liberty," for the evils that the clause was designed to prevent involved interferences with the freedom from personal restraint. Nor does the so-called "two-clause" theory provide a satisfactory justification. Professor Corwin formulates that theory in these terms:

> [I]t will be generally found that words which refer to governing institutions, like "jury," "legislature," "election," have been given their strictly historical meaning, while words defining the subject-matter of power or of rights like "commerce," "liberty," "property," have been deliberately moulded to the views of contemporary society.[69]

This "two-clause" theory has won significant judicial and academic acceptance as an accurate representation of the Framers' intent.[70]

---

[64] L. Levy, American Constitutional Law 1 (1966).

[65] Wechsler, *The Courts And The Constitution*, 65 Colum. L. Rev. 1001, 1009-10 (1965).

[66] *See* Monaghan, *supra* note 61, at 1363 n.3. *See also* Rehnquist, *The Notion of a Living Constitution*, 54 Texas L. Rev. 693 (1976).

[67] *See generally* Ely, *supra* note 11, at 928-37. On the relationship between text and structure, see Monaghan, *supra* note 5, at 13 n.72 (commenting on C. Black, Structure and Relationship in Constitutional Law (1969)).

[68] Ely, *supra* note 11, at 929. *See* Gaffney, *History and Legal Interpretation: The Early Distortion of the Fourteenth Amendment by the Gilded Age Court*, 25 Cath. U.L. Rev. 207, 215-16 (1976).

[69] Corwin, *Judicial Review in Action*, 74 U. Pa. L. Rev. 639, 659-60 (1926), *quoted in* P. Brest, The Process of Constitutional Decision-making 117 (1975).

[70] *See, e.g.*, Williams v. Florida, 399 U.S. 78, 125 n.11 (1970) (dissenting opinion, Harlan, J.); P. Brest, *supra* note 69, at 117-18. *See also* Board of Regents v. Roth, 408 U.S. 564, 571-72 (1972).

But in the area of substantive due process, it ignores the crucial fact that the broad definition of "liberty" (and therefore of due process) is wholly a *judicial* creation. Charles Curtis writes:

> Take the phrase "due process of law." It is perhaps the prime example of a large generality in our Constitution which has gathered meaning from experience. But who made it a large generality? Not they. We did. When they put it into the Fifth Amendment, its meaning was as fixed and definite as the common law could make a phrase. . . . We turned the legal phrase into common speech and raised its meaning into the similitude of justice itself.[71]

If one agrees with Professor Corwin, that the "debates in Congress on the [fourteenth] amendment leave one in little doubt of the intention of its framers to nationalize civil liberty in the United States"[72] through the privileges and immunities clause, then ascribing a substantive content to due process is perhaps a defensible way of correcting the original sin of the *Slaughter-House Cases*.[73] But if one finds the opposite conclusion far more probable,[74] then expanding "liberty" beyond freedom from personal restraint poses one of the most unsettling problems in constitutional theory. How can this extension be justified as a legitimate mode of constitutional interpretation?[75] I do not know. But, like others,[76] I must accept reality: this judicial expansion of "liberty" is now far too central a part of our constitutional order to admit of reassessment. Indeed, loosened from the fetters of original intent and fortified by judicial precedent, I readily accept *Roth*'s proposition that "[i]n a Constitution for a free people, there can be no doubt that the meaning of 'liberty' must be broad indeed."[77]

C. *Substantive Due Process As Equal Protection*

Substantive due process fell on hard times in the New Deal days, but not because of any general dissatisfaction with an expansive concept of "liberty." The objections were, rather, that the courts

---

[71] Curtis, *Review and Majority Rule*, in SUPREME COURT AND SUPREME LAW 177 (E. Cahn ed. 1954).

[72] E. CORWIN, *supra* note 2, at 118.

[73] 83 U.S. (16 Wall.) 36 (1872).

[74] *See, e.g.*, Bickel, *Citizenship In The American Constitution*, 15 ARIZ. L. REV. 369, 373-80 (1973).

[75] *See* G. GUNTHER, *supra* note 4, at 567.

[76] *See, e.g.*, Whitney v. California, 274 U.S. 357, 373 (1927) (concurring opinion, Brandeis, J.); P. BREST, *supra* note 69, at 169-70.

[77] 408 U.S. at 572.

continually rejected completely rational state justifications for legislation that interfered with an admitted liberty to engage in free enterprise.[78] The Warren Court's invocation of the equal protection clause as the dominant textual vehicle for expressing its constitutional doctrines was, of course, partly influenced by the stench then surrounding the whole concept of substantive due process.[79] But there was more to it than that. The equal protection clause possessed a unique appeal because egalitarian notions underlay so much of the Warren Court's thinking about the nature of both the substantive and procedural restraints imposed by the Constitution.[80]

Once freed from its historical moorings in race discrimination,[81] the language of the equal protection clause apparently obviates any threshold need for inquiry into the nature of the interests it protects. Equal protection analysis traditionally, and still dominantly, focuses on the adequacy of the justification offered for state classifications affecting (principally) state-created interests.[82] The common understanding is that the acceptability of the means-end connection is ascertained by federal standards alone.[83]

---

[78] For representative comments see the articles collected in ASSOCIATION OF AMERICAN LAW SCHOOLS, 2 SELECTED ESSAYS ON CONSTITUTIONAL LAW 693-732 (1938). *See also* McCloskey, *Economic Due Process and the Supreme Court: An Exhumation and Reburial*, 1962 SUP. CT. REV. 34. It is useful to compare these articles with the earlier attacks on viewing "liberty" as dealing with anything beyond freedom from personal restraint. *See, e.g.*, Shattuck, *supra* note 38; Warren, *supra* note 46, at 439-40.

[79] But the Warren Court invoked due process when that was the only avenue to reach the desired result. *See, e.g.*, Aptheker v. Secretary of State, 378 U.S. 500 (1964); Bolling v. Sharpe, 347 U.S. 497 (1954).

[80] A. COX, THE WARREN COURT 5-8 (1968). *See also* P. KURLAND, POLITICS, THE CONSTITUTION, AND THE WARREN COURT 98-169 (1970). The language of the moribund privileges and immunities clause could have provided the doctrinal foundation for the developments associated with due process and equal protection. But the clause long ago became an "idle provision." *Compare* McGovney, *Privileges or Immunities Clause, Fourteenth Amendment*, 4 IOWA L. BULL. 219, 220-21 (1918), *with* Kurland, *The Privileges or Immunities Clause: "Its Hour Come Round at Last"?*, 1972 WASH. U.L.Q. 405.

[81] Slaughter-House Cases, 83 U.S. (16 Wall.) 36 (1872). The Court noted: "We doubt very much whether any action of a State not directed by way of discrimination against the negroes as a class, or on account of their race, will ever be held to come within the purview of this provision." *Id.* at 81.

[82] For recent examples of the traditional analysis, see Massachusetts Bd. of Retirement v. Murgia, 96 S. Ct. 2562 (1976); City of New Orleans v. Duke, 96 S. Ct. 2513 (1976); City of Charlotte v. Local 660, Int'l Ass'n of Firefighters, 426 U.S. 283 (1976), *But see* G. GUNTHER, *supra* note 4, at 657-65. State interference with interests created by federal law can more comfortably be analyzed in preemption terms; a state's interference with the law of another state may be analyzed in terms of the full faith and credit and commerce clauses. *See* Monaghan, *supra* note 5, at 14 n.78, 17.

[83] *See* Massachusetts Bd. of Retirement v. Murgia, 96 S. Ct. 2562, 2569-70 (1976) (cases cited in dissenting opinion of Marshall, J.).

The Warren Court's most enduring equal protection legacy was the addition of a "second tier" to the traditional analysis, a tier where a rigorous justification for challenged state classifications was demanded.[84] Whatever its merits, the second tier's "fundamental right-fundamental interest" strand did require an analysis of the interests protected by the clause, and raised some interesting questions about the relationship between state and federal law.

"Fundamental rights" were, of course, not conceived of as interests having their source in state law. The sole office of the equal protection clause in this context was to trigger strict scrutiny. But whatever the ideological appeal in invoking the mesmerizing language of equal protection, there was, analytically, no necessity for doing so. If the right, such as freedom of speech, constituted part of the "liberty" protected by the due process clause, inadequately justified discriminatory state law would, as Mr. Justice Harlan noted, violate due process.[85] If the federal right bound the states prior to the adoption of the fourteenth amendment, as did the right to travel, any conflicting state law would be displaced by the supremacy clause without the need for an intermediate reference to the fourteenth amendment.[86]

The "fundamental interest" strand is more complex. The Court has now firmly shut the door on efforts to subject state legislation affecting housing, welfare, education, and so forth, to the rigors of "strict scrutiny."[87] Our concern here is with the nature of the rejected interests. Perceptive commentators assert that the claims made were not viewed as involving independent constitutional "rights," such as freedom of speech or religion, but rather as implicating fundamental "interests."[88] To a considerable extent this framework imposes a retrospective unity on untidy data. The claims were advanced in different forms. Sometimes they were asserted to be "rights" having the same status as the textually specified ones.[89] Sometimes they were viewed somewhat less grandly as adopted stepchildren of acknowledged constitutional

[84] The second tier legacy is still with us. *See, e.g.*, Massachusetts Bd. of Retirement v. Murgia, 96 S. Ct. 2562, 2566-67 (1976); Mathews v. Lucas, 96 S. Ct. 2755, 2761-63 (1976).

[85] Shapiro v. Thompson, 394 U.S. 618, 659 (1969) (dissenting opinion, Harlan, J.).

[86] Crandall v. Nevada, 73 U.S. (6 Wall.) 35 (1867).

[87] San Antonio Ind. Sch. Dist. v. Rodriguez, 411 U.S. 1 (1973), and Dandridge v. Williams, 397 U.S. 471 (1970), are the decisive precedents.

[88] *See, e.g.*, G. GUNTHER, *supra* note 4, at 659; P. BREST, *supra* note 69, at 805, 809.

[89] *E.g.*, Harper v. Virginia Bd. of Elections, 383 U.S. 663 (1966) (voting in state election).

rights.[90] And sometimes the claims were made in terms of constitutionally created fundamental "interests."[91] Interestingly, no one seems to have argued that although the "fundamental" character of various "interests" is determined by federal standards, those interests must have been initially created by state law.[92] The Court has now promised not to invent new nontextually oriented or nonstructurally based rights,[93] and so the Court is not likely to cast further light on the nature of these "fundamental interests" in the near future.[94]

Many recent equal protection cases have arisen from controversies involving voting in state elections.[95] The constitutional framework seemed to treat the right to vote in state elections as one created by state law, with various constitutional amendments prohibiting specified types of discriminations.[96] But despite Mr. Justice Harlan's protestations,[97] the equal protection clause has been used as a general warrant for invalidating restrictions not covered by the specific voting amendments.[98] This has generated several interesting theories which wholly or partially free voting in state elections from its moorings in state law. Mr. Justice Stewart asserts that the equal protection clause itself creates "the substan-

---

[90] San Antonio Ind. Sch. Dist. v. Rodriguez, 411 U.S. 1, 35 (1973).

[91] Lindsey v. Normet, 405 U.S. 56, 73 (1972).

[92] Professor Michelman's "minimum protection for just wants" theory seems to me to proceed on the premise that these wants are not only to be determined by wholly federal standards but indeed have their origin in the fourteenth amendment. Michelman, *The Supreme Court, 1968 Term—Foreword: On Protecting the Poor Through The Fourteenth Amendment*, 83 HARV. L. REV. 7 (1969).

[93] San Antonio Ind. Sch. Dist. v. Rodriguez, 411 U.S. 1, 33 (1973). *Rodriguez*, of course, follows Roe v. Wade, 410 U.S. 113 (1973). *See also* Massachusetts Bd. of Retirement v. Murgia, 96 S. Ct. 2562, 2566 (1976).

[94] Fundamental interest analysis is not entirely a matter of historical interest. It appears again in somewhat modified form in Mr. Justice Marshall's famous "sliding scale" approach to equal protection analysis, which requires judicial assessment of the importance of the interest affected by state actions. *See, e.g.*, Massachusetts Bd. of Retirement v. Murgia, 96 S. Ct. 2562, 2568-73 (1976) (dissenting opinion, Marshall, J.). *See also* Coven & Fersh, *Equal Protection, Social Welfare Litigation, and the Burger Court*, 51 NOTRE DAME LAW. 873 (1976). At one point or another, a majority of the Court's present members had apparently endorsed this test in one form or another. *See* G. GUNTHER, *supra* note 4, at 660-61 & n.9. But recent equal protection clause cases pay it no heed. *See, e.g.*, cases cited in note 82 *supra*.

[95] For a comprehensive collection of materials, see T. EMERSON, D. HABER & N. DORSEN, POLITICAL AND CIVIL RIGHTS IN THE UNITED STATES 1481-1606 (3d ed. 1967).

[96] *See, e.g.*, Pope v. Williams, 193 U.S. 621, 632 (1904). The Court stated: "The privilege to vote in any State is not given by the Federal Constitution, or by any of its amendments."

[97] *See* Oregon v. Mitchell, 400 U.S. 112, 152 (1970) (Harlan, J., dissenting in part).

[98] *E.g.*, Kramer v. Union Free Sch. Dist., 395 U.S. 621 (1969).

tive right to participate on an equal basis with other qualified voters whenever the State has adopted an electoral process"[99] of representation, a theory bred from an interesting mating of federal and state laws. Several decisions refer to voting as a "fundamental right," without indicating how such a right can properly be inferred from the text, or from the structure and relationships created by the Constitution.[100] In any event, a "fundamental right" analysis makes reference to the equal protection clause unnecessary, as do the occasional suggestions that the right to vote is a "penumbral" aspect of the constitutional guarantee of freedom of speech.[101]

State law, therefore, plays no significant role in the interpretation of the equal protection clause: even where interests are created by state law, their importance for equal protection purposes and the adequacy of the justifications for the state law are assessed by federal standards. This may have importance in the future because the equal protection clause, unlike due process, does not require an initial showing that "life, liberty, or property" is at stake.

D. *The Narrowing of Liberty: "The Gradual Process of . . . Exclusion"*

After three decades, it is once again fashionable to invoke the language of substantive due process.[102] And, following *Goldberg v. Kelly*,[103] there has been an enormous explosion of litigation raising issues of procedural due process.[104] It comes as no real surprise, therefore, that judicial effort to limit the reach of the due process clause should, in part, find expression in limiting conceptions as to the nature of the "liberty" the clause protects.

Board of Regents v. Roth[105] began that process in earnest. A nontenured teacher asserted that the lack of procedural safeguards governing the decision whether to rehire him violated due process. The Court began its examination of his claim by quoting *Meyer*'s broad definition of liberty,[106] and added grandly that "[i]n a Con-

---

[99] San Antonio Ind. Sch. Dist. v. Rodriguez, 411 U.S. 1, 59 n.2 (1973) (concurring opinion, Stewart, J.). *See also id.* at 34 n.74 (opinion of the Court).

[100] *But see* Pope v. Williams, 193 U.S. 621, 632 (1904).

[101] *See* T. EMERSON, D. HABER & N. DORSEN, *supra* note 95, at 848-49. *See also* Buckley v. Valeo, 424 U.S. 1 (1976).

[102] *See* note 8 and accompanying text *supra*.

[103] 397 U.S. 254 (1970).

[104] For a summary of most of the major Supreme Court cases, see K. DAVIS, ADMINISTRATIVE LAW OF THE 1970's 241-76 (1976).

[105] 408 U.S. 564 (1972).

[106] *See* notes 55-57 and accompanying text *supra*.

stitution for a free people, there can be no doubt that the meaning of 'liberty' must be broad indeed."[107] Broad—but, as previously noted, not "infinite."[108] The gradual process of exclusion had begun. *Roth* rejected the contention that, standing alone, termination of a specific public employment interfered with either "liberty" or "property." As to the "liberty" claim, said the Court, no stigma had been imposed by the decision not to rehire, nor had the Regents "invoke[d] any regulations to bar the respondent from all other public employment in state universities."[109] The Court concluded that "[i]t stretches the concept too far to suggest that a person is deprived of 'liberty' when he simply is not rehired in one job but remains as free as before to seek another."[110]

Roth permits the states to operate a probationary system of public employment, free from claims that decisions made in the day-to-day operation of the system constitute deprivations of the due process rights of individuals affected by those decisions. That result is certainly defensible. Judgments concerning retention of probationary employees are often highly personal and subjective, and the imposition, in the name of due process, of an adversary procedure into that retention process is a dubious proposition.[111] But the road taken by the Court opens to broader and more difficult vistas. *Roth*'s logic necessarily applies to substantive due process even though it is a procedural due process case in form. Since the probationary employee lacks a "liberty" or "property" interest, there is no basis under the due process clause for a substantive due process requirement that a state's conduct meet even the "base line requirement of rationality." This problem, perhaps, is not acute when a state is involved, given the existence of the equal protection clause. But what of probationary employees of the national government? The textual basis for imposition of the rational basis standard in such a case is not apparent.[112]

---

[107] 408 U.S. at 572.

[108] *Id*. at 570.

[109] *Id*. at 573.

[110] *Id*. at 575. *Roth* may profitably be compared with Greene v. McElroy, 360 U.S. 474 (1959), where the Court stated: "The right to hold specific private employment . . . [is] 'liberty' and 'property' . . . ." *Id*. at 492.

[111] This is an area where, in part, we may prefer to operate without rules and formal structures. *See generally* L. JAFFE, JUDICIAL CONTROL OF ADMINISTRATIVE ACTION 490-94 (1965). *See also* Meachum v. Fano, 96 S. Ct. 2532, 2540 (1976).

[112] To say that there is an independent substantive right (or liberty) to be free from "arbitrary" governmental action is unconvincing. One could just as readily assert that there is an independent substantive right (or liberty) to be free from unfair procedures. More importantly, this argument confuses the scope of review under the due process clause with

Roth's importance, however, should not be overstated. *Roth*'s companion case, *Perry v. Sindermann*,[113] emphasized that public employees are deprived of "liberty" if discharged for reasons that would violate *specific* constitutional guarantees, such as freedom of speech, a position from which the Court has not wavered.[114] More importantly, *Hampton v. Mow Sun Wong*,[115] following the *Roth* caveat, held the due process clause to be applicable to a civil service regulation barring aliens from access to a class of public employment. Unfortunately, the Court has not adequately explained why the discharge of a specific public employee does not activate the due process clause, while "a rule which deprives a discrete class of persons of an interest in liberty on a wholesale basis" does.[116] One is tempted to say that the liberty protected by due process operates only at wholesale, not retail.[117] But even that comfortable generalization would fail as a description so long as the holding of *Greene v. McElroy*,[118] that "the right to hold *specific* private employment . . . free from unreasonable governmental interference comes within the 'liberty' and 'property' concepts of [due process]," survives *Roth*.[119] In any event, in the public sector the Court perceives a material distinction between the right to seek employment and the right to hold a job forever.[120]

Liberty, then, although not confined simply to a negative freedom from personal restraint, is not synonymous with the freedom to do everything one wishes, at least where the wish is that the government continue to provide one with money, property, or employment. Still, *Roth* raised no serious question about *Butler v.*

---

the initial question of whether the clause is applicable at all. The Court is, however, apparently unconcerned with all of this. *See, e.g.*, Mathews v. De Castro, 97 S. Ct. 431, 432 n.1 (1976).

[113] 408 U.S. 593 (1972).

[114] *See, e.g.*, Elrod v. Burns, 96 S. Ct. 2673 (1976); Paul v. Davis, 424 U.S. 693, 710 n.5, *rehearing denied*, 425 U.S. 985 (1976).

[115] 426 U.S. 88 (1976).

[116] *Id.* at 102-03. *See also* Examining Bd. v. Flores de Otero, 426 U.S. 572 (1976). In Mathews v. Diaz, 426 U.S. 67 (1976), the Court unanimously upheld the exclusion of certain aliens from supplemental medical insurance under medicare. The Court assumed, without discussion, that an interest sufficient to trigger due process scrutiny was involved.

[117] Board of Regents v. Roth, 408 U.S. 564, 573-74 (1972), asserts that in such cases the "injury" is greater. But once the focus shifts from the "importance" of the individual interest to the "nature" of that interest it is not clear why the extent of the injury matters.

[118] 360 U.S. 474 (1959).

[119] *Id.* at 492 (emphasis added). *See also* Hampton v. Mow Sun Wong, 426 U.S. 88, 120 (1976) (dissenting opinion, Rehnquist, J.).

[120] *See* text accompanying notes 91-100 *supra*.

Perry's[121] conception of "liberty" as a negative "right to be let alone," an idea embracing all the interests in personal security (including freedom from defamation), which had been protected from private interference by the common-law courts. Continued governmental employment, after all, hardly constituted one of those "fundamental rights long recognized under the common law system."[122] But other decisions have begun to weaken *Butler*. In *Kelley v. Johnson*,[123] the Court, speaking through Mr. Justice Rehnquist, only assumed arguendo that "liberty" was implicated by a requirement that a policeman's hair be trimmed as a condition of his employment.[124] Then *Paul v. Davis*[125] was decided.

E. *Paul v. Davis*

In *Paul* the plaintiff complained that a circular sent by local police officials to stores during the Christmas season defamed him by describing him as an "active shoplifter." The plaintiff asserted that this conduct denied him procedural due process because he had not been given notice and a hearing before the circular was sent. The court of appeals upheld the claim, relying upon the Supreme Court's decisions in *Roth* and *Wisconsin v. Constantineau*[126] to support the proposition that state defamation of a private person implicated a constitutional "liberty." In *Constantineau* the Court had invalidated on due process grounds a state statute that allowed a sheriff to label publicly an individual an alcoholic by posting his name in a public place, without giving him prior notice and a hearing. The Court noted that the challenged procedure denied the individual more than just the opportunity to purchase alcoholic beverages within city limits: the posting was an act of defama-

[121] 240 U.S. 328 (1916).

[122] Massachusetts Bd. of Retirement v. Murgia, 96 S. Ct. 2562 (1976).

[123] 425 U.S. 238 (1976).

[124] *Id.* at 244. Since the Court was not required to pass on the question, there was no discussion of whether such a requirement as a condition of employment would at least implicate fundamental rights long recognized by the common law, at least when the common law is read with the doctrine of unconstitutional conditions. If *Kelley* really does not involve a protected interest, there will be some anomalies for the layman. Hair-length regulations in public schools may still be reviewed as an arbitrary restriction on the student's "property" right to attend school. *See* Goss v. Lopez, 419 U.S. 565 (1975). *Cf.* New Rider v. Board of Educ., 414 U.S. 1097 (1973), *denying cert. to* 480 F.2d 693 (10th Cir.) (dissenting opinion, Douglas, J.) (suggesting hair-length regulations violate students' first amendment right of free speech).

[125] 424 U.S. 693, *rehearing denied*, 425 U.S. 985 (1976).

[126] 400 U.S. 433 (1971).

tion.[127] In language subsequently quoted with approval in *Roth*,[128] the Court said that "[w]here a person's good name, reputation, honor, or integrity is at stake because of what the government is doing to him, notice and an opportunity to be heard are essential."[129]

But in *Paul*, the Court characterized this same language as ambiguous and supportive of the respondent's claim only if "read that way."[130] The majority then proceeded to distinguish a long line of decisions which had recognized the standing of a plaintiff to complain about governmental defamation. The Court concluded that in all those cases the defamation standing alone was insufficient to implicate a liberty interest; instead, all involved an interference with some specific constitutional guarantee *or with some other "more tangible" interest created by state law*. The Court cavalierly distinguished *Constantineau* by noting that the state defamation there involved—posting by the sheriff—had the legal effect of cutting off the plaintiff's prior state-created right to buy liquor, a factor which, the Court failed to add, played an obviously trivial role in the decision of that case.[131] The Court's re-rationalization of the earlier cases is wholly startling to anyone familiar with those precedents. In many ways I find this *Paul*'s most disturbing aspect. Fair treatment by the Court of its own precedents is an indispensable condition of judicial legitimacy.

Taken at face value, *Paul* would radically reorient thinking about the nature of the "liberty" protected by the due process clause. The case's rationale would confine the *federal content* of "liberty" to specific constitutional guarantees and to the *Roe* right of privacy, and, perhaps, to the Framers' understanding of liberty as freedom from personal restraint.[132] Otherwise, interests "attain this constitutional status [as liberty] by virtue of the fact that they

---

[127] *Id.* at 435-36. It had generally been assumed as the clearest case that a plaintiff had standing to complain of governmental action if the wrong would have amounted to a tort if committed by a private person. Indeed, defamation was cited in the leading work as a prototypical example. *See* P. BATOR, P. MISHKIN, D. SHAPIRO, & H. WECHSLER, HART & WECHSLER'S THE FEDERAL COURTS AND THE FEDERAL SYSTEM 154 (2d ed. 1973) [hereinafter cited as HART & WECHSLER]. Presumably, that line of authority remains intact, so long as a constitutionally protected right or an independent "tangible" interest is at stake.

[128] 408 U.S. at 573. *See also* Goss v. Lopez, 419 U.S. 565, 574-75 (1975).

[129] 400 U.S. at 437.

[130] 424 U.S. at 708. *But see* Codd v. Velger, 45 U.S.L.W. 4175, (U.S. Feb. 27, 1977) (apparently preserving *Roth* holding).

[131] *Id.* at 707. For additional criticism, see Shapiro, *supra* note 33, at 326; *The Supreme Court, 1975 Term*, 90 HARV. L. REV. 58, 93 n.44 (1976).

[132] 424 U.S. at 710 n.5 (bill of rights); *id.* at 712-13 (privacy).

have been initially recognized and protected by state law,"[133] and it is only state conduct "officially removing the interest from the recognition and protection previously afforded by the State, which [is] sufficient to invoke [due process] procedural guarantees."[134] This language suggests that any state conduct *imposing a new legal disability* on any prior freedom (including a presumably general right to be let alone) would implicate "liberty" in the constitutional sense. For instance, under this new theory, freedom of contract claims would still implicate due process liberty but under a different rationale. Heretofore, that freedom had been viewed as part of the "liberty" independently created by the due process clause. Under *Paul*, however, a state action interfering with that liberty could be challenged only if a new state-imposed disability "officially remov[ed] the interest from the recognition and protection previously afforded"[135] it by state law. But standing alone, defamation does not qualify as such a "liberty" because the victim of the defamation suffers no additional legal disabilities.[136] The plaintiff in *Paul* could vote, drive his vehicle, and buy liquor—all just as before the defamatory act.[137]

Paul's rule might also exclude claims by victims of physical assault by state officers, since the victim labors under no new legal disabilities. There is the possibility that the detention necessary for the assault will be viewed as an interference with the historical Blackstonian definition of "liberty" as freedom from personal restraint. But even if the detention is held to implicate "liberty," can a

---

[133] *Id.* at 710.

[134] *Id.* at 711. Of course, the liberty interest could be created by federal statutory or decisional law.

[135] *Id.* In theory the challenge would be available only to those who had the right before the challenged restriction came into effect. Thus, children born after a restriction became effective could not claim an interference with their liberty.

[136] The Court argued that:

> Kentucky law does not extend to respondent any legal guarantee of present enjoyment of reputation which has been altered as a result of petitioners' actions. Rather his interest in reputation is simply one of a number which the State may protect against injury by virtue of its tort law, providing a forum for vindication of those interests by means of damages actions. And any harm or injury to that interest . . . [has not] worked any change of respondent's status as theretofore recognized under the State's laws.

Id. at 711-12. This is not well put by the Court. I think that state libel law is a "guarantee of present enjoyment of reputation," the unjustified invasion of which results in tort damages. And I do not see that this is any less true simply because there is no "change of respondent's status"—at least in the Court's sense that the respondent suffered no new legal disabilities. The real explanation for the result is in the last sentence of the quotation.

[137] *See also* Sullivan v. Brown, 544 F.2d 279, 283-84 (6th Cir. 1976); Edelberg v. Illinois Racing Bd., 540 F.2d 279, 285 (7th Cir. 1976).

court then award damages for the accompanying assault? If so, the assault damages are parasitic in character, and it is hardly satisfying to rationalize their award on these terms. Long ago, a noted commentator observed that "[t]he treatment of any element of damage as a parasitic factor belongs essentially to a transitory stage of legal evolution. A factor which is to-day recognized as parasitic will, forsooth, to-morrow be recognized as an independent basis of liability."[138] An alternative theory—that the assault constitutes the imposition of punishment without trial[139] and therefore violates a specific constitutional right—is open to the objection that such reasoning rests on a patent fiction. Moreover, such reasoning inadequately distinguishes *Paul*, since defamation could just as easily be characterized as punishment without trial.

However read, *Paul*'s difficulties are deep ones. Even if the Court was free to view the question before it as an open one, it was surely not compelled to reject freedom from defamation as a protected interest. And, in a "Constitution for a free people," it is an unsettling conception of "liberty" that protects an individual against state interference with his access to liquor but not with his reputation in the community.[140] To the extent that this is an area for judicial exercise of the "sovereign prerogative of choice,"[141] the Court's choice seems to cut sharply against the grain of our political-constitutional order with its central emphasis on individual dignity. One does not need the authority of Blackstone for the proposition that without one's reputation "it is impossible to have the perfect enjoyment of any other advantage or right."[142] Moreover, the Court's reasoning ignores the social nature of human personality. For, as Isaiah Berlin observed in a famous essay on the meaning of "liberty," "am I not what I am, to some degree, in virtue of what others think and feel me to be?"[143] Finally, and most importantly, the Court's theory ignores the spiritual character of human personality. Defamation is a serious

[138] T. STREET, 1 THE FOUNDATIONS OF LEGAL LIABILITY 470 (1906).

[139] Screws v. United States, 325 U.S. 91 (1945).

[140] It may well be that a state could constitutionally abolish all defamation actions in suits between private parties. It does not follow that a state which has taken such a step could then itself engage in defamation without implicating fourteenth amendment values.

[141] O. HOLMES, *Law in Science and Science in Law*, in COLLECTED LEGAL PAPERS 210, 239 (1920).

[142] W. BLACKSTONE, *supra* note 39, at *134. For the effect of the defamation at issue in the *Paul* case on the plaintiff, see *The Supreme Court, 1975 Term*, 90 HARV. L. REV. 100-01 n.85 (1976), in which Davis is quoted as stating: "Now, five years later . . . I am broke, without employment, emotionally sick and in a state of anxiety."

[143] I. BERLIN, FOUR ESSAYS ON LIBERTY 155 (1969).

assault upon an individual's sense of "self-identity," and has from ancient times been viewed as "psychic mayhem."[144] Accordingly, the Court's conclusion that such an assault implicates no constitutionally protected interest stands wholly at odds with our ethical, political, and constitutional assumption about the worth of each individual.

Mr. Justice Rehnquist's opinion does more than repudiate the long-standing tradition of an expansive reading of the word "liberty" as a matter of federal law. The opinion seems to have completely reversed the logic of *Butler*,[145] and instead to have proceeded from the premise that if the challenged conduct would constitute a common-law tort by a private person, it cannot constitute an interference with the "liberty" protected by the fourteenth amendment. Thus, the more reprehensible and subject to legal redress the conduct, the freer the state is to engage in it—at least until that conduct bumps up against some specific constitutional guarantee or the hodge-podge right of privacy. Indeed, unless those latter rights are implicated, the state need not even comply with the base line requirement of rationality, until, that is, the state's conduct imposes some new legal disability, however trivial.

Mr. Justice Rehnquist begins his opinion by observing that if Paul's complaint had been made against a private party there "would have [been] nothing more than a claim for defamation under state law."[146] He then frames the central issue in the case as whether the due process clause "should *ex proprio vigore* extend to him [the plaintiff] a right to be free of injury wherever the State may be characterized as the tortfeasor."[147] To state the thesis, he argues, is enough to condemn it, for it "would make of the Fourteenth Amendment a font of tort law to be superimposed upon whatever systems may already be administered by the States."[148] The thrust of Justice Rehnquist's concern is unclear. He seems to assume that the tortious character of the state official's conduct, if proved, would of necessity *establish* a constitutional violation. Thus, he writes: "Respondent's construction would seem almost necessarily to result in every legally cognizable [state-inflicted] injury . . .

---

[144] Cahn, *Jurisprudence*, 30 N.Y.U. L. Rev. 150, 158 (1955). The meaning of personal identity is a central concern of much modern philosophical and psychological writing. *See, e.g.*, Note, *The Limits of State Intervention: Personal Identity and Ultra-Risky Actions*, 85 Yale L.J. 826, 834-42 (1976).

[145] *See* text accompanying note 54 *supra*.

[146] 424 U.S. at 698.

[147] *Id.* at 701.

[148] *Id.*

establishing a violation of the Fourteenth Amendment."[149] This is plainly wrong. An invasion of a common-law interest only *implicates* a constitutional "liberty." Whether, once implicated, there has been an impermissible deprivation of that interest is an entirely separate question. Resolution of that question depends not on the law of torts, but on such matters as the nature of the invasion, its magnitude, and the character of the justification asserted. Thus, ordinarily, negligent conduct by the state would implicate liberty or property interests but would not, given the fourteenth amendment's concern with protecting the individual from the *abuse* of governmental power, constitute a deprivation of these interests.[150] In any event, whether or not the conduct complained of was illegal under state law—or under the common law of torts—would not be dispositive of the merits of the constitutional claim, a point which Mr. Justice Rehnquist himself expressly notes at the beginning of his opinion.[151]

Meachum v. Fano[152] followed *Paul*. At issue was a challenge to the constitutional sufficiency of the procedures surrounding the transfer of a state prisoner to a more restrictive prison. The challenge was rejected. The Court observed that the prisoner had not urged that any specific constitutional right had been violated; that the generalized "liberty" of due process was no longer implicated after the lawfulness of the original decision to commit was established;[153] and finally, that state law created no independent liberty interest.[154]

Precisely where these decisions leave us is by no means clear. *Roth*, *Paul*, and *Meachum* have narrowed the content of "liberty." Taken together, they seem to have some common core: loss of a specific job, of a specific prison location, or of reputation does not, *given the countervailing interests at stake*, materially impede an individual's "freedom to do what he wants." But the victim of defamation finds his options closed in fact, if not in theory; and jobs are not fungible, except perhaps in economics textbooks. I do not

[149] *Id.* at 699.

[150] Thus the negligent destruction of property, as in Dalehite v. United States, 346 U.S. 15 (1953), while implicating a constitutional interest, would not ordinarily constitute a "deprivation" of that interest within the meaning of the due process clause. *But see* Fox v. Sullivan, 539 F.2d 1065 (5th Cir. 1976).

[151] 424 U.S. at 699-701. *See also* Cooper v. California, 386 U.S. 58, 60-61 (1967) (legality of seizure under state law not dispositive of constitutional issues); *accord*, South Dakota v. Opperman, 96 S. Ct. 3092, 3098 (1976).

[152] 96 S. Ct. 2532 (1976).

[153] *Id.* at 2538.

[154] *Id.* at 2538-40.

doubt that the Justices realize all this. Nonetheless, the pressure to keep these cases out of the federal courts was great, and so a compromise was struck. Rather than facing the balancing question at the merits stage, the Court struck a compromise at the definitional stage. But it has struck this balance on the uncritical assumption that every federal interference with state government undermines the values embodied by federalism. This is hardly self-evident. A constitutional norm that denies the states power to defame unjustly their citizens does not seem to undercut any important federalism value,[155] particularly since federalism as an institutional arrangement is concerned with the maximization of individual liberty.[156] There are, indeed, instances when federal intervention might constitute a "positive instrument of federalism."[157] In any event, even if Supreme Court intervention in some way diminishes federalism, those costs must be weighed against any resulting gains. A constitutional norm prohibiting state defamation positively reinforces the fundamental fourteenth amendment concern for individual dignity. Moreover, that amendment was intended to alter the previous federal-state balance, a point which Mr. Justice Rehnquist expressly recognized for a unanimous Court later in the term in *Fitzpatrick v. Bitzer*.[158]

F. *The "New Liberty"*

The Burger Court's attempt to formulate postulates of self-denial is understandable, if not acceptable. But why the Court has embarked on this difficult route of constitutional exegesis remains unclear. Surely, when read in light of its historical origins and the demands of "Our Federalism," section 1983 could have been read less than literally—read so as not to embrace all the interests encompassed by the "liberty" (and "property") of the due process clause.[159] Nor would *Bivens v. Six Unknown Named Agents of Federal*

---

[155] Federalism is one of the major devices by which our ocean-spanning continent hopes to "reconcile unity with diversity." Abraham, *Effectiveness of Governmental Operations*, 426 ANNALS AM. ACAD. POLITICAL & SOC. SCI. 81, 94 (1976).

[156] For a description of the importance the Founders placed on "liberty," see Diamond, *The Declaration and the Constitution: liberty, democracy & the Founders*, 41 THE PUBLIC INTEREST 39 (1975).

[157] *See* Note, *Theories of Federalism and Civil Rights*, 75 YALE L.J. 1007, 1017-24, 1029-33 (1966).

[158] 96 S. Ct. 2666, 2670-71 (1976). The Court there discussed the increased powers of Congress over the states, but of course the amendment also augments judicial power.

[159] *See* Shapo, *Constitutional Tort: Monroe v. Pape, and the Frontiers Beyond*, 60 NW. U.L. REV. 277 (1965). Professor Shapo was criticized in McCormack, *Federalism and Section 1983:*

Bureau of Narcotics[160] compel the Court to fashion "common law" damage or equitable remedies against state and municipal officials.[161] In the short run, the level of federal interference with state and municipal conduct would be reduced by closing the doors of the federal trial courts to plaintiffs asserting certain types of claims.[162] This, in turn, would give legal scholars time to probe the ultimate constitutional questions involved. The scholars, of course, could not "solve" the ultimate problems, but their research and analysis might help by more clearly focusing debate on the underlying problems and their alternative solutions.

This stop-gap solution would not permanently avoid the underlying constitutional questions. Plaintiffs excluded from federal trial courts would sue in the state courts complaining that the state's conduct had unconstitutionally deprived them of the due process guarantee of "liberty" (or "property"). Eventually the Court would be forced to pass upon the constitutional decisions made by the state courts. This leads me to express my views on the ultimate issues.

The real difficulty perceived by the Court is not so much with the intrusions into the province of the states by the federal trial courts as institutions, but rather with two related substantive constitutional concerns. The first concern has more relevance in cases dealing with "property" than with "liberty," but is applicable to both. This concern grows out of *Goldberg v. Kelly*'s [163] much criticized insistence upon adversary proceedings, absent exigent cir-

---

Limitations on Judicial Enforcement of Constitutional Protections (pt. 1), 60 VA. L. REV. 1, 8-10 (1974). I recognize that the present Court shows no disposition to read the post-Civil War statutes narrowly. *See, e.g.*, Runyon v. McCrary, 96 S. Ct. 2586 (1976). Nonetheless, statutory language cast in constitutional terms need not be read to embody the full range of constitutional interests. *E.g.*, HART & WECHSLER, *supra* note 127, at 870-73; Note, *The Indian Bill of Rights and the Constitutional Status of Tribal Governments*, 82 HARV. L. REV. 1343, 1353-55 (1969).

[160] 403 U.S. 388 (1971). *See also* Monaghan, *supra* note 5, at 24 & n.125.

[161] *See* Aldinger v. Howard, 96 S. Ct. 2413 (1976). *See also* Note, *Damage Remedies Against Municipalities For Constitutional Violations*, 89 HARV. L. REV. 922, 935-51 (1976). If § 1983 preempts judicial remedial power, the difficult question remains as to whether the congressional denial of the remedy is unconstitutional, and the extent to which the answer to this question is affected by the fact that state courts provide an alternative forum. These questions are, of course, beyond the compass of this Article.

[162] Jurisdiction could not be grounded on the basis of Smith v. Kansas City Title & Trust Co., 255 U.S. 180 (1921), because § 1983 and other civil rights statutes would, by implication, be taken to limit the full scope of any otherwise existing nondiversity jurisdiction authority of the federal courts. *But see* Wheeldin v. Wheeler, 373 U.S. 647, 659-60 (1963) (dissenting opinion, Brennan, J.). *See also* Aldinger v. Howard, 96 S. Ct. 2413 (1976).

[163] 397 U.S. 254 (1970).

cumstances, *before* governmental actions adversely affecting individual interests occur.[164] Although the Court has, for all practical purposes, repudiated the broad scope of the hearings apparently mandated by *Goldberg*,[165] it remains obsessed with the notion of "some kind" of a prior hearing. "When protected interests are implicated," said the *Roth* Court, "the right to some kind of prior hearing is paramount."[166] But prior hearings might well be dispensed with in many circumstances in which the state's conduct, if not adequately justified, would constitute a common-law tort. This would leave the injured plaintiff in precisely the same posture as a common-law plaintiff, and this procedural consequence would be quite harmonious with the substantive view that the fourteenth amendment encompasses the same liberties as those protected by the common law.[167] This view, if accepted, would have disposed of the procedural due process objection in *Paul*.[168] And it would require overruling *Constantineau*, since, in my view, the heart of the complaint was defamation, not restriction of access to liquor.[169] Moreover, it may be, as Judge Friendly has observed, that the whole concept of prior hearing in the area of mass administrative justice should be reconsidered, at least where there are other "non-adversary" internal administraitve controls to monitor and check administrative abuse.[170] Due process might mean no process, at least no formal adversary process.[171]

I do not pursue these inquiries here because they are wide of my primary concern. I mention them only because I think that *Goldberg*'s insistence upon prior hearings is at the root of a consid-

---

[164] For a useful general summary of most of the cases and relevant articles, see K. Davis, *supra* note 104, at 242-47, 260-68. *See also* Monaghan, *supra* note 5, at 24-26.

[165] *See* Mathews v. Eldridge, 424 U.S. 319 (1976); Goss v. Lopez, 419 U.S. 565 (1975).

[166] 408 U.S. at 569-70 (footnote omitted). *But see* Mathews v. Eldridge, 424 U.S. 319, 333-34 (1976).

[167] Monaghan, *supra* note 61, at 1366 n.18.

[168] 424 U.S. 693, *rehearing denied*, 424 U.S. 985 (1976).

[169] The common–law courts were most reluctant to grant an injunction when the legal question was whether the circulation of defamatory material constituted defamation. Thus, they generally denied injunctive relief against such conduct. By analogy, no prior administrative hearings would be required.

[170] Friendly, *"Some Kind of Hearing"*, 123 U. Pa. L. Rev. 1267 (1975). *See* K. Davis, *supra* note 104, at 702; Kirp, *Proceduralism and Bureaucracy: Due Process in the School Setting*, 28 Stan. L. Rev. 841, 864-70 (1976).

[171] This concept is, in fact, already solidly reflected in our thinking. Some infractions of liberty or property are too minor to require any process whatever. *See* Goss v. Lopez, 419 U.S. 565, 587-89 (1975) (dissenting opinion, Powell, J.). *See also* K. Davis, *supra* note 104, at 266-67; *The Supreme Court, 1975 Term*, 90 Harv. L. Rev. 58, 102-03 (1976). *But see* Wilkinson, *Goss v. Lopez: The Supreme Court As School Superintendent*, 1975 Sup. Ct. Rev. 25, 35-36.

erable part of the Court's concern. But alteration of our present conceptions of procedural due process will alleviate only part of the Court's doubts, for substantive due process is also at stake. In *Paul*, for example, the plaintiff could have waived any procedural objections and argued that the false and defamatory character of the police circular constituted a denial of substantive due process. When considered in substantive due process terms, *Paul*'s analysis discloses its strongest appeal, at least as long as section 1983 is assumed to incorporate the full range of constitutionally protected interests. Surely the fourteenth amendment cannot require that state officials be right in all cases at all times. To continue the development of section 1983 privilege defenses will not solve this problem, for they are applicable only to damage claims and not to requests for injunctive relief.[172] Moreover, unless the privilege is absolute, some litigation is necessary, and *Paul* seems animated by the desire to avoid *any* litigation of these claims.

But *Paul*'s apparent solution—to make constitutional protection attach only if the invasion implicates some trivial state-created interest—does not have much to commend it in terms of the underlying postulates of our political and constitutional order. *Paul*'s solution involves far too costly a sacrifice of important values. In a "Constitution for a free people," *Paul* provides an unacceptable answer to the question of the *constitutional* status of a person who is a victim of intentional, unjustified defamatory statements perpetrated by state officials,[173] and, perhaps more generally, to the question of the constitutional status of the citizens' Blackstonian right of personal security.[174] Despite the high premium I place on stare decisis even in constitutional cases, I think that *Paul* should be overruled. The Court could fashion a constitutional law of public defamation, drawn in part from the complex state of the common-law rules, as it has done with respect to defamation of public figures.

If not overruled, *Paul* should be read as narrowly as possible. However, I cannot confidently proffer a satisfactorily principled

[172] *See* Barr v. Matteo, 360 U.S. 564 (1959); Howard v. Lyons, 360 U.S. 593 (1959). *See generally* Davis, *supra* note 104, at 573-604. *Paul* contained a prayer for injunctive relief.

[173] *Paul*, it should be recalled, was decided against the backdrop of *state* law that presumably provided some basis for relief against wholly unjustified state-sponsored defamation.

[174] The constitutional right of privacy can, of course, protect much of the ground previously occupied by the law of defamation. Note also the possibility of expanding the largely group-based rule of Yick Wo v. Hopkins, 118 U.S. 356 (1886), to cases of individual discrimination. *See generally* Oyler v. Boles, 368 U.S. 448 (1962); Note, *The Right to Nondiscriminatory Enforcement of State Penal Laws*, 61 COLUM. L. REV. 1103 (1961).

limiting conception. Perhaps *Paul* can be held inapplicable where the injury to the "right of personal security" is more than imposition of a stigma. Perhaps wholly unjustified defamation of an individual with the purpose and effect of inflicting unjustifiable mental suffering can still be treated as an invasion of the "liberty" of "personal security" within the ambit of the due process clause. The crucial wrong is not so much in reducing a man's reputation —which is all that the common law protected[175]—but in its additional impact upon his personality. If interference with an individual's bodily integrity implicates "liberty," I see very little justification for the conclusion that interference with an individual's psychic integrity—his personality—is not also protected, at least if we seriously believe that "[i]n a Constitution for a free people . . . the meaning of 'liberty' must be broad indeed."[176]

The word "liberty" could and, given our constitutional traditions, should be read to embrace intangible interests beyond that of privacy. More specifically, it should be read to embrace what the tort law is now in the process of proscribing: namely, *any* governmental conduct which so invades a decent respect for a person's personal integrity that, if not fairly justified, the result would outrage public sensibility.[177] Dean Prosser puts it well: "One who, by extreme and outrageous conduct, intentionally or recklessly causes severe emotional distress . . . is subject to liability . . . ."[178] That the statements are defamatory may constitute evidence of the invasion, but this is not decisive; indeed, even true statements gratuitously publicized might invade an individual's right of personal security. This standard is simply a modern embodiment of the once widely accepted principle that the Constitution prohibits all governmental conduct contrary to fundamental principles of "ordered liberty."[179] Applied in a disciplined manner, this standard would not give the Court a roving commission to impose nonconstitutionally based values on the states.[180] Nor would it convert the due process clause into a body of federal tort law.[181] And measured against this standard, the plaintiff in *Paul* arguably did not

---

[175] "The law [of defamation] went wrong from the beginning in making the damage and not the insult the cause of action." F. POLLOCK, TORTS 181 (15th ed. 1951).

[176] Board of Regents v. Roth, 408 U.S. 564, 572 (1972).

[177] H. KALVEN & C. GREGORY, TORTS 974-75 (2d ed. 1969).

[178] Prosser, *Insult and Outrage*, 44 CALIF. L. REV. 40, 43 (1956). *See also* RESTATEMENT (SECOND) OF TORTS § 46 (1965).

[179] Palko v. Connecticut, 302 U.S. 319, 325 (1937).

[180] Monaghan, *supra* note 5, at 44-45.

[181] Professor Shapo has advanced a similar view of § 1983. *See* Shapo, *supra* note 159, at 320-29.

state a prima facie case.[182] The wording of the particular police circular left something to be desired, but a case can be made for the proposition that it does not violate fundamental traditions of our law for the police to notify businesses during the Christmas season that a person is suspected of being an active shoplifter.

II

Property

A. *In General*

One need not be a disciple of Charles Beard to recognize the Framers' enchantment with the "rights of property."[183] But it is apparent that the Framers hoped to secure those rights less by constitutional prohibitions than by the creation of a strong national government with control over commerce.[184] The new government, moreover, was to have a representative structure designed to secure a considerable place for the "responsible sort" in the Senate, the Presidency, and the national courts.[185] But this scheme proved insufficient to meet the increasing interference with the "rights of property" that occurred at the state level as the nineteenth century passed, and thus the rise of substantive due process doctrines designed to protect those property rights followed.[186] Interestingly, during this period social and political theorists increasingly emphasized that the protection of economic interests was an aspect of "liberty,"[187] rather than "property," a conception ultimately adopted by the Supreme Court.[188] The right to acquire, own, and use

---

[182] Accordingly, no question of privilege arose. *See generally* Hochman, *"Outrageousness" and Privilege in the Law of Emotional Distress—A Suggestion*, 47 CORNELL L.Q. 61 (1961).

[183] For an illuminating discussion of the Beard view, see ESSAYS ON THE MAKING OF THE CONSTITUTION (L. Levy ed. 1965).

[184] *See* the materials excerpted in W. LOCKHART, Y. KAMISAR & J. CHOPER, THE AMERICAN CONSTITUTION 177-81 (4th ed. 1975).

[185] Greene, *Values and Society in Revolutionary America*, 426 ANNALS AM. ACAD. POLITICAL & SOC. SCI. 53, 60-61 (1976). For a comprehensive treatment see G. WOOD, THE CREATION OF THE AMERICAN REPUBLIC 1776-1787, at 471-564 (1969).

[186] *See* notes 45-46 and accompanying text *supra*.

[187] Coker, *American Traditions Concerning Property and Liberty*, 30 AM. POLITICAL SCI. REV. 1 (1936).

[188] Freedom of contract was, for example, part of the "liberty" protected by due process. Lochner v. New York, 198 U.S. 45 (1905). Freedom of contract was, however, also treated as "property." *E.g.*, Coppage v. Kansas, 236 U.S. 1, 14 (1915); Adair v. United States, 208 U.S. 161, 172 (1908); Holden v. Hardy, 169 U.S. 366, 391 (1898).

property became an aspect of the broad "liberty" secured by due process.[189]

Given this history, it is hardly surprising that in the past little attention has been paid to the definition of "property" for due process purposes. Although there are cases which can be read to the contrary, time seems to have yielded a consensus that the due process clause itself does not "create" any property interests.[190] Those interests must be located in some other source, principally state law. Like the contract clause,[191] therefore, the due process clause threw a federal constitutional shield around property interests initially created by state law.[192]

The existence, *vel non*, of "property" seldom raised any issue reaching the Supreme Court in the first half of the twentieth century. In the few cases raising the question, the Court accepted the state court's determination as to whether certain interests had been created by state law, as long as that determination had a "fair and substantial" basis in state law.[193] This limited review ensured that federal constitutional protection for state-created interests was not undermined by state court manipulation of legal doctrine.

The "fair and substantial basis" rule, it is important to emphasize, is entirely consistent with the principle that there is a federal *content* to the word "property." To be sure, the *interests* must be initially created by state law,[194] and on that question the state court's assessment is nearly, although not absolutely, controlling. But the state court's *characterization* of those "interests" is another matter altogether. The difference between the existence of an interest—a matter of state law—and its significance—a matter of federal law—is firmly established in other areas of law.[195] In the past, this distinction has received little explicit attention in constitutional cases.[196] It is the implicit premise of the now discredited

[189] "As late as the turn of the last century justices were not yet distinguishing between liberty and property; in the universes beneath their hats liberty was still the opportunity to acquire property." Hamilton, *Property—According to Locke*, 41 YALE L.J. 864, 877 (1932).

[190] Demorest v. City Bank Farmers Trust Co., 321 U.S. 36 (1944).

[191] U.S. CONST. art. 1, § 10.

[192] HART & WECHSLER, *supra* note 127, at 500-02. The contrary view of the cases expressed in Tushnet, *supra* note 8, at 267-77, rejecting any role for state law seems to me to be in error both on the basis of principle and authority.

[193] Demorest v. City Bank Farmers Trust Co., 321 U.S. 36, 42-43 (1944); HART & WECHSLER, *supra* note 127, at 502-04.

[194] The "interests" could also be created by some other source, such as federal law, or that of a foreign state.

[195] HART & WECHSLER, *supra* note 127, at 489-94.

[196] For a recent example, see City of Madison, Joint Sch. Dist. No. 8 v. Wisconsin Employment Relations Comm'n, 97 S. Ct. 421, 425 n.5 (1976).

"freedom of contract cases," which clearly assumed a federal content of the word in holding that a person's interest in gainful employment constituted "property" (as well as "liberty").[197] But those cases, it must be admitted, hardly focus on the relevant issues here.[198] More in point are the cases that marked the demise of the "right-privilege" distinction. Although some of the interests asserted in those cases may not have fitted very comfortably within the common-law conceptions of property, they nonetheless constituted part of the system of "entitlements" so important in the twentieth century. And given the purposes behind the protection of "property," the word may fairly be held to embrace new forms of property as they emerge.[199] However the "new property"[200] interests might have been characterized by state law, the Court correctly proceeded on the implicit premise that they were substantial enough to qualify as "property" for due process purposes.[201]

Recent decisions of the Supreme Court address the underlying issue more directly. The problem first arose in *Roth*,[202] where the Court held that nontenured teachers have a sufficient "property" interest in their employment to entitle them to some kind of pro-

---

[197] *See* cases cited in note 188 *supra*.

[198] An examination of these cases shows that they proceed on the premise that it is "obvious" that a property interest is involved. *See also* City of Eastlake v. Forest City Enterprises, Inc., 426 U.S. 668, 680 (1976) (dissenting opinion, Stevens, J.):

> [T]hroughout this litigation everyone has assumed, without discussing the problem, that the Due Process Clause does apply [and thus property is involved]. Both reason and authority support that assumption.
>
> Subject to limitations imposed by the common law of nuisance and zoning restrictions, the owner of real property has the right to develop his land to his own economic advantage.

Id. at 681 (footnote omitted).

[199] Monaghan, *supra* note 61, at 1380.

[200] Reich, *The New Property*, 73 YALE L.J. 733 (1964). *See also* Grey, *Property and Need: The Welfare State and Theories of Distributive Justice*, 28 STAN. L. REV. 877 (1976).

[201] *See also* contract clause cases cited in note 188 *supra*. In those cases the Court recognized that, although state law creates contract interests, it can make an independent judgment on what the state law is. The question is whether the Court is under an obligation to treat as contract under art. 1, § 10, all agreements that state law treats as contracts. With respect to "quasi contracts," the answer is clear. Kauper, *What is a "Contract" Under the Contracts Clause of the Federal Constitution*, 31 MICH. L. REV. 187, 193-97 (1932). But if the contract is a valid consensual agreement under state law, the answer is uncertain. The authorities cited in Merrill, *Application of the Obligation of Contract Clause to State Promises*, 80 U. PA. L. REV. 639 (1932), seem to support the view that some consensual agreements valid under state law are not contracts within art. 1, § 10. But some of the contracts therein discussed were void under federal law, and as to the remainder the Court seemed, in large part, to be either interpreting state law or applying general contract law theories. The latter approach does not survive Erie R.R. v. Tompkins, 304 U.S. 64 (1938).

[202] 408 U.S. 564 (1972).

cedural due process only if state law has created "a legitimate claim of entitlement."[203] This results, said the Court, because property interests "are not created by the Constitution. Rather, they are created and their dimensions are defined by existing rules or understandings that stem from an independent source such as state law . . . ."[204] *Bell v. Burson*'s[205] focus on the "importance" of the interest, a criterion easily satisfied by terminated public employees, no longer sufficed.

Roth's analytical foundation is defensible, for the Court apparently proceeded on the premise that although interests are created by state law, their characterization as "property" for due process purposes is determined by federal standards.[206] And *Roth*'s companion case, *Perry v. Sindermann*,[207] emphasized that "property" in the constitutional sense embraces the broad range of interests secured by "existing rules or understandings."[208] Moreover, a person's interest in a "benefit" qualifies "if there are such rules or mutually explicit understandings that support his claim of entitlement to the benefit."[209]

Claims of entitlement were readily found. In *Arnett v. Kennedy*,[210] a federal employee who could be discharged only for "just cause," challenged the procedural sufficiency of his pretermination hearings. A divided Court sustained the procedures, although no individual opinion commanded the assent of more than three Justices. Significantly, however, all nine Justices agreed that the employee had a sufficient property interest to trigger due process scrutiny. In *Goss v. Lopez*,[211] a majority of the Court concluded that a student's right to attend public school was a "legitimate entitlement" sufficient to constitute "property"—thereby subjecting school suspension procedures to due process scrutiny.[212]

---

[203] *Id.* at 577.

[204] *Id.*

[205] 402 U.S. 535 (1971). *See* text accompanying note 15 *supra*.

[206] The "words 'liberty' and 'property' . . . must be given some meaning." 408 U.S. at 572.

[207] 408 U.S. 593 (1972).

[208] *Id.* at 601.

[209] *Id.* This view seems to treat the crucial issue of legitimate entitlements as a question of law, rather than one of constitutional fact. Thus, I do not believe that the Court is really concerned with the expectations of the holder of the entitlement. *But see The Supreme Court, 1975 Term*, 90 HARV. L. REV. 58, 98-99 (1976).

[210] 416 U.S. 134 (1974).

[211] 419 U.S. 565 (1975).

[212] *Id.* at 574. The dissent apparently did not dispute that technically a "property" interest was at stake. *Id.* at 585-86 (dissenting opinion, Powell, J.). *See* Wilkinson, *supra* note 171, at 25, 48-50.

And finally, in *Mathews v. Eldridge*,[213] the Court, in rejecting a procedural due process challenge to pre-termination procedures for social security disability payments, said: "[T]he interest of an individual in continued receipt of these benefits is a statutorily created 'property' interest protected by the Fifth Amendment."[214]

The foregoing decisions apparently absorbed as constitutional "property" most of the twentieth century entitlements. The sole exception was that a state could, under *Roth*, create a probationary period in public employment (and perhaps elsewhere) without thereby creating a "property" (or "liberty") interest. This exception allowed the states a procedural flexibility unhampered by federally prescribed notice and hearing requirements. Mr. Justice Rehnquist's three-man plurality opinion in *Arnett*, however, suggested additional possibilities. In form, his opinion was not directed to the definition of the word "property" but only to the scope of the procedural protection for what was admittedly a property interest. It advanced the startling view that an entitlement derived from a statute is inherently limited by the procedures for its termination contained in the statute creating the entitlement.[215] The thrust of this analysis, however, is to break down any distinction between substance and procedure and to assert that, in some contexts at least, procedural safeguards are themselves indispensable aspects of the "property" itself. There is probably nothing inherently illogical in this approach. "Property" may be viewed as merely a series of discrete rights and powers, the property teacher's "bundle of sticks." And there is no a priori reason to exclude "procedural sticks" from the bundle.[216] But our legal traditions strongly oppose this mode of analysis. In countless contexts we distinguish between substance and procedure, and subject the procedural aspects of "property" rights to independent constitutional scrutiny.[217] Moreover, the fundamental premises behind the treating of "entitlements" as property argue against disregarding

---

[213] 424 U.S. 319 (1976).

[214] *Id.* at 332. *See also* Hortonville Joint Sch. Dist. No. 1 v. Hortonville Educ. Ass'n, 426 U.S. 482, 488 n.2 (1976).

[215] 416 U.S. at 152-55. Prior to the Civil War, however, there was much support for the view that due process and legislative process were synonymous forms. Corwin, *The Doctrine of Due Process of Law Before the Civil War*, 24 HARV. L. REV. 366, 460 (1911). Thus, properly enacted statutes that limited the scope of a property right would have been prima facie constitutional under the due process clause. This view, that the clause was only a restriction on the executive and the courts, has long since gone by the boards.

[216] Van Alstyne, *supra* note 14, at 1451-54.

[217] Mr. Justice Rehnquist's view still does not command a majority. *See, e.g.*, Mathews v. Eldridge, 424 U.S. 319 (1976); Goss v. Lopez, 419 U.S. 565, 573-74 (1975).

distinctions between substance and procedure. Be that as it may, it is not far removed from Mr. Justice Rehnquist's mode of thinking to conclude that an individual can have no "substantive" property interest under state law, but at best only an interest that certain prescribed procedures be followed.[218] *Bishop v. Wood*,[219] decided last term, comes close to so holding.

B. *Bishop v. Wood*

In *Bishop* petitioner alleged he was a permanent employee within the meaning of a local ordinance, and brought a section 1983 action in federal court complaining that he had been discharged without receiving procedural due process. The terms of the local ordinance provided:

> *Dismissal. A permanent employee whose work is not satisfactory over a period of time shall be notified in what way his work is deficient and what he must do if his work is to be satisfactory.* If a permanent employee fails to perform work up to the standard of the classification held, or continues to be negligent, inefficient, or unfit to perform his duties, he may be dismissed by the City Manager. Any discharged employee shall be given written notice of his discharge setting forth the effective date and reasons for his discharge if he shall request such a notice.[220]

Despite this language the district court concluded, on the basis of the sparsest state court authority, that under North Carolina law the petitioner "held this position at the will and pleasure of the city."[221] The Fourth Circuit affirmed by an equally divided court,[222] and its decision was affirmed by the Supreme Court by a narrow five to four majority.

Mr. Justice Stevens framed the decisive constitutional issue in the following terms: "[*T*]*he sufficiency of the claim of entitlement must be decided by reference to state law*. . . . Whether such a guarantee has been given can be determined only by an examination of the particular statute or ordinance in question."[223] He admitted that "[o]n

---

[218] But I do not see that there is a federal right to have the procedures followed. *See* Ryan v. Aurora Bd. of Educ., 540 F.2d 222, 228-29 (6th Cir. 1976).

[219] 426 U.S. 341 (1976).

[220] *Id.* at 344 n.5 (quoting MARION, N.C., PERSONNEL ORDINANCE, art. II, § 6) (emphasis added).

[221] *Id.* at 345 (quoting Bishop v. Wood, 377 F. Supp. 501, 504 (W.D.N.C. 1973). The case would seem to have been an obvious one for abstention. *See* Bellotti v. Baird, 96 S. Ct. 2857 (1976).

[222] Bishop v. Wood, 498 F.2d 1341 (4th Cir. 1974).

[223] 426 U.S. at 344-45 (emphasis added) (footnote omitted).

its face the ordinance on which petitioner relies may fairly be read as conferring such a guarantee," but he relied on the courts below for the alternative conclusion that the state law created "*no right to continued employment* but merely condition[ed] an employee's removal on compliance with certain specified procedures."[224] To the majority, that proved fatal to petitioner's case.

Under *Bishop* there should in principle be no constitutional barrier to prevent a state, by clear statement, from denying the existence of a "right to continued" public employment, attendance at public schools, or welfare benefits and from then asserting that the procedures actually afforded by the state with respect to any discontinuance are all that it need accord. Indeed, lacking any substantive interest, it seems, for example, that any discontinued employee or welfare recipient would not possess an independent constitutional due process right to insist that the state comply with its own specified procedures. If so, the "right-privilege" distinction is back in full bloom.

Bishop is wrongly reasoned, or at least wrongly phrased. The Court erred in thinking that the "sufficiency of the claim of entitlement must be decided by reference to state law." The nature and character of the entitlement is surely "decided by reference to state law," but not its "sufficiency" to constitute a "legitimate" entitlement and therefore "property" in the constitutional sense. An illustration clarifies this. Suppose that a state motor vehicle statute invested automobiles with all the attributes of property as that term is generally understood, but also provided that no person who bought a car after the statute was passed would be deemed to have a "right to continued" ownership as against the state. If the state were suddenly to confiscate automobiles for revenue purposes, surely the Supreme Court, upon assessing the state law, would conclude that the owner's interest had sufficient attributes of "property" at least to implicate the due process clause.[225]

The entitlement cases are no different. A state-funded welfare or pension system can qualify as "property," as *Mathews v. Eldridge*[226] reaffirms. That an entitlement can constitute "property" is not altered, as *Bishop* seems to assume, simply because the state law

[224] *Id.* at 345 (emphasis added).

[225] *E.g.*, Calero-Toledo v. Pearson Yacht Leasing Co., 416 U.S. 663 (1974). See also the line of cases commencing with Fuentes v. Shevin, 407 U.S. 67 (1972), holding that the right to a hearing before repossession of a chattel does not turn upon who has title under state law.

[226] 424 U.S. 319 (1976).

also provides that there is "no right to continued receipt." There are few, if any, "continued" rights to receive entitlements. Welfare programs and public jobs can be abolished, after all. *But while they are in general existence*, they can constitute "property" for the individual. *Flemming v. Nestor*,[227] a case involving the validity of a termination of social security benefits, proves particularly instructive in this regard. The Court there declined to hold that individual interests in these programs constituted "accrued property rights," because to do so would deprive the Social Security System "of the flexibility and boldness in adjustment to ever-changing conditions which it demands."[228] But the absence of a right to continued receipt of the benefits did not mean that the interest was not within the ambit of the due process clause: "The interest of a covered employee . . . is of sufficient substance to fall within the protection from arbitrary governmental action afforded by the Due Process Clause."[229]

The absence of a "continuing right" is not, therefore, entitled to the weight attached to it by the Court. Still, the case of public employment is perhaps the hardest analytically, since even now we are not accustomed to viewing continuance in specific public employment as an entitlement of the same order as welfare payments. It would, indeed, have been possible to say that such an interest in specific public employment could never constitute "property" in the constitutional sense, but *Roth*, *Perry*, and *Arnett* foreclose any such categorical position. *Roth* formulated a different mode of analysis by analogizing interests in public employment to other forms of entitlements. Like its counterparts in the "liberty" area, *Roth* does reflect some balancing, with the Court making a normative judgment based upon the reasonable expectations of the public employee and the state's need for flexibility in areas where judgments are often intuitive. But the mode of analysis is the application of independent federal standards to state-created interests.

Bishop poses a unique problem—a state law which on the surface has an essentially contradictory character. The first two sentences of the *Bishop* ordinance look remarkably like the "just cause" statute in *Arnett*.[230] So viewed, *Bishop* raises several important issues. The conversion of a "just cause" provision into its opposite as a matter of state law raises substantial issues under the traditional

---

[227] 363 U.S. 603 (1966).

[228] *Id*. at 610.

[229] *Id*. at 611.

[230] 5 U.S.C. § 7501(a) (1970), *quoted in* Arnett v. Kennedy, 416 U.S. 134, 140 (1974).

"fair and substantial support" test, at least where the employee gains his nonprobationary status before the "conversion." In this aspect, therefore, *Bishop* raises the question of the Supreme Court's scope to independently determine the content of state law in order to enforce federal constitutional guarantees.[231] But such an inquiry need not be undertaken. It is enough to focus on the *significance* of the state law as it stood at the time *Bishop* was decided. The state had, in effect, denied "tenure" protection to a class of persons not normally viewed as "probationary." *Bishop* mistakenly assumed that the statutory language providing that there was "no continued right to its receipt" was decisive. But that should be only one factor in a principled analysis. Unless a state court had held that the ordinance's term "permanent" meant "probationary," the Supreme Court could have properly reasoned that the interest in *Bishop* was of sufficient magnitude to constitute "property." Such an employee was, after all, different from the employee in *Roth* who was hired for a fixed period; he had reached a step in state employment that for some purposes presumably differentiated him from the purely probationary employee. That additional stature seems to me to be enough to constitute "property."

C. *The Implications of Bishop v. Wood*

If *Bishop* is to be followed, it seems to stand for the following proposition: a statute or ordinance which, facially or as construed, requires only that an employee receive a "statement of reasons" does not, as a matter of federal constitutional law, give him an interest significantly distinguishable from *Roth* to constitute "property" within the meaning of the due process clause. The only point at which such an interest reaches the "property" level for constitutional purposes occurs when the state law restricts termination to grounds of "individualized cause," as in *Arnett*.[232] Even if read this

---

[231] The Court has thus far concluded that, unlike the "independent judgment" rule of the contract clause cases, its authority is restricted to the "fair and substantial basis" rule, unless perhaps a contract claim is made under the due process clause or contract clause. *See* HART & WECHSLER, *supra* not 127, at 501-05. In practice the tests come close to converging, because in contract clause cases great deference is paid to the view of the state court. *Id.* at 501-02.

[232] *See* Hortonville Joint Sch. Dist. No. 1 v. Hortonville Educ. Ass'n, 426 U.S. 482, 488 n.2 (1976). Thurston v. Delke, 531 F.2d 1264, 1272 (5th Cir. 1976); Huntley v. Community Sch. Bd., 543 F.2d 979 (2d Cir. 1976).

I am most reluctant to conclude that the existence of state-provided procedural safeguards is enough to show that a "property" interest has been created. Where the government is not under a constitutional obligation to provide procedural protections because of the absence of a "property" interest, the provision of sensible safeguards ought not to

narrowly, however, the case could have far-reaching consequences. It might be argued that under *Bishop* the state would be restrained by generalized procedural due process only with respect to existing relationships interruptible only for cause.[233] A state eager to maximize its freedom from due process scrutiny in the public sector (for example, with respect to public welfare or public employment), arguably need only restructure any program along temporal lines. At the expiration of a specific period the "property" interest would end, and accordingly, a state decision not to continue the benefit—or more accurately, not to recommence it—would seemingly not involve any "property" interest.

I doubt, however, that such a danger will materialize. The Court's doctrine is still flexible enough to permit a holding that a present legal relationship, interruptible only for cause, plus a practical expectancy of its continuance, might constitute "property." *Bishop*, after all, involved a relationship which, *at all times*, was one that existed only at will. But if the state legislature is willing to go further and to restructure its programs so that they are entirely "at will" under state law, *Bishop*'s logic cannot be escaped. No "property" interest has been created, and thus no due process is required unless some "liberty" interest is also threatened. I hope that the political process can act partially to restrain the state legislatures from redesigning their programs in "at will" terms,[234] and I believe that the state courts are not likely to seize upon ambiguous state law to reach such a result with respect to interests that sensible men value. Moreover, the "liberty" protected by the due process clause will, as we have seen, often be involved even if "property" is not.

Conclusion

The Court's present "gradual process of exclusion" probably has not resulted in much narrowing of the "liberty" and "property" protected by due process. Indeed, it may only result in the creation of a technical barrier, infrequently and erratically invoked to exclude cases from the Court's docket, so that the rules will in time be perceived as arbitrary.[235] But the cases are capable of broader

---

result in the penalty (in the state's view) of triggering the applicability of the due process clause. Plainly, any such theory might be counter-productive, for the state's only option in that case would be to provide no procedural safeguards whatsoever.

[233] *See, e.g.*, note 124 *supra*.

[234] *E.g.*, Moody v. Daggett, 97 S. Ct. 274, 282 n.8 (1976) (noting that Congress has provided statutory right to parole revocation hearing).

[235] Codd v. Velger, 45 U.S.L.W. 4175 (U.S. Feb. 27, 1977), apparently assumes that a probationary public employee has a right to a name-clearing administrative hearing

mischief,[236] particularly *Bishop v. Wood*. They are capable of generating doctrine and results that are inconsistent with the long-standing conceptions about the meaning of "liberty" and "property" in a "Constitution for a free people." Accordingly, I hope that the Court will not proceed much further in the direction suggested by *Paul* and *Bishop*.

---

where defamation is alleged. Among the difficulties with the holding is that the Court does not explain how the *Roth* nationale survives *Paul*. *See* note 130 and accompanying text *supra*. Since a probationary employee has no "liberty" interest in *specific* public employment, it is not clear how he differs from an ordinary citizen when he complains of defamation.

[236] *See* Van Alstyne, *supra* note 14, at 1458-64.

DEEDS UNDER A DOCTRINE: CIVIL LIBERTIES IN THE 1963 TERM*

WALTER F. MURPHY
Princeton University

Judged by any standards the 1963 term of the United States Supreme Court was one of momentous importance to the future of the American political system. Most immediately, the Justices once again found themselves embroiled in political controversy, their decisions attacked by the Republican party platform, by the Republican presidential candidate and by many members of Congress.

Among the more notable deeds of the 1963 term were decisions writing into the margins of the Constitution the formula "one man, one vote" as the proper rule for apportioning electoral districts for the House of Representatives and for both houses of state legislatures. The Court also invalidated two acts of Congress, and in the field of criminal justice introduced several new principles while overturning supposedly settled law. In addition the Court again struck down officially sanctioned prayers in public schools.

For its part, Congress seriously considered constitutional amendments to reverse the school prayer decisions of this and previous terms, and to modify the doctrine of the reapportionment cases.[1] The House went so far as to pass a bill to remove from federal courts jurisdiction to hear apportionment suits. After a quasi-filibuster by liberal senators had beaten down a stronger measure, the Senate then adopted a resolution urging federal judges to allow state legislators ample time to redistrict their states. This resolution was adopted as an amendment to the foreign aid bill, but was deleted in conference.

The most personal and perhaps the most stinging congressional rebuke to the Justices came on a money matter. In June 1964 the House passed a general pay raise for federal employees, including $7500 for the Justices. Four days later the Court handed down the bulk of the term's state legislative districting cases. During floor debate in the Senate, Gordon Allott, Republican of Colorado—and Colorado was one of the states whose districting had just been declared unconstitutional—proposed cutting the Justices' raise to $2500. While Senator Allott disclaimed any effort "to slap them in the face, or anything of that sort,"[2] some of his colleagues were more candid about their intention to punish judicial law-making. In any event, the Senate adopted Allott's amendment, 46–40. The conference settled on a $4500 increase, and much to the disgust of some Court foes both houses agreed to the compromise. Three thousand dollars a year poorer because of their work in recent terms, the Justices were reminded of one use for congressional control of the purse strings.

This paper will first summarize the more important deeds of the Court's 1963 term in the field of civil liberties. The second section analyzes the divisions among the Justices on these issues, and the third section examines some of the larger doctrinal implications of recent decisions as well as their possible political effects.

I. DEEDS

As has typically occurred in the last quarter century, questions of civil liberties formed the most significant part of the business of the 1963 term of the Court. These decisions will be analyzed here under three sub-headings, Criminal Justice, Freedom of Political Expression and Association, and Discrimination against Insular Minorities. Reasons for the choice of these categories will be fully explained in Section III of this paper.

Criminal Justice. A large number of cases related to procedural and substantive guarantees in criminal trials, and these were generally decided in favor of the rights of the accused.[3] Two

* I am indebted to my colleagues, William M. Beaney and Robert K. Faulkner, and my research assistant, Irving Faber, for reading the manuscript and making many helpful suggestions.

[1] For the school prayer amendments see Edward Beiser and William Beaney, "Prayers and Politics: The Impact of *Engel* and *Schempp* on the Governmental Process," 13 *Journal of Public Law* (1965). Among the more important of the proposed amendments to modify the reapportionment decisions were: H. J. Res. 1055 (McCulloch), S. J. Res. 181 (Stennis), and S. J. Res. 185 (Dirksen), all 88th Cong., 2d sess. Within a few weeks of the term's reapportionment decisions, at least 51 modifying constitutional amendments were introduced in Congress.

[2] 110 *Cong. Rec.* 15312 (daily ed.).

[3] The major exceptions were: Rugendorf v. United States, 376 U. S. 528 (1964); Ungar v. Sarafite, 376 U. S. 575 (1964); United States v. Barnett, 376 U.S. 681 (1964); United States v.

cases reversed convictions because of systematic exclusion of Negroes from juries;[4] another overruled *Stein* v. *New York* and held that, in a state court, the voluntariness of a confession must be determined by the trial judge and may not be submitted to the jury along with the question of guilt or innocence.[5] *Malloy* v. *Hogan*[6] buried the 56-year-old doctrine of *Twining* v. *New Jersey*[7] and applied to the states the Fifth Amendment's prohibition against self-incrimination. On the other hand, six Justices held that protection against double jeopardy does not bar the federal government from retrying a defendant who was earlier coerced into entering a guilty plea.[8]

The Court also rejected Governor Ross Barnett's request for protection of his asserted civil rights. A five-judge majority, over dissents from Warren, Black, Douglas, and Goldberg, reaffirmed the old rule that a defendant accused of contempt may be tried without a jury. However, some of the majority Justices undermined much of the effect of this traditional rule by adding the Delphic qualification that the punishment imposed under such circumstances could not exceed that usually accorded to "petty" offenses.[9] In another contempt case, six Justices found no violation of due process where the judge who presided at the contempt trial was the same judge who had presided over the main trial at which the defendant had been cited for contempt.[10] A third contempt decision held that before trial in a federal court, a defendant was entitled to a hearing on his attorney's allegation that he had been mentally ill during the period in which the contemptuous acts were committed.[11]

In three state search-and-seizure cases, the Justices tried to make it clear that *Mapp* v. *Ohio*[12] imposed on state courts an obligation to follow the same rules as federal courts in denying admission of unconstitutionally obtained evidence.[13] A fourth search-and-seizure decision reversed a conviction obtained in a federal court on the basis of evidence secured by state officials in a search without a warrant.[14]

Two right-to-counsel cases established new protections for defendants. *Massiah* v. *United States*[15] held inadmissible in a federal court incriminating statements voluntarily made by a man under indictment. Federal officers, the majority said, could question a defendant under such circumstances, but they could not use evidence so obtained *against him* unless his lawyer had been present at the interrogation. *Escobedo* v. *Illinois* tried to begin to solve one of the problems raised by *Gideon* v. *Wainwright*:[16] at what stage of a criminal prosecution does the right to counsel begin? In essaying an answer, the majority reverted to a "special circumstances" rule. After stressing that in this case the accused was a young man of Mexican descent with no previous record of experience with the police, the Court said: "We hold only that when the process shifts from investigatory to accusatory—when its focus is on the accused and its purpose is to elicit a confession—our adversary system begins to operate, and, under the circumstances here, the accused must be permitted to consult with his lawyer."[17]

In reversing a series of sit-in convictions,

Healy, 376 U.S. 75 (1964); United States v. Tateo, 377 U.S. 463 (1964); United States v. Welden, 377 U.S. 95 (1964).

In this article I have not tried to summarize every civil liberties decision of the 1963 term. Tables I, II, and III below list all of these decisions, at least those decided by full opinion. For a more complete discussion see Note, "The Supreme Court, 1963 Term," 78 *Harvard Law Review* 177 (1964).

[4] Arnold v. North Carolina, 376 U.S. 773 (1964); Coleman v. Alabama, 377 U.S. 129 (1964).

[5] Jackson v. Denno, 378 U.S. 368 (1964). Except for two sentences in White's majority opinion, one might have said that constitutional standards would be met if a state required a jury to return a special verdict regarding the voluntariness of a confession. The two sentences read: "Jackson's position before the District Court, and here, is that the issue of his confession should not have been decided by the convicting jury but should have been determined in a proceeding separate and apart from the body trying guilt and innocence. So far we agree and hold that he is now entitled to such a hearing in the state court." *Ibid.*, at p. 394.

[6] 378 U.S. 1 (1964). See also Murphy v. Waterfront Commission, 378 U.S. 52 (1964).

[7] 211 U.S. 78 (1908).

[8] United States v. Tateo, *supra* note 3.

[9] So Justice Clark said in his opinion for the Court. United States v. Barnett, *supra* note 3 at 695 n.

[10] Ungar v. Sarafite, *supra* note 3.

[11] Panico v. United States, 375 U.S. 29 (1963).

[12] 367 U.S. 643 (1961).

[13] Fahy v. Connecticut, 375 U.S. 85 (1963); Stoner v. California, 376 U.S. 483 (1964); Aguilar v. Texas, 378 U.S. 39 (1964).

[14] Preston v. United States, 376 U.S. 364 (1964).

[15] 377 U.S. 201 (1964).

[16] 372 U.S. 335 (1963).

[17] 378 U.S. 478, 492 (1964).

three Justices (Clark, Brennan and Stewart) demonstrated considerable virtuosity not only in avoiding basic constitutional issues themselves, but also in preventing any official Court pronouncement on those issues, even though six of their colleagues wanted the Court to rule on the fundamental questions of constitutional law. In two cases the Court found state action in the form of official encouragement of segregation policies by merchants;[18] in another the Court applied the *ex post facto* prohibition to judicial interpretations of law and set aside the convictions because South Carolina courts had changed their interpretations of South Carolina's criminal trespass law.[19] In still another case from South Carolina the Court again used the *ex post facto* rationale to reverse criminal trespass convictions and found there was insufficient evidence to justify charges of breach of peace.[20] In *Bell* v. *Maryland* the Court reversed other sit-in convictions to permit the Maryland courts to reconsider the cases in the light of subsequent state passage of an equal accommodations law.[21]

Avoidance of fundamental issues did not appeal to the Chief Justice or to Justices Douglas and Goldberg. They joined in the Court's opinion, but in concurring opinions written by Goldberg and Douglas these three put forth an argument that, if ever successful in commanding a majority of the Court, would render redundant the controversial public accommodations title of the 1964 Civil Rights Act. Reasoning along lines similar to the first Justice Harlan's dissent in the old *Civil Rights Cases*,[22] Goldberg and Douglas concluded that the Fourteenth Amendment forbids innkeepers to discriminate on the basis of race.

Black, Harlan, and White would also have reached the basic constitutional issues. These Justices dissented in four of the five sit-in cases; three of their dissents were written by Black, one by Harlan. They rejected the theory of the elder Harlan's dissent in the *Civil Rights Cases*, denied that anyone could have been misled by previous state court interpretations of state law, and found no state action in a merchant's obtaining police assistance—absent an official policy commanding or actively encouraging segregation—in removing unwanted persons from his property.

Freedom of Expression and Association. The 1963 term had more than its annual share of voting and speech cases. In the 1962 term, a majority of the Court had held in *NAACP* v. *Button* that an interest group had a First Amendment right to use—and to urge its members to use—the judicial process to accomplish its policy aims.[23] *Brotherhood* v. *Virginia*[24] extended the *Button* doctrine by ruling that a union had a constitutionally protected right to advise its members to seek, in employer liability cases, the counsel of particular lawyers. Three decisions sustained the right of unions to picket in labor disputes;[25] two other decisions, based largely on *Edwards* v. *South Carolina*,[26] upheld the right of Negro demonstrators to protest publicly against state-sanctioned segregation policies.[27] Two cases involving allegations of obscenity and counter-allegations of police censorship found the Justices coming down once more in favor of freedom of expression.[28] But on neither occasion could a majority agree on an opinion for the Court, and one of these cases produced the odd result of Warren and Clark joining in protest against a libertarian decision.[29]

In a series of decisions more directly related to political expression, a unanimous Court once again affirmed the right of NAACP members to freedom of association and for the fourth time reversed Alabama's efforts to prevent the NAACP from doing business in the state.[30] The Court also held that provisions

[18] Robinson v. Florida, 378 U.S. 153 (1964); Griffin v. Maryland, 378 U.S. 130 (1964). The ability of three Justices to impose their will on the other six may be the result of the so-called paradox of voting. See my *Elements of Judicial Strategy* (University of Chicago Press, 1964), pp. 85–7.

[19] Bouie v. Columbia, 378 U.S. 347 (1964).

[20] Barr v. Columbia, 378 U.S. 146 (1964).

[21] 378 U.S. 226 (1964).

[22] 109 U.S. 3 (1883).

[23] 371 U.S. 415 (1963). For a full analysis of this case, see Robert Birkby and Walter Murphy, "Interest Group Conflict in the Judicial Arena," 42 *Texas Law Review* 1018 (1964).

[24] 377 U.S. 1 (1964).

[25] Liner v. Jafco, 375 U.S. 301 (1964); NLRB v. Fruit & Veg. Local, 377 U.S. 58 (1964); United Steelworkers v. NLRB, 376 U.S. 492 (1964).

[26] 372 U.S. 229 (1963).

[27] Henry v. Rock Hill, 375 U.S. 6 (1963); Fields v. South Carolina, 375 U.S. 44 (1963).

[28] A Quantity of Books v. Kansas, 378 U.S. 205 (1964); Jacobellis v. Ohio, 378 U.S. 184 (1964).

[29] Jacobellis v. Ohio, *supra* note 28.

[30] NAACP v. Alabama, 377 U.S. 288 (1964). This time the Court's decision stuck and the injunction was lifted. *Southern School News* (October 1964), p. 7. For a discussion of the background of this litigation see Birkby and Murphy,

of Washington loyalty oaths were void for vagueness. Where the "sensitive" field of dissemination of ideas was involved, so White wrote for a seven-judge majority, restrictive regulations must meet high standards of definiteness.[31]

New York Times v. *Sullivan* reversed a libel judgment against the *Times* for publishing an advertisement that accused Montgomery, Alabama, officials of interfering with the civil rights of Negroes. The *Times*, though claiming the advertisement was generally accurate, admitted it contained some false information. Black, Douglas, and Goldberg would have conferred absolute immunity on newspapers to criticize public officials, but the other six Justices would not go so far. In an opinion written by Justice Brennan, the majority held that in order to be outside the protection of the First and Fourteenth Amendments a newspaper's criticism of a public official had to be malicious as well as false. "The constitutional guarantees require," Brennan said, "a federal rule that prohibits a public official from recovering damages for defamatory falsehood relating to his official conduct unless he proves that the statement was made with 'actual malice'—that is, with knowledge that it was false or with reckless disregard of whether it was false or not."[32]

In a democratic society, one of the principal uses of freedom of expression and association is to influence electoral behavior, and the Court made the most significant decisions of its 1963 term in this area. The Justices decided eleven districting cases, nine involving apportionment of state legislatures and two congressional districting. Felix Frankfurter had earlier warned that to enter the reapportionment controversy was to throw the Court into a political thicket. His brethren, however, accepted that risk, realizing perhaps that like nine Br'er Rabbits they have historically thrived in that briar patch.

In all nine of the state cases[33] and the one congressional case[34] where the proper apportioning formula was at issue, a six-judge majority—Warren, Black, Douglas, Brennan, White, and Goldberg—firmly endorsed the principle of "one man, one vote." These Justices also interpreted that principle to require substantially equal populations in electoral districts for the national House of Representatives and for both houses of state legislatures. Stewart and Clark preferred a more flexible approach than the one man, one vote formula, but both agreed in four of the nine state cases[35] that the legislatures were sufficiently malapportioned to warrant correction by judicial action. Clark came to this conclusion in two of the other cases.[36] Only Harlan adhered to the view that legislative districting is a political rather than a justiciable matter.

The eleventh apportionment case, *Wright* v. *Rockefeller*,[37] revolved around the question whether New York had gerrymandered some congressional districts. Over dissents from Douglas and Goldberg, the Court held that the plaintiffs had failed to prove deliberate rigging of district lines for forbidden purposes. In a relatively minor decision, *Anderson* v. *Martin*,[38] a unanimous Court ruled that it was a denial of equal protection for Lousiana to require that a candidate's race be indicated on the ballot.

Discrimination against Insular Minorities. The term "insular minority," discussed in Section III below, is not easily defined. Whatever criteria one might use, however, would probably bring under this rubric cases involving Indians, aliens, denaturalized citizens, members of relatively small religious sects holding to controversial beliefs or practices, conscientious objectors to prayers in public schools, procedural rights of alleged security risks, rights of Communists (at least other than those in the First Amendment), and possibly school integration in the Deep South. The 1963 term settled no cases involving the civil rights of Indians, but representatives of each of these other beleaguered minority groups

---

op. cit. supra note 23 and my "The South Counter-Attacks," 12 *Western Political Quarterly*, 371 (1959).

[31] Baggett v. Bullitt, 377 U.S. 360 (1964).

[32] 376 U.S. 254, 279–80 (1964). See also Garrison v. Louisiana, 379 U.S. 64 (1964), and Harry Kalven, Jr., "The New York Times Case: A Note on 'The Central Meaning of the First Amendment,' " 1964 *Supreme Court Review* 191.

[33] Davis v. Mann, 377 U.S. 678 (1964); Lucas v. Colorado, 377 U.S. 713 (1964); Maryland Commission v. Tawes, 377 U.S. 656 (1964); Reynolds v. Sims, 377 U.S. 533 (1964); Roman v. Sincock, 377 U.S. 695 (1964); WMCA v. Lomenzo, 377 U.S. 633 (1964); Swann v. Adams, 378 U.S. 553 (1964); Meyers v. Thigpen, 378 U.S. 554 (1964); Williams v. Moss, 378 U.S. 558 (1964).

[34] Wesberry v. Sanders, 376 U.S. 1 (1964).

[35] Davis v. Mann, Reynolds v. Sims, Roman v. Sincock, Williams v. Moss, all *supra* note 33.

[36] Maryland Commission v. Tawes and Meyers v. Thigpen, both *supra* note 33.

[37] 376 U.S. 52 (1964).

[38] 375 U.S. 399 (1964).

had their day—and with only one exception[39] a successful day—in court.

Even when they did not have a day before the Supreme Court, these minorities sometimes won. *United States* v. *Communist Party*, for instance, denied review of a Court of Appeals decision that communist party officers could not be required to register under the Internal Security Act of 1950 because the government had failed to prove that any party official could carry out the registration procedure without incriminating himself under the clause of the Smith Act that makes knowing party membership a crime.[40]

Chamberlin v. *Dade County*[41] upheld the claim of those offended by public prayers, by invalidating Florida's Bible-reading requirements for public schools. *Schneider* v. *Rusk*[42] reversed a denaturalization order, and in so doing held unconstitutional as an unreasonable discrimination against naturalized citizens that section of the Immigration and Nationality Act of 1952 providing for denaturalization of a naturalized citizen who resides in his former country for seven years. In another denaturalization case, a six-judge majority halted the deportation of the notorious Frank Costello. The Court interpreted the congressional statute authorizing deportation of an alien twice convicted of crimes involving moral turpitude as not applying to a denaturalized alien when the criminal acts had been committed while he was a citizen.[43] On a more technical but less obscure point, *Foti* v. *Immigration Service* ruled that Courts of Appeals have jurisdiction to review administrative denials of suspensions of deportation proceedings.[44]

A third deportation case brought back to the Court the troublesome question of when an American national can be held to have lost his citizenship. At issue was the constitutionality of that portion of the Immigration and Nationality Act of 1952 which provides that an American national loses his citizenship by serving in the armed forces of a foreign nation without obtaining authorization from the Secretaries of State and Defense. The Court of Appeals for the Second Circuit had reluctantly ruled that Herman Marks was a deportable alien because he had lost his citizenship by serving as a captain in Castro's army after the revolutionaries had taken over the Cuban government.[45] With Brennan not participating, the Justices divided 4–4 and thereby affirmed the decision of the Court of Appeals.[46]

The alleged security risk seeking judicial protection was William L. Greene, whose earlier litigation had been the occasion for a 1959 Supreme Court decision that neither Congress nor the President had authorized in the Industrial Security Program a denial of the right of confrontation of hostile witnesses.[47] This time Greene asked that the government be ordered to give him monetary restitution under the regulations in effect when he began his initial action rather than under later and more restrictive regulations. Seven Justices, over dissents by Harlan and White, agreed that Greene was entitled to collect under the earlier regulations.[48]

On the final day of the term, a group of Communist Party officers succeeded in their efforts to strike down the passport provisions of the Subversive Activities Control Act of 1950. Justice Black would have held the entire act unconstitutional, but the majority invalidated only the passport section. For the Court, Goldberg wrote that in excluding members of communist-dominated organizations from passports and in making it a crime for them even to apply for passports, the statute "too broadly and indiscriminantly restricts the right to travel and thereby abridges the liberty guaranteed by the Fifth Amendment."[49] Clark, Harlan, and White dissented.

Earlier in the term the Justices in a unanimous *per curiam* opinion again emphasized their growing impatience with the slow progress of school desegregation.[50] And in what promises to be one of the last stages of the Prince Edward County case—one of the original school suits brought in 1951—seven members of the Court held that a federal district judge could: (1) enjoin state officials from paying tuition grants to parents of children attending "pri-

[39] Mrvica v. Esperdy, 376 U.S. 560 (1964), held that an alien had interrupted his residence in the United States and did not qualify as a permanent resident.

[40] Communist Party v. United States, 331 F. 2d 807 (1964); *cert. den.*, 377 U.S. 968 (1964). *Cf.* Communist Party v. Subversive Activities Control Board, 367 U.S. 1 (1961).

[41] 377 U.S. 402 (1964).

[42] 377 U.S. 163 (1964).

[43] Costello v. Immigration and Naturalization Service, 376 U.S. 120 (1964).

[44] 375 U.S. 217 (1963).

[45] 315 F. 2d 673 (1963). See John P. Roche, "The Expatriation Cases," 1963 *Supreme Court Review* 325.

[46] Marks v. Esperdy, 377 U.S. 214 (1964).

[47] Greene v. McElroy, 360 U.S. 474 (1959).

[48] Greene v. United States, 376 U.S. 149 (1964).

[49] Aptheker v. Rusk, 378 U.S. 500, 514 (1964).

[50] Calhoun v. Latimer, 377 U.S. 263 (1964).

vate" schools established to avoid integration; and (2) order those officials to reopen the county's public schools, closed since 1959. Justices Clark and Harlan dissented against the latter part of the ruling but otherwise agreed with the majority that Virginia was denying Negro children equal protection.[51]

In *Cooper* v. *Pate* a Black Muslim in the Illinois state penitentiary tried to sue the warden for denying him his civil rights. The Muslim claimed that he was in effect segregated from the rest of the prisoners, and while they were allowed religious literature he was not permitted to obtain a copy of the "*Quran.*" Illinois replied that the Muslims were more than a religious group: they were also a political organization dedicated to "Black Supremacy." More particularly their record in instigating prison riots justified special treatment. The district court and the Court of Appeals for the Seventh Circuit agreed with state officials and dismissed the case as not stating a cause of action. In ruling that there had been no abridgment of civil rights, both courts relied heavily on what they described as sociological evidence—a study by the Chicago police department linking Muslims to prison disorders.[52] In a terse and unanimous *per curiam* opinion the Supreme Court reversed and sent the case back for a trial on the merits.[53]

II. DIVISIONS

The decisions of the 1963 term were overwhelmingly libertarian. Whatever the number and range of factors the Justices weighed in making their decisions, they usually managed to tip the scales in favor of the claim of civil liberties, as the data in Tables I, II, and III demonstrate. Of the 64 cases[54] involving civil liberties claims, 56 (over 87 per cent) were decided in favor of the claimant, and 21 of these 56 decisions (37 per cent), were unanimous.

In recent years Black, Douglas, Warren, and Brennan have tended to vote together. In 1962 Arthur Goldberg came to the Court and immediately joined the libertarian wing. Even on the more difficult cases, this group of five Justices was often able to pick up an additional vote from Stewart or White and not infrequently from Clark. Thus in more than half of the decisions that divided the Court, there were six or more votes for a libertarian result.

No matter what the specific nature of the case, Justice Douglas voted for the civil liberties claim in all but two instances and Justice Goldberg in all but three. In contrast, in all but two of the cases that divided the Court, Justice Harlan found a compelling reason—considerations of federalism or the doctrine of political questions, for example—for voting against a libertarian result.

The data in Tables I, II, and III also qualify any characterization of Justice White as being relatively unsympathetic to civil liberties. In criminal justice and insular minority cases only Harlan was less apt to decide for the claimant; but in cases involving freedom of expression or association, White voted for a libertarian result as often as Black or Brennan and more often than Warren.

One of the more interesting sidelights of these voting records is Hugo Black's relatively frequent votes for what is here classified as a non-libertarian result. Part of the problem, of course, as with all schemes of classification, lies in categorizing a particular vote as for or against civil liberties. In many instances a vote may clearly fall within one or the other category; but in other instances the choice is not so obvious. The issue may not be for or against civil liberties, but rather for or against one of two competing claims to personal freedom.[55] The most salient examples of the latter situation were the sit-in cases. There Black several times voted against Negroes' claims to freedom

[51] Griffin v. Prince Edward County, 377 U.S. 218 (1964).

[52] Cooper v. Pate, 324 F. 2d. 165 (1963).

[53] 378 U.S. 546 (1964).

[54] Marks v. Esperdy, *supra* note 45, is not counted here since it was a 4-4 decision, nor is Dresner v. Tallahassee, 378 U.S. 539 (1964), because it was not a decision on the merits, only a determination that there had not been a final decision by the highest state court. The cases in these three tables may be found in volumes 375–378 of the U.S. Reports. I have not listed here those decisions listed under "Memorandum Cases" by the Lawyers Cooperative Publishing Co. This classification does not always coincide with that used by the official reporter of the Supreme Court.

[55] In Jackson v. Denno, *supra* note 5, for example, I have counted Black as voting for the civil liberties claim even though he filed a dissenting opinion. I did so because Black said he would have ruled the confession inadmissible because it was obtained under inherently coercive circumstances. Black also dissented from the majority view that a judge would be a better protector than a jury, in such cases, of the civil rights of a defendant. He took a similar position on the question of whether the judge or the jury should determine the existence of a clear and present danger. Dennis v. United States, 341 U.S. 494 (1951).

TABLE I. CRIMINAL JUSTICE CASES

Case	Vote	Do	Go	Wa	Br	Bl	St	Cl	Wh	Ha
Coleman v. Alabama	9–0	+	+	+	+	+	+	+	+	+
Arnold v. No. Car.	9–0	+	+	+	+	+	+	+	+	+
Preston v. U.S.	9–0	+	+	+	+	+	+	+	+	+
Smith v. Pa.	9–0	+	+	+	+	+	+	+	+	+
Leonard v. U.S.	9–0	+	+	+	+	+	+	+	+	+
Nagelberg v. U.S.	9–0	+	+	+	+	+	+	+	+	+
Michaels v. U.S.	9–0	+	+	+	+	+	+	+	+	+
U.S. v. Behrens	9–0	+	+	+	+	+	+	+	+	+
Murphy v. Commission	9–0	+	+	+	+	+	+	+	+	+
Robinson v. Florida	9–0	+	+	+	+	+	+	+	+	+
Fallen v. U.S.	9–0	+	+	+	+	+	+	+	+	+
Stoner v. California	8–1	+	+	+	+	+	+	+	+	−
Corey v. U.S.	8–1	+	+	+	+	+	+	+	+	−
Hardy v. U.S.	8–1	+	+	+	+	+	+	+	+	−
Panico v. U.S.	7–2	+	+	+	+	+	+	−	+	−
Aguilar v. Texas	6–3	+	+	+	+	−	−	−	+	+
Massiah v. U.S.	6–3	+	+	+	+	+	+	−	−	−
Bartone v. U.S.	6–3	+	+	+	+	+	+	−	−	−
Bouie v. Columbia	6–3	+	+	+	+	−	+	+	−	−
Barr v. Columbia	6–3	+	+	+	+	−	+	+	−	−
Bell v. Maryland	6–3	+	+	+	+	−	+	+	−	−
Griffin v. Maryland	6–3	+	+	+	+	−	+	+	−	−
Jackson v. Denno	6–3	+	+	+	+	+	−	−	+	−
Fahy v. Connecticut	5–4	+	+	+	+	+	−	−	−	−
Malloy v. Hogan	5–4	+	+	+	+	+	−	−	−	−
Escobedo v. Illinois	5–4	+	+	+	+	+	−	−	−	−
Rugendorf v. U.S.	4–5	+	+	+	+	−	−	−	−	−
Barnett v. U.S.	4–5	+	+	+	−	+	−	−	−	−
Ungar v. Sarafite	3–6	+	+	−	−	+	−	−	−	−
U.S. v. Tateo	3–6	+	+	−	−	+	−	−	−	−
U.S. v. Welden	2–7	+	−	−	−	+	−	−	−	−
U.S. v. Healy	0–9	−	−	−	−	−	−	−	−	−
Pro civil liberties in non-unanimous decisions:		20–0	19–1	17–3	16–4	14–6	10–10	7–13	6–14	1–19

+ = Vote for civil liberties claim.
− = Vote against civil liberties claim.
0 = Took no part in decision.

from discrimination in eating places open to the public and in favor of the freedom of restaurant owners—in the absence of statutory prohibitions—to select their own clientele.

There is room for reasonable men to differ about which result in the sit-in cases was truly libertarian. Through Black's dissents in these cases, however, runs a theme of deep concern for the effect on public order if a state could not enforce criminal trespass laws against civil rights demonstrators who remain on private property after being told by the owner to leave. Usually when demands of public order have clashed with demands of freedom of expression—and basically these sit-ins are political expression cases, though the majority of the Court did not choose to treat them as such—Black has finally voted in favor of freedom of expression.[56] Moreover, Black's insistence on the primacy of private control

[56] See his position in Beauharnais v. Illinois, 343 U.S. 250 (1952); Cantwell v. Connecticut, 310 U.S. 296 (1940); Feiner v. New York, 340 U.S. 315 (1951); and Terminiello v. Chicago, 337 U.S. 1 (1949). See also "Justice Black and First Amendment 'Absolutes': A Public Interview," 37 *New York University Law Review* 549 (1962).

TABLE II. POLITICAL FREEDOM CASES

Cases	Vote	Go	Do	Bl	Br	Wh	Wa	St	Cl	Ha
Liner v. Jafco	9–0	+	+	+	+	+	+	+	+	+
Anderson v. Martin	9–0	+	+	+	+	+	+	+	+	+
N.Y.T. v. Sullivan	9–0	+	+	+	+	+	+	+	+	+
Henry v. Rock Hill	9–0	+	+	+	+	+	+	+	+	+
NAACP v. Alabama	9–0	+	+	+	+	+	+	+	+	+
Steelworkers v. NLRB	8–0	0	+	+	+	+	+	+	+	+
Roman v. Sincock	8–1	+	+	+	+	+	+	+	+	–
Davis v. Mann	8–1	+	+	+	+	+	+	+	+	–
Williams v. Moss	8–1	+	+	+	+	+	+	+	+	–
Reynolds v. Sims	8–1	+	+	+	+	+	+	+	+	–
Md. Comm. v. Tawes	7–2	+	+	+	+	+	+	–	+	–
Meyers v. Thigpen	7–2	+	+	+	+	+	+	–	+	–
Baggett v. Bullitt	7–2	+	+	+	+	+	+	+	–	–
Books v. Kansas	7–2	+	+	+	+	+	+	+	–	–
NLRB v. Packers	6–2	+	0	+	+	+	+	–	+	–
Trainmen v. Virginia	6–2	+	+	+	+	+	+	0	–	–
Wesberry v. Sanders	6–3	+	+	+	+	+	+	–	–	–
WMCA v. Lomenzo	6–3	+	+	+	+	+	+	–	–	–
Lucas v. Colorado	6–3	+	+	+	+	+	+	–	–	–
Jacobellis v. Ohio	6–3	+	+	+	+	+	–	+	–	–
Wright v. Rockefeller	2–7	+	+	–	–	–	–	–	–	–
Rabinowitz v. Kennedy	0–9	–	–	–	–	–	–	–	–	–
Pro civil liberties in non-unanimous decisions:		15–0	14–0	14–1	14–1	14–1	13–2	7–7	7–8	0–15

+ = Vote for civil liberties claim.
– = Vote against civil liberties claim.
0 = Took no part in decision.

TABLE III. INSULAR MINORITY CASES

Case	Vote	Do	Bl	Go	Wa	Br	St	Cl	Wh	Ha
Calhoun v. Latimer	9–0	+	+	+	+	+	–	+	+	+
Cooper v. Pate	9–0	+	+	+	+	+	+	+	+	+
Foti v. Immigration	9–0	+	+	+	+	+	+	+	+	+
Griffin v. Pr. Edw.	9–0	+	+	+	+	+	+	+	+	+
Chamberlin v. Dade	8–1	+	+	+	+	+	–	+	+	+
Greene v. U.S.	7–2	+	+	+	+	+	+	+	–	–
Costello v. Immigrat'n	6–2	+	+	+	+	+	+	–	–	0
Aptheker v. Rusk	6–3	+	+	+	+	+	+	–	–	–
Schneider v. Rusk	5–3	+	+	+	+	0	+	–	–	–
Mrvica v. Esperdy	3–6	+	+	+	–	–	–	–	–	–
Pro civil liberties in non-unanimous decisions:		6–0	6–0	6–0	5–1	4–1	4–2	2–4	1–5	1–5

+ = Vote for civil liberties claim.
– = Vote against civil liberties claim.
0 = Took no part in decision.

over property open to the public does not evidence the same sort of value hierarchy as did his opinion for the Court in *Marsh* v. *Alabama*.[57]

Black's votes in earlier cases tell a story of a consistent preference, one that makes his sit-in votes seem somewhat strange. But Black's votes do not reveal the entire man; nor do his published opinions. Apparently there has been for some time a strong tension within his jurisprudence. For instance, in *Martin* v. *Struthers*,[58] the 1943 Jehovah's Witness case involving the constitutionality of an anti-doorbell ringing ordinance, Black originally voted to sustain the ordinance. At conference and in the opinion he first circulated—as senior majority Justice, Black had assigned to himself the task of writing the opinion of the Court—he stressed that the case involved a conflict of rights, and that the ordinance was a valid means of protecting the privacy of the home. At conference he had emphasized the necessity of guarding the integrity of private property and had expressed fear that the Witnesses would soon be invading Catholic churches to distribute their literature—with predictable results. Black later had second thoughts, withdrew his opinion, and switched his vote. Stone then graciously allowed him to write a new opinion for the Court, this one vindicating Stone's position at conference that the ordinance was an abridgment of freedom of speech.[59]

III. DOCTRINES

Protesting against what he felt was too rigid a solution to problems of legislative districting, Potter Stewart charged that the majority Justices were pursuing a particular political theory.[60] Undoubtedly Stewart was correct, though candor should have required him to add that he, too, was following a political theory, albeit a different one from the majority's. The great difficulty, given the vagueness of many Supreme Court opinions on fundamental principles of jurisprudence and political theory, is to discover the precise nature and implications of doctrines currently dominant within the Court.

Thus it should be said at the outset that problems of evidence require a cautious approach to any jurisprudential interpretation of Supreme Court decisions. The student of judicial behavior is at least as apt to impose his own categories, substitute his personal judgments, and construct subjectively attractive causal links between concepts when he is analyzing opinions as when he is classifying votes. Determining the significance of a pattern of dicta is no less difficult than categorizing, for example, the reapportionment decisions as basically involving questions of protection of "minority" rights or of free access to the political processes. The willingness of the Justices to compromise their views—and occasionally to change their votes[61]—to gain in intra-Court bargaining or to cope with matters of power politics complicates both kinds of analysis, as do problems of literary style and the pragmatic approach to legal issues that American judges so often take.

One might even go so far as to question whether Supreme Court Justices have a jurisprudence in the academic sense of that term. Perhaps "doctrine" would be less pretentious as well as more descriptive, but as Cardozo once observed, each judge is subject to "a stream of tendency, whether you choose to call it philosophy or not, which gives coherence and direction in thought and action."[62]

Insofar as the majority Justices of the Warren Court, more particularly Black, Douglas, Warren, Brennan and Goldberg, can be said to have accepted any jurisprudential doctrine, it is a revision of that of Harlan F. Stone.[63] Widely known as the Preferred Position Theory, Stone's ideas were first articulated in a footnote to the *Carolene Products* case in 1938.[64] The doctrine was originally drafted by Stone's clerk, Louis Lusky, and edited and amended by Charles Evans Hughes.[65] In later cases Stone elaborated his ideas; and after his death, his biographer, Alpheus T. Mason, brought the Justice's thoughts together into a more coherent theory than Stone had had an

[57] 326 U.S. 501 (1946).

[58] 319 U.S. 141 (1943).

[59] The Frank Murphy Papers, Michigan Historical Collections, University of Michigan.

[60] Lucas v. Colorado, *supra* note 33 at p. 748.

[61] See my *Elements of Judicial Strategy, supra* note 18.

[62] *The Nature of the Judicial Process* (Yale University Press, 1921), p. 12.

[63] Arthur Miller contends that it is the political theory of Thomas Hill Green that is now triumphant on the Court. "An Affirmative Thrust to Due Process of Law," 30 *George Washington Law Review* 399, 416–19 (1962). While I do not agree with Miller on this point, I would like to express my general intellectual debt to this very suggestive article.

[64] United States v. Carolene Products, 304 U.S. 144 (1938).

[65] The details are given in Alpheus T. Mason, *Harlan Fiske Stone: Pillar of the Law* (New York, 1956), ch. 31.

opportunity—or an inclination—to do during his own life.[66]

As published in 1938, Stone's doctrine listed three kinds of cases in which the Court would relax its usual presumption that challenged legislation is constitutional: (1) where a statute appears to fall within the specific prohibitions of the Bill of Rights itself or as made applicable to the states by the Fourteenth Amendment; (2) where a statute restricts access to the political processes; (3) where a statute is directed against specific religious, national, or racial groups, or against any "insular" minority so subject to prejudice that it could not have a meaningful voice in the political process.

The civil liberties decisions of the 1963 term can be viewed as falling under these three categories, and they were so arranged in the first section of this paper, though the titles of the categories were somewhat changed. Not only can the decisions be placed in the pattern prescribed by Stone, but much of the language of recent opinions is reminiscent of the Roosevelt Court in its libertarian prime. In the 1962 term *NAACP* v. *Button* spoke of First Amendment freedoms as "supremely precious" as well as "delicate and vulnerable" and therefore demanding and deserving the most careful judicial protection.[67] In the 1963 term *Baggett* v. *Bullitt*,[68] in striking down Washington's loyalty oaths, emphasized the sensitivity of "basic First Amendment freedoms." In *Wesberry* v. *Sanders*, Black paraphrased his earlier panegyric[69] of the First Amendment to describe the right to vote: "No right is more precious in a free country than that of having a voice in the election of those who make the laws. . . . Other rights, even the most basic, are illusory if the right to vote is undermined."[70] In *Schneider* v. *Rusk*, Douglas quoted with approval the statement by a lower court judge—who in turn was quoting Justice Goldberg speaking for the Court—that citizenship is "a most precious right."[71]

There appears to be either some confusion about which rights are most precious or overgenerous use of the superlative. Moreover it is difficult to distinguish rights under the first eight amendments (category 1 of Stone's doctrine) from First Amendment rights under freedom of access to the political process (category 2).[72] Perhaps the Justices could reduce the problems if they never again used the misleading title "Preferred Freedoms" (to my knowledge the Warren Court Justices have not used it in recent years) and if they restated Stone's doctrine along the following lines:

> First, as the highest tribunal in the nation the Supreme Court must be alert to maintain the integrity of the judicial process, to insure that, where officials from other branches of government undertake to use the judicial process to achieve policy aims, judges will proceed with a scrupulous regard for procedural fairness.
>
> Second, if judges are to presume constitutional legislation affecting economic arrangements, they have a heavy obligation to insure the truly democratic nature of the political process by which such laws are enacted. Courts must thus play a special role in guarding the right to vote and more broadly ensuring that freedom of communication—speech and press—as well as freedom of association are available equally to dissidents as to those espousing currently popular causes.

This rephrasing eases rather than eliminates problems.[73] Stone's third category, for instance, is the vaguest of the three. How does a judge determine that a group in a highly pluralistic society is an insular minority? Numbers alone would hardly constitute an adequate criterion of insularity. The du Ponts, Harrimans, Rockefellers, and Kennedys taken together form only the tiniest fraction of the population; yet from time to time they give evidence of being able to stand on their own feet politically.

Race may not be a very useful criterion either. At one time it might have made sense to put most of the Negro cases under this third rubric. Since 1954, however, much racial litigation could just as logically be classed under the Court's role of protecting the democratic nature of the political process. Indeed, one authoritative commentator has suggested that the basic justification for judicial action to end publicly sanctioned segregation can be found under Stone's second category: free access to

[66] See especially Alpheus T. Mason, *The Supreme Court from Taft to Warren* (Baton Rouge, Louisiana State University Press, 1958), chs. 5–6, and *The Supreme Court: Palladium of Freedom* (University of Michigan Press, 1962).

[67] *Supra* note 23.

[68] *Supra* note 31.

[69] Milk Wagon Drivers Union v. Meadowmoor Dairies, 317 U.S. 287, 302 (1941).

[70] *Supra* note 34 at p. 17.

[71] 377 U.S. 163, 167 (1964). Goldberg had made this statement in Kennedy v. Mendoza-Martinez, 372 U.S. 144, 159 (1963).

[72] The reason for this overlap is explained in Mason, *Harlan Fiske Stone*, ch. 31.

[73] For a perceptive critique of Stone's doctrine, see George Braden, "The Search for Objectivity in Constitutional Law," 57 *Yale Law Journal* 571 (1948).

political process can have no real meaning in a society where government authority imposes caste lines among citizens.[74]

Some of the difficulties of this third category could be lessened if it were rephrased to read:

> Courts have a third special obligation, that of making sure that regulations affecting social or political freedom, particularly where the freedom of specific groups is immediately involved, meet the highest standards of equal protection of the law. In applying these standards the Court will be obliged to look carefully at the actual impact of a regulation, as *Yick Wo* v. *Hopkins*[75] so eloquently promised.

There are still other problems inherent in any rejuvenation of Stone's doctrine. First, it does not provide a set of objective standards to guide decision-making. Even those who accept the doctrine may differ fundamentally about important kinds of decisions it requires. Stone, for instance, was adamant in insisting that courts should keep out of the apportionment controversy. At the conference discussion of *Colegrove* v. *Green*,[76] so Justice Murphy recorded in his notes, Stone said that judicial intervention in legislative districting "would create confusion in each state. It isn't court business." Again according to Murphy's notes, Justices Black and Rutledge at first agreed with Stone. The original vote on *Colegrove* was 6–1, with Murphy "passing," Jackson not participating and Douglas dissenting alone.[77] Black and to some extent Rutledge later changed their minds. Stone did not live to do so.

A jurisprudence is not, to be sure, a rigid set of formulae designed to supply quick answers to specific and complex social conflicts. It is to a large extent a means of ordering values —and hopefully shaping attitudes and behavior—in terms of ends that are justified by relatively abstract, morally desirable, and intellectually defensible principles. Nevertheless one may charge that, even as restated here, Stone's doctrine is still defective: insofar as it orders values it does so more in terms of desired procedures than of general goals. If this is a defect, it is one shared by much of American political thought.[78]

A more practical difficulty is that Stone's doctrine offers a role for the Court in only one part, although an important part, of its work. The doctrine offers no help at all in fields where the questions do not involve basic constitutional issues, where for example Congress has formulated only vague general statements of policy and left it to judges or administrators to fill in the wide policy gaps. Does deference to Congress require the Court to make such policy, or does self-restraint require the Justices to override congressional judgment? A complete role theory would have to offer guidelines here, for this kind of problem arises rather often, and it goes to the heart of the function of the Court in the political system.[79]

Whatever the shortcomings of Stone's doctrine, if the Justices have decided to accept it, scholars can do little beyond writing critical articles and books in an effort to steer the Court onto more promising jurisprudential paths. Other public officials, however, may make the Justices pay a high price for following Stone's doctrine, for it prescribes a very controversial role for the Court, one beset with political no less than with intellectual pitfalls.

Most responsible people would concede that protecting the integrity of the judicial process is a proper task for an appellate tribunal, though there might be—and with the Supreme Court there often is—deep and widespread doubt that a particular court is playing that role properly. On the other hand, there is more widespread and far deeper doubt that protecting the democratic character of the political process is a proper role for the judiciary. Moreover, protection of unpopular and insular minorities—however insular is defined—is by definition likely to be itself an unpopular task. By embarking on a libertarian course that to many people appears to be unduly technical

[74] Mason, *The Supreme Court from Taft to Warren*, chs. 5–6.

[75] 118 U.S. 356, 373–74 (1886).

[76] 328 U.S. 549 (1946).

[77] Murphy Papers and the Harold H. Burton Papers, the Library of Congress, Washington, D. C. I am indebted to Mr. Edward Beiser of Princeton for this latter reference. My interpretation of Murphy's notes was that he first voted with Stone; but Burton's docket book records Murphy as passing and Burton's conference notes report Murphy voted with Douglas. These discrepancies indicate the difficulties the Justices must face in determining their colleagues' views, and serve also as a warning about the historical value of notes jotted down during a lively debate.

[78] Yves Simon, *The Philosophy of Democratic Government* (University of Chicago Press, 1951), p. 123, says that in a democratic society "deliberation is about means and presupposes that the problem of ends has been settled."

[79] See Martin Shapiro, *Law and Politics in the Supreme Court* (New York, 1964); and my "Congressional Reliance on Judicial Law-Making," a paper delivered at the 1963 meetings of the American Political Science Association.

in protecting the rights of persons accused of crime, by being solicitous of the political rights of "radicals" and "subversives," and by being acutely sensitive to the civil rights of minorities who wish to rise above their "place" in society, the Justices may invite, as they did in 1954–58, the formation of a powerful coalition determined to overturn a number of individual decisions if not to curb the very authority of the Court.[80]

One might speculate, therefore, that a libertarian Justice or group of Justices might recognize the dangers confronting their doctrine and might decide that the most prudent course would be to alter the political climate within which the Court operates. In a sense every judicial opinion is an effort to create or maintain a favorable climate of opinion by offering a reasoned explanation for a given decision. The Justices have open to them other means of influencing public opinion,[81] but they might also decide to strike directly at their opponents. Thus a brash observer might see the reapportionment cases as both a part of the Court's general libertarian orientation and as a means to translate that orientation into viable public policy. The majority Justices, this observer might reason, have decided to alter in a drastic way the power of the people most likely to oppose the Court's policies. That is, by their reapportionment decisions, the Justices may have deliberately set out to revamp the political processes and to change the character of the interests and segments of opinion that a majority of legislators are likely to represent.

First of all it must be said that the direct evidence in support of this power-politics interpretation is just about nonexistent. It is true that the reapportionment decisions endorsing the one man, one vote formula occurred only after Warren, Black, Douglas, and Brennan had experienced severe difficulties with Congress and state legislatures and had seen their majority within the Court on some civil liberties issues temporarily wither away. It is also true that as men of considerable political experience—and acumen—the majority Justices must have been aware of the hostile attitudes of many other public officials toward recent libertarian decisions and aware as well of the potential effect of the reapportionment decisions on the structure of political power in this country.

Nevertheless, experience and awareness are not sufficient of themselves to prove or even strongly indicate intent. There is also a time problem here. For years before the Warren Court's problems with other public officials, Black and Douglas had been urging the Court to decide reapportionment cases on their merits.[82] And for some time the Chief Justice and Justice Brennan had been indicating that they, too, thought the Court should be hearing such cases.[83] Furthermore, Justice White, who joined in the reapportionment decisions and in most of the other political freedom rulings, was much more often than not opposed to a libertarian result in non-unanimous criminal justice and insular minority cases. One would not, therefore, expect him to be anxious to join in an effort to weaken the chances of some of his own views becoming viable public policy, unless of course those particular views were relatively unimportant to him.[84]

While this power interpretation has no direct evidential support at this time, it is worth pursuing because considerations of political power can never be very far removed from analysis of Supreme Court decisions. This explanation has at least the merit of directing attention to the impact of judicial decisions on public policy and more particularly to the ability of a court to change the nature of the political system within which it operates. That change may be no less significant because the judges did not think through the implications of their decisions and did not deliberately plot a revolution by judicial fiat. No serious student of public law has ever doubted the immense power of the Justices, but this power has usually been viewed in terms of a capacity to limit the authority of other public officials or, less frequently, of increasing their authority by validating controversial courses of action.[85] These are significant exer-

[80] See my *Congress and the Court* (University of Chicago Press, 1962).

[81] See my *Elements of Judicial Strategy*.

[82] For example: Colegrove v. Green, *supra* note 76; MacDougal v. Green, 325 U.S. 281 (1948); and South v. Peters, 339 U.S. 276 (1950). The other decisions are summarized in Jo Desha Lucas, "Dragon in the Thicket," 1961 *Supreme Court Review* 194.

[83] Hartsfield v. Sloan, 357 U.S. 916 (1958).

[84] It is very possible that in the sit-in cases White's values in the criminal justice field clashed with his values in the political freedom field. White voted to affirm the sit-in convictions in each decision that divided the Court.

[85] See Robert Dahl, "Decision-Making in a Democracy: The Supreme Court as a National Policy-Maker," 6 *Journal of Public Law* 279 (1957); and Charles Black, *The People and the Court* (New York, 1960).

cises of power, but hardly as significant as the capacity of the Court to change the character of our entire system of representation.

Without denying the potentially revolutionary effect of the reapportionment decisions—again whether intended or not—one might question whether that effect may not be so gradual as to be evolutionary rather than revolutionary. At the outset, one cannot say with any degree of certainty what immediate impact these cases will have. No doubt urban and suburban areas currently are badly underrepresented in Congress as well as in most state legislatures. But how much and exactly how these areas will gain politically depends on how electoral lines are redrawn. Linking of suburban and rural areas in the same districts could have a very different effect from linking suburban and urban areas, or from carving new districts from within urban or suburban regions.

It must also be remembered that new electoral lines will be drawn by legislators chosen under the old—and unfair—system. And it is possible to gerrymander districts of equal population. Indeed, given a pluralistic society, it is probably impossible to construct any representation lines that do not give advantages to one party or to one kind of interest over another. How judges can distinguish inevitable advantage from subtle deliberate rigging, and what they will be able to do about gerrymandering if they detect it, remain to be seen. Here, certainly, is an area in which there are few established judicial standards of judgment.[86] *Gomillion* v. *Lightfoot*[87] did invalidate a crude effort by Alabama officials to gerrymander Tuskegee, but in that situation race was the sole criterion for districting used by the state. When legislators are less crass, judicial difficulties will increase, as indicated by the Court's refusal to grapple with gerrymandering in *Wright* v. *Rockefeller*.[88]

Second, insofar as the Justices have increased urban political power, they may have weakened or at best have done nothing to increase political support for civil rights. Put quite simply, support for the welfare state does not automatically carry with it respect for the rights of dissenters or tolerance toward other minorities. Available evidence, while hardly conclusive, indicates that although urban working classes may be economically liberal, they are hardly libertarian.[89] They may be somewhat more so than farmers; but by being more exposed to political communication, blue collar workers may also be more vulnerable to rabble-rousing and may choose representatives who are less sympathetic to civil liberties than rural conservatives would be. Cries like "Wipe out crime in the streets!" may strike closer to home in the cities and are not likely to generate support for libertarian decisions in the criminal justice field. The Court's decision in *New York Times* v. *Sullivan*,[90] while it did free the *Times* from what was clearly political oppression, formulated a general doctrine of constitutional law that will make it more difficult to control political smears and reckless campaign charges. In fact one of the first uses of the *Times* decision was to reverse a libel judgment growing out of an irresponsible campaign slur. Washington state representative John Goldmark had obtained a $40,000 verdict against a group who had called him a subversive during the 1962 campaign, but the superior court judge ordered a new trial on the ground that the instructions to the jury had not conformed to the standards laid down in the *Times* opinion.[91]

On the other hand, it is probable that the reapportionment decisions will also increase the political influence of the suburbs, perhaps more so than that of the old urban centers. In the middle and upper income groups that

[86] State courts have applied such standards as contiguity and compactness to districting, but these would hardly seem to make gerrymandering very difficult. See Anthony Lewis, "Legislative Apportionment and the Federal Courts," 71 *Harvard Law Review* 1057, 1066–70 (1958). For an analysis of some of the more commonly used apportioning formulae and suggestions for improvement, see: Alan L. Clem, "Measuring Legislative Malapportionment: In Search of a Better Yardstick," 7 *Midwest Journal of Political Science* 125 (1963).

[87] 364 U.S. 339 (1960).

[88] *Supra* note 37.

[89] Much of the available evidence is summarized in Seymour M. Lipset, *Political Man* (New York, 1960), ch. 4.

[90] *Supra* note 32.

[91] *New York Times*, December 10, 1964, 23: 1. See also Talley v. California, 362 U.S. 60 (1960), invalidating a Los Angeles ordinance requiring that handbills disclose the name of the publisher and the distributor. For discussions of the serious nature of the problem of securing intelligent and thoughtful political debate, consult the two books by Stanley Kelley, Jr., *Professional Public Relations and Political Power* (The Johns Hopkins University Press, 1956), and *Political Campaigning* (Washington, D.C., The Brookings Institution, 1960); and Frank Jonas, "The Art of Political Dynamiting," 10 *Western Political Quarterly* 374 (1957).

populate the suburbs, the Justices may well find greater support for libertarian decisions, especially for those whose impact does not immediately occur next door. But the Justices are also children of the New Deal—in one or two cases the relationship is avuncular—and economic liberalism is almost as much a part of their background as is devotion to civil liberties. Insofar as the reapportionment decisions increase the political influence of the suburbs, their effect may run counter to economic liberalism in many respects. Suburbanites are apt to back government spending policies from which they benefit, such as improved highways and subsidies to commuter railroads. It is questionable how these people will react to other aspects of the welfare state.[92]

Third, it does seem very probable that Negro political influence will be increased, particularly in the South, since it is apparently more difficult to discriminate against Negro voters in urban areas.[93] This change may to some extent cut down the incidence of race-baiting, though alone it will by no means end such demagoguery. And while increased representation in southern state legislatures will not automatically bring about the collapse of resistance to integration, such representation will at least turn these legislatures into a forum in which both sides will be heard.[94]

Increased Negro political influence will certainly help ease some racial problems; but, judging from past experience, it is not at all improbable that Negroes will be as callous toward the rights of other minority groups as whites have been toward those of the Negro. Perhaps more significant than scattered indications among Negroes of anti-semitism[95] and more overt hostility toward Puerto Ricans, is the past behavior of white ethnic groups. A recent status as a member of a lower caste group does not appear to have made whites more tolerant of newer immigrants into American society. Irish resentment of Poles and Italians has been as bitter as Yankee disdain for the Irish; and outside the South, white opposition to civil rights legislation—though obviously not against Lyndon Johnson—seems to have its strongest emotional base in working class neighborhoods of first and second generation Americans.[96]

Fourth, it is naive to think that changing the nature of electoral districts will immediately change the nature of the legislative process. Because of public ignorance and apathy on many issues, legislators have considerable leeway in voting for or against measures and far wider freedom in allowing themselves to be placed in a position not to vote at all. The fundamental fact here may be that a legislature is a social system as well as a political institution, a social system in which the character of constituents is an important factor, but only one of many operative factors.[97]

Furthermore, although dramatic civil liberties issues are occasionally fought out in the legislative arena, probably the more usual context for these problems, whether of discrimination against minorities, criminal justice, or political freedom, is within the jurisdiction of local police and local prosecutors. It is true that these officials may be applying statutes formally passed by state legislatures or ordinances that technically owe their legality to legislative sufferance; but these regulations typically allow broad administrative discretion,

[92] See James Q. Wilson and Edward C. Banfield, "Public-Regardingness as a Value Premise in Voting Behavior," this REVIEW, Vol. 58 (Dec. 1964), pp. 876–887.

[93] See *1961 U.S. Commission on Civil Rights Report* (Washington, D.C., G.P.O., 1961), Bk I.

[94] Georgia, for instance, in 1962 elected to its state legislature the first Negro since Reconstruction. Albert Saye, "Revolution by Judicial Action in Georgia," 17 *Western Political Quarterly* 10 (1964).

[95] The New York office of the Anti-Defamation League has a thick file of newspaper reports and analyses of anti-semitism among Negroes. While this evidence is not conclusive in proving the widespread existence of anti-semitism among Negroes, it is still disconcerting to those who had hoped that the Negro would learn and profit from the experience of his white brethren. These reports would come as no surprise to those who accept the thesis of E. Franklin Frazier in his *Black Bourgeoisie* (New York, 1957).

For discussions of Negro-Jewish relations, see especially: Kenneth B. Clark, "Candor about Negro-Jewish Relations," 1 *Commentary* 8 (Feb., 1946); James Baldwin, "The Harlem Ghetto: Winter 1948," 5 *Commentary* 165 (Feb., 1948); Nathan Glazer, "Negroes and Jews: The New Challenge to Pluralism," 38 *Commentary* (Dec., 1964); and R. C. Hertz, "Rising Tide of Negro-Jewish Tensions," 20 *Ebony* 117 (Dec., 1964).

[96] Direct evidence here is lacking. I say "seems" and base this statement on numerous newspaper stories in *The New York Times* and *The Washington Post and Times-Herald* during the fall of 1964 and on my own experience in working for the U.S. Civil Rights Commission in New Jersey.

[97] See John Wahlke, Heinz Eulau, William Buchanan, and LeRoy Ferguson, *The Legislative System* (New York, 1962).

and it is difficult to see how they could be otherwise drawn, given the complexity of the problems with which they deal. Ordinary breach of the peace regulations provide ample discretion for local officials to do a thorough job of curtailing civil liberties.

It is also true that strong legislative support for or against certain actions may influence police and prosecutor decisions. This influence, however, may trickle down rather slowly, and a few strategically placed legislators who are hostile to libertarian judicial decisions may encourage police to persist in practices of which judges disapprove.

IV. TOWARD A NEW JURISPRUDENCE

The work of the 1963 term reveals a libertarian majority solidly in control of the Court. Insofar as these Justices have adopted a revised version of Stone's jurisprudence, they are applying it in a more positive fashion than Stone envisioned.[98] Instead of merely checking governmental action—though they are doing that in many instances—the Justices are also pushing and shaping governmental action to cope with the problems of twentieth century American society. They have accepted the necessity of big government to help run the complex economy of an urban, industrialized society. But as intellectual heirs of a liberal tradition, the Justices have not lost their fear of government as an oppressor of personal freedom. Nor have they lost their fear of the dangers to personal freedom from non-governmental action.

Edward S. Corwin once showed that historically the basic doctrine of American constitutional law had been one of vested rights[99] —a doctrine that eventually asserted an almost unrestricted liberty to use, dispose of, and contract for property and labor. That doctrine died in 1937. Since then the Justices have been formulating, not always deliberately or perhaps even consciously, a new jurisprudence for the welfare state. This new jurisprudence has many facets, but its core, I believe, is composed of two concepts: freedom and social equality. "Freedom" here has been modified to mean political not economic freedom, for the Court has encouraged—not merely tolerated—government regulation of the economy.[100] For its part, the concept of equality includes but goes far beyond the old common law standard of equal justice within the courtroom between rich and poor. The new concept is much broader in scope and more activist in effect. It requires judges as well as other government officials to foster equality within society as a whole.[101] The Justices have deemed this aspect of constitutional law so important as to incorporate the Fourteenth Amendment's equal protection clause into the Bill of Rights.[102]

The old jurisprudence was subject to serious tensions, and judicial inability to adjust the doctrine of vested rights to a mass, industrialized society led to its downfall. The new jurisprudence, too, is not without its tensions, as the discussion of the possible impact of the reapportionment decisions tried to illustrate. A more fundamental tension, despite a recent denial by Mr. Justice Goldberg,[103] is that between social equality and political freedom. In a society of men of unequal talent, ambition, and character, political freedom may be as dangerous to social equality as economic freedom was. This is not to deny that the Justices may be able to find a way that will allow much of both values to become operational, only to caution that their mutual existence may depend on a delicate process of reconciliation.

The Justices may lack a fully articulated theory of politics to explain and justify their role, or their variety of roles, in the American

[98] For a related but somewhat different thesis, see Miller, *op. cit., supra* note 63.

[99] "The Basic Doctrine of American Constitutional Law," 12 *Michigan Law Review* 247 (1914).

[100] For example: American Power & Light Co. v. SEC, 329 U.S. 90 (1946); Ferguson v. Skrupa, 372 U.S. 726 (1963); Interstate Natural Gas Co. v. FPC, 331 U.S. 682 (1947); Phillips Petroleum Co. v. Wisconsin, 347 U.S. 672 (1954); Wickard v. Filburn, 317 U.S. 111 (1942).

[101] See, for example: Steele v. L. & N. Rr., 323 U.S. 192 (1944); Tunstall v. Brotherhood, 323 U.S. 210 (1944); Shelley v. Kraemer, 334 U.S. 1 (1948); Graham v. Brotherhood, 338 U.S. 232 (1949); Trainmen v. Howard, 343 U.S. 768 (1952); Barrows v. Jackson, 346 U.S. 249 (1953); Brown v. Board, 347 U.S. 483 (1954).

[102] Bolling v. Sharpe, 347 U.S. 497 (1954).

[103] "Equality in Governmental Action," 39 *New York University Law Review* 205 (1964). At one point Goldberg stated that he believes the framers of the Constitution "naturally assumed that [equality] was encompassed within the concept of liberty." *Ibid.*, p. 207. On this point, Philip Kurland, "Equal in Origin and Equal in Title to the Legislative and Executive Branches of Government," 78 *Harvard Law Review* 143 (1964), has angrily lashed back at Goldberg in particular and the recent work of the Court in general.

political system. They may also lack a coherent philosophy of law to balance liberty against equality and to direct governmental action into socially beneficial channels with a minimum of flooding onto the plains of personal freedom. Yet the Justices do not seem to lack a sense of political direction. Their positive approach to problems of law and policy may mean that they are making different kinds of law than they were thirty years ago; they are hardly making less important law—or less important policy.

Introduction—Is Freedom of the Press A Redundancy: What Does it Add To Freedom of Speech?

By MELVILLE B. NIMMER*

BEFORE turning to the provocative issues posed in this symposium on the First Amendment and the Media, it may be well to pause by way of introduction to consider a preliminary constitutional issue. In the voluminous discussions, judicial and otherwise, of the rights of the media, one issue appears to have been virtually ignored.[1] That the First Amendment guarantee of freedom of expression, whatever its scope, may be claimed not just for newspapers and other printed publications, but also for motion pictures,[2] and radio and television broadcasts[3] is clear enough. Freedom of the press amounts to freedom of "the media."[4] But the constitutional text protects against "abridging the freedom of speech, or of the press."[5] Why this duality? Is any freedom conferred upon "the press" by the freedom of the press clause which would not be available to it (as well as to nonmedia speakers) by the freedom of speech clause? Alternatively, may it be argued that a separate press clause implies that speech via the press is subject to some restraints that would not be applicable to other speech? If each of these inquiries is to be answered in the negative, does this mean

---

* Professor of Law, University of California, Los Angeles.

1. Since this text was written, it has come to the author's attention that Mr. Justice Potter Stewart, in a recent speech at the Yale Law School, focused upon the same issue as that posed in this introduction, reaching somewhat different conclusions. The reader is fortunate in being able to consider for himself Justice Stewart's insightful views by turning to page 631 of this issue.

2. Joseph Burstyn, Inc. v. Wilson, 343 U.S. 495 (1952).

3. Columbia Broadcasting Sys., Inc. v. Democratic Nat'l Comm., 412 U.S. 94 (1973).

4. *See* Gertz v. Robert Welch, Inc., 94 S. Ct. 2997 (1974); United States v. Paramount Pictures, Inc., 334 U.S. 131, 166 (1948).

5. U.S. CONST. amend. I.

that "freedom of the press" is a meaningless appendage to the speech clause?

As nature abhors a vacuum, the law cannot abide a redundancy. The presumption is strong that language used in a legal instrument, be it a constitution, a statute, or a contract, has meaning, else it would not have been employed.[6] In the real world we know that even lawyers sometimes employ unnecessary phrases.[7] But the legal presumption against futile verbiage is itself a part of the real world, and must be taken into account. Apart from the force of the canons of construction, we are beginning to observe a tension between the rights of the press and of those who would speak although they do not command the press. It may well be, then, that the courts will ultimately reach for some independent meaning in the freedom of the press clause. It is the purpose of this introduction preliminarily to explore that issue.

History casts little light on the question here posed. The foremost historian of the First Amendment tells us that prior to and contemporaneous with its adoption "[m]ost writers, including Addison, Cato, and Alexander, who employed the term 'freedom of speech' with great frequency, used it synonymously with freedom of the press."[8] Insofar as a few writers did distinguish the two concepts, it was based upon the now discarded theory that for purposes of defamation "speech was free so long as it was truthful, while truth was not a defense to a charge of libelous publication."[9] Nothing in the fragmentary records of debate attending the adoption of the First Amendment suggests that the Founding Fathers had this, or, indeed, any other distinction in mind, when they chose to protect both freedom of speech and of the press against abridgment. It may be surmised that to some this duality was deemed necessary because the reference to "speech" might be construed to protect only oral expression, so that the reference to "the press" was added in order explicitly to protect written expression.

This rationale is somewhat remotely suggested by the language of Pennsylvania's first constitution, adopted in 1776. It provided: "That the people have a right to freedom of speech, and of writing, and publishing their sentiments; therefore the freedom of the press ought not to be restrained."[10] But only the state constitutions of Pennsylvania

6. *E.g.*, United States v. Howell, 78 U.S. (11 Wall.) 432, 436 (1871); *see* CAL. CIV. CODE § 3541 (West 1970); *cf.* Cole v. Richardson, 405 U.S. 676 (1972).

7. *See* D. MELLINKOFF, THE LANGUAGE OF THE LAW 349, 404 (1963).

8. L. LEVY, LEGACY OF SUPPRESSION 174 (1960).

9. *Id.*

10. PA. CONST. art. XII (1776) (Declaration of Rights), *quoted in* 5 THE FEDERAL

and Vermont at the time of the adoption of the First Amendment purported to protect freedom of speech as such, while all but four of the states at that time expressly provided constitutional protection for freedom of the press.[11] This fact, when combined with the prevailing rhetoric in the post-Revolutionary period recognizing freedom of speech, tends to support Professor Levy's conclusion that freedom of speech and of the press were at that time thought of as interchangeable.

But as we have seen in other constitutional contexts, the original understanding of the Founders is not necessarily controlling. It is what they said, and not necessarily what they meant, that in the last analysis may be determinative. This is particularly true when constitutional language is subjected to tensions not anticipated when the text was written. During the past term of the Supreme Court, several cases were decided which suggest that just such a tension is building between the rights of speech and of the press.

The Prison Visitation Cases

There are, for example, the prison visitation cases, *Pell v. Procunier*[12] and *Saxbe v. Washington Post Co.*,[13] which, although not articulated as such, may be said to pose the issue of whether those who assert claims under the freedom of the press clause are entitled to greater rights than those who claim under the freedom of speech clause. In both of the cases members of the press challenged prison regulations which forbade press and other media interviews with specific individual inmates.[14] In each instance the challenge was based upon the freedom of the press clause. In *Pell* there was a companion case in which the same regulations were challenged by a group of prisoners, relying upon the freedom of speech clause.

The Court first disposed of the freedom of speech issue. Proceeding upon "the hypothesis that under some circumstances the right of free speech includes a right to communicate a person's views to any willing listener, including a willing representative of the press for the purpose of publication by a willing publisher,"[15] the Court nevertheless

AND STATE CONSTITUTIONS, COLONIAL CHARTERS, AND OTHER ORGANIC LAWS 3083 (F. Thorpe ed. 1909).

11. L. LEVY, LEGACY OF SUPPRESSION 183-85 (1960).

12. 94 S. Ct. 2800, 2827 (1974).

13. *Id.* at 2811, 2827 (1974).

14. Visitation with prisoners was limited to the inmate's family, friends, attorneys and clergy. *See id.* at 2808 n.8, 2813.

15. *Id.* at 2804.

denied the free speech claim. It found that the applicable countervailing interests, especially that of internal security within the corrections facilities, outweighed any speech interests asserted by the prisoners, particularly in view of the alternative modes of communications open to prisoners.[16]

The media representatives asserted a freedom of the press claim that markedly differed from the free speech position of the prisoners. They argued that freedom of the press includes a right of access to the sources of newsworthy information.[17] The Court, borrowing from its opinion in the reporter privilege case, *Branzburg v. Hayes*,[18] acknowledged that " 'news gathering is not without its First Amendment protections' . . . for 'without some protection for seeking out the news, freedom of the press could be eviscerated.' "[19] By this concession, the Court appeared to recognize a right under freedom of the press not available under freedom of speech. But the concession was quickly withdrawn by the further statement that "[t]he Constitution does not, however, require government to accord the press special access to information not shared by members of the public generally."[20] Since members of the public[21] were denied visitation rights, the Court denied such rights to the press. The proposition that the press may claim greater rights than the public generally, said the Court, "finds no support in the words of the Constitution or in any decision of this Court."[22]

This is as clear a statement as has thus far emerged from any decision of the Court that those words in the Constitution which speak of "freedom of the press" do not carry any meaning beyond that contained in the reference to "freedom of speech." Yet, the Court's reasoning in the *Pell* and *Saxbe* opinions raises doubts that are not entirely set at rest by the decisions. The Court reacknowledged that "without

16. *Id.* at 2806-07. These were found to include communications by mail, and via those persons who were permitted visitation rights. See note 14 *supra.*

17. The media plaintiffs contended "that, irrespective of what First Amendment liberties may or may not be retained by prison inmates, members of the press have a constitutional right to interview any inmate who is willing to speak with them, in the absence of an individualized determination that the particular interview might create a clear and present danger to prison security or to some other substantial interest served by the corrections system." 94 S. Ct. at 2807.

18. 408 U.S. 665, 707 (1972). For a discussion of this case, see note 24 *infra.*

19. 94 S. Ct. at 2809 (citations omitted), *quoting* Branzburg v. Hayes, 408 U.S. 665, 681, 707 (1972).

20. 94 S. Ct. at 2810.

21. Other than a limited group previously known to the prisoner. See note 14 *supra.*

22. 94 S. Ct. at 2810.

some protection for seeking out the news, freedom of the press could be eviscerated."[23] Can it be said, in the same sense, that without some protection for seeking out the news, freedom of speech could be eviscerated?[24] Even the restrictive prison regulations challenged in both *Pell* and *Saxbe* accorded greater visitation rights to the press than to members of the public. For example, the California prison regulations involved in *Pell* permit newsmen (but not general members of the public) to enter prisons to interview inmates selected at random by the corrections officials from the prison population. They also permit newsmen to sit in on group meetings in connection with prison programs, and to interview inmate participants. In the federal system, the subject of *Saxbe*, newsmen (but not members of the public) are permitted to tour the premises, to photograph prison facilities, and to interview inmates who may be encountered in such a tour. The Court made a point of noting these greater rights for the press,[25] but apparently found

23. *Id.* at 2809, *quoting* Branzburg v. Hayes, 408 U.S. 665, 681 (1972).

24. *Compare* Zemel v. Rusk, 381 U.S. 1 (1965), *with* Branzburg v. Hayes, 408 U.S. 665 (1972). In *Zemel* the Court affirmed denial of a passport to Cuba where the claimant's stated purpose was " 'to satisfy my curiosity about the state of affairs in Cuba and to make me a better informed citizen.' " 381 U.S. at 4. In denying Zemel's First Amendment claim, the Court stated: "The right to speak and publish does not carry with it the unrestrained right to gather information." *Id.* at 17. But Zemel did not allege a purpose to publish, only to gather information for himself. This is, then, at most, a "speech" and not a "press" claim. Only two of the Justices (Douglas and Goldberg) dissented on First Amendment grounds.

Contrast this with *Branzburg,* where the reporters asserted a right to gather information for press purposes. Although a majority of the Court denied this claim as well (insofar as it impliedly granted a privilege against disclosure of sources), four of the Justices dissented on First Amendment grounds: Mr. Justice Douglas argued, "The press has a preferred position in our constitutional scheme . . . . The function of the press is to explore and investigate events . . . ." 408 U.S. at 721-22. Mr. Justice Stewart (joined by Justices Brennan and Marshall) premised his dissent on "the critical role of an independent press in our society." *Id.* at 725. Mr. Justice Powell joined the majority in a special concurrence which suggested that under other facts he might join with the dissenters in finding a reporter's privilege. "The asserted claim to privilege should be judged [in each case] on its facts by the striking of a proper balance between *freedom of the press* and the obligation of all citizens to give relevant testimony with respect to criminal conduct." *Id.* at 710 (emphasis added).

Taking *Zemel* and *Branzburg* together, it is arguable that a majority of the Justices would find no "speech" right to seek out information, but that, at least in some circumstances, there is a "press" right to seek out news. The quoted passage from *Zemel,* particularly with the gloss cast by *Branzburg,* suggests by "necessary implication" that the right to "speak *and* publish" [provided both functions are involved] does carry with it a "restrained" right to gather information. *Id.* at 728 n.4 (Stewart, J., dissenting) (emphasis added). But see also a "speech" right to obtain information upheld in Lamont v. Postmaster General, 381 U.S. 301 (1965) and Procunier v. Martinez, 94 S. Ct. 1800 (1974). Cf. Kleindienst v. Mandel, 408 U.S. 753 (1972).

25. 94 S. Ct. at 2813-14.

them of no constitutional significance.

One may wonder, however, had the prison regulations in fact granted no greater rights to the press than to members of the public, whether the Court would as easily have concluded that freedom of the press confers no rights beyond those of freedom of speech. The question is particularly pertinent since even where the press enjoyed greater de facto rights than the general public, as in *Pell* and *Saxbe*, only five justices were prepared to deny the press still greater constitutional rights and to concur in the stated equating of press and speech rights. In a case involving the reporting of news where press and public are in fact equally restricted, it is not difficult to envisage at least one member of the *Pell-Saxbe* majority shifting sides so as to produce a constitutionally cognizable freedom of the press that goes beyond freedom of speech.[26]

The Right of Access Cases

Pell and *Saxbe* were cases in which both freedom of the press and freedom of speech were invoked in support of the same objective. What of a case where the freedoms of press and speech may be said to be in conflict? What is to prevail?

The day after the decisions in *Pell* and *Saxbe* the Supreme Court handed down a decision which may be viewed as just such a case. In *Miami Herald Publishing Co. v. Tornillo*[27] the validity of a Florida right of reply statute was put in issue. The *Miami Herald* argued that the statute, by requiring a newspaper to grant political candidates a right to equal space in order to answer such newspaper's criticism, violated the freedom of the press guarantee. The Florida circuit court upheld the *Herald's* position, expressly holding the statute unconstitutional under the freedom of the press clause.[28] On direct appeal, the Florida Supreme Court reversed, ruling that "free speech" was enhanced rather than abridged by the right of reply statute.[29] It may be said that both of the Florida courts were correct in their conclusions, but each ignored the competing right involved. The circuit court properly concluded

26. In this regard it may not be without significance that Mr. Justice Stewart, who has evidenced a profound understanding of First Amendment theory in numerous opinions upholding speech claims, and who advocated a constitutional right of the press to seek out news in his dissent in *Branzburg* (*see* 408 U.S. at 728 n.4), was the author of the Court's opinions in *Pell* and *Saxbe*.

27. 94 S. Ct. 2831 (1974).

28. 38 Fla. Supp. 80 (Cir. Ct. 1972).

29. 287 So. 2d 78 (Fla. 1973).

that the operation of the right of reply statute served to limit freedom of the press, while the Florida Supreme Court was equally correct in deciding that the same statute enhanced the public's freedom of speech. The largely unarticulated but crucial issue presented to the United States Supreme Court was as to which of these rights is to prevail when they are in conflict.

Chief Justice Burger, speaking for the Court, stated that "[c]ompelling editors or publishers to publish that which "reason" tells them should not be published' is what is at issue in this case."[30] With the issue thus characterized, the Court had no difficulty in concluding that the right of reply statute was violative of the freedom of the press guarantee.[31] Nowhere does the *Tornillo* opinion explicitly acknowledge a confrontation between the rights of speech and press, but implicit recognition of the speech interest may be found in the Court's reference to the "access advocates'" argument that, given the present semi-monopolistic posture of the press, speech can be effective and therefore free only if enhanced by devices such as a right of reply statute.[32] The Court in accepting the press clause argument in effect necessarily found it to be superior to any competing speech clause claims.

Still, the appellee in *Tornillo* did not assert that a right of access was required by the freedom of speech clause, but only that the Florida statute which provided such a right was not a violation of the freedom of press clause. Without such a statute it would have been necessary to invoke the speech clause as a sword against the shield of the press clause. That was precisely the nature of the claim in *Columbia Broadcasting System, Inc. v. Democratic National Committee*.[33] In that case the complainants argued that they had a First Amendment right to purchase television advertising time in order to comment on public issues

30. 94 S. Ct. at 2839.

31. *Cf.* Pittsburgh Press Co. v. Pittsburgh Comm'n on Human Relations, 413 U.S. 376 (1973). In *Pittsburgh Press* the freedom of a newspaper to determine the content of its publication was held to be subordinate to a city ordinance which forbade sex-designated columns in help-wanted advertisements. The Court emphasized the commercial nature of the advertisements, and made the point that its decision did not "authorize any restriction whatever, whether of content or layout, on stories or commentary originated by Pittsburgh Press, its columnists, or its contributors." *Id.* at 391. The same might be said of material appearing in a newspaper pursuant to a right of reply statute, yet the Court in *Tornillo* concluded that freedom of the press precluded injection of material not originated or consented to by the newspaper. Is it significant that in *Pittsburgh Press* the interest competing with freedom of the press was not freedom of speech, but rather sex equality in employment practices?

32. 94 S. Ct. at 2835-37.

33. 412 U.S. 94 (1973).

without regard to whether the broadcaster had complied with the Federal Comunications Commission's "fairness doctrine."

Since both the speech and press clauses of the First Amendment only protect against governmental abridgment, *i.e.*, "state action," an issue not posed in *Tornillo* was presented in *Democratic National Committee.* In *Tornillo* the right of reply statute both constituted state action with respect to the newspaper's defense under the press clause and at the same time obviated any need for the plaintiff to establish state action as a basis of claim under the speech clause.[34] The complainants' reliance in *Democratic National Committee* upon the speech clause as the source of a right of access apart from the commands of any statute[35] required a showing that the broadcaster's refusal to accord such access constituted state action. A majority of the Court in denying the public such right of access to television nevertheless assumed that the network's refusal of access constituted state action.[36] This decision then may be said to be predicated, like *Tornillo*, upon a determination that the rights of the media, under the press clause, outweigh the speech clause rights of those who do not control the media.

In reaching its decision, the Court in *Democratic National Committee* recognized that it was "[b]alancing the various First Amendment interests involved in the broadcast media and determining what best serves the public's right to be informed."[37] What was *not* acknowledged was that it was the press clause which was being weighed

34. In another case in which the right of access was denied by the Court during the past term, Lehman v. City of Shaker Heights, 94 S. Ct. 2714 (1974), state action was present in that the defendant city was the operator of a rapid transit system. The city was upheld in its refusal to carry in its cars advertising of a political nature. The Court noted that "a newspaper or periodical, or even a radio or television station, need not accept every proffer of advertising from the general public," but because in the present case "state action exists . . . the policies and practices governing access to the transit system's advertising space must not be arbitrary, capricious or invidious." *Id.* at 2717. The Court concluded that defendant's policies and practices could not be so characterized.

35. The complaintants relied upon a construction of the Federal Communications Act in addition to an independent First Amendment right of access. 412 U.S. at 98.

36. Only Chief Justice Burger and Justices Stewart and Rehnquist found an absence of state action. *Id.* at 114-21. Of course, absent a right of reply statute it would be more difficult to find that a newspaper's activities constitute state action than to find that a broadcaster's activities may be so characterized. *See* Lehman v. City of Shaker Heights, 94 S. Ct. 2714 (1974); Associates & Aldrich Co. v. Times Mirror Co., 440 F.2d 133 (9th Cir. 1971); Chicago Amal. Clothing Workers v. Chicago Tribune Co., 435 F.2d 470 (7th Cir. 1970); T. EMERSON, THE SYSTEM OF FREEDOM OF EXPRESSION 678 (1970); *cf.* Barron, *Access to the Press—A New First Amendment Right,* 80 HARV. L. REV. 1641, 1669 (1967).

37. 412 U.S. at 102.

against the speech clause. In essence, however, the Court's decision may be seen as drawing just such a balance,[38] and finding in favor of "the press."[39]

The Defamation Cases

Nowhere has the Supreme Court's failure to discern or articulate a distinction between the freedoms of speech and the press been more evident than in the libel cases. In its latest venture into this field, *Gertz v. Robert Welch, Inc.*,[40] the Court both limited and extended the application of *New York Times v. Sullivan*.[41] *Times* had enunciated a standard whereby defamatory statements against public officials were protected by the First Amendment provided such statements were neither knowingly false nor made with reckless disregard of their truth. That rule was subsequently extended to defamatory statements made against public figures as well as public officials.[42] In *Rosenbloom v. Metromedia, Inc.*[43] a plurality opinion extended the doctrine still further by invoking First Amendment immunity for defamatory statements relating to matters "of public or general interest."[44]

The majority opinion in *Gertz* retreated from the farthest reaches of *Rosenbloom* by restricting application of the *Times* doctrine to statements against public officials or figures. But while limiting the First Amendment impact upon the law of defamation in this respect, in another respect it greatly increased that impact. The Court in *Gertz* for the first time[45] formulated, as a constitutional matter, rules governing recoverable damages even for defamatory utterances against private individuals.[46] These constitute sweeping changes in the law of defama-

38. "In the delicate balancing historically followed in the regulation of broadcasting Congress and the Commission could appropriately conclude that the allocation of journalistic priorities should be concentrated in the licensee rather than diffused among many." *Id.* at 125.

39. The *Democratic National Committee* opinion does suggest that a statute might constitutionally provide for a right of access to broadcasting (*see id.* at 131), but this option may have been removed by the subsequent decision in *Tornillo*, unless broadcasting is to be distinguished from newspapers in this respect.

40. 94 S. Ct. 2997 (1974).

41. 376 U.S. 254 (1964).

42. Greenbelt Cooperative Publ. Ass'n v. Bresler, 398 U.S. 6 (1970); *see* Curtis Publ. Co. v. Butts, 388 U.S. 130 (1967).

43. 403 U.S. 29 (1971).

44. *Id.* at 43-44.

45. *But see id.* at 62 (Harlan, J., dissenting) *and id.* at 78 (Marshall, J., dissenting).

46. The rules set out by the Court may be summarized as follows: No longer may there be any recovery without fault in defamation actions; the plaintiff must at least of-

tion, and much can be said both for and against the Court's new rules. Such is not the intent of this commentary. What should be here pointed out is the ambiguity in the sweep of the *Gertz* damage rules resulting from the Court's failure to acknowledge that speech and press represent two separable interests.

Mr. Justice Powell, at the beginning of the Court's opinion in *Gertz*, spoke of the need to accommodate "the law of defamation" on the one hand, and "the freedoms of speech and press" on the other.[47] From this is might appear that no distinction was intended as between speech and press in the application of the doctrine which was to follow. Later, however, the court stated that "[t]he principal issue in this case is whether a *newspaper or broadcaster* that publishes defamatory falsehoods about an individual who is neither a public official nor a public figure may claim a constitutional privilege against liability for the injury inflicted by those statements."[48] Since for constitutional purposes a broadcaster is no less a part of "the press" than is a newspaper, the above statement of "the principal issue" seems to relate exclusively to freedom of the press. Further, the opinion stated "that a rule of strict liability that compels a *publisher or broadcaster* to guarantee the accuracy of his factual assertions may lead to intolerable self-censorship."[49]

That the term "publisher" was not here used in the broad sense of anyone who causes a "publication" within the meaning of the law of defamation[50] is evident from the sentence which immediately followed: "Allowing *the media* to avoid liability only by proving the truth of all injurious statements does not accord adequate protection to First Amendment liberties."[51] Later the Court apparently spoke interchangeably of the needs of "the press"[52] and of "the communications media."[53] In enunciating the new damage limitations, the Court

fer proof of negligence by the defendant. Further, the damage award must be limited to compensation for actual injury in such cases; there is to be no recovery of presumed or punitive damages, at least in the absence of a showing of knowing falsity or reckless disregard of the truth.

47. 94 S. Ct. at 3000.

48. *Id.* at 3003 (emphasis added).

49. *Id.* at 3007 (emphasis added).

50. "Publication of defamatory matter is its communication intentionally or by a negligent act to one other than the person defamed." RESTATEMENT (FIRST) OF TORTS § 577 (1938).

51. 94 S. Ct. at 3007 (emphasis added).

52. *Id.* at 3009.

53. *Id.* at 3010.

stated: "We hold that, so long as they do not impose liability without fault, the States may define for themselves the appropriate standard of liability for a *publisher or broadcaster* of defamatory falsehood injurious to a private individual,"[54] adding that it thus "shields the *press and broadcast media* from the rigors of strict liability for defamation."[55] At one point Justice Powell restated the balance referred to at the beginning of the opinion, but this time characterized it as "the balance between the needs of *the press* and the individual's claim to compensation for wrongful injury."[56]

It seems fair, then, to conclude that the *Gertz* opinion formulates doctrine applicable only to defamatory statements made by newspapers and broadcasters, *i.e.*, "the media." If the Court's opinion is thus to be read literally, it leaves untouched a significant area of defamation involving written and spoken statements *not* uttered via the media.[57] Yet, one is left with the uneasy feeling that the Court's application of the new doctrine to what may be regarded as the freedom of the press arena, and its unarticulated exclusion of other "speech," may have been inadvertent, and that, further, the inadvertence was due precisely to the failure of the Court to recognize that the freedoms of speech and press are not necessarily coextensive. This failure to distinguish between the two concepts may be even more evident in Mr. Justice White's dissent in *Gertz*. He there characterized the majority opinion as applicable to

54. *Id.* (emphasis added).

55. *Id.* at 3011 (emphasis added).

56. *Id.* at 3009 (emphasis added).

57. The lower courts have generally applied the *New York Times* doctrine to non-media defamation cases. *See, e.g.*, Scott v. McDonnell Douglas Corp., 37 Cal. App. 3d 277, 112 Cal. Rptr. 609 (1974) (letter charging misconduct); McCunn v. California Teachers Ass'n, 3 Cal. App. 3d 956, 83 Cal. Rptr. 846 (1970) (investigatory report concerning an employee); Roemer v. Retail Credit Co., 3 Cal. App. 3d 368, 83 Cal. Rptr. 540 (1970) (credit reports); Moriarty v. Lippe, 162 Conn. 371, 294 A.2d 326 (1972) (statement of police misconduct); Ryan v. Dionne, 28 Conn. Supp. 35, 248 A.2d 583 (Super. Ct. 1968) (statement concerning misconduct of tax collector); Filliben v. Jackson, 247 A.2d 913 (Del. 1968), *cert. denied*, 394 U.S. 906 (1969) (letter charging police misconduct); Flannery v. Allyn, 75 Ill. App. 2d 365, 221 N.E.2d 89 (1966), *cert. denied*, 388 U.S. 912 (1967) (letter regarding police misconduct); Sas Jaworsky v. Padfield, 211 So. 2d 122 (La. Ct. App. 1968) (statement calling plaintiff a communist); Rice v. Winkelman Bros. Apparel, Inc., 13 Mich. App. 281, 164 N.W.2d 417 (1968) (credit report); Beatty v. Ellings, 285 Minn. 293, 173 N.W.2d 12 (1969), *cert. denied*, 398 U.S. 904 (1970) (statement at town meeting); Anderson v. New York Telephone Co., 42 App. Div. 2d 151, 345 N.Y.S.2d 740 (1973) (recorded telephone statements); Silbowitz v. Lepper, 32 App. Div. 2d 520 (N.Y. 1969) (letter regarding postal employee); Fox v. Kahn, 421 Pa. 563, 221 A.2d 181, *cert. denied*, 385 U.S. 935 (1966) (statement at public meeting). But *cf.* Hollander v. Pan American World Airways, Inc., 382 F. Supp. 96 (D. Md. 1973).

"each and every defamation action,"[58] and "to all defamation actions,"[59] thus seeming to ignore the majority's repeated and apparently limiting references to defamations by newspapers and broadcasters.

The point here made is not that the majority and Justice White were necessarily in disagreement as to the scope of the majority opinion. It is rather that neither appears to have been aware that there is a contradiction between the Court's stated scope of its opinion and the description of that scope in the White dissent. The majority assumed without explanation that only "the press" was implicated in its holding, while Justice White, equally without discussion, asserted that all defamatory "speech" was involved.

Other areas of actual or potential tension between speech and press could be noted.[60] Enough has been said, perhaps, to point up the need to articulate unstated and perhaps unconscious premises as to the relationship between these two forms of expression. When such premises are made explicit it may be that the Court will decide to treat freedom of speech and freedom of the press as coextensive and as merely alternative descriptions of a unitary concept. But this need not be the conclusion to be drawn. It may be that for some purposes freedom of the press should confer greater rights than does freedom of speech, and for other purposes lesser rights.

"The Press": Defining the Physical Scope

A first step in making this determination must be a clarification as to what physical acts are referred to under the concept of freedom of the press, and how, if at all, these differ from the acts encompassed under freedom of speech. These First Amendment principles are not self-defining, so that it is open to the Court to supply definitions.[61] If "speech" is held to refer to all forms of expression, it would include speech by newspapers and other segments of "the press," and freedom of the press would be a meaningless redundancy. At the other polar

58. 94 S. Ct. at 3022.

59. *Id.* at 3031.

60. It has been suggested that the issue of a reporter's privilege remains live notwithstanding the denial of the privilege in Branzburg v. Hayes, 408 U.S. 665 (1972). See note 24 *supra.* This raises the question of defining "those categories of newsmen who [are] qualified for the privilege." 408 U.S. at 704. This, in turn, requires a definition of "the press." See text accompanying notes 68-71 *infra.*

61. On the propriety and desirability of the Court engaging in such definitional balancing, see Nimmer, *The Right to Speak from Times to Time: First Amendment Theory Applied to Libel and Misapplied to Privacy,* 56 CALIF. L. REV. 935 (1968) [hereinafter cited as *Right to Speak*].

extreme "speech" could be held to be limited to spoken, and perhaps symbolic,[62] expression, leaving the protection of written expression to the freedom of the press clause. Such a construction might find some support in early First Amendment history.[63]

But such a definition of "the press" would be odd because it is both too narrow and too broad. It is too narrow in that it would exclude from "the press" those components of the media which deal in spoken rather than written expression. Television and motion pictures consist in large part, and radio in its entirety, in spoken rather than visual expression. If any substantive distinction is to be made between the rights of speech and press, in most contexts it would make little sense to vary the rights to be accorded various components of the media depending upon whether they deal in the spoken or the written word.[64] This conclusion is implicit in the Supreme Court's acknowledgment that broadcasters in particular, and "the media" in general are entitled to claim freedom of "the press."[65]

But to regard "the press" as relating to all written expression would also constitute an unduly broad definition. It is true that the Supreme Court has said that "[t]he liberty of the press is not confined to newspapers and periodicals. It necessarily embraces pamphlets and leaflets. . . . The press in its historic connotation comprehends every sort of publication which affords a vehicle of information and opinion,"[66] and, further, that it includes "the right of the lonely pamphleteer

62. *See* Nimmer, *The Meaning of Symbolic Speech Under the First Amendment*, 21 U.C.L.A.L. Rev. 29 (1973).

63. See text accompanying note 10 *supra*.

64. A defamatory statement if written is libel, and if spoken is slander (Restatement (First) of Torts § 568 (1938)), with varying consequences flowing from this distinction. There is, however, a split of authority on whether radio and television broadcasts constitute libel or slander. *Compare* Coffey v. Midland Broadcasting Co., 8 F. Supp. 889 (W.D. Mo. 1934), Sorensen v. Wood, 123 Neb. 348, 243 N.W. 82 (1932), Hartmann v. Winchell, 296 N.Y. 296, 73 N.E.2d 30 (1947) (note particularly the opinion of Fuld, J., concurring, discussing the varying views in detail, *id.* at 300-05, 73 N.E.2d at 32-34), *and* Shor v. Billingsley, 4 Misc. 2d 857, 158 N.Y.S.2d 476 (Sup. Ct. 1956), *with* Cal. Civ. Code § 46 (West 1954). Retraction statutes (for whatever vitality they may retain post-*Gertz*) may apply to both written and spoken defamation by the media. *See, e.g., id.* § 48a (applicable to both newspapers and radio).

In another context, the doctrine which asserts "a heavy presumption" against the constitutionality of prior restraints (*see, e.g.*, New York Times Co. v. United States, 403 U.S. 713, 714 (1971)) may be seen as the favoring of "press" over "speech" since generally it is only the former which may be the subject of prior restraint.

65. *See, e.g.*, Gertz v. Robert Welch, Inc., 94 S. Ct. 2997 (1974); United States v. Paramount Pictures, Inc., 334 U.S. 131, 166 (1948).

66. Lovell v. City of Griffin, 303 U.S. 444, 452 (1938).

who uses carbon paper or a mimeograph as much as of the large metropolitan publisher who utilizes the latest photocomposition methods."[67] Flexible as this concept may be in terms of sophistication of equipment and production cost, it would seem that something more is called for than the mere act of applying words to paper, even if followed by a transfer of the paper to a given individual. As the above quoted passage suggests, at the very least in order to qualify as a part of "the press" there must be a "publication." That is, there must be an act of publishing in the copyright sense, *i.e.*, copies of the work must be made available to members of the public.[68]

One who duplicates a document and then passes it on to an agent of a foreign government is in a sense engaged in an act of "speech" (whether or not protected by "freedom of speech"),[69] but it would be strange indeed to regard the actor as performing a function of "the press." If the actor turns the same document over to the representative of a newspaper, which proceeds to publish it, we may well then regard the entire process as within the sphere of "press" activities. This distinction does not in itself tell us whether either the former or the latter act should be regarded as constitutionally protected, although I will argue below that at least in some circumstances the latter act should be protected when the former is not.[70] The point here to be made is that we both forego the possibility of analytical distinctions and do violence to the plain meaning of language if we indiscriminately regard any dissemination of printed material as an activity of "the press." Whether the distinction is to turn on the copyright definition of publication or on some other standard,[71] it is clear that accepted usage already distinguishes between visual materials which comprise a part of press activities and those which are speech but not press.

67. Branzburg v. Hayes, 408 U.S. 665, 704 (1972).

68. *See* M. NIMMER, NIMMER ON COPYRIGHT § 49 (1974).

69. *Cf.* United States v. Rosenberg, 195 F.2d 583, 591-92 (2d Cir.), *cert. denied*, 344 U.S. 838 (1952).

70. See note 81 & accompanying text *infra*.

71. In his dissent in *Saxbe*, Justice Powell pointed out that the Federal Bureau of Prisons employs a workable definition of "the press" for prison visitation purposes as including " '[a] newspaper entitled to second class mailing privileges; a magazine or periodical of general distribution; a national or international news service; a radio or television network or station.' " 94 S. Ct. at 2826. For a collection of 17 state statutes which provide for a "newsman's" privilege, see Branzburg v. Hayes, 408 U.S. 665, 689 n.27 (1972). Later in the *Branzburg* opinion, however, the Court discusses the difficulty of defining "those categories of newsmen who qualified for the privilege." *Id.* at 704.

The Functions of Speech and Press

Having concluded that it is possible to distinguish between press and speech activities, the question remains as to whether the "freedom" of the press should differ substantively from that accorded to speech. This introduction is intended only as the beginning of that inquiry. No more will be attempted here than to suggest certain guidelines and directions that may be helpful in delineating the constitutional relationship between press and speech.

An understanding of the press-speech relationship must begin with a brief review of the reasons why freedom of speech is important, in order to determine whether those reasons are equally applicable to freedom of the press. Mr. Justice Brandeis, in his concurring opinion in *Whitney v. California*,[72] summed up the three major justifications for freedom of speech. First, free speech is a necessary concomitant of a democratic society. We cannot intelligently make decisions required of a self-governing people unless we are permitted to hear all possible views bearing upon such decisions. This is sometimes called the democratic dialogue function. Second, quite apart from its utility in the democratic process, freedom of expression is an end in itself. Self-expression is a part of self-fulfillment, or as Justice Brandeis suggested, liberty is "the secret of happiness."[73] Third, freedom of speech is a necessary safety valve. Those who are not permitted to express themselves in words are more likely to seek expression in violent deeds. There may be other justifications for freedom of speech but these are sufficient for our purposes.[74]

Are these purposes equally applicable to freedom of the press? Speech on a one-to-one basis between friends, neighbors and fellow workers may sometimes prove more significant than the media in the shaping of public opinion. This is occasionally the case in a political context, and somewhat more frequently in other contexts, as with respect to critical reviews of books and films. The *succes d'estime* is a phenomenon sufficiently familiar to have been given a name. Still, these are the exception. The democratic dialogue rationale is eminently applicable to the press. The informing and opinion-shaping function of the press is unquestioned. Most would agree that generally speech via the press is much more significant as a contribution to the democratic dialogue than is speech through nonmedia channels.

72. 274 U.S. 357, 372 (1927).

73. *Id.* at 375.

74. For a more expanded treatment of these justifications, see *Right to Speak*, *supra* note 61.

The self-fulfillment function of speech finds little counterpart in relation to the press.[75] To be sure, the individual contributor to the press may experience self-fulfillment by the publication of his work. But for the press *qua* press, apart from the individual pamphleteer, it is unlikely that this is a significant factor. Even less relevant to the press is the safety valve aspect of speech.

In evaluating the significance of the differences between the speech and press functions, it is helpful to consider separately those situations in which the forces of speech and press pull in the same direction, and those in which they are antithetical. The prison visitation and defamation cases and, indeed, most First Amendment issues, fall in the former category. The access cases are an example of the latter. In *Pell* and *Saxbe* both the prisoners' speech claim and the media's press claim sought the same result, *i.e.*, prisoner interviews by the media. Moreover, the speech claim was not asserted independently of the press claim; both the prisoners and the media wanted the prisoners' speech to be disseminated via the press. In such circumstances the substantial democratic dialogue function of the press is combined with the prisoners' self-fulfillment and safety valve functions, as well as their own contribution to the democratic dialogue. The combined weight of the speech-press interests is considerable.

Against this the Court weighed the interests in prison administration, and found in particular that "security considerations"[76] outweighed the First Amendment interests. In concluding that the press should have no greater visitation rights than do members of the public, the Court ignored the separate and substantial democratic dialogue function of the press not present when prisoner speech is addressed simply to members of the public.[77] It also ignored the fact that security precautions against visitation abuses are much more feasible if only the press, and not the public generally, is permitted to designate given prisoners for interview. This is not to suggest that on balance the speech-press interest necessarily outweighs the prison administration interest. The point is, rather, that the Court cannot properly weigh these respective

75. *But see* Branzburg v. Hayes, 408 U.S. 665, 726-27 (1972) (Stewart, J., dissenting) ("the press enhance[s] personal self-fulfillment by providing the people with the widest possible range of fact and opinion").

76. 94 S. Ct. at 2806, 2808.

77. In his dissent in *Saxbe*, Mr. Justice Powell stated: "For most citizens the prospect of personal familiarity with newsworthy events is hopelessly unrealistic. In seeking out the news the press therefore acts as an agent of the public at large. . . . The press is the necessary representative of the public's interest in this context . . . ." 94 S. Ct. at 2821-22.

interests without examining separately the respective claims of speech and press. Either interest alone might not outweigh the prison administration interest, while the combined speech-press interests might. It is, then, submitted that the Court was wrong in blithely concluding in *Saxbe* that "it is unnecessary to engage in any delicate balancing [because] the sole limitation imposed on newsgathering . . . is no more than a particularized application of the general rule that nobody may enter the prison and designate an inmate whom he would like to visit, unless the prospective visitor is a lawyer, clergyman, relative, or friend of that inmate."[78]

In the defamation cases the speech and press interests again pull in the same direction, *i.e.*, immunizing defamatory expression against the counter-interest in reputation.[79] But here, unlike the prisoner visitation cases, the speech and press interests are not necessarily combined. If Mr. Justice White's characterization of the scope of the majority opinion in *Gertz* is correct, then the Court has articulated a First Amendment rule of immunity for defamatory expression regardless of whether such expression is channeled through the media. The majority opinion itself, however, appears to be limited to media expression. One could construct an argument, based upon an evaluation of the speech and press interests outlined above, as to why the *Gertz* doctrine should be limited to media expression.

Defamatory statements appearing in the media generally consist of expressions by persons not themselves connected with the media, quoted in the media as "news." In such circumstances the speech values of self-fulfillment and, to some extent, democratic dialogue and safety valve which pertain to the speech of the person quoted are combined with the considerable democratic dialogue press interest. Together these may be said to outweigh the counter-interest in reputation. The balance might shift in favor of reputation if the democratic dialogue press interest is removed, as would be the case in nonmedia defamatory speech. The point, once again, is not that these respective balances are necessarily correct; it is only that the Court cannot properly assess the balance in each situation without distinguishing between the separable press and speech interests.

There is, moreover, an additional concomitant of media expression which may at times justify extending First Amendment protection to

78. *Id.* at 2814.

79. For an analysis of the speech and reputation interests which collide in a defamation action, see *Right to Speak*, *supra* note 61.

it though not to the same communication expressed through nonmedia channels. This relates to the public nature of media communication. Justice Brandeis told us: "If there be time . . . to avert the evil . . . the remedy to be applied is . . . not enforced silence."[80] Objectionable public statements via the media generally may be countered with "more speech." This is not usually the case with respect to nonmedia speech, wherein the fact of the communication itself may not be known until it is too late to counter it by corrective speech or other action. The application of this principle to the law of defamation is obvious, and it is clear that the injury to reputation may be no less devastating where there is a nonmedia defamatory communication.

Similarly, disclosure of governmental "secrets" to a foreign agent will not be known by the government, and hence corrective action by the government will not be possible. Disclosure to and publication by a newspaper will sometimes permit of such corrective action (this is in addition to the fact that the democratic dialogue interest of the public is served by newspaper disclosure and not by foreign agent disclosure). This is surely not to suggest that disclosure of governmental secrets to newspapers is necessarily protected by the First Amendment. Rather, it is to argue that in some circumstances the First Amendment line should be drawn differently depending upon whether there is a press disclosure or a nonmedia speech disclosure.[81]

Finally, we may consider those instances in which speech and press interests are in conflict. The access cases are a paradigm example. Unlike prison visitation and defamation, here the pull of press and of (nonmedia) speech is not in the same direction. The press does not wish to communicate the same expression as that urged by members of the nonmedia public. The Supreme Court in *Tornillo* and in *Democratic National Committee* opted in favor of "press," and in effect,

80. Whitney v. California, 274 U.S. 357, 377 (1927) (concurring opinion).

81. In this sense, the alleged disclosure by Daniel Ellsberg to the *New York Times* and *Washington Post* may be distinguished from the disclosures by Julius and Ethel Rosenberg and Alger Hiss. Some "secrets," no matter to whom they are disclosed, will give rise to criminal liability, as for example the atomic bomb information allegedly passed on by the Rosenbergs. But other information may be of a different order of sensitivity. The celebrated "pumpkin papers" in the Hiss case, for example, consisted for the most part of documents from the internal file of the Trade Agreements Section of the State Department. A. COOKE, A GENERATION ON TRIAL 162 (2d ed. 1952). As to less sensitive materials, whatever the statutory "classification," for First Amendment purposes a distinction may be made depending upon whether the dissemination is via secret "speech" or public "press." For a general discussion of the First Amendment status of governmental "secrets," see Nimmer, *National Security v. Free Speech: The Issues Left Undecided in the Ellsberg Case*, 26 STAN. L. REV. 311 (1974).

but not explicitly, against "speech." One wonders whether the Court would have reached this same result had the nature of the opposing forces been more squarely faced. The impact on the democratic dialogue function is essentially the same regardless of whether a given matter appearing in a newspaper originated from its editorial staff or from outsiders who gain access to the press by reason of a right of reply statute or some similar device. But that dialogue is in fact furthered if proponents of more than one side of an issue are allowed to address the same media audience. Moreover, the self-fulfillment and safety valve functions are more readily applicable to the outsiders who seek access than to those within the confines of the editorial room. Thus, in these circumstances the claims of "speech" may actually outweigh those of "press."

There are, of course, counterarguments to be made. Serious questions of governmental control of the media and of the watering down of media messages that may result from state-enforced access requirements are not without substance.[82] But the issue cannot be resolved merely by noting, as did the Court in *Tornillo*, that a right of reply statute "constitutes the [state] exercise of editorial control and judgment."[83] This is but one half of the equation. The Court in *Tornillo* ignored the strong conflicting claims of "speech." Perhaps on

---

82. See the thoughtful concurring opinion of Mr. Justice Douglas in Columbia Broadcasting Sys., Inc. v. Democratic Nat'l Comm., 412 U.S. 94, 148 (1973). For a most effective presentation of the case against access both in the broadcasting and newspaper contexts, see Lange, *The Role of the Access Doctrine in the Regulation of the Mass Media*, 52 N.C.L. REV. 1 (1974). This writer, however, is not convinced that state-imposed access rules applicable to broadcasters or newspapers would necessarily result in state control of media content. That has not been the experience in the application of those access rules known as parade ordinances. *See* Walker v. City of Birmingham, 388 U.S. 307 (1967). Media access is, of course, much more complex, but given speech rights to be weighed against press rights, it is not clear that the press has the more persuasive case.

Professor Lange describes as "the access doctrine's most obvious cost: the possibility that the state may exercise its power to deny enforcement in some particular case. In conceptual terms the power to enforce also necessarily imports the power to withhold enforcement. Thus an obvious but nonetheless necessary cost of the access doctrine is that the state must acquire new powers not only to require particular publications but also to suppress them." Lange, *The Role of the Access Doctrine in the Regulation of the Mass Media*, 52 N.C.L. REV. 1, 73 (1974). It is not clear to me how state denial of a right of access to a given work constitutes state "suppression" of that work unless the only means of publication in a given medium is via a state-imposed access route. Absent such an access monopoly, a given work which has been denied a state right of access retains substantially as much or as little opportunity for voluntary media publication as would have been the case without state access machinery.

83. 94 S. Ct. at 2840.

balance the press should still prevail, but those who doubt the efficacy of such a result are hardly persuaded by an approach that apparently fails to recognize that any balancing of speech and press rights is required.

In sum, the last term of the Supreme Court provided vivid illustrations of the variety of circumstances in which the First Amendment freedoms of speech and of the press may represent different interests, be they harmonious or discordant. Whatever the eventual results of any rebalancing of First Amendment rights in light of such a differentiation, freedom of the press as a right recognizably distinct from that of freedom of speech is an idea whose time is past due.

KENNETH B. O'BRIEN JR.
Colgate University

Education, Americanization and the Supreme Court: The 1920's

IN 1917 RICHARD CAMPBELL, UNITED STATES COMMISSIONER OF NATURALIZATION, called foreign-speaking aliens within a community "fester spots on the body politic" of that community.[1] By the following year his hysteria had mounted to the point where he not only advocated the elimination of the teaching of any language other than English from the secondary schools, but also suggested that the teaching of Central European tongues in college for scientific use was not valid since most scientific research of any consequence was being done in America rather than in Europe.[2]

Campbell's feelings were shared by countless others. World War I and the Russian Revolution brought to the surface all the latent fears of the immigrant engendered by the "new" immigration from South and Central Europe.[3] Nationalism and xenophobia were intensified and hyphenate Americans became subjects for assimilation rather than settlement. Americans called upon the Federal Government to finance Americanization programs, but because of a lack of funds all the Federal Bureau of Education and the Federal Bureau of Naturalization could do was to provide leadership in the form of advice and organizational facilities.[4]

1 *Annual Report of the Commissioner of Naturalization,* 1917, p. 37.

2 *Ibid.,* 1918, pp. 25-26.

3 For an excellent survey of this problem see John Higham, *Strangers in the Land: Patterns of American Nativism, 1860-1925* (New Brunswick, N. J.: Rutgers University Press, 1955), chaps. viii and ix. Oscar Handlin, in a provocative essay, points to the fallacies of the view that the "new" immigrants were unassimilable into the patterns of American society, and to the unscientific and biased nature of the famous Immigration Commission forty-two-volume study on immigration published in 1910; a study which furnished the basis of much of the restrictive legislation. See Handlin, *Race and Nationality in American Life* (Boston, 1957), chap. v.

4 Higham, *Strangers in the Land,* pp. 242-43. See also Edward G. Hartmann, *The Movement to Americanize the Immigrant* (New York: Columbia University Press, 1948), pp. 225-36.

Before the end of the war a few small voices had been raised in protest to the idea of a common language crusade being able to solve the problems of the nation. Frank V. Thompson, Superintendent of the Boston Public Schools, called this method one the Germans had tried without success, and he insisted that habits of thinking and feeling could not be manufactured by force and decree.[5] Thompson's anxiety was shared by the foreign language press and other immigrant associations. The more courageous of these groups began to find their tongues before the war ended.[6] Steven Hattala, manager of the New York Hungarian daily newspaper, the *Amerikai Magyar Nepszava,* pledged the use of his newspaper to the quest for Americanization, but he took exception to the compulsory English language program. Hattala pointed out that a man who knew many languages was an intelligent man; "it is not the language that makes a good American citizen, but the character and the spirit." [7] Their protests were swallowed up, however, in the mounting tide of compulsory English language advocates.

With the end of the war many restraints were loosened and the nation plunged eagerly into an intensified campaign for unity. Three things made this movement particularly virile. In the first place, fears engendered by radical ideas spreading from the Bolshevist experiment in Russia magnified immigrant differences.[8] Secondly, the rural, anti-foreign segments of the progressive movement, who had seen many of their reforms come to fruition under the Wilson administration, returned to moral crusades such as prohibition and 100% Americanism; ideas which had long been submerged beneath the crust of populism and progressivism.[9] A third reason, at least one stressed by the United States Com-

[5] *Immigration and Americanization: Selected Readings,* ed. and comp. Philip Davis (Boston: Ginn & Co., 1920), pp. 582-90.

[6] Both Higham and Hartmann maintain that it was not until the war was over that these groups began to protest. Some of them did so, however, before the war ended. See Higham, *Strangers in the Land,* p. 254; Hartmann, *Movement to Americanize the Immigrant,* pp. 253-58.

[7] Hattala to Dr. P. P. Claxton, July 10, 1918. Records of the Council of National Defense, File 13 J-A3 (National Archives).

[8] For the most recent and comprehensive survey of the "Big Red Scare" see Robert K. Murray, *Red Scare: A Study in National Hysteria, 1919-1920* (Minneapolis, Minn.: University of Minnesota Press, 1955).

[9] Richard Hofstadter effectively draws out the incongruities of this type of sentiment within progressivism as contrasted with its drive for political reform; the clash between the rural and urban elements within and outside of the populist-progressive elements of the population. See Hofstadter, *The Age of Reform: From Bryan to F.D.R.* (New York: Alfred A. Knopf, 1955). See also Higham, *Strangers in the Land,* pp. 265-66. This is also borne out by an examination, by the author, of the Papers of William Jennings Bryan (Division of Manuscripts, Library of Congress).

missioner of Education, was the discovery in the draft tests of the high rate of illiteracy. This revelation awakened leaders of education to the fact that the "melting pot" had been essentially a figment of their imagination.[10]

The solution seemed to be the public school. If American youth, especially those from foreign language speaking homes, could be insulated from the "demoralizing" effects of foreign languages, particularly German, then perhaps they would be strengthened in their devotion to America. As a result many states passed laws stressing the learning of English as the major element in their Americanization programs, and several states specifically passed laws prohibiting the teaching of German below the high school level.[11]

This legislation quite naturally antagonized German-American groups, who resented the association of the German language with Prussianism or with a lack of patriotism.[12] It was not surprising, therefore, that the question of language coercion came to the United States Supreme Court from Nebraska, a state with a large German-American population.[13]

In 1919 the Nebraska Legislature passed a law prohibiting any person or teacher in a private, denominational, parochial or public school to teach any language other than English to children who had not successfully passed the eighth grade. As a consequence, the District Court for Hamilton County, Nebraska, convicted a teacher in the Zion Parochial School of unlawfully teaching a student to read German, before this

10 *Report of the Commissioner of Education*, 1919, pp. 43-45. This was also the last time during the 1920's that a major section on Americanization appeared in these reports.

11 Francis G. Blair, "The American Melting Pot," *National Education Association, Proceedings*, LXV (1927), 38; William C. Bagley, "Federal Aid for Public Schools," *N.E.A., Proceedings*, LIX (1921), 619. In 1919 sixteen states prohibited the teaching of foreign languages in all public and private primary schools. These were Alabama, Arkansas, Colorado, Delaware, Illinois, Idaho, Iowa, Kansas, Michigan, Minnesota, Nebraska, Nevada, New Hampshire, Ohio, Oklahoma and Oregon. See Hartmann, *Movement to Americanize the Immigrant*, pp. 253-54; Higham, *Strangers in the Land*, pp. 259-60.

12 Elihu Root made this charge as early as the spring of 1917:

> . . . one does not intentionally introduce the young to bad company, or subject them to demoralizing influences that can be avoided. The Prussianizing of the German people has been a process of demoralization until they have become exponents and their language the vehicle for the expression of a gross and brutal philosophy of life which involves a negation of the Christian morality of modern civilization. The influence of Germany and the prevailing German thought of our time are demoralizing in a high degree, and we have no right to facilitate exercise of that influence upon the youth of America.

Root to Richard J. Biggs, May 31, 1918, Eilhu Root Papers (Division of Manuscripts, Library of Congress).

13 *Meyer v. the State of Nebraska*, 262 U.S. 390 (1923).

student had passed the eighth grade.[14] In their argument before the Supreme Court the attorneys for Nebraska freely admitted that the legislation had been passed with the sole purpose of creating "an enlightened American citizenship in sympathy with the principles and ideals of this country," and to prevent children from being trained in foreign languages and cultures before they had an opportunity to learn English and "observe American ideals." In addition they maintained that it was fully within the police power of the state to regulate its own educational system.[15]

Justice James C. McReynolds read the majority opinion. He began with a brief dissertation on the value of education to the American people. McReynolds pointed out that parents had a natural duty and right to educate their children in a manner suitable "to their station in life." [16] This statement was interesting for two reasons. In the first place, it indicated McReynolds' recognition of a basic inequality in social attitudes in America which permitted different types of educational facilities for people in varying walks of life. In the second place, this was the first case in which the Court categorically affirmed primary parental rights in American education.[17]

McReynolds then turned to an examination of the particulars of the case. Since German had been a desirable subject in the schools up until World War I, he argued that mere knowledge of the language could not now be regarded as harmful. He pointed out that even if the end result of giving all the youth of the nation a knowledge of English was desirable, it still could not be coerced by methods which conflicted with the Constitution. Comparing this type of legislation, somewhat erroneously, with the patterns of Plato's *Republic* and the Spartan political system wherein inferior citizens were submerged and ideal ones developed, he charged that a similar American restriction would violate the letter and spirit of the Constitution. In addition McReynolds pointed out that no immediate emergency existed which rendered knowledge of a language other than English so clearly harmful as to justify its prohibition with the consequent infringement of previously enjoyed rights. Thus, the majority of the Court declared the Nebraska legislation to be arbitrary and without reasonable relation to any end within the competence of

[14] *Ibid.*, pp. 396-97.

[15] *Ibid.*, pp. 393-95.

[16] *Ibid.*, p. 400.

[17] Sister M. Bernard Francis Loughery, *Parental Rights in American Educational Law: Their Bases and Limitations* (Washington, D.C.: Catholic University Press, 1952), p. 124.

the state.[18] The principle expressed in this decision was also used to rule against similar state legislation in Iowa and Ohio.[19]

Justice Oliver Wendell Holmes, with Justice George Sutherland concurring, registered a dissent to the majority. Holmes felt that it was desirable for all citizens of the United States to speak a common tongue. He pointed out that familiarity with a language was established in childhood and that if a child heard only a foreign language in the home, it was not unreasonable to require that he should hear and speak only English at school. The major factor in his dissent was that these cases presented a question "upon which men reasonably might differ," and he felt that the United States Constitution would permit an experiment of this sort to be tried.[20]

For the first time a Supreme Court decision aroused considerable discussion as to the place of the Court in determining educational policy. Many people who had been firmly convinced that the state legitimately could provide uniform language requirements in the schools, were disturbed by the decision. They insisted that the Court had overstepped its bounds in declaring the acts unconstitutional. Ellwood P. Cubberley, Dean of the Stanford University School of Education and a noted educational author, thought the decision to be "almost incomprehensible." He maintained that assimilating the foreigner was one of the leading problems in the schools, and the justices had merely compounded the difficulty by this decision. Cubberley wondered how the Court could conclude that "such an important nationalizing requirement" interfered with guarantees of individual and family freedom.[21] More significant was the recognition by educators of the controlling influence of Supreme Court decisions on education. I. N. Edwards, Professor of Education at the University of Chicago, declared that the decision in the Meyer case reversed an important educational policy followed by approximately

18 262 U.S. 390, pp. 400-3.

19 *Bartels* v. *Iowa; Bohning* v. *Ohio; Pohl* v. *Ohio; Nebraska District of Evangelical Lutheran Synod of Missouri, Ohio, et al.* v. *McKelvie et al.*, 226 U.S. 404 (1923).

20 *Ibid.*, p. 412. Max Lerner noted that many people expressed surprise at Holmes's dissent in this case, feeling that his liberal views would have caused him to side with the majority. Lerner, however, pointed out that Holmes was being consistent. Holmes believed in judicial tolerance of state legislative action, especially in a situation of this nature where he thought that a desirable end could be achieved through means which were not unreasonable. *The Mind and Faith of Justice Holmes: His Speeches, Essays, Letters and Judicial Opinions*, ed. Max Lerner (Boston: Little, Brown & Co., 1943), p. 318.

21 Ellwood P. Cubberley, "The American School Program from the Standpoint of the Nation," *N.E.A., Proceedings*, LXI (1923), 181.

one-fourth of the states.[22] Edwards criticized this power, maintaining that education was essentially local in character, that state educational policy was not a matter of law but one of opinion. With this in mind the Court should make a greater effort to respect state legislative policy.[23]

The real or fancied problem of assimilating the foreign born was thrust before the American public with even more force in the famous Oregon School case.[24] In November 1922, the people of Oregon, prodded by the Ku Klux Klan, passed an initiative measure requiring parents to send their children to the public primary schools controlled by the state. According to the attorneys for the state the law had several objectives. In the first place, they argued that the increase in juvenile crime in the United States was connected to the growth of parochial schools. Because these schools took pupils out of the public schools the lawyers contended that the students were segregated into special groups and so developed antisocial attitudes. Secondly, they expressed their alarm at the rising tide of religious suspicion in the schools, which they claimed came from putting children in special religious schools. Last, and most important, they wanted to assimilate immigrant children (the vast majority of whom they claimed did not attend public schools) in order to mingle children of different sects and races to guard against "further internal dissensions and consequent weakening of the community against foreign dangers."[25]

The Oregon school law directly resulted from the nativist sentiment which arose in full force in the early years of the twenties. Strong backing for the measure came from the Scottish Rite Masons, the Federated Patriotic Societies and the Ku Klux Klan, all of which were extremely influential in Oregon politics in 1922.[26] The Klan had been reorganized after the war to campaign against alien races, creeds and radical social ideas. It was, as well, a dying gasp of fundamentalist Protestantism, striking out at secularism and Roman Catholicism. Membership in the Klan

[22] I. N. Edwards, "State Educational Policy and the Supreme Court of the United States," *The Elementary School Journal*, XXVI (1925), 25.

[23] *Ibid.*, p. 29.

[24] *Pierce* v. *Society of Sisters; Pierce* v. *Hill Military Academy*, 268 U.S. 510 (1925).

[25] *Ibid.*, pp. 524-25. See also Robert W. Bruere, "The Supreme Court on Educational Freedom," *The Survey*, July 1, 1925, p. 379. This Americanization argument loses some force in the light of the fact that Oregon, as late as 1922, had not created any statewide program to provide for immigrant education or Americanization; this would indicate that there was no need for such a program. See the report from J. A. Churchill, Superintendent of Public Instruction, State of Oregon, to the Bureau of Naturalization, 1922, in Records of the Immigration and Naturalization Service, Americanization Section, File E27671 (National Archives).

[26] *School and Society*, August 11, 1923, pp. 177-78; *ibid.*, April 12, 1924, p. 430; *The Literary Digest*, June 13, 1925, p. 71.

boomed, and by 1925 it included some four or five million persons.[27] The Klan was particularly strong in Oregon where, it was charged, Governor Pierce, a Democrat, was elected by successfully courting the Klan's support. The Governor, in return for this support, agreed to help the Klan pass its compulsory public school law; this was done with virtually no protest from the press, the pulpit or the public in the state.[28]

Two corporations tested the law. One, the Society of Sisters, maintained several academies and schools designed to teach the usual school subjects and the tenets of the Roman Catholic Church. The other corporation, the Hill Military Academy (a private school), taught military training in addition to the customary subjects. These two organizations claimed that the compulsory school law diminished their enrollments. This caused their property to depreciate, they charged, and so interfered with the protection of rights and property guaranteed by the Fourteenth Amendment.[29]

In addition to the constitutional arguments the lawyers for the Society of Sisters delivered a lengthy discourse on the traditional values of private and religious education. They pointed out that the leaders of the Revolution and those who drafted the Constitution were products of private or religious schools. If the law was upheld the attorneys argued that an important and essential portion of the nation's educational system would be destroyed.[30]

As in the Meyer case, Justice McReynolds delivered the opinion of the Court. Basing his decision on the principle established in the Meyer case, McReynolds maintained that the Oregon law unreasonably interfered with the liberty of parents to direct the education of their children. (Apparently Justice Holmes felt that this type of restriction was one which all reasonable men would reject because he joined the unanimous Court in declaring the Oregon law unconstitutional.) McReynolds went on to point out that the law, in attempting to standardize children by forcing them into the public schools, ran counter to the fundamental theory of liberty upon which the nation rested. The child was not the

27 Preston W. Slosson, *The Great Crusade and After, 1914-1928* (New York: The Macmillan Co., 1930), pp. 307-8. See also Higham, *Strangers in the Land*, pp. 293-94; Murray, *Red Scare*, p. 265; Hofstadter, *The Age of Reform*, p. 295.

28 Waldo Roberts, "The Ku Kluxing of Oregon," *The Outlook*, March 14, 1923, pp. 490-91. Other Klan bills were introduced which attempted to remove the Catholic Chaplain from the state penitentiary, prevent the wearing of Catholic garb in any school in the state and amend the ecclesiastical privilege of sacramental wine. *Ibid.*, p. 491.

29 268 U.S. 510, pp. 532-33.

30 *Ibid.*, pp. 514-15.

"mere creature of the state," and parents had the right and duty to "direct his destiny." [31]

National reaction to this case was extensive and favorable. Newspaper opinion was virtually unanimous in support of the decision.[32] The editors of the New York *Times,* who noted that few Court decisions in recent years had attracted as much attention as this one, welcomed the ruling as an asset in helping to stamp out "one of the most hateful by-products of the Ku Klux movement." [33] They also viewed the decision as a happy omen as to what the Court would do when and if the Tennessee anti-evolution law reached that body.[34] Interestingly, William Jennings Bryan, the great protagonist of the anti-evolution crusade, interpreted the Oregon decision as sanctioning the anti-evolution laws. He confidently predicted, throughout the course of the Scopes trial, that the Oregon ruling would support his position in defense of the Tennessee law:

> The Oregon case affirms the right of the parent to guard the religious welfare of the child and this, I think, is decisive in our case. The Oregon case also affirms the right of the state to control the schools to the extent of compelling the teaching of anything that the state deems necessary, and explicitly declaring the right of the state to prohibit the teaching of anything 'manifestly inimical' to the public welfare. The words 'manifestly inimical' might be in a large way open for construction, but certainly the state legislature or the state Supreme Court, rather than the United States Supreme Court, would be the power to decide what is 'manifestly inimical.' [35]

Bryan was joined in this sentiment by large segments of the fundamentalist Protestant community. An exultant cry burst forth from *The Methodist* which hailed the decision as a new "Magna Charta" in American education, as well as one of the "high points in American history." Legislation would ensue which would put all private schools under strict state supervision for the great moral benefit of all concerned; this would give the leaders of church and moral reform a "magnificent new field

[31] *Ibid.,* pp. 534-35.

[32] Robert F. Drinan, "Parental Rights and American Law—the Oregon School Case Twenty-five Years After," *The Catholic World,* CLXXII (1950), 22.

[33] New York *Times,* June 2, 1925, 22:1.

[34] *Ibid.*

[35] Bryan to Austin Peay, June 27, and Bryan to Samuel Untermeyer, June 11, 1925, Bryan Papers. See also William J. and Mary B. Bryan, *Memoirs of William Jennings Bryan* (Philadelphia: John C. Winston Co., 1925), pp. 480, 530. It was evident from these statements that Bryan had not seen, or understood, the implications of the Meyer decision which made it clear that the United States Supreme Court could decide what was "manifestly inimical" to the public welfare in the field of public education.

of operation," and they concluded, enthusiastically, "it is a great and wonderful decision for us." [36]

Many others praised the decision for slightly different reasons than those of the Great Commoner and fundamentalist groups. Arthur Dean, one of the editors of *Industrial Education Magazine,* said that this was the most important Supreme Court decision on education. The ruling brought back something that educators were forgetting, he insisted, namely that "children belong primarily to parents and only to a limited extent to the state." [37] The *Political Science Quarterly* indicated that the case revealed the constitutional obstacle "over which bigotry or mistaken patriotism must fall when legislatures attempt to control private education." [38] Editorials in leading periodicals called the Oregon law arbitrary and lauded the Supreme Court for maintaining "liberty" by restricting such laws.[39] Felix Frankfurter, however, issued a word of caution as to the apparent "liberalism" of the Court in this case. To be sure he praised the decision, along with that in the Meyer case, as putting an end to "two striking manifestations of post war obscurantism"; nevertheless he pointed out that by the time of the decision in the Oregon case public opinion opposed the compulsory school law, and so the Court merely reflected the general drift of public opinion.[40]

The lack of protest on the part of educators and laymen indicated that the public, too, was more inclined to view with favor attempts to break down conformity. This was not because of any sudden liberalism on the part of great segments of the population but rather because nativist sentiment, and the anti-Catholic activities of the Ku Klux Klan, were dying or were very nearly dead by 1925. Immigration restriction had broken down the unreasonable fear of the immigrant and so the public could view, with more equanimity, decisions such as that delivered in the Oregon case.

36 *Christian Fundamentals in School and Church,* VII (1925), 33-34.

37 Arthur Dean, "A Far Reaching Decision," *Industrial Education Magazine,* XXVII (1925), 38.

38 *Political Science Quarterly,* XLI (1926), 60.

39 For editorial comment see *The Outlook,* June 10, 1925, p. 205; *The Literary Digest,* April 18, 1925, p. 32; *The Commonweal,* Feb. 19, 1930, p. 433.

40 Felix Frankfurter, "Can the Supreme Court Guarantee Toleration?" *The New Republic,* June 17, 1925, pp. 86-87. Perhaps more credit can be given the Court for the Meyer decision since it came when nativist fervor was still fairly high. The Court during the twenties, however, was not thought of as being liberal. Even in the field of educational litigation the Taft Court refused to modify *Plessy* v. *Ferguson* / 163 U.S. 537 (1986) / and, in the case of *Gong Lum* v. *Rice* / 275 U.S. 78 (1927) /, ruled that the state could provide "separate but equal" school facilities for Chinese as well as for Negro pupils.

Constitutionally the Oregon decision was significant in assuring the continued existence of private schools and in protecting parental and teachers' rights. It also helped to pave the way for the incorporation of the Federal Bill of Rights into the Fourteenth Amendment. The Court, by construing liberty to include the right of parents to direct the education of their children, opened the way for federal protection of liberty of thought against state encroachments under the Fourteenth Amendment.[41]

The third and final case concerned with the problems of Americanization and assimilation of the foreign born in the twenties was *Farrington* v. *Tokushige*.[42] In 1920, 1923 and 1925 the Hawaii Legislature passed laws to regulate the conduct of foreign-language schools and the teaching of foreign languages, "in order that the Americanism of the pupils may be promoted."[43] Under the provisions of these acts, children in Hawaii were required to have completed at least the third grade before entering a foreign-language school. The law empowered the Department of Public Instruction to certify, inspect and prescribe courses for these schools.[44]

The problem of assimilating the foreign born was a very real one in Hawaii. There were 163 foreign-language schools in the Territory, of which 147 were Japanese. The Japanese schools had twenty thousand pupils and three hundred teachers. In fact, in the public schools of Hawaii, Japanese students represented almost one-half of the school population.[45] One writer praised the laws regulating these schools; the problem of Americanizing the Japanese, many of whom came from rural areas of Japan and were therefore doubly hard to assimilate, was a serious charge upon the Territory, he argued.[46] The operators of the foreign-language schools, encouraged by the decisions in the Meyer and Oregon cases, appealed for an injunction against the acts on the grounds that they deprived them of their liberty and property as safeguarded by the Fifth Amendment.[47]

Justice McReynolds, who by now had been established as an expert in litigation of this nature, read the majority decision. He based his opinion on the Meyer and Oregon cases, and asserted that the Hawaiian laws would destroy most of the foreign-language schools and deprive

[41] Zechariah Chafee, Jr., *Free Speech in the United States* (Cambridge: Harvard University Press, 1941), pp. 321-22.

[42] 273 U.S. 248 (1927).

[43] *Ibid.*, p. 293.

[44] *Ibid.*, p. 294.

[45] *Ibid.*, pp. 290-91.

[46] Henry B. Swartz, "The Foreign Language Schools of Hawaii," *School and Society*, January 23, 1926, p. 102.

[47] 273 U.S. 248, p. 290.

parents of a fair opportunity to procure instruction for their children.

McReynolds pointed out that all the provisions of the acts seemed to be designed as a deliberate plan to bring the foreign-language schools under strict governmental control, for which there was no adequate reason. Thus, the Court upheld the injunction against the Hawaiian laws granted by the Circuit Court of Appeals on the grounds that the laws violated the Fifth Amendment.[48]

The American public, feeling much more secure now that quota legislation had diminished the immigrant problem, reacted favorably to this decision. Educators and laymen realized that, even though the problem of assimilation was more pronounced in Hawaii, the Supreme Court, in line with the Meyer and Oregon opinions, had to rule in favor of parental and private school rights.[49] A writer in *School and Society,* however, pointed out that the judgment would increase the Japanese problem in Hawaii, but the gain in friendly relations between Japan and America as a result of the decision would more than compensate for any problems that it might create.[50]

It is difficult to overestimate the import of the Meyer, Society of Sisters and Farrington cases. In the first place, the idea of the priority of the rights of the parent to supervise the education of his children was emphatically reaffirmed. In the second place, and in keeping with the general political and social trends in the 1920's, the Court overruled state action when it attempted to limit the rights and powers of individuals, especially individuals as property holders. Finally, and perhaps more significant, these cases dealt with matters upon which there was a considerable amount of public discussion. Americanization, assimilation of the foreign born and the combatting of foreign languages and ideals representated areas of very real concern to many Americans. Thus, when a conservative Court in a conservative decade seemed to exhibit liberal, perhaps even radical, ideas in declaring unconstitutional legislation designed to combat foreign ideas, educators and the general public suddenly became aware of the power of the Court in educational affairs.

48 *Ibid.,* pp. 298-99.

49 *The Elementary School Journal,* XXVII (1927), 561-64; *The Literary Digest,* March 26, 1927, p. 10.

50 *School and Society,* March 5, 1927, p. 289.

COURT, CONSTITUTION AND PRAYER

Leo Pfeffer *

I. Introduction

Supreme Court decisions that arouse furor are hardly unprecedented. Throughout its history, the Court has witnessed reactions of outrage to this or that decision, generally accompanied by demands to amend the Constitution, impeach the Justices or restrict the powers or jurisdiction of the Court.[1] The furor, however, which greeted the *Engel v. Vitale*[2] invalidation of the public school recitation of the New York Regents' prayer, though apparently short-lived, was probably unusual in its intensity. The decision was deplored and damned on and off the floor of Congress,[3] and Senators and Representatives rushed to sponsor resolutions for amendments to the Constitution to nullify the decision.[4] The Governors' Conference, which happened to be meeting about that time, adopted a resolution, with only the governor of New York abstaining, deploring the decision and calling for a constitutional amendment to overrule it.[5] Representative George W. Andrews of Alabama, combining his displeasure with *The Prayer Case* and with *The School Segregation Cases*,[6] stated: "They put the Negroes in the schools, and now they've driven God out."[7]

---

* General Counsel, American Jewish Congress; Visiting Professor of Constitutional Law, Yeshiva University.

1. See Warren, The Supreme Court in United States History *passim* (1922).
2. 82 Sup. Ct. 1261 (1962).
3. See, *e.g.*, 108 Cong. Rec. 10883–85, 10897–98, 11102–08. Statements off the floor of Congress included the following: Cardinal Spellman: "I am shocked and frightened that the Supreme Court has declared unconstitutional a simple and voluntary declaration of belief in God by public school children. The decision strikes at the very heart of the Godly tradition in which America's children have for so long been raised." N.Y. Times, July 1, 1962, § 4, p. 9, col. 3. Evangelist Billy Graham: "This is another step toward the secularization of the United States. . . . The framers of our Constitution meant we were to have freedom of religion, not freedom from religion." N.Y. Times, July 1, 1962, § 4, p. 9, col. 3–4. Senator Robert C. Byrd: "Can it be that we, too, are ready to embrace the foul concept of atheism. . . . Is this not in fact the first step on the road to prompting atheistic and agnostic beliefs? . . . Somebody is tampering with America's soul. I leave it to you who that somebody is." N.Y. Times, July 1, 1962, § 4, p. 9, col. 6. Rev. L. Mendel Rivers: "The court has now officially stated its disbelief in God Almighty." Washington Post, July 7, 1962.
4. See, *e.g.*, S.J. Res. 204, 205, 206, 207, H.S. Res. 752, 753, 754, 755, 756, 757, 89th Cong. 2d Sess. (1962).
5. N.Y. Times, July 4, 1962, p. 1, col. 2.
6. Brown v. Board of Educ., 347 U.S. 483 (1954).
7. A.P. dispatch from Washington, June 26, 1962, N.Y. Times, July 1, 1962, § 4, p. 1, col. 6.

Congressman Andrews' grievance against the Supreme Court is more valid in respect to the decision that put the Negroes in than the one that drove God out. *The School Segregation Cases* overruled a long standing precedent, one going back to 1896.[8] *The Prayer Case* overruled no precedent, but was completely consistent with and, indeed, required by all the Court's decisions[9] under the no-establishment clause of the first amendment.[10] However, before this assertion is considered, something should be said about the background of the case and about the decision itself.

In November 1951 the New York State Board of Regents proposed what it considered a truly non-sectarian prayer for daily recitation in the public schools of the state. It issued a "policy statement" that asserted that American people have always been religious, that a program of religious inspiration in the schools will assure that the children will acquire "respect for lawful authority and obedience to law [and that] each of them will be properly prepared to follow the faith of his or her father, as he or she receives the same at mother's knee or father's side and as such faith is expounded and strengthened by his or her religious leaders." [11]

The "policy statement" then said: "We believe that at the commencement of each school day the act of allegiance to the flag might well be joined with this act of reverence to God: 'Almighty God, we acknowledge our dependence upon Thee, and we beg Thy blessings upon us, our parents, our teachers and our country.' " [12]

The announcement aroused a storm of controversy. The proposal was opposed by the leading Protestant weekly, *The Christian Century*, which deemed the practice ineffectual, and the prayer "likely to deteriorate quickly into an empty formality with little, if any, spiritual significance." [13] The leaders of the Lutheran Church of Our Redeemer in Peekskill, New York, charged that Christ's name had "deliberately been omitted to mollify non-Christian elements," and that the prayer "therefore is a denial of Christ and His prescription for a proper prayer. As such it is not a prayer but an abomination and a blasphemy." [14]

Opposition, but of course for different reasons, was also voiced by all the major Jewish organizations, including the American Jewish Congress, the Synagogue Council of America and the New York Board

8. Plessy v. Ferguson, 163 U.S. 537 (1896).

9. Even Zorach v. Clauson, 343 U.S. 306 (1952) which was not in harmony in its specific holding with the other decisions before and after it.

10. "Congress shall make no law respecting an establishment of religion. . . ."

11. N.Y. Times, December 1, 1951, p. 6, col. 5.

12. *Ibid.*

13. N.Y. Times, January 9, 1952.

14. Peekskill Evening Star, January 16, 1952.

of Rabbis,[15] as well as such non-sectarian organizations as the American Civil Liberties Union, the New York Teachers Guild, the United Parents Association and the Citizens Union.[16]

On the other hand, strong support came from many Protestant and Catholic church leaders, such as The Rev. Norman Vincent Peale, Dr. Ralph Sockman, Charles H. Tuttle, Bishop William Scully of Albany and Msgr. John S. Middleton, secretary for education of the Archdiocese of New York.[17] *The Tablet,* official organ of the Brooklyn Catholic Diocese, quickly became the most passionate defender of the proposal, and John F. Brosnan, a member of the Board of Regents, speaking before the Friendly Sons of St. Patrick, charged that "the only criticism came from those who do not believe in God." [18]

The Regents' proposal was not mandatory; it was merely a recommendation which local school boards were free to adopt or not. In New York City, after a stormy public hearing, the Board of Education decided not to institute recitation of the prayer in the public schools of the city, but instead, compromised by providing for the daily recitation of the fourth stanza of the patriotic hymn, *America.* ("Our fathers' God, to Thee, Author of Liberty, to Thee we sing. Long may our land be bright with freedom's holy light, protect us by Thy might, great God our King.") [19]

No survey appears to have been taken to determine how many school boards did adopt the Regents' prayer. A reasonable estimate is that not more than ten percent of them did so. However, among those that did was the school board in New Hyde Park, a Long Island suburb of New York. With the aid of the New York Civil Liberties Union, a group of parents of children in the public schools of that community brought suit in the state courts to declare the practice unconstitutional.

The New York Supreme Court, in a lengthy and scholarly decision,[20] upheld the action of the New Hyde Park School Board, although it required the school authorities to promulgate regulations to assure that participation by the children would be entirely voluntary and that nonparticipation would not be penalized; suggesting, for example, a regulation which would permit nonparticipating pupils to arrive at school after the exercise. The Appellate Division, expressing agreement with

---

15. N.Y. Times, December 15, 1951, January 4, 1952, p. 12, col. 2, January 17, 1952; N.Y. Herald Tribune, December 19, 1951, January 4, 1952.

16. N.Y. Times, December 10, 1951, p. 23, col. 5; N.Y. Herald Tribune, December 18, 1951, p. 00, col. 0; N.Y. Compass, February 10, 1952.

17. The Tablet, December 8, 1951; N.Y. Times, December 1, 1951, p. 6, col. 5. January 13, 1952, p. 67, col. 3.

18. N.Y. Herald Tribune, March 18, 1952.

19. For further details of the Regents' prayer controversy, see PFEFFER, CHURCH, STATE AND FREEDOM, 395–398 (1953).

20. Engel v. Vitale, 18 Misc.2d 659, 191 N.Y.S.2d 453 (Sup. Ct. 1959).

the views contained in the decision, affirmed,[21] and by a vote of five to two the Court of Appeals affirmed the action of the Appellate Division.[22] In the Court of Appeals, however, three separate opinions for affirmance were written, no one of which received the acceptance of a majority of the court. Therefore, it is not possible to state precisely on what particular ground the action of the school board was sustained. As best as can be judged from the various opinions, the action was sustained on four separate but somewhat related grounds:

(1) The prayer formulated by the Board of Regents is "non-sectarian," *i.e.*, it is acceptable to all faiths and is preferential to none. Its recitation in concert by the children may constitutionally be made part of the daily public school program since the purpose of the first amendment is only to preclude preferential treatment of some religions over others.

(2) Since provision is made in the lower court's decision to assure complete freedom of nonparticipation on the part of any child, there is no infringement on the first amendment.

(3) The first amendment is made applicable to the states by virtue of the due process clause of the fourteenth. Public school recitation of prayer is a long-standing practice. A practice which has continued so long in time cannot be held to be wanting in due process.

(4) We are a religious people. Those who wrote our Constitution were friends of religion. Exclusion of prayer from the public school curriculum manifests a hostility to religion, and such motivation cannot reasonably be ascribed to the framers of our Constitution.

Unsuccessful in the New York courts, the plaintiffs applied to the United States Supreme Court for certiorari, and to the surprise of many, including the present writer, the Court granted the writ.[23]

II. The Decision of the Supreme Court

By a vote of six to one (Mr. Justice Frankfurter was ill and Mr. Justice White was not yet on the bench when the case was argued), the

21. 11 App. Div.2d 340, 206 N.Y.S.2d 183 (1960).

22. 10 N.Y.2d 174, 176 N.E.2d 579, 218 N.Y.S.2d 659 (1961).

23. 368 U.S. 924 (1961). In Schempp v. School Dist. of Abington Township, 177 F. Supp. 398 (E.D.Pa. 1959), the court invalidated as violative of both the establishment and free exercise clauses of the first amendment, a Pennsylvania statute requiring daily reading from the Bible in the public schools. After an appeal from the decision had been filed, the state legislature amended the statute to provide for the excusal from participation of any child whose parents so requested. Thereupon, on motion, the Supreme Court vacated the district court's decision and remanded the case for reconsideration in the light of the statutory amendment, School Dist. v. Schempp, 364 U.S. 298 (1960), this although, as McCollum v. Board of Educ., 333 U.S. 203 (1948) had shown in the past, and the instant case was to show in the future (see *infra*, p. 750), the voluntariness of participation has no relevance to the issue of constitutionality under the establishment clause. See also, Pfeffer, *Some Current Issues in Church and State*, 13 W. Res. L. Rev. 9, 18–21 (1961).

Supreme Court overruled the New York court and held the practice unconstitutional as violative of the first amendment's ban on establishment of religion. The majority opinion was written by Mr. Justice Black, who had written the majority opinions in *Everson v. Board of Educ.*,[24] *McCollum v. Board of Educ.*,[25] and *Torcaso v. Watkins*,[26] and who had dissented in *Zorach v. Clauson*.[27]

"We think," said Mr. Justice Black for the majority, "that by using its public school system to encourage recitation of the Regents' prayer, the State of New York has adopted a practice wholly inconsistent with the Establishment Clause. There can, of course, be no doubt that New York's program of daily classroom invocation of God's blessings as prescribed in the Regents' prayer is a religious activity. It is a solemn avowal of divine faith and supplication for the blessings of the Almightly." [28]

The state laws requiring or permitting use of the prayer, continued Mr. Justice Black, must be struck down because "the constitutional prohibition against laws respecting an establishment of religion must at least mean that in this country it is no part of the business of government to compose official prayers for any group of the American people to recite as part of a religious program carried on by the government." [29]

The history of government-sponsored prayer both in the Old World and the New has been a history of oppression, coercion and conflict. When our Constitution was written, Mr. Justice Black stated:

> [The] people knew, some of them from bitter personal experience, that one of the greatest dangers to freedom of the individual to worship in his own way lay in the Government's placing its official stamp of approval upon one particular kind of prayer or one particular form of religious services. . . . The First Amendment was added to the Constitution to stand as a guarantee that neither the power nor the prestige of the Federal Government would be used to control, support or influence the kinds of prayer the American people can say. . . . Under that Amendment's prohibition against governmental establishment of religion, as reinforced by the provisions of the Fourteenth Amendment, government in this country, be it state or federal, is without power to prescribe by law any particular form of prayer which is to be used as an official prayer in carrying on any program of governmentally-sponsored religious activity.[30]

The Court rejected the argument that since the prayer is "non-de-

---

24. 330 U.S. 1 (1947) (upholding parochial school bus transportation at public expense).

25. *Supra* note 21 (invalidating released time programs for religious instruction on public school premises).

26. 367 U.S. 488 (1961) (invalidating religious tests for public offices).

27. *Supra* note 9 (upholding released time programs held off public school premises).

28. 82 Sup. Ct. 1261, 1263–64 (1962).

29. *Id.* at 1264.

30. *Supra* note 28 at 1266.

nominational" and since pupils may remain silent or be excused from the room if they request, there is no constitutional violation, and stated:

> Neither the fact that the prayer may be denominationally neutral, nor the fact that its observance on the part of the students is voluntary can serve to free it from the limitations of the Establishment Clause, as it might from the Free Exercise Clause of the First Amendment, both of which are operative against the States by virtue of the Fourteenth Amendment. . . . The Establishment Clause, unlike the Free Exercise Clause, does not depend upon any showing of direct governmental compulsion and is violated by the enactment of laws which establish an official religion whether those laws operate directly to coerce nonobserving individuals or not. . . . The Establishment Clause . . . stands as an expression of principle on the part of the Founders of our Constitution that religion is too personal, too sacred, too holy, to permit its 'unhallowed perversion' by a civil magistrate. Another purpose of the Establishment Clause rested upon an awareness of the historical fact that governmentally-established religions and religious persecutions go hand in hand. . . . The New York laws officially prescribing the Regents' prayer are inconsistent with both the purposes of the Establishment Clause and with the Establishment Clause itself.[31]

Nothing, according to Mr. Justice Black, could be more wrong than the argument that to apply the Constitution in such a way as to prohibit state laws respecting an establishment of religious services in public schools is to indicate a hostility toward religion or toward prayer. Men who had faith in the power of prayer were the leaders of the fight for the adoption of our Constitution and Bill of Rights. "It is neither sacreligious nor anti-religious to say that each separate government in this country should stay out of the business of writing or sanctioning official prayers and leave that purely religious function to the people themselves and to those the people choose to look to for religious guidance." [32]

Mr. Justice Black concluded the opinion by disposing of the assertion that the recitation of the Regents' prayer constituted at most a minor infringement on the separation of church and state.

> 'It is true, that New York's establishment of its Regents' prayer as an officially approved religious doctrine of that state does not amount to a total establishment of one particular religious sect to the exclusion of all others—that, indeed, the governmental endorsement of that prayer seems relatively insignificant when compared to the governmental encroachments upon religion which were commonplace 200 years ago. To those who may subscribe to the view that because the Regents' official prayer is so brief and general there can be no danger to religious freedom in its governmental establishment, however, it may be appropriate to say in the words of James Madison, the author of the First Amendment:

---

31. *Id.* at 1266–68.
32. *Id.* at 1269.

It is proper to take alarm at the first experiment on our liberties. . . . Who does not see that the same authority which can establish Christianity in exclusion of all other religions may establish with the same ease any particular sect of Christians, in exclusion of all other sects? That the same authority which can force a citizen to contribute three pence only of his property for the support of any one establishment, may force him to conform to any other establishment in all cases whatsoever?' [33]

III. Mr. Justice Douglas' Concurrence

In *Zorach v. Clauson,*[34] it was Mr. Justice Douglas who wrote the majority opinion, in which he cited "prayers in our legislative halls; the appeals to the Almighty in the messages of the Chief Executive; the proclamation making Thanksgiving Day a holiday; 'so help me God' in our courtroom oaths . . . and all other references to the Almighty that run through our laws, our ceremonies" as evidence that the "First Amendment . . . does not say that in every and all respects there shall be a separation of Church and State." Were that so, he said, a "fastidious atheist or agnostic could even object to the supplication with which the Court opens each session: 'God save the United States and this Honorable Court'. . . ." [35] To him, these practices supported the majority conclusion that released time religious instruction during public school hours was not unconstitutional if held off public school premises.

In *Engel v. Vitale,* Mr. Justice Douglas refused to accept practices as proof of constitutionality. Indeed, his concurring opinion contains the first statement by a Justice of the Supreme Court that the many forms of governmental aid to religion, so often cited to support further aid, may themselves be unconstitutional.

"The point for decision," he said, "is whether the Government can constitutionally finance a religious exercise. Our system at the federal and state levels is presently honeycombed with such financing." [36] Among others cited by him in footnotes,[37] are chaplaincies in Congress and the armed forces, presidential issuance of religious proclamations, use of the Bible in the administration of oaths, the applicability of the the G.I. bill to religious schools, the use of the slogan "In God We Trust," the addition of "under God" to the pledge of allegiance, Bible reading in the public schools of the District of Columbia and tax deductibility for contributions to religious organizations. "Nevertheless," he continued, "I think it is an unconstitutional undertaking whatever form it takes." [38]

---

33. *Id.* at 1269–70.
34. *Supra* note 1.
35. *Id.* at 312–13.
36. *Supra* note 2 at 1271.
37. *Id.* at 1270 n.1, 1272 n.5.
38. *Id.* at 1270.

Mr. Justice Douglas stated:

> In New York the teacher who leads in prayer is on the public payroll; and the time she takes seems minuscule as compared with the salaries appropriated by state legislatures and Congress for chaplains to conduct prayers in legislative halls. Only a bare fraction of the teacher's time is given to reciting the short 22-word prayer, about the same . . . time that our Marshal spends announcing the opening of our sessions and offering a prayer for this Court. Yet for me the principle is the same, no matter how briefly the prayer is said, for in each of the instances given the person praying is a public official on the public payroll, performing a religious exercise in a governmental institution.[39]

What is also noteworthy about Mr. Justice Douglas' opinion is the intimation that he now considers use of public funds for parochial school transportation to be unconstitutional. "My problem today," he said, "would be uncomplicated but for *Everson v. Board of Education, . . .* which allowed taxpayers' money to be used to pay 'the bus fares of parochial school pupils as a part of a general program under which' the fares of pupils attending public and other schools were also paid. The *Everson* case seems in retrospect to be out of line with the First Amendment." [40]

It should be noted that the *Everson* case was decided by a vote of five to four, and that Mr. Justice Douglas was one of the majority. Had he then held the views expressed in this decision, the *Everson* case would have been decided the other way. Of course, this is no indication that a majority of the present Court would hold differently from *Everson.* In 1961, with only Mr. Justice Frankfurter and Mr. Justice Douglas noting dissent, the Court dismissed for want of a substantial federal issue, an appeal from a Connecticut decision which upheld bus transportation to parochial schools at taxpayers' expense.[41]

IV. Mr. Justice Stewart's Dissent

The sole dissenter in *Engel v. Vitale* was Mr. Justice Stewart. In his view, the Court "misapplied a great constitutional principle." [42] He could not see how an official religion is established by letting those who want to say a prayer say it. He too, noted that the Court opens its sessions with a prayer, as do the Senate and the House of Representatives. He also referred to the numerous presidential religious proclamations, the addition of "under God" to the pledge of allegiance, the slogan "In God We Trust" on our coins, etc. But he reached a conclusion opposite to that reached by Mr. Justice Douglas. To him, these practices indi-

39. *Id.* at 1272–73.
40. *Id.* at 1273–74.
41. Snyder v. Town of Newton, 365 U.S. 299 (1961) dismissing appeal from 147 Conn. 347, 161 A.2d 770 (1960).
42. *Supra* note 2 at 1274.

cated that public school recitation of the Regents' prayer is not unconstitutional. "I do not believe," he said, "that this Court, or the Congress, or the President has by the actions and practices I have mentioned established an 'official religion' in violation of the Constitution. And I do not believe the State of New York has done so in this case. . . . I dissent." [43]

V. What Does No Establishment Mean?

In the *Everson* case, Mr. Justice Black, speaking for the majority of the Court, spelled out the meaning of the no establishment clause in the following definitive terms:

> The 'establishment of religion' clause of the First Amendment means at least this: Neither a state nor the Federal Government can set up a church. Neither can pass laws which aid one religion, aid all religions, or prefer one religion over another. Neither can force nor influence a person to go to or remain away from church against his will or profess a belief or disbelief in any religion. No person can be punished for entertaining or professing religious beliefs, for church attendance or non–attendance. No tax in any amount, large or small, can be levied to support religious activities or institutions, whatever they may be called, or whatever form they may adopt to teach or practice religion. Neither a state nor the Federal Government can, openly or secretly, participate in the affairs of any religious organizations or groups and vice versa. In the words of Jefferson, the clause against establishment of religion by law was intended to erect 'a wall of separation between church and State.' [44]

In the *McCollum* case,[45] Mr. Justice Black reiterated this paragraph in his opinion for the majority. In *McGowan v. Maryland,*[46] the paragraph was again set forth in the majority opinion, this time written by Mr. Chief Justice Warren. Finally, in *Torcaso v. Watkins,*[47] the paragraph was once more set forth in the Court's opinion, again written by Mr. Justice Black. In *Engel v. Vitale,* it was Mr. Justice Black who once more spoke for the Court, but curiously he did not this time reiterate the paragraph which can be said almost to have become part of the first amendment itself. But perhaps even more curious is the fact that, in his entire opinion in *Engel v. Vitale,* Mr. Justice Black does not cite a single decision as authority for any proposition.[48]

Wherein lies the explanation for these rather curious omissions? This writer suggests it is to be found in the implicit assumption that the

---

43. *Id.* at 1277.
44. *Supra* note 22 at 15, 16.
45. *Supra* note 21 at 210, 211.
46. 366 U.S. 420, 443 (1961) (upholding Sunday closing laws).
47. 367 U.S. 488, 493 (1961).
48. Footnote 11 cites *Everson,* but only as a source for the history of the enactment of the Virginia Bill for Religious Liberty.

meaning of the no establishment clause is now so well settled and known that even a decent respect to *stare decisis* did not require citation of judicial authorities. Lawyers frequently—and judges sometimes—will assert assuredly that "it requires no citation of authority" to establish a certain point, when in fact they were unable to find authorities to support the point. In the present case, however, I think Mr. Justice Black could have used the formula with reasonable justification.

I suggest that, with the exception of *Zorach,* the Court, even before *Everson,* has been consistent in its interpretation of the no establishment clause, although not necessarily in its application of the interpretation to the facts before it. Under these decisions, the first amendment, which merely makes explicit what is implicit in the Constitution itself, requires government in the United States to be secular. Its ends must be exclusively secular and in achieving them, it may use only secular means. The Preamble to the Constitution sets forth the purposes for which the new republic on the western hemisphere was established, and all are secular: "form a more perfect union, establish justice, insure domestic tranquility, provide for the common defense, promote the general welfare, and secure the blessings of liberty. . . ."

In governmental effectuation of its secular purposes, its action may, as an incidental by-product, affect religion, either beneficially or detrimentally—indeed, one would assume that this would generally be so—and that fact, the Court has consistently held, does not restrict government in the manner in which it effects its purposes. Thus, as in the *Everson* case, a state may seek to achieve its secular purpose of protecting children from the hazards of traffic, either by providing them with free transportation to the schools they attend or by requiring the schools to provide such transportation, just as it requires them to provide safe and sanitary buildings for the children. If it adopts the former method, an incidental by-product benefits religion by relieving parochial schools of what might otherwise be a necessary part of their budget. If it adopts the latter method, the incidental by-product injures religion by imposing a cost which the parochial schools might not otherwise assume. So long as the state's choice cannot be said to be arbitrary, the first amendment is not violated by the fact that it chooses one or the other method. Those who quarrel with the *Everson* decision do so, not on the basis of the underlying principle, but on its application. They contend that the real purpose of such legislation is not to protect children from traffic hazards but to enable them to get to school in order to be educated, and if the education is religious, the real governmental purpose is religious.

So, too, in pursuing its secular purpose of assuring to every person one day a week for rest, relaxation and family togetherness, the state may require businesses to close down on Sundays, even though the

Christian religion, or that part of it which observes Sunday as the Sabbath, is incidentally benefitted thereby, while those faiths which observe Saturday as the Sabbath are detrimentally affected.[49] Here, too, disagreement is not with the principle, but with its application, *i.e.*, with the assumption that Sunday laws, concededly religious in their origin, have now become secular in their purpose.

On the other hand, if the governmental purpose is to aid religion, its action transgresses the limits of its power prescribed by the Constitution and the first amendment. As Mr. Chief Justice Warren, speaking for the majority in one of the Sunday law cases, said: "We do not hold that Sunday legislation may not be a violation of the 'Establishment' Clause if it can be demonstrated that its purposes—evidenced either on the face of the legislation, in conjunction with its legislative history, or in its operative effect—is to use the State's coercive power to aid religion." [50]

For that reason, the Court, with only Mr. Justice Reed dissenting, invalidated a program of released time which involved "a utilization of the tax-established and tax-supported public school system to aid religious groups to spread their faiths." [51] For the same reason, the Court, with no dissent, invalidated a requirement in a state constitution that all public officers, as a condition to qualification, take an oath that they believe in the existence of God.[52]

The same underlying principle would forbid government to employ its power to punish or censor expression [53] so as to protect religious orthodoxy from heresy or religion from such attack as falls short of the "fighting words" type,[54] for it would thereby be using governmental instrumentalities to achieve a religious end—the preservation of religious beliefs.[55] While the decision of the Supreme Court in *Burstyn v. Wilson* [56] was based on the narrow ground that the term "sacrilege" was too indefinite to accord with due process, the tenor of both the Court's opinion and Mr. Justice Frankfurter's concurrence indicates that, even were the licensing statute worded in language which clearly encompassed films such as "The Miracle" (which impugned the virgin birth of Jesus), it, nevertheless, would have been held unconstitutional.

Moreover, in pursuing secular ends, government may use only secular means. One of the arguments stated by Madison in his monumental

---

49. McGowan v. Maryland, *supra* note 44; Two Guys v. McGinley, 366 U.S. 582 (1961); Gallagher v. Crown Kosher Market, 366 U.S. 617 (1961); Braunfeld v. Brown, 366 U.S. 599 (1961).

50. McGowan v. Maryland, *supra* note 44 at 453.

51. McCollum v. Board of Educ., 333 U.S. 203 (1948).

52. Torcaso v. Watkins, *supra* note 24.

53. Under the latest decision of the Supreme Court, government has the power to censor motion pictures. Times Film Corp. v. Chicago, 365 U.S. 43 (1961).

54. Chaplinsky v. New Hampshire, 315 U.S. 568 (1942).

55. See Cantwell v. Connecticut, 310 U.S. 296 (1940).

56. 343 U.S. 495 (1952).

Memorial and Remonstrance Against Religious Assessments in opposition to taxation for religious purposes, was that government's employment of "Religion as an engine of Civil policy . . . [is] an unhallowed perversion of the means of salvation." [57] A great statesman and jurist, Jeremiah S. Black, stated that the fathers of our Constitution "built up a wall of complete and perfect partition" between church and state in order that "one should never be used as an engine for the purposes of the other." [58]

To hold that government may employ religion as a means to effect secular ends that are properly within governmental competence would make the first amendment meaningless. Practically every defense of religious instruction in public schools is expressly predicated on the not unreasonable assertion that religious education leads to morality and good citizenship. If religion could be used to achieve the obviously secular goal of morality and good citizenship, it would follow not only that religion could constitutionally be taught in the public schools, but also that tax-raised funds could be used to finance religion and religious education. Moreover, the government could reasonably find that some religions, such as Protestantism, Catholicism and Judaism, are more likely to inculcate morality and good citizenship than others (Jehovah's Witnesses, for example) and, therefore, could aid the former and not the latter—a conclusion which the Supreme Court has expressly rejected [59] and which even the proponents of narrow interpretation of the no establishment clause do not defend.[60]

Because religion may not be employed by government as a means to achieve secular ends, the Supreme Court turned a deaf ear to the argument of the State of Maryland in *Torcaso v. Watkins* [61] that believers in God make better public officials than do non-believers. The same reason explains the Court's decision in *Bradfield v. Roberts*,[62] wherein the Court upheld a grant of public funds for the erection of a hospital to be operated by a corporation composed exclusively of Catholic nuns. The end sought to be achieved—the healing of the sick—is obviously secular, and, the Court held, the means employed to achieve it are likewise secular, for a corporation is an entity created by law and distinct

57. II WRITINGS OF MADISON 183, 185–86. Added as an appendix to Everson v. Board of Educ. The Court in *Everson* declared it to be part of the legislative history of the first amendment, *supra* note 22 at 13.

58. BLACK, ESSAYS AND SPEECHES 53 (1885).

59. Fowler v. Rhode Island, 345 U.S. 67 (1953).

60. See O'NEIL, RELIGION AND EDUCATION UNDER THE CONSTITUTION *passim* (1949); Corwin, *The Supreme Court as a National School Board,* 14 LAW & CONTEMP. PROB. 3 (1949); PARSONS, THE FIRST FREEDOM 30–49 (1948); BRADY, CONFUSION TWICE CONFOUNDED *passim* (1954). While all these deny that the first amendment imposes a mandate of neutrality between religion and non-religion or that it forbids governmental aid conferred equally upon all faiths, all agree that it does preclude preferential treatment by government of some religions over others.

61. *Supra* note 45.

62. 175 U.S. 291 (1899).

from its stockholders and is, therefore, a secular institution.[63] Here again disagreement with the decision rests not on the underlying principle but on its application—specifically, upon the use of the fiction of corporate distinctiveness to evade a fundamental constitutional restriction.[64]

This writer suggests too, that *Kedroff v. St. Nicholas Cathedral*[65] is encompassed by the principle that religious means may not constitutionally be employed to achieve secular ends. An examination of the background of the extended controversy culminating in this decision[66] indicates that what the State of New York was seeking to do was to employ control of the temporal assets of the Russian Orthodox Greek Catholic Church as an instrument in the cold war against the Soviet Union.

Measured by these standards, the action of the New York State Regents was twice–vulnerable and the decision of the Supreme Court in *Engel v. Vitale* was inevitable. Perhaps more surprising than the Court's decision is the fact that one Justice dissented.[67] The Regents sought to achieve both a religious end and a secular end through the use of religious means. By sponsoring recitation of their prayer they sought to assure, in their somewhat inelegantly-styled policy statement, that "each of them [public school children] will be properly prepared to follow the faith of his or her father, as he or she receives the same at mother's knee or father's side and as such faith is expounded and strengthened by his or her religious leaders."[68] This is obviously a religious purpose and, therefore, beyond the constitutional competence of government. The second purpose sought to be achieved by the Regents was to assure that public school children will acquire "respect for lawful authority and obedience to law."[69] This, of course, is a secular end, but its effectuation could not constitutionally be sought through a religious activity.[70]

The one decision that cannot be squared with the principle that the Constitution limits government to the achievement of secular ends through secular means is *Zorach*. On the facts, the case was easily distinguishable from *McCollum*. In the latter case, the religious instruc-

63. "That the influence of any particular church may be powerful over the members of a non-sectarian and secular corporation, incorporated for a certain defined purpose and with clearly stated powers, is surely not sufficient to convert such a corporation into a religious or sectarian body." *Id.* at 298.

64. *Cf.*, Everson v. Board of Educ., *supra* note 22 at 44 (dissenting opinion).

65. 344 U.S. 94 (1952).

66. And in Kreshik v. St. Nicholas Cathedral, 363 U.S. 190 (1960).

67. As in *McCollum*, when, however, the meaning of the establishment clause had not become so well settled.

68. N.Y. Times, December 1, 1951, at 6, col. 5.

69. *Ibid.*

70. "There can, of course, be no doubt that New York's program of daily classroom invocation of God's blessings as prescribed in the Regents' prayer is a religious activity." Engel v. Vitale, 82 Sup. Ct. 1261, 1264 (1962).

tion was conducted within the public school and with considerable supervision and other involvement by public school officials. In the former case, the authorities did no more than release from their secular studies those children wishing to participate in religious instruction off school premises and without any public school involvement. Mr. Justice Douglas, speaking for the majority in *Zorach,* stressed the differences.[71] *McCollum* was not to be deemed overruled. On the contrary, Douglas said unqualifiedly, "we follow the *McCollum* case." Moreover, "Government may not finance religious groups nor undertake religious instruction nor blend secular and sectarian education nor use secular institutions to force one or some religion on any person." [72] Hence, even *Zorach* would not have justified a contrary decision in *Engel v. Vitale.*

However, unless government is forbidden to utilize religious means or pursue religious ends, there appears to be no reason why it may not do these things. And if it is so forbidden, it may not utilize the public school system to aid religious instruction even if it be given off school premises. Mr. Justice Douglas and his associates did not repudiate the principle underlying *Everson* and *McCollum;* they simply disregarded it, or perhaps, more charitably, misapplied it. They treated the situation as if it involved no more than adjusting public school schedules so that children might have time to take religious instruction if they so desired, in the same way that they might want to take piano or dancing lessons. But, as Mr. Justice Frankfurter pointed out acutely in his dissent, this is not what was happening. The public schools were not closing their doors to accommodate pupils nor even releasing those pupils who wished to be released to attend to private matters, including religious instruction. It kept the school in full session and released only those who undertook to use the time in acquiring religious indoctrination.[73]

In his dissent, Mr. Justice Jackson suggested that the Court's judgment would "be more interesting to students of psychology and of the judicial processes than to students of constitutional law." [74] What he meant to imply by this is not quite certain, but it is suggested that the

71. "In the *McCollum* case the classrooms were used for religious instruction and the force of the public school was used to promote that instruction. Here, as we have said, the public schools do no more than accommodate their schedules to a program of outside religious instruction." Zorach v. Clauson, 343 U.S. 306, 315 (1952).

72. *Id.* at 314.

73. "The pith of the case is that formalized religious instruction is substituted for other school activity which those who do not participate in the released-time program are compelled to attend. The school system is very much in operation during this kind of released time. If its doors are closed, they are closed upon those students who do not attend the religious instruction, in order to keep them within the school. This is the very thing which raises the constitutional issue. It is not met by disregarding it. Failure to discuss this issue does not take it out of the case." *Id.* at 321 (dissenting opinion).

74. *Id.* at 325.

explanation for the decision is to be found outside the boundaries of constitutional law, at least as defined by stare decisis. *Zorach* cannot be understood except in the background of the temper of the time in which it was decided and the four years of attack and villification that followed *McCollum.*

Zorach was a sport which left no offspring. Mr. Justice Frankfurter was not merely optimistic but prophetic in his statement:

> The result in the McCollum case . . . was based on principles that received unanimous acceptance by this Court, barring only a single vote. I agree with Mr. Justice Black that those principles are disregarded in reaching the result in this case. Happily they are not disavowed by the Court. From this I draw the hope that in future variations of the problem which are bound to come here, these principles may again be honored in the observance.[75]

Burstyn, Kedroff, Torcaso and, finally, *Engel,* all of which followed *Zorach,* validated Mr. Justice Frankfurter's hope. Whatever may have happened in *Zorach,* today the principle is established, as firmly as anything can be said to be in constitutional law, that government in the United States is secular, that it may seek to achieve only secular ends, and that, in doing so, it may employ only secular means.

VI. What Means *Engel v. Vitale?*

Subject to sports such as *Zorach,* which may arise at any time without notice, and assuming the continued operation of stare decisis, at least to the extent that it is operative in constitutional law, it is suggested that the following conclusions can reasonably be drawn from *Engel v. Vitale:*

(1) Once again, the Court has made it clear that the first amendment does not merely forbid preferential treatment of one religion over others, but forbids any governmental involvement in religious affairs and imposes upon government a mandate of neutrality not only as among competing faiths, but as between religion and non-religion.

(2) Again, too, the Court has made it clear that this mandate of neutrality is as binding upon the states under the fourteenth amendment as it is upon the federal government under the first.

(3) It follows from this that non-denominational religious practices in the public schools are as unconstitutional as those which are frankly sectarian. Accordingly, the discussions in various state court cases as to whether the "Lord's Prayer" is sectarian or nonsectarian are now academic. As far as the United States Constitution is concerned, the "Lord's Prayer" may not be recited in the public schools whether or not it is sectarian. Of course, the decision does not forbid children to engage in private or individual prayer of any kind during school hours

75. *Id.* at 322–23.

in a manner which does not interfere with the regular conduct of school operations.

Heard often after the decision, particularly from sectarian sources hostile to it and school officials reluctant to change existing practices, was the assertion that it invalidated recitation only of prayers composed by public officials and not, for example, the "Lord's Prayer." This is analogous to the assertion that the mere fact that a bridge collapsed under a horse does not prove that it would have collapsed under an elephant. The Regents' prayer is as innocuous, nonsectarian and universal as theistic prayer can be, and, if such a prayer may not be recited in the public schools, it is more than difficult to see how a Christian prayer taken from the New Testament may be.

(4) What is true of prayer is true also of devotional reading of the Bible. It is constitutionally immaterial which version of the Bible is used, the King James (Protestant), Douay (Catholic) or Jewish Publication Society version. Nor is it material that the readings may be taken from the Old, rather than the New Testament. In each case, the necessary consequence of *Engel v. Vitale* is that devotional reading from the Bible in the public schools is unconstitutional.

This does not mean that the Bible may not be read or studied as a work of literature, even though such study may lead some to accept or others to reject it religiously. The study of literature is a secular activity and is not proscribed to public school students, even if an incidental by-product of the activity may be benefit or harm to religion.

(5) The decision, likewise, requires the conclusion that religious holiday observances in the public schools, Christmas, Hanukah, Easter or Passover, are unconstitutional. This had already been held in *Chamberlin v. Dade County Bd. of Public Instruction.*[76]

(6) Religious hymns may not be sung in the public schools as an act of devotion. They may, however, be learned and sung as part of a course in music, since this is a secular activity. For the same reason patriotic hymns, such as "America" may be sung even though some of the stanzas may have a religious content.

(7) The fact that no coercion is employed and that children are free to refrain from participation, or even from being present, is immaterial. The ban on establishment of religion, unlike that on laws prohibiting its free exercise, forbids any governmental activity in furtherance of religious purposes even if no direct compulsion is shown.

(8) One of the most significant aspects of the decision is its relation to the *de minimis* rule. In the *McCollum* case, the Supreme Court of Illinois ruled that the incidental expense incurred by the state through the use of its public school facilities in the course of released-time religious instruction was so small as to fall within the *de minimis* rule.[77]

76. 17 Fla. Supp. 183 (1961), *aff'd,* 143 So. 2d 21 (Fla. 1962).
77. McCollum v. Board of Educ., 396 Ill. 14, 71 N.E.2d 161 (1947).

In a brief presented to the United States Supreme Court on appeal from the Illinois court's decision, this writer challenged the assertion that the cost was small, and urged, in addition, that in cases involving religious liberty or establishment of religion, the *de minimis* doctrine is inapplicable.[78] This argument was criticized by Professor Arthur E. Sutherland, Jr. in the following language:

> [T]o say . . . that there is no place at all for *de minimis* may turn out to be embarrassingly extreme, for the number of small instances of government support, or at least favorable recognition, of religious activity is so great that they go unnoticed until attention is drawn to them.
>
> Among mankind there are always enthusiasts for all causes, and it is well that this is so; but one conquest only adds zeal for the next, and the Supreme Court may yet be glad to have available a doctrine that some matters are really so trifling that they do not set in motion the somewhat ponderous machinery of the Federal Government. . . .[79]

If there ever was an occasion for the Court to avail itself of the protection afforded by the *de minimis* rule it was in *Engel v. Vitale*. Nothing can be more *de minimis* than the inoffensive twenty-two word prayer that takes less than ten seconds to recite. Yet the Court quite firmly refused the protection. It quite clearly held that, in cases involving the religion clauses of the first amendment, it is not the degree, but the fact of governmental invasion that is controlling.

I do not mean to imply that the Court may not in the future, particularly in "pocketbook" cases, *i.e.*, where the violation of the first amendment consists only in an expenditure of public funds rather than in engaging in a religious exercise, necessarily set aside a state court's refusal to exercise jurisdiction where the expenditure of public funds is minimal. I mean only that, assuming stare decisis to be operative, if it does so its abstention will be based upon its general policy of taking only such cases as it deems of general importance and not because the minimal expenditure does not violate the Constitution.

VII. Conclusion

It was perhaps too much to expect that Mr. Justice Black's disavowal of anti-religious motivation would deter attacks upon the decision as atheistic, or the fact that none of the six Justices concurring in it is non-Christian would avert charges that it is an assault upon Christianity. The easy identification of opposition to government-sponsored religion with opposition to religion itself was echoed and re-echoed in the stridency of the reaction to the decision. Yet, examined dispas-

78. Brief for the Synagogue Council of America and the National Community Relations Advisory Council as *Amici Curiae*, pp. 30, 31; McCollum v. Board of Educ., 333 U.S. 203 (1948).

79. Sutherland, *Due Process and Disestablishment*, 62 HARV. L. REV. 1343 (1949).

sionately in the light of history, the decision—as the American principle of separation which required it—was an act of friendliness, rather than hostility, to religion. It is state-sanctioned prayer, not the banning of it, that is harmful to religion.

State-sanctioned prayer has a long and ignoble history. From the early days of persecuted Christianity in Rome to the twentieth century in Russia when the Jews were compelled to recite in synagogue every Sabbath a prayer for the welfare of the very Tsarist government that instigated and encouraged terrible pogroms against them, the consequence of state-sponsored prayer has been martyrdom or insincerity.

It was not so long ago that England experienced an event which vividly illustrated the fact that state sponsorship of prayer is not beneficial, but harmful to religion and conscience. In 1927, the Church of England wished to revise the Anglican Prayer Book. Since it is the established church, it could not do so without the approval of Parliament. In that year, and again in the following year, it petitioned Parliament to permit the change but in each year the proposal was rejected by the House of Commons because it was felt that the proposed revisions manifested too much Roman Catholic influence. The result is that, for the past thirty-five years, Anglicans have been praying in a manner which does not fully accord with their conscience only because the government possesses the power to formulate prayer.[80]

The lesson of history is clear. It supports fully the statement in the Court's opinion in *Engel v. Vitale* that the first amendment "rested on the belief that a union of government and religion tends to destroy government and degrade religion," that "whenever government had allied itself with one particular form of religion, the inevitable result had been that it had incurred the hatred, disrespect and even contempt of those who held contrary beliefs," and that "many people had lost their respect for any religion that had relied upon the support of government to spread its faith." [81]

It was for that reason that the deeply religious fathers of our Constitution wrote a preamble which carefully refrained from listing among the purposes of government any power or obligation to promote religious ends and deliberately kept out of the Constitution itself, not only any prayer or invocation to God, but even any mention of God at all. The decision of the Supreme Court in outlawing public school recitation of prayer is consistent not only with its own prior decisions, but with the intent of the founders of our republic and with the cause of religious liberty.

---

80. See Pfeffer, Church, State and Freedom 46.
81. *Supra* note 68 at 1267.

ILLEGAL ENFORCEMENT OF THE LAW

William T. Plumb, Jr.*

"I think it a less evil that some criminals should escape than that the Government should play an ignoble part."

Justice Holmes

So spoke the Great Dissenter in *Olmstead v. United States.*[1] His words might well be the watchword of the struggle to curb illegal enforcement of the law.

Illegal enforcement in this country is an evil of no small proportions. Inefficient, delinquent or merely impatient police officers, who are frequently ill-trained, occasionally abuse their powers, sometimes from excessive but misguided zeal, sometimes to placate the popular clamor for the solution of a crime by producing a victim by fair means or foul. In their zeal to accomplish results, government officials may lose sight of the fact that they are the servants of the law, peculiarly charged with a duty to observe its spirit and its letter. Yet they must beware the sinister sophism that the end justifies the employment of illegal means to bring offenders to justice. The public respect for law, which is the fundamental prerequisite of law observance, can hardly be expected of people generally if the officers charged with its enforcement do not set the example of obedience to its precepts.[2]

Illegal arrests, both inside the state where the crime occurred and beyond its borders, are a major example of illegal enforcement. Corollary to this are illegal searches and seizures and tapping of wires. The practice of the "third degree" is a still more serious instance. The wrongfulness of all of these practices is generally conceded, and direct remedies of civil and perhaps criminal actions are regularly provided for such abuses. This article will be confined to the abuses named,[3] and to the question of indirect checks upon them—*i.e.,* when the illegal act has been done and the accused is before the court, held under illegal process or incriminated by evidence illegally obtained, will the court disregard the wrongful act and retain the case or admit the evidence?

I. Illegal Arrests

The law, in order to secure freedom from illegal restraint for trivial causes, provides that, except where the gravity of the offense seems to

---

*The writer wishes to express his deep appreciation for the many helpful suggestions and criticisms of Professor Lyman P. Wilson of the Cornell Law School.

[1] 277 U. S. 438, 470, 48 Sup. Ct. 564, 575 (1928).

[2] See National Commission on Law Observance and Enforcement, Report on Lawlessness in Law Enforcement (Government Printing Office 1931).

[3] Others that might be mentioned include entrapment and unfair tactics in the conduct of the trial. On the latter, see *op. cit. supra* note 2, at page 263.

justify an immediate arrest without a warrant or a crime has been committed in the presence of the person making the arrest, no arrest may lawfully be made unless a warrant has been issued after formal charge filed with the proper court.[4] But a considerable number of arrests are made illegally, because to arrest without a warrant is often more convenient, saving time and trouble. Again, there is in many cases a natural temptation or an actual necessity to seize a suspect while it is yet possible, rather than to give him an opportunity to escape while the officer takes time to draw up an information and apply for and obtain a warrant.

When the accused has fled from the state, it becomes necessary to apply to the governor of the state where the crime occurred for a requisition directed to the executive of the state to which the accused has fled, demanding the fugitive's return. But the processes of extradition are slow, complicated, and inefficient. In these days of rapid transportation a criminal often can keep several jumps ahead of the law if extradition is attempted.

Furthermore, when the crime is one committed by the accused when he was not physically present in the state where it took effect, he is not extraditable under the Constitution[5] and the federal act which implements it,[6] for he has not *fled* from the state. Thus, there are a number of crimes for which one may not be extradited to the state where the crime was consummated yet for which he may not be punished in the state where he did the acts because no crime took effect therein. The classic example is *State v. Hall.*[7] Hall and his accomplice shot a man. Being well advised or just lucky, they were standing in North Carolina, while the deceased was over the line in Tennessee. Upon a trial for murder in North Carolina, it was held that no murder had been committed in that state, and that one state cannot enforce the criminal laws of another or punish crimes against another state. Thereupon Tennessee demanded extradition, but the defendants were released on *habeas corpus* because they had not been in Tennessee and were not *fugitives* from its justice.[8] As a result, they were immune from any punishment so long as they stayed out of Tennessee.

[4]On the general subject of the necessity for a warrant, see 2 R. C. L. 446-464; 2 Am. Jur. 7-36; 5 C. J. 389-421; 6 C. J. S. 575-608; Bohlen and Shulman, *Arrest With and Without a Warrant* (1927) 75 U. of Pa. L. Rev. 485; Hall, *Legal and Social Aspects of Arrest Without a Warrant* (1936) 39 Harv. L. Rev. 566; Waite, *Public Policy and the Arrest of Felons* (1933) 31 Mich. L. Rev. 749; Wilgus, *Arrest Without a Warrant* (1924) 20 Mich. L. Rev. 541, 673, 798.

[5]U. S. Const. Art. IV § 2, Cl. 2: "A person charged in any state with treason, felony, or other crime, who shall flee from justice, and be found in another state, shall on demand of the executive authority of the state from which he fled, be delivered up to be removed to the state having jurisdiction of the crime."

[6]18 U. S. C. A. § 662 (1927).

[7]114 N. C. 909, 19 S. E. 602 (1894) (murder trial); 115 N. C. 811, 20 S. E. 729 (1894) (extradition); note (1895) 7 Green Bag 201. In the extradition case, there was a vigorous dissent pointing out the danger involved in such a rule.

[8]That this is the construction of the federal law was settled by Hyatt v. Corkran, 188 U. S. 691, 23 Sup. Ct. 456 (1903).

Less striking but more frequent cases in the same class are the procurement of a crime to be committed by another in a different state, frauds carried on by mail,[9] bombs and poison sent through the mail, and non-support of one's family which is then resident in another state.

Another cause of dissatisfaction with the extradition process is that, for one reason or another, governors sometimes elect to disregard the plain duty laid down by the law, and refuse to surrender a fugitive. It is settled that the governor of the state where the fugitive is found has no discretion to refuse to extradite, if he is satisfied simply that the accused is charged with a crime under the laws of the demanding state, that he is a fugitive from justice, and that he is the man sought.[10] But if the governor refuses to issue a warrant, it is equally well settled that it is beyond the power of the courts to compel him to do so.[11]

As a result of these defects in the extradition procedure, there is a serious

---

[9]Use of the mails to defraud is now a federal offense, 18 U. S. C. A. § 318 (1927), so this large class of crimes is taken care of.

[10]Biddinger v. Comm'r of Police, 245 U. S. 128, 134, 38 Sup. Ct. 41 (1917).

[11]In Kentucky v. Dennison, 24 How. 66 (U. S. 1861), Chief Justice Taney declared that the Constitutional provision was not a mere compact of peace and comity between nations who had no claim upon each other for mutual support, but a compact binding them to aid each other in executing their laws, and that harmony between the states required that one state should not harbor and protect another's criminals; that the duty to surrender fugitives was absolute, subject to no discretion on the part of the state where they are found; that the provision is substantially identical with that in the Articles of Confederation, when the Confederation was a league of separate sovereignties, under which provision, by analogy to international rendition, the executive of the state was the one of whom the demand was made, and upon whom the duty rested; that although the Constitution does not specify what officer shall be bound to surrender the fugitive (see *supra* note 5), it impliedly adopted the same procedure when it adopted the language of the Articles, and this was the construction placed upon it by Congress in enacting the Extradition Act (*supra* note 6). Having thus concluded that the Constitution should be construed as imposing an absolute duty on the governor, the Court then turns around and holds that it is only a moral duty and that there is no power to compel him to act; for if the General Government could impose any duty on the officers of a state, as such, and compel them to perform it, it would be within the power of Congress to load state officials with duties, which might be incompatible with their rank and dignity and so heavy as to disable them from performing their obligations to the state; that Congress may authorize a state officer to perform a duty, but cannot compel it. This seems the most fatuous reasoning that ever emanated from the Court before the days of social legislation. For if, as was clearly stated, the Constitution itself impliedly imposed the duty on the governor, there is nothing unconstitutional in an act of Congress implementing this provision; although Congress may not impose duties on the states, surely the Constitution can! The truth probably is that this is another instance of hard cases making bad law. The fugitive in this case was accused of aiding the escape of slaves. The Governor of Ohio had refused to return him to Kentucky for trial. And March of 1861 was no time for the Supreme Court to appear to line itself up on the wrong side of the slavery question!

Since state laws implementing the federal act also impose such a duty on the governor, it might be possible to mandamus the governor in the state court. No case has been found in which this was attempted, however. The authorities are in conflict on the power of the courts to compel the exercise of ministerial duties by the governor. It is denied in New York, People *ex rel.* Broderick v. Morton, 156 N. Y. 136, 50 N. E. 791 (1898), but there is no weight of authority. The cases are collected in a complete annotation in (1936) 105 A. L. R. 1124. But even if mandamus is granted, it merely changes the form of the duty, and there is no way to enforce it.

temptation to ignore its requirements and forcibly return the fugitive to the offended state, frequently with the open connivance of the officers of the state where he is found. In a number of cases, this summary action has been accompanied by violence and a flagrant disregard of the criminal law by those charged with its enforcement.[12] Cases of this nature frequently gain great notoriety in the press and tend to lower public respect for the law, to say nothing of the individual wrong to the accused.

Illegal arrests, within and without the state, must be discouraged. Direct remedies, civil and criminal, are said to be ineffective. Shall we, then, as the only practical means to safeguard individual liberties, deny to the court the right to try a defendant who has been illegally arrested? With substantial unanimity the courts have refused to impose this additional sanction upon illegal arrests, even when the question was duly raised by *habeas corpus* or a plea to the jurisdiction,[13] although a small number of

---

[12]It must, however, be borne in mind that most of these cases came up on demurrers to the accused's allegations and his necessarily highly colored account was taken as true for purposes of the decision.

[13]*Illegal arrest within the jurisdiction: In re* Johnson, 167 U. S. 120, 17 Sup. Ct. 735 (1897) (defendant held even though he raised question on *habeas corpus* before trial); Albrecht v. United States, 273 U. S. 1, 47 Sup. Ct. 250 (1927); People v. Brown, 368 Ill. 177, 13 N. E. (2d) 272 (1938) (issue not raised in trial court); State v. May, 57 Kan. 428, 46 Pac. 709 (1896); Commonwealth v. Tay, 170 Mass. 192, 48 N. E. 1086 (1898); Commonwealth v. Gorman, 288 Mass. 294, 192 N. E. 618 (1934); People v. Miller, 235 Mich. 340, 209 N. W. 81 (1926); State *ex rel.* Brown v. Fitzgerald, 51 Minn. 534, 53 N. W. 799 (1892); State v. DeHart, 129 Atl. 427 (N. J. C. P. 1925) (preliminary motion to the jurisdiction); People v. Eberspacher, 79 Hun 410, 29 N. Y. Supp. 796 (Gen'l Term, 2d Dep't 1894); People v. Iverson, 46 App. Div. 301, 61 N. Y. Supp. 220 (2d Dep't 1899); *In re* Durant, 60 Vt. 176, 12 Atl. 650 (1888); *Ex parte* Krans, 1 B. & C. 258, 107 Eng. Rep. 96 (K. B. 1823); Rex v. Marks, 3 East 157, 102 Eng. Rep. 557 (K. B. 1802) (both on *habeas corpus*); Rex v. Hughes, 4 Q. B. D. 614, 14 Cox Crim. 284 (1879) (no preliminary objection); Rex v. Iaci, [1924] 3 D. L. R. 321 (Br. Col. Sup. Ct.); Rex v. McLatchy, [1923] 3 D. L. R. 291 (New Bruns. Sup. Ct. App. Div.); Rex v. Flavin, 56 D. L. R 666 (Nova Scotia Sup. Ct. 1921). *Cf. In re* Johnson, 40 Cal. App. 242, 180 Pac. 644 (1919) (rule applied to administrative agencies; petitioner arrested without warrant, found to have contagious disease, so confined by health officer, *habeas corpus* denied).

Illegal arrest in and removal from another state: Mahon v. Justice, 127 U. S. 700, 8 Sup. Ct. 1204 (1888) (*habeas corpus*); Cook v. Hart, 146 U. S. 183, 13 Sup. Ct. 40 (1892); Pettibone v. Nichols, 203 U. S. 192, 27 Sup. Ct. 111, 7 Ann. Cas. 1047 (1906) (*habeas corpus*); *Ex parte* Barker, 87 Ala. 4, 6 So. 7 (1888) (*habeas corpus*); State v. Chapin, 17 Ark. 561 (1856); *In re* Moyer, 12 Ida. 250, 85 Pac. 897, 12 L. R. A. (N.S.) 227 (1906) (*habeas corpus*); State v. Ross, 21 Iowa 467 (1866); State v. Chandler, 158 Minn. 447, 197 N. W. 847 (1924); Balbo v. People, 80 N. Y. 484, 499 (1880); Mathews v. State, 19 Okla. Cr. 153, 198 Pac. 112 (1921); State v. Owen, 119 Ore. 15, 244 Pac. 516 (1926); Dow's Case, 18 Pa. 37 (1851, per Gibson, C. J.) (*habeas corpus*); State v. Smith, 1 Bailey Law 283, 19 Am. Dec. 679 (S. C. 1829) (*habeas corpus*); Brookin v. State, 26 Tex. App. 121, 9 S. W. 735 (1888); *In re* Miles, 52 Vt. 609 and note (1875); State v. McAninch, 95 W. Va. 362, 121 S. E. 161 (1924); Kingen v. Kelley, 3 Wyo. 566, 28 Pac. 36, 15 L. R. A. 117 (1891).

Illegal arrest in and removal from a foreign country: Ker v. Illinois, 119 U. S. 436, 7 Sup. Ct. 225 (1886); United States v. Unverzagt, 299 Fed. 1015 (W. D. Wash. 1924), *aff'd on other grounds, sub nom.* Unverzagt v. Benn, 5 F. (2d) 492 (C. C. A. 9th 1925), *cert. denied,* 269 U. S. 566, 46 Sup. Ct. 24 (1925), note (1924) 13 GEO. L. J. 70 (apparently the first case holding that the federal courts themselves would take advantage of an illegal arrest abroad; earlier cases merely held that a trial by the *state*

courts have held that such an arrest was a bar to prosecution, at least where raised by a preliminary plea to the jurisdiction.[14]

The question of the effect of lack of extradition first reached the United States Supreme Court, final arbiter of the meaning of the Constitution and the federal statute and treaties involved, in *Ker v. Illinois*.[15] The accused had fled to Peru, and the President had issued an extradition warrant to an officer, who went after him. But instead of presenting his papers to the

---

violated no constitutional rights); United States v. Insull, 8 Fed. Supp. 310 (N. D. Ill. 1934) (the same); People v. Pratt, 78 Cal. 345, 20 Pac. 731 (1889); Ker v. People, 110 Ill. 627 (1884); People v. Rowe, 4 Parker Cr. 253 (N. Y. Super. Ct. 1858) (motion to quash indictment); Lagrave's Case, 14 Abb. Pr. N. S. 333 note, 45 How. Pr. 301 (N. Y. Sup. Ct. 1873); State v. Brewster, 7 Vt. 118 (1835); *Ex parte* Scott, 9 B. & C. 446, 109 Eng. Rep. 168 (K. B. 1829) (*habeas corpus*); *Re* Walton, 11 Ont. L. R. 94, 6 Ont. Week. R. 905 (1905) (*habeas corpus*).

Cf. United States *ex rel.* Voight v. Toombs, 67 F. (2d) 744 (C. C. A. 5th 1933), *appeal dismissed,* 291 U. S. 686, 54 Sup. Ct. 442 (1934) (illegal removal between federal judicial districts).

An interesting variant is the question whether one illegally brought *into* a state is subject to extradition *from* there to the state whose agent brought him that far without extradition. *Ex parte* Ponzi, 106 Tex. Cr. 58, 290 S. W. 170 (1926) (interstate arrest; *habeas corpus* denied); see *contra, In re* Jones, 54 Cal. App. 423, 201 Pac. 944 (1921) (removal from Mexico to California, extradition to Oklahoma; strong dictum, but removal was found to have been lawful).

[14]As to courts of general jurisdiction, the cases are rare, and vary as to whether the unlawfulness of the arrest must be seasonably raised or is fatal to the jurisdiction (only *dicta* can be found on the latter rule, for in all these cases the issue appears to have been duly raised). Tennessee v. Jackson, 36 Fed. 258, 1 L. R. A. 370 (E. D. Tenn. 1888) (*habeas corpus*: federal court released state prisoner; the case is undoubtedly overruled by later Supreme Court cases); State v. Simmons, 39 Kan. 262, 18 Pac. 177 (1888) (later strictly confined to violations of interstate comity, the general rule being applied to illegal arrests within the state: State v. May, 57 Kan. 428, 46 Pac. 709 [1896]); *Re* Robinson, 29 Neb. 135, 45 N. W. 267 (1890) (*habeas corpus*). These latter cases are not controlled by the United States Supreme Court decisions, which held only that no rights under the Federal Constitution and laws would be violated by trying a person so arrested.

In England, although a long line of King's (and Queen's) Bench cases followed the majority view (*supra* note 13), the Court of Exchequer went to the other extreme and held that a person unlawfully arrested must be released, and that no subsequent lawful arrest during such custody can cure the defect. Att'y-Gen'l v. Cass, 11 Price 345, 147 Eng. Rep. 494 (1822). An article in (1896) 32 CAN. L. J. 534 states that this is the general English and Canadian view, but the only cases there cited are cases of civil arrests, with which the writer of that note is unable to see a distinction (see *infra* note 30). In Dixon v. Wells, 25 Q. B. D. 249 (1890), Lord Chief Justice Coleridge expresses regret that his dictum in Rex v. Hughes, *supra* note 13, and other cases had been so broad as to exclude a preliminary objection to the jurisdiction, but he does not upset the rule, resting the case rather upon a special ground (see *infra*).

In Canada, the Provinces are in conflict, some of them following the majority view (the cases are cited *supra* note 13) and others holding squarely that they will release on preliminary motion. Rex v. Linder, [1924] 3 D. L. R. 505 (Alta. Sup. Ct. App. Div.); Rex v. Suchaki, [1924] 1 D. L. R. 971 (Man. Ct. App. 1923).

Statutes creating certain courts of limited jurisdiction, such as justice courts, may be construed as making a proper warrant a condition precedent to the court's jurisdiction. People *ex rel.* Lawton v. Snell, 216 N. Y. 527, 111 N. E. 50 (1916); Harris County v. Stewart, 91 Tex. 133, 41 S. W. 650 (1897); Dixon v. Wells, 25 Q. B. D. 249 (1890); see State v. Wenzel, 77 Ind. 428 (1881). But even in this case the requirement is waived by pleading, People v. Burns, 19 Misc. 680, 44 N. Y. Supp. 1106 (Co. Ct. 1897), and is cured by a subsequent lawful arrest while in custody. People v. Bradley, 58 Misc. 507, 111 N. Y. Supp. 625 (Co. Ct. 1908).

[15]119 U. S. 436, 7 Sup. Ct. 225 (1886), *aff'g* 110 Ill. 627 (1884).

Peruvian government, the officer and other armed men kidnapped the defendant and placed him on a naval vessel. He was taken to California, from which he was duly extradited to Illinois. Defendant pleaded to the jurisdiction, but his plea was overruled. He was convicted and appealed to the Illinois Supreme Court and finally to the United States Supreme Court. In each case he lost. It was held that the illegality of the arrest does not oust the jurisdiction of a court before which the accused is brought, or give him immunity from trial for a crime with which he is charged in a regular indictment. To his claim that the extradition treaty with Peru gave him a right of asylum, a positive right that he should be free from molestation and not forcibly removed except in accordance with the treaty, it was replied that the treaty merely restricts a country's freedom voluntarily to give him an asylum, but gives the individual no right to insist upon security there. The laws of Peru were violated in his capture, but that is a matter between that nation and the officer, who may himself be extradited and tried for the kidnapping.[15a] But since the officer did not profess to act under the treaty, for he kept the extradition papers in his pocket, the defendant can claim no rights under it. The violation of the sovereignty of Peru by a federal officer is a political matter concerning only the two governments, in which the courts have no concern. It was *not* held, however, that the kidnapping might not give rise to an *international* obligation on the part of the United States to restore the kidnapped fugitive if the offended government demands it. It has long been the custom of our government to return kidnapped fugitives on the demand of the offended nation,[16] and to demand the return of those so kidnapped from this country.[17] A complication arises when the victim of the kidnapping is held by a state court, for the federal government has no authority to order the prisoner's release and the states frequently have been unwilling to honor a request to that effect.[18]

[15a]Villareal v. Hammond, 74 F. (2d) 503 (C. C. A. 5th 1934) (granting extradition to Mexico of the officer who returned a prisoner without extradition).

[16]John Bassett Moore, in his TREATISE ON EXTRADITION (1891) vol. I, 282 ff., gives a number of illustrations gathered from State Department correspondence. Thus, in 1872, this government, on demand of the Canadian authorities, released a Dr. Bratton, who had been illegally seized in Canada and returned for trial on a federal charge. (p. 283). On the other hand, in 1906, the State Department cited the *Ker* case—although that case had not passed on the point—as authority for refusing a similar request from Mexico. [1906] 2 FOREIGN RELATIONS 1121-22.

[17]In 1841, one Grogan, who had been seized in Vermont by British soldiers and taken to Canada, was returned at the request of our government. I MOORE, EXTRADITION (1891) 282. Again in 1876, England granted our demand, although the man had been seized here not by English officers but by a private individual, acting in connivance with American officials, and although the prisoner had already been convicted in England. (p. 285, case of Blair). The case of Martin was more extreme: a naturalized citizen of this country was convicted in northern British Columbia; to get him to the jail at Victoria, he had to be taken through Alaska; the State Department demanded and obtained his release because of this violation of our sovereignty (p. 285).

[18]In 1850, England requested the return of one Bullock, who had been unlawfully seized in England by a Georgia sheriff and returned to Georgia for trial. The State

The holding in the *Ker* case that the defendant is subject to the jurisdiction of the court when he is brought before it, by whatever means, and may not himself raise the issue of the wrong to the foreign government, must be read in connection with the case of *United States v. Rauscher,*[19] decided at the same time. There the fugitive was legally returned under an extradition treaty, but was tried for another crime than that for which he was extradited. It was held, in effect, that his surrender under the treaty was conditional and for a special purpose, and that the treaty impliedly forbade his trial for any other crime without his first being given an opportunity to return.[20] Here the individual was permitted to set up the rights of the foreign government under the treaty, and it is ably argued by Professor Dickinson[21] that the same principle which applies to arrests in violation of a treaty should apply to arrests in violation of international law, and that the individual prisoner should in each case be permitted to raise the question of good faith toward the nation wronged. The Constitution makes a treaty part of the law of the land,[22] and thus Rauscher was able to raise the question of its violation. But international law is part of our law as well[23] and Professor Dickinson asserts that the same rule should apply. However, if the offended nation makes no objection and if there is no treaty stipulation violated, it is difficult to see that any principle of international law requires the return of the fugitive.[24]

Department referred it to the governor of Georgia, who refused to intervene, saying it was a judicial matter. I MOORE, EXTRADITION (1891) 291. Likewise, in 1879, one Cahill was abducted from Canada and tried in the Buffalo Superior Court. His return was demanded and the State Department referred it to the governor of New York and to the trial judge. But the prisoner was convicted and served his sentence (p. 292)

[19]119 U. S. 407, 7 Sup. Ct. 234 (1886).

[20]In England, it is now provided by law that a fugitive shall not be surrendered unless provision is made, by the law of the foreign state or by arrangement, that he shall be detained for no offense committed prior to extradition, other than the one for which he is surrendered, without first being given an opportunity to return. EXTRADITION ACT OF 1870 (33 & 34 Vict., c. 52), 8 HALSBURY'S STAT. ENG. 452, § 3 (2). A like immunity is given fugitives returned from other countries. *Id.* § 19. See also Article III of the Extradition Convention between the United States and Great Britain, 1889. (It may be found most conveniently on page 932 of *Gilbert's New York Criminal Code,* 1938.)

[21]Dickinson, *Jurisdiction Following Seizure or Arrest in Violation of International Law* (1934) 28 AM. J. INT. LAW 231. But see note (1935) 29 AM. J. INT. LAW 502.

[22]U. S. CONST. Art. VI, cl. 2.

[23]"International law is part of our law, and must be ascertained and administered by the courts of justice of appropriate jurisdiction, as often as questions of right depending upon it are duly presented for their determination." The Paquete Habana, 175 U. S. 677, 700, 20 Sup. Ct. 290, 299 (1900).

[24]Even in the treaty cases, the lack of jurisdiction is waived by pleading to the indictment. Ford v. United States, 273 U. S. 593, 47 Sup. Ct. 531 (1927) (British liquor ship and men seized outside three-mile limit, in violation of treaty).

A unique variant of the treaty cases is Dominguez v. State, 90 Tex. Cr. 92, 234 S. W. 79 (1921), notes (1922) 18 A. L. R. 503, (1922) 20 MICH. L. REV. 536, (1922) 31 YALE L. J. 443. American soldiers, acting under orders from the War Department, pursued bandits across the Mexican border and brought them back; the defendant was brought back in the mistaken belief that he was one of them; on discovery of the mistake, he was turned over to the police to answer a prior charge of murder. The

The principle that one who is extradited under a treaty is immune from prosecution for any offense but the one for which he is extradited has no application to fugitives extradited between states under the Constitution.[25] In respect to fugitives, states do not occupy the relation of foreign nations. Interstate rendition is not effected by contract on which conditions may be imposed, but is required unconditionally by the supreme law of the land. It is not a favor which the state may withhold or grant conditionally. So, there being no law or treaty provision to the contrary, the general rule applies that one found within the jurisdiction may be tried for any crime charged to have been committed there, no matter how his presence was obtained. *A fortiori,* the principle of the *Ker* case would apply to persons illegally arrested in another state and brought back without extradition.[26]

But a number of early cases had intimated that if the state whose sovereignty was violated by the kidnapping should demand the return of the accused, the demand would have to be granted.[27] This question shortly

State claimed that defendant was kidnapped and that the *Ker* case applied. But the court preferred to presume that the War Department was not ordering unlawful invasions but was acting under some privilege from Mexico, however informal, and if the terms of this privilege were violated by bringing back one other than the bandits being pursued, it was like a treaty violation and the *Rauscher* case applied. Therefore he must be returned.

The companion principles of the *Ker* and *Rauscher* cases apply to penal forfeitures of property. Thus, in an early case, the facts were that three American slave ships set sail from Havana to Pensacola in Spanish Florida, but upon their arrival they were greeted by the American army (General Jackson's Seminole expedition) which seized the ships and took them to Mobile, where they were libeled for forfeiture, having violated the law against American ships engaging in such trade, even wholly between foreign ports. As with persons wrongfully arrested, it does not now avail the ship or its owner that the seizure violated the sovereignty of a peaceful nation, for it is before the court and has violated the law. The Merino, 9 Wheat. 391 (U. S. 1824). Accord: The Ship Richmond v. United States, 9 Cranch 102 (U. S. 1815, Marshall, C. J.); The Tenyu Maru, 4 Alaska 129 (1910) (Japanese sealing schooner, whose crew had killed female seals in violation of law within the three-mile limit, was seized outside the limit and brought to port; forfeiture upheld). A like principle has been applied to forfeitures under the Prohibition and Revenue Acts, where automobiles and boats are seized without authority but the seizure is then adopted by the proper authorities. Dodge v. United States, 272 U. S. 530, 47 Sup. Ct. 191 (1926), in which Justice Holmes was careful to emphasize, without explaining, the distinction between forfeiture of property unlawfully seized and its use in evidence (see *infra* note 204).

A recent case has demonstrated that here, too, there is a *Rauscher* principle, and that if the seizure is not merely in violation of a foreign sovereignty but of a treaty, which is the law of the land, the ordinary incidents of the court's possession of the property yield to the treaty, and a forfeiture is not allowed. Cook v. United States, 288 U. S. 102, 53 Sup. Ct. 305 (1933). See Dickinson, *loc. cit. supra* note 21.

[25]Lascelles v. Georgia, 148 U. S. 537, 13 Sup. Ct. 687 (1893), resolving a conflict among state decisions. However, the case holds only that no right under the Federal Constitution is involved, and a state is still free to refuse to try the defendant for another crime, as a matter of local policy. A substantial majority now follow the *Lascelles* case. See note (1922) 21 A. L. R. 1418.

[26]See *supra* notes 13 and 14.

[27]*Ex parte* Barker, 87 Ala. 4, 6 So. 7 (1888); Dow's Case, 18 Pa. 37 (1851); Kingen v. Kelley, 3 Wyo. 566, 577, 28 Pac. 36, 38 (1891). On the authority of the dictum of Chief Justice Gibson, "a greater judge than whom never lived," in *Dow's Case,* a Pennsylvania Common Pleas judge released a prisoner who had been kidnapped in New York after being decoyed from Canada. Governor Cleveland of New York had demanded

came before the United States Supreme Court in *Mahon v. Justice*.[28] This case arose out of the most famous blood-feud in American history. The Hatfields of West Virginia and the McCoys of Kentucky lived on opposite sides of the mountain stream that marks the state line. One August day in 1882, a Hatfield was mortally wounded by two of the McCoys in an election fight. The Hatfield clan took the two McCoys and their young brother into custody and held them in close confinement on the West Virginia side until the victim's death was announced. Thereupon, the McCoys were taken back to Kentucky and brutally murdered. Indictments were found, in Kentucky, against twenty-three members of the Hatfield clan, but they were safe at home over the line. They continued to make forays over the line, harassing the McCoys but always armed and in such numbers that prudent officers considered it advisable to return their warrants with the report "not found". Rich rewards were offered by the state but none was so bold as to seek to earn them. Finally, giving up hope of arresting them in Kentucky, the Governor requisitioned the Governor of West Virginia for their extradition. One Frank Phillips, a deputy sheriff, was appointed to receive the men when they should be surrendered by West Virginia, but the Governor of West Virginia, for reasons never satisfactorily explained, refused extradition, resulting in perhaps the most bitter exchange of correspondence that has ever passed between two governors. The outrages of the Hatfields continuing and growing more vicious, Phillips took matters into his own hands, gathered a band of armed men together and struck rapid and unexpected blows at the Hatfields, returning a number of them to jail in Kentucky. The Governor of West Virginia, shocked at this affront to his sovereignty, sued out a writ of *habeas corpus* in the federal court. It was refused and the Supreme Court affirmed, holding that although the fugitive, while in West Virginia, had the right not to be surrendered except in accordance with the extradition law, his presence in Kentucky and his detention under lawful process gave jurisdiction to the Kentucky court to try him for a crime committed within that state.[29] Of

---

his return, and the demand was granted at the instance of Pennsylvania's governor, not as a constitutional right of the accused but as a matter of comity. Commonwealth *ex rel.* Norton v. Shaw, 15 Weekly Notes 395, 6 Crim. L. Mag. 245 (Pa. C. P. 1884).

[28]127 U. S. 700, 8 Sup. Ct. 1204 (1888).

[29]Two justices dissented, saying that the Constitution provides a peaceable means of procuring the return of fugitives, with the object of preventing friction between the states both from their giving asylum to each other's criminals and from violent invasions for the purpose of returning them; that while it is purely the concern of the offended state when its sovereignty is thus violated, its demand for the fugitive's return should be honored if made.

The prisoners were subsequently convicted and sentenced to life imprisonment. Hatfield v. Commonwealth, 11 Ky. L. Rep. 468, 82 S. W. 309 (1889). In retaliation, Deputy Sheriff Phillips was indicted in West Virginia and tried for kidnapping, but he was freed after a long court battle—from which it may well be argued that the difficulty with direct remedies for illegal law enforcement is that juries judge the act by its results, and if a real criminal has been brought to justice, however illegally, few

course, the decision was only to the effect that no federal question was involved under the extradition laws. The state might still honor the demand as a matter of comity.

One important question remained: suppose that not an individual (and an officer acting without authority is no more) but the state itself, its governor and its militia, becomes the kidnapper, using the forms of extradition but conniving to evade its requirements. This is a different thing than for the state merely to insist that it will try an accused criminal found within its borders, irrespective of any wrongs done him by individuals. And many cases, in so holding, in effect reserved this other question. For, in pointing out the contrast with civil cases, in which a plaintiff is not allowed to take advantage of his own wrong in obtaining service,[30] they emphasized

---

juries would punish the offending officer. But would justice have been better served in this case by letting the Hatfields go free?

For a full account of the Hatfield-McCoy feud (from a McCoy viewpoint), see MUTZENBERG, KENTUCKY'S FAMOUS FEUDS AND TRAGEDIES (1917) 29-110.

[30]The courts will usually set aside service of civil process procured by force or trick. Snelling v. Watrous, 2 Paige Ch. 314 (N. Y. 1830) (civil arrest by trick); Bernstein v. Hakim, 126 Misc. 582, 214 N. Y. Supp. 82 (A. T. 1st Dep't 1926) (service of summons by trick); Anderson v. Abeel, 96 App. Div. 370, 89 N. Y. Supp. 254 (1st Dep't 1904) (service by assault); Birch v. Prodger, 1 Bos. & P. (N. R.) 136, 127 Eng. Rep. 410 (1804) (plaintiff met defendant on the street and forcibly detained him until process could be procured); see note, Ann. Cas. 1916C, 612, 616. New York has now changed its rule as to service by fraud not involving enticement into the jurisdiction. Gumperz v. Hofmann, 245 App. Div. 622, 283 N. Y. Supp. 823 (1st Dep't 1935), *aff'd,* 271 N. Y. 544, 2 N. E. (2d) 687 (1936).

This is particularly important in cases where the civil defendant has been kidnapped or decoyed from his home into another jurisdiction, for "it is the right of a party defendant in a civil action to be sued in the forum of his domicile, though he may be sued in personal action in a foreign forum, if found there, if he went there voluntarily. If his presence there was procured by fraud or force, it does not subject him to a civil suit, or to the service of any civil process there." Kingen v. Kelly, 3 Wyo. 566, 570, 28 Pac. 36, 37 (1891) (dictum). *Accord*: Commercial Mut. Acc. Co. v. Davis, 213 U. S. 245, 256, 29 Sup. Ct. 445, 448 (1909) (dictum); Hill v. Goodrich, 32 Conn. 588 (1858); Williams ads. Reed, 29 N. J. L. 385 (1862); Carpenter v. Spooner, 2 Sand. 717 (N. Y. Super: Ct. 1850); Metcalf v. Clark, 41 Barb. 45 (N. Y. Sup. Ct. 1864) (creditor arranged to meet his Canadian debtor for a conference in a store just over the line in Canada; he suggested that the debtor hitch his horse in a nearby shed—over the state line, where a process server was lurking); Baker v. Wales, 14 Abb. Pr. N. S. 331 (N. Y. Super. Ct. 1873) (plaintiff asked defendant to come in from Connecticut to negotiate a settlement; when the negotiations failed, he filled out a blank summons and served it; this would be all right if *bona fide,* but the court saw a general plan in the fact that a supply of blank summonses was kept in the office, so it was held a deceit); Lagrave's Case, 14 Abb. Pr. N. S. 333, 45 How. Pr. 301 (N. Y. Sup. Ct. 1873) (creditors obtained extradition of a storekeeper who had absconded to France by falsely representing that he was charged with burglary; on his return he was served with civil process; at that time, and until the enactment of CODE CRIM. PROC. § 855 in 1936, which restricts the right in certain cases, New York permitted service of civil process on persons brought there by extradition, Adriance v. Lagrave, 59 N. Y. 110 [1874]; but since the extradition was fraudulently procured, the creditors who participated in the fraud were prevented from serving him); Garabettian v. Garabettian, 206 App. Div. 502, 201 N. Y. Supp. 548 (1st Dep't 1923); Stein v. Valkenhuysen, El. Bl. & El. 65, 120 Eng. Rep. 431 (1858). *Cf.* Phelps v. Goddard, 1 Tyler 60 (Vt. 1801) (damages allowed against those who decoyed a debtor into New York where he was sued in a civil action which was barred by lapse of time in Vermont but not in New York).

The same rule applies to civil proceedings *in rem.* In Moynahan v. Wilson, Fed. Cas.

that the state was guilty of no wrong.[31]

This question came before the Supreme Court in *Pettibone v. Nichols.*[32] Like the *Mahon* case, this arose out of an era of unbridled lawlessness, a long drawn out labor war in which murder seems to have been the normal and usual weapon of both sides. Ex-Governor Steunenberg of Idaho, who had used troops to suppress a mine strike during his term, was killed by a bomb planted in his gate. The man who planted the bomb was captured and told a lurid tale of a great plot to murder governors, judges and others who had opposed the union. He accused Haywood, Moyer and Pettibone of complicity in the plot. These men were leaders of the radical Western Federation of Miners and had been in Colorado at the time of the crime, hence were not legally extraditable as "fugitives" from Idaho. But the Idaho authorities presented incorrect affidavits[33] to their governor to the effect that these men had been in Idaho and were fugitives from its justice. The Governor of Idaho, though later charged with knowledge of the falsity, made demand on the Governor of Colorado, who also was said to have been well aware of the truth. The arrest of the men on the extradition warrants was delayed until Saturday night, when judges and lawyers were not readily available—for as long as the men were in Colorado, they could be released on proof in court that the requisites of extradition had not been

---

No. 9897, 2 Flip. 130 (C. C. E. D. Mich. 1887), defendant had brought plaintiff's horse from a bailee; plaintiff wrote defendant that he had already arranged a match race and would lose a substantial wager unless defendant brought the mare into the state for the race; defendant was a good fellow, and he sent the horse, which was attached in replevin upon its arrival; the attachment was set aside. In Houghton v. May, 22 Ont. L. R. 434 (1910), a judgment creditor in Canada procured the setting adrift of his debtor's steamer on the American side, and he levied execution when it floated to the other bank. The levy was set aside. See also (1929) 42 HARV. L. REV. 439.

[31]Mahon v. Justice, 127 U. S. 700, 706, 8 Sup. Ct. 1204, 1207 (1888); State v. Ross, 21 Iowa 467, 471 (1866); People v. Rowe, 4 Parker Cr. 253, 254 (N. Y. Super. Ct. 1858); Lagrave's Case, 14 Abb. Pr. N. S. 333, 343 (N. Y. Sup. Ct. 1873); Kingen v. Kelley, 3 Wyo. 566, 570-1, 28 Pac. 36, 37-38, 15 L. R. A. 177 (1891).

[32]203 U. S. 192, 27 Sup. Ct. 111, 7 Ann. Cas. 1047 (1906), noted (1907) 16 YALE L. J. 347. *Habeas corpus* proceedings were brought in both the state and federal courts, and the release of the prisoners was denied in each case. Appeals from both actions were argued together in the Supreme Court. The state court decision is *In re* Moyer, 12 Ida. 250, 85 Pac. 897, 12 L. R. A. (N. S.) 227 (1906).

With this case, compare People v. Pratt, 78 Cal. 345, 20 Pac. 731 (1889), in which the accused escaped to Japan. The United States had no extradition treaty with Japan, and its policy in such a case was not to request extradition. So the Governor, who concededly had no authority to deal with foreign nations, made the request himself, and it was granted. The court held that even conceding that a wrong was done the defendant by the Governor, he may be tried by the court when found within the state. "The Governor of the state cannot oust the courts . . . of their right to try an individual charged with an offense over which they have jurisdiction, because of the fact that he has been instrumental in having the defendant there, by violation of his personal rights. It will not do to say that a fugitive from justice can escape the punishment for his crime because the Governor of a state may have violated some law. The people of a state are not bound by the illegal act of their Governor, nor should they be." 78 Cal. at 349.

[33]The allegations of the petition for *habeas corpus* were taken as true for purposes of this appeal.

met.[34] It was claimed that they were rushed out of the state on a special train guarded by the militia, before any court action could be taken to protect them.

The case attracted nation-wide attention. The prisoners engaged Clarence Darrow as their chief counsel, and William E. Borah, then a newly elected Senator about to take his seat, led the prosecution. The first move of the defense, the only one which concerns us here, was a test of the state's right to hold the prisoners for trial when the state itself was the kidnapper. Denied release by both state and federal courts, appeals were taken to the Supreme Court,[35] but the Court held that once the accused is within the jurisdiction in which he is charged with crime, the extradition warrant, if any, has served its function and the court will not look to the manner of his arrest and rendition. This is equally true when the power of the state effects the illegal arrest and when it is done by an individual. The crime of the accused is not purged thereby, and when before the court he must stand trial.[36]

Thus it is apparent that, by the great weight of authority, the court before which a defendant is brought, however illegally he may have been seized, locally or abroad, will not hesitate to take advantage of his presence and will try him. The interest of society requires that crime be punished, and all that the defendant is entitled to demand is a fair trial by a court having jurisdiction of the subject matter, in which he has an opportunity of knowing the charge and of being fully heard.[37]

When a resident is indicted or is brought before the committing magistrate, the one really material inquiry is whether there is probable cause for

---

[34]Either in the federal court, Roberts v. Reilly, 116 U. S. 80, 94, 6 Sup. Ct. 291, 299 (1885), or in the state court, Robb v. Connolly, 111 U. S. 624, 4 Sup. Ct. 544 (1884).

[35]*Supra* note 32. Justice McKenna dissented.

[36]Haywood and Pettibone were acquitted, the terrorist's confession being the only substantial evidence against them. The prosecution of Moyer was then dropped. DARROW, THE STORY OF MY LIFE (1932) 155, 169, 171.

Radicals asserted that the Supreme Court in the *Pettibone* case had legalized the kidnapping of fugitives from justice, and the editor of the Socialist *Appeal to Reason* decided to test the question "whether there is one law for the rich corporation and another for the poor man". For his test, he selected the case of ex-Governor Taylor of Kentucky. Taylor had been removed as Governor by the Legislature, under a law put through by his defeated rival, who thereupon was named Governor; but before the latter (Gov. Goebel) took over, he was shot by a person unknown, from the State House window; Taylor was accused of complicity, fled to Indiana; the Governor of Indiana refused extradition. The editor, one Warren, placed on his mailing envelopes an offer of $1,000 reward to anyone who would kidnap Taylor and return him to Kentucky. His "test" ran afoul of the law against placing defamatory matter on the outside of mailing matter, and Warren was convicted. Warren v. United States, 183 Fed. 718, 33 L. R. A. (N. S.) 800 (C. C. A. 8th 1910). Darrow defended, but withdrew from the case and let Warren argue for himself, when the latter insisted on pressing the argument that kidnapping of fugitives had been legalized (but the court wholly ignored this point). The case has interest as demonstrating the false impression that the public may get when the courts take advantage of illegal acts of those charged with law enforcement.

[37]Ker v. Illinois, 119 U. S. 436, 7 Sup. Ct. 225 (1886); Regina v. Hughes, 4 Q. B. D. 614, 14 Cox Crim. 284 (1879).

his commitment and trial. This is the same inquiry that would have been made if a warrant had been sought before bringing him in, and no more is necessary for the protection of the accused. A stronger practical argument on the other side can be made where the accused is brought illegally from another state. For, until trial, we must presume him innocent and, unlike a resident, he has been brought to trial before a foreign tribunal, governed by laws unknown to him, separated from his friends, from his witnesses, confined among strangers who know him only as an accused outlander whatever his reputation may have been at home.[38] To continue the presumption of innocence, he may never have been in the state where he stands accused, yet he has had no opportunity to demonstrate this to his own governor or his home courts. At first blush there is force in this argument, but it must be borne in mind that if he had been extradited, he would be in the same position, for these objections are inherent in our system which requires that the criminal defendant, unlike the civil defendant, must be tried where the crime is alleged to have occurred. An indictment duly found is all the protection a resident or a non-resident can claim even when all is lawful, for (apart from "discretionary" abuses by the governor) extradition is then virtually automatic.[39]

II. Illegally Obtained Evidence

While it is almost universally held that a person illegally arrested, by no matter how gross a violation of personal liberty and the public peace, will not be released on this account if probable cause for his detention appears, the admissibility of evidence obtained by a violation of law is not so freely conceded. Rather, it is a subject on which the most bitter controversy has raged for a quarter of a century. We should hesitate to add to the already great volume of legal literature on the subject had it not once more become a burning question in New York.[40]

A. *Scope of the Constitutional Provision*

It is a basic principle of Anglo-American liberty that our "persons, houses, papers, and effects" shall be secure from *unreasonable* search and seizure.[41] Under certain circumstances, no search warrant is required, when a search

[38]See *Ex parte* Smith, 3 McLean 121, 136 (C. C. D. Ill. 1842).

[39]It must be conceded, however, that on the one question of establishing his identity, the position of the accused is rendered worse by his removal without extradition.

[40]The Constitutional Convention of 1938 bitterly debated the question, finally refused to exclude such evidence. The Legislature by the time this appears should have passed one of the bills referred to, *infra* note 94, adopting completely or partially the rule excluding illegally obtained evidence. (Note: Both bills have been shelved for this session.)

[41]U. S. Const., 4th Amendment. Similar language is now found in the constitution of every state. New York was the last to adopt it (Const. 1938, Art. I, § 12), having previously relegated this principle to a statute (Civil Rights Law § 8).

without a warrant is reasonable.[42] When a warrant is necessary, it must be duly issued by a court, upon an affidavit that there is probable cause to believe that certain described property will be found. General warrants to search for and seize books and papers and other things lawfully possessed, though of evidential value, are not reasonable or lawful.[43] Warrants are justified only where a right of search and seizure may be found in the interest of the public or of the complainant in the property to be seized, or where a valid exercise of the police power makes possession of the property unlawful.[44]

One's person may be searched only upon a warrant, except that when one is lawfully arrested, an officer may then search him and seize anything on his person or under his immediate control which may be useful as evidence of the crime for which he is arrested.[45] An arrest unlawful in its inception, however, is not made lawful by what is discovered by searching,[46] and a search pursuant to an unlawful arrest is likewise unlawful.

---

[42]See the full discussion in United States v. Snyder, 278 Fed. 650 (N. D. W. Va. 1922).

[43]Entick v. Carrington, 19 How. St. Tr. 1029, 95 Eng. Rep. 807 (1765); Gouled v. United States, 255 U. S. 298, 41 Sup. Ct. 261 (1921); State v. Sheridan, 121 Iowa 164, 96 N. W. 730 (1903). Warrants to tap wires, such as are now provided for in New York, are inconsistent with this principle but have express constitutional authorization. N. Y. CONST. (1938) Art. I, § 12.

[44]See Gouled v. United States, *supra* note 43. The Court gives as examples: burglar tools, weapons, stolen or forfeited property, property subject to tax and the books required by law to be kept as to them, counterfeit money, and gambling implements. See also Lefkowitz v. United States, 52 F. (2d) 52 (C. C. A. 2d 1931), *aff'd*, 285 U. S. 452, 52 Sup. Ct. 420 (1932).

See the statutory enumerations in 18 U. S. C. A. § 612 and N. Y. CODE CRIM. PROC. § 792.

[45]People v. Chiagles, 237 N. Y. 193, 142 N. E. 583 (1923). Although a search warrant may not issue for purely evidentiary articles (see *supra* note 43), a search in the course of an arrest may properly result in the seizure of evidence. Judge Cardozo thus rationalizes the rule: An officer making a lawful arrest may properly disarm his prisoner; for this purpose a search is necessary and lawful; and whatever is found by a *lawful* search he may retain if it is connected with the crime.

A general exploratory search of the room where the arrest is made is not justified under this principle. Lefkowitz v. United States, *supra* note 44. But articles exposed to view in the room may be seized if the officers are present pursuant to a lawful arrest. Marron v. United States, 275 U. S. 192, 48 Sup. Ct. 74 (1927).

[46]The American Law Institute's Model Code of Criminal Procedure, however, in § 21 (b) makes an arrest *lawful* if a felony has in fact been committed by the one arrested, irrespective of the officer's probable cause for believing it at the time. This section is in force, in substance, in at least seventeen states: ALA. CODE ANN. (Michie 1928) § 3263; ARIZ. REV. CODE ANN. (Struckmeyer 1938) § 4937; CAL. PEN. CODE (Deering 1937) § 836; IDA. CODE ANN. (1932) § 19-603; LA. CODE CRIM. PROC. ANN. (Dart 1932) art. 60: MICH. COMP. LAWS (1929) § 17149; MINN. STAT. (Mason 1927) § 10570; MISS. CODE ANN. (1930) § 1227; MONT. REV. CODES ANN. (Anderson & McFarland 1935) § 11753; NEV. COMP. LAWS (Hillyer 1929) § 10751; N. Y. CODE CRIM. PROC. § 177; N. D. COMP. LAWS ANN. (1913) § 10567; OKLA. STAT. ANN. (1937) tit. 27, § 196; ORE. CODE ANN. (1930) § 13-2111; S. D. COMP. LAWS (1929) § 4553; TENN. CODE ANN. (Williams 1934) § 11536; UTAH REV. STAT. ANN. (1933) § 105-13-3. The same rule is adopted by case law in Missouri. State v. Whitley, 183 S. W. 317 (1916), but such cases are rare. The rule does not apply to misdemeanors.

Where this rule is inapplicable, it is held that "although the defendant ought to have been arrested, and in fact was arrested, such arrest was not warranted" because the officer lacked probable cause for the arrest when he made it.

The question of whether the constitutional meaning of "reasonable search" will

A house or place of business may not be searched without a warrant.[47] This principle has been repeatedly enunciated by champions of liberty, notably by Lord Chatham in Parliament just before the American Revolution: "A man's house is his castle;[48] it may be a straw hut, the wind may whistle around it, the rain may enter it, but the King cannot."[49]

A mere trespass to land, other than the building where one dwells or does business, or the immediate surroundings thereof, is not a search within the meaning of the Constitution.[50] Therefore, officers trespassing in open fields, orchards, stables, and the like may be liable for damages, but they are not guilty of an unconstitutional search—a rule which is of great importance where evidence secured by a technical "search" is excluded.[51] Furthermore, a "search" implies a prying into hidden places for what is concealed, and when actions or articles are visible to the eye, no "search" is committed in their discovery, even though the officer be guilty of the most reprehensible spying and window-peeping.[52] It is immaterial that a flashlight or search-

---

expand to meet this expanded statutory meaning of "lawful arrest" is fully considered in Waite, *Public Policy and the Arrest of Felons* (1933) 31 MICH. L. REV. 749.

[47]Agnello v. United States, 269 U. S. 20, 46 Sup. Ct. 4 (1925) (it is not enough that the officer have probable cause; a warrant is necessary); Silverthorne Lumber Co. v. United States, 251 U. S. 385, 40 Sup. Ct. 182 (1920) (place of business) (even though the papers could have been *subpoenaed* because the corporation could not claim privilege, the *seizure* was unlawful).

[48]This expression is likewise found in the famous speech of James Otis in 1761, quoted in 2 WATSON, THE CONSTITUTION (1910) 1416, at 1418. It probably originated with Lord Coke. Semayne's Case, 5 Co. Rep. 91a, 77 Eng. Rep. 194 (1605).

[49]Nevertheless, it has been judicially declared that a nudist camp in a clearing in the forest is *not* one's castle. People v. Ring, 267 Mich. 657, 255 N. W. 373 (1934). But compare Chapin v. State, 107 Tex. Cr. 477, 296 S. W. 1095 (1927) (tent held to be a dwelling house).

[50]The protected area is defined as the house or place of business and those things immediately connected therewith (gardens, outhouses, and appurtenances necessary for the domestic comfort of the dwelling or place of business), sometimes called the "curtilage". Worth v. State, 111 Tex. Cr. 288, 12 S. W. (2d) 582 (1928).

[51]Hester v. United States, 265 U. S. 57, 44 Sup. Ct. 445 (1924) (open field); United States v. McBride, 287 Fed. 214 (S. D. Ala. 1922), *cert. den.*, 261 U. S. 614, 43 Sup. Ct. 359 (1923) (stable); Guaresimo v. United States, 13 F. (2d) 848 (C. C. A. 6th 1926) (garage and barns, not proved appurtenant to house); Koth v. United States, 16 F. (2d) 61 (C. C. A. 9th 1926) (still found quarter mile from house); Dulek v. United States, 16 F. (2d) 275 (C. C. A. 6th 1926) (cabin in swamp, not used as dwelling); Schnorenberg v. United States, 23 F. (2d) 38 (C. C. A. 7th 1927) (barn and chicken coop); Brent v. Commonwealth, 194 Ky. 504, 240 S. W. 45 (1922) (still in woods); State v. Ladue, 73 Mont. 535, 237 Pac. 495 (1925) (still in the open); Eversole v. State, 106 Tex. Cr. 567, 294 S. W. 210 (1927) (barn). But compare People v. Lind, 18 N. E. (2d) 189 (Ill. 1938) (hen-house); People v. Brocamp, 307 Ill. 448, 138 N. E. 728 (1923) (officers dug in passage-way under cottage).

[52]United States v. Lee, 274 U. S. 559, 563, 47 Sup. Ct. 746 (1927) (examination of boat by searchlight before boarding it, revealing that smuggling was being committed, made the subsequent arrest and search proper); Smith v. United States, 2 F. (2d) 715 (C. C. A. 4th 1924) (flashlight turned on rear floor of parked automobile); Cohn v. State, 120 Tenn. 61, 109 S. W. 451 (1907) (officers removed brick in saloon wall and looked through); Hunter v. State, 111 Tex. Cr. 252, 12 S. W. (2d) 581 (1929) (window-peeping by officer); State v. Basil, 126 Wash. 155, 217 Pac. 720 (1923) (window).

"The eye cannot by the law of England be guilty of a trespass." Lord Camden in Entick v. Carrington, 19 How. St. Tr. 1029, 1066 (1765).

light is used, for there is no right in the privacy afforded by darkness.[53] Eavesdropping also is not a "search".[54]

Likewise, the doctrine of the *Six Carpenters' Case,*[55] although it operates to make the officers civilly liable as trespassers *ab initio* when they enter a building under a valid search warrant and abuse their authority, does not have the effect of making the search and seizure unconstitutional.[56] The constitutional guaranty is not co-extensive with the definition of a civil trespass.

Automobiles and vessels may be searched without a warrant, provided the officer had probable cause.[57] For such vehicles are mobile and may be far away before a warrant can be obtained.[58]

Sealed letters and sealed packages in the mail are as fully guarded from inspection, except as to their outward appearance, and are as fully protected as if retained in the sender's possession, and may be opened only pursuant to a proper warrant.[59]

But the constitutional protection has been held not to extend to such intangible things as messages traveling on telegraph or telephone wires,[60] on the theory that there is no "search" or "seizure" but a simple use of the sense of hearing. Although there was a *physical* tapping of the wires, the Court refused to indulge in the fiction that a wire leading many miles from a home or office was a part of it. Wire-tapping might be made unlawful by statute, but it is not unconstitutional. It is a penal offense in many states, as is the revelation of information thereby discovered.[61] When Congress

---

[53]United States v. Lee, and Smith v. United States, *supra* note 52.

[54]People v. Cotta, 49 Cal. 166 (1874); Commonwealth v. Everson, 123 Ky. 330, 96 S. W. 460 (1906) (the landlady at the keyhole); DeLore v. Smith, 67 Ore. 304, 136 Pac. 13 (1913) (party line); Hunter v. State, 111 Tex. Cr. 252, 12 S. W. (2d) 581 (1929) (officer listening at window).

[55]8 Coke 146a, 77 Eng. Rep. 695 (1611).

[56]McGuire v. United States, 273 U. S. 95, 47 Sup. Ct. 259 (1927) (liquor seized under *valid* search warrant; officers, by an "illegal and oppressive act", destroyed all except some samples; held that the fiction is only applied as a rule of civil liability, and it will not be extended to exclude the use of evidence by the Government; the opinion is most instructive as showing how the Court sometimes gags on its own rule, for everything said in this opinion could be applied to the rule as a whole!) The contrary had been held in United States v. Cooper, 295 Fed. 709 (D. Mass. 1924).

[57]Carroll v. United States, 267 U. S. 132, 45 Sup. Ct. 280 (1925); People v. Schaub, 279 Mich. 457, 272 N. W. 867 (1937). It would be unreasonable to permit automobiles to be searched without probable cause, so such searches are unlawful. Gambino v. United States, 275 U. S. 310, 48 Sup. Ct. 137 (1927); Hughes v. State 145 Tenn. 544, 238 S. W. 588 (1922).

[58]Because of the greater sanctity of persons and houses, the courts are unwilling to apply this reasoning to them, although persons and articles in houses may be just as mobile. Agnello v. United States, 269 U. S. 20, 46 Sup. Ct. 4 (1925).

[59]*Ex parte* Jackson, 96 U. S. 727, 733 (1877).

[60]Olmstead v. United States, 277 U. S. 438, 48 Sup. Ct. 564 (1928).

[61]*E.g.* N. Y. PENAL LAW § 1423(6). Since this is in the article on Malicious Mischief, it has generally been assumed not to apply to police officers, and it was so held in People v. Hebbard, 96 Misc. 617, 620, 162 N. Y. Supp. 80 (Sup. Ct. 1916). *Cf.* Wass v. Stephens, 128 N. Y. 123, 28 N. E. 21 (1891), construing another subdivision of the same section.

took over the regulation of wire communications in 1934, it adopted such a provision,[62] which makes criminal, subject to severe penalties,[63] the interception of such communications by any person, including an officer.[64] No provision is made for warrants; it is unlawful under all circumstances. In New York, where wire-tapping by officers had formerly been unrestricted,[65] the 1938 Constitutional Convention adopted a provision requiring a court order to be obtained for tapping wires, the order to be granted upon showing reasonable cause to believe that evidence of crime may thus be obtained.[66] But there remains the anomaly that officers acting under a lawful state warrant will be committing a federal felony![67]

The constitutional provisions as to search and seizure are restrictions on the government, not on individuals, and hence trespasses by private individuals do not violate the Constitution, if not instigated or participated in by officers.[68] The Federal Bill of Rights does not apply to state governments,[69] so state officers do not violate the Federal Constitution when they search,[70] unless they act in concert with federal authorities;[71] nor do federal

---

[62]Communications Act of 1934, § 605; 47 U. S. C. A. § 605 (Supp. 1938).

[63]Maximum fine of $10,000, imprisonment of two years, or both. 47 U. S. C. A. § 501 (Supp. 1938).

[64]Nardone v. United States, 302 U. S. 379, 58 Sup. Ct. 275 (1937), *rev'g* 90 F. (2d) 630 (C. C. A. 2d 1937).

[65]*Supra* note 61.

[66]N. Y. CONST. (1938) Art. I, § 12. Contrast the fact that *search* warrants may not be issued solely for the purpose of getting evidence, *supra* note 43.

[67]Whether this clause of the federal act applies only to interstate communications is still in dispute. But since it is not the nature of the wire but that of the communication that is material, an officer would in any case risk tapping into a communication with someone outside the state. Prosecution would be doubtful, however.

[68]Burdeau v. McDowell, 256 U. S. 465, 41 Sup. Ct. 574 (1921) (employer broke into desk and safe and seized papers for purpose of prosecution); Bacon v. United States, 97 Fed. 35 (C. C. A. 8th 1899); Imboden v. People, 40 Colo. 142, 180, 90 Pac. 608, 619 (1907); Gindrat v. People, 138 Ill. 103, 27 N. E. 1085 (1891) (private detective); Commonwealth v. Everson, 123 Ky. 330, 96 S. W. 460 (1906) (landlady); State v. Mathers, 64 Vt. 101, 23 Atl. 590 (1892) (letter taken from pocket by daughter); Barrett v. Fish, 72 Vt. 18, 47 Atl. 174 (1899) (letters between petitioner and co-adulterer given to agent to be burned; agent, in breach of faith, gave letters to prosecutor); Ware v. State, 201 Wis. 425, 230 N. W. 80 (1930) (husband stole wife's diary, used in prosecution for adultery). The *statutory* provision against wire-tapping, however, applies to *all* persons, 47 U. S. C. A. § 605 (Supp. 1938).

[69]Barron v. Baltimore, 7 Peters 243 (U. S. 1833). The "due process" and "privileges and immunities" clauses of the Fourteenth Amendment do not incorporate all of these rights, as restrictions on the states. Walker v. Sauvinet, 92 U. S. 90 (1875) (trial by jury); Twining v. New Jersey, 211 U. S. 78, 29 Sup. Ct. 14 (1908) (self-incrimination).

[70]Weeks v. United States, 232 U. S. 383, 34 Sup. Ct. 341 (1914) (admitting evidence furnished by *local* officers). *Cf.* Pederson v. United States, 271 Fed. 187 (C. C. A. 2d 1921) (evidence seized by *British* officers).

[71]Byars v. United States, 273 U. S. 28, 47 Sup. Ct. 248 (1927) (search by local police who invited federal officer to join them; held that *mere* participation in a state search by a federal officer is not enough, unless he participates in his official capacity; but the courts will scrutinize such arrangements for indirect violations, and one was found here); Gambino v. United States, 275 U. S. 310, 48 Sup. Ct. 137 (1927) (state officers, not directed by federal authority but still enforcing the Federal Prohibition Law, of which there was no state counterpart; held to be a violation, since done solely on behalf of Federal Government, if it ratifies it by prosecuting); Flagg v. United States, 233 Fed.

officers violate state constitutions by anything *they* may do.[72]

B. *Admissibility of Illegally Obtained Evidence*

When property is obtained by an unreasonable search and seizure, as here defined, may the evidence be used in court? The earliest known case is *Bishop Atterbury's Trial,*[73] in the House of Lords in 1723. Certain letters were taken from the defendant's person by violence,[74] while others were intercepted in the mails.[75] These letters were admitted without permitting inquiry as to the authority by which they were seized.

In America, the question was first raised by a dictum of the Massachusetts court in *Commonwealth v. Dana,*[76] in 1841. The court had held the seizure lawful, but it went on to say, "There is another conclusive answer," that even if it were illegally seized, the evidence was nevertheless admissible.[77] This half-page dictum became the basis of a rule that was, at one time or another, adopted by most of the states.[78] It was never questioned until the United States Supreme Court countered with an even more gratuitous dictum,[79] in *Boyd v. United States,*[80] in 1886.

The *Boyd* case, taking what was decided and not what was said, was probably correctly determined.[81] Under *court order,* defendant produced certain papers. The Court held that the order violated the Fifth Amendment by compelling defendant to be a witness against himself, and that the evidence could not be used. But the Court went on and assimilated such compulsory

481 (C. C. A. 2d 1916) (local officers seized books and papers, taken at once to federal prosecutor; court indulged presumption that prosecutor had read the *Weeks* case not wisely but too well); United States v. Welch, 247 Fed. 239 (S. D. N. Y. 1917), *aff'd,* 267 Fed. 819 (C. C. A. 2d 1920), *cert. den.,* 254 U. S. 637, 41 Sup. Ct. 9 (1920) (steamship detective acting for customs officer in his temporary absence).

Where local officers are actually engaged in enforcing a state statute, and are not coöperating with federal authorities, there is no violation of the Federal Constitution and federal courts will admit the evidence. Gowling v. United States, 64 F. (2d) 796 (C. C. A. 6th 1933).

[72]State v. Gardner, 77 Mont. 8, 249 Pac. 574 (1926) (seizure by federal officers without knowledge of state authorities; it was for a crime under both laws, so prosecuted in state court—the dual system comes in handy!)

[73]16 Howell State Trials 323 (1723). The authority of this case is weakened by the fact that it was a bill of attainder, this procedure being adopted expressly to avoid another rule of evidence (requiring two witnesses for treason), so it should not be accepted too readily as establishing any rule of evidence. See pages 489 and 660 of the report.

[74]*Id.* at 490-493.

[75]*Id.* at 430, 433, 495-96, 629-30.

[76]2 Metc. 329, 337 (Mass. 1841).

[77]Citing two English *civil* cases where court records, obtained without a proper order, were admitted in evidence. Jordan v. Lewis, 14 East 305 note, 104 Eng. Rep. 618 (1740); Legatt v. Tollervey, 14 East 302, 104 Eng. Rep. 617 (1811).

[78]The first square holding is in State v. Flynn, 36 N. H. 64 (1858).

[79]It has been said, with some force, that two-thirds of our law stems originally from dicta.

[80]116 U. S. 616, 6 Sup. Ct. 524 (1886). There was an earlier dictum, more directly in point, in *Ex parte* Jackson, 96 U. S. 727, 733 (1877).

[81]The contrary has been suggested by Edgerton, *The Incidence of Judicial Control Over Congress* (1937) 22 CORNELL L. Q. 299, 302.

production of papers to a search and seizure, both of which force evidence from a person. Seizure of evidence was thus declared to be equivalent to compelling a man to be a witness against himself. Two justices, concurring in result, were unable to stomach this line of reasoning, but they were snowed under.

The *Boyd* case caused some stir in the state courts, but most of them recognized it as dictum, and distinguished it in search cases.[82] The Supreme Court itself was not fully prepared to follow its rule, for in *Adams v. New York,*[83] in 1904, it indicated that the self-incrimination provision had no application to search and seizure, and that violations of the latter guaranty would not be punished indirectly by excluding the evidence, drawing an analogy to the *Ker* and *Mahon* cases.[84] While later cases sought to distinguish it on several grounds,[85] the case contains strong language. It distinguishes the *Boyd* case, cites and quotes from every leading case for admissibility, and declares unequivocally for that rule.[86] A few courts, however, even after the *Adams* case, found the *Boyd* dictum "too good to be untrue",[87] and declared for the first time that if evidence was obtained in violation of the constitution, it could not be used in court.[88]

It took a more definite pronouncement by the highest court than it had made in the *Boyd* case, to really fertilize the "seeds of a dangerous heresy" that the *Boyd* case had sown. And in 1914 came *Weeks v. United States,*[89] in answer to the defense lawyers' prayer. The Court suddenly discovered that it had admitted the evidence in the *Adams* case, not for the reasons indicated in the opinion, but because no motion for the return of the property and

[82]See Starchman v. State, 62 Ark. 538, 36 S. W. 940 (1896); People v. LeDoux, 155 Cal. 535, 102 Pac. 517 (1909); State v. Pomeroy, 130 Mo. 489, 32 S. W. 1002 (1895); State v. Atkinson, 40 S. C. 363, 18 S. E. 1021 (1894); and many others.

[83]192 U. S. 585, 24 Sup. Ct. 372 (1904), *aff'g* People v. Adams, 176 N. Y. 351, 68 N. E. 636 (1903).

[84]*Supra* notes 15 and 28.

[85]That the seizure was (apparently) lawful, that no preliminary motion was made, and that it was a seizure by state officers (*supra* note 70). Only the first of these is even suggested in the opinion as a possible second ground of decision.

[86]If this was dictum, at least the same cannot be said of the short but clear holding in Hyde v. United States, 225 U. S. 347, 380, 32 Sup. Ct. 793, 807 (1912), where evidence that certain letters used in evidence were obtained by officers "robbing the mails" was excluded as irrelevant. "We cannot see how proof of 'a greater crime . . . in robbing the mails' was relevant to a decision of the charge then under consideration."

[87]Hammock v. State, 1 Ga. App. 126, 128, 58 S. E. 66, 67 (1907).

[88]Hammock v. State, 1 Ga. App. 126, 58 S. E. 66 (1907) (distinguishing Williams v. State, 100 Ga. 511, 28 S. E. 624 [1897], which had also come after the *Boyd* case but had admitted the evidence, on the basis that a search of the *person* compels him to be a witness against himself, while a search of his premises does not!); State v. Sheridan, 121 Iowa 164, 96 N. W. 730 (1903); State v. Slamon, 73 Vt. 212, 50 Atl. 1097 (1901) (but the court refused to extend the rule to contraband: State v. Krinski, 78 Vt. 162, 62 Atl. 37 [1905]). It is noteworthy that not one of these three states now follows the federal rule. The *Hammock* case was repudiated in Calhoun v. State, 144 Ga. 679, 87 S. E. 893 (1916); the *Sheridan* case in State v. Tonn, 195 Iowa 94, 191 N. W. 530 (1923); the *Slamon* case in State v. Stacy, 104 Vt. 379, 401, 160 Atl. 257, 266 (1932).

[89]232 U. S. 383, 34 Sup. Ct. 341 (1914).

the suppression of the evidence had been made before trial. Early cases and text-writers had made an unfortunate choice of language when they said that the court would not "stop the trial" to try a "collateral" issue. A collateral issue, properly, is one that has no bearing on the merits of the case, in short, one that is irrelevant. It is no less collateral when it is raised in advance of trial than when it is raised at any other time. But when the Court at last decided to read into the Constitution the requirement that the evidence be excluded, it seized on these words as the basis for distinguishing past holdings, and read into it also a rule of practice found in no constitution, in no statute,[90] and in no analogous rule of evidence! As to all other rules of evidence, courts universally stop the trial, exclude the jury if necessary, and determine the admissibility of the evidence—the confession of a prisoner, the qualifications of an expert or of a child witness, and a myriad others. If the court in the *Adams* case had really thought the evidence improper, it would have determined the facts on the trial and excluded the evidence. But Justice Day, who delivered the opinions in both cases, insisted that the lack of a preliminary motion was a distinguishing fact.

Then the parade began. The fervent rhetoric in the *Weeks* case influenced one court after another to follow the new rule, just as fast as defense lawyers discovered the magic formula whereby older cases might be distinguished. No matter how strong and how sweeping the language in the older cases, no matter how little they rested on an unwillingness to "stop the trial", courts found that this was the true basis of the older cases, and distinguished them.[91] A rare few definitely overruled their former holdings,[92] and others

[90]Since 1917, there has been statutory sanction for this procedure. 40 STAT. 229, 18 U. S. C. A. § 626. But there was none at the time. It appears first to have been attempted in United States v. Wilson, 163 Fed. 338 (C. C. S. D. N. Y. 1908), where the practice was approved but the motion was denied on the ground that the evidence was admissible (following the *Adams* case). It was first successful in United States v. Mills, 185 Fed. 318 (C. C. S. D. N. Y. 1911), *app. dismissed sub nom.* Wise v. Mills, 220 U. S. 549, 31 Sup. Ct. 597 (1911), which followed the *Boyd* case, obscurely distinguishing the *Adams* case.

[91]The lack of a motion was given as the ground of distinguishing in People v. Marxhausen, 204 Mich. 559, 171 N. W. 557 (1919) (distinguishing People v. Aldorfer, 164 Mich. 676, 130 N. W. 351 [1911]); State v. Owens, 302 Mo. 348, 259 S. W. 100 (1924) (distinguishing State v. Pomeroy, 130 Mo. 489. 32 S. W. 1002 [1895]); State *ex rel.* Thibodeau v. District Court, 70 Mont. 202, 224 Pac. 866 (1924) (distinguishing State v. Reed, 53 Mont. 292, 163 Pac. 477 [1917]); State v. McDaniel, 115 Ore. 187, 231 Pac. 965 (1925) (distinguishing State v. Ware, 79 Ore. 367, 154 Pac. 905, 155 Pac. 364 [1916]); State v. Gibbons, 118 Wash. 171, 203 Pac. 390 (1922) (ignoring State v. Royce, 38 Wash. 111, 80 Pac. 268 [1905], but the cases are distinguishable on this ground). Other grounds for distinguishing cases were found in People v. Brocamp, 307 Ill. 448, 138 N. E. 728 (1923) (distinguishing a one-time leading case, Gindrat v. People, 138 Ill. 103, 27 N. E. 1085 [1891], and other cases, on the ground that the seizure was by a private detective); and in Hughes v. State, 145 Tenn. 544, 238 S. W. 588 (1922) (distinguishing Cohn v. State, 120 Tenn. 61, 109 S. W. 451 [1907] on the ground that there was no technical search when officers made a peep-hole in defendant's wall).

[92]State v. Arregui, 44 Ida. 43, 254 Pac. 788 (1927) (overruling State v. Anderson, 31 Ida. 514, 174 Pac. 124 [1918], which was indistinguishable because a motion was

simply overlooked them.[93] At present, by decision or by statute, the federal rule is adopted in twenty-one states, in complete or modified form.[94] These states are concentrated in two principal areas, a solid belt from north to south throughout the Middle West (excluding only Alabama), and the north-

---

there made and denied); Nicholas v. City of Cleveland, 125 Ohio St. 474, 182 N. E. 26 (1932) (the latest convert, repudiating strong dicta in Rosanski v. State, 106 Ohio St. 442, 140 N. E. 370 [1922]); Gore v. State, 24 Okla. Cr. 394, 218 Pac. 545 (1923) (overruling Silva v. State, 6 Okla. Cr. 97, 116 Pac. 199 [1911]); State v. Gooder, 57 S. D. 619, 234 N. W. 610 (1931) (overruling City of Sioux Falls v. Walser, 45 S. D. 417, 187 N. W. 821 [1922]); State v. Wills, 91 W. Va. 659, 114 S. E. 261 (1922) (rejecting strong dicta in State v. Edwards, 51 W. Va. 220, 41 S. E. 429 [1902] and State v. Sutter, 71 W. Va. 371, 76 S. E. 811 [1912]; completely ignoring the only square case, State v. Douglas, 20 W. Va. 770 [1882]).

[93] Tucker v. State, 128 Miss. 211, 90 So. 845 (1922) (ignoring Pringle v. State, 108 Miss. 802, 67 So. 455 [1915]); Town of Blacksburg v. Beam, 104 S. C. 146, 88 S. E. 441 (1916) (citing no cases at all, overlooking State v. Atkinson, 40 S. C. 363, 18 S. E. 1021 [1894]; the *Blacksburg* case was in turn overruled and admissibility restored in State v. Prescott, 125 S. C. 22, 117 S. E. 637 [1923]).

[94] United States v. Giovanetti, 6 Alaska 454 (1921); Gildrie v. State, 94 Fla. 134, 113 So. 704 (1927); State v. Arregui, 44 Ida. 43, 254 Pac. 788 (1927); People v. Castree, 311 Ill. 392, 143 N. E. 112 (1924); People v. Lind, 18 N. E. (2d) 189 (Ill. 1938); Callender v. State, 193 Ind. 91, 136 N. E. 10, 138 N. E. 817 (1922); Youman v. Commonwealth, 189 Ky. 152, 224 S. W. 860 (1920); People v. Marxhausen, 204 Mich. 559, 171 N. W. 557 (1919); Tucker v. State, 128 Miss. 211, 90 So. 845 (1922); State v. Owens, 302 Mo. 348, 259 S. W. 100 (1924); State *ex rel.* Thibodeau v. District Court, 70 Mont. 202, 224 Pac. 866 (1924); Nicholas v. City of Cleveland, 125 Ohio St. 474, 182 N. E. 26 (1932); Gore v. State, 24 Okla. Cr. 394, 218 Pac. 545 (1923); State v. McDaniel, 115 Ore. 187, 231 Pac. 965 (1925); State v. Gooder, 57 S. D. 619, 234 N. W. 610 (1931); Hughes v. State, 145 Tenn. 544, 238 S. W. 588 (1922); Odenthal v. State, 106 Tex. Cr. 1, 290 S. W. 743 (1927) (under statute, CODE CRIM. PROC. [Vernon 1925] § 727a, changing the rule announced in Welchek v. State, 93 Tex. Cr. 271, 247 S. W. 524 [1922]); State v. Gibbons, 118 Wash. 171, 203 Pac. 390 (1922); State v. Wills, 91 W. Va. 659, 114 S. E. 261 (1922); Hoyer v. State, 180 Wis. 407, 193 N. W. 89 (1923); State v. Peterson, 27 Wyo. 185, 194 Pac. 342 (1920).

In North Carolina, an attempt was made to adopt the federal rule by statute in 1937 (N. C. CODE ANN. [Michie Supp. 1937] § 4530 [1]), but poor drafting immediately led to the anomalous result that evidence obtained under an illegal warrant is inadmissible, but evidence obtained *without* a warrant is still admitted. State v. McGee, 198 S. E. 616 (N. C. 1938).

In Maryland and Michigan, compromises have been adopted in the interest of public safety. In Maryland, where the evidence formerly was admissible (Lawrence v. State, 103 Md. 17, 63 Atl. 96 [1906]), the Legislature was unwilling to go the whole route, and declared in 1929 that such evidence should be inadmissible in misdemeanor trials but admissible in felony cases. MD. ANN. CODE (Flack Supp. 1935) Art. 35, § 4A. Michigan had followed the rule of inadmissibility, which, resting on supposed constitutional grounds, could not be changed by statute. But crime conditions got sufficiently serious (see the study by Waite, *Public Policy and the Arrest of Felons* [1933] 31 MICH. L. REV. 749) that the Legislature proposed a constitutional amendment excepting dangerous weapons from this rule, if seized "outside the curtilage of any dwelling house". It was accepted by the voters in 1936, and will be found in Mich. Pub. Acts. 1937, p. 876.

Two attempts to write the federal rule into state constitutions have been defeated. A convention in Louisiana in 1921 rejected the rule (see State v. Fleckinger, 152 La. 337, 341, 93 So. 115, 116 [1922]), and the New York convention in 1938 did likewise after a long and bitter debate. A compromise similar to the Michigan amendment was proposed by Delegate Poletti (now Lieutenant Governor), but was also rejected. CONVENTION RECORD (N. Y. 1938) p. 617. The fight is now going on in the Legislature, and before this article appears, New York will probably be completely or partially in the federal camp, because a compromise has already been proposed by the admissibility adherents, which would reject evidence obtained by illegal wire-tapping, but not other illegally obtained evidence. N. Y. Times, Feb. 3, 1939, p. 1, col. 1.

west corner of the country. Outside of these two areas, there are only three concurring states in the Southwest and three on the South Atlantic seaboard (two of the latter having statutes in restricted form). The rule of admissibility is followed in the remaining twenty-seven states (three of them by dictum),[95] and in three of the federal rule states the evidence is admissible in certain cases.[96] The evidence is admitted in England[97] and Canada,[98] on common law principles.

---

[95]In some of these states, the question of whether the evidence will be excluded on preliminary motion has never been raised, and the cases are still subject to be distinguished on this ground. But the courts in most of these states have reviewed their prior decisions with the federal rule before them and have not rested their decisions on so narrow a ground. The cases in which a motion has been made and denied are starred; in these states the question appears closed. Where possible, a leading early case has been supported by a later case reviewing the question after the *Weeks* decision. The cases admitting illegally seized evidence are: Shields v. State, 104 Ala. 35, 16 So. 85 (1893); Banks v. State, 207 Ala. 179, 93 So. 293 (1921), *cert. den.*, 260 U. S. 736, 43 Sup. Ct. 96 (1922); Argetakis v. State, 24 Ariz. 599, 212 Pac. 372 (1923) (dictum); Starchman v. State, 62 Ark. 538, 36 S. W. 940 (1896); Venable v. State, 156 Ark. 564, 246 S. W. 860 (1923); People v. LeDoux, 155 Cal. 535, 102 Pac. 517 (1909); People v. Mayen*, 188 Cal. 237, 205 Pac. 435 (1922); Massantonio v. People*, 77 Colo. 392, 236 Pac. 1019 (1925); State v. Reynolds, 101 Conn. 224, 125 Atl. 636 (1924) (dictum, but thorough discussion); State v. Chuchola*, 32 Del. 133, 120 Atl. 212 (Ct. Gen. Sess. 1922); Williams v. State, 100 Ga. 511, 28 S. E. 624 (1897); Herndon v. State, 178 Ga. 832, 174 S. E. 597 (1934); Territory v. Soga, 20 Hawaii 71 (1910); State v. Tonn*, 195 Iowa 94, 191 N. W. 530 (1923); State v. Miller, 63 Kan. 62, 64 Pac. 1033 (1901); State v. Johnson*, 116 Kan. 58, 226 Pac. 245 (1924); State v. Fleckinger*, 152 La. 337, 93 So. 115 (1922); State v. Burroughs, 72 Me. 479 (1881); Commonwealth v. Tibbetts, 157 Mass. 519, 32 N. E. 910 (1893); Commonwealth v. Wilkins*, 243 Mass. 356, 138 N. E. 11 (1923); State v. Hesse, 154 Minn. 89, 191 N. W. 267 (1922); Georgis v. State*, 110 Neb. 352, 193 N. W. 713 (1923); State v. Chin Gim*, 47 Nev. 431, 224 Pac. 798 (1924); State v. Flynn, 36 N. H. 64 (1858); State v. Agalos, 79 N. H. 241, 107 Atl. 314 (1919) (dictum); State v. Lyons, 99 N. J. L. 301, 122 Atl. 758 (1923); State v. First Criminal Judicial District*, 10 N. J. Misc. 715, 160 Atl. 672 (Sup. Ct. 1932); State v. Dillon*, 34 N. M. 366, 281 Pac. 474, 88 A. L. R. 340 (1929); People v. Adams, 176 N. Y. 351, 68 N. E. 636 (1903), *aff'd sub nom.* Adams v. New York, 192 U. S. 585, 24 Sup. Ct. 372 (1904); People v. Defore*, 242 N. Y. 13, 150 N. E. 585 (1926), *cert. den.*, 270 U. S. 657, 46 Sup. Ct. 353 (1926); State v. Fahn*, 53 N. D. 203, 205 N. W. 67 (1925); Commonwealth v. Dabbierio*, 290 Pa. 174, 138 Atl. 679 (1927) (this report does not say whether there was a pre-trial motion, but the report below in 89 Pa. Super. Ct. 435 [1926] reveals that a motion was duly made and denied); State v. Chester, 46 R. I. 485, 129 Atl. 596 (1925) (dictum); State v. Atkinson, 40 S. C. 363, 18 S. E. 1021 (1894); State v. Prescott, 125 S. C. 22, 117 S. E. 637 (1923); State v. Aime*, 62 Utah 476, 220 Pac. 704 (1923); State v. Krinski, 78 Vt. 162, 62 Atl. 37 (1905); State v. Stacy, 104 Vt. 379, 160 Atl. 257 (1932); Lucchesi v. Commonwealth*, 122 Va. 872, 94 S. E. 925 (1918) (dictum); Hall v. Commonwealth, 138 Va. 727, 121 S. E. 154 (1924).

This rule is ably defended by Prof. Wigmore in 4 EVIDENCE (2d ed. 1923) §§ 2183, 2184.

Whereas the legislature is empowered to abandon or modify this rule by statute, it is impossible to *adopt* this rule by statute when the courts have followed the federal rule. It was attempted in Mississippi (L. 1924, c. 244, § 3, relating only to Prohibition cases), but the statute was declared unconstitutional. Orick v. State, 140 Miss. 184, 105 So. 465 (1925).

[96]Maryland, Michigan, North Carolina. *Supra* note 94.

[97]Bishop Atterbury's Trial, 16 How. St. Tr. 323 (H. L. 1723); Regina v. Granatelli, 7 St. Tr. (N. S.) 979, 987 (Cent. Crim. Ct. 1849). No later cases have been found, but it is stated to be the law of England as recently as (1922) 86 JUST. P. 173.

[98]Rex v. Moore, 17 Alta. 503, 63 Dom. L. R. 472 (App. Div. 1922); Regina v. Doyle, 12 Ont. Rep. 347 (1886); Rex v. Honan, 26 Ont. L. R. 484, 6 Dom. L. R. 276 (C. A.

The fact that the federal rule grew up by a process of distinguishing former cases has saddled the rule with a court-made rule of practice that it has not yet shaken off. If, as these courts maintain, the Constitution forbids the use of evidence obtained in violation of its provisions, it surely should have been treated like other rules of evidence with a less sanctified origin, with objection permitted on the trial, and there is no constitutional authority permitting a court to impose restrictions not clearly implied in the implied provision of the Constitution.[99] A few courts, lacking or sweeping aside contrary precedents, recognized this argument and declared that this rule shall be treated like any other rule of evidence, with objection to be raised on trial.[100] So far as there is any justification for the rule of exclusion, this seems the preferable view.[101]

But other courts, loath to dispense with earlier precedents, have retained the above requirement and will admit the evidence if no preliminary motion is made.[102] It has been assumed by many courts and writers that the

---

1912); Rex. v. Hawkins, 35 Que. K. B. 96 (1923); Rex v. Gilchrist, [1936] 3 Dom. L. R. 238 (Sask. K. B.).

By a curious inversion of the federal rule, the Canadian courts will admit the evidence but deny a forfeiture. Rex v. Moore, *supra; Ex parte* Kavanaugh, 2 Can. C. C. 267 (N. B. 1896). *Cf.* Dodge v. United States, 272 U. S. 530, 47 Sup. Ct. 191 (1926), and see *supra* note 24.

[99]It is surely heaping fiction on fiction to read in both the bar of the evidence and the unusual procedural restriction on this implied bar!

[100]*Kentucky*: No motion required. Youman v. Commonwealth, 189 Ky. 152, 224 S. W. 860 (1920). A motion before trial is properly overruled, for the issue can *only* be raised on the trial. Commonwealth v. Meiner, 196 Ky. 840, 245 S. W. 890 (1922). A motion to strike out, at the close of all the evidence, is timely although no objection had been made. Wathen v. Commonwealth, 211 Ky. 586, 277 S. W. 839 (1925).

Maryland: No motion required, under statute. Gorman v. State, 161 Md. 700, 158 Atl. 903 (1932).

Mississippi: Irrespective of motion, no seized evidence can be admitted on the trial without showing a warrant or justifying the lack of one. King v. State, 147 Miss. 31, 113 So. 173 (1927). But objection must be made to the offer of the evidence, not after it has come in. McNutt v. State, 143 Miss. 347, 108 So. 721 (1926).

North Carolina: No motion specified in statute. N. C. CODE ANN. (Michie Supp. 1937) § 4530(1).

Oklahoma: No motion required. Gore v. State, 24 Okla. Cr. 394, 218 Pac. 545 (1923). But defendant must "object at the first opportunity". Webb v. State, 33 Okla. Cr. 77, 242 Pac. 784 (1926) (failed to object to offer of evidence; this language does not impose the requirement of a motion). A motion is sanctioned, however. Committi v. State, 28 Okla. Cr. 380, 231 Pac. 316 (1924).

Tennessee: No motion required. State v. Bass, 153 Tenn. 162, 281 S. W. 936 (1926).

Texas: Under statute, no motion required. Odenthal v. State, 106 Tex. Cr. 1, 290 S. W. 743 (1927). Nor is it permitted. Gentry v. State, 105 Tex. Cr. 385, 288 S. W. 213 (1926).

West Virginia: No motion required. State v. Wills, 91 W. Va. 659, 114 S. E. 261 (1922).

[101]One sound reason for the requirement, however—though it would apply equally to many rules of pleading and evidence in which it is *not* applied,—is that it prevents surprise of the prosecutor, who may not know of the illegality of the seizure. Atkinson, *Prohibition and the Weeks case* (1925) 23 MICH. L. REV. 748, 751.

[102]State v. Wansgaard, 46 Ida. 20, 265 Pac. 671 (1928) (motion after jury impaneled is too late; *cf.* State v. Arregui, 44 Ida. 43, 254 Pac. 788 [1927], motion after plea but before jury impaneled held timely); People v. Winn, 324 Ill. 428, 155 N. E. 337 (1927); McSwain v. State, 89 Ind. App. 592, 166 N. E. 444, 167 N. E. 568 (1929)

federal courts had abandoned the requirement,[103] because of the language used in and the results of a series of leading cases that followed the *Weeks* case.[104] But later federal cases, following a significant dictum in *Segurola v. United States,*[105] have held that the requirement of a motion is still maintained, although subject to undefined "exceptions".[106] Analyzing the cases in which it has been held unnecessary, it is difficult to be sure whether the rule rests on waiver or on trial convenience. In *Gouled v. United States,*[107] defendant had no knowledge before the trial that the particular evidence had been illegally seized. In *Amos v. United States*[108] and *Agnello v. United States,*[109] the fact of illegal seizure was not in controversy but was brought out on cross-examination of the witness who offered the evidence. It is probable that in the courts which recognize the latter exception, there is no question of waiver by failure

(but *cf.* an earlier case in a higher court, where no mention is made of a motion having been made yet the evidence was excluded. Callender v. State, 193 Ind. 91, 136 N. E. 10, 138 N. E. 817 [1922]); People v. Vulje, 223 Mich. 656, 194 N. W. 582 (1923) (motion after impaneling of jury had begun, too late); People v. Boyd, 228 Mich. 57, 199 N. W. 662 (1924) (notice of motion served two days before trial date; rules required four days notice, and the evidence was given before the motion could be heard; admissible) (but *cf.* People v. Van Vorce, 240 Mich. 75, 215 N. W. 5 [1927], in which the notice was served before trial but the case was pushed to trial too soon; held, the court's refusal to grant a continuance or shorten the time of notice was an abuse of discretion); State v. Wagner, 311 Mo. 391, 279 S. W. 23 (1926); State v. Gotta, 71 Mont. 288, 229 Pac. 405 (1924); Ciano v. State, 105 Ohio St. 229, 137 N. E. 10 (1922) (this case preceded the express adoption of the rule in Ohio, but it contains dicta indicating that the court already inclined that way); State v. Harris, 119 Ore. 422, 249 Pac. 1046 (1926); United States v. Cerecedo, 6 Porto Rico Fed. 607 (1914); State v. Dersiy, 121 Wash. 455, 209 Pac. 837 (1922) (motion immediately after calling of case for trial, before jury impaneled, too late).

The making of an unsuccessful motion before trial does not relieve of the need to object at the trial. Robertson v. State, 94 Fla. 770, 114 So. 534 (1927). *Contra*: Giles v. United States, 284 Fed. 208 (C. C. A. 1st 1922) (but *cf.* Segurola v. United States, 275 U. S. 106, 48 Sup. Ct. 77 [1927]).

[103]The lower federal courts were in confusion on this question. Motion *required*: Youngblood v. United States, 266 Fed. 795 (C. C. A. 8th 1920); Wiggins v. United States, 272 Fed. 41 (C. C. A. 2d 1921); Armstrong v. United States, 16 F. (2d) 62 (C. C. A. 9th 1926), *cert. den.,* 273 U. S. 766, 47 Sup. Ct. 571 (1927). *No* motion required: Ganci v. United States, 287 Fed. 60 (C. C. A. 2d 1923) (even though no objection to evidence, motion to strike timely at any time before verdict); Rizzo v. United States, 275 Fed. 49 (C. C. A. 4th 1921) (no objection or motion to strike; held properly raised by motion for directed verdict).

[104]Gouled v. United States, 255 U. S. 298, 41 Sup. Ct. 261 (1921); Amos v. United States, 255 U. S. 313, 41 Sup. Ct. 266 (1921); Agnello v. United States, 269 U. S. 20, 46 Sup. Ct. 4 (1925). In none of these cases was a preliminary motion made, and in the *Gouled* case, at p. 313, the Court said, "A rule of practice must not be allowed for any technical reason to prevail over a constitutional right."

[105]275 U. S. 106, 112, 48 Sup. Ct. 77, 79-80 (1927). In this case, there was no objection on the trial, so it is not too strong an authority for the necessity of raising it *before* trial, but there is a dictum to that effect, citing the *Adams* case, *supra* note 83. The dictum is quoted in Cogen v. United States, 278 U. S. 221, 223, 49 Sup. Ct. 118 (1929).

[106]Rocchia v. United States, 78 F. (2d) 966 (C. C. A. 9th 1935); Peters v. United States, 97 F. (2d) 500 (C. C. A. 9th 1938).

[107]*Supra* note 104. In People v. Bass, 235 Mich. 588, 209 N. W. 926 (1926), where defendant knew of the seizure but his attorney did not, the court denied objection on the trial, saying it was defendant's duty to tell his attorney.

[108]*Supra* note 104.

[109]*Supra* note 104.

to move, but if that is the case, the defendant's rights are made to hang on the district attorney's decision to make an issue of it; if the officer denies the key facts (for example, probable cause for obtaining the warrant), the court will not determine the issue. It becomes, then, purely a question of trial convenience, which will be waived when there was no opportunity to raise the issue before trial and will be inapplicable where the facts are undisputed or where the illegality appears upon the face of the warrant or affidavits so that a pure question of law is presented.[110]

The motion which is customarily made is not merely for the return of the evidence but also for the suppression of all oral evidence of what the officers saw in the course of the unlawful search.[111] Furthermore, the officers can make no use *whatever* of the knowledge gained by the illegal search. In *Silverthorne Lumber Company v. United States,*[112] officers seized the books of a corporation. They were returned on motion. Thereupon, since corporations cannot assert the privilege against self-incrimination,[113] the books were subpoenaed. The case came up on contempt for disobeying the subpoena, and it was held that the government could not use its tainted knowledge even to found a regular and legal proceeding. Presumably, therefore, a new search warrant likewise could not be founded upon "probable cause" derived from such knowledge. In the *Gouled* case,[114] a contention was made but not expressly passed on (the Court deciding generally for the defendant) that certain duplicate originals of a seized contract, lawfully obtained from the other party to the contract, should be suppressed on the ground that its existence was inferred as a result of discovering the original unlawfully. Nevertheless, the information does not become sacred and inaccessible, but the officers must put the search out of mind and hustle around for inde-

---

[110]The rules are thus stated in Robertson v. State, 94 Fla. 770, 114 So. 534 (1927); State v. Dersiy, on rehearing, 121 Wash. 455, 461, 215 Pac. 34 (1923); State v. Warfield, 184 Wis. 56, 198 N. W. 854 (1924) (applying the second rule).

In any event, it is discretionary with the trial court, if a motion is made, to withhold consideration until the facts are developed on the trial. Panzich v. United States, 285 Fed. 871 (C. C. A. 9th 1922).

[111]United States v. Kraus, 270 Fed. 578 (S. D. N. Y. 1921); Flagg v. United States, 233 Fed. 481 (C. C. A. 2d 1916); Carignano v. State, 31 Okla. Cr. 228, 238 Pac. 507 (1925) (no motion there required, but excluded oral evidence). Where the property is possessed by revenue officers, not officers of the court and not acting pursuant to judicial process, they cannot be bound by a motion to return, but an independent proceeding must be brought to regain the property; but a motion to suppress the evidence would be proper. United States v. Hee, 219 Fed. 1019 (D. N. J. 1915).

Where the property seized is contraband, its possession being unlawful, it is subject to forfeiture (see *supra* note 24), so a motion to suppress or destroy the evidence would be made. See *infra* note 137. And see full discussion in United States v. Goodhues, 53 F. (2d) 696 (D. Md. 1931).

[112]251 U. S. 385, 40 Sup. Ct. 182 (1920).

[113]Hale v. Henkel, 201 U. S. 43, 74, 26 Sup. Ct. 370, 378 (1906); Essgee Co. of China v. United States, 262 U. S. 151, 43 Sup. Ct. 514 (1923).

[114]*Supra* note 104.

pendent sources of the same information, in no way traceable to their prior misdeeds.[115]

The rule of exclusion, as manifested in the federal and state courts, is honeycombed with exceptions, some resulting from the limitations of the constitutional guaranty, as heretofore outlined, and some from an attempt to distinguish prior cases (admitting the evidence) by confining them to their facts. The most important exceptions result from the fact that the rule itself is regarded as an exception to the general rule that illegality in obtaining evidence does not operate to exclude it unless some constitutional right has been violated.[116] Hence it is universally agreed[117] that evidence is not to be excluded because obtained by the wrong of a private individual.[118] It is also agreed that evidence wrongfully obtained by officers of a different government than that conducting the prosecution might be admitted without violating the constitution,[119] provided there was no collusion between such officers and those of the prosecuting government;[120] but, irrespective of the constitutional question, a number of courts and one legislature have doubted the propriety of accepting such evidence from other officers as a matter of public policy.[121] This exception has been subjected to a great deal of criticism, particularly by judges holding the contrary view who utilize the familiar device of *reductio ad absurdum*.[122] The exception has probably

[115]The procedure on a motion in such a case was outlined by Judge Learned Hand in United States v. Kraus, 270 Fed. 578 (S. D. N. Y. 1921): the order of the court provides that *all information contained* in the seized papers, shall be suppressed, unless the officers can show that they learned it independently of their wrongful possession of the papers; this issue is settled by reference to a master, to whom proof of independent information is presented.

For an example of evidence subsequently obtained as a result of knowledge from sources independent of the prior seizure, see Safarik v. United States, 62 F. (2d) 892 (C. C. A. 8th 1933).

[116]Fraenkel, *Recent Developments in the Law of Search and Seizure* (1920) 13 MINN. L. REV. 1, 13, submits that *all* illegally obtained evidence should now be excluded, since what he considers the sole reason for the common law rule, the desire to avoid collateral issues on the trial, has been eliminated by the invention of the motion. But it is the thesis of this article that there are more important reasons than this for the rule of admissibility and that few if any of the leading cases that established that rule ever went off on this ground. It became merely a convenient peg on which to hang a new rule when a court changed its mind.

But, irrespective of reasons, Fraenkel is not without support in high places. See dissent of Justices Brandeis and Holmes in Burdeau v. McDowell, 256 U. S. 465, 476, 41 Sup. Ct. 574 (1921) (private individual seized papers).

[117]Brandeis and Holmes dissenting. See *supra* note 116.

[118]Cases cited *supra* note 68.

[119]*Supra* notes 70 and 72.

[120]*Supra* note 71.

[121]Evidence of federal officers *rejected* in state courts: State v. Arregui, 44 Ida. 43, 254 Pac. 788 (1927); Wathen v. Commonwealth, 211 Ky. 586, 277 S. W. 839 (1925) (without discussion of the point); Ramirez v. State, 123 Tex. Cr. 254, 58 S. W. (2d) 829 (1933) (under statute expressly excluding evidence obtained by an officer *or other person* in violation of the constitution *or laws* of Texas or the *Federal* Constitution, a provision which would seem broad enough to exclude the results even of private trespasses, although no case in point has been found. TEX. CODE CRIM. PROC. [Vernon 1925] § 727a). *Contra*: State v. Gardner, 77 Mont. 8, 249 Pac. 574 (1926).

[122]In People v. Defore, 242 N. Y. 13, 22, 150 N. E. 585, 588 (1926), Judge Cardozo

been overemphasized, for the courts have been astute to discover collusion.

There is another exception of major importance, although it has never come squarely before the Supreme Court. It is uniformly held that a defendant cannot object to the seizure of another's property, for no constitutional right of the *defendant* has been violated.[123] The immunity from search and seizure is a personal one. The third party whose property was seized may move for its return,[124] but he may not have oral evidence concerning it suppressed except as against himself.[125] A proprietary or possessory interest in either the premises searched or the things seized would appear to be sufficient,[126] although there are cases in the circuit courts of appeals that suggest that if the defendant's own property is searched but articles belonging to another are seized, the defendant can make no complaint. These cases seem of doubtful validity, however, for *his* constitutional rights were violated by the search of his property, and *whatever* was found was a direct result of this violation.[127] The owner of property leased to another

---

attacks the federal rule as "either too strict or too lax", for the prosecutor who, in using the results of his own officers' wrongs, is said to ratify the means, need not be so scrupulous about evidence brought to him by others. "We exalt form above substance when we hold that the use is made lawful because the intruder is without a badge of office."

In State v. Fahn, 53 N. D. 203, 210, 205 N. W. 67, 70 (1925), it is said that the result of the federal rule is that if one enters a house with felonious intent, the evidence of what he saw and took away is admitted; but if he enter as an officer, his eyes, ears, and lips are sealed.

The vitriolic dissenter in State v. Gooder, 57 S. D. 619, 633, 234 N. W. 610, 616 (1930), regards it as a "mystic and incomprehensible honor that accepts and shares the dishonorable conduct of faithless and disobedient officers of the particular jurisdiction in which the case is to be tried, but which honor refuses to be sullied by the unlawful acts of citizens or officers of another jurisdiction."

[123]Tsuie Shee v. Backus, 243 Fed. 551 (C. C. A. 9th 1917); Connolly v. Medalie, 58 F. (2d) 629 (C. C. A. 2d 1932), citing cases from every circuit except the first.

[124]United States v. Spallino, 21 F. (2d) 567 (W. D. N. Y. 1927).

[125]*In re* Dooley, 48 F. (2d) 121 (C. C. A. 2d 1931). The court leaves open the question whether the evidence might, after return, be subpoenaed for use against the other defendants; since the process is directed against the one wronged, even though the evidence is not to be used against him, a subpoena might be denied if based on knowledge gained by the search. *Cf.* Silverthorne Lumber Co. v. United States, *supra* note 112.

[126]Gilliland v. Commonwealth, 224 Ky. 453, 6 S. W. (2d) 467 (1928). See Safarik v. United States, 62 F. (2d) 892, 895 (C. C. A. 8th 1933) (stating that, to raise the issue, defendant must own, lease, control, occupy, possess, or have an interest in the property).

Apparently the sender and recipient of telegrams have sufficient interest in the copies filed with the telegraph company to object to their unlawful *seizure*. See Hearst v. Black, 66 App. D. C. 313, 87 F. (2d) 68 (1936) (the court denied relief on the special grounds that it could not control the Senate Committee, and that the Communications Commission contemplated no further seizures and had turned over the spoils to the Senators). But such telegrams are subject to subpoena for a proper purpose, since such process is not directed against a party and does not compel *him* to give evidence. Newfield v. Ryan, 91 F. (2d) 700 (C. C. A. 5th 1937), *cert. den.*, 302 U. S. 729, 58 Sup. Ct. 54 (1937); State v. Sawtelle, 66 N. H. 488, 32 Atl. 831 (1891); *cf.* McMann v. Securities and Exchange Comm., 87 F. (2d) 377 (C. C. A. 2d 1937), *cert. den.*, 301 U. S. 684, 57 Sup. Ct. 785 (1937) (defendant's brokerage account may be subpoenaed).

[127]Hurwitz v. United States, 299 Fed. 449 (C. C. A. 8th 1924) (narcotics illegally seized in defendant's car; since two of the bottles had been previously sold to a third party, they were admitted in evidence with the admonition to the jury that they

cannot complain of a search, for he has no right to possession.[128] A lessee or other lawful occupant, has a sufficient interest to raise the issue.[129] But one having merely the custody of the property as an employee is not protected;[130] the evidence may be used against the workman at the still, but the head bootlegger must be protected in his constitutional right of privacy. There is some doubt as to the *officers* of a corporation. In the *Silverthorne* case,[131] corporate officers were protected against unlawful seizure and use of corporate papers, which raises some doubt as to whether the Supreme Court, if squarely presented with the question, would not repudiate the whole third party exception. However, the lower courts have regularly applied the exception, and have refused protection even to officers of corporations and associations,[132] distinguishing the *Silverthorne* case if it was raised at all.[133] If the defendant disclaims ownership or possession of the property, he has no standing to demand its return or suppression;[134] but

---

should disregard them unless they found an executed sale had been consummated!); Lewis v. United States, 92 F. (2d) 952 (C. C. A. 10th 1937) (memorandum book of prostitute taken from white slaver's baggage, held admissible because not his property); State v. Goldstein, 111 Ore. 221, 224 Pac. 1087 (1924) (stolen goods taken from defendant's shop, held admissible). *Contra*: People v. Galnt, 235 Mich. 646, 209 N. W. 915 (1926) (possessor of liquor in his own dwelling may suppress evidence although he does not own the liquor).

Would it be amiss to suggest that courts shrink from their vaunted "liberal" interpretation of the Bill of Rights when confronted with a drug peddler, a white slaver, or a thief, instead of a Prohibition or revenue violator?

[128]Hardwig v. United States, 23 F. (2d) 992 (C. C. A. 6th 1928). The fact that the trespassing officers passed through parts of the premises occupied by defendant is immaterial if the search and seizure occurred in leased portions. United States v. Muscarelle, 63 F. (2d) 806 (C. C. A. 2d) (1933).

[129]Alvau v. United States, 33 F. (2d) 467 (C. C. A. 9th 1929) (one actually domiciled in residence, as a guest or employee, may claim protection); Gilliland v. Commonwealth, 224 Ky. 453, 6 S. W. (2d) 467 (1928) (lessee). But a trespasser, using an abandoned farm building as a still and as a residence, is not protected. Stakich v. United States, 24 F. (2d) 701 (C. C. A. 9th 1928) (as trespassers, their *possessio pedis* was protected to the extent of *actual* occupancy—the building itself—but by the time the officers got that close they *saw* the crime in process, and made a lawful arrest and search).

[130]Connolly v. Medalie, 58 F. (2d) 629 (C. C. A. 2d 1932) (watchman and workers at still); Whitcombe v. United States, 90 F. (2d) 290 (C. C. A. 3rd 1937) (driver of liquor truck and workers).

[131]251 U. S. 385, 40 Sup. Ct. 182 (1920).

[132]Haywood v. United States, 268 Fed. 795 (C. C. A. 7th 1920), *cert. den.*, 256 U. S. 689, 41 Sup. Ct. 449 (1921) (voluntary association regarded as entity distinct from its members for all purposes except contract liability, so its officers could not assert its constitutional immunity from search); Newingham v. United States, 4 F. (2d) 490 (C. C. A. 3rd 1925) (officers and sole owners of corporation not protected).

[133]The *Haywood* case, *supra* note 132, refers to the *Silverthorne* case and says that if "proper parties"—presumably the same officers in their capacity as such, instead of as individuals—had applied, the evidence would have been returned and no subpoena could have been enforced (unless founded on independent knowledge). In the *Dooley* case, *supra* note 125, the court distinguishes the *Silverthorne* case by treating corporate officers as *sui generis*, sharing the immunity of their corporation on grounds of policy, for there would be little to discourage the police from illegal raids on corporations if all they lost was the corporation's fine, its officers still being punishable.

[134]Gowling v. United States, 64 F. (2d) 796 (1933); and the same is implicit in the cases cited *supra* notes 123 *et seq.*

if he alleges ownership or possession in affidavits on the motion, these damaging admissions, having resulted wholly from the exigency of the unlawful search, are excluded from evidence.[135]

Somewhat related to this exception is another one once clearly the rule in a few courts and frequently recognized by dicta during the "growing pains" of the federal rule, by courts hesitant to accept its full implications. This rule is that illegally seized evidence is excluded unless it is contraband or is "the *corpus delicti*".[136] Under this rule, evidence unlawfully seized could be used if it was stolen property, property the possession of which was unlawful, or forfeitable property, on the same theory that property belonging to a third party could be used, since forfeiture of contraband property occurs automatically upon the commission of the forbidden act, the later judicial declaration of forfeiture relating back to that time, and it was regarded as a seizure of *government* property.[137] But, except in Vermont and some lower federal courts, no jurisdiction has ever produced two decisions, one holding contraband admissible and the other holding non-contraband inadmissible, and those jurisdictions, moving in opposite directions, have since repudiated the distinction. Therefore, while some dicta remain to haunt a few courts, it may be said that the contraband exception is virtually a dead

---

[135]Safarik v. United States, 62 F. (2d) 892 (C. C. A. 8th 1933). *Contra*: Vaught v. United States, 7 F. (2d) 370 (C. C. A. 9th 1925) (without discussion).

[136]United States v. Welch, 247 Fed. 239 (S. D. N. Y. 1917), *aff'd*, 267 Fed. 819 (C. C. A. 2d 1920), *cert. den.*, 254 U. S. 637, 41 Sup. Ct. 9(1920) (letter used in aiding the enemy, held to be the *corpus delicti* so admissible) ; United States v. Fenton, 268 Fed. 221 (D. Mont. 1920) (liquor and automobile seized; as they were forfeitable, held to be a seizure of *government's* property, of which defendant cannot complain) ; Pasch v. People, 72 Colo. 92, 209 Pac. 639 (1922) (liquor; court rests it on basis of contraband, but in a later liquor case the court unequivocally adopted the rule of complete admissibility. Massantonio v. People, 77 Colo. 392, 236 Pac. 1019 [1925]) ; State v. Chuchola, 32 Del. 133, 120 Atl. 212 (Ct. Gen. Sess. 1922) (liquor case, held admissible; "it may be" that the rule would be different if not contraband, but no case has so held) ; Matter of Horschler, 116 Misc. 243, 190 N. Y. Supp. 355 (Co. Ct. 1921) (non-contraband held inadmissible, using this basis to distinguish the *Adams* case) ; State v. Simmons, 183 N. C. 684, 110 S. E. 591 (1922) (liquor; dictum thus distinguishes *Weeks* case) ; Rosanski v. State, 106 Ohio St. 442, 140 N. E. 370 (1922) (rests on contraband rule, but vigorous dictum for general admissibility; overruled on both points, Nicholas v. City of Cleveland, 125 Ohio St. 474, 182 N. E. 26 [1932]) ; State v. Chester, 46 R. I. 485, 129 Atl. 596 (1925) (dictum) ; City of Sioux Falls v. Walser, 45 S. D. 417, 187 N. W. 821 (1922) (liquor admissible; overruled in State v. Gooder, 57 S. D. 619, 234 N. W. 610 [1931]) ; State v. Krinski, 78 Vt. 162, 62 Atl. 37 (1905) (Vermont had adopted the rule of exclusion in State v. Slamon, 73 Vt. 212, 50 Atl. 1097 [1901], as to letters, but the court here refused to apply it to liquor; the *Slamon* case was repudiated in State v. Stacy, 104 Vt. 379, 401, 160 Atl. 257, 266 [1932], and Vermont now admits *all* such evidence).

[137]United States v. Stowell, 133 U. S. 1, 16, 10 Sup. Ct. 244, 247 (1890). It is also suggested in some cases that the distinction rests upon the fact that the government *might have* obtained a warrant for such property but could not have obtained one for non-contraband property, so it is placed in the same positions as if a warrant had been applied for. The fact that possession could not be restored, when possession was unlawful, had some weight when the motion to return was the regular practice, the motion to suppress evidence without returning the property being a later growth. Rosanski v. State, *supra* note 136.

letter. Most courts never drew such a distinction, and the United States Supreme Court has repeatedly rejected it.[138]

At one time the Georgia courts, attempting to reconcile inconsistent decisions on related questions, declared that a seizure from one's *person* compelled him to give evidence against himself, whereas other seizures did not.[139] But this distinction has been eliminated in favor of general admissibility.[140]

Another exception covers evidence obtained by wire-tapping. The constitutional protection against search and seizure has been held inapplicable to wire-tapping so even where wire-tapping is unlawful by statute, the evidence is admissible under the rule that illegally obtained evidence is competent if no constitutional right is violated.[141] This was accepted even in the federal courts, in the *Olmstead* case,[142] until 1937, when an astute criminal lawyer seized upon an obscure provision of the Communications Act of 1934 and persuaded a majority of the Court that Congress had thus expressed its "intent" not merely to forbid wire-tapping but to ban the evidence obtained thereby.[143] Although the language is concededly susceptible of such interpretation, it is extremely doubtful that Congress realized that it was dealing with probably the most controversial rule of evidence of modern times. The Communications Act was designed "to provide for the regulation of interstate and foreign communication by wire or radio, and for other purposes".[144] The debates in Congress were entirely concerned with the communications "monopoly", and there was no specific

[138]Agnello v. United States, 269 U. S. 20, 46 Sup. Ct. 4 (1925) (narcotics inadmissible); Byars v. United States, 273 U. S. 28, 47 Sup. Ct. 248 (1927) (counterfeit stamps); Gambino v. United States, 275 U. S. 310, 48 Sup. Ct. 137 (1927) (liquor). See also People v. Defore, 242 N. Y. 13, 18, 150 N. E. 585, 586 (1926); Gore v. State, 24 Okla Cr. 394, 405, 218 Pac. 545, 549 (1923); State v. McDaniel, 115 Ore. 187, 231 Pac. 965 (1925).

"A search prosecuted in violation of the Constitution is not made lawful by what it brings to light." Byars v. United States, *supra*.

[139]Hammock v. State, 1 Ga. App. 126, 58 S. E. 66 (1907), followed by a long line of Georgia Court of Appeals decisions.

[140]Calhoun v. State, 144 Ga. 679, 87 S. E. 893 (1916); Herndon v. State, 178 Ga. 832, 174 S. E. 597 (1934) (property unlawfully seized from *person* admitted).

[141]Olmstead v. United States, 277 U. S. 438, 48 Sup. Ct. 564 (1928); People v. McDonald, 177 App. Div. 806, 165 N. Y. Supp. 41 (2d Dep't 1917) (although it is probable that the New York statute did not apply to the police, the court makes no decision on this point, holding the evidence admissible regardless); Rowan v. State, 3 Atl. (2d) 753 (Md. 1939) (admit wire-tapping evidence although its revelation in or out of court is now a federal felony). *Cf.* Matter of J. Richard ("Dixie") Davis, 252 App. Div. 591, 299 N. Y. Supp. 632 (1st Dep't 1937) (admitted in disbarment proceeding). And *cf.* State v. Hester, 137 S. C. 145, 134 S. E. 885 (1926) (dictaphone).

[142]*Supra* note 141.

[143]47 U. S. C. A. § 605 (Supp. 1938). The pertinent clause is that "no person not being authorized by the sender shall intercept any communication and divulge or publish the existence, contents, substance, purport, effect, or meaning of such intercepted communication to any person." The case is Nardone v. United States, 302 U. S. 379, 58 Sup. Ct. 275 (1937), *rev'g* 90 F. (2d) 630 (C. C. A. 2d 1937).

[144]Title of the Act, 48 STAT. 1064 (1934). See also §§ 1 and 2, on the scope and application of the Act.

reference to this section, tucked away among the "Miscellaneous Provisions" with the repealer section and other odds and ends.[145] The committee report hardly mentions it.[146] It is probable that Congress simply intended, as an incident to taking over the regulation of communications, to adopt penal provisions such as are found in most states, which had never been held to call for banning the evidence obtained by their violation. Congress itself was not too pleased to learn that it had expressed this intent, and a few months after this decision Senator Wheeler introduced a bill to permit wire-tapping by officers if the *head* of any executive department or independent establishment of the government certifies that he reasonably believes a violation of a federal criminal statute which he is charged with enforcing will be discovered by such means.[147] The bill passed the Senate, and it passed the House on the last day of the session, but was amended there and died in the closing hours.[148]

But whatever Congress intended, the rule is now established. It makes no provision for warrants to tap wires upon "probable cause", although Justice Sutherland, in dissent, warns that we have enabled "the most depraved criminals to further their criminal plans over the telephone, in the secure knowledge that even if these plans involve kidnapping and murder, their telephone conversations can never be intercepted by officers of the law and revealed in court."[149] Although it is conceded that it would be equivalent to a search warrant for *evidence,* such as is never permitted as to tangible things, it would seem that the balance of policy should favor the granting of a restricted privilege under court supervision. Lacking that, the temptation to indiscriminate tapping is enormous, for many clues may

[145]When Senator Dill was explaining the provisions of the Act, he said, "In Title VI will be found the miscellaneous provisions which are to provide for the transfer of employees and the records and property of the Radio Commission. . . ." 78 CONG. REC. 8826 (1934). There was no mention of the particular section. There was not even this much in the House.

[146]SEN. REP. No. 781, 73rd Cong., 2d Sess. (1934) 11. "Section 605, prohibiting unauthorized publication of communications, is based upon Section 27 of the Radio Act and extends it to wire communications." The section referred to, formerly 47 U. S. C. A. § 107, under which there were no decisions, was enacted without mention either in debates or committee reports. See SEN. REP. No. 772, 69th Cong., 1st Sess. (1926); H. R. REP. No. 464, 69th Cong., 1st Sess. (1926); H. R. REP. No. 1886, 69th Cong., 2d Sess. (1927). And it obviously was not concerned with rules of evidence, for radio communications would not likely be used for criminal purposes.

In 1932, bills designed expressly to exclude evidence obtained by wire-tapping had been introduced but had died in committee. S. 1396 and H. R. 5305 (72d Cong., 1st Sess.). In 1933, there was inserted in the appropriation act for Prohibition enforcement a proviso that none of the appropriation should be expended for wire-tapping, but there was no suggestion of excluding the evidence. 47 STAT. 1381 (1933).

[147]S. 3756. It was reported by unanimous committees of both houses. SEN. REP. No. 1798 and H. R. REP. 2656, 75th Cong., 2d Sess. (1938).

[148]The amendment imposed heavy penalties on officers tapping wires without proper authority. The tragedy is that this committee amendment which resulted in the death of the bill was simply repetitive of identical general provisions in § 501, and added nothing whatever.

[149]Nardone v. United States, 302 U. S. 379, 385, 58 Sup. Ct. 275, 278 (1937).

be uncovered thereby even if they cannot be used in court. Better to provide a way to do it legally when the court is satisfied of the necessity, and then to provide effective sanctions to keep the police within these reasonable limits. But of that more later.

The Act, as thus interpreted, plainly excludes the evidence even though obtained by a private individual,[150] which is unlike the rule as to ordinary search and seizure.[151] There is a conflict among the lower federal courts, seeking vainly for the details of that imaginary Congressional intent, as to whether the ban applies only to *interstate* communications intercepted, or to *all* communications.[152] The second question has yet to come before the Supreme Court, which has only ruled on the former.[153]

Thus it must be conceded that the exceptions to the federal rule, although some of them are sufficiently inconsistent to tend to discredit the rule, are on the whole not of great significance.[154] Argument founded on these

---

[150]See *supra* note 143. "No person. . . ."

[151]*Supra* notes 68 and 118.

[152]The First and Fifth Circuits have squarely held that the Act only applies to interstate messages, and have admitted evidence of tapped local communications. Valli v. United States, 94 F. (2d) 687 (C. C. A. 1st 1938); Ginsberg v. United States, 96 F. (2d) 433 (C. C. A. 5th 1938). The Second Circuit has just held such evidence admissible. N. Y. *Times,* April 11, 1939, p. 46, col. 2 (the official title of the case is not given; the defendants were Goldstein, Krupp, Weiss, and Gross).

But the contrary view, justified by the language of the section if not by the purported scope of the Act, has also been expressed. United States v. Plisco, 22 Fed. Supp. 242 (D. D. C. 1938); Sablowski v. United States, 101 F. (2d) 183 (C. C. A. 3rd, Dec. 9, 1938).

[153]The *Nardone* case concerned interstate messages. Although *certiorari* was granted in the *Valli* case, 58 Sup. Ct. 760 (1938), the petitioner dismissed his appeal, 58 Sup. Ct. 1053 (1938).

[154]One more "exception", if such it can be called, is the universally recognized principle that illegally obtained evidence is admissible in a civil action, for no question of violation of constitutional rights is there involved. Generally it is immaterial that it was obtanied by the party's own wrong. Mossman v. Thorson, 118 Ill. App. 574 (1905) (admitting papers which one party induced the other to send to her P. O. box by fraud); Sullivan v. Nicoulin, 113 Iowa 76, 84 N. W. 978 (1901) (defendant claimed plaintiff's plastering job defective but would not let his witnesses inspect it; they got in under an unlawful court order but were allowed to testify); Cluett v. Rosenthal, 100 Mich. 193, 58 N. W. 1009 (1894) (copies of defendant's books made while held under a void attachment; plaintiff's attorney had made the attachment and copies while employed by another person; the Supreme Court had ordered him to return the copies to right an abuse of process, Rosenthal v. Muskegon Circuit Judge, 98 Mich. 208, 57 N. W. 112 [1893], but meanwhile he had taken the copies to this plaintiff, been retained, and used them in evidence; held admissible because there was no abuse of process by this plaintiff—other cases do not seem to regard the plaintiff's wrong as material); Matter of Davis, 252 App. Div. 591, 299 N. Y. Supp. 632 (1st Dep't 1937) (wire-tapped evidence admitted in disbarment proceedings; wires were tapped by police, and the court suggests that "a very serious situation" would arise if it had been done by the petitioner); DeLore v. Smith, 67 Ore. 304, 136 Pac. 13 (1913) (defendant testified to conversation between plaintiff and daughter on a country party line telephone); Stockfleth v. DeTastet, 4 Camp. 10, 171 Eng. Rep. 4 (N. P. 1814) (plaintiff's attorney, when acting for the bankruptcy commissioners, had improperly examined defendant about plaintiff's claim; Lord Ellenborough admitted the evidence although the attorney had abused the authority of the Great Seal).

Many of the cases have arisen where court records, and the like, were removed from

inconsistencies is weak, in that the best answer to such argument would be to plug the gaps by statute. The rule must be attacked on broader grounds.

III. Pro and Con

What, then, are the arguments? When a person is illegally arrested or his property illegally seized, what course is more consonant with sound public policy? Although most of these arguments would apply equally to arrest and to search and seizure, the controversy has centered around the latter and we shall discuss the problem with special reference to search and seizure.

The question is one upon which reasonable and honest men may differ, and none be heard to say that the one group is seeking to set at naught our constitutional liberties or that the other is seeking advantage for the criminal classes.[155] Although there has been an effort to separate the sheep from the goats, to call the rule of exclusion the liberal view, no liberal need apologize for espousing either view when we find three great liberal jurists in disagreement, Holmes and Brandeis[156] on the one side, Cardozo[157] on

---

the files surreptitiously, without a proper court order. They are invariably held admissible. Stevison v. Earnest, 80 Ill. 513 (1875); Citizens' National Bank of Pocomoke City v. Custis, 153 Md. 235, 138 Atl. 261 (1927); Jordan v. Lewis, 14 East 305 note, 104 Eng. Rep. 618 (1740); Legatt v. Tollervey, 14 East 302, 104 Eng. Rep. 617 (1811). *Cf.* People v. Alden, 113 Cal. 264, 45 Pac. 327 (1896) (criminal case).

The same rule has been applied in a *civil* proceeding by the *government* to abate a nuisance, even though there was an unconstitutional seizure. McColl v. Hardin *ex rel.* State, 70 S. W. (2d) 327 (Tex. Civ. App. 1934). But that rests on interpretation of the word "criminal" in a statute, for exclusion of the evidence does not rest on the constitution in Texas. The federal rule has recently been extended to exclude the evidence in civil proceedings by the government to recover taxes. Rogers v. United States, 97 F. (2d) 691 (C. C. A. 1st 1938), noted (1938) 6 U. of Chi. L. Rev. 113; *Contra:* Camden County Beverage Co. v. Blair, 46 F. (2d) 648 (D. N. J. 1930), *app. dismissed,* 46 F. (2d) 655 (C. C. A. 3rd 1931) (revocation of license).

The rule in civil cases is a strange inversion of the criminal rules. A civil plaintiff may not take advantage of his wrong in obtaining jurisdiction (*supra* note 30), but may use evidence illegally obtained; the state may take advantage of its officers' wrongs in arresting defendants, but the federal rule will not permit the use of evidence illegally obtained by them!

[155]"For some reason not easily ascertainable, a great deal of asperity appears in the writings on the subject, particularly among those who can write free from any responsibility except the judgment of their readers." Finch, J., in People v. Defore, 213 App. Div. 643, 652, 211 N. Y. Supp. 134, 142 (1st Dep't 1925).

[156]See particularly their dissents in the *Olmstead* case, *supra* note 141. Even Justice Holmes did not always feel as strongly as he later did, for when on the Massachusetts bench he declared, "The mode in which the officer got his knowledge of what the girl had in her hand [by an unlawful search of her person] did not make the fact inadmissible." Commonwealth v. Welch, 163 Mass. 372, 40 N. E. 103 (1895). Conceded that he was faced with a long line of precedents, still Justice Holmes was not one to state a rule he disapproved without at least mentioning that fact.

[157]See People v. Defore, 242 N. Y. 13, 150 N. E. 585 (1926). It is true that he was faced with the precedent of the *Adams* case, *supra* note 83, but a preliminary motion was made by Defore, a basis on which many lesser judges had been able to cast aside contrary precedents; Judge Cardozo's hands were free, and his ringing words reveal that he and New York's greatest Court of Appeals made a free choice after a thorough reexamination of the whole question. It has been suggested that Cardozo had been converted before his death, for he joined the majority in the *Nardone* case, *supra* note

the other. It is not a choice between a good principle and a bad principle but between two good principles, and the problem is to strike a balance.

When the weight of the federal courts is thrown onto the scales—though their criminal jurisdiction is comparatively limited—the nation's courts are about evenly divided. It has been said that the rule of admissibility is a dying doctrine, because over a dozen states have been converted from that rule to the rule of exclusion.[158] But it was inevitable that a doctrine arising at a very late date, with the prestige of the Supreme Court behind it, should cause defections among the followers of an established rule. On the other hand, four states, whose appellate courts had adopted the federal rule even before the Supreme Court had made up its mind, re-examined the federal rule after the *Weeks* case [159] and cast it aside.[160] And about nine states, considering the question for the first time, faced with the *Weeks* case and free to choose, chose the rule of admissibility.[161] A number of the other courts that had long followed the rule of admissibility as a matter of course were moved to re-examine the rule and declared unequivocally that the rule should not be changed.[162]

The one all-inclusive argument for admitting evidence irrespective of how it was obtained is that the manner of obtaining the evidence is immaterial to the merits of the question before the court, namely the guilt or innocence of the accused.[163] And this is true whether the issue is raised before or at the trial.[164] When a court is presented with the question of a defendant's guilt, it needs all relevant reliable evidence, and it is illogical to suppress any such evidence, either as compensation for a trespass or as punishment

149, but it must be remembered that no question of constitutional law or of policy was before the Court. Congress had spoken, and the sole question was what it had intended to say.

[158]Idaho, Illinois, Michigan, Mississippi, Missouri, Montana, Ohio, Oklahoma, Oregon, South Dakota, Tennessee, Washington, and West Virginia. See cases cited *supra* notes 91, 92 and 93. The others adopting the federal rule had had no earlier cases on the point.

[159]*Supra* note 89.

[160]Georgia, Iowa, South Carolina, and Vermont. The cases are cited *supra* notes 88 and 93.

[161]Colorado, Delaware, Nevada, New Jersey, New Mexico, North Dakota, Pennsylvania, Utah, and Virginia. See cases cited *supra* note 95.

[162]See the more recent of the cases from these states, cited *supra* note 95: Alabama, California, Kansas, Louisiana, Massachusetts, New York, South Carolina, and a few others. These courts in particular do not speak like courts following a precedent because of *stare decisis*. They have now heard the new arguments introduced by the *Weeks* case, and they are unconvinced. Some of these opinions, like several of those in the preceding footnote, are classics of their kind.

[163]"The defendant is released, not because he is innocent, but because the postal inspector secured without instead of with a warrant the proofs of his guilt." Flagg v. United States, 233 Fed. 481, 487 (C. C. A. 2d 1916) (reluctant concurring opinion of Veeder, J.).

"Are the letters less criminal, if the person who stopped them did not punctually observe the directions of that statute?" Bishop Atterbury's Trial, 16 How. St. Tr. 323, 630 (1723) (argument of counsel, adopted by the House of Lords).

[164]See State v. Fahn, 53 N. D. 203, 209, 205 N. W. 67, 69 (1925).

of the officers for "dirty business".[165] The rejection of the evidence will not punish the offending officer; it will punish all society.[166] As was said by Judge Finch,

> "To be unable to find a murderer guilty, although competent evidence is before the court to warrant a conviction, for the reason that someone else is guilty of petit larceny in connection with obtaining such evidence, seems a handicap rather than a help to the administration of justice."[167]

The rules of evidence are designed to reach the truth and to secure a fair trial to one accused of crime.[168] Evidence is no less reliable, no less true, because obtained by other than nice ethical conduct—obtained, if you will, by gross invasions of constitutional rights. If a criminal's arsenal is discovered by an illegal search on mere suspicion, is the criminal to go free, to resume his preying on society? True, he would have remained free if the officer had observed the constitutional restraints, and not even a court order could legalize such a search on mere suspicion—so much is necessary to protect the innocent from lawless invasions of their privacy. But when the invasion *has* occurred, when the court can look back and see that the victim of the invasion was *not* innocent, then, although the officer's wrong is the same and should be punished accordingly, the protection of the *innocent* does not require the exclusion of evidence of guilt.[169]

This is not like the "third degree". Evidence extorted by such means is inherently unreliable, since a person under such pressure would say anything to buy peace. But the gun which is seized is just as much a gun, and is just as much in the defendant's possession, whether it is seized legally or illegally. A conversation heard upon a tapped wire is just as reliable as one heard on the street—probably more so today, with modern recording devices.[170]

---

[165]See State v. Dillon, 34 N. M. 366, 376-7, 281 Pac. 474, 478-9 (1929).

And there is remarkable language from the Supreme Court itself, in rejecting an extension of the rule, which could well be used against the whole federal rule: "We are concerned not with their [the officers'] liability but with the interest of the government in securing the benefit of the evidence seized." McGuire v. United States, 273 U. S. 95, 99, 47 Sup. Ct. 259 (1927).

[166]"The criminal is to go free because the constable has blundered." Cardozo, J., in People v. Defore, 242 N. Y. 13, 21, 150 N. E. 585, 587 (1926).

"The sins of the [officer], for which the person aggrieved has not chosen to seek redress or punishment, are visited upon the only party whose claim to consideration is unimpeachable, namely the United States." Flagg v. United States, 233 Fed. 481 (C. C. A. 2d 1916) (reluctant concurring opinion of Veeder, J.).

See also Chief Justice Taft's language in Olmstead v. United States, 277 U. S. 438, 468, 48 Sup. Ct. 564, 569 (1928).

[167]People v. Defore, 213 App. Div. 643, 652, 211 N. Y. Supp. 134, 142 (1st Dep't 1925).

[168]See State v. Reynolds, 101 Conn. 224, 235, 125 Atl. 636, 639 (1924); People v. Esposito, 118 Misc. 867, 873, 194 N. Y. Supp. 326, 333 (Ct. Sp. Sess. 1922).

[169]As stated in State v. Chin Gim, 47 Nev. 431, 441, 224 Pac. 798, 800 (1924), by the contrary holding "the sanctity of the castle is converted into a sanctity for crime."

[170]In the brief of the American Civil Liberties Union against the admissibility of

There is some suggestion that the admission of illegally obtained evidence violates the presumption of innocence, in that the accused is considered guilty and left to prove his way out.[171] But the victim of an illegal seizure is not, any more than any other accused, "considered guilty". The evidence thus obtained is presented to the jury just as is any other competent evidence, and the defendant, as in all cases, must raise a reasonable doubt of his guilt. The presumption of innocence does not go so far as to exclude proofs tending to show the defendant's guilt! We must not pervert it to mean that a man is conclusively presumed innocent until he gives himself away.

The issue then becomes whether there is a policy, some public necessity, sufficiently strong to warrant excluding such evidence in spite of its tendency to reach the truth. Certain "privileges" are recognized where such a public policy exists, for "truth, like all the good things, may be loved unwisely, may be pursued too keenly, may cost too much."[172] Mr. Justice Brandeis has expressed great concern for the privacy of what is "whispered in the closet".[173] But crime operates by means of just such "whispers in the closet". And when an officer, however unlawfully, has discovered positive evidence of crime conducted by means of such "whispers", is there any public policy that requires that its secrecy be preserved? Does it not rather demand that the secret be dragged into the light? Whatever is "proper and confidential", to use again the words of Justice Brandeis, will not be exposed in court, for if it is thus "proper", no crime being revealed thereby, it will never appear in court. Likewise there should be no privilege for the private arsenal or for other tangible evidences of crime.

In this connection, a fear has been expressed that freedom of opinion will be endangered if such evidence may be received.[173a] A system of espionage of the Old World variety is visioned, wherein one's privately expressed opinions and his copy of Marx behind the door in the library[174] will be ferreted out and used in evidence against him—for just what crime is not

wire-tapped evidence, there is given a shocking account of inaccurate and perjured evidence given by the officers who tapped the wires in the *Olmstead* case. But this argument has nothing to do with the illegal means of obtaining the evidence. Dishonest witnesses can perjure one kind of evidence as well as another. Courts will always receive conversations overheard on the street by casual bystanders, months after they occurred, the inaccuracy of their hearing or their memory and the honesty of their report going to the credibility of the testimony but not operating to exclude it.

[171]Delegate Dyett thus expressed himself in the Constitutional Convention. CONVENTION RECORD (N. Y. 1938) 548-9.

[172]Pearse v. Pearse, 1 DeG. & Sm. 12, 28, 63 Eng. Rep. 950, 957 (1846), referring to the attorney-client privilege.

[173]"Subtler and more far-reaching means of invading privacy have become available to the Government. Discovery and invention have made it possible for the Government, by means far more effective than stretching upon the rack, to obtain disclosure in court of what is whispered in the closet." Olmstead v. United States, 277 U. S. 438, 473, 48 Sup. Ct. 564 (1928).

[173a]See speech of Governor Lehman. N. Y. Times, June 18, 1938, p. 1, col. 2.

[174]His copy of *Das Kapital* gave much concern to one of the delegates to the New York Convention.

made clear. So long as we have no political crimes, we need not fear that such evidence will be used to our hurt. Some fear, perhaps justifiably, that we may see again the Sedition Acts of old, and they feel that we should begin now to exclude illegally obtained evidence and not set a precedent which may be availed of at that time. But the government that so far breaks with our time-honored traditions of freedom of speech and opinion, that so far ignores Constitutional restrictions[175] as to make one's views criminal, will not be deterred by another tradition a quarter of a century old! If we are to have political crimes, the necessary rules of evidence will come in as their hand-maidens, even though we exclude them now. Therefore, we need not fear that we are setting dangerous precedents for those who will need none. The question is properly considered in the light of what we, today, recognize as crimes. If the guardians of liberty will focus their attention on the substantive law, they need not fear that any innocent man will suffer from the admission of any reliable evidence.

Is there anything in the state or federal constitutions that requires that the courts recognize such a privilege? None of them expressly so provide, but efforts have been made so to construe several of the clauses of the constitutions. It has universally been recognized that the admission of the evidence does not violate the "due process" clause of the Fourteenth Amendment. As applied to judicial proceedings, due process requires only that the accused have sufficient notice and adequate opportunity to defend.[176]

Defense attorneys seeking a constitutional theory upon which to rest their demands dug up and dusted off the gratuitous dictum of Justice Bradley in the *Boyd* case,[177] which had been but scotched in the *Adams* case,[178] and persuaded the Supreme Court that when evidence was obtained by a violation of the Fourth Amendment, its use in court was a violation of the Fifth in that it compelled the defendant to "be a witness against himself". The result is the same to the defendant, it was said, whether he is obliged himself to supply the evidence or whether it is taken from him by an illegal seizure; in either case he is the unwilling source of the evidence.[179] The government could not lawfully compel the defendant to produce the evidence, so it cannot do so unlawfully.[180] But this argument proceeds upon the premise that the Constitution confers an immunity from conviction upon evidence which a person is able to conceal from open view or from

[175]Prof. R. E. Cushman, in 1 ENCY. SOC. SCI. (1930) 635, expresses the opinion that the Sedition Act was unconstitutional. The Supreme Court never passed upon it. *Cf.* Herndon v. Lowry, 301 U. S. 242, 57 Sup. Ct. 732 (1937).

[176]Banks v. State, 207 Ala. 179, 186, 93 So. 293, 303 (1921) (full discussion); People v. Defore, 242 N. Y. 13, 28, 150 N. E. 585, 590 (1926). *Cf.* Twining v. New Jersey, 211 U. S. 78, 29 Sup. Ct. 14 (1908).

[177]116 U. S. 616, 6 Sup. Ct. 524 (1886).

[178]192 U. S. 585, 24 Sup. Ct. 372 (1904).

[179]See particularly Gouled v. United States, 255 U. S. 298, 306, 41 Sup. Ct. 261 (1921).

[180]See State v. Wills, 91 W. Va. 659, 669, 114 S. E. 261, 265 (1922).

lawful process—that it would be unfair to make a defendant the instrument of his own destruction. This is a doctrine as dangerous as it is questionable. The federal cases look to *Entick v. Carrington*[181] as their guide—but it was there said by Lord Camden that the prohibition against compelling self-incrimination rests on the fact that "The *necessary means of compelling self-accusation,* falling upon the innocent as well as the guilty, would be both cruel and unjust." There is no suggestion that all evidence of which the defendant is the "unwilling source" is to be excluded. And it might be added that the defendant is as much the "unwilling source" of evidence seized under *lawful* warrant, yet it has never been suggested (except in the *Boyd* dictum) that evidence so obtained could not be used.[182] Professor Wigmore declares,[183] and the cases support him,[184] that the Fifth Amendment concerns only testimonial compulsion, statements and evidence which one is compelled to make or produce under court process directed against him as a witness, either before or at the trial. When the defendant is not himself compelled to produce the evidence, when it is seized by an officer lawfully or unlawfully, the evidence given on the stand is not his but is the evidence of the officer testifying about his own observations; and the real evidence, the article seized, speaks for itself and is not evidence given by the accused.[185]

But the privilege against self-incrimination is no protection to a corporation.[186] So a new trick was pulled out of the bag in the *Silverthorne* case,[187] which rested the federal rule on a new ground: that the prohibition against unreasonable search and seizure extends not only to the *fact* of search and seizure but to every incident of it.[188] Since the purpose of the search was to obtain evidence, it is pure sophistry to declare, as courts frequently have done,[189] that the search and the subsequent use of the evidence are distinct

---

[181]19 How. St. Tr. 1029 (1765).

[182]That such evidence could be used was the clearest holding in Adams v. New York, *supra* note 178, and this much of the *Boyd* dictum has never recovered. See also Commonwealth v. Dabbierio, 290 Pa. 174, 178-9, 138 Atl. 679, 681 (1927), and dissent in State v. Owens, 302 Mo. 348, 397, 259 S. W. 100, 115 (1924).

[183]4 WIGMORE, EVIDENCE (2d ed. 1923) §§ 2263 ff.

[184]See, on its application to search and seizure, Banks v. State, Commonwealth v. Dabbierio, and other cases cited *infra* note 185.

[185]Banks v. State, 207 Ala. 179, 93 So. 293 (1921), *cert. den.,* 260 U. S. 736, 43 Sup. Ct. 96 (1922); People v. LeDoux, 155 Cal. 535, 102 Pac. 517 (1909); State v. Reynolds, 101 Conn. 224, 125 Atl. 636 (1924); State v. Johnson, 116 Kan. 58, 226 Pac. 245 (1924); State v. Rogne, 115 Minn. 204, 132 N. W. 5 (1911); Pringle v. State, 108 Miss. 802, 67 So. 455 (1915); State v. Pomeroy, 130 Mo. 489, 32 S. W. 1002 (1895); State v. Flynn, 36 N. H. 64 (1858); Commonwealth v. Dabbierio, 290 Pa. 174, 138 Atl. 679 (1927); State v. Atkinson, 40 S. C. 363, 18 S. E. 1021 (1894). *Cf.* State v. Miller, 71 N. J. L. 527, 60 Atl. 202 (1905), and Matter of Schmidt v. District Attorney, 255 App. Div. 353, 8 N. Y. Supp. (2d) 787 (4th Dep't 1938) (medical examination). See note in this issue, (1939) 24 CORNELL L. Q. 437.

[186]Hale v. Henkel, 201 U. S. 43, 74, 26 Sup. Ct. 370, 378 (1906).

[187]251 U. S. 385, 40 Sup. Ct. 182 (1920).

[188]See dissent in State v. Prescott, 125 S. C. 22, 117 S. E. 637 (1923).

[189]See People v. Mayen, 188 Cal. 237, 205 Pac. 435 (1922); State v. Reynolds, 101 Conn. 224, 125 Atl. 636 (1924); State v. Chuchola, 32 Del. 133, 120 Atl. 212 (Ct. Gen.

transactions. But, distinct transaction or no, there is much room to question whether it was ever intended to impose this additional sanction. The provision operates upon legislatures to bar them forever from making unreasonable searches and seizures lawful, upon executives to bar them from enforcing such laws, and upon the courts to bind them to punish such searches and seizures whether made with or without legislative sanction.[190] But the Constitution lays down no rule of evidence. This provision was "designed to protect the intimate sanctity of the person and the home from invasion by the state. . . . The Constitution and the laws of the land are not solicitous to aid persons charged with crime to conceal or sequester evidence of their iniquity."[191] When the invasion of the home has been effected, the violation of the Constitution is complete. It is neither the possession of property nor the use of evidence, but the sanctity of homes, that is the concern of the Constitutional guaranty.

This surely is the correct view historically. For while the proponents of the rule of exclusion look fondly back to *Entick v. Carrington*[192] as the parent of their rule, that case is far from authority for them. It granted *damages* to Entick against the instigator of the search, but nowhere in the opinion is there a suggestion that the evidence should be suppressed and the officers be compelled to purge their minds of all knowledge gained thereby.[193] Nor did James Otis, when he made his great speech in Boston denouncing the writs of assistance, concern himself with the use of the evidence; it was the invasion of homes that prompted him to make his attack.[194] It was never the law of England, of the Colonies, or of any state in the Union until more than a century after the Revolution, yet we are glibly told that it is a fundamental right of Englishmen that no evidence illegally taken from them may be used against them!

But it is said that excluding the evidence is the only practical means of making the Constitutional guaranty effective. Reserving the question of the ineffectiveness of other remedies, just what does this "more effective"

Sess. 1922); State v. Johnson, 116 Kan. 58, 226 Pac. 245 (1924); State v. Dillon, 34 N. M. 366, 281 Pac. 474 (1929).

[190]Judge Lumpkin in Williams v. State, 100 Ga. 511, 28 S. E. 624 (1897). See also Adams v. New York, *supra* note 178.

[191]People v. Mayen, 188 Cal. 237, 249, 251, 205 Pac. 435, 440 (1922).

[192]19 How. St. Tr. 1029 (1765).

[193]Lord Camden gives as the reason for the privilege against self-incrimination that "the necessary means of compelling self-accusation, falling upon the innocent as well as the guilty, would be both cruel and unjust." The same reason is implicit in the bar of a general search for evidence. But a search could only be "cruel and unjust" to the innocent at the time of the invasion of the home, not at the admission of the evidence. The search of the innocent would reveal no incriminating evidence, and there would be none to admit; the hardship, if any, would fall only on the guilty. Only the obtaining, not the subsequent use, is cruel and unjust to the *innocent*. See State v. Dillon, 34 N. M. 366, 373, 281 Pac. 474, 477 (1929).

[194]The significant portion of the speech will be found in 2 WATSON, THE CONSTITUTION (1910) 1416.

remedy add? To the rights of the innocent man it would add not one iota. The speeches in the New York Constitutional Convention are replete with harrowing stories of innocent victims of vicious searches in which no evidence was found.[195] The speakers then go on to say that the constitutional guaranty is meaningless if the evidence is admissible. But they fail utterly to connect up these two points and show how the innocent victim is helped in the slightest by the fact that the evidence which was *not* found would be inadmissible! As a means of reparation for a wrong done an innocent man, the exclusion of evidence is no help.[196]

The only person benefitted by the suppression of incriminating evidence is the guilty man with something to conceal.[197] True, *his* constitutional rights have been violated, but are we justified in providing an additional remedy, above those ordinarily granted to individuals who have been wronged, a remedy useful only to a law-violator? It has been said by Judge Learned Hand that "the Constitution protects the guilty along with the innocent."[198] It might more accurately be said, as in the *Weeks* case,[199] that it protects those *accused of crime,* because of the possibility—the presumption—that they are innocent. But should it be so interpreted as to shield those faced with actual evidence of their guilt from just punishment therefor? Judge Seabury well expressed the thought a few years ago:

> "As we look at some of the uses which the criminal classes have made of constitutional provisions, one might suppose that the far-seeing barons who wrung the great charter from King John at Runnymede were intent upon safeguarding the twentieth century racketeer, gangster, kidnapper, gunman and corrupt political leader in the prosecution of their sinister vocations. It ought to be possible to find a way, by judicial interpretation, to use these constitutional provisions for the protection of liberty without giving them such fanciful and far-fetched interpretations as to convert them into a weapon by which criminals can make war safely upon organized society and its law-abiding members."[200]

---

[195]See particularly pages 487-92 of the Convention Record.

[196]Whether it will help the innocent victims indirectly by discouraging *further* searches will be considered presently.

[197]"It would have been consoling and gratifying to the defendant, of course, if the judge had . . . [returned] his whisky, with an apology, and without allowing the state to prove that the whisky was found in the defendant's possession. Perhaps that would have atoned for the sheriff's wrongdoing as far as the defendant was concerned, but how about the law-abiding public? They are . . . the complainants in both accusations." State v. Eddins, 161 La. 240, 247, 108 So. 468, 470 (1926).

[198]United States v. Casino, 286 Fed. 976, 978 (S. D. N. Y. 1923).

[199]232 U. S. 383, 392, 34 Sup. Ct. 341, 344 (1914).

[200]Address at annual dinner of American Law Institute, May 7, 1932. (1932) 18 A. B. A. J. 371.

Cf. the language of Chief Justice Marshall of Ohio in Rosanski v. State, 106 Ohio St. 442, 462, 140 N. E. 370, 376 (1922): "If all the doctrines which are being urged by attorneys representing . . . law violators should be adopted by the courts as the true interpretation of our sacred Bill of Rights, it would no longer be recognized as a charter of government and as a guaranty of protection of the weak against the aggressions of the strong, but rather as a charter of unbridled license and a certificate of character to the criminal classes."

There is another argument that is made, apart from all questions of constitutional construction. It is the argument of public policy, that the court should not ratify the illegal search by receiving the evidence obtained thereby. Although it is conceded that no officer is authorized to commit a crime on behalf of the government, and an officer's illegal acts are beyond the scope of his authority, yet it is argued that if the government, through the courts, avails itself of the fruits of the officer's crime, it thereby sanctions the illegal means by which the evidence was obtained.[201] The fact that evidence of crime was found by a search unlawful in its inception does not purge the search of its illegality. This much must be admitted.[202] For we cannot accept the philosophy that the end justifies the means, that the law-violating officer is to be excused if his offense reveals another.[203] But does it follow that the court, in accepting the evidence, is "allowing such iniquities to succeed"?[204] Both the officers and the courts are peculiarly charged with the duty of enforcing the Constitution and the laws. When one of these agencies fails this duty and itself violates the law, the other is derelict in its duty if it then refuses to enforce the law. It should not be within the power of one of these agencies, the officers, to tie the hands of the other, the

---

[201]See Weeks v. United States, 232 U. S. 383, 34 Sup. Ct. 341 (1914); State v. Arregui, 44 Ida. 43, 254 Pac. 788, 792 (1927); Gore v. State, 24 Okla. Cr. 394, 218 Pac. 545, 550 (1923); State v. Wills, 91 W. Va. 659, 114 S. E. 261 (1922); Hoyer v. State, 180 Wis. 407, 193 N. W. 89 (1923).

The same argument was made in connection with illegal arrest, but was almost universally rejected, even by the United States Supreme Court. Two state cases and a since discredited federal case accepted the argument. State v. Simmons, 39 Kan. 262, 18 Pac. 177 (1888); *Re* Robinson, 29 Neb. 135, 45 N. W. 267 (1890); Tennessee v. Jackson, 36 Fed. 258, 1 L. R. A. 370 (E. D. Tenn. 1888).

[202]Nevertheless, some eighteen states, including nine which adopt the federal rule as to search and seizure, have declared by statute or decision that an *arrest,* even without any justification whatever, may become lawful if it develops that a felony has in fact been committed. See *supra* note 46.

And those who throw up their hands in holy horror at the idea of judging an officer's crime by its results should be reminded that this concept is no stranger to our law. A simple assault may become a far graver offense if the victim happens to land on his head, and driving seventy miles an hour through a school zone is a misdemeanor or a felony, depending upon its results. However, we shall not labor this point, for there are less debatable grounds upon which to rest the argument.

[203]"To declare that in the administration of the criminal law the end justifies the means—to declare that the Government may commit crimes in order to secure the conviction of a private criminal—would bring terrible retribution." Justice Brandeis' dissent in Olmstead v. United States, 277 U. S. 438, 485, 48 Sup. Ct. 564 (1928).

See also Byars v. United States, 273 U. S. 28, 29, 47 Sup. Ct. 248 (1927); Town of Blacksburg v. Beam, 104 S. C. 146, 88 S. E. 441 (1916).

[204]Justice Holmes dissenting in Olmstead v. United States, *supra* note 203 at 470.

Just why the government is permitted to "*adopt* the unlawful seizure" in *forfeiture* cases yet may not do so for the purpose of using the evidence is hard to fathom. But Justice Holmes says that they rest upon a different footing. Dodge v. United States, 272 U. S. 530, 47 Sup. Ct. 191 (1926). Canada likewise draws a distinction—and reaches opposite results on each point! *Supra* note 98.

Furthermore, the court just as much takes advantage of a wrong when it uses evidence wrongfully obtained by a private individual, but of all the judicial votaries of the federal rule only Justices Holmes and Brandeis have seen this. See their dissent in Burdeau v. McDowell, 256 U. S. 465, 41 Sup. Ct. 574 (1921).

courts, and thus confer a virtual immunity upon an offender against society. Two wrongs do not make a right, and the courts do not ratify or condone one wrong by refusing to apply to it indirect sanctions that operate not to punish that wrongdoer but to release another in the face of evidence of his guilt! The plain duty of the court is to punish every wrong that is brought to its attention, and if existing sanctions for this purpose are inadequate, the energies of the Legislature should be directed to devising more effective direct remedies.[205]

For the same reason, the "unclean hands" argument, which is occasionally raised,[206] must be rejected. Equity, so far as it has as its object the redress of private wrongs, can afford to refuse its extraordinary aid to those who have acted unfairly in connection with the transaction. But criminal courts exist for the protection of society, and they fail this purpose, this duty, if they release a prisoner in the face of evidence of his guilt because another has failed the same duty.

There is another important argument of public policy which must be met. It is best expressed by Justice Brandeis:

> "In a government of laws, the existence of the government will be imperilled if it fails to observe the law scrupulously. Our Government is the potent, the omnipresent teacher. For good or for ill, it teaches the whole people by its example. Crime is contagious. If the Government becomes a lawbreaker, it breeds contempt for law; it invites every man to become a law unto himself; it invites anarchy."[207]

It is true that public respect for law is gravely impaired when the police disregard constitutional safeguards. But public confidence is equally betrayed when criminals escape punishment for demonstrable guilt. Far better it would be to provide effective means to punish both the offending officer and the criminal whose crime is thus fortuitously revealed.

In this connection we are told that conviction of a person by such evidence "shocks the common man's sense of decency and fair play".[208] This is what old Jeremy Bentham so aptly labeled the Fox-Hunter's Reason, introducing into criminal law the sportsman's concept of fairness.[209] Not every man has pursued the wily fox, but every fair-minded citizen, when he was a child

[205]The argument of the federal courts on this point is best repudiated in Williams v. State, 100 Ga. 211, 28 S. E. 624 (1897); State v. Eddins, 161 La. 240, 108 So. 468 (1926); Commonwealth v. Wilkins, 243 Mass. 356, 138 N. E. 11 (1923); Hall v. Commonwealth, 138 Va. 727, 121 S. E. 154 (1924).

[206]See Justice Brandeis' dissent in Olmstead v. United States, *supra* note 203 at 483.

[207]Dissent in Olmstead v. United States, *supra* note 203 at 485.

"The shock to the sensibilities of the average citizen when his government violates a constitutional right of another is far more evil in its effect than the escape of any criminal through the courts' observance of those rights." State v. Arregui, 44 Ida. 43, 58, 254 Pac. 788, 792 (1927).

[208]Brandeis, J., dissenting in Burdeau v. McDowell, 256 U. S. 465, 477, 41 Sup. Ct. 574 (1921).

[209]BENTHAM, *Rationale of Judicial Evidence* in 7 WORKS (Bowring's ed. 1843) 452 ff.

playing "cops and robbers",[210] knew that if the "cops" took unfair advantage of the "robbers", the captured robbers had to be released and given a new chance to hide. And this admirable spirit of fair play is carried over in the minds of many citizens and is applied by them to the real-life "cops and robbers" situation. But we must remember that this is not a harmless game engaged in by equals, and that there are other factors to be considered besides the wrong done by one group of children to another—that the robbers released will not run harmlessly off to hide under Mrs. O'Leary's back porch, but will resume their real-life killing and thieving. The rules of sport are conducive to the end sought—amusement—but they are ill-adapted to the enforcement of the criminal law.[211] And if the application of the rule could be divorced from popular prejudices concerning the liquor, gambling, and revenue laws, in the enforcement of which the federal rule saw its greatest growth,[212] and if a murderer, bank robber, or kidnapper[213] should go free in the face of evidence of his guilt, the public would surely arise and condemn the helplessness of the courts against the depredations of the outlaws.[214]

The final argument for the federal rule is that all direct remedies are ineffective to discourage those charged with law enforcement from seeking evidence by illegal means. It has already been pointed out that, as an additional means of reparation for a wrong *done,* the suppression of incriminating evidence can benefit only the guilty. As a punishment of the officer, the release of his quarry is of doubtful value. But it may have a very real effect in discouraging the authorities from using such means in the first instance, if they are not to be able to use the product of their acts.[215] If it has this effect, it cannot be denied that innocent as well as guilty will benefit. But here we have two vital social needs, the need that crime be repressed and the need "that the law shall not be flouted by the insolence of office".[216]

[210]Now called "G-men and racketeers."

[211]It hardly seems cricket to borrow words from the Supreme Court to support this thesis, but in 1927 Justice Stone declared: "A criminal prosecution is more than a game in which the Government may be checkmated and the game lost merely because its officers have not played according to rule." McGuire v. United States, 273 U. S. 95, 99, 47 Sup. Ct. 259 (1927) (in refusing to extend the federal rule).

[212]An extensive sampling of cases following the federal rule reveals that the great majority of these cases involved seizure of liquor.

[213]The evidence used against Hauptmann, the kidnapper of the Lindbergh baby, was seized without a warrant; would it have served the cause of justice—and would public respect for law have been enhanced—if this evidence had been excluded? (The source of this information is the speech of Justice Lewis in the New York Constitutional Convention of 1938. RECORD, p. 470. Since the law is settled in New Jersey, it is not mentioned in the report of the case. State v. Hauptmann, 115 N. J. L. 412, 180 Atl. 809 [1935]).

[214]See Roberts v. People, 78 Colo. 55, 243 Pac. 544, 545 (1926).

[215]The federal rule does not follow this policy to its logical conclusion. It has already been pointed out that the evidence so obtained may be used to convict the truck-driver and the still-tender. It is the "higher-up" who owns the property who is protected. Connolly v. Medalie, 58 F. (2d) 629 (C. C. A. 2d 1932).

[216]People v. Defore, 242 N. Y. 13, 24, 150 N. E. 585, 589 (1926).

When these vital needs come in conflict, we must move cautiously, lest in our zeal to promote one, we neglect the other. It is much to be doubted, in any event, whether the evil is as widespread as many judges and speakers would have us believe; no factual study has been found. However, in the absence of a factual study of our own, we must meet the problem as if illegal searches and seizures were every bit as prevalent as is claimed.[217]

Has this rule, then, had the effect of discouraging such methods? The large number of cases of illegal searches that continue to arise long after the federal rule is well established in a jurisdiction casts substantial doubt upon its efficacy.[218] The well-meaning over-zealous officer will not, of course, be deterred by such a rule, for he is probably unaware that his act is unreasonable. And the officer who wilfully abuses his power to show his authority will hardly be deterred by a sanction not directed at him personally. The beneficial effect of the rule, if any it has, must be with respect to police departments whose settled policy is to get evidence in such manner—and if this is their policy, it will continue, for the value of the raid on suspicion and the tapping of wires is fully as great for "getting a lead" as it is for getting evidence useful in court. With the clues thus obtained, which might be sufficient in themselves to convince any jury, the police are thus better armed to go through the formality of seeking out further evidence that a court will accept. Such "fishing expeditions" will not be checked by any such indirect means as rejecting the evidence in court. Therefore, it is to be questioned whether the bare possibility of deterring official lawlessness by this indirect means is sufficient to overweigh the certainty of turning criminals loose.

Justices Cardozo and Holmes both recognized that this is a question of balancing social interests, and they reached opposite conclusions as to which is the lesser evil. The argument of each is wholly speculative, neither appearing to rest on a factual study. This question, like many questions of law, rests ultimately on a question of fact, yet not one of the courts that have passed on it has ever indicated that it had made the factual study that must underlie its conclusion that this remedy will or will not be effective, that one or the other is the lesser evil. Wise judgments cannot be based on mere

[217]King John, in *Magna Charta* (clause 55), pledged: "We will not make any justices, constables, sheriffs or bailiffs, but of such as know the law of the realm, *and mean duly to observe it.*" But it is certain that, to an unknown extent, some officers are not of that caliber. THE POLICEMAN'S POCKET LAW BOOK (1924) 101 contains the following words: "What is the highest law? The law of necessity is the highest law known to man—it is supreme even over the written Constitution." See LAWLESSNESS IN LAW ENFORCEMENT, *infra* note 223, at 106; unfortunately the study does not cover the application of this "legal principle" to search and seizure or to arrest.

[218]The latest A. L. R. annotation cites some 300 such cases, over a six-year period, reaching appellate courts in jurisdictions where the federal rule was well settled—and a correspondingly large number of cases probably arose in trial courts that were not appealed because the exclusion of the evidence prevented a conviction. See (1934) 88 A. L. R. 340.

speculation and unproved assumptions.[219] There is one factual study that has been made of the effect of the federal rule upon law enforcement in Detroit.[220] Professor Waite of Michigan found that at least one-quarter of those arrested in Detroit for unlawfully carrying concealed weapons were discharged not because they were innocent but because the weapon—indisputable evidence of guilt—had been unlawfully discovered. There were 1,347 armed robberies in Detroit in the year studied, and the gun-toters who were released no doubt had their part in them. This seems a high price to pay for a rule that *may* possibly discourage illegal enforcement.[221]

The argument that the federal rule hampers efficient law enforcement must be most closely scrutinized, however. For, as Connor Hall so aptly pointed out in one of the early forays in this great battle,[222] if the *direct* remedies against the officers are as effective as their advocates claim, then equally will criminals go free and law enforcement be inefficient. However, if illegal enforcement is thereby checked, it will be a real boon to the innocent citizen, and to gain this benefit we may tolerate some inefficiency in law enforcement. Yet there will always be some over-zealous and some brutal officers, who are no more checked by direct remedies than by indirect, but at least the *direct* remedy punishes *them,* not society; and when, by whatever means, a court is presented with evidence of two crimes, it should punish both, whereas today under the federal rule it may punish neither. In Detroit and probably elsewhere, the "indirect remedy" *has not* discouraged illegal enforcement. It *has* released known criminals in the face of evidence of their guilt.

Let us consider for a moment how these principles have been applied to confessions unlawfully extorted.[223] Of course, no court will receive confessions obtained as a result of torture or fear, and most courts will reject them if motivated by hope of any material benefit.[224] The nature and degree of the hope or fear which is necessary to exclude the confession need not

[219]"Knowledge is essential to understanding, and the understanding should precede judging." Dissent of Justice Brandeis in Burns Baking Co. v. Bryan, 264 U. S. 504, 520, 44 Sup. Ct. 412 (1924).

[220]Waite, *Public Policy and the Arrest of Felons* (1933) 31 MICH. L. REV. 749, 763 ff.

[221]Since this study was published, Michigan has retreated from the federal rule to the extent of making *weapons* admissible. *Supra* note 94.

Professor Waite states, further, that in his observation the rule *encourages* illegal practices, for if the police cannot prosecute an arrested lawbreaker even on positive evidence which they have found, they tend to take the punishment into their own hands—which at least discourages the lawbreaker and silences press criticism of ineffective enforcement.

[222]Hall, *Evidence and the Fourth Amendment* (1922) 8 A. B. A. J. 646, 647.

[223]A full study of the prevalence of the "third degree" is found in NATIONAL COMMISSION ON LAW OBSERVANCE AND ENFORCEMENT, REPORT ON LAWLESSNESS IN LAW ENFORCEMENT (Government Printing Office 1931) 13.

[224]Under N. Y. CODE CRIM. PROC. § 395, a confession is not rendered inadmissible by the fact that it was induced by hope of benefit except where a promise of immunity has been made by or by the authority of the district attorney. But this is not the law in most states.

concern us here.[225] The important fact to note is that, with rare exceptions, the courts have recognized that the rejection of such evidence is grounded not upon the constitutional privilege against self-incrimination, not upon any policy against ratifying the unlawful means or against encouraging such practices, but squarely and solely upon the ground that a confession so induced is unreliable.[226] This distinction in theory is vitally important when the extorted confession leads to the discovery of independent facts, such as the location of stolen property or of the victim's body.[227] No case has ever refused to receive evidence of these independent facts,[228] and the great

[225]Here again there may be said to be a federal rule, which follows the earlier English cases in excluding anything but the spontaneous outpourings of a troubled conscience. The least urging or inducement will exclude the confession. Bram v. United States, 168 U. S. 532, 18 Sup. Ct. 183 (1897); Ziang Sung Wan v. United States, 266 U. S. 1, 45 Sup. Ct. 1 (1924); State v. Brick, 2 Harring. 530 (Del. 1835); Green v. State, 88 Ga. 518, 15 S. E. 10 (1891); and many cases cited in the *Bram* case, *supra*. Under this rule, "It would be best to tell the truth" is sufficient to exclude the evidence. *Contra*: People v. Randazzio, 194 N. Y. 147, 155, 87 N. E. 112, 115 (1909); King v. State, 40 Ala. 314 (1867).

The courts vary on how much is necessary to exclude the confession. Rough handling is generally sufficient. Lang v. State, 178 Wis. 114, 189 N. W. 558 (1922). But in New York it is simply considered on the basic question of voluntariness. People v. Trybus, 219 N. Y. 18, 113 N. E. 538 (1916). Fear of mob violence is sufficient to exclude the confession. Taylor v. Commonwealth, 19 Ky. L. Rep. 836, 42 S. W. 1125 (1897); Walker v. State, 2 Tex. App. 326 (1877). Agitation resulting from being shown his father's mangled body is not sufficient. State v. Crank, 2 Bailey Law 66, 77 (S. C. 1831). Placing the accused in a "sweat box" or dark, airless cell will exclude the resultant confession. Ammons v. State, 80 Miss. 592, 32 So. 9 (1902).

The courts disagree on whether illegally prolonged custody or questioning will exclude the confession. It is material to the question of voluntariness, but is usually held not sufficient in itself to exclude the confession. People v. Mummiani, 258 N. Y. 394, 180 N. E. 94 (1932); State v. Kirby, 1 Strob. 378 (S. C. 1847). *Contra*: Regina v. Berriman, 6 Cox Crim. 388 (N. P. 1854). In Kentucky, a statute excludes confessions obtained by "plying" with questions while in custody. KY. STAT. ANN. (Baldwin 1936) § 1649b; Commonwealth v. McClanahan, 153 Ky. 412, 155 S. W. 1131 (1913). This statute does not refer to a single question but to persistent, repeated questions. Commonwealth v. Long, 171 Ky. 132, 188 S. W. 334 (1916).

[226]The constitutional privilege relates only to testimonial compulsion directed against the defendant as a witness, and has no connection with extra-judicial confessions. See 2 WIGMORE, EVIDENCE (2d ed. 1923) § 823; State v. Turner, 82 Kan. 787, 109 Pac. 654 (1910); Baughman v. Commonwealth, 206 Ky. 441, 267 S. W. 681 (1924); People v. Mahon, 15 N. Y. 384, 386 (1857); Duffy v. People, 26 N. Y. 589 (1863).

But courts have frequently confused these very similar principles and rested on the ground of self-incrimination. Bram v. United States, 168 U. S. 532, 18 Sup. Ct. 183 (1897); People v. Loper, 159 Cal. 6, 112 Pac. 720 (1910); Evans v. State, 106 Ga. 519, 32 S. E. 659 (1899); State v. Simpson, 157 La. 614, 102 So. 810 (1925); Jordan v. State, 32 Miss. 382 (1856) (promptly repudiated in Belote v. State, 36 Miss. 96 [1858]); State v. Thomas, 250 Mo. 189, 157 S. W. 330 (1913); Lang v. State, 178 Wis. 114, 189 N. W. 558 (1922).

[227]A closely related problem is involved in the cases on compulsory medical examinations and forcible comparison of shoe tracks, discussed in a note in this issue. (1939) 24 CORNELL L. Q. 437.

[228]This statement is just a little too strong. Jordan v. State, 32 Miss. 382 (1856), which rested its holding upon self-incrimination, brought out the whole armory of reasons which were later used for the federal rule on search and seizure—the constitutional protection extending to every incident of the violation, the court sanctioning the means, etc. The case was promptly overruled in Belote v. State, 36 Miss. 96 (1858), in which counsel cited the case but the court did not. In time even defense counsel

weight of authority will receive in addition so much of the confession as is thereby shown to be true, as evidence of defendant's knowledge of the criminatory facts, which he is then left to reconcile with his innocence if he can.[229] Similarly, if a confession is procured by means of the most

---

tired of citing it. In spite of the adoption of the federal rule in Mississippi, it still adheres to the prevailing view on this related question. Smith v. State, 166 Miss. 893, 144 So. 471 (1932).

[229]The prevailing view admits the facts found and so much of the confession as relates strictly to those facts and is explanatory of the discovery. Thus, the fact that the property or body was found as a result of defendant's information will be admitted to show his knowledge of the location. Lewis v. State, 220 Ala. 461, 125 So. 802 (1930); Shufflin v. State, 122 Ark. 606, 184 S. W. 454 (1916); People v. Hoy Yen, 34 Cal. 176 (1867); Osborne v. People, 83 Colo. 4, 262 Pac. 892 (1927); State v. Brick, 2 Harring. 530 (Del. 1835); Rusher v. State, 94 Ga. 366, 21 S. E. 593 (1894); People v. Ascey, 304 Ill. 404, 136 N. E. 766 (1922); State v. Moran, 131 Iowa 645, 109 N. W. 187 (1906); State v. Turner, 82 Kan. 787, 109 Pac. 654 (1910); Baughman v. Commonwealth, 206 Ky. 441, 267 S. W. 681 (1924); Commonwealth v. Knapp, 9 Pick. 496, 511 (Mass. 1830); Smith v. State, 166 Miss. 893, 144 So. 471 (1932); State v. Simas, 25 Nev. 432, 62 Pac. 242 (1900); State v. Due, 27 N. H. (7 Foster) 256 (1853); Duffy v. People, 26 N. Y. 589 (1863), *aff'g* 5 Park. Cr. 321 (Sup. Ct. 1862); State v. Lowry, 170 N. C. 730, 87 S. E. 62 (1915); Laros v. Commonwealth, 84 Pa. 200 (1877); Dupuis v. State, 14 Ohio App. 67 (1918); State v. Danelly, 116 S. C. 113, 107 S. E. 149 (1921); Collins v. State, 169 Tenn. 393, 88 S. W. (2d) 452 (1935); State v. Conklin, 109 Vt.—, 194 Atl. 378 (1937); United States v. Richard, Fed. Cas. No. 16154 (C. C. D. C. 1823) (the last case on the point in any federal court!); Rex v. Lockhart, 1 Leach C. C. 386, 168 Eng. Rep. 295 (1785); see 2 EAST P. C. (1803) 658.

Under this view, it is improper to admit defendant's admission that he *stole* the goods or *placed* them in the place where they were found, since nothing but his *knowledge* of the location is corroborated by the discovery. And the goods must be *identified* independently of the confession, because the accused might have given up money or property of his own to buy peace. Whitley v. State, 78 Miss. 255, 28 So. 852 (1900); State v. Due, *supra* (both reversing on this ground; the rule is so stated in the other cases above).

Profs. Wigmore and Chamberlayne have attacked these limitations on the rule, believing that the partial corroboration is sufficient to give some credit to the confession as a whole. 2 WIGMORE, EVIDENCE (2d ed. 1923) § 858; 2 CHAMBERLAYNE, MODERN LAW OF EVIDENCE (1911) § 1614. Their view is adopted by statute in Texas, TEX. CODE CRIM. PROC. (Vernon 1926) § 727; Greer v. State, 116 Tex. Cr. 491, 32 S. W. (2d) 845 (1930). It has had occasional support in the cases. Frederick v. State, 3 W. Va. 695 (1869); Rex v. Griffin, Russ. & R. 151, 168 Eng. Rep. 732 (1809) (Lord Ellenborough, admitting the money surrendered by the accused, without independent identification; the same court on the same day, by a slight realignment of the judges, "Ellenborough *dubitante*", went the other way in Rex v. Jones, Russ. & R. 152, 168 Eng. Rep. 733 [1809]; the ground of distinction is difficult to perceive); Regina v. Gould, 9 Car. & P. 364, 173 Eng. Rep. 870 (N. P. 1840) (admitting statement that he had *placed* the lantern where it was found). And see dissent in Berry v. United States, 2 Colo. 186 (1873).

A few English decisions have gone to the other extreme from the *Griffin* case, *supra*, and, while admitting the facts found, refuse to permit any reference to the confession or any showing that the defendant had knowledge. Rex v. Warickshall, 1 Leach C. C. 263, 168 Eng. Rep. 234 (1783); Rex v. Harvey, 2 East P. C. 658 (1800); Regina v. Berriman, 6 Cox Crim. 388 (N. P. 1854). Only one jurisdiction in the United States follows this rule. State v. Simpson, 157 La. 614, 102 So. 810 (1925) (resting on self-incrimination but avoiding the logical conclusion that the *facts* found thereby should also be excluded).

It was suggested in Rusher v. State, 94 Ga. 366, 21 S. E. 593 (1894) that if *violence* had been used on the defendant instead of mere fear, all the fruits would be suppressed as a matter of public policy, but this dictum has never been applied and its validity has been questioned in Williams v. State, 100 Ga. 511, 28 S. E. 624 (1897). The rule in Georgia is already confused enough without this. For a series of incon-

reprehensible of deception, it is fully admissible if the deception was not such as might make the confession untrue.[230] This is perfectly defensible on the theory that the extorted confession is excluded only because and to the extent that it is unreliable. But where are all the fine arguments of public policy that many of these same courts expressed when the issue involved evidence obtained by illegal search and seizure? Is there not an equal need to discourage "third degree" methods, by excluding not only the complete confession but also all knowledge gained as a result of it?[231] Does not the court "ratify the illegal means" when it receives evidence discovered as a result of an extorted confession or receives confessions procured by trickery? Could it be significant that this rule grew up almost entirely in murder and robbery cases, while the federal rule, in its greatest growth, was the step-child of Prohibition?

But in a leading case on the confession question in the United States Supreme Court, *Bram v. United States*,[232] the Court sowed the seeds from which there yet may grow another "dangerous heresy". For, with a remarkable lack of historical accuracy, the Court declared that the exclusion of confessions (other than spontaneous utterances made to relieve the conscience) results from the Constitutional privilege against self-incrimination. The case, on its facts, appears to be a square holding that a confession induced by a trick will be excluded.[233] But there are still deeper implications to be found in the opinion and in its adoption of the self-incrimination theory. It may require only a Supreme Court decision, following out these implications, to start the parade for a new "federal rule" excluding not only the entire

sistent cases on analogous points leave this anomalous result: If an officer unlawfully *searches* a man and finds a gun, it is admissible. Williams v. State, *supra*. If he compels the man to tell him that he has a gun, and then finds it, it is admissible. Rusher v. State, *supra*. But if he forces the man to *hand over* the gun, it is forcing him to give evidence against himself and is excluded! Evans v. State, 106 Ga. 519, 32 S. E. 659 (1899).

[230]McKinney v. State, 134 Ala. 134, 32 So. 726 (1902); State v. McKean, 36 Iowa 343 (1873); People v. Barker, 60 Mich. 277, 27 N. W. 539 (1886); Heldt v. State, 20 Neb. 492, 30 N. W. 626 (1886); Commonwealth v. Spardute, 278 Pa. 37, 122 Atl. 161 (1923); Wright v. State, 7 Tex. App. 574 (1880).

There is some doubt as to the federal courts. Bram v. United States, 168 U. S. 532, 18 Sup. Ct. 183 (1897), which excluded a confession, could be interpreted as a deception case, since it declares that if, but for inducement, defendant would have remained silent, the communication is inadmissible even though it takes the form of a denial ("He could not have seen me") from which guilt is inferred. *Cf.* Lefkowitz v. United States, 52 F. (2d) 52 (C. C. A. 2d 1931), in which an officer induced a prisoner to write her name without revealing that it was to be used in evidence; the court doubts, but does not pass upon, its admissibility.

And see Smith v. State, 88 Ga. 628, 15 S. E. 675 (1895) (doubting the inadmissibility of a tricked confession, but finding other evidence sufficient).

Similarly, the fact that a confession reaches the court through a gross breach of faith by an agent or confidant does not exclude it. Rex v. Derrington, 2 Car. & P. 418, 172 Eng. Rep. 189 (1826); Rex v. Shaw, 6 Car. & P. 372, 172 Eng. Rep. 1282 (1834).

[231]*Cf.* Silverthorne Lumber Co. v. United States, 251 U. S. 383, 40 Sup. Ct. 182 (1920).

[232]168 U. S. 532, 18 Sup. Ct. 183 (1897).

[233]See *supra* note 230. *Cf.* Gouled v. United States, 255 U. S. 298, 41 Sup. Ct. 261 (1921) (search procured by means of fraud is equivalent to one with force).

statement of the defendant but also the facts discovered thereby.[234] There are already a few lonesome bell-ringers for this rule in those courts which exclude the results of compulsory medical examinations and forcible comparison of shoe tracks with the defendant's feet or shoes.[235] The *Bram* case contains the seeds of a heresy fully as dangerous as did the *Boyd* case.[236] Let us hope that it has fallen upon barren ground, as now seems to be the case.[237]

It appears, therefore, that none of the arguments so eloquently propounded in the search and seizure cases have been accepted by the courts of a great majority of jurisdictions when the question of illegal arrest or extorted confession was before them.[238] When a person is unlawfully arrested, whether within or without the state, whether the kidnapping is effected by private persons or by the connivance of the governor himself, a federal court and nearly every state court will take jurisdiction if the person is before it. When a person is brutally beaten by the police and a confession is extorted which leads to discovery of other facts, all courts will receive these facts. But when the question is search and seizure, nearly half the courts of this country declare that they will not receive either the evidence so obtained or any evidence discovered as a result thereof! We submit that the courts should recognize in these latter cases, as they have in the others, that two evils cannot be set off against each other.

IV. Remedies

Repeated reference has been made to "direct remedies" which will be more appropriate to prevent and to punish illegal enforcement. But it is said that these remedies are ineffective. If so, the Legislature or its good right arm, the Law Revision Commission, should make a thorough study of the problem of devising effective direct remedies, to make the constitutional guaranty "a real, not an empty blessing". We can here only make suggestions, for we have made no study.

Let us look first to the civil remedy. If it is true, as the *Weeks* case[239]

---

[234]No federal case squarely in point has been found in the digests later than 1823. United States v. Richard, Fed. Cas. No. 16154 (C. C. D. C. 1823) (following the orthodox view).

[235]See note in this issue. (1939) 24 Cornell L. Q. 437.

[236]Boyd v. United States, 116 U. S. 616, 6 Sup. Ct. 524 (1886).

[237]A ray of hope may be seen in Holt v. United States, 218 U. S. 245, 31 Sup. Ct. 2 (1910), holding (per Justice Holmes) that the privilege against self-incrimination does not exclude testimony as to the forcible trying on of a blouse. But the case relies on the *Adams* case, and much water has passed under the bridge since then.

[238]It is not readily understandable why the courts should line up as they do on these three closely related questions. Not one of the courts that exclude search and seizure evidence is found among the few that dissent on the other rules, while the dissenters on the arrest question (Kansas and Nebraska) and on the question of showing knowledge by confessions (Louisiana and possibly Georgia) are all among those that *admit* evidence obtained by illegal search and seizure!

[239]*Supra* note 89.

insists, that (unless the indirect remedy is applied) the Constitutional protection "is of no value" and "might as well be stricken from the Constitution", then likewise the common law sanctions for the trespasses of private individuals are "of no value".[240] For the remedy is identical. When a man is illegally arrested, when his home is illegally invaded and his property seized, when the police abuse him in an effort to extort a confession, he is entitled to the same civil remedies as any other person whose rights have been violated. The officer who arrests or searches without a warrant, or who abuses a prisoner, the prosecutor who connives at such acts, and the person who swears out a warrant without probable cause may all be sued for damages, and punitive damages may be awarded.[241] This is the right of innocent and guilty alike, but it is obvious that a jury will not render any substantial verdict against an officer if he is lucky enough to uncover a crime by his unlawful acts. But is it not true that, in actions for damages, an act is always judged by its results? Socially speaking, the criminal whose crime is revealed has not suffered the same damages as the law-abiding citizen who has been subjected to the indignities of an arrest and a search of his home.[242] When a man who later proves to be guilty is arrested or searched, the jury may render a small verdict (if any), which will have little effect in discouraging the officers, although it may cover all the socially recognized damage suffered by the victim.[243] But when the rights of an innocent man are wilfully violated by police and prosecutors, it is not to be supposed that jurors are so lacking in respect for the sanctity of personal liberty that they will not do adequate justice and make the offender regret his acts so that he will seriously consider a change in policy.[244]

But, unfortunately, few police officers accumulate very substantial fortunes, and judgments against them may avail little. Garnishment of the government

---

[240]See State v. Dillon, 34 N. M. 366, 370, 281 Pac. 474, 476 (1929).

[241]The clasic cases are Entick v. Carrington, 19 How. St. Tr. 1029, 95 Eng. Rep. 807 (1765); Wilkes v. Wood, 19 How. St. Tr. 1153, 98 Eng. Rep. 489 (1763); Leach v. Money, 19 How. St. Tr. 1001 (1765). The largest verdict in these cases was one for £5000 against Lord Halifax, who issued the illegal warrants.

See also Snead v. Bonnoil, 166 N. Y. 325, 59 N. E. 899 (1901) ($500 verdict against officer making an illegal arrest upheld); Johnson v. Comstock, 14 Hun 238 (1878) (officer protected by warrant fair on its face, but person who swore out search warrant without cause held liable for $1000 punitive damages).

[242]"He who has voluntarily made his home a den of thieves, a distillery for the manufacture of contraband liquor, a warehouse for infernal machines, or a safety deposit box for forged documents or counterfeit coins, *has not sustained the same damages* when its sanctity is invaded, as has the citizen who has maintained that sanctity." Massantonio v. People, 77 Colo. 392, 236 Pac. 1019, 1021 (1925) (italics supplied).

[243]At least eighteen states have gone so far as to say that an arrest is not unlawful at all if it develops that the one arrested has committed a felony, even though the arresting officer was ignorant of it at the time. See *supra* note 46.

[244]"We do not know whether the public, represented by its juries, is today more indifferent to its liberties than it was when the immunity was born." Cardozo, J., in People v. Defore, 242 N. Y. 13, 24, 150 N. E. 585, 589 (1926).

by which they are employed is generally not allowed, in the absence of special statutory provision.[245] The government cannot be sued for the tort of a police officer or prosecutor, for their duties are governmental and the rule of *respondeat superior* does not apply.[246] Where official bonds are required to be filed, there is a possibility of an action on the bond, but strict construction of the bonds and narrow views as to the parties for whose benefit the bond was given have generally frustrated such action.[247]

We must devise more effective means of enforcing civil judgments against the officers, by garnishment or otherwise.[248] An overhauling of official bonds and the statutes relating thereto might give a more valuable remedy; the terms of the bonds might well be adjusted so that the officer will be indemnified for violations in good faith but will bear the ultimate liability, to the limit of his means, if he wilfully violates the law.[249] This would make possible reparation to the victim of the wrong in all cases, would discourage officers from committing wilful wrongs, but would not compel them to act at their peril in performing their duties in good faith.

An alternative would be to provide a remedy against the government by which the officer is employed.[250] Difficulties might be encountered with principles of agency, unless the remedial law were so expressed as to assume responsibility for acts in excess of authority. This would provide reparation, but it would hardly discourage the officer, for there would be a tendency for the government to absorb the loss and not pass it on to the offending officer or prosecutor. A private bondsman would feel no such inhibitions and the cost of wilful law violation would fall where it should.

The individual wronged has a right, in addition, to sue for the return of his property, whether it was lawfully or unlawfully seized. But if it is held

---

[245]6 McQUILLIN, MUNICIPAL CORPORATIONS (2d ed. 1937) § 2681; Hall, *The Law of Arrest in Relation to Contemporary Social Problems* (1936) 3 U. OF CHI. L. REV. 345, 346-7. See cases cited in both sources.

[246]6 McQUILLIN, *op. cit. supra* note 245, § 2591; Borchard, *Government Liability in Tort* (1925) 34 YALE L. J. 229, 240-1; David, *Municipal Liability in Tort in California* (1934) 7 SO. CAL. L. REV. 295, 302-4; Hall, *loc. cit. supra* note 245 at 347-8; (1925) 11 VA. L. REV. 315. Recovery has been allowed in Canada. McSorley v. City of St. John, 6 Can. Sup. Ct. 531 (1881).

[247]It is not the purpose of this article to go deeply into these matters. For a full discussion, see Hall, *loc. cit. supra* note 245 at 346-53. In general, where the abuse is most flagrant—arrest without process—the officer is held to be acting individually and his bondsman is not liable. 6 McQUILLIN, *op. cit. supra* note 245, § 2592.

[248]Some states, by statute, permit garnishment of their salaries. ARIZ. REV. CODE (Courtright Supp. 1934) §§ 4277 a-e; COLO. STAT. ANN. (Michie 1935), CODE CIV. PROC. C. 7, §§ 131-132 A.

[249]Combining, that is, some features of both liability insurance, in which the bondsman would bear the loss, and a surety bond, in which he recovers over against the officer.

[250]See N. Y. CT. CLAIMS ACT § 12-a (waiver of immunity by state for torts of officers). *Cf.* Matter of Evans v. Berry, 262 N. Y. 61, 186 N. E. 203 (1933) (New York City ordinance authorizing Board of Estimate to make awards, in its discretion, to those injured by police in making arrests; held constitutional as recognition of a moral obligation, not a gratuity; but it rests upon grace and does not confer legal right to compel compensation).

in good faith to be used as evidence in a criminal proceeding, the individual's right of possession is postponed until the needs of justice are satisfied.[251] He may at once recover whatever property is not found by the court to be of evidentiary value, but must await the final disposition of the case before he can recover the balance (except under the federal rule, where his possessory right is made superior to the requirements of criminal justice unless the original seizure was proper).

The criminal penalties which are provided for oppressive acts of enforcement officers are often, on paper, very severe.[252] But prosecutions are rare.[253] The problem, therefore, is to translate the paper remedy into effective actuality. In all too many cases, the acts of which the officer is guilty were done in pursuance of the established policy of the enforcement office, and it is not to be expected that the prosecutor will proceed against him under such circumstances. But a study should be made of the possibility of devising some summary proceeding in the nature of contempt, in which the court would take the initiative, upon affidavits of the offended party calling the wrong to its attention, and upon a hearing of the officer, without the intervention of the prosecutor.[254] There would be procedural questions to be

---

[251]United States v. Wilson, 163 Fed. 338 (C. C. S. D. N. Y. 1908); State v. Magnano, 97 Conn. 543, 117 Atl. 550 (1922); Azparren v. Ferrel, 44 Nev. 157, 191 Pac. 571 (1920); Simpson v. St. John, 93 N. Y. 363 (1883); Smith v. Jerome, 42 Misc. 22, 93 N. Y. Supp. 202 (Sup. Ct. 1905) (Gaynor, J.); Welchek v. State, 93 Tex. Cr. 271, 247 S. W. 524 (1922).

[252]Arrests and seizures without a warrant (or justification for acting without one), and abuse of authority in executing a warrant are misdemeanors in New York. PENAL LAW §§ 1846, 1847. The maximum penalty is one year in jail, $500 fine, or both. PENAL LAW § 1937.

For searches (without a warrant) of private dwellings (or of any other property if done maliciously and without probable cause), the federal law provides $1000 maximum fine; and for a second offense, the same fine or a year in jail, or both. 18 U. S. C. A. § 53a (Supp. 1938). For exceeding authority in executing a warrant, $1000 fine or one year or both. 18 U. S. C. A. § 631 (1927).

Wire-tapping by any person, including a federal or state officer, is now a federal felony punishable by a maximum fine of $10,000 or two years in jail, or both. 47 U. S. C. A. §§ 501, 605 (Supp. 1938).

Unlawful arrest abroad and return to this country without extradition was held to be a kidnapping, irrespective of its purpose to return the fugitive to justice, and extradition of the offending officer to Mexico for prosecution for this offense was allowed in Villareal v. Hammond, 74 F. (2d) 503 (C. C. A. 5th 1934). By Statute in New York, it is further made a felony for an officer of this state to *turn a man over* to the agents of another state, even under a valid extradition warrant, until he has first been taken before a court, been informed of the charges and of his rights, and been given an opportunity to contest the legality of the proceeding if he will. N. Y. CODE CRIM. PROC. §§ 838, 839; UNIFORM CRIMINAL EXTRADITION ACT §§ 10, 11 (see *infra* note 268 for states which have adopted this act). A mandatory one-year sentence is provided.

[253]In State v. Wagstaff, 115 S. C. 198, 105 S. E. 283 (1920), a police officer, and the chief who stood by, were convicted of criminal assault for seizing a grip and searching it unlawfully. This is probably an unusual case; and the punishment decreed is not stated in the report.

Annotations to the statutes imposing such penalties are conspicuous by their absence.

[254]For an illustration of the use of the contempt procedure where practical reasons make criminal punishment impossible, see United States v. Shipp, 203 U. S. 563, 27

determined, as to just what formalities and safeguards would be desired. And, while abuses in the execution of warrants of the court are probably within the constitutional scope of contempt of court,[255] arrests and searches without any warrant would seem not to be (despite one dictum suggesting the contrary[256]). The question would then have to be studied whether this summary proceeding, without formal indictment or information, could constitutionally be applied to such acts by means of a statutory implication of a waiver of this guaranty by persons becoming or continuing members of the police force.

Probably a fine would be more effective than imprisonment as a remedy, in any case, for if a sentence were imposed, there are "very serious doubts whether the marshall would ever be compelled to live upon jail fare".[257] It should be provided in that event that the fine imposed might not be paid directly or indirectly from the budget of the enforcement office.

Another effective remedy, if means can be devised for enforcing it independently of the prosecutor's control, would be forfeiture of the office or employment of anyone, from the prosecutor on down, who wilfully and habitually engages in illegal practices, and ineligibility for later election or employment in the enforcement office.[258] But how this may be enforced is a problem that would require study. We can only pose the problems. The Legislature might better study these problems than seek to provide "indirect remedies" of doubtful effectiveness and propriety.

But there is one type of "indirect remedy" that is to be encouraged. That is to strike at the very roots of the problem and remove some of the causes of illegal enforcement, particularly with respect to arrest. We need a realistic reappraisal of long outmoded rules as to arrest.[259] When it is recognized just what arrests represent true abuses of the police power, it will be more

Sup. Ct. 165 (1906); s. c., 214 U. S. 386, 29 Sup. Ct. 637 (1909) (original contempt proceeding in Supreme Court against leaders of mob which lynched prisoner after Supreme Court had granted an appeal).

[255] *Cf.* United States v. Hoffman, 13 F. (2d) 269 (N. D. Ill. 1925), *aff'd,* 13 F. (2d) 278 (C. C. A. 7th 1926); Westbrook v. United States, 13 F. (2d) 280 (C. C. A. 7th 1926). In these cases, the sheriff to whom federal prisoners had been committed under a court order, and the jailer (although acting under the sheriff's orders), were adjudged guilty of a contempt in permitting the prisoners to leave the jail. It would seem that improper execution of a search warrant or of a warrant of arrest would fall in the same category. And see *In re* Chin K. Shue, 199 Fed. 282 (D. Mass. 1912), which implies that such a remedy would be available except that the offenders there were customs officers executing a warrant issued by the revenue commissioner and not by the court.

[256] See State v. Reynolds, 101 Conn. 224, 238, 125 Atl. 636, 640 (1924).

[257] Hall, *Evidence and the Fourth Amendment* (1922) 8 A. B. A. J. 646, 647.

[258] The exclusion camp in the late Constitutional Convention, as a dying gesture or perhaps as a test of the good faith of their opponents, proposed such an amendment but it was defeated on the ground that it was a matter for the Legislature to decide. Convention Record (N. Y. 1938) 620.

[259] See articles cited *supra* notes 4 and 186.

possible to cope with the problem, and the present too general contempt of the police for the rules may be overcome.

In the field of interstate crime, much progress has been made toward the ideal of "free trade" in criminals.[260] The Uniform Fresh Pursuit Act, adopted in at least half the states,[261] permits officers of another state, provided it makes reciprocal provisions, to continue a close pursuit over a state line after a fleeing felon and to have the same authority to make the arrest that a local officer would have if the crime had been committed in his own state, provided the captive is taken immediately before a magistrate to determine, not his guilt or innocence, but the lawfulness of the arrest. But it is still necessary to obtain extradition, except that New York, as to the states which make reciprocal provisions, permits immediate removal after the hearing before the magistrate, eliminating extradition entirely in the case of close pursuit.[262] This is a step in the right direction, for the simpler the extradition process is made, preserving its safeguards but eliminating the "red tape", the less the temptation to ignore it entirely. The permission to out-of-state officers to make arrests would have shocked an earlier age, when such acts were looked upon as little short of an armed invasion. Today, when criminals range freely among the states, we must give "full faith and credit" to the officers of our neighbors, provided they do what they would have to do at home, take the prisoner at once before a magistrate.

An attack on the same problem from another angle has been made by Congress in the Fleeing Felon Law,[263] which makes it a federal offense to travel in interstate commerce with intent to avoid prosecution for certain named felonies.[264] Thus, the renowned "G-Men" take up at the state line the chase of those wanted for the more serious crimes. The statute provides for trial where the original crime was alleged to have been committed, so, by the process of removal from one federal judicial district to another, much simpler and more certain than extradition,[265] the fugitive is returned to

[260]See Osler, J., in *In re* Parker, 9 Ont. Prac. R. 332, 335 (1882).

[261]See (1938) 38 COL. L. REV. 705. The Act was not proposed by the Commissioners on Uniform Laws, but by the Interstate Commission on Crime, and hence the text is not found in the U. L. A.

[262]N. Y. CODE CRIM. PROC. § 860, adopted in 1936. No states making reciprocal provisions have been found, however. New York also broadened the act as to crimes covered —all acts which are crimes under our laws, rather than just felonies.

The same result has been achieved by interstate compact, under the permission of Congress, 18 U. S. C. A. § 420 (Supp. 1938), among Colorado, New Mexico, and Wyoming, permitting each other's officers to arrest fugitives with no formalities but their own authority, waiving all requirements of extradition. Although Kansas did not accept this part of the compact, the full text is found in KANS. GEN. STAT. (1935) § 62-2503.

[263]18 U. S. C. A. § 408c (Supp. 1938), 48 STAT. 782 (1934).

[264]Murder, kidnapping, burglary, robbery, mayhem, rape, assault with a dangerous weapon, or extortion accompanied by threats of violence, or attempt to commit any of these crimes.

[265]18 U. S. C. A. § 591 (1927). Removal between federal districts is very informal.

the state where he is wanted for the original crime. And it is tacitly understood that upon his return he will be turned over to the state authorities for prosecution for the original, more serious offense.[266]

The simplification of interstate arrest under these various statutes—which preserve the safeguard of an immediate hearing where the accused is found—removes much of the temptation to unlawful arrests in other states. Another major temptation, resulting from the non-extraditability of those who were not in the state where the crime was consummated, has been attacked from two angles. Under the leadership of Wisconsin[267] and the sponsorship of the Commissioners on Uniform State Laws,[268] the gap in the Constitution has been filled by state statutes providing for the extradition of non-fugitives. Thus, the man who shoots across the state line or defrauds another without entering the state may be returned under the forms of law and is no longer granted an immunity that could be overcome only by kidnapping him. Alternatively, or in addition, some statutes now provide that where a force is set in motion or a duty omitted, within the state, which results in the consummation of a crime in another state, it is punishable in the former state just as if the whole crime had been completed there.[269] Thus, the

---

The prisoner is identified as the person named in a federal indictment, and the district judge signs a removal order, the indictment itself being *prima facie* evidence that the prisoner is charged with crime in another state.

[266]See United States v. McClure, 15 Fed. Supp. 931 (E. D. Tenn. 1936). On the constitutionality of the Act, see Brabner-Smith, *The Commerce Clause and the New Federal "Extradition" Statute* (1934) 29 ILL. L. REV. 335. The practice of removal to the jurisdiction for a federal offense followed by trial in the state court for another crime was justified by analogy to the *Lascelles* case, *supra* note 25, in *In re* Little, 129 Mich. 454, 89 N. W. 38, 57 L. R. A. 295 (1902).

[267]L. 1919, c. 559. Wisconsin modified its statute in accordance with the Uniform Act in 1933. WIS. STAT. (1933) § 364.06.

[268]UNIFORM CRIMINAL EXTRADITION ACT § 6, adopted in Alabama, Arkansas, Arizona, California, Delaware, Idaho, Indiana, Kansas, Maine, Maryland, Massachusetts, Montana, Nebraska, New Hampshire, New Jersey, New Mexico, New York, North Carolina, Ohio, Oregon, Pennsylvania, South Dakota, Utah, Vermont, West Virginia, Wisconsin, Wyoming. But New York, to protect residents who had not been in the demanding state, added a proviso that the crime charged must be such as would be a crime under its own laws and that the Governor may, in his discretion, make the surrender conditional on the granting of immunity from prosecution for other crimes until the prisoner has had an opportunity to leave after aquittal or after serving his term; and its section does not apply to libel. N. Y. CODE CRIM. PROC. § 834. The Uniform Act changes the rule of the *second* case of State v. Hall, 115 N. C. 811 (1899), *supra* note 7.

[269]This changes the rule of the *first* case of State v. Hall, 114 N. C. 909 (1904), *supra* note 7. A pioneer in this regard was California. People v. Botkin, 132 Cal. 231, 64 Pac. 286 (1901) (poisoned candy mailed from California to Delaware, where recipient ate it and died; held to be a murder triable in California). See *e.g.*, ALA. CODE ANN. (Michie 1928) § 4893; CAL. PENAL CODE (Deering 1937) § 27; MICH. COMP. LAWS (1929) § 17126; N. Y. PENAL LAW § 1930; WIS. STAT. (1937) § 353.29. Larremore, *Inadequacy of the Present Federal Statute Regulating Interstate Rendition* (1910) 10 COL. L. REV. 208, n. 2, says that a majority of the states have so provided. Reid, *Interstate Rendition for Extra-Territorial Crimes* (1920) A. B. A. REP. 432, expresses the view that this is the less effective of the two remedies, for those most interested in a prosecution are far away.

absentee criminal, immune from extradition in the absence of special statute, becomes liable to prosecution in the state of his residence.

Perhaps the most effective remedy of all has yet to be mentioned. Law enforcement officers are peculiarly sensitive to the power of the press. When newspapers begin to editorialize on their failure to solve a notorious crime, the police "get on their toes". (Sometimes, in their anxiety to "solve" the crime and placate the clamor of the press, they also get on the toes of innocent victims.) Of late the press has been demanding in editorials that these criminals be released in the face of evidence of their guilt, if the seizure of such evidence was improper. If the newspapers would devote their energies and their facilities to an unbiased investigation of the true situation in illegal enforcement in each city—illegal arrests, search and seizure, and the "third degree"—and would then concentrate on arousing public opinion by turning the white light of publicity on the practices, wherever and if ever they exist, if they would put pressure on prosecutors to cease encouraging such practices and to discharge or discipline offending officers, and if they would tell the public at election time whether the prosecutor has been careless of individual rights and liberties, they could accomplish a great and constructive public service. At present the public may only make its choice between highly dramatized but poorly supported assertions on the one side and categorical denials of the prosecutors on the other.[270] Facts and figures, gathered and presented by newspapers respected for their integrity, and driven home to the public in an active campaign to improve the quality of law enforcement, could do much to end the practices if and where they exist or to still the clamor of the exclusionists if the evil is not all that is claimed.

If these remedies, or some of them, were applied and proved effective, the question of using evidence illegally obtained or of trying the prisoner illegally arrested would seldom arise. But when it did arise, there could be only one answer. The release of one criminal in the face of evidence of his guilt is *never* a *proper* remedy for the wrong of another. If effective direct remedies are devised, as we believe they can be, none can claim that it is a *necessary* remedy. Its indirect effect in discouraging illegal enforcement may—or may not—be of great value. But the consequences to society of releasing accused criminals, not because they have been denied a fair trial but because of the wholly collateral wrong committed in apprehending them

[270] *Cf.* People v. Mummiani, 258 N. Y. 394, 398-403, 180 N. E. 94, 95-98 (1932), in which Judge Lehman (Cardozo, C. J., and Pound, J., concurring) declares that it is the prosecutor's duty to explain the circumstances of the obtaining of a confession and not leave the jury to choose blindly between the highly interested assertions of the accused and the categorical denials of the police. (The case presents an interesting dilemma, for these three judges voted to reverse on this ground, while one, disagreeing on this point, found another error. The case was reversed, four to three, but no majority agreed on any particular error. What was the trial court to do?)

or in discovering their crime, are too great to justify this indirect attack on the problem.

Our conclusion could not be better expressed than in the language of the late Justice Cardozo:

> "The law . . . is sedulous in maintaining for a defendant charged with crime whatever forms of procedure are of the essence of an *opportunity to defend.* Privileges so fundamental as to be inherent in every concept of a fair trial that could be acceptable to the thought of reasonable men will be kept inviolate and inviolable, however crushing may be the pressure of incriminating proof. But justice, though due to the accused, is due to the accuser also. The concept of fairness must not be strained until it is narrowed to a filament. *We must keep the balance true.*"[271]

[271]Snyder v. Massachusetts, 291 U. S. 97, 122, 54 Sup. Ct. 330, 338 (1934) (the case held due process was not denied when defendant was not present at a "view"). Italics the writer's.

COLUMBIA LAW REVIEW

VOL. 82 | OCTOBER 1982 | NO. 6

Carolene Products Revisited*

Lewis F. Powell, Jr.**

I

Columbia honored me with a degree in 1978. I therefore am particularly pleased to be on *our* campus again. I also am proud to join the distinguished company who have given prior Harlan Fiske Stone lectures.

My topic this evening comes from one of Stone's own opinions—or, more precisely, from one of Stone's footnotes: Footnote 4 of the *Carolene Products* case,[1] decided in 1938, in which Stone gave birth to the term "discrete and insular minorities." And may I say at the outset—in an after-dinner talk—that I speak necessarily in generalities, leaving much unsaid.

From today's perspective, *United States v. Carolene Products* seems an unremarkable, even an easy, case. At issue was the constitutionality of a piece of economic regulatory legislation, of a kind now passed routinely by Congress. Writing for the Court, Justice Stone held that the legislation was entitled to a presumption of constitutionality, and that it should be upheld if supported by any rational basis.[2] Under that standard the statute easily withstood review.[3]

Carolene Products retains its fascination solely because of Footnote 4—the most celebrated footnote in constitutional law.[4] In it, Stone reserved for

* With only minor modifications, the text of this article was prepared and delivered as the Harlan Fiske Stone Lecture, Columbia University, New York, New York, May 11, 1982. Its structure and content continue to reflect the occasion and the forum for which it was written.

** Associate Justice, Supreme Court of the United States.

1. United States v. Carolene Products Co., 304 U.S. 144, 152 n. 4 (1938).

2. Id. at 152–54.

3. The statute expressed a congressional prohibition against the interstate shipment of "filled milk" (i.e., skimmed milk mixed with nonmilk fats).

4. Professor Fiss, for example, has termed Footnote 4 of *Carolene Products* "the great and modern charter for ordering the relations between judges and other agencies of government." Fiss, The Supreme Court, 1978 Term—Foreword: The Forms of Justice, 93 Harv. L. Rev. 1, 6 (1979). And, according to Professor Gunther, it has had a "pervasive influence," which can be seen in the two-tiered model of equal protection analysis under which the Court regularly has invalidated legislation involving so-called "suspect classifications." See G. Gunther, Cases and Materials on Constitutional Law 542 (10th ed. 1980). As Professor Gunther's reference suggests, the influence of Footnote 4 cannot be measured accurately by simple enumeration of cases in which it has been cited. Nonetheless, I have counted at least 28 cases in which Footnote 4 has been cited in either a majority, concurring, or dissenting opinion of the Supreme Court.

The scholarly literature on Footnote 4 is voluminous. For a somewhat dated survey of the academic responses, see Ball, Judicial Protection of Powerless Minorities, 59 Iowa L. Rev. 1059, 1060–64 (1974). Much of the recent work has taken the form of responses to *Democracy and Distrust,* Professor John Hart Ely's elaboration of his reading of Footnote 4 into a comprehensive

another day the standard of review appropriate in certain other cases not before the Court. In one short paragraph he noted that it was "unnecessary to consider now" the standard the Court should apply to "legislation which restricts those political processes which can ordinarily be expected to bring about repeal of undesirable legislation." Another paragraph was more provocative. It consisted of a single sentence, broken by a colon, in which Stone first reserved the standard applicable in reviewing "statutes directed at particular religious, . . . or national, . . . or racial minorities . . . ." The reservation, as explained following the colon, was:

> whether prejudice against discrete and insular minorities may be a special condition which tends seriously to curtail the operation of those political processes ordinarily to be relied upon to protect minorities, and which may call for a correspondingly more searching judicial inquiry.[5]

This footnote now is recognized as a primary source of "strict scrutiny" judicial review.[6] Indeed, many scholars think it actually commenced a new era in constitutional law. The footnote also is thought to have provided its own theoretical justification. The theory properly extracted from Footnote 4, as expressed by more than a few prominent scholars, is roughly as follows: The fundamental character of our government is democratic. Our constitution

---

theory of constitutional adjudication. See, e.g., Estreicher, Platonic Guardians of Democracy: John Hart Ely's Role for the Supreme Court in the Constitution's Open Texture, 56 N.Y.U. L. Rev. 547 (1981).

5. Footnote 4 provides in full:

> There may be narrower scope for operation of the presumption of constitutionality when legislation appears on its face to be within a specific prohibition of the Constitution, such as those of the first ten amendments, which are deemed equally specific when held to be embraced within the Fourteenth. See *Stromberg v. California*, 283 U.S. 359, 369-370; *Lovell v. Griffin*, 303 U.S. 444, 452.
>
> It is unnecessary to consider now whether legislation which restricts those political processes which can ordinarily be expected to bring about repeal of undesirable legislation, is to be subjected to more exacting judicial scrutiny under the general prohibitions of the Fourteenth Amendment than are most other types of legislation. On restrictions upon the right to vote, see *Nixon v. Herndon*, 273 U.S. 536; *Nixon v. Condon*, 286 U.S. 73; on restraints upon the dissemination of information, see *Near v. Minnesota ex rel Olson*, 283 U.S. 697, 713-714, 718-720, 722; *Grosjean v. American Press Co.*, 297 U.S. 233; *Lovell v. Griffin*, supra; on interferences with political organizations, see *Stromberg v. California*, supra, 369; *Fiske v. Kansas*, 274 U.S. 380; *Whitney v. California*, 274 U.S. 357, 373-378; *Herndon v. Lowry*, 301 U.S. 242; and see Holmes, J., in *Gitlow v. New York*, 268 U.S. 652, 673; as to prohibition of peaceable assembly, see *DeJonge v. Oregon*, 299 U.S. 353, 365.
>
> Nor need we enquire whether similar considerations enter into the review of statutes directed at particular religious, *Pierce v. Society of Sisters*, 268 U.S. 510, or national, *Meyer v. Nebraska*, 262 U.S. 390; *Bartels v. Iowa*, 262 U.S. 404; *Farrington v. Tokushige*, 273 U.S. 484, or racial minorities, *Nixon v. Herndon*, supra, *Nixon v. Condon*, supra: whether prejudice against discrete and insular minorities may be a special condition, which tends seriously to curtail the operation of those political processes ordinarily to be relied upon to protect minorities, and which may call for a correspondingly more searching judicial inquiry. Compare *McCulloch v. Maryland*, 4 Wheat. 316, 428; *South Carolina v. Barnwell Bros.*, 303 U.S. 177, 184 n.2, and cases cited.

304 U.S. at 152-53 n.4.

6. See G. Gunther, supra note 4, at 542.

assumes that majorities should rule and that the government should be able to govern. Therefore, for the most part, Congress and the state legislatures should be allowed to do as they choose. But there are certain groups that cannot participate effectively in the political process. And the political process therefore cannot be trusted to protect these groups in the way it protects most of us. Consistent with these premises, the theory continues, the Supreme Court has two special missions in our scheme of government:

First, to clear away impediments to participation, and ensure that all groups can engage equally in the political process; and

Second, to review with heightened scrutiny legislation inimical to discrete and insular minorities who are unable to protect themselves in the legislative process.

I do not embrace this theory one hundred percent; nor do I condemn it. I do wish to say a few words about the theory, and to suggest that—even when accepted—it leaves open many of the hardest questions of judicial competence faced by courts today.

II

Harlan Fiske Stone stands as one of the great transitional figures in Supreme Court history. Appointed by President Calvin Coolidge in 1925, Stone came to the Court in what scholars now recall as the *Lochner* era,[7] or the era of substantive due process. During this period the Court repeatedly invalidated social welfare legislation passed by Congress and state legislatures. A majority of the Court viewed such legislation as interfering impermissibly with freedom of contract and with traditional rights of liberty and property. Stone, however, disagreed. No judicial activist, Stone generally was reluctant to interfere with legislative decisions. When the Court invalidated legislation, Stone frequently joined the Court's aging giants, Holmes and Brandeis, in dissent.[8]

Unlike Holmes, Stone lived to see—and indeed helped to preside over—the passing of the *Lochner* era. The well-known turning point came in 1937, when the Court upheld the constitutionality of a state miminum wage law for women.[9] *Carolene Products* was an otherwise unremarkable decision in the same line. But Footnote 4, as interpreted by many commentators, represented a radical departure of its own. Far from initiating a jurisprudence of judicial deference to political judgments by the legislature, Footnote 4—on this view—undertook to substitute one activist judicial mission for another. Where once the Court had championed rights of property, now—according to some—it should view its special function as the identification and protection of "dis-

---

7. See Lochner v. New York, 198 U.S. 45 (1905) (invalidating New York's maximum hours law for bakers).

8. See, e.g., Tyson & Bro. v. Banton, 273 U.S. 418 (1927); DiSanto v. Pennsylvania, 273 U.S. 34 (1927).

9. West Coast Hotel Co. v. Parrish, 300 U.S. 379 (1937).

crete and insular minorities." Where the Court before had used the substantive due process clause to protect property rights, now it should use the equal protection clause—a generally forgotten provision that Holmes once dismissed as "the usual last resort of constitutional arguments"[10]—as a sword with which to promote the liberty interests of groups disadvantaged by political decisions.

The difference—or so runs the argument—is that protection of minority rights occurs in the name of correcting defects of *process*, defects that may have prevented minorities from gaining for themselves a fair bargain in the political arena. The theory is that the court—in so protecting minority interests—does not risk imposing its own substantive values and distributive preferences on the Constitution and on the people of the United States.

III

Occasionally I think that Stone should be defended, not from his detractors, but from some of his admirers. Footnote 4 is a fertile starting place for constitutional theory. Generally, it has been a constructive influence in the development of modern constitutional doctrine. But it is not a developed theory in itself. Nor is there reason to think that Stone intended it to be. He did not state that it *was* the special function of the Court to identify and protect "discrete and insular minorities." He merely reserved the question of how the Court should review legislation "directed at" minority groups. The reservation undoubtedly was portentous. Yet, to reserve a question is not necessarily to imply an answer—and certainly not to imply a simplistic answer.

According to Stone's biographer, Professor Alpheus Mason, Stone occasionally liked to use footnotes to spark debate over ideas that he had not developed fully.[11] And, looking only at the footnote itself, it seems quite likely that Stone was doing just this in Footnote 4. Far from suggesting that he had developed a comprehensive theory of constitutional adjudication, Stone's cryptic language frames more questions than it implies answers. What *did* Stone have in mind when he used the phrase "discrete and insular" minorities? What did he mean when he spoke of impediments to their participation in the political process?

The definitional question is not simple. Today interest groups are legion. Yet, in one sense, any group that loses a legislative battle can be regarded as both "discrete" and "insular." It is discrete because it supported or opposed legislation not supported or opposed by the majority. It is insular because it was unable to form coalitions with other groups that would have enabled it to achieve its desired ends through the political process. On this view the drug cult—or for that matter public utilities—could be considered discrete and

10. Buck v. Bell, 274 U.S. 200, 208 (1927).
11. See A. Mason, Harlan Fiske Stone: Pillar of the Law 513 (1956).

insular.[12] But, as the cases cited make clear, these are not the types of groups that Stone had in mind.

As I have mentioned, Stone referred to discrete and insular minorities in a sentence, divided by a colon, in which he had referred earlier to racial, ethnic, and religious groups. Examining the textual evidence only, I think it would be a plausible reading that these are the only kinds of groups to which the term "discrete and insular" was intended to refer. In the normal operation of the political process, the term then would suggest that *some* racial, religious, and ethnic groups are not treated fairly and equally. Courts therefore should apply strict scrutiny to laws "directed at" these disadvantaged groups.

This idea has intuitive appeal, and it has been widely accepted. But it too may require some form of limitation in its application. In our uniquely heterogeneous society there are countless groups with some claim to being racial, ethnic, or religious. Over our history many have been minorities, ineffective in politics, and often discriminated against. But these conditions do not remain static. Immigrant groups that once were neglected have become influential participants in the political process. One reasonably may doubt the capacity of courts to distinguish wisely among them or determine which groups—at a given time and place—operate effectively within our politics. One also must inquire how far a court may go in determining when a law, nondiscriminatory on its face, fairly may be considered as "directed at" a particular group.

The problem is this: in a democratic society there inevitably are both winners and losers. The fact that one group is disadvantaged by a particular piece of legislation, or action of government, therefore does not prove that the process has failed to function properly. To infer otherwise—that the process has been corrupted by invidious discrimination—a judge must have some *substantive* vision of what results the process should have yielded. Otherwise he has no way to know that the process was unfair.

Here I must pause to wonder. If I am correct about the implicit link between a substantive judgment and a malfunction of process, then one may inquire whether we have not returned in some cases to a kind of substantive due process. And one also may wonder what Stone—who had fought so vigorously against substantive due process—would have had to say about this.

IV

As you will have noted, I have raised a number of questions here tonight. You may be relieved to learn that I have no intention of trying to answer them. These are the kinds of questions with which the Court must deal on a regular basis. And as they seem to grow more difficult each year, I have

12. Cf. Sugarman v. Dougall, 413 U.S. 634, 657 (1973) (Rehnquist, J., dissenting) ("Our society, consisting of over 200 million individuals of multitudinous origins, customs, tongues, beliefs, and cultures is, to say the least, diverse. It would hardly take extraordinary ingenuity for a lawyer to find 'insular and discrete' minorities at every turn in the road.").

learned it is a mistake to try to answer the hard ones without the benefit of full briefing and argument and a careful examination of the factual record.

Nonetheless, reflecting on the difficulty of these and similar questions, I can better appreciate Stone's prescience and insight by recalling that these are the kinds of questions that he *reserved*. I am reasonably confident that Stone himself would have had little patience with the suggestion that Footnote 4 provided some neat formula for constitutional adjudication. It was far more his character to deal with legal questions in all their complexity and their inconvenient detail. Dr. Mason has recorded Stone's impatience with an opinion written by Justice Holmes, then almost ninety years of age and nearing retirement. Holmes's analysis, Stone said, read brilliantly; the problem was that it had omitted the most difficult facts and the most troublesome arguments.[13]

Stone was critical because of his relentless honesty, his demand for principle, and his insistence on reckoning with frequently unknowable and intractable social realities. This attitude of judicial mind is Harlan Stone's greatest legacy. And it is in the context of this legacy that I would read Footnote 4—perhaps the most farsighted dictum in our modern judicial heritage. But, after all, it is *dictum* and was intended to be no more.

---

13. See A. Mason, supra note 11, at 327.

California Law Review

VOL. 48 AUGUST 1960 No. 3

Privacy

*William L. Prosser**

IN THE YEAR 1890 Mrs. Samuel D. Warren, a young matron of Boston, which is a large city in Massachusetts, held at her home a series of social entertainments on an elaborate scale. She was the daughter of Senator Bayard of Delaware, and her husband was a wealthy young paper manufacturer, who only the year before had given up the practice of law to devote himself to an inherited business. Socially Mrs. Warren was among the èlite; and the newspapers of Boston, and in particular the *Saturday Evening Gazette*, which specialized in "blue blood" items, covered her parties in highly personal and embarrassing detail. It was the era of "yellow journalism," when the press had begun to resort to excesses in the way of prying that have become more or less commonplace today;[1] and Boston was perhaps, of all of the cities in the country, the one in which a lady and a gentleman kept their names and their personal affairs out of the papers. The matter came to a head when the newspapers had a field day on the occasion of the wedding of a daughter, and Mr. Warren became annoyed.[2] It was an annoyance for which the press, the advertisers and the entertainment industry of America were to pay dearly over the next seventy years.

Mr. Warren turned to his recent law partner, Louis D. Brandeis, who was destined not to be unknown to history. The result was a noted article, *The Right to Privacy*,[3] in the *Harvard Law Review*, upon which the two men collaborated. It has come to be regarded as the outstanding example of the influence of legal periodicals upon the American law. In the Harvard

* Dean, University of California School of Law, Berkeley.

1 "The press is overstepping in every direction the obvious bounds of propriety and of decency. Gossip is no longer the resource of the idle and of the vicious, but has become a trade, which is pursued with industry as well as effrontery. To satisfy a prurient taste the details of sexual relations are spread broadcast in the columns of the daily papers. To occupy the indolent, column upon column is filled with idle gossip, which can only be procured by intrusion upon the domestic circle. The intensity and complexity of life, attendant upon advancing civilization, have rendered necessary some retreat from the world, and man, under the refining influence of culture, has become more sensitive to publicity, so that solitude and privacy have become more essential to the individual; but modern enterprise and invention have, through invasions upon his privacy, subjected him to mental pain and distress, far greater than could be inflicted by mere bodily injury." Warren and Brandeis, *The Right to Privacy*, 4 HARV. L. REV. 193, 196 (1890).

2 MASON, BRANDEIS, A FREE MAN'S LIFE 70 (1946).

3 4 HARV. L. REV. 193 (1890).

Law School class of 1877 the two authors had stood respectively second and first, and both of them were gifted with scholarship, imagination, and ability. Internal evidences of style, and the probabilities of the situation, suggest that the writing, and perhaps most of the research, was done by Brandeis; but it was undoubtedly a joint effort, to which both men contributed their ideas.

Piecing together old decisions in which relief had been afforded on the basis of defamation, or the invasion of some property right,[4] or a breach of confidence or an implied contract,[5] the article concluded that such cases were in reality based upon a broader principle which was entitled to separate recognition. This principle they called the right to privacy; and they contended that the growing abuses of the press made a remedy upon such a distinct ground essential to the protection of private individuals against the outrageous and unjustifiable infliction of mental distress. This was the first of a long line of law review discussions of the right of privacy,[6] of which this is to be yet one more. With very few exceptions,[7] the writers have agreed, expressly or tacitly, with Warren and Brandeis.

The article had little immediate effect upon the law. The first case to

---

[4] Woolsey v. Judd, 4 Duer (11 N.Y. Super.) 379, 11 How. Pr. 49 (N.Y. 1855) (publication of private letters); Gee v. Pritchard, 2 Swans. 402, 36 Eng. Rep. 670 (1818) (same); Prince Albert v. Strange, 2 De G. & Sm. 652, 41 Eng. Rep. 1171, 1 Mac. & G. 25, 64 Eng. Rep. 293 (1849) (exhibition of etchings and publication of catalogue).

[5] Yovatt v. Winyard, 1 Jac. & W. 394, 37 Eng. Rep. 425 (1820) (publication of recipes surreptitiously obtained by employee); Abernethy v. Hutchinson, 3 L.J. Ch. 209 (1825) (publication of lectures to class of which defendant was a member); Pollard v. Photographic Co., 40 Ch. D. 345 (1888) (publication of plaintiff's picture made by defendant).

[6] Larremore, *The Law of Privacy*, 12 COLUM. L. REV. 693 (1912); Ragland, *The Right of Privacy*, 17 KY. L.J. 101 (1929); Winfield, *Privacy*, 47 L.Q. REV. 23 (1931); Green, *The Right of Privacy*, 27 ILL. L. REV. 237 (1932); Kacedan, *The Right of Privacy*, 12 B.U.L. REV. 353, 600 (1932); Dickler, *The Right of Privacy*, 70 U.S.L. REV. 435 (1936); Harper & McNeely, *A Re-examination of the Basis for Liability for Emotional Distress*, [1938] WIS. L. REV. 426; Nizer, *The Right of Privacy*, 39 MICH. L. REV. 526 (1941); Feinberg, *Recent Developments in the Law of Privacy*, 48 COLUM. L. REV. 713 (1948); Ludwig, *"Peace of Mind" in 48 Pieces vs. Uniform Right of Privacy*, 32 MINN. L. REV. 734 (1948); Yankwich, *The Right of Privacy*, 27 NOTRE DAME LAW. 429 (1952); Daims, *What Do We Mean by "Right to Privacy,"* 4 S.D.L. REV. 1 (1959).

Also Notes in 8 MICH. L. REV. 221 (1909); 12 COLUM. L. REV. 1 (1912); 43 HARV. L. REV. 297 (1929); 7 N.C.L. REV. 435 (1929); 26 ILL. L. REV. 63 (1931); 81 U. PA. L. REV. 324 (1933); 33 ILL. L. REV. 87 (1938); 13 SO. CAL. L. REV. 81 (1939); 15 TEMP. L.Q. 148 (1941); 25 MINN. L. REV. 619 (1941); 30 CORNELL L.Q. 398 (1945); 48 COLUM. L. REV. 713 (1948); 15 U. CHI. L. REV. 926 (1948); 6 ARK. L. REV. 459 (1952); 38 VA. L. REV. 117 (1952); 28 IND. L.J. 179 (1953); 27 MISS. L.J. 256 (1956); 44 VA. L. REV. 1303 (1958); 31 MISS. L.J. 191 (1960).

The foreign law is discussed in Gutteridge, *The Comparative Law of the Right to Privacy*, 47 L.Q. REV. 203 (1931); Walton, *The Comparative Law of the Right to Privacy*, 47 L.Q. REV. 219 (1931).

[7] O'Brien, *The Right of Privacy*, 2 COLUM. L. REV. 437 (1902); Lisle, *The Right of Privacy (A Contra View)*, 19 KY. L.J. 137 (1931); Notes, 2 COLUM. L. REV. 437 (1902); 64 ALBANY L.J. 428 (1902); 29 LAW NOTES 64 (1925); 43 HARV. L. REV. 297 (1929); 26 ILL. L. REV. 63 (1931).

allow recovery upon the independent basis of the right of privacy was an unreported decision[8] of a New York trial judge, when an actress very scandalously, for those days, appeared upon the stage in tights, and the defendant snapped her picture from a box, and was enjoined from publishing it. This was followed by three reported cases in New York,[9] and one in a federal court in Massachusetts,[10] in which the courts appeared to be quite ready to accept the principle. Progress was brought to an abrupt halt, however, when the Michigan court flatly rejected the whole idea, in a case[11] where a brand of cigars was named after a deceased public figure. In 1902 the question reached the Court of Appeals of New York, in the case of *Roberson v. Rochester Folding Box Co.*[12] in which the defendant made use of the picture of a pulchritudinous young lady without her consent to advertise flour, along with the legend, "The Flour of the Family." One might think that the feebleness of the pun might have been enough in itself to predispose the court in favor of recovery; but in a four-to-three decision, over a most vigorous dissent, it rejected Warren and Brandeis and declared that the right of privacy did not exist, and that the plaintiff was entitled to no protection whatever against such conduct. The reasons offered were the lack of precedent, the purely mental character of the injury, the "vast amount of litigation" that might be expected to ensue, the difficulty of drawing any line between public and private figures, and the fear of undue restriction of the freedom of the press.

The immediate result of the *Roberson* case was a storm of public disapproval, which led one of the concurring judges to take the unprecedented step of publishing a law review article in defense of the decision.[13] In consequence the next New York Legislature enacted a statute[14] making it both a misdemeanor and a tort to make use of the name, portrait or picture of any person for "advertising purposes or for the purposes of trade" without his written consent. This act remains the law of New York, where there have been upwards of a hundred decisions dealing with it. Except as the statute itself limits the extent of the right, the New York decisions are quite

[8] Manola v. Stevens (N.Y. Sup. Ct. 1890), in N.Y. Times, June 15, 18, 21, 1890.

[9] Mackenzie v. Soden Mineral Springs Co., 27 Abb. N. Cas. 402, 18 N.Y.S. 240 (Sup. Ct. 1891) (use of name of physician in advertising patent medicine enjoined); Marks v. Jaffa, 6 Misc. 290, 26 N.Y.S. 908 (Super. Ct. N.Y. City 1893) (entering actor in embarrassing popularity contest); Schuyler v. Curtis, 147 N.Y. 434, 42 N.E. 22 (1895) (erection of statue as memorial to deceased; relief denied only because he was dead).

[10] Corliss v. E. W. Walker Co., 64 Fed. 280 (D. Mass. 1894) (portrait to be inserted in biographical sketch of plaintiff; relief denied because he was a public figure).

[11] Atkinson v. John E. Doherty & Co., 121 Mich. 372, 80 N.W. 285 (1899). The man was dead, and in any case a public figure; and on either ground the same decision would probably result today. See *infra*, text at notes 205, 218–32.

[12] 171 N.Y. 538, 64 N.E. 442 (1902).

[13] O'Brien, *The Right of Privacy*, 2 Colum. L. Rev. 437 (1902).

[14] N.Y. Sess. Laws 1903, ch. 132, §§ 1–2. Now, as amended in 1921, N.Y. Civ. Rights Law, §§ 50–51. Held constitutional in Rhodes v. Sperry & Hutchinson Co., 193 N.Y. 223, 85 N.E. 1097 (1908), *aff'd*, 220 U.S. 502 (1911). See generally, Hofstadter, The Development of the Right of Privacy in New York (1954).

consistent with the common law as it has been worked out in other states, and they are customarily cited in privacy cases throughout the country.

Three years later the supreme court of Georgia had much the same question presented in *Pavesich v. New England Life Insurance Co.*,[15] when the defendant's insurance advertising made use of the plaintiff's name and picture, as well as a spurious testimonial from him. With the example of New York before it, the Georgia court in turn rejected the *Roberson* case, accepted the views of Warren and Brandeis, and recognized the existence of a distinct right of privacy. This became the leading case.

For the next thirty years there was a continued dispute as to whether the right of privacy existed at all, as the courts elected to follow the *Roberson* or the *Pavesich* case. Along in the thirties, with the benediction of the *Restatement of Torts*,[16] the tide set in strongly in favor of recognition, and the rejecting decisions began to be overruled. At the present time the right of privacy, in one form or another, is declared to exist by the overwhelming majority of the American courts. It is recognized in Alabama,[17] Alaska,[18] Arizona,[19] California,[20] Connecticut,[21] the District of Columbia,[22] Florida,[23] Georgia,[24] Illinois,[25] Indiana,[26] Iowa,[27] Kansas,[28] Kentucky,[29] Louisiana,[30]

---

[15] 122 Ga. 190, 50 S.E. 68 (1905).

[16] RESTATEMENT, TORTS § 867 (1939).

[17] Smith v. Doss, 251 Ala. 250, 37 So. 2d 118 (1948); Birmingham Broadcasting Co. v. Bell, 259 Ala. 656, 68 So. 2d 314 (1953), *later appeal,* 266 Ala. 266, 96 So. 2d 263 (1957).

[18] Smith v. Suratt, 7 Alaska 416 (1926).

[19] Reed v. Real Detective Pub. Co., 63 Ariz. 294, 162 P.2d 133 (1945).

[20] Melvin v. Reid, 112 Cal. App. 285, 297 Pac. 91 (1931); Kerby v. Hal Roach Studios, 53 Cal. App. 2d 207, 127 P.2d 577 (1942); Stryker v. Republic Pictures Corp., 108 Cal. App. 2d 191, 238 P.2d 670 (1951); Gill v. Curtis Pub. Co., 38 Cal. 2d 273, 239 P.2d 630 (1952); Linehan v. Linehan, 134 Cal. App. 2d 250, 285 P.2d 326 (1955); Fairfield v. American Photocopy Equipment Co., 138 Cal. App. 2d 82, 291 P.2d 194 (1955).

[21] Korn v. Rennison, 156 A.2d 476 (Conn. Super. 1959).

[22] Peay v. Curtis Pub. Co., 78 F. Supp. 305 (D.D.C. 1948).

[23] Cason v. Baskin, 155 Fla. 198, 20 So. 2d 243 (1944), *second appeal,* 159 Fla. 31, 30 So. 2d 635 (1947); and see Jacova v. Southern Radio & Television Co., 83 So. 2d 34 (Fla. 1955).

[24] Pavesich v. New England Life Ins. Co., 122 Ga. 190, 50 S.E. 68 (1905); Bazemore v. Savannah Hospital, 171 Ga. 257, 155 S.E. 194 (1930); McDaniel v. Atlanta Coca Cola Bottling Co., 60 Ga. App. 92, 2 S.E.2d 810 (1939); Walker v. Whittle, 83 Ga. App. 445, 64 S.E.2d 87 (1951); Gouldman-Taber Pontiac, Inc. v. Zerbst, 96 Ga. App. 48, 99 S.E.2d 475 (1957).

[25] Eick v. Perk Dog Food Co., 347 Ill. App. 293, 106 N.E.2d 742 (1952); Annerino v. Dell Pub. Co., 17 Ill. App. 2d 205, 149 N.E.2d 761 (1958).

[26] Continental Optical Co. v. Reed, 119 Ind. App. 643, 86 N.E.2d 306 (1949). See also Estill v. Hearst Pub. Co., 186 F.2d 1017 (7th Cir. 1951).

[27] Bremmer v. Journal-Tribune Co., 247 Iowa 817, 76 N.W.2d 762 (1956).

[28] Kunz v. Allen, 102 Kan. 883, 172 Pac. 532 (1918). See also Johnson v. Boeing Airplane Co., 175 Kan. 275, 262 P.2d 808 (1953).

[29] Foster-Milburn Co. v. Chinn, 134 Ky. 424, 120 S.W. 364 (1909); Douglas v. Stokes, 149 Ky. 506, 149 S.W. 849 (1912); Brents v. Morgan, 221 Ky. 765, 299 S.W. 967 (1927); Rhodes v. Graham, 238 Ky. 225, 37 S.W.2d 46 (1931); Trammell v. Citizens News Co., 285 Ky. 529, 148 S.W.2d 708 (1941).

[30] Itzkovitch v. Whitaker, 115 La. 479, 39 So. 499 (1905); Schwartz v. Edrington, 133 La. 235, 62 So. 660 (1913); Hamilton v. Lumbermen's Mut. Cas. Co., 82 So. 2d 61 (La. App. 1955); Souder v. Pendleton Detectives, 88 So. 2d 716 (La. App. 1956).

Michigan,[31] Mississippi,[32] Missouri,[33] Montana,[34] Nevada,[35] New Jersey,[36] North Carolina,[37] Ohio,[38] Oregon,[39] Pennsylvania,[40] South Carolina,[41] Tennessee,[42] and West Virginia.[43] It will in all probability be recognized in Delaware[44] and Maryland,[45] where a federal and a lower court have accepted it; and also in Arkansas,[46] Colorado,[47] Massachusetts,[48] Minnesota,[49] and Washington,[50] where the courts at least have refrained from holding

---

31 Pallas v. Crowley, Milner & Co., 322 Mich. 411, 33 N.W.2d 911 (1948).

32 Martin v. Dorton, 210 Miss. 668, 50 So. 2d 391 (1951). See Note, 27 MISS. L.J. 256 (1956).

33 Munden v. Harris, 153 Mo. App. 652, 134 S.W. 1076 (1911); Barber v. Time, Inc., 348 Mo. 1199, 159 S.W.2d 291 (1942); State *ex rel.* Clemens v. Witthaus, 228 S.W.2d 4 (Mo. 1950); Biederman's of Springfield, Inc. v. Wright, 322 S.W.2d 892 (Mo. 1959).

34 Welsh v. Pritchard, 125 Mont. 517, 241 P.2d 816 (1952).

35 Norman v. City of Las Vegas, 64 Nev. 38, 177 P.2d 442 (1947).

36 Vanderbilt v. Mitchell, 72 N.J. Eq. 910, 67 Atl. (Ct. Err. & App. 1907); Edison v. Edison Polyform Mfg. Co., 73 N.J. Eq. 136, 67 Atl. 392 (Ch. 1907); Frey v. Dixon, 141 N.J. Eq. 481, 58 A.2d 86 (Ch. 1948); Ettore v. Philco Television Broadcasting Co., 229 F.2d 481 (3d Cir. 1956).

37 Flake v. Greensboro News Co., 212 N.C. 780, 195 S.E. 55 (1938).

38 Friedman v. Cincinnati Local Joint Exec. Board, 6 Ohio Supp. 276, 20 Ohio Op. 473 (C.P. 1941); Housh v. Peth, 165 Ohio St. 35, 133 N.E.2d 340 (1956).

39 Hinish v. Meier & Frank Co., 166 Ore. 482, 113 P.2d 438 (1941).

40 Clayman v. Bernstein, 38 Pa. D. & C. 543 (C.P. 1940); Bennett v. Norban, 396 Pa. 94, 151 A.2d 476 (1959); Aquino v. Bulletin Co., 154 A.2d 422 (Pa. Super. 1959); Jenkins v. Dell Pub. Co., 251 F.2d 447 (3d Cir. 1958).

41 Holloman v. Life Ins. Co. of Va., 192 S.C. 454, 7 S.E.2d 169 (1940); Meetze v. Associated Press, 230 S.C. 330, 95 S.E.2d 606 (1956); Frith v. Associated Press, 176 F. Supp. 671 (E.D.S.C. 1959).

42 Langford v. Vanderbilt University, 199 Tenn. 389, 287 S.W.2d 32 (1956).

43 Roach v. Harper, 105 S.E.2d 564 (W. Va. 1958); Sutherland v. Kroger Co., 110 S.E.2d 716 (W. Va. 1959).

44 Miller v. National Broadcasting Co., 157 F. Supp. 240 (D. Del. 1957).

45 Graham v. Baltimore Post Co., (Baltimore Super. Ct. 1932), reported in 22 KY. L.J. 108 (1933).

46 Mabry v. Kettering, 89 Ark. 551, 117 S.W. 746 (1909), *second appeal,* 92 Ark. 81, 122 S.W. 115 (1909).

47 Fitzsimmons v. Olinger Mortuary Ass'n, 91 Colo. 544, 17 P.2d 535 (1932); McCreery v. Miller's Grocerteria Co., 99 Colo. 499, 64 P.2d 803 (1936). In the last named case the dissent indicates that an opinion recognizing the right of privacy was written, but withdrawn.

48 Marek v. Zanol Products Co., 298 Mass. 1, 9 N.E.2d 393 (1937); Thayer v. Worcester Post Pub. Co., 284 Mass. 160, 187 N.E. 292 (1933); Themo v. New England Newspaper Pub. Co., 306 Mass. 54, 27 N.E.2d 753 (1940). In Wright v. R.K.O. Radio Pictures, 55 F. Supp. 639 (D. Mass. 1944), the court considered that the state had rejected the right of privacy; but in Kelley v. Post Pub. Co., 327 Mass. 275, 98 N.E.2d 286 (1951), the question was said to be still open. See also Hazlitt v. Fawcett Publications, 116 F. Supp. 538 (D. Conn. 1953).

49 Berg v. Minneapolis Star & Tribune Co. 79 F. Supp. 957 (D. Minn. 1948). See also Hazlitt v. Fawcett Publications, 116 F. Supp. 538 (D. Conn. 1953).

50 In Hillman v. Star Pub. Co., 64 Wash. 691, 117 Pac. 594 (1911), the right of privacy was rejected, and said to be a matter for legislation. In State *ex rel.* La Follette v. Hinkle, 131 Wash. 86, 229 Pac. 317 (1924), it was apparently recognized; but in Lewis v. Physicians & Dentists Credit Bureau, 27 Wash. 2d 267, 177 P.2d 896 (1947), the question was said to be

that it does not exist, but the decisions have gone off on other grounds. It is recognized in a limited form by the New York statute,[51] and by similar acts adopted in Oklahoma,[52] Utah,[53] and Virginia.[54]

At the time of writing the right of privacy stands rejected only by a 1909 decision in Rhode Island,[55] and by more recent ones in Nebraska,[56] Texas,[57] and Wisconsin,[58] which have said that any change in the old common law must be for the legislature, and which have not gone without criticism.

In nearly every jurisdiction the first decisions were understandably preoccupied with the question whether the right of privacy existed at all, and gave little or no consideration to what it would amount to if it did. It is only in recent years, and largely through the legal writers, that there has been any attempt to inquire what interests are we protecting, and against what conduct. Today, with something over three hundred cases in the books,

---

still open in Washington. See also Hazlitt v. Fawcett Publications, 116 F. Supp. 538 (D. Conn. 1953).

Writers have added South Dakota and Wyoming. Davis, *What Do We Mean by "Right to Privacy,"* 4 S.D.L. Rev. 1 (1959), considers that rather vague constitutional provisions in South Dakota will lead to recognition of the right; and the Note, 11 Wyo. L.J. 184 (1957), believes that the same result may follow on the basis of the Wyoming constitutional provision that truth is a defense to libel.

[51] See *supra,* note 14.

[52] Okla. Stat. Ann. tit. 21, §§ 839–40 (1958). Before the statute there were numerous indications that Oklahoma would recognize the right of privacy without it. Bartholomew v. Workman, 197 Okl. 267, 169 P.2d 1012 (1946); McKinzie v. Huckaby, 112 F. Supp. 642 (W.D. Okl. 1953); Lyles v. State, 330 P.2d 734 (Okl. Cr. 1958); Paramount Pictures v. Leader Press, 24 F. Supp. (W.D. Okl. 1938), *rev'd on other grounds* in 106 F.2d 229 (10th Cir. 1939; Banks v. King Features Syndicate, 30 F. Supp. 352 (S.D.N.Y. 1939, Oklahoma law); Hazlitt v. Fawcett Publications, 116 F. Supp. 538 (D. Conn. 1953, Oklahoma law). The Note in 10 Okl. L. Rev. 353 (1957), considers that there is still some doubt as to whether the common law right may not be recognized, in addition to the statutory one. The New York statute has been held to be exclusive. Kimmerle v. New York Evening Journal Co., 262 N.Y. 99, 186 N.E. 217 (1933).

[53] Utah Code Ann. §§ 76–4–8 and 76–4–9 (1953).

[54] Va. Code Ann. § 8–650 (1957). See Notes, 38 Va. L. Rev. 117 (1952); 44 Va. L. Rev. 1303 (1958).

[55] Henry v. Cherry & Webb, 30 R.I. 13, 73 Atl. 97 (1909).

[56] Brunson v. Ranks Army Store, 161 Neb. 519, 73 N.W.2d 803 (1955). See also Schnieding v. American Farmers Mut. Ins. Co., 138 F. Supp. 167 (D. Neb. 1955).

[57] Milner v. Red River Valley Pub. Co., 249 S.W.2d 227 (Tex. Civ. App. 1952); McCullagh v. Houston Chronicle Pub. Co., 211 F.2d 4 (5th Cir. 1954). See Seavey, *Can Texas Courts Protect Newly Discovered Interests,* 31 Texas L. Rev. 309 (1953).

[58] Judevine v. Benzies-Montanye Fuel & Warehouse Co., 222 Wis. 512, 269 N.W. 295 (1936); State *ex rel.* Distenfeld v. Neelen, 255 Wis. 214, 38 N.W.2d 703 (1949); see Note, [1952] Wis. L. Rev. 507. The last decision, in Yoeckel v. Samonig, 272 Wis. 430, 75 N.W.2d 925 (1956), involved a particularly outrageous invasion, when the defendant intruded into a ladies' rest room, photographed the plaintiff there, and exhibited the picture to patrons in a restaurant. The court bowed to the fact that a bill providing for the right of privacy had failed to pass in the last legislature. The case is nevertheless an atrocity.

the holes in the jigsaw puzzle have been largely filled in, and some rather definite conclusions are possible.

What has emerged from the decisions is no simple matter. It is not one tort, but a complex of four. The law of privacy comprises four distinct kinds of invasion of four different interests of the plaintiff, which are tied together by the common name, but otherwise have almost nothing in common except that each represents an interference with the right of the plaintiff, in the phrase coined by Judge Cooley,[59] "to be let alone." Without any attempt to exact definition, these four torts may be described as follows:

1. Intrusion upon the plaintiff's seclusion or solitude, or into his private affairs.
2. Public disclosure of embarrassing private facts about the plaintiff.
3. Publicity which places the plaintiff in a false light in the public eye.
4. Appropriation, for the defendant's advantage, of the plaintiff's name or likeness.

It should be obvious at once that these four types of invasion may be subject, in some respects at least, to different rules; and that when what is said as to any one of them is carried over to another, it may not be at all applicable, and confusion may follow.

The four may be considered in detail, in order.

I

INTRUSION

Warren and Brandeis, who were concerned with the evils of publication, do not appear to have had in mind any such thing as intrusion upon the plaintiff's seclusion or solitude. Nine years before their article was published there had been a Michigan case[60] in which a young man had intruded upon a woman in childbirth, and the court, invalidating her consent because of fraud, had allowed recovery without specifying the ground, which may have been trespass or battery. In retrospect, at least, this was a privacy case. Others have followed, in which the defendant has been held liable for intruding into the plaintiff's home,[61] his hotel room,[62] and a woman's stateroom on a steamboat,[63] and for an illegal search of her shopping bag in a store.[64] The privacy action which has been allowed in such cases will evi-

[59] COOLEY, TORTS 29 (2d ed. 1888).

[60] De May v. Roberts, 46 Mich. 160, 9 N.W. 146 (1881).

[61] Young v. Western & A. R. Co., 39 Ga. App. 761, 148 S.E. 414 (1929) (search without warrant); Walker v. Whittle, 83 Ga. App. 445, 64 S.E.2d 87 (1951) (entry without legal authority to arrest husband); Welsh v. Pritchard, 125 Mont. 517, 241 P.2d 816 (1952) (landlord moving in on tenant).

[62] Newcomb Hotel Co. v. Corbett, 27 Ga. App. 365, 108 S.E. 309 (1921).

[63] Byfield v. Candler, 33 Ga. App. 275, 125 S.E. 905 (1924).

[64] Sutherland v. Kroger Co., 110 S.E.2d 716 (W. Va. 1959).

dently overlap, to a considerable extent at least, the action for trespass to land or chattels.

The principle was, however, soon carried beyond such physical intrusion. It was extended to eavesdropping upon private conversations by means of wire tapping[65] and microphones;[66] and there are three decisions,[67] the last of them aided by a Louisiana criminal statute, which have applied the same principle to peering into the windows of a home. The supreme court of Ohio, which seems to be virtually alone among our courts in refusing to recognize the independent tort of the intentional infliction of mental distress by outrageous conduct,[68] has accomplished the same result[69] under the name of privacy, in a case where a creditor hounded the debtor for a considerable length of time with telephone calls at his home and his place of employment.[70] The tort has been found in the case of unauthorized prying into the plaintiff's bank account,[71] and the same principle has been used to invalidate a blanket subpoena duces tecum requiring the production of all of his books and documents,[72] and an illegal compulsory blood test.[73]

It is clear, however, that there must be something in the nature of prying or intrusion, and mere noises which disturb a church congregation,[74] or bad manners, harsh names and insulting gestures in public,[75] have been held not to be enough. It is also clear that the intrusion must be

---

65 Rhodes v. Graham, 238 Ky. 225, 37 S.W.2d 46 (1931).

66 McDaniel v. Atlanta Coca Cola Bottling Co., 60 Ga. App. 92, 2 S.E.2d 810 (1939); Roach v. Harper, 105 S.E.2d 564 (W. Va. 1958). The same conclusion was reached, on the basis of a criminal statute, in People v. Trieber, 28 Cal. 2d 657, 163 P.2d 492, 171 P.2d 1 (1946).

67 Moore v. New York Elevated R. Co., 130 N.Y. 523, 29 N.E. 997 (1892) (looking into windows from elevated railway; plaintiff compensated under eminent domain); Pritchett v. Board of Commissioners of Knox County, 42 Ind. App. 3, 85 N.E. 32 (1908) (relief on the basis of nuisance); Souder v. Pendleton Detectives, 88 So. 2d 716 (La. App. 1956) (spying into windows).

This topic gave rise to a possible nomination for the all-time prize law review title, in the Note, *Crimination of Peeping Toms and Other Men of Vision*, 5 Ark. L. Rev. 388 (1951).

68 Bartow v. Smith, 149 Ohio St. 301, 78 N.E.2d 735 (1948).

69 *Cf.* Duty v. General Finance Co., 154 Tex. 16, 273 S.W.2d 64 (1954).

70 House v. Peth, 165 Ohio St. 35, 133 N.E.2d 340 (1956), *affirming* 99 Ohio App. 485, 135 N.E.2d 440 (1955). *Accord,* on the ground of "nuisance," Wiggins v. Moskins Credit Clothing Store, 137 F. Supp. 764 (E.D.S.C. 1956).

71 Brex v. Smith, 104 N.J. Eq. 386, 146 Atl. 34 (Ch. 1929); Zimmerman v. Wilson, 81 F.2d 847 (3d Cir. 1936).

72 Frey v. Dixon, 141 N.J. Eq. 481, 58 A.2d 86 (Ch. 1948); State *ex rel.* Clemens v. Witthaus, 228 S.W.2d 4 (Mo. 1950) (court order).

73 Bednarik v. Bednarik, 18 N.J. Misc. 633, 16 A.2d 80 (Ch. 1940). *Cf.* Hawkins v. Kuhne, 153 App. Div. 216, 137 N.Y.S. 1090 (1912), *aff'd,* 208 N.Y. 555, 101 N.E. 1104 (1913) (illegal photographing and measuring by police called an "assault").

74 Owens v. Henman, 1 W. & S. 548, 37 Am. Dec. 481 (Pa. 1841).

75 Lisowski v. Jaskiewicz, 76 Pa. D. & C. 79 (C.P. 1950); Christie v. Greenleaf, 78 Pa. D. & C. 191 (C.P. 1951).

something which would be offensive or objectionable to a reasonable man, and that there is no tort when the landlord stops by on Sunday morning to ask for the rent.[76]

It is clear also that the thing into which there is prying or intrusion must be, and be entitled to be, private. The plaintiff has no right to complain when his pre-trial testimony is recorded,[77] or when the police, acting within their powers, take his photograph, fingerprints or measurements,[78] or when there is inspection and public disclosure of corporate records which he is required by law to keep and make available.[79] On the public street, or in any other public place, the plaintiff has no right to be alone, and it is no invasion of his privacy to do no more than follow him about.[80] Neither is it such an invasion to take his photograph in such a place,[81] since

---

[76] Horstman v. Newman, 291 S.W.2d 567 (Ky. 1956).

[77] Gotthelf v. Hillcrest Lumber Co., 280 App. Div. 668, 116 N.Y.S.2d 873 (1952).

[78] Voelker v. Tyndall, 226 Ind. 43, 75 N.E.2d 548 (1947); McGovern v. Van Riper, 140 N.J. Eq. 341, 54 A.2d 469 (Ch. 1947), *affirming* 137 N.J. Eq. 548, 45 A.2d 842 (Ct. Err. & App. 1946), *which reversed* 137 N.J. Eq. 24, 43 A.2d 514 (Ch. 1945); State *ex rel.* Mavity v. Tyndall, 224 Ind. 364, 66 N.E.2d 755 (1946); Bartletta v. McFeeley, 107 N.J. Eq. 141, 152 Atl. 17 (Ch. 1930), *aff'd,* 109 N.J. Eq. 241, 156 Atl. 658 (Ct. Err. & App. 1931); Fernicola v. Keenan, 136 N.J. Eq. 9, 39 A.2d 851 (Ch. 1944); Norman v. City of Las Vegas, 64 Nev. 38, 177 P.2d 442 (1947); Mabry v. Kettering, 89 Ark. 551, 117 S.W. 746 (1909), *second appeal,* 92 Ark. 81, 122 S.W. 115 (1909); Hodgeman v. Olson, 86 Wash. 615, 150 Pac. 1122 (1915); *cf.* Sellers v. Henry, 329 S.W.2d 214 (Ky. 1959). As to the use made of police photographs, see *infra,* text at notes 143–45.

In Anthony v. Anthony, 9 N.J. Super. 411, 74 A.2d 919 (Ch. 1950), a compulsory blood test in a paternity suit was held to be justified, and not to invade any right of privacy.

Such cases, of course, usually turn on constitutional rights.

[79] Bowles v. Misle, 64 F. Supp. 835 (D. Neb. 1946); United States v. Alabama Highway Express Co., 46 F. Supp. 450 (D. Ala. 1942); Alabama State Federation of Labor v. McAdory, 246 Ala. 1, 18 So. 2d 810 (1944).

[80] Chappell v. Stewart, 82 Md. 323, 33 Atl. 542 (1896). *Cf.* McKinzie v. Huckaby, 112 F. Supp. 642 (W.D. Okl. 1953), where the defendant, calling at the plaintiff's home, brought along a policeman, who remained outside in the car.

In Schultz v. Frankfort Marine, Accident & Plate Glass Ins. Co., 151 Wis. 537, 139 N.W. 386 (1913), "rough shadowing" which was visible to onlookers, was held to be actionable as slander.

[81] Gill v. Hearst Pub. Co., 40 Cal. 2d 224, 253 P.2d 441 (1953); Berg v. Minneapolis Star & Tribune Co., 79 F. Supp. 957 (D. Minn. 1948) (courtroom); Lyles v. State, 330 P.2d 734 (Okl. Cr. 1958) (television in court). *Cf.* Gautier v. Pro-Football, Inc., 304 N.Y. 354, 107 N.E.2d 485 (1952); Sports & General Press Agency v. "Our Dogs" Pub. Co., [1916] 2 K.B. 880; and cases cited *infra,* note 104. See Fitzpatrick, *Unauthorized Photographs,* 20 GEO. L.J. 134 (1932). In United States v. Gugel, 119 F. Supp. 897 (E.D. Ky. 1954), the right to take such pictures was said to be protected by the Constitution of the United States.

The same type of reasoning, that the record does not differ from a written report, was applied to the recording of a private telephone conversation between plaintiff and defendant, in Chaplin v. National Broadcasting Co., 15 F.R.D. 134 (S.D.N.Y. 1953).

As to publication, see *infra,* text at notes 102–08.

In Friedman v. Cincinnati Local Joint Executive Board, 6 Ohio Supp. 276, 20 Ohio Op. 473 (C.P. 1941), a labor union which had taken pictures of customers crossing a picket line was enjoined from making use of them for purposes of retaliation.

this amounts to nothing more than making a record, not differing essentially from a full written description, of a public sight which any one present would be free to see. On the other hand, when he is confined to a hospital bed,[82] and in all probability when he is merely in the seclusion of his home, the making of a photograph without his consent is an invasion of a private right, of which he is entitled to complain.

It appears obvious that the interest protected by this branch of the tort is primarily a mental one. It has been useful chiefly to fill in the gaps left by trespass, nuisance, the intentional infliction of mental distress, and whatever remedies there may be for the invasion of constitutional rights.

II

PUBLIC DISCLOSURE OF PRIVATE FACTS

Because of its background of personal annoyance from the press, the article of Warren and Brandeis was primarily concerned with the second form of the tort, which consists of public disclosure of embarrassing private facts about the plaintiff. Actually this was rather slow to appear in the decisions. Although there were earlier instances,[83] in which other elements were involved, its first real separate application was in a Kentucky case[84] in 1927, in which the defendant put up a notice in the window of his garage announcing to the world that the defendant owed him money and would not pay it. But the decision which has become the leading case, largely because of its spectacular facts, is *Melvin v. Reid*,[85] in California in 1931. The plaintiff, whose original name was Gabrielle Darley, had been a prostitute, and the defendant in a sensational murder trial. After her acquittal she had abandoned her life of shame, become rehabilitated, married a man named Melvin, and in a manner reminiscent of the plays of Arthur Wing Pinero, had led a life of rectitude in respectable society, among friends and associates who were unaware of her earlier career. Seven years afterward the defendant made and exhibited a motion picture, called "The Red Kimono," which enacted the true story, used the name of Gabrielle Darley, and ruined her new life by revealing her past to the world and her friends. Relying in part upon a vague constitutional provi-

[82] Barber v. Time, Inc., 348 Mo. 1199, 159 S.W.2d 291 (1942). *Cf.* Clayman v. Bernstein, 38 Pa. D. & C. 543 (C.P. 1940) (picture of semi-conscious patient taken by physician).

[83] Douglas v. Stokes, 149 Ky. 506, 149 S.W. 849 (1912) (publication of picture by photographer, breach of implied contract); Thompson v. Adelberg & Berman, 181 Ky. 487, 205 S.W. 558 (1918) (publication of debt, libel); Feeney v. Young, 191 App. Div. 501, 181 N.Y.S. 481 (1920) (exhibition of pictures of caesarian operation, breach of trust and implied contract); Peed v. Washington Times, 55 Wash. L. Rep. 182 (D.C. 1927) (publication of stolen picture).

[84] Brents v. Morgan, 221 Ky. 765, 299 S.W. 967 (1927). "Dr. W. R. Morgan owes an account here of $49.67. And if promises would pay an account this account would have been settled long ago. This account will be advertised as long as it remains unpaid."

[85] 112 Cal. App. 285, 297 Pac. 91 (1931).

sion that all men have the inalienable right of "pursuing and obtaining happiness," which has since disappeared from the California cases, the court held that this was an actionable invasion of her right of privacy.

Other decisions have followed, involving the use of the plaintiff's name in a radio dramatization of a robbery of which he was the victim,[86] and publicity given to his debts,[87] to medical pictures of his anatomy,[88] and to embarrassing details of a woman's masculine characteristics, her domineering tendencies, her habits of profanity, and incidents of her personal conduct toward her friends and neighbors.[89] Some limits, at least, of this branch of the right of privacy appear to be fairly well marked out, as follows:

First, the disclosure of the private facts must be a public disclosure, and not a private one. There must be, in other words, publicity. It is an invasion of the right to publish in a newspaper that the plaintiff does not pay his debts,[90] or to post a notice to that effect in a window on the public street[91] or cry it aloud in the highway;[92] but, except for one decision of a lower Georgia court which was reversed on other grounds,[93] it has been agreed that it is no invasion to communicate that fact to the plaintiff's employer,[94] or to any other individual, or even to a small group,[95] unless

[86] Mau v. Rio Grande Oil, Inc., 28 F. Supp. 845 (N.D. Cal. 1939).

[87] Trammell v. Citizens News Co., Inc., 285 Ky. 529, 148 S.W.2d 708 (1941); Biederman's of Springfield, Inc. v. Wright, 322 S.W.2d 892 (Mo. 1959). *Cf.* Bennett v. Norban, 396 Pa. 94, 151 A.2d 476 (1959).

In Maysville Transit Co. v. Ort, 296 Ky. 524, 177 S.W.2d 369 (1944), it was held that a corporation had no right of privacy, but that there could be recovery for disclosure of its tax returns on the basis of violation of a statute.

[88] Banks v. King Features Syndicate, 30 F. Supp. 352 (S.D.N.Y. 1939) (Oklahoma law; newspaper publication of X-rays of woman's pelvic region); Griffin v. Medical Society, 11 N.Y.S.2d 109 (Sup. Ct. 1939) (publication in medical journal of pictures of plaintiff's deformed nose); Feeney v. Young, 191 App. Div. 501, 181 N.Y.S. 481 (1920) (public exhibition of films of caesarian operation). *Cf.* Clayman v. Bernstein, 38 Pa. D. & C. 543 (C.P. 1940) (doctor enjoined from using pictures of facial disfigurement taken while patient was semi-conscious).

[89] Cason v. Baskin, 155 Fla. 198, 20 So. 2d 243 (1945), *second appeal*, 159 Fla. 31, 30 So. 2d 635 (1947).

[90] Trammell v. Citizens News Co., 285 Ky. 529, 148 S.W.2d 708 (1941). *Cf.* Thompson v. Adelberg & Berman, Inc., 181 Ky. 487, 205 SW. 558 (1918).

[91] Brents v. Morgan, 221 Ky. 765, 299 S.W. 967 (1927).

[92] Bennett v. Norban, 396 Pa. 94, 151 A.2d 476 (1959). *Cf.* Biederman's of Springfield, Inc. v. Wright, 322 S.W.2d 892 (Mo. 1959) (public restaurant).

[93] Gouldman-Taber Pontiac, Inc. v. Zerbst, 96 Ga. App. 48, 99 S.E.2d 475 (1957), *reversed in* 213 Ga. 682, 100 S.E.2d 881 (1957), on the ground that the communication was privileged.

[94] Patton v. Jacobs, 118 Ind. App. 358, 78 N.E.2d 789 (1948); Voneye v. Turner, 240 S.W.2d 588 (Ky. 1951); Lucas v. Moskins Stores, 262 S.W.2d 679 (Ky. 1953); Hawley v. Professional Credit Bureau, Inc., 345 Mich. 500, 76 N.W.2d 835 (1956); Lewis v. Physicians & Dentists Credit Bureau, 27 Wash. 2d 267, 177 P.2d 896 (1947). *Cf.* Davis. v. General Finance & Thrift Corp., 80 Ga. App. 708, 57 SE.2d 225 (1950) (telegram to plaintiff); Perry v. Moskins Stores, 249 S.W.2d 812 (Ky. 1952) (postcard to plaintiff).

[95] Gregory v. Bryan-Hunt Co., 295 Ky. 345, 174 S.W.2d 510 (1943) (oral accusation of

there is some breach of contract, trust or confidential relation which will afford an independent basis for relief.[96] Warren and Brandeis[97] thought that the publication would have to be written or printed unless special damage could be shown; and there have been decisions[98] that the action will not lie for oral publicity; but the growth of radio alone has been enough to make this obsolete,[99] and there now can be little doubt that writing is not required.[100]

Second, the facts disclosed to the public must be private facts, and not public ones. Certainly no one can complain when publicity is given to information about him which he himself leaves open to the public eye, such as the appearance of the house in which he lives, or to the business in which he is engaged. Thus it has been held that a public school teacher has no action for a compulsory disclosure of her war work and other outside activities.[101]

Here two troublesome questions arise. One is whether any individual, by appearing upon the public highway, or in any other public place, makes his appearance public, so that any one may take and publish a picture of him as he is at the time. What if an utterly obscure citizen, reeling along drunk on the main street, is snapped by an enterprising reporter, and the picture given to the world? Is his privacy invaded? The cases have been much involved with the privilege of reporting news and other matters of public interest,[102] and for that reason cannot be regarded as very conclusive; but the answer appears to be that it is not. The decisions indicate that anything visible in a public place may be recorded and given circulation by means of a photograph, to the same extent as by a written descrip-

theft). On the other hand, in Kerby v. Hal Roach Studios, 53 Cal. App. 2d 207, 127 P.2d 577 (1942), the distribution of a letter to a thousand persons was held, without discussion, to make it public.

[96] Berry v. Moench, 8 Utah 2d 191, 331 P.2d 814 (1958); *cf.* Simonsen v. Swenson, 104 Neb. 224, 177 N.W. 831 (1920); and see Note, 43 MINN. L. REV. 943 (1959).

[97] Warren and Brandeis, *The Right to Privacy*, 4 HARV. L. REV. 193, 217 (1890).

[98] Martin v. F.I.Y. Theatre Co., 10 Ohio Op. 338 (Ohio C.P. 1938); Gregory v. Bryan-Hunt Co., 295 Ky. 345, 174 S.W.2d 510 (1943); Pangallo v. Murphy, 243 S.W.2d 496 (Ky. 1951); Lewis v. Physicians & Dentists Credit Bureau, 27 Wash. 2d 267, 177 P.2d 896 (1947).

[99] Mau v. Rio Grande Oil, Inc., 28 F. Supp. 845 (N.D. Cal. 1939) (radio); Strickler v. National Broadcasting Co., 167 F. Supp. 68 (S.D. Cal. 1958) (television); Binns v. Vitagraph Co. of America, 210 N.Y. 51, 103 N.E. 1108 (1913) (motion picture); Donohue v. Warner Bros. Pictures, 194 F.2d 6 (10th Cir. 1952) (same); Ettore v. Philco Television Broadcasting Co., 229 F.2d 481 (3d Cir. 1956) (motion picture film on television).

[100] Bennett v. Norban, 396 Pa. 94, 151 A.2d 476 (1959); Biederman's of Springfield, Inc. v. Wright, 322 S.W.2d 892 (Mo. 1959); Linehan v. Linehan, 134 Cal. App. 2d 250, 285 P.2d 326 (1955).

[101] Reed v. Orleans Parish Schoolboard, 21 So. 2d 895 (La. App. 1945). Compare the cases of disclosure of corporate records, *supra* note 79.

[102] See *infra*, text at notes 218–63.

tion,[103] since this amounts to nothing more than giving publicity to what is already public and what any one present would be free to see.[104] Outstanding is the California case[105] in which the plaintiff, photographed while embracing his wife in the market place, was held to have no action when the picture was published. It has been contended[106] that when an individual is thus singled out from the public scene, and undue attention is focused upon him, there is an invasion of his private rights; and there is one New York decision to that effect.[107] It was, however, later explained upon the basis of the introduction of an element of fiction into the accompanying narrative.[108]

On the other hand, it seems clear that when a picture is taken surrepetitiously, or over the plaintiff's objection, in a private place,[109] or one already made is stolen,[110] or obtained by bribery or other inducement of breach of trust,[111] the plaintiff's appearance which is thus made public is at the time still a private thing, and there is an invasion of a private right, for which an action will lie.

The other question is as to the effect of the fact that the matter made public is already one of public record. If the record is a confidential one,

---

103 In Chaplin v. National Broadcasting Co., 15 F.R.D. 134 (S.D.N.Y. 1953), the same reasoning was applied to the broadcast of a recorded private telephone conversation between plaintiff and defendant. The case looks wrong, since one element, the sound of Chaplin's voice, was not then public, and was expected to be private to the recipient.

104 Sports & General Press Agency v. "Our Dogs" Pub. Co., [1916] 2 K.B. 880; Humiston v. Universal Film Mfg. Co., 189 App. Div. 467, 178 N.Y.S. 752 (1919); Merle v. Sociological Research Film Corp., 166 App. Div. 376, 152 N.Y.S. 829 (1915); Berg v. Minneapolis Star & Tribune Co., 79 F. Supp. 957 (D. Minn. 1948) (courtroom); Lyles v. State, 330 P.2d 734 (Okl. Cr. 1958) (television in courtroom). *Cf.* Gautier v. Pro-Football, Inc., 304 N.Y. 354, 107 N.E.2d 485 (1952) (football game); Jacova v. Southern Radio & Television Co., 83 So. 2d 34 (Fla. 1955) (cigar store raid).

It may be suggested, however, that a man may still be private in a public place. Suppose that a citizen responds to a call of nature in the bushes in a public park?

105 Gill v. Hearst Pub. Co., 40 Cal. 2d 224, 253 P.2d 441 (1953).

106 Note, 44 Va. L. Rev. 1303 (1958).

107 Blumenthal v. Picture Classics, 235 App. Div. 570, 257 N.Y.S. 800 (1932), *aff'd*, 261 N.Y. 504, 185 N.E. 713 (1933).

108 In Sarat Lahiri v. Daily Mirror, 162 Misc. 776, 295 N.Y.S. 382 (Sup. Ct. 1937).

109 Barber v. Time, Inc., 348 Mo. 1199, 159 S.W.2d 291 (1942) (hospital bed). *Cf.* Clayman v. Bernstein, 38 Pa. D. & C. 543 (C.P. 1940) (picture of semi-conscious patient taken by physician).

110 Peed v. Washington Times, 55 Wash. L. Rep. 182 (D.C. 1927).

In Metter v. Los Angeles Examiner, 35 Cal. App. 2d 304, 95 P.2d 491 (1939), the newspaper appears to have gotten away with a great deal. After plaintiff's wife had committed suicide, the screen of his kitchen window was forced open, and a photograph of his wife disappeared from his table. The same day the same photograph appeared in the paper. The court considered that there was no evidence that the defendant had stolen it. The actual decision can be justified, however, on the ground that the woman was dead. See *infra*, text at note 205.

111 Bazemore v. Savannah Hospital, 171 Ga. 257, 155 S.E. 194 (1930) (picture of deformed child born to plaintiff, obtained from hospital attendants). *Cf.* Douglas v. Stokes, 149 Ky. 506, 149 S.W. 849 (1912) (breach of implied contract by photographer).

not open to public inspection, as in the case of income tax returns,[112] it is not public, and there can be no doubt that there is an invasion of privacy. But it has been held that no one is entitled to complain when there is publication of his recorded date of birth or his marriage,[113] or his military service record;[114] and the same must certainly be true of his admission to the bar or to the practice of medicine, or the fact that he is driving a taxicab. The difficult question is as to the effect of lapse of time, and the extent to which forgotten records, as for example of a criminal conviction, may be dredged up in after years and given more general publicity. As in the case of news,[115] with which the problem may be inextricably interwoven, it has been held that the memory of the events covered by the record, such as a criminal trial,[116] can be revived as still a matter of legitimate public interest. But there is the leading case of *Melyvin v. Reid,*[117] which held that the unnecessary use of the plaintiff's name, and the revelation of her history to new friends and associates, introduced an element which was in itself a transgression of her right of privacy. The answer may be that the existence of a public record is a factor of a good deal of importance, which will normally prevent the matter from being private, but that under some special circumstances it is not necessarily conclusive.

Third, the matter made public must be one which would be offensive and objectionable to a reasonable man of ordinary sensibilities.[118] All of us, to some extent, lead lives exposed to the public gaze or to public inquiry, and complete privacy does not exist in this world except for the eremite in the desert. Any one who is not a hermit must expect the more or less casual

[112] *Cf.* Maysville Transit Co. v. Ort, 296 Ky. 524, 177 S.W.2d 369 (1944); Munzer v. Blaisdell, 183 Misc. 773, 49 N.Y.S.2d 915 (Sup. Ct. 1944), *aff'd,* 269 App. Div. 970, 58 N.Y.S.2d 360 (1945) (records of mental institution); Sellers v. Henry, 329 S.W.2d 214 (Ky. 1959) (police photograph; liability dependent upon use).

[113] Meetze v. Associated Press, 230 S.C. 330, 95 S.E.2d 606 (1956).

[114] Stryker v. Republic Pictures Corp., 108 Cal. App. 2d 191, 238 P.2d 670 (1951); Continental Optical Co. v. Reed, 119 Ind. App. 643, 86 N.E.2d 306 (1949).

In Thompson v. Curtis Pub. Co., 193 F.2d 953 (3d Cir. 1952), a patent obtained by the plaintiff was held to be a public matter, "as fully as a play, a book, or a song."

[115] See *infra,* text at notes 285–88.

[116] Bernstein v. National Broadcasing Co., 129 F. Supp. 817 (D.D.C. 1955), *aff'd,* 232 F.2d 369 (D.C. Cir. 1956) (murder trial used in broadcast); Smith v. National Broadcasting Co., 138 Cal. App. 2d 807, 292 P.2d 600 (1956) (false report to police of escape of black panther). In both cases the name of the plaintiff was not used.

[117] 112 Cal. App. 285, 297 Pac. 91 (1931) (see *supra,* text at note 85). *Accord,* Mau v. Rio Grande Oil, Inc., 28 F. Supp. 845 (N.D. Cal 1939); and see cases cited in the preceding note. The Melvin and Mau cases were explained on the basis of the use of the name in the Smith case.

[118] Reed v. Real Detective Pub. Co., 63 Ariz. 294, 162 P.2d 133 (1945); Davis. v. General Finance & Thrift Corp., 80 Ga. App. 708, 57 S.E.2d 225 (1950); Gill v. Hearst Pub. Co. 40 Cal. 2d 224, 253 P.2d 441 (1953); Samuel v. Curtis Pub. Co., 122 F. Supp. 327 (N.D. Cal. 1954).

observation of his neighbors and the passing public as to what he is and does, and some reporting of his daily activities. The ordinary reasonable man does not take offense at mention in a newspaper of the fact that he has returned from a visit, or gone camping in the woods, or that he has given a party at his house for his friends; and very probably Mr. Warren would never have had any action for the reports of his daughter's wedding. The law of privacy is not intended for the protection of any shrinking soul who is abnormally sensitive about such publicity.[119] It is quite a different matter when the details of sexual relations are spread before the public gaze,[120] or there is highly personal portrayal of his intimate private characteristics or conduct.[121]

Here the outstanding case is *Sidis v. F-R Publishing Corporation.*[122] The plaintiff, William James Sidis, had been an infant prodigy, who had graduated from Harvard at sixteen, and at the age of eleven had lectured to eminent mathematicians on the fourth dimension. When he arrived at adolescence he underwent some unusual psychological change, which brought about a complete revulsion toward mathematics, and toward the publicity he had received. He disappeared, led an obscure life as a bookkeeper, and occupied himself in collecting street car transfers, and studying the lore of the Okamakammessett Indians. The *New Yorker* magazine sought him out, and published a not unsympathetic account of his career, revealing his present whereabouts and activities. The effect upon Sidis was devastating, and the article unquestionably contributed to his early death. The case involved the privilege of reporting on matters of public interest;[123] but the decision that there was no cause of action rested upon the ground that there was nothing in the article which would be objectionable to any normal person. When this case is compared with *Melvin v. Reid,*[124] with its revelation of the past of a prostitute and a murder defendant, what emerges is something in the nature of a "mores" test,[125] by which there will be liability only for publicity given to those things which the customs and ordinary views of the community will not tolerate.

---

119 Meetze v. Associated Press, 230 S.C. 330, 95 S.E.2d 606 (1956) (report of birth of child to girl twelve years old).

120 Garner v. Triangle Publications, 97 F. Supp. 546 (S.D.N.Y. 1951). *Cf.* Myers v. U.S. Camera Pub. Corp., 9 Misc. 2d 765, 167 N.Y.S.2d 771 (N.Y. City Ct. 1957) (nude full body photograph of model); Feeney v. Young, 191 App. Div. 501, 181 N.Y.S. 481 (1920) (exhibition of film of caesarian operation); Banks v. King Features Syndicate, 30 F. Supp. 352 (S.D.N.Y. 1939) (X-rays of woman's pelvic region).

121 Cason v. Baskin, 155 Fla. 198, 20 So. 2d 243 (1944), *second appeal,* 159 Fla. 31, 30 So. 2d 635 (1947). *Cf.* Stryker v. Republic Pictures Corp., 108 Cal. App. 2d 191, 238 P.2d 670 (1951).

122 113 F.2d 806 (2d Cir. 1940), *affirming* 34 F. Supp. 19 (S.D.N.Y. 1938).

123 See *infra,* text at notes 218–63.

124 See *supra,* text at note 85.

125 Suggested by the lower court in Sidis v. F–R Pub. Corp., 34 F. Supp. 19 (S.D.N.Y. 1938).

This branch of the tort is evidently something quite distinct from intrusion. The interest protected is that of reputation, with the same overtones of mental distress that are present in libel and slander. It is in reality an extension of defamation, into the field of publications that do not fall within the narrow limits of the old torts, with the elimination of the defense of truth.[126] As such, it has no doubt gone far to remedy the deficiencies of the defamation actions, hampered as they are by technical rules inherited from ancient and long forgotten jurisdictional conflicts, and to provide a remedy for a few real and serious wrongs that were not previously actionable.

III

FALSE LIGHT IN THE PUBLIC EYE

The third form of invasion of privacy, which Warren and Brandeis again do not appear to have had in mind at all, consists of publicity that places the plaintiff in a false light in the public eye. It seems to have made its first appearance in 1816, when Lord Byron succeeded in enjoining the circulation of a spurious and inferior poem attributed to his pen.[127] The principle frequently, over a good many years, has made a rather nebulous appearance in a line of decisions[128] in which falsity or fiction has been held to defeat the privilege of reporting news and other matters of public interest, or of giving further publicity to already public figures. It is only in late years that it has begun to receive any independent recognition of its own.

One form in which it occasionally appears, as in Byron's case, is that of publicity falsely attributing to the plaintiff some opinion or utterance.[129] A good illustration of this might be the fictitious testimonial used in advertising,[130] or the Oregon case[131] in which the name of the plaintiff was signed to a telegram to the governor urging political action which it would have been illegal for him, as a state employee, to advocate. More typical are spurious books and articles, or ideas expressed in them, which

[126] See *infra*, text at note 290.

[127] Lord Byron v. Johnston, 2 Mer. 29, 35 Eng. Rep. 851 (1816).

[128] See *infra*, text at notes 260–63, 271–73.

[129] See Wigmore, *The Right Against False Attribution of Belief or Utterance*, 4 Ky. L.J. No. 8, p. 3 (1916).

[130] *Cf.* Pavesich v. New England Life Ins. Co., 122 Ga. 190, 50 S.E. 68 (1905); Manger v. Kree Institute of Electrolysis, 233 F.2d 5 (2d Cir. 1956); Foster-Milburn Co. v. Chinn, 134 Ky. 424, 120 S.W. 364 (1909); Fairfield v. American Photocopy Equipment Co., 138 Cal. App. 2d 82, 291 P.2d 194 (1955).

[131] Hinish v. Meier & Frank Co., 166 Ore. 482, 113 P.2d 438 (1941). *Accord*, Schwartz v. Edrington, 133 La. 235, 62 So. 660 (1913) (continued circulation of petition after plaintiff had withdrawn his signature).

purport to emanate from the plaintiff.[132] In the same category are the unauthorized use of his name as a candidate for office,[133] or to advertise for witnesses of an accident,[134] or the entry of an actor, without his consent, in a popularity contest of an embarrassing kind.[135]

Another form in which this branch of the tort frequently has made its appearance is the use of the plaintiff's picture to illustrate a book or an article with which he has no reasonable connection. As remains to be seen,[136] public interest may justify a use for appropriate and pertinent illustration. But when the face of some quite innocent and unrelated citizen is employed to ornament an article on the cheating propensities of taxi drivers,[137] the negligence of children,[138] profane love,[139] "man hungry" women,[140] juvenile delinquents,[141] or the peddling of narcotics,[142] there is an obvious innuendo that the article applies to him, which places him in a false light before the public, and is actionable.

Still another form in which the tort occurs is the inclusion of the plaintiff's name, photograph and fingerprints in a public "rogues' gallery" of convicted criminals, when he has not in fact been convicted of any crime.[143] Although the police are clearly privileged to make such a record in the first instance, and to use it for any legitimate purpose pending trial,[144] or even

---

132 D'Altomonte v. New York Herald Co., 154 App. Div. 453, 139 N.Y.S. 200 (1913), *modified*, however, as not within the New York statute, in 208 N.Y. 596, 102 N.E. 1101 (1913) (authorship of absurd travel story); Hogan v. A. S. Barnes & Co., 114 U.S.P.Q. 314 (Pa. C.P. 1957) (book on golf purporting to give information from plaintiff about his game).

133 State *ex rel.* La Follette v. Hinkle, 131 Wash. 86, 229 Pac. 317 (1924).

134 Hamilton v. Lumbermen's Mutual Cas. Co., 82 So. 2d 61 (La. App. 1955).

135 Marks v. Jaffa, 6 Misc. 290, 26 N.Y.S. 908 (Super. Ct. N.Y. City 1893).

136 *Infra*, text at notes 258–59.

137 Peay v. Curtis Pub. Co., 78 F. Supp. 305 (D.D.C. 1948).

138 Leverton v. Curtis Pub. Co., 192 F.2d 974 (3d Cir. 1951).

139 Gill v. Curtis Pub. Co., 38 Cal. 2d 273, 239 P.2d 630 (1952).

140 Martin v. Johnson Pub. Co., 157 N.Y.S.2d 409 (Sup. Ct. 1956). *Accord*, Semler v. Ultem Publications, 170 Misc. 551, 9 N.Y.S.2d 319 (N.Y. City Ct. 1938) (pictures of model in sensational sex magazine); Russell v. Marboro Books, 18 Misc. 2d 166, 183 N.Y.S.2d 8 (Sup. Ct. 1959) (picture of model used in bawdy advertisement for bed sheets).

141 Metzger v. Dell Pub. Co., 207 Misc. 182, 136 N.Y.S.2d 888 (Sup. Ct. 1955).

More doubtful is Callas v. Whisper, Inc., 198 Misc. 829 (1950), *affirmed*, 278 App. Div. 974, 105 N.Y.S.2d 1001 (1951), where the picture of a minor, obtained by fraudulent representations, was used as background in a night club, with the innuendo that she was in a disreputable place. It was held that she had no cause of action. The facts, however, are by no means entirely clear from the summary of the pleading.

142 Thompson v. Close-Up, Inc., 277 App. Div. 848, 98 N.Y.S.2d 300 (1950).

143 Itzkovitch v. Whitaker, 115 La. 479, 39 So. 499 (1950); and see Downs v. Swann, 111 Md. 53, 73 Atl. 653 (1909); State *ex rel.* Mavity v. Tyndall, 224 Ind. 364, 66 N.E.2d 755 (1946); Norman v. City of Las Vegas, 64 Nev. 38, 177 P.2d 442 (1947). *Cf.* Vanderbilt v. Mitchell, 72 N.J. Eq. 910, 67 Atl. 97 (Ct. Err. & App. 1907) (birth certificate naming plaintiff as father of child).

144 Mabry v. Kettering, 89 Ark. 551, 117 S.W. 746 (1909), *second appeal*, 92 Ark. 81, 122 S.W. 115 (1909); State *ex rel.* Mavity v. Tyndall, 224 Ind. 364, 66 N.E.2d 755 (1946);

after conviction,[145] the element of false publicity in the inclusion among the convicted goes beyond the privilege.

The false light need not necessarily be a defamatory one, although it very often is,[146] and a defamation action will also lie. It seems clear, however, that it must be something that would be objectionable to the ordinary reasonable man under the circumstances, and that, as in the case of disclosure,[147] the hypersensitive individual will not be protected.[148] Thus minor and unimportant errors in an otherwise accurate biography, as to dates and place, and incidents of no significance, do not entitle the subject of the book to recover,[149] nor does the erroneous description of the plaintiff as a cigarette girl when an inquiring photographer interviews her on the street.[150] Again, in all probability, something of a "mores" test must be applied.

The false light cases obviously differ from those of intrusion, or disclosure of private facts. The interest protected is clearly that of reputation, with the same overtones of mental distress as in defamation. There is a resemblance to disclosure; but the two differ in that one involves truth and the other lies, one private or secret facts and the other invention. Both require publicity. There has been a good deal of overlapping of defamation in the false light cases, and apparently either action, or both, will very often lie. The privacy cases do go considerably beyond the

---

Norman v. City of Las Vegas, 64 Nev. 38, 177 P.2d 442 (1947); Bartletta v. McFeeley, 107 N.J. Eq. 141, 152 Atl. 17 (Ch. 1930), *affirmed,* 109 N.J. Eq. 241, 156 Atl. 658 (Ct. Err. & App. 1931); McGovern v. Van Riper, 140 N.J. Eq. 341, 54 A.2d 469 (Ch. 1947); Downs v. Swann, 111 Md. 53, 73 Atl. 653 (1909).

145 Hodgeman v. Olsen, 86 Wash. 615, 150 Pac. 1122 (1915) (convict); Fernicola v. Keenan, 136 N.J. Eq. 9, 39 A.2d 851 (Ch. 1944).

146 *Cf.* Bennett v. Norban, 396 Pa. 94, 151 A.2d 476 (1959) (accusation of theft upon the street); Linehan v. Linehan, 134 Cal. App. 2d 250, 285 P.2d 326 (1955) (public accusation that plaintiff was not the lawful wife of defendant's ex-husband); D'Altomonte v. New York Herald, 154 App. Div. 453, 139 N.Y.S. 200 (1913), *modified,* 208 N.Y. 596, 102 N.E. 1101 (1913) (imputing authorship of absurd travel story); Peay v. Curtis Pub. Co., 78 F. Supp. 305 (D.D.C. 1948) (imputing cheating practices to taxi driver); Martin v. Johnson Pub. Co., 157 N.Y.S.2d 409 (Sup. Ct. 1956) (use of picture with article on "man hungry" women); Russell v. Marlboro Books, 18 Misc. 2d 166, 183 N.Y.S.2d 8 (Sup. Ct. 1959) (picture used in bawdy advertisement).

147 See *supra,* text at notes 118–25.

148 In Strickler v. National Broadcasting Co., 167 F. Supp. 68 (S.D. Cal. 1958), it was left to the jury to decide whether fictitious details of plaintiff's conduct in an airplane crisis, as portrayed in a broadcast, would be objectionable to a reasonable man.

149 Koussevitzky v. Allen, Towne & Heath, 188 Misc. 479, 68 N.Y.S.2d 779 (Sup. Ct.), *aff'd,* 272 App. Div. 759, 69 N.Y.S.2d 432 (1947).

150 Middleton v. News Syndicate Co., 162 Misc. 516, 295 N.Y.S. 120 (Sup. Ct. 1937).

It would appear, however, that this was carried entirely too far in Jones v. Herald Post Co., 230 Ky. 227, 18 S.W.2d 972 (1929). There was a newspaper report of the murder of plaintiff's husband in her presence, and false and sensational statements were attributed to her: that she had fought with the criminals, and would have killed them if she could.

narrow limits of defamation, and no doubt have succeeded in affording a needed remedy in a good many instances not covered by the other tort.

It is here, however, that one disposed to alarm might express the greatest concern over where privacy may be going. The question may well be raised, and apparently still is unanswered, whether this branch of the tort is not capable of swallowing up and engulfing the whole law of public defamation; and whether there is any false libel printed, for example, in a newspaper, which cannot be redressed upon the alternative ground. If that turns out to be the case, it may well be asked, what of the numerous restrictions and limitations which have hedged defamation about for many years, in the interest of freedom of the press and the discouragement of trivial and extortionate claims? Are they of so little consequence that they may be circumvented in so casual and cavalier a fashion?

IV

APPROPRIATION

There is little indication that Warren and Brandeis intended to direct their article at the fourth branch of the tort, the exploitation of attributes of the plaintiff's identity. The first decision[151] had relied upon breach of an implied contract, where a photographer who had taken the plaintiff's picture proceeded to put it on sale; and this is still one basis upon which liability continues to be found.[152] By reason of its early appearance in the *Roberson* case,[153] and the resulting New York statute,[154] this form of invasion has bulked rather large in the law of privacy. It consists of the appropriation, for the defendant's benefit or advantage, of the plaintiff's name or likeness.[155] Thus in New York, as well as in many other states, there are a great many decisions in which the plaintiff has recovered when his name[156] or picture,[157] or other likeness,[158] has been used without his

---

151 Pollard v. Photographic Co., 40 Ch. D. 345 (1888).

152 Holmes v. Underwood & Underwood, 225 App. Div. 360, 233 N.Y.S. 153 (1929); Klug v. Sheriffs, 129 Wis. 468, 109 N.W. 656 (1906); Fitzsimmons v. Olinger Mortuary Ass'n, 91 Colo. 544, 17 P.2d 535 (1932); McCreery v. Miller's Grocerteria Co., 99 Colo. 499, 64 P.2d 803 (1936); Bennett v. Gusdorf, 101 Mont. 39, 53 P.2d 91 (1935).

153 *Supra*, text at note 12.

154 *Supra*, note 14.

155 It is not impossible that there might be appropriation of the plaintiff's identity, as by impersonation, without the use of either his name or his likeness, and that this would be an invasion of his right of privacy. No such case appears to have arisen.

156 Mackenzie v. Soden Mineral Springs Co., 27 Abb. N. Cas. 402, 18 N.Y.S. 240 (Sup. Ct. 1891); Eliot v. Jones, 66 Misc. 95, 120 N.Y.S. 989 (Sup. Ct. 1910), *aff'd*, 140 App. Div. 911, 125 N.Y.S. 1119 (1910); Thompson v. Tillford, 152 App. Div. 928, 137 N.Y.S. 523 (1912); Brociner v. Radio Wire Television, Inc., 15 Misc. 2d 843, 183 N.Y.S.2d 743 (Sup. Ct. 1959) (use in union drive for membership held advertising); Birmingham Broadcasting Co. v. Bell, 259 Ala. 656, 68 So. 2d 314 (1953), *later appeal*, 266 Ala. 266, 96 So. 2d 263 (1957); Kerby v.

consent to advertise the defendant's product, or to accompany an article sold,[159] to add luster to the name of a corporation,[160] or for other business purposes.[161] The statute in New York,[162] and the others patterned after

Hal Roach Studios, 53 Cal. App. 2d 207, 127 P.2d 577 (1942); Fairfield v. American Photocopy Equipment Co., 138 Cal. App. 2d 82, 291 P.2d 194 (1955).

In the cases cited in the next note, the plaintiff's name accompanied the picture.

[157] Fisher v. Murray M. Rosenberg, Inc., 175 Misc. 370, 23 N.Y.S.2d 677 (Sup. Ct. 1940); Russell v. Marboro Books, 18 Misc. 2d 166, 183 N.Y.S.2d 8 (Sup. Ct. 1959); Flores v. Mosler Safe Co., 7 N.Y.2d 276, 164 N.E.2d 853 (1959), *affirming* 7 App. Div. 2d 226, 182 N.Y.S.2d 126 (1959); Korn v. Rennison, 156 A.2d 476 (Conn. Super. 1959); Pavesich v. New England Life Ins. Co., 122 Ga. 190, 50 S.E. 68 (1905); Colgate-Palmolive Co. v. Tullos, 219 F.2d 617 (5th Cir. 1955) (Georgia law); Eick v. Perk Dog Food Co., 347 Ill. App. 293, 106 N.E.2d 742 (1952); Continental Optical Co. v. Reed, 119 Ind. App. 643, 86 N.E.2d 306 (1949); Kunz v. Allen, 102 Kan. 883, 172 Pac. 532 (1918); Foster-Milburn Co. v. Chinn, 134 Ky. 424, 120 S.W. 364 (1909); Pallas v. Crowley, Milner & Co., 322 Mich. 411, 33 N.W.2d 911 (1948); Munden v. Harris, 153 Mo. App. 652, 134 S.W. 1076 (1911); Flake v. Greensboro News Co., 212 N.C. 780, 195 S.E. 55 (1938).

[158] Young v. Greneker Studios, 175 Misc. 1027, 26 N.Y.S.2d 357 (Sup. Ct. 1941) (manikin). In Freed v. Loew's, Inc., 175 Misc. 616, 24 N.Y.S.2d 679 (Sup. Ct. 1940), an artist used the plaintiff's figure as a base, but improved it, and it was held not to be a "portrait or picture" within the New York statute. But in Loftus v. Greenwich Lithographing Co., 192 App. Div. 251, 182 N.Y.S. 428 (1920), the artist used the plaintiff's picture in designing a poster, but made some changes, and the result was held not to fall within the statute. The difference between the two cases may have been one of the extent of the resemblance.

[159] Neyland v. Home Pattern Co., 65 F.2d 363 (2d Cir. 1933) (patterns); Lane v. F. W. Woolworth Co., 171 Misc. 66, 11 N.Y.S.2d 199 (Sup. Ct. 1939), *aff'd,* 256 App. Div. 1065, 12 N.Y.S.2d 352 (1939) (lockets); McNulty v. Press Pub. Co., 136 Misc. 833, 241 N.Y.S. 29 (Sup. Ct. 1930) (cartoon containing photograph); Jansen v. Hilo Packing Co., 202 Misc. 900, 118 N.Y.S.2d 162 (Sup. Ct. 1952), *aff'd,* 282 App. Div. 935, 125 N.Y.S2d 648 (1952) (popcorn); Miller v. Madison Square Garden Corp., 176 Misc. 714, 28 N.Y.S.2d 811 (Sup. Ct. 1941) (booklet sold at bicycle races).

Also, of course, when there is an unauthorized sale of the picture itself. Kunz v. Boselman, 131 App. Div. 288, 115 N.Y.S. 650 (1909); Wyatt v. James McCreery Co., 126 App. Div. 650, 111 N.Y.S. 86 (1908); Holmes v. Underwood & Underwood, 225 App. Div. 360, 233 N.Y.S. 153 (1929).

[160] Von Thodorovich v. Franz Josef Beneficial Ass'n, 154 Fed. 911 (E.D. Pa. 1907); Edison v. Edison Polyform Mfg. Co., 73 N.J. Eq. 136, 67 Atl. 392 (Ch. 1907). *Cf.* U.S. Life Ins. Co. v. Hamilton, 238 S.W.2d 289 (Tex. Civ. App. 1951), where the use of an employee's name on company letterhead after termination of his employment was said not to invade his right of privacy (not recognized in Texas), but was held to be actionable anyway.

[161] Hogan v. A. S. Barnes Co., 114 U.S.P.Q. 314 (1957) (book); Binns v. Vitagraph Co. of America, 210 N.Y. 51, 103 N.E. 1108 (1913) (motion picture); Redmond v. Columbia Pictures Corp., 277 N.Y. 707, 14 N.E.2d 636 (1938), *affirming* 253 App. Div. 708, 1 N.Y.S.2d 643 (same); Stryker v. Republic Pictures Corp., 108 Cal. App. 2d 191, 238 P.2d 670 (1951) (same); Ettore v. Philco Television Broadcasting Co., 229 F.2d 481 (3d Cir. 1956) (motion picture exhibited on television); Almind v. Sea Beach Co., 78 Misc. 445, 139 N.Y.S. 559 (Sup. Ct. 1912), *aff'd,* 157 App. Div. 927, 142 N.Y.S. 1106 (1913) (picture of plaintiff entering or leaving street car used to teach other passengers how to do it).

In Donahue v. Warner Bros. Pictures, 194 F.2d 6 (10th Cir. 1952), it was held that a motion picture, based upon the life of a deceased celebrity but partly fictional, and using his name, came within the Utah statute. But in Donahue v. Warner Bros. Pictures Distributing Corp., 2 Utah 2d 256, 272 P.2d 177 (1954), the state court rejected this decision, and indicated that the statute was to be limited to the use of name or likeness in advertising, or the sale of "some collateral commodity." The effect of this is to nullify the federal decision.

[162] *Supra,* text at note 14.

it[163] are limited by their terms to use for advertising or for "purposes of trade," and for that reason must be somewhat more narrow in their scope than the common law of the other states;[164] but in general, there has been no significant difference in their application in the field that they cover.

It is the plaintiff's name as a symbol of his identity that is involved here, and not his name as a mere name. There is, as a good many thousand John Smiths can bear witness, no such thing as an exclusive right to the use of any name. Unless there is some tortious use made of it, any one can be given or assume any name he likes.[165] The Kabotznicks may call themselves Cabots, and the Lovelskis become Lowells, and the ancient proper Bostonian houses can do nothing about it but grieve. Any one may call himself Dwight D. Eisenhower, Henry Ford, Nelson Rockefeller, Eleanor Roosevelt, or Willie Mays, without any liability whatever. It is when he makes use of the name to pirate the plaintiff's identity for some advantage of his own, as by impersonation to obtain credit or secret information,[166] or by posing as the plaintiff's wife,[167] or providing a father for a child on a birth certificate,[168] that he becomes liable. It is in this sense that "appropriation" must be understood.

On this basis, the question before the courts has been first of all whether there has been appropriation of an aspect of the plaintiff's identity. It is not enough that a name which is the same as his is used in a novel,[169] a comic strip,[170] or the title of a corporation,[171] unless the context or the

---

163 In Oklahoma, Utah and Virginia. See *supra* notes 52–54.

164 See, as illustrations of possible differences: Cardy v. Maxwell, 9 Misc. 2d 329, 169 N.Y.S.2d 547 (Sup. Ct. 1957) (use of name and publicity to extort money not a commercial use within the statute); Hamilton v. Lumbermen's Mutual Cas. Co., 82 So. 2d 61 (La. App. 1955) (advertising in name of plaintiff for witnesses of accident); State *ex rel.* La Follette v. Hinkle, 131 Wash. 86, 229 Pac. 317 (1924) (use of name as candidate for office by political party). See also the cases cited *infra,* notes 167 and 168.

165 Du Boulay v. Du Boulay, L.R. 2 P.C. 430 (1869); Cowley v. Cowley, [1901] A.C. 450; Brown Chemical Co. v. Meyer, 139 U.S. 540 (1891); Smith v. United States Casualty Co., 197 N.Y. 420, 90 N.E. 947 (1910); Baumann v. Baumann, 250 N.Y. 382, 165 N.E. 819 (1929); Bartholomew v. Workman, 197 Okla. 267, 169 P.2d 1012 (1946).

166 "While I know of no instance, it can safely be assumed that should *A,* by the use of *B*'s name, together with other characteristics of *B,* successfully impersonate *B,* and thereby obtain valuable recognition or benefits from a third person, a suit by *B* against *A* could be maintained." Green, *The Right of Privacy,* 27 ILL. L. REV. 237, 243–44 (1932).

Three years after these words were published, recovery was allowed in such a case. Goodyear Tire & Rubber Co. v. Vandergriff, 52 Ga. App. 662, 184 S.E. 452 (1936), in which defendant, impersonating plaintiff's agent, obtained confidential information from dealers about tire prices.

167 Burns v. Stevens, 236 Mich. 443, 210 N.W. 482 (1926). *Contra,* Baumann v. Baumann, 250 N.Y. 382, 165 N.E. 819 (1929); *but cf.* Niver v. Niver, 200 Misc. 993, 111 N.Y.S.2d 889 (Sup. Ct. 1951).

168 Vanderbilt v. Mitchell, 72 N.J. Eq. 910, 67 Atl. 97 (Ct. Err. & App. 1907).

169 Swacker v. Wright, 154 Misc. 822, 277 N.Y.S. 296 (Sup. Ct. 1935); People v. Charles Scribner's Sons, 205 Misc. 818, 130 N.Y.S.2d 514 (N.Y. City Magis. Ct. 1954).

170 Nebb v. Bell Syndicate, 41 F. Supp. 929 (S.D.N.Y. 1941).

171 Pfaudler v. Pfaudler Co., 114 Misc. 477, 186 N.Y.S. 725 (Sup. Ct. 1920).

circumstances,[172] or the addition of some other element,[173] indicate that the name is that of the plaintiff. It seems clear that a stage or other fictitious name can be so identified with the plaintiff that he is entitled to protection against its use.[174] On the other hand, there is no liability for the publication of a picture of his hand, leg and foot,[175] his dwelling

[172] In Uproar Co. v. National Broadcasting Co., 8 F. Supp. 358 (D. Mass. 1934), *affirmed as modified,* 81 F.2d 373 (1st Cir. 1936), the comedian Ed Wynn published, in pamphlet form, humorous skits which he had performed on the radio, in which he made frequent mention of "Graham." It was held that the public would reasonably understand this to refer to Graham McNamee, a radio announcer who had been his foil.

In Kerby v. Hal Roach Studios, 53 Cal. App. 2d 207, 127 P.2d 577 (1942), defendant, advertising a motion picture, made use of the name Marion Kerby, which was signed to a letter apparently suggesting an assignation. Plaintiff, an actress named Marion Kerby, was the only person of that name listed in the city directory and the telephone book. She had in fact a large number of telephone calls about the letter. It was held that it might reasonably be understood to refer to her.

In Krieger v. Popular Publications, 167 Misc. 5, 3 N.Y.S.2d 480 (Sup. Ct. 1938), a complaint alleging that the plaintiff was a professional boxer, and that the defendant had appropriated his name by publishing a story about such a boxer of the same name, which appeared more than a hundred times in twenty pages, was held sufficient to state a cause of action.

On the other hand, in Levey v. Warner Bros. Pictures, 57 F. Supp. 40 (S.D.N.Y. 1944), the plaintiff, whose name was Mary, was the divorced first wife of the actor George M. Cohan. The defendant made a motion picture of his life, in which the part of the wife, named Mary, was played by an actress. The part was almost entirely fictional, and there was no mention of the divorce. It was held that this could not reasonably be understood to be a portrayal of the plaintiff.

In such cases the test appears to be that usually applied in cases of defamation, as to whether a reasonable man would understand the name to identify the plaintiff. Compare Harrison v. Smith, 20 L.T.R. (n.s.) 713 (1869); Clare v. Farrell, 70 F. Supp. 276 (D. Minn. 1947); Macfadden's Publications v. Turner, 95 S.W.2d 1027 (Tex. Civ. App. 1936); Landau v. Columbia Broadcasting System, 205 Misc. 357, 128 N.Y.S.2d 254 (Sup. Ct. 1954); Newton v. Grubb, 155 Ky. 479, 159 S.W. 994 (1913).

[173] Mackenzie v. Soden Mineral Springs Co., 27 Abb. N. Cas. 402, 18 N.Y.S. 240 (Sup. Ct. 1891) (signature); Orsini v. Eastern Wine Corp., 190 Misc. 235, 73 N.Y.S.2d 426 (Sup. Ct. 1947), *aff'd,* 273 App. Div. 947, 78 N.Y.S.2d 224 (1948), *appeal denied,* 273 App. Div. 996, 79 N.Y.S.2d 870 (1948) (plaintiff's coat of arms).

[174] The only cases have involved construction of the New York statute, as to the use of the plaintiff's "name." In Davis v. R.K.O. Radio Pictures, 16 F. Supp. 195 (S.D.N.Y. 1936), where a clairvoyant made use of the name "Cassandra," it was held that this was limited to genuine names. In Gardella v. Log Cabin Products Co., 89 F.2d 891 (2d Cir. 1937), a trade mark case, a dictum disagreed, and said that the statute would cover a stage name. In People v. Charles Scribner's Sons, 205 Misc. 818, 130 N.Y.S.2d 514 (N.Y. City Magis. Ct. 1954), it was said that there was no protection of an "assumed" name, and doubt as to a "stage name." In the unreported case of Van Duren v. Fawcett Publications, No. 13114, S.D. Cal. 1952, the court regarded the *Davis* case as controlling New York law, and disregarded the *Gardella* case as dictum.

Apart from statutory language, however, it is suggested that the text statement is correct. The suggestion, for example, that Samuel L. Clemens would have a cause of action when that name was used in advertising, but not for the use of "Mark Twain," fully speaks for itself.

[175] Brewer v. Hearst Pub. Co., 185 F.2d 846 (7th Cir. 1950). *Cf.* Sellers v. Henry, 329 S.W.2d 214 (Ky. 1959), and Waters v. Fleetwood, 212 Ga. 161, 91 S.E.2d 344 (1956), where there were photographs of unidentifiable dead bodies.

house,[176] his automobile,[177] or his dog,[178] with nothing to indicate whose they are. Nor is there any liability when the plaintiff's character, occupation, and the general outline of his career, with many real incidents in his life, are used as the basis for a figure in a novel who is still clearly a fictional one.[179]

Once the plaintiff is identified, there is the further question whether the defendant has appropriated the name or likeness for his own advantage. Under the statutes this must be a pecuniary advantage; but the common law is very probably not so limited.[180] The New York courts were faced very early with the obvious fact that newspapers and magazines, to say nothing of radio, television and motion pictures, are by no means philanthropic institutions, but are operated for profit. As against the contention that everything published by these agencies must necessarily be "for purposes of trade," they were compelled to hold that there must be some closer and more direct connection, beyond the mere fact that the newspaper is sold; and that the presence of advertising matter in adjacent columns does not make any difference.[181] Any other conclusion would undoubtedly have been an unconstitutional interference with the freedom of the press.[182] Accordingly, it has been held that the mere incidental mention of the plaintiff's name in a book[183] or a motion picture[184] or even in a commentary upon news which is part of an advertisement,[185] is not an invasion of his privacy;

---

176 Rozhon v. Triangle Publications, 230 F.2d 359 (7th Cir. 1956). In accord is the unreported case of Cole v. Goodyear Tire & Rubber Co., App. Dept. Superior Court, San Francisco, Calif., Nov. 21, 1955.

177 Branson v. Fawcett Publications, 124 F. Supp. 429 (E.D. Ill. 1954).

178 Lawrence v. Ylla, 184 Misc. 807, 55 N.Y.S.2d 343 (Sup. Ct. 1945).

179 Toscani v. Hersey, 271 App. Div. 445, 65 N.Y.S.2d 814 (1946). *Cf.* Bernstein v. National Broadcasting Co., 129 F. Supp. 817 (D.D.C. 1955), *aff'd*, 232 F.2d 369 (D.C. Cir. 1956); Miller v. National Broadcasting Co., 157 F. Supp. 240 (D. Del. 1957); Levey v. Warner Bros. Pictures, 57 F. Supp. 40 (S.D.N.Y. 1944).

180 See, for example, State *ex rel.* La Follette v. Hinkle, 131 Wash. 86, 229 Pac. 317 (1924) (use of name as candidate by political party); Hinish v. Meier & Frank Co., 166 Ore. 482, 113 P.2d 438 (1941) (name signed to telegram urging governor to veto a bill); Schwartz v. Edrington, 133 La. 235, 62 So. 660 (1913) (name signed to petition); Vanderbilt v. Mitchell, 72 N.J. Eq. 910, 67 Atl. 97 (Ct. Err. & App. 1907) (birth certificate naming plaintiff as father); Burns v. Stevens, 236 Mich. 443, 210 N.W. 482 (1926) (posing as plaintiff's common law wife).

181 Colyer v. Richard K. Fox Pub. Co., 162 App. Div. 297, 146 N.Y.S. 999 (1914).

182 See Donahue v. Warner Bros. Picture Distributing Corp., 2 Utah 2d 256, 272 Pac. 177 (1954).

183 Damron v. Doubleday, Doran & Co., 133 Misc. 302, 231 N.Y.S. 444 (Sup. Ct. 1928), *aff'd*, 226 App. Div. 796, 234 N.Y.S. 773 (1929); Shubert v. Columbia Pictures Corp., 189 Misc. 734, 72 N.Y.S.2d 851 (Sup. Ct. 1947), *aff'd*, 274 App. Div. 571, 80 N.Y.S.2d 724 (1948), *appeal denied*, 274 App. Div. 880, 83 N.Y.S.2d 233 (1948).

184 Stillman v. Paramount Pictures Corp., 1 Misc. 2d 108, 147 N.Y.S.2d 504 (Sup. Ct. 1956), *aff'd*, 2 App. Div. 2d 18, 153 N.Y.S.2d 190 (1956), *appeal denied*, 2 App. Div. 2d 886, 157 N.Y.S.2d 899 (1956).

185 Wallach v. Bacharach, 192 Misc. 979, 80 N.Y.S.2d 37 (Sup. Ct. 1948), *aff'd*, 274 App. Div. 919, 84 N.Y.S.2d 894 (1948).

In accord is O'Brien v. Pabst Sales Co., 124 F.2d 167 (5th Cir. 1941), where the court

nor is the publication of a photograph[186] or a newsreel[187] in which he incidentally appears.

This liberality toward the publishers was brought to an abrupt termination, however, when cases began to appear in which false statements were made. It was held quite early in New York[188] that the publication of fiction concerning a man is a use of his name for purposes of trade, and that in such a case the mere sale of the article is enough in itself to provide the commercial element. It follows that when the name or the likeness is accompanied by false statements about the plaintiff,[189] or he is placed in a false light before the public,[190] there is such a use. The result of this rule for the encouragement of accuracy in the press is that the New York court has in fact recognized and applied the third form of invasion of privacy[191] under a statute which was directed only at the fourth.

It seems sufficiently evident that appropriation is quite a different matter from intrusion, disclosure of private facts, or a false light in the public eye. The interest protected is not so much a mental as a proprietary one, in the exclusive use of the plaintiff's name and likeness as an aspect of his identity. It seems quite pointless to dispute over whether such a right is to be classified as "property."[192] If it is not, it is at least, once it is protected by the law, a right of value upon which the plaintiff can capitalize by selling licenses. Its proprietary nature is clearly indicated by a decision of the Second Circuit[193] that an exclusive license has what has been called

---

refused to find a commercial use in the publication of the pictures of an all-American football team on a calendar advertising the defendant's beer, with no suggestion that the team endorsed it.

186 Dallessandro v. Henry Holt & Co., 4 App. Div. 2d 470, 166 N.Y.S.2d 805 (1957) (plaintiff's photograph while conversing with a priest who was the subject of the book).

187 Humiston v. Universal Film Mfg. Co., 189 App. Div. 467, 178 N.Y.S. 752 (1919); Merle v. Sociological Research Film Corp., 166 App. Div. 376, 152 N.Y.S. 829 (1915) (picture of plaintiff's factory showing his name).

188 Binns v. Vitagraph Co. of America, 147 App. Div. 783, 132 N.Y.S. 237 (1911), *aff'd,* 210 N.Y. 51, 103 N.E. 1108 (1913).

189 Holmes v. Underwood & Underwood, 225 App. Div. 360, 233 N.Y.S. 153 (1929); Sutton v. Hearst Corp., 277 App. Div. 155, 98 N.Y.S.2d 233 (1950), *appeal denied,* 297 App. Div. 873, 98 N.Y.S.2d 589 (1950); Garner v. Triangle Publications, 97 F. Supp. 546 (S.D.N.Y. 1951).

190 Semler v. Ultem Publications, 170 Misc. 551, 9 N.Y.S.2d 319 (N.Y. City Ct. 1938); Thompson v. Close-Up, Inc., 277 App. Div. 848, 98 N.Y.S.2d 300 (1950); Metzger v. Dell Pub. Co., 207 Misc. 182, 136 N.Y.S.2d 888 (Sup. Ct. 1955); Martin v. Johnson Pub. Co., 157 N.Y.S.2d 409 (Sup. Ct. 1956). These were all cases involving the use of plaintiff's picture to illustrate articles with which he had no connection.

191 *Supra,* text at notes 126–50.

192 See Rhodes v. Sperry & Hutchinson Co., 193 N.Y. 223, 85 N.E. 1097 (1908); Gautier v. Pro-Football, Inc., 304 N.Y. 354, 107 N.E.2d 485 (1952); Mau v. Rio Grande Oil, Inc., 28 F. Supp. 845 (N.D. Cal. 1939); Hull v. Curtis Pub. Co., 182 Pa. Super. 86, 125 A.2d 644 (1956); Metter v. Los Angeles Examiner, 35 Cal. App. 2d 304, 95 P.2d 491 (1939); Ludwig, *"Peace of Mind" in 48 Pieces vs. Uniform Right of Privacy,* 32 MINN. L. REV. 734 (1948).

193 Haelan Laboratories v. Topps Chewing Gum, Inc., 202 F.2d 866 (2d Cir. 1953), *reversing* Bowman Gum Co. v. Topps Chewing Gum, Inc., 103 F. Supp. 944 (E.D.N.Y. 1952).

a "right of publicity,"[194] which entitles him to enjoin the use of the name or likeness by a third person. Although this decision has not yet been followed,[195] it would seem clearly to be justified.

V

COMMON FEATURES

Judge Biggs has described the present state of the law of privacy as "still that of a haystack in a hurricane."[196] Disarray there certainly is; but almost all of the confusion is due to a failure to separate and distinguish these four forms of invasion, and to realize that they call for different things. Typical is the bewilderment which a good many members of the bar have expressed over the holdings in the two *Gill* cases in California. Both of them involved publicity given to the same photograph, taken while the plaintiff was embracing his wife in the Farmers' Market in Los Angeles. In one of them,[197] which involved only the question of disclosure by publishing the picture, it was held that there was nothing private about it, since it was a part of the public scene in a public place. In the other,[198] which involved the use of the picture to illustrate an article on the right and the wrong kind of love, with the innuendo that this was the wrong kind, liability was found for placing the plaintiff in a false light in the public eye. The two conclusions were based entirely upon the difference between the two branches of the tort.

Taking them in order—intrusion, disclosure, false light, and appropriation—the first and second require the invasion of something secret, secluded or private pertaining to the plaintiff; the third and fourth do not. The second and third depend upon publicity, while the first does not, nor does the fourth, although it usually involves it. The third requires falsity or fiction; the other three do not. The fourth involves a use for the defendant's advantage, which is not true of the rest. Obviously this is an area in

194 Nimmer, *The Right of Publicity,* 19 LAW & CONTEMP. PROB. 203 (1954); Notes, 62 YALE L.J. 1123 (1953); 41 GEO. L.J. 583 (1953).

195 The "right of publicity" was held not to exist in California in Strickler v. National Broadcasting Co., 167 F. Supp. 68 (S.D. Cal. 1958). It was rejected in Pekas Co. v. Leslie, 52 N.Y.L.J. 1864 (Sup. Ct. 1915).

It appears to have been foreshadowed when relief was granted on other grounds in Uproar Co. v. National Broadcasting Co., 8 F. Supp. 358 (D. Mass. 1934), *modified* in 81 F.2d 373 (1st Cir. 1936); Liebig's Extract of Meat Co. v. Liebig Extract Co., 180 Fed. 68 (2d Cir. 1910). See also Madison Square Garden Corp. v. Universal Pictures Co., 255 App. Div. 459, 7 N.Y.S.2d 845 (1938).

196 In Ettore v. Philco Television Broadcasting Co., 229 F.2d 481 (3d Cir. 1956).

197 Gill v. Hearst Pub. Co., 40 Cal. 2d 224, 253 P.2d 441 (1953). The complaint alleged the publication of the picture in connection with the article involved in the other case, but failed to plead that the defendant had authorized it. A demurrer was sustained, but the plaintiff was permitted to amend.

198 Gill v. Curtis Pub. Co., 38 Cal. 2d 273, 239 P.2d 630 (1952).

which one must tread warily and be on the lookout for bogs. Nor is the difficulty decreased by the fact that quite often two or more of these forms of invasion may be found in the same case, and quite conceivably all four.[199]

There has nevertheless been a good deal of consistency in the rules that have been applied to the four disparate torts under the common name. As to any one of the four, it is agreed that the plaintiff's right is a personal one, which does not extend to the members of his family,[200] unless, as is obviously possible,[201] their own privacy is invaded along with his. The right is not assignable;[202] and while the cause of action may[203] or may not[204] survive after his death, according to the survival rules of the particular state, there is no common law right of action for a publication concerning one who is already dead.[205] The statutes of Oklahoma, Utah and Virginia,[206] however, expressly provide for such an action. It seems to be generally agreed that the right of privacy is one pertaining only to indi-

---

199 *E.g.*, the defendant breaks into the plaintiff's home, steals his photograph, and publishes it with false statements about the plaintiff in his advertising.

200 Murray v. Gast Lithographic & Engraving Co., 8 Misc. 36, 28 N.Y.S. 271 (N.Y.C.P. 1894); Rozhon v. Triangle Publications, 230 F.2d 359 (7th Cir. 1956); Waters v. Fleetwood, 212 Ga. 161, 91 S.E.2d 344 (1956); Bremmer v. Journal-Tribune Co., 247 Iowa 817, 76 N.W.2d 762 (1956); Kelly v. Johnson Pub. Co., 160 Cal. App. 2d 718, 325 P.2d 659 (1958). See also the cases cited *infra*, note 202.

201 Walker v. Whittle, 83 Ga. App. 445, 64 S.E.2d 87 (1951) (intrusion into home to arrest husband). See Coverstone v. Davies, 38 Cal. 2d 315, 239 P.2d 876 (1952); Smith v. Doss, 251 Ala. 250, 37 So. 2d 118 (1948); and *cf.* Bazemore v. Savannah Hospital, 171 Ga. 257, 155 S.E. 195 (1930); Douglas v. Stokes, 149 Ky. 506, 149 S.W. 849 (1912).

202 Hanna Mfg. Co. v. Hillerich & Bradsby Co., 78 F.2d 763 (5th Cir. 1939); Wyatt v. Hall's Portrait Studios, 71 Misc. 199, 128 N.Y.S. 247 (Sup. Ct. 1911); Murray v. Gast Lithographic & Engraving Co., 8 Misc. 36, 28 N.Y.S. 271 (N.Y.C.P. 1894); Rhodes v. Sperry & Hutchinson Co., 193 N.Y. 223, 85 N.E. 1097 (1908). *Cf.* Von Thodorovich v. Franz Josef Beneficial Ass'n, 154 Fed. 911 (E.D. Pa. 1907) (Austrian diplomat cannot maintain action on behalf of Emperor of Austria).

203 Reed v. Real Detective Pub. Co., 63 Ariz. 294, 162 P.2d 133 (1945).

204 Wyatt v. Hall's Portrait Studios, 71 Misc. 199, 128 N.Y.S. 247 (Sup. Ct. 1911); Lunceford v. Wilcox, 88 N.Y.S.2d 225 (N.Y. City Ct. 1949).

205 Schuyler v. Curtis, 147 N.Y. 434, 42 N.E. 22 (1895); *In re* Hart's Estate, 193 Misc. 884, 83 N.Y.S.2d 635 (Surr. Ct. 1948); Schumann v. Loew's, Inc., 199 Misc. 38, 102 N.Y.S.2d 572 (Sup. Ct. 1951), *aff'd*, 135 N.Y.S.2d 361 (Sup. Ct. 1954); Rozhon v. Triangle Publications, 230 F.2d 359 (7th Cir. 1956); Abernathy v. Thornton, 263 Ala. 496, 83 So. 2d 235 (1955); Metter v. Los Angeles Examiner, 35 Cal. App. 2d 304, 95 P.2d 491 (1939); Kelly v. Johnson Pub. Co., 160 Cal. App. 2d 718, 325 P.2d 659 (1958); James v. Screen Gems, Inc., 174 Cal. App. 2d 650, 344 P.2d 799 (1959); Kelley v. Post Pub. Co., 327 Mass. 275, 98 N.E.2d 286 (1951); Bartholomew v. Workman, 197 Okl. 267, 169 P.2d 1012 (1946). *Cf.* Atkinson v. John E. Doherty & Co., 121 Mich. 372, 80 N.W. 285 (1899).

As in the case of living persons, however, a publication concerning one who is dead may invade the separate right of privacy of surviving relatives. See the last three cases cited *supra* and note 198.

206 *Supra*, notes 52–54. See Donahue v. Warner Bros. Pictures, 194 F.2d 6 (10th Cir. 1952); Donahue v. Warner Bros. Pictures Distributing Corp., 2 Utah 2d 256, 272 P.2d 177 (1954).

viduals, and that a corporation[207] or a partnership[208] cannot claim it as such, although either may have an exclusive right to the use of its name, which may be protected upon some other basis such as that of unfair competition.[209]

So far as damages are concerned, there is general agreement that the plaintiff need not plead or prove special damages,[210] and that in this respect the action resembles one for libel or slander per se. The difficulty of measuring the damages is no more reason for denying relief here than in a defamation action.[211] Substantial damages may be awarded for the presumed mental distress inflicted, and other probable harm, without proof.[212] If there is evidence of special damage, such as resulting illness, or unjust enrichment of the defendant,[213] or harm to the plaintiff's own commercial interests,[214] it can be recovered. Punitive damages can be awarded upon the same basis as in other torts, where a wrongful motive or state of mind appears,[215] but not in cases where the defendant has acted innocently, as for example in the belief that the plaintiff has given his consent.[216]

---

[207] Jaggard v. R.H. Macy & Co., 176 Misc. 88, 26 N.Y.S.2d 829 (Sup. Ct. 1941), *aff'd,* 265 App. Div. 15, 37 N.Y.S.2d 570 (1942); Shubert v. Columbia Pictures Corp., 189 Misc. 734, 72 N.Y.S.2d 851 (Sup. Ct. 1947), *aff'd,* 274 App. Div. 571, 80 N.Y.S.2d 724 (1948), *appeal denied,* 274 App. Div. 880, 83 N.Y.S.2d 233 (1948); Maysville Transit Co. v. Ort, 296 Ky. 524, 177 S.W.2d 369 (1944); United States v. Morton, 338 U.S. 632 (1950).

[208] Rosenwasser v. Ogoglia, 172 App. Div. 107, 158 N.Y.S. 56 (1916).

[209] Vassar College v. Loose-Wiles Biscuit Co., 197 Fed. 982 (W.D. Mo. 1912).

[210] Reed v. Real Detective Pub. Co., 63 Ariz. 294, 162 P.2d 133 (1945); Fairfield v. American Photocopy Equipment Co., 138 Cal. App. 2d 82, 291 P.2d 194 (1955); Cason v. Baskin, 155 Fla. 198, 20 So. 2d 243 (1945); Pavesich v. New England Life Ins. Co., 122 Ga. 190, 50 S.E. 68 (1905); Kunz v. Allen, 102 Kan. 883, 172 Pac. 532 (1918); Foster-Milburn Co. v. Chinn, 134 Ky. 424, 120 S.W. 364 (1909); Munden v. Harris, 153 Mo. App. 652, 134 S.W. 1076 (1911); Flake v. Greensboro News Co., 212 N.C. 780, 195 S.E. 55 (1938).

[211] Brents v. Morgan, 221 Ky. 765, 299 S.W. 967 (1927); Rhodes v. Graham, 238 Ky. 225, 37 S.W.2d 46 (1951); Hinish v. Meier & Frank Co., 166 Ore. 482, 113 P.2d 438 (1941); Fairfield v. American Photocopy Equipment Co., 138 Cal. App. 2d 82, 291 P.2d 194 (1955).

[212] Pavesich v. New England Life Ins. Co., 122 Ga. 190, 50 S.E. 68 (1905); Sutherland v. Kroger Co., 110 S.E.2d 716 (W. Va. 1959). In Cason v. Baskin, 159 Fla. 31, 30 So. 2d 635 (1947), where there was evidence that the plaintiff had suffered no great distress, and had gained weight, the recovery was limited to nominal damages.

[213] Bunnell v. Keystone Varnish Co., 254 App. Div. 885, 5 N.Y.S.2d 415 (1938), *affirming* 167 Misc. 707, 4 N.Y.S.2d 601 (Sup. Ct. 1938).

[214] Continental Optical Co. v. Reed, 119 Ind. App. 643, 86 N.E.2d 306 (1949); Manger v. Kree Institute of Electrolysis, 233 F.2d 5 (2d Cir. 1956); Hogan v. A. S. Barnes & Co., Inc., 114 U.S.P.Q. 314 (Pa. C.P. 1957). Likewise, the fact that the plaintiff has benefited in his profession by the publicity may be considered in mitigation, and may reduce his recovery to nominal damages. Harris v. H. W. Gossard Co., 194 App. Div. 688, 185 N.Y.S. 861 (1921).

[215] Munden v. Harris, 153 Mo. App. 652, 134 S.W. 1076 (1911); Hinish v. Meier & Frank Co., 166 Ore. 482, 113 P.2d 438 (1941); Welsh v. Pritchard, 125 Mont. 517, 241 P.2d 816 (1952).

[216] Fisher v. Murray M. Rosenberg, Inc., 175 Misc. 370, 23 N.Y.S.2d 677 (Sup. Ct. 1940); Barber v. Time, Inc., 348 Mo. 1199, 159 S.W.2d 291 (1942). But in Myers v. U.S. Camera

At an early stage of its existence, the right of privacy came into head-on collision with the constitutional guaranty of freedom of the press. The result was the slow evolution of a compromise between the two. Much of the litigation over privacy has been concerned with this compromise, which has involved two closely related, special and limited privileges arising out of the rights of the press.[217] One of these is the privilege of giving further publicity to already public figures. The other is that of giving publicity to news, and other matters of public interest. The one primarily concerns the person to whom publicity is given; the other the event, fact or other subject-matter. They are, however, obviously only different phases of the same thing.

VI

PUBLIC FIGURES AND PUBLIC INTEREST

A public figure has been defined as a person who, by his accomplishments, fame, or mode of living, or by adopting a profession or calling which gives the public a legitimate interest in his doings, his affairs, and his character, has become a "public personage."[218] He is, in other words, a celebrity—one who by his own voluntary efforts has succeeded in placing himself in the public eye. Obviously to be included in this category are those who have achieved at least some degree of reputation[219] by appearing before the public, as in the case of an actor,[220] a professional baseball

---

Pub. Corp., 9 Misc. 2d 765, 167 N.Y.S.2d 771 (N.Y. City Ct. 1957), punitive damages were allowed where the defendant "knew or should have known."

In Harlow v. Buno Co., 36 Pa. D.&C. 101 (C.P. 1939), the fact that the defendant had acted in good faith under a forged consent was held to defeat the action entirely. This appears to be wrong. *Cf.* Kerby v. Hal Roach Studios, 53 Cal. App. 2d 207, 127 P.2d 577 (1942), where the defendant made use of the plaintiff's name without even being aware of her existence.

[217] In Themo v. New England Newspaper Pub. Co., 306 Mass. 54, 27 N.E.2d 753 (1940), it was said that these privileges are not technically defenses, and the absence of a privileged occasion must be pleaded and proved by the plaintiff. This is the only case found bearing on the question; but it may be doubted that other jurisdictions will agree.

[218] Cason v. Baskin, 159 Fla. 31, 30 So. 2d 635, 638 (1947).

[219] The question of degree has not been discussed in the cases. In Kerby v. Hal Roach Studios, 53 Cal. App. 2d 207, 127 P.2d 577 (1942), the plaintiff was an actress, concert singer and monologist, so obscure that the defendant's studio had never heard of her. She was allowed to recover for appropriation of her name and a false light before the public, without mention of whether she was a public figure, which obviously would have made no difference in the decision. It may be suggested that even an obscure entertainer may be a public figure to some limited extent, but that the field in which she may be given further publicity may be more narrowly limited. See *infra,* text at notes 282–84.

[220] Paramount Pictures v. Leader Press, 24 F. Supp. 1004 (W.D. Okl. 1938), *reversed on other grounds* in 106 F.2d 229 (10th Cir. 1939); Chaplin v. National Broadcasting Co., 15 F.R.D. 134 (S.D.N.Y. 1953).

player,[221] a pugilist,[222] or any other entertainer.[223] The list is, however, broader than this. It includes public officers,[224] famous inventors[225] and explorers,[226] war heroes[227] and even ordinary soldiers,[228] an infant prodigy,[229] and no less a personage than the Grand Exalted Ruler of a lodge.[230] It includes, in short, any one who has arrived at a position where public attention is focused upon him as a person. It seems clear, however, that such public stature must already exist before there can be any privilege arising out of it, and that the defendant, by directing attention to one who is obscure and unknown, cannot himself create a public figure.[231]

Such public figures are held to have lost, to some extent at least, their right of privacy. Three reasons are given, more or less indiscriminately, in the decisions: that they have sought publicity and consented to it, and so cannot complain of it; that their personalities and their affairs already have become public, and can no longer be regarded as their own private business; and that the press has a privilege, guaranteed by the Constitution, to inform the public about those who have become legitimate matters of public interest. On one or another of these grounds, and sometimes all, it is held that there is no liability when they are given additional publicity,

---

221 Ruth v. Educational Films, 194 App. Div. 893, 184 N.Y.S. 948 (1920); see Jansen v. Hilo Packing Co., 202 Misc. 900, 118 N.Y.S.2d 162 (Sup. Ct. 1952), *aff'd,* 282 App. Div. 935, 125 N.Y.S.2d 648 (1953). *Cf.* O'Brien v. Pabst Sales Co., 124 F.2d 167 (5th Cir. 1941) (all-American football player).

222 Jeffries v. New York Evening Journal Pub. Co., 67 Misc. 570, 124 N.Y.S.780 (Sup. Ct. 1910); Cohen v. Marx, 94 Cal. App. 2d 704, 211 P.2d 320 (1950); Oma v. Hillman Periodicals, 281 App. Div. 240, 118 N.Y.S.2d 720 (1953).

223 Colyer v. Richard K. Fox Pub. Co., 162 App. Div. 297, 146 N.Y.S. 999 (1914) (high diver); Koussevitzky v. Allen, Towne & Heath, 188 Misc. 479, 68 N.Y.S.2d 779 (Sup. Ct. 1947), *aff'd,* 272 App. Div. 759, 69 N.Y.S.2d 432 (1947) (symphony conductor); Gavrilov v. Duell, Sloan & Pierce, 84 N.Y.S.2d 320 (Sup. Ct. 1948) (dancer); Redmond v. Columbia Pictures Corp., 277 N.Y. 707, 14 N.E.2d 636 (1938), *affirming* 253 App. Div. 708, 1 N.Y.S.2d 643 (trick shot golfer). *Cf.* Gautier v. Pro-Football, Inc., 304 N.Y. 354, 107 N.E.2d 485 (1952) (performing animal act at football game); Goelet v. Confidential, Inc., 5 App. Div. 2d 226, 171 N.Y.S.2d 223 (1958) (unspecified).

224 Martin v. Dorton, 210 Miss. 668, 50 So. 2d 391 (1951) (sheriff); Hull v. Curtis Pub. Co., 182 Pa. Super. 86, 125 A.2d 644 (1956) (arrest by policeman).

225 Corliss v. E. W. Walker Co., 64 Fed. 280 (D. Mass. 1894). *Cf.* Thompson v. Curtis Pub. Co., 193 F.2d 953 (3d Cir. 1952).

226 Smith v. Suratt, 7 Alaska 416 (1926).

227 Stryker v. Republic Pictures Corp., 108 Cal. App. 2d 191, 238 P.2d 670 (1951). *Accord,* Molony v. Boy Comics Publishers, 277 App. Div. 166, 98 N.Y.S.2d 119 (1950), *reversing* 188 Misc. 450, 65 N.Y.S.2d 173 (Sup. Ct. 1946) (hero in disaster).

228 See Continental Optical Co. v. Reed, 119 Ind. App. 643, 86 N.E.2d 306 (1949).

229 Sidis v. F-R Pub. Corp., 113 F.2d 806 (2d Cir. 1940), *affirming* 34 F. Supp. 19 (S.D. N.Y. 1938).

230 Wilson v. Brown, 189 Misc. 79, 73 N.Y.S.2d 587 (Sup. Ct. 1947).

231 Cason v. Baskin, 155 Fla. 198, 20 So. 2d 243 (1945), *second appeal,* 159 Fla. 31, 30 So. 2d 635 (1947). A book, *Cross Creek,* which became a best seller, was written about the back woods people of Florida, and an obscure local woman was described in embarrassing personal detail. It was held that she did not became a public figure.

as to matters reasonably within the scope of the public interest which they have aroused.[232]

The privilege of giving publicity to news, and other matters of public interest, arises out of the desire and the right of the public to know what is going on in the world, and the freedom of the press and other agencies of information to tell them. "News" includes all events and items of information which are out of the ordinary humdrum routine, and which have "that indefinable quality of information which arouses public attention."[233] To a very great extent the press, with its experience or instinct as to what its readers will want, has succeeded in making its own definition of news. A glance at any morning newspaper will sufficiently indicate the content of the term. It includes homicide[234] and other crimes,[235] arrests[236] and police raids,[237] suicides,[238] marriages[239] and divorces,[240] accidents,[241] a death from the use of narcotics,[242] a woman with a rare disease,[243] the birth of a child to a twelve year old girl,[244] the filing of a libel suit,[245] a report to the police concerning the escape of a black panther,[246] the reappearance of one supposed to have been murdered years ago,[247] and undoubtedly many other similar matters of genuine, if more or less deplorable, popular appeal.[248]

---

[232] See cases cited *supra,* notes 221–31.

[233] Sweenek v. Pathe News, 16 F. Supp. 746, 747 (E.D.N.Y. 1936).

[234] Jones v. Herald Post Co., 230 Ky. 227, 18 S.W.2d 972 (1929); Bremmer v. Journal-Tribune Co., 247 Iowa 817, 76 N.W.2d 762 (1956); Waters v. Fleetwood, 212 Ga. 161, 91 S.E.2d 344 (1956); Jenkins v. Dell Pub. Co., 143 F. Supp. 953 (W.D. Pa. 1956), *aff'd,* 251 F.2d 447 (3d Cir. 1958); Bernstein v. National Broadcasting Co., 129 F. Supp. 817 (D.D.C. 1955), *aff'd,* 232 F.2d 369 (D.C. Cir. 1956).

[235] Elmhurst v. Pearson, 153 F.2d 467 (D.C. Cir. 1946) (sedition); Miller v. National Broadcasting Co., 157 F. Supp 240 (D. Del. 1957) (robbery); Hillman v. Star Pub. Co., 64 Wash. 691, 117 Pac. 594 (1911) (mail fraud).

[236] Frith v. Associated Press, 176 F. Supp. 671 (E.D.S.C. 1959) (mob action); Coverstone v. Davies, 38 Cal. 2d 315, 239 P.2d 876 (1952) ("hot-rod" race); Hull v. Curtis Pub. Co., 182 Pa. Super. 86, 125 A.2d 644 (1956).

[237] Jacova v. Southern Radio & Television Co., 83 So. 2d 34 (Fla. 1955). *Cf.* Schnabel v. Meredith, 378 Pa. 609, 107 A.2d 860 (1954).

[238] Metter v. Los Angeles Examiner, 35 Cal. App. 2d 304, 95 P.2d 491 (1939); and see Samuel v. Curtis Pub. Co., 122 F. Supp. 327 (N.D. Cal. 1954).

[239] Aquino v. Bulletin Co., 154 A.2d 422, 190 Pa. Super. 528 (1959).

[240] Berg v. Minneapolis Star & Tribune Co., 79 F. Supp. 957 (D. Minn. 1948); Aquino v. Bulletin Co., 154 A.2d 422, 190 Pa. Super. 528 (1959).

[241] Kelley v. Post Pub. Co., 327 Mass. 275, 98 N.E.2d 286 (1951). *Cf.* Strickler v. National Broadcasting Co., 167 F. Supp. 68 (S.D. Cal. 1958) (crisis in airplane).

[242] Rozhon v. Triangle Publications, 230 F.2d 539 (7th Cir. 1956). *Cf.* Abernathy v. Thornton, 263 Ala. 496, 83 So. 2d 235 (1955) (death of criminal paroled for federal offense).

[243] See Barber v. Time, Inc., 348 Mo. 1199, 159 S.W.2d 291 (1942).

[244] Meetze v. Associated Press, 230 S.C. 330, 95 S.E.2d 606 (1956).

[245] Langford v. Vanderbilt University, 199 Tenn. 389, 287 S.W.2d 32 (1956).

[246] Smith v. National Broadcasting Co., 138 Cal. App. 2d 807, 292 P.2d 600 (1956).

[247] Smith v. Doss, 251 Ala. 250, 37 So. 2d 118 (1948).

[248] See, as to unspecified news, Moser v. Press Pub. Co., 59 Misc. 78, 109 N.Y.S. 963 (Sup. Ct. 1908); Themo v. New England Newspaper Pub. Co., 306 Mass. 54, 27 N.E.2d 753 (1940).

The privilege of enlightening the public is not, however, limited to the dissemination of news in the sense of current events. It extends also to information or education, or even entertainment and amusement,[249] by books, articles, pictures, films and broadcasts concerning interesting phases of human activity in general,[250] and the reproduction of the public scene as in newsreels and travelogues.[251] In determining where to draw the line the courts have been invited to exercise nothing less than a power of censorship over what the public may be permitted to read; and they have been understandably liberal in allowing the benefit of the doubt.

Caught up and entangled in this web of news and public interest are a great many people who have not sought publicity, but indeed, as in the case of the accused criminal, have tried assiduously to avoid it. They have nevertheless lost some part of their right of privacy. The misfortunes of the frantic woman whose husband is murdered before her eyes,[252] or the innocent bystander who is caught in a raid on a cigar store and mistaken by the police for the proprietor,[253] can be broadcast to the world, and they have no remedy. Such individuals become public figures[254] for a season; and "until they have reverted to the lawful and unexciting life led by the great bulk of the community, they are subject to the privileges which publishers have to satisfy the curiosity of the public as to their leaders, heroes, villains

---

249 Ruth v. Educational Films, 194 App. Div. 893, 184 N.Y.S. 948 (1920) (baseball); Sweenek v. Pathe News, 16 F. Supp. 746 (E.D.N.Y. 1936) (group of fat women reducing with novel and comical apparatus); and see Jenkins v. Dell Pub. Co., 143 F. Supp. 953 (W.D. Pa. 1956), *aff'd*, 251 F.2d 447 (3d Cir. 1958).

250 People *ex rel.* Stern v. Robert M. McBride & Co., 159 Misc. 5, 288 N.Y.S. 501 (N.Y. City Magis. Ct. 1936) (strike-breaking); Kline v. Robert M. McBride & Co., 170 Misc. 974, 11 N.Y.S.2d 674 (Sup. Ct. 1939) (same); Samuel v. Curtis Pub. Co., 122 F. Supp. 327 (N.D. Cal. 1954) (suicide); Hogan v. A. S. Barnes Co., 114 U.S.P.Q. 314 (Pa. C.P. 1957) (golf); Oma v. Hillman Periodicals, 281 App. Div. 240, 118 NY.S.2d 720 (1953) (boxing); Delinger v. American News Co., 6 App. Div. 2d 1027, 178 N.Y.S.2d 231 (1958) (muscular development and virility).

251 Humiston v. Universal Film Mfg. Co., 189 App. Div. 467, 178 N.Y.S. 752 (1919). *Cf.* Gill v. Hearst Pub. Co., 40 Cal. 2d 224, 253 P.2d 441 (1953) (market place); Berg. v. Minneapolis Star & Tribune Co., 79 F. Supp. 957 (D. Minn. 1948) (photograph in courtroom); Lyles v. State, 330 P.2d 734 (Okl. Cr. 1958) (television in courtroom); Middleton v. News Syndicate Co., 162 Misc. 516, 295 N.Y.S. 120 (Sup. Ct. 1937) ("inquiring photographer" on the street).

252 Jones v. Herald Post Co., 230 Ky. 227, 18 S.W.2d 972 (1929).

253 Jacova v. Southern Radio & Television Co., 83 So. 2d 34 (Fla. 1955).

254 In theory the privilege as to public figures is to depict the person, while that as to news is to report the event. In practice the two often become so merged as to be inseparable. See, for example, Elmhurst v. Pearson, 153 F.2d 467 (D.D.C. 1946) (place of employment of defendant in sedition trial); Martin v. Dorton, 210 Miss. 668, 50 So. 2d 391 (1951) (mass meeting complaining of conduct of sheriff); Stryker v. Republic Pictures Corp., 108 Cal. App. 2d 191, 238 P.2d 670 (1951) (military career of war hero); Molony v. Boy Comics Publishers, 277 App. Div. 166, 98 N.Y.S.2d 119 (1950), *reversing* 188 Misc. 450, 65 N.Y.S.2d 173 (Sup. Ct. 1946) (conduct of hero in disaster). The outstanding example in our time has been the popular interest in Charles A. Lindbergh, after he flew the Atlantic.

and victims."[255] The privilege extends even to identification and some reasonable depiction of the individual's family,[256] although there must certainly be limits as to their own private lives into which the publisher cannot go.[257]

What is called for, in short, is some logical connection between the plaintiff and the matter of public interest. The most extreme cases of the privilege are those in which the likeness of an individual is used to illustrate a book or an article on some general topic, rather than any specific event. Where this is appropriate and pertinent, as where the picture of a strike-breaker is used to illustrate a book on strike-breaking,[258] or that of a Hindu illusionist is employed to illustrate an article on the Indian rope trick,[259] it has been held that there is no liability, since the public interest justifies any invasion of privacy. On the other hand, where the illustration is not pertinent, and a connection is suggested which does not exist, as where the face of an honest taxi driver appears in connection with an article on the cheating practices of the trade,[260] or the picture of a decent model illustrates one on "man hungry" women,[261] the plaintiff is placed in a false light, and may recover on that basis. The difference is well brought out by two cases in California and New York. In one of them[262]

---

255 RESTATEMENT, TORTS § 867, comment *c* (1939).

256 Smith v. Doss, 251 Ala. 250, 37 So. 2d 118 (1948) (family of man who disappeared, was believed murdered, died, and his body was brought home); Coverstone v. Davies, 38 Cal. 2d 315, 239 P.2d 876 (1952) (father of boy arrested for "hot-rod" race); Kelly v. Post Pub. Co., 327 Mass. 275, 98 N.E.2d 286 (1951) (parents of girl killed in accident); Aquino v. Bulletin Co., 190 Pa. Super. 528, 154 A.2d 422 (1959) (parents of girl secretly married and then divorced); Jenkins v. Dell Pub. Co., 143 F. Supp. 952 (W.D. Pa. 1956), *aff'd,* 251 F.2d 447 (3d Cir. 1958) (family of boy kicked to death by hoodlums); Hillman v. Star Pub. Co., 64 Wash. 691, 117 Pac. 594 (1911) (son of man arrested for mail fraud). *Cf.* Milner v. Red River Valley Pub. Co., 249 S.W.2d 227 (Tex. Civ. App. 1952) (family of man killed in accident).

257 Such a limitation is indicated in Martin v. New Metropolitan Fiction, 139 Misc. 290, 248 N.Y.S. 359 (Sup. Ct. 1931), *aff'd,* 234 App. Div. 904, 254 N.Y.S. 1015 (1931), where a mother, attending her son's criminal trial, was depicted as broken-hearted in a news story. On the pleadings, the court refused to dismiss because it could not say that evidence could not be produced which would go beyond the privilege.

258 People *ex rel.* Stern v. Robert M. McBride & Co., 159 Misc. 5, 288 N.Y.S. 501 (N.Y. City Magis. Ct. 1936); Kline v. Robert M. McBride & Co., 170 Misc. 974, 11 N.Y.S.2d 674 (Sup. Ct. 1939).

259 Sarat Lahiri v. Daily Mirror, 162 Misc. 776, 295 N.Y.S. 382 (Sup. Ct. 1937). *Accord,* Delinger v. American News Co., 6 App. Div. 2d 1027, 178 N.Y.S.2d 231 (1958) (physical training instructor, article on relation of muscular development and virility); Dallessandro v. Henry Holt & Co., 4 App. Div. 2d 470, 166 N.Y.S.2d 805 (1957) (picture of plaintiff conversing with priest who was subject of book); Oma v. Hillman Periodicals, 281 App. Div. 240, 118 N.Y.S.2d 720 (1953) (boxer, article on boxing); Gavrilov v. Duell, Sloan & Pierce, 84 N.Y.S.2d 320 (Sup. Ct. 1948), *aff'd,* 276 App. Div. 826, 93 N.Y.S.2d 715 (dancer, book on dancing).

260 Peay v. Curtis Pub. Co., 78 F. Supp. 305 (D.D.C. 1948).

261 Martin v. Johnson Pub. Co., 157 N.Y.S.2d 409 (Sup. Ct. 1956). For other examples, see *supra* notes 137–42.

262 Samuel v. Curtis Pub. Co., 122 F. Supp. 327 (N.D. Cal. 1954).

a photograph of the plaintiff arguing with a would-be suicide on a bridge was held properly used to illustrate an article on suicide. In the other[263] the picture of a boy in the slums, taken while he was innocently talking baseball on the street, was used with an artice about juvenile delinquency, entitled "Gang Boy," and he was allowed to recover.

VII

LIMITATIONS

It is clear, however, that the public figure loses his right of privacy only to a limited extent,[264] and that the privilege of reporting news and matters of public interest is likewise limited. The decisions indicate very definitely that both privileges apply only to one branch of the tort, that of disclosure of private facts about the individual. The famous motion picture acrtess who "vants to be alone"[265] unquestionably has as much right as any one else to be free from intrusion into her home or her bank account; and so has the individual whose divorce is the sensation of the day.[266] The celebrity can undoubtedly complain of the appropriation of his name or likeness for purposes of advertising, or the sale of a product,[267] and so can the victim of an accident.[268] It was once held that even the Emperor of Austria had a right to object when his name was bestowed on an insurance company.[269] And while it seems to be agreed that the courts are not arbiters of taste, and the fact that a publication is morbid, grue-

---

263 Metzger v. Dell Pub. Co., 207 Misc. 182, 136 N.Y.S.2d 888 (Sup. Ct. 1955).

264 Discussed in Spiegel, *Public Celebrity v. Scandal Magazine—The Celebrity's Right to Privacy*, 30 So. Cal. L. Rev. 280 (1957).

265 Attributed to Greta Garbo.

266 This seems to be clear from the cases holding that the publication of stolen or surreptitiously obtained pictures is actionable, even though the plaintiff is "news." See *supra* notes 109–11.

267 Eliot v. Jones, 66 Misc. 95, 120 N.Y.S. 989 (Sup. Ct. 1910), *aff'd*, 140 App. Div. 911, 125 N.Y.S. 1119 (1910) (name of president of Harvard used to sell books); Lane v. F. W. Woolworth Co., 171 Misc. 66, 11 N.Y.S.2d 199 (Sup. Ct. 1939), *aff'd*, 256 App. Div. 1065, 12 N.Y.S.2d 352 (1939) (picture of actress sold in lockets); Birmingham Broadcasting Co. v. Bell, 259 Ala. 656, 68 So. 2d 314 (1953), *later appeal*, 69 So. 2d 263 (Ala. 1957) (name of sports broadcaster used to advertise program with which he had no connection); Continental Optical Co. v. Reed, 119 Ind. App. 643, 86 N.E.2d 306 (1949) (picture of soldier used to advertise optical goods); Jansen v. Hilo Packing Co., 202 Misc. 900, 118 N.Y.S.2d 162 (Sup. Ct. 1952), *aff'd*, 282 App. Div. 935, 125 N.Y.S.2d 648 (1953) (picture of baseball player sold with popcorn). *Cf.* Kerby v. Hal Roach Studios, 53 Cal. App. 2d 207, 127 P.2d 577 (1942) (name of actress used to advertise motion picture); State *ex rel.* La Follette v. Hinkle, 131 Wash. 86, 229 Pac. 317 (1924) (use of name of politician as candidate by political party).

268 Flores v. Mosler Safe Co., 7 N.Y.2d 276, 164 N.E.2d 853 (1959), *affirming* 7 App. Div. 2d 226, 182 N.Y.S.2d 126 (1959) (picture and news story of man who accidentally set a fire used to advertise safes).

269 Von Thodorovich v. Franz Josef Beneficial Ass'n, 154 Fed. 911 (E.D. Pa. 1907). *Accord*, Edison v. Edison Polyform Mfg. Co., 73 N.J. Eq. 136, 67 Atl. 392 (Ch. 1907) (Thomas Edison).

some, lurid, sensational, immoral, and altogether cheap and despicable will not forfeit the privilege,[270] it is also clear that either the public figure[271] or the man in the news[272] can maintain an action when false or fictitious statements are published about him, or when his picture is used with an innuendo which places him in a false light before the public.[273]

But even as to the disclosure of private facts, it appears that there must be some rather undefined limits upon these privileges. Warren and Brandeis[274] thought that even a celebrity was entitled to his private life, and that he would become a public figure only as to matters already public and those which directly bore upon them. The development of the law has not been so narrow. It has recognized a legitimate public curiosity about the personalities of celebrities, and about a great deal of otherwise private

[270] Goelet v. Confidential, Inc., 5 App. Div. 2d 226, 171 N.Y.S.2d 223 (1958); Bremmer v. Journal-Tribune Pub. Co., 247 Iowa 817, 76 N.W.2d 762 (1956); Jenkins v. Dell Pub. Co., 143 F. Supp. 953 (W.D. Pa. 1956), *aff'd,* 251 F.2d 447 (3d Cir. 1958); Aquino v. Bulletin Co., 190 Pa. Super. 528, 154 A.2d 422 (1959); Waters v. Fleetwood, 212 Ga. 161, 91 S.E.2d 344 (1956).

Two cases sometimes cited to the contrary, Douglas v. Stokes, 149 Ky. 506, 149 S.W. 849 (1912), and Bazemore v. Savannah Hospital, 171 Ga. 257, 155 S.E. 194 (1930), are apparently to be explained on the basis of pictures obtained by inducing breach of trust.

It may nevertheless be suggested that there must be some as yet undefined limits of common decency as to what can be published about anyone; and that a photograph of indecent exposure, for example, can never be legitimate "news."

[271] Hazlitt v. Fawcett Publications, 116 F. Supp. 539 (D. Conn. 1953) (fictional account of stunt driver, tried for homicide); Sutton v. Hearst Corp., 277 App. Div. 155, 98 N.Y.S.2d 233 (1950), *appeal denied,* 277 App. Div. 873, 98 N.Y.S.2d 589 (1950) (fictional story about turret gunner); Hogan v. A. S. Barnes Co., 114 U.S.P.Q. 314 (Pa. C.P. 1957) (book purporting to give information from plaintiff about his golf game); Stryker v. Republic Pictures Corp., 108 Cal. App. 2d 191, 238 P.2d 670 (1951) (fiction in motion picture about war hero); Binns v. Vitagraph Co. of America, 147 App. Div. 783, 132 N.Y.S. 237 (1911), *aff'd,* 210 N.Y. 51, 103 N.E. 1108 (1913) (fiction in motion picture about radio operator hero); Donahue v. Warner Bros. Pictures, 194 F.2d 6 (10th Cir. 1952) (fiction in motion picture about entertainer); D'Altomonte v. New York Herald Co., 154 App. Div. 953, 139 N.Y.S. 200 (1913), *modified* as not within the New York statute in 208 N.Y. 596, 102 N.E. 1101 (1913) (authorship of absurd story attributed to well known writer). See also the last two cases cited *supra,* note 267.

[272] Garner v. Triangle Publications, 97 F. Supp. 546, (S.D.N.Y. 1951) (fiction added to murder story); Reed v. Real Detective Pub. Co., 63 Ariz. 294, 162 P.2d 133 (1945) (false statements in story of crime); Annerino v. Dell Pub. Co., 11 Ill. App. 2d 205, 149 N.E.2d 761 (1958) (fiction in account of murder of plaintiff's husband); Strickler v. National Broadcasting Co., 167 F. Supp. 68 (S.D. Cal. 1958) (false details in story of plaintiff's conduct in airplane crisis); Aquino v. Bulletin Co., 190 Pa. Super. 528, 154 A.2d 422 (1959) (reporter of secret marriage and subsequent divorce drew on his imagination).

[273] See the cases of pictures used to illustrate articles, *supra,* notes 137–42.

[274] "In general, then, the matters of which the publication should be repressed may be described as those which concern the private life, habits, acts and relations of an individual, and have no legitimate connection with his fitness for a public office which he seeks or for which he is suggested, and have no legitimate relation to or bearing upon any act done by him in a public or quasi public capacity." Warren and Brandeis, *The Right to Privacy,* 4 HARV. L. REV. 193, 215 (1890).

and personal information concerning them. Their biographies can be written,[275] and their life histories and their characters set forth before the world in unflattering detail. Discreditable facts about them can be exposed.[276] And as our newspapers demonstrate daily, the public can be treated to an enormous amount of petty gossip as to what they eat for breakfast, wear, read, do with their spare time, or say to their friends.

Some boundaries, however, still remain; and one may venture the guess that the private sex relations of actresses and baseball players, to say nothing of inventors and the victims of automobile accidents, are still not in the public domain.[277] As some evidence of popular feeling in such matters, one might look to the statutes in several states[278] prohibiting the public disclosure of the names of victims of sex crimes. The private letters, even of celebrities, cannot be published without their consent;[279] and the good Prince Albert was once held to have an action when his private etchings were exhibited to all comers.[280] An excellent illustration of the privacy of a public figure is a case[281] in a trial court in Los Angeles, not officially reported, in which the actor Kirk Douglas, after engaging in some undignified antics before a home motion picture camera for his friends, was held to have a cause of action when the film was put upon public exhibition.

Very probably there is some rough proportion to be looked for, between the importance of the public figure or the man in the news, and of the occasion for the public interest in him, and the nature of the private facts revealed. Perhaps there is very little in the way of information about the President of the United States, or any candidate for that high office,[282] that is not a matter of legitimate public concern; but when a mere member of the armed forces is in question, the line is drawn at his military service,

---

[275] Jeffries v. New York Evening Journal Co., 67 Misc. 570, 124 N.Y.S. 780 (Sup. Ct. 1910); Koussevitzky v. Allen, Towne & Heath, 188 Misc. 479, 68 N.Y.S.2d 779 (1947), *aff'd*, 272 App. Div. 759, 69 N.Y.S.2d 432 (1947). *Cf.* Corliss v. E. W. Walker Co., 64 Fed. 280 (D. Mass. 1894).

[276] Smith v. Suratt, 7 Alaska 416 (1926) (Dr. Cook).

[277] *Cf.* Garner v. Triangle Publications, 97 F. Supp. 546 (S.D.N.Y. 1951) (relations, partly fictional, between participants in murder).

[278] For example, FLA. STAT. § 794.03 (1957); WIS. STAT. ANN. § 942.02 (1958).

[279] Pope v. Curl, 2 Atk. 341; 26 Eng. Rep. 608 (1741); Roberts v. McKee, 29 Ga. 161 (1859); Woolsey v. Judd, 4 Duer 379 (11 N.Y. Super. 1855); Denis v. Leclerc, 1 Mart. (o.s.) 297 (La. 1811); Baker v. Libbie, 210 Mass. 599, 97 N.E. 109 (1912). Usually this has been put upon the ground of a property right in the letter itself, or literary property in its contents. See Note, 44 IOWA L. REV. 705 (1959).

[280] Prince Albert v. Strange, 1 Mac. & G. 25, 64 Eng. Rep. 293 (1848), *aff'd*, 2 De. G. & Sm. 652, 41 Eng. Rep. 1171 (1849).

[281] Douglas v. Disney Productions, reported in Los Angeles Daily Journal Rep., Dec. 31, 1956, p. 27, col. 3.

[282] Witness the disclosure, in the election of 1884, of Grover Cleveland's parentage of an illegitimate child, many years before.

and those things that more or less directly bear upon it.[283] And no doubt the defendant in a spectacular murder trial which draws national attention can expect a good deal less in the way of privacy than an ordinary citizen who is arrested for ignoring a parking ticket. But thus far there is very little in the cases to indicate just where such lines are to be drawn.

One troublesome question, which cannot be said to have been fully resolved, is that of the effect of lapse of time, during which the plaintiff has returned to obscurity. There can be no doubt that one quite legitimate function of the press is that of educating or reminding the public as to past history, and that the recall of former public figures, the revival of past events that once were news, can properly be a matter of present public interest. If it is only the event itself which is recalled, without the use of the plaintiff's name, there seems to be no doubt that even a great lapse of time does not destroy the privilege.[284] Most of the cases have held that even the use of his name[285] or likeness[286] is not enough in itself to lead to liability. Thus a luckless prosecuting attorney who once made the mistake of allowing himself to be photographed with his arm around a noted criminal was held to have no remedy when the picture was republished fifteen years later in connection with a story of the criminal's career.[287] Such decisions indicate that once a man has become a public figure, or news, he remains a matter of legitimate recall to the public mind to the end of his days.

There is, however, *Melvin v. Reid*,[288] in which it was held that the use

---

283 Stryker v. Republic Pictures Corp., 108 Cal. App. 2d 191, 238 P.2d 670 (1951); and see Continental Optical Co. v. Reed, 119 Ind. App. 643, 86 N.E.2d 306 (1949).

284 Bernstein v. National Broadcasting Co., 129 F. Supp. 817 (D.D.C. 1955), *affd*, 232 F.2d 369 (D.C. Cir. 1956) (murder and trial); Smith v. National Broadcasting Co., 138 Cal. App. 2d 807, 282 P.2d 600 (1956) (false report to police of escape of black panther).

285 Cohen v. Marx, 94 Cal. App. 2d 704, 211 P.2d 320 (1950) (pugilist, ten years); Sidis v. F-R Pub. Corp., 113 F.2d 806 (2d Cir. 1940), *affirming* 34 F. Supp. 19 (S.D.N.Y. 1938) (infant prodigy, seven years); Schnabel v. Meredith, 378 Pa. 609, 107 A.2d 860 (1954) (slot machines found on plaintiff's premises, six months).

286 Jenkins v. Dell Pub. Co., 143 F. Supp. 953 (W.D. Pa. 1956), *aff'd*, 251 F.2d 447 (3d Cir. 1958) (family of murdered boy, three months). *Accord*, as to pictures illustrating articles, Samuel v. Curtis Pub. Co., 122 F. Supp. 327 (N.D. Cal. 1954) (arguing with suicide, twenty-two months); and see Leverton v. Curtis Pub. Co., 192 F.2d 974 (3d Cir. 1951) (child struck by car, two years).

287 Estill v. Hearst Pub. Co., 186 F.2d 1017 (7th Cir. 1951).

The case of Smith v. Doss, 251 Ala. 250, 37 So. 2d 118 (1948), where a man who had disappeared and was believed to have been murdered died in a distant state, and his body was brought back to town, is probably to be distinguished on the basis that the later event was itself "news," and so justified the revival of the story.

288 112 Cal. App. 285, 297 Pac. 91 (1931).

The report of the case leaves the facts in some doubt. It came up on the plaintiff's pleading, which alleged that the defendant made use of the plaintiff's maiden name of Gabrielle Darley, and that "by the production and showing of the picture, friends of appellant learned for the first time of the unsavory incidents of her early life." It is difficult to see how this was accomplished, unless the picture also revealed her present identity under her married name of Melvin. At least the allegation is not to be ignored in interpreting the case.

of the name of a former prostitute and murder defendant made the publisher liable when a motion picture narrated her story; and there are a few other cases[289] that look in the same direction. One may speculate that the real reason for the decision in the *Melvin* case was not the use of the name in connection with past history, but the disclosure of the plaintiff's whereabouts and identity, which were no part of the revived "news," or perhaps that the explanation lay in the shocking enormity of the revelation of a woman's past when she was trying to lead a decent life, and that again something in the nature of a "mores" test is to be applied. There is, however, almost nothing in the cases to throw any satisfactory light upon such speculations. All that can be said is that there appear to be situations in which ancient history cannot safely be revived.

VIII

DEFENSES

Next in order are the various defenses to the claim of invasion of privacy. It is clear first of all that the truth of the matter published does not arise in the cases of intrusion, and can be no defense to the appropriation of name or likeness, nor to the public disclosure of private facts.[290] It may, however, be in issue where the third form of the tort is involved, that of putting the plaintiff in a false light in the public eye,[291] and to that extent it has some limited importance, and cannot be entirely ruled out.

Chief among the available defenses is that of the plaintiff's consent to the invasion, which will bar his recovery as in the case of any other tort.[292] It may be given expressly, or by conduct, such as posing for a picture with knowledge of the purposes for which it is to be used,[293] or industriously

[289] Mau v. Rio Grande Oil, Inc., 28 F. Supp. 845 (N.D. Cal. 1939) (radio dramatization of robbery); and see the cases cited *supra*, note 284.

In Barber v. Time, Inc., 348 Mo. 1199, 159 S.W.2d 291 (1942), the court laid stress upon the "unnecessary" use of the name in even a current report, concerning a woman suffering from a rare disease. The decision, however, appears rather to rest upon the intrusion of taking her picture in bed in a hospital.

[290] Brents v. Morgan, 221 Ky. 765, 299 S.W. 967 (1927); Melvin v. Reid, 112 Cal. App. 285, 297 Pac. 91 (1931); Mau v. Rio Grande Oil, Inc., 28 F. Supp. 845 (N.D. Cal. 1939); Barber v. Time, Inc., 348 Mo. 1199, 159 S.W.2d 291 (1942); Cason v. Baskin, 155 Fla. 198, 20 So. 2d 243 (1945), *second appeal*, 159 Fla. 31, 30 So. 2d 635 (1947); Themo v. New England Newspaper Pub. Co., 306 Mass. 54, 27 N.E.2d 753 (1940).

[291] See *supra*, text at notes 127–50.

[292] Grossman v. Frederick Bros. Acceptance Corp., 34 N.Y.S.2d 785 (Sup. Ct., App. T. 1942) (written consent a complete defense under the New York statute); Jenkins v. Dell Pub. Co., 143 F. Supp. 953 (W.D. Pa. 1956), *aff'd*, 250 F.2d 447 (3d Cir. 1958); Reitmeister v. Reitmeister, 162 F.2d 691 (2d Cir. 1947); Tanner-Brice Co. v. Sims, 174 Ga. 13, 161 S.E. 819 (1931).

In Porter v. American Tobacco Co., 140 App. Div. 871, 125 N.Y.S. 710 (1910), it was held that consent must be pleaded and proved as a defense.

[293] Gill v. Hearst Pub. Co., 40 Cal. 2d 224, 253 P.2d 441 (1953); Thayer v. Worcester Post Co., 284 Mass. 160, 187 N.E. 292 (1933); Wendell v. Conduit Machine Co., 74 Misc. 201, 133 N.Y.S. 758 (Sup. Ct. 1911); Johnson v. Boeing Airplane Co., 175 Kan. 275, 262 P.2d 808 (1953).

seeking publicity of the same kind.[294] A gratuitous consent can be revoked at any time before the invasion;[295] but if the agreement is a matter of contract it is normally irrevocable, and there is no liability for any publicity or appropriation within its terms.[296] But if the actual invasion goes beyond the contract, fairly construed, as by alteration of the plaintiff's picture,[297] or publicity materially differing in kind or in extent from that contemplated,[298] the consent is not effective to avoid liability. The statutes[299] all require that the consent be given in writing. As against the contention that this can still be "waived" by consent given orally, the rule which has emerged in New York is that the oral consent will not bar the cause of action, but is to be taken into account in mitigation of damages.[300]

---

[294] In O'Brien v. Pabst Sales Co., 124 F.2d 167 (5th Cir. 1941), the fact that the plaintiff had gone to great lengths to get himself named as an all-American football player was held to prevent any recovery for publicity given to him in that capacity. *Cf.* Gautier v. Pro-Football, Inc., 304 N.Y. 354, 107 N.E.2d 485 (1952) (television broadcast of performing animal act at football game).

See also Schmieding v. American Farmers Mut. Ins. Co., 138 F. Supp. 167 (D. Neb. 1955), where the plaintiff failed to object to continued use of his rubber-stamp signature after termination of his employment.

[295] Garden v. Parfumerie Rigaud, 151 Misc. 692, 271 N.Y.S. 187 (Sup. Ct. 1933); State *ex rel.* La Follette v. Hinkle, 131 Wash. 86, 229 Pac. 317 (1924).

[296] Lillie v. Warner Bros. Pictures, 139 Cal. App. 724, 34 P.2d 835 (1934) (motion picture contract includes use of "shorts"); Long v. Decca Records, 76 N.Y.S.2d 133 (Sup. Ct. 1947) (contract to make records held to include use of name and picture in advertising); Fairbanks v. Winik, 119 Misc. 809, 198 N.Y.S. 299 (Sup. Ct. 1922) (motion picture actor surrenders right to use of film); Wendell v. Conduit Machine Co., 74 Misc. 201, 133 N.Y.S. 758 (Sup. Ct. 1911) (use of employee's picture in business after termination of employment); Marek v. Zanol Products Co., 298 Mass. 1, 9 N.E.2d 393 (1937) (contract consent to use of name); Sharaga v. Sinram Bros., 275 App. Div. 967, 90 N.Y.S.2d 705 (1949) (use of salesman's name after termination of employment); Johnson v. Boeing Airplane Co., 175 Kan. 275, 262 P.2d 808 (1953) (consent to picture in house organ held to include national publication).

In Bell v. Birmingham Broadcasting Co., 263 Ala. 355, 82 So. 2d 345 (1955), it was held that a custom of giving consent was proper evidence bearing on the interpretation of the contract.

[297] *Cf.* Manger v. Kree Institute of Electrolysis, 233 F.2d 5 (2d Cir. 1956) (letter altered to make it testimonial); Myers v. Afro-American Pub. Co., 168 Misc. 429, 5 N.Y.S.2d 223 (Sup. Ct. 1938), *aff'd*, 255 App. Div. 838, 7 N.Y.S.2d 662 (1938) (consent to use of semi-nude picture on condition that nudity be covered up).

[298] Ettore v. Philco Television Broadcasting Co., 229 F.2d 481 (3d Cir. 1956) (motion picture contract held not to include use of the film on television, subsequently developed); Colgate-Palmolive Co. v. Tullos, 219 F.2d 617 (5th Cir. 1955) (use of employee's picture in advertising after termination of employment); Sinclair v. Postal Tel. & Cable Co., 72 N.Y.S.2d 841 (Sup. Ct. 1935) (picture of actor putting him in undignified light); Russell v. Marboro Books, 18 Misc. 2d 166, 183 N.Y.S.2d 8 (Sup. Ct. 1959) (picture of model used in bawdy advertisement of bed sheets).

[299] *Supra*, notes 14, 52–54. It has been held that the consent of an infant is ineffective under the New York statute and that of the parent must be obtained. Semler v. Ultem Publications, 170 Misc. 551, 9 N.Y.S.2d 319 (N.Y. City Ct. 1938); Wyatt v. James McCreery Co., 126 App. Div. 650, 111 N.Y.S. 86 (1908).

[300] Buschelle v. Conde Nast Publications, 173 Misc. 674, 19 N.Y.S.2d 129 (Sup. Ct. 1940); Hammond v. Crowell Pub. Co., 253 App. Div. 205, 1 N.Y.S.2d 728 (1938); Miller v. Madison

Other defenses have appeared only infrequently. Warren and Brandeis[301] thought that the action for invasion of privacy must be subject to any privilege which would justify the publication of libel or slander, reasoning that that which is true should be no less privileged than that which is false. There is still no reason to doubt this conclusion, since the absolute privilege of a witness,[302] and the qualified one to report the filing of a nominating petition for office[303] or the pleadings in a civil suit[304] have both been recognized. The privilege of the defendant to protect or further his own legitimate interests has appeared in a case or two, where a telephone company has been permitted to monitor calls,[305] and the defendant was allowed to make use of the plaintiff's name in insuring his wife without his consent.[306] It has been held that where uncopyrighted literature is in the public domain, and the defendant is free to publish it, the name of the plaintiff may be used to indicate its authorship,[307] and that when the plaintiff has designed dresses for the defendant it is no invasion of his privacy to disclose his connection with the product in advertising.[308]

The conflict of laws, so far as the right of privacy is concerned, is in the same state of bewildered confusion as that which surrounds the law of defamation. The writer has attempted to deal with it elsewhere,[309] and will not repeat it here.

Square Garden Corp., 176 Misc. 714, 28 N.Y.S.2d 811 (Sup. Ct. 1941) (reduced to nominal damages); Lane v. F. W. Woolworth Co., 171 Misc. 66, 11 N.Y.S.2d 199 (Sup. Ct. 1939), *aff'd,* 256 App. Div. 1065, 12 N.Y.S.2d 352 (1939); Harris v. H. W. Gossard Co., 194 App. Div. 688, 185 N.Y.S. 861 (1921).

301 Warren and Brandeis, *The Right to Privacy,* 4 HARV. L. REV. 193, 216 (1890).

302 Application of Tiene, 19 N.J. 149, 115 A.2d 543 (1955).

303 Johnson v. Scripps Pub. Co., 18 Ohio Op. 372 (C.P. 1940).

304 Langford v. Vanderbilt University, 199 Tenn. 389, 287 S.W.2d 32 (1956). *Cf.* Lyles v. State, 330 P.2d 734 (Okl. Cr. 1958) (television in courtroom); Berg v. Minneapolis Star & Tribune Co., 79 F. Supp. 957 (D. Minn. 1948) (photograph taken in courtroom).

305 Schmukler v. Ohio-Bell Tel. Co., 116 N.E.2d 819 (Ohio C.P. 1953). *Accord,* People v. Appelbaum, 277 App. Div. 43, 97 N.Y.S.2d 807 (1950), *aff'd,* 301 N.Y. 738, 95 N.E.2d 410 (1950) (subscriber tapping his own telephone to protect his interests). *Cf.* Davis v. General Finance & Thrift Co., 80 Ga. App. 708, 57 S.E.2d 225 (1950) (creditor's telegram to debtor threatening suit); Gouldman-Taber Pontiac, Inc. v. Zerbst, 213 Ga. 682, 100 S.E.2d 881 (1957) (creditor's complaint to debtor's employer).

306 Holloman v. Life Ins. Co. of Va., 192 S.C. 454, 7 S.E.2d 169 (1940).

307 Ellis v. Hurst, 70 Misc. 122, 128 N.Y.S. 144 (Sup. Ct. 1910); Shostakovitch v. Twentieth-Century Fox Film Corp., 196 Misc. 67, 80 N.Y.S.2d 575 (Sup. Ct. 1948), *aff'd,* 275 App. Div. 692, 87 N.Y.S.2d 430 (1949).

Cf. White v. William G. White Co., 160 App. Div. 709, 145 N.Y.S. 743 (1914), where the plaintiff's sale of a corporation bearing his name was held to convey the right to continue to use it.

308 Brociner v. Radio Wire Television, Inc., 15 Misc. 2d 843, 183 N.Y.S.2d 743 (Sup. Ct. 1959).

309 Prosser, *Interstate Publication,* 51 MICH. L. REV. 959 (1953), reprinted in PROSSER, SELECTED TOPICS ON THE LAW OF TORTS 70–134 (1953).

CONCLUSION

It is evident from the foregoing that, by the use of a single word supplied by Warren and Brandeis, the courts have created an independent basis of liability, which is a complex of four distinct and only loosely related torts; and that this has been expanded by slow degrees to invade, overlap, and encroach upon a number of other fields. So far as appears from the decisions, the process has gone on without any plan, without much realization of what is happening or its significance, and without any consideration of its dangers. They are nonetheless sufficiently obvious, and not to be overlooked.

One cannot fail to be aware, in reading privacy cases, of the extent to which defenses, limitations and safeguards established for the protection of the defendant in other tort fields have been jettisoned, disregarded, or ignored. Taking intrusion first, the gist of the wrong is clearly the intentional infliction of mental distress, which is now in itself a recognized basis of tort liability.[310] Where such mental disturbance stands on its own feet, the courts have insisted upon extreme outrage, rejecting all liability for trivialities, and upon genuine and serious mental harm, attested by physical illness, or by the circumstances of the case. But once "privacy" gets into the picture, and the fact of intrusion is added, such guarantees apparently are no longer required. No doubt the cases thus far have been sufficiently extreme; but the question may well be raised whether there are not some limits, and whether, for example, a lady who insists upon sun-bathing in the nude in her own back yard should really have a cause of action for her humiliation when the neighbors examine her with appreciation and binoculars.

The public disclosure of private facts, and putting the plaintiff in a false light in the public eye, both concern the interest in reputation, and move into the field occupied by defamation. Here, as a result of some centuries of conflict, there have been jealous safeguards thrown about the freedom of speech and of the press, which are now turned on the left flank. Gone is the defense of truth, and the defendant is held liable for the publication of entirely accurate statements of fact, without any wrongful motive. Gone also is the requirement of special damage where what is said is not libel or slander "per se"—which, however antiquated and unreasonable the rigid categories may be, has at least served some useful purpose in the discouragement of trivial and extortionate claims. Gone even is the need for any defamatory innuendo at all, since the publication of nondefamatory facts, or of even laudatory fiction concerning the plaintiff, may be enough. The retraction statutes, with their provision for demand

310 Discussed at length in Prosser, *Insult and Outrage*, 44 CALIF. L. REV. 40 (1956).

upon the defendant, and the limitation to proved special damage if a demand is not made, or is complied with, are circumvented; and so are the statutes requiring the filing of a bond for costs before a defamation action can be begun. These are major inroads upon a right to which there has always been much sentimental devotion in our land; and they have gone almost entirely unremarked. Perhaps more important still is the extent to which, under any test of "ordinary sensibilities," or the "mores" of the community as to what is acceptable and proper, the courts, although cautiously and reluctantly, have accepted a power of censorship over what the public may be permitted to read, extending very much beyond that which they have always had under the law of defamation.

As for the appropriation cases, they create in effect, for every individual, a common law trade name, his own, and a common law trade mark in his likeness. They confer upon him rights much more extensive than those which any corporation engaged in business can expect under the law of unfair competition. These rights are subject to the verdict of a jury. And there has been no hint that they are in any way affected by any of the limitations which have been considered necessary and desirable in the ordinary law of trade marks and trade names.

This is not to say that the developments in the law of privacy are wrong. Undoubtedly they have been supported by genuine public demand and lively public feeling, and made necessary by real abuses on the part of defendants who have brought it all upon themselves. It is to say rather that it is high time that we realize what we are doing, and give some consideration to the question of where, if anywhere, we are to call a halt.

All this is a most marvelous tree to grow from the wedding of the daughter of Mr. Samuel D. Warren. One is tempted to surmise that she must have been a very beautiful girl. Resembling, perhaps, that fabulous creature, the daughter of a Mr. Very, a confectioner in Regent Street, who was so wondrous fair that her presence in the shop caused three or four hundred people to assemble every day in the street before the window to look at her, so that her father was forced to send her out of town, and counsel was led to inquire whether she might not be indicted as a public nuisance.[311] This was the face that launched a thousand lawsuits.

311 Reported in a note to Rex v. Carlisle, 6 Car. & P. 636, 172 Eng. Rep. 1397 (1834).

Portrait of a Civil Libertarian: The Faith and Fear of Zechariah Chafee, Jr.

JONATHAN PRUDE

"NEVER in the history of our country, since the Alien and Sedition Acts of 1798," announced a concerned young Harvard law professor, Zechariah Chafee, Jr., "has the meaning of free speech been the subject of such sharp controversy as today." Appearing as it did in a 1919 *Harvard Law Review* article,[1] amidst the unreasoning suspicion of dissent which pervaded the country during and just after World War I, this assessment, despite its somewhat dramatic tone, was not unwarranted. The xenophobia aroused by President Woodrow Wilson's call to arms, together with the fear and confusion engendered by the Bolshevik Revolution, had created an atmosphere in which the guarantees of the First Amendment were ignored by private citizen and public official alike. By the time the essay appeared, the Wisconsin socialist Victor Berger had been banned from Congress, *Masses* had been excluded from the mails, and more than 800 persons had been convicted in the federal courts under the most severe espionage and sedition legislation enacted in more than a century.[2]

In the face of such widespread disregard for free speech, the recommendation offered by Chafee was sensible enough. What was needed, he observed, was "to determine the true limits of freedom of expression, so that speakers and writers may know how much they can properly say, and governments may be sure how much they can lawfully and wisely suppress."[3]

Although he did not then know it, and although he would subsequently have cause to regret it, Zechariah Chafee, Jr.—at the age of thirty-three—

Jonathan Prude is a graduate student in history at Harvard University.

[1] Zechariah Chafee, Jr., "Freedom of Speech in War Time," *Harvard Law Review*, XXXII (June 1919), 932.

[2] See Zechariah Chafee, Jr., *Free Speech in the United States* (Cambridge, Mass., 1941), 247-69, 42-52.

[3] Chafee, "Freedom of Speech in War Time," 933.

had found his life's work. Throughout the next forty years, in books, articles, pamphlets, and occasionally in speeches, he would repeatedly return to the problem of determining the true limits of freedom of expression. His interest in free speech was as unexpected as it was prolonged. Neither as a law student nor as a member of a prestigious Rhode Island law firm, which he had joined after receiving his degree, had Chafee evidenced even the slightest curiosity about questions of civil liberty.[4] It was only with the sedition and espionage trials during the war that he seems to have realized that tolerance was less a social axiom in America than a principle badly in need of defense.

Chafee quickly demonstrated, however, an extraordinary skill at framing shrewd and persuasive arguments on behalf of free expression. By the time he retired from the Harvard faculty in 1956, his work had won him widespread public recognition as an advocate of free speech; lawyers and legal scholars, even when they disagreed with him, could not deny that he had emerged as one of the country's distinguished civil libertarians.

Chafee, of course, was not the only attorney to think about the problem. The years spanned by his career saw many legal authorities, both on and off the bench, consider issues relating to free expression. This was a crucial period in the development of American libertarian consciousness, not so much because any questions were finally resolved but because during these years civil liberty, and free speech in particular, attracted attention in quarters where it had hitherto been largely ignored and won the support of identifiable interest groups which had not previously existed.

Chafee's initiation into the whole subject of free speech just after World War I coincided with the Supreme Court's first real attempt to interpret the First Amendment. Prior to the Espionage Act of 1917 and its even more draconian successor, the so-called Sedition Act of 1918, the federal government had made no direct attempt to limit free speech since the fiasco of the Alien and Sedition Acts.[5] As a result, the Supreme Court, which had not passed on the 1798 laws and which, after 1833, had refused to regard the

[4] Zechariah Chafee, Jr., *Thirty-five Years with Freedom of Speech* (New York, 1952), 1-2. When Zechariah Chafee thought about the subject at all, he had simply assumed that the whole prewar era was a time when "[a]ll possibilities were open to examination, under the guiding principle, 'Prove all things; hold fast that which is good.' " Z[echariah] C[hafee], Jr., "Harold Laski and the *Harvard Law Review*," *Harvard Law Review*, LXIII (June 1950), 1398.

[5] Giles J. Patterson, *Free Speech and a Free Press* (Boston, 1939), 146; Alfred Kelly, "Constitutional Liberty and the Law of Libel: A Historian's View," *American Historical Review*, LXXIV (Dec. 1968), 443. The conspiracy sections of the criminal code passed during the Civil War might be seen as an exception to this statement. See 18 U.S.C.A. [United States Code Annotated] section 2384 (1970). See also Chafee, *Free Speech in the United States*, 146-48, 507.

Bill of Rights as binding on state legislation,[6] had found little opportunity to explore the constitutional implications of free speech until appeals from convictions under the World War I statutes appeared on its docket.[7] Predictably, the decisions handed down in these cases and in others arising over the next several decades did not resolve all the questions surrounding free speech, but simply by beginning to deal with the First Amendment directly the Court inevitably helped to clarify the issues. By the end of the 1920s, moreover, the Bill of Rights had been extended to cover state laws,[8] and Justices Oliver Wendell Holmes and Louis D. Brandeis had used several of their opinions as occasions for resonant and persuasive defenses for free expression.[9] The civil libertarian—judge, lawyer, or layman—could thus measure his legal arguments against the opinions of the Court and bolster his philosophic rationale with Holmes' rhetoric.

The same World War I sedition trials which stirred Chafee and the Court into action led Roger Baldwin to start the National Civil Liberties Bureau, which soon evolved into its more famous successor, the American Civil Liberties Union (ACLU).[10] As a private national defense organization, ACLU divided its energies between aiding particular citizens whose rights it felt were being violated and organizing publicity campaigns aimed at building within the general public a firm libertarian constituency. In effect, Baldwin

[6] For the doctrine that state laws could not be judged by the standard of the federal Bill of Rights, see *Barron* v. *Baltimore*, 7 Peters 243 (1833).

[7] The Court was occasionally called on to render decisions upon libel law. For example, it turned back in 1911 "what amounted to a federal criminal common law [libel] suit" initiated by "two overenthusiastic district attorneys" determined to defend the Taft administration against criticism of its Panama Canal policy. Kelly, "Constitutional Liberty and the Law of Libel," 433n, 443; *United States* v. *Smith*, 173 F. 227 (D. Ind. 1909). The Court in 1907 was asked to rule on the trial and conviction of an editor for his criticism of the Colorado state supreme court. The defendants insisted that the privileges and immunities guaranteed by the Fourteenth Amendment necessarily included the rights of free speech and a free press. The Court, however, was not at this point ready to consider this extension of the First Amendment and sustained the conviction on the grounds "that the State court had the power to punish publications which it regarded as tending to interfere with the administration of justice. . . ." *Patterson* v. *Colorado*, 205 U.S. 454 (1907). See Patterson, *Free Speech and a Free Press*, 146-47.

[8] The Court in 1925 held that under the liberty clause of the Fourteenth Amendment, state laws could be held liable to the federal Constitution. In the specific case at hand, however, the majority did not find that the state law had violated the First Amendment. *Gitlow* v. *New York*, 268 U.S. 652 (1925).

[9] Oliver Wendell Holmes' career does not reveal the continuous devotion to civil liberties that historians have sometimes read into it. Nevertheless, by the early 1920s several of his opinions, even those which he may not have originally intended as pro-free speech, provided highly useful phrases and rules of law for adamant libertarians. Fred D. Ragan, "Justice Oliver Wendell Holmes, Jr., Zechariah Chafee, Jr., and the Clear and Present Danger Test for Free Speech: The First Year, 1919," *Journal of American History*, LVIII (June 1971), 24-45.

[10] See Donald Johnson, *The Challenge to American Freedoms: World War I and the Rise of the American Civil Liberties Union* ([Lexington], 1963), x.

and his colleagues represented the emergence of the non-judicial civil libertarian into a new social and intellectual type. They were full-time professional activist-advocates, for whom defending the Bill of Rights inevitably involved direct engagement in controversy and whose method of defense moved easily from the declaration of abstract principles to pitched courtroom battles and even to public protests.

Chafee drew on the men and ideas around him. Baldwin was a personal friend and Holmes was an authority to whom he frequently referred in his writings. At the same time, however, Chafee's work retained its own particular identity. It was not only that his arguments often took a distinctive tack on substantive issues but also that his whole approach to civil liberty questions had a unique tone and emphasis.

Although he was deeply committed to arousing interest in free speech, he wished to do so only through argumentation—not action—and only through argumentation that was sober and rational. He was, after all, a scholar. He had left a lucrative law practice in 1916 to accept a teaching position at Harvard, and he took seriously his identity as a man devoted to calm and detached reflection.[11] As he was willing to admit, his temperament was that of an observer, not a reformer; and he viewed his role as that of an "investigator and advisor, always ready to express an opinion but reluctant to campaign."[12] Like many other brilliant law students who began increasingly to teach law rather than practice it in the years after World War I, Chafee found special pleasure in the mix of theory and hard reality afforded by legal scholarship and the opportunity it offered to "be a scholar without living in an ivory tower."[13] The problem with free speech, however, was that it threatened constantly to escape the boundaries of reasoned discussion and to evolve into endless and ill-formed debates based on mere righteousness. Whenever that happened, Chafee bridled and declared that the whole topic annoyed him, that he preferred subjects which could be dealt with clearly and dispassionately. He never actually ceased to write about civil liberty, but whenever he did take it up he did so on his own terms. Advocacy to Chafee never involved a loud voice.[14]

[11] For discussion of the place occupied by scholars like Chafee within the legal profession, see Jerold Auerbach, "Enmity and Amity: Law Teachers and Practitioners, 1900-1922," *Perspectives in American History*, V (1971), 551-601.

[12] Chafee to John S. Codman, June 4, 1920, File 20, Box XXX, Zechariah Chafee Papers (Law Library, Harvard University).

[13] Chafee to Felix Frankfurter, April 25, 1944, File 15, Box IV, Chafee Papers.

[14] Chafee went so far as to hold up the clear logic of insurance law as a model and to claim that his most important contribution was not his work on free speech but his effort to help legislators formulate the 1936 Interpleader Act under which millions of dollars in unclaimed insurance claims were speedily ajudicated. Zechariah Chafee, Jr., *The Free and the Brave* (New York, 1950), 2.

If the tone with which free speech was frequently discussed tended to make Chafee a rather reluctant libertarian, so did the fact that many of the men whose free speech he championed were far to the left of him politically. The heir to an established Rhode Island family, the son of a prominent Providence businessman, and ultimately the chairman of a substantial corporation, Chafee was hardly a radical. He had a deep and abiding faith in the sanctity of order and the justice of the American status quo. In 1921, when a group of prominent Harvard Law School alumni attempted to have him fired for his overzealous interest in the rights of radicals, Chafee successfully defended himself by declaring, "My people have been business people for generations. . . . My family is a family that has money. I believe in property and I believe in making money. . . ."[15] He did not deny the existence of problems or the necessity of reform. When the time came, he cheerfully accepted the New Deal. But that was as far as he was willing to go. He was never touched, as Baldwin sometimes was, by a desire for wholesale revision. Indeed, a basic tenet of his philosophy was that free speech should be permitted precisely because it was an important part of an ongoing society and diminished the chances of sudden and drastic upheavals. The fact that, despite all his declarations to the contrary, he was still often dubbed an extremist was infuriating to Chafee and provided yet another reason for his periodic expressions of impatience with free speech discussions.

But if Chafee was clearly not a freewheeling libertarian propagandist, he was not quite the patrician he has sometimes been made out to be.[16] To be sure, in both his intellectual style and basic political sympathies, he demonstrated many similarities to the confident, often condescending manner of a thinker like Holmes. For the most part he viewed the radical defendants in free speech cases with a sort of complacent *noblesse oblige*, a subtle blend of compassion and outright disdain. If Holmes could speak of them as "poor devils," Chafee could as easily call them "the very queer people."[17]

[15] Quoted in Harlan B. Phillips, *Felix Frankfurter Reminisces* (New York, 1960), 197. See also Arthur E. Sutherland, *The Law at Harvard: A History of Ideas and Men, 1817-1967* (Cambridge, Mass., 1967), 255-56. A letter signed by Austen G. Fox and twenty other graduates of the law school was sent to Harvard President Abbott Lawrence Lowell in 1920 protesting that Chafee's essay, "A Contemporary State Trial—The United States *versus* Jacob Abrams *et al.*," (*Harvard Law Review*, XXXIII [April 1920], 747-74), was substantively inaccurate and reflected views which made its author unfit to "be entrusted with the training of youth." Chafee was acquitted of the charges by a Special Committee created by the Board of Overseers by a vote of 6-5. Sutherland, *Law at Harvard*, 250-59.

[16] Jerold Auerbach, "The Patrician as Libertarian: Zechariah Chafee, Jr. and Freedom of Speech," *New England Quarterly*, XLII (Dec. 1969), 521-22.

[17] Mark DeWolfe Howe, ed., *Holmes-Laski Letters: The Correspondence of Mr. Justice Holmes and Harold J. Laski, 1916-1935* (2 vols., Cambridge, Mass., 1953), I, 203; Chafee to Daniel Doherty, April 21, 1941, File 3, Box XXXI, Chafee Papers.

For Chafee, however, this rather smug attitude was coupled with, and often overbalanced by, a suspicion that his confidence in America was misplaced. Beneath his commitment to the nation's institutions and traditions was a deep fear that the citizenry could at any moment succumb to irrational fears and suspicions and do away with civil liberty altogether. The sedition trials of World War I always represented for Chafee a particularly powerful demonstration of precisely this phenomenon, and throughout the remainder of his career his single greatest concern was that reason might again someday give way to mindless repression. Ironically, his own temperament, his commitment to rational debate and order—the very qualities which often made him seem aloof and stolidly uncritical of American society—only served to aggravate this anxiety. He was simply unequipped to see the waves of intolerance, which swept through the American people several times during his lifetime, as developments to be analyzed and understood. To him, such occurrences were simply incomprehensible disasters.

Faith in the justice of American society and fear of its vulnerability to irrational behavior in effect established two poles toward which Chafee's mind, sometimes confident, sometimes skeptical, was alternately attracted. And it is precisely the presence of these two themes in his thought—the faith and the fear—which make Chafee a distinctive and important figure. He was not simply defending free speech in America; he was also inquiring into its very possibility.

The first public expression of Chafee's thinking on free speech was an article appearing in the *New Republic* in 1918 attacking the sedition trials then being conducted by the government.[18] The same topic was treated in far greater detail the following year when Chafee published his classic essay "Freedom of Speech in War Time" in the *Harvard Law Review* and commenced in earnest his life-long effort to locate the "true limits of free expression."[19] In 1920, he wrote another article, this one sharply critical of the government's position in *United States* v. *Jacob Abrams et al.*, a case in which six young Russian immigrants were convicted for protesting the American armed intervention in Russia.[20] These last two articles were both included in *Freedom of Speech*, Chafee's definitive effort in this area of the law and a landmark in the literature of American civil liberties. By the time the book was expanded and republished in 1941 (under the title *Free*

[18] Zechariah Chafee, Jr., "Freedom of Speech," *New Republic*, XVII (Nov. 16, 1918), 66-69.

[19] Chafee, "Freedom of Speech in War Time," 932-73.

[20] Zechariah Chafee, Jr., "A Contemporary State Trial—Jacob Abrams *et al.*," *Harvard Law Review*, XXXIII (April 1920), 747-74.

Speech in the United States), it was regarded as a veritable bible for lawyers interested in the issue.[21]

Part of the persuasiveness of all Chafee's writing, at least in its treatment of the more purely legal issues surrounding free speech, was its consistency. His understanding of how (or whether) free speech functioned in American society varied considerably over the years, but from the earliest articles to the last edition of *Free Speech in the United States* his formulation of the legal questions remained essentially unaltered. For Chafee, the basic legal problem was the difficulty of establishing a clear and flexible test by which courts might determine whether or not a given statement passed beyond the protection afforded by the First Amendment. He never suggested that free speech was an absolute or unlimited right. He always maintained that the government "has affirmative power to protect its own life and the lives of its officers, not only from revolution and assassination but also from attempts and solicitation directed toward these ends. . . ."[22] Meanwhile, however, Chafee rejected Blackstone's contention that "the liberty of the press . . . consists in laying no *previous* restraints upon publications and not in freedom from censure for criminal matter when published."[23] To grant a man the freedom to say anything at all while simultaneously granting the government the freedom to punish a speaker after he had said anything at all was, in Chafee's view, a meager freedom.

The proper definition of free speech was somewhere between these extremes and could be formulated only by balancing opposing interests and powers. The individual has the right to speak and the community has the right to hear him, but the community also has the right to set limits on what he says. A principle was needed by which to judge the conflicting rights, and by 1919 Chafee was arguing that the true "boundary line of free speech . . . is fixed close to the point where words will give rise to unlawful acts."[24] By 1920, when *Freedom of Speech* was published, he was prepared to adopt the classic test put forward by Holmes in *United States* v. *Schenck* as "substantially" affirming the same "boundary line":

> *The question in every case* [Holmes wrote for a unimous Court] *is whether the words used are used in such circumstances and are of such a nature as to create a clear and present danger that they will bring about the substantive evils that Congress has a right to prevent.*[25]

[21] Zechariah Chafee, Jr., *Freedom of Speech* (New York, 1920); Zechariah Chafee, Jr., *Free Speech in the United States* (Cambridge, Mass., 1941).

[22] Chafee, *Free Speech in the United States*, 171.

[23] *Ibid.*, 9.

[24] Chafee, "Freedom of Speech in War Time," 960.

[25] Quoted in Chafee, *Freedom of Speech*, 88, with italics supplied by Chafee.

For Chafee, the fact that the Schenck decision had upheld the defendant's conviction was far outweighed by the persuasiveness of the "clear and present danger" test. He interpreted the formula to mean that the state would not prosecute a man on the grounds that his words or deeds might have a remote "tendency" to cause an evil. He was adamant on this point because he was convinced that it was prosecution for the "bad tendency" of words, rather than their actual "danger," which had constituted "the very essence of sedition as defined by the English courts during the eighteenth century" and which had worked to stifle freedom of speech and of the press in both the colonies and England.[26] It was also the inclination to punish "tendency" that represented in Chafee's mind the single greatest source of legal error during the World War I trials.[27] What had been forgotten in the courts during these years was that even in wartime, when the problem of national security was so directly at stake, the boundary line of free speech must be fixed close to the point where "the interest of public safety is really imperiled, and not, as many believe, when it is barely conceivable that it may be slightly affected."[28]

But although he used the Schenck doctrine, Chafee was not blind to its limitations. Holmes, as Chafee pointed out, had initially been quite reluctant to use the test as a forceful libertarian weapon or, for that matter, even to use it consistently. Only weeks after the Schenck decision, Holmes had written the Court's opinion upholding the conviction of Eugene Debs on grounds that were at most, in Chafee's view, "bad tendency." Indeed, Holmes' career as a civil libertarian did not really begin until the Abrams case reached the Court. It was only then that Holmes, joined in his eloquent dissent by Brandeis, first started to oppose the majority and to use the "clear and present danger" formula as a positive rule to defend free speech.[29]

[26] Chafee, *Free Speech in the United States*, 392.

[27] Chafee's critique of these trials did not directly attack the various sedition and espionage laws under which the defendants were being tried. In his view, the Federal Espionage Act of 1917, which forbade interference with the armed forces when the nation was at war, the Sedition Act of 1918, which extended the earlier law to include, in part, prohibitions against "scurrilous or abusive language" directed toward the government, the Constitution, the flag, or the military uniform, and the scores of state laws which were enacted during these years were probably all constitutional and did not in themselves obviate free speech. Saddled with a "bad tendency" interpretation, however, these statutes became lethal barriers to dissent. See Chafee, *Free Speech in the United States*, 84-85, 101, 136.

[28] *Ibid.*, 35.

[29] *Ibid.*, 84-86. Chafee was generous enough to suggest that Holmes may have been simply biding his time, hoping to avoid alienating his more conservative colleagues by moving cautiously himself. For an analysis of Holmes' thought between the Schenck and Abrams decisions, see Ragan, "Justice Oliver Wendell Holmes, Jr., Zechariah Chafee, Jr., and the Clear and Present Danger Test for Free Speech." Ragan suggests that Chafee may have been instrumental in pushing Holmes to see the libertarian implications of the Schenck test. *Ibid.*, 42-43.

But even after Abrams, Chafee had reservations; the Schenck test in effect made "the nature of the words only one element of danger" and did not require "that the utterances . . . themselves satisfy an objective standard."[30] Chafee, in fact, seems to have always preferred the test put forward by District Court Judge Learned Hand in the *Masses* trial of 1917, which limited prosecutions only to "direct incitement to violent resistance."[31]

Whatever its faults, however, the Holmes formula had the crucial advantage of having been unanimously accepted by the Court. For this reason, if for no other, Chafee was content to make the test the core of his legal position on free speech and to find considerable encouragement in the Court's continued—albeit sporadic[32]—use of the rule in the period between the wars. Ironically, however, it was during these same years that Chafee constantly and emphatically expressed the conviction that the ultimate guarantee of civil liberty in America did not rest with the judiciary at all. The numerous instances during and after World War I of courts enforcing public alarm rather than the law—instances exhaustively described in both editions of *Freedom of Speech*—had convinced him that no court, not even the United States Supreme Court, could offer permanent protection to personal freedom when there was an "almost total absence . . . of any genuine belief in the usefulness of the open expression of unpopular ideas."[33] "The law," he concluded soberly in 1941, "plays only a small part in either suppression or freedom. In the long run the public gets just as much freedom of speech as it really wants."[34]

Such a notion might easily have degenerated into a cliché, but Chafee took it very seriously. If the people and not the courts were really the final arbiter of civil liberty then the only secure safeguard of that freedom was a general understanding among the American people that such freedom was valuable to society. The aim of Chafee's books was educational, and to that end his arguments appealed less to technical legal precedent than to the

[30] Chafee, *Free Speech in the United States*, 82.

[31] *Masses Pub. Co.* v. *Patten*, 244 F. 535 (S.D.N.Y. 1917); Zechariah Chafee, Jr., *The Blessings of Liberty* (Philadelphia, 1956), 70.

[32] Holmes had first presented the formula for a unanimous Court in *Schenck* v. *United States*, 249 U.S. 47 (1919), but it was not used to reverse the defendant's conviction. Later in the same year, when *Abrams et al.* v. *United States*, 250 U.S. 616 (1919) finally reached the court, Holmes and Louis Brandeis wrote a dissenting opinion upholding the test and claiming the convictions should be overturned. In *Gitlow* v. *New York*, 268 U.S. 652 (1925) Holmes and Brandeis, again in dissent, held that the Schenck test could be applied to upset state convictions under the liberty clause of the Fourteenth Amendment. This last step was finally taken by the full Court in *Stromberg* v. *California*, 283 U.S. 359 (1931). Despite these decisions, however, the Court's use of the test throughout the 1930s and 1940s remained highly unpredictable. See Wallace Mendelson, "Clear and Present Danger—From Schenck to Dennis," *Columbia Law Review*, LII (March 1952), 313-33.

[33] Zechariah Chafee, Jr., *The Inquiring Mind* (New York, 1928), 53.

[34] Chafee, *Free Speech in the United States*, 563-64.

pragmatic, commonsense considerations of self-interest which he felt any intelligent citizen could understand and support. He did not defend free speech because it was in keeping with the Constitution, for what was constitutional was no more than what five justices thought on a complicated issue on a given day.[35] Nor did he justify it as an absolute or natural right. Rather, drawing on Holmes' "legal realism," which insisted that principles governing human conduct could be evaluated solely by their ability to meet real and pressing social needs, and on the general utilitarian outlook of John Stuart Mill, whose essay "On Liberty" he frequently cited, Chafee consistently, almost stubbornly, defended free speech simply because it was "wise," because the practical consequences of free discussion would be beneficial.

Specifically, Chafee suggested that free speech serves to spread information and to build the "critical public" necessary for a democracy. Through unfettered dialogue, different interest groups can express their needs in the public arena. When apprised of pressing issues, the general polity can move to deal with them, thus preventing violence and gradually ameliorating the general level of living in the nation.[36] He did not deny the individual's interest in being able to speak freely which Mill had so emphasized, but Chafee was convinced that free speech would never be safe unless its social value was also understood. Thus he stressed that the constant discussion of fundamental issues, far from interfering with the political process, actually provided the driving energy for the gradual social changes which he called progress. It was not the capacity of a single idea to cause a "conflagration" that worried Chafee, but the "dry rot" which arose whenever a society refused to discuss publicly its problems—"The clash of ideas is to be welcomed . . . even if it occasionally involves the . . . exhortations of a manifesto."[37]

Superficially, this line of argument seems little more than a gloss on the classic liberal notion of tolerance as proposed by Mill. Actually, the fact that Chafee had shifted the focus of the discussion from the relation between free speech and the individual to the relation between free speech and the social collectivity suggested a crucial difference in the way the two men viewed the ultimate value of free expression. For Mill, tolerance was important because it allowed individual citizens to fulfill themselves in "in-

[35] Chafee, *Blessings of Liberty*, 90-91.
[36] Chafee, *Inquiring Mind*, 15-16; Chafee, *Free Speech in the United States*, 31.
[37] Chafee, *Inquiring Mind*, 107; Chafee, *Free Speech in the United States*, 33.

numerable and conflicting ways";[38] for Chafee, free speech was vital because it lessened the possibility that differences between individuals would lead to conflict. For Mill, the purpose of all civil liberty was to insure the possibility of individual variety; for Chafee, free speech provided a way for society to grow and change fast enough to prevent the competition of various interest groups within society from becoming hardened ideological conflicts.

Chafee's stance was reasonable, but it left unresolved one large problem. He was obviously not a thoroughgoing relativist. "I believe in property and I believe in making money . . . ," he had assured the Harvard Law School alumni in 1921.[39] But if that were true, and if he defended free speech because it exposed problems and provided the momentum for orderly social advancement, how could he justify using the First Amendment to protect people who—as he admitted—had absolutely nothing to teach the country, who represented no real constituency, who exposed no real problems, and who offered no meaningful solutions?

Mill had taken great pains to suggest that the process of refuting even totally wrong ideas could be educational, but for Chafee the answer was found elsewhere. He simply wanted his side to "fight fair."[40] Even if most dissenters had nothing valuable to say, it was still unseemly for America to repress their opinions forcibly. Rather let them be confronted honorably by better men with better arguments. But beyond this gentlemanly desire for tolerance was another far more important consideration. The real problem with stifling radical voices was that the process of repression would silence others as well:

> My contention is that the pertinacious orators and writers who get hauled up are merely extremist spokesmen for a mass of more thoughtful and more retiring men and women, who share in varying degrees the same critical attitude toward prevailing policies and institutions. When you put the hotheads in jail, these cooler people do not get arrested—they just keep quiet. And so we lose the things they could tell us, which would be very advantageous for the future course of the nation.[41]

[38] John Stuart Mill, "On Liberty," Max Lerner, ed., *The Essential Mill* (New York, 1961), 305. To be sure, Mill had asserted: "for such actions are prejudicial to the interests of others, the individual is accountable, and may be subjected either to social or to legal punishments." But within these limits the basic rationale for free speech was the development of individual variety. *Ibid.*, 340.

[39] Quoted in Phillips, *Felix Frankfurter Reminisces*, 177. See also Sutherland, *Law at Harvard*, 256.

[40] *Ibid.*

[41] Chafee, *Free Speech in the United States*, 561.

There was a potential risk to tolerating shrill demagogues, even if the tolerance proved only a means of protecting a more genuine wisdom. It was questionable, for example, whether the Kerensky government ought to have tolerated criticism from the Bolsheviks. "Given enough time, we ought to have faith that truth will win," he wrote in 1931. "The difficulty is that the process does not always operate rapidly and meanwhile harm may be done by fallacious arguments." The United States, however, had little to fear, for here "the government is so firmly established in the approval of the citizens that there is no real danger at all . . ." from radical dissent.[42] America's manifest justice, wealth, and good sense, he was sure, would always work to prevent the growth of any large number of malcontents who might listen seriously to inflammatory critiques. It was even possible that when exposed to the full richness of the American system, the dissenters themselves might be seduced away from their narrow ideologies. This was the line he took in 1941 when he opposed a number of state laws which would have excluded Communist candidates from the ballot. The New Deal reforms, he was convinced, would go far to erode the bitterness and "dilute the violent ideas" of even the most passionate Marxist, for even "their resentment can be gradually removed by high wages, an electric refrigerator, and a second-hand Ford." Allowing such people to participate in electoral politics, he argued, would only further integrate them into the American way of life.[43] Tolerance was thus justified not only by the need of a pluralist society for new ideas, but also by the ability of the American system to dissolve the extremes of that pluralism. Ultimately, the "clash of ideas" was as harmless as it was helpful.

There was an exception to Chafee's image of America as a society invulnerable to revolutionary rabble-rousing. The situation of the American Negro, particularly the southern Negro, constituted a problem so grievous as to render free speech on the issue too dangerous to permit. Chafee did not often mention Negroes. His interest, as he explained to Lincoln Steffens when he refused to help in the Scottsboro trial, was in political trials, and civil rights cases did not seem to him to be particularly political.[44]

In his commentary on *Herndon* v. *Lowry*, however, Chafee finally confronted the issue of black America directly. Herndon, a Negro Communist, was arrested in Georgia for distributing pamphlets urging that several southern states should be made into a "Black Belt" ruled by a Negro majority. The law under which he was indicted and later convicted had originally

[42] Chafee to Jonathan S. England, May 16, 1931, File 9, Box XXX, Chafee Papers.
[43] Chafee, *Free Speech in the United States*, 492.
[44] Chafee to Lincoln Steffens, June 1, 1931, File 9, Box XXX, Chafee Papers.

been a pre-Civil War statute designed to prevent slave uprisings. In 1937 the United States Supreme Court reversed Herndon's conviction by reaffirming the Schenck test and by charging that the Georgia law (and the state court's construction of it) had allowed mere tendency to be the standard of guilt.[45]

Chafee applauded the decision, but noted that for him this case represented one of the only sedition trials which might have had some legitimacy:

> Not that there was clear and present danger of the insurrection for which he was indicted. Not that the Black Belt Free State could have suddenly emerged into being. But, given the unrest of Negroes, . . . [Herndon's] demands for equal racial rights, lavish relief, and the virtual abolition of debts might have produced some sort of disorder in the near future. Smoking is all right, but not in a powder magazine.[46]

This remark raised eyebrows in liberal circles,[47] and Chafee himself recognized the perverse implications of his position. "In short," he admitted, "the very conditions that cause the grievances render agitation to remove the grievances dangerous." In the end, the contradictions actually proved too painful and Chafee concluded his ambivalent, troubled discussion of the case with the suggestion that even in the South, "sedition prosecutions are only likely to make matters worse."[48]

But the most important aspect of Chafee's treatment of this case is that even as he recognized the existence of a "powder magazine" in American society he was quick to label it an anomaly. The situation in the South was a bizarre departure from the normal American process of "accomplishing reforms through political channels," a problem deserving of concern but incapable of justifying apocalyptic solutions. Nothing about *Herndon* v. *Lowry*, neither the trial itself nor the social pathology which had motivated Herndon to speak, seems to have shaken his commitment to order and gradual reform, or weakened his scorn for men who tried to disrupt the prevailing status quo.[49]

Chafee's belief in the justice of American society was further bolstered by his reading of American history. He insisted, incorrectly it now appears, that the First Amendment had been "intended to wipe out the common law

[45] Chafee, *Free Speech in the United States*, 388-97; *Herndon* v. *Lowry*, 301 U.S. 242 (1937).

[46] *Ibid.*, 397.

[47] Leonard Boudin, "The First Amendment," a review of Chafee's *Free Speech in the United States*, *New Republic*, CVI (Jan. 26, 1942), 121-22.

[48] Chafee, *Free Speech in the United States*, 397-98.

[49] *Ibid.*

of sedition, and make further prosecutions for criticism of the government, without any incitement to law-breaking, forever impossible in the United States. . . ."[50] In Chafee's view this initial inspiration had by and large shaped the American attitude toward free speech and made tolerance one of "the great traditions of our race."[51] By treating the Alien and Sedition Acts as an exception from which the country learned a painful lesson, and by deliberately excluding from consideration all "acts by mobs or by officials, police, and soldiers, committed under old laws or no laws at all," he was able to point to the lack of explicit sedition legislation during the nineteenth century as proof that throughout most of its history the country had shown a consistent determination to permit open discussion.[52] Only recently had the people and their leaders succumbed to the temptation of repressing all dissent. The fact that for Chafee this development represented a senseless declension from a proven and admirable heritage made it all the more incomprehensible.

Between 1920 and 1940, Chafee oscillated between confidence and fear. He drew considerable comfort from the apparent mellowing of public feelings toward dissent in the years following the Red Scare. The increasing appreciation with which Chafee's own works were received was indicative of just this shift and could only have appeared as a hopeful sign to him. In 1921 he had been an extremist, and *Freedom of Speech* had been dismissed as illustrative of merely a "passing phase of incorrigible sentimentality."[53] By 1928 the New York *Times* could suggest that "Americans would be prouder of their land . . . if .[there were] more men of the calibre of Chafee,"[54] and a decade later even the conservative Boston *Herald Traveler* could conclude in a review of Chafee's essays that although "most free speech defendants are pretty scabby characters . . . [and] a few may be real or potential traitors . . . [nonetheless] if fools are locked up . . . wise men are less likely to speak. . . ."[55] At the same time, however, the appeals for aid and advice addressed to Chafee during the 1920s and 1930s by school teachers, Communists, and union lawyers—nearly all of whom Chafee felt had suffered some abridgement of their civil liberties—were proof that free speech was far from secure. "The unrational is all around

[50] *Ibid.*, 21. See also Leonard Levy, *Legacy of Suppression: Freedom of Speech and Press in Early American History* (Cambridge, Mass., 1960).

[51] Chafee, "Freedom of Speech in War Time," 973.

[52] Chafee, *Free Speech in the United States*, 506-07.

[53] Archibald E. Stevenson, "The World War and Freedom of Speech," New York *Times*, Feb. 13, 1921.

[54] Unsigned review of Chafee's *Inquiring Mind*, New York *Times*, July 8, 1928.

[55] Boston *Herald Traveler*, Oct. 20, 1941.

me," he admitted sadly in 1936, "and I see that reason plays less part than I hoped."[56]

As World War II approached, Chafee's anxiety became more intense. He knew that war tested a nation's commitment to tolerance most severely, and he feared that the dreary precedents set by World War I would be re-enacted. In 1940, when Congress passed the Smith Act—the first peacetime sedition law since 1798—all his fears seemed justified.

The government, however, adopted a relatively relaxed posture toward free speech, and its reluctance to prosecute cases under the Smith Act soon made the law practically a dead letter for the duration of the war.[57] For Chafee, this policy of restraint was obviously a welcome surprise; and the relief he felt may even explain his mild response to the government's internment of Japanese-Americans during these years. Commenting in 1942, Chafee argued that the policy of forced relocation was in itself not necessarily unwise for "No doubt there is cause for apprehension" from some native-born Japanese. These people, furthermore, were "so different from ourselves" that it would be very difficult to identify and restrict only "the undesirable" among them. He was quick to concede that the implications of these measures posed "grave dangers," for what started as "regulation of freedom of movement" among "second generation Japanese" might easily become "regulation of freedom of speech" among "ninth generation English, and any of us who voice vigorous disapproval" of governmental policies. Moreover, the fact that the internments were planned as simply administrative procedures to be implemented without the formal safeguards of judicial review seemed especially ominous. Still, after reviewing the whole situation and urging that the administration of the policy be made accessible to the courts, Chafee could go on to define the internments as simply one of "the inevitable hardships of war." For him, the outstanding fact was that the "free speech problem has thus far been almost non-existent" and "It begins to look as if we might get through this war without a Debs case or an Abrams case."[58]

[56] Zechariah Chafee, Jr., "Some New Ideas About Law," *Indiana Law Journal*, XI (Aug. 1936), 523.

[57] The only wartime prosecutions under the act were against a group of Minneapolis Trotskyites who were tried in 1941 and twenty-eight Nazis who were brought to court in Washington in 1943.

[58] Unpublished article by Chafee, March 1, 1942, File 10, Box IX, Chafee Papers. Chafee compared the internment to the administrative arrests carried out in 1862 by Lincoln against southern sympathizers in Baltimore. The legality of these measures, Chafee conceded, was "hotly argued at the time, though I suppose that Lincoln's action is now regarded as proper." Chafee to Douglas Arant, June 13, 1942, File 10, Box IX, Chafee Papers.

In a sense he was right. Feelings against resident Germans and Japanese found many ugly modes of expression during the war years, but they were never translated into the sedition trials which Chafee so abhorred. Nevertheless, his optimism proved naïve. The frenzy against Communism after World War II convinced him that the devastating syndrome of fear and repression was still very much alive in America. In fact, developments in the late 1940s and early 1950s appeared so threatening to Chafee, so deeply disturbing, that his doubts about the American people seem finally to have triumphed, obliging him to make a subtle but significant change in his defense of civil liberties.

The specific development which first triggered Chafee's concern in the years after World War II was President Truman's Executive Order in March 1947 establishing an "employees loyalty program in the executive branch of the government."[59] Chafee believed the rash of security checks and loyalty oaths were both foolish and dangerous. The chance that this procedure would actually turn up spies was very remote, for obviously any bona fide traitor would protect himself against this sort of elementary investigation.[60] The danger arising from this program, however, would be incalculable. The consequence, Chafee argued, would be to drive from the government precisely the men the country most needed, the men "with strong and vigorous minds, who are capable of individual thinking," men who "without being disloyal . . . have ideas which are unpopular in certain conservative quarters."[61] It was—as always—the unorthodox but wise men that Chafee labored to protect.

But Chafee was battling against the tide. Truman's loyalty program was instituted, and in 1950 the American Bar Association proposed its own anticommunist loyalty oath for lawyers. No state bar association accepted the suggested formula, but even the recommendation was enough to convince Chafee that the country's major professional legal organization was spiritually bankrupt.[62] It might well be, as his law school colleague and friend Felix Frankfurter had once suggested, that lawyers "serve as leaven-

[59] See Roger S. Abbot, "The Federal Loyalty Program: Background and Problems," *American Political Science Review*, XLII (June 1948), 486-99.

[60] Chafee memo to Mrs. Maxwell C. Huntoon, Feb. 13, 1948, File 9, Box XXXIV, Chafee Papers.

[61] *Ibid.*

[62] Chafee, *Blessings of Liberty*, 157-60. Part of Chafee's dismay undoubtedly arose from the fact that he sat on the American Bar Association's Special Committee on the Bill of Rights, and it had been this committee which had recommended in 1948 that subversion and sedition be fully prosecuted, that Communist organizations be compelled to register with the government, and that all Communists and all those practicing its teachings should be banned from all government service. See Chafee to Granville Clark, June 14, 1949, File 19, XXXIV, Chafee Papers.

ing centers of calm and responsible thinking"[63] in times of trouble, but the association's drive for unquestioning orthodoxy among its members was hardly conducive to such a role. "[T]here is no depth of folly to which the American Bar Association will not stoop," Chafee wrote in 1952; "If this organization under its present leadership had existed in 1789 it would have overwhelmingly resolved to reject the Constitution, just as the Daughters of the American Revolution would have been against the Revolution."[64]

In the context of the postwar era, however, loyalty oaths were only a minor expression of the passions at work. Even as he opposed Truman's Executive Order, Chafee had conceded that the President might well have been trying to forestall an even more brutal investigation by Congress, for it was the legislative branch that was emerging as the real "distorting factor" and the source of the most serious dangers to free speech.[65] The introduction of the Mundt-Nixon bill in 1949 seemed to prove this point in a painfully clear manner. The main operating clauses of the bill called for registration of all Communist and "Communist-front" organizations—including their complete membership lists—with the attorney general's office. The power to decide which groups fell into these categories was left to a Subversive Activities Control Board to be appointed by the President.[66] Characteristically, Chafee opposed the act on pragmatic not constitutional grounds. In a pamphlet he wrote for ACLU in 1950, Chafee argued that the small number of Communists in the country did not constitute an internal danger necessitating such drastic action.[67] Moreover, the so-called Communist-front organizations were exactly those progressive groups that Chafee saw as providing the creative tension in America, the source of vaguely disturbing ideas which urged the country to grow and change.[68]

At first, the arguments which Chafee and others presented against the bill seemed to prevail. It failed to pass during the 1949 session of Congress. The following year, however, the McCarren Act, as the Mundt-Nixon bill was now named, was voted into law over President Truman's veto. The event was deeply disturbing to Chafee, not only because of the law itself but also because he felt the act was emblematic of the nation's mood. It was an ugly mood, hostile to change, imagination, and even intelligence, and capable of many kinds of repression. It had produced the Dies Committee, the Hiss trial, the Oppenheimer affair, and the numerous con-

[63] Frankfurter to Chafee, Feb. 13, 1952, File 16, Box IV, Chafee Papers.
[64] Chafee to Frankfurter, May 2, 1952, *ibid.*
[65] Chafee memo to Mrs. Huntoon, Feb. 13, 1948, File 9, Box XXXIV, *ibid.*
[66] Chafee, *Free and the Brave*, 22.
[67] *Ibid.*, 7.
[68] *Ibid.*, 30-31.

gressional investigations of liberal intellectuals both within and without the professional academy. The McCarthy era, in fact, drove Chafee to express a depth of despair which he had never before acknowledged. He continued to write books and articles professing his belief in America; he continued to explicate patiently the utility of free speech and the wisdom of the "clear and present danger test." But increasingly he felt obliged to conclude these efforts with sad conviction that "probably the only cure for all this trouble is time."[69]

In part, Chafee's despondency during this period may have been due simply to the realization that he no longer had the energy to "deal with all the oppressions that are done under the sun."[70] He was sixty-four in 1950 and was frequently hospitalized in the years preceding his death seven years later. But the basis of his depression was far deeper than mere physical or even intellectual exhaustion. He felt deserted and complained that there were not nearly as many people willing to help him in 1950 as there had been in 1920.[71] Hostility from the right was, of course, to be expected. Anyone who helped raise money for Alger Hiss and petitioned Truman to pardon the Rosenbergs could hardly be surprised that a confirmed anti-Stalinist like Sidney Hook considered his views "frightening,"[72] or even that several congressional committees had marked him as belonging to five "subversive groups."[73] More unexpected, however, and more disturbing too, were the warnings he was beginning to receive from several supposedly staunch liberals that he was aligning himself too closely with "fellow travellers" and risked being contaminated.

It was Chafee's alliance with a small ad hoc group called the National Committee to Defeat the Mundt-Nixon Bill which particularly aroused concern among his more cautious liberal colleagues. In June 1949, Arthur Schlesinger, Jr., then at Harvard, urged Chafee to resign from the National Committee to Defeat the Mundt-Nixon Bill because it was "clearly a Communist controlled outfit." Soon after hearing from Schlesinger, Chafee received letters from Baldwin of ACLU and Joseph L. Rauh, Jr., chairman of Americans for Democratic Action (ADA), both of whom reiterated Schlesinger's warning. "It hurts me," wrote Rauh, "to see persons who do not share your devotion to civil liberties exploit your reputation and your integrity to their own ends. . . . We would very much like to have you

[69] Chafee to Harold Harowitz, Sept. 29, 1954, File 13, Box XXXIV, Chafee Papers.
[70] Chafee to John Caughey, April 8, 1952, File 10, Box XXXV, *ibid.*
[71] Chafee, *Blessings of Liberty*, 82-83.
[72] Sidney Hook, *Political Power and Personal Freedom* (New York, 1959), 259.
[73] Chafee to Frank Graham, March 23, 1950, File 18, Box XXXIII, Chafee Papers.

working with us. . . ."[74] Chafee's response was immediate and indignant. It was not that he condoned all the views of the National Committee to Defeat the Mundt-Nixon Bill or the frequently shrill tones of its membership. The real issue, as he wrote in identical letters to all three men, was that this organization had been the "first in the field to get in touch with me," and "When there is a big fire raging, I do not inquire meticulously into all the political and economic views of the man who is carrying a bucket of water beside me."[75]

It was a splendid gesture, but not too much more than that. Actually Chafee was always, if not meticulous, at least very careful with whom he collaborated. He had dropped out of the Civil Legion in 1926 and the Progressive Citizen's Committee in 1947 precisely because he did not wish to associate too closely with extreme views of either the right or the left.[76] Moreover after 1949, when organizations like ACLU and ADA began their own large-scale campaigns against the Mundt-Nixon bill, Chafee, despite his harsh words to Schlesinger, Baldwin, and Rauh, rechannelled most of his energy into their efforts.

The reason for such circumspection, particularly in the last decade of his life, is obvious. As much as Chafee hated loyalty oaths and congressional investigations, he loathed equally the self-righteous moralism into which the opposition to those oaths and investigations so often degenerated. Indeed, the deepest cause of the sense of isolation which he experienced during this last period of his life arose from his own insistent attempt to steer a middle course between anticommunist paranoia and anti-McCarthy propaganda. He wanted to oppose McCarthy just as he had always opposed needless repression: rationally, calmly, and pragmatically.[77] And he wrote the playwright Arthur Miller that now, as always, "the opposition [to McCarthy] should be put on the grounds of wisdom and American traditions, rather than on Constitutionality. . . ."[78] Moreover, in correspondence with the philosopher Alexander Meikeljohn, a thinker sympathetic to arguments rooted in the sanctity of the human conscience, Chafee pointed out that McCarthy too was operating under a higher law. Appeals to super-legal authority simply were not practical; for "[s]urely we cannot rely only on the inner

[74] Arthur Schlesinger, Jr., to Chafee, June 10, 1949, File 12, Box XXXIII, *ibid.*; Joseph L. Rauh, Jr., to Chafee, June 13, 1949, File 13, Box XXXIII, *ibid.*

[75] Chafee to Schlesinger, Rauh, and Roger N. Baldwin, June 17, 1949, File 12, Box XXXIII, *ibid.*

[76] Chafee to Civil Legion, April 6, 1920, File 2, Box XXX, Chafee Papers; Chafee to Harlow Shapley, Progressive Citizens of America, Oct. 16, 1947, File 23, Box XXXV, *ibid.*

[77] Chafee to Bernard Freyd, Oct. 26, 1951, File 16, Box IV, *ibid.*

[78] Chafee to Arthur Miller, June 9, 1950, File 14, Box XXXIV, *ibid.*

light of the individual as the proof of what the higher law is, which supersedes the obligation of duly enacted statutes and judicial decisions. . . ." After all, to Chafee the purpose of argumentation was not to disclaim on moral absolutes but to persuade people to change their opinions and their actions. "I am not going to bang my head against a stone wall," he wrote to Meikeljohn, "even for the sake of feeling good when I stop. So I have tried to argue about things as to which I have some chance of winning and getting action."[79]

But as Chafee looked around the country, he began to wonder whether in fact his defense of free speech had any chance of "winning and getting action." His calm style of argumentation was not simply isolating him, it was also beginning to appear totally ineffective. Up to this point, the ultimate rationale for appealing to wisdom and common sense had been his conviction that the American people, the real source of civil liberty, could be won over by logic. Now he was not so sure. The fact that Congress, the branch of government closest to the people, was the major source of this new intolerance seems to have been taken by Chafee as an indication that the people themselves had finally succumbed to their worst instincts. Looking back from the early 1950s, it was clear that whatever progress had been made since 1920 had not been because the man in the street was more tolerant but merely because he had momentarily become "more indifferent and less frightened." "When the fear returned," as it did in the confused years after World War II, "suppression . . . [returned] with it."[80] Chafee's one great anxiety about America was thus confirmed: the "irrational" had at last triumphed and "the public," upon whose good sense he had counted so heavily, was eager to silence all dissent. His unanswerable logic had been rejected. And not only his: Holmes, Brandeis, Hand, even the dreary experiences of World War I—all had been forgotten. Chafee was in the impossible position of a pragmatist whose audience was living according to a different and far less rational calculus.

Therefore, Chafee began to add a footnote to his argument. Tolerance was still the obviously "wise" policy, but if the executive branch instituted loyalty programs, if the legislature became the chief source of repression, if the people themselves could no longer be trusted, then clearly the only area of the federal government capable of recognizing wisdom was the judiciary. "Even though we should like to have legislatures and other lawmaking

[79] Chafee to Alexander Meikeljohn, June 14, 1954, File 16, Box XII, *ibid.* See also Chafee's review of Alexander Meiklejohn, *Free Speech: And Its Relation to Self-Government* (New York, 1948), *Harvard Law Review*, LXII (March 1949), 891-901.

[80] Chafee, *Blessings of Liberty*, 80.

bodies protect our civil rights," Chafee wrote in 1949, "we must in these times of pressure and not to say hysteria look to the courts to guarantee them for us."[81]

To suddenly regard the courts as the last safeguard of civil liberty in America obviously constituted a sharp break with Chafee's previous views. No one had been more painstaking than he to point up precisely how the courts had failed during and after World War I, how they had repeatedly fallen prey to public prejudices and imposed stiff penalties upon trivial or even nonexistent crimes. But now the situation looked different. One reason the McCarran Act was so abhorrent to Chafee was because the Subversive Activities Control Board effectively bypassed the courts in deciding which organizations would go on the attorney general's list. Even at their worst, Chafee argued, sedition and espionage trials were preferable to this administrative repression because a court proceeding inevitably guaranteed certain safeguards. Trial by jury, the possibility of review and appeal, the necessity of establishing the violation of a specific statute—all these are "conspicuously lacking in the novel methods of suppression which have recently sprung up."[82] The dangers from this non-judicial repression thus represented a profound threat for free speech in America. The only hope lay with the courts, specifically the United States Supreme Court, which could strike down the laws creating this "subtle repression" and ensure the survival of personal freedom.

Chafee's new reliance on the courts, however, was not only inconsistent with his own past writings but also defied the belief held by many distinguished jurists and political philosophers that the American courts must refrain from inflicting their own views upon the whole country. "While the courts must exercise a judgment of their own," Holmes had written, "it by no means is true that every law is void which may seem to the judges who pass upon it excessive, unsuited to its ostensible end, or based upon conceptions of morality with which they disagree."[83] Holmes and thinkers so different as Hook and Frankfurter held that civil liberty in America was guarded as much by the legislature as by the courts and that the supreme law of the land must reflect equally the nation's "legislative will" and "judicial will."[84] Earlier in his career this had been more or less Chafee's own view. The lesson of the Abrams case, he had written, "is that Congress alone can effectively safeguard minority .opinion in times of excitement.

[81] Irving Dillard to Chafee, Dec. 27, 1949, File 16, Box XXXIII, Chafee Papers.
[82] Chafee, *Blessings of Liberty*, 83, 143-44.
[83] *Otis* v. *Parker*, 187 U.S. 606 (1903), 608.
[84] Hook, *Political Power and Personal Freedom*, 252-57.

Once a sedition statute is on the books . . . Trial judges will be found to adopt a free construction of the act so as to reach objectionable doctrines and the Supreme Court will probably be unable to afford relief."[85] By 1950, however, the excesses of Congress had convinced him that it was no longer wise to trust the legislature. "I suppose that you still agree with Holmes that Congress is the guardian of the liberties of the people as well as the courts," he wrote Frankfurter in that year. "I am beginning to doubt whether Holmes was right."[86] Frankfurter had no doubt whatsoever. His experience as a working judge had demonstrated to his satisfaction that even the highest court was not above excesses, shortsightedness, or even outright error. Chafee's new-found respect for the judiciary struck Frankfurter as painfully naïve and ultimately foolish.

> I am all for your indulging a *jeu d'esprit* as often as the spirit moves you. But my sense of humor has its limits; they are reached when you put the weight of your authority behind the assumption that judges are the great saviors of liberty and welfare. It is no answer to refer to this court's decision in some "civil liberties" cases. Look at the whole record![87]

The fact that the Supreme Court did on occasion move to protect individual freedom, he lectured Chafee, did not mean that the process of judicial review functioned according to logic. "If I told you how some opinions over which you throw your hat in the air came to pass," he confided, "I should shock you out of your boots."[88]

But Chafee knew that to urge the courts to take a more active role was to grasp at straws. It was not the habit of the high court to fight Congress on policy issues like national security, and Chafee was well aware of this. As early as 1951, in the Dennis case, the Court had upheld the Smith Act and in Chafee's view reduced the First Amendment to mean simply that "Congress shall make no law abridging the freedom of speech and of the press unless Congress does make a law abridging the freedom of speech and of the press."[89] But even if the judges had wished to oppose Congress, their decisions, which depended so frequently on "distinctions as thin as a hair," could never have fully constituted a recovery of freedom. In a moment of total candor, Chafee admitted in 1953 that the ultimate solution lay where it always had, with the people, and the only realistic hope he could muster

[85] Chafee, *Free Speech in the United States*, 139.
[86] Chafee to Frankfurter, June 15, 1950, File 17, Box IV, Chafee Papers.
[87] Frankfurter to Chafee, Nov. 19, 1956, *ibid.*
[88] Frankfurter to Chafee, Dec. 17, 1952, *ibid.*
[89] Chafee, *Blessings of Liberty*, 85.

was that McCarthyism would "die out because people are sick of it, the way censorship expired in 1695 in England."[90]

In a sense Chafee was right. By the time he died in 1957 McCarthy had fallen from power and the anticommunist frenzy which he had led had begun to dissipate. As Chafee had foreseen, moreover, the transformation from intolerance to moderation was due less to the Court, which continued to avoid opposing Congress, than to a shift in the basic political sympathies of the country. Despite the accuracy of this prediction, however, the process by which the public moved to a more tolerant attitude remained incomprehensible to him. And that was the central irony which governed all his efforts. He believed in America, yet he realized that his knowledge of the country, and his faith in it as well, was far from complete. The unpredictability of public emotions, the imponderable interplay of fact and reason with suspicion and prejudice, he knew to be terribly important, but all this was beyond what he was willing or able to analyze. As a result, these powerful forces remained mysterious to him, limiting his confidence and threatening constantly to demonstrate the foolishness of his position.

What, then, is to be made of Chafee? Was he simply a naïve spokesman for an honorable cause, a patient, thoroughly decent man whose views, while always sensible and frequently incisive, were ultimately insufficiently penetrating to be of lasting interest? Such an appraisal is far too harsh. The enormous influence Chafee had over civil libertarians between 1920 and the mid-1950s cannot be doubted. "No single piece of writing," commented the eminent legal scholar Mark DeWolfe Howe at the time of Chafee's death, "did more than Chafee's *Freedom of Speech* to define the nature of personal liberty and to measure the scope of governmental power to restrict its exercise."[91] The exact impact of a book is obviously difficult to measure, but Howe's judgment does not seem an exaggeration. Two generations of free speech advocates looked to the work as the starting point for all their discussions and debates. And if his final years presented Chafee with a crisis for which he had no satisfactory response, it remains true nonetheless that the arguments he put forward even during this period were of considerable help to those organizations and individuals intent on resisting the attack on civil liberties implicit in McCarthyism.

But there is another more symbolic significance to be derived from

[90] Quoted in Ernest Angell, "Zechariah Chafee, Jr.: Individual Freedoms," *Harvard Law Review*, LXX (June 1957), 1343.

[91] Mark DeWolfe Howe, "Zechariah Chafee, Jr. (1885-1957)," *Nation*, CLXXXIV (March 2, 1957), 183.

Chafee's career. It is a modern demonstration of how in America libertarian sympathies can often be yoked to strongly conservative convictions. The very fact that free speech is formally guaranteed in the Constitution has frequently made it possible to conceive that right as simply part of the prevailing political arrangement, part of the American heritage which must be preserved. The libertarian committed to the status quo is, of course, not a phenomenon unique to this nation's history, but a conservative conception of free speech has clearly had a deep influence on the way Americans have come to view the First Amendment. Seen in the context of this tradition, moreover, the difficulty Chafee had in reconciling himself to the dynamics of American society appears less as an expression of ignorance or naïveté than as a function of dilemmas which have frequently emerged to trouble proponents of conservative liberalism in this country. He was committed to the notion that there were no really fundamental contradictions in American society, but at the same time forced to admit that Americans frequently turned upon themselves with a ferocity indicative of just such contradictions. He believed that the ultimate authority should be vested in the people, but could not help observing how the exercise of the popular will often destroyed freedom. He believed in democracy, but doubted whether the public possessed the maturity to make the system feasible.

In the final analysis, however, Chafee's real importance does not rest with any particular book he wrote or even with his place in the history of American libertarian thought. His most important contribution was simply to have sensitized the country to the fact that free speech in modern America cannot be regarded as automatically guaranteed by the First Amendment but must be the object of a concerted effort by all levels of society.

Historians tend to treat free speech advocates with considerable condescension, accepting their arguments uncritically and viewing their mere existence as proof that the libertarian viewpoint has never been without its champion in America. To treat Chafee in this way, however, would be the final irony. To take Chafee's career as proof that civil liberty was secure during the first half of the twentieth century is to misunderstand his whole effort to make America realize that free speech can easily disappear without constant and imaginative attention. That events ultimately forced him to realize how tenuous the country's commitment to tolerance really was during this period serves only to emphasize the truth of this central lesson and increase its relevance for future advocates of civil liberty in America.

Harvard Civil Rights-Civil Liberties Law Review

Volume 12, Number 1 Winter, 1977

AN INDEPENDENT RIGHT TO FREEDOM OF ASSOCIATION

*By Reena Raggi**

In a number of cases over the last thirty years, the Supreme Court has invoked "freedom of association" to overturn various state actions.[1] The opinions in these cases have led individuals to believe that the decision to join with others in pursuit of a common goal is a fundamental aspect of their liberty. A close examination of the opinions in the leading association cases reveals, however, that the Court actually has never been committed to the protection of freedom of association as an independent and unique right. In fact, "freedom of association" has been little more than a shorthand phrase used by the Court to protect traditional first amendment rights of speech and petition as exercised by individuals in groups. Occasionally, opinions have hinted at the possibility of a freedom distinct from traditional first amendment rights.[2] However, in the one recent case which clearly presented the opportunity for a full and careful exploration of the scope of freedom of association outside the bounds of speech and petition, the Court established its commitment to the narrower position by summarily rejecting the right.[3]

*Law Clerk, Judge Thomas E. Fairchild, United States Court of Appeals, 7th Cir.; J.D. Harvard Law School, 1976; B.A. Wellesley College, 1973.

[1] *See, e.g.*, Buckley v. Valeo, 424 U.S. 1 (1976); United Mine Workers v. Illinois State Bar Ass'n, 389 U.S. 217 (1967); Griswold v. Connecticut, 381 U.S. 479 (1965); Brotherhood of R.R. Trainmen v. Virginia *ex rel.* Va. State Bar, 377 U.S. 1 (1964); NAACP v. Button, 371 U.S. 415 (1963); Shelton v. Tucker, 364 U.S. 479 (1960); Bates v. City of Little Rock, 361 U.S. 516 (1960); NAACP v. Alabama *ex rel.* Patterson, 357 U.S. 449 (1958).

[2] *See* Buckley v. Valeo, 424 U.S. 1 (1976); Village of Belle Terre v. Boraas, 416 U.S. 1, 12-20 (1974) (Marshall, J., dissenting); United States Dep't. of Agriculture v. Moreno, 413 U.S. 528, 538-45 (1973) (Douglas, J., concurring); Griswold v. Connecticut, 381 U.S. 479 (1965).

[3] *See* Garcia v. Texas State Bd. of Medical Examiners, 384 F. Supp. 434 (W.D. Tex. 1974), *aff'd mem.*, 421 U.S. 995 (1975).

Rather than candidly admitting that freedom of speech or petition is the basis for its decisions, the Court consistently has invoked the "freedom of association" language, indicating that the concept may retain a broader scope. As the law has begun to move beyond the post-*Lochner* era,[4] individuals have reconsidered the possibility that their liberty is something broader than the few fundamental rights expressly safeguarded in the Constitution.[5] It is now appropriate to reconsider the potential of an independent doctrine of freedom of association to determine what role it can play in the promotion of human dignity and independence, and accordingly, to formulate for the Court a theory broad enough to ensure that the doctrine serves this purpose.

I. FREEDOM OF ASSOCIATION: THE PROTECTION OF FIRST AMENDMENT RIGHTS EXERCISED THROUGH A GROUP

Traditionally, freedom of association has been tied to the first amendment rights of speech, petition, and assembly. This historical basis provides a framework within which the nature of the right may be analyzed, but if association is now to serve as a vehicle for expanding human liberty, a new formulation of the right is necessary. Such formulation must begin with an examination of the traditional cases.

NAACP v. Alabama ex rel. Patterson[6] often is hailed as the first Supreme Court decision to recognize freedom of association as a constitutional right.[7] The NAACP had been found guilty of contempt for refusing to comply with an Alabama court order to produce various records, including those containing the names and addresses of all its Alabama members.[8] Justice Harlan reversed the contempt order, noting, "It is hardly a novel perception that compelled disclosure of affiliation with groups engaged in advocacy may constitute . . . a restraint on freedom of association. . . ."[9] Although it was such language which earned the case its reputation as the first to recognize freedom of association, other lan-

---

[4] *See generally* Tribe, *Structural Due Process*, 10 HARV. C.R.-C.L. L. REV. 269 (1975); Grey, *Do We Have an Unwritten Constitution?*, 27 STAN. L. REV. 703 (1975), suggesting alternative approaches to the due process clause as a source of rights.

[5] *See* Tribe, *supra* note 4; Grey, *supra* note 4.

[6] 357 U.S. 449 (1958).

[7] *See, e.g.*, Emerson, *Freedom of Association and Freedom of Expression*, 74 YALE L.J. 1 (1964).

[8] NAACP v. Alabama *ex rel.* Patterson, 357 U.S. 449, 451-54 (1958).

[9] *Id.* at 462.

guage in the decision made it clear that the emphasis was not on "freedom of association" as an independent right, but rather on association as a vehicle for the advocacy of beliefs and ideas.[10] Of concern to Justice Harlan and the Court, then, was not "association" in any abstract sense, but the possibility that Alabama, by discouraging certain associations, was burdening the first amendment rights of individual members to speak and advocate ideas.[11]

This recognition of the value of association in the context of first amendment advocacy had been approved by the Court in earlier decisions. In *Sweezy v. New Hampshire*,[12] for example, Chief Justice Warren explicitly linked political expression and association as fundamental to our system of government.[13] That "political" advocacy, an element of freedom of speech, might be the essence of any association claim certainly was recognized by the NAACP when it framed its argument in *Patterson*.[14] The Court's decision, however, suggests that this focus would be unnecessary. Indeed, the primary innovation of Justice Harlan's decision in the *Patterson* case was not that it recognized a freedom of association independent of the first amendment, for indeed it did not, but rather that it broadened the scope of protected first amendment expression

---

[10] "Effective *advocacy* of both public and private points of view, particularly controversial ones, is undeniably enhanced by group association, as this Court has more than once recognized by remarking on the close nexus between the freedoms of *speech* and *assembly*." *Id.* at 460. (emphasis added).

[11] As conceived of by Justice Harlan, freedom of association was protected to the extent the associational purpose was "the advancement of beliefs and ideas," in short, so long as the associational aims were in some manner "expressional." In concluding that such freedom of association is an "aspect of the 'liberty' assured by the Due Process Clause of the Fourteenth Amendment," Justice Harlan immediately added "which embraces freedom of speech," thereby putting an end to all doubt as to the source of the right. *Id.* at 460.

[12] 354 U.S. 234 (1957). *See also* United States v. CIO, 335 U.S. 106, 143-44 (Rutledge, J., concurring).

[13] "Our form of government is built on the premise that every citizen shall have the right to engage in *political expression* and *association*. This right was enshrined in the First Amendment of the Bill of Rights. . . . All political ideas cannot and should not be channeled into the programs of our two major parties. History has amply proved the virtue of political activity by minority, dissident groups, who innumerable times have been in the vanguard of democratic thought and whose programs were ultimately accepted. Mere unorthodoxy or dissent from the prevailing mores is not to be condemned. The absence of such voices would be a symptom of grave illness in our society." Sweezy v. New Hampshire, 354 U.S. 234, 250-51 (1957) (emphasis added).

[14] "While petitioner eschews partisan politics, it seeks to influence public opinion and affect [sic] the political structure to achieve its objectives. As such it is a political organization in the true sense. . ." Brief for Petitioner at 23, NAACP v. Alabama *ex rel.* Patterson, 357 U.S. 449 (1958).

"enhanced by group association" beyond the realm of the political. In noting that "it is immaterial whether the beliefs sought to be advanced by association pertain to political, economic, religious or cultural matters,"[15] the Court indicated that associations would be allowed to claim the same first amendment right of speech as individuals could claim, regardless of the content of that speech.[16]

In *Bates v. City of Little Rock*,[17] another case involving the NAACP, the Court also discussed freedom of association in a first amendment context. Justice Stewart, writing for the Court, noted:

> Like freedom of speech and a free press, the right of peaceable assembly was considered by the Framers of our Constitution to lie at the foundation of a government based upon the consent of an informed citizenry. . . . And it is now beyond dispute that freedom of *association for the purpose of advancing ideas and airing grievances* is protected by the Due Process Clause of the Fourteenth Amendment.[18]

If the two sentences must be read in conjunction to appreciate the common first amendment origins of all the rights enunciated by Justice Stewart, no such effort is required to appreciate the formulation of Justice Black's and Justice Douglas' concurrence: "freedom of assembly, includes of course freedom of association; and it is entitled to no less protection than any other First Amendment right. . . ."[19]

---

[15] NAACP v. Alabama *ex rel.* Patterson, 357 U.S. 449, 460 (1958).

[16] This recognition that an association can sue on behalf of its members to secure fundamental first amendment rights is the real significance of the decision in NAACP v. Alabama *ex rel.* Patterson. Although cases such as Sweezy v. New Hampshire, 354 U.S. 234 (1957), had established that the first amendment protected one's right not to divulge the associations in which one was a member, it was not yet clear whether an association could assert this right on behalf of its members or whether the issue had to be raised by individuals. Brief for Respondent at 26-27 and Brief for Petitioner at 32, NAACP v. Alabama *ex rel.* Patterson, 357 U.S. 449 (1958). Justice Harlan settled the issue: "If petitioner's rank-and-file members are constitutionally entitled to withhold their connection with the Association despite the production order, it is manifest that this right is properly assertable by the Association. To require that it be claimed by the members themselves would result in nullification of the right at the very moment of its assertion. Petitioner is the appropriate party to assert these rights, because it and its members are in every practical sense identical. The Association . . . is but the medium through which its individual members seek to make more effective the expression of their own views." 357 U.S. at 459.

[17] 361 U.S. 516 (1960).

[18] *Id.* 522-23 (emphasis added) (citations omitted).

[19] *Id.* at 528.

In three cases, *NAACP v. Button*,[20] *Brotherhood of Railroad Trainmen v. Virginia ex rel. Virginia State Bar*,[21] and *United Mine Workers v. Illinois State Bar Association*,[22] the Court did seem to safeguard associational activities not strictly linked to free speech or assembly. All three cases concerned an individual's ability to obtain legal counsel through an organization rather than his right to express his beliefs and ideals through membership. While in each of the cases the Court approved the organization's legal efforts,[23] the significant feature of the decisions for the instant analysis is not so much their outcome as their minimal reliance on any right of association for the realization of that outcome. Counsel in their briefs hardly mentioned the right,[24] and the dissenters never actually focused on it.[25] Rather, all the discussion cen-

---

[20] 371 U.S. 415 (1963).

[21] 377 U.S. 1 (1964).

[22] 389 U.S. 217 (1967).

[23] *Button* involved a plan by which the association paid attorneys on a per diem basis to litigate the civil rights claims of individual members. The Court approved the plan on the grounds that "litigation . . . is . . . a form of political expression." 371 U.S. at 429. The reliance on the term "political expression" suggested a possible limitation of the right of association when petition rather than speech was the underlying express first amendment right. The question of whether legal assistance obtained through an association had to be related to the attainment of "political goals" was raised in Brotherhood of R.R. Trainmen v. Virginia *ex rel.* Va. State Bar, 377 U.S. 1 (1964). In that case the Brotherhood advised members as to attorneys who might best pursue FELA claims. The Virginia Bar charged the Brotherhood with barratry, distinguishing *Button* precisely because the membership claims there involved civil, that is, "political" rights. The Court, however, chose to uphold the association's plan of legal assistance, noting that first amendment rights of petition and assembly necessarily included the right to consult with others regarding the best means of exercising those rights. 377 U.S. 1, 5-6 (1964).

In United Mine Workers v. Illinois State Bar Ass'n, 389 U.S. 217 (1967), where the union not only advised its members regarding legal action but actually hired an attorney on a salaried basis to pursue members' workmen's compensation claims, the Court went even further in negating any attempt to narrow the first amendment right of petition to the realm of the political.

[24] Brief for Petitioner at 37, NAACP v. Gray, *decided sub nom.* NAACP v. Button, 371 U.S. 415 (1963); Brief for Petitioner at 41, Brotherhood of R.R. Trainmen v. Virginia *ex rel.* Va. State Bar, 377 U.S. 1 (1964). In both briefs only the slightest mention of a right of association is made in support of petitioner's argument. Indeed, no reliance was placed on such a right in the briefs filed in United Mine Workers v. Illinois State Bar Ass'n, 389 U.S. 217 (1967).

[25] *See* NAACP v. Button, 371 U.S. 415, 448 (1963) (Harlan, J., with Clark and Stewart, JJ., dissenting). Interestingly, although Justice Harlan cited his own opinion in NAACP v. Alabama *ex rel.* Patterson, 357 U.S. 449, 453 (1958), he cited it for its recognition of the "freedom of expression" rather than any freedom of association. *See also* Brotherhood of R.R. Trainmen v. Virginia *ex rel.* Va. State Bar, 377 U.S. 1, 10 (1964) (Clark, J., with Harlan, J., dissenting); United Mine Workers v. Illinois State Bar Ass'n, 389 U.S. 217, 226 (1967) (Harlan, J., dissenting).

tered on the scope of the express first amendment right to petition the government for a redress of grievances.

But in *Button* the Court did invoke the association shorthand.

> We need not, in order to find constitutional protection for the kind of cooperative organizational activity disclosed by this record, . . . subsume such activity under a narrow, literal conception of freedom of speech, petition or assembly. For there is no longer any doubt that the First and Fourteenth Amendments protect certain forms of orderly group activity. Thus we have affirmed the right "to engage in association for the advancement of beliefs and ideas."[26]

By refusing to deal with the case under the "literal conception of . . . petition," and by instead invoking freedom of association, the Court only added to the ambiguity of the independent status of associational rights. The impression created by this language was that association is a first amendment right apart from speech or petition, but this does not represent the Court's decision in *Button* and other cases thus far considered here.

The Court's decision in *Griswold v. Connecticut*[27] created further confusion. Although the primary focus of the appellants' brief was on the constitutional right of privacy as it could be derived from the first, third and fourth amendments,[28] and although the bulk of the opinions in the case focused on this right,[29] Justice Douglas, writing for the Court, chose to close his decision with a comment on marital privacy and association.

> Marriage is a coming together for better or worse, hopefully enduring, and intimate to the degree of being sacred. It is an association that promotes a way of life, not causes; a harmony in living, not political faiths, a bilateral loyalty, not commercial or social projects. Yet it is an association for as noble a purpose as any involved in our prior decisions.[30]

---

[26] NAACP v. Button, 371 U.S. 415, 430 (1963).

[27] 381 U.S. 479 (1965) (striking down Connecticut statutes banning the use of contraceptives).

[28] Brief for Appellants at 79-89, Griswold v. Connecticut, 381 U.S. 479 (1965).

[29] Griswold v. Connecticut, 381 U.S. at 484-86, 486-87, 494-99 (Goldberg, J., concurring); *id.* at 508-10 (Black, J., with Stewart, J., dissenting); *id.* at 530 (Stewart, J., with Black, J., dissenting).

[30] *Id.* at 486.

Elsewhere in the decision, Justice Douglas had ascribed the right of association to the "penumbra of the First Amendment,"[31] which hardly departs from the line of cases already considered. This closing dicta, however, is the first suggestion that, although the right owes its origins to the first amendment, its scope is somehow larger. This is the first invocation of the freedom that would seem to safeguard an association without requiring its aims or goals to be related in any way to the more express first amendment rights of speech, petition, and assembly.

Justice Douglas continued to explore the possibility of an expanded freedom of association in *United States Department of Agriculture v. Moreno*.[32] This case challenged the constitutionality of the 1964 Food Stamp Act on grounds that its denial of food stamps to households containing unrelated individuals was a denial of due process. Although the majority struck down the law as violative of equal protection[33] because the implementing regulation was not "rationally related" to the statutory purpose of ensuring adequate food to the needy,[34] Justice Douglas, in concurrence, wrote:

> This case involves desperately poor people with acute problems who, though unrelated, come together for mutual help and assistance. The choice of one's associates for social, political, race or religious purposes is basic in our constitutional scheme. . . . I suppose that no one would doubt that an association of people working in the poverty field would be entitled to the same constitutional protection as those working in the racial, banking or agricultural field. I suppose poor people holding a meeting or convention would be under the same constitutional umbrella as others. . . . As the facts of this case show, the poor are congregating in households where they can better meet the adversities of poverty. This banding together is an *expression of the right of freedom of association* that is very deep in our traditions.[35]

Justice Douglas remained in the main-stream of association cases in noting the rights of the poor to meet, convene, and associate "for the

---

[31] *Id.* at 484.

[32] 413 U.S. 528 (1973).

[33] Once again, the Court acted without any prompting by the briefs filed in the case.

[34] United States Dep't of Agriculture v. Moreno, 413 U.S. 528, 536-38 (1973).

[35] *Id.* at 541 (emphasis added) (citations omitted).

advancement of beliefs and ideas." But he moved to a different plane in shifting from recognizing the right to *express oneself through an association* to recognizing the "*expression of the right of freedom of association.*" In the former case, an association is protected only because of its connection to some underlying fundamental right, while in the latter case, it is the association itself, regardless of its reason for being, that is given constitutional recognition.

Clearly this is a significant departure from the traditional association cases. It suggests that the importance lies not in an activity's being expressional, but in its being communal. Although freedom of association thus no longer was confined by the express terms of the first amendment, the precise limits of the formulation remained unclear.

In *Village of Belle Terre v. Boraas*,[36] the Court considerd a local zoning ordinance prohibiting three or more unrelated persons from living together. Despite certain factual parallels that could be drawn to *Moreno*, Justice Douglas, speaking for the Court, found the case to involve "no 'fundamental' right guaranteed by the Constitution, such as . . . the right of association. . . ."[37] In upholding the ordinance, the Court reverted to the more traditional associational analysis of the earlier cases, noting that the statute's prohibition on living together did not preclude a group's meeting together.[38] In short, the statute did not seriously impinge on the ability to advocate beliefs and ideas, the crucial element of the pre-*Griswold* association decisions.[39]

---

[36] 416 U.S. 1 (1974).

[37] *Id.* at 7. Justice Douglas chose to dismiss any freedom of association issue in the case although appellees did not rely on the freedom in their brief. Instead, they chose to argue rights of privacy and travel. Brief for Appellees at 60-67, Village of Belle Terre v. Boraas, 416 U.S. 1 (1974). *But see* Brief for Appellant at 14-24, *Village of Belle Terre*, *id.*

[38] *Id.* at 8. This is somewhat at odds with the statement in *Griswold* that "[t]he right of association . . . is more than the right to attend a meeting. . . ." Griswold v. Connecticut, 381 U.S. 479, 483 (1965).

[39] Justice Marshall's dissent in the case merits attention. He clearly saw a freedom of association issue in the case, for in his opinion "freedom of association is often inextricably entwined with the constitutionally guaranteed right of privacy. . . . The choice of household companions — of whether a person's 'intellectual and emotional needs' are best met by living with family, friends, professional associates or others — involves deeply personal considerations as to the kind and quality of intimate relationships within the home. That decision surely falls within the ambit of the right of privacy protected by the Constitution." Village of Belle Terre v. Boraas, 416 U.S. 1, 15-16 (1974). This link between association and privacy had been recognized by the Court in previous cases. Indeed, in NAACP v. Alabama *ex rel.* Patterson, 357 U.S. 449 (1958), Justice Harlan noted the "vital relationship between freedom to associate and privacy in one's association. . . . Inviolability of privacy in group association may in many circumstances be indispensable to preservation of freedom of association. . . ." *Id.* at 462. There is no precise analogy between the prevention of the chilling effect of public disclosure of membership in

To appreciate how completely the Court abandoned the expansive formulation of freedom of association suggested by Justice Douglas in *Griswold* and *Moreno*, one need look only to its recent summary affirmance of the district court's decision in *Garcia v. Texas State Board of Medical Examiners*.[40] In that case, a group of indigents challenged the constitutionality of a Texas statute requiring any medical corporation to have all-doctor boards of directors. Plaintiffs, participants in a pre-paid health plan, charged that the law violated their right of association, for only a lay group would form a pre-paid health plan and hire a doctor on a salaried basis to provide meaningful medical care to the poor. The situation here was analogous to that in *Moreno*,[41] yet the Supreme Court, without opinion, affirmed the lower court's ruling that freedom of association would warrant recognition only in the context of express first amendment rights.

The Court's recent discussion of freedom of association in *Buckley v. Valeo*,[42] insofar as it affirmatively strengthens the link between freedom of association and traditional first amendment rights, further weakens the status of freedom of association as an independent right. The case involved challenges to the constitutionality of various sections of the Federal Election Campaign Act of 1971 as amended in 1974.[43] In a

---

an association and the protection of "private" and "intimate" choices and decisions. But, as most association cases have been speech, petition, or assembly cases involving a group, this dissent may also be viewed as invoking a safeguard for privacy when a group is involved rather than an independent right of association.

[40] 421 U.S. 995 (1975), *aff'g mem.*, 384 F. Supp. 434 (W.D. Tex. 1974).

[41] Certainly *Garcia* as much as *Moreno* involved "desperately poor people," people who have come together and pooled their resources with the aim "better [to] meet the adversities of poverty." United States Dep't of Agriculture v. Moreno, 413 U.S. 528, 541 (1973) (Douglas, J., concurring). Another analogy is United Mine Workers v. Illinois State Bar Ass'n, 389 U.S. 217 (1967). The only difference between the hiring of a lawyer on a salaried basis and the hiring of a doctor proves to be a crucial one. The Mine Workers were facilitating the means by which their members could petition the courts, a right expressly safeguarded by the first admendment, but while the Court has recognized the importance of medical care as a necessity of life, *see* Memorial Hosp. v. Maricopa County, 415 U.S. 250, 259 (1974), it has yet to recognize it as a constitutionally protected right. And without some underlying constitutional right, specifically without some underlying first amendment right, a group has not been able to gain Court recognition of its freedom of association.

[42] 424 U.S. 1 (1976).

[43] 18 U.S.C. § 591 (1971), *as amended by* Federal Election Campaign Act Amendments of 1974, Pub. L. No. 93-443, 88 Stat. 1267, 1268, 1304. Specifically challenged were provisions (1) limiting political contributions to candidates for federal office by an individual or group to $1,000 and by a political committee to $5,000 for any single candidate per election, with an overall annual limitation of $25,000 for an individual contributor, (2) limiting expenditures by individuals or groups "relative to a clearly identified candidate" to $1,000 per candidate per election, and by a candidate from his personal

lengthy *per curiam* decision, the Court struck down the section of the Act limiting campaign expenditures to $1,000 per candidate per election on the ground that such limitation impermissibly burdened the "right to engage in 'vigorous advocacy,' " a part of freedom of speech protected by the first amendment.[44] The Court went on to find that the law impinged on "protected associational freedoms" to "amplif[y] the voice of the adherents."[45] The Court protected association insofar as it contributes to effective exercise of the first amendment right of speech, returning to the traditional conception of the freedom.

The most recent Supreme Court discussion of freedom of association continues to uphold the tradition. In *Runyon v. McCrary*,[46] respondents brought a class action arguing that certain Virginia private schools violated 42 U.S.C. § 1981 by refusing to admit them because of their race. On behalf of the parents who patronized the schools, petitioners invoked freedom of association as a part of their defense. Justice Stewart, returning to the point made in *NAACP v. Alabama ex rel. Patterson* that the first amendment recognized a right " 'to engage in association for the advancement of beliefs and ideas. . .', "[47] admitted that the parents did have a right to join together to advocate segregation. but noted that the effective group *advocacy* of such an idea did not necessarily include Court protection of the effective group *implementation* of that idea.[48]

The inescapable conclusion is that the Court is now applying a limited conception of the right of association: whenever men may speak as individuals, they may speak in and through groups; if they may assem-

---

or family funds to various specified annual amounts depending on the office sought, (3) requiring political committees to keep detailed records of contributions and expenditures including, in some cases, the names, addresses, and places of business of contributors and to report same to the Federal Election Commission, and (4) creating the Federal Election Commission.

[44] Buckley v. Valeo, 424 U.S. 1, 48 (1976), *quoting* New York Times Co. v. Sullivan, 376 U.S. 254, 269 (1964), *quoting* Bridges v. California, 314 U.S. 252, 270 (1941) and NAACP v. Button, 371 U.S. 415, 429 (1963).

[45] "[T]he Act's $1,000 limitation on independent expenditures 'relative to a clearly identified candidate' precludes most associations from effectively *amplifying the voice of their adherents*, the original basis for the recognition of First Amendment protection of the freedom of association. *See* NAACP v. Alabama, 357 U.S. at 460." Buckley v. Valeo, 424 U.S. 1, 22 (1976) (emphasis added).

[46] 96 S. Ct. 2586 (1976).

[47] *Id.* at 2596, *quoting* NAACP v. Alabama *ex rel.* Patterson, 357 U.S. 449, 460 (1958).

[48] "[I]t may be assumed that parents have a First Amendment right to send their children to educational institutions that promote the belief that racial segregation is desirable, and that the children have an equal right to attend such institutions. But it does not follow that the *practice* of excluding racial minorities from such institutions is also protected by the same principle." *Id.*

ble and petition, they may associate in such a way as to facilitate such petitioning. Despite the seeming expansion of the right by Justice Douglas in *Griswold* and *Moreno*, and by Justice Marshall dissenting in *Belle Terre*, the cases taken together provide no basis for a broader reading. If freedom of association is to move beyond the traditional scope of the first amendment, then, it is clear that a completely new formulation of the right is needed.

II. FREEDOM OF ASSOCIATION: THE BASIS FOR AN INDEPENDENT FORMULATION

Freedom of association has traditionally been little more than a shorthand for safeguarding an individual's rights of speech and petition when he exercises them through a group. Were courts to acknowledge this and explicitly ground their decisions on the underlying rights,[49] more candid adjudication might be achieved, but no independent basis for freedom of association would necessarily be accepted. Without such a basis, however, non-expressional associations such as the one involved in *Garcia* cannot be constitutionally protected. Therefore, the rationale for a doctrine of association which operates beyond the traditional realm of the first amendment must be detailed.[50]

The fundamental reason for developing an independent, non-expressional formulation of freedom of association is that most associations are not formed solely to express ideas or to petition the government, but to take action to implement those ideas. The basic value of this associational action is that it allows an individual to achieve through collective effort what he might not otherwise be able to achieve for himself.

The realization that great things and small can frequently be attained only through association has made the urge to associate a natural impulse of man. Over a century ago, Alexis de Tocqueville observed:

> The most natural privilege of man, next to the right of acting for himself, is that of combining his exertions with those of his fellow creatures and of acting in common with them. The right of association therefore appears . . . almost as inalienable in its nature as the right of personal liberty. No legislator can attack it without impairing the foundations of society.[51]

---

[49] For example, NAACP v. Alabama *ex rel.* Patterson, 357 U.S. 449 (1958), would be cited simply *pro forma* as authority that rights of speech and petition are to be protected whether a person exercises them individually or through a group.

[50] The suggested formulation of the doctrine is considered at pp. 15-18 *infra*.

[51] 1 A. de Tocqueville, Democracy in America 196 (P. Bradley, ed. 1945).

De Tocqueville noted that this "almost inalienable" right could serve the instrumental purpose of promoting individual independence, at least as against the power of government,[52] but he also recognized that in a democracy, as opposed to an aristocracy, it was almost impossible for man to achieve anything by himself.[53] Thus the alternatives seemed clear: the individual either must rely on government or join with others in group endeavors. Americans early on chose the latter course.[54]

It has been suggested that Emerson's conception of individual independence and self-reliance stands in contrast to the idea of voluntary association.[55] Associational activity, it is said, cripples individuality.[56] However, because as a nation we have grown larger and less flexible since Emerson wrote, self-reliance in its purest sense has become almost impossible. Yet a hybrid self-reliance, based in part on voluntary associations and having as its goal the maximization of individual independence of government power, does seem attainable. Groups which promote the common good of their members help the individual to realize his goals by functioning as intermediaries between him and the government.[57] The

---

[52] "The citizen of the United States is taught from infancy to rely upon his own exertions in order to resist the evils and the difficulties of life; he looks upon the social authority with an eye of mistrust and anxiety, and he claims its assistance only when he is unable to do without it." *Id.* at 191.

[53] II A. DE TOCQUEVILLE, DEMOCRACY IN AMERICA 118-19 (P. Bradley, ed. 1945).

[54] "Whenever at the head of some new undertaking you see the government in France, or a man of rank in England, in the United States you will be sure to find an association." *Id.* at 106. De Tocqueville's buoyant confidence in the American reliance on associations is not, however, without its critics. George Kateb has observed that "everything has changed its scale since he wrote." Kateb, *Some Remarks on de Tocqueville's View of Voluntary Associations*, XI NOMOS 138, 141, Y.B. AM. SOC'Y FOR POL. AND LEGAL PHILOSOPHY (1969). And certainly de Tocqueville, in his nineteenth century championship of collective economic pursuits, could not have foreseen that uniquely twentieth century "association," the conglomerate, having at its disposal enormous amounts of money and thus wielding enormous quantities of power. Nor could he have foreseen that labor unions, then just struggling for recognition of their legitimacy, *see, e.g.*, Commonwealth v. Hunt, 45 Mass. (4 Met.) 111 (1842), would grow into forces to be reckoned with. But it does not follow, as Kateb suggests, that de Tocqueville failed to appreciate the oligarchic tendencies of associations. Kateb, *supra*, at 141-43. At least with respect to political associations, de Tocqueville observed: "I doubt whether, in any country or in any age, it is wise to set no limits to freedom of association." DE TOCQUEVILLE, *supra* note 51, at 131. It is necessary to note, then, that in urging a reformulation of freedom of association, this article seeks no absolute freedom. Rather it seeks a judicial awareness that associational action, as well as expression, can serve a valuable function in a society committed to the development of individual self-reliance.

[55] Kateb, *supra* note 54, at 143.

[56] *Id.*

[57] "More and more the individual, in order to realize his own capacities or to stand up to the institutionalized forces that surround him, has found it imperative to join with others

recognition of an independent right of freedom of association will ensure the continued existence of such essential groups.

Although the Constitution nowhere explicitly recognizes such an independent principle, the Court has been willing to recognize other rights which are not expressly mentioned but which are necessary either to the full realization of express rights or to the protection of fundamental principles underlying civil society.[58] Various members of the Court, in discussing the concept of due process, have repeatedly urged the protection of basic values "implicit in the concept of ordered liberty,"[59] values "that underlie our society,"[60] values ascertained as a result of "respect for the teaching of history. . . ."[61]

The notion of society is one of men joining together to further common goals. Definitions of such basic principles often are derived from the philosophy of inalienable and natural rights relied on by the framers of the Constitution. Because the framers found certain rights in the laws of nature rather than merely in the law or constitutions of men,[62] the Constitution gave legitimacy to a gov-

---

of like mind in pursuit of common objectives. . . . In a society governed by democratic principles it is the individual who is the ultimate concern of the social order. His interests and his rights are paramount. Association is an extension of individual freedom. It is a method of making more effective, of giving greater depth and scope to, the individual's needs, aspirations and liberties." Emerson, *Freedom of Association and Freedom of Expression*, 74 YALE L.J. 1, 4 (1964). *See* Rice, *The Constitutional Right of Association*, 16 HASTINGS L.J. 491, 499 (1965); Schlesinger, *Biography of a Nation of Joiners*, 50 AM. HIST. REV. 1 (1944). *See generally* D. FELLMAN, THE CONSTITUTIONAL RIGHT OF ASSOCIATION (1963); R. HORN, GROUPS AND THE CONSTITUTION (1956); C. SMITH, VOLUNTARY ASSOCIATIONS: PERSPECTIVES ON THE LITERATURE (1973) (bibliography of the area). *See also* A. SCHLESINGER, THE RISE OF THE CITY 1878–1898 (1933). Americans became the "world's greatest joiners" out of necessity. For individuals whose sense of self-importance was bruised by the anonymity of life amidst increasingly larger crowds, associations served to restore both self-identity and self-confidence. *Id.* at 288-90.

[58] *See, e.g.*, Griswold v. Connecticut, 381 U.S. 479 (1965) (right to privacy); Crandall v. Nevada, 73 U.S. (6 Wall) 35 (1868) (right to travel).

[59] Palko v. Connecticut, 302 U.S. 319, 325 (1937) (Cardozo, J.).

[60] Griswold v. Connecticut, 381 U.S. 479, 501 (1965) (Harlan, J., concurring).

[61] Adamson v. California, 332 U.S. 46, 59 (1947) (Frankfurter, J., concurring).

[62] The commitment to "natural rights" is evident throughout the works of the framers. *See* Corwin, *The "Higher Law" Background of American Constitutional Law*, (pts. 1-2), 42 HARV. L. REV. 149, 365 (1928); W. SOLBERG, INTRODUCTION TO THE FEDERAL CONVENTION AND THE FORMATION OF THE UNION OF THE AMERICAN STATES (W. Solberg, ed. 1958). It is clear that Locke, Harrington, and Montesquieu, all exponents of the theory that man's inalienable rights precede government, exercised far more of an influence on the Revolutionary generation than did Hobbes and Rousseau who denied the existence of natural rights. *Id.*

For further evidence of the commitment to natural law by the founding generation, see also Humphreys, *The Rule of Law and the American Revolution*, and Gay, *Enlightenment*

ernment ordained to secure these rights, not to create or limit them.[63]

Freedom of association as a principle which is implicit in the concept of ordered liberty, basic to our democratic society, with roots deep in our history, should be recognized as an independent right.[64] There is precedent to support recognition as a fundamental right of an activity which at one time was protected only because of its ties to some more traditional right. The right to travel, nowhere expressly mentioned in the Constitution, was first recognized because it was necessary to the full enjoyment of other Constitutional rights, such as the right to travel to and petition at the seat of government,[65] but it has since come to protect a citizen's right to travel for whatever reason.[66] So should freedom of association, long recognized as a valuable vehicle for the exercise of the first amendment rights of speech and petition, now be seen as protecting associational activity that is non-speech or non-petition related as well. The following formulation proposes guidelines to ensure meaningful exercise of the right.

Thought and the American Revolution, in THE ROLE OF IDEOLOGY IN THE AMERICAN REVOLUTION (J. Howe, Jr., ed. 1970); Grey, *Do We Have an Unwritten Constitution?*, 27 STAN. L. REV. 703, 715, 717 (1975).

[63] The classical American expression on the subject comes from Jefferson and is captured in the opening sentences of the Declaration of Independence: "[M]en are created . . . with certain unalienable Rights. . . . [T]o secure these rights, Governments are instituted among Men. . . ." Close to fifty years later, Jefferson's faith remained unshaken: "Nothing then is unchangeable but the inherent and unalienable rights of man." Letter to John Cartwright (June 5, 1824), *reprinted in* 16 THE WRITINGS OF THOMAS JEFFERSON 42, 48 (A. Lipscomb & A. Bergh, eds. 1905).

When critics attacked the Constitution for its failure to include a bill of rights, the framers replied that a bill of rights was unnecessary, for *natural* rights could not be alienated by government. *See generally* MADISON, I ANNALS OF CONGRESS 456 (J. Gales ed. 1834); II STORY, COMMENTARIES ON THE CONSTITUTION OF THE UNITED STATES 626-27 (5th ed. 1891); Calder v. Bull, 3 Dall. 386, 399 (1789) (Iredell, J., concurring); W. SOLBERG, INTRODUCTION TO THE FEDERAL CONVENTION AND THE FORMATION OF THE UNION OF THE AMERICAN STATES at cix (W. Solberg, ed. 1958).

[64] *See generally* R. HORN, GROUPS AND THE CONSTITUTION (1956), for a development of the premise that freedom of association, while not to be found in the text of the Constitution, is one of the most important civil liberties implicitly guaranteed by our constitutional system of government. *See also* D. FELLMAN, THE CONSTITUTIONAL RIGHT OF ASSOCIATION (1963), considering the preservation of particular associational rights and the notion that a fundamental right of association may be derived from the Constitution.

[65] Crandall v. Nevada, 73 U.S. (6 Wall) 35 (1868).

[66] *E.g.*, Shapiro v. Thompson, 394 U.S. 618 (1969); United States v. Guest, 383 U.S. 745 (1966); Aptheker v. Secretary of State, 378 U.S. 500 (1964); Kent v. Dulles, 357 U.S. 116 (1958).

III. PROTECTING FREEDOM OF ASSOCIATION: A GUIDE FOR THE COURTS

The basic principle for which recognition will be sought in the formulation of an independent constitutional right of association is that whatever action a person can pursue as an individual, freedom of association must ensure he can pursue with others. Only such a principle assures man that, in his struggle to be independent of government control, he will not be crippled simply because on occasion he strives to achieve that independence with the help of others.

Thus in any situation in which an individual finds his endeavors hampered because he has chosen to pursue them through an association, the courts should intervene by posing a number of questions to the government. The first must be whether, under the Constitution, the government could bar or hamper a sole individual engaging in the same pursuit. If the answer is "no" because the individual's freedom of speech or petition would be chilled, because his right of privacy would be invaded, or because any Constitutional right would be infringed, then the state cannot so bar or hamper the association. It is not freedom of association which protects the group activity in such a case but rather the fundamental constitutional right that each member, acting alone, could invoke.

Returning to the intitial query, if instead the answer is "yes," that is, if the state could act to bar or hamper a lone individual in such pursuit, a second question must be asked: has the state so acted? If the answer is "yes" then the right of association, as it is here formulated, would afford no protection. For an association and its members "are in every practical sense identical."[67] Therefore, if an individual may not act on his own, he should not be able to act through an association.

This notion that an association is no more than the sum of its individual members seems essential in a society in which it is "the individual who is the ultimate concern of the social order."[68] In such a society it would hardly seem possible that an abstract entity such as an association should enjoy rights apart from and indeed greater than its individual members;[69] to hold otherwise would contradict the equality of opportu-

---

[67] NAACP v. Alabama *ex rel.* Patterson, 357 U.S. 449, 459 (1958). The Court referred to this identity in connection with the issue of the NAACP's standing to assert the injuries of its members, but the principle can have a more general application.

[68] Emerson, *supra* note 7, at 4.

[69] An exception might have to be made in the case of associations so unique that what the individual seeks to pursue through membership can be achieved only through the group. One example is the goal of procreation within the marital association, discussed by the

nity which is at the heart of this argument for freedom of association. Thus to the extent the state can bar individuals from certain activities, once it has done so it has the unquestioned power to bar associations from similar activities.

Freedom of association as an independent right thus actually comes into play under this formulation only when the state has chosen not to bar or hamper an individual from engaging in an activity, despite the state's ability to do so. In such a case, freedom of association would create a presumption of invalidity regarding the state action affecting only the association. The presumption arises from the underlying principle of freedom of association proposed.[70]

This presumption of invalidity would place a definite burden on the state. Where the state had acted against an association but not against the individual, courts would engage in "strict scrutiny" of the state's actions. They would require a showing that the associational activity involved in such a case posed a greater threat to some legitimate social goal than that posed by the similar activity of an individual, and that the state

---

Court in Griswold v. Connecticut, 381 U.S. 479 (1965). The rights of such a group may indeed be different from those enjoyed by individual citizens. This Article, however, deals with associational rights only insofar as they promote their goals sought by members as discrete individuals.

Another example in this regard is drawn from labor law. Through the collective strength of unions, individuals achieve benefits which they could seek on their own, but which they do not have the power to obtain as single actors. The National Labor Relations Act, 29 U.S.C. §§ 141-197 (1970), 49 Stat. 449, *as amended by* 61 Stat. 136 and 73 Stat. 519, was enacted to preserve such individual rights through association. Although it may be argued that the size and influence of modern unions enable them to attain goals which no individual could legitimately pursue, the basis of their statutory power is the rights of the individual. These rights can be obtained effectively only through association, but the grounding of these rights in the individual and the restrictions on union abuses of power embodied in the federal regulatory scheme should ensure unions' survival under any theory of freedom of association.

[70] It is reasonable to inquire as to the basis of a formulation which presumes the invalidity of state action taken against an association, but which would not presume the invalidity of the same state action if it were taken against an individual. The explanation rests on the strong tradition of association in the American experience outlined in pp. 11-14 *supra*, as well as the concept of "rights" as existing apart from explicit constitutional provisions also discussed *supra*. In this context, it is possible to argue that freedom of association is not meant to secure greater rights for groups than for individuals, but rather that it is meant to ensure that those activities which the state concedes individuals have the "right" to pursue may be pursued whether individuals act alone or in groups.

Freedom of association does not protect individuals against infringement of their liberties by the state. Rather, it ensures that, once the state has recognized rights, any attempt to limit the pur uit of those rights in a group will be carefully scrutinized by the courts.

had chosen the least restrictive means to cope with the increased threat. Courts engaging in such scrutiny should not be satisfied by a mere showing that an association enhances the ability of its members to secure some goal, for indeed every association would then qualify for state regulation. Rather, a court's inquiry should focus on whether the association has acquired power for its individual members greater than that which the law allows any individual, regardless of wealth or talent, to acquire.[71] Only if this were shown could individuals acting through associations be treated differently than individuals acting alone. Such a rule would leave the government free to safeguard against the oligarchic tendencies of some groups while continuing to recognize that as a general rule associational action requires protection lest individuals be helpless to better themselves in light of an increasingly industrialized status quo.

Perhaps the greatest impact such a formulation of freedom of association would have would be in those areas of economic legislation where the Court has tended to require no more than a showing of "rational relationship" to an acceptable state purpose for a law to be deemed valid.[72] What is now urged is that whenever a court finds that a law bars an association from engaging in an activity which an individual may pursue, be that activity expressional, social, or economic in nature, it demand a compelling reason for the difference in treatment. Some critics might deem this a return to the *Lochner* era.[73] Strictly speaking, its scope is too narrow for such a characterization. To the extent state laws affect all citizens, either as individuals acting alone or as members of an association, there would be no judicial second-guessing of the legislature. Only in the very narrow area of cases where a law makes it more difficult for an individual to achieve a legitimate goal by combining his efforts with

---

Thus, the formulation at times may appear to be phrased in the language of equal protection. In fact there are strong parallels, almost as if it is those individuals who join in associations who form the "suspect class." However, the Court has not been receptive to efforts to expand the categories of individuals who can invoke equal protection, and so this analysis relies on the special reasons for affording protection in association cases that are not present in other instances of discrimination. The high standards of review proposed do not reflect an attempt to impose an equal protection analysis, but rather a borrowing of strict scrutiny to protect special rights.

[71] In this regard it might be useful to consider, as an example, the Sherman Act's § 1 prohibition on conspiracies in furtherance of a monopoly. 15 U.S.C. § 1 (1974). It does no more than prevent a group from doing what § 2 prevents an individual from doing, *i.e.*, acquiring a monopoly.

[72] *See, e.g.*, North Dakota State Bd. of Pharmacy v. Synder's Drug Stores, 414 U.S. 156 (1973); Williamson v. Lee Optical Co., 348 U.S. 483 (1955).

[73] *See, e.g.*, Lochner v. New York, 198 U.S. 45 (1905); Coppage v. Kansas, 236 U.S. 1 (1915); Adkins v. Children's Hosp., 261 U.S. 525 (1923).

others than by struggling, perhaps hopelessly, on his own, would the state have to show a compelling reason for the difference. There would be no *Lochner*-like second-guessing, for the state, by allowing individuals to engage in the activity at issue, already would have decided that the goal is one permissible to pursue.

Accordingly, under the proposed formulation both antitrust and conspiracy laws would remain viable. Admittedly, the state would have to justify such laws by showing that when it sought to treat groups differently from individuals it was because the group threatened either the economic model or the existence of the government in a way no individual could. But this would merely mean more carefully written laws and greater legislative inquiry into probable effects.[74] If the legislature is doing no more than guessing as to effect, then courts will be free to invoke freedom of association to strike down the unnecessary intrusion on liberty. Surely no one can support laws imposing limits on individuals who can better themselves only through collective activity when there is no showing by the state of a particular need for such limits.

IV. FREEDOM OF ASSOCIATION: APPLYING THE PROPOSED FORMULATION

The proposed doctrine of freedom of association would operate in fact only in a small and discrete atmosphere. Its application to several recent decisions evidences this point.

In *Buckley v. Valeo*,[75] the Supreme Court invoked freedom of association to strike down the expenditure limitation in the Campaign

[74] This is not to suggest that every antitrust or conspiracy action will be plagued by the government's continually having to justify the compelling interest it has in a given law, for admittedly the formulation proposed aims at a balancing between the interests of the members of a group and the interests of the state. Requiring the government to demonstrate evidence of its interests in a few cases will probably encourage the legislature to be more specific about its rationale for different treatment of individual and group activity in future legislation. *See* Gunther, *The Supreme Court, 1971 Term — Foreword: In Search of Evolving Doctrine of a Changing Court: A Model for a Newer Equal Protection*, 86 HARV. L. REV. 1, 20-24 (1972). A clear presentation of the policy behind such a statute will obviate the need, in many cases, for detailed inquiry into justification at trial. Legislatures have already demonstrated a willingness to do this in the area of labor law, where lengthy hearings and long debates have characterized the passage of laws such as the Taft-Hartley Act, 61 Stat. 136, amending 29 U.S.C. §§ 141-197 (1970) regulating union activity. Of course, the Court will have to be persuaded that the chosen state policy is the least restrictive alternative to achieving the compelling state interest before an abridgment of freedom of association is tolerated. But more careful legislative definition of the interest and the means chosen to deal with it cannot but expedite the Court's task in this regard.

[75] 424 U.S. 1 (1976).

Finance Act. Under the first prong of the proposed formulation of freedom of association, such invocation would be unnecessary. Once the Court decides, as it did, that the state lacks the power to limit the expenditures of a private individual lest his first amendment right of speech be infringed, then it necessarily follows that this same constitutional right of speech invalidates any such limitation on the expenditures of an association. Moreover, once the Court decides, as it did, that limiting contributions, as opposed to expenditures, has only a negligible effect on an individual's freedom of speech,[76] there would be, under the first part of the proposed formulation, no need to discuss any possible "associational" right to limitless contribution.

In the *Buckley* decision, the Court did discuss this right, finding that contribution limits as well as expenditure limits impinge on associational freedoms: "Making a contribution . . . enables like-minded persons to pool their resources in furtherance of common political goals."[77] However, the Court did not consider this sufficient to warrant overturning the law, because the contributor remained "free to become a member of any political association and to assist personally in the association's efforts on behalf of candidates."[78] In essence, what the Court seemed to be saying was that denial of opportunity to contribute limitlessly through a group is not a constitutionally cognizable deprivation given that the individual can still express his support, that is, exercise his right of speech, through direct expenditures. The crucial distinction, then, is between expenditures and contributions insofar as limits on either affect freedom of speech and expression. Admittedly the Court recognized the need for establishing this distinction, but by invoking freedom of association and then refusing to recognize it as an independent dispositive right,[79] the Court only added unnecessary confusion.

Use of the proposed formulation would have resulted in a clearer decision. Under the first guideline, if there is a particular constitutional right, such as freedom of speech, which prevents the state from limiting some individual activity such as campaign expenditures, then that right rather than any notion of freedom of association prevents the state from so

---

[76] "A contribution serves as a general expression of support for the candidate and his views, but does not communicate the underlying basis for the support. The quantity of communication by the contributor does not increase perceptibly with the size of his contribution, since the expression rests solely on the undifferentiated, symbolic act of contributing. . . . While contributions may result in political expression if spent by a candidate or an association to present views to the voters, the transformation of contributions into political debate involves speech by someone other than the contributor." *Id.* at 21.

[77] *Id.*

[78] *Id.*

[79] *Id.* at 57-59.

limiting the activity of an association. Under the second guideline, once the Court finds that the state can prohibit certain individual activity such as making campaign contributions, and has in fact done so, it need not entertain an association claim that a group, because it is a group, should not be barred from that activity.[80]

More troubling in its result is the discussion of freedom of association in *Aguayo v. Richardson*.[81] The case involved a challenge under the Civil Rights Act, 42 U.S.C. § 1983, to experimental work projects for recipients of Aid to Families with Dependent Children (AFDC). It was

---

[80] Reconsidering the concerns which underlie the proposed formulation of freedom of association, it becomes clearer how inappropriate discussion of any associational claim is in the contribution aspect of the *Buckley* case. Freedom of association is valuable, it has been argued, because it allows an individual to achieve through collective effort what he might not be able to achieve by himself. *See* pp. 11-14 *supra*. By spending money for, or contributing to, the campaign of a chosen candidate, the individual strives to achieve communication of support for the candidate and his ideas in the short run, and election of that candidate in the long run. If wealthy individuals acting independently are free to spend as much as they want lest their freedom of speech be abridged, it necessarily follows that groups of individuals must have the same freedom. Otherwise, their speech may have less effect than that of wealthy individuals acting independently merely because of the inability of the group to pool what may be quite modest resources and to focus the manner in which these are spent.

But if wealthy individuals are limited in the amount they can contribute to a candidate, a less affluent individual cannot assert that by similarly limiting the amount an association of which he is a member can contribute to a candidate, he is denied the opportunity to achieve a goal which he could legitimately pursue individually. For example, the law as approved by the Court in *Buckley* would allow an individual to contribute $1,000 per candidate. If twenty-five members of an association which is not a political committee each have $100 which they can afford to contribute to a candidate, the $1,000 limit on associational contributions does not deny the members an opportunity to achieve a goal which they legitimately could pursue, *i.e.*, a total contribution of $25,000. It simply means that only $1,000 of their currently available $2,500 can be contributed through the association. The remaining $1,500, and indeed any further funds up to $25,000 still can be contributed by the members, but only in their individual capacity.

Indeed, to a certain extent the Campaign Finance Act favors associations insofar as it does not require contributors to deduct from their individual contribution limits the amounts that they have contributed through associations not linked to a "clearly identifiable candidate." To the extent these associations enjoy benefits and rights seemingly greater than individuals, the premise of the proposed formulation, that associations are no more than vehicles by which individuals maximize their potential, is weakened. It should be noted, however, that there are requirements as to the number of contributors in associations, especially "political committees," which may contribute as much as $5,000, and these may ensure that associations do not become vehicles by which individuals evade the applicable contribution limitation.

[81] 473 F.2d 1090 (2d Cir. 1973), *cert. denied*, 414 U.S. 1146 (1974).

brought by a number of AFDC recipients, seven welfare rights organizations, and others, but the Second Circuit dismissed the welfare organizations from the suit on the grounds that only individuals have standing to sue under § 1983. Judge Friendly relied on the language of § 1983, which confers a cause of action on " '*any citizen* of the United States or other person . . .' who has been deprived under color of state law 'of any rights, privileges, or immunities,' " as evidence that an association could not sue on behalf of its members.[82]

Anticipating a possible challenge on grounds of freedom of association, Judge Friendly went on to note:

> We do not regard the line of decisions beginning with *NAACP v. Alabama ex rel. Patterson*, . . . and continuing through . . . *NAACP v. Button*, . . . as having altered that principle. [T]he statements in those opinions that the organization has standing to assert the rights of its members were made in the context of . . . the constitutional right of association.[83]

In short, Judge Friendly would grant protection under the freedom of association doctrine only if the association itself were threatened. This reading of even the traditional association cases, with its complete concentration on some abstract creature — the association — ignores the strong concern for individual rights and individual fulfillment that lies at the heart of freedom of association. Although traditional association cases at times focused on protection of the association itself, all in fact were concerned with the free and full exercise of first amendment rights of speech and petition by the association's *members*.[84] All drew on the

[82] *Id.* at 1099 (emphasis added).

[83] *Id.* at 1099-1100 (citations omitted). Judge Friendly continued: "While the Court said in Sierra Club v. Morton, [405 U.S. at 739,] '[i]t is clear that an organization whose members are injured may represent those members in a proceeding for judicial review,' followed by a citation to *Button*, we think this must be limited to the issue there *sub judice*, standing to seek review of the action of federal officers, and not as broadening the standing of organizations as plaintiffs under the Civil Rights Act." 473 F.2d at 1100 (1973).

Judge Friendly's narrow and perhaps even wooden reading of the scope of § 1983 has not been approved by the Supreme Court. Indeed, in Warth v. Seldin, 422 U.S. 490 (1975), the Court, citing *Sierra Club*, suggested that so long as an association could allege that its members, or any one of them, "are suffering immediate or threatened injury as a result of the challenged action of the sort that would make out a justiciable case had the members themselves brought suit," and so long as the nature of the claim and the relief sought do not require the individual participation of each injured party, an association may indeed maintain a § 1983 suit on behalf of its members. 422 U.S. at 511.

[84] *See* pp. 2-10 *supra*.

initial observation of Justice Harlan in *NAACP v. Alabama ex rel. Patterson*, that an "[a]ssociation . . . is but the medium through which its individual members seek to make more effective the expression of their own views."[85] The proposed formulation draws on this observation, by asserting that associations are but the instruments through which members seek more effectively to make numerous endeavors and hence should be protected so that individuals can achieve their maximum potential.

Applying the guidelines to determine whether an association could pursue the claims of its members in a § 1983 action, the following analysis might result. At the first level, although Congress can constitutionally prevent an individual from bringing a civil rights claim in federal court,[86] it has not. Indeed, Congress expressly enacted 42 U.S.C. § 1983 to provide "a federal right in federal courts,"[87] when civil rights are at stake. *Aguayo* could thus be viewed as a true association case in which an individual acting through a group is barred from a pursuit permitted to an individual acting alone. The court then would require the government to prove that the association in question wields a power greater than its collective members before acceding to any suggestion that the association not be allowed to pursue members' claims.

In fact, however, such an analysis might be too facile, and the reliance on freedom of association premature. What is really at stake in considering whether an association may bring a § 1983 claim on behalf of its members is whether those members will be able to exercise meaningfully their fundamental right of petition. If a grant of federal jurisdiction like § 1983 is a congressional definition of the scope of petition, then a case like *Aguayo* need proceed no further than the first level of consideration. Having included within the fundamental right of petition the right to initiate civil rights actions in federal courts, Congress cannot limit the right by burdening an individual's exercise of it.[88] Accordingly, the state

---

[85] 357 U.S. 449, 459 (1958).

[86] *See* Sheldon v. Sill, 49 U.S. (8 How.) 441 (1850), which makes clear that the federal courts enjoy only such original jurisdiction as Congress expressly vests in them by statute. Thus, Congress was under no obligation to provide a federal forum to hear individuals' civil rights claims and if it had not, there would have been no constitutional right to such a forum. *See also* P. BATOR, P. MISHKIN, D. SHAPIRO & H. WECHSLER, HART & WECHSLER'S THE FEDERAL COURTS AND THE FEDERAL SYSTEM, 330-75 (2d ed. 1973).

[87] Munroe v. Pape, 365 U.S. 167, 180 (1961).

[88] *See* Arnett v. Kennedy, 416 U.S. 134 (1974). In *Arnett* six members of the Court took the position that the power of Congress to define the scope of rights does not always include the power to limit their exercise within that scope. *But see* Bishop v. Wood, 96 S. Ct. 2074 (1976).

cannot burden individual exercise by limiting the right of petition through an association.[89]

Two cases do, at first glance, seem to offer the opportunity to move beyond the first level of inquiry and to invoke the proposed formulation of freedom of association. *United States Department of Agriculture v. Moreno*[90] and *Village of Belle Terre v. Boraas*[91] both involve situations in which associations were formed to better enable the individual members to attain a particular goal. Both involve state action against associational pursuit of that goal, but not against individual pursuit.

In *Moreno*,[92] the proposed formulation would place on the government the burden of showing why unrelated recipients of food stamps who maintained group households were so much more likely to be guilty of fraudulent receipt of stamps than unrelated recipients who maintained separate households that it was necessary to deny the benefits of the program to all such group recipients. Given the poignant facts which drove many of the unrelated plaintiffs to establish common households,[93] it seems highly unlikely that the government could adequately support the need for such a sweeping exclusion.

In *Belle Terre*[94] the proposed formulation would place on the government the burden of showing why unrelated members of group households posed greater threats to "family values, . . . quiet seclusion and clean air"[95] than did the unrelated individuals who were allowed to maintain separate residences in the town. In this case, it is not inconceivable that the government could have sustained its burden by persuading the Court that when any group of individuals, related or unrelated, lives

---

[89] Although Judge Friendly in Aguayo v. Richardson, 473 F.2d 1090 (2d Cir. 1973), *cert. denied*, 414 U.S. 1146 (1974), seemed willing to allow an association to bring a § 1983 suit on its own behalf if it can show that the association has itself suffered deprivation of a constitutional right, and though this indeed seems to be the prevailing rule, *see* Warth v. Seldin, 422 U.S. 490, 511 (1975), such a position is difficult to justify unless one equates the rights of the members with the rights of the association. *See* NAACP v. Alabama *ex rel.* Patterson, 357 U.S. 449, 459 (1958). To suggest, as does Judge Friendly, a distinction between the rights of members of an association and of an association itself and to allow the association to protect only the latter is to suggest that, by joining together, individuals may create an abstract entity with the ability to guarantee its own rights, but that in so doing the individuals have not meaningfully guaranteed their own rights. Such a distinction renders association virtually useless to the individual seeking to better himself, and is completely incompatible with the formulation here proposed.

[90] 413 U.S. 528 (1973).

[91] 416 U.S. 1 (1974).

[92] 413 U.S. 528 (1973).

[93] *Id.* at 531-32.

[94] 416 U.S. 1 (1974).

[95] *Id.* at 9.

in a given confined area they pose more of a noise and sanitation problem than when any one individual lives in that same area. The government could have argued that this was a circumstance in which groups were more powerful and posed more of a threat than any individual and hence, regulation was appropriate.

And yet the very realities of the case make such an analysis seem too simple. The fact that the ordinance placed no limit on how many related members of a group could reside together shows that the village of Belle Terre really was not concerned with population density. The real discrimination here was between related groups and unrelated groups; the real issue was whether this distinction was valid.

In a number of ways then, *Belle Terre* is a most difficult case, for it suggests that association cases may involve two different forms of discrimination. The first is between individuals, who are allowed to engage in a given activity, and associations, which are not. The second is between associations, that is, between those groups which are permitted to engage in a given activity and those groups which are not. In applying the proposed formulation, it is essential to realize that the two discriminations are actually not different. In both, individuals who choose to pursue goals through groups find that they are hampered in ways that individuals pursuing those same goals singly, or in "particular" groups, are not.

Thus, in *Belle Terre* it was incumbent upon the state to show a compelling interest in its decision to treat individuals in groups differently from individuals acting singly. The state should also have been forced to justify its decision to treat groups of related individuals differently from groups of unrelated individuals.

Although the village of Belle Terre did not make the argument, it is possible to find a competing associational interest in the case: that of the townspeople in living in and maintaining a community that practiced a certain lifestyle. There was no state prohibition in Belle Terre of individual married couples raising their children in single-family suburban dwellings. Accordingly, it could be argued that the state, acting through its courts, should not be allowed to prevent groups of married couples (or at most two single individuals) from joining together to ensure the continuance of that lifestyle.

In fact, however, each resident who joined in enacting the zoning ordinance acquired considerably greater power than any individual could exercise independently. Through the ordinance, each resident was able to ensure not only that no unwanted group would move into his home, but also that no unwanted group would move into any home in the community. Individuals have always enjoyed the power to determine the disposition of their own property, whether by sale, gift or lease. Yet while the absolute right of one person, or a majority of persons, to dictate the disposal of another's property has never been recognized, that is precisely what the residents of Belle Terre would have been claiming had they invoked freedom of association.[96]

More troubling, perhaps, are the possible implications the proposed formulation would have in the private academy cases such as *Runyon v. McCrary*.[97] In that case, the lower court ordered that the admissions policies of certain private schools become color-blind. The Supreme Court, on review of the order, found no violation of the white parents' freedom to associate as they remained free to advocate segregation.

In *Runyon*, the parental association certainly was as concerned with the actual composition of the student bodies at the schools in question as with being able to advocate segregation of those student bodies. The Court, however, because it had so long conceived of association only in terms of speech and expression, was able to avoid the more fundamental association claim: the whites' asserted right to have no association with blacks in the process of acquiring an education.

Under the proposed formulation, the inquiry into such a right would proceed in the following way. First, the court would ask whether the state leaves each parent free to remove his child from the integrated public schools and enter into a contract for him to be tutored privately. The answer, in all probability, would be "yes."[98] The court would then ask if allowing a group of parents to join in an association which pools resources to provide for private tutoring, indeed which provides a whole private school system, threatens valid state interests more seriously than if each individual hires his own tutor. In refusing to cope with the real associational interests of the parents in *Runyon*, the Court never addressed this question.

Even discussing this question under the proposed formulation, however, does not dispose of the case. While each parent whose child at-

---

[96] See the discussion of the association claim by a group that has acquired more power than an individual could, or would be permitted to exercise, pp. 17-18 *supra*. As regards *Belle Terre*, it is important to note that all zoning ordinances involve an association, the community, dictating to individuals how they can and cannot dispose of their property. While most zoning ordinances would be upheld, it is one thing to uphold a zoning ordinance as a rational exercise of the police power and quite another to claim its passage is a constitutionally-protected exercise of freedom of association. As conceived by the formulation here advanced, the right of association is an instrument meant to assist individuals in achieving goals, not to give them some superpower over their fellow citizens.

[97] 96 S. Ct. 2586 (1976).

[98] *Compare* Wisconsin v. Yoder, 406 U.S. 205 (1972) *with* Pierce v. Society of Sisters, 268 U.S. 510 (1925), and Meyer v. Nebraska, 262 U.S. 390 (1923).

tended one of the schools involved in *Runyon* had a right to engage a private tutor for his child, and thus to avoid the integrated public schools, the tutor who accepted that child would nonetheless be bound by 42 U.S.C. § 1981 not to discriminate on the basis of race in offering his tutorial services. Therefore, the fact that the white parents associated to support a school, rather than paying for a tutor on an individual basis to provide an alternative to the integrated public schools, is irrelevant to any determination of whether the white school officials can be shown to have violated § 1981 by their complete unwillingness to enter into contracts with blacks.

Since the parents' right of association was not involved there would have been no difference in outcome under the proposed formulation. However, rather than twisting the associational goal of the parents in the case in order to show that "freedom of association" was not being impinged, the Court, under the proposed formulation, could have stated candidly that the mere presence of an associational interest in a case does not grant immunity from liability for violations of the law committed in pursuit of that interest.

It is in *Garcia v. Texas State Board of Medical Examiners*[99] that use of the proposed formulation of freedom of association would have made the most immediate and positive difference in outcome. Plaintiffs, a number of low-income residents of San Antonio, Texas, had formed a consumer-controlled health maintenance association which planned to use its members' pooled financial resources to provide low-cost, quality medical care to these members. One of the primary reasons for the plaintiffs' inability to get adequate medical care was the prohibitive cost of the fee-for-service solo-practitioner system of health care delivery.[100] Plaintiffs sought to mitigate this problem by using their pooled resources to hire doctors on a salaried basis. The problem was that certain Texas statutes barred the operation of any such consumer health organization unless all administrative control over non-medical as well as medical matters was in the hands of an independent contractor who was a doctor, or a board of directors comprised entirely of licensed doctors.[101] In fact, all of the "all-doctor board" organizations existing in Texas continued to

---

[99] 421 U.S. 995 (1975), *aff'g mem.*, 384 F. Supp. 434 (W.D. Tex. 1974).

[100] The fee-for-service system, generally practiced throughout the United States, allows doctors to place whatever value they think the market will bear on the services they perform for patients.

[101] TEX. REV. CIV. STAT. arts. 4498.1, 4505(12), 4505(15), 4506, 4509a, 4510a, 4510b (Supp. 1974).

demand payment on a fee-for-service basis.[102] Plaintiffs argued that only if consumers, rather than doctors, were the administrative heads of such an organization would a non fee-for-service plan be put into effect.

If the case is thought of simply as one involving the police power over public health, and if the legal analysis therefore proceeds under equal protection, it is clear that plaintiffs must lose. Control over medical services is a traditional exercise of such police power,[103] and the decision to place doctors in charge of medical organizations hardly seems irrational with respect to the promotion of good public health.

Moreover, any attempt to suggest that interferences with self-determination over the mode of access to health services constitutes a violation of the right of privacy would not succeed. In their jurisdictional statement to the Supreme Court, plaintiffs made such an argument,[104] only to have the Court summarily affirm the lower court's adverse holding in the case. As the Seventh Circuit explained in a decision last year, while some medical choices might involve private decisions, the manner in which these decisions are implemented is properly left to state determination.[105] Plaintiffs in their jurisdictional statement tied their association argument quite closely to their privacy argument. They submitted that since determining the mode of access to health care was a decision protected by the right of privacy, the right of association meant that individuals had the right to join together and assist themselves in exercising that underlying fundamental right.[106] Of course, this meant that the rejection of the appellants' privacy claim necessarily meant rejection of any association claim as well.

Under the proposed formulation of freedom of association, however, this would not be the case. The absence of any state infringement of an individual's right of privacy, or any other constitutional right, would mean no more than that the mode of access to health care was within the sphere of activities subject to possible state regulation. Texas was willing to allow wealthy individuals to opt out of the fee-for-service system by

---

[102] Jurisdictional Statement of Appellant, Garcia v. Texas State Bd. of Medical Examiners, 421 U.S. 995 (1975).

[103] *See* Lambert v. Yellowley, 272 U.S. 581 (1926); Douglas v. Noble, 261 U.S. 165 (1923); Dent v. West Virginia, 129 U.S. 114 (1889). *See also* Garcia v. Texas State Bd. of Medical Examiners, 384 F. Supp. 434 (W.D. Tex. 1974), *aff'd mem.*, 421 U.S. 995 (1975).

[104] Jurisdictional Statement of Appellants at 21-22, Garcia v. Texas State Bd. of Medical Examiners, 421 U.S. 995 (1975).

[105] *See* Fitzgerald v. Porter Mem. Hosp., 523 F.2d 716, 721 (7th Cir. 1975).

[106] *See generally* Jurisdictional Statement of Appellants at 21-23, Garcia v. Texas State Bd. of Medical Examiners, 421 U.S. 995 (1975).

purchasing full-time services of a physician on a retainer basis. Yet it denied individuals grouped together the right to do this. This distinction, it is suggested, must trigger a court's strict scrutiny. The individuals who were members of plaintiffs' health maintenance association had as much right to seek medical care as any other individual in the community. The organization's hiring of a doctor to serve its members was no more detrimental than an individual's hiring a doctor to serve his personal needs. It did not impede a valid state goal in a way no individual could. In short, this organization was no different from an individual, and Texas could advance no compelling state interest for the distinction. Freedom of association demands that any such unexplained discrimination between group and individual be invalidated.

The state might argue that in fact the group is very different from an individual, for while an individual chooses his own doctor, plaintiffs would have their doctor chosen for them by their representatives. This is not, however, a sufficiently compelling reason to support the state ban on consumer-sponsored health organizations. While Texas does prohibit an individual from hiring an intermediary whose responsibility would be the selection of a doctor, it does not bar an individual from seeking the advice of a friend regarding a doctor and agreeing to follow that advice.[107]

Texas might also argue that when a group, as opposed to an individual, is involved in hiring a doctor, there is a greater risk that the group

---

[107] Of course the "friend" in the case turns out to be the expression of the majority will of the members of the health cooperative. Here it may be helpful to distinguish this analysis from that of *Belle Terre*. Assume hypothetically that when each member of the health cooperative joined with the others and agreed to be bound by the common will, he did no more than seek and agree to follow the advice of a friend. It might then be argued that when the residents of Belle Terre moved into that community, and agreed to be bound by the decision of the majority regarding what kinds of individuals or groups would be allowed to live in the community, they were doing no more than acting as friends advising each other as to how to dispose of property. But there is a critical difference, and it goes to the heart of the proposed formulation. The residents of Belle Terre primarily were concerned with controlling their neighbors' property dispositions. This was why the "community" passed the ordinance. There was nothing each resident acquired for himself that he had been striving for singly. But in *Garcia*, the power the majority acquired to select doctors for all members really was only incidental to the main goal sought by the members, that is, adequate and affordable health care for each individual. Any court confronted with a claim of associational rights thus should have to consider whether the "majority power," which necessarily will be a part of every association, is the primary end of the association and therefore a means by which certain individuals achieve extraordinary power over their fellows, or whether the "majority power" is a necessary means by which to achieve benefits sought by each member. *See, e.g.*, note 69 *supra*.

will select a poorly-qualified doctor, and hence force the state to assume a regulatory role that could be financially burdensome. There are at least two responses to that argument. First, the presumption of the Supreme Court has been that group communication generally results in better rather than poorer choices.[108] And, in any event, the power to ensure that only qualified doctors serve the medical needs of the citizens of the state would in no way be impeded by protecting the associational rights in this case. The state would remain free to set requirements in licensing doctors who practice medicine within its borders. Second, the state's claim of fiscal harm as a result of additional regulation seems conjectural at best. There is no reason to assume that individuals like those in *Garcia*, who receive virtually no medical care, would be in so much more threatened a position in receiving some minimal care through a health cooperative that vast sums of state money would have to be used to police the association. It is precisely such conjecture which courts should find insufficient to warrant denial of individual betterment through associative action. *Garcia* thus seems a case that may well have warranted more than the summary affirmance the Supreme Court gave it.[109]

---

[108] *Compare* United Mine Workers v. Illinois State Bar Ass'n, 389 U.S. 217 (1967) *with* Brotherhood of R.R. Trainmen v. Virginia *ex rel.* Va. State Bar, 377 U.S. 1 (1964).

[109] It is interesting to speculate as to how much the Court was influenced in *Garcia* by its recent decision in North Dakota State Bd. of Pharmacy v. Snyder's Drug Stores, 414 U.S. 156 (1973). In fact, reliance on that case would be most inapposite under the proposed formulation. North Dakota law required that the majority of all the stock in corporations qualified for pharmaceutical permits be owned by registered pharmacists. Respondent did not meet this stock ownership requirement and brought suit challenging its constitutionality. The Court found the requirement rationally related to a valid state purpose and ruled for the petitioners. The notable difference between this case and *Garcia* is that the corporation in *Snyder's Drug Stores* was seeking to do what no individual could do: hire a pharmacist and set up a business. This, then, was not a case in which individuals attempted to engage in an activity which they could have pursued singly. As a group they were being denied a permit for the identical reason they could have been denied permits as individuals.

Texas courts have held that when a corporation employs a licensed physician to treat patients and itself receives the fees, paying the physician a salary, the corporation is unlawfully engaged in the practice of medicine. *See* Watt v. State Bd. of Medical Examiners, 303 S.W.2d 884 (Tex. Civ. App. 1957), *cert. denied*, 356 U.S. 912 (1958); Rockett v. State Bd. of Medical Examiners, 287 S.W.2d 190 (Tex. Civ. App. 1956). But a distinction seems necessary between cooperatives which receive fees only insofar as such come from their members, and which are therefore akin to an individual of means hiring a physician on salary, and corporations which receive fees and offer services to non-members. The *Rockett/Watt* position might be more acceptable in the latter circumstance given that Texas would not allow an individual to hire a doctor on salary to provide services for a third-party from whom the individual received fees.

CONCLUSION

The refusal to protect the right of association as it has been proposed here meant that in at least one case individuals needlessly were denied access to necessary medical care for no reason other than that, because of their economic condition, they sought to achieve through cooperative effort what was legitimate for others to achieve singly. In light of the increasingly institutionalized nature of our society and the long American tradition of voluntary associations and cooperatives to secure valid ends, one cannot expect the average citizen to accept such a summary denial of his endeavors to better himself.

Certainly there are many areas in which the state may act and in which the courts cannot second-guess. But where the state has not acted, where it has not expressed concern for a matter by regulating it with respect to all citizens, whether acting as individuals or as members of associations, then it is appropriate for the courts to become involved. Close to forty years ago, Justice Cardozo observed that "the law [is] guided by a robust common sense which assumes the freedom of the will as a working hypothesis."[110] The proposed formulation of freedom of association would not involve the courts in second-guessing the legislature as much as it would have them return such common sense and free will to those areas of cooperative human endeavor in which the state actually has no compelling interest.

---

[110] Steward Machine Co. v. Davis, 301 U.S. 548, 590 (1937).

The FCC and the First Amendment: Observations on 40 Years of Radio and Television Regulation

Glen O. Robinson*

INTRODUCTION

Congress created the first system of regulation of radio and television with its enactment of the Radio Act of 1927.[1] Although considered a drastic measure at that time,[2] today, some forty years after its creation, comprehensive regulation of radio and television communications has for the most part become an accepted phenomenon. Although regulatory policy has yet to mature completely, the essential features of the policy have been outlined. With this coming of age, it seems appropriate to reflect on an aspect of radio regulation which has been of critical importance from the earliest time: the first amendment implications of the various facets of radio and television regulation.

Virtually everyone accepts the proposition that the first amendment does apply to radio and television. Whatever doubts might once have existed about the applicability of the first amendment to mass communications media were dispelled in *United States v. Paramount Pictures*[3] where the Supreme Court stated that it had "no doubt" that radio, newspapers, and moving pictures were covered by the first amendment. Even the Federal Communications Commission, which has never shown itself to be keenly aware of the finer points of constitutional limitations, has recognized the applicability of the first amendment as at least some kind of general curb on its regulatory actions which are intended to limit or to aid free speech.[4]

Despite this agreement on its general applicability, there continues to be very considerable doubt on the part of many, including the FCC, whether the first amendment really has the same scope in the field of radio and television as it does in the

---

* Associate Professor of Law, University of Minnesota.

1. 47 U.S.C. §§ 81-83 (1964).

2. *See* J. Herring & G. Gross, Telecommunications, Economics and Regulation 226 (1936).

3. 334 U.S. 131, 166 (1948). *See also* American Broadcasting Co. v. United States, 110 F. Supp. 374, 389 (S.D.N.Y. 1953), *aff'd*, 347 U.S. 284 (1954).

4. *E.g., Report and Statement of Policy Re: Commission En Banc Programming Inquiry*, 20 P & F Radio Reg. 1902, 1907 (1960).

case of other communications media. This doubt is founded on the persistent and widely held, but almost never critically analyzed, assumption that broadcasting is somehow different or unique.

For example, one of the assumed unique characteristics of radio and television is the fact that for technical and economic reasons access to these communications media is limited. Since only a few thousand persons can use the airwaves, it follows that some form of regulation is essential. Many assume that this regulation must include some form of regulation of programming in order to compensate for the supposed monopoly power given to the fortunate few who obtain licenses to use the airwaves. When viewed in this light, there are relatively few outside the industry who are very much concerned about FCC regulation of program operations, even where it represents an intrusion which would be bitterly attacked outside the field of radio and television. So long as the broadcast licensee is regarded as a monopolist who, were it not for regulation, would be able to run free, it is he who is portrayed as the censor and not the Commission. Indeed, the Commission can pass itself off as the champion of free speech, dedicated to ensuring that the licensee gives the fullest expression to all possible viewpoints and addresses itself to all possible tastes. There is no doubt that the Commission is aided in playing this role by dissatisfaction with the average quality of programming, particularly among intellectuals who would be most likely to express concern about infringements on free speech. The Commission's repeated exhortations to broadcasters to upgrade the quality of programming and its efforts to encourage, cajole, or even coerce broadcasters to present better programming "in the public interest," add to the pattern. When the Commission is joined by the newspapers and the irrepressible complaints of the public, it is not surprising that the broadcaster attracts little sympathy.

There is more than a little discrimination and a very noticeable absence of critical judgment in this treatment of broadcasting. Most of those who rail against the poor quality of television programming fare have never given a second thought to the equally poor quality of the newspapers, magazines, and books which flood the newsstands and bookstalls. Those who are disturbed that there are only three television stations in their city, or only three television networks, are not generally as disturbed over the fact that there are only one, or perhaps two, daily newspapers in the same city, and at most a handful of weekly news magazines. These same people are probably not at all disturbed that there are only two major political parties.

But despite first appearances this Article is not intended as an apology for the cause of broadcasters. It is, rather, an attempt to discuss comprehensively the constitutional limits on governmental regulation of radio and television under the first amendment. It is important to emphasize at the outset that the primary concern of this Article is not with the entire scope of the first amendment with regard to mass communications media of all kinds. The principal aims here are to focus on those restraints on radio and television which are clearly extraordinary, to point out those restraints which, though they may appear to be of great moment, clearly are not extraordinary or are not, in any event, unique to radio and television, and to evaluate the first amendment implications of such restraints.

I. REGULATION OF ENTRY AND CONTROL OF ECONOMIC CONCENTRATION

A. THE ALLOCATIONS AND LICENSING SCHEME

It is impossible to present a full history and description of the complex system of allocations and licensing as it has been developed for radio and television. However, a brief outline of the scheme will suffice to set the framework for analyzing the first amendment problems of Commission regulation.

The Radio Act of 1927 and its successor, the Communications Act of 1934, both of which gave the Commission broad licensing and regulatory powers over radio communications, were the outgrowth of a breakdown of the law during the early 1920's[5] which had permitted the emerging commercial radio industry to develop in chaos. Because of the lack of effective regulation prior to 1927, radio stations were free to begin operation when and where

5. The Radio Act of 1912, 37 Stat. 302, granted to the Secretary of Commerce authority to deal with regulatory problems presented by the private use of radio channels for broadcasting including authority to license radio broadcast stations. However, the Secretary's authority to regulate under the Act was virtually destroyed by subsequent judicial interpretation. In Hoover v. Intercity Radio Co., 286 F. 1003 (D.C. Cir. 1923), *appeal dismissed per stipulation*, 266 U.S. 636 (1924), the court held that the Secretary lacked discretion to refuse to renew a license on the grounds of interference. Subsequently in United States v. Zenith Radio Corp., 12 F.2d 614 (N.D. Ill. 1926), a district court held that licensees were not bound by nonstatutory regulations and could operate on any frequency despite the Secretary's regulations to the contrary. Following *Zenith* the Secretary abandoned all efforts to regulate and urged, in vain, self-regulation.

they chose. The new stations used any frequency they desired, changed frequencies, and increased power without regard to interference caused to others. The result was a great waste of radio frequencies because "with everybody on the air, nobody could be heard."[6] The primary purposes of the 1927 Act were to ensure adequate technical service to the public by establishing regulations designed to eliminate objectionable interference and to promote optimum utilization of the radio spectrum through fair, efficient, and equitable distribution of facilities.[7]

To accomplish these objectives, the Commission has allocated different portions of the radio spectrum to different kinds of uses, such as radio and television broadcast, citizens radio, and safety and special services. Secondly, it has allocated the available broadcasting channels on a geographic basis in an attempt to achieve optimum utilization with minimal electrical interference and a fair and equitable distribution of the frequencies.[8]

The most flexible system of allocation is the allocation and distribution of AM frequencies and stations. Standard broadcast (AM) stations are broken down into four major classes.[9] Each class of stations is given its own normally protected contour within which its signal is intended to be free of objectionable interference from co-channel and adjacent channel stations.[10] Although some effort has been made to develop a reasonably equitable distribution of the AM facilities to all parts of the

---

6. NBC v. United States, 319 U.S. 190, 212 (1943). For a more extensive history of this early period, the failure of regulation under the Radio Act of 1912, and enactment of the Acts of 1927 and 1934, see L. White, The American Radio 126-54 (1947); Office of Network Study, FCC, Second Interim Report on Television Network Procurement pt. II, 59-69 (1965).

7. *See* NBC v. United States, 319 U.S. 190 (1943); W. Jones, Report to the Administrative Conference, Licensing of Major Broadcast Facilities by the Federal Communications Commission 3-6 (1962).

8. For a useful summary of these two types of allocation of the radio spectrum and of the principal components of the economic structure of the broadcasting industry, see W. Jones, Cases and Materials on Regulated Industries 1032-63 (1967).

9. 47 C.F.R. § 73.21 (1967).

10. The normally protected contour concept is far too technical and complex for discussion here. It is sufficient to note that the concept of normally protected contour involves a relationship between (a) a signal by the protected station of specified strength (for most AM stations, the 0.5 millivolt/meter ground wave signal is protected during the day) and (b) the interfering signal of another station which exceeds a specified strength (which varies depending on whether the signal is co-channel or adjacent channel) such that the desired station's service in those areas which it is designed to serve is free of objectionable interference from the undesired station.

country, no fixed assignment scheme, such as has been adopted for FM or television, has ever been established for AM radio.

The FM allocation system was originally the same as that for AM stations. Recently, however, the Commission abandoned the flexible AM approach and, in lieu of the normally protected contour approach, established a system of allocation based on minimum mileage separation between facilities and on specific assignments of FM frequencies to specific communities.[11] The current FM allocation system is patterned on the allocation scheme for television. At the time when the Commission came to consider allocation of frequencies for television use, it had the benefit of some twenty years experience with its AM broadcast allocations scheme, a system which, due to excessive flexibility, had permitted the spectrum to become overcrowded and, as a result, had failed in its primary purpose of preventing objectionable interference. To guard against overcrowding and the resultant erosion of service because of objectionable interference, the Commission in its *Sixth Report and Order* in 1962[12] set forth a comprehensive scheme for allocating all television channels on a fixed basis across the country.[13] The heart of the allocations scheme is a table of assignments which assigns all television channels to specific communities. The table is based on a system of minimum mileage separations between stations, designed to eliminate in advance the possibility of objectionable interference in the service areas of existing and potential television stations.

Although the table of assignments is fixed, it is not rigid. Changes in allocations have been made on a selective basis. Although the Commission has generally adhered to the minimum mileage separation requirements and refused to authorize short-spaced assignments,[14] since 1952 it has granted numerous peti-

11. 47 C.F.R. §§ 73.202-03 (1967). *See Revision of FM Broadcast Rules*, 23 P & F RADIO REG. 1859 (1963).

12. *Sixth Report on Television Allocations*, 1 P & F RADIO REG. pt. 3, at 91:601 (1952).

13. 47 C.F.R. §§ 73.606-07 (1967).

14. The Commission in *Interim Policy on VHF-TV Channel Assignments*, 21 P & F RADIO REG. 1695 (1961), undertook consideration of short-spaced VHF assignments in certain specified markets in which only two VHF stations then operated, but refused to adopt a policy under which it would authorize further short-spaced VHF assignments in markets having "serious shortages" of channels. Subsequently, in *VHF Drop-ins*, 25 P & F RADIO REG. 1687 (1963), the Commission rejected most of the limited drop-in proposals which had been held for consideration under its prior *Report and Order* in 21 P & F RADIO REG. 1695 (1961).

tions to amend the table and has reassigned channels to different locations.[15]

Within this general allocations framework, the Commission controls entry into broadcasting by a system of licenses renewable every three years.[16] Leaving aside those cases involving comparative choice between two or more mutually exclusive applications, licenses for available frequencies are granted subject to a showing by the applicant that it has complied with the Commission's technical regulations and standards, that it possesses the necessary character,[17] financial,[18] and legal[19] qualifications, and that its program operations will serve the public interest.[20]

---

15. *E.g., VHF Channel Assignments in Nevada,* 7 P & F RADIO REG. 2d 1589 (1966); *Channel Assignment in Rhinelander, Wisc.,* 3 P & F RADIO REG. 2d 1683 (1964). The FM table of assignments possesses the same flexibility and reassignments can be made on petition of interested party or on the Commission's motion. *E.g., FM Channel Assignments,* 1 P & F RADIO REG. 2d 1545 (1963).

16. 48 Stat. 1081 (1934), 47 U.S.C. § 301 (1964). Although in the field of radio and television the Commission's authority to regulate entry was originally considered to be limited to radio and television *broadcast* stations, the Commission has now extended its authority to limit and control entry into the nonbroadcast radio and television area of community antenna television, discussed below. However, the Commission's "regulation" of entry into the field of community antenna television is limited and is incidental to its licensing of radio and television broadcast stations.

17. This is a negative qualification and the applicant need not affirmatively allege good character. Typically a finding of "bad" character relates to willful refusal to disclose or misrepresentations to the Commission. *See, e.g.,* WMOZ, Inc., 1 P & F RADIO REG. 2d 801 (1964). But it may involve virtually any activity which bears on character, *e.g.,* violation of the Communications Act, FCC regulations, or other laws. *See, e.g.,* General Electric Co., 2 P & F RADIO REG. 2d 1038 (1964) (violation of antitrust laws considered). *See generally* Brown, *Character and Candor Requirements for FCC Licensees,* 22 LAW & CONTEMP. PROB. 644 (1957).

18. Traditionally, applicants were required to show financial resources sufficient to build the station and operate it for three months without advertising revenue. Recently, however, the Commission has established a requirement that all stations demonstrate financial ability to construct and meet fixed and operating costs for one year without revenue or to establish convincingly that such revenue will be forthcoming in an amount sufficient to continue operation. Ultravision Broadcasting Co., 5 P & F RADIO REG. 2d 343 (1965).

19. Legal qualifications relate chiefly to § 310(a) of the Act, forbidding licenses to aliens, *e.g.,* United Artists Broadcasting. Inc., 7 P & F RADIO REG. 2d 7 (1966), and to compliance with the Commission's multiple ownership rules. See the discussion of multiple ownership rules in text accompanying notes 26-27 *infra.*

20. For a discussion of program regulation, see Part II *infra.*

B. General Outline of Economic Regulation

Unlike most other federal regulatory schemes, the Communications Act does not contemplate a system of economic regulation and, accordingly, does not authorize the Commission either to fix the rates charged by the licensed stations or to engage in other general economic regulation.[21] Notwithstanding this supposed limitation on its authority, the Commission has, in fact, exercised its regulatory powers to control certain economic aspects of radio and television to a considerable degree.

1. Monopoly, Diversification, and Chain Broadcasting

Although the Commission does not have power to enforce the antitrust laws as such,[22] it has long undertaken economic regulation along essentially antitrust lines, relying on its general authority to protect the public interest. The Commission's multiple ownership rules, its regulation of certain network practices, and its policy of favoring diversification of control in the mass communications media all reflect economic policy substantially similar to the policies of the federal antitrust laws.

The genesis of the Commission's regulation of economic concentration is its *Report on Chain Broadcasting*,[23] released in 1941 after some three years of intensive study of problems posed principally by the networks. The present scope of the rules and policies which grew out of this original study[24] can be summarized very generally. The rules prohibit or limit various types of exclusive dealing practices between networks and affiliated stations and network ownership of stations under circumstances where it would restrain competition.[25] In addition, mul-

21. *E.g.*, FCC v. Sanders Bros. Radio Station, 309 U.S. 470 (1940). For a brief discussion of the similarities and differences as to the economic characteristics of broadcasting and public utility fields where there is extensive economic regulation, see Levin, *Federal Control of Entry in the Broadcast Industry*, 5 J. Law & Econ. 49, 52-56 (1962).

22. United States v. RCA, 358 U.S. 334, 343 (1959).

23. FCC, Report on Chain Broadcasting (1941).

24. The fullest treatment of the problem of economic concentration in radio and television, although now considerably out of date, is the so-called *Barrow Report*, House Comm. on Interstate and Foreign Commerce, Report on Network Broadcasting, H.R. Rep. No. 1297, 85th Cong., 1st Sess. (1958) [hereinafter cited Network Broadcasting]. *See also* Hale & Hale, *Competition or Control II: Radio and Television Broadcasting*, 107 U. Pa. L. Rev. 585 (1959).

25. These rules, generally referred to as the "chain broadcasting rules," are substantially identical for radio and television. *See* 47 C.F.R. §§ 73.131-.138 (AM), .231-.238 (FM), .658 (TV) (1967).

For a comprehensive history of the rules up to 1958, see Network

tiple ownership rules limit the total number of stations which can be held under common ownership or under common control[26] and prohibit "duopoly," the common ownership or control of two or more stations of the same class in the same area.[27]

The Commission's original chain broadcasting regulations were upheld in *National Broadcasting Company v. United States*,[28] against a challenge that they were beyond the Commission's statutory powers. The Commission's multiple ownership rules were subsequently upheld against a rather feeble attack

---

BROADCASTING. The principal changes in the rules since 1958 have been the prohibition of television option time, *see Television Option Time*, 25 P & F RADIO REG. 1651 (1963), and the prohibition of network's representation of affiliated stations in selling national spot sales, *see Network Spot Sales Representation*, 19 P & F RADIO REG. 1501 (1960), *aff'd sub nom.* Metropolitan Television Co. v. FCC, 289 F.2d 874 (D.C. Cir. 1961).

26. Again the rules are substantially identical for radio and television. *See* 47 C.F.R. §§ 73.35 (AM), .240 (FM), .636 (TV) (1967). With respect to AM and FM stations, the rules place an upper limit on common ownership, interest in, or control of seven stations. With respect to television stations, the upper limit is again seven stations, no more than five of which may be VHF stations. For a brief outline of the history of these rules, see NETWORK BROADCASTING 84.

In 1965 the Commission proposed a further amendment to the multiple ownership rule to limit common ownership of television stations in the "top 50" markets to a total of one UHF and two VHF stations. *Television Multiple Ownership Rules*, 5 P & F RADIO REG. 2d 1609 (1965). Pending such amendment, it adopted an "interim policy" under which it would, in the absence of a compelling showing, designate for hearing any application to acquire a VHF station in the top 50 television markets by a party already having one or more such stations or by a new party to acquire more than one such station. Although this interim policy was undoubtedly intended to have some restraining effect in itself, this effect was almost certainly weakened by the Commission's subsequent refusal to order a hearing on an application by a Chicago station licensee to take over and operate a station in Denver, one of the top 50 markets. Channel 2 Corp., 6 P & F RADIO REG. 2d 885 (1966).

27. The "duopoly" rules formerly prohibited common ownership, interest in or control of another station in the same class where both would serve "substantially the same area." Under this approach a number of different factors were considered in determining whether two stations would serve substantially the same area. *See, e.g.*, Sheffield Broadcasting Co., 21 P & F RADIO REG. 514j (1962). The current rules, however, have established fixed boundaries to this "area" by proscribing common ownership, interest in, or control of two or more stations where there would result any overlap of specified contours of the respective stations. In AM and FM, any overlap of the respective 1 mv/m contours is proscribed; in television, overlap of Grade B contours is proscribed. 47 C.F.R. §§ 73.35 (AM), .240 (FM), .636 (TV) (1967).

28. 319 U.S. 190 (1943). The *NBC* case also considered and rejected a first amendment challenge to the regulations, discussed at note 73 *infra*.

in *United States v. Storer Broadcasting Company.*[29]

Apart from the chain broadcasting and multiple ownership rules, the Commission has long purported to follow a general licensing policy of promoting diversification of ownership of all mass communications media[30] in evaluating the respective merits of competing applicants in a comparative hearing.[31] This policy has never been crystallized into written regulations, and, like most of the factors assessed in comparative hearings, it has not been vigorously or consistently applied.[32]

2. *Economic Injury Through Competition*

Ignoring dicta in several early circuit court opinions,[33] the the Commission persistently refused, until recent years, to consider competitive economic injury to existing licensees as a basis for refusing to license new stations. This policy was approved in *FCC v. Sanders Brothers Radio Station,*[34] where the Supreme Court held that the Commission was not bound to consider economic injury as such in determining whether or not to grant an application for a new station. However, the Court did

29. 351 U.S. 192 (1956).

30. The other media interests generally involved besides radio and television are newspaper interests. However, while ownership, interest in, or control of a newspaper is a comparative "demerit" against an applicant in theory, the fact remains that common ownership of newspapers and broadcast stations is so prevalent as to indicate that newspaper ownership is not a serious liability. *See, e.g.*, the comprehensive list of broadcast stations identified with newspaper and magazine ownership in 1966 BROADCASTING YEARBOOK, at A-92-99.

31. In noncomparative cases the Commission has only rarely considered an applicant's ownership or control of other communications media where the applicant meets the multiple ownership rules. *See* NETWORK BROADCASTING 112-13. A rare exception is Laurence W. Harry, 13 F.C.C. 23 (1948), *aff'd sub nom.* Mansfield Journal Co. v. FCC, 180 F.2d 28 (D.C. Cir. 1950).

32. As to newspapers, see note 30 *supra*, and Heckman, *Diversification of Control of the Media of Mass Communication—Policy or Fallacy?*, 42 GEO. L.J. 378 (1954) (which argues, however, that the diversification policy should not be pursued except to prevent monopoly). For a general criticism of the policy as applied both with respect to newspaper and other radio ownership, see NETWORK BROADCASTING 121-24; Note, *Diversification and the Public Interest: Administrative Responsibility of the FCC*, 66 YALE L.J. 365 (1957).

The Commission's new *Policy Statement on Comparative Broadcast Hearings*, 5 P & F RADIO REG. 2d 1901 (1965) suggests a somewhat greater stress on the factor of diversification than has been stressed in the past cases. To what extent this stress in a general policy statement will carry over to actual decision, however, is anyone's guess.

33. *E.g.*, WOKO, Inc. v. FCC, 109 F.2d 665, 666-68 (D.C. Cir. 1939); Tri-State Broadcasting Co. v. FCC, 107 F.2d 956, 957-58 (D.C. Cir. 1939).

34. 309 U.S. 470 (1940).

indicate that under some circumstances economic injury could be taken into account where it might have an important bearing on the ability of the new station or the existing station to render adequate service.[35] Following *Sanders,* the Commission continued to disclaim any power to refuse licenses on the grounds of competitive injury, or that, if it had such power, it would be in the public interest to exercise it.[36]

In 1958, the policy of refusing to consider competitive injury even where the competitive injury might lead to disruption of service was sharply reversed in *Carroll Broadcasting Company v. FCC.*[37] The court held that the Commission had misread the *Sanders* case and that, while the Commission could not consider competitive, economic injury merely for the purpose of protecting the revenue of an existing station, it could and must take it into account where it threatens the ability of the existing station to provide adequate service to the public. Although the primary concern of the court in *Carroll* seems to have been with competitive injury which would so drastically curtail an existing station's revenues as to cause it to leave the air, it seems clear that the decision was not intended to be limited to such extreme situations. Thus, for example, economic injury which might lead to curtailment of high-cost, local live programming would justify refusal to license a new station.

The Commission's refusal to consider competitive injury in the licensing of new stations prior to the *Carroll* case was motivated principally by a fear of being deluged by similar protests against every new applicant. The Commission was unwilling to undertake the difficult task of sorting out the valid protests. The Commission explained its refusal to consider economic injury by disclaiming the power to make any such economic determinations, but this seems to have been more of a rationalization than a reason, since the Commission has long rendered economic judgments in converse situations involving economic concentration. The most notable example of the Commission's willingness to consider economic injury on a broad, general plane in which *it* could choose the time and place to apply economic judgment and policy is its deintermixture proceedings during the 1950's,

35. *Id.* at 476.

36. *See* Voice of Cullman, 14 F.C.C. 770 (1950); Southeastern Enterprises, 13 P & F RADIO REG. 139 (1957). For a vigorous criticism of the latter case and the Commission's policy of refusing to consider competitive injury, see Note, *Economic Injury in FCC Licensing: The Public Interest Ignored,* 67 YALE L.J. 135 (1957).

37. 258 F.2d 440 (D.C. Cir. 1958).

in which it decided to reallocate VHF and UHF channels to different television markets because of the inability of UHF stations to compete effectively with VHF stations in the same market.[38] Although the Commission has now declared a moratorium on its deintermixture policy because of the enactment of

38. VHF and UHF channels were intermixed in the same markets in *Sixth Report on Television Allocation*, 1 P & F RADIO REG. pt. 3, at 91:601 (1952). It was not long after the lifting of the television "freeze" that it became apparent that UHF stations suffered a very substantial competitive disadvantage in comparison to VHF, due mainly to (a) inferior propagation characteristics of UHF and a very restricted service area in the case of UHF stations as compared with VHF stations and (b) the manufacture of VHF-only receivers by television set manufacturers.

To correct the situation, the Commission instituted five rulemaking cases looking towards the deintermixture of five specific communities. On further study of the problem, the Commission determined that the problem was too widespread to be materially affected by deintermixture in only five markets and terminated the earlier proposals, *First Report on Deintermixture*, 13 P & F RADIO REG. 1511 (1955). Subsequently, the Commission instituted rulemaking looking toward solution of the problem on a broad, nationwide basis, as a result of which it concluded that the most promising solution to the problem would be to transfer all television stations to UHF frequencies, *Second Report on Deintermixture*, 13 P & F RADIO REG. 1571, 1577 (1956). As an "interim" measure, it instituted proceedings looking toward deintermixture in certain specified communities. *Id.* at 1581, 1583-84. Following the release of its *Second Report*, the Commission deintermixed a number of communities, *e.g.*, Elmira Deintermixture Case, 15 P & F RADIO REG. 1515 (1957); Fresno Deintermixture Case, 15 P & F RADIO REG. 1586i (1957), *modified*, 18 P & F RADIO REG. 1733 (1959), *modified further*, 19 P & F RADIO REG. 1598a (1960).

The Commission's proposal to transfer all television stations to UHF announced in 1956 failed to jell. In April, 1959, the Commission reported to Congress, in substance, that it was still "studying" the problem. It reported its conclusion that deintermixture either on a selective community or area basis was ineffective but that, as an "interim policy," it had decided to add VHF channels to some large population centers. The VHF additions were short-spaced drop-ins which were supposed to alleviate the shortage of service in those areas by adding a third VHF station—obviously on the assumption that UHF in those areas could not be made to work. *See Hearings on Television Allocations Before the Senate Comm. on Interstate and Foreign Commerce*, 86th Cong., 2d Sess. 4585-611 (1960) (Statement of FCC Chairman Doerfer).

The 1959 report to Congress notwithstanding, the Commission subsequently proposed deintermixture on a selective basis in eight specified communities, *Expanded Use of UHF Channels*, 21 P & F RADIO REG. 1711, 1714 (1961). However, the deintermixture proposals were met by fierce opposition from the strongest elements in the industry. At the same time that it released its interim policy in 1961, the Commission proposed to Congress that it enact all-channel receiver legislation which would require all receivers shipped in interstate commerce to be capable of receiving both VHF and UHF channels. At that time it seems evident that the Commission viewed all-channel receiver legislation as a means for paving the way to an eventual shift of all VHF

the all-channel receiver legislation,[39] this does not represent an abandonment of the type of economic regulation represented by its deintermixture efforts, but simply the choice of a different remedy: legislation requiring television receivers to be compatible with both UHF and VHF reception.

3. *Regulation of Community Antenna Television*

Without question the most extensive economic regulation yet undertaken by the Commission is its controversial regulation of community antenna television (CATV).[40] Because of its rela-

---

stations to the UHF spectrum. *See id.* at 1714-15. The all-channel receiver legislation proved to be a promising way out of the deintermixture controversy for both the Commission and the industry. The industry opponents of deintermixture agreed to support the all-channel receiver legislation but insisted that Congress exact from the Commission a commitment that its interim policy on deintermixture and its intention to pursue an all-UHF system would be abandoned for at least a sufficient period of time to permit the all-channel receiver legislation to cure the competitive imbalance between UHF and VHF, which it was thought that the all-channel receiver legislation could do. On the representation by the Commission that it would terminate its deintermixture efforts, the all-channel receiver legislation was enacted in 1962 as § 303(s) of the Communications Act. *See* H.R. Rep. No. 1559, 87th Cong., 2d Sess. 18-26 (1962); S. Rep. No. 1526, 86th Cong., 2d Sess. 13-19 (1962). As a result, the Commission declared a moratorium on its deintermixture proposals. Deintermixture Cases, 23 P & F Radio Reg. 1645 (1962).

39. See note 38 *supra*.

40. Reduced to its basic elements, a CATV system consists of two basic components: (a) a "head-end" system consisting of receiving antennae and related equipment (*e.g.*, amplifiers), usually of high gain capability and generally situated in a location best suited for receiving usable signals from broadcast stations; and (b) a distribution system consisting of coaxial cable, which transmits the signal from the head-end system to the subscriber, and amplifiers to compensate for signal attenuation through the cable. Although the CATV system itself *transmits* entirely by wire, most larger systems today make use of microwave relay facilities which permit a signal to be picked up by a receiving antenna near its point of origin, converted to microwave frequencies and transmitted virtually any distance to another receiving antenna from which it is converted back to video-audio frequencies and transmitted by cable to the subscriber. For a brief description, see *Hearings on Regulation of Community Antenna Television Before the Subcomm. on Communications and Power of the House Comm. on Interstate and Foreign Commerce*, 89th Cong., 1st Sess., ser. 89-16, 4-5 (1965) [hereinafter cited as *1965 Hearings on CATV Regulation*].

For general surveys of the CATV regulation problem, see Note, *The Wire Mire: The FCC and CATV*, 79 Harv. L. Rev. 366 (1965); Note, *Community Antenna Television: Survey of a Regulatory Problem*, 52 Geo. L.J. 136 (1963). An economic analysis of the CATV industry, commissioned by the FCC, is M. Seiden, An Economic Analysis of Community Antenna Television Systems and the Television Broadcast Industry (1965) [hereinafter cited as Seiden Report]. Al-

tive newness and far-reaching importance, and because it serves as an ideal vehicle for considering what limitations, if any, the first amendment places on economic regulation by the Commission the Commission's regulatory efforts to control CATV warrant somewhat greater attention than other areas of FCC economic regulation.

Begun as relatively crude facilities designed to bring television broadcast signals into topographic pockets and other geographical areas where an adequate number of satisfactory signals could not be received, CATV has now become a major rival of the broadcast industry.[41] In the six year period between 1959, when the Commission first considered CATV regulation,[42] and 1965, when it first adopted comprehensive regulations governing CATV operations,[43] the number of CATV systems more than trebled.[44] Instead of the old "Mom and Pop" type of community facility, bringing in perhaps three to five nearby signals, CATV systems now boast of twenty or more channels and, with the aid of microwave, can take the signals virtually any distance and into any size or type of community.[45] With this extraordinary development and growth it was inevitable that there would be a confrontation between CATV owners and broadcasters, for although CATV does not generally compete with broadcast stations for advertising revenues,[46] it does compete for the audience on which their advertising revenue depends.[47]

---

though the SEIDEN REPORT contains a number of dubious conclusions, resulting partly from now out-of-date statistics, it provides a useful general description of the industry and its structure as of that time.

41. On the growth of CATV, see authorities cited note 40 *supra*.

42. *CATV Systems and Auxiliary Television Services*, 18 P & F RADIO REG. 1573 (1959).

43. *First Report on CATV Regulation*, 4 P & F RADIO REG. 2d 1725 (1965) [hereinafter cited as *First Report*].

44. *Second Report on CATV Regulation*, 6 P & F RADIO REG. 2d 1717, 1772-79 (1966) [hereinafter cited as *Second Report*].

45. *Id.*

46. Some CATV systems have carried local advertising but not to the degree that it has become a serious competitor for advertising revenues. The Commission's new rules prohibit deletion of advertising of the station whose signal is carried. *Id.* at 1757. However, they apparently do not prohibit carriage of advertising by CATV in addition to the station's advertising.

47. The existence or probable existence *vel non* of economic injury is really at the heart of the entire controversy between CATV, broadcasters, and the Commission. CATV interests have persistently denied that there has been (or that there is sufficient evidence that there will be) any serious impairment to broadcast revenues resulting from CATV competition. *See, e.g., 1965 Hearings on CATV Regulation* 132-33, 213-15 (statements of President of NCTA and President of Jerrold Corp.). The broadcast opponents of CATV on the other hand have

The history of CATV regulation began with the Commission's termination of an inquiry into the economic impact of CATV systems and other auxiliary facilities such as translators on broadcast stations.[48] The Commission in 1959 found insufficient economic impact by CATV systems at that stage of their development to justify taking jurisdiction over these all-wire facilities.[49] However, it was not long before it became apparent

---

contended essentially that the past impact has been understated but, in any event, the *past* experience with CATV, based on its operations as a small service, is an inadequate guide to the future and that current trends show demonstrable tendencies towards economic impact. *See, e.g., id.* at 357-59, 389-94; *Appendix to Reply Comments of NAB*, in FCC Dkt. Nos. 14895 and 15233, Oct. 26, 1964 (the "Fisher Report"). The Commission, wavering somewhat at first, has now sided with the latter view that CATV would, absent regulation, have strong economic impact on all broadcast stations. *Second Report* 1772-80.

48. *CATV Systems and Auxiliary Television Services,* 18 P & F RADIO REG. 1573 (1959). Translators are low power, auxiliary *broadcast* stations designed, as CATV systems were originally designed, to fill in topographic "pockets" and sparsely settled areas where adequate off-the-air service cannot be received from regular broadcast stations. For a brief description of their history and use, see SEIDEN REPORT 18-22. Historically, translator operations have been severely restricted by Commission regulation, primarily to avoid a very troublesome problem of interference which it has been thought would result from too free licensing of such facilities. However, the Commission has in recent years taken some steps to liberalize translator licensing and has under consideration other proposals. *See Second Report* 1757-61. Without question, considerable impetus for this liberalization policy stems from the desire to provide an auxiliary *broadcast* facility as a competitive substitute for CATV.

49. *CATV Systems and Auxiliary Television Services,* 18 P & F RADIO REG. 1573, 1595-97, 1602 (1959). Although the Commission did not pass directly on its statutory power to control CATV in the event it were shown that CATV had a marked economic impact on broadcasting, it did reject other bases of jurisdiction. It held that it had no power to assert jurisdiction over CATV systems as common carriers under part II of the Act, following its prior decision in Frontier Broadcasting v. Collier, 16 P & F RADIO REG. 1005 (1958). 18 P & F RADIO REG. at 1599. It further held that it had no statutory power to *license* CATV systems under § 301 of the Act because CATV did not come within the definition of "radio station" or "broadcasting" to which § 301 applies. *Id.* at 1600-01. The Commission stated that it had no plenary authority to regulate CATV simply because it was related to or affected broadcasting, which was within its jurisdiction. *Id.* at 1600. Finally, it held that it had no power to regulate CATV indirectly through its admitted jurisdiction over microwave facilities which serve CATV. *Id.* at 1603-05. On this latter position, the Commission subsequently changed its mind and was upheld on appeal in Carter Mountain Transmission Corp. v. FCC, 321 F.2d 359 (D.C. Cir.), *cert. denied,* 375 U.S. 951 (1963).

Although the Commission reserved judgment on its authority to regulate CATV where it could be shown to impair its regulatory scheme for broadcasting, it seems evident that the Commission did not

that CATV was a rapidly growing phenomenon which, unless regulated before it grew too large, might escape regulation until after it had had a severe economic impact on broadcast stations. In 1962 the Commission, in *Carter Mountain Transmission Corporation,*[50] denied a microwave carrier's application for a license to improve service to CATV customers because of probable economic injury to a local station in competition with CATV. However, the carrier was given leave to reapply on a showing that the CATV system would carry the local station on its cable and that it would not carry programs of stations which duplicated the local station's programs. This type of protection is generally referred to as "non-duplication" or, more euphemistically, "exclusivity." Later in 1962 the Commission instituted rulemaking proceedings to consider adopting the *Carter Mountain* type of conditions of carriage and nonduplication as permanent rules for all common carrier licensees. The proposal was extended a year later to noncommon carrier licensees as well.[51] These proposals culminated in the Commission's *First Report on CATV Regulation*[52] in 1965, adopting rules requiring mandatory carriage and nonduplication for all microwave-served CATV systems.[53]

The carriage and nonduplication rules implemented by the Commission's *First Report* followed the regulatory mode of *Carter Mountain.* No jurisdiction was asserted directly over the CATV systems themselves, but only over those served by microwave facilities. While this disposed of virtually all of the larger systems and those capable of having the greatest economic impact on broadcast stations, the mode of regulation could hardly be considered completely effective from the point of view of the Com-

---

believe there was any basis for asserting jurisdiction even if economic injury were substantiated.

50. 22 P & F RADIO REG. 193 (1962), *aff'd,* 321 F.2d 359 (D.C. Cir.), *cert. denied,* 375 U.S. 951 (1963).

51. *See* 1965 FCC ANN. REP. 82-83.

52. Note 43 *supra.*

53. The most controversial aspect of the nonduplication rules was, and has continued to be, the question of the duration of the nonduplication protection. Over the bitter opposition of CATV interests, who wanted no more than simultaneous or at least no more than "same-day" nonduplication protection, the Commission adopted a period of 30 days protection, 15 days before broadcast and 15 days after. *See e.g., 1965 Hearings on CATV Regulation* 133-53 (testimony of President of NCTA). The extra period was thought essential to protect delayed network broadcasts and, to a degree, syndicated film broadcasts by local stations. *First Report* 1768-71. However, the Commission subsequently reduced the protection period down to "same-day" protection. *Second Report* 1747-51.

mission, or very evenhanded from the point of view of those regulated. Moreover, the carriage and nonduplication rules, originally the ultimate goal of CATV regulation, had become merely a stopgap measure in the view of the broadcast opponents of CATV and the Commission. At best they helped correct an unfair competitive advantage which CATV was considered to have[54] and alleviated some of its economic impact. These rules did not, however, correct the basic economic problem which was posed by CATV, *i.e.*, simple dilution of audience as a result of an increased number of available signals.

Believing that this problem could not be met without more comprehensive control exercised directly over CATV systems, and not merely over microwave carriers, the Commission simultaneously issued in its *First Report,* a notice of further inquiry[55] which proposed, in addition to carriage and nonduplication requirements, broad scale restrictions on CATV operations. In 1966 the Commission released its *Second Report on CATV Regulation*[56] in which it asserted jurisdiction and regulatory authority over CATV systems directly, irrespective of whether they used microwave facilities, extended carriage and nonduplication rules to all CATV systems, and issued comprehensive regulations controlling CATV entry which were aimed principally at distant carriage of signals by CATV into markets far removed from those served by the stations whose signals were carried.[57] The Commission asserted its jurisdiction over all CATV systems on the grounds that its authority under the Act is not confined to regulation of common carriers and licensing of radio stations, but

54. One of the chief grounds relied on by the Commission in its *First Report* was that the CATV system has an unfair competitive edge because: (a) in those homes in which it is hooked up, it can effectively preclude reception of competitive off-the-air signals, a problem which was overcome by requiring carriage on the cable; and (b) unlike the broadcast station, CATV does not pay for the programs which it takes from broadcast stations and sells in competition with such stations. This latter problem was alleviated in part by the nonduplication rules and the carriage rules. *See First Report* 1747-52.

55. *Notice of Inquiry and Notice of Proposed Rule-Making,* 4 P & F RADIO REG. 2d 1680 (1965).

56. Note 44 *supra.*

57. The principal purpose served by this type of "distant carriage" restriction, as opposed to other forms of restriction, is that it enables the Commission to conform CATV operations to its basic geographical scheme of allocations for television broadcast stations; and it effectively limits the attractiveness and, hence, growth potential of CATV systems since, except as permitted within the strict geographical limits, the CATV system cannot bring in much more than subscribers already have.

extends beyond these areas to activities in interstate commerce[58] which are an integral part of the radio and television system and which have an immediate and substantial disruptive effect on the scheme of regulation adopted by the Commission and approved by Congress and the courts.[59]

The ultimate effect of the Commission's regulation of CATV is still uncertain despite the adoption of its *Second Report.* As may be expected of any undertaking of this magnitude, it will be many years before the scope of the rules is fully developed, and not until this occurs can their true effects be known. Although plainly more far-reaching insofar as a greater number of persons are involved, the CATV rules are not unique in their ultimate purpose or effect. The basic theory behind them is essentially that underlying the *Carroll* case:[60] Unrestrained competition can severely curtail the economic support of radio and television stations causing injured stations to cut back more expensive programming (which by a somewhat dubious hypotheses is deemed "better" programming) to leave the air permanently, resulting in a loss of broadcast service to the public.

4. *Proposed Authorization and Regulation of Subscription TV*

Whether to authorize subscription television (STV) on a permanent basis has been one of the enduring problems of the Commission since the earliest days of television. In 1955 the Commission instituted proposed rulemaking to inquire into its power under the Communications Act to authorize subscription television and to determine whether such authorization would be in the public interest.[61] After prolonged delay, experimental operations were licensed in Hartford, Connecticut.[62] At the ter-

---

58. Although the question whether CATV systems which operate in the confines of one state operate in interstate commerce was the subject of considerable dispute by CATV interests, this seems the least troublesome aspect of the problem. *See* Idaho Microwave, Inc. v. FCC, 352 F.2d 729 (D.C. Cir. 1965); Ward v. Northern Ohio Tel. Co., 300 F.2d 816 (6th Cir.), *cert. denied*, 371 U.S. 820 (1962).

59. *See Second Report* 1725-32; *Notice of Inquiry and Notice of Proposed Rule-Making, Regulation of CATV*, 4 P & F RADIO REG. 2d 1680, 1707-12 (1965). On congressional and judicial approval, *see* H.R. REP. No. 1559, 87th Cong., 2d Sess. 3 (1962) (approving the system of service through diverse local stations); Logansport Broadcasting Corp. v. United States, 210 F.2d 24 (D.C. Cir. 1954) (upholding the Commission's *Sixth Report and Order*).

60. 258 F.2d 440 (D.C. Cir. 1958).

61. 20 Fed. Reg. 988 (1955).

62. Hartford Phonevision Co., 20 P & F RADIO REG. 754 (1961), *aff'd*, Connecticut Comm. Against Pay TV v. FCC, 301 F.2d 835 (D.C. Cir.), *cert. denied*, 371 U.S. 816 (1962).

mination of the trial period in Hartford, further proceedings were commenced to study the question anew in light of the results of this test.[63]

To make an initial investigation and prepare a report on the question, three commissioners were appointed as a Subscription Television Committee. After some two years of further rule-making proceedings, the STV Committee has recently submitted its report in which it proposes for adoption by the full Commission permanent authorization of STV, but with numerous restrictions and limitations.[64] The full Commission, apparently still undecided, has declined to act without still further comment and argument from the industry and other interested parties.[65] Accordingly, the matter is still pending and, after twelve years in limbo, the fate of STV is still undecided.

The central issue on which regulatory policy has been and is being debated is analogous to the issue raised by the sudden rapid growth of CATV: the problem of economic impact on free television broadcasting. The manner of economic impact is, however, distinct. Although there would be direct diversion of audience from free television to pay television, the principal impact of STV, according to its opponents, is the possible diversion or siphoning of programs and talent from free television. This siphoning argument is based on the conclusion that STV could outbid conventional television's advertising sponsors for program talent. Of principal concern is the supposed ability of STV to outbid free television for movies and major sports events. With this type of programming lost to STV, free television would be unable to generate sufficient advertising revenues to compete for an audience and would eventually lose out to STV. At that point, according to the STV opponents, all television would become pay television.[66]

The primary concerns of the STV Committee with regard to the economic impact of STV are two: the possible preemption of broadcast time by STV operations, particularly in prime-time viewing hours;[67] and the siphoning of programs and program talent from free television to STV.[68] As protection against these

63. *Further Notice of Proposed Rule Making and Notice of Inquiry*, 7 P & F RADIO REG. 2d 1501 (1966).

64. *Report of the Subscription Television Committee to the FCC*, 10 P & F RADIO REG. 2d 1617 (1967) [hereinafter cited as *STV Report*].

65. 10 P & F RADIO REG. 2d 1617 (1967). FCC 67-819 (July 14, 1967).

66. *See STV Report* 1654-57.

67. *Id.* at 1660-61, 1668-79.

68. *Id.* at 1661.

dangers to free television, the Committee has proposed that a number of restrictions be placed on STV market entry and STV operations. In order to ensure that at least three network services and one independent service could be received in such markets and to minimize the number of hours of free television which would be preempted, the Committee would first restrict STV operations to markets receiving Grade A commercial service from five stations, of which the STV station may be one.[69] Further, it would permit only one STV operation in any market.[70] To protect against program and talent siphoning, the STV Committee has proposed regulations which have greater constitutional implications insofar as they are aimed directly at the kind of programming STV may present. The Committee has proposed prohibiting STV from presenting feature films older than two years from the time of first release to theatres on the rationale that movies newer than two years are not generally available to free television. In addition, it has proposed prohibiting STV from carrying current sports events which were regularly carried live on free television in the community in which the STV operates, and prohibiting STV from presenting continuing series programs which are a mainstay of free television. Finally, it proposes limiting the total percentage of time which STV may devote to feature films and sports to no more than ninety per cent of a station's STV programming annually and no more than ninety-five per cent monthly.[71]

As in the case of the restrictions on CATV market entry and operations, the central policy of the above regulations is to restrict competition to the extent deemed necessary to preserve the continuation of free television broadcast service. Essentially, it is a reflection of the principles of the *Carroll* case. It is in these terms that the constitutional implications of the Commission's regulation of CATV and pay television and its economic regulation in general must be considered.

C. First Amendment Implications of Economic Regulation

The foregoing discussion of the general regulatory framework within which the Commission operates is not intended to suggest that the entire regulatory scheme under the Communications Act has serious first amendment implications. All aspects of Commission regulation, whether they be technical, so-

69. *Id.* at 1668-73; proposed rules, § 73.642, *id.* at 1738.
70. *Id.* at 1678-79; proposed rules, § 73.642, *id.* at 1738.
71. *Id.* at 1702-14; proposed rules, § 73.643, *id.* at 1740, app. D.

cial, or economic, have some measure of impact on free speech. However, no one would seriously contend today that the Commission is without constitutional power to license the use of radio frequencies, and, as part of such a licensing scheme, to impose such technical restraints and limitations as are necessary to ensure a fair, equitable, and efficient distribution and use of such frequencies. Minimum restraints through licensing are necessary in order that there be any effective radio communication, a fact made clear by the experience of the 1920's. To this extent the cliché that Commission regulation makes possible the exercise of free speech in radio communications is fair and accurate.

Moreover, beyond the very narrow engineering aspects of allocation of frequencies, it must be accepted that the Commission may set a very broad limit on the type of use to which frequencies may be put. Thus, it seems clearly appropriate to require licensees in the Aviation Radio Service to restrict their communications to those having some relationship to aviation. Nor does it do violence to the first amendment to restrict their use still further and to prohibit private chit-chat.[72]

However, to concede all this sheds little light on the problem, for what is at issue here is not whether the Commission should have and does have the constitutional power to act as a traffic cop of the airways. The question here is to what extent the Commission may constitutionally restrain free speech on radio and television by regulating economic conditions in the industry.

The *NBC* case[73] is generally regarded as the touchstone for measuring the constitutionality of Commission regulation. Indeed, in the field of economic and program regulation of radio and television, the *NBC* opinion affirming the Commission's power to regulate chain broadcasting has become the *vade mecum* of the Commission in exercising regulatory powers in nontechnical areas. One can scarcely pick up a single case in which the Commission's regulatory authority is in question where some portion of Justice Frankfurter's opinion is not quoted as a talisman to dispel all doubts about the Commission's statutory and constitutional power.[74]

---

72. *See* Lafayette Radio Electronics Corp. v. United States, 345 F.2d 278, 281 (2d Cir. 1965) (Friendly, J.), upholding against first amendment challenge Commission regulations prohibiting the use of radio facilities in the Citizens Radio Service as a "hobby" or a "diversion."

73. National Broadcasting Co. v. United States, 319 U.S. 190 (1943).

74. The Commission is not alone in so regarding *NBC*. *See, e.g.,*

The importance of the *NBC* case lies not in the nature of the specific regulation upheld but in Justice Frankfurter's sweeping pronouncements on the comprehensive powers[75] with which Congress endowed the Commission and his almost equally broad pronouncements on the constitutionality of Commission exercise of such powers. Of primary importance, of course, is the scope of the latter. Rejecting a challenge to the regulations based on the first amendment, Justice Frankfurter concluded for the majority:

> The Regulations, even if valid in all other respects, must fall because they abridge, say the appellants, their right of free speech. If that be so, it would follow that every person whose application for a license to operate a station is denied by the Commission is thereby denied his constitutional right of free speech. Freedom of utterance is abridged to many who wish to use the limited facilities of radio. Unlike other modes of expression, radio inherently is not available to all. That is its unique characteristic, and that is why, unlike other modes of expression, it is subject to governmental regulation. Because it cannot be used by all, some who wish to use it must be denied. But Congress did not authorize the Commission to choose among applicants upon the basis of their political, economic or social views, or upon any other capricious basis. If it did, or if the Commission by these Regulations proposed a choice among applicants upon some such basis, the issue before us would be wholly different. . . . The right of free speech does not include, however, the right to use the facilities of radio without a license. The licensing system established by Congress in the Communications Act of 1934 was a proper exercise of its power over commerce. The standard it provided for the licensing of stations was the 'public interest, convenience, or necessity.' Denial of a station license on that ground, if valid under the Act, is not a denial of free speech.[76]

Accepting this opinion at face value, it is difficult to find any significant first amendment limitations on the authority of the Commission to regulate radio and television broadcasting, at least in the area of economic regulation,[77] so long as it can be

---

Barron, *The Federal Communications Commission's Fairness Doctrine: An Evaluation*, 30 GEO. WASH. L. REV. 1, 2 n.6 (1961): "The [*NBC*] opinion . . . is generally regarded as having sounded the death knell for the argument that government regulation of broadcasting violated the licensee's right of free expression guaranteed by the First Amendment." Although this statement of the effect of *NBC* in silencing first amendment objections to broadcast regulation is plain hyperbole, it is nevertheless indicative of a widespread, if wholly uncritical, acceptance of *NBC* as dispositive of constitutional issues in broadcast regulation.

75. 319 U.S. at 217.

76. *Id.* at 226-27.

77. However, *NBC* is read as broadly permissive in the case of program regulation as well as economic regulation. This is discussed in Parts II & III *infra*.

found that the standard of public interest, convenience, or necessity is satisfied. At the same time, however, Justice Frankfurter's opinion seems fundamentally wrong insofar as it suggests an unacceptably broad license for Commission regulation, particularly in the field of programming. At the heart of Frankfurter's reasoning is the classic cliche: "Unlike other modes of expression, radio inherently is not available to all. That is its unique characteristic, and that is why, unlike other modes of expression, it is subject to governmental regulation."[78]

This argument, which has been assiduously trotted out on every appropriate occasion, has several major defects.[78a] First, contrary to common assumption, the radio broadcast spectrum is not now, and may never be, saturated. While the technical limitations on entry into broadcasting are real enough, the economic limitations are probably more restrictive. The economic barriers to entry into radio broadcasting are, however, far less restrictive than in the case of media such as newspapers, which lie essentially beyond public control. Second, there are more competitive outlets for expression in radio and television than there are in the newspaper media—or probably in all major publications media combined. This disparity between the number of different radio and television outlets and the number of newsprint media is increasing. Third, the mere fact that there are barriers to entry into the communications media, be it newspapers or radio and television, does not in itself resolve the problem of the kinds of control that are permissible and how narrow the focus on restraint of free speech may be.

The defect of Justice Frankfurter's approach to the constitutional issue is illustrated by the Commission's regulation of community antenna television. The CATV regulations prohibiting duplication of the programs of local broadcast stations by programs carried on CATV systems have been twice upheld against constitutional challenge. In the *Carter Mountain* case[79] the court rejected the argument that the Commission's nonduplication protection for local television stations contravened the first amendment. Essentially the court reasoned that since some restraint on complete freedom is inherent in all licensing regulation of radio communications,

> it may be assumed that any denial of a license to transmit radio or television programs keeps off the air, and hence de-

78. 319 U.S. at 226.

78a. *See generally* Part III *infra*.

79. Carter Mountain Transmission Corp. v. FCC, 321 F.2d 359 (D.C. Cir.), *cert. denied*, 375 U.S. 951 (1963).

> prives the public of, the material which the applicant desires to communicate. But that does not mean that the Commission must grant every license which is requested. Nor does it mean that the whole statutory system of regulation is invalid. Quite the contrary is true: a denial of a station license, validly made because the standard of 'public interest, convenience, or necessity' has not been met, is not a denial of free speech.[80]

On the same reasoning, the court again upheld the nonduplication rules against first amendment challenge in *Idaho Microwave, Inc. v. FCC.*[81]

Neither decision deals with the constitutional issue in a satisfactory way. To be sure, licensing of radio communications involves a degree of restraint. The mere fact that some restraint may be inherent in legitimate licensing does not in itself, however, justify this particular form of regulation nor, indeed, does it bestow a constitutional carte blanche on all forms and all degrees of regulation.[82] Not even the FCC would contend, for example, that the licensing power includes the power to direct every aspect of the licensee's operations, including the particular programs presented. Moreover the reasoning is inapposite in the case of direct regulation of CATV where there is no prevailing scheme of licensing to which regulation can be said to be an incidental restraint.

While the constitutional issue was inadequately analyzed in *Carter Mountain* and *Idaho Microwave,* it was almost ignored in *Buckeye Cablevision, Inc. v. FCC.*[83] In *Buckeye* the court upheld the CATV regulations restricting carriage by the system of distant signals. Unlike *Carter Mountain* and *Idaho Microwave* the rules here were directed against CATV systems themselves and were not confined to regulating microwave carriers within the licensing jurisdiction of the Commission. The two principal challenges to the rules were that the Commission was without statutory jurisdiction to regulate CATV and, more fundamentally, that the rules violated the first amendment insofar as they precluded the system from carrying signals originating beyond a specified distance from the CATV station. Affirming the Commission's jurisdiction to regulate CATV systems directly, the court gave little more than the back of its hand to the first amendment challenge, stating that "the restraint imposed by the rules is no more than is reasonably required to effectuate the

80. *Id.* at 364.
81. 352 F.2d 729 (D.C. Cir. 1965).
82. *Cf.* Sherbert v. Verner, 374 U.S. 398 (1963).
83. 10 P & F RADIO REG. 2d 2029 (D.C. Cir. 1967).

public interest requirements of the Act."[84] The court then cited *NBC* and *Carter Mountain* for support.

Taken at face value, this rather offhand statement suggests the preposterous conclusion that the Constitution is circumscribed by an act of Congress and that, so long as the Commission's actions are within the scope of its legislative mandate, there are no first amendment restrictions. Undoubtedly the court did not intend such a sweeping abdication to Congress of the judicial power to determine the scope of the first amendment. However, its refusal to go beyond the question of the legislatively created public interest standard to resolve the constitutional issue suggests just such an abdication.

The court's failure to deal with the first amendment issue is not corrected by its reliance on the *Carter Mountain* and *NBC* cases. As previously noted, the reasoning of *Carter Mountain* is entirely inadequate since the validity of some types and degrees of restraint does not justify all types and all degrees of restraint. Nor is the issue resolved by citing *NBC*. Even if the technical barriers to entry and the fact that radio is inherently not available to all justify Commission regulation of radio and television broadcasting, this clearly does not support regulation of CATV. Unlike broadcasting, CATV transmits its signals entirely by wire, and except to a negligible degree[85] transmission by wire does not interfere with other stations. From a technical viewpoint, CATV is available to all. If, therefore, Justice Frankfurter's scarcity argument is relied on as the constitutional basis for regulating radio and television, it follows that CATV is no more constitutionally subject to regulation of entry than newspapers, magazines, or other communications media. The *NBC* case, far from providing support for Commission regulation, as concluded by the Commission,[86] really supports the opposite re-

84. *Id.* at 2034. *Buckeye* conflicts with an earlier decision in the Ninth Circuit, Southwestern Cable Co. v. United States, 378 F.2d 118 (9th Cir. 1967), *petition for cert. filed*, 36 U.S.L.W. 3068 (U.S. July 13, 1967), holding that the commission had no statutory jurisdiction over non-microwave CATV.

85. Even radio transmissions by wire emit some degree of spurious radiation which may interfere with radio broadcast signals. These spurious emissions are not of major significance, however, and can be practically eliminated by use of heavy cable. The Commission's regulations have long provided for control of such spurious emissions long before CATV itself was regulated. *See* 47 C.F.R. § 15.1 (1967).

86. *See Notice of Inquiry and Notice of Proposed Rule-Making, Regulation of CATV*, 4 P & F RADIO REG. 2d 1679, 1709-10 (1965); *see also CATV Regulation (Petition for Reconsideration of Second Report)*, 8 P & F RADIO REG. 2d 1677, 1681-82 (1967) (rejecting argument that

sult. Following Justice Frankfurter's scarcity argument to its logical conclusion, it must be seen that abandonment of CATV regulation and the supplanting of broadcasting with CATV and other forms of wire communication would do away with the entire problem of spectrum scarcity and with it the entire ostensible basis for the regulatory scheme established by the Communications Act of 1934.

Notwithstanding what seem to be obvious fallacies in the reasoning underlying the *NBC, Carter Mountain,* and *Buckeye* cases, it does not necessarily follow that the economic regulation sustained in those decisions is unconstitutional. The problem is not that these decisions have reached the wrong result but that they have traveled the wrong path. On grounds other than those advanced in the decisions, the Commission's economic regulation and its proposed subscription television regulations seem defensible even under the strictest application of the first amendment.

Radio, television, newspaper publication, and theatre are, within limits, subject to general economic restraints and regulations. For example, no one doubts any longer that communications media, whether or not their facilities are inherently available to all, are subject to the antitrust laws. In *Associated Press v. United States* [87] the Court, per Justice Black, held that the antitrust laws prohibited the Associated Press from restricting member newspapers from furnishing news to nonmember newspapers. The Court rejected the contention that this application of the antitrust laws to a news media was in violation of the first amendment.

> It would be strange indeed, however, if the grave concern for freedom of the press which prompted adoption of the First Amendment should be read as a command that the government was without power to protect that freedom. The First Amendment, far from providing an argument against application of the Sherman Act, here provides powerful reasons to the contrary. That Amendment rests on the assumption that the widest possible dissemination of information from diverse and antagonistic sources is essential to the welfare of the public, that a free press is a condition of a free society. Surely a command that the government itself shall not impede the free flow of ideas does not afford non-governmental combinations a refuge if they impose restraints upon that constitutionally guaranteed freedom. Freedom to publish means freedom for all and not for some. Freedom to publish is guaranteed by the Constitution, but freedom to combine to keep others from pub-

---

regulation unconstitutionally restrains free speech, relying in part on *NBC*).

87. 326 U.S. 1 (1945).

lishing is not. Freedom of the press from governmental interference under the First Amendment does not sanction repression of that freedom by private interests. The First Amendment affords not the slightest support for the contention that a combination to restrain trade in news and views has any constitutional immunity.[88]

It may be argued that the *AP* antitrust case disposes of the constitutional challenge to regulations against monopoly but not of the converse, *i.e.*, regulations which have the effect of *furthering* economic concentration, and economic regulation of the kind reflected in *Carroll*, CATV regulation, and the proposed regulation of STV operations is directly contrary to regulation of the type upheld in the *AP* case since the effect really is a measure of protection of economic concentration.

One critic of the policy of imposing barriers to entry on economic grounds has contended that this latter type of economic regulation, in contrast to antimonopoly regulation, is unconstitutional.[89] He concludes that the chain broadcasting rules upheld in *NBC* flow logically from the Court's recognition of the scarcity of available frequencies,[90] but economic regulation of entry does not. But this distinction between regulatory limits on entry and regulatory limits on monopoly simply reflects a bias in favor of strong competition at all costs. However sound this view may be as a matter of economic or social policy, it seems rather far-fetched to give it constitutional stature.

While it is true that economic regulation of the type considered in the *Carroll* case, the Commission's CATV regulation or its proposed regulation of STV may in a very real sense be economic protectionism,[91] it is nevertheless a protectionism undertaken to effect the purpose the antitrust laws were supposed

88. *Id.* at 20 (footnote omitted). The Court also relied in part on its decision in Associated Press v. NLRB, 301 U.S. 103 (1937), in which it upheld against first amendment challenge the application of the National Labor Relations Act to AP. *See* note 272 *infra* and accompanying text. It also relied on its prior decision in Indiana Farmer's Guide Co. v. Prairie Farmer Co., 293 U.S. 268 (1934), involving the application of the antitrust laws to a newspaper. However, in *Prairie Farmer* the first amendment issue was not raised or discussed.

89. Givens, *Refusal of Radio and Television Licenses on Economic Grounds*, 46 VA. L. REV. 1391, 1400-03 (1960). *Cf.* Weaver v. Jordan, 64 Cal. 2d 235, 49 Cal. Rptr. 537, 411 P.2d 289 (1966), which invalidated a state statute banning subscription television (by wire) and distinguished *NBC* on grounds that the rules there were designed to eliminate monopoly whereas the statute here fostered monopoly.

90. Givens, *supra* note 89, at 1401-02.

91. *See* Cole, *Community Antenna Television, The Broadcaster Establishment, and the Federal Regulator,* 14 AM. U.L. REV. 124-25, 142-45 (1965).

by the Court in the *AP* case to serve—diversity of opinion. The rationale expressed by the Commission for its regulation of CATV is that CATV, left to itself, may seriously curtail if not destroy many of the local broadcast outlets whose continued existence is necessary to maintain diversified sources of free speech and opinion.

More fundamentally, the constitutionality of general economic regulation does not necessarily turn on whether the regulation has the purpose or effect of benefiting free speech itself. This is clearly the necessary conclusion to be drawn from *Associated Press v. NLRB*[92] which upheld the constitutionality of the National Labor Relations Act as applied to the press. Here the NLRB had entered a cease and desist order against AP under section 7 of the Act ordering it, among other things, to reinstate a member of its editorial staff whom it had discharged. AP argued that the Act, as applied to it in this manner, violated the first amendment. AP contended that in hiring and firing

> it must have absolute and unrestricted freedom to employ and to discharge those who, like Watson, [the discharged employee] edit the news . . . and that the Associated Press cannot be free to furnish unbiased and impartial news reports unless it is equally free to determine for itself the partiality or bias of editorial employees. . . . [A]ny regulation protective of union activities, or the right collectively to bargain on the part of such employees, is necessarily an invalid invasion of the freedom of the press.[93]

The Court rejected the contention as irrelevant since no bias on the part of the employee had been shown. The contention was also rejected as an unsound generalization, the Court noting

> [t]he business of the Associated Press is not immune from regulation because it is an agency of the press. The publisher of a newspaper has no special immunity from the application of general laws.[94]

---

92. 301 U.S. 103 (1937).

93. *Id.* at 131.

94. *Id.* at 132. For an extended treatment of "general legislation" to which the "press," including radio, is subject, see 2 Z. CHAFEE, GOVERNMENT AND MASS COMMUNICATIONS 500-678 (Comm'n on Freedom of the Press ed. 1953). Chafee identifies five types of "general burdens" in this regard: (1) taxation, (2) laws against unfair competition, (3) rationing of paper (not, of course, applicable to radio), (4) labor laws, and (5) antitrust laws. *Id.* at 501. Of all of these general burdens, Chafee regards the application of the antitrust laws to communications industries as the most troublesome in its potential for interference with freedom of the press. *Id.* at 666-74. Chafee's concern in this respect seems unjustified. As he himself recognizes, the antitrust laws have not been applied to communications industries in such a manner as to raise any imminent threat to freedom of speech and the press. Nor is there anything which suggests that such an application is likely in the future.

Unlike the *AP* antitrust case discussed above, the *AP* labor case does not in any respect turn on a presumed, ultimate benefit to the goal of free speech. It cannot be said, for example, that application of the labor laws, unlike the antitrust laws, has the effect of fostering diversity. The rationale of the *AP* labor case is, very simply, that communications media as commercial enterprises are no less subject to general social regulation merely because they are in the business of dissemination of news and opinion.

The same rationale, which seems quite obviously sound as a principle of constitutional law, applies to radio and television as well as to newspapers. It applies regardless of whether radio and television is distributed through a spectrum which is inherently not available to all or by means of wire which is.[95]

It is important to stress that acceptance of this rationale in support of the constitutionality of the Commission's regulations is not necessarily an acceptance of the Commission's statutory power. It is particularly necessary to distinguish statutory from constitutional authority in the CATV area.[96] Moreover, in order to accept this rationale, one need not accept the necessity or the wisdom of the Commission's regulatory policy in all respects. In the case of CATV regulation one might take the view that the Commission's regulation goes too far. One can even take the extreme view that the Commission's regulatory policies in this area are the handiwork of the economically and politi-

---

95. *But see* Weaver v. Jordan, 64 Cal. 2d 235, 49 Cal. Rptr. 537, 411 P.2d 289 (1966), holding unconstitutional under the state constitution and the first amendment a statute banning subscription television. The result seems dubious. Even though the statute seemed ill-advised, it does not seem unconstitutional to proscribe certain methods of communications on general economic or other grounds not going to the content of the speech. *See* cases discussed in text above; *cf.* Kovacs v. Cooper, 336 U.S. 77 (1949). The court conceded the validity of general regulatory restraints of the type upheld in *Kovacs* or in the *AP* cases, but struck down the statute here because it went beyond regulation and banned subscription television entirely. But the distinction seems thin. The Act did not ban all television communications but only the business of charging directly for television. Query whether the extent of the restraint on such an incident of communications and not directed to the content of the communications goes any further than the restraint upheld in *Kovacs* or restraints imposed in applying general economic regulation of the type sustained in the *AP* cases.

96. That is, statutory authority in the *jurisdictional* sense. Of course, since § 326 of the Act, 47 U.S.C. § 326 (1964), is in substance an incorporation of the first amendment's prohibition of "censorship," anything which unconstitutionally interferes with free speech also violates § 326.

cally influential members of the industry.[97] Similarly one might conclude that the proposed restrictions on STV operations, such as limiting STV to markets having five or more commercial services, are unnecessary and overly protectionistic. But an unwise or unnecessary policy does not become transformed into an unconstitutional policy merely because free expression is in some way involved. If this were the case, there are many antitrust, labor, social, and economic measures in effect today which might well be unconstitutional as applied to any form of communications media.

While it might be granted that the Commission could limit or proscribe altogether a CATV system's competition with broadcast stations in certain markets where this is deemed necessary to the public interest, it is arguable that the Commission cannot achieve this same result by proscribing certain types of CATV programming and that it therefore cannot impose restrictions simply because the CATV programs duplicate local programming or because they originate in a "distant market." In the abstract, the argument has a certain persuasiveness. Certainly the power to achieve a given economic result such as protection from "disruptive" competition does not include the power to achieve it by any and all means. Assuming the power of the Commission to preclude CATV entry into certain markets entirely,[98] it clearly cannot impose unconstitutional restrictions or conditions on entry.[99] Plainly the Commission could not tell a CATV system that it could operate in a given locale, but only on the condition that it carry such particular programs as the Commission approved as suitable for the residents of that locale.

However, the mere fact that a particular program classification is used to implement the regulatory objective does not necessarily indicate that the Commission is engaged in censorship. The Commission's CATV program nonduplication rules which, in general, preclude a CATV system from carring television programs which duplicate the programs carried on the same day by local broadcast stations, illustrate the problem. Although the effect might be to proscribe a particular classification of programming, the classification is a neutral one, based not on program content or quality but simply on the timing and manner of presentation. The

97. *See* Cole, *supra* note 91.

98. *But see* Weaver v. Jordan, 64 Cal. 2d 235, 49 Cal. Rptr. 537, 411 P.2d 289 (1966).

99. *E.g.*, Sherbert v. Verner, 374 U.S. 398 (1963); Hannegan v. Esquire, Inc., 327 U.S. 146, 156 (1946); Terral v. Burke Constr. Co., 257 U.S. 529 (1922).

effect is not to keep such programming from being presented but to restrict the number of entirely duplicative presentations at substantially the same time. Thus, what is really involved here is not a true classification of programs but a classification of signals. If it is accepted that economic regulation in general is constitutional, then given a justifiable economic objective such as the elimination of duplicate programming, such restraints as the CATV nonduplication rule seem constitutional.[100]

An analogous albeit somewhat more troublesome problem is presented by the new subscription television regulations proposed by the Commission's STV Committee. The proposal to prohibit broadcast of feature films which are more than two years old, current sports events regularly carried live on local conventional stations, series-type programs, and combined feature film and sports totaling more than ninety per cent of a station's annual STV programming would appear to go beyond the kind of CATV nonduplication protection previously discussed. Here certain types of programs, not merely the manner of their presentation, are singled out and forbidden to be carried on STV. Such predetermination of allowable program types would seem clearly unconstitutional if imposed as a flat restraint against presentation on television altogether.

However, such a conclusion is not dispositive here. By prohibiting STV from carrying movies which are more than two years old, the Commission would not be attempting to make a program judgment about the relative quality or acceptability *vel non* of older movies. It would instead be acting on the economic prediction that presentation of older films by STV would siphon such programming away from free television thereby impairing the vitality of the latter.[101] The same economic judgment underlies the proposed regulation which would prohibit STV from carrying current sports events, regularly carried live on free television,[102] and from carrying series-type programs,[103] which, along with movies, have been a mainstay of free televi-

100. The same reasoning would hold true of the CATV rules restricting carriage of "distant" signals, *i.e.*, signals originating beyond a certain distance from the community served by the CATV system. Here regulation is again drawn on a classification of program signals, a differentiation between local and distant signals. Like nonduplication, the classification is not based on a judgment of program quality or desirability but on the purely neutral factor of distance (which again is used as a means of achieving a measure of economic protection).

101. *See STV Report* 1705-07.

102. *See id.* at 1707-13.

103. *See id.* at 1714.

sion. As in the case of CATV nonduplication regulation, the aim of these rules is not to render judgment on particular types of programs but rather to achieve certain economic goals based on classifications which relate to programming types. As the STV Committee Report points out, such a structuring of the channels of distribution seems entirely consistent with the first amendment, even though it necessarily places some limitation on the dissemination of speech.[104]

The foregoing does not mean, of course, that the Commission has a constitutionally free rein to do as it pleases in the field of economic regulation. More particularly, it does not mean that, under the guise of economic or social regulation fostering diversity of speech, it can control the speech itself to ensure that the dissemination of ideas is sufficiently diverse according to its judgment. In this respect, the STV Committee's proposal to restrict a station's annual STV programming to not more than ninety per cent feature film and sports programs clearly seems to go beyond any general economic regulation. The sole basis for such a rule is to force STV to present cultural programming.[105] Such a rule is based squarely on a judgment as to the type of programming deemed to be desirable, a judgment which goes beyond general economic regulation and enters, subtly but surely, into the area of program regulation, where the Commission's regulatory policies and actions seem to be of far more doubtful constitutional validity.

II. REGULATION AND CONTROL OF PROGRAMMING

While the first amendment implications of the Commission's activity in the field of economic regulation have received relatively little attention, the Commission's regulatory efforts in the field of programming have provoked considerable comment. This is understandable in view of the far more doubtful constitutionality of many of its activities and policies in program regulation. The analysis of the constitutional implications of the Commission's regulation of programming has, however, tended to be undiscriminating. Little attention has been given to the different regulatory measures which control or influence programming and to the distinct effects of and the different constitutional problems raised by such measures.

---

104. *Id.* at 1705. Accepting this argument, however, I do not, for reasons previously set forth at length, subscribe to the Committee's reliance on the sweeping pronouncements laid down in the *NBC* case as support for its proposed regulation. *See id.* at 1704-05.

105. *See id.* at 1712-13.

A. Direct Restraints Against Illegal, Harmful, or Offensive Programming

1. *Commission Actions From Dr. Brinkley to Pacifica*

To date the Commission has instituted direct action against a station for broadcast of particular programs in only a few cases. These include defamatory programs,[106] programs involving improper and harmful medical advice[107] or medical advertising,[108] broadcasts relating to illegal lotteries,[109] broadcasts of certain horseracing information,[110] broadcasts of fraudulent contests,[111] and "offensive" programming.[112] In several such cases, however, although the Commission instituted action by issuing a show cause order or by instituting a hearing on license revocation or renewal, it has taken no final action either because it was persuaded that the programming was in fact satisfactory[113] or because it was satisfied that the licensee's "bad" performance would not be repeated.[114]

The earliest case involving direct restraint in the regulation of programming is the *Dr. Brinkley* case.[115] While much has been made of this famous case, more attention has been given to the atrocious opinion by the court of appeals in affirming the Radio Commission's action than to the facts which led the Commission to refuse to renew Dr. Brinkley's license for a radio station. Dr. Brinkley controlled a radio station, a pharmaceutical associa-

106. Trinity Methodist Church, South v. Federal Radio Comm'n, 62 F.2d 850 (D.C. Cir. 1932), *cert. denied*, 288 U.S. 599 (1932).

107. KFKB Broadcasting Ass'n v. Federal Radio Comm'n, 47 F.2d 670 (D.C. Cir. 1931).

108. *See* WSBC, Inc., 2 F.C.C. 293 (1936).

109. WRBL Radio Station, Inc., 2 F.C.C. 687 (1936).

110. Community Broadcasting Serv., Inc., 13 P & F Radio Reg. 179 (1955).

111. KWK Radio, Inc., 25 P & F. Radio Reg. 577 (1963); *cf.* Melody Music, Inc., 6 P & F. Radio Reg. 2d 973 (1966) (involvement in fixed quiz show not involving station considered as bearing on "character" of renewal applicant); Eleven Ten Broadcasting, 22 P & F Radio Reg. 699 (1962) (also involving other matters, however, such as program log falsification).

112. Mile High Stations, Inc., 20 P & F Radio Reg. 345 (1960); Pacifica Foundation, 1 P & F Radio Reg. 2d 747 (1964) (licensee exonerated); *cf.* Palmetto Broadcasting Co., 23 P & F Radio Reg. 483 (1961), *aff'd sub nom.* Robinson v. FCC, 334 F.2d 534 (D.C. Cir.), *cert. denied*, 379 U.S. 843 (1964) (also involved, however, misrepresentations to Commission).

113. *See* Pacifica Foundation, 1 P & F Radio Reg. 2d 747 (1964).

114. *See* Mile High Stations, 20 P & F Radio Reg. 345 (1960).

115. KFKB Broadcasting Ass'n v. Federal Radio Comm'n, 47 F.2d 670 (D.C. Cir. 1931).

tion, and a hospital which he operated in a common interest. The hospital was advertised over the station and paid a substantial amount to the station each month for this advertising. The pharmaceutical association was composed of druggists who dispensed medical preparations prepared according to Brinkley's formulas. Each member of the association paid a nominal fee to the station for use of the formulas. For three and one-half hours *daily*, Brinkley personally broadcast a program over the station devoted to diagnosing and prescribing treatment for cases from symptoms given in letters addressed to Brinkley or the station. Predictably, the good doctor's treatment was in almost all cases to prescribe one of his prepared tonics.

It was against this background that the Radio Commission denied Brinkley's application for renewal. On appeal the decision was affirmed by the court of appeals on the grounds that: (a) the operations of KFKB were being used for the purely private purpose of furthering Dr. Brinkley's other business and professional interests with no regard for the public interest; and (b) that use of the station for diagnosing the problems of and prescribing treatment for patients whom Brinkley had never even seen was inimical to the public health and safety and, therefore, was not in the public interest.

In 1936 the Commission set down for hearing a renewal application by a licensee which had carried advertisements of two medical preparations. One of these was prepared and sponsored by a person convicted of practicing medicine without a license, while the other was prepared and sponsored by a person convicted of violating the Food and Drug Act and of fraudulent use of the mails in promoting the advertised preparations. However, because the licensee had previously cancelled the advertisements, apparently after learning of these facts regarding the sponsors, and had an otherwise good record, the license was renewed.[116]

Shortly after the Radio Commission had refused to permit Dr. Brinkley to continue to use radio frequencies to further his "organized charlatanism," it was confronted with the Reverend Doctor Shuler, another "doctor," of similarly doubtful character.[117] The Radio Commission refused to renew Shuler's broadcast license based on findings that he was using his licensed frequency for defamatory broadcasts and for obstructing the orderly

116. WSBC, Inc., 2 F.C.C. 293 (1936).

117. Trinity Methodist Church, South v. Federal Radio Comm'n, 62 F.2d 850 (D.C. Cir.), *cert. denied*, 288 U.S. 599 (1932).

administration of public justice. As in the *Brinkley* case, the Commission's action seems clearly justified on the facts. Shuler's defamatory broadcasts evidently consisted of more than an occasional lapse of caution and judgment in criticizing individuals. In reviewing the evidence on which the Commission made its finding, the court of appeals noted that Shuler

> not satisfied with attacking the judges of the courts in cases then pending before them, attacked the bar association for its activities in recommending judges, charging it with ulterior and sinister purposes. With no more justification, he charged particular judges with sundry immoral acts. He made defamatory statements against the board of health. He charged that the labor temple in Los Angeles was a bootlegging and gambling joint. . . . On one occasion he announced over the radio that he had certain damaging information against a prominent unnamed man which, unless a contribution (presumably to the church) of a hundred dollars was forthcoming, he would disclose . . . . He alluded slightingly to the Jews as a race, and made frequent and bitter attacks on the Roman Catholic religion and its relations to government.[118]

On these findings the court of appeals, not surprisingly, held that the Commission's refusal to renew Shuler's license was not a violation of the first amendment.

Pursuant to section 1304 of the United States Criminal Code,[119] the Commission has long scrutinized broadcasts of information about prize-giving schemes and taken action against those found to be lotteries. The Commission's power, indeed, its duty to enforce the mandate of section 1304 and to implement it by means of general rule or individual decisions was expressly affirmed in *FCC v. American Broadcasting Company.*[120]

The Commission has also proscribed the broadcast of horse-racing information in a manner and under such circumstances that it is evident that the information is being used by bookmakers and others for illegal gambling purposes.[121]

---

118. 62 F.2d at 852.

119. 18 U.S.C. § 1304 (1964), *formerly* § 316 of the Communications Act of 1934:

> Whoever broadcasts by means of any radio station for which a license is required by any law of the United States, or whoever, operating any such station, knowingly permits the broadcasting of, any advertisement of or information concerning any lottery, gift enterprise, or similar scheme, offering prizes dependent in whole or in part upon lot or chance, or any list of the prizes drawn or awarded by means of any such lottery, gift enterprise, or scheme, whether said list contains any part or all of such prizes, shall be fined not more than $1,000 or imprisoned not more than one year, or both. Each day's broadcasting shall constitute a separate offense.

120. 347 U.S. 284, 289 (1954). The Court held, however, that the rules there adopted by the Commission were too broad.

121. *See* Community Broadcasting Serv., Inc., 13 P & F RADIO REG.

An extension of its action in the *Brinkley* case and its action in lottery and horseracing cases is the action taken by the Commission against programs involving some form of fraudulent contest. In *Eleven Ten Broadcasting Corp.*[122] the Commission denied the renewal of a station's license on findings that the licensee had, among other things, conducted "fraudulent" contests over its station. Although the Commission evidently considered the fraudulent contest alone sufficient to support denial of the license, it relied on other grounds, including deliberate falsification of the station's program logs and other misrepresentations to support its action. Subsequently, in *KWK Radio, Inc.*,[123] the Commission was confronted with a similar fraudulent contest, except that the "fraudulent" program itself was the only matter before it. The Commission revoked the station's license on the basis of findings that it had conducted fraudulent contests which, the Commission found, resulted in deception to the public, inconvenience, "public disorder," and in some instances actual property damage.[124]

Related to the *KWK* case is the Commission's more recent action in making a short-term renewal grant in *Melody Music, Inc.*,[125] which grew out of the famous quiz show scandal of 1959 in which some contestants on a popular quiz program were given the answers to the questions beforehand. There, however, the matter was considered in a context somewhat different from that in *KWK*. In *Melody Music* the station itself had not been held responsible for the deceptive quiz program. One of the two principals of the station had, however, been involved in the rigged contest. As a result the Commission set the renewal application down for a hearing on the character qualifications of the two principals. In its first opinion[126] the Commission denied the renewal application of the station on these grounds. On appeal, the court of appeals for the District of Columbia reversed,[127] stating that the Commission had treated the licensee differently

---

179 (1955) (also discussing other cases). A brief statement of Commission policy guidelines as to the types of horseracing broadcasts which are considered questionable by the Commission was subsequently issued in *Broadcast of Horse Racing Information*, 22 P & F RADIO REG. 417 (1961), *reaff'd, Broadcast of Horse Racing Information*, 2 P & F RADIO REG. 2d 1609 (1964).

122. 22 P & F RADIO REG. 699 (1962).
123. 25 P & F RADIO REG. 577 (1963).
124. *Id.* at 581-82.
125. 6 P & F RADIO REG. 2d 973 (1966).
126. 2 P & F RADIO REG. 2d 571 (1964).
127. 345 F.2d 730 (D.C. Cir. 1965).

here than it had in *NBC*,[128] where the Commission had renewed NBC's license notwithstanding the fact that its parent corporation (RCA) had violated the antitrust laws. The evident discrimination was made even more patent by the fact that in *Melody*, unlike *NBC* where a violation of law was involved, the rigging of quiz shows was not *at that time* a violation of law.[129] On remand the Commission was able to avoid the impossible task of distinguishing the case from other cases in which it renewed the licenses of applicants convicted of violating the antitrust laws. The principals had applied to assign the license to other, presumably untainted, persons. Seizing this opportunity to rescue itself from a bad position, the Commission granted a short-term renewal on condition that the present licensee divest itself of its broadcast interest.

The foregoing cases all dealt with programs which were fraudulent, illegal, or at least patently harmful. Several recent cases focus on a more difficult problem: control of programming deemed to be improper, indecent, or offensive. At the present time, there remains some uncertainty whether the Commission will attempt any direct restraint on programming which it deems merely offensive and, if it does, what circumstances might prompt it to take direct action against such programming.

In *Mile High Stations, Inc.*,[130] the Commission issued an order to show cause why an AM license should not be revoked where the station's announcer had made a number of offcolor remarks over a period of several months. Although the Commission regarded the remarks as sufficiently offensive to warrant license revocation, it declined to take such action and instead simply issued a cease and desist order against further broadcast announcements of this kind.

The problem of what action could be taken against such programming was posed again in *Palmetto Broadcasting Company*.[131] The Commission, in response to complaints received concerning programs which were allegedly vulgar and suggestive, requested from the licensee a statement concerning the complaints. In response to the request, the licensee stated that he was unaware

128. 345 F.2d at 732; *see also* General Electric Co., 2 P & F RADIO REG. 2d 1038 (1964); Westinghouse Broadcasting Co., 22 P & F RADIO REG. 1023 (1962).

129. Rigged quiz shows are now proscribed by 47 U.S.C. § 509 (1964).

130. 20 P & F RADIO REG. 345 (1960).

131. 23 P & F RADIO REG. 483 (1962), *aff'd sub nom.* Robinson v. FCC, 334 F.2d 534 (D.C. Cir.), *cert. denied*, 379 U.S. 843 (1964).

at the time that such offensive statements were made. Subsequently, the Commission designated the licensee's application for renewal of its license and for construction of an antenna system for a hearing on the issues, among others, of whether the licensee had misrepresented facts to the Commission or was otherwise lacking in candor, whether the programming was "coarse, vulgar, suggestive and susceptible of indecent, double meaning," whether the licensee had permitted such program material, and whether, in light of those facts determined on these issues, the applications should be permitted. The hearing examiner found against the licensee on all of these issues and concluded that it had not, therefore, served the interests of the community. He proposed that the applications be denied. The Commission affirmed the examiner's findings but modified his conclusions of law, holding that the licensee's misrepresentations and false statements, *in and of themselves,* constituted grounds for denial of the applications. On appeal, the court of appeals affirmed on the narrow grounds that because of the licensee's concealment of material facts, the Commission was justified in its conclusion that the licensee did not possess the requisite character qualifications and was, therefore, justified in refusing to renew the license.

Subsequently, in *Pacifica Foundation,*[132] the Commission was again confronted at renewal time with complaints directed at several programs which were said to be of questionable taste. This time the Commission refused to take any action, holding that even if the programs were of questionable taste, they were isolated instances spread out over a four year period and did not demonstrate any persistent lapse of taste, and that the programs were not so egregiously offensive as to warrant Commission action.

2. *First Amendment Implications*

In the relatively few cases in which the Commission has singled out for review or taken direct action against particular programs, the constitutional implications of the Commission's actions are largely self-evident. Because the restraint exercised in these cases is directed at particular program content, some form of censorship is necessarily involved. The issue then becomes simply whether or not, on the particular facts, such censorship is constitutional.

---

132. 1 P & F RADIO REG. 2d 747 (1964).

While it is not difficult to envision circumstances in which action of the type reflected in the previously discussed cases might well be unconstitutional, it is difficult to find any unconstitutionality in the few cases decided to date, although several recent Commission cases give rise to some concern. Consider first, for example, the Commission's refusal to renew Dr. Brinkley's broadcast license. On the facts of that case, this action can scarcely be considered extraordinary or patently unreasonable. The Commission imposed no greater restraint than could constitutionally have been imposed by other, even more direct means wholly without regard to Brinkley's use of a radio station. Surely a law which outlawed unethical medical practice and which was enforced by means of revocation of a license to practice could not be considered an unconstitutional abridgment of free speech.[133] The refusal to renew Brinkley's broadcast license seems no more unconstitutional than the action taken by the state of Kansas in suspending his medical license for unethical conduct.[134] Surely the Commission's refusal of a license to Brinkley because of his fraudulent practices is no more unconstitutional than the actions of the Food and Drug Administration or the Federal Trade Commission in enforcing provisions of the Food, Drug and Cosmetic Act, the Federal Trade Commission Act, and other acts which regulate labeling and other representations of drugs and medical preparations which are of doubtful safety or efficacy. So far as is known, no one has ever seriously suggested that these acts constitute an unconstitutional abridgment of free speech.

Unfortunately, in discussions about the *Brinkley* case today, attention is focused less on the extraordinary facts which underlie the Commission's actions than on some sweeping and foolish language in the opinion of the court of appeals in affirming. Despite defensible grounds for affirming the Radio Commission's actions, the court of appeals reasoned that there was no censorship and no first amendment violation because there had been no attempt at a prior restraint.

> In considering the question whether the public interest, convenience or necessity will be served by renewal of . . . [this]

133. This is not to say, of course, that there may not be constitutional requirements for adherence to certain procedures, *e.g.*, an adjudicatory hearing to be followed in revoking a license.

134. At the time of the proceedings before the Radio Commission, Brinkley was also before the Kansas State Medical Examination Board in a proceeding to revoke his medical license for "having acted according to the ethical standards of an imposter" and for "organized charlatanism." Brinkley v. Hassig, 130 Kan. 874, 289 P. 64 (affirming denial of an injunction against medical board proceedings), *appeal dismissed*, 282 U.S. 800 (1930).

license, the commission has merely exercised its undoubted right to take note of . . . past conduct, which is not censorship.[135]

It scarcely needs pointing out that this reasoning would give the Commission a constitutional carte blanche to take virtually any action it chose against station practices, particular types of programming, or particular programs which it deemed not in the public interest. Fortunately, it is unnecessary to pursue the parade of evils which might ensue from the court of appeals' opinion in the *Brinkley* case since its reasoning was clearly rejected by the Supreme Court's opinion in *Near v. Minnesota*,[136] handed down only a few months after the *Brinkley* case, which made it clear that the reach of the first amendment was not confined to restraints imposed prior to the exercise of speech. Thus, the court of appeals' opinion is of doubtful significance today. Nevertheless, on its special facts, the *Brinkley* case should be and is good law today. The mere fact that the court affirmed on unacceptable grounds should not obscure the fact that this was an extraordinary case which warranted the drastic action taken.

Essentially the same considerations which justified the Commission's actions against Brinkley hold true of the *Shuler* case, although perhaps to a less compelling degree. The restraint imposed by the Commission in this latter case seems not materially different in kind or effect from restraints imposed by courts in actions for defamation or for contempt of court. With few exceptions, these latter restraints have been generally accepted as constitutionally permissible. For example, a civil action for an injunction or damages against Shuler for his defamatory utterances would probably have been constitutional at the time when the Commission refused renewal of his license, although some of his remarks against public officials would probably now be protected under the *Sullivan* case doctrine.[137]

One critic of the decision has concluded that the essential facts of the *Shuler* case are indistinguishable from those of *Near v. Minnesota* and that the decision is irreconcilable with *Near*.[138] However, it seems extreme to say that the cases are irreconcilable. *Near* does not proscribe all attempts to curb defamatory utterances. It did not say that it could never be constitutional to refuse to permit a person to operate a communications medium

135. 47 F.2d at 672 (D.C. Cir. 1931).
136. 283 U.S. 697 (1931).
137. New York Times Co. v. Sullivan, 376 U.S. 254 (1964).
138. Sullivan, *Editorials and Controversy: The Broadcaster's Dilemma*, 32 GEO. WASH. L. REV. 719, 758 (1964).

which had repeatedly engaged in defaming persons and obstructing justice. The primary evil of the statute struck down in *Near* was its broad and vague scope. It applied not merely to defamatory utterances but to publication of scandalous matter. Moreover, the statute in effect placed the burden of proof on the newspaper, since it was not necessary to prove the falsity of the defamatory utterances before a court could enjoin them. While the facts as reported in the *Shuler* case do not permit a detailed comparison of all of the facts and circumstances, these evils do not appear to have been present in that case. This is not to say, of course, that Commission actions in this area are not subject to the same constitutional scrutiny as applied in *Near*.

The constitutional implications of the Commission's actions in restraining the use of broadcast facilities for broadcasting lottery and other illegal gambling information are in substance no different from those raised by the Commission's actions in the *Brinkley* case. Once again the action of the Commission is not essentially different from that of other agencies such as the Post Office or the Justice departments. So far as is known, no one has seriously challenged those provisions of the United States Criminal Code which proscribe the dissemination of lottery information or other information which aids and abets gambling[139] as being unconstitutional. The Supreme Court in the *American Broadcasting* case gave no indication that antilottery laws, reasonably construed, pose any serious first amendment problems. The same basic considerations apply to restraints against the broadcast of fraudulent contests such as that involved in the *KWK* case.[140] In restraining fraudulent or deceptive practices, the Commission is doing very little more than is done, for example, by the FTC[141] or the Post Office Department[142] or, in a more restricted area, the SEC[143] or the FDA,[144] and the constitutionality of these

139. In 1961 Congress made it a crime to use wire communications facilities for the transmission of wagering information by persons engaged in the business of betting or wagering. *See* 18 U.S.C. § 1084 (1964).

140. 25 P & F Radio Reg. 577 (1963); *see also* Eleven Ten Broadcasting Corp., 22 P & F Radio Reg. 699 (1962).

141. 15 U.S.C. §§ 52, 53a, 54a (1964); *see, e.g.*, Koch v. FTC, 206 F.2d 311 (6th Cir. 1953).

142. 39 U.S.C. § 4005 (1964); *see, e.g.*, Donaldson v. Read Magazine, Inc., 333 U.S. 178 (1948).

143. *See* § 17 of the Securities Act of 1933, 48 Stat. 84 (1933), *as amended*, 15 U.S.C. § 77q (1964); § 15 of the Securities Exchange Act of 1934, 48 Stat. 895 (1934), *as amended*, 15 U.S.C. § 780 (1964); SEC Rule 10b-5, 7 C.F.R. § 240.10b-5; 3 L. Loss, Securities Regulation 1423-30 (2d ed. 1961).

"antifraud" measures can scarcely be seriously questioned.[145] This is not, however, to suggest that there are *no* first amendment problems here. There are surely some outer constitutional limits on what the Commission can restrain in the name of "fraud." These limits are suggested by the rigged quiz show scandal where relatively harmless deception, done for the chief purpose of enhancing entertainment value, was equated with fraud by both the Commission[146] and Congress.[147] This particular problem in defining fraud is unique to Commission regulation since, outside the field of Commission regulation, civil, criminal, and regulatory actions against fraud and misrepresentation are confined to cases which have long been accepted as actionable at common law or at least those in which it is likely to cause ascertainable public harm. The Commission, however, does not need to look to the traditional definitions of or limitations on actions for fraud. It can, in its view, always proceed under the all-encompassing cloak of "public interest."[148] It is here that the real problem lies.

More troublesome than the potentially broad exercise of power to proscribe "fraud" which is not really fraud is the exercise of power by the Commission to proscribe "offensive" programming. The Commission's action in *Mile High Stations,*[149] although the result was favorable to the licensee, indicates the need for concern over the exercise of sweeping powers to proscribe programming which the Commission finds offensive or improper. *Mile High Stations* did not attract particularly wide attention, probably because the licensee did not contest the constitutional issue but simply pleaded ignorance of the station announcer's offensive remarks. Since the Commission forgave the licensee this one trespass and terminated the show cause proceed-

---

144. 21 U.S.C. §§ 321(k), (m) (1964); *see, e.g.*, Kordel v. United States, 335 U.S. 345 (1948).

145. *See* Donaldson v. Read Magazine, Inc., 333 U.S. 178, 189-92 (1948), where the Court affirmed the power of Congress to control fraudulent practices (here under the postal fraud statutes): "[T]he constitutional guarantees of freedom of speech and freedom of the press [do not] include complete freedom, uncontrollable by Congress, to use the mails for perpetration of swindling schemes." *Id.* at 191.

146. *See* Melody Music, Inc., 6 P & F RADIO REG. 2d 973 (1966).

147. *See* 47 U.S.C. § 509 (1964).

148. It may be that in the narrow area of quiz programs the Commission would be limited by the statutory requirements of § 509 of the Act. However, § 509 would presumably not be interpreted as a limitation on the Commission's power under the Act to take action in the "public interest" against other types of "fraud."

149. 20 P & F RADIO REG. 345 (1960).

ing with a warning, apparently few were concerned with the action of the Commission which raises a serious question of whether restraint of the speech in that case was constitutional.

The Commission's subsequent action in the *Palmetto*[150] case has attracted wider attention. In one sense, however, the action in *Palmetto* is less troublesome than the action in *Mile High Stations.* The Commission's actions in *Palmetto* have been criticized as being, in substance, direct censorship of program content notwithstanding the Commission's unwillingness to rest its decision on the grounds that the program content was vulgar, indecent, and offensive.[151] While this may be, it is important to note that on its facts *Palmetto* is somewhat of an exceptional case in that there were misrepresentations of material fact which could be said to bear on the character of the licensee. Clearly the Commission has some latitude in passing on the character of licensees even though the Commission's findings as to character qualifications may in some instances be connected with or related to program issues.

This is not to say that the Commission would be constitutionally justified in using character qualifications as a dodge to evade the constitutional issues which are confronted when particular programming is called into question.[152] For example, it would clearly be improper and unconstitutional for the Commission to examine a particular program or type of program, decide for itself that the program is bad, and then take action against the licensee, not on the basis of the particular program, but on the basis of the licensee's lack of character qualifications as indicated by the bad programming. *Palmetto* itself, however, does not necessarily indicate that the Commission is disposed to proceed in such a manner, since in *Palmetto* there were misrepresentations to the Commission as to circumstances surrounding the programming.

The fears raised by the Commission's action in *Palmetto* have been at least partly allayed by its subsequent decision in the *Pacifica* case.[153] Perhaps most significant is the reason given by the Commission for refusing to take action against the licensee for broadcasts which had occasioned many public complaints.

---

150. 23 P & F RADIO REG. 483 (1961), *aff'd sub nom.* Robinson v. FCC, 334 F.2d 534 (D.C. Cir.), *cert. denied,* 379 U.S. 843 (1964).

151. Note, *Regulation of Program Content by the FCC,* 77 HARV. L. REV. 701, 712-14 (1964).

152. *See* Brown, *Character and Candor Requirements for FCC Licensees,* 22 LAW & CONTEMP. PROB. 644, 654-55 (1957).

153. 1 P & F RADIO REG. 2d 747 (1964).

> We recognize that, as shown by the complaints here, such provocative programming as here involved may offend some listeners. But this does not mean that those offended have the right, through the Commission's licensing power, to rule such programming off the airway. Were this the case, only the wholly inoffensive, the bland, could gain access to the radio microphone or TV camera. No such drastic curtailment can be countenanced under the Constitution, the Communications Act, or the Commission's policy. . . .[154]

Even if *Pacifica* does not entirely set to rest all fears raised by *Palmetto* and *Mile High Stations,* it does suggest that the Commission intends to proceed cautiously in this area.

While the Commission's authority to impose direct restraints on obscene, defamatory, or other socially harmful programming poses significant first amendment problems, the actions of the Commission to date probably do not warrant grave concern since they have been fairly circumscribed within the ambit of restraints constitutionally justifiable and permitted for nonregulated communications media.

3. *Control of Advertising: A Note in Passing*

Until its recent "fairness doctrine" ruling that stations advertising cigarettes must devote time to expression of the view that smoking is a health hazard,[154a] the Commission's attempts to "regulate" the advertising practices, as such, of broadcast stations had been minimal, limited, and largely ineffectual. Leaving direct supervision and control of deceptive advertising practices to the Federal Trade Commission,[155] the FCC has traditionally confined its concern almost exclusively to excessive advertising, with an occasional foray into advertising of certain products[156]

154. *Id.* at 750.

154a. Letter to WCBS-TV, 9 P & F RADIO REG. 2d 1423, *petition for reconsideration denied,* 11 P & F RADIO REG. 2d 1901 (1967). See text accompanying notes 259-63 *infra.*

155. The Commission has established a "liaison" with the FTC whereby the latter advises the FCC of "questionable advertising" broadcast over radio and television stations. Any determination of deceptive advertising—or perhaps even "questionable" advertising—is taken into account by the FCC in weighing whether the licensee is operating "in the public interest." *Liaison Between FCC and FTC Relating to False and Misleading Radio and TV Advertising,* P & F RADIO REG., Current Service vol. 1, at 11:201 (1957); *see generally Developments in the Law—Deceptive Advertising,* 80 HARV. L. REV. 1005, 1019-27, 1063-1101 (1967).

156. Knickerbocker Broadcasting Co., 2 F.C.C. 76 (1935) (advertising of birth control product). In the case of liquor, the Commission has confined its activities to approval of the self-regulation standards of the NAB codes which prohibit advertising hard liquor, NAB, THE TELEVISION CODE 14 (§ IX, ¶ 5) (11th ed. 1966), and impose other re-

or overly loud commercials.[157] With respect to excessive advertising, although the Commission did at one time propose to adopt fixed rules imposing time limitations similar to those of the NAB Codes, the proposal was abandoned principally as a result of a strong congressional opposition.[158] As a result, the Commission's efforts in this area have been made largely through "scrutiny" at renewal time[159] and the usual panoply of techniques incident to renewal, including admonitory letters to offending licensees[160] and short-term renewals.[161]

It is difficult to know how to assess, from a first amendment viewpoint, the Commission's efforts in the field of advertising controls, since it is doubtful that commercial advertising is "speech" protected by the first amendment.[162] While this reflects a rather circumscribed view of the first amendment, which deserves to receive more critical analysis than it has thus far received, it is beyond the scope of the present article. Even if commercial advertising were within first amendment protection, it is doubtful whether those of the Commission's regulatory ac-

---

strictions on advertising methods, *see Developments in the Law, supra* note 155, at 1155.

157. *See Objectionable Loudness of Commercials*, 5 P & F RADIO REG. 2d 1621-22 (1965), making certain revisions in regulations to control loudness and adopting a "Statement of Policy" concerning loud commercials proscribing certain practices in commercial announcements.

158. *Commercial Advertising Standards*, 1 P & F RADIO REG. 2d 1606 (1964); *see also Commercial Practices of Broadcast Licensees*, 2 P & F RADIO REG. 2d 885 (1964) (dissent of Chairman Henry). Congressional opposition was manifested, among other ways, in a bill introduced at the time to strip the Commission of its power to prescribe rules governing the length and frequency of advertisements. *See id.* at 890. Although the Commission in 1964 declined to adopt fixed standards along the lines of those set by the NAB, it recently did announce a policy of requiring licensees to justify a failure to observe NAB Code limits on commercial time (18 minutes per hour for radio, 16 minutes per hour for television). *See* BROADCASTING MAGAZINE, March 6, 1967, at 36-37.

159. Overcommercialization has on relatively rare occasions occurred in the context of initial applications. *See, e.g.*, Michigan Broadcasting Co., 20 P & F RADIO REG. 667 (1960) (designation for hearing on issues relating to number and length of commercials); Sheffield Broadcasting Co., 21 P & F RADIO REG. 507 (1961) (comparative demerit for overcommercialization); Travelers Broadcasting Serv. Corp., 6 F.C.C. 456 (1938) (application for assignment of license denied).

160. *See* BROADCASTING MAGAZINE, March 6, 1967, at 36-37.

161. Gordon County Broadcasting Co., 24 P & F RADIO REG. 315 (1962); Mississippi Arkansas Broadcasting Co., 22 P & F RADIO REG. 305 (1961).

162. *See* Valentine v. Chrestensen, 316 U.S. 52 (1942). For an excellent treatment of the constitutional question, see *Developments in the Law, supra* note 155, at 1027-38.

tions which impose *direct* restraints on advertising practices involve any serious encroachment on such first amendment protection as is accorded to advertising. Curbs on overcommercialization and on certain techniques of advertising such as overloudness seem generally justifiable in the context of radio and television to the same extent they are in comparable situations outside the field of radio and television.[163] And, of course, curbs on false or fraudulent advertising are clearly constitutional under established authority.[164] The constitutional implications of the *indirect* restraints on cigarette advertising imposed by the Commission's recent fairness doctrine decision will be discussed below.

B. General Program Regulation Through the Licensing Process

1. *General Program Standards*

The Commission's regulation of programming is, of course, by no means confined to direct proscription of undesirable programs. More often the nature of the FCC's action is indirect, tending to influence the broadcast of certain programming by imposition of general standards or through informal oversight of the licensee's programming policies. While the Commission's actions in the area of direct restraint have been relatively circumspect to date, its indirect influence on program policies evidences a greater control of program choice and this poses far greater constitutional problems.

Typically, the Commission attempts to achieve what it euphemistically refers to as "program balance" and "programming in the public interest." The first comprehensive statement of Commission policy on programming balance and on the responsibility of broadcasters to program in the public interest was the Commission's famous *Blue Book*:

> In issuing and in renewing the licenses of broadcast stations the Commission proposes to give particular consideration to four program service factors relevant to the public interest. . . . (1) the carrying of sustaining programs, including network sustaining programs, with particular reference to the retention by licensees of a proper discretion and responsibility for maintaining a well-balanced program structure; (2) the carrying of local live programs; (3) the carrying of programs devoted to the discussion of public issues; and (4) the elimination of advertising excesses.[165]

---

163. *Cf.* Kovacs v. Cooper, 336 U.S. 77 (1949).

164. Donaldson v. Read Magazine, Inc., 333 U.S. 178 (1948); Regina Corp. v. FTC, 322 F.2d 765, 770 (3d Cir. 1963).

165. FCC, Public Service Responsibility of Broadcast Licensees 55 (1946). For an excellent discussion of the background of the *Blue*

Although its policies were invoked in several cases to question renewal applications not meeting the announced standards,[166] the *Blue Book*, as such, never assumed the permanent substantial importance that it was undoubtedly intended to have. Today it is all but forgotten as anything more than an historical source of Commission policy, and is never directly relied on.

However, the basic policies outlined in the *Blue Book* have not been abandoned. The same "program service factors" continue to occupy the Commission's attention although the Commission, learning from its experience with the *Blue Book*, has attempted to avoid stating its standards in terms of absolute demands. Basically the same emphasis on "balanced programming," but with somewhat less emphasis on "sustaining" versus "commercial" programs and the same emphasis on public service programming are inherent in the Commission's "modern" policy statement,[167] and in its current practices. Neither its concern for "local live" programming[168] nor its concern over excessive advertising[169] has in any way abated.

Book, see L. WHITE, THE AMERICAN RADIO 182-99 (Comm'n on Freedom of the Press ed. 1947); *see also* 2 Z. CHAFEE, GOVERNMENT AND MASS COMMUNICATIONS 689-94 (Comm'n on Freedom of the Press ed. 1947). The *Blue Book* evoked strong condemnation from the broadcast industry. Illustrative is the statement of the Chairman of CBS who denounced it as "government program-censorship" and "the most direct threat yet made by government to interfere with programming." Paley, "Radio and Its Critics," Address to NAB, October 22, 1946, *quoted in* 2 Z. CHAFEE, *supra* at 636.

Strong criticism was also voiced from outside the industry, both on grounds of regulatory wisdom as well as doubtful constitutionality. *See* L. WHITE, *supra* at 193-99, 229-30. Without getting into the question of wisdom, Chafee did not view the *Blue Book* as posing a serious first amendment problem. 2 Z. CHAFEE, *supra* at 637-38.

166. The Community Broadcasting Co., 12 F.C.C. 85 (1947); Howard W. Davis, 12 F.C.C. 91 (1947); Eugene Roth, 12 F.C.C. 102 (1947).

167. *Statement of Policy on Programming*, 20 P & F RADIO REG. 1901 (1960). On program balance and service, the following oft-quoted statement is generally the point of departure for the Commission:

> The major elements usually necessary to meet the public interest, needs and desires of the community in which the station is located as developed by the industry, and recognized by the Commission, have included: (1) Opportunity for Local Self-Expression, (2) The Development and Use of Local Talent, (3) Programs for Children, (4) Religious Programs, (5) Educational Programs, (6) Public Affairs Programs, (7) Editorializing by Licensees, (8) Political Broadcasts, (9) Agricultural Programs, (10) News Programs, (11) Weather and Market Reports, (12) Sports Programs, (13) Service to Minority Groups, (14) Entertainment Programming.

Id. at 1913.

168. *See* note 175 *infra* and accompanying text.

169. *See* notes 155-161 *supra* and accompanying text.

Program balance and programming in the public interest are determined by the Commission principally on the basis of an analysis of past or proposed programming in terms of categories established by the Commission as representative of all of the major different types, and on the basis of an assessment of whether the programs meet the needs, tastes, and interests of the station's service area. Of critical significance in the latter regard is the applicant's efforts to ascertain those needs, tastes, or interests.

Part IV, "Statement of Program Service," of the broadcast applications required for new stations, major changes in facilities, transfer of control, and assignment or renewal of license, is the heart of the Commission's direct regulatory oversight of programming. A detailed statement as to the amount and percentage of *proposed* programming is required and, in cases of renewal or assignment and transfer, a detailed statement supported by station program logs showing the *past* programming in each of the specified program categories is mandatory.[170]

The particular classifications used by the Commission have long been widely criticized in the industry as being arbitrary, vague, meaningless, needlessly detailed, and burdensome to the station. Each station is required (a) to maintain detailed logs in which each of the programs is carefully recorded in one of the categories, and (b) to analyze the logs at renewal time to obtain the information required in the renewal application. Even the Commission has recognized the validity of the criticism directed at the arbitrariness and vagueness of the categories. In 1965 it revised the AM-FM program classifications, and in 1966 it adopted similar changes for television.[171] The validity of the other criticisms has not been recognized. Indeed, the new forms are, if anything, more detailed and more burdensome. The Commission's expanding concern with the nature of the program service presented and its apparent use of program classification as a means of influencing stations to provide programming of a

---

170. The Commission's recently revised programming forms for AM, FM, and television prescribe the following primary categories of programming: agricultural, entertainment, news, public affairs, religious, instructional, sports, and others. Three secondary categories are established: editorials, political programs, and educational institution programs. Under this revised procedure, a station maintains logs classifying each program into the above categories but is required to show overall amounts of programming only in the following: news, public affairs, and all other programs exclusive of entertainment and sports.

171. *AM-FM Program Forms*, 5 P & F RADIO REG. 2d 1773 (1965); *Television Program Forms*, 8 P & F RADIO REG. 2d 1512 (1966).

certain type have, however, raised even more troublesome questions.

While the effort of a broadcast station applicant to seek out community interests has long been one of the criteria taken into account in comparative hearings,[172] it did not play a major role in the Commission's consideration of individual applicants until the 1961 *Suburban Broadcasters* decision.[173] Since that time, however, the Commission has given increased attention to the efforts made by an applicant or licensee to become familiar with and to demonstrate how its programming will serve the service area's tastes, needs, and interests.[174] This policy, while theoretically applicable to all programming, has in recent years been reflected principally as a concern for increased local live programming, especially during "prime time" hours.[175]

2. *Licensing New Facilities: Single Applicant*

Despite constant protests by the Commission that it is not concerned with the content of particular programs or that it does not require a station to broadcast a certain amount of any type of programming, its actions belie these disclaimers. This is most clearly indicated in the Commission's practice of pressing all applicants onto the procrustean bed of "acceptable" program categories.

A seeming exception to this attitude might be seen in the fact that the Commission has been willing to allow AM and FM stations to engage in specialized programming in one or a few of the standard program categories, on a showing that overall pro-

---

172. Under the so-called "planning and preparation" criteria. *E.g.*, WHDH, Inc., 13 P & F RADIO REG. 507, 555-59, 576-77 (1957), *remanded on other grounds sub nom.* Massachusetts Bay Telecasters, Inc. v. FCC, 261 F.2d 55 (D.C. Cir. 1958).

173. 20 P & F RADIO REG. 951 (1961), *aff'd sub nom.* Henry v. FCC, 302 F.2d 191 (D.C. Cir.), *cert. denied,* 371 U.S. 821 (1962). The decision was purportedly based on the comprehensive program policy announced a year earlier in its *Statement of Policy on Programming,* 20 P & F RADIO REG. 1901 (1960), which emphasized the preeminent importance of a "diligent, positive and continuing effort [by the licensee] to discover and fulfill the tastes, needs and desires of the service area."

174. *E.g.*, Washington Broadcasting Co., 5 P & F RADIO REG. 2d 653 (1965) (assignment of license); Chapman Radio & Television Co., 4 P & F RADIO REG. 2d 532 (1965) (application for new facilities); WCSC, Inc., 1 P & F RADIO REG. 2d 619 (1964) (dissent to renewal without hearing).

175. *See, e.g.*, Address by Commissioner Ford, Virginia Association of Broadcasters, June 20, 1963, reprinted in FCC Release No. 37,118; *Omaha Local Television Programming Inquiry,* 1 P & F RADIO REG. 2d 1901 (1963); WCSC, Inc., 1 P & F RADIO REG. 2d 619 (1964) (dissent).

gram balance is provided by complementary program schedules.[176] However, the exception only proves the rule. Absent very special circumstances, the broadcaster who fails to provide a respectable percentage of programming in the categories which the Commission has selected as representative of balanced programming in the public interest does so, or, what is substantially the same, reasonably believes that he does so, at his peril.

The Commission's decision in *Lee Roy McCourry*[177] illustrates this. In *McCourry* the applicant applied for a license for a new UHF television station, proposing a specialized programming format comprised of seventy per cent entertainment and thirty per cent educational programs. Based principally[178] on the applicant's failure to offer any special justification for not providing for religious, agricultural, news, discussion, or similar programming,[179] the Commission set the application down for hearing on the issues, *inter alia,* of whether the applicant had investigated community needs and whether the applicant's specialized format would meet these needs. The immediate effect of the Commission's action was simply to require McCourry to justify his programming. However, as noted by the dissent, this was virtually tantamount to denial of the application in this case or was, in any event, a heavy sanction for failing to conform to the Commission's idea of a proper pattern of programming.[180]

The *McCourry* case is certainly no *cause celebre.* Despite a strong dissent, the case probably cannot be regarded as a significant departure from the Commission's longstanding insistence on the ascertainment of community needs and on basic conformity to a balanced program format in the context of comparative hearings and renewal proceedings.

3. *Licensing New Facilities: The Comparative Hearing*

The Commission's procedure for determining which of two

176. *See, e.g.,* Herbert Muschel, 23 P & F RADIO REG. 1059 (1962). At least a theoretical distinction should be drawn between specialized programming in this sense and programming oriented towards the special needs of a minority group in the station's service area which may still be accomplished by adherence to a "balanced" program schedule with programs in each of the various categories. The Commission has also approved this type of "special audience" programming. *See* Voice of Charlotte Broadcasting, 6 P & F RADIO REG. 2d 355 (1965).

177. 2 P & F RADIO REG. 895 (1964).

178. In addition to the programming issue, issues as to adequacy of staffing, financial qualifications, and main studio location were involved. *Id.* at 897.

179. *Id.* at 896.

180. *Id.* at 901-02.

or more applicants for the same facility[181] is by comparison more deserving of a broadcast permit has long been held up by critics as a classic example of the administrative process at its worst.[182] Inadequately guided by Commission procedures and standards, the prodigious efforts by the parties to compile a complete and comparatively superior record produce little more than staggering records.[183]

It is not the purpose of this Article, however, to criticize the comparative hearing process or the comparative criteria. The concern here is only with those aspects of the comparative hearing process which relate to program regulation and its constitutional implications.

The Commission's focus on an applicant's proposed programming in a comparative hearing is not essentially different from its examination of the program proposals of a noncomparative single applicant. The Commission typically evaluates comparative applicants on the basis of their efforts to survey and ascertain community needs and interests and on the basis of a quanti-

---

181. The term "comparative hearing" is often used, inaccurately, to designate all hearings on mutually inconsistent applications. There are significant differences, however, between the scope of a true comparative hearing involving two or more applicants for the *same* frequency in the *same* location and a hearing on mutually inconsistent applications for stations in different communities which propose the mutually incompatible use of co-channel or adjacent channel frequencies —generally referred to as a "307(b) hearing." The comparative hearing is focused on the so-called "standard comparative issue," a broad issue encompassing comparisons between *applicants* on numerous criteria. *See* note 187 *infra.* However, the more limited 307(b) hearing is focused on a comparison of the service needs of the respective communities and considerations of relative efficiency in the utilization of frequencies. *See, e.g.*, Bible Institute of Los Angeles, Inc., 24 P & F RADIO REG. 205 (1962). Thus, the 307(b) hearing does not contemplate a comparison of the respective proposed programming or program-related operations (such as staffing, etc.), although under certain circumstances programming issues may be added. *See, e.g.*, Saul M. Miller, 24 P & F RADIO REG. 550 (1962); Granite City Broadcasting Co., 18 P & F RADIO REG. 852 (1959).

182. *E.g.*, W. JONES, LICENSING OF MAJOR BROADCAST FACILITIES BY THE FEDERAL COMMUNICATIONS COMMISSION, REPORT TO THE ADMINISTRATIVE CONFERENCE OF THE UNITED STATES, COMMITTEE ON LICENSES AND AUTHORIZATIONS 198-204 (1962); Friendly, *The Federal Administrative Agencies: The Need For Better Definition of Standards*, 75 HARV. L. REV. 1055, 1065-72 (1962); Schwartz, *Comparative Television and the Chancellor's Foot*, 47 GEO. L.J. 655 (1959).

183. WHDH, Inc., FCC 66 D-47, at 264 (1966). Some idea of the magnitude of the hearing in *WHDH* (resulting from the reopening of a decision based on earlier hearings held in 1954-1955!) may be gleaned from the size of the examiner's opinion, 252 pages of which are devoted to findings of fact alone.

tative evaluation of each applicant's program balance based on the respective percentages of time to be devoted the various program types defined by the Commission.[184] Where the applicants each show respectable balance in the various categories,[185] the Commission is quick to deny any judgment of *qualitative* difference between particular programs.[186]

It is true, however, that the comparative hearing has a somewhat different impact on program discretion than does the hearing in a noncomparative situation. Unlike the *McCourry* type of situation, for example, there is no occasion here for setting an application for hearing on the basis of insufficient balance or other assumed defects in proposed programming, since mutually inconsistent applications must go to hearing anyway. Every application set for a comparative hearing is set for a hearing on the standard comparative issue.[187]

---

184. *See, e.g.*, Central Coast Television, 1 P & F RADIO REG. 2d 237, 247 (1963); Jefferson Standard Broadcasting Co., 24 P & F RADIO REG. 319, 331-32 (1962); Florida Gulfccast Broadcasters, Inc., 23 P & F RADIO REG. 1, 8 (1962).

185. *E.g.*, *Policy Statement on Comparative Broadcast Hearings*, 5 P & F RADIO REG. 2d 1901 (1965); Sunbeam Television Corp., 5 P & F RADIO REG. 2d 85, 87 (1965); Florida Gulfcoast Broadcasters, 23 P & F RADIO REG. 1, 8 (1962).

186. *E.g.*, Jefferson Standard Broadcasting Co., 24 P & F RADIO REG. 319, 332 (1962). The Commission's eschewing of "qualitative" comparisons is criticized in Irion, *FCC Criteria for Evaluating Competing Applicants*, 43 MINN. L. REV. 479, 492-94 (1959). It is perhaps significant that Irion, one of the most highly regarded FCC hearing examiners, evidently sees no major first amendment problem involved in the evaluation of the quality of particular programming and program proposals.

187. The "standard comparative issue" is an exceedingly broad statement of the key issue in *comparative* hearings (not in "307(b) hearings"). The formulation of the standard comparative issue is as follows:

> To determine on a comparative basis which of the operations proposed in the above-entitled applications would best serve the public interest, convenience, and necessity in light of the record made with respect to the significant differences between the applicants as to:
>
> (a) The background and experience of each of the above-named applicants having a bearing on its ability to own and operate the proposed television station.
>
> (b) The proposals of each of the above-named applicants with respect to the management and operation of the proposed station.
>
> (c) The programming service proposed in each of the above-entitled applications.

WHDH, Inc., 13 P & F RADIO REG. 507, 515 (1957).

Within this broad formulation, criteria have crystallized which are supposed to be relevant in deciding among applicants (although many of these criteria are petty and not conceivably important and several are mutually contradictory). Prior to the Commission's 1965 *Policy*

On the other hand, the Commission may add other issues directed to specific questionable aspects of a party's application.[188] An applicant proposing what the Commission regards as questionable program policies may have the application set for a hearing on the so-called "Suburban issue," theoretically designed to investigate what efforts the applicant has made to determine and satisfy the needs and interests of its proposed service area. Although the standard comparative issue substantially includes this investigation, the significance of the additional "Suburban issue" is that it is a potentially disqualifying issue unrelated to the *comparative* merits of the applicants. If one applicant buys out or merges with competing applicants, the standard comparative issue becomes moot, but the disqualifying issue does not.[189] In such a case, the Commission will insist on investigating whether the remaining applicant has met its burden on the disqualifying issues.

4. *Renewal of License: In Terrorem Control*

The discussion above focused on the method by which the Commission controls programming by setting standards to which a broadcast applicant must conform if he is to succeed in obtaining a license. The process of license renewal every three years adds a new dimension to this control. The renewal process is the primary tool used by the Commission to enforce continuing compliance with the demands initially made on an applicant. Without this instrument it would be difficult if not impossible to effect any real control of programming operations. If a licensee fails to adhere to the standards of its promised perform-

Statement on Comparative Broadcast Hearings, the accepted criteria were: (1) local residence; (2) civic participation; (3) diversification of occupations of principals; (4) experience; (5) integration of ownership with management; (6) past broadcast record; (7) planning and preparation; (8) program policies; (9) program proposals; (10) studio and equipment; (11) staff; (12) diversification of ownership of mass communications media. WHDH, Inc., *supra* at 566-85. *See generally*, Irion, *FCC Criteria for Evaluating Competing Applicants*, 43 MINN. L. REV. 479 (1959). The 1965 *Policy Statement* retains most of these criteria but purports to establish some degree of priority among them and explain their proper implementation. Whether the 1965 *Policy Statement* has really clarified or resolved the contradictions and erased any of the nonsense that has characterized the interpretation and implementation of these criteria remains to be seen.

188. These may be added on the Commission's own motion or by motion of the parties to enlarge issues. *See, e.g.*, Springfield Telecasting Co., 3 P & F RADIO REG. 2d 727 (1964).

189. *See, e.g.*, Tri-Cities Broadcasting Co., 6 P & F RADIO REG. 2d 1, 2 (1965).

ance, the Commission may, of course, revoke the license. Such a procedure is, however, too cumbersome to be practical. A license revocation proceeding entails initiation by the Commission of a formal hearing in which the Commission must bear the burden of proof of noncompliance with the law or unsatisfactory performance by the licensee.[190] The procedural burdens of a revocation proceeding would impede and deter Commission enforcement, and would eliminate any real *in terrorem* effect from the threat of revocation.

The effectiveness of the renewal process in influencing a licensee's operations, including his program operations, arises from two facts. First, the *licensee* has the burden of coming forth, in a formal application, to show compliance with Commission standards and fulfillment of prior promises;[191] second, this process is routine and relatively frequent, thereby eliminating any doubt that the Commission will scrutinize the actual performance of the station in relation to the performance promised.

The manner in which the renewal process is carried out by the Commission makes it far more than merely a periodic inspection. Rather the renewal process has become the primary method through which the Commission exercises day-by-day control over virtually all broadcast operations, and particularly over program practices and program operations. Thus, the fact that the licensee must go through the trial and prove himself every three years is in a very real sense a "Sword of Damocles" over the broadcaster's head. If the sword does not often fall, neither is it ever lifted and the *in terrorem* effect of the sword's presence enables the Commission to exercise far-reaching powers of control over the licensee's operations.

It is this *in terrorem* aspect of periodic renewal which one former FCC Commissioner labeled "regulation by the lifted eyebrow,"[192] a label which has since gained considerable currency in the field of administrative regulation. A letter to the station from the Commission or even a telephone call to the station's Washington attorney from the Commission's staff indicating the Commission's "concern" over a particular practice of the licensee and asking for the licensee's justification will generally be all

190. *See* 48 Stat. 1086 (1934), *as amended*, 47 U.S.C. § 312(c) (1964).

191. In the event the application is set down for hearing, the licensee has the burden of proof. *E.g.*, Office of Communication of the United Church of Christ v. FCC, 359 F.2d 994 (D.C. Cir. 1966).

192. Commissioner Doerfer dissenting in Miami Broadcasting Co. (WQAM), 14 P & F RADIO REG. 125, 128 (1956).

that is necessary to bring the licensee around to the Commission's way of thinking. If not cultivated, the technique is at least used to great advantage by the Commission, which almost invariably makes a point of informing the licensee that its inquiry and the licensee's response will be associated with the licensee's file and given "due consideration" upon his next application for renewal.

If a Commission inquiry or expression of concern over a licensee's practices can be expected to have an influential effect on the licensee, the effect is even greater when the Commission makes such inquiry at renewal time or notifies the licensee that it is deferring action on pending renewal applications until it has received answers to its questions. An example is the Commission's action in *Local Live Programming of Television Stations*[193] where the Commission sent letters to five stations deferring renewal applications because of an inadequate showing of local live programming in prime time and requesting information as to local live programming presentations and plans and efforts to ascertain community needs. In spite of the Commission's request for further information, it is extremely doubtful whether the Commission really expected to receive any information which would add meaningfully to what the licensee had already reported. What the Commission seeks in such cases is not information but assurance that future operations will conform to Commission standards; and it would be incredible if the experienced broadcaster or his Washington counsel would mistake the Commission's handwriting on the wall.[194]

For the more recalcitrant, there are stronger methods short of revocation. One is the frequently employed short-term re-

---

193. 25 P & F RADIO REG. 482 (1963).

194. *Cf.* Pierson, *The Need for Modification of Section 326*, 18 FED. COM. B.J. 15, 19-20 (1963):

> The lawyer [advising his client as to type of program] has a number of guides. First, in his day-to-day dealings with the Commission and its staff, he learns of their attitudes toward various kinds of proposals. He knows that certain program proposals are accepted and favorably processed with alacrity. Other program proposals create problems not only of getting expeditious action but of getting favorable action. On occasion his client is almost directly threatened with costly litigation unless program proposals are changed. In addition, Commission decisions, statements of policy and the public statements of its members afford insight into Commission attitudes toward various types of programming. With these as guides, the lawyer can quite unerringly outline to his client the programs that the Commission favors and disfavors . . . . To deny that this constraint exists is to indulge pure myth. To say that . . . an applicant proposes or 'promises' programs on the basis of his independent judgment of the needs and wants of his area compounds the myth.

newal (generally for one year) during which time the licensee is made aware that he is "on probation."[195]

The practice of informal control over or influence on individual licensee practices is also followed on an industry-wide basis through statements of Commission concern over particular practices or announcements of proposed action.[196] This is enhanced by speeches of individual commissioners. Former Chairman Minow's famous "Wasteland Speech" is a classic example.[197] However, less sweeping and dramatic speeches in which some comment is made on program policies have become almost a matter of routine. While some of these speeches are inconsequential, there can be no doubt that many are valuable as a source of at least one commissioner's thinking on a given subject.

5. *First Amendment Implications*

The Commission's insistence on the licensee's presenting "balanced" programming, although done in the name of promoting diversity, has had largely the opposite effect. Notwithstanding repeated criticism by various commissioners of the undeniable sameness of programming among broadcasters, the Commission's own policies do little to encourage diversity or originality either in the style or content of individual programs or in the overall format of a station's program operations. Indeed, its policies have, if anything, added to the inherent tendency of broadcasters to conform to safe, established patterns of operation and programming.

Insistence by the Commission that the licensee maintain respectable percentages of its total programming in the various program categories is one example of such a policy. Adherence to these categories by the licensee does not necessarily fix the content of specific programs within each category. The un-

---

195. *See, e.g.*, Lamar Life Broadcasting Co., 5 P & F RADIO REG. 2d 205 (1965) (one year renewal because of questionable "fairness" in presenting views on controversial public issues); Loyola Univ., 24 P & F RADIO REG. 766 (1962) (one year renewal because of significant deviations from previous program promises).

196. *See, e.g.*, 6 TELEVISION DIGEST 2-3 (1966) (press report that staff "reportedly" urges Commission to send letters to ten AM stations inquiring as to their failure to carry political broadcasts); 6 TELEVISION DIGEST 2 (1966) (report of staff proposing to send letters to nineteen AM stations which proposed to devote less than 5% of their time to "public affairs" and "other," *i.e.*, agricultural, religious, and similar nonentertainment categories programming).

197. Address to the 39th Annual Convention of the National Association of Broadcasters, May 9, 1961.

mistakable result of prescribing categories in which all licensees are expected to present some programming is, however, sameness of program formats among licensees. Following the Commission's guidelines, for example, *each* station will generally present a religious discussion program or coverage of a church service at least one Sunday a month; a regularly scheduled farm news or discussion program, no matter how urban the area; and, to satisfy the ambiguous category of "talks," a "homemaker" show at least once a week. There emerges a pattern of sameness in conformity with safe and acceptable standards bearing the FCC seal of approval. While the licensee may decide the particular content of programs within each accepted category, he must maintain a balance among the accepted categories. He deviates at his peril as is illustrated by the *McCourry*[198] case where the applicant was required to justify, in a formal hearing, his deviation from the Commission's standard of "balance" because of his failure to conform to the pattern of programming in each of the accepted categories.

Commissioner Cox, one of the most vigorous and articulate defenders of the Commission's programming policy, has attempted to justify the Commission's action in *McCourry* on the ground that the Commission has the responsibility to ensure that licensees ascertain and serve the needs and interests of their service areas, and the failure of the applicant in *McCourry* to justify its failure to show "balanced" programming fully warranted and indeed required the Commission to hold a hearing to determine whether the applicant would serve the public interest.[199] This simply begs the question.

Even under the most expansive interpretation of the first amendment, the Commission is not forbidden to insist that an applicant show that it has made an effort to ascertain the general needs and interests of the community to be served and that its operations will serve those needs and interests. Moreover, it does not seem either unconstitutional or unreasonable for the Commission to require that, in attempting to ascertain and serve the needs of the community, the *licensee* must apply his own judgment, not that of the network or some other program supplier. *Simmons v. FCC*[200] illustrates this problem. There the Commission denied an application on the ground that a proposal

198. 2 P & F RADIO REG. 2d 895 (1964).

199. Cox, *The FCC, the Constitution and Religious Broadcast Programming*, 34 GEO. WASH. L. REV. 196, 207 (1965).

200. 169 F.2d 670 (D.C. Cir. 1948); *cf.* Churchill Tabernacle v. FCC, 160 F.2d 244 (D.C. Cir. 1947).

to broadcast the complete, unaltered CBS network schedule would be an abdication of licensee responsibility and would not serve the public interest. In affirming, the court held that there was no censorship involved.[201]

But it is one thing to require an applicant or licensee to demonstrate that it has made, by *itself*, a good faith, reasonable effort to ascertain and serve the needs of the public; it is quite another for the Commission to set forth a catalogue of the types of programs which it considers the public interest to require, and then to require that an applicant or licensee conform its programming to these standards unless it can offer compelling reasons for a varying format. Notwithstanding the fact that this action was purported to be merely an inquiry into whether McCourry had really investigated the needs of his prospective service area and whether his programming would serve those needs, no one familiar with FCC practice could doubt that the action was intended to influence McCourry—and other future applicants who could be counted on to take due note of the Commission's actions—to modify the program format to conform with the Commission's concept of balanced programming.

That the threat of an agency hearing is in itself, regardless of potential outcome, an effective method of imposing program standards is even more persuasively demonstrated in cases involving applications for renewal of existing licenses. The threat of a hearing on renewal is virtually certain to induce the licensee to conform to the established standards of balanced programming, except in those cases where, for good cause shown, the Commission has approved specialized programming.

The conformity principle can also be seen at work in the comparative hearing process. Here, however, the effect of an evaluation of the applicants' respective program proposals is not immediately apparent. Although the program proposals, formats, and policies of the applicants are among the criteria for choosing between them, the Commission never gives express decisional importance to the superiority of one applicant's program proposals, even in "quantitative" terms. Indeed, it is unusual to find a decision in which the Commission even awards a preference to one applicant in the area of programming. Generally, any preferences granted in the area of programming are expressed as preferences for a superior showing as to an applicant's efforts to survey and ascertain community needs. On the basis

201. 169 F.2d at 672.

of the Commission's decisions, then, it might appear that there is no problem of restraint, since the Commission purports to give so little attention to a comparative evaluation of programming proposals. But appearances are deceptive, as are the Commission's published decisions.

In many, if not most cases, no preference could be granted on the basis of program proposals since there is no discernible difference of substance between them. This sameness is largely attributable to similar network program fare, particularly where both propose an affiliation with the same network. To some extent, sameness of programming is also attributable to the fact that radio and television stations, like other commercial enterprises, generally strive to meet the widest possible market. To a significant degree, however, the sameness is also attributable to the Commission's own efforts to supervise programming operations. The trend to conformity and sameness is inherent in the Commission's insistence on adherence to "balance," defined as devoting respectable percentages of program time to each of the categories prescribed by the Commission. The trend to conformity and sameness is particularly encouraged by the comparative hearing process itself.[202]

It takes relatively little imagination on the part of an applicant competing for a license to realize that he must develop a format of balanced programming which will pass muster under the Commission's examination. It takes even less imagination, talent, or creativity to put such a format into effect. It is small wonder then that most applicants, with the help of Washington counsel, develop program proposals which will pass the balance test and which will compare, neither more nor less favorably, with any other applicant's balanced proposals.[203] The Commission encourages this practice. If some applicant gets carried away with the idea of something special in the way of programming, the Commission is likely to discount his proposals as impractical and unlikely to be effectuated.[204]

In defense of the Commission's use of program types, Commissioner Cox has suggested that the program categories are not the Commission's creation but that they reflect the basic program interests of the public, as reported by broadcasters be-

202. *See* Pierson, *The Need for Modification of Section 326*, 18 FED. COM. B.J. 15, 19-21 (1963).
203. *Id.*
204. *See, e.g.*, Veterans Broadcasting Co., 4 P & F RADIO REG. 2d 375 (1965).

fore the time when such categories were established. According to this argument, the categories were developed simply for convenience to broadcasters in reporting the programming which they presented and for ease of processing applications by the Commission.[205] The thrust of this argument is that the use of specified program categories is simply a convenient method of getting information.

It may be that the mere requirement that a licensee report his programming in the various categories, as an incident to recordkeeping activities by the Commission does not raise any significant first amendment problem. But Commissioner Cox's suggestion that the licensee's report of programming is purely a recordkeeping exercise seems to be less than a candid explanation of the purpose of the report and the use to which it is put, and as the Supreme Court has on more than one occasion emphasized, the fact that an inquiry can be justified as merely routine cannot be accepted as a cloak which shields such activity from constitutional objection if the character of the inquiry, or the manner and circumstances in which it is done, accomplish a restraint on free speech.[206]

Perhaps more basically troublesome than the encouragement of conformity is the fact that it is impossible to tell whether the Commission is in fact making value judgments about programming while its published opinions deny that it is doing so. One can scarcely accept the gratuitous and self-serving statements made by the Commission in its opinions that it has not recognized or given any decisive significance to any difference between program proposals. Since the Commission is not wholly oblivious to the constitutional implications of the close supervision of programming, it is not surprising that the opinions, written to be as "appeal-proof" as possible, attempt to show an abundance of caution and restraint in this area.

It is sometimes suggested that, whatever the constitutional limits on direct program regulation or even on indirect program influence, the Commission has full constitutional authority to consider and pass judgment on the programming of two or more applicants in a comparative hearing, as a basis for choosing between them. Such a distinction between comparative program

---

205. Cox, *supra* note 199, at 199-201.

206. *See, e.g.*, Talley v. California, 362 U.S. 60 (1960); Bates v. Little Rock, 361 U.S. 516 (1960); NAACP v. Alabama, 357 U.S. 449 (1958); *cf.* Brown, *Character and Candor Requirements for FCC Licensees*, 22 LAW & CONTEMP. PROB. 644, 654-55 (1957).

evaluation and other forms of program regulation is suggested by two of the leading cases on FCC regulatory authority in the field of programming, *Bay State Beacon, Inc. v. FCC*[207] and *Johnston Broadcasting Company v. FCC.*[208] In *Bay State* the court held it was not a violation of the first amendment or section 326[209] for the Commission to consider, as a factor in selecting one comparative applicant over another, a quantitative analysis of the amount of time to be devoted by the respective applicants to commercial vis-a-vis noncommercial programs. The court reasoned that the program analysis merely indicated how the applicant would perform in the public interest and that, if the Commission could not make such an inquiry as to programming, it would be unable to perform its duty to ensure that the public interest, convenience, and necessity were being served. The court went on to state that if denial of a license to the unsuccessful applicant on the basis of inferior program proposals violated the first amendment, "then every unsuccessful applicant would have the right of free speech throttled and abridged."[210] In *Johnston* the court again approved the Commission's preference for one comparative applicant over another on the basis of program proposals. The court reasoned

> It is true that the Commission cannot choose on the basis of political, economic or social views of an applicant. But in a comparative consideration, it is well recognized that comparative service to the listening public, is the vital element and programs are the essence of that service. So, while the Commission cannot prescribe any type of program (except for prohibition against obscenity, profanity, etc.), it can make a comparison on the basis of public interest and, therefore, of public service.[211]

Insofar as the courts in *Bay State* and *Johnston* intended to distinguish between evaluation of programming in the context of comparative hearings and other forms of direct or indirect program supervision by the Commission, the reasoning is something less than clear. Implicit in the suggested distinction is the assumption that because there must be *some* basis for selection between applicants it is proper, indeed necessary, to weigh the comparative merits of the applicant's respective program proposals.

As to any supposed *necessity* for choosing between applicants on the basis of program proposals, it is sufficient first to

207. 171 F.2d 826 (D.C. Cir. 1948).
208. 175 F.2d 351 (D.C. Cir. 1949).
209. 47 U.S.C. § 326 (1948).
210. 171 F.2d 826, 827 (D.C. Cir. 1948).
211. 175 F.2d 351, 359 (D.C. Cir. 1949).

note the numerous other bases for comparative evaluation which in no way involve judgments as to programming. There is scarcely any inherent necessity in basing a selection on an evaluation of program proposals. Second, the convenience or even necessity of evaluating program proposals to fulfill the *statutory* mandate of effecting the public interest, convenience, and necessity can scarcely warrant an intrusion into constitutionally prohibited areas. In the final analysis there is no basis whatsoever for singling out the comparative hearing process as some special justification for control of program choice. The Commission's program regulation policies are just as questionable in this area as in a noncomparative hearing context.

The ultimate ostensible aim of the Commission's emphasis on program balance and its general insistence on programming in all of the key program categories is the advancement of diversity of viewpoints, ideas, and entertainment. This same general aim is the underlying rationale for regulation of more direct impact and more far-reaching implications: regulation of the broadcasting of political and controversial public issues. It is here that the constitutional problems of the Commission's program regulation are brought most sharply into focus.

C. Regulation of Political Broadcasts and Controversial Public Issues Programming

Few areas of broadcast regulation have been as controversial as the regulation of political broadcasts and controversial public issues programming. Acting under the equal time requirements of section 315 of the Communications Act of 1934 and pursuant to its so-called "fairness doctrine," the Commission has come under increasingly heavy criticism from the industry, Congress, and even some of its own members because of its interference with broadcasters' discretion and responsibility in this area of programming.[212] Although political broadcasts and controversial public issues programming may appear in many respects to pose but a single regulatory problem, they in fact pose two distinct, though related, problems with distinct, and somewhat different, constitutional implications.

212. *See, e.g., Hearings on Equal Time Before the Subcomm. on Communications of the Senate Comm. on Commerce*, 88th Cong., 1st Sess., ser. 29 (1963); *Hearings on Political Broadcasting before the Communications Subcomm. of the Senate Comm. on Interstate and Foreign Commerce*, 86th Cong., 1st Sess. (1959); *see also* Dean, *Political Broadcasting: The Communications Act of 1934 Reviewed*, 20 Fed. Com. B.J. 16, 38-43 (1966).

1. Equal Time

Section 315 of the Communications Act of 1934 provides:

> (a) If any licensee shall permit any person who is a legally qualified candidate for any public office to use a broadcasting station, he shall afford equal opportunities to all other such candidates for that office in the use of such broadcasting station . . . .
>
> (b) The charges made for the use of any broadcasting station for any of the purposes set forth in this section shall not exceed the charges made for comparable use of such station for other purposes.
>
> (c) The Commission shall prescribe appropriate rules and regulations to carry out the provisions of this section.[213]

An exception from the equal time requirement is provided for appearances by candidates on bona fide news, interview, or documentary programs, so long as the licensee continues "to operate in the public interest and to afford reasonable opportunity for the discussion of conflicting views on issues of public importance."[214]

The concept of equal time in itself is essentially a simple one, and in most cases its requirements are relatively clear and direct.[215] The Commission's key rulings on the principal problems of scope and interpretation are summarized in its *Equal Time Primer*[216] and have been quite fully explored by others.[217] It is, therefore, sufficient here merely to sketch the outline of the equal time requirements. The equal time requirements are much more limited than is popularly supposed. First of all, the duty to provide equal opportunity arises only when a legally qualified,[218] bona fide candidate *himself*[219] makes an appearance on the station either live or on tape for any purpose[220] except

---

213. 48 Stat. 1088 (1934), *as amended*, 47 U.S.C. § 315 (1964).

214. 48 Stat. 1088 (1934), *as amended*, 47 U.S.C. § 315(a)(4) (1964).

215. Those problems of construction which have been raised in the application of equal time can be generally summarized under the following questions: (1) who are legally qualified candidates?; (2) what constitutes "equal" opportunity?; (3) what constitutes a "use" by a political candidate?; and (4) what is a bona fide "newscast," "news interview," "news documentary," or "news events"?

216. *Political Broadcasts*, 24 P & F RADIO REG. 1901 (1962) (incorporating earlier summaries).

217. *E.g.*, Friedenthal & Medalie, *The Impact of Federal Regulation on Political Broadcasting: Section 315 of the Communications Act*, 72 HARV. L. REV. 445 (1959); Comment, 30 GEO. WASH. L. REV. 63 (1961).

218. *See Political Broadcasts*, 24 P & F RADIO REG. 1901, 1913-15 (1962).

219. Equal time is not required where another person appears on behalf of the candidate. Felix v. Westinghouse Radio, 186 F.2d 1 (3d Cir. 1950), *cert. denied*, 341 U.S. 909 (1951).

220. The Commission has ruled in numerous instances that a candi-

an appearance in connection with a news program or interview.[221] There is no specific obligation on the station to carry political broadcasts in the first instance, although a refusal to carry any political broadcasting may be considered against the licensee at renewal time when the Commission decides whether the station has been operated in the public interest.[222] In addition, the station is not required to seek out the opposing candidates. The initiative is on the opposing candidate to request equal time[223] within one week of the broadcast.[224]

Enforcement of section 315 generally arises on complaint[225] to the Commission by a candidate who has been denied equal time. The licensee is notified of the complaint and given time to reply. Once an order is issued, the order can be enforced through the usual means of fines, cease and desist orders, and even denial of license renewal or license revocation for willful and repeated violations.[226] However, the issuance of a ruling that a candidate is entitled to equal time has apparently sufficed in all or virtually all cases. No case has been found in which any formal sanctions were invoked. The reason for this is obvious since compliance, or attempted compliance in good faith with a prior ruling is all that is required. Since judicial review can be had from the informal ruling,[227] a refusal to comply in order to test the correctness or the constitutionality of the ruling is unnecessary. In any event, the sanctions risked by noncom-

---

date who appears for any purpose or in any capacity, even in that of a station announcer, is a use by the candidate requiring equal time. *See Political Broadcasts*, 24 P & F RADIO REG. 1901, 1908-12 (1962). *But see* Brigham v. FCC, 276 F.2d 828 (5th Cir. 1960), where the Fifth Circuit held that a station weatherman's appearance on a program to present the weather report was not a use although the weatherman was also a candidate. This may be rationalized, however, on the exemption for bona fide news broadcasts rather than any exemption for candidates who make appearances for nonpolitical purposes.

221. 47 U.S.C. § 315 (1964); *see Political Broadcasts*, 24 P & F RADIO REG. 1901, 1908-13 (1962).

222. *Licensee's Obligation to Carry Political Broadcasts*, 25 P & F RADIO REG. 1731 (1963).

223. "Equivalent" time means equivalent in terms of rates charged (or absence of rates), length of time, desirability of the time spot offered, and any other conditions of use. *See Political Broadcasts*, 24 P & F RADIO REG. 1901, 1919-21 (1962).

224. 47 C.F.R. § 13.657(e) (Supp. 1966).

225. The Commission does, when asked, also render declaratory decisions without any complaint. *E.g.*, Columbia Broadcasting Sys., 3 P & F RADIO REG. 2d 623 (1964).

226. *See* 47 U.S.C. §§ 307(d), 312(a) & (b), 504(b) (1964).

227. *See* Felix v. Westinghouse Radio, 186 F.2d 1 (3d Cir. 1950), *cert. denied*, 341 U.S. 909 (1951).

pliance are quite evidently regarded as more important to the broadcaster than his right not to accord equal time.

Notwithstanding the fact that section 315 is quite limited, not only as to the period in which it is operative but also as to the scope of the obligation imposed, the equal time requirements have been the subject of unrelenting criticism over the years, and a number of attempts have been made to modify or repeal section 315.[228] Probably the most severe attacks have been aimed at the Commission's interpretation of section 315, which has generally tended to expand the scope of the section. The classic example is the Commission's *Lar Daly*[229] decision, holding that the appearance of an incumbent political candidate on a newscast and a separate announcement on behalf of the March of Dimes constituted a "use" entitling all other candidates to equal time. This remarkably obtuse decision called forth a flood of criticism which was quickly followed by congressional reversal of the decision, and the present exemptions for bona fide news events.

Despite this swift reversal the Commission has continued to adhere to an extremely broad interpretation of the word "use." Thus it insists that any appearance by a candidate for any purpose whatsoever, other than in connection with a bona fide news program, constitutes a use irrespective of whether the appearance has any bearing on his political candidacy.[230] This interpretation is based on the rather tenuous theory that any exposure of a candidate over radio or television ultimately accrues to the candidate's benefit or that, in any event, the licensee should not be permitted to judge whether the candidate has benefited from the appearance.[231] Consistent with their expansive reading of section 315, the Commission has also placed some rather narrow interpretations on the news exemption established by Congress in 1959 with respect to such appearances as press conferences

228. *See, e.g.*, S. 1010, 89th Cong., 1st Sess. (1965); S. 1696, 88th Cong., 1st Sess. (1963). For criticism before Congress of § 315, see *Hearings on Equal Time before the Subcomm. on Communications of the Senate Comm. on Commerce*, 88th Cong., 1st Sess., ser. 29 (1963). The critics of § 315 include at least one former Commissioner. *See Hearings on Political Broadcasting before the Communications Subcomm. of the Senate Comm. on Interstate and Foreign Commerce*, 86th Cong., 1st Sess. 81 (1959) (testimony of Commissioner Ford).

229. CBS, Inc., 18 P & F RADIO REG. 701 (1959). For industry criticisms of the *Lar Daly* case, see *Hearings on Political Broadcasting Before the Communications Subcomm. of the Senate Comm. on Interstate and Foreign Commerce*, 86th Cong., 1st Sess. (1959).

230. *See* note 219 *supra*.

231. *See* WMCA, Inc., 7 P & F RADIO REG. 1132 (1952).

and reports from Congressmen.[232] These limited interpretations have justifiably invoked criticism from members of the Commission as well as the industry.[233]

While the Commission has been severely criticized on many occasions for its interpretation of section 315, probably as much criticism has been levied at the statutory requirements themselves. This criticism has centered chiefly on the problem of giving equal time to minority candidates. Although Congress suspended section 315 for presidential and vice-presidential candidates in 1960,[234] every attempt thus far to modify or repeal section 315 permanently[235] has failed. An attempt to suspend section 315 again for presidential and vice-presidential candidates in the 1964 election campaign failed despite some strong support for following the 1960 pattern.

2. *The Fairness Doctrine*

Closely akin to, but distinct from the equal time requirements is the Commission's so-called "fairness doctrine." Stated most generally, the fairness doctrine is an obligation imposed on the broadcaster to present contrasting responsible points of view on controversial issues of public importance.[236]

The history of the fairness doctrine is rather uncertain since it depends on how one defines what now passes for a doctrine. The Commission maintains that the fairness doctrine has, in essence, been in effect from the first days of regulation by the Federal Radio Commission.[237] A statement in the 1929 *Annual*

232. *See, e.g.*, Columbia Broadcasting Sys., 3 P & F RADIO REG. 2d 623 (1964); Letter to Congressman Thompson, 23 P & F RADIO REG. 178 (1962).

233. *See, e.g.*, dissenting opinions of Commissioners Ford and Loevinger in Columbia Broadcasting Sys., 3 P & F RADIO REG. 2d 623, 630-31 (1964).

234. Act of Aug. 24, 1960, Pub. L. No. 86-677, 74 Stat. 554.

235. *See, e.g.*, S. 252; S. 1696; *Hearings on Equal Time Before the Communications Subcomm. of the Senate Comm. on Commerce*, 88th Cong., 1st Sess., ser. 29 (1963).

236. *Fairness Doctrine*, 2 P & F RADIO REG. 2d 1901, 1904 (1964). For extensive comments on the fairness doctrine reflecting different attitudes toward it, see Barron, *The Federal Communications Commission's Fairness Doctrine: An Evaluation*, 30 GEO. WASH. L. REV. 1 (1961); Sullivan, *Editorials and Controversy: The Broadcaster's Dilemma*, 32 GEO. WASH. L. REV. 719 (1964).

237. *See Fairness Doctrine*, 2 P & F RADIO REG. 2d 1901, 1903 (1964). The Commission also interprets § 315, as amended in 1959, to give statutory sanction for the doctrine. *See id.* But this seems a somewhat dubious interpretation of congressional intent. *See* text accompanying notes 250-51 *infra*.

Report of the Federal Radio Commission does suggest an early origin of the doctrine:

> It would not be fair, indeed, it would not be good service to the public, to allow a one-sided presentation of political issues of a campaign. Insofar as the program consists of discussion of public questions, public interest requires ample play for the fair and free competition of opposing views, and the Commission believes that the principle applies not only to addresses of political candidates but to discussion of issues of importance to the public.[238]

While a general obligation to be fair in presenting opposing viewpoints on controversial issues may be inherent in the broadcaster's duty to serve the public interest, there is an important difference between a general moral responsibility—enforceable, if at all, only by self-regulation—and a specific legal requirement enforceable by Commission sanction.[239] Despite the Commission's early insistence that the broadcaster is obligated to present all sides of a controversial issue, it was really not until the Commission's opinion in *Mayflower Broadcasting Company*[240] in 1940, which imposed a ban on broadcast editorializing as inherently unfair, that the Commission articulated something like the fairness doctrine, enforceable by direct sanction or specific admonishment, as it is now understood.[241] The *Mayflower* decision represents a crude first attempt on the part of the Commission to enforce fairness in the treatment of controversial issues by broadcasters. The case did not, however, lay down any specific requirements other than the negative commandment: thou shalt not be an advocate. Apart from condemning editor-

---

238. 1929 FRC ANN. REP. 33.

239. Sullivan, *supra* note 236, at 728.

240. 8 F.C.C. 333 (1940).

241. In Red Lion Broadcasting Co. v. FCC, 10 P & F RADIO REG. 2d 2001, 2011 (D.C. Cir. 1967), the court attempts to give an earlier genesis for the fairness doctrine by finding it in such cases as *Shuler* and *Brinkley*. Trinity Methodist Church, South v. Federal Radio Comm'n, 62 F.2d 850 (D.C. Cir. 1932), *cert. denied*, 288 U.S. 599 (1933); KFKB Broadcasting Ass'n v. Federal Radio Comm'n, 47 F.2d 670 (D.C. Cir. 1931). However, the denial of licenses in these cases was based on a far more flagrant conduct than simple failure to present both sides of a public controversy and neither was grounded on any articulated fairness doctrine as that term is understood today. So also the Commission's refusal to license the applicant in Young People's Ass'n for the Propogation of the Gospel, 6 F.C.C. 178 (1938), which announced its intention to pursue a flat, general policy of not permitting use of its facilities for presenting *any* view differing from that of the applicant, bears but slight resemblance to the fairness doctrine today but is more akin to the *Brinkley* and *Shuler* cases and the principle that a licensee cannot operate the station in its purely private interests to the exclusion of any public interest.

ializing, it spoke only in very sweeping and general terms:

> Freedom of speech on the radio must be broad enough to provide full and equal opportunity for the presentation to the public of all sides of public issues. Indeed, as one licensed to operate in a public domain, the licensee has assumed the obligation of presenting all sides of important public questions, fairly, objectively and without bias.[242]

The scope of the licensee's obligation to ensure the fair presentation of all sides of controversial issues and the manner in which the Commission intended to enforce that obligation remained as vague as the broadcaster's duty to serve the public interest. Few stations were hurt by the ban on editorializing, since the practice was not widespread in the industry and was generally frowned upon.[243] Thus, the *Mayflower* opinion did not evoke as overwhelming a protest from the industry as might have been expected.

Apart from the flat ban on editorializing, little effort was made by the Commission to clarify the scope of the licensee's obligation to be fair or to set forth any guidelines as to what would be deemed controversial or what was required in order to be fair. In fact, the Commission quite evidently did not really know what fairness meant. Thus, in 1946 it decided not to require a station to give an atheist opportunity to "give the other side" of views reflected in the station's religious programs, while at the same time instructing the station to be fair in presenting religious issues even though this would require the station to permit expression of highly unpopular minority views including those of atheists.[244] The confusingly vague scope of the fairness obligation was compounded by the fact that the Commission had, in 1945, issued a statement of policy to the effect that stations could not avoid the problem by refusing to carry programs dealing with controversial public issues.[245]

In 1947 the Commission, prompted by the evident need to clarify the fairness obligation with respect to controversial public issues generally, instituted hearings on the relationships between editorializing and a broadcaster's obligations under the Act. These culminated in the Commission's *Report on Editorializing by Broadcast Licensees*,[246] released in 1949, in which the Commission reversed *Mayflower* and reestablished the right of the broadcaster to editorialize. In addition, this report dealt

242. 8 F.C.C. 333, 340 (1940).
243. Sullivan, *supra* note 236, at 730-32.
244. Robert Harold Scott, 3 P & F Radio Reg. 259 (1946).
245. United Broadcasting Co., 10 F.C.C. 515 (1945).
246. 1 P & F Radio Reg. 91:201 (1949).

generally with the licensee's overall duty of fairness in treating controversial issues. It set forth the licensee's twofold obligation: first, to speak out on controversial public issues, although not necessarily in the format of station editorials; and, second, an affirmative obligation to ascertain and seek out all responsible viewpoints on controversial issues and to afford the opportunity for such contrasting viewpoints to be heard.[247] It is this twofold obligation which constitutes the modern fairness doctrine.

The 1949 *Editorializing Report* remains the basic expression of policy for the fairness doctrine. Congress recognized the fairness doctrine in its 1959 amendments to section 315. Amended section 315, after establishing the exemption for bona fide news broadcasts, provides:

> Nothing in the foregoing sentence shall be construed as relieving broadcasters, in connection with the presentation of newscasts, news interviews, news documentaries, and on-the-spot coverage of news events, from the obligation imposed upon them under this chapter to operate in the public interest and to afford reasonable opportunity for the discussion of conflicting views on issues of public importance.[248]

Although the Commission has read the above provision as a ratification of the fairness doctrine, it seems doubtful that Congress, in amending section 315, actually intended to give specific statutory sanction to the Commission's fairness doctrine. More probably, Congress intended neither approval nor disapproval of it, but merely intended to ensure that section 315 would not interfere with it. There was no other consideration of the fairness doctrine as such and no consideration was given to the statutory authority for the doctrine as then applied.[249]

In recent years the Commission has attempted to furnish some more specific guidance in its *Fairness Primer*, a collection of ad hoc rulings implementing the fairness doctrine.[250] The Commission's ad hoc rulings are at best an uncertain guideline. In order to set forth the basic theory of the fairness doctrine and to distinguish it from section 315, a few generalizations may be made.

Unlike section 315, the fairness doctrine does not necessarily require a station to grant *equal* time to all opposing viewpoints. A ten-minute commentary by the station on one side of a con-

247. *Id.* at 91:206.

248. 48 Stat. 1088 (1934), *as amended*, 47 U.S.C. § 315(a)4 (1964).

249. For a brief discussion of the question see Dean, *Political Broadcasting: The Communications Act of 1934 Reviewed*, 20 FED. COMM. B.J. 16, 29-31 (1966).

250. *Fairness Doctrine*, 2 P & F RADIO REG. 2d 1901 (1964).

troversial school bond issue, for example, does not necessarily require that the station grant ten minutes to all other sides. This flows from the fact that the obligation is to ensure *fair* treatment, not necessarily precisely equal time, to the various sides. Moreover, unlike section 315, the fairness doctrine does not necessarily require the station to offer time to any outside person, group, or agency. If the station's programming is such that fairness is accorded to all sides *over a reasonable period of time,* then the station's obligations are at least theoretically met.

An exception to the above is the so-called "personal attack" rule which requires that, where a station makes a personal attack on a specific individual or group, it must provide the individual attacked with a script or tape of the broadcast prior to or at the time of the broadcast and with a specific offer of time to reply.[251] This rule has now been codified into specific regulations which have extended it not only to require opportunity to reply to personal attacks but also to require the station to offer rebuttal time in the case of editorial endorsements of or opposition to qualified political candidates.[252] These rules reflect an evolving crystallization, if not rigidification, of the fairness doctrine from a general obligation of responsibility into fixed regulations prescribing specific licensee duties. The wisdom of such regulatory policy is certainly open to question.

The Commission's enforcement of the fairness doctrine is substantially similar to its enforcement of section 315, except that it is possibly even more informal. Upon complaint that a licensee has not accorded fair coverage to a controversial public issue, the Commission forwards the complaint to the licensee and demands a reply. If the reply does not satisfy the Commission, it informs the station of the error of its ways, indicating perhaps that the matter may be considered at renewal time.[253] In addition, it may demand from the licensee a statement of how it will comply with the fairness doctrine in the future.[254]

A notification to the applicant that the matter will be con-

---

251. Billings Broadcasting Co., 23 P & F RADIO REG. 951 (1962); Clayton W. Mapoles, 23 P & F RADIO REG. 586 (1962); Times-Mirror Broadcasting Co., 24 P & F RADIO REG. 404, 407 (1962).

252. *Fairness Doctrine Rules*, 10 P & F RADIO REG. 2d 1901, 1903 (1967). Appeals challenging the rules have been taken in the Second and Seventh Circuit Courts of Appeals. BROADCASTING MAGAZINE, July 31, 1967, at 23-24.

253. *See* 1965 FCC ANN. REP. 89-92.

254. *E.g.*, Letters to Taft Broadcasting Co. and WBRE-TV, Public Notice-G No. 73,787 (Sept. 24, 1965); New Broadcasting Co. (WLIB), 6 P & F RADIO REG. 258 (1950).

sidered at renewal time is precisely the kind of "lifted eyebrow" technique which the Commission has successfully employed in other aspects of broadcast regulation. Generally, it is not so much the possible loss of its license as the possibility of being forced through the ordeal of a hearing which makes the informal letter-telegram procedure effective. To reinforce this informal procedure, the Commission has in one recent case issued a one-year renewal where a station's presentation of controversial public issues had been of questionable fairness.[255] Finally, if the fairness doctrine has been incorporated into section 315, then enforcement methods such as cease and desist orders and fines should be at least theoretically available. The Commission has not as yet resorted to these methods although it may well do so in the future, particularly in enforcing its new personal attack regulations.[256]

2. *First Amendment Implications*

The operation of the equal time rule imposes a significant restraint on broadcasters' discretion and responsibility in choice of programming. Its effects are to compel the licensee to offer time for political programs which, if left to his own discretion, he might not otherwise broadcast, and to compel the licensee to refuse to present programs which he would otherwise broadcast in order to avoid the burden of complying or the risk of not complying with this requirement. The latter restraint is probably the more significant because it is here that the requirement for equal time to all candidates, including minority and fringe candidates, has its most immediate impact upon political broadcasting. CBS President Frank Stanton, one of the most persistent and vocal critics of section 315, has contended that

> The inescapable conclusion is that Section 315 does far more harm than good, and that its result is neither to increase diversity of opinion nor expand free speech but rather as a practical matter of practical necessity is compelled suppression and blackout. This compulsion is as simple as it is obvious: Time and time again radio and television have been unable to present candidates to the American people because broadcasters have known that under Section 315 a half hour to a Democratic or

255. Lamar Life Broadcasting Co., 5 P & F RADIO REG. 2d 205 (1965).

256. A major purpose for the Commission's recent codification of the "personal attack" rule is to crystallize its policy sufficiently that it can be enforced by specific sanction such as fine. *See Fairness Doctrine Rules*, 10 P & F RADIO REG. 2d 1901, 1904 (1967).

> Republican candidate can mean a total of 4, 8 or 16 half hours to obscure and unknown opponents. So when a half hour has had to be multiplied to 8 hours, we have had to forego the half hour, the result has been less, not more, broadcasting in the public interest.[257]

Congress recognized the significant restraint imposed on broadcasters by the equal time requirements in 1960 when it suspended section 315 for presidential and vice-presidential candidates.[258]

As in the case of the equal time requirements of section 315, it seems undeniable that the fairness doctrine acts as a significant restraint on the broadcaster's choice of programming and represents a substantial intrusion by the Commission into the area of program selection. While the nature of the restraints imposed is basically similar for both the equal time requirements and the fairness doctrine, there are important substantive differences.

First, the equal time requirement focuses on personalities rather than directly on program content, though it may indirectly affect program content to some extent. There is no requirement, for example, that the Commission examine the content of a particular broadcast to determine whether its standards are met in the case of equal time. On the other hand, the fairness doctrine is predicated on just such an examination, evaluation, and judgment by the Commission of specific program content. The fairness doctrine cannot be applied without the Commission making a determination that the content of the program is of such nature as in its judgment requires opportunity for presentation of opposing views. This aspect of the fairness doctrine is crucial from a first amendment viewpoint since the restraint on free speech grows directly out of an examination and judgment by the Commission of program content.

Second, unlike the equal time requirement, which has a narrow scope and correspondingly imposes only a limited degree of restraint, the scope of the general fairness doctrine is sweepingly broad. While equal time is limited to a relatively short period prior to elections, the fairness doctrine is always applicable. While equal time affects only programs involving a legally qualified candidate for public office, the fairness doctrine

---

257. *Hearings on Political Broadcasting Before the Communications Subcomm. of the Senate Comm. on Interstate and Foreign Commerce*, 86th Cong., 1st Sess. 97 (1959) (statement of Frank Stanton, President of CBS).

258. Pub. L. No. 86-677, 74 Stat. 554 (1960).

affects all programming which involves controversial public issues. Thus the effect upon program choice is infinitely greater in the case of the fairness doctrine. A broadcaster, faced with the possibility that he may have to give time to candidates *B, C,* and *D* if he makes time available to candidate *A* may well forego giving time to *A*. The program choice foreclosed is limited. Compare, however, the alternatives faced by a broadcaster who is considering a public discussion program, a commentary series, or editorials. He is met at the outset with the possibility that if he touches on any significant public issue, even if *he* does not judge it to be controversial, it may give rise to an obligation to provide time to opposing viewpoints. The problem will not arise just once or twice, but may arise on hundreds of occasions. Virtually every topic which might be worth discussing or commenting upon is likely to be considered by the Commission to be a controversial issue of public importance which obligates him to seek out and provide an opportunity for the expression of opposing viewpoints. The most conscientious broadcaster may well have very substantial qualms about presenting controversial public issues when he is required to be fair by someone else's standards, particularly if the someone else happens to be the government.

The almost infinite reach of the fairness doctrine is most graphically illustrated by the Commission's recent ruling that a station which presents cigarette advertising "has the duty of informing its audience of the other side of this controversial issue of public importance—that however enjoyable, such smoking may be a hazard to the smoker's health."[259] This is the first time the fairness doctrine has been held applicable to routine advertising. To say the least, such an application of the doctrine raises a question whether there is any kind of broadcast message

---

259. Letter to WCBS-TV, 9 P & F RADIO REG. 2d 1423, 1424, *petition for reconsideration denied*, 11 P & F RADIO REG. 2d 1921 (1967). The ruling was issued on complaint. An appeal has been filed by the NAB on behalf of the broadcasting industry (and, by reasonable assumption, on behalf of the cigarette industry) in the Fourth Circuit challenging the ruling on essentially the following grounds: (1) it conflicts with the Cigarette Labeling and Advertising Act of 1965, (2) it exceeds the Commission's statutory authority, (3) it violates the first and fifth amendments, and (4) it is procedurally defective. These are the same grounds urged before the Commission in seeking reconsideration. *See* BROADCASTING MAGAZINE, Sept. 18, 1967, at 34-38. Complainant, a lawyer in the vein of Ralph Nader, has also filed an appeal in the District of Columbia Circuit claiming that the ruling does not go far enough. *Id.* The latter appeal is an obvious race-to-the-courthouse attempt to get review in a sympathetic court.

which, in any context, touches even tangentially on a controversial issue to which the fairness doctrine does not apply. For example, does the advertising of automobiles give rise to an obligation to permit Ralph Nader to present his views on automotive safety?[260] The Commission rejected such implications of its ruling as simply a "parade of horribles" and emphasized that here the decisive criteria were the "governmental and private reports and congressional action" stressing the danger of smoking and urging persons to cease.[261] But the distinction seems paper-thin, particularly since nothing in the way the fairness doctrine has been applied in other contexts suggests that the presence or absence of governmental action or concern is of decisive importance. And even if it is, the ruling still has potentially limitless ramifications considering the range of issues with which the government is concerned. For example, does the advertising of vitamin supplements require a station to give air time to Dr. Goddard to present the FDA's views[262] on the questionable need for such supplements?

Perhaps the most startling thing about the cigarette ruling is that it requires *continuing* presentations by the station of the viewpoint that smoking is a health hazard because cigarette commercials are presented on a continuing basis. The Commission made clear that the station must allocate sufficient time to the opposing viewpoint each week. Moreover, the obligation to present the opposing view extends to giving time on the air without charge if that is necessary to achieve the requisite fairness. Indeed, it is evident from the Commission's letter-opinion that it contemplated that the obligation would be met at least partially by public service announcements of the American Cancer Society or HEW in this field.[263] Thus the impact which can logically be expected from this ruling is a continuing one.

However, notwithstanding the above objections, it is possible that on the present state of the law the ruling is immune from first amendment attack insofar as it involves advertising, although arguably this should make no difference here where the Commission is applying a rule applicable generally to the dissemination of ideas regardless of whether the particular ideas

260. *See* R. NADER, UNSAFE AT ANY SPEED (1965).
261. 11 P & F RADIO REG. 2d at 1929-30 (1967).
262. *See, e.g.*, "Health and the Consumer," Address by Goddard, Annual Meeting of the Food Industries of the Nutrition Foundation, June 8, 1967.
263. 9 P & F RADIO REG. 2d 1423 (June 2, 1967).

happen to be embodied in an advertising message.[263a] The restraining effect of the fairness doctrine is compounded for the broadcaster by its vague and indefinite standards. The vagueness and uncertainty are inherent first in the definition of what constitutes a controversial public issue giving rise to the obligation to be fair. The cigarette advertising ruling is an illustration of the potential sweeping inclusiveness of this element. There is also uncertainty as to what fairness requires the licensee to do in any particular circumstances. Uncertainty as to the elements of the doctrine and what it requires must inevitably cause a greater restraint on broadcaster discretion than would otherwise be the case. Thus the broadcaster may forego a wider range of programming in order to guard against the *possibility* that the fairness doctrine might apply, or he may broadcast programs expressing viewpoints opposing those of an original broadcast where it may not actually be necessary under a reasonable interpretation of the doctrine. The fairness doctrine is likely to have a particularly dampening effect on the quality of station advocacy such as editorializing. Advocacy by its nature seldom involves a complete and unbiased exposure of all contrasting views by the advocate. Were every advocate required to give such a full and unbiased treatment of all views, few would find advocacy and controversy worth the effort.

Under these circumstances, it is not surprising that many broadcasters forego controversial public issue programming, being content to play it safe with planned, noncontroversial subjects of the "mother-and-home" variety. But even this alternative may not avoid trouble since the Commission takes the position that the presentation of controversial public issues programming is an affirmative duty of every licensee.[264]

A distinction somewhat similar to that between equal time and the fairness doctrine can arguably be made between the fairness doctrine as it is applied to controversial public issues and the so-called personal attack principle,[265] which has developed out of the fairness doctrine. The personal attack principle represents a considerable extension of the fairness doctrine as traditionally applied insofar as it fixes an absolute duty to offer

263a. *See* note 162 and accompanying text *supra*. The Commission only noted in passing the question of whether advertising is protected speech, but did not rule that it is not protected. 11 P & F RADIO REG. 2d at 1908 n.4 (1967).

264. *Editorializing by Licensees*, 1 P & F RADIO REG. 91:201, 91:206 (1949).

265. *See* text accompanying notes 251-52 *supra*.

to the person attacked an opportunity to reply. It is in this respect basically similar to the equal time requirements of section 315, except that it is not confined to political candidates. While the personal attack principle is an extended application of the fairness doctrine, it does not represent quite the same constitutional problems. The vagaries and sweeping scope of the fairness doctrine are not inherent in the personal attack principle. Correspondingly, the compulsion to present ideas and speech which the broadcaster would otherwise not present is far less sweeping, and the inhibition on ideas and speech is far less broad where the broadcaster is required to afford the right to reply only to one who is personally attacked than where the broadcaster is required to give a fair presentation of controversial public issues. Moreover, a case can be made for the right to reply to a personal attack, at least where the attack is libelous, near-libelous, or arguably libelous. Professor Chafee persuasively argued that in such cases a legislative requirement imposing a duty to permit a reply to such statements is preferable to punishing or inhibiting defamation through libel and slander suits, and probably no more unconstitutional.[266] It should be emphasized, however, that this argument does not single out radio and television stations: it applies equally to newspapers and other mass communication media.[267] Indeed, one state has a statute imposing such a duty on newspapers.[268] However, even this limited right to reply to defamatory statements, whether applied to broadcasters or newspapers, seems to be of questionable wisdom and even more doubtful constitutionality. Moreover, even if its constitutionality were recognized, it would not justify either the fairness doctrine as it is generally applied or the rule which requires stations to afford an opportunity to reply to editorial endorsement of or opposition to political candidates. In the case of the personal attack principle, justification and constitutional sanction might be found in a long tradition of remedying defamation, antedating the first amendment. No such tradition affords a remedy in the case of one who merely takes a stand on controversial public issues. No such tradition compels one always to give all sides of the story.

---

266. 1 Z. CHAFEE, GOVERNMENT AND MASS COMMUNICATIONS MEDIA 172, 184-90 (Comm'n on Freedom of the Press ed. 1947). Professor Chafee points out, however, that there are some very serious difficulties with and objections to a legislative command to afford a right of reply. *Id.* at 180-84.

267. *Id.* at 184-90.

268. NEV. REV. STAT. ch. 200.570 (1965).

The basic rationalization for the Commission's fairness doctrine, as for its general standards for presenting "balanced" programming, is that the licensee, bound by statutory policy to serve the public interest, must fairly present balanced and diversified programming so as to meet the needs and interests of all of the public. This rationalization rests on the assumption that, because the licensee has something of a monopoly in regard to access to and use of broadcast facilities, it is necessary and justifiable to compensate for this monopoly by requiring that he present all types of programming and all points of view which, by hypothesis, would be presented if there were no technological barriers to entry into broadcasting.

On this assumption, the Commission generally refuses to acknowledge any of the significant first amendment implications posed by its regulation of programming. Perhaps the most succinct single statement of its view is set forth in its 1949 *Editorializing Report:*[269]

> We believe . . . that a requirement that broadcast licensees utilize their franchises in a manner in which the listening public may be assured of hearing varying opinions on the paramount issues facing the American people is within both the spirit and letter of the First Amendment. [T]he Supreme Court of the United States . . . pointed [this] out in the Associated Press monopoly case. (*Associated Press v. United States,* 326 U.S. 1, 20).
>
> * * *
>
> We fully recognize that freedom of the radio is included among the freedoms protected against governmental abridgment by the First Amendment. . . . But this does not mean that the freedom of the people as a whole to enjoy the maximum possible utilization of this medium of mass communication may be subordinated to the freedom of any single person to exploit the medium for his own private interest.

Despite this army of high-sounding words and phrases, the basic premise on which the Commission justifies its intrusion into the program field is simply too tenuous to sustain such potentially far-reaching powers. Notwithstanding the Commission's rationalization in terms of the right of the public to receive diversified and balanced presentation of public issues, it has refused to consider whether or not, on a given issue, the public has received such a balanced presentation from all the various public media taken as a whole. It has ruled that each licensee must present all sides of a public issue irrespective of what other media and other radio and television stations pre-

269. *Editorializing by Licensees,* 1 P & F RADIO REG. 91:201, 91:210-11 (1949).

sent.[270] If the right of the public to receive diverse and balanced viewpoints is the decisive desideratum, it is curious, to say the least, that the Commission purposely insists on ignoring the question of whether the public is in fact receiving diverse and balanced presentations from existing communications media as a whole.

Moreover, the Commission's concern over licensees' use of public facilities for private purposes at the expense of the public is something of a red herring. The real issue is not whether the licensee has a right to exploit his license or to abuse its privileges, for example, by using the station to broadcast his own private views or to promote his own biases or interests, ignoring all public interests and needs. Those who oppose the Commission's fairness doctrine are not arguing for the rights of the licensee to be unfair or to use licensed facilitiees for a purely personal cause or aim. The question is who should have the responsibility; whose concept of fairness should be applied? If it is "unfair" for an advocate to put forward his own views without giving full and unbiased exposure to other opposing views, one may wonder whether any true advocacy is or can ever be "fair."

Finally, the Commission's reliance on the *AP* antitrust case is misplaced. As previously discussed,[271] the first amendment does not proscribe general economic and social regulation of the type involved in the *AP* antitrust case and the *AP* labor law case.[272] There is, however, a marked difference between regulation of the economic structure of a communications industry which is designed to protect the basic minimum conditions in which free, diversified speech may develop and regulation which attempts directly to ensure such diversified speech by examining the speech itself to see if it meets the tests of balance, fairness, and diversity. It seems more than doubtful that Justice Black, who wrote the majority opinion in the *AP* antitrust case, or indeed any of the justices who joined him, supposed that by affirming the application of the Sherman Act to newspapers, he was affirming the power of the government to pass upon the balance, diversity, or fairness of newspapers, even those enjoying a natural monopoly position. The *NBC* case is no more dispositive than the *AP* case. Despite the Court's rather sweeping opinion which suggests sanction for all manner of Commission

270. *See* Jorgensen, Schwartz & Woods, *Programming Diversity in Proposals for New Broadcast Licenses*, 32 GEO. WASH. L. REV. 769 (1964).
271. *See* Part I *supra*.
272. Associated Press v. NLRB, 301 U.S. 103 (1937).

regulation in the public interest, the issue before the Court was the Commission's power to adopt essentially economic regulations similar in substance and purpose to the antitrust law sustained in the *AP* antitrust case. In both cases the difference between such broad socio-economic regulation and direct regulation of programming is obvious. To pass from the former to the latter without distinction is to pass beyond the elusive but nevertheless important line which separates speech in a free, open society from speech controlled by the government in the public interest—the earmark of a closed society.[273]

3. *The Red Lion Case*

Although a number of court decisions previously discussed[274] have upheld the constitutionality of various aspects of Commission program regulation, some in rather sweeping terms, the constitutionality of the Commission's fairness doctrine went unchallenged in the courts until the recent decision in *Red Lion Broadcasting Company v. FCC*[275] involving personal attacks by a licensee.

Following the 1964 presidential elections petitioner-licensee broadcast a program which included a discussion of the election and a book by a Mr. Cook about the Republican campaign. The personal attack consisted of a charge that Cook, a newspaperman, had been fired for having made a false charge against an unnamed New York City official. Contrary to the Commission's personal attack policy, the licensee failed to notify Cook of

---

273. The phrases "open society" and "closed society" are borrowed from K. Popper, The Open Society And Its Enemies (4th ed. 1963).

To some the association of the Commission's regulation of radio and television programming with the attitude of the closed society will undoubtedly seem hyperbole. Some—those believing in the good intentions and motivations of the Commission in this concededly difficult and delicate area—will perhaps even treat this association with derision. There should not be any doubt that the Commission has acted on the highest of motivations and good intentions and it has not been altogether insensitive, at least as to some of the more obvious constitutional problems in this area. The fact remains, however, that the first amendment was designed to protect against well-intentioned, well-motivated interference with free speech as well as that which stems from a less well-intentioned social philosophy.

274. *See, e.g.*, Johnston Broadcasting Co. v. FCC, 175 F.2d 351 (D.C. Cir. 1949); Trinity Methodist Church, South v. Federal Radio Comm'n, 62 F.2d 850 (D.C. Cir. 1932), *cert. denied*, 288 U.S. 599 (1933); KFKB Broadcasting Ass'n v. Federal Radio Comm'n, 47 F.2d 670 (D.C. Cir. 1931); text accompanying notes 115-18, 133-35, 208-11 *supra*.

275. 10 P & F Radio Reg. 2d 2001 (D.C. Cir.), *petition for cert. filed*, 36 U.S.L.W. 3100 (U.S. Sept. 11, 1967).

the attack or to furnish him with a transcript of the program and refused Cook's request for free time to respond to the attack. Following receipt of the complaint from Cook, the Commission issued a letter to the licensee ruling that it had violated the fairness doctrine and requested it to advise the Commission of its "plans to comply with the 'fairness doctrine'."[276] In response to the licensee's request for a ruling, the Commission affirmed the constitutionality of the fairness doctrine as it was applied to this situation.

On appeal the licensee challenged the constitutionality of the fairness doctrine on four grounds: (1) section 315 of the Act, the chief statutory authority for the fairness doctrine, constitutes an unconstitutional delegation of legislative power; (2) the fairness doctrine is unconstitutionally vague; (3) the fairness doctrine infringes upon the ninth and tenth amendments insofar as it violates the licensee's right to engage in political activity and insofar as it infringes upon powers reserved to the people; and (4) the fairness doctrine violates the first amendment.[277] Each ground was rejected by the court.

As to the first ground, the question of delegation in itself adds virtually nothing to the arguments that the fairness doctrine is unconstitutionally vague and unconstitutionally restrictive of free speech. If the latter arguments can be satisfactorily resolved there seems no tenable basis for attacking the delegation itself and, of course, if either of the latter arguments is upheld, the delegation question loses any significance.[278] As to the argument based on the ninth and tenth amendments, it is

---

276. *Id.* at 2006-08.

277. *Id.* at 2004.

278. Setting aside the issue of free speech, or the issue of vagueness such as would offend due process, the question of the constitutionality of the delegation seems fully disposed of by a line of authority too long to recite in its entirety. The standards of § 315 which were challenged,—"reasonable opportunity," "sufficient time for full discussion," "controversial issues of public importance," and others, *id.* at 2014—may indeed be broad and uncertain, but *considered under the issue of delegability* they are quite obviously no broader or more uncertain than standards which have been repeatedly upheld. *See, e.g.*, Lichter v. United States, 334 U.S. 742 (1948) (authorizing recovery of "excess profits" under the Renegotiation Act); Federal Radio Comm'n v. Nelson Bros. Bond & Mortgage Co., 289 U.S. 266, 285 (1933) (regulation of licenses under the standard of "public interest, convenience, and necessity" under the Radio Act of 1927); Yakus v. United States, 321 U.S. 414, 423-5 (1944) (administrator under Emergency Price Control Act of 1942 given power to fix prices which "in his judgment will be generally fair and equitable and will effectuate the purposes of this Act").

difficult to know what to make of the licensee's contentions. Reliance on the ninth and tenth amendments was evidently predicated on Justice Goldberg's concurring opinion in *Griswold v. Connecticut*,[279] and the theory that the ninth and tenth amendments constitute some kind of residuum of protected rights not elsewhere enumerated in the Constitution. The court's rejection of this argument in *Red Lion* seems undeniably correct. There is neither historical authority nor solid constitutional precedent for the proposition that the ninth and tenth amendments embody any specific constitutional rights. While, as Justice Goldberg pointed out, the ninth and tenth amendments indicate that the first eight amendments are not preclusive of other fundamental rights not enumerated, it is impossible to find in them any hint of what such other fundamental rights might be. Moreover, Justice Goldberg's use of the ninth and tenth amendments was dubious enough when applied in *Griswold* as a basis for "filling in" the interstices between specific constitutional guarantees. It would be even more dubious to apply the two amendments to the *Red Lion* situation where other *specific* constitutional provisions are directly in issue. Such an interpretation of the ninth and tenth amendments would cause the entire Bill of Rights to be all but swallowed up in these two virtually forgotten amendments.

The licensee's vagueness argument appears on its face to be somewhat more persuasive. Viewing the fairness doctrine in general, it can hardly be denied that it is vague and uncertain in its scope and application. However, the vagueness argument seems misdirected here.

In the sense in which it is most widely understood and applied, the void-for-vagueness doctrine is based on the need to give fair notice to the individual as to what is unlawful. The evils sought to be eliminated are twofold: the subjection of a person to threat of punishment when he cannot know that his conduct is unlawful,[280] and the restraint of a person from engaging in protected conduct because of the threat that the broad and vague reach of the statute may proscribe such conduct.[281] In addition to the notice aspect, the vagueness doctrine has been

279. 381 U.S. 479, 486 (1965).

280. *See, e.g.*, Lanzetta v. New Jersey, 306 U.S. 451 (1939); Connally v. General Constr. Co., 269 U.S. 385 (1926).

281. *See, e.g.*, Herndon v. Lowry, 301 U.S. 242 (1937). On the distinction between the two evils inherent in "fair notice" cases, see Note, *The Void-for-Vagueness Doctrine in the Supreme Court*, 109 U. PA. L. REV. 67, 76 (1960).

applied as a limitation on the discretionary powers which may be given to a lower court, an administrative agency, or official.[282] In this latter aspect the doctrine assumes a somewhat broader scope and limits grants of overly broad discretion to trial judges and agencies to impose restraints without clear standards by which the lawfulness of their decisions or possible intrusions into areas of protected conduct may be tested.[283]

The court's opinion in *Red Lion* does not analyze the differing applications of the vagueness doctrine. It appears to have regarded the issue as solely a question of fair notice to the individual.[284] But, despite this blurring of important distinctions, the court's rejection of the vagueness doctrine may be justified since none of the evils which the doctrine is intended to correct were present in this case. While absence of fair notice and the evil of overbroadness may well be present in the fairness doctrine generally, there is no problem of fair notice as to what constitutes a controversial public issue in the personal attack type of case. It would strain credulity for the licensee to assert that it could not determine with fair certainty whether it was engaged in a personal attack. Neither is the standard overbroad in that it gives too much discretion to the agency; the standard of "personal attack" is no more elusive or vague for the agency to apply than it is for the licensee to understand. The same is true of the particular obligations imposed on the licensee here. Unlike the case of the general fairness doctrine, as applied to controversial issues, the personal attack principle is quite definite in the obligations which it imposes on licensees and the standard to be enforced by the agency. Like the equal time requirement of section 315, the personal attack principle requires

---

282. *See* Giaccio v. Pennsylvania, 382 U.S. 399, 402-03 (1966). *See also* Joseph Burstyn, Inc. v. Wilson, 343 U.S. 495 (1952); Hague v. C.I.O., 307 U.S. 496 (1939). For a persuasive and well-documented exposition of this and related aspects of the vagueness doctrine see Note, *The Void-for-Vagueness Doctrine in the Supreme Court*, 109 U. PA. L. REV. 67 (1960).

283. Obviously at some point as the vagueness doctrine is applied to strike down broad authorizations by the legislatures to the courts or agencies, it becomes almost impossible to distinguish the vagueness doctrine from the substantive rights, such as free speech, which are ultimately being protected. However, to the extent the vagueness doctrine has any independent significance, such a distinction must be recognized. The court in *Red Lion* appears not to have done so since its opinion tends to fuse the vagueness problem with the free speech question itself.

284. The licensee relied on Connally v. General Constr. Co., 269 U.S. 385 (1926), a "notice case," and the court dealt with the argument essentially on that basis. 10 P & F RADIO REG. 2d at 2017-20 (1967).

in all cases a specific offer of rebuttal time. The licensee's duty and the court's mandate under this requirement seem sufficiently clear.

There remains, however, the first amendment issue, and here the court's opinion is clearly less satisfying. Predictably, the Commission in its argument pointed out the public nature of the frequencies, the broadcaster's fiduciary responsibility to present all viewpoints, its duty to serve the public interest and recited the usual cases. In substance the court approved these arguments in rejecting the first amendment challenge.[285]

However, the court did not rest its decision simply on the licensee's duties and public responsibilities, but went on to conclude that the application of the personal attack principle, or the fairness doctrine in general, did not in fact restrain the licensee's freedom of speech. At one place the court noted that

> petitioners are not prohibited from broadcasting any program which petitioners think suitable . . . . [they] are not furnished with a mandatory program format, nor does the Doctrine define which, if any, controversial issues are to be the subject of broadcasting.[286]

Elsewhere it stated:

> The petitioners are in no manner exposed to or subject to any prior censorship of their broadcasts. Their latitude in the selection of program material, program substance, program format, and identity of program format, and identity of program personnel is bounded only by their own determination of the public interest appeal of their end product.[287]

In response to the assertion that a fear of punishment may act as a restraint upon free speech the court stated:

> The remedial provisions of Title 47 U.S.C., the Administrative Procedure Act, and the accessibility of the courts guarantee petitioners full redress from illegal, arbitrary, or capricious conduct on the part of the Commission.[288]

This reasoning is a mixture of naiveté, incorrect facts, and faulty legal analysis. The court's assumption that the broadcaster has complete discretion in selection of programming is simply incorrect. Apart from the restrictions discussed in some detail previously,[289] there is the Commission's fairness doctrine itself, one command of which is that the licensee must present controversial public issues programming as part of its duty to

285. *Id.* at 2022-25; *see also* 2018-20.
286. *Id.* at 2018.
287. *Id.* at 2024.
288. *Id.* at 2025.
289. See discussion, *supra*, Part II: A, B, and C.

serve the public interest.[290] The court's evident conclusion that because there is no direct control and no prior restraint of programming, there is no restraint resulting from the Commission's fairness doctrine is unrealistic and legally erroneous. To the extent the free exercise of speech is conditioned upon the speaker's doing something which he would not otherwise do because of the threat of incurring some penalty, there is a clear restraint. The court's conclusion to the contrary and its apparent insistence on some form of prior restraint is directly contrary to the constitutional principles settled more than thirty-five years ago in *Near v. Minnesota*.[291] Finally, the court's conclusion that the alleged restraint resulting from Commission sanctions and from the fear of punishment is somehow dissolved by the availability of judicial review and adequate safeguards against arbitrary Commission action is naive. Although the availability of review and the applicability of standards may be relevant in deciding whether a restraint is a permissible one, the restraint is no less real by reason of its being reviewable, and no less substantial because it is not arbitrarily imposed. A court cannot avoid its responsibility of deciding whether the action of the agency, including agency sanctions or the threat of such sanctions, constitutes an impermissible restraint on speech merely because it can review the agency's actions. Obviously once the review is made, a decision must be made at least with respect to the agency's action in the case before it. Undoubtedly the court did not mean to suggest that there could never be an impermissible restraint merely because of the availability of judicial review. Yet it seems to have used the availability of review as an excuse for refusing to consider the permissible extent of the restraint imposed by the application of the Commission's fairness doctrine.

The *Red Lion* opinion is simply inadequate. One might argue that whether the general fairness doctrine is valid or not, the personal attack principle is sufficiently different in purpose, scope, and effect to be upheld.[292] Had the court confined itself to the personal attack rules and attempted to so limit the scope of its holding, its decision might be at least defensible, even if questionable. Unfortunately, the court recognized no distinction between the broad scope of the fairness doctrine and the more limited personal attack rule. On the contrary, the court couched

290. Editorializing by Licensees, 1 P & F RADIO REG. 91:201, 206 (1949).

291. 283 U.S. 697 (1931).

292. See text accompanying notes 265-68 *supra*.

its opinion in the broadest terms, reaching conclusions which are not merely unconvincing but plainly erroneous in their generality. The larger questions were passed over too easily with irrelevancies and facile reasoning.

Most notably the court's opinion makes no effort to penetrate the basic assumption on which the Commission's arguments and conclusions rest and which is central to the entire first amendment issue: the assumption that radio communication is unique and, being unique, is subject to interference with freedom of speech that the court would never tolerate if applied to other communications media.

III. TOWARDS A GENERAL RATIONALE FOR REGULATION: SENSE AND NONSENSE ABOUT THE NATURE OF RADIO AND TELEVISION

The Commission, as has been seen, has little if any well defined policy or philosophy of program regulation as such. Indeed, it has persistently refused to acknowledge that it "regulates" programming or that its actions are in any significant way a restraint of or an interference with free speech. About all one can say is that the Commission requires that: (a) a broadcaster must not permit his station to be used for broadcasting indecent, defamatory, or otherwise unlawful program material; (b) a broadcaster must at least take some steps to ascertain local programming interests and to meet such interests in a responsible manner; (c) a broadcaster must present "balanced" programming in accordance with certain general standards (set by the Commission); and (d) a broadcaster must be "fair" in presenting controversial issues or political broadcasts. These are standards which in themselves may seem difficult to oppose. Indeed, to take issue with them seems almost like attacking the Boy Scout Oath. But the issue here is not whether these standards are acceptable standards of conduct. The question is whether or not the FCC has any right to impose such standards.

Ultimately, the justification advanced for the Commission's vaguely conceived and dimly illumined policies toward nontechnical regulation, particularly in the area of programming, centers around the basic assumption that, whatever may be the application of the first amendment to common forms of expression or to other mass communications media, the rules are different for radio and television because they are unique. There are varying explanations given by the courts, by the Commission, and by critical observers as to why radio and television are unique. The principal explanations can be fairly summarized into four basic arguments:[293] (1) unlike other communications media, private or public, the means of communications which radio and television use are publicly owned;[294] (2) radio and television communications are uniquely affected with the public interest, and the use of airways is a *privilege* to be granted to broadcasters only so long as they continue to serve the public;[295] (3) radio and television are uniquely influential and powerful as communications media;[296] and (4) unlike other communications media, private or public, there are physical and technical limitations imposed on access to and the use of the radio and television media.[297] Without question each of these notions contains some germ of the truth. The problem is that they have become more than just arguments to be analyzed and critically evaluated. They have become ideologies which have taken the place of thoughtful reasoning. Comment about the "unique" nature of broadcasting has become so far removed from practical considerations that it has become a kind of modern-day analogue to the medieval discourses on the number of angels that can stand on the head of a pin.

One of the most persistent of modern shibboleths used in support of virtually every form of FCC regulation has been the proposition that the airways and broadcast spectrum are owned by the public, that is, they are "public domain" administered in trust for the public by the FCC. According to this theory, the broadcast licensee is permitted to use this public domain only so long as it serves the public interest, as determined by the FCC.[298] Because of this public ownership, the Commission has a broad regulatory authority and even a duty to oversee all aspects of the licensee's use of such public property. According to

---

293. For a good, brief discussion of the principal arguments, see Sullivan, *Editorials and Controversy: The Broadcaster's Dilemma*, 32 GEO. WASH. L. REV. 719, 757-66 (1964). *See also* Pierson, *The Need for Modification of Section 326*, 18 FED. COM. B.J. 15, 25-26 (1963); Note, *Regulation of Program Content by the FCC*, 77 HARV. L. REV. 701, 713 (1964).

294. *See, e.g.*, H.R. REP. No. 281, 88th Cong., 1st Sess. 205-07 (1963).

295. *See* Television Corp. v. FCC, 294 F.2d 730, 733-34 (D.C. Cir. 1961); S. REP. No. 994, 87th Cong., 1st Sess., pt. 6, 1 (1962).

296. *See, e.g., Hearings on S. 1898 Before the Communications Subcomm. of the Senate Comm. on Interstate and Foreign Commerce*, 86th Cong., 2d Sess. 18 (1960).

297. *See, e.g.*, National Broadcasting Co. v. United States, 319 U.S. 190, 215-16 (1943); KFKB Broadcasting Ass'n v. Federal Radio Comm'n, 47 F.2d 670, 672 (D.C. Cir. 1931).

298. H.R. REP. No. 281, 88th Cong., 1st Sess. 205-07 (1963).

proponents of this argument, this necessarily includes overseeing the station's program operations.

As is true of so many of the concepts which have become encrusted on the law, there is a superficial appeal in the public domain idea which makes it hard to dispel, even in the minds of those whom one would not assume disposed to the type of constitutional intrusions which it is used to support.[299] Little effort has ever been made to look beneath the superficiality of the concept of public ownership of the broadcast spectrum to determine whether it has any practical logic or meaning. Logically the concept is meaningless. To say that the airways or spectrum can be owned by anyone is simply to indulge in fantasy. Surely no one seriously supposes that the airways are a thing of nature which can be possessed, occcupied, or used in any normal sense of the word. In actuality, "airways" is merely convenient shorthand, an abstraction for a phenomenon created as a result of the use of privately owned transmission facilities. The "spectrum" is a purely artificial construct of the Commission itself. To give this construct an independent nature and then attempt to justify the regulation itself in those terms is entirely circular. It is like saying that the Commission owns the frequencies because it has the power to regulate their use, and that it has the power to regulate their use because it owns them.

One may perhaps speak with some sense about public ownership of air rights or space through which electrical impulses are transmitted, but this is quite different. Moreover, even this concept will not support any claim for rightful regulation. All such air space is not publicly owned. And even if it were all publicly owned, this would not support regulation of broadcast communications or speech as distinguished from any other

---

299. Justice Douglas, whom few would accuse of being an apologist for regulation of free speech under any pretext, appears to have accepted the public domain theory in conjunction with the "spectrum scarcity" argument, as justifying different rules for radio and television:

> We have, of course, a system of licensing for radio and television stations. But the problem there is quite different. The channels all lie in the public domain, the air space above the earth being under the exclusive control of Congress. The channels are restricted in number. It is necessary to regulate all if interference is to be kept at a minimum and service is to be efficient. What the government owns or controls in the airways it can regulate as it sees fit.

W. DOUGLAS, RIGHT OF THE PEOPLE 76-77 (1958).

A more extreme statement of the case for plenary regulation by the FCC could scarcely have been made by the FCC itself. It should be emphasized, however, that the loose, even offhand, observations in a book are not the same as a carefully considered judicial decision.

kind of communication or speech. If, for example, this hypothetical public ownership of air space is a basis for regulating broadcast speech, is it not also a basis for regulating virtually all types of speech that similarly use air space—in short, all forms of oral communications from loudspeaker announcements to backyard gossip? This is an absurd proposition, but how would the distinguishing line between broadcasting and other forms of speech be drawn? Clearly reliance on the ownership concept itself provides no basis for such a distinction.

In any event the public ownership concept is plainly insufficient justification for government interference with free speech under well-established constitutional doctrine. The Supreme Court has made it emphatically clear, for example, that public ownership of postal facilities does not justify censorship of the content of private correspondence or other printed matter sent through the mail.[300] Nor does public ownership of parks, streets, or other property justify otherwise unconstitutional restraints on free speech.[301] Public ownership of the airways, whatever it may mean, is surely no exception.

In substance, the public ownership argument seems really to be a paraphrase of a widely held, seldom well-stated assumption that because broadcasting is an activity "affected with a public interest," restraints which would not otherwise be permitted in a purely private sector of society are warranted and even necessary.[302]

While few would dispute that broadcasting is affected with a public interest, this fact does not justify any intrusion on free speech which would not otherwise be permissible. It is, therefore, neither controlling nor even particularly pertinent that Congress concluded that broadcasting is affected with a public interest, provided for periodic licensing of broadcast facilities, and stated that a license to broadcast is purely a privilege and not a right.[303] The Supreme Court has made it emphatically

---

300. Hannegan v. Esquire, 327 U.S. 146 (1946).

301. *See, e.g.*, Kunz v. New York, 340 U.S. 290, 293-4 (1951); Saia v. New York, 334 U.S. 558 (1948) (by implication); Hague v. CIO, 307 U.S. 496, 515-16 (1939).

302. Television Corp. of Michigan, Inc. v. FCC, 294 F.2d 730 (D.C. Cir. 1961). It should be pointed out that the context in which this statement was made was not one involving any constitutional or even statutory question of Commission authority. Rather, it was a wholly gratuitous remark made in the course of admonishing the licensee and the FCC that broadcasting must serve the public.

303. S. Rep. No. 994, 87th Cong., 1st Sess., pt. 6, 1 (1962) (emphasis in last sentence added). For the concurring view of former FCC

clear that the right to license does not carry with it the right to place unconstitutional limitations or conditions on the license and particularly that it confers no authority to censor or interfere with free speech, whether or not the license be characterized as a mere privilege.[304] Indeed, far from expanding an agency's powers with respect to first amendment freedoms, the authority to license is a basis for even closer scrutiny of the agency's actions in this respect. Recognizing that a degree of censorship may be an inherent tendency in the exercise of administrative licensing powers, the Court has indicated it will scrutinize such licensing activities with particular care to ensure that they are not used to override first amendment guarantees.[305]

Implicit in many, if not most, of the arguments advanced for a greater governmental interference with broadcast speech than is permitted for other types of communications media is the usually unarticulated assumption that broadcasting is uniquely influential and powerful as a medium of communication.

There is perhaps a degree of truth in this belief, at least in the case of television.[306] First, there is the immediacy of a televised message as compared with the printed word. For example, few who watched the classic televised political campaign debates between Kennedy and Nixon in 1960 would seriously question that television had a far greater impact on each viewer than any verbatim newspaper coverage would have. This is not to say that news, editorials, and other public affairs information are necessarily more effectively covered by broadcasting. But item for item, a well-done television program is likely to have far greater impact on the average person than is a comparable newspaper article.[307] Second, the impact of radio and

---

Chairman Minow, see FREEDOM AND RESPONSIBILITY IN BROADCASTING 173 (Coons ed. 1961).

304. *E.g.*, Sherbert v. Verner, 374 U.S. 398 (1963); Hannegan v. Esquire, 327 U.S. 146, 156 (1946); Terral v. Burke Constr. Co., 257 U.S. 529 (1922); *see generally* Note, *Unconstitutional Conditions*, 73 HARV. L. REV. 1595 (1960).

305. *See* Saia v. New York, 334 U.S. 558 (1948); Hannegan v. Esquire, 327 U.S. 146, 156 (1946); Hague v. CIO, 307 U.S. 496 (1939).

306. I would be inclined to doubt that the impact of a radio message is anywhere near as strong as that of a well-written newspaper or magazine story.

307. See Fairly, *Can You Believe Your Eyes?*, IX HORIZON 24 (1967), for a persuasive commentary on the impact of television news programming. However, it must be admitted that the presumed impact of television can be and sometimes is highly exaggerated. To many people, television has, like radio, become largely a background of music, speech, or simply noise, a part of the din of civilization which many need to hear but not necessarily pay any attention to.

television in terms of the size of audience far exceeds that of any other mass communications medium. Consider, for example, a well known, regularly scheduled network news program, the "Huntley-Brinkley Report." Nielson audience ratings for January 1967 indicate that during this period each broadcast reached an average of nearly ten million homes.[308] This is more than three times the combined average daily circulation of the *New York Times*, the *Washington Post*, the *Chicago Tribune*, the *Los Angeles Times* and the *St. Louis Post Dispatch*,[309] five of the largest and most influential newspapers in the country. Obviously it cannot be denied that television is an influential and powerful communications medium.

It remains to be seen, however, whether adequate justification has been shown for greater government interference with speech in the case of broadcasting than in the case of less powerful media. Although television may have a great effect in terms of its immediacy and the extent of its audience, radio is not nearly so effective. Yet no one has suggested that radio and television might be regulated in differing degrees. In addition, the influence and importance of any single television station, which is the basic regulatory unit, has been misunderstood and exaggerated. The audience test mentioned above, for example, does not take into account that the audience reached by the program is not the result of a single, monolithic voice but actually the voices of more than 700 individual stations.[310] Even narrowing this number down to take into account those stations under common ownership, it is apparent that there are a substantial number of different entities responsible. It may be argued that since most local stations are merely outlets for the three major networks and a handful of program suppliers that it is the net effect of broadcasting as an industry which is the essential fact in determining to what extent the FCC should interfere with programming. But if this approach is accepted, one must alter the comparative picture since newspapers, too, have their networks. Like broadcast stations, newspapers often speak with one voice—that of the Associated Press, United Press

---

308. BROADCASTING MAGAZINE, February 13, 1967, at 68. An entertainment special covered by the same reporting period, "The Bob Hope Christmas Show," reached nearly 21 million homes. *Id.* at 66.

309. Based on the then current ABC circulation data, AYER & SONS, DIRECTORY OF NEWSPAPERS AND PERIODICALS 106, 189, 284, 600, 767 (1965), indicates the combined average daily circulation of these newspapers to be 3,087,547.

310. 1966 FCC ANN. REP. 116-18 shows 721 television stations operating as of June 30, 1966.

or other news service or, more accurately, that of the originating source. The relative impact of television would thus seem comparable not to one newspaper or even five, but more realistically, to all newspapers subscribing to a major news wire service.

Even if one unrealistically aggregates all of the television stations under four headings according to their affiliation with one of the three major networks or their independent status, and even if one considers this as a potential of four distinct and potentially different voices accounting for all broadcast programming, is this in itself grounds for government interference with programming? Is it constitutionally necessary, in short, to have at least a possibility of more than four distinct voices on all subjects? We have only two national political parties which, based on the same theory which leads us to believe that there are only four potentially distinct broadcast voices, give us only two political viewpoints. Does this warrant some form of government interference with political speech or perhaps government subsidization of a third party point of view? In all but a handful of American cities there are, at the most, two daily newspapers and thus, in theory, only two distinct and potentially different viewpoints from the daily press. Does this perhaps warrant government interference through subsidizing more local newspapers or controlling the content of those newspapers which do exist?

In the final anlaysis it is doubtful that the Supreme Court would ever hold that the application of the first amendment's protection of free speech depends on any subtle and tenuous evaluation of the influence of the speaker. Justice Douglas, concurring in *Superior Films v. Department of Education* stated:

> Motion pictures are of course a different medium of expression than the public speech, the radio, the stage, the novel, or the magazine. But the First Amendment draws no distinction between the various methods of communicating ideas. On occasion one may be more powerful or effective than another . . . . Which medium will give the most excitement and have the most enduring effect will vary with the theme and the actors. It is not for the censor to determine in any case.[311]

Although all of these various rationalizations concerning the uniqueness of radio and television have occupied an important place in the ideology of broadcast regulation, ultimately the rationale to which almost all return is that of "spectrum scarcity." As Justice Frankfurter stated in the *NBC*[312] case, "Un-

311. 346 U.S. 587, 589 (1954) (concurring opinion).

312. National Broadcasting Co. v. United States, 319 U.S. 190, 226 (1943). For an excellent critical analysis of *NBC* and the spectrum

like other modes of expression, radio inherently is not available to all . . . and that is why, unlike other modes of expression, it is subject to governmental regulation."

The most obvious shortcoming of Justice Frankfurter's logic is that, notwithstanding conceded physical limitations on frequency availability and the corresponding limitation on the number of broadcast facilities which can be operated, the fact remains that radio and television stations are more numerous than any of the other competing mass communications media. For example, as of June 30, 1966, there were 5,881 radio and 721 television stations operating.[313] The number of radio and television stations is substantially greater than, for example, the number of daily newspapers, of which there were 1,751 operating as of January 1, 1966.[314] The disparity between the number of newspapers and the number of radio and television stations is most strikingly evident when it is noted that only the largest cities can boast two or more daily newspapers not under common ownership.[315] By contrast virtually every city large enough to have a daily newspaper is served by at least two television stations and several radio stations.[316] While the number of daily newspapers has slowly declined, the number of competing radio

---

scarcity argument, see Sullivan, *Editorials and Controversy: The Broadcaster's Dilemma*, 32 GEO. WASH. L. REV. 719, 757-66 (1964).

313. 1966 FCC ANN. REP. 116-18. This figure does not include television translators and boosters. As of that date, there were an additional 318 radio and 158 television stations (exclusive of translators and boosters) authorized but not operating. Most of these latter are stations which had received construction permits but had not then received licenses or "program test authority."

314. U.S. BUREAU OF THE CENSUS, STATISTICAL ABSTRACT OF THE UNITED STATES 523 (87th ed. 1966).

315. *See* AYER & SONS, *supra* note 309, at 1250-71 (1965).

316. *See* 1967 TELEVISION FACTBOOK; 1967 BROADCASTING YEARBOOK. Although, except as the information is set forth throughout the above standard references, there is no single published source which clearly identifies the number of radio and television services which each city receives, a fair idea of the multiple television service available is given in a 1960 Nielson study, *Television '60*, which shows that some 94% of all television homes (94% of all homes in the United States, *see* 1967 BROADCASTING YEARBOOK 18) can receive at least three television stations and some 81% can receive at least four. No distinction is drawn here between a city to which a station is licensed and a city which receives service. Drawing such a distinction as a general proposition is unrealistic, at least so far as television is concerned. As a practical matter, a station need not be physically located in or technically assigned to a city in order to serve that city adequately, particularly where the cities are part of the same culturally and socially integrated metropolitan area.

and television stations has rapidly increased and continues to increase.[317]

It is often said that the limitations on access to and use of the newspaper medium is an economic limitation, not a technical one. The distinction, however, is entirely specious. Contrary to common assumption, the spectrum is not nearly saturated. There are few, if any, areas of the country today where additional radio and television stations are not technically possible.[318] Moreover, it is at least doubtful whether, given the present structure of the industry, the spectrum will ever be competely saturated with radio and television stations.[319] Although there is currently a trend towards an increased number of stations, particularly UHF television stations, it seems unlikely that the trend will continue to the technical saturation point. In almost all radio and television markets, economic barriers to entry will come into play before the technical barriers. The economic limitations have already become the dispositive factor in the growth of radio and television stations in many, if not most, small and medium-sized markets. The barrier to entry to further stations in those areas is not the technical unavailability of frequencies, but rather the economic inability of the area to support an additional station and the unavailability of sources of programming different from that which is already being provided by the existing stations. This situation then is identical to

317. From 1950 to June 30, 1966, the number of radio stations on the air more than doubled from 2,897 to 5,881; and the number of television stations (exclusive of translators and boosters) increased seven times, from 104 to 721. 1966 FCC ANN. REP. 116-18. By contrast, from 1950 to January 1, 1966, the number of daily newspapers declined from 1,772 to 1,751. U.S. BUREAU OF THE CENSUS, STATISTICAL ABSTRACT OF THE UNITED STATES 523 (87th ed. 1966).

318. On February 9, 1966, the Commission adopted its newly revised, computer-determined Table of Assignments for television channels. *Fifth Report, UHF Channel Assignments*, 6 P & F RADIO REG. 2d 1643 (1966). The revised Table at that date provided for 1,756 fixed VHF and UHF assignments (in 792 cities). *Id.* at 1667. However, the Table made only two assignments in the upper UHF frequency band, Channels 70-83, these channels proposed to be used for small "community" stations on an ad hoc basis. *Id.* at 1666. Thus, the 1,756 assignments (stations) do not include some 17% of the spectrum. Moreover, even as to channels below 70, the Table is not "saturated" and thus there is space for additional assignments over and above the 1,756 reflected in the Table. *Id.* at 1649, 1673-74. *See, e.g., UHF Channel Assignments in Palm Springs*, 8 P & F RADIO REG. 2d 1533 (1966) (adding another UHF channel to Palm Springs). In short, even with present technology, there is, at a *conservative* estimate, room for three or more times the 721 stations operating as of June 30, 1966. *See* note 318 *supra*.

319. *See Second Report* 1772.

the situation in all large mass communications media. It is impossible, therefore, to distinguish radio and television from newspapers, movie theaters, or magazine and book publishers on this basis. If barriers to entry and limitations on access to the use of mass communications media are to be relied on as a basis for imposing regulation of free speech which would not otherwise be justified, such regulation should not discriminate against radio and television but should extend to all communications media.

One commentator, recognizing that the natural barriers to entry into and the limitations on access to the newspaper industry are as great as those which surround broadcasting, has recently proposed that newspapers should also be subject to some kind of general editorial regulation, similar to the fairness doctrine, to ensure that a diversity of viewpoints is presented to the public.[320] According to this proposal, by Professor Barron, such regulation would not only be consistent with the first amendment but it would promote the essential spirit of the first amendment which, in his view, was not designed to protect the right to speak freely so much as to protect the right of the public to hear a diversity of viewpoints.[321] Since barriers to entry and limitations on access effectively limit the right of the public to receive such a diversity of views, newspapers and presumably all other mass media should be required to present all sides of an issue. Despite a certain superficial appeal, Professor Barron's proposition is unsupportable. His theory fits well with John Stuart Mill's utilitarian defense of free speech and with the traditional thinking which conceives of free speech as a surer way to the truth,[322] but it is inadequate as an exposition of the meaning and thrust of the first amendment and free speech today. One major justification for free speech is, of course, the

---

320. Barron, *Access to the Press—A New First Amendment Right*, 80 HARV. L. REV. 1641 (1967).

321. *Id.* at 1648-49.

322. Were an opinion a personal possession of no value except to the owner; if to be obstructed in the enjoyment of it were simply a private injury, it would make some difference whether the injury was inflicted only on a few persons or on many. But the peculiar evil of silencing the expression of an opinion is, that it is robbing the human race; posterity as well as the existing generation; those who dissent from the opinion, still more than those who hold it. If the opinion is right, they are deprived of the opportunity of exchanging error for truth: if wrong, they lose, what is almost as great a benefit, the clearer perception and livelier impression of truth, produced by its collision with error.

J. S. MILL, ON LIBERTY, in UTILITARIANISM, LIBERTY AND REPRESENTATIVE GOVERNMENT 104 (Everyman Lib. 1951). *Compare* Justice Holmes' dissent in Abrams v. United States, 250 U.S. 616, 630 (1919).

benefit which the public at large derives from hearing a diversity of viewpoints and ideas. But if the sole or even the paramount aim of the first amendment is merely to ensure that the public is able to hear a Babel of voices, the first amendment is not the great libertarian principle it has been thought to be. Freedom of speech is a justifiable aim in itself insofar as it helps to create the individual freedom and security essential to a free society. It need not be buttressed by any apologies that it will assure the dissemination of a diversity of viewpoints, that it will ensure a free marketplace for ideas, or that it is a surer means of advancing truth.

It is suggested that if the government does not place some direct editorial control on mass communications media, it is in essence allowing them to be censors,[323] given the effective limits on entry into such media. According to Barron, this problem cannot be met by general legislation such as the antitrust laws, but must be dealt with by some kind of direct editorial control.[324] In short, we are told to replace the private censor with a government censor. The portrayal of the mass media as all-powerful private censors, subject to no one's influence but their own, is greatly exaggerated. Moreover, the supposed inability of the antitrust laws or, in the case of broadcasting, the various diversification policies and multiple ownership rules to increase competition is due more to the manner in which they are presently being applied than to any inherent deficiency in their approach.

Finally, if it is true that the barriers to entry and the limitations on access to the use of mass communications media give too much control to the mass media, this still does not resolve the problem. The question of what kinds of corrective regulation should be provided and how much government supervision should be permitted remain. What are we to conclude from the fact that there are, for example, not sufficient finances to provide every city of a quarter million population with more than three local television stations or two local newspapers? Do we infer from this fact that the government must take upon itself the responsibility of guiding, if not controlling, the program policies of these stations or the editorial policies of the newspapers? If so, does this extend equally to stations in communities which have ten stations and four newspapers? What kind or degree of control would be permitted on this basis? At what point is the line drawn between complete control and mere "influence" of

323. Barron, *supra* note 320, at 1648.
324. *Id.* at 1654.

program choice? What standard shall underlie the Commission's judgment in acting on such matters? If, for example, audience surveys show that eighty-five per cent of the population in a given market prefers light entertainment, should the Commission be guided by this or must it take upon itself the role of a "leader" in guiding popular choice by setting down more elevated, "enlightened" standards? I would agree with those who strongly protest the slavish attitudes with which most broadcasters follow the lowest common denominator of public taste, as represented by audience ratings. I emphatically agree with the idea, as expressed by one critic, that "the first task of the purveyors of entertainment and intelligence is to anticipate, gamble on, whet, stimulate, elevate, and/or broaden the public taste."[325] But how can this responsibility be adequately enforced by a government agency without seriously compromising the first amendment?

Neither society as a whole, Congress, nor the FCC has ever formulated any principles which satisfactorily guide judgment on such matters consistent with the aims of an open society. There have developed, in a long Anglo-American tradition of legal and social thinking, various controls on the abuse of free speech, but nowhere in this tradition has there been any developed thinking going beyond sporadic and occasional restraints, such as prohibition of defamatory speech, obscenity, fraud, and otherwise patently harmful or socially disrupting speech. There is no tradition of establishing, for example, standards of "fairness," "diversity," or "balance." These are judgments which, for better or for worse, have been left to the admittedly sometimes quixotic judgment of the public, unguided by their "enlightened" cultural, social, or political leaders.

There may be little reason to trust the judgment of broadcasters or the managers of other mass communications media, but is there any more reason to have an abiding faith in the judgment of the FCC or any other governmental agency? The probability of the mass media's being responsive to public needs is, I think, as great, if not greater than the probability that the FCC's judgment will adequately reflect those needs. And ultimately, the danger to a free society from a reliance on the judgment of private broadcasters is less than from a reliance on the judgment of the FCC. Barron has expressed a realistic concern over the tendency of the mass media to avoid the controversial,

325. L. White, The American Radio 221 (Comm'n on Freedom of the Press ed. 1947).

novel, and heretical ideas whose expression is so crucial to a vital growing society.[326] It is, however, naive in the extreme to suppose that government supervision, through the fairness doctrine or other means, would ultimately promote heterodoxy. As has been pointed out above, government intervention in broadcast programming has in fact been a major impetus toward conformity and orthodoxy.

Where does the foregoing evaluation, if correct, lead us? There are undoubtedly some who would conclude that these considerations must lead ineluctably to the conclusion that the Congress and the Commission should be allowed to regulate only the technological aspects of radio and television. This conclusion, however, seems as extreme in principle as it is naive. There is no constitutional principle which says that, merely because some forms of regulation of free speech are unconstitutional, all forms of regulation which might affect or in some manner restrain free speech are similarly unconstitutional. The first amendment does not forbid the Commission from going beyond its role as "traffic cop" of the airways. Radio and television are certainly not constitutionally exempt from general social and economic regulation merely because their business is the business of communication.

Thus radio and television, like newspapers, are subject to the general laws which bind all persons, institutions, and businesses, such as the antitrust laws, labor laws, and laws governing libel, slander, fraud, and other socially disruptive conduct and speech. Concededly there are first amendment limitations on the application of such laws, but the limitations are not unique to radio and television. They extend as well to newspapers, movie theaters, or soap box orators.

Moreover, it does not necessarily follow that because the Commission may not constitutionally impose its own standards of orthodox programming or its own standards of balance, fairness, and diversity that it may not in general insist that a licensee investigate and be responsive to demonstrated needs of his community. The first amendment does not require that a licensee must be permitted to operate a radio facility purely in his private and selfish interest with no concern for public needs and interests. The first amendment comes into play, however, when the Commission, in the name of reviewing a licensee's responsiveness, begins to concern itself with programming or pro-

326. Barron, *supra* note 320, at 1645-47.

gram operations to the point of establishing standards of acceptable and nonacceptable programming. It has already reached and gone beyond this point.

Although some supporters of strong Commission regulation predict dire consequences in the event the Commission should relinquish any of its regulatory oversight of licensee program operations, it is doubtful that the Republic will falter should the Commission's thus far unfettered powers in this area be curbed to conform to the first amendment as interpreted for and applied to other communications media. On the basis of the first forty years of regulation, it may be difficult to say that the cause of free speech has suffered egregiously at the hands of the FCC. But there is every indication that the problem is serious and becoming increasingly more so. The fairness doctrine which the Commission seems bent on applying and interpreting with increasing rigidity, cases such as *Palmetto*, and an increasing preoccupation with, if not fetish for, balanced programming are three very strong reasons for taking a less sanguine view of FCC regulation in the next forty years and for implementing more vigorous first amendment limitations on regulation in this field.

Mr. Justice Holmes: A Dissenting Opinion—The Speech Cases

Yosal Rogat*
James M. O'Fallon**

Preface

When Walton Hamilton wrote, in 1941, that it had "taken a decade to elevate Mr. Justice Holmes from deity to mortality,"[1] he spoke with wisdom on his subject, but he spoke too soon. The champions of Holmes' apotheosis were not finished: Those who would assign him to a warmer eternity were just beginning.[2]

By 1962, when the *Stanford Law Review* published the first part of Yosal Rogat's *Mr. Justice Holmes: A Dissenting Opinion,*[3] scholars had begun a sober reconsideration of Holmes. As Saul Touster, whose own work has been of central importance to that reconsideration,[4] said:

> By this time a sense of the ambiguities and double-facedness of Holmes, what Boorstin called the elusiveness of the man, had already surfaced. Commentary on [Mark De Wolfe] Howe's work reflected this by more cautious judgments on Holmes and his influences as a legal theorist and judge. One such essay, by the late Yosal Rogat, was a powerfully argued and documented critique of Holmes' work on the Supreme Court in which Holmes' callousness to civil liberties, exemplified by his consistent denial of the constitutional claims of Negroes and aliens,

* Late Associate Professor of Law and Political Science, Stanford University.

** Professor of Law, University of Oregon. I thank Yosal's children, Paul and Anne, for permitting me to use his manuscript. I have had the support and encouragement of many of Yosal's friends, especially Gerald Gunther, Saul Touster, and Ellen Hawkes, but it does not denigrate their contributions to remark that the opportunity to once again engage this extraordinary mind, teacher, and friend was itself support enough for my effort.

1. Hamilton, *On Dating Mr. Justice Holmes,* 9 U. Chi. L. Rev. 1, 1 (1941).

2. For a general account of attitudes towards Holmes, including the attack on Holmes as the forerunner of fascism, see White, *The Rise and Fall of Justice Holmes,* 39 U. Chi. L. Rev. 51 (1971).

3. Rogat, *Mr. Justice Holmes: A Dissenting Opinion,* 15 Stan. L. Rev. 3, 254 (1962–63).

4. *See* Touster, *In Search of Holmes from Within,* 18 Vand. L. Rev. 437 (1965); Touster, *Holmes: The Years of* The Common Law, 64 Colum. L. Rev. 230 (1964).

was explored. Rogat's work was important in providing a lasting corrective to the myth of Holmes as one of " 'the most liberty-alert Justices of all time.' " Perhaps more important was Rogat's analysis of Holmes' reasoning. He revealed how Holmes—who had magisterially told us "[t]he life of the law has not been logic: it has been experience"— continously resorted to a legalistic logic rather than the counsels of human experience in liberty-sensitive matters.[5]

In his first article Rogat announced a plan to publish two additional articles, "one considering the speech cases—which are, of course, [Holmes'] best known in the area of civil liberties—the other considering the general area of defendants' rights."[6] The plan was never executed. In 1964, Rogat published *The Judge as Spectator*, [7] an essay that Gerald Gunther called "the most provocative and intellectually satisfying stimulus to the modern reexamination of Holmes."[8] It was Rogat's last published contribution to Holmes scholarship. The centerpiece of the essay was a comparative study of Holmes, Henry Adams, and Henry James, which employed the three friends' shared attitudes and similar responses to situations to illuminate the characteristic that most distinguished Holmes from other judges—his detachment.[9]

This article is the second of the three announced in Rogat's original plan. Its core is an extensive manuscript, which he diffidently entitled "Some Notes on Case Stuff." While I cannot date the manuscript precisely, extrinsic evidence suggests that Rogat probably wrote it not too long after the 1964 article. Some of the discussion is anticipated in *The Judge as Spectator*. Yosal discussed other aspects of it in his courses at Stanford in the late 1960s and

5. Touster, *Holmes a Hundred Years Ago:* The Common Law *and Legal Theory,* 10 HOFSTRA L. REV. 673, 679 (1982) (citations omitted).

Professor White has argued that the attack on Holmes' "liberalism" is ahistorical—finding Holmes wanting by the standards of a different time than his own. White, *supra* note 2, at 72–74. It may be that if one limits comparison to other justices of the Supreme Court, Holmes was a cut above a generally retrograde lot. But, as David Rabban has demonstrated, some of the scholarly literature on free speech during Holmes' time had a notably modern "liberal" cast. Rabban, *The First Amendment in Its Forgotten Years,* 90 YALE L.J. 514 (1981).

6. Rogat, *supra* note 3, at 10.

7. Rogat, *The Judge as Spectator,* 31 U. CHI. L. REV. 213 (1964).

8. Gunther, *Learned Hand and the Origins of Modern First Amendment Doctrine: Some Fragments of History,* 27 STAN. L. REV. 719, 720 n.4 (1975).

9. Rogat, *supra* note 7, at 254. That study prefigured the intellectual endeavor which would be the primary focus of the remainder of Yosal's working life—an effort to redraw the boundaries of modernism along lines suggested by Wittgenstein's concept of family resemblances.

early 1970s. For the most part, the task of bringing the manuscript to publication has been editorial. (One can only admire the elan of a writer who executes a sixty-page manuscript without identifying the location of a single reference, particularly when one of the sources has a five-foot bookshelf to himself.[10]) The major addition to the original manuscript is the discussion of Learned Hand's *Masses* alternative to Holmes' "clear and present danger" doctrine.[11] Yosal had not discussed that, although comments in the manuscript and a note to Professor Gunther clearly indicate his belief that it was necessary. Of course, the task was very much eased by Professor Gunther's work on Hand and *Masses*.[12]

Professor Rogat's technique was to analyze Holmes' participation in every nonunanimous civil liberties decision during his thirty years on the bench. The opinions are illuminated by Holmes' underlying ideology, and compared to Holmes' reputation as one of the two most "liberty-alert Justices of all time." As Professor Rogat noted in the introduction to his first article, this technique presents several practical difficulties. First, it is sometimes difficult to identify the civil liberties interest in any particular case. Second, Holmes' opinions are among the tersest and most elliptical in the history of the Supreme Court. This contributes to their rhetorical power, but it also makes them particularly difficult to construe, and open to diverse interpretations. "One has no alternative," Yosal wrote, "but to offer one's own."[13]

Nearly a generation has passed since this article was initially conceived. The idea that Holmes was not the great liberal he was once thought to be is by now a part of conventional wisdom. Yet we still have much to learn, as recent pathbreaking work by Saul Touster[14] and Robert Gordon[15] amply demonstrates. Though twenty years late, Yosal Rogat's analysis of Holmes' free speech opinions deepens our understanding of Holmes, and reminds us how much of that understanding we owe to Rogat.

---

10. *See* note 59 *infra*.

11. Masses Publishing Co. v. Patten, 244 F. 535 (S.D.N.Y. 1917), *rev'd*, 246 F. 24 (2d Cir. 1917). *See* notes 121–139 *infra* and accompanying text.

12. Gunther, *supra* note 8.

13. This paragraph is drawn from the introduction to the first article. Rogat, *supra* note 3, at 3–10.

14. Touster, *supra* note 5.

15. Gordon, *Holmes'* Common Law *as Legal and Social Science*, 10 Hofstra L. Rev. 719 (1982).

I. The "Early," Pre-*Schenck* Cases

While on the Massachusetts Supreme Court, Holmes wrote the majority opinions in *McAuliffe v. Mayor of New Bedford*[16] and *Commonwealth v. Davis*.[17] In *McAuliffe,* New Bedford had fired a police officer for political activities. The controlling statute provided that policemen should hold office during good behavior, subject to removal by the mayor for sufficient cause. A New Bedford police regulation read: "No member of the department shall be allowed to solicit money or any aid, on any pretense, for any political purpose whatever."[18] Membership on a political committee was also prohibited.

At the initial hearing before the mayor, the City offered testimony to show that McAuliffe had been at the headquarters of a political party prior to an election, and that he had attended a conference as a member of a political committee. During the trial, however, the mayor could not recall which specific acts he had deemed "soliciting aid" within the prohibition of the rule. McAuliffe had not solicited money or other material aid, but he had "talked politics"; the mayor would not state, however, that McAuliffe had done so while on duty.[19] McAuliffe petitioned the Massachusetts Supreme Court to restore him to his job, arguing that the mayor's finding did not warrant the removal, and that the rule restricted his right to express his political opinions.

In the best known part of his opinion, Holmes said:

> The petitioner may have a constitutional right to talk politics, but he has no constitutional right to be a policeman. There are few employments for hire in which the servant does not agree to suspend his constitutional right of free speech, as well as of idleness, by the implied terms of his contract. The servant cannot complain, as he takes the employment on the terms which are offered him. On the same principle, the city may impose any reasonable condition upon holding offices within its control.[20]

Holmes gave no indication of what kinds of conditions were "reasonable." He simply concluded: "This condition seems to us reasonable, if that be a question open to revision here."[21]

---

16. 155 Mass. 216, 29 N.E. 517 (1892).
17. 162 Mass. 510, 39 N.E. 113 (1895).
18. *McAuliffe,* 155 Mass. at 220, 29 N.E. at 517.
19. *Id.* at 218–19, 29 N.E. at 517.
20. *Id.* at 220, 29 N.E. at 517–18.
21. *Id.* at 220, 29 N.E. at 518. The paragraph containing the famous dictum begins:

In *Commonwealth v. Davis*[22], the defendant was convicted of violating a Boston city ordinance which prohibited making any public address on any public ground without a permit from the mayor. Apparently, Davis claimed that the ordinance was unconstitutional, although the precise grounds are not clear from the opinion. Holmes said:

> The argument . . . involves the same kind of fallacy that was dealt with in *McAuliffe v. New Bedford* . . . . It assumes that the ordinance is directed against free speech generally . . . whereas in fact it is directed toward the modes in which Boston Common may be used. There is no evidence before us to show that the power of the Legislature over the Common is less than its power over any other park dedicated to the use of the public, or over public streets the legal title to which is in a city or town . . . . For the Legislature absolutely or conditionally to forbid public speaking in a highway or public park is no more an infringement of the rights of a member of the public than for the owner of a private house to forbid it in his house. When no proprietary right interferes, the Legislature may end the right of the public to enter upon the public place by putting an end to the dedication to public uses. So it may take the lesser step

---

> One answer to [McAuliffe's] argument, assuming that the statute does not make the mayor the final judge of what cause is sufficient, and that we have a right to consider it, (*Ham v. Boston Board of Police,* 142 Mass. 90, 95 [1886] and *Osgood v. Nelson,* L.R. 5 H.L. 636, 649 [1872]), is that there is nothing in the Constitution or the statute to prevent the city from attaching obedience to this rule as a condition to the office of policeman, and making it part of the good conduct required.

Id. at 220, 29 N.E. at 517. In *Ham,* the Supreme Judicial Court noticed the absence of any express statutory provision for revising a determination of cause for removal of a police officer, and went on to say "there would appear to be no opportunity for such revision, unless perhaps by the courts, in case of an arbitrary exercise of the power, for a cause which is unreasonable and in law insufficient; as, for example, for refusing to contribute money for political purposes." 142 Mass. 90, 95 (1886). Holmes was a member of the court when *Ham* was decided, but did not participate in the decision.

The *Osgood* citation refers, apparently with approval, to the fact that the court of Queen's Bench had always considered itself empowered, in cases of removal from office, to correct the removing power's decision "if it should be found that such persons have disregarded any of the essentials of justice in the course of their inquiry, before making that removal, or if it should be found that in the place of reasonable cause those persons have acted obviously upon mere individual caprice." 5 L.R.–E. & I. App. at 649 (1872).

Holmes' caution in asserting the court's authority, both at the beginning and the end of the noted paragraph, may be nothing more than careful reservation of questions not yet decided. But Holmes was conceptually troubled with the very idea of legal limits on the power of the sovereign, Rogat, *supra* note 3, at 10–18, and his failure to give significant consideration to the first amendment claims in *McAuliffe* may be a product of his general view on sovereign power.

22. 162 Mass. 510, 39 N.E. 113 (1895).

of limiting the public use to certain purposes.[23]

Holmes said the constitutionality of the ordinance was "implied by the former decision [against Davis] and does not appear to us open to doubt." The earlier *Davis* opinion contains no discussion of the constitutional issue.[24]

It is instructive that Holmes refuses, on the slim basis of an unstated premise of judgment in a prior case, to accord the constitutional question the dignity of an issue open to debate. A similar position was recorded some forty years later in a letter to Harold Laski.

> Do you know that I really am bothered by the old difference between us, if there is one, as to sovereignty, because as I understand the question it seems to me one that does not admit of argument . . . . I can't understand how anyone should think that an instrumentality [the Supreme Court] established by the United States to carry out its will, and that it can depose upon a failure to do so, should undertake to enforce something that *ex hypothesi* is against its will. It seems to me like shaking one's fist at the sky, when the sky furnishes the energy that enables one to raise the fist.[25]

Thus, in *Davis*, the city's ownership of the park seemed conclusive to Holmes. The simplicity of this view characterized his opinions in both cases.[26] How much is Holmes' *Davis* analogy stretched by inferring that a municipality might exclude speakers from parks as capriciously as an individual might exclude someone from his home: Might the municipality exclude anyone in particular, or anyone of a given age or hair color? Both *Davis* and *McAuliffe* succeed stylistically because of their breadth and lack of qualification. These very same qualities, however, make them potential support for arbitrary action.

In neither opinion did Holmes seriously consider the risk of inhibiting speech or the social interest in free expression. He therefore recognized no rights; he saw only privileges which government need not grant at all, privileges to which it seemingly could attach any conditions whatsoever.[27]

23. Davis, 162 Mass. at 511, 39 N.E. at 113 (citations omitted).

24. Commonwealth v. Davis, 140 Mass. 485, 4 N.E. 577 (1886) upheld Davis' conviction against objections that the ordinance had been enacted by an improper procedure.

25. Letter from O.W. Holmes, Jr. to Harold Laski (Jan. 29, 1926), in 2 HOLMES-LASKI LETTERS 822 (M. Howe ed. 1953).

26. The "greater includes the lesser power" form of argument was a standard in Holmes' arsenal. Rogat, *supra* note 3, at 14–18, 281–82, 300.

27. While in *McAuliffe* Holmes suggested that the power to remove the policeman

Patterson v. Colorado[28] was the first case in which Holmes addressed a first amendment claim for the Supreme Court.[29] The

---

from office might be subject to judicial review for arbitrariness, no similar qualifying language appears in *Davis*.

It appears that Davis also advanced an "as applied" argument against the ordinance.

> It is argued that the ordinance really is directed especially against free preaching of the Gospel in public places, as certain Western ordinances seemingly general have been held to be directed against the Chinese. But we have no reason to believe, and do not believe, that this ordinance was passed for any other than its ostensible purpose, namely, as a proper regulation of the use of public grounds.

162 Mass. at 512, 39 N.E. at 113. If, as seems likely, Holmes's mention of "Western ordinances" was an oblique reference to Yick Wo v. Hopkins, 118 U.S. 356 (1886), his way of disposing of the claim, by focusing on the purpose for which the ordinance was passed, totally misrepresents the point of that case, which deals with the discriminatory enforcement of a facially neutral statute. Counsel for Davis on appeal to the U.S. Supreme Court relied on *Yick Wo* and other cases protecting Chinese immigrants from discrimination at the hands of municipal authorities. Rabban, *supra* note 5, at 530 n.62. It is unlikely that Holmes misunderstood *Yick Wo*. Rather, Holmes plainly rejected the statement of political principle on which Justice Matthews had based his analysis.

> Sovereignty itself is, of course, not subject to law, for it is the author and source of law; but in our system, while sovereign powers are delegated to the agencies of government, sovereignty itself remains with the people, by whom and for whom all government exists and acts. And the law is the definition and limitation of power. It is, indeed, quite true, that there must always be lodged somewhere, and in some person or body, the authority of final decision; and in many cases of mere administration the reponsibility is purely political, no appeal lying except to the ultimate tribunal of the public judgment, exercised either in the pressure of opinion or by means of the suffrage. But the fundamental rights to life, liberty and pursuit of happiness, considered as individual possessions, are secured by those maxims of constitutional law which are the monuments showing the victorious progress of the race in securing to men the blessings of civilization under the reign of just and equal laws . . . . [T]he very idea that one man may be compelled to hold his life, or the means of living, or any material right essential to the enjoyment of life, at the mere will of another, seems to be intolerable in any country where freedom prevails, as being the essence of slavery itself.

118 U.S. at 370. Given this theoretical predicate for *Yick Wo,* it is not surprising that Holmes did not rush to embrace it in *Davis*. *See* notes 21, 25 *supra* and accompanying text.

The United States Supreme Court accepted Holmes' view of the matter in Davis v. Massachusetts, 167 U.S. 43, 47–48 (1897). *But cf.* Hague v. C.I.O., 307 U.S. 496, 514–16 (1939) (opinion of Roberts, J.) (privilege of using streets and parks for communication may be regulated in general interest, but cannot be denied or abridged under guise of regulation).

28. 205 U.S. 454 (1907).

29. Rabban has recently demonstrated the error in the view that modern first amendment history sprang from a void with the Espionage Act of 1917 and the litigation that it spawned. Rabban, *supra* note 5. Between the time that Holmes took his seat on the Supreme Court in 1902 and *Patterson,* the Court decided a number of cases concerning the authority of the Postmaster General to determine the mailability of material, and

Court dismissed an appeal of a contempt judgment imposed by the Colorado Supreme Court. Patterson, who published articles and a cartoon allegedly reflecting upon the Colorado court's conduct in cases that were still before it, claimed that he had a constitutional right to prove the truth of the articles, and that he had published them in pursuance of a public duty. Holmes disposed of most of Patterson's appeal on the jurisdictional ground that it raised issues of local law, not reviewable by the Supreme Court.[30]

---

the qualifications for second class mailing privileges that implicitly involved first amendment issues. *See* Rabban, *supra* note 5, at 526–28.

The Court explicitly addressed the first amendment claims of an Englishman deported for his anarchist views in Turner v. Williams, 194 U.S. 279 (1904). Turner had been arrested after giving a lecture in New York in which he had discussed a general strike of workers. *Id.* at 283. Chief Justice Fuller's opinion said only, "We are at a loss to understand in what way the act is obnoxious to [the first amendment]." *Id.* at 292. Part of the discussion resonates with Holmes' views on the constitutional protection accorded aliens, discussed in Rogat, *supra* note 3, at 10–44. Fuller said:

> To appeal to the Constitution is to concede that this is a land governed by that supreme law, and as under it the power to exclude has been determined to exist, those who are excluded cannot assert the rights in general obtaining in a land to which they do not belong as citizens or otherwise.

Turner, 194 U.S. at 292.

In addressing the claim that the statute excluding alien anarchists was unconstitutional because it would include mere political philosophers, as well as advocates of government overthrow, Fuller showed great deference to congressional authority.

> If the word "anarchists" should be interpreted as including aliens whose anarchistic views are professed as those of political philosophers innocent of evil intent, it would follow that Congress was of [the] opinion that the tendency of the general exploitation of such views is so dangerous to the public weal that aliens who hold and advocate them would be undesirable additions to our population, whether permanently or temporarily, whether many or few, and, in the light of previous decisions, the act, even in this aspect, would not be unconstitutional, or as applicable to any alien who is opposed to all organized government.
>
> We are not to be understood as depreciating the vital importance of freedom of speech and of the press, or as suggesting limitations on the spirit of liberty . . . but this case does not involve those considerations.

Id. at 294.

Holmes did not disagree with this statement of first amendment doctrine. Given his willingness to allow the government nearly absolute discretion in withholding the privilege of entry from aliens, *see* Rogat, *supra* note 3, this may reveal very little of his view of the substance of the first amendment claim. He did not join Justice Brewer's concurring opinion, which indicated concern for the claim of the philosophical anarchist by pointing out that Turner had offered no rebuttal to the evidence that *he* was an advocate of overthrowing the government. 194 U.S. at 296.

30. Patterson evidently argued that the Colorado court's proceedings in his case involved departures from well-settled precedents. Holmes deprecated this argument by saying "this allegation is regarded as giving some sort of constitutional right to the plaintiff in error," but "[t]here is no constitutional right to have all general propositions of law once adopted remain unchanged." 205 U.S. at 460–61. Later courts, sensitive to

Rather than deciding the then open question of whether the fourteenth amendment imposed on the states a prohibition similar to the first amendment's restriction on the federal government, Holmes reached out to decide the "easier" free speech claim. Holmes' deprecatory view of the first amendment came close to eliminating the claims of free expression altogether. Relying on an analogy to the law of criminal libel, he asserted that the Constitution does not prevent subsequent punishment for expression: While the government cannot enjoin or censor words before they are expressed, it is free to punish them afterwards:

> But even if we were to assume that freedom of speech and freedom of the press were protected from abridgment on the part not only of the United States but also of the States . . . the main purpose of such constitutional provisions is "to prevent all such *previous restraints* upon publications as had been practiced by other governments," and they do not prevent the subsequent punishment of such as may be deemed contrary to the public welfare. The preliminary freedom extends as well to the false as to the true; the subsequent punishment may extend as well to the true as to the false. This was the law of criminal libel apart from statute in most cases, if not in all.[31]

He also dismissed the publication's lack of actual effect as irrelevant by saying, "if a court regards, as it may, publication concerning a matter of law pending before it, as *tending* toward [an interference with the exercise of judgment], it may punish it . . . ."[32] Long before 1907, prior licensing had ceased to be the primary danger to freedom of expression.[33] A narrow interpretation like Holmes' would have rendered the first amendment insignificant. As Chafee said, under this kind of theory, "liberty of

---

the possibility that a state court might manipulate state law so as to insulate violations of federal rights from Supreme Court review, have been more receptive to arguments like Patterson's. *See e.g.*, Indiana *ex rel.* Anderson v. Brand, 303 U.S. 95 (1938) (refusal to accept state court's contract law judgment, in case raising impairment of obligation of contract claim); Williams v. Georgia, 349 U.S. 375 (1955) (state court refusal to entertain constitutional challenge on procedural grounds no bar to Supreme Court jurisdiction on merits, where independent review of state law reveals that relief from procedural failure is discretionary); Henry v. Mississippi, 379 U.S. 443 (1965) (procedural defaults in state proceedings do not prevent vindication of federal rights unless state's insistence on compliance with procedural rule serves legitimate state interest).

31. 205 U.S. at 462 (emphasis in original) (citations omitted).

32. *Id.* at 463 (emphasis added).

33. *See* 2 T. COOLEY, CONSTITUTIONAL LIMITATIONS 883–85 (8th ed. 1927). *See generally* L. LEVY, LEGACY OF SUPPRESSION (1960); Anderson, *The Formative Period of First Amendment Theory, 1870–1915,* 24 AM. J. LEGAL HIST. 56 (1980); Rabban, *supra* note 5.

the press means opportunity for blackmailers and no protection for political criticisms."[34] Furthermore, by this time many states had rejected the English rule that truth was no defense in criminal libel.[35]

Holmes' later reputation for unique sensitivity to free speech claims was certainly not built on *Patterson*. Justice Harlan—whom Holmes later derided as having a mind like "a powerful vise the jaws of which couldn't be got nearer than two inches to each other"[36]—dissented:

> I cannot assent . . . if it be meant that the legislature may impair or abridge the rights of a free press and of free speech whenever it thinks that the public welfare requires that to be done. The public welfare cannot override constitutional privileges . . . . In my judgment the action of the court below was in violation of the rights of free speech and a free press as guaranteed by the Constitution.[37]

In *Patterson,* the vice was Holmes'.

Holmes again spoke for the Court in *Fox v. Washington.*[38] Fox belonged to a nudist group whose members had been charged with indecent exposure; two had been imprisoned. Fox published an article entitled *The Nude and the Prudes,* castigating the "few prudes" who had denounced the nudists to the police, and urging a boycott of those interfering with the nudist community's freedom.

> And the perpetrators of this vile action wonder why they are being boycotted . . . . The first step in the way of subjecting the [nudist] community to all the persecution of the outside has been taken. If this was let go without resistance the progress of the prudes would be easy . . . . The boycott will be pushed until these invaders will come to see the brutal mistake of their

34. Z. Chafee, Jr., Free Speech in the United States 9 (1941).

35. *Id.* at 5 n.2.

36. 2 Holmes-Pollock Letters 8 (M. Howe ed. 1941).

37. 205 U.S. at 465 (Harlan, J., dissenting).

38. 236 U.S. 273 (1915).

Between *Patterson* and *Fox,* the Court avoided a potential first amendment challenge to New York's criminal libel statute by narrowly construing the Federal Assimilative Crimes Act of 1898 in United States v. Press Publishing Co., 219 U.S. 1 (1911). It also rejected a first amendment objection to a statute requiring that publications seeking second-class mailing privileges divulge information regarding ownership, and label advertising as such, on the ground that the requirements were reasonable and incidental conditions on the privilege of subsidized mailing. Lewis Publishing Co. v. Morgan, 229 U.S. 288, 313–16 (1913). Both opinions were unanimous. For further discussion, see Rabban, *supra* note 5, at 528–29, 540.

action and so inform the people.[39]

Fox was convicted of editing printed matter tending "to encourage or advocate disrespect for law" under a Washington statute making it a gross misdemeanor to willfully print or knowingly circulate any matter "advocating, encouraging or inciting, or having a tendency to encourage or incite the commission of any crime, breach of the peace or act of violence, or which shall tend to encourage or advocate disrespect for law or for any court or courts of justice."[40]

Fox argued that the Court should void the law because of what later came to be called overbreadth and vagueness. He maintained that the reach of the law was not certain enough, and that a state could not constitutionally punish utterances that merely "tend to encourage or advocate disrespect for law."[41] The statute contained no language requiring "proximity" to success, but spoke only of "a tendency."

In his opinion for the Court, Justice Holmes admitted that Fox's article incited only "by indirection." However, he had only the following to say about liberty of expression:

> We understand the state court by implication at least to have read the statute as confined to encouraging an actual breach of law. Therefore the argument that this act is both an unjustifiable restriction of liberty and too vague for a criminal law must fail. It does not appear and is not likely that the statute will be construed to prevent publications merely because they tend to produce unfavorable opinions of a particular statute or of law in general.[42]

The only basis for Holmes' remark about the reading of the statute was that the Washington court had said, "The article is not a criticism of the law, but was calculated to, and did, incite the violation of law. . . ."[43] But there was no indication whatsoever that the Washington Supreme Court believed it constitutionally necessary to limit the application of the law to "an actual breach of law," or thought that the law would not apply to more ambiguous facts. The opinion contains very general language such as "it is not meant [by the constitutional guarantee of free speech] that persons may with impunity advocate disregard of

39. *Fox,* 236 U.S. at 276–77 (quoting from Fox's article).

40. *Id.* at 275 (quoting from the statute).

41. *Id.* at 275.

42. *Id.* at 277.

43. State v. Fox, 71 Wash. 185, 187, 127 P. 1111, 1112 (1912).

law."[44] Furthermore, an incitement theory was inconsistent with the facts in *Fox*. Fox's article does not on its face incite a breach of the laws against exposure; it merely threatens certain people with a "boycott." Fox could have been convicted for encouraging disrespect for the law only by advocating the ostracism of the "public minded" citizens who reported violations of the law. But this is not the same as affirmatively encouraging violations of law.

Even if this were not the case, Holmes seemed to take the position that a law may on its face validly provide for the punishment of constitutionally immune acts by punishing those who publish material which merely tends to encourage disrespect for law, so long as a court thinks it is "not likely" to be applied to those acts. Yet eight months earlier, the Court in *International Harvester Co. of America v. Kentucky*[45] had for the first time struck down a criminal statute for uncertainty, holding unconstitutional a Kentucky statute regulating price-fixing combinations. Holmes, writing for the Court, saw those affected as having to "guess on peril of indictment" and "divine prophetically,"[46] whether their behavior was unlawful. Because a "vague" law may inhibit constitutionally protected behavior, a court should consider the importance of the actions that may be inhibited. The two decisions reveal something of Holmes' attitude toward these two activities. Although he considered the risk of inhibiting lawful price-fixing schemes in *International Harvester,* Holmes did not consider the risk of inhibiting lawful criticism of a statute in *Fox*. Nor did he consider the relative unimportance of the state's interest in prosecuting Fox, though, as even clothing manufacturers would agree, it was not a matter of national security. He said, in typical fashion, "Of course we have nothing to do with the wisdom of the defendant, the prosecution, or the act."[47] At this time, four years before his *Schenck* opinion, Holmes certainly showed no special concern about the expression of dissident social views.[48]

---

44. *Id.* at 186, 127 P. at 1112.

45. 234 U.S. 216 (1914).

46. *Id.* at 223.

47. *Fox,* 236 U.S. at 278.

48. On the same day that *Fox* was decided, a unanimous Court rejected the claim that motion pictures were within the ambit of first amendment protection, upholding censorship programs in Ohio and Kansas. Mutual Film Corp. v. Industrial Comm'n of Ohio, 236 U.S. 230 (1915); Mutual Film Corp. of Missouri v. Hodges, 236 U.S. 248 (1915).

II. Political Thought, Legal Thought, and the Origin of "Clear and Present Danger"

Zechariah Chafee said, "The real issue in every free speech controversy is this: whether the state can punish all words which have some tendency, however remote, to bring about acts in violation of law, or only words which directly incite to acts in violation of law."[49] Despite the results reached in these early cases, the clear and present danger doctrine—the linchpin of Holmes' reputation as a liberal—was on the "liberal" side of the basic dividing line. It was taken up for thirty years by those arguing for fewer restraints on expression, and came to symbolize this effort. From a historical point of view, this fact is more important than the possibility that they might have been more successful with a more definite test.

Holmes' formulations of a concept with these "liberal" *potentialities* need not be considered fortuitous in relation to his political thought. To explain the connection, however, we must inquire into the genesis of the "clear and present danger" doctrine as well as summarize his political thinking.

A. *Holmes' Theory of Attempts*

A relationship between the clear and present danger test and Holmes' theory of attempts has been noted but not adequately explicated.[50] That relationship, illuminated by Holmes' total political outlook, demonstrates that the "liberal" and desirable aspects of the clear and present danger concept were intimately connected with, and almost a direct result of, the very way in which Holmes was mistaken about and consistently exaggerated the "objectivity" of the laws.

Holmes' account of legal phenomena was fundamentally impoverished; it suffered from a failure to distinguish a crude system of social control resting on naked force from a distinctively legal method of control.[51] He thought of a legal system as simply

---

49. Z. Chafee, Jr., *supra* note 34, at 23.

50. *See* Ragan, *Justice Oliver Wendell Holmes, Jr., Zechariah Chafee, Jr., and the Clear and Present Danger Test for Free Speech: The First Year, 1919*, 58 J. Am. Hist. 24, 29–31 (1971); Green, *Liberty Under the Fourteenth Amendment*, 27 Wash. U.L.Q. 497, 539–40 (1942); Hall, *The Substantive Law of Crimes, 1887–1936*, 50 Harv. L. Rev. 616, 621 (1937).

51. [I]t seems to me clear that the *ultima ratio*, not only *regum*, but of private persons, is force, and that at the bottom of all private relations, however tempered by sympathy and all the social feelings, is a justifiable self-preference. If a man is on a plank in the deep sea which will only float one, and a stranger lays

a mechanism to enforce in any manner the desires of the dominant group as if a "reign of terror" were merely a subspecies of "legal system" rather than a fundamentally contrasting concept.[52]

Given this view of a legal system, Holmes concentrated his legal theory, like his political theory, on eliminating obstacles to the will of the dominant class.[53] For Holmes, the most important obstacle was the habit of associating legal rules with moral ideas. If a court modified a concrete expression of the sovereign will in the light of moral ideas, it imputed independent legal relevance to those ideas apart from any command of the sovereign. Holmes recognized that many legal words had been taken from a moral context and often retained their original moral meaning. He therefore acknowledged that it would be difficult to see them only as technical, neutral expressions, to dissociate them completely from morals, to realize that legal rules were simple "statement[s] of the circumstances in which the public force will be brought to bear upon men through the courts."[54] To accomplish this, Holmes suggested that we somehow lift ourselves up (drag ourselves down?) by our own malevolence, and look at the law through the eyes of a "bad man," who wanted to know only what he could get away with: to prophesy "what the courts will do."[55]

Holmes used his "external standard" theory to separate law from morality. He said that the law was radically "objective," that it was not concerned with internal phenomena but only with external compliance.[56] By objectivity, Holmes meant the law was behaviorist: It regarded only observable evidence—"bodily motions and rests"[57]—even when it appeared to refer to mental phenomena.[58] The observable was not only evidence of internal

---

hold of it, he will thrust him off if he can. When the state finds itself in a similar position, it does the same thing.

O.W. HOLMES, THE COMMON LAW 38 (M. Howe ed. 1963).

52. "[A]ll law means I will kill you if necessary to make you conform to my requirements." 1 HOLMES-LASKI LETTERS 16 (M. Howe ed. 1953).

53. "The first requirement of a sound body of law is, that it should correspond with the actual feelings and demands of the community, whether right or wrong." O.W. HOLMES, *supra* note 51, at 36.

54. 2 HOLMES-POLLOCK LETTERS 212 (M. Howe ed. 1941).

55. O.W. HOLMES, *The Path of the Law,* in COLLECTED LEGAL PAPERS 167, 171, 173 (1952).

56. O.W. HOLMES, *supra* note 51, at 33.

57. *Id.* at 88.

58. "[A]ll reference to the state of his consciousness is misleading if it means any-

phenomena, but itself the very criterion of legal decision. Holmes thus adopted the position that W.S. Holdsworth has criticized as a "confus[ion] [of] the evidence for a proposition with the proposition proved by that evidence."[59] While this part of the theory seemed to center on what it is possible to ascertain, Holmes also argued that the law did, and should, adopt a definite policy of requiring only outward conformity. He asserted that although the law had originally based liability on moral blameworthiness, it had discarded its moral bases. Now the law took moral considerations into account "only for the purpose of drawing a line between such bodily motions and rests as it permits, and such as it does not." The law had become "wholly indifferent to the internal phenomena of conscience."[60]

This ubiquitous issue of "subjectivity" versus "objectivity" is particularly acute in the law of attempts. Two of the elements used to distinguish noncriminal "preparation" from a criminal "attempt" have been, first, the specific intent to bring about the consequences which legally constitute the crime, and second, actions which get "pretty near" to the crime, or, in another view, are unequivocally directed at the doing of a criminal act.[61]

Exaggerated "objectivity" concentrates on purely external events as the criteria of punishment, and minimizes the importance of the actor's actual intentions. This approach risks injustice, since socially dangerous and morally culpable individuals may benefit simply because a fortuitous event prevents the consummation of an intended crime, while others may be punished for unintended harm. At the other extreme, concentration on the actor's intention would "treat" potentially antisocial personalities rather than punish actions.

It has generally been said that intent is "the essence of an attempt." Most analysts have followed Austin, who concluded that criminal attempt punished intention, with the act constituting evidence of a firm intention.[62] Holmes, however, predictably assigned intent a strictly subsidiary role. In contrast to Austin, he

---

thing more than that the circumstances in connection with which the tendency of his act is judged are the circumstances known to him." *Id.* at 61.

59. 3 W.S. Holdsworth, A History of English Law 375 (3d ed. 1923).

60. O.W. Holmes, *supra* note 51, at 88.

61. *See* Wechsler, Jones & Korn, *The Treatment of Inchoate Crimes in the Model Penal Code of the American Law Institute: Attempt, Solicitation, and Conspiracy,* 61 Colum. L. Rev. 571, 586–95 (1961).

62. 1 J. Austin, Lectures on Jurisprudence 440–41 (Campbell ed. 1885).

set out to reduce the law of attempt to objective probability: "[I]f the views which I have advanced as to murder and manslaughter are sound, the same principles ought logically to determine the criminality of acts in general. Acts should be judged by their tendency under the known circumstances, not by the actual intent which accompanies them."[63]

Holmes asserted that "an act is punishable as an attempt, if, supposing it to have produced its natural and probable effect, it would have amounted to a substantive crime."[64] However, he specified one exception where actual intent was necessary: where acts could not have effected a crime unless followed by other acts. It was then necessary to show that the actor, had he not been interrupted, would have chosen to do them. In this special category, the law gave intent its "common meaning." As he said in *Swift & Co. v. United States,*[65] "[w]here acts are not sufficient in themselves to produce a result . . . but require further acts in addition to the mere forces of nature . . . an intent to bring it to pass is necessary in order to produce a dangerous probability that it will happen."[66]

Yet even in these special cases, Holmes stressed that intent was relevant only because it indicated the probability of harm: "because the intent raises a strong probability that an act, innocent in itself, will be followed by other acts or events in connection with which it will accomplish the result sought to be prevented by the law."[67] These cases, where "intent" was to be given a "common meaning," were also, therefore, part of Holmes' general theory, applicable to all of the criminal law—namely, that wherever intent was an element of a crime, it was only an index to the probability of future external acts.[68] Fully conscious of the issue of "objectivity," Holmes maintained that the law does not look at the character of the actor, but at his actions. "The importance of the intent is not to show that the act was wicked, but to show that it was likely to be followed by hurtful consequences."[69] Holmes was also consistent in treating at-

63. O.W. HOLMES, *supra* note 51, at 54.

64. *Id.* at 55.

65. 196 U.S. 375 (1905).

66. *Id.* at 396. *See* notes 153–157 *infra* and accompanying text.

67. O.W. HOLMES, *supra* note 51, at 62.

68. *See, e.g., id.* at 59. ("In theft the intent to deprive the owner of his property establishes that the thief would have retained . . . the stolen goods.")

69. *Id.* at 56.

tempts in terms of the "external standard." He wanted to draw a line and to punish all those whose acts for whatever reason crossed it. He was as willing to ignore what society learned about the dangerousness of those who, because of accident, fell short of the line, as he was to punish those who sought to cause consequences which did not constitute a crime.

This view of attempt raises serious difficulties. Courts have long stressed "intent," and not only where some future act remained to be done. The law does not consider only the "tendency under the known circumstances"; the most negligent acts, with the greatest probability of harm, may not suffice.[70]

Holmes' approach to the law of attempts anticipated the clear and present danger doctrine, which is akin to the "proximity rule," requiring that "[t]here must be dangerous proximity to success"[71] before attempts are punished. He himself associated the external standard theory and clear and present danger language when he said, "As the aim of the law is not to punish sins, but is to prevent certain external results, the act done must come pretty near to accomplishing that result before the law will notice it."[72]

In *Schenck,* Holmes had to apply a statute which punished willfully causing or attempting to cause military insubordination and disruption of recruiting. Ordinarily, a defendant would be prosecuted for criminal attempt only if his utterances had brought his unlawful intention somewhere close to success. It is therefore not surprising that the war situation and the statute in *Schenck* evoked the clear and present danger doctrine; Holmes' language represented, in large part, a habitual response in terms of concepts he had expressed since at least 1881.

Holmes' external standard approach is especially suited to the needs of the speech area, where the very desideratum is Holmes' professed general objective: indifference to "internal phenomena of conscience." A liberal desire to protect a wide range of expression would very likely demand evidence of both "proximity" and consequences. This approach at least guards against the

70. Wechsler, Jones & Korn, *supra* note 61, at 587, criticize Holmes' approach as "based on the assumption that the purpose of punishing attempts is to deter undesirable behavior," rather than to neutralize dangerous individuals.

71. Hyde & Schneider v. United States, 225 U.S. 347, 388 (1912) (Holmes, J., dissenting).

72. Commonwealth v. Kennedy, 170 Mass. 18, 20, 48 N.E. 770 (1897).

greatest danger: punishing for thoughts. Thus, the "liberal" aspect of the clear and present danger doctrine resulted from the very way in which Holmes' approach to the problem of externality was generally wrong.

B. *Authoritarianism vs. Totalitarianism*

The liberal political implications of Holmes' doctrine expressed, in this area of the law, the politically attractive aspect of Holmes' Social Darwinism. To explain this, it is necessary to summarize a certain important strand of Holmes' political ideas and to distinguish between "authoritarian" and "totalitarian" thought.

A small group of Holmes' critics has called him "totalitarian."[73] Yet, although Holmes consistently deprecated the role of both reason and custom, vesting authority almost solely in force, his "authoritarian" style of thought is, in a sense, the very opposite of "totalitarian" thought. His assertion that a man "rightly" preferred his own self-interest, along with his lack of concern about internal phenomena, differs completely from totalitarianism's attack on individual privacy and its demand for complete loyalty and constant affirmation. Totalitarianism attempts to transform the individual by forcing him to abandon all private concerns and partial-group loyalties. Attaining moral freedom by merging with the whole, the individual receives his "life and being" thereafter as a part of it. Where totalitarian thought uses the word "freedom" to mean something very close to what we ordinarily mean by "discipline," Holmes, like Hobbes, never meant anything but an absence of restraint. Since reason, because of Holmes' "skepticism," did not establish obligation for him, and since he did not recognize any meaningful conception of the "general interest," dominating social groups could never claim to represent an individual's actual interest. They could coerce him, but they had to call it coercion. Holmes' ruling class could not demand internal affirmation, but only external compliance.

Totalitarianism takes a position exactly opposite to Holmes' by minimizing the importance of the legal act itself and stressing motivation and the nature of the actor. We may criticize Holmes

73. *E.g.*, Palmer, *The Totalitarianism of Mr. Justice Holmes: Another Chapter in the Controversy*, 37 A.B.A. J. 809 (1951). For other examples, see Kurland, Book Review, 25 U. CHI. L. REV. 206, 206 n.4 (1957).

for exaggerating the toughness and amorality of the common law, but we cannot simultaneously accuse him of holding a theory which thinks only of preventing antisocial potentialities, which attacks all individualism by identifying crime with disease, and which assumes that man is completely knowable and completely malleable. Holmes' image of a legal system comes close to a bill of fare on which a price has been attached to each act by an impersonal management almost indifferent to what the customer himself decides; totalitarianism sees law as a system of prophylaxis based on knowledge and anticipation of what and how the patients are likely to decide.

Further, because Holmes saw all activity as purposeless, he refused to justify any effort instrumentally. Nevertheless, he displayed a thoroughly attractive intrinsic appreciation of art, scholarship, and privacy. Totalitarianism, on the other hand, with demonic fervor, subordinates everything, including life itself, to making its vision real. Thus, where Holmes completely separated morals from politics and from law, totalitarianism insists on their absolute identification. Not only does every legal duty become a moral duty, but every moral duty must be legally enforced. The state must not merely provide an opportunity for men to lead a good life, but must make certain they lead it. Most fundamentally, totalitarianism opposes Holmes' acceptance of men as he found them. It is horrified by them, and obsessed with the desire to transform them.

In short, the question of how much "radical" expression government should permit did not directly touch the inhumane, overly "tough" amoralism of Holmes' outlook. Rather, it revealed the other aspect which stressed that anyone was "free" (subject to subsequent punishment) to do even that which was strictly forbidden, as determined exclusively by matching an external act with a rule.

C. *Skepticism*

One other factor also led Holmes to a liberal position on speech. This was his concern that judges should not impede the avenues of social change.[74] The history of the law reflected a series of wars between social groups. Law should somehow not

74. *See* O.W. HOLMES, *The Path of the Law*, *supra* note 55, at 184; O.W. HOLMES, *Law in Science and Science in Law*, *supra* note 55, at 239.

participate in that ongoing conflict, but should remain a passive observer until each particular battle has at least temporarily ended. As he said:

> [I]t is as it should be, that the law is behind the times . . . . As law embodies beliefs that have triumphed in the battle of ideas and then have translated themselves into action, while there still is doubt, while opposite convictions still keep a battle front against each other, the time for law has not come . . . .[75]

Since Holmes was skeptical of absolute "truth," believing instead that there were only degrees of probability, he focused his attention on the clash of conflicting beliefs, and ended by accepting whatever won out and commanded the most force. He felt courts should not clog that struggle by placing impediments in the way of "the natural outcome of a dominant opinion."[76] Ultimate strength was a curiously predestined condition for Holmes, apparently unaffected by conscious governmental attempts to impede some groups or to assist others. Judges should become neutral, friction-free transmission belts, making political rights exactly equivalent to societal power. The curious fatalism he expressed in his *Gitlow* dissent reflects this outlook: "If in the long run the beliefs expressed in proletarian dictatorship are destined to be accepted by the dominant forces of the community, the only meaning of free speech is that they should be given their chance and have their way."[77]

This background helps to relate Holmes' view of the world to the judicial doctrine he created.

III. *SCHENCK* AND ITS COMPANION CASES

A. Schenk, Frohwerk, *and* Debs

In a series of cases decided shortly after World War I, the Court, essentially for the first time, considered federal legislation in relation to the constitutional right of "free speech." Holmes wrote the opinions for a unanimous Court in three cases that sustained convictions under the Espionage Act of 1917. It is essential to consider the opinion in *Schenck v. United States*,[78] in which the phrase "clear and present danger" first appeared,[79] together

75. O.W. HOLMES, *Law and the Court, supra* note 55, at 294–95.
76. Lochner v. New York, 198 U.S. 45, 76 (1905) (Holmes, J., dissenting).
77. Gitlow v. New York, 268 U.S. 652, 673 (1925) (Holmes, J., dissenting).
78. 249 U.S. 47 (1919).
79. *Id.* at 52.

with the *Frohwerk*[80] and *Debs*[81] opinions that Holmes read the following Monday.

The Espionage Act of 1917 made it criminal, while the United States was at war, (1) to make false statements with intent to interfere with the operation of the services or to promote the success of the enemy; (2) to cause or attempt to cause disloyalty or insubordination in the army or navy; or (3) to willfully obstruct recruiting and enlistment.[82] In *Schenck,* the court affirmed the conviction of the General–Secretary of the Socialist Party of Philadelphia for conspiracy to obstruct enlistment and to cause and attempt to cause insubordination in the armed services. He was found responsible for sending a circular to men called and accepted for military service that urged them to assert constitutional rights allegedly violated by the conscription act. As Holmes described it, the circular

> recited the first section of the Thirteenth Amendment, said that the idea embodied in it was violated by the Conscription Act and that a conscript is little better than a convict . . . . [I]t intimated that conscription was despotism in its worst form and a monstrous wrong against humanity in the interest of Wall Street's chosen few. It said: "Do not submit to intimidation"; but in form at least confined itself to peaceful measures such as petition for the repeal of the act. . . . It stated reasons for alleging that any one violated the Constitution when he refused to recognize "your right to assert your opposition to the draft," and went on "If you do not assert and support your rights, you are helping to deny or disparage rights which it is the solemn duty of all citizens and residents of the United States to retain. . . . You must do your share to maintain, support, and uphold the rights of the people of this country."[83]

The statute was not directed against speech. It did not prohibit designated utterances as such, but only (except for false statements) when they were part of certain prohibited acts—interference, and attempts to interfere, with military affairs. The Court therefore had to consider the conditions under which a statute could validly be applied to utterances when it did not on its face prohibit them. To answer this question and to determine whether the act could be applied to these facts, Holmes employed the clear and present danger standard. He first asserted

80. Frohwerk v. United States, 249 U.S. 204 (1919).

81. Debs v. United States, 249 U.S. 211 (1919).

82. Espionage Act of June 15, 1917, ch. 30, § 3, 40 Stat. 217, 219 (repealed 1948).

83. *Schenck,* 249 U.S. at 50–51.

that the constitutional right of free speech was neither absolute nor invariable.

> [T]he character of every act depends upon the circumstances in which it is done. The most stringent protection of free speech would not protect a man in falsely shouting fire in a theatre and causing a panic. It does not even protect a man from an injunction against uttering words that may have all the effect of force. The question in every case is whether the words used are used in such circumstances and are of such a nature as to create a clear and present danger that they will bring about the substantive evils that Congress has a right to prevent. It is a question of proximity and degree. When a nation is at war many things that might be said in time of peace are such a hindrance to its effort that their utterance will not be endured so long as men fight and that no Court could regard them as protected by any constitutional right.[84]

The language of the statute, which punished successful interference—and attempts to interfere— with the war, combined with some of Holmes' most deeply ingrained responses, to lead him to formulate a standard of liability resembling his approach to criminal attempt. That is, the words uttered had to approach—"come dangerously near"—"success." They had to bring about a clear and present danger of those interferences with the war that Congress had prohibited.

When, however, the standard is considered in the context of Holmes' entire opinion,[85] much of the language in *Schenck* is simply inconsistent with any satisfactory protection of speech. At one point, Holmes says: "Of course the document would not have been sent unless it had been intended to have some effect, and we do not see what effect it could be expected to have upon persons subject to the draft except to influence them to obstruct the carrying of it out."[86] This would seem to endorse intention as sufficient for liability. At another point Holmes says that "[i]f the act . . . its tendency and the intent with which it is done are the same, we perceive no ground for saying that success alone

84. *Id.* at 52 (citations omitted).

85. He started by saying that he was discussing freedom of speech only because it might be thought that subsequent punishment could infringe upon it. "It well may be that the prohibition of laws abridging the freedom of speech is not confined to previous restraints, although to prevent them may have been the main purpose, as intimated in *Patterson v. Colorado.*" *Id.* at 51–52 (citation omitted). Thus he backed away from but did not altogether repudiate his own statement in *Patterson* that the first amendment did not prevent subsequent punishment.

86. *Id.* at 51.

warrants making the act a crime."[87] A "tendency" to produce an act can hardly be equated with a "clear and present danger" that the act will result. In any case, the *Schenck* leaflet confined itself to urging lawful measures, and it is not clear it could talk anyone into anything. The government had presented no evidence of probable or even possible effects. Although *Schenck* used the phrase "clear and present danger," it is hard to see how a clear and present danger test of any substance was there applied.

Moreover, as Justice Vinson later pointed out,[88] Holmes' use of precedent in *Schenck* considerably weakened the force of the phrase. For example, he cited *Goldman v. United States*,[89] saying that case alone "might be said to dispose of the present contention if the precedent covers all *media concludendi*. But as the right to free speech was not referred to specially, we have thought fit to add a few words."[90] *Goldman* had involved the prosecution of Emma Goldman and Alexander Berkman for conspiracy to induce refusal to register for the draft. The trial judge insisted, in his charge to the jury, that the constitutional guarantee of free speech was not involved in the case.[91] Even though the overt acts charged consisted of speeches and publications opposing the draft, counsel did not pursue first amendment objections to the convictions, and the Supreme Court did not address the subject.[92]

Holmes cited *Gompers v. Bucks Stove & Range Co.*[93] for the proposition that the guarantee of free speech "does not even protect a man from an injunction against uttering words that may have all the effect of force."[94] But the *Gompers* Court had refused to discuss the first amendment argument, saying that the injunction against Gompers "did not, in terms, restrain any form of publication"[95] and that, under the circumstances of an illegal boycott, words take on "a force not inhering in the words themselves . . . therefore exceeding any possible right of speech." The words

87. *Id.* at 52 (citation omitted).

88. Dennis v. United States, 341 U.S. 494, 504 (1951).

89. 245 U.S. 474 (1918) (involving a prosecution under the Selective Draft Law of 1917). *See* The Selective Draft Law Cases, 245 U.S. 366 (1918).

90. *Schenck,* 249 U.S. at 52.

91. Dept. of Justice Bull., Interpretation of War Statutes, 41 at 2, 10.

92. Rabban, *supra* note 5, at 581–82.

93. 221 U.S. 418 (1911) (involving union publications associated with boycott activities).

94. *Schenck,* 249 U.S. at 52 (citation omitted).

95. *Gompers,* 221 U.S. at 436–37.

"become . . . 'verbal acts' . . . as much subject to injunction as the use of any other force."[96] Holmes' reliance on these cases fit his epigrammatic style. It did not reflect a serious concern with first amendment issues.

Nor are these the only problems with the *Schenck* opinion. Even the well-known remark, "[t]he most stringent protection of free speech would not protect a man in falsely shouting fire in a theatre and causing a panic,"[97] either presents an inappropriate analogy or slides over a serious difficulty. The ambiguous remark might suggest either a statement intended to be a falsehood or one subsequently found to be false. But "falsely shouting" could not mean willful falsehood when applied to sincerely held radical political views. The writers of the pamphlet obviously thought there really was a "fire," and it is not criminal to say mistakenly, but in good faith, that one sees a fire. The only alternative is that "falsely" means that which the Court subsequently proclaims to be false—the Court saying officially that there really was no "fire." But aside from the profound illiberality of this alternative, it is almost impossible for Holmes to have meant this. Justice Pitney once said, "Common knowledge . . . would have sufficed to show at least that the statements [about World War I being a Morgan war] were grossly false; and such common knowledge went to prove also that defendants knew they were untrue."[98] But Holmes was the last person likely to impose upon the Supreme Court the duty of determining the truth or falsity of politically controversial statements; it is well known that he claimed to have difficulty even with the "truth" of the sum of two and two.

Frohwerk and *Debs*, however, raise even more difficult problems about Holmes' approach to the first amendment. Frohwerk was convicted of preparing and circulating twelve newspaper articles as part of a conspiracy to obstruct recruiting, and was fined and sentenced to ten years imprisonment. The articles were very critical of America's entry into the war, the purposes of the war, and the constitutionality and merits of the draft. Holmes summarized the most extreme language: " 'that a few men and corporations might amass unprecedented fortunes we sold our honor, our very soul,' with the usual repetition that we

96. *Id.* at 439.

97. *Schenck,* 249 U.S. at 52.

98. Pierce v. United States, 252 U.S. 239, 251 (1920).

went to war to protect the loans of Wall Street. Later, after more similar discourse, comes 'We say therefore, cease firing.' "[99]

Holmes decided *Frohwerk* without referring to "clear and present danger" or to any question of consequences, saying, "[W]e have decided in *Schenck v. United States,* that a person may be convicted of a conspiracy to obstruct recruiting by words of persuasion."[100] He said:

> [T]he First Amendment . . . cannot have been, and obviously was not, intended to give immunity for every possible use of language. We venture to believe that neither Hamilton nor Madison, nor any other competent person then or later, ever supposed that to make criminal the counselling of a murder within the jurisdiction of Congress would be an unconstitutional interference with free speech.[101]

Holmes seemed to assume that the *Frohwerk* article contained language which would incite crimes. He did not mention probability of harm, except for the following remarkable comment:

> [O]n [the] record it is impossible to say that it might not have been found that the circulation of the paper was in quarters where a little breath would be enough to kindle a flame and that the fact was known and relied upon by those who sent the paper out.[102]

The *Schenck* circulars were mailed to men already passed by draft boards, but only the limited audience of the *Missouri Staats Zeitung* read these publications.

---

99. *Frohwerk,* 249 U.S. at 207.

100. *Id.* at 206.

101. *Id.*

102. *Id.* at 209. It would have been more accurate to say "because of the lack of an evidentiary record it is impossible to say . . . ." The trial judge, after refusing to sign a bill of exceptions proposed by defendant, approved one which omitted exceptions which would have brought the trial record before the Supreme Court. Brief for Plaintiff in Error 5–6, *Frohwerk.* Frohwerk sought to correct the record by writ of mandamus, a procedure approved by Chief Justice Marshall in *Ex parte* Crane, 30 U.S. (5 Pet.) 190 (1831), but the writ was denied without explanation. *In re* Frohwerk, 248 U.S. 540 (1918).

Holmes' taste for the memorable metaphor was turned against his own later efforts to stiffen "clear and present danger" as a speech-protective doctrine. In Gitlow v. New York, 268 U.S. 652, 669 (1925), Justice Sanford said:

> A single revolutionary spark may kindle a fire that, smouldering for a time, may burst into a sweeping and destructive conflagration. It cannot be said that the state is acting arbitrarily or unreasonably when . . . it seeks to extinguish the spark without waiting until it has enkindled the flame or blazed into the conflagration.

Holmes, of course, dissented in *Gitlow, see* text accompanying notes 223–225 *infra,* as much, one may imagine, from the hyperbolic abuse of his phrase as from the result.

But it is the *Debs* opinion which is most incompatible with any meaningful clear and present danger standard. To adopt Chafee's summary:

> Debs was convicted of an attempt to cause insubordination in the army and obstruct recruiting, yet no provocation to any such definite and particular acts was proved. He spoke to a convention of Socialists in support of their economic views, instancing the war as the supreme curse of capitalism. In a few sentences he approved the conduct of persons convicted of like offenses, saying, for example, that if Mrs. Stokes was guilty so was he. Her conviction has since been reversed. Not one word was designed for soldiers, not one word urged his hearers to resist the draft, objectionable as he considered it.[103]

As Chafee concluded, "Judge Westenhaver's charge gave the jury such a wide scope that Debs was probably convicted for an exposition of socialism, merely because the jury thought his speech had some tendency to bring about resistance to the draft."[104]

It was alleged that Debs "caused and incited and attempted to cause and incite insubordination, disloyalty, mutiny, and refusal of duty in the military . . . and with intent so to do delivered . . . a public speech" and "obstructed and attempted to obstruct the recruiting and enlistment service," and "with that intent delivered the same speech."[105] All Debs had done was talk. Yet, despite the necessity of establishing a connection between talking and obstructing recruiting, Holmes did not suggest any standard like "clear and present danger." Instead, he said, the jury could find:

> [T]hat one purpose of the speech, whether incidental or not does not matter, was to oppose not only war in general, but this war, and that the opposition was so expressed that its *natural and intended* effect would be to obstruct recruiting. If that was intended, and if . . . that would be its probable effect, it would not be protected . . . .[106]

Holmes added that it was permissible to introduce at the trial an "Anti-war Proclamation and Program" adopted at the Socialist convention, of which Debs approved. It was:

> [e]vidence that if in that speech he used words *tending* to obstruct the recruiting service he meant that they should have that effect. . . . [T]he [members of the] jury were most carefully in-

103. Z. CHAFEE, *supra* note 34, at 85.

104. *Id.* at 84.

105. *Debs*, 249 U.S. at 212.

106. *Id.* at 214-15 (emphasis added).

> structed that they could not find the defendant guilty for advocacy of any of his opinions unless the words used had as their *natural tendency* and *reasonably probable effect* to obstruct the recruiting service . . . and unless the defendant had the specific intent to do so in his mind.[107]

The facts of *Debs* seem almost designed to illustrate the distinction between "advocacy" and "incitement," which is rarely useful precisely because most cases, unlike *Debs*, fall into a blurred middle area. But Holmes slides over this problem with words like "natural," "tending to," "natural tendency," and "reasonably probable effect" that suggest a vague seditious libel approach—the dead opposite of any significant clear and present danger doctrine.[108]

In *Debs*, Holmes came close to equating "specific intent"—the doing of one thing for the purpose of doing another, or for causing another to take place— with what the defendant would not be displeased to have happen. Although the government introduced into evidence statements that Debs had made on another occasion, it provided no direct evidence that the defendant was then trying to bring about insubordination, refusal of duty, or interference with enlistment. Holmes assumed that the "specific intent" thus "established" made it unnecessary to show that the talk had had any actual effect, or at most he allowed the jury to assume some "probable effect" from what he called "specific intent." But this kind of reasoning could convict someone who complained of cigarette smoke in a theatre. A finding that the mention of smoke "tended" to panic an audience, together with evidence that the defendant had once turned in a false alarm, could support an inference of intent to cause panic. Tendency plus intent would be sufficient for liability. Was this "the most stringent protection of free speech" then conceivable by Holmes?

---

107. *Id.* at 216 (emphasis added).

108. As Ernst Freund said at the time:

> [T]he jury was permitted to find a tendency and an intent to obstruct recruiting. There was nothing to show actual obstruction or an attempt to interfere with any of the processes of recruiting.
>
> . . . .
>
> . . . [T]o be permitted to agitate at your own peril, subject to a jury's guessing at motive, tendency and possible effect, makes the right of free speech a precarious gift. . . . Justice Holmes takes the very essentials of the entire problem for granted.

Freund, *The* Debs *Case and Freedom of Speech,* 19 THE NEW REPUBLIC 13, 13–14 (1919), *reprinted in* 40 U. CHI. L. REV. 239, 239–40 (1973).

In discussing the clear and present danger decisions, Justice Frankfurter has said, "Since the significance of every expression of thought derives from the circumstances evoking it, results reached rather than language employed give the vital meaning."[109] But in *Frohwerk* and *Debs*, as well as in *Schenck*, any kind of clear and present danger requirement would probably have meant reversing the convictions. These three decisions not only laid down wide and illiberal standards capable of restricting expression, but also applied these standards to uphold convictions. It was no accident that in *Abrams*[110] and the cases that followed it, when Holmes became more conscious of the implications of his phrase, he had to dissent from majority holdings that relied on words he himself had used in *Patterson*, *Fox*, *Schenck*, *Frohwerk*, and *Debs*.

Professor Chafee presents a quite different view of Holmes' outlook at the time of these cases. He says:

> These three decisions . . . came as a great shock to forward-looking men and women . . . . They were especially grieved that the opinions which dashed [the] hope [that the Espionage Act would be invalidated] were written by the Justice who for their eyes had long taken on heroic dimensions. Looking backward, however, we see that Justice Holmes was biding his time until the Court should have before it a conviction so clearly wrong as to let him speak out his deepest thoughts about the First Amendment.[111]

With all respect to Professor Chafee, this is indeed to look at it "backwards." To impute to Holmes the desire to wait for a more appropriate case is to make a nonhistorical assumption on an order with "Goodbye, I'm off to the Thirty Years' War." If Holmes thought these decisions were wrong, but not "so clearly wrong," why did he vote as he did? Of course, for the sake of unanimity a judge may refrain from dissenting. Or he may think that a solitary dissent would have little influence on the development of the law. He might even agree to write for the Court in order to influence doctrine, since changes in the law are often facilitated by opinions that sap a rule while ostensibly endorsing it. But such an explanation is inconsistent with Holmes' *Frohwerk* and *Debs* opinions, for the criteria he suggested were the very opposite of a

109. Dennis v. United States, 341 U.S. 494, 528 (1951) (Frankfurter, J., concurring in result).

110. Abrams v. United States, 250 U.S. 616 (1919).

111. Z. CHAFEE, *supra* note 34, at 86.

"danger" approach. This simply cannot be squared with "biding his time." Nor is it obvious that *Abrams* is significantly worse than *Debs*, if "proximity and degree" are considered objectively. Finally, it would have been most uncharacteristic of Holmes—who was deeply opposed to judicial "renovation" of the law and suspicious of all reformers—to undertake the long range strategy which Chafee suggests.[112]

In fact, there is ample evidence that Holmes did not think *Schenck*, *Frohwerk*, and *Debs* wrong. In a letter to Sir Frederick Pollock he wrote:

> I am beginning to get stupid letters of protest against a decision that Debs, a noted agitator, was rightly convicted of obstructing the recruiting service so far as the law was concerned. I wondered that the Government should press the case to a hearing before us, as the inevitable result was that fools, knaves, and ignorant persons were bound to say he was convicted because he was a dangerous agitator and that obstructing the draft was a pretence. How it was with the Jury of course I don't know, but of course the talk is silly as to us. There was a lot of jaw about free speech, which I dealt with somewhat summarily in an earlier case—*Schenck v. U.S.* . . . also *Frohwerk v. U.S.* . . . As it happens I should go farther probably than the majority in favor of it, and I dare say it was partly on that account that the C.J. assigned the case to me.[113]

Again to Pollock he said: "Of course there were people who pitched into the Court for sending Debs to prison under the espionage act, but there was no doubt that the Jury was warranted in finding him guilty or that the act was Constitutional."[114]

Shortly thereafter he wrote, but did not send, a letter to the editor of *The New Republic* responding to a highly critical article on the *Debs* case by Ernst Freund.[115] In it, Holmes agreed with an earlier *New Republic* note that had acknowledged the legality of Deb's conviction while urging commutation of his sentence.[116] He went on to attack the Freund article, saying:

> The constitutionality of the act so far as the clauses concerning obstructing the recruiting service are involved was passed upon

112. *See, e.g.*, O.W. HOLMES, *Law in Science and Science in Law*, in COLLECTED LEGAL PAPERS 239 (1952); 2 HOLMES-LASKI LETTERS 42 (M. Howe ed. 1953); 2 HOLMES-LASKI LETTERS 942 (M. Howe ed. 1953); 1 HOLMES-LASKI LETTERS 243–44 (M. Howe ed. 1941).

113. 2 HOLMES-POLLOCK LETTERS 7 (M. Howe ed. 1941) (footnotes omitted).

114. *Id.* at 11.

115. *See* note 108 *supra*.

116. *Editorial Note*, 18 THE NEW REPUBLIC 362 (1919).

> in *Schenck v. U.S.* and so all that was needed in the *Debs* case was to refer to that decision, and, given the finding of the jury, in my opinion it was impossible to have a rational doubt about the law. Freund's objection to a jury "guessing at motive, tendency and possible effect" is an objection to pretty much the whole body of the law, which for thirty years I have made my brethren smile by insisting to be everywhere a matter of degree . . . . Moreover I think the *clauses under consideration* not only were constitutional but were proper enough while the war was on. When people are putting out all their energies in battle I don't think it unreasonable to say we won't have obstacles intentionally put in the way of raising troops—by persuasion any more than by force.[117]

Finally, he wrote to Pollock again: "It is one of the ironies that I, who probably take the extremest [sic] view in favor of free speech (in which, in the abstract, I have no very enthusiastic belief, though I hope I would die for it), that I should have been selected for blowing up."[118]

Professor Ragan has suggested that Chafee himself, at a tea arranged by Harold Laski, may have convinced Holmes of the need for more stringent protection of speech.[119] It may also be that Holmes was moved by finding among the "fools and knaves" who took issue with *Debs* many of the young men whose friendship and respect he greatly valued. Whatever the explanation for his later shift, the evidence strongly suggests that what Professor Kalven said of *Debs* was true of all these cases—"It was for Holmes a routine criminal appeal."[120]

B. *The* Masses *Alternative*

As evidence of the *Schenck* defendants' intent, the government argued that the second side of the leaflet, entitled "Assert Your Rights," was printed after the decision was made to target draftees. The government characterized the message as "a frank, bitter, passionate appeal for resistance to the Selective Service Law."[121]

One might reasonably question that characterization. Beginning with the title call to "assert your rights," the message had a

117. 1 HOLMES-LASKI LETTERS 203–04 (M. Howe ed. 1953).

118. 2 HOLMES-POLLOCK LETTERS 29 (M. Howe ed. 1941).

119. Ragan, *supra* note 50, at 43.

120. Kalven, *Professor Ernst Freund and* Debs v. United States, 40 U. CHI. L. REV. 235, 238 (1973).

121. Brief for Appellee at 13, *Schenck*.

distinct flavor of legalism. It spoke of officers entrusted with administration of the draft laws who "violate the provisions of the United States Constitution . . . when they refuse to recognize your right to assert your opposition to the draft," and insisted that exemptions for clergy and Quakers constituted discrimination. It deplored a "tacit or silent consent to the conscription law" instead of assertion of rights. It asserted a lack of power, delegated by the people, to enter the war, and asked its readers if they were "willing to submit to the degradation of having the Constitution of the United States treated as a 'mere scrap of paper.' " Finally, the leaflet was published and distributed in August, 1917; the Selective Draft Law did not receive the Supreme Court's stamp of constitutional approval until January, 1918.[122] This suggests that the legalism of the leaflet cannot be dismissed as mere subterfuge.

It is arguable that Congress never intended its ban on obstruction of the recruiting and enlistment service to include raising legal objections to the service's validity. The *Schenck* leaflet can be read as doing nothing more. Holmes apparently missed this point.[123]

Holmes failed to perceive both the possibility of a speech-protective approach based on the content of the utterance under examination, and the potential for destructiveness in a lax application of his own formula. This is especially noteworthy since he had been explicitly confronted with Judge Learned Hand's alternative approach, which held the promise of much more protection for speech.

Judge Hand presented the alternative in *Masses Pub. Co. v. Patten*.[124] Masses sought to enjoin the Postmaster of the City of New York from refusing to accept its magazine, *The Masses*, for mailing. The Postmaster based his refusal on the Espionage Act of June 15, 1917,[125] which forbade willfully making or conveying false reports or false statements with intent to interfere with the success of the war effort, and willfully causing or attempting to cause insubordination or obstruction of the recruiting and enlistment service. Publications in violation of the act were not legally mailable.

---

122. *The Selective Draft Cases,* 245 U.S. 366 (1918).
123. *See* text accompanying note 86 *supra*.
124. 244 F. 535 (S.D.N.Y. 1917).
125. Ch. 30, § 3, 40 Stat. 217 (repealed 1948).

Judge Hand approached the problem as a matter of statutory construction: The issue was not how far Congress might go in suppressing hostile comment under its war powers, but how far it had gone.[126] He excluded all statements of opinion from the provision forbidding willfully false statements: "That phrase properly includes only a statement of fact which the utterer knows to be false . . . ."[127]

The prohibition on willfully causing insubordination, etc., could not, in Hand's view, be understood to reach everything which might "arouse discontent and dissaffection [sic] among the people with the prosecution of the war and with the draft."[128] Admitting the tendency of the utterances to lead to unhappy consequences, Hand maintained that such a broad interpretation of "cause" would "involve necessarily as a consequence the suppression of all hostile criticism, and of all opinion except what encouraged and supported the existing policies" and would "contradict the normal assumption of democratic government that the suppression of hostile criticism does not turn upon the justice of its substance or the decency and propriety of its temper."[129]

Hand drew the line with regard to prosecutable utterances between "keys of persuasion" and "triggers of action" having "no purport but to counsel the violation of law. . . . To counsel or advise a man to an act is to urge upon him either that it is his interest or his duty to do it."[130] He eloquently stated the reasons for so drawing the line.

> Political agitation, by the passions it arouses or the convictions it engenders, may in fact stimulate men to the violation of law. Detestation of existing policies is easily transformed into forcible resistance of the authority which puts them in execution, and it would be folly to disregard the causal relation between the two. Yet to assimilate agitation, legitimate as such, with direct incitement to violent resistance, is to disregard the tolerance of all methods of political agitation which in normal times is a safeguard of free government. The distinction is not a scholastic subterfuge, but a hard-bought acquisition in the fight for freedom, and the purpose to disregard it must be evident when the power exists. If one stops short of urging upon

126. *Masses,* 244 F. at 538.
127. *Id.* at 539.
128. *Id.*
129. *Id.* at 539, 540.
130. *Id.* at 540.

> others that it is their duty or their interest to resist the law, it seems to me that one should not be held to have attempted to cause its violation. If that be not the test, I can see no escape from the conclusion that under this section every political agitation which can be shown to be apt to create a seditious temper is illegal. I am confident that by such languge Congress had no such revolutionary purpose in view.[131]

Hand believed his approach established "a qualitative formula, hard, conventional, difficult to evade," while Holmes' clear and present danger doctrine was simply a matter of degree that could be manipulated by administrators hostile to minority views.[132]

Holmes was clearly aware of Judge Hand's approach when he wrote *Schenck*, *Frohwerk* and *Debs*. Counsel for Schenck cited it, quoting from the section of the opinion set out above.[133] More important, Holmes and Hand discussed the problem of a majority's right to suppress dissent, both in person and by letter, before *Schenck* was decided. Just one week before *Schenck* was handed down, Holmes acknowledged that he had read Hand's *Masses* decision.[134]

One of the more attractive aspects of Judge Hand's approach, from a speech-protective point of view, is the warrant it provides for taking a case away from the jury on the ground that the lan-

---

131. *Id.*

132. Letter from Learned Hand to Zechariah Chafee, Jr. (Jan. 2, 1921), *reprinted in* Gunther, *supra* note 8, at 770.

133. Brief for Appellant at 7, 12, *Schenck.* There might be some room for doubt on this point if the brief were the only evidence. The brief cites Hand in two places. The first citation reads: "Judge Hand in the 'Masses' case (U.S. vs. Eastman, 252 Fed. 232), says: —." The second reference reads: "In United States vs. Eastman (Masses Publishing Co., *et. al.* 252 Fed. 232" and goes on to give an extensive quotation from Hand which does not appear in the report of that case, but apparently is from a later stage of that Espionage Act prosecution. *Masses* and *Eastman* were different cases. If all Justice Holmes knew of Hand's position was what could be gleaned from the case cited in the brief, one could understand Holmes' professed inability to distinguish Hand's approach from his own in *Schenck.* Letter from Oliver Wendell Holmes, Jr. to Learned Hand (Apr. 3, 1919), *reprinted in* Gunther, *supra* note 8, at 760. In *Eastman*, Hand says, "The principle now established . . . depends upon the likelihood of the words to produce the result, coupled with the specific intent." 252 F. 233 (S.D.N.Y. 1918). The principle had been established in the Court of Appeals reversal of Hand's *Masses* judgment. Masses Pub. Co. v. Patten, 246 F. 24 (2d Cir. 1917). That court had taken the unusual step of staying Hand's injunction during the pendency of the appeal. Hand was chagrined at the professional reception given his *Masses* opinion, *see* Gunther, *supra* note 8, at 729, 759, 760, 765, 767, 768, but would not allow that to intrude upon his judicial function, *id.* at 765.

134. Gunther, *supra* note 8, at 732, 755–58.

guage used did not directly counsel violation of law. Compare Holmes' laconic comment in *Schenck* that "defendants do not deny that the jury might find against them" on the question of whether sending the leaflet to men subject to the draft evidenced an intent to influence them to violate the draft law.[135]

The "hard, conventional" element of Hand's test would appear to hold some intrinsic attraction for one as attached as Holmes was to external standards of liability. But there is an essential tension, never adequately resolved in Holmes' work, between the insistence on external standards of liability and the insistence that law reflect the wishes of the dominant social forces. Holmes was quite adamant that the fixing of legal standards was a matter for judges, not juries.[136] But any judge who imposes standards while the forces are in motion runs the risk of interfering with the outcome of the battle. The alternative, represented by the practice of turning over questions of negligence to the jury, is an abandonment of law in the sense of standards of behavior. It is resort to "whim" and "popular prejudice."[137] Holmes' approval of this use of juries shows that his failure to distinguish between law and force threatens his legal theory with incoherence.

One must suppose that these inconsistent views never came together in Holmes' mind in the form of a contradiction. One must have been present to the exclusion of the other when he was considering any particular problem. When he chose the uncertain metric of "clear and present danger" over Hand's "objective" incitement test, his deference to dominant social forces prevailed. Given Holmes' attachment to metaphors of battle and death in discussions of social issues, and the war context of the Espionage Act, this should come as no surprise.

Holmes and Hand shared a profound skepticism with regard to the existence of absolute truths, and neither thought much of courts that sought to hold legislatures within boundaries of the courts' making. But the practice of judicial review of legislative acts did not contain for Hand any inherent conflict with his theory of law. Indeed, just because law was to be taken seriously, as a mediation of the passions of the moment, Hand could rest his

135. *Schenck,* 249 U.S. at 51.

136. O.W. HOLMES, *Law in Science and Science in Law,* in COLLECTED LEGAL PAPERS, *supra* note 74, at 232–34.

137. *Id.* at 235, 237–38.

effort to protect dissent not on a constitutional ruling, but on a carefully crafted statutory interpretation. It is doubtful that Hand would have placed much stock in the capacity of a court to stop a determined majority from taking the country down the road to hell.[138] But it is impossible to conceive of Hand saying, as Holmes did, "[I]f my fellow citizens want to go to Hell I will help them. It's my job."[139]

V. The Vitalization of "Clear and Present Danger"

A. *The* Abrams *Dissent*

It was only after *Schenk*, *Frohwerk*, and *Debs* that clear and present danger emerged as a useful free speech standard. The following November, Holmes wrote his intense and brilliant dissenting opinion in *Abrams*.[140] It and the *Lochner*[141] dissent may be his best-known opinions. He argued that his clear and present danger dictum in *Schenk* should be taken seriously and promoted to a legal principle. In March 1920, he reaffirmed that position by concurring with Justice Brandeis' dissents in *Schaefer*[142] and *Pierce*[143].

The defendants in *Abrams* supported the new revolutionary regime in Russia. In August 1918, they threw about 5,000 leaflets from the window of a New York hat factory, some in English and some in Yiddish. The English leaflets, written in turn-of-the-century radical vernacular, protested the sending of American troops to Siberia. The Yiddish leaflets said that any munitions produced might be used against the Soviets, and supported, without details or preconditions, the idea of a general strike. There was no evidence that anyone engaged in war work read the leaflets. However, conviction arguably could be sustained under a clear and present danger requirement more easily in *Abrams* than in *Debs*. The defendants, and perhaps some of their readers, were in an excited state because of the events leading up to the October revolution in Russia. The pamphlets contained at least

---

138. L. Hand, The Bill of Rights 76 (1958) (quoting Benjamin Franklin: "[This Government] can only end in Despotism . . . when the people have become so corrupted as to need despotic Government.")

139. 1 Holmes-Laski Letters 249 (M. Howe ed. 1953).

140. Abrams v. United States, 250 U.S. 616, 624 (1919) (Holmes, J., dissenting).

141. Lochner v. New York, 198 U.S. 45, 74 (1905) (Holmes, J., dissenting).

142. Schaefer v. New York, 251 U.S. 466, 482 (1920) (Brandeis, J., dissenting).

143. Pierce v. United States, 252 U.S. 239, 253 (1920) (Brandeis, J., dissenting).

some threat of violence. Furthermore, the absence of legal sanctions for quitting work might make such a result more likely than would resistance to the draft, where the resister would face a jail sentence.

The case differed from the three earlier decisions because the 1918 amendments to the Espionage Act had made it criminal, when the United States was at war, to "willfully . . . urge, incite, or advocate any curtailment of production . . . *with intent* . . . to cripple or hinder the United States in the prosecution of the war. . . ."[144] The question before the Court— whether the evidence was sufficient to sustain the guilty verdict—turned in large part on this 1918 requirement of specific intent to interfere with the war against Germany. The defendants insisted on their hostility to Germany. One of the pamphlets had said, "It is absurd to call us pro-German. We hate and despise German militarism . . . ."[145] The government therefore had to prove that the defendants' desire to interfere with the expedition to Russia entailed an intention to obstruct the war with Germany, even though they claimed that they did not want to obstruct *that* war.

Mr. Justice Clarke, writing for the majority, met this difficulty by saying:

> It will not do to say . . . that the only intent of these defendants was to prevent injury to the Russian cause. Men must be held to have intended, and to be accountable for, the effects which their acts were likely to produce. Even if their primary purpose and intent was to aid the cause of the Russian Revolution, the plan of action . . . necessarily involved . . . defeat of the war program of the United States . . . .[146]

The basis for the maxim that "men must be held to have intended . . . the effects which their acts were likely to produce"—or, as it is sometimes put, "the natural and probable consequences of their acts"—would seem to be that we see normal human action as intentional. We usually say that someone acted intentionally only to refute some suggestion that he did not. It is as natural, in speaking of what we see men do, for us to incorporate a reference to some mental element, as it is unnatural to do so in describing the motions of an inanimate object.

Justice Clarke's reliance upon this cliche is both disturbingly

144. Espionage Act of June 15, 1917, ch. 30, § 3, 40 Stat. 219 (amended 1918, repealed 1948) (emphasis added).

145. *Abrams,* 250 U.S. at 625.

146. *Id.* at 621.

general and inappropriate. It is disturbingly general because courts make many significant exceptions to it. As Glanville Williams said, "It is not true in fact that a man necessarily intends the natural consequences of his acts: and, it is not true in law that he is compellingly presumed to do so."[147] It is inappropriate because Justice Clarke is not dealing with a general requirement of an intentional act, but with a statutory requirement of "specific intent." When a statute specifically requires an intent to cause a particular injury, the defendant must as a rule be found to have actually had that consequence in mind. Courts have often considered as good defenses an unconcern with, or inattention to, or unawareness of, or occasionally even disregard of, the probability of certain consequences following upon acts.[148]

Of course, in certain extreme cases the law may regard something close to certainty that particular consequences will follow as equivalent to a specific intention to bring them about. Thus, an Aztec would not be heard to say that he did not want to kill, but only to collect a heart; it is no answer to an indictment for assault with intent to disfigure by biting off an ear that there was intention to injure but not to disfigure.[149] J.F. Stephen discusses the defendant who cuts off a person's head because he thinks it will be great fun seeing him look for it when he awakes.[150] These kinds of cases involve a perception of reality so distorted that a person does not "know" what he is doing. To allege that inevitable consequences were not intended is to claim some sort of freakish breakdown, not, as in a hallucination, of what is seen, but rather of what is generally known—for example, that humans bleed.

Justice Clarke's loose and summary statement avoided the real question: whether the relationship between the pamphlet and obstructing the war against Germany was like the relationship between the act and its forbidden, inevitable consequences in the Aztec example. It would seem to have been far from it. As Holmes pointed out in dissent, giving Justice Clarke's meaning to "natural and probable" made it criminal for someone mistakenly to believe and advocate that a change in the types or number of

147. G. Williams, Criminal Law: The General Part 89 (2d ed. 1961).

148. *Id.* at 51–52, 78, 90–91, 140–41.

149. State v. Clark, 69 Iowa 196 (1886), *discussed in* Z. Chafee, *supra* note 34, at 131.

150. J. Stephen, A History of the Criminal Law of England 166 (1883).

weapons produced would aid the war effort.[151] And, as Chafee noted, the pamphlet conceivably could have helped bring about a change in governmetal policy toward Russia, which, in turn, could have led to more enthusiastic support of the war against Germany.[152]

In his dissent, Holmes directly challenged Justice Clarke's interpretation of "with intent." Holmes first advanced his general, external standard definition of "intent:" "A man may have to pay damages, may be sent to prison, at common law might be hanged, if at the time of his act he knew facts from which common experience showed that the consequences would follow, whether he individually could forsee them or not."[153]

Normally, of course, Holmes minimized the importance of a mental state as a requirement of a crime. Here, however, he placed the statutory requirement of specific intent into his limited category where words received their "common meaning." As in the special class of attempts mentioned previously, where it was necessary to establish the likelihood that the acts done would be followed by other acts, "intent" was to be read literally.[154] Therefore, Holmes said,

> [W]hen words are used exactly, a deed is not done with intent to produce a consequence unless that consequence is the aim of the deed . . . . [h]e does not do the act with intent to produce it unless the aim to produce it is the proximate motive of the specific act, although there may be some deeper motive behind.[155]

And, referring to the passage in his *Swift* opinion where he discussed his special category of literal meaning[156] he said:

> An actual intent . . . is necessary to constitute an attempt, where a further act of the same individual is required to complete the substantive crime, for reasons given in *Swift & Co. v. United States* . . . . It is necessary where the success of the attempt depends upon others because if that intent is not present the actor's aim may be accomplished without bringing about

151. *Abrams,* 250 U.S. at 627.

152. Z. CHAFEE, *supra* note 34, at 132–33.

153. *Abrams,* 250 U.S. at 626–27.

154. In Hartzell v. United States, 322 U.S. 680 (1944), a World War II prosecution under the 1917 Espionage Act, the Court followed Holmes' *Abrams* dissent in requiring proof of a "specific intent . . . to cause insubordination or disloyalty in the armed forces or to obstruct the recruiting and enlistment service." *Id.* at 686.

155. *Abrams,* 250 U.S. at 627.

156. Swift & Co. v. United States, 196 U.S. 375, 396 (1905); *see* note 66 *supra* and accompanying text.

> the evils sought to be checked. An intent to prevent interference with the revolution in Russia might have been satisfied without any hindrance to carrying on the war in which we were engaged.[157]

Holmes assumed in *Abrams* that *Schenck*, *Frohwerk*, and *Debs* had somehow established a clear and present danger principle. Curiously, his description of the principle seems to assert not only that intent plays a crucial evidentiary role in establishing a probability of harm, but that intent is a sufficient alternative to proof of that probability. He assumed that proof of an intent to bring about an evil made proof that the publication had any effect whatsoever unnecessary.

> I have never seen reason to doubt that the questions of law . . . before this Court in . . . *Schenk*, *Frohwerk* and *Debs* . . . were rightly decided . . . . [B]y the same reasoning that would justify punishing persuasion to murder, the United States constitutionally may punish speech that produces *or* is intended to produce a clear and imminent danger that it will bring about forthwith certain substantive evils that the United States constitutionally may seek to prevent . . . .
>
> It is only the present danger of immediate evil *or an intent to bring it about* that warrants Congress in setting a limit to the expression of opinion where private rights are not concerned.[158]

This would negate the very principle Holmes tried so often to establish: If intent is an independent and sufficient alternative, it is not necessary to show any probable effect. Holmes overlooks the very requirement of probable success he himself so often emphasized, indeed overemphasized. His language appears to sanction what he would be the last person to allow: punishment of absolutely futile thoughts. Thus one may justifiably doubt that Holmes had yet worked out a coherent principle of clear and present danger, even for himself.

Holmes concluded his opinion with the brilliant discussion of liberty of expression that has been called "the greatest utterance of intellectual freedom by an American, ranking in the English tongue with Milton and Mill:"[159]

> Persecution for the expression of opinions seems to me perfectly logical. If you have no doubt of your premises or your power and want a certain result with all your heart you naturally express your wishes in law and sweep away all opposition. To

157. *Abrams*, 250 U.S. at 628.
158. *Id.* at 627–28 (emphasis added).
159. The Mind and Faith of Justice Holmes 306 (M. Lerner ed. 1943).

> allow opposition by speech seems to indicate that you think the speech impotent, as when a man says that he has squared the circle, or that you do not care whole-heartedly for the result, or that you doubt either your power or your premises. But when men have realized that time has upset many fighting faiths, they may come to believe even more than they believe the very foundations of their own conduct that the ultimate good desired is better reached by free trade in ideas—that the best test of truth is the power of the thought to get itself accepted in the competition of the market, and that truth is the only ground upon which their wishes safely can be carried out. That at any rate is the theory of our Constitution. It is an experiment, as all life is an experiment. Every year if not every day we have to wager our salvation upon some prophecy based upon imperfect knowledge. While that experiment is part of our system I think that we should be eternally vigilant against attempts to check the expression of opinions that we loathe and believe to be fraught with death, unless they so imminently threaten immediate interference with the lawful and pressing purposes of the law that an immediate check is required to save the country. I wholly disagree with the argument of the Government that the First Amendment left the common law as to seditious libel in force . . . . Only the emergency that makes it immediately dangerous to leave the correction of evil counsels to time warrants making any exception to the sweeping command, 'Congress shall make no law . . . abridging the freedom of speech.' Of course I am speaking only of expressions of opinion and exhortations, which were all that were uttered here, but I regret that I cannot put into more impressive words my belief that in their conviction upon this indictment the defendants were deprived of their rights under the Constitution of the United States.[160]

Holmes' acerbic intensity is moving. *Abrams* brought out the attractive political aspects of his Social Darwinism. His style derived from the language he had always used to talk about the truth; one can think the paragraph impressive, and, in the circumstances of the case, admirable. At the same time, one might believe that diversity ánd the expression of dissident views is intrinsically desirable, and thus disagree with Holmes' extreme positions that "persecution" is "perfectly logical," that when one has no doubt one "naturally" sweeps away all opposition, and that "to allow opposition by speech" necessarily is to think it "impotent" or doubt one's "power or premises." Despite these questionable manifestations of Holmes' thought about "truth"

160. *Abrams,* 250 U.S. at 630–31.

and "power," it is easy to understand why the *Abrams* dissent added immeasurably to his already unique stature. His very name became laden, through processes not completely secular, with connotations of concern for liberty; only with the greatest difficulty could he from that time on be seen as merely a man.

B. *With Brandeis in Dissent*

In the early part of 1920 Holmes joined Justice Brandeis' dissents in *Schaefer*[161] and *Pierce*.[162] These two cases turned on the clause of the 1917 Espionage Act prohibiting the publication of willfully false reports and statements "with intent to interfere with the operation or success of the military or naval forces of the United States or promote the success of its enemies."[163] In *Schaefer* the Court sustained the convictions of three defendants for printing false and distorted accounts of the war in a German language newspaper, *The Philadelphia Tageblatt*. The newspaper could not afford telegraphic service, so it printed clippings from other newspapers, cutting and summarizing both headlines and text. The government did not allege that the articles were intentionally false in fact, but rather that the original article had been altered or mistranslated so as to evoke negative responses and attitudes toward the allies and the war effort. Justice McKenna said in the majority opinion, "Their effect or the persons affected could not be shown, nor was it necessary. The tendency of the articles and their efficacy were enough for offense . . . ."[164] On the first amendment challenge, he wrote that the Constitution, "that great ordinance of . . . orderly liberty," had been invoked to justify the activities of anarchy or of the enemies of the United States, and by a strange perversion of its precepts it was adduced against itself."[165]

In dissent, Justice Brandeis added greatly to the stature, explicitness and clarity of the clear and present danger doctrine. He disagreed about the extent to which the court could allow a jury to decide the probable effect of the articles under the clear and present danger test, and maintained that a judge must withhold the case from the jury when it could not reasonably find that

161. Schaefer v. New York, 251 U.S. 466, 482 (1920) (Brandeis, J., dissenting).
162. Pierce v. United States, 252 U.S. 239, 253 (1920) (Brandeis, J., dissenting).
163. Espionage Act of 1917, ch. 30, § 3, 40 Stat. 217, 219 (repealed 1948).
164. *Schaefer*, 251 U.S. at 477.
165. *Id.* at 477.

the words had created a "clear and present danger."[166] Anticipating his *Whitney v. California*[167] concurrence, where he explicitly asserted that the clear and present danger test limited legislatures, Justice Brandeis spoke of a "rule of reason" capable of preserving free speech from "tyrannous, well-meaning majorities."[168]

In *Pierce*, the defendants distributed a four-page leaflet, written by a prominent Episcopalian clergyman, which asserted that the miseries of war resulted from capitalism. The defendants received the pamphlet from the Socialist Party headquarters, but did not distribute it until a Maryland judge ordered an acquittal in a case involving the very same pamphlet. They were nevertheless arrested and convicted. The Supreme Court affirmed the conviction. Justice Pitney said that the question to be decided by the jury was "[w]hether the statements in the pamphlet had a natural tendency to produce the forbidden consequences."[169] He added that distribution of the pamphlet "with full understanding of its contents . . . itself furnished a ground for attributing to them an intent to bring about, and for finding that they attempted to bring about, any and all such consequences as reasonably might be anticipated from its distribution."[170]

Justice Brandeis concentrated on the assumption that statements like those about the effect of Morgan's loans on the United States entry into the war were capable of being proved false when made. He said:

> To hold that a jury may make punishable statements of conclusions or of opinion, like those here involved, by declaring them to be statements of facts and to be false would practically deny members of small political parties freedom of criticism and of discussion in times when feelings run high and the questions involved are deemed fundamental.[171]

Justice Brandeis also insisted that the prosecution had not proved a specific intent to interfere with the war effort, as required by the statute.[172] Thus, Justice Holmes' language was kept alive, though the method displayed by Justice Brandeis in

166. *Id.* at 482–83 (Brandeis, J., dissenting).
167. Whitney v. California, 274 U.S. 357, 372 (1927) (Brandeis, J., concurring).
168. *Schaefer*, 251 U.S. at 482.
169. *Pierce*, 252 U.S. at 244.
170. *Id.* at 249.
171. *Id.* at 269.
172. *Id.* at 271–72.

Pierce has more in common with the careful craftsmanship of Judge Hand in *Masses* than with the master rhetorician of *Schenck* and *Abrams*.

The next year, in *Gilbert v. Minnesota,*[173] Justices Brandeis and White dissented when the Court sustained a conviction under a Minnesota law which made it unlawful to advocate "that men should not enlist in the military or naval forces of the United States or the state of Minnesota," or "that the citizens of this state should not aid or assist the United States in prosecuting or carrying on war with the public enemies of the United States."[174] Gilbert was indicted and convicted for the following words:

> We are going over to Europe to make the world safe for democracy, but I tell you we had better make America safe for democracy first. You say, what is the matter with our democracy . . . . Have you had anything to say as to who should be president? . . . [W]ho should be Governor . . . ? [W]hether we would go into this war? You know you have not. If this is such a great democracy, for Heaven's sake why should we not vote on conscription of men. We were stampeded into this war by newspaper rot to pull England's chestnuts out of the fire for her. I tell you if they conscripted wealth like they have conscripted men, this war would not last over forty-eight hours.[175]

The defendants argued that the statute was within the exclusive legislative power of Congress, which had occupied the field, and that it violated an alleged right of free speech. Justice McKenna, speaking for the Court, rejected both contentions. He conceded, without deciding, that the freedom asserted might be secured, presumably against the state, by the United States Constitution.[176] But then he brushed aside the issue of free speech, quoting, in passing, from *Schenck* and *Frohwerk:*

> [E]very word that he uttered in denunciation of the war was false, was deliberate misrepresentation of the motives which impelled it, and the objects for which it was prosecuted. He could have had no purpose other than that of which he was charged. It would be a travesty on the constitutional privilege he invokes to assign him its protection.[177]

Chief Justice White dissented separately on the grounds that

173. 254 U.S. 325 (1921).

174. *Id.* at 326–27.

175. *Id.* at 327.

176. *Id.* at 332.

177. *Id.* at 333. Holmes's inapt fire metaphor from *Schenck* was turned against Gilbert's free speech claim: "[T]he asserted freedom . . . is not absolute . . . . In *Schenck v. United States* . . . we distinguished times and occasions and said that 'the most strin-

Congress had occupied the field.[178] In his rather scattered dissent, Justice Brandeis also took up this position.[179] In addition, however, he anticipated *Gitlow*[180] by arguing that the statute and its application denied "privileges and immunities" and the "liberty" guaranteed by the fourteenth amendment.[181] Justice Brandeis stressed that the statute was much broader and potentially more repressive than the Espionage Act, and that it did not come close to meeting the requirements of the clear and present danger doctrine.[182] He asserted that in substance it prevented teaching that the abolition of war was possible, disregarded the defendant's motive, intention, or purpose, and invaded the "privacy and freedom of the home."[183]

Justice Holmes did not join Justice Brandeis in dissent but rather concurred "in the result."[184] Thus, one can only guess at his reasons. To sustain the conviction, he first had to believe that Congress had not occupied the field, although, in line with his belief in a strong national government, he often came to the opposite conclusion when dealing with areas of much more legitimate state concern than preserving government or conducting war.[185] In addition, he then either had to refuse to find any constitutional protection for freedom of speech against the states, or concede the possibility of protection but see nothing unconstitutional in the Minnesota law or its application. Since Holmes might well have refused to take the necessary first step of thinking that the Constitution protected freedom of speech against state action,[186] his concurrence does not tell us whether he applied the standards of the first amendment to the Minnesota law.

In *Milwaukee Publishing Co. v. Burleson,*[187] with Justices Holmes

---

gent protection of free speech would not protect a man in falsely shouting fire in a theater and causing panic.'" *Gilbert,* 254 U.S. at 332 (quoting *Schenck,* 249 U.S. at 52).

178. *Id.* at 334.

179. *Id.* at 341–42.

180. Gitlow v. New York, 268 U.S. 652 (1925).

181. *Gilbert,* 254 U.S. at 336.

182. *Id.* at 336, 340.

183. *Id.* at 334–35.

184. *Id.* at 334.

185. In Johnson v. Maryland, 254 U.S. 51 (1920), decided just a month before *Gilbert,* Holmes wrote the Court's opinion upholding a claim that the Constitution precluded the state from requiring an employee of the post office to have a state driver's license while driving a mail truck on state roads. Justice Brandeis' dissent in *Gilbert* cited the *Johnson* opinion in support of its view on state preclusion. *Gilbert,* 254 U.S. at 341.

186. *See* Patterson v. Colorado, 205 U.S. 454 (1907).

187. 255 U.S. 407 (1921).

and Brandeis dissenting, the Court upheld the Postmaster General's order revoking the second-class mailing rates of the company's *Social Democratic Milwaukee Leader.* The question was one of statutory construction. The order applied not only to issues which had violated provisions of the Espionage Act, but to all future issues as well, even though Congress had not provided in the Act for barring future issues of a publication. The Postmaster General relied in part on an argument that was as ingenious as it was artificial: Past violations of the 1917 Espionage Act provisions had kept the publication from being "regularly issued," a requirement for second-class privileges under the 1879 law.[188]

Justice Clarke, in a rather intemperate opinion for the Court, said that Congress had "practically plenary power over the mails" and that the second-class permit was specifically revocable upon determination by the postal department that the publication did not conform to the law. Furthermore, the postmaster could reasonably presume that the publication would continue to be nonmailable.[189]

In his dissent, Justice Brandeis said: "If the construction urged by the Postmaster General is rejected, these [constitutional] questions need not be answered; but it seems appropriate to indicate why the doubts raised by them are grave."[190] Then, acting on his magnificent conception of the Supreme Court as a vital educating force, he discussed the fallacies involved in the idea that the government was free from constitutional limitations in choosing whether to grant or withhold a "privilege."[191]

Justice Holmes filed a separate short dissent, expressing his agreement "in substance" with Justice Brandeis' view. Perhaps because he doubted the propriety of Justice Brandeis' extended dicta, Holmes said, "The question of the rate has nothing to do with the question whether the matter is mailable . . . . [A]s my brother Brandeis has pointed out, the conditions attached to the second-class rate by the statute cannot be made to justify the Postmaster's action except by a quibble."[192]

While he withheld explicit comment on constitutional issues

---

188. *Id.* at 425–26 (Brandeis, J., dissenting).

189. *Id.* at 411, 416.

190. *Id.* at 430.

191. *Id.* at 430–36.

192. *Id.* at 437.

which might be raised by a different view of the statutory issue, Justice Holmes stated that

> The United States may give up the Post Office when it sees fit, but while it carries it on the use of the mails is almost as much a part of free speech as the right to use our tongues, and it would take very strong language to convince me that Congress ever intended to give such a practically despotic power to any one man.[193]

It is noteworthy that in a case which could easily have elicited a *McAuliffe-Davis*[194] resort to the right/privilege distinction, Justice Holmes at least hinted that the government's choice was between giving up the business or observing constitutional limitations. For Justice Holmes, whose published correspondence fills volumes, this may have been a case that "hit him where he lived."[195]

C. *Deference to the Legislature*

Meyer v. Nebraska[196] does not directly concern speech, but rather involves innominate fourteenth amendment rights. It illustrates well, however, how much Justice Holmes deferred to legislative judgments— how far, in his view, majorities could constitutionally go even when civil liberties were at stake—and it is significant in light of the problem faced by the Court in *Gitlow*.

Shortly after World War I a number of states passed similar statutes prohibiting the teaching of any modern language except English to children below the eighth grade in any school, private or public.[197] Teachers in Nebraska, Iowa, and Ohio were convicted of violating these statutes and the convictions were upheld in the respective state supreme courts. On appeal, the Supreme Court, with Justices Holmes and Sutherland dissenting, held that the laws unconstitutionally deprived teachers and parents of liberty without due process.

The cases raised the most fundamental issues of majority prerogatives and minority rights. That Justice McReynolds, speaking for the Court, was moved to discuss the Platonic and the Spartan relationship between the community and the individual itself suggests how insistently the facts forced the Court to the

---

193. *Id.*
194. *See* notes 16–27 *supra* and accompanying text.
195. 1 HOLMES-LASKI LETTERS 127 (M. Howe ed. 1941).
196. 262 U.S. 390 (1923).
197. *Id.* at 395.

consideration of basic issues.[198] In dissent, Justice Holmes, characteristically, said:

> I cannot . . . believe that in some circumstances, and circumstances existing it is said in Nebraska, the statute might not be regarded as a reasonable or even necessary method of reaching the desired result [a common tongue] . . . . No one would doubt that a teacher might be forbidden to teach many things, and the only criterion of his liberty under the Constitution that I can think of is 'whether, considering the end in view, the statute passes the bounds of reason and assumes the character of a mere arbitrary fiat.'[199]

Justice Holmes' position here, which freed legislatures from judicial supervision, was completely congruent with his most basic political assumptions. But consider how easy it is to satisfy his conditions of constitutionality. In saying "in some circumstances . . . [it] . . . might . . . be regarded as . . . reasonable or even necessary," he demands a finding by the Court that the statute could not be regarded as reasonable in any circumstances. Instead of suggesting inquiry into the actual circumstances, he says only "circumstances existing *it is said* in Nebraska," thus, a mere allegation can satisfy the requirements of "some circumstances." Holmes substitutes a loose reference to prevailing attitudes, "popular speech," or what "is said," for a detailed investigation of the impact of the law on constitutionally protected interests.

This approach resembles his solution of a similar problem in *Patsone v. Pennsylvania*.[200] In discussing a legislative assumption that resident aliens were peculiarly liable to kill wildlife, he said that "this court ought to be very slow to declare that the state legislature was wrong in its facts . . . . If we might trust popular speech . . . it was right—but it is enough that this Court has no such knowledge of local conditions as to be able to say that it was manifestly wrong."[201] This also seems to be a test which cannot be failed. How could this kind of approach lead to a conclusion that a statute could *not* be regarded as reasonable? Did Holmes equate, as elsewhere he said he did, "reasonableness" with "believed-by-some opinion"? Yet a law has always been passed by a majority of a legislature and can always, therefore, be taken as representing not merely substantial opinion, but the "dominant

---

198. *Id.* at 401–02.

199. *Id.* at 412 (citations omitted).

200. 232 U.S. 138 (1914). For further discussion of what *Patsone* reveals of Justice Holmes' views on civil liberties issues, see Rogat, *supra* note 3, at 41–44.

201. *Patsone,* 232 U.S. at 144–45.

opinion" of which he said, "I think that the word liberty in the Fourteenth Amendment is perverted when it is held to prevent the natural outcome of a dominant opinion . . . ."[202]

Justice Holmes' dissent in *Gitlow*,[203] the first peacetime prosecution for criminal anarchy, was the last opinion he wrote directly involving the first amendment.[204] In 1919 Gitlow had published a "Left Wing Manifesto"—a kind of bringing-up-to-date of the Communist Manifesto. It described the past and the present in order to demonstrate the inevitability of a proletarian revolution and a Communist reconstruction of society. Remarkably turgid, even by the standards of its genre, it could have served as an acid test for revolutionary zeal and fortitude. There was no evidence that it had any effect whatsoever.[205] Gitlow was convicted, under the New York Criminal Anarchy Act of 1902, which defined criminal anarchy as the "doctrine that organized government should be overthrown by force or violence . . . or by any unlawful means" and provided punishment for the advocacy of such a doctrine.[206]

The statute raised the question of how the constitutionality of a conviction based on utterances should be affected by a legislative judgment that a certain class of utterances produced a risk of serious danger. Justice Sanford, writing for the majority, did not deny the necessity of a connection between the publication and a

202. Lochner v. New York, 198 U.S. 45, 76 (1905) (Holmes, J., dissenting). In *Meyer*, Holmes did concur, without explanation, with the majority's rejection of an Ohio provision singling out the German language for specially disfavored treatment. 262 U.S. at 413. One can surmise that Holmes found no rational relationship between the objective of a "common tongue" and the special treatment of German, or perhaps that discrimination brought into play the proviso Holmes attached to the just quoted statement from *Lochner*: "unless it can be said that a rational and fair man necessarily would admit that the statute proposed would infringe fundamental principles as they have been understood by the traditions of our people and our law." *Lochner*, 198 U.S. at 76.

203. Gitlow v. New York, 268 U.S. 652 (1925).

204. Holmes joined Justice Brandeis' concurrence in Whitney v. California, 274 U.S. 357 (1927). *See* text accompanying note 213 *infra*. He was with a unanimous Court in Fiske v. Kansas, 274 U.S. 380 (1927), which reversed a conviction under the Kansas Criminal Syndicalism Act on the due process ground that the conviction was unsupported by evidence of prohibited behavior. He was in a 7–2 majority in Stromberg v. California, 283 U.S. 359 (1931), which declared unconstitutional a California statute insofar as it permitted conviction for display of a red flag as part of peaceful and orderly political activity. Finally, he joined Chief Justice Hughes' majority opinion in Near v. Minnesota, 283 U.S. 697 (1931), finding that a Minnesota statute which permitted enjoining of malicious, scandalous, and defamatory publications constituted an invalid prior restraint; Justices Butler, Van Devanter, McReynolds and Sutherland dissented.

205. *Gitlow*, 268 U.S. at 656.

206. *Id.* at 654.

risk reasonably apprehended and legitimately prohibited.[207] Rather, he accepted as conclusive the legislative judgment that a specified type of utterance was dangerous and could be suppressed.

> [T]he state has determined . . . that utterances advocating the overthrow of organized government . . . are so inimical to the general welfare, and involve such danger of substantive evil, that they may be penalized in the exercise of its police power. That determination must be given great weight. Every presumption is to be indulged in favor of the validity of the statute.[208]

This was the standard of reasonableness which, at least in theory, limited the exercise of the police power. Since the legislative determination could not be considered arbitrary, and the particular utterance fell within the prohibited class, the judicial function was effectively at an end.[209]

> [W]hen the legislative body has determined generally . . . that utterances of a certain kind involve such danger of substantive evil that they may be punished, the question whether any specific utterance coming within the prohibited class is likely, in and of itself, to bring about the substantive evil, is not open to consideration. It is sufficient that the statute itself be constitutional and that the use of the language comes within its prohibition.[210]

Justice Sanford concluded his argument by saying that the "general statement" in *Schenck* of the clear and present danger rule "has no application . . . where the legislative body itself has previously determined the danger of substantive evil arising from utterances of a specified character."[211] He limited the application of the clear and present danger rule—which he rendered in the much-criticized phrase, "natural tendency and probable effect"—to cases where the statute

> merely prohibits certain acts involving the danger of substantive evil, without any reference to language itself, and it is sought to apply its provisions to language used by the defendant . . . . There . . . it must necessarily be found . . . whether the specific language used involved such likelihood of bringing about the substantive evil as to deprive it of the constitutional

207. *Id.* at 664–65.
208. *Id.* at 668.
209. *Id.* at 669–70.
210. *Id.* at 670.
211. *Id.* at 671.

protection.[212]

Although Sanford's opinion has been justly criticized (while unjustly singled out on other grounds), it became the standard textbook example of the "bad tendency" rule.[213] Certainly a "bad tendency" approach risks unwise and unconstitutional suppression of ideas because of the danger of seeing revolutionary oaks in jejune acorns. But the most criticized portions of Justice Sanford's opinion were very much like opinions that had been written years earlier by Holmes. True, Justice Sanford said that "[a] single revolutionary spark may kindle a fire that, smouldering for a time, may burst into a sweeping and destructive conflagration."[214] But Holmes, as noted above, had said in *Frohwerk*, "it is impossible to say that it might not have been found that the circulation of the paper was in quarters where a little breath would be enough to kindle a flame . . . ."[215]

Another favorite symbol of the uniquely retrograde characteristics of the opinion is Justice Sanford's phrase, "natural tendency and probable effect." But in his *Debs* opinion, Holmes had said "natural tendency and reasonably probable effect."[216] In that same opinion he also spoke of "probable effect," "tending to obstruct," and "natural and intended effect." Recall also his *Patterson* position: "[I]f a court regards . . . a publication concerning a matter of law pending before it, as *tending* toward such an interference, it may punish it,"[217] and his use of "its tendency" in *Schenck*.[218]

Furthermore, Justice Sanford's basic assertion was that the clear and present danger test did *not* apply here. This mattered much more than *how* he described the test. His description might become significant in the future, but would have no effect so long as the test itself was considered irrelevant. It was somewhat like the announcement in the old vaudeville routine: "You can't have it without chocolate sauce. We're all out of chocolate sauce. You'll have to have it without strawberry sauce."

Justice Sanford's opinion, however, did raise the basic issue of

---

212. *Id.* at 670–71.

213. *See, e.g.*, Cushman, *Some Constitutional Problems of Civil Liberty*, 23 B.U.L. REV. 335, 340 (1943) (distinguishing "bad tendency" and "clear and present danger").

214. *Gitlow*, 268 U.S. at 669.

215. *Frohwerk*, 249 U.S. at 209; *see* text accompanying note 102 *supra*.

216. *Debs*, 249 U.S. at 214–16; *see* text accompanying notes 106–107 *supra*.

217. *Patterson*, 205 U.S. at 463; *see* text accompanying note 31 *supra*.

218. *Schenck*, 249 U.S. at 52; *see* text accompanying note 87 *supra*.

deference to the legislative judgment. This problem is a subspecies of the most difficult question raised by the Supreme Court's role in the American governmental system: its relationship to the legislature. Precisely because it raised this issue, *Gitlow* promised resolution of some of the important ambiguities of the clear and present danger doctrine.

Justice Sanford, relying on previous uses of the doctrine, asserted that it only bridged the gap between speech and the general prohibitions of a statute not directly concerned with expression. It had no place, he said, when the legislature, in a reasonable exercise of its police power, designated a category of speech as dangerous, and the court found that a particular publication fell within that category. There was then no further basis for considering the validity of the conviction. This approach reflected a reasonable reading of prior decisions: With the exception of Justice Brandeis' opinion in *Gilbert*,[219] no one, and certainly not Holmes, had suggested that the clear and present danger doctrine should test the validity of legislation. It had been used only to require a relationship between words and forbidden acts.

Nor did Justice Sanford have to rely on precedent alone. His distinction between bridging the gap between speech and acts prohibited by statute, as opposed to a legislative judgment that certain speech in itself was so dangerous that it must be prohibited, revealed that the clear and present danger doctrine, as it had developed so far, was conceptually inadequate to handle the second class of cases. The doctrine still bore the marks of its origins in the law of attempts. It had originated as a standard governing the relationship between a publication and the nearly successful interference with the war required by the attempt-like 1917 Espionage Act. The doctrine asked whether someone, by using words, had come close enough to the specified prohibited consequences. It required, as did the law of attempts, "dangerous proximity to success."

The *Gitlow* type of statute presents an altogether different problem. Since it prohibits specified language, there is no act to approach, no question of nearness to success. There is no relationship between language and prohibited consequences to be measured: *The legislature has itself designated the point at which words*

219. *See* notes 173–186 *supra* and accompanying text.

become unlawful. The components of the crime, therefore, do not resemble those of the law of attempts; the model is closer to criminal solicitation—urging a person to commit a crime. One is guilty of solicitation if he counsels that another commit an act which is criminal. Here, also, there is no question of success, of proximity to any act; the words of exhortation themselves are punished although the other party promptly rejects the solicitation without committing any act.[220]

In response to the latter kind of statute, prohibiting not "any words which do X," but "words urging X," a court can protect a wide range of free expression only by establishing conditions to be met before these words can be designated as unlawful—by restricting *what* may be made criminal.[221] When a legislature asserts the right to prohibit political speech, a doctrine like clear and present danger can remain meaningful only if courts say that the legislature may constitutionally punish only the use of language which presents a clear and present danger of some significant evil. But this will not be sufficient unless the *courts* retain the power to decide whether the legislature has inhibited expression at a constitutionally permissible point. Otherwise, a legislature could prohibit the use of given words, regardless of the circumstances in which they were used, by the simple assertion that the words themselves constitute a clear and present danger. This is what Justice Brandeis meant by saying in *Whitney:* "[W]here a statute is valid only in case certain conditions exist, the enactment of the statute cannot alone establish the facts which are essential to its validity."[222]

Thus a latent antagonism exists between constitutional limitations on the regulation of expression, and statutes modeled on the crime of solicitation. Since these cases force courts to consider ultimate questions of constitutionality, they subjected Holmes in particular to acute conflict. Holmes was anxious not to interfere with the possible growth of dissident social groups, but he also believed, in accordance with his most deeply felt views of the relation between politics and law, in an almost unqualified judicial deference to legislative decisions. When faced

220. R. Perkins, Criminal Law 649 (3d ed. 1969).

221. This may include an absolute barrier to laws which make utterances illegal. *See* Linde, *"Clear and Present Danger" Reexamined: Dissonance in the Brandenburg Concerto,* 22 Stan. L. Rev. 1163, 1183 (1970).

222. Whitney v. California, 274 U.S. 352, 374 (1927) (Brandeis, J., concurring).

with an attempt-like statute, he could comfortably reconcile the two: He gave great deference to the legislature and used clear and present danger as a standard for the application of an act. But in the *Gitlow* type of case, the clear and present danger doctrine, if it were to be significant, had to be used to determine the validity of the statute itself. To disagree squarely with Justice Sanford, it was necessary to take the hard view that the Court may, and indeed must, sometimes reject the type of legislative determination it considered in *Gitlow*. Since Holmes declined to take this step, he provided no substantial answer to Justice Sanford's assertion that the doctrine did not apply.

Holmes instead wrote the short, stirring dissent which has since received so much praise. Its style evoked the last paragraph of *Abrams*, arguing in an appealing way that it was necessary, perhaps inevitable, to allow dissident groups an opportunity to be heard and a chance to become dominant. Achieving this stylistic brilliance would have been more difficult if Holmes, instead of disagreeing enigmatically about the application of the statute, had dealt squarely with the relationship between the legislature and the Court. He said:

> If what I think the correct test is applied, it is manifest that there was no present danger of an attempt to overthrow the government by force on the part of the admittedly small minority who shared the defendant's views. It is said that this manifesto was more than a theory, that it was an incitement. Every idea is an incitement. It offers itself for belief, and, if believed, it is acted on unless some other belief outweighs it, or some failure of energy stifles the movement at its birth. The only difference between the expression of an opinion and an incitement in the narrower sense is the speaker's enthusiasm for the result. Eloquence may set fire to reason. But whatever may be thought of the redundant discourse before us, it had no chance of starting a present conflagration. If, in the long run, the beliefs expressed in proletarian dictatorship are destined to be accepted by the dominant forces of the community, the only meaning of free speech is that they should be given their chance and have their way.
>
> If the publication . . . had been laid as an attempt to induce an uprising . . . at once . . . it would have presented a different question. The object would have been one with which the law might deal, subject to the doubt whether . . . the publication could produce any result; or, in other words, whether it was not futile and too remote from possible consequences. But the in-

dictment alleges the publication and nothing more.[223]

Holmes' dissent is too compressed to be clear. He started from the factual situation, and since he saw no present danger from either the publication in question or from the activities of the small group, he argued that the statute could not validly be applied. He did not use the clear and present danger standard to question the constitutionality of the statute itself. Yet he clearly did not agree with Justice Sanford that the Court always had to accept as conclusive a legislative determination of the danger likely from statements which advocated "anarchy."

Holmes not only failed to mark out the appropriate degree of judicial deference to the legislative judgment. He also completely avoided discussing the extent to which the Court can independently determine the likelihood of danger from a particular expression. Judging from his opinion, his position might have been that a court *at times* could still consider whether a particular publication presented any reasonable expectation of harm, and that, in terms of the clear and present danger standard, it was unconstitutional to apply the statute to the particular facts of *Gitlow*. In any case, one would think that the desire to influence future decisons, to guide those eager to follow his lead on this question, would have led him to clarify the basis of his position, to demonstrate that it answered the problem posed by the New York law.

Justice Sanford had also drawn Holmes' fire by saying, "[t]his is not the expression of philosophical abstraction, the mere prediction of future events; it is the language of direct incitement."[224] Justice Holmes' response that "every idea is an incitement"—an epigram in the sense of a half-truth aimed at someone who believes the other half—paradoxically stated the difficulty of drawing a line between advocacy and incitement, and asserted the possibility of potential incitement even where statements seem to shade over into abstract discussion. Although the difference is generally too vague to be of much use, it can very often serve as a useful initial distinction. If Holmes is saying anything, it is that since every idea is an incitement, none is ever only mere abstract doctrine. Even if this is partially valid psychologically, legally it is completely false. Not every incitement constitutes the crime of "incitement," and Justices Sanford and

223. *Gitlow,* 268 U.S. at 673 (Holmes, J., dissenting).
224. *Id.* at 665.

Holmes each spoke within a legal context, referring to the crime of "incitement."[225]

The extreme sociological fatalism of Holmes' remarks should also be noticed. Holmes assumes here, as he always did, that government itself lacks control or even influence, that it is a passive instrument on which social forces play. By saying, "destined to be accepted," he reveals that he has no basis for opposing the ascendency of any beliefs which "might" prevail. What is perhaps even more fascinating, Holmes does not seem to conceive of a court decision—or perhaps any other event—helping to decide whether the beliefs "have their way." Instead, he turns the relationship around—it is the potential future dominance of beliefs which requires giving them a "chance."

The response to Justice Sanford's opinion in *Gitlow* had to await Justice Brandeis' brilliant concurring opinion in *Whitney,*[226] in which Holmes joined. Anita Whitney, who had helped organize the Communist Labor Party in California, had been found guilty of violating California's Criminal Syndicalism Law, which made it a felony to organize or knowingly become a member of an organization formed to advocate, teach, or aid and abet criminal syndicalism.[227] Justice Brandeis felt compelled to sustain the conviction because the constitutional issue had not been raised at the trial, and could therefore not be reached by the Supreme Court in exercising its limited power of review in state criminal cases.[228] He did, however, take the opportunity to give new clarity and a different significance to the clear and present danger doctrine.

> This court has not yet fixed the standard by which to determine when a danger shall be deemed clear; how remote the danger may be and yet be deemed present; and what degree of evil shall be deemed sufficiently substantial to justify resort to abridgement of free speech and assembly as the means of protection.[229]

Justice Brandeis went on to illuminate these issues, arguing, "There must be reasonable ground to believe that the danger

225. Corwin, *Bowing Out "Clear and Present Danger,"* 27 NOTRE DAME LAW. 325, 340 (1952).

226. *Whitney,* 274 U.S. at 372 (Brandeis, J., concurring).

227. *Id.* at 360.

228. *Id.* at 379–80.

229. *Id.* at 374.

apprehended is imminent."[230] Going far beyond Holmes' original formulation, he said that "[t]he fact that speech is likely to result in some violence or in destruction of property is not enough to justify its suppression. There must be the probability of serious injury to the State."[231] Justice Brandeis thus raised for the first time the question of the importance of the interests that justified repression. He discussed the value of free discussion—the basic justification for limiting government action in this area—and specifically linked, in a way it is difficult to imagine Holmes doing, the protection of the first amendment to "the occasional tyrannies of governing majorities."[232] And he anticipated the Court's resolution in *Brandenburg v. Ohio*,[233] by linking the incitement test of *Masses* with the imminence of serious harm.[234]

On the issue of legislative limitations, he answered Sanford's opinion in *Gitlow*: "Where a statute is valid only in case certain conditions exist, the enactment of the statute cannot alone establish the facts which are essential to its validity."[235] And,

> [w]henever the fundamental rights of free speech and assembly are alleged to have been invaded, it must remain open to a defendant to present the issue whether there actually did exist at the time a clear danger; whether the danger, if any, was imminent; and whether the evil apprehended was one so substantial as to justify the stringent restriction interposed by the legislature. The legislative declaration, like the fact that the statute was passed and was sustained by the highest court of the state, creates merely a rebuttable presumption that these conditions have been satisfied.[236]

The legislature's assertion that certain words were in and of themselves sufficiently dangerous to be repressed could not bar a court from examining whether, in a particular situation the words did in fact constitute such a danger. When Justice Brandeis took that last step, he gave the "clear and present danger" doctrine the full potentialities exploited during its brief heyday.

---

230. *Id.* at 376.
231. *Id.* at 378.
232. *Id.* at 376.
233. 395 U.S. 444 (1969).
234. *Whitney,* 274 U.S. at 375–76.
235. *Id.* at 374.
236. *Id.* at 378–79.

VI. Epilogue

United States v. Schwimmer,[237] which did not concern speech directly, is one of Holmes' most attractive opinions. Rosika Schwimmer, fifty years old and a well-known pacifist, applied for naturalization, but refused to swear that she would bear arms in case of war. Her application was denied because she had not demonstrated that she was, in the language of the statutory requirement, "attached to the principles of the Constitution of the United States and well disposed to the good order and happiness of the same" and would "support and defend the Constitution and laws of the United States against all enemies, foreign and domestic."[238] The court of appeals reversed the decree and was reversed in turn by the Supreme Court. Justice Butler, speaking for the Court, said that citizenship was properly denied in these circumstances. He said, "Citizenship is a high privilege and when doubts exist . . . they should be resolved . . . against the claimant."[239]

Holmes dissented. He used characteristically general language, which was, however, appropriate and quite superb in these circumstances. At 88, after a life-long opposition to pacifism and a preoccupation with war reflected in the imagery and very texture of his speech, Holmes' intense attack on the decision is unusually moving.

Referring to his skepticism about the abolition of war, he wrote that Mrs. Schwimmer believes "that war will disappear and the impending destiny of man is to unite in peaceful leagues. I do not share that optimism nor do I think that a philosophic view of the world would regard war as absurd."[240] He continued,

> Some of her answers might excite popular prejudice, but if there is any principle of the Constitution that more imperatively calls for attachment than any other it is the principle of free thought—not free thought for those who agree with us but freedom for the thought that we hate . . . . And, recurring to the opinion that bars this applicant's way, I would suggest that the Quakers have done their share to make the country what it is, that many citizens agree with the applicant's belief, and that I had not supposed hitherto that we regretted our inability to ex-

237. 279 U.S. 644 (1929).

238. Naturalization Act of 1906, 8 U.S.C. §§ 381, 382 (repealed 1940).

239. *Schwimmer,* 279 U.S. at 649–50 (quoting United States v. Manzi, 276 U.S. 463, 467 (1928)). For a discussion of *Manzi,* see Rogat, *supra* note 3, at 37.

240. *Schwimmer,* 279 U.S. at 654 (Holmes, J., dissenting).

> pel them because they believe more than some of us do in the teachings of the Sermon on the Mount.[241]

On reading, in January 1930, that Holmes was ill, Mrs. Schwimmer wrote to him. While acknowledging that the letter was written against advice that one does not thank a judge,[242] she expressed gratitude for his dissent in her case. Justice Holmes replied that a decision which deserved thanks would demonstrate a failure to do one's duty.

> A case is simply a problem to be solved, although the considerations are more complex than those of mathematics. Even when as in your case it was only to interpret a statute, Madame, you appreciate that the opinion of the majority simply meant that they did the sum differently—that duty and reason seemed to them to require a different answer from that which the minority reached.[243]

Justice Holmes did his "sums" elegantly. That elegance was put to good use by Chafee and others whose dedication to a liberal conception of free speech is clear. But the response to Mrs. Schwimmer, reflecting as it does Justice Holmes' celebrated detachment, calls to mind another line. In it, we may find the ultimate answer to those who would canonize Holmes for his defense of free speech—"in which, in the abstract, I have no very enthusiastic belief, though I hope I would die for it."[244]

---

241. *Id.* at 654–55.

242. Letter from Rosika Schwimmer to Oliver Wendell Holmes (Jan. 28, 1930) (Schwimmer-Lloyd Collection, Box G–11, Rare Books and Manuscripts Division, The New York Public Library, Astor, Lenox and Tilden Foundations).

243. Letter from Oliver Wendell Holmes to Rosika Schwimmer (Jan. 30, 1930) (Schwimmer-Lloyd Collection, Box G–11, Rare Books and Manuscript Divison, New York Public Library, Astor, Lenox and Tilden Foundations).

244. 2 Holmes-Pollock Letters 29 (M. Howe ed. 1941).

THE RIGHT TO PRIVACY IN NINETEENTH CENTURY AMERICA

On December 15, 1890, Samuel D. Warren and Louis D. Brandeis, two young Boston law partners, published an article in the *Harvard Law Review* entitled *The Right to Privacy.*[1] In that article, they proposed a remedy for invasions of personal privacy by the press.[2] More than ninety years later, protection of privacy has become a major concern of the law. Legal scholars have organized the extensive body of case law into a coherent common law of privacy;[3] the Supreme Court has enshrined the right to privacy in the "penumbra" of the Bill of Rights;[4] and Congress has enacted additional safeguards.[5]

This increased recognition of a right to privacy has brought corresponding praise for Warren and Brandeis as the originators of a new legal right.[6] At the same time, their contribution has been criticized as having lacked sufficient legal[7] and factual[8] basis for the right they are credited with launching. One recent commentator surveyed the English precedents cited in *The Right to Privacy* and concluded that "before 1890 no court had protected inviolate personality . . . or a right to privacy, independent of property rights."[9] A more fundamental critique of privacy law in general attempts to reduce this "new" right to its component interests and then to assess whether these interests deserve legal protection.[10] Finding some aspects

---

[1] Warren & Brandeis, *The Right to Privacy*, 4 HARV. L. REV. 193 (1890).

[2] *Id.* at 219.

[3] *See* RESTATEMENT (SECOND) OF TORTS §§ 652B–652E (1977); Prosser, *Privacy*, 48 CALIF. L. REV. 383, 389 (1960).

[4] *See, e.g.*, Griswold v. Connecticut, 381 U.S. 479, 483–86 (1965).

[5] *See, e.g.*, Privacy Act of 1974, 5 U.S.C. § 552a (1976); Freedom of Information Act of 1974, § 2(b), 5 U.S.C. § 552(b)(7)(C) (1976) (privacy exception).

[6] *See, e.g.*, P. DIONISOPOULOS & C. DUCAT, THE RIGHT TO PRIVACY 20 (1976); Prosser, *supra* note 3, at 383.

[7] *See, e.g.*, Pratt, *The Warren and Brandeis Argument for a Right to Privacy*, 1975 PUB. L. 161, 179.

[8] *See, e.g.*, Barron, *Warren and Brandeis,* The Right to Privacy, *4 Harv. L. Rev. 193 (1890): Demystifying a Landmark Citation*, 13 SUFFOLK U.L. REV. 875 (1979).

[9] Pratt, *supra* note 7, at 176. A similar criticism that property rights were the only rights protected by injunctions in equity was advanced in Hadley, *The Right to Privacy*, 3 NW. L. REV. 1, 3–4 (1894), and later recanted in Hadley, *Can the Publication of a Libel Be Enjoined?*, 4 NW. L. REV. 137, 145–46 (1896).

[10] *See, e.g.*, Davis, *What Do We Mean by "Right to Privacy"?*, 4 S.D.L. REV. 1 (1959); Kalven, *Privacy in Tort Law — Were Warren and Brandeis Wrong?*, 31 LAW & CONTEMP. PROB. 326 (1966); Posner, *Privacy, Secrecy, and Reputation*, 28 BUFFALO L. REV. 1 (1979); Posner, *The Right to Privacy*, 12 GA. L. REV. 393 (1978) (economic analysis of the right of privacy).

of privacy to be, for example, merely extensions of property and reputation, the reductionist approach suggests that what Warren and Brandeis invented did not constitute an independently protectible right.[11]

Both praise and criticism proceed on the assumption, shared by modern courts,[12] commentators,[13] and legal historians,[14] that "courts had not prior to 1890 granted relief expressly for invasion of [a] right of privacy."[15] Warren and Brandeis, however, deserve neither full credit nor blame for the law's recognition of privacy as a protectible interest. They did not purport to add a novel right to the legal universe, but instead drew upon some of the established legal doctrines protecting personal privacy to propose an extension of remedies against the press.[16] Readers of their article in 1890 would

---

[11] *See, e.g.*, Davis, *supra* note 10, at 7–12; Kalven, *supra* note 10, at 339–41.

[12] *See, e.g.*, Flores v. Mosler Safe Co., 7 N.Y.2d 276, 280, 164 N.E.2d 853, 854–55, 196 N.Y.S.2d 975, 978 (1959); Nader v. General Motors Corp., 31 A.D.2d 392, 397, 298 N.Y.S.2d 137, 143 (1969) (Steuer, J., dissenting) ("Prior to 1890, if the phrase ['right of privacy'] was used at all it represented, at least logically, an amorphous concept somewhat in the nature of 'the pursuit of happiness', something to which we had a right; but reducing that right to enforcible proportions was not even imagined."), *aff'd*, 25 N.Y.2d 560, 255 N.E.2d 765, 307 N.Y.S.2d 647 (1970); Billings v. Atkinson, 489 S.W.2d 858, 859 (Tex. 1973).

[13] *See, e.g.*, A. MILLER, THE ASSAULT ON PRIVACY 169 (1971) ("As the last century drew to an end, it was relatively simple to evaluate the legal position of a man whose privacy had been invaded — the doors of the courthouse were closed to him." (footnote omitted)); W. PROSSER, HANDBOOK OF THE LAW OF TORTS § 117, at 802 (4th ed. 1971); Davis, *supra* note 10, at 3.

[14] *See, e.g.*, L. FRIEDMAN, A HISTORY OF AMERICAN LAW 548 (1973); O'Connor, *The Right to Privacy in Historical Perspective*, 53 MASS. L.Q. 101, 109–10 (1968).

Among the first commentators to reject this assumption were Alan Westin and David Flaherty. *See* D. FLAHERTY, PRIVACY IN COLONIAL NEW ENGLAND 248 (1972) ("[A] right to privacy existed . . . that was both traditional and customary."); A. WESTIN, PRIVACY AND FREEDOM 330–38 (1967). Recently, historians have begun to concede the existence of some wider concern for privacy shortly before 1890. *See* M. KELLER, AFFAIRS OF STATE 519–21 (1977); G. WHITE, TORT LAW IN AMERICA 173 (1980).

[15] Billings v. Atkinson, 489 S.W.2d 858, 859 (Tex. 1973).

[16] Their article recognized that "the existing law afford[ed] a principle which may be invoked to protect the privacy of the individual from invasion." Warren & Brandeis, *supra* note 1, at 206. The "next step" they proposed was a small but difficult one, extending this principle from its secure grounding to a direct confrontation with a robust "yellow press" that jealously guarded its first amendment privileges. *Id.* at 195; *see* Bloustein, *Privacy, Tort Law, and the Constitution: Is Warren and Brandeis' Tort Petty and Unconstitutional as Well?*, 46 TEX. L. REV. 611 (1968). The authors reasoned in part from contractual and equitable doctrines, Warren & Brandeis, *supra* note 1, at 207–13, but primarily from the law of intellectual property. Courts, in preventing the publication of private letters, *see* p. 1900 *infra*, had recognized a right to "inviolate personality" or had at least strayed so far from conventional notions of property that recognition of a property interest in personal information could logically follow. *Id.* at 204–05. *But see* p. 1904 *infra*.

have recognized that the law already afforded many explicit protections against other invasions of privacy.[17]

This Note examines the extent to which nineteenth century American courts and legislatures recognized privacy as an independent interest. Part I sets out the legal doctrines protecting the home and the privacy associated with it. Part II deals with the protection of confidential communication, which had much less to do with conventional notions of property than did the rights associated with the home. Part III describes how information about individuals, information that was not property at all, was protected by limiting access to public records and preventing unwanted publications. The picture that emerges by 1890 is one of ample and explicit protection of privacy in its own right.

I. PRIVATE PROPERTY

The legal maxim and popular proverb that "a man's house is his castle" had wide application in the nineteenth century.[18] American courts administered criminal penalties[19] and civil remedies to safeguard "the sanctity and inviolability of one's house,"[20] the householder's right to "quiet and peaceable possession,"[21] and the dwellinghouse as "the place of family re-

[17] For contemporary reviews of the Warren and Brandeis article that make this point, see *The Right to Privacy*, 51 NATION 496 (1890); 17 LIFE 4 (1891) (brief commentary); 9 SCRIBNER'S MAGAZINE 261 (1891) (same).

[18] For examples of nonlegal appearances of the phrase, see A. TAYLOR & B. WHITING, A DICTIONARY OF AMERICAN PROVERBS AND PROVERBIAL PHRASES, 1820–1880, at 193 (1958); B. WHITING, EARLY AMERICAN PROVERBS AND PROVERBIAL PHRASES 226–27 (1977). The principal English authority for the maxim is Semayne's Case, 5 Co. Rep. 91a, 91b, 77 Eng. Rep. 194, 195 (1605). An earlier mention can be found in Y.B. Mich. 21 Hen. 7, f. 39, pl. 50 (1499), *noted in* 2 THE REPORTS OF SIR JOHN SPELMAN *316* & n.2 (94 Selden Society, J. Baker ed. 1978).

[19] On this basis, Sir William Blackstone justified the criminal punishment of burglary, arson, nuisance, and eavesdropping, as well as the rule that sheriffs or bailiffs could not break down doors for the execution of any civil process. 4 W. BLACKSTONE, COMMENTARIES ON THE LAWS OF ENGLAND *223 (The law has "so particular and tender a regard to the immunity of a man's house that it stiles it his castle, and will never suffer it to be violated with impunity."). American courts echoed Blackstone's sentiments. *See, e.g.*, Snydacker v. Brosse, 51 Ill. 357, 359–60 (1869) (no authority to break outer doors in the execution of civil process); Mitchell v. Commonwealth, 88 Ky. 349, 353, 11 S.W. 209, 210 (1889) (dictum) (severe punishment for crimes against the "peculiar sanctity" of the dwelling-house) (superseded on other grounds by KY. R. CRIM. PROC. 6.12, 6.16, *see* Luna v. Commonwealth, 571 S.W.2d 88 (Ky. Ct. App. 1977), *remanded*, 574 S.W.2d 227 (Ky. 1978)); Armour v. State, 22 Tenn. (3 Hum.) 379, 384 (1842).

[20] Christian v. State, 96 Ala. 89, 91, 11 So. 338, 338–39 (1892).

[21] Foye v. Sewell, 21 Abb. N. Cas. 15, 17 (N.Y. Ct. C.P. 1888).

pose."[22] In particular, the law of trespass and the constitutional prohibition of unreasonable search and seizure were interpreted as safeguards of privacy interests against official and unofficial intrusion.

The ability to exclude others, a central feature of private property,[23] was absolute when the family home was the property in question and domestic privacy the interest at stake. Even the property rights of others yielded before the householder's "right of shutting his own door."[24] Landlords entering to make repairs,[25] owners of goods seeking to retrieve them,[26] and creditors sending sheriffs to execute valid judgments[27] could all be held liable for intrusion upon the repose and tranquillity of families within the dwellinghouse."[28] Further, a Vermont court upheld a houseguest's "right of quiet occupancy and privacy" against the unwelcome intrusion of her host into the bedroom he had provided for her,[29] and a Michigan court found a sacred "right of privacy" violated when a doctor brought an unqualified assistant into the bedchamber of a woman in childbirth.[30] Whether the plaintiff was a property owner or a guest, and whether the defendant gained entry by force or by false pretenses, the trespass remedy protected domestic privacy. Moreover, damages in trespass were not limited to the plaintiff's pecuniary loss, but included, in the words of a New York court, compensation for "injury, insult, invasion of the privacy, and interference with the comfort of the plaintiff and his family."[31]

---

[22] Mitchell v. Commonwealth, 88 Ky. 349, 353, 11 S.W. 209, 210 (1889) (emphasis omitted) (superseded on other grounds by KY. R. CRIM. PROC. 6.12, 6.16, *see* Luna v. Commonwealth, 571 S.W.2d 88 (Ky. Ct. App. 1977), *remanded*, 574 S.W.2d 227 (Ky. 1978)).

[23] *See* 2 W. BLACKSTONE, *supra* note 19, at *2.

[24] State v. Armfield, 9 N.C. (2 Hawks) 246, 247 (1822).

[25] Wien v. Simpson, 2 Phila. 158, 158–59 (Pa. Dist. Ct. 1857).

[26] *See* Hobbs v. Geiss, 13 Serg. & Rawl. 417, 418–19 (Pa. 1826). *But see* Keith v. Johnson, 31 Ky. (1 Dana) 604, 605 (1833) (statute permitted forcible entry to recover a slave adjudged to belong to the plaintiff).

[27] *See, e.g.*, Ilsley v. Nichols, 29 Mass. (12 Pick.) 270, 277 (1832) (deputy sheriff making attachment of goods); Oystead v. Shed, 13 Mass. 520, 523 (1816) (deputy sheriff making arrest); State v. Armfield, 9 N.C. (2 Hawks) 246, 247 (1822) (constable executing civil process).

[28] Oystead v. Shed, 13 Mass. 520, 523 (1816).

[29] Newell v. Whitcher, 53 Vt. 589, 591 (1880). The concern of the court may have been to avenge the honor of a defenseless woman, but the language of privacy protection provided the legal rationale for recovery.

[30] De May v. Roberts, 46 Mich. 160, 165–66, 9 N.W. 146, 149 (1881).

[31] Ives v. Humphrey, 1 E.D. Smith 196, 201–02 (N.Y. Ct. C.P. 1851) (emphasis omitted).

Invasions of domestic privacy that fell short of physical trespass were dealt with by the criminal law. Eavesdropping, a common law crime noted by Blackstone,[32] was prosecuted in America on the ground that "no man has a right . . . to pry into your secrecy in your own house."[33] Although never numerous, indictments for eavesdropping occurred throughout the nineteenth century under common law and statute.[34] In addition, "peeping Toms" could be punished under state statutes and city ordinances.[35] These sanctions against curious eyes and ears augmented the trespass remedy, giving householders a right to be free from unwanted observation from without. In 1892, trespass itself was extended to this type of conduct by the New York Court of Appeals. The court awarded damages for "loss of privacy" to a plaintiff whose rooms were exposed to observation when the defendant constructed an elevated train platform.[36] By the late nineteenth century, the law had erected high walls around the family home by extending criminal penalties for and civil remedies against intrusion by strangers.

Official intrusions into the home were also narrowly restricted in the interest of privacy. In 1791, with colonial writs of assistance and general warrants an all-too-recent memory, the independent states added the fourth amendment to the federal Constitution, preserving the "right of the people to be secure in their persons, houses, papers, and effects" from warrantless search and seizure by agents of the new national government.[37] Thomas Cooley, a leading constitutional authority, linked the fourth amendment to the common law principle that "a man's house is his castle," a guarantee of the citizen's "immunity in his home against the prying eyes of the

---

[32] 4 W. BLACKSTONE, *supra* note 19, at *169 (defining the offense as "listen[ing] under walls or windows, or the eaves of a house, to hearken after discourse, and thereupon to frame slanderous and mischievous tales").

[33] Commonwealth v. Lovett, 6 Pa. L.J.R. 226, 227 (1831); *see id.* at 228 (discussing *Commonwealth v. Mengelt*, unpublished Pennsylvania decision of 1818); State v. Pennington, 40 Tenn. (3 Head) 299 (1859); State v. Williams, 2 Tenn. (2 Overt.) 108 (1808).

[34] *See* State v. Davis, 139 N.C. 547, 547–48, 51 S.E. 897, 897 (1905); N.Y. PEN. CODE § 436 (1881); *Indicted for Eavesdropping*, 9 CRIM. L. MAGAZINE 941 (1887).

[35] City of Grand Rapids v. Williams, 112 Mich. 247, 250, 70 N.W. 547, 547–48 (1897) (violation of ordinance against "indecent, insulting, or immoral conduct").

[36] Moore v. New York Elevated R.R., 130 N.Y. 523, 527–28, 29 N.E. 997, 997–98 (1892). The court here grounded the action on continuing trespass in the nature of a loss of easement.

[37] U.S. CONST. amend. IV. *See generally* N. LASSON, THE HISTORY AND DEVELOPMENT OF THE FOURTH AMENDMENT TO THE UNITED STATES CONSTITUTION (1937).

government."[38] Each state adopted a parallel provision in its own constitution,[39] and much early development of search and seizure doctrine took place in state courts.[40] As a state judge, Cooley interpreted Michigan's search and seizure provision "to make sacred the privacy of the citizen's dwelling and person against everything but process issued upon a showing of legal cause for invading it."[41]

Boyd v. United States,[42] one of the first Supreme Court decisions to interpret the fourth amendment,[43] expressed a similar view of the purpose of this constitutional safeguard.[44] Relying on the English precedent of *Entick v. Carrington*,[45] the Court recognized an "indefeasible right of personal secu-

---

[38] The earliest appearances of a search and seizure provision in state constitutions are collected in Harris v. United States, 331 U.S. 145, 160 n.5 (1947) (Frankfurter, J., dissenting), *overruled*, Chimel v. California, 395 U.S. 752 (1969). New York, the only state Justice Frankfurter omits, enacted such a provision in a 1787 "Bill of Rights." *See* Hitchcock, *The Inviolability of Telegrams*, 2 PROC. A.B.A. 93, 110 n.* (1879).

[39] *See, e.g.*, Larthet v. Forgay, 2 La. Ann. 524, 525–26 (1847) (constitutional protection of "the domestic repose of the citizen" permitted recovery for "injury to the plaintiff's feelings, and the disturbance of his family" caused by entrance without a valid warrant); Bell v. Clapp, 10 Johns. 263, 264–65 (N.Y. 1813). *See generally* A. WESTIN, *supra* note 14, at 333.

[40] T. COOLEY, A TREATISE ON THE CONSTITUTIONAL LIMITATIONS 299–300 (Boston 1868). This language was adopted by a federal court in United States v. Three Tons of Coal, 28 F. Cas. 149, 151 (E.D. Wis. 1875). *See also* 1 F. LIEBER, ON CIVIL LIBERTY AND SELF-GOVERNMENT 46 (Philadelphia 1853) (fourth amendment guarantee of "individual security" against "police government"); H. VON HOLST, THE CONSTITUTIONAL LAW OF THE UNITED STATES OF AMERICA 257 (A. Mason trans. 1887) (fourth amendment protection against "arbitrary acts of the public power"). Outside the ambit of criminal prosecution, protections of the castle were invoked against censustakers. *Trials of the Census-Taker*, N.Y. Times, July 19, 1875, at 4, col. 4. Members of Congress were even reluctant to permit entry into homes by the District of Columbia water board. *See* 10 CONG. REC. 3170 (1880) (remarks of Sen. Ingalls).

[41] Weimer v. Bunbury, 30 Mich. 201, 208 (1874).

[42] 116 U.S. 616 (1886) (holding unconstitutional a statute compelling production of private papers).

[43] *Boyd* and *Ex parte* Jackson, 96 U.S. 727 (1878), *discussed at* pp. 1899–900 *infra*, provided the first substantial opportunities for the Court to develop a fourth amendment jurisprudence. *See* Note, *Formalism, Legal Realism, and Constitutionally Protected Privacy under the Fourth and Fifth Amendments*, 90 HARV. L. REV. 945, 952 n.42 (1977).

[44] *See* L. BETH, THE DEVELOPMENT OF THE AMERICAN CONSTITUTION, 1877–1917, at 200–01 (1971). The *Boyd* Court's broad interpretation of the scope of the fourth and fifth amendments, *see* pp. 1899–900, 1903 *infra*, has not been equalled in the 20th century. *See* United States v. Abrams, 615 F.2d 541, 547 (1st Cir. 1980) (stating that Warden v. Hayden, 387 U.S. 294 (1967), "wounded *Boyd* mortally"); Note, *supra* note 43.

[45] 19 How. St. Tr. 1029 (C.P. 1765).

rity, personal liberty and private property"[46] against "all invasions on the part of the government and its employés of the sanctity of a man's home and the privacies of life."[47]

Although judicial protection of privacy was substantial, resort to the courts was not the first line of defense for the homeowner faced with official or unofficial intrusion. The principal means of protecting privacy subsumed under the maxim "a man's house is his castle" was the willingness of nineteenth century Americans to resort to force — quite often deadly force — in the defense of their homes. The acquittal of one vehement householder in 1890 received national attention:

> "A man's house is his castle"; in it he is supposed to be safe; privacy is sacred in the eyes of civilization, and no individual has the right to violate the privacy of another; ergo, has not the right to enter his house without his consent for any purpose whatsoever. . . . The courts have so decided, and a fresh decision by Judge Collins has brought to notice the danger of violation of the principle: "A man's house is his castle." Officer John Mahoney went to the house of Thomas Bailey, and, without warrant, forcibly entered. Bailey shot him, as he had a perfect right to do, and the court acquitted him. Any citizen has a right to defend his privacy to whatever extent he may find necessary, save against recognized and accredited officers of the law with the official order of the community in the shape of a warrant to justify their intrusion.[48]

Among the available legal remedies for invasion of domestic privacy must be counted the law's provision for this extraordinary measure of individual self-help. In court, defense of the castle may have had its limits, but in public opinion it was an absolute right.

---

[46] 116 U.S. at 630. Justice Bradley echoed the words of Joseph Story who, in his treatise on the Constitution, declared the fourth amendment's protections to be "indispensable to the full enjoyment of the rights of personal security, personal liberty, and private property." 3 J. STORY, COMMENTARIES ON THE CONSTITUTION OF THE UNITED STATES § 1895, at 748 (Boston 1833). For an adoption of Justice Story's extrajudicial pronouncement by a state court, see Larthet v. Forgay, 2 La. Ann. 524, 516 (1847).

[47] 116 U.S. at 630. This language reappeared in ICC v. Brimson, 154 U.S. 447, 479 (1894) (Harlan, J.).

[48] *A Man's House His Castle*, 9 PUB. OPINION 342 (1890) (reprinted from *Chicago Mail*).

II. Confidential Communications

Nineteenth century public opinion regarded the "sanctity of the mails" as absolute in the same way it esteemed the inviolability of the home.[49] A special agent of the Post Office explained in 1855 that "[t]he laws of the land are intended not only to preserve the person and material property of every citizen sacred from intrusion, but to secure the privacy of his thoughts, so far as he sees fit to withhold them from others."[50] Legal protection of private letters and other confidential communications from interception, publication, and forced disclosure depended on notions of personal privacy often unattached to any property interest.

Although a letter was considered the property of the sender while in transit, unauthorized opening and reading of its contents was neither theft nor damage to property. Congress nevertheless made interception intended "to pry into another's business or secrets" a criminal offense.[51] Whether this or any other prohibition prevented the federal government, acting officially, from opening sealed letters in the custody of its post office was unsettled[52] until 1878. In *Ex parte Jackson*,[53] the Supreme Court held that a statute banning lottery information from the mails could not be enforced by federal officers' opening letters and sealed packages, unless upon the authority of

---

[49] *See, e.g.*, F. Currier, Postal Communication, Past and Present 3–4 (1894) (quoting remarks of Ralph Waldo Emerson); 1 F. Lieber, *supra* note 40, at 109 ("the sacredness of epistolary communion"); *Lotteries and Letters*, N.Y. Times, Mar. 23, 1858, at 4, col. 3.

[50] J. Holbrook, Ten Years Among the Mail Bags xviii (Philadelphia 1855).

[51] Act of Mar. 3, 1825, ch. 64, § 22, 4 Stat. 102 (penalty against any person opening letters en route) (believed to have been drafted chiefly by Daniel Webster, *see* 5 Cong. Rec. 444 (1877) (remarks of Sen. Conkling)); *see* Act of Feb. 20, 1792, ch. 7, § 16, 1 Stat. 232 (penalty against postal employees who "unlawfully" opened, delayed, or detained the mails). Similar provisions had been enacted by the Continental Congress, 21 Journals of the Continental Congress, 1774–1789, at 671 (W. Ford ed. 1782). For state cases involving accusations of letter opening, see Hillhouse v. Peck, 2 Stew. & P. 395, 395 (Ala. 1832); McCuen v. Ludlum, 17 N.J. L. 12 (1839).

[52] *See* D. Wells, The Relation of the Government to the Telegraph 49–50 (1873). In the 19th century, the government itself opened private correspondence only on rare occasions and for specific purposes: (1) the protection of military secrets, *see* J. Randall, Constitutional Problems Under Lincoln 500 (1926); *cf.* 5 Cong. Rec. 350 (1876) (remarks of Rep. Kasson) (the degree of wartime censorship was later minimized); (2) the prevention of fraud, *see Ex parte* Jackson, 96 U.S. 727 (1878); *Lotteries and Letters*, N.Y. Times, Mar. 23, 1858, at 4, col. 3; (3) the eradication of obscene literature, *see* Act of Mar. 3, 1865, ch. 89, § 16, 13 Stat. 504; Cong. Globe, 38th Cong., 2d Sess. 660–62 (1865) (debate); *Suppression of Obscene Literature*, N.Y. Times, July 3, 1873, at 8, col. 2.

[53] 96 U.S. 727 (1878).

a warrant issued in compliance with the fourth amendment.[54] "The constitutional guaranty," wrote Justice Field, "of the right of the people to be secure in their papers against unreasonable searches and seizures extends to their papers, thus closed against inspection, wherever they may be."[55] This decision, coupled with a statutory mandate that postal officials not detain or delay letters,[56] ensured virtually absolute protection against official tampering.[57]

The privacy of letters once delivered was protected by state law. Criminal penalties for "the violation of epistolary correspondence" were proposed[58] and enacted[59] in some jurisdictions. In addition, courts of equity would issue injunctions to prevent publication of private letters contrary to the sender's wishes. Despite some early doubts,[60] American courts, led by Justice Joseph Story,[61] refused to limit this relief to letters of "literary merit" in which the sender might have a pecuniary or proprietary interest.[62]

When produced in court, letters again received special treatment. According to one description of late nineteenth century practice, letters were handed quietly to the judge, who read them privately and without disclosure to the parties or to the jury, "unless they be of that nature falling within the restrictions of the law which commits them to the record as evidence in the case."[63] What was not relevant or material,

---

[54] *Id.* at 735; *cf.* Coltzhausen v. Nazro, 107 U.S. 215 (1883) (opening of sealed letter does not render customs agent liable).

[55] 96 U.S. at 733.

[56] Act of Feb. 20, 1792, ch. 7, § 16, 1 Stat. 232.

[57] *See* U.S. POST OFFICE DEP'T, POSTAL LAWS AND REGULATIONS § 506 (1887) ("the absolute sanctity of the seal" could not be broken, even to furnish evidence of criminal matters).

[58] Edward Livingston, an early reformer and codifier of the criminal law, proposed fines and imprisonment for unauthorized opening, malicious publication, and taking of private letters. Draft Code of Crimes and Punishments art. 621 (1824), *reprinted in* 2 E. LIVINGSTON, COMPLETE WORKS 166 (1873); *see* 1 *id.* at 322.

[59] *See, e.g.*, CAL. PEN. CODE § 618 (1872).

[60] *See* Hoyt v. Mackenzie, 3 Barb. Ch. 320, 324–25 (N.Y. Ch. 1848); Wetmore v. Scovell, 3 Edw. Ch. 515, 527–28 (N.Y. Ch. 1842).

[61] Folsom v. Marsh, 9 F. Cas. 342, 346 (C.C.D. Mass. 1841) (Story, J.); 2 J. STORY, COMMENTARIES ON EQUITY JURISPRUDENCE §§ 944–949 (Boston 1836).

[62] *See* Rice v. Williams, 32 F. 437, 439 (C.C.E.D. Wis. 1887) (sale of letters relating to medical afflictions was "grossly disreputable business"); Folsom v. Marsh, 9 F. Cas. 342, 346 (C.C.D. Mass. 1841); Denis v. Leclerc, 1 Mart. 297, 313 (Terr. Orleans 1811); Woolsey v. Judd, 4 Duer 379, 406, 11 How. Pr. 49, 78 (N.Y. Super. Ct. 1855); Dock v. Dock, 180 Pa. 14, 22, 36 A. 411, 412 (1897); *cf.* Eyre v. Higbee, 22 How. Pr. 198 (N.Y. Sup. Ct. 1861) (personal and business letters in hands of executor are not assets subject to sale).

[63] 5 CONG. REC. 444 (1877) (remarks of Sen. Conkling).

and especially what might be "injurious to the feelings or interest of third persons," was left unrevealed.[64]

The telegraph posed additional problems of privacy protection because messages were necessarily read by the operators who sent and received them. Wiretapping, a practice learned by military telegraphers during the Civil War,[65] was made a crime in some states;[66] elsewhere it was effectively prohibited by laws against interference with telegraph company property.[67] Disclosure by employees, including operators and those with access to messages retained in office files, was prohibited by company rules[68] and by statute in nearly every state.[69] According to one early judicial interpretation, these laws were intended "to prevent the betrayal of private affairs . . . for the promotion of private gain or the gratification of idle gossip."[70]

Whether such statutes also prevented government investigators from demanding the production of telegrams was much debated.[71] Western Union firmly opposed and resisted legislative as well as judicial subpoenas,[72] and newspapers characterized congressional dragnet subpoenas of telegraph office files as "unconstitutional and indecent."[73] Debate over the privacy of the telegraph reached its height in the aftermath of

---

[64] *Id*; 1 S. GREENLEAF, A TREATISE ON THE LAW OF EVIDENCE § 253 (Boston 1842) (emphasis omitted).

[65] *See* S. DASH, R. SCHWARTZ & R. KNOWLTON, THE EAVESDROPPERS 23 (1959).

[66] *See, e.g.*, CAL. PEN. CODE § 640 (1872); 1895 Ill. Laws 157.

[67] *See, e.g.*, 1868 Me. Laws 97; Rosenzweig, *The Law of Wire Tapping*, 33 CORNELL L.Q. 73, 73 (1947); Westin, *The Wire-Tapping Problem: An Analysis and a Legislative Proposal*, 52 COLUM. L. REV. 165, 182–83 (1952).

[68] *See, e.g.*, WESTERN UNION TELEGRAPH CO., RULES, REGULATIONS, AND INSTRUCTIONS no. 128, at 55 (Cleveland 1866).

[69] Statutes are cited in M. GRAY, A TREATISE ON COMMUNICATION BY TELEGRAPH § 120, at 213 nn.1–3 (1885); Hitchcock, *supra* note 38, at 114–19.

[70] Henisler v. Freedman, 2 Pars. Eq. Cas. 274 (Pa. Ct. C.P. 1851).

[71] As an emergency war measure in 1861, President Lincoln's War Office seized files of telegrams in all the major cities. *See* A. HARLOW, OLD WIRES AND NEW WAVES 264–65 (1936); 1 W. PLUM, THE MILITARY TELEGRAPH DURING THE CIVIL WAR IN THE UNITED STATES 69 (1882); *cf.* D. BATES, LINCOLN IN THE TELEGRAPH OFFICE 235–36 (1907) (privacy protest of a New York City office manager in 1864).

After the war, the Reconstruction Congress took the initiative, issuing dragnet subpoenas of telegraph company files to fuel its investigative activities. *See, e.g.*, CONG. GLOBE, 40th Cong., 2d Sess. supp., at 89–92 (1868) (impeachment trial of Andrew Johnson); 4 CONG. REC. pt. 7, at 216 (1876) (impeachment trial of William Belknap).

[72] In 1873, Western Union ordered employees not to comply with subpoenas for telegraph messages in the company's possession. Exec. Order No. 147 (1873), *reprinted in* 5 CONG. REC. 453 (1877).

[73] *Washington — Secrets of the Telegraph*, N.Y. Times, June 24, 1876, at 4, col. 7; *see Glover's Raid for Telegrams*, N.Y. Tribune, Dec. 20, 1876, at 1, col. 2.

the contested presidential election of 1876.[74] Judge Cooley again took a strongly protective stance, favoring judicial recognition of the absolute "inviolability" of telegraphic correspondence.[75] Western Union pressed for specific legislation affording telegrams the same protection as letters in the mail.[76] Ultimately the issue was settled by the courts, which required that subpoenas specify the date and subject of the particular telegrams sought.[77] Dragnet searches of the files, whether by legislative or by judicial authority, would no longer be tolerated.[78]

Other private conversations and sensitive items of personal information were also protected from disclosure in courtroom testimony and in official records of legal proceedings.[79] The common law rule of evidence that excluded spousal testimony and confidential communications between husband and wife, though rooted in antiquated notions of the couple's single legal identity,[80] acquired a new justification in the nineteenth century: preserving "the sacred privacy of domestic life."[81]

---

[74] Opponents of the subpoenas in Congress invoked the "rights of private citizens," 5 CONG. REC. 327 (1876) (remarks of Rep. McCrary), to "intrust their most sacredly private affairs to the telegraph compan[y] under the seal of its confidence," *id.* at 328–29 (remarks of Rep. Garfield), against "the invasion of their privacy by their servants, the House of Representatives," *id.* at 328; *see id.* at 326 (remarks of Rep. Hurd); *id.* at 442 (1877) (remarks of Sen. Sherman). *See also* A. Westin, Privacy and American Law: The Search for Lost Doctrine in the Computer Age 64–70 (1965) (unpublished manuscript in the Harvard Law School Library).

[75] Cooley, *Inviolability of Telegraphic Correspondence*, 18 AM. L. REG. (n.s.) 65 (1879); *see* T. COOLEY, *supra* note 40, at 375 n.2 (4th ed. 1878); *cf.* Hitchcock, *supra* note 38, at 140 (advocating a legislative solution).

[76] H.R. 5101, 46th Cong., 2d Sess. (1880), *reprinted in* N.Y. Tribune, Jan. 11, 1880, at 5, col. 3.

[77] *See, e.g.*, United States v. Babcock, 24 F. Cas. 908, 909 (C.C.E.D. Mo. 1876); United States v. Hunter, 15 F. 712, 714–15 (N.D. Miss. 1882); *Ex parte* Jaynes, 70 Cal. 638, 639, 12 P. 117, 117 (1886); *Ex parte* Brown, 72 Mo. 83, 94–95 (1880); Henisler v. Freedman, 2 Pars. Eq. Cas. 274 (Pa. Ct. C.P. 1851); *cf.* State v. Litchfield, 58 Me. 267 (1870) (operator may testify to specific message in criminal proceeding); National Bank v. National Bank, 7 W. Va. 544 (1874) (specific telegrams not privileged in civil proceeding).

[78] On the general limitations imposed on legislative investigations, see Kilbourn v. Thompson, 103 U.S. 168, 195 (1880); *In re* Pacific Ry. Comm'n, 32 F. 241, 250 (C.C.N.D. Cal. 1887).

[79] The privacy of jury deliberations was protected in Rickard v. State, 74 Ind. 275, 277 (1881); People v. Knapp, 42 Mich. 267, 270–71, 3 N.W. 927, 929 (1879).

[80] *See* 1 E. COKE, THE FIRST PART OF THE INSTITUTES OF THE LAWES OF ENGLAND 6b (London 1628). The changing rationales of the rules are discussed in 8 J. WIGMORE, A TREATISE ON THE LAW OF EVIDENCE §§ 2228, 2332–2333 (rev. ed. J. McNaughton 1961).

[81] Johnson v. State, 63 Miss. 313, 317 (1885); *see* Collins v. Mack, 31 Ark. 684, 689 (1877); Stanford v. Murphy, 63 Ga. 410, 416 (1879); People v. Hayes, 140 N.Y. 484, 495–96, 35 N.E. 951, 954 (1894).

Courts went far to avoid "embarrassing questions" that would "tear . . . away the veil, which hides from public gaze the sacred confidences which subsist between husband and wife."[82] The value of confidentiality was emphasized again in the common law privilege for attorney-client communications[83] and in nineteenth century extension of similar protection to disclosures from patient to doctor[84] and from penitent to priest.[85]

Nineteenth century jurisprudence also recognized a privacy component in the fifth amendment safeguard against self-incrimination.[86] Until the close of the century, "incrimination" was read broadly to include "infamy and disgrace" in addition to liability to criminal prosecution.[87] One purpose of the amendment, it was argued, was to avoid "compel[ling] a man who has fought his way from obscurity to dignity and honor to reveal crimes of which he had repented and of which the world was ignorant."[88] It prevented the compulsory production of personal papers[89] and permitted defendants to refuse to act, speak, or wear clothing for purposes of courtroom identification.[90]

Further constitutional underpinning for the privacy of communications was sought by nineteenth century jurists in the

---

[82] Owen v. State, 78 Ala. 425, 429–30 (1885); *see* Kelley v. Proctor, 41 N.H. 139, 141, 144 (1860).

[83] *See, e.g.*, Denver Tramway Co. v. Owens, 20 Colo. 107, 36 P. 848 (1894); Wheeler v. Hill, 16 Me. 329, 333 (1839); Hatton v. Robinson, 31 Mass. (14 Pick.) 416, 422 (1833).

[84] *See, e.g.*, Masonic Mutual Benefit Ass'n v. Beck, 77 Ind. 203, 209–10 (1881); Edington v. Mutual Life Ins. Co., 67 N.Y.185, 194 (1876); 2 N.Y. REV. STATS. pt. 3., ch. 7, tit. 3, art. 9, § 73 (1828).

[85] *See* 1 E. LIVINGSTON, *supra* note 58, at 467–68.

[86] The connection was recognized in a case involving the marital privilege: "It would be as wrong to make them reveal their private conversations, as admissions against interest, as it would be to charge them with their thoughts." Sumner v. Cooke, 51 Ala. 521, 521 (1874).

[87] Brown v. Walker, 161 U.S. 591, 636–37 (1896) (Field, J., dissenting); United States v. James, 60 F. 257, 260–61, 265 (N.D. Ill. 1894); *Ex parte* Rowe, 7 Cal. 184 (1857); Zanone v. State, 97 Tenn. 101, 118, 36 S.W. 711, 715 (1896), *overruled*, State v. Morgan, 541 S.W.2d 385 (Tenn. 1976); Carroll v. State, 32 Tex. Crim. 431, 24 S.W. 100 (1893); Kendrick v. Commonwealth, 78 Va. 490 (1884). *See generally* 3A J. WIGMORE, *supra* note 80, §§ 984, 986–987 (rev. ed. J. Chadbourn 1976).

[88] Brown v. Walker, 161 U.S. 591, 632 (1896) (Field, J., dissenting).

[89] Boyd v. United States, 116 U.S. 616 (1886) (holding unconstitutional a statute compelling production of private papers).

[90] *See, e.g.*, Cooper v. State, 86 Ala. 610, 611–12, 6 So. 110, 111 (1888), *overruled*, Hubbard v. State, 283 Ala. 183, 215 So. 2d 261 (1968), *vacated on other grounds*, 408 U.S. 934 (1972); People v. McCoy, 45 How. Pr. 216, 217 (N.Y. Sup. Ct. 1873); Stokes v. State, 64 Tenn. 619, 621 (1875).

"freedom of communion" guaranteed by the first amendment.[91] The "chilling effect" of public disclosure on private expression was best explained by Justice Story. The publication of private letters

> strikes at the root of all that free and mutual interchange of advice, opinions, and sentiments, between relatives and friends, and correspondents, which is so essential to the well-being of society, and to the spirit of a liberal courtesy and refinement. It may involve whole families in great distress, from the public display of facts and circumstances, which were reposed in the bosoms of others under the deepest and most affecting confidence, that they should forever remain inviolable secrets. It may do more; and compel every one, in self-defence, to write, even to his dearest friends, with the cold and formal severity, with which he would write to his wariest opponents, or his most implacable enemies.[92]

The law's protection of confidential communications from interception, publication, and compulsory disclosure served to preserve the privacy without which free interchange was considered impossible.

III. Personal Information

"Mind your own business" was an eleventh commandment in nineteenth century America.[93] Toward the end of the century, however, more and more of people's personal "business" found its way into public records and into the gossip columns of an enterprising "yellow press."[94] Although common law doctrines protecting property and reputation often failed to prevent unwanted disclosure, personal information did not go unprotected. Courts and legislatures both restricted access to information that individuals were required to supply to the government and applied broad civil and criminal libel remedies against the press.

The first United States census in 1790 sought little more than the constitutionally required enumeration of persons, slave and free.[95] Decade by decade, the scope of inquiry

---

[91] Hitchcock, *supra* note 38, at 139. *See also* 1 F. Lieber, *supra* note 40, at 109.

[92] 2 J. Story, *supra* note 61, § 946.

[93] *See* A. Taylor & B. Whiting, *supra* note 18, at 49. *See also* B. Whiting, *supra* note 18, at 51.

[94] *See* D. Boorstin, The Americans: The Democratic Experience 168–73 (1973); D. Pember, Privacy and the Press 10–15 (1972).

[95] U.S. Const. art. 1, § 2, cl. 3. Even so, the first enumeration was opposed on privacy grounds. 1 Annals of Cong. 1107–08 (J. Gales ed. 1790) (remarks of Reps. Livermore and Page); *see* Merriam, *The Evolution of American Census-Taking*, 65 Century 831, 834 (1903).

increased to encompass physical and mental defects, national origin, literacy, value of real property, and a number of other details.[96] Citizens' concerns about the privacy of their returns increased apace,[97] and, beginning in 1840, instructions to census takers ordered that individual returns be treated as confidential.[98] Congressman James A. Garfield, the principal advocate of a statutory penalty for disclosure of census data, feared that "[t]he citizen is not adequately protected from the danger, or rather the apprehension, that his private affairs, the secrets of his family and his business, will be disclosed to his neighbors" or, at the central office, be "made the quarry of bookmakers and pamphleteers."[99] In 1889, a penalty for such disclosure was enacted.[100]

Even with guarantees of confidentiality, there were subjects about which Americans felt the government had no right to ask. For example, new questions about secret diseases and home mortgages were added to the census schedule in 1890, arousing a storm of public protest that such questions were impertinent, illegal, and unconstitutional.[101] Lawyers as eminent as David Dudley Field took to the national press, advising citizens not to answer.[102] The Superintendent of the Census prudently determined not to prosecute those who followed such advice,[103] but a large number refused to give any census

---

[96] *See* C. WRIGHT & W. HUNT, THE HISTORY AND GROWTH OF THE UNITED STATES CENSUS 85 (1900).

[97] *See, e.g.*, LETTERS ADDRESSED TO THE HON. JOHN DAVIS, S. MISC. DOC. NO. 64, 30th Cong., 2d Sess. 21–22 (1849).

[98] *See* C. WRIGHT & W. HUNT, *supra* note 96, at 145, 150; Davis, *Confidentiality and the Census, 1790–1929*, in U.S. DEP'T OF HEALTH, EDUCATION & WELFARE, RECORDS, COMPUTERS, AND THE RIGHTS OF CITIZENS 178, 187 (1973). In 1870 the instructions read: "No graver offense can be committed by Assistant Marshals than to divulge information acquired in the discharge of their duty. All disclosures should be treated as strictly confidential . . . . The Department is determined to protect the citizen in all his rights in the present Census." CENSUS OFFICE, DEP'T OF THE INTERIOR, INSTRUCTIONS TO ASSISTANT MARSHALS 7 (1870).

[99] HOUSE COMM. ON THE NINTH CENSUS, NINTH CENSUS, H.R. REP. NO. 3, 41st Cong., 2d Sess. 49 (1870); Garfield, *The American Census*, 2 J. SOC. SCI. 31, 42 (1870).

[100] Act of Mar. 1, 1889, ch. 319, §§ 8, 13, 25 Stat. 760 ($500 fine for enumerators); *see* Davis, *supra* note 98, at 178. For an investigation of offenses under the Act, see H.R. REP. NO. 1933, 52d Cong., 1st Sess. 122, 125 (1892).

[101] *See, e.g.*, 21 CONG. REC. 5158 (1890) (resolution introduced by Rep. McAdoo).

[102] Letter from David Dudley Field (May 29, 1890), in 70 FRANK LESLIE'S ILLUSTRATED NEWSPAPER 395 (1890); *see* Atlanta Const., May 30, 1890, at 4, cols. 1–2; New Orleans Daily Picayune, June 5, 1890, at 4, col. 4; N.Y. Times, May 26, 1890, at 4, col. 3.

[103] *See* Boston Evening Transcript, June 2, 1890, at 4, col. 1; Wash. Post, May 28, 1890, at 4, col. 4. The penalty for refusing to answer was upheld by the courts. United States v. Moriarity, 106 F. 886, 891–92 (C.C.S.D.N.Y. 1901); United States

information whatsoever.[104] For the time being, the federal government had reached the limit of its inquiry; hidden diseases and debts joined political party and religious affiliation as subjects effectively barred from direct inquiry.[105]

"[T]he 'natural and inalienable right' of everybody to keep his affairs to himself"[106] was also asserted in opposition to other recordkeeping enterprises begun in the late nineteenth century.[107] Records of individual financial affairs, required for collection of the Civil War income tax, were initially kept confidential,[108] but so much revenue was lost through fraud and evasion that later legislation threw open the assessors' returns to the newspapers.[109] This public disclosure engendered sufficient hostility to kill the tax and, later, to prevent any attempt to reinstitute it.[110] Local records of land titles were open for inspection, but many state courts required that those inspecting titles have an "interest" in the particular piece of property.[111] Inquiries motivated by "idle curiosity" were

---

v. Sarle, 45 F. 191, 193 (C.C.D.R.I. 1891). *But cf.* United States v. Mitchell, 58 F. 993, 999 (N.D. Ohio 1893) (if a census required disclosure of trade secrets, "it may be equivalent to the appropriation of private property").

[104] *See* Chicago Tribune, June 4, 1890, at 1, col. 5; N.Y. Times, June 1, 1890, at 12, cols. 1–2.

[105] On nineteenth century American sensitivity about medical examination, see Union Pac. Ry. v. Botsford, 141 U.S. 250, 252 (1891) (compulsory surgical examination invades "inviolability of the person").

[106] *The Way It Ought Not to Be Collected*, 9 NATION 453, 453 (1869).

[107] Charitable organizations began to keep central records of their recipients in what was called from the outset a "confidential exchange." F. BRUNO, TRENDS IN SOCIAL WORK, 1874–1956, at 105 (1957). Even prison officials opposed "marking men" by copious records, lest "our penal institutions would become nothing more than Pinkerton detectives." NATIONAL PRISON ASS'N, PROCEEDINGS OF THE ANNUAL CONGRESS, 1890, at 65 (1891). The communications of an early credit reporting agency were found "grossly libellous" in Muetze v. Tuteur, 77 Wis. 236, 244, 246, 46 N.W. 123, 125, 126 (1890), *overruled on other grounds*, Judevine v. Benzies-Montanye Fuel & Warehouse Co., 222 Wis. 512, 269 N.W. 295 (1936), *overruled on other grounds*, Martin v. Outboard Marine Corp., 15 Wis. 2d 452, 113 N.W.2d 135 (1962).

[108] *See* Howe, *The Federal Revenues and the Income Tax*, 4 ANNALS 64, 71 (1894).

[109] *See id.* at 74–75; *The Way It Ought Not to Be Collected*, 9 NATION 453 (1869).

[110] *See* CONG. GLOBE, 41st Cong., 2d Sess. 2937 (1870) (remarks of Rep. Wood) ("[I]nconsistent with the personal liberty of the citizen," the tax "authorizes the assessor to intrude into the household, the private business affairs, the domestic relations of every individual."); *id.* at 3994–95 (remarks of Reps. Kelley and Butler); *id.* at 4031–32 (remarks of Rep. Davis); Howe, *supra* note 108, at 75.

[111] Webber v. Townley, 43 Mich. 534, 537, 5 N.W. 971, 972 (1880). Courts were beginning to require a similar showing before allowing stockholders to examine corporate records. *See* People *ex rel.* Field v. Northern Pac. R.R., 50 N.Y. Super. Ct. (18 Jones & Spen.) 456, 459–60 (1884); Phoenix Iron Co. v. Commonwealth *ex rel.* Sellers, 113 Pa. 563, 572, 6 A. 75, 79 (1886).

not permitted,[112] lest inspection, copying, and possible later publication "make unnecessarily public men's private affairs, which the law, for the purposes of fairness, requires them to put upon record."[113] Thus, as more and more personal and financial information was required by expanding government enterprises, courts and legislatures demanded greater confidentiality from recordkeepers and attempted to limit the access of others to such information.

The law of libel governed disclosure of information about individuals to the public at large. In theory, invasion of privacy by the press could be distinguished from defamation; in a civil action for libel, the truth of the matter published was a complete defense,[114] but the sting of an invasion of privacy was precisely that the personal information published was true.[115] In practice, however, courts effectively extended the civil libel remedy to substantially true accounts by insisting on the exact truth of every detail of information published[116] and on publication of the "whole truth."[117] The damages a successful plaintiff recovered could include compensation for emotional distress as well as for loss of reputation.[118] As long as a newspaper account contained some inaccuracies or omissions, both loss of privacy and loss of reputation could be remedied by a libel suit.

Nineteenth century Americans fiercely resented attack and exposure by the press. A publication so outrageous or offensive that it incited breaches of the peace could be prosecuted

---

[112] Randolph v. State *ex rel.* Collier, Pinckard & Gruber, 82 Ala. 527, 529, 2 So. 714, 716 (1887) ("idle curiosity"); Buck v. Collins, 51 Ga. 391, 397 (1874); Cormack v. Wolcott, 37 Kan. 391, 397, 15 P. 245, 247 (1887).

[113] Buck v. Collins, 51 Ga. 391, 397 (1874).

[114] *See* 3 W. BLACKSTONE, *supra* note 19, at *126; W. PROSSER, *supra* note 13, § 116, at 796–97.

[115] *But see* Gavison, *Privacy and the Limits of Law*, 89 YALE L.J. 421, 431–32 & n.33 (1980).

[116] *See, e.g.*, Sharpe v. Stephenson, 34 N.C. (12 Ired.) 348, 350 (1851).

[117] *See, e.g.*, McAllister v. Detroit Free Press Co., 76 Mich. 338, 354, 43 N.W. 431, 437 (1889) (highly colorful report of an arrest held libelous when the suspect had been discharged before it was published). In reaching its conclusion the Michigan Supreme Court added:

> [T]he reporter of a newspaper has no more right to collect the stories on the street, or even to gather information from policemen or magistrates out of court, about a citizen, and to his detriment, and publish such stories and information as facts in a newspaper, than has a person not connected with a newspaper to whisper from ear to ear the gossip and scandal of the street.

Id. at 356, 43 N.W. at 437.

[118] *See* Adams v. Smith, 58 Ill. 417 (1871); *cf.* Terwilliger v. Wands, 17 N.Y. 54 (1858) (damage other than mental distress required).

as a criminal libel.[119] The truth of the matter published was no bar to such prosecution; indeed, the maxim was "the greater the truth, the greater the libel."[120] At first, criminal prosecutions for this offense did not even allow evidence of the truth to be offered.[121] Even when the states by statute and constitutional provision allowed such evidence to be given,[122] truth was still not a complete defense unless published "with good motives and for justifiable ends."[123] "Indeed," said a Louisiana court, permitting truth as an absolute defense "would be a barbarous doctrine which would grant to the evil-disposed the liberty of ransacking the lives of others to drag forth and expose follies, faults or crimes long since forgotten, and perhaps expiated by years of remorse and sincere reform."[124]

Although available to victims of privacy invasion, libel remedies often were inadequate; libel suits compounded unwanted publicity and focused the trial on the issue of truth or falsity of a damaging disclosure.[125] Libel doctrines also did not reach new invasions of privacy made possible by advances in photography in the late 1880's, such as the taking of "can-

---

[119] *See* State v. Burnham, 9 N.H. 34, 42 (1837).

[120] *See, e.g., id.* at 41; People v. Croswell, 3 Johns. Cas. 337 (N.Y. Sup. Ct. 1804). *See generally "The Greater the Truth, the Greater the Libel"*, 26 CAN. L. TIMES 394, 394–95 (1906).

[121] Territory v. Nugent, 1 Mart. 108, 111 (Terr. Orleans 1810); State v. Lehre, 4 S.C.L. (2 Brev.) 446, 447–48 (1811); Smith v. State, 32 Tex. 594, 597–98 (1870).

[122] *See* A. HATCH, STATUTES AND CONSTITUTIONAL PROVISIONS OF THE UNITED STATES AND THE STATUTES OF ENGLAND ON LIBEL AND SLANDER (1895).

[123] Respublica v. Dennie, 4 Yeates 267, 270 (Pa. 1805) (the formulation was apparently originated by Alexander Hamilton); *see* Delaware State Fire & Marine Ins. Co. v. Croasdale, 11 Del. (6 Houst.) 181, 210–11 (Super. Ct. 1880); Castle v. Houston, 19 Kan. 417, 428 (1877); Barthelmy v. People, 2 Hill 248, 259 (N.Y. Sup. Ct. 1842); Commonwealth v. Odell, 3 Pittsb. R. 449, 452 (Pa. Ct. Quar. Sess. 1867); *cf.* Commonwealth v. Damon, 136 Mass. 441, 447 (1884) (if truth is shown, state must prove "actual malicious intention"); Commonwealth v. Blanding, 20 Mass. (3 Pick.) 304, 314 (1826) (truth is a defense in the "public interests"); Commonwealth v. Clap, 4 Mass. 163, 169 (1808) ("justifiable purpose" is a defense, but truth is not).

[124] State v. Bienvenu, 36 La. Ann. 378, 382 (1884); *see* Delaware State Fire & Marine Ins. Co. v. Croasdale, 11 Del. (6 Houst.) 181, 194–95 (Super Ct. 1880) ("[I]t would be a gross abuse of the constitutional privilege of printing upon any subject, to drag before the public the private character of a person, for the malicious purpose of injuring or destroying it." (emphasis omitted)); Commonwealth v. Blanding, 20 Mass. (3 Pick.) 304, 312 (1826) ("No state of society would be more deplorable than that which would admit an indiscriminate right in every citizen to arraign the conduct of every other, before the public, in newspapers, handbills or other modes of publication, not only for crimes, but for faults, foibles, deformities of mind or person, even admitting all such allegations to be true.").

[125] *See* Godkin, *Libel and Its Legal Remedy*, 12 J. SOC. SCI. 69, 80, 82 (1880).

did" photographs without the subject's knowledge[126] and subsequent printing of these photos in newspapers.[127] Widespread public dissatisfaction with the lack of effective legal recourse led to many demands for improved remedies.[128] Just as "[n]ew conditions both of law and customs were called for as safeguards against the collisions of railroads," wrote a university president in 1884, it was time that "new defenses should be set up in behalf of the individual" against "the omnipresent press."[129]

IV. CONCLUSION

Newspaper disclosures of personal information were not the only invasions of privacy to be remedied by nineteenth century American law, nor the first to receive the law's attention. When Warren and Brandeis wrote in 1890, restraint of the press was among the least developed areas of privacy protection. The principle they invoked had been expressed by E.L. Godkin in 1880:

> [N]othing is better worthy of legal protection than private life, or, in other words, the right of every man to keep his affairs to himself, and to decide for himself to what extent they shall be the subject of public observation and discussion.
>
> . . . The press has no longer anything to fear from legal restriction of any kind, as regards its influence or material prosperity; while the community has a good deal to fear from what may be called excessive publicity, or rather from the loss by individuals of the right of privacy.[130]

---

[126] *See* A. WESTIN, *supra* note 14, at 172, 338; Speed, *The Right of Privacy*, 163 N. AM. REV. 64, 73 (1896); *The Kodak Fiend*, Boston Evening Transcript, June 2, 1890, at 6, col. 4.

[127] *See* Manola v. Stevens, N.Y. Times, June 21, 1890, at 2, col. 2 (N.Y. Sup. Ct. June 20, 1890); *Photographed in Tights*, N.Y. Times, June 15, 1890, at 2, col. 3; *Manola Gets an Injunction*, N.Y. Times, June 18, 1890, at 3, col. 2. *See also* Moore v. Rugg, 44 Minn. 28, 46 N.W. 141 (1890) ("highly improper" use of photograph held breach of implied contract by photographer); *The Photographic Nuisance*, 50 NATION 154 (1890) (anticipates the Warren-Brandeis proposal); *Liberty vs. License*, N.Y. Tribune, Jan. 26, 1890, at 6, col. 4 (verbal description as invasive as photographic depiction).

[128] *See, e.g.*, Bascom, *Public Press and Personal Rights*, 4 EDUC. 604, 604–05 (1884); Field, *The Newspaper Press and the Law of Libel*, 3 INT'L REV. 479, 484–86 (1876); Godkin, *supra* note 125, at 80, 82; Godkin, *The Rights of the Citizen. — IV. — To His Own Reputation*, 8 SCRIBNER'S MAGAZINE 58, 62–63, 67 (1890); Proffatt, *The Law of Newspaper Libel*, 131 N. AM. REV. 109, 110, 121–22 (1880); *The Law of Libel*, 48 NATION 173 (1889).

[129] Bascom, *supra* note 128, at 604–05.

[130] Godkin, *supra* note 125, at 80, 82.

Doctrines already well established protected personal privacy more directly, so that no reporter could intrude upon the domestic castle, read private letters, or obtain individual census data. In an effort to improve the legal remedy for publication of private matters, Warren and Brandeis needed to set against the newspapers' jealously guarded first amendment rights a countervailing right on the part of individuals, an explicit "right to privacy."[131]

Did the many legal protections afforded to private property, confidential communications, and personal information testify to the existence of a "right to privacy"? Certainly, nineteenth century Americans thought so. Legal and popular writers frequently invoked a right to privacy,[132] even a constitutional right to privacy,[133] before Warren and Brandeis adopted the phrase. Courts and legislatures explicitly recognized that privacy was a legally protected interest.[134] The *Harvard Law Review* article by Warren and Brandeis, which has been credited with so much, must be read against this existing background of common law, constitutional, and statutory protection.

---

[131] *See* note 16 *supra*.

[132] *See, e.g.*, M. GRAY, *supra* note 69, at 217; Godkin, *supra* note 125, at 82; *The Way It Ought Not to Be Collected*, 9 NATION 453 (1869); Boston Sunday Globe, May 25, 1890, at 1, cols. 6–8.

[133] *See, e.g.*, J. BONHAM, RAILWAY SECRECY AND TRUSTS 38, 41 (1890); Book Review, 9 PUB. OPINION 45 (1890).

[134] *See* O. HANDLIN & M. HANDLIN, THE DIMENSIONS OF LIBERTY 60 (1961) (the right "was respected in advance of any direct protection"); A. WESTIN, *supra* note 14, at 330–38; G. WHITE, *supra* note 14, at 175 ("[P]rivacy became a significant value in American society, beginning in the latter part of the nineteenth century.").

YALE LAW JOURNAL

Subscription price, $4.50 a year *Single copy, 80 cents*
Canadian subscription price is $5.00 a year; foreign, $5.25 a year.

YALE LAW JOURNAL COMPANY, INC., Yale Station, New Haven, Connecticut
Publication Office, P. O. Box 552, Albany, N. Y.

THE SUPREME COURT'S ATTITUDE TOWARD LIBERTY OF CONTRACT AND FREEDOM OF SPEECH

A NEW JERSEY insurance agency succeeded in bringing to the Supreme Court of the United States its complaint that a New Jersey statute, prohibiting insurance companies from paying to any local agent commissions in excess of those paid to any other local agent, infringed upon its "liberty" to contract about its affairs in violation of the Fourteenth Amendment.[1] The complaint was appealing. Agency and principals had agreed upon a 25% commission as "reasonable" within the terms of their contracts. Both desired that the contracts be performed. The only obstacle was that another broker had agreed to accept a 20% commission. The latter made no complaint. Nothing stood in the way of performance of the contract, except the company's reluctance to disobey the statute. Four Justices of

[1] O'Gorman & Young, Inc. v. Hartford Ins. Co., 282 U. S. 251, 51 Sup. Ct. 130 (1931). This was a consolidation of two actions at law against two separate insurance companies to recover commissions alleged to be due under similar contracts with both. The companies pleaded the statute in defense.

the Court [2] recognized the obvious infringement of the parties' liberty, recalled the Court's prior insistence that "freedom of contract is the general rule, restraint the exception," and, having been given no grounds to justify the exception in the case before them, concluded, of necessity, that the statute was unconstitutional. But five Justices [3] took seriously what had hitherto come to be meaningless bromides, that the judicial annulment of legislative enactments is, at best, a dangerous business, that the power to that end is to be exercised only in the "clearest" cases, that statutes are not to be annulled unless invalidity is clearly proved by a presentation of the underlying facts which condition constitutionality. Since no "factual foundation of record for overthrowing the statute" was presented, and since it did "not appear upon the face of the statute, or from any facts of which the court must take judicial notice," that evils "did not exist" for which this statute was "an appropriate remedy" "the presumption of constitutionality" had, of necessity, to prevail.[4] The long list of cases cited by the four dissenters in which the "general rule" of liberty of contract was used to overthrow legislation even in the face of a factual foundation in favor of validity was simply ignored.

Less than one month after these opinions were read from the Bench, *Near v. Minnesota* [5] was argued before the same court. Near complained that a Minnesota statute which authorized a permanent injunction, issued by a Minnesota court, restraining him from publishing a newspaper containing "malicious, scandalous and defamatory matter" deprived him of "liberty" in violation of the Fourteenth Amendment. His complaint was not at all appealing. The nine issues of the newspaper which he had published prior to the injunction proceedings were part of the record in the case.[6] They were devoted in large part to scandalous charges against certain public officers of the county, private individuals, leading newspapers of the city, and the Jewish race. The articles were written in the vernacular

[2] Van Devanter, McReynolds, Sutherland and Butler, J. J.

[3] Hughes, C. J., Holmes, Brandeis, Stone and Roberts, J. J.

[4] In several later cases, attacks on legislation failed for similar lack of "factual foundation." See Notes (1931) 31 COL. L. REV. 1136, (1931) 40 YALE L. J. 657; Hamilton, *The Jurist's Art* (1931) 31 COL. L. REV. 1073.

[5] 283 U. S. 697, 51 Sup. Ct. 625 (1931).

[6] The suit for injunction was brought by the County Attorney pursuant to the authority conferred by the statute for the institution of such suit by him, or on his failure or refusal, by the Attorney General, or on his failure or refusal, by any citizen of the county. As interpreted by the State Court, the statute left all other civil and criminal remedies in force and was aimed not at the redress of private wrongs but at the suppression, for "the protection of the public welfare," of newspapers continually publishing scandalous and defamatory charges, with regard to private persons, or against public officers, of corruption, malfeasance in office or neglect of duty.

of the street, with bold-faced, large type generously interspersed for emphasis. The language was undoubtedly scurrilous. Style and language were obviously focused on appeals to prejudice and passion, even if truth were written. Near's associates in a prior enterprise of the same kind had concededly used that newspaper for blackmail purposes. Near made no attempt to prove the truth of any of his charges or that his "motives" were good.[7] He relied on his "freedom" to publish even false charges, conceding possible liability to subsequent punishment.

The Court again divided, exactly as in the *O'Gorman* case. Mr. Justice Butler, of Minnesota, wrote an opinion in which the three Justices who were with him in the *O'Gorman* case concurred. They agreed with the rest of the Court that "freedom of speech and of the press" was a "liberty" protected by the Fourteenth Amendment, but that it was nevertheless subject to some control by the State. The Minnesota courts had, "in due course of judicial procedure" adjudged that Near was engaged in the "business of publishing" "malicious, scandalous and defamatory matter" and abated it as a "public nuisance." The statute authorizing this measure was passed "in the exertion of the State's power of police" and the Supreme Court, "by well established rule," must assume "until the contrary is clearly made to appear, that there exists in Minnesota a state of affairs that justifies this measure for the preservation of the peace and good order of the State." And they pointed, *inter alia,* to chapter and verse in the *O'Gorman* case. Not only did Near's attack lack "factual foundation," but the presumption of validity was bolstered by the obvious scurrility of the articles, by the history of Near's previous enterprise, by the shootings which Near himself attributed to his publications.

The five Justices, whose teaching in the *O'Gorman* case had thus been absorbed, were willing to accede to these characterizations of Near's business and publications. They were willing to assume the falsity of his charges,—to admit that the persons involved in them were "impeccable." But they found in the "general conception" of "liberty of the press, historically considered and taken up by the Federal Constitution," the "essential attribute" of freedom from "previous restraint" which they thought was violated by the statute. While recognizing as "undoubtedly true" that "the protection even as to previous restraint is not absolutely unlimited," the limitations were of such "exceptional nature" as only to clarify the "general conception" and were "not applicable" to the case at bar. Charges

[7] The statute made "available the defense that the truth was published with good motives and for justifiable ends." Whether the same defense would be available in contempt proceedings for violation of the injunction was left in doubt both by the statute and by the State Court.

like those made by Near "unquestionably create a public scandal, but the theory of the constitutional guaranty is that even a more serious public evil would be caused by authority to prevent publication." That the liberty of the press may be abused by "miscreant purveyors of scandal" does not lessen the necessity of immunity of the press from previous restraint "when dealing with official misconduct," even as the existence of abuses in "the wide field of activity in the making of contracts," which is otherwise "subject to legislative supervision," had been held by the Court to be insufficient to justify interference "with what are deemed to be certain indispensable requirements" of the "liberty of contract," "notably with respect to the fixing of prices and wages." The *O'Gorman* case, and the reliance on it by the minority, was not mentioned. The statute was declared invalid and the decree granting the injunction reversed.

Thus was the conflict between the two groups thrown into sharp relief. Every member of the Court changed his attitude, shifting from one rule of presumption in the one case to an opposite rule of presumption in the other. But the two cases do more than illustrate the opportunistic use of precedents and logic. They do more than distinguish the five Justices who constituted the majority in both. They are a hopeful sign pointing in the direction of the ideal of freedom.

The ideal of freedom, has been termed "the holy grail of social progress." [8] The way to its acquisition may be blocked by the tyranny of government. But governmental restraints are not the sole obstruction. The path may be blocked even more effectively by physical barriers, or by our whole complex social and economic organization. Even in the absence of governmental restraint, one is not free to grow plants in rock; nor is a miner free to join a union when the cost is loss of his job and inability to secure another. Our state and federal governments have attempted, therefore, to secure greater freedom to individuals by compelling the removal of compulsions incident to our social and economic organization, by limiting the power of some to dominate the choice of others. Such attempts were the minimum wage laws, the hours of labor laws, the yellow dog contract, employment agencies and ticket-scalping legislation. When the constitutionality of this legislation was challenged, the Supreme Court postulated the existence and maintenance of the economic organization in which we happened to find ourselves. When it invalidated these statutes in the name of "liberty" protected by the Fourteenth Amendment, it frankly meant the liberty to maintain, promote and exploit advantages

[8] Hamilton, "*Freedom and Economic Necessity*," in KALLEN, FREEDOM IN THE MODERN WORLD (1928) 25.

which some had secured as a result of that organization.[9] The "liberty" protected was liberty from governmental attempts to relax human, economic constraints on freedom. Of course, that protection had not always been accorded. The full potentialities of the due process clauses in this regard were slow in being recognized.[10] But after recognition, the clauses became a bar to be hurdled only by legislation supported by a strong showing of appropriateness under the "police power." The presumption of constitutional validity always received a verbal bow; the real embraces were given the presumption of constitutional invalidity.

The change in the Court's affections, displayed by the majority in the *O'Gorman* case, can undoubtedly be justified simply by the ugly appearance of the record. The case was confessedly a test suit. Yet, no party interested in upholding the statute was joined or appeared. The respondents, like the petitioner, were willing, perhaps even anxious, to have the statute invalidated. The issues had been joined by motions to dismiss the defendants' answers based on the statute. Apparently no evidence was offered or introduced at the hearing on the motions. The record before the Supreme Court comprised but forty-two pages and consisted wholly of the formal pleadings in the two cases, captions, formal notices between counsel and the formal papers on appeal. Not a line in the record added anything to the words of the statute by way of light for the determination of the issue of constitutionality. While the petitioner in the Supreme Court filed a thirty-nine page brief in opposition to the act, in addition to the "statement as to jurisdiction on appeal," a single attorney filed but one four page brief for both insurance companies in its defense. He cited four cases and filled two pages of the brief with quotations of general statements from them.[11] Even if the fate of this legis-

---

9 See Pitney, J. in Coppage v. Kansas, 236 U. S. 1, 17, 35 Sup. Ct. 240, 244 (1915): "No doubt, wherever the right of private property exists, there must and will be inequalities of fortune; and thus it naturally happens that parties negotiating about a contract are not equally unhampered by circumstances."

10 See Warren, *The New "Liberty" Under the Fourteenth Amendment*, (1926) 39 HARV. L. REV. 431, 422 *et seq.*

11 After argument, pursuant to the Court's permission, he filed "supplemental memoranda" of three and one-half pages in which he set forth for the first time somewhat similar legislation of Missisippi and Louisiana relating to commissions of insurance agencies. He had also "gathered from questions addressed by members of the Court that doubt was entertained as to the good faith of the defendants. . . . in defending the statute" and he attempted to quiet the doubt. While the companies were willing to pay the petitioners the commissions agreed upon, if the statute did not prohibit, they were "desirous of final determination as to [its] constitutionality." The particular "form by which the constitutionality was being tested" was chosen, in preference to suit for injunction against the state officers, not in

lation were ordinarily to be settled by a struggle with the presumption of invalidity, pure sportsmanship could hardly permit the award of victory to the presumption when the statute's cause was championed by a straw gladiator.[12] But the majority's opinion shows more than sportsmanship. Recent developments have indicated that our economic organization has not the skill of conveniently curing its ills. Governmental aid appears inevitable. Man is not born into our society free of economic constraints. Legislation relaxing them may more likely be an enhancement of than a restriction upon the "liberty of contract." The Court is not to stand in the way of experimentation. The addition of two vigorous thinkers to the Bench has carried the day for pragmatism and liberal tolerance of legislative experiment with control for the purpose of advancing a larger capacity for individual freedom.

Personal liberties, freedom of speech and of the press, received constitutional protection earlier than the "liberty of contract," but the protecting cloak of the Fourteenth Amendment was not thrown over them till after that liberty had become firmly established.[13] The Federal Constitution contains in the First Amendment the absolute prohibition that "Congress shall make no law . . . abridging the freedom of speech, or of the press." The state constitutions generally qualify the similar prohibition on state legislatures with a clause saving power to impose responsibility for abuse of the freedom thus guaranteed. But the difference in phraseology is apparently nothing more than that. Judicial interpretation has engrafted even on the absolute prohibition a limitation in favor of a power "inherent" in government to protect itself and to maintain "peace and order." After the abortive Alien and Sedition Laws of 1798, Congress has not directly restrained freedom of speech and of the press until the Espionage Acts of the World War period. Long prior to the war, however, the states had imposed restraints and the patriotic fervor of the war brought on a further avalanche.[14]

The Espionage Acts survived attack based on the First Amend-

---

bad faith, but simply to avoid procedural difficulties in the New Jersey practice which might have hindered "decision on the real question in issue." The parties' unusual preferment of the state courts over the federal district court, in which this test suit could have been prosecuted either originally or by removal, apparently needed no explanation, although federal jurisdiction existed both on federal question and diversity of citizenship grounds. In conclusion, counsel expressed the belief "that every case that can throw light on the subject has been presented to this court."

[12] A test case staged like the O'Gorman case involves even greater evils than those feared from advisory opinions and declaratory judgments. See Frankfurter, *Note on Advisory Opinions* (1924) 37 HARV. L. REV. 970.

[13] See Warren, op. cit. *supra* note 10.

[14] See CHAFEE, FREEDOM OF SPEECH (1920) c. 1 and 4.

ment, but with the important qualification, laid down for a unanimous court by Mr. Justice Holmes, that "the question in every case is whether the words used are used in such circumstances and are of such a nature as to create a clear and present danger that they will bring about the substantive evils that Congress has a right to prevent." The Court assumed that the prohibition of laws abridging the freedom of speech was "not confined to previous restraints, although to prevent them may have been the main purpose." [15] With one possible exception,[16] state restraints, until the last term, met with similar success. The battle was waged on the front of the "privileges and immunities" and "due process" clauses of the Fourteenth Amendment. The statutes imposed punishment for talk not censorship. The Court "assumed" for the purposes of the cases before them that freedom of speech was a "liberty" and that the due process clause limited the power to punish as well as the power to impose previous restraint.[17] It found that the restraints imposed were within "implied exceptions" to the prohibition.[18]

In *Stromberg v. California* [19] and *Near v. Minnesota,* the Court

[15] Schenk v. United States, 249 U. S. 47, 52, 39 Sup. Ct. 247, 249 (1919). See Note (1931) 31 COL. L. REV. 1148 and CHAFEE, op. cit. *supra.* note 14, for sources as to freedom of speech and previous restraint.

[16] Fiske v. Kansas, 274 U. S. 380, 47 Sup. Ct. 655 (1927).

[17] Gitlow v. New York, 268 U. S. 652, 666, 45 Sup. Ct. 625, 630 (1925). As late as 1922, in answering a contention that freedom of speech included a "freedom of silence," which was infringed by a state statute requiring employers to give "service letters" to discharged employees, the Court said that "neither the Fourteenth Amendment nor any other provision of the Constitution of the United States imposes upon the States any restriction about 'freedom of speech'." Prudential Ins. Co. v. Check, 259 U. S. 530, 543, 42 Sup. Ct. 516, 522 (1922).

[18] But in reviewing cases under state acts, the Court was not to be governed by the considerations announced in the Espionage cases. Those were deemed to refer only to the interpretation of the Espionage Acts—not to the issue of constitutionality. In reviewing cases from state courts, the Court was not to consider whether "in each case" the words were spoken under "such circumstances" and were "of such a nature" as to create "a clear and present danger" that they would bring about the "substantive evils" that the states have "a right to prevent." It was to consider only whether the legislature could have determined reasonably that the "class" of language prohibited by the statute, as verbally interpreted, rather than as effectively administered, created a reasonable danger of such substantive evils. And of this, the mere enactment of the statute would be weighty proof. Gitlow v. New York, 268 U. S. 652, 670, 45 Sup. Ct. 625, 631 (1925). But compare Brandeis' dissent in Whitney v. California, 274 U. S. 357, 372, 374, 47 Sup. Ct. 641, 647 (1927), and the last paragraph of the Court's opinion in the Stromberg case, *infra* note 19.

[19] 283 U. S. 359, 51 Sup. Ct. 532 (1931). The Court declared invalid the provision in the California Penal Code making it a felony to display a red flag "as a sign . . . of opposition to organized government." Since Miss Stromberg's conviction might have been based on that provision alone, the Court found it unnecessary to pass upon the provisions making felonious the

held affirmatively, rather than assumed *ad hoc,* that freedom of speech was a "liberty" within the due process clause. In both cases, the plaintiff's interests could well have been regarded as interests of substance, of "property", just as in *Meyer v. Nebraska* [20] and *Pierce v. Society of Sisters* [21] freedom to teach was referred to the teacher's calling and to the school's business—"property-liberty" protected by the Fourteenth Amendment. Instead, the legislation was invalidated on the ground that "liberty" was taken without due process. Personal liberty. Liberty without material value. In authorizing an injunction with the power to punish for contempt, the statute in the *Near* case was deemed to impose a censorship by the equity court—a *previous* restraint on speech. The statute was therefore declared invalid, not because restraint was unjustified but because the form in which it was to be exerted was not permissible.

The difference between previous restraint and subsequent punishment does not, of course, determine the effectiveness of the restraint. As has been suggested, a death penalty for publication would be a more effective preventive than censorship. The injunction issued in the *Near* case was phrased in the exact words of the statute. It was no more definite or vague in its prohibitions than was the statute. If the statute had provided only for criminal punishment for the proscribed publications, Near would have been under exactly the same restraint arising from the statute itself as he was under the injunction. With one difference. A violation of the supposed statute would have resulted in a criminal prosecution before a judge and probably also a jury. A violation of the injunction would have resulted in summary contempt proceedings before the equity judge. The difference is striking in view of the historic struggle for greater jury powers in criminal libel cases.[22] But it wanes considerably in view of the Supreme Court's holding that the Federal Constitution contains no guaranty of jury trial in state courts.[23] It would

---

display of a flag as "an invitation or stimulus to anarchistic action or as an aid to propaganda that is of a seditious character." It did not have "to review the historic controversy with respect to 'sedition laws' or to consider the question as to the validity of a statute dealing broadly and vaguely with what is termed seditious conduct, without any limiting interpretation either by the statute itself or by judicial construction." *Cf.* the opinion of Brandeis, J. in the Whitney case, *supra* note 18. The death gasp of the doubt as to whether "liberty" in the Fourteenth Amendment includes freedom of speed and of the press is uttered in the dissenting opinion of Mr. Justice Butler in the Stromberg case.

[20] 262 U. S. 390, 43 Sup. Ct. 625 (1923).

[21] 268 U. S. 510, 45 Sup. Ct. 571 (1925).

[22] See CHAFEE, *op. cit. supra* note 14, c. 1; Pound, *Equitable Relief Against Defamation* (1916) 29 HARV. L. REV. 640, 655.

[23] See Note (1931) 31 COL. L. REV. 468. The doubt as to whether truth

have been more gratifying if the inarticulate dislike of legislation which imposes so vague and so dangerous a restraint upon freedom of speech had been made articulate.

But, by whatever means, the Court has removed an obstruction to freedom of speech and of the press. Only commendation can be given to the majority's refusal to yield to the importunities of the minority in the *Stromberg* and *Near* cases, that procedural difficulties and technical faults in the conduct of the litigation below prevented consideration of the larger issues on which the decisions were based. Review by the Supreme Court, even if its members were of one mind, is a weak safeguard of personal liberty. It can review only a very small fraction of the cases litigated. For the most part, this liberty is at the mercy of executive and administrative officers and trial courts. But while personal liberty must thus look for protection to our generally becoming "more civilized," the Supreme Court can set a brilliant example.[24]

The existing capacities for freedom of speech and of the press, its impingement on the liberty of others and the incidence of the legislation thereon differ widely from that of the freedom of contract sought to be protected against hours of labor, minimum wage, "yellow dog contract", and similar laws. "Freedom to think as you will and to speak as you think" is the vehicle to more general liberty; its complete exercise by some does not infringe upon the like liberty of others, whatever other evils it may

---

would be a defense in contempt proceedings should be mentioned as a further possible difference.

[24] Innumerable restraints on freedom of thought and speech exist with only the remotest, if any, possibility of Supreme Court review: in the enforcement of laws relating to immigration, naturalization, deportation, the mails (*cf.* Milwaukee Pub. Co. v. Burleson, 255 U. S. 407, 41 Sup. Ct. 352 (1921)) the tariff, radio broadcasting, the theatre, public assembly, street speaking and all manner of local police ordinances with avowed objects such as facilitation of traffic, *etc.* See Comment (1931) 40 YALE L. J. 967; Note (1931) 31 COL. L. REV. 1148; Grant and Angoff, *Massachusetts and Censorship* (1930) 10 BOSTON U. L. REV. 36, 147. Mr. Justice Butler's attempt in the Near case to assimilate scandalous charges against public officers with "obscene" publications overlooks obvious differences, as would also an assimilation of such charges, and of discussions of political, social or economic problems, with invasions of privacy by the publication of matters concerning only an individual's private affairs and having no public interest other than the satisfaction of curiosity. Compare the English equity jurisdiction to restrain publication of certain libels on candidates for public office on the eve of an election, DAWSON, LAW OF THE PRESS (1927) 197.

The serious abridgments of freedom of speech and other personal liberties by labor injunctions issued for the avowed purpose of protecting private property, without regard to the public interest involved, cries for courageous action. See the dissenting opinion of Judge Maxey in Kraemer Hosiery Co. v. Schmidt, Supreme Court of Pennsylvania, Oct. 9, 1931.

cause. But freedom to contract as you will and impose whatever conditions you can may be a sure means of oppression; its complete exercise by some often results in the curtailment of the like freedom of others. A larger capacity for liberty to contract in our economic organization may well need governmental control of the power to exert economic compulsion.[25] But a larger capacity for the liberty of speech needs primarily absence of governmental restraint on speech. Legislation designed to promote a larger capacity for freedom by the relaxation of economic compulsion may, indeed, be presumed valid. But a contrary presumption seems eminently proper when legislation constricts the existing larger capacity by imposing new governmental restraints.

H. S.

EDITORIAL NOTES

FREEDOM OF ASSOCIATION—A NEW AND FUNDAMENTAL CIVIL RIGHT

*Myron W. Solter**

I. Introduction

With the decision of *NAACP v. Alabama,*[1] there has emerged from the due process clause of the fourteenth amendment[2] a new constitutional freedom—the freedom of association.

The penultimate stage in the evolution of this new freedom was reached in 1957, when the United States Supreme Court delivered its decision in *Sweezy v. New Hampshire.*[3] During an investigation by the Attorney General of New Hampshire, conducted pursuant to a resolution[4] of the state legislature authorizing him to investigate violations of the New Hampshire Subversives Act[5] and to determine whether subversive persons were present within the state, Sweezy, a university professor, refused to answer questions concerning the Progressive Party and its adherents. He again refused to answer the same questions when propounded by a state superior court upon the petition of the Attorney General, whereupon he was adjudged in contempt. The conviction was upheld by the New Hampshire Supreme Court.[6] The United States Supreme Court granted certiorari and reversed the conviction.

Writing for the majority, Mr. Chief Justice Warren held that the resolution was too broadly framed and that consequently the Attorney General had no legislative authority to ask the questions.[7] Justices Frankfurter and Harlan, concurring in the result, would have held that the questions infringed Sweezy's constitutionally protected academic and political freedoms and that the state had failed to show that the in-

* Member, The George Washington Law Review; A.B. 1950, The George Washington University.

1 NAACP v. Alabama *ex rel.* Patterson, 357 U.S. 449 (1958).

2 U.S. Const. amend. XIV, § 1: ". . . nor shall any State deprive any person of life, liberty, or property, without due process of law. . . ."

3 354 U.S. 234 (1957).

4 N. H. Laws ch. 307 (1953).

5 N. H. Rev. Stat. Ann. ch. 588, §§ 1-16 (1955).

6 Wyman v. Sweezy, 100 N.H. 103, 121 A.2d 783 (1956).

7 Sweezy v. New Hampshire, *supra* note 3, at 251-52.

fringement was justified in the protection of state interests.[8] Although the majority did not reach the question of impairment of constitutional freedoms, Chief Justice Warren significantly presaged *NAACP v. Alabama* when, in setting forth the necessity for definiteness in legislation authorizing investigations into political beliefs and activities, he spoke in the following language:

> It is particularly important that the exercise of the power of compulsory process be carefully circumscribed when the investigative process tends to impinge upon such highly sensitive areas as freedom of speech or press, freedom of political association. . . .[9]
>
> . . . .
>
> Equally manifest as a fundamental principle of a democratic society is political freedom of the individual. Our form of government is built on the premise that every citizen shall have the right to engage in political expression and association. This right was enshrined in the First Amendment of the Bill of Rights. Exercise of these basic freedoms in America has traditionally been through the media of political associations. Any interference with the freedom of a party is simultaneously an interference with the freedom of its adherents.[10]

Thus was the stage set while *NAACP v. Alabama* was evolving. The state of Alabama sought, in a state court, to enjoin the National Association for the Advancement of Colored People from further activity within Alabama, asserting that it had failed to comply with the Alabama Foreign Corporation Registration Act.[11] Upon the state's motion, the court ordered the NAACP to produce its membership list as relevant to the issue of violation of the act; the NAACP refused to comply on the ground that production of the list would infringe its constitutionally protected rights, whereupon it was adjudged in contempt. The NAACP's petitions for certiorari to the Alabama Supreme Court were twice denied.[12]

The question was thus presented squarely to the United States Supreme Court whether there was in fact a right of association protected by the fourteenth amendment from impairment by state action, and whether, if there were such a right, the state's interest in ordering the production of the membership list was sufficiently compelling to justify the interference.

[8] *Id.* at 265, 267.

[9] *Id.* at 245.

[10] *Id.* at 250.

[11] ALA. CODE, Tit. 10, §§ 192-98 (1940).

[12] *Ex parte* NAACP, 265 Ala. 349, 91 So.2d 214; 265 Ala. 699, 91 So.2d 221 (1956).

In a unanimous decision delivered by Mr. Justice Harlan, the Court confirmed the implication of *Sweezy v. New Hampshire* and held expressly that freedom to engage in association for the advancement of beliefs and ideas is an inseparable aspect of the "liberty" assured by the due process clause of the fourteenth amendment, and that it is immaterial whether the beliefs sought to be advanced by the association pertain to political, economic, religious, or cultural matters.[13] It further said that compelled disclosure may constitute an effective restraint on the freedom of association and that in the instant case there was no overriding state interest to justify the disclosure.[14]

II. The Emergence of a Fully Enunciated "Freedom of Association"

Mr. Justice Harlan prefaces the court's enunciation of the new freedom in *NAACP v. Alabama* with the statement:

> Effective advocacy of both public and private points of view, particularly controversial ones, is undeniably enhanced by group association, as this Court has more than once recognized by remarking the close nexus between the freedoms of speech and assembly.[15]

He went on to remark that it is "beyond debate" that freedom to engage in association for the advancement of beliefs and ideas is an inseparable part of fourteenth amendment liberty.[16]

The assertion that it is "beyond debate," however, was unsupported by citation of a single Supreme Court decision establishing freedom of association. In 1927, Justice Sanford, speaking for the majority, held that a California syndicalism act was not repugnant to the due process clause of the fourteenth amendment "as a restraint of the rights of free speech, assembly, and *association*" (emphasis added).[17] But here it must be noted that Justice Brandeis, concurring, limited his exposition to free speech and assembly, without mentioning a freedom of association.[18] Not for twenty-two years, until 1949, is mention again made of a "right of association," this time by Justice Frankfurter.[19] The Court next, in *American Communications Association v. Douds*,[20]

---

13 NAACP v. Alabama, *supra* note 1, at 460.
14 *Id.* at 465.
15 *Id.* at 460.
16 *Ibid.*
17 Whitney v. California, 274 U.S. 357, 371 (1927).
18 *Id.* at 372-80.
19 AFL v. American Sash Co., 335 U.S. 538, 546 (1949).
20 339 U.S. 382, 409 (1950).

assumed, arguendo, a "freedom of association" but did not explain or define it. Following upon *Douds* came *Sweezy v. New Hampshire* and *Watkins v. United States*.[21] In the latter, Chief Justice Warren held that Congress in the exercise of its investigatory powers may not abridge "the First Amendment freedoms of speech, press, religion, or *political belief and association*" (emphasis added).[22]

It must be concluded that this freedom of association is in truth a cognate of the enumerated first amendment freedoms and is essential to their untrammeled exercise. The "close nexus" between association and these freedoms has indeed been recognized by the Court. The right of the people peaceably to assembly for lawful purposes existed long before the Constitution, and it has always been one of the attributes of citizenship under a free government.[23] "Liberty" includes the right to enjoy those privileges long recognized at common law as essential to the orderly pursuit of happiness by free men.[24] The right of peaceable assembly is a right inseparable from those of free speech and free press and is equally fundamental.[25] It is in the American tradition to allow the widest room for discussion, the narrowest range for its restriction, particularly when this right is exercised in conjunction with peaceable assembly; it was not by accident or coincidence that the rights to freedom in speech and press were coupled in a single guaranty with the right of the people peaceably to assembly and to petition for redress of grievance.[26]

The close connection between the enumerated first amendment freedoms and freedom of association has also been recognized in the states. Statutes or ordinances prohibiting the organization of labor unions and the solicitation of members have been held unconstitutional denials of the right of freedom of speech.[27] Included in the rights of assembly and petition is the right of exercising them in union with others through membership in organizations seeking political or economic change.[28] Life, liberty, and property include the right to all our liberties, personal, civil, and political.[29] Liberty of press is also enjoyed by associations of individuals, such as labor unions and corporations, and is protected under the due process clause.[30]

---

[21] 354 U.S. 178 (1957).

[22] *Id.* at 188.

[23] United States v. Cruikshank, 92 U.S. 542 (1875).

[24] Meyer v. Nebraska, 262 U.S. 390 (1923).

[25] De Jonge v. Oregon, 299 U.S. 253 (1937).

[26] Thomas v. Collins, 323 U.S. 516 (1945).

[27] AFL v. Reilly, 113 Colo. 90, 155 P.2d 145 (1945).

[28] Lawson v. Housing Authority, 270 Wis. 269, 70 N.W.2d 605; *cert. denied* 350 U.S. 882 (1955).

[29] *In re* Flukes, 157 Mo. 125, 57 S.W. 545 (1900).

[30] Bowe v. Secretary of Commonwealth, 320 Mass. 230, 69 N.E.2d 115 (1946).

Hence, the first amendment and the due process clause of the fourteenth amendment have been enriched by an articulate freedom of association. Fully emerged, it appears as the right to associate with others for the advancement of beliefs and ideas whether they pertain to political, economic, religious, or cultural matters. It is part of the enumerated first amendment freedoms and is equally fundamental to the concept of ordered liberty.[31]

The advent of this newly defined freedom necessitates an examination of its impact on several areas of the law—regulation of Communism, political activity by employees of the federal government, and political activity by labor unions. Entailed in this examination is a consideration of several problems respecting the essential nature of freedom of association itself: the extent to which it may be justifiably limited by congressional enactment; whether it is no more than a synonym of free speech, press, assembly, and petition, or whether it is fundamentally a constitutional innovation, importing a scope of protective coverage beyond that of the enumerated freedoms; and whether the right is the possession primarily of the association or of the individuals composing the association.

III. Communism and Freedom of Association

The Smith Act[32] makes it unlawful to conspire or attempt to organize to teach, advocate, or encourage the overthrow of the Government by force or violence.[33] It is directed to suppressing the advocacy of certain beliefs and ideas,[34] and, by its very nature, against association for the advocacy of such beliefs and ideas. These prohibited activities are clearly within the protective reach of freedom of association. This freedom, rising, as it does, to the preferred position of the first amendment freedoms, may accordingly offer a basis for challenging the constitutionality of these portions of the Smith Act.

The ready reply to a challenge so grounded is the limitation on the exercise of first amendment freedoms found in the power of Congress

---

[31] Justice Frankfurter, discussing liberty of political autonomy, states: "The implications of the U.S. Constitution for national elections and the 'concept of ordered liberty' implicit in the Due Process Clause of the Fourteenth Amendment as against the States . . . were not frozen as of 1789 or 1868, respectively." Sweezy v. New Hampshire, *supra,* note 3, at 266.

[32] 18 U.S.C. § 2385 (1952), as amended, (Supp. IV, 1957).

[33] 18 U.S.C. § 2385 (1952). The third paragraph provides, "Whoever organizes or helps or attempts to organize any society, group, or assembly of persons who teach, advocate, or encourage the overthrow or destruction of any such government by force or violence; or becomes or is a member of, or affiliates with, any such society, group, or assembly of persons, knowing the purposes thereof. . . ."

[34] Dennis v. United States, 341 U.S. 494 (1951), Justice Douglas dissenting at page 584.

to protect the Government from forcible overthrow, subject to the clear and present danger test.[35]

The principal case upholding the constitutionality of the Smith Act is *Dennis v. United States*,[36] wherein Chief Justice Vinson, for the majority, traced the evolution of the clear and present danger rule, concluding that success or probability of success is not the criterion,[37] and adopting the rule as stated by Chief Judge Learned Hand: "In each case [the courts] must ask whether the gravity of the 'evil,' discounted by its improbability, justifies such invasion of free speech as is necessary to avoid the danger." [38] It has been said that this is not the clear and present danger test at all, and that if it is, it is nevertheless a misapplication of it.[39]

Yates v. United States,[40] without actually repudiating the *Dennis* decision, does limit it and does restore to the clear and present danger doctrine some of its earlier meaning. Writing for the majority, Mr. Justice Harlan narrowly construes "organize" and limits it to the time of actual organization, thus bringing it within the three-year statute of limitations.[41] More generally, the Court adopts the construction that the Smith Act does not prohibit advocacy and teaching of forcible overthrow as an abstract principle, divorced from any effort to instigate action to that end, even if such advocacy is engaged in with evil intent, and the Court distinguishes, in principle, between advocacy of "abstract doctrine" and advocacy "directed at promoting unlawful action." [42]

Most probably, freedom of association will not affect the constitutionality of the Smith Act. All the prohibitions of this act have been tested, through the *Dennis* and *Yates* cases, against the guarantees of free speech, assembly, and petition, and have been found to be justified by the government's power to protect itself from overthrow by unconstitutional means, within the bounds of the clear and present danger doctrine as enunciated by these two decisions. Although freedom of association is coordinate with the enumerated first amendment freedoms, it does not rise above them,[43] and appears to be subject to the same limiting

---

[35] Schenk v. United States, 249 U.S. 47, 52 (1919).

[36] Dennis v. United States, *supra* note 34.

[37] *Id.* at 510.

[38] *Ibid.*

[39] Berns, Freedom, Virtue, and the First Amendment, Louisiana State Univ. Press (1957), 204. *Cf.* Boudin, *"Seditious Doctrines" and the "Clear and Present Danger" Rule,* Pt. II, 38 Va. L. Rev. 315, 356, (1952).

[40] 354 U.S. 298, 331 (1957).

[41] *Id.* at 310-311.

[42] *Id.* at 318.

[43] Justice Frankfurter, concurring, in AFL v. American Sash Co., *supra* note 19, at 546. "The right of association, like any other right carried to its extreme, encounters limiting principles."

principles.[44] Nonetheless, some of the Smith Act prohibitions do impinge upon the area protected by freedom of association, and in future Smith Act prosecutions, association may appropriately be included in the array of basic freedoms asserted and should serve equally as a restriction on the applicability of the Smith Act within the same bounds of clear and present danger.

Another area in which freedom of association may have possible impact is that defined by the Internal Security Act of 1950.[45] This act, directed primarily at curbing the Communist Party, requires that any organization found by the Subversive Activities Control Board (SACB) to be a "Communist-action organization"[46] register annually with the Attorney General, and that the registration be accompanied by a list of the names and addresses of all individual members of that organization.[47] If the organization fails to register as directed, within 30 days each member is required to register individually;[48] failure of the individual so to register is made a felony.[49] Any publication circulated by the organization through the mails or in interstate or foreign commerce must be stamped with the words: "Disseminated by ———, a Communist organization;" radio and television broadcasts must be preceded by the announcement: "The following program is sponsored by ———, a Communist organization."[50] The act authorizes the SACB, in determining whether an organization is a "Communist-action organization," to take into consideration the fact that its members refuse to acknowledge membership.[51] One clause states that the act shall not be construed to infringe upon freedom of press or speech.[52]

Both the constitutionality of the Internal Security Act and its ap-

---

[44] NAACP v. Alabama, *supra* note 1, at 463-466. This is evidently the assumption underlying Justice Harlan's finding that the interest of Alabama was not "compelling" or "overriding."

[45] 64 Stat. 987 (1950), 50 U.S.C. §§ 781-826 (1952).

[46] 64 Stat. 989 (1950), 50 U.S.C. § 782(3)(a) and (b) (1952). Defined as follows:

> (a) any organization in the United States (other than a diplomatic representative or mission of a foreign government accredited as such by the Department of State) which (i) is substantially directed, dominated, or controlled by the foreign government or foreign organization controlling the world Communist movement . . . and (ii) operates primarily to advance the objectives of such world Communist movement . . .; and
>
> (b) any section, branch, faction, or cell of any organization defined in subparagraph (a) of this paragraph which has not complied with the registration requirements of this subchapter.

[47] 64 Stat. 994 (1950), 50 U.S.C. § 786(a), (d)(4) (1952).

[48] 64 Stat. 995 (1950), 50 U.S.C. § 787(a), (b) (1952).

[49] 64 Stat. 1602 (1950), 50 U.S.C. § 794(a)(2) (1952).

[50] 64 Stat. 996 (1950), 50 U.S.C. § 789(1), (2) (1952).

[51] 64 Stat. 999 (1950), 50 U.S.C. § 792(e)(7) (1952).

[52] 64 Stat. 1605 (1950), 50 U.S.C. § 798 (1952).

plicability to the Communist Party have been upheld by the Court of Appeals of the District of Columbia[53] but have not yet been considered by the Supreme Court. After lengthy hearings held upon the petition of the Attorney General, the SACB issued in 1953 a decision finding the Communist Party of the United States to be a Communist action organization within the meaning of the act and ordered it to comply with the registration and identification provisions. Pursuant to the judicial review provision of the act,[54] the Communist Party petitioned the Court of Appeals for the District of Columbia to set aside the order, contending, among other things, that the registration and identification provisions violated the first amendment.

Judge Prettyman, speaking for the majority of the Court of Appeals,[55]

---

[53] Communist Party of the United States v. Subversive Activities Control Board, 223 F.2d 531 (D.C. Cir. 1954). The Supreme Court remanded the case to the Board to reassess the credibility of two Government witnesses. 351 U.S. 115 (1956). When it again came before the Court of Appeals, that court reaffirmed its earlier opinion on the constitutional issues and remanded for the production of reports made by one of the witnesses to the FBI. 254 F.2d 314 (D.C. Cir. 1958). On February 9, 1959, the SACB for the second time reaffirmed its findings. Eventually the constitutionality of the act is certain to reach the Supreme Court.

[54] 64 Stat. 1001 (1950), 50 U.S.C. § 793 (1952). The presence of this provision in the act renders unnecessary a detailed analysis of the question of the standing of the Party to assert, in a representative capacity, the rights of its members in connection with this case. With regard to other restrictive legislation, however, a potential problem is presented by the Communist Control Act of 1954, 68 Stat. 775 (1954), 50 U.S.C. § 842 (Supp. IV, 1957), wherein it is stated:

> The Communist Party of the United States . . . [is] not entitled to any of the rights, privileges, and immunities attendant upon legal bodies created under the jurisdiction of the laws of the United States or any political subdivision thereof. . . .

This would appear to have the effect of outlawing the Communist Party and depriving it of the right to assert freedom of association, as well as the other freedoms, against various restrictive enactments. Extreme doubt would attach to any assertion that Congress has the power to prevent judicial review of any statute by depriving those affected by it of the right to sue (including review of the Communist Control Act.) This question, however, is probably not involved here, for the rights, privileges, and immunities created by the first amendment are not necessarily those "attendant upon legal bodies created under the jurisdiction of the United States of any political subdivision thereof"; the standing of an unincorporated association to assert constitutional freedoms appears to be a judicial creation derivative of the rights possessed by its individual members. Joint Anti-Fascist Committee v. McGrath, 341 U.S. 123 (1951), especially the concurring opinion of Justice Jackson at 186-87; NAACP v. Alabama, *supra* note 1, at 458-59. Accordingly, except in a situation wherein the individual rights of a member of the Communist Party could be vindicated only by the Party as plaintiff, the disability imposed by the Communist Control Act of 1954 may operate to preclude the Party from asserting the right to freedom of association. Any such disability on the Party, however, can certainly not be made to extend to individual Communists. At least one United States District Court has held that the specific findings of Congress in the Communist Control Act, standing alone, create no law or presumption of law as regards Smith Act prosecutions. United States v. Blumberg, 136 F. Supp. 269 (E.D. Pa. 1955).

[55] Judge Bazelon dissented and would hold that the act violates the fifth amendment prohibition that "no person shall be compelled in any criminal case to be a witness against himself" on the authority of Blau v. United States, 340 U.S. 159 (1950). Communist Party v. SACB, *supra* note 53, at 576.

held that the Government has the power to require identification of the activities proscribed by the act,[56] and that although there is impingement upon the area of first amendment freedoms, nevertheless there is a clear and present danger that permits the Government to exercise its prohibitive power.[57] The court saw "no difficulty" in upholding the registration requirement and likened it to the registration and identification requirements imposed by the states upon persons participating in political activities.[58] Similar summary dismissal was accorded the challenge directed to the act's labelling requirement,[59] although mail thus identified and addressed to members of a communist organization doubtless violates the "privacy . . . indispensable to preservation of freedom of association. . . ." [60]

---

[56] *Id.* at 543. "It seems clear beyond question that, if the conditions described in this statute do actually exist, the presently existing Federal Government has power to prohibit within its borders activity of the sort described; *a fortiori* it has power to require indentification of such activities and to impose conditions short of proscription."

[57] *Id.* at 544. "The activities of a world Communist movement such as that described in this statute and of organizations in this country devoted to its objectives constitute a clear and present danger within the meaning of any definition of the point at which freedom of speech gives way to the requirements of government security."

[58] *Id.* at 555. The state political identification statutes are distinguishable. The duty of registration and disclosure of affiliation is imposed only upon those who choose to participate positively in political activities, *i.e.,* become a candidate for office, participate in conventions, and vote in primaries. There exists thus a privilege of election between being active and being identified and remaining passive and remaining unidentified, although still engaging in numerous lesser political activities. Moreover, in most cases, failure to register is not made a felony.

[59] *Id.* at 556.

[60] NAACP v. Alabama, *supra* note 1, at 462. If the Communist Party is ultimately compelled so to label its mail, such mail, when addressed to non-communists or even to anti-communists, can produce a result, intended or fortuitous, that is harmful to the addressee. It is not difficult to see how public hostility could be thus brought down upon innocent persons to their considerable detriment. In this situation, does freedom of association import a correlative freedom of "non-association," that is, a freedom from being falsely or mistakenly identified with communist organizations? Such would doubtless constitute a private wrong, perhaps remediable against the Party, but can it be said to be a public wrong growing out of the requirements of the statutory provision here in question?

The negative answer may be that the injury to such persons would be too remote from the public act. But, again, that the impairment stemmed only indirectly from a public act did not preclude the vindication of freedom of association in NAACP v. Alabama, the Court saying at 463:

> It is not sufficient to answer, as the State does here, that whatever repressive effect compulsory disclosure of names of petitioner's members may have upon participation by Alabama citizens in petitioner's activities follows not from *state* action but from *private* community pressures [emphasis by the Court]. The crucial factor is the interplay of governmental and private action, for it is only after the initial exertion of state power represented by the production order that private action takes hold.

The procedural means of testing this question exists in the Administrative Procedure Act, 60 Stat. 243 (1946), 5 U.S.C. § 1009(a) (1952):

> Any person suffering legal wrong because of any agency action, or adversely

Significantly, the Communist Party contended, with probable truth, that if its members were identified, they would be jeopardized in their livelihood and liberty. The court rejected this contention:

> [A] statutory requirement is not valid merely because of results which may flow from the unpopularity of the cause affected. . . . Unpopular causes are entitled to the privilege of the public arena, but they must sustain the severe burdens of that arena. So long as they are not denied the privilege, they cannot complain that their unpopularity frustrates them or that the observing public visits upon them its displeasure. Stoutness is indeed a requisite for those who would contest in that arena.[61]

The position thus taken by the Court of Appeals is at variance with the view of the Supreme Court, expressed in *NAACP v. Alabama*, that such results of identification work a substantial restraint on the right to freedom of association. The Court said:

> We think that the production order [to produce membership lists] . . . must be regarded as entailing the likelihood of a substantial restraint upon the exercise by petitioner's members of their right to freedom of association. Petitioner has made an uncontroverted showing that on past occasions revelation of the identity of its rank-and-file members has exposed these members to economic reprisal, loss of employment, threat of physical coercion, and other manifestations of public hostility. Under these circumstances, we think it apparent that compelled disclosure of petitioner's Alabama membership is likely to affect adversely the ability of petitioner and its members to pursue their collective effort to foster beliefs which they admittedly have the right to advocate, in that it may induce members to withdraw from the Association and dissuade others from joining it because of fear of exposure of their beliefs shown through their associations and of the consequences of this exposure.[62]

Accordingly, it appears that the Party's contention respecting the consequences to its members of public identification merits more weight than was given it by the Court of Appeals.

One effect of the provisions of the Internal Security Act of 1950 under consideration is to harass and hinder the Communist Party by

---

> affected or aggrieved by such action within the meaning of any relevant statute, shall be entitled to judicial review thereof.

The A.P.A. is made applicable to the Internal Security Act by § 795 of that act.

61 Communist Party v. SACB, *supra* note 53, at 558.

62 NAACP v. Alabama, *supra* note 1, at 462-463.

directing public hostility against its individual members through publicly identifying them with their associations; on the other hand, the spirit of *NAACP v. Alabama* is to foster association for the advocacy of beliefs and ideas by protecting individual members from public hostility resulting from identification. As suggested by the language of *NAACP v. Alabama* quoted above, the question turns ultimately, not on whether reprisals induced by public hostility violate freedom of association, but rather on whether the members of an association have a right to advocate the beliefs and ideas they espouse. Whether communists have such a right depends on the power of Congress to restrain the fundamental right of the individual communist to freedom of association in the interest of safeguarding the government from forcible overthrow and the establishment of a totalitarian dictatorship under foreign domination.[63] As has been seen above, Congress does have this power with respect to freedom of association, equally as to the enumerated first amendment freedoms, if the acts of the communists complained of present a clear and present danger that the government will be forcibly overthrown. Congress, in its preamble to the act, finds the existence of clear and present danger;[64] the Court of Appeals concludes that clear and present danger does exist, largely in the sense of *Dennis v. United States*. Nevertheless, it appears likely that this infringement of freedom of association will have to meet the strengthened clear and present danger test applied to the Smith Act in the *Yates* case; recalling that infringed here is the right, not of the Party, but of its individual members to freedom of association, the Government will have to show that the advocacy of the in-

---

63 The test contained in the criminal offense provision, § 783, is "any act which would substantially contribute to the establishment within the United States of a totalitarian dictatorship . . . the direction and control of which is to be vested in, or exercised by or under the domination or control of, any foreign government, foreign organization, or foreign individual . . . ," which language suggests the evil the act seeks to strike down. Since in order to establish such a totalitarian dictatorship, by definition (§ 782 (15)) the presently constituted government must be overturned by unconstitutional means, we are in actuality dealing here with the familiar forcible and violent overthrow problem.

64 Internal Security Act, 64 Stat. 987 (1950), 50 U.S.C. § 781(15) (1952). "The Communist organization in the United States . . . and the nature and control of the world Communist movement itself, present a clear and present danger to the security of the United States and to the existence of free American institutions, and make it necessary that Congress . . . enact appropriate legislation . . . ." It is to be noted that this is an application by Congress of a test evolved by the judiciary for testing just such congressional enactments. It raises the problem, a discussion of which is without the scope of this note, of the extent to which judicial notice should be taken of such legislative findings. In this connection, it is interesting that the Court, in *NAACP v. Alabama,* distinguished *Bryant v. Zimmerman,* 278 U.S. 63 (1928), wherein the State of New York was held entitled to compel the disclosure of the membership of a Ku Klux Klan organization, in this language: "The decision was based on the particular character of the Klan's activities, involving acts of unlawful intimidation and violence, which the Court assumed was before the state legislature when it enacted the statute, and of which the Court itself took judicial notice." *Supra* note 1, at 465.

dividual communists is not divorced from any effort to instigate action directed toward forcible overthrow, even if such advocacy is engaged in with evil intent.[65] Accordingly, it is not at all certain that, even should the constitutionality of these provisions be upheld, the Supreme Court will sustain its application in this case.

IV. The Hatch Act and Freedom of Association

The second sentence of the Hatch Act[66] reads:

> No officer or employee in the executive branch of the Federal Government, or in any agency or department thereof, shall take any active part in political management or in political campaigns. All such persons shall retain the right to vote as they may choose and to express their opinions on all political subjects and candidates.

Violation of this commandment is punishable by immediate dismissal from employment. This near-blanket prohibition on political activity collides directly and forcefully with freedom of association as perhaps no other enactment does.

The constitutionality of this act was upheld in 1947 by a narrow and much criticized decision—*United Public Workers v. Mitchell.*[67] Mr. Justice Reed, for the majority, found that the act did infringe the first amendment, as well as the ninth and tenth amendments,[68] but asserted that the "essential rights of the first amendment in some instances are subject to the elemental need for order without which the guarantees of civil rights to others would be a mockery."[69] The Court viewed the problem as one of balancing "the extent of the guarantees of freedom against a congressional enactment to protect a democratic society against the supposed evil of political partisanship by classified employees of the government."[70] Relying heavily upon several cases not particularly in point[71] and an exposition of the evils that might be inflicted upon

---

65 Yates v. United States, *supra* note 40, at 318.

66 53 Stat. 1148 (1939), 54 Stat. 767 (1940) and 56 Stat. 181 (1942), 5 U.S.C. § 118i (1952).

67 330 U.S. 75 (1947). The decision was four to three. Justices Murphy and Jackson did not participate. The majority comprised Chief Justice Vinson and Justices Reed, Frankfurter, and Burton. Justices Rutledge, Douglas, and Black dissented. Much of the criticism of the case has enlarged upon the arguments of Justice Black at 105-115 and of Justice Douglas at 121-126.

68 U.S. Const. amend. IX. "The enumeration in the Constitution, of certain rights, shall not be construed to deny or disparage others retained by the people."

U.S. Const. amend. X. "The powers not delegated to the United States by the Constitution, nor prohibited by it to the States, are reserved to the States respectively, or to the people."

69 United Public Workers v. Mitchell, *supra* note 67, at 95.

70 *Id.* at 96.

71 *Ex parte* Curtis, 106 U.S. 371 (1882) held constitutional a statute forbidding

the nation should this provision of the act not be applied, the Court accepted with perhaps undue homage Congress' own estimate of its power thus to circumscribe fundamental liberties[72] and concluded that the restriction was not repugnant to the Constitution.

NAACP v. Alabama raises several problems necessitating a reappraisal of this case. Chief among these is the difficulty posed by the Court's determination, in *United Public Workers v. Mitchell,* with respect to the degree of seriousness of the evil sought to be prohibited. In concluding that Congress has the power to impose the restriction, it accepted as a fact that the suppression of political partisanship in the civil service would not be indispensable to the operation of constitutional government.[73] This appears to mean that this admittedly lesser species of evil, presenting little of the compelling and imperative necessity of, say, a threat of forcible overthrow, nevertheless justifies an invasion of first amendment freedoms. In view of the Court's omission of any mention of clear and present danger,[74] it is most probable that it considered the invasion of fundamental liberties, occasioned by this provision of the Hatch Act, to be less serious, or certainly not more serious,[75] than the

---

certain classes of federal employees from giving or receiving money for political purposes to or from other federal employees. Even further afield, *United States v. Wurzbach,* 280 U.S. 396 (1930) upheld the constitutionality of a provision prohibiting members of Congress from receiving contributions for any political purpose from other federal employees.

72 For a criticism of the Court's acceptance of the congressional purpose, see 15 GEO. WASH. L. REV. 443.

73 United Public Workers v. Mitchell, *supra* note 67, at 100. "The argument that political neutrality is not indispensable to a merit system for federal employees may be accepted. But because it is not indispensable does not mean that it is not desirable or permissible."

74 It may be that, in eschewing clear and present danger, the Court had in mind the implication of the words of Mr. Justice Black, writing for the majority, in *Bridges v. California,* 314 U.S. 252 at 262, 63 (1941):

> [T]he 'clear and present danger' language in the Schenk case has afforded practical guidance in a great variety of cases in which the scope of constitutional protection of freedom of expression was in issue. . . . the likelihood, however great, that a substantive evil will result cannot alone justify a restriction upon freedom of speech or the press. The evil itself must be 'substantial' . . . it must be 'serious' . . . . and even the expression of 'legislative preferences or beliefs' cannot transform minor matters of public inconvenience or annoyance into substantive evils of sufficient weight to warrant the curtailment of liberty of expression. . . . What finally emerges from the 'clear and present danger' cases is a working principle that the substantive evil must be extremely serious and the degree of imminence extremely high before utterances can be punished."

75 "[The act] leaves untouched full participation by employees in political decisions at the ballot box and forbids only the partisan activity of federal personnel deemed offensive to efficiency. With that limitation only, employees may make their contributions to public affairs or protect their own interests, as before the passage of the Act" (at 99). But contrast this with Justice Black's view that "the section of the Act here held valid reduces the constitutionally protected liberty of several million citizens to less than a shadow of its substance" (at 115).

lesser danger held to justify the invasion. The Court has in effect said concededly, that the evil sought to be prevented does not present a grave threat, but neither are fundamental liberties seriously abridged by the regulatory act. The fundamental liberties before the Court in this case were freedom of speech, press, assembly, and petition; these were the preserves held not to be seriously trespassed by the Hatch Act.

Accordingly, there emerges a rather significant question—does freedom of association stand as a mere synonym for the enumerated first amendment freedoms, or does it represent an innovation in our constitutional law? Is it an addition to the first amendment and does it import a scope of its own, extending its protection to areas and activities not protected directly or not hitherto protected at all by the enumerated freedoms?

Significant to the elucidation of this question is the fact that the briefs for petitioner in *NAACP v. Alabama* grounded its case on both freedom of speech and freedom of association. The Court had not before held that the precise activity there sought to be protected was within the reach of freedom of speech or assembly. When faced with the issue, it chose not to further extend free speech, already broadened by numerous decisions to protect peaceful picketing and certain aspects of labor organizing; instead it adopted the freedom of association alternative, appearing thus to mark the opening of a new area of fundamental constitutional protection.

Perhaps most significant, however, is the manner in which the Court interpreted, in *NAACP v. Alabama*, its holdings in *United States v. Rumely*[76] and *United States v. Harriss:*[77]

> Similar recognition of possible unconstitutional intimidation of the free exercise of the right to advocate [i. e., freedom of association] underlay this Court's narrow construction of the authority of a congressional committee investigating lobbying, *although in neither case was there an effort to suppress speech* [emphasis added].[78]

There are thus reasonable grounds for concluding that the Court intends freedom of association to be additional to the traditional fundamental freedoms and to extend its protection to areas not hitherto covered, at least by free speech. *Sweezy v. New Hampshire* and *NAACP v. Alabama* appear to have staked out a broader area for freedom of association, at least as respects political activity, and however little the

[76] 345 U.S. 41 (1953).

[77] 347 U.S. 612 (1954).

[78] NAACP v. Alabama, *supra* note 1, at 461.

Hatch Act may have trespassed upon the enumerated freedoms, it seems now to represent a major invasion of the new freedom. Among the activities prohibited by various determinations of the Civil Service Commission, incorporated by reference by § 118 (1) of the act, are: serving as an election officer; publicly expressing political views at a party caucus or political gathering for or against any candidate or cause identified with a party; soliciting votes for a candidate or party; participating in a political parade; writing for publication or publishing any letter or article, signed or unsigned, in favor or against any political party, candidate, or faction; initiating, or canvassing for signatures on, community petitions or petitions to Congress.[79]

A possibility of distinguishing the applicability of *NAACP v. Alabama* to the Hatch Act may be found in the fact that the act is a restraint not on an association for the advocacy of beliefs and ideas or on the members of such an association, but rather is a restraint on a non-homogeneous group whose component individuals, if they were to be active in political management and campaigns, would constitute only partial memberships of diverse associations. This argument, however, overlooks the fact that freedom of association may be primarily the right of the individual, rather than of the association, and that the association may assert the right only on behalf of its members.[80] Moreover, to grant this argument would be a long step toward materializing the horrendous specter evoked by Mr. Justice Douglas in his dissent to the *Mitchell* case—that of an eventually socialized United States where the federal government would be the employer of large numbers of politically impotent workers.[81]

Accordingly, in any future litigation raising its constitutionality, the Hatch Act will face a sterner test than that applied in *United Public Workers v. Mitchell*, for this act appears to represent a much graver invasion of freedom of association than of speech and assembly. Certainly a politically nonpartisan civil service is a desirable feature of government, and Congress has the power to regulate the conditions of federal employment to that end. But the balance struck in the *Mitchell* case, between a lesser danger to the nation and a lesser abridgement of liberty, is probably no longer valid. Congress may well be constrained to undertake legislation more narrowly drawn to accord with the lesser dimensions of this evil.

---

[79] United Public Workers v. Mitchell, *supra* note 67, cited in dissent of Justice Black at 107-08.

[80] This question is considered at length in Section V, *infra*.

[81] United Public Workers v. Mitchell, *supra* note 67, at 125-26.

V. Political Activity by Labor Unions and Freedom of Association

The Corrupt Practices Act[82] bans labor unions from making any "contribution or expenditure" in connection with any federal election. The violating union is subject to fine and a consenting officer is guilty of a misdemeanor. Appraisal of the effect of freedom of association upon the constitutionality of this law necessitates an examination of the question of in whom the right fundamentally resides.

The Supreme Court has not yet determined the constitutionality of this provision; the two cases that have been before it have resulted in no more than a construction of "expenditure." *United States v. CIO*[83] presented the question whether an indictment, charging the union with having supported a congressional candidate in the union newspaper, stated an offense under the act. The Court said:

> If § 313 [§ 610] were construed to prohibit the publication, by corporations and unions in the regular course of their affairs, of periodicals advising their members, stockholders, or customers of danger or disadvantage to their interests from the adoption of measures or the election to office of men espousing such measures, the gravest doubt would arise in our minds as to its constitutionality,[84]

and held that this type of activity does not come under the ban of the statute.

United States v. Auto Workers[85] arose on a somewhat broader situation. There the United Automobile Workers had sponsored television broadcasts designed to influence the electorate at large in connection with an impending congressional election, thus extending its political advocacy beyond the confines of its membership. The Court held this activity to be within the prohibition. In both cases the Court "took the smooth handle for the sake of repose," [86] declining decision of the constitutional issues for the reason that dismissals of the indictments in the trial courts had foreclosed proper refinement of the facts and issues.

The purpose of the act is to prevent large aggregations of wealth from exerting undue and disproportionate influence on the electoral process. Moreover, as Mr. Justice Frankfurter stated it, its purpose is not only

[82] 18 U.S.C. § 610 (1952). Political activity by corporations is also prohibited by this enactment.

[83] United States v. CIO, 335 U.S. 106 (1948).

[84] *Id.* at 121.

[85] 352 U.S. 567 (1957).

[86] *Id.*, at 591. The Court's alluding thus to its own declining of the constitutional issues refers to a letter by Mr. Justice Catron to President Buchanan in connection with the *Dred Scott* case, which is set out in a footnote at 591.

"to prevent the subversion of the integrity of the electoral process. Its underlying philosophy is to sustain the active, alert responsibility of the individual citizen in a democracy for the wise conduct of government." [87] On the other hand, the act abridges most if not all of the first amendment freedoms, as was pointed out in both dissents, and particularly freedom of association. Justice Douglas stated it thus:

> The principle at stake is not peculiar to unions. It is applicable as well to associations of manufacturers, retail and wholesale trade groups, consumers' leagues, farmers' unions, religious groups, and every other association representing a segment of American life and taking an active part in our political campaigns and discussions.[88]

The specific and grevious impairment of freedom of association inherent in this prohibition appears to afford an even stronger ground for assailing the act's constitutionality than do the enumerated freedoms, for the ban on political activity by labor unions negates the very rationale of freedom of association.

There has been a manifest tendency to regard labor unions as "separate functioning institutions," with a resultant theory that treats the union's rights of free speech, press, and assembly as distinct and severable from those of its component members. The most succinct judicial statement of this doctrine is contained in *AF of L v. Mann,* wherein was upheld the constitutionality of a Texas statute, similar to 18 USC § 610, prohibiting "contributions" by labor unions in connection with elections:

> Being regulatory, rather than prohibitory in nature, the test to be applied to the Act in determining its validity is that of its reasonableness, and not the 'clear and present danger doctrine' applicable to prohibitions or restraints upon the exercise by *individuals* [emphasis by the court] of freedom of speech, of the press, and of religion. . . . It is now well settled that as to labor unions, though voluntary unincorporated associations, regulations [sic] of unions as such is severable from and does not constitute a regulation of the individuals composing the union. As 'separate functioning institutions' they have been granted many substantive rights applicable to them as such, separate and distinct from the individuals composing the membership, and also imposing upon them as unions regulations and responsibilities, not applicable to individuals.[89]

---

[87] United States v. Auto Workers, *supra* note 85, at 575.

[88] *Id.* Douglas's dissenting at 593.

[89] 188 S.W.2d 276,282 (Tex. Civ. App. 1945).

The Massachusetts Supreme Court, in *Bowe v. Commonwealth*,[90] struck from an initiative ballot as inconsistent with the Massachusetts Declaration of Rights a proposed law that would have proscribed all political activity by labor unions; although declaring the proposed law unconstitutional, the court's treatment of the question of whose rights were affected followed this same doctrine. The court said:

> The liberty of the press is enjoyed, not only by individuals, but also by associations of individuals such as labor unions. . . .
>
> . . . .
>
> Deprived of the right to pay any sum of money for [political activities], a union could not carry on any substantial and effective political activity. It could not get its message to the electorate. Its rights of freedom of the press and of peaceable assembly would be crippled.[91]

In the only federal case upholding the constitutionality of 18 U.S.C. § 610, *United States v. Painters Local Union No. 481*,[92] the District Court said:

> These reflections suggest that an aggregation may be subjected to more stringent regulation in the exercise of its freedoms than an individual.[93]

Accordingly, the defense of the constitutionality of this provision of the Corrupt Practices Act proceeds from Congress' power to regulate the circumstances of federal elections, and on the theory that if the act abridges the rights of freedom of speech, press, and assembly, it is the less preferred rights of the union as a "separate functioning institution" that are affected, and not those of the individual members, whose rights continue to enjoy their preferred position. Can this defense prevail against a charge of abridgement of freedom of association?

---

[90] Bowe v. Commonwealth, *supra* note 30.

[91] *Id.* at 130-31. On the subordinate question of whether such a prohibition does in fact invade fundamental freedoms, the Massachusetts court said at 130:

> One of the chief reasons for freedom of the press is to insure freedom, on the part of individuals and associations of individuals at least, of political discussion of men and measures, in order that the electorate at the polls may express the genuine and informed will of the people. . . . Individuals seldom impress their views upon the electorate without organization. They have a right to organize into parties, and even into what are called 'pressure groups,' for the purpose of advancing causes in which they believe. They have a right to engage in printing and circulating their views, and in advocating their cause in public assemblies and over the radio. All this costs money, and if all use of money were to be denied them the result would be to abridge even to the vanishing point any effective freedom of speech, liberty of the press, and the right of peaceable assembly.

[92] United States v. Painters Local Union No. 481, 79 F. Supp. 516 (D.C. Conn.), *rev'd* on other grounds 172 F.2d 854 (2d Cir. 1949).

[93] *Id.* at 523.

Freedom of association, by its essential nature, is the possession primarily of the individual rather than of the association. This view threads throughout *NAACP v. Alabama*, as is evidenced by the Court's statements that the right is "freedom to engage in association for the advancement of beliefs and ideas,"[94] that it is the "right of petitioner's members to associate freely,"[95] and that the restraint was upon "the exercise by petitioner's members of their right to freedom of association"[96] and upon "the free exercise by petitioner's members of their constitutionally protected right of association."[97] Emphasis thus is placed on the rights of the members, and not upon the rights of the association. This being so, serious doubt therefore arises as to the validity of the "separate functioning institution" doctrine as a defense to a challenge grounded on freedom of association.

The rationale of freedom of association is plainly that individuals of like persuasion may associate to accomplish in concert what they may be too weak to accomplish acting alone. Such has been historically the *raison d'etre* of the labor unions. The right of association being not the right to advocate beliefs and ideas, which is free speech, but the right to *associate* for such advocacy, any interference with the exercise by the association of the privileges attendant upon freedom of association, i.e., advocacy of beliefs and ideas, must destroy the very right itself at its source—the individual. This is the significance of *NAACP v. Alabama.*

Accordingly, whatever the validity of the "separate functioning institution" doctrine as regards freedom of speech, press, and assembly as applied to labor unions, that validity is reduced to extremely doubtful proportions when confronted with the fundamental nature of freedom of association.[98] It must be concluded that the prohibition on "expendi-

---

94 NAACP v. Alabama, *supra* note 1, at 460.

95 *Id.* at 461.

96 *Id.* at 462.

97 *Id.* at 463.

98 Union democracy and minority rights arise, however, as necessary collateral problems in connection with this consequence of freedom of association. The power, wealth, and influence upon the community attained by the labor unions, which considerations led to the inclusion of the unions in the Corrupt Practices Act, require assurance that the exercise by the unions of their members' right to freedom of association will not be diverted from the legitimate ends of that freedom and subverted in the hands of self-perpetuating autocracies on union "bosses." This consideration, too, has been marshalled in defense of the constitutionality of the ban on "expenditures"; but though substantial as a threat, it would nevertheless appear to lack the substance necessary to stifle the exercise of freedom of association. Minority rights may be protected in ways other than through 18 U.S.C. § 610, for "this way of doing it is, indeed, burning down the house to roast the pig." (Dissent by Justice Douglas, *United States v. Auto Workers, supra* note 85, at 596). Moreover, the fact that union democracy is amenable to rule of law dissolves any substance the autocratic union management argument may have as a defense. Currently in progress is various legislation narrowly drawn to meet this specific evil, including the Kennedy-Ervin Bill, S. 1555, 86th Cong., 1st Sess. (1959). Space does not permit analysis of the

tures" of 18 USC § 610, as construed by the Supreme Court and applied to labor unions in *United States v. Auto Workers*, is subject to grave constitutional doubt as an unjustified abridgement of union members' right to freedom of association.

VI. Conclusion

There emerge from the foregoing analysis several conclusions respecting the essential nature of freedom of association, which, it is submitted, merits recognition as a new civil liberty with probable significant impact on regulatory restrictions directed to controlling the exercise of other fundamental liberties through the medium of association.[99]

Not all rights protected from impairment by state action by the due process clause of the fourteenth amendment rise to the preferred position of the first amendment freedoms. A reading of *NAACP v. Alabama* in conjunction with *Sweezy v. New Hampshire*, however, affords more than adequate support for the conclusion that the new freedom of association is a cognate of these first amendment freedoms and enjoys coordinately their preferred status. In consequence, it may be asserted not only against restrictive actions by the states, but equally against federal abridgement.

As described and applied in *NAACP v. Alabama*, this freedom may be said to be an innovation in our constitutional law. It imports a protective scope of its own not coincidental with that of the other first amendment freedoms, and it displays a malleability well suited to the tradition of enlarging constitutional concepts to meet the increasingly complex needs of American society.

Finally, it is more than apparent from the circumstances of its emergence that freedom of association, though exercised by associations of individuals acting in concert, is nevertheless primarily the right of the individual, a fact of considerable constitutional significance to the regulation of associations.

---

legislative measures under consideration; these are reviewed, however, in Cox, *The Role of Law in Preserving Union Democracy*, 72 Harv. L. Rev. 609.

[99] As this note went to print, the Supreme Court announced two decisions further defining the scope of freedom of association.

In Uphaus v. Wyman, 27 U.S.L. Week 4394 (U.S. June 8, 1959), the Court, treating the same resolution of the New Hampshire legislature involved in Sweezy v. New Hampshire, held that "the governmental interest in self-preservation is sufficiently compelling to subordinate the interest in associational privacy of persons who, at least to the extent of the guest registration statute, made public at the inception of the association they now wish to keep private" (at 4396). Query: was this gathering at a summer camp an association or an assembly? If it was an assembly, is there a right to privacy in assembly, as there is in association?

In Barenblatt v. United States, 27 U.S.L. Week 4366 (U.S. June 9, 1959), the Court held that "associational relationships" may be disclosed by a congressional investigation, if the inquiry is related to a valid legislative purpose, thus bringing freedom of association within the rule of Watkins v. United States.

The Puzzling Persistence of Process-Based Constitutional Theories

Laurence H. Tribe†

In deciding constitutional cases, the Supreme Court has often invoked a vision of how politics should work, justifying judicial intervention as a response to supposed gaps between that vision and political reality. Legislation or other governmental action is of constitutional concern, the Court suggests, when it seems to obstruct political representation and accountability—by blocking speech or voting, for example—or when it reveals the existence of past or present obstructions—by distributing the law's benefits and burdens in ways that show a particular group to have been denied fair representation.[1] By invalidating legislative or administrative acts of this sort, the Court can reason, it avoids controversial judgments about substantive issues left open by the Constitution's text and history, and safeguards the representative character of the political process.

It is easy to see why courts would be attracted to this way of describing the content and role of constitutional law. Such an account permits courts to perceive and portray themselves as servants of democracy even as they strike down the actions of supposedly democratic governments.[2]

† Professor of Law, Harvard University. A.B., Harvard, 1962; J.D. 1966. I would like to acknowledge the extensive help of Professor Patrick O. Gudridge of the University of Miami Law School. Professor Gudridge and I are collaborating on what we hope will be a series of essays on the foundations of constitutional law. This Article is the introduction to that joint enterprise.

1. The best known statement of this view by the Supreme Court was written by Justice Stone in United States v. Carolene Prods. Co., 304 U.S. 144, 152 n.4 (1938):

> It is unnecessary to consider now whether legislation which restricts those political processes which can ordinarily be expected to bring about repeal of undesirable legislation, is to be subjected to more exacting judicial scrutiny under the general prohibitions of the Fourteenth Amendment than are most other types of legislation . . . .
>
> Nor need we enquire whether similar considerations enter into the review of statutes directed at particular religious, . . . or national, . . . or racial minorities, . . .; whether prejudice against discrete and insular minorities may be a special condition, which tends seriously to curtail the operation of those political processes ordinarily to be relied upon to protect minorities, and which may call for a correspondingly more searching judicial inquiry.

2. The doctrinal forms in which the Supreme Court expresses its decisions at least sometimes support the view that the Court is attempting to portray itself as working

But other constitutional theorists, unencumbered by the judiciary's rhetorical needs, also find the idea of perfecting process, and process alone, to be powerfully magnetic.[3] In the most recent and lucid argument for a process-perfecting view of constitutional law, John Ely's *Democracy and Distrust*, the vision is boldly stated:

> [C]ontrary to the standard characterization of the Constitution as "an eduring but evolving statement of general values," . . . in fact the selection and accommodation of substantive values is left almost entirely to the political process and instead the document is overwhelmingly concerned, on the one hand, with procedural fairness in the resolution of individual disputes (process writ small), and on the other, with what might capaciously be designated process writ large—with ensuring broad participation in the processes and distributions of government.[4]

Yet it is not difficult to show that the constitutional theme of perfecting the processes of governmental decision is radically indeterminate and fundamentally incomplete. The process theme by itself determines almost nothing unless its presuppositions are specified, and its content supplemented, by a full theory of substantive rights and values—the very sort of theory the process-perfecters are at such pains to avoid. If that proposition, which this Article seeks to elaborate, is correct, it leaves us with a puzzle: why do thoughtful judges and scholars con-

with, or at least not *against*, Congress or state legislatures. Judicial review should continue to leave room for legislative action or so, at least, Justice Jackson suggested in defending equal protection analysis. *See* Railway Express Agency v. New York, 336 U.S. 106, 111-12 (1949) (Jackson, J., concurring) (preferring use of equal protection clause to use of due process clause to invalidate legislation, as former leaves government option of drafting more equitably framed legislation to regulate conduct). Some commentators have thought that a similar idea partly explained the appeal (for a time) of the First Amendment overbreadth doctrine. *See, e.g.*, G. GUNTHER, CONSTITUTIONAL LAW 1134 (1975).

3. *See, e.g.*, L. LUSKY, BY WHAT RIGHT? (1975); Ball, *Judicial Protection of Powerless Minorities*, 59 IOWA L. REV. 1059 (1974); Black, *The Unfinished Business of the Warren Court*, 46 WASH. L. REV. 3, 8-9 (1970); Brest, *The Supreme Court, 1975 Term—Foreword: In Defense of the Antidiscrimination Principle*, 90 HARV. L. REV. 1, 6-12 (1976); Fiss, *Groups and the Equal Protection Clause*, in EQUALITY AND PREFERENTIAL TREATMENT 85, 130 (M. Cohen, T. Nagel & T. Scanlon eds. 1977); Karst, *The Supreme Court, 1976 Term—Foreword: Equal Citizenship Under the Fourteenth Amendment*, 91 HARV. L. REV. 1, 8-10, 24-26 (1977); Tribe, *Structural Due Process*, 10 HARV. C.R.-C.L. L. REV. 269 (1975); Note, *Mental Illness: A Suspect Classification?*, 83 YALE L.J. 1237 (1974). *See generally* Rostow, *The Democratic Character of Judicial Review*, 66 HARV. L. REV. 193 (1952). Sometimes the concern for process is coupled with an effort to ground constitutional law in fundamental values, such as respect for individual dignity. *See, e.g.*, Brest, *supra*, at 11 (prevention of stigmatic harms to particular individuals supports antidiscrimination principle in equal protection doctrine); Karst, *supra*, at 8 (participation in community decisionmaking processes contributes to self-respect).

4. J. ELY, DEMOCRACY AND DISTRUST 87 (1980) (footnotes omitted) [hereinafter cited as ELY].

tinue to put forth process-perfecting theories as though such theories could banish divisive controversies over substantive values from the realm of constitutional discourse by relegating those controversies to the unruly world of power?

I. The Constitution's Openly Substantive Commitments

One difficulty that immediately confronts process theories is the stubbornly substantive character of so many of the Constitution's most crucial commitments: commitments defining the values that we as a society, acting politically, must respect. Plainly, the First Amendment's guarantee of religious liberty and its prohibition of religious establishment are substantive in this sense.[5] So, too, is the Thirteenth Amendment, in its abolition of slavery and repudiation of the Constitution's earlier, ostensibly procedural, protections of that institution.[6]

In many of its parts, the Constitution also evinces a substantive commitment to the institution of private property and to the contractual expectations that surround it. The just compensation clause of the Fifth Amendment is an obvious example.[7] The contracts clause of article I, section 10 is another.[8] The old substantive due process, which is obviously an important part of our constitutional history and thus significant for our understanding of what the Constitution is

5. *See* B. Bailyn, The Ideological Origins of the American Revolution 246-72 (1967).

6. *See* Note, *The Thirteenth Amendment and Private Affirmative Action*, 89 Yale L.J. 399, 406 (1979) (framers of amendment intended to guarantee blacks "meaningful freedom" by obliterating all vestiges of slavery). To say that the nation's experience with slavery shows the folly of incorporating substantive matters in the Constitution, *see* Ely, *supra* note 4, at 93, 100, 226 n.68, is simply to invert the lessons of our history.

7. Just compensation cases, arising under the Constitution or under statutes that Congress and the state legislatures have adopted in response to constitutional requirements, are a steady and continuing part of the business of the courts. *See generally* B. Ackerman, Private Property and the Constitution (1977).

8. Contracts clause cases, rarer than just compensation cases, are thought to be less important because the clause itself imposes no significant restriction. The conventional view is that the Supreme Court, in limiting the clause's protection to that against retroactive legislation, *see* Ogden v. Saunders, 25 U.S. (12 Wheat.) 213, 303 (1827), rendered the clause less significant. The traditional learning holds that whatever residual importance the clause retained has disappeared. *See* Home Bldg. & Loan Ass'n v. Blaisdell, 290 U.S. 398 (1934) (reasonable legislation, even if retroactive, disturbs no legitimate expectation interest of contracting parties). The Court, however, has on some 100 occasions since *Ogden* voided state statutes and municipal ordinances under the clause. Moreover, the Court that decided *Blaisdell* did not act as if that decision vitiated the clause. *See, e.g.*, Wood v. Lovett, 313 U.S. 362 (1941) (state law that removed procedural rights from purchasers at a tax sale violates clause); Indiana *ex rel.* Anderson v. Brand, 303 U.S. 95 (1938) (state teacher tenure law held to have created a binding obligation under clause). Indeed, the Court has very recently invalidated state legislation under the contracts clause. *See, e.g.*, Allied Structural Steel Co. v. Spannaus, 438 U.S. 234 (1978); United States Trust Co. v. New Jersey, 431 U.S. 1 (1977).

about, also served to protect the transactions and expectations to which the institution of private property gives rise.[9] Whatever our views of the substantive due process heyday, most of us would readily concede that the framers of the 1787 Constitution adopted a federal system of government organization in order to, among other goals, help secure the institution of private property.[10] When Madison, in his theory of faction, suggested that shifting the legislative responsibility for certain problems from the state to the national level could help assure that majorities would not trample minority rights,[11] the problems he had

9. *See, e.g.*, Coppage v. Kansas, 236 U.S. 1 (1915) (protecting employer's constitutional right under due process clause to choose not to hire union member employees); Lochner v. New York, 198 U.S. 45 (1905) (invalidating maximum hour work laws as violative of contractual liberties protected by Constitution).

A number of critics have charged that the old substantive due process is inconsistent with the language of the due process clause itself. *See, e.g.*, Whitney v. California, 274 U.S. 357, 373 (1927) (Brandeis, J., concurring); ELY, *supra* note 4, at 18 ("[T]here is simply no avoiding the fact that the word that follows 'due' is 'process.' "). But the words that follow "due process" are "of law," and the word "law" seems to have been the textual point of departure for substantive due process. *See, e.g.*, Hurtado v. California, 110 U.S. 516, 535-36 (1884):

> It is not every act, legislative in form, that is law. Law is something more than mere will exerted as an act of power. It must not be a special rule for a particular person or a particular case, . . . thus excluding, as not due process of law, acts of attainder, bills of pains and penalties, acts of confiscation, acts reversing judgments, and acts directly transferring one man's estate to another, legislative judgments and decrees, and other similar special, partial and arbitrary exertions of power under the forms of legislation.

The form that substantive due process analysis took has recently begun to receive scholarly attention. *See* Kennedy, *The Structure of Blackstone's Commentaries*, 28 BUFFALO L. REV. 205 (1979); Miller, *The Forest of Due Process of Law: The American Constitutional Tradition*, in DUE PROCESS: NOMOS XVIII 3 (J. Pennock & J. Chapman eds. 1977). "Due process *of law*" was elaborated through a theory of legislation founded upon ideals of separation of powers. The theory distinguished legislation from adjudication by assigning to adjudication the task of rearranging vested rights; it distinguished among types of legislation by asking whether the various types infringed vested rights; and it identified vested rights by treating the common law as a mirror of individual expectations, by regarding that which the common law protected—liberty of contract, for example—as something that individuals rightly presupposed, and upon which individuals justifiably relied. *See* T. COOLEY, CONSTITUTIONAL LIMITATIONS 500-75 (7th ed. 1903).

The form of the old substantive due process doctrine is important here for two reasons. That the doctrine *had* form—and a form that drew upon such traditional sources of legal principles as ideas about the common law and separation of powers—suggests that the substantive due process cases were not some mad judicial tear, which we may today safely and gladly forget. *See* L. TRIBE, AMERICAN CONSTITUTIONAL LAW 434-36 (1978). Moreover, the fact that the form of the doctrine drew in part upon separation of powers concepts illustrates a more general point: the Constitution may *appear* in large part to address the structure and arrangement of government—process writ large and small—but the concerns that *underlie* and *explain* the structures and arrangements ordained by the Constitution are themselves undeniably substantive.

10. *See* Wood, *Rhetoric and Reality in the American Revolution*, 23 WM. & MARY Q. 3 (3d Ser. 1966).

11. *See, e.g.*, THE FEDERALIST No. 10 (J. Madison).

in mind were largely economic;[12] the minority rights the federal system would protect were, for the most part, rights of property and contract.[13]

Religious freedom, antislavery, private property: much of our constitutional history can be written by reference to just these social institutions and substantive values. That the Constitution has long addressed such matters, and often with beneficial effect, ought to surprise no one. What is puzzling is that anyone can say, in the face of this reality, that the Constitution is or should be predominantly concerned with *process* and *not* substance.

But our constitutional reality poses even deeper problems for process theorists. Even the Constitution's most procedural prescriptions cannot be adequately understood, much less applied, in the absence of a developed theory of fundamental rights that are secured to persons against the state—a theory whose derivation demands precisely the kinds of controversial substantive choices that the process proponents are so anxious to leave to the electorate and its representatives.

II. The Substantive Roots of Procedural Norms

Much of the Constitution does indeed appear to address matters of procedure. Sometimes the subject is *adjudicative* process—the process due to individuals who become defendants in criminal or civil litigation or targets of administrative actions. Elsewhere, the Constitu-

12. For example, witness which responsibilities the framers gave to the federal government—particularly the power to regulate interstate and foreign commerce. U.S. CONST., art. I, § 8, cl. 3. Many of the prohibitions of article I, § 10, also have an economic cast:

> No State shall . . . coin Money; emit Bills of Credit; make any Thing but gold and silver Coin a Tender in Payment of Debts; pass any . . . Law impairing the Obligation of Contracts . . . .
>
> No State shall, without the Consent of the Congress, lay any Imposts or Duties on Imports or Exports . . . .
>
> No State shall, without the Consent of Congress, lay any Duty of Tonnage . . . .

13. *See* THE FEDERALIST No. 10, at 79 (C. Rossiter ed. 1961) ("But the most common and durable source of factions has been the various and unequal distribution of property. Those who hold, and those who are without property, have ever formed distinct interests in society. Those who are creditors, and those who are debtors, fall under a like discrimination."); G. WOOD, THE CREATION OF THE AMERICAN REPUBLIC 503-04 (1969) (federal bicameralism as means of protecting minority property rights).

It is a mistake to view the concern of the Federalists with property rights in contemporary terms. Property rights in the late 18th century partook more of status than of exchange; debtor legislation was perceived as threatening not only because it represented the loss of wealth but also because it portended the triumph of the "licentious," the disruption of an order of virtue and merit in society. *See id.* at 393-425. Yet, even if the concern with property is recast in 18th-century terms, the protection of individual property rights remains intact as an aim of the Constitution. *See id.* at 609 ("The liberty that was now emphasized was personal or private, the protection of individual rights against all governmental encroachments, particularly by the legislature . . . . Government was no longer designed merely to promote the collective happiness of the people, but also . . . 'to protect citizens in their personal liberty and their property' . . . .")

tion focuses on *representative* process—including the process that governs the election of Congress,[14] of the President,[15] or of state representative bodies.[16] That the *subject* in all these cases is procedure, however, is not to say that the *meaning* and *purpose* of the Constitution's prescriptions on each such subject are themselves merely procedural. There is no reason to suppose that "constitutive" rules—rules defining the basic structure of political and legal relations—can or should be essentially neutral on matters of substantive value.

The very dichotomy just drawn—between adjudicative and representative process—would prove incoherent without a substantive theory. How do we decide which *form* of participation the complaining individual may claim: the right to be heard as a litigant, or the right to be counted as a voter? The question whether individuals may insist on being heard by rulemakers, for whom they have already (directly or indirectly) voted, has bedeviled administrative law since the turn of the century.[17] How the government chooses to deal with individuals—as individuals or *en masse*—cannot be dispositive. For, at least sometimes, government action that purports to deal with groups is unconstitutional precisely because it does *not* deal with individuals as such: the conclusive presumption decisions[18] and the mandatory death penalty cases,[19] however opaque they might otherwise be, establish this much, as does Justice Powell's opinion in *Regents of the University of California v. Bakke*.[20] Conversely, in at least some circumstances, there is

14. *See, e.g.*, U.S. CONST., art. I, §§ 2, 3.

15. *See, e.g.*, *id.*, art. II, § 1.

16. *See, e.g.*, Reynolds v. Sims, 377 U.S. 533, 568 (1964) (equal protection clause requires apportionment of state legislative seats by population).

17. *See, e.g.*, Bi-Metallic Inv. Co. v. State Bd. of Equalization, 239 U.S. 441 (1915) (no hearing necessary before assessments of all taxable property uniformly increased); Londoner v. City of Denver, 210 U.S. 373 (1908) (hearing required before costs of local improvements are assessed to property owners on the basis of relative benefit).

18. *See, e.g.*, Cleveland Bd. of Educ. v. LaFleur, 414 U.S. 632, 645 (1974) (mandatory maternity-leave rules creating an irrebuttable presumption violate due process clause in failing to recognize individual differences); Stanley v. Illinois, 405 U.S. 645, 656-57 (1972) (statute containing irrebuttable presumption that all unmarried fathers are incompetent to raise children is unconstitutionally overbroad). For a discussion of these and related cases, see L. TRIBE, *supra* note 9, at 1092-97.

19. *See, e.g.*, Lockett v. Ohio, 438 U.S. 586, 605 (1978) (Eighth and Fourteenth Amendments require death penalty statutes to permit individualized consideration of mitigating factors for each defendant); Woodson v. North Carolina, 428 U.S. 280, 304 (1976) (opinion of Stewart, Powell, and Stevens, JJ.) (process must treat offenders on individualized basis in capital cases); Gregg v. Georgia, 428 U.S. 153, 197-98 (1976) (death penalty held constitutional when statute is drafted to ensure jury consideration of individual circumstances of crime and offender).

20. 438 U.S. 265, 320 (1978) (Powell, J., announcing judgment of the Court) (relying on "personal rights" theory of equal protection clause to invalidate racial quotas in medical school admissions); *see* Tribe, *Perspectives on* Bakke: *Equal Protection, Procedural Fairness, or Structural Justice?*, 92 HARV. L. REV. 864, 867 (1979).

no constitutional infirmity in relying only on representative, or even directly democratic, processes to deal with individuated grievances: individual zoning variances may be made the subject of local referendum;[21] and unions, as delegatees of federal power,[22] may bind members of bargaining units to the terms of wage bargains or, indeed, of individual grievance negotiations, even though the unions do not act as representatives of individuals *as individuals*.[23]

The question of whether adjudicative or representative process is required in a given context simply cannot be analyzed in terms of how fairly and accurately various participatory processes reflect the interests and inputs of those governed by them. Deciding what *kind* of participation the Constitution demands requires analysis not only of the efficacy of alternative processes but also of the character and importance of the interest at stake—its role in the life of the individual as an individual. That analysis, in turn, requires a theory of values and rights as plainly substantive as, and seemingly of a piece with, the theories of values and rights that underlie the Constitution's provisions addressing religion, slavery, and property.

Once one has decided whether the Constitution requires adjudicative or representative process in a particular setting, one must again rely on substantive values in elaborating the requirements of either procedural form. Consider first the problem of adjudicative process. Certainly the Fifth Amendment's self-incrimination and double jeopardy clauses embody concerns for protecting individual dignity in the criminal process.[24] A substantive concern for individual "privacy" necessarily underpins the Fourth Amendment.[25] Other superficially procedural

21. *See, e.g.*, City of Eastlake v. Forest City Enterprises, Inc., 426 U.S. 668, 676-77 (1976). *But see* L. TRIBE, *supra* note 9, at 493-95.

22. *See* Steele v. Louisville & N.R.R., 323 U.S. 192, 202 (1944).

23. *See, e.g.*, Hines v. Anchor Motor Freight, Inc., 424 U.S. 554, 563-64 (1976); Vaca v. Sipes, 386 U.S. 171, 182 (1967).

24. *See, e.g.*, Miranda v. Arizona, 384 U.S. 436, 457-58 (1966) ("incommunicado interrogation" is "destructive of human dignity" and conflicts with privilege against self-incrimination); Green v. United States, 355 U.S. 184, 187 (1957) ("underlying idea" behind guarantee against double jeopardy "is that the State . . . should not be allowed to make repeated attempts to convict an individual for an alleged offense, thereby subjecting him to embarrassment, expense and ordeal and compelling him to live in a continuing state of anxiety and insecurity").

25. Payton v. New York, 48 U.S.L.W. 4375, 4380, 4383 (U.S. April 15, 1980) (No. 78-5420) (absent exigent circumstances, Fourth Amendment requires warrant to arrest person in home even with probable cause); Griswold v. Connecticut, 381 U.S. 479, 485 (1965) (Fourth Amendment implies "right to privacy"); Boyd v. United States, 116 U.S. 616, 630 (1886) (Fourth Amendment applies to all government invasions of "the sanctity of a man's home and the privacies of life"). That privacy alone cannot account for the Fourth Amendment, *see* ELY, *supra* note 4, at 96, 172, obviously does not show that procedural concerns alone—such as limiting official discretion—can suffice to explain it. *But see id.* at 97.

provisions of the Constitution, such as the rights to counsel, confrontation, bail, and jury trial, echo similar themes; they function, often at some cost to the efficiency and accuracy of fact-finding,[26] to prevent the government from treating individuals in the criminal process as though they were objects.[27]

Even outside the criminal context, elaborating rights of adjudicative process requires recourse to a substantive theory. Procedural due process rights are not simply means of protecting whatever "entitlements" happen to be conferred by legislation or administrative regulation. Otherwise, the drafters of an entitlement could frame it in the procedural terms of their choice, and the constitutional guarantee would be reduced to a right to receive whatever process the drafters had defined as due.[28] But that view has been repeatedly rejected by the Supreme Court, which has never fully embraced a purely positivist theory of procedural due process.[29] The only alternative theories, however, are ones that posit a right to individual dignity, or some similarly substantive norm, as the base on which conceptions of procedural fairness are constructed.[30]

If process is constitutionally valued, therefore, it must be valued not only as a means to some independent end, but for its intrinsic characteristics: being heard is part of what it means to be a person.[31] Pro-

26. *See generally* Packer, *Two Models of the Criminal Process*, 113 U. PA. L. REV. 1, 6-23 (1964) (tension in criminal process between crime control model, seeking efficient, expeditious and reliable screening and disposition of persons suspected of crimes, and due process model, seeking maintenance of dignity and autonomy of individual).

27. *See generally* C. FRIED, AN ANATOMY OF VALUES 125-32 (1970) (criminal procedure has "expressive aspects" and implicitly evidences societal ends).

28. One difficulty with a positivist theory of entitlements is that, if the Constitution requires government to deliver *only* what it promises, government is likely to respond by promising little. The present confusion in the law of procedural due process is strikingly illustrated by the Supreme Court's failure to require even the government to honor its procedural commitments. *See, e.g.*, United States v. Caceres, 440 U.S. 741 (1979) (evidence obtained by method contrary to agency regulations not excluded under exclusionary rule).

29. *See, e.g.*, Vitek v. Jones, 100 S. Ct. 1254, 1261-62 (1980); Carey v. Piphus, 435 U.S. 247, 266 (1978); Arnett v. Kennedy, 416 U.S. 134 (1974).

30. *See, e.g.*, Michelman, *Formal and Associational Aims in Procedural Due Process*, in DUE PROCESS: NOMOS XVIII 126, 127 (J. Pennock & J. Chapman eds. 1977) (due process vindicates substantive values of "participation" and "revelation"); Saphire, *Specifying Due Process Values: Toward a More Responsive Approach to Procedural Protection*, 127 U. PA. L. REV. 111, 117-25 (1978) (due process standard should measure whether conduct in question comports with basic notions of fairness and dignity). Values like accuracy do not by themselves justify a constitutional right to procedural due process. "Accuracy" is inevitably an instrumental concept. To give it content, to decide which procedures a concern for accuracy requires, we must look to the entitlement in question. The legislature, in drafting the statute conferring the entitlement, may deliberately define it in ambiguous terms. If the entitlement is not precisely defined, a concern for accuracy presumably would not result in elaborate procedure. Thus an instrumentalist approach leaves an opening for positivism.

31. What process is due depends upon what is at stake in a given case. The interest at

cess itself, therefore, becomes substantive. There is a curious irony here. One who holds that constitutional law should aim chiefly to perfect process is apparently unable to treat process as *itself* valuable. For, to see why process would itself be valuable—intrinsically so—is to see why the Constitution is inevitably substantive. Instead, the process-perfecter must treat process as ultimately instrumental, as but a means to other ends, and thus must regard as secondary what he would at the same time celebrate as primary.[32]

The process theorist is similarly confounded by questions about the right to vote—the quintessential procedural right in the realm of politics. Voting-rights issues commonly take one of two forms. One set of issues concerns *who* votes. Is the electorate to include racial minorities, women, District of Columbia residents, eighteen-year-olds?[33] Is it to include only property owners, only property owners and parents, only residents, only citizens?[34] What of the disenfranchisement of children?[35] Who votes, it turns out, is a profoundly substantive question.[36] For *who* participates—who counts—in the electoral process is a question that must precede any inquiry into the fairness of the process itself. The issue goes not to fairness procedurally, but to our sense of who constitutes a political community, and of which relations in society must be horizontal rather than vertical, fraternal rather than hierarchical. And if *any* question is plainly substantive, that question is fundamentally so.[37]

The second set of issues concerns how voting power is to be *allocated* among those who are included within an electoral constituency. Sometimes, in this context, the Supreme Court looks to whether the election

stake is pertinent to what procedures, in a given circumstance, are consistent with individual dignity. *See, e.g.*, Cafeteria & Restaurant Workers Local 473 v. McElroy, 367 U.S. 886, 895 (1961) (consideration of what procedures due process may require under any given set of circumstances must begin with determination of private interest affected); Note, *Specifying the Procedures Required by Due Process: Toward Limits on the Use of Interest Balancing*, 88 Harv. L. Rev. 1510, 1528-30 (1975) (process due depends on interest at stake).

32. *See* Ely, *supra* note 4, at 95-96.

33. *See* U.S. Const. amends. XV, XIX, XXIII, XXVI.

34. *See* City of Phoenix v. Kolodziejski, 399 U.S. 204 (1970) (franchise cannot be limited to property owners); Kramer v. Union Free School Dist. No. 15, 395 U.S. 621 (1969) (franchise in school board election cannot be limited to property owners and parents); Holt Civic Club v. City of Tuscaloosa, 439 U.S. 60 (1978) (nonresidents can be denied vote even in jurisdiction that taxes and regulates them); Rosberg, *Aliens and Equal Protection: Why Not the Right to Vote?*, 75 Mich. L. Rev. 1092 (1977).

35. *See Developments in the Law—The Constitution and the Family*, 93 Harv. L. Rev. 1156, 1201-02, 1221-42, 1350-83 (1980) [hereinafter cited as *Developments*].

36. Conventionally, it is treated as if it were a matter of procedure. *See, e.g.*, Ely, *supra* note 4, at 98-99.

37. Consider the question whether fetuses are persons with rights, a question raised by the right-to-life critique of Roe v. Wade, 410 U.S. 113 (1973). *See* L. Tribe, *supra* note 9, at 926-29.

is one that chooses representatives or one that resolves a one-shot issue,[38] or whether voters are voting as individuals or as, say, property owners.[39] But generally, the Court has enforced the famous rule announced in the reapportionment cases: one person, one vote.[40] The obvious substantive underpinnings of this rule—its role as an expression of the equal respect in which we as a society aspire to hold each individual[41]—all of this the theorists of perfecting process must ignore. They can defend the rule only hesitantly, claiming, for example, that it is merely a matter of administrative convenience.[42] Again we observe the irony already revealed in the adjudicative process cases: because embracing process for its own sake means embracing process as substance—as an expression of the value in which we would hold individuals—theorists who would defend constitutional law as ultimately reducible to the quest for perfection of process cannot themselves treat process as primary.[43] Again the puzzle deepens: as the next section will show, theorists of perfecting process are not only undercut by their inability affirmatively to advocate process as such, but their negative critique of obstructed process is stunted as well.

III. The Quandary of Whom to Protect

For those who would fill the gaps left by the Constitution's ambiguities and silences with representation-reinforcing principles, perhaps the core "process value" is the value of protecting certain minorities from perennial defeat in the political arena. The theme was anticipated by John Marshall;[44] it assumed a central role for Harlan Fiske Stone;[45]

38. *See* Town of Lockport v. Citizens for Community Action at the Local Level, Inc., 430 U.S. 259 (1977) (sustaining constitutionality of electoral procedures requiring concurrent majorities for restructuring constituent political units).

39. *See* Salyer Land Co. v. Tulare Lake Basin Water Storage Dist., 410 U.S. 719 (1973) (sustaining rule tantamount to "one acre, one vote" in composition of special water districts).

40. *See, e.g.*, Reynolds v. Sims, 377 U.S. 533, 567-68 (1964).

41. *See* R. DWORKIN, TAKING RIGHTS SERIOUSLY 273 (1977).

42. *See, e.g.*, ELY, *supra* note 4, at 124.

43. Nor can such theorists rest with a view that accepts a purely instrumental role for procedural norms and defends the constitutional plan as an indirect scheme for implementing substantive values that are not authoritatively established by the Constitution itself. For if the realization of such substantive values is the Constitution's aim, then their elaboration is appropriately the task of all who would interpret the Constitution.

44. *See* McCulloch v. Maryland, 17 U.S. (4 Wheat.) 316, 435-36 (1819) (state has no power to tax federal instrumentality because it would thereby act on national population, not represented in its legislature).

45. United States v. Carolene Prods. Co., 304 U.S. 144, 152 n.4 (1938) (strict judicial review for statutes that are directed against "discrete and insular minorities"); South Carolina State Highway Dep't v. Barnwell Bros., 303 U.S. 177, 184 n.2 (1938) (commerce clause may prohibit legislation burdening political outsiders).

it signally motivated Earl Warren;[46] and it has been elaborated by numerous scholars,[47] most powerfully in the work of John Ely.[48] The idea seems as simple as it sounds reasonable: governmental action that burdens groups effectively excluded from the political process is constitutionally suspect. In its most sophisticated form, the resulting judicial scrutiny is seen as a way of invalidating governmental classifications and distributions that turn out to have been motivated either by prejudiced hostility or by self-serving stereotypes.[49]

It all sounds pretty good—until we ask how we are supposed to distinguish such "prejudice" from principled, if "wrong," disapproval. Which groups are to count as "discrete and insular minorities"? Which are instead to be deemed appropriate losers in the ongoing struggle for political acceptance and ascendancy?

To begin with, of course, the theory must clearly distinguish itself from its *reductio ad absurdum*: "whichever group happens to lose the political struggle or fails to command the attention of the legislature . . . is—by that fact alone—a discrete and insular minority."[50] How about focusing on immutability, discreteness, insularity? For the process theorist, all such features might seem helpful in suggesting why a legislature would regard some groups as "different" and thus fall prey to cruel or self-servingly careless stereotyping. Or such features may signal why other groups would fail to interact with a group considered "different," or to engage in the usual protective logrolling.

But features like immutability are neither sufficient[51] nor necessary.[52]

46. *See* Ely, *The Chief*, 88 HARV. L. REV. 11, 12 (1974) (Warren sought to ensure that machinery of democratic process does not become self-serving organ of privileged class).

47. *See, e.g.*, L. LUSKY, *supra* note 3, at 11-12; L. TRIBE, *supra* note 9, *passim*.

48. *See* ELY, *supra* note 4, at 135-79.

49. *See id.* at 153-70.

50. Fiss, *The Supreme Court, 1978 Term—Foreword: The Forms of Justice*, 93 HARV. L. REV. 1, 8 (1979); *see* Sugarman v. Dougall, 413 U.S. 634, 657 (1973) (Rehnquist, J., dissenting) (no "extraordinary ingenuity" needed for lawyers to "find 'insular and discrete' minorities at every turn in the road").

51. Immutability by itself is plainly not sufficient. Intelligence, height, and strength are all immutable for a particular individual, but legislation that distinguishes on the basis of these criteria is not generally thought to be constitutionally suspect. Discreteness and insularity are also insufficient: chiropractors may be a discrete and insular minority, but legislation that singles them out would not be subject to strict scrutiny on that basis alone. Even all three factors in combination may not be sufficient. Old age is an immutable characteristic, and the elderly may well be a discrete and insular minority. However, age is not *per se* a suspect criterion of classification. *See* Massachusetts Bd. of Retirement v. Murgia, 427 U.S. 307 (1976) (per curiam). For background discussion, see L. TRIBE, *supra* note 9, at 1077-82.

52. Alienage is properly treated as a classification at least partially suspect, despite its mutable character. *See, e.g.*, Nyquist v. Mauclet, 432 U.S. 1 (1977) (denying state scholar-

For in looking at social attitudes toward groups, one cannot simply play Linnaeus and engage in taxonomy. One cannot speak of "groups" as though society were objectively subdivided along lines that are just there to be discerned.[53] Instead, people *draw* lines, attribute differences, as a way of ordering social existence—of deciding who may occupy what place, play what role, engage in what activity. Thus, in order to justify the role of chattel that blacks initially played in our society, we may have differentiated that role by describing it in terms of the most obvious distinguishing feature of the people who played it, thus equating race and role.[54] This equation, and thus the "group," survived the Civil War and the Thirteenth Amendment. It did so not simply by reason of confusion or inertia, but because the role that society allowed blacks remained partly unchanged; thus the need to justify the role by differentiating it, by seeing not the role but the group—"inferior" blacks capable of nothing better anyway—persisted.[55]

The temptation to think of groups as simply given is exacerbated by the complex interaction between social attitudes and those identified as group members. Individuals who find themselves so identified may indeed see themselves as group members; because they approve of the options that society leaves them and want to protect those options, they identify the options with themselves, the differentiated "group."[56] Alternatively, assertion of group status may be a form of internal exile, a way of repudiating the limited possibilities for action that the larger social structure would allow, a choice of "exit" rather than "voice."[57]

ship aid to resident aliens who choose to remain noncitizens violates equal protection). And even if race or gender became readily mutable by biomedical means, I would suppose that laws burdening those who choose to remain black or female would properly remain constitutionally suspect.

53. This point is neatly illustrated by a passage quoted by Foucault, in which Borges cites a Chinese encyclopedia's assertion that "animals are divided into: (a) belonging to the Emperor, (b) embalmed, (c) tame, (d) sucking pigs, (e) sirens, (f) fabulous, (g) stray dogs, (h) included in the present classification, (i) frenzied, (j) innumerable, (k) drawn with a very fine camelhair brush, (l) *et cetera*, (m) just having broken the water pitcher, (n) that from a long way off look like flies." M. FOUCAULT, THE ORDER OF THINGS xv (1970).

54. *See* W. JORDAN, WHITE OVER BLACK (1968).

55. *See* C. V. WOODWARD, THE STRANGE CAREER OF JIM CROW (2d ed. 1966).

56. Individuals who disapprove of the options that society presents them may nevertheless accept their treatment as a differentiated group, and accept as natural or inevitable their inferior status. Even individuals with options more favorable than those of most group members may accept the social characterization of the group in order to differentiate themselves from the group. *See* Castaneda v. Partida, 430 U.S. 482, 503 (1977) (Marshall, J., concurring); *cf.* G. WEINBERG, SOCIETY AND THE HEALTHY HOMOSEXUAL 74-82 (1972) (homosexual self-loathing, contempt, and prejudice parallel societal attitudes).

57. Thus, some blacks may differentiate themselves as a way of rejecting, or of expressing a critical judgment about, the options with which society at large leaves them.

This way of thinking about groups, I believe, captures not only much of the dynamics of race, but also much of the social significance of religion, alienage, gender, sexual preference, legitimacy, wealth—traits we as a society commonly use in separating out groups.[58] Views about the "differentness" of groups generally, therefore, may reflect an interacting set of judgments about activities or options or roles, expressed sometimes harmoniously and sometimes dialectically by *both* "we" and "they."[59] If so, the conclusion that a legislative classification reveals prejudicial stereotypes must, at bottom, spring from *a disagreement with the judgments that lie behind the stereotype*: judgments about the propriety of the options left to individuals or the burdens imposed on them.

Consider several illustrations. Burglars are subject to widespread hostility: indeed, the activity that defines the group is everywhere legislatively prohibited. Are burglars therefore a "suspect class"? Of course not. Suspect status is unthinkable—but only because of the substantive value we attach to personal security, and the importance for us of the system of private property and its rules of transfer, which the burglary prohibition preserves.[60] If we speak of burglars as a class, we do so as a way of giving form to our view that burglary *is* a "different" activity, different not so much because burglars visibly define a group as because we disapprove of the activity, deny it any claim to protection as a right.

Homosexuals, too, are subject to widespread hostility; legislation penalizing homosexuals and homosexual practices is common.[61] Homosexuals often do not identify themselves by sexual preference when acting politically, and generally do not "come out of the closet" to refute the traditional stereotypes.[62] But even if they did, legislation might be unaltered. Coming out of the closet could dispel ignorance, but it may not alter belief. Legislators may see homosexuals as "dif-

Cf. A. Hirschman, Exit, Voice, and Loyalty 108-12 (1970) (American black power movement advocates collective program for blacks as group and rejects traditional pattern of upward social mobility for individual, selected blacks).

58. *See* Fiss, *supra* note 3, at 124-33; *cf.* G. Myrdal, An American Dilemma 27-30 (1944).

59. *See* Ely, *The Constitutionality of Reverse Racial Discrimination*, 41 U. Chi. L. Rev. 723, 732 (1974).

60. *See* Ely, *supra* note 4, at 154.

61. *See* Rivera, *Our Straight-Laced Judges: The Legal Position of Homosexual Persons in the United States*, 30 Hastings L.J. 799 (1979).

62. *See* Ely, *supra* note 4, at 163 ("serious social costs" of encountering prejudice upon admission); C. Reich, The Sorcerer of Bolinas Reef 71-73 (1976) (fear of societal opprobrium caused repression of homosexuality). *But see* L. Humphreys, Out of the Closets (1972) (chronicling recent organizational activism, political action, and violence by homosexuals in response to oppression).

ferent" not out of ignorance, but on principle—on the basis of a morality that treats certain sexual practices as repugnant to a particular view of humanity, and thus regards people who engage in those practices as "other."[63] Such legislation can be rejected only on the basis of a principle that is equally substantive: a view of what it means to be a person, and to have a sexual identity.[64] Process and prejudice thus seem profoundly beside the point. Any constitutional distinction between laws burdening homosexuals and laws burdening exhibitionists, between laws burdening Catholics and laws burdening pickpockets, must depend on a substantive theory of which groups are exercising fundamental rights and which are not.[65]

Indeed, even laws putting blacks and women "in their place"—banning racial intermarriage, say, or excluding women from combat—are likely to reflect neither simple hostility nor self-serving blindness but *a substantive vision of proper conduct*—a vision that no amount of attention to flaws in the political process could condemn or correct. Accordingly, the idea of blacks or women as properly segregated beings can be rejected *only* by finding a constitutional basis for concluding that, in our society, such hierarchical visions are substantively out of bounds, at least as a justification for government action.[66] And such a finding would in turn entail a theory of unenumerated substantive rights, rights at best *suggested* by constitutional text and history, rights whose necessarily controversial elaboration the process theorists seek to eschew.[67]

63. *See, e.g.*, Doe v. Commonwealth's Attorney for City of Richmond, 403 F. Supp. 1199, 1202 (E.D. Va. 1975), *aff'd mem.*, 425 U.S. 901 (1976) ("ancestry" of state statute prohibiting sodomy goes back to Judaic and Christian law); Barrett, *Legal Homophobia and the Christian Church*, 30 HASTINGS L.J. 1019 (1979) (arguing that Christian morality is responsible for legal homophobia).

64. *See* Karst, *The Freedom of Intimate Association*, 89 YALE L.J. 624, 633-35 (1980).

65. *See Developments, supra* note 35, at 1176 n.119.

66. *See, e.g.*, Craig v. Boren, 429 U.S. 190, 210 n.23 (1976) (dictum) (disapproving earlier decision that upheld occupational exclusions of women); Loving v. Virginia, 388 U.S. 1 (1967) (invalidating ban on racial intermarriage). If, as some suggest, *see, e.g.*, ELY, *supra* note 4, at 256 n.92, a governmental decision to impose a burden could be defended simply by showing that the decision reflects "a bona fide feeling that [the burdened choice] is immoral," *id.*, then even racial segregation would be sustainable.

67. Even assuming that laws burdening groups such as women are founded on no moral convictions, a process-based analysis is still fatally inadequate. Although legislation discriminating against women does not, at least superficially, reflect hostility toward women, and despite the fact that women are not a minority, there is nonetheless reason, a process theorist might argue, for strict judicial scrutiny of such legislation. Male legislators no doubt frequently regard women as "they" rather than "we." *See* ELY, *supra* note 4, at 164. In process terms, however, this is a weak case. Arguably, all that keeps women from full participation is the fact that many women (as well as men) accept a view of society in which women are subject to men or are otherwise inappropriate participants in public life. But that view of society is increasingly controversial. To

Process-Based Theories

The crux of any determination that a law unjustly discriminates against a group—blacks, or women, or even men[68]—is not that the law emerges from a flawed process, or that the burden it imposes affects an independently fundamental right,[69] but that the law is part of a pattern that denies those subject to it a meaningful opportunity to realize their humanity. Necessarily, such an approach must look beyond process to identify and proclaim fundamental substantive rights. Whatever difficulties this may entail, it seems plain that important aspects of constitutional law, including the determination of which groups deserve special protection, can be given significant content in no other way. Thus it is puzzling indeed that process-based approaches—designed to deny the need for, and legitimacy of, any such substantive theory—should nonetheless continue to find such articulate proponents and persist in attracting such perceptive adherents.

IV. The Closed Circle of Political Openness

If protecting minorities requires a theory of substantive rights, might another value, that of "political openness"—of clearing the channels for change through speech and voting—be salvaged as a unifying theme for the process-minded?[70] First Amendment theorists such as Alexander Meiklejohn have pursued this general line, with varying degrees of success.[71] But there are at least three fundamental difficulties with any effort to reduce substantive rights to mere mechanisms for channel-clearing. The first problem is the inherently incomplete nature of channel-clearing as an aim. Why *should* politics be open to equal

conclude today that women are an "excluded" group is simply to challenge the support of many women and men for contemporary legislation. Thus only sexist laws enacted long enough ago may be struck down as mere expressions of prejudicial stereotypes. *See id.* at 166-67.

Disputes over the place of women, however, are hardly a recent development. *See* E. Pagels, The Gnostic Gospels 59-63 (1979) (tracing Gnostic treatment of women as equals); A. Kelly, Eleanor of Aquitaine and the Four Kings 163-64 (1950) (women of late 12th-century Poitevin court sat in judgment upon points of courtly love). The fact of contemporary dispute is thus not necessarily a sign of progress. But if the idea of equal rights for women is a perpetually contested concept, then the constitutionality of legislation that treats men and women differently cannot turn, as process theorists might argue, on whether such legislation preceded or followed dispute about the status of women.

68. *See, e.g.*, Orr v. Orr, 440 U.S. 268 (1979) (state statutory scheme cannot exempt women from alimony obligations imposed on men).

69. Neither drinking age, *see* Craig v. Boren, 429 U.S. 190 (1976), nor age of expiration of parental support obligations, *see* Stanton v. Stanton, 421 U.S. 7 (1975), involve independently fundamental rights—but in both areas the Supreme Court has invalidated gender-based lines that lock the sexes into their traditional roles.

70. *See* Ely, *supra* note 4, at 105-34.

71. *See* A. Meiklejohn, Free Speech and Its Relation to Self-Government 27 (1948).

participation by all? Doesn't that norm itself presuppose some substantive vision of human rights? Why wouldn't a vision rich enough to support a reasonably complete theory of political openness also suffice to generate a theory of which substantive claims individuals may make against the majority?

The second problem is the absence of any plausible stopping point for channel-clearing theories. If the system must be open to change through peaceful persuasion, how do we distinguish between example and advocacy or between demonstration and assertion as forms of persuasion? If we do not draw some such distinction, life-style choices that seek to convince by demonstration—communal living arrangements or homosexual marriage, for example—are entitled to constitutionally protected status. Surely that is not what process theorists have in mind! Efforts to draw the necessary distinctions, however, are inevitably unsatisfactory. To accord special protection to advocacy alone is to censor those messages that can be conveyed only by example. Moreover, dichotomies such as speech and conduct, expression and action, or persuasion and instruction, do not in truth separate.[72]

If the acts of individuals may be demonstrations, and hence forms of persuasion, may not the same be said of the acts of government?[73] The actions of government define expectations, confer legitimacy, establish a status quo, and thus necessarily shape the nature and distribution of interests and attitudes in society itself. The state shapes society almost as much as society shapes the state: this is the third problem that any channel-clearing theory must confront—but cannot surmount without losing its "procedural" status.

Government subsidies to "major" political parties, for example, or the failure of state governments to provide funds to compensate school districts lacking "rich" property tax bases, are government actions that affirm some aspects of the status quo as desirable, and others as inevitable. Such government actions are at present constitutional,[74] as are governmental decisions that inculcate the young with the standard public virtues and defeat the self-defining, value-forming, and power-amassing efforts of all but the more standard social groupings.[75] Unable

72. *See, e.g.*, L. TRIBE, *supra* note 9, at 598-601; ELY, *supra* note 4, at 113 n.*.

73. *See* Yudof, *When Governments Speak: Toward A Theory of Government Expression and the First Amendment*, 57 TEX. L. REV. 863 (1979).

74. *See* Buckley v. Valeo, 424 U.S. 1 (1976); San Antonio Independent School Dist. v. Rodriguez, 411 U.S. 1 (1973). *But see* Serrano v. Priest, 5 Cal. 3d 584, 487 P.2d 1241, 96 Cal. Rptr. 601 (1971) (interpreting state constitution as creating a cause of action for violation of equal protection in suit to invalidate property tax funding of public schools).

75. *Compare, e.g.*, Moore v. City of East Cleveland, 431 U.S. 494 (1977) (protecting extended families) *with* Village of Belle Terre v. Boraas, 416 U.S. 1 (1974) (households of

to support a challenge to such exercises of power, a truly procedural channel-clearing theory seems doomed to irrelevance, for without such challenge government may well be able to shape the "will" of the governed in the image of those who govern,[76] reducing consent and representation to all but empty ideals.

This should not seem too surprising: that domination can appear in the guise of democracy is hardly a novel observation in the late twentieth century. The puzzle is that the failure of process-based theories even to speak to this danger should be so readily and persistently excused or overlooked.

V. A Broader Role for Constitutional Theory

One final and closely related puzzle—a puzzle that may follow from the very aspiration of process-based theories to purge constitutional discourse of inevitably controversial claims about substantive rights and values—is the willingness of so many to embrace process-based theories in the face of their virtually total incapacity to inform the *content* of public discussion, debate, and decision. One can perhaps understand the appeal to judges of a theory purporting to instruct them that they are to construe the Constitution so as to reinforce representation, that is, fill in the blanks so as to perfect democracy. But what can be the appeal of such a theory to an elected representative—especially one who regards the Constitution as addressed to *all* who govern,[77] and who accordingly wonders whether some of the "interests" of his constituents ought, as a constitutional matter, to be resisted rather than represented?[78] And what can be the appeal of such a theory to a citizen who regards the Constitution as addressed to the people at large, and who, accordingly, asks which of his preferences—for exploiting the poor, perhaps, or for denigrating ethnic minorities—the citizen ought to suppress or even change?

unrelated individuals not protected); *compare* NAACP v. Button, 371 U.S. 415 (1963) (group legal services protected) *with* Garcia v. Texas State Bd. of Medical Examiners, 384 F. Supp. 434 (W.D. Tex. 1974), *aff'd mem.*, 421 U.S. 995 (1975) (group health plans not).

76. Ely notes this phenomenon in connection with his discussion of the idea of progress as an organizing basis for constitutional law: "[T]oday's judicial decision (no matter what its source of judgment) will inevitably have an important influence on the values of tomorrow's majority." ELY, *supra* note 4, at 70. *Cf. id.* at 165 (societal stereotypes accepted by the stereotyped). He does not, however, generalize this insight to government action generally.

77. *See* Linde, *"Clear and Present Danger" Reexamined: Dissonance in the* Brandenburg *Concerto*, 22 STAN. L. REV. 1163 (1970); Linde, *Due Process of Lawmaking*, 55 NEB. L. REV. 197 (1976).

78. *See* H. PITKIN, THE CONCEPT OF REPRESENTATION (1967).

Perhaps the impoverished relevance of the Constitution for everyone *except* judges under a process-based theory is to be offset in some way by the theory's supposed ability to improve constitutional argument, analysis, and adjudication in the judicial branch. But are we really to believe that the way judges decide cases will be powerfully and beneficially affected by theories linking the judiciary's constitutional role to the supposed failures of political process? Might not the care and humility that we are entitled to expect of judges be *undermined* if judges were indeed persuaded that much judicial activism is simply a corollary of democracy?

Most process-based theorists and their followers evidently have seen little point in analyzing what the general acceptance of their views would be likely to do to the actual course of constitutional argument and decision.[79] The views they espouse apparently strike chords so responsive, accord with beliefs so deep, that inquiry into probable effects—like close attention to counter-examples and logical gaps—seems beside the point. But if this is so, then we are left with a final puzzle, one to be explored in a later essay: what does it say about our situation, and about the prospect for constitutional theory, that views so deeply problematic continue to exert so powerful a grip upon our thought?

79. *But see* ELY, *supra* note 4, at 102 n.* (concern over effect of theory on protection of civil liberties).

THE RECRUDESCENCE OF PROPERTY RIGHTS AS THE FOREMOST PRINCIPLE OF CIVIL LIBERTIES: THE FIRST DECADE OF THE BURGER COURT*

WILLIAM W. VAN ALSTYNE†

> The great and chief end, therefore, of men's uniting into commonwealths and putting themselves under government is the preservation of their property, to which in the state of nature there are many things lacking.
>
> —John Locke[1]

> [T]he dichotomy between personal liberties and property rights is a false one. Property does not have rights. People have rights. The right to enjoy property without unlawful deprivation, no less than the right to speak or the right to travel, is in truth a "personal" right. * * * In fact, a fundamental interdependence exists between the personal right to liberty and the personal right in property. Neither could have any meaning without the other. That rights in property are basic civil liberties has long been recognized.
>
> —*Lynch v. Household Finance Corp.*[2]

I
INTRODUCTION: IN SEARCH OF A SYNECDOCHE

A "synecdoche" is a figure of speech which uses a less inclusive term in lieu of a more inclusive term. In addressing the work of the Supreme Court in relation to individual liberty during this past decade, it would obviously be helpful to have a synecdoche: some single word to stand in place of the Court's libertarian jurisprudence otherwise scattered among the several hundred opinions of the last ten years of U.S. Reports.

Despite the volume of published reviews of the Court's work, however, for a considerable time it seemed to me that no suitably accurate, single-word description could be found. It could not be located in the use of any one Justice's name, as an unhurried review of the Court's civil liberties decisions does not suggest that the results or the reasoning are characteristically marked by the constitutional jurisprudence of one dominant figure. Clearly we do not have an equivalent, for instance, of "The Marshall Court" in which, despite the great brilliance of other individuals such as Justice Story, it was nonetheless possible to speak usefully of a dominant jurisprudence conveniently

† William R. Perkins and Thomas C. Perkins Professor of Law, Duke University.

1. J. Locke, *Of the Ends of Political Society and Government*, in SECOND TREATISE OF CIVIL GOVERNMENT (1690).

2. 405 U.S. 538, 552 (1972).

identified to the Chief Justice. Ostensibly, neither do we have a pattern of decisions that are sufficiently all-of-a-piece that the various civil liberties cases of the past decade can, with not unreasonable oversimplification, be captured in a single, conventional, political adjective or noun. This has not been a "radical" Court, surely, but neither has it been "reactionary" in its applications of the Bill of Rights. It does not even appear quite serviceable to denominate it a Court of "retrenchment." Rather, on first impression, it appears more eclectic and individuated with no strong single jurisprudential signature evident in either some general orientation of result (e.g., favoring the government or favoring the individual) or of analytic mode (e.g., favoring a textual literalism or favoring a "purpose" perspective of various constitutional clauses).

In matters of criminal procedure, there has undoubtedly been an arrest of rights and some actual diminution in safeguards previously thought to be secured in the Bill of Rights.[3] In matters of religious freedom, prerogatives of free exercise have been rather generously construed[4] albeit, as Professor Grey quite rightly observes, principally for claims of conventional virtue and of established morality.[5] Insofar as individual liberty may be enhanced by the establishment clause, on the other hand, the results are assuredly more mixed: incentives have been newly furnished to sectarian establishments seeking financial relief through the public treasury[6] and no formula has yet been devised to check the enactment of fundamentalist beliefs. In respect to freedom of speech and of the press, there has been at the least an arrest of the expansionary protections characteristic of the preceding decade[7] and, in certain

3. *See, e.g.*, Williams v. Florida, 399 U.S. 78 (1970) (twelve person jury not required in state criminal trials); Apodaca v. Oregon, 406 U.S. 404, and Johnson v. Louisiana, 406 U.S. 356 (1972) (less-than-unanimous jury verdicts sufficient in state criminal trials); Harris v. New York, 401 U.S. 222 (1971), Oregon v. Hass, 429 U.S. 714 (1975), and Rakas v. Illinois, 99 S. Ct. 421 (1978) (exclusionary rule of Miranda v. Arizona, 384 U.S. 436 (1966) restricted); Stone v. Powell, 428 U.S. 465 (1976) and United States v. Calandra, 414 U.S. 338 (1971) (exclusionary rule further restricted); Kirby v. Illinois, 406 U.S. 682 (1972) (due process requisites of suspect identification, United States v. Wade, 388 U.S. 218 (1967) limited); United States v. Martinez-Fuerte, 428 U.S. 543 (1976) and Smith v. Maryland, 99 S. Ct. 2577 (1979) (fourth amendment search warrant requirements held inapplicable); Scott v. Illinois, 440 U.S. 367 (1979) (jury trial requirements of Argersinger v. Hamlin, 407 U.S. 25 (1972) reduced).

4. *See, e.g.*, Wisconsin v. Yoder, 406 U.S. 205 (1972). *Cf.* Prince v. Massachusetts, 321 U.S. 158 (1944).

5. Thus, in *Yoder*, Chief Justice Burger extolled the sturdy, agrarian, self-reliant virtues of the Amish and declared:

> It cannot be overemphasized that we are not dealing with a way of life and mode of education by a group claiming to have recently discovered some "progressive" or more enlightened process for rearing children for modern life.

406 U.S. at 235. He concludes that "probably few other religious groups or sects could make" the same sort of "convincing showing" sufficient to render the compulsory attendance law invalid as applied to the Amish. *Id.* at 236.

6. *See, e.g.*, Wolman v. Walter, 433 U.S. 229 (1977), Roemer v. Board of Public Works, 426 U.S. 736 (1976), and Hunt v. McNair, 413 U.S. 734 (1973) (varieties of state financial assistance to distinctly sectarian schools sustained).

7. *See, e.g.*, Time, Inc. v. Firestone, 424 U.S. 448 (1976) and Gertz v. Robert Welch, Inc., 418

respects, a net diminution in the boundary of the free speech clause for those without money to pay[8] as against the enlarged prerogatives of those with the means to advertise.[9] The nascent revolution of Millian autonomy has been altogether checked and the "penumbras" of rights "emanating" from the ninth amendment have been reined in.[10] Most conspicuously, the procedural due process explosion in administrative law has bumped up against a very tough doctrinal barrier: entitlements to some kind of hearing are newly dependent upon a fulcrum of "property," and, evidently, what constitutes property depends upon the pleasure of the state.[11]

On the other hand, the *Bivens* case[12]—which held that the Bill of Rights provides private causes of action—is unquestionably one of the most significant positive-law developments in the entire history of the Bill of Rights. Though it appeared early in the decade, it was nonetheless a feature of this decade of constitutional law. Similarly, the abortion decisions were also civil liberties decisions of the 1970s.[13] Judging them merely from the criticism levelled by moderates of constitutional law alone,[14] they may reasonably be described as resting far from a conservative view of the Bill of Rights. Finally,

---

U.S. 323 (1974) (libel standards eased); Gannet Co. v. DePasquale, 99 S. Ct. 2898 (1979), Houchins v. KQED, 438 U.S. 1 (1978), and Lehman v. City of Shaker Heights, 418 U.S. 298 (1974) (speech-access restricted).

8. *See, e.g.*, Greer v. Spock, 424 U.S. 828 (1976) (handbilling on government property limited); Hudgens v. NLRB, 424 U.S. 507 (1976) (picketing on private property limited); Miami Herald Pub. Co. v. Tornillo, 418 U.S. 241 (1974) (newspaper right-of-reply statute held invalid). *Cf.* Flower v. United States, 407 U.S. 197 (1972) (handbilling on military base protected); Amalgamated Food Employees Union v. Logan Valley Plaza, 391 U.S. 308 (1968) (picketing on private property protected); Red Lion Broadcasting Co. v. FCC, 395 U.S. 367 (1969) (FCC right-of-reply regulation sustained).

9. *See, e.g.*, First National Bank v. Bellotti, 435 U.S. 765 (1978) (corporate funds to campaign against ballot issues protected); Buckley v. Valeo, 424 U.S. 1 (1976) (restrictions on personal electioneering expenditures invalidated); Virginia State Bd. of Pharmacy v. Virginia Citizens Council, Inc., 425 U.S. 748 (1976), and Bates v. State Bar, 433 U.S. 350 (1977) (commercial advertising protected).

10. *See, e.g.*, Doe v. Commonwealth's Attorney, 425 U.S. 901 (1976), *aff'g mem.*, 403 F. Supp. 1199 (E.D. Va. 1975); Wainwright v. Stone, 414 U.S. 21 (1973). Chief Justice Burger provides a nearly explicit denunciation in Paris Adult Theatre I v. Slaton, 413 U.S. 49 (1973). It is fair to note, by way of passing interest, that parts of Holmes's famous dissenting opinion in Lochner v. New York, 198 U.S. 45 (1905) are similar. *See, e.g.*, *id.* at 75 where Holmes derides "[t]he liberty of the citizen to do as he likes so long as he does not interfere with the liberty of others to do the same," as "a shibboleth for some well-known writers."

11. *See, e.g.*, Meachum v. Fano, 429 U.S. 215 (1976); Bishop v. Wood, 426 U.S. 341 (1976); Board of Regents v. Roth, 408 U.S. 564 (1972).

12. Bivens v. Six Unknown Named Agents, 403 U.S. 388 (1971). The original implications of the case are described in Dellinger, *Of Rights and Remedies: The Constitution as a Sword*, 85 HARV. L. REV. 1532 (1972). An excellent recent review of its operational limitations is provided by a Note, *"Damages or Nothing"—The Efficacy of the Bivens-Type Remedy*, 64 CORNELL L. REV. 667 (1979).

13. Roe v. Wade, 410 U.S. 113 (1973); Doe v. Bolton, 410 U.S. 179 (1973). *But see* the retrenchment more recently evident in Maher v. Roe, 432 U.S. 464 (1977).

14. *See, e.g.*, Ely, *The Wages of Crying Wolf: A Comment on* Roe v. Wade, 82 YALE L.J. 920 (1973).

if one judges these matters not alone from pure constitutional decisions, (i.e., those involving interpretations of particular clauses in the Constitution itself), but from the perspective of practical recourse against government infringements of those liberties, the statutory rendering of our most important Civil Rights Act (42 U.S.C. § 1983) in the *Monnell*[15] case is an exceedingly liberal opinion—providing money recourse against the deep pockets of cities and counties for violations of fourteenth amendment liberties.

This artless, thumbnail, skimming review is not meant to be complete by any means. To the contrary, I recognize that it but cavalierly restates what has been more systematically reviewed elsewhere. I have reiterated it only to demonstrate the difficulty, and perhaps the foolishness, of looking for a synecdoche—a lesser inclusive term useful to represent the more inclusive term of the Supreme Court and liberties during the preceding decade of constitutional law.

One may try other kinds of comparisons, but they, too, lack both novelty and importance. In comparison with the last decade of the Warren Court, for instance, without doubt the work of this decade has been less aggressive. In comparison with nearly any other decade of Bill of Rights interpretations, on the other hand, this last one is probably virtually as generous as any previous ten years of decisions (and, of course, the "jurisprudence" of the Warren Court has been the object of intense criticism). In the thoughtfulness, care, and professional excellence of the Justices, so close are we to each decision as it comes down that our own parsing of its logic prematurely leads us to the supposition that the members of this court may somehow be less learned, less careful, or less judicious in superintending the Constitution than their predecessors. I personally do not think that this is so. To the contrary, I am inclined to believe that with only a few exceptions of the past, the ability, acuity, and detachment of the twelve Justices who have served since 1969 will, on sober comparison, overall compare very well. The well publicized voyeurism of *The Brethren*,[16] incidentally, may be unintentionally instructive that there is nothing fundamentally amiss on the Court in this regard. Despite myriad personal revelations and despite the glimpses of private utterance and of unkind epithet, it is interesting that no scandal, no single instance of corruption, no incident of wrongdoing was unearthed. Even more, the revealed maneuvers of one Justice to influence another, to secure opinion-writing prerogatives, etc., are inadvertently reassuring: the Judges evidently care a great deal about their work and they do not regard the adjudication of constitutional law lightly. If studies of other departments of our national government were so ultimately empty of disturbing findings as were the best investigative efforts

15. Monell v. Department of Social Services, 436 U.S. 658 (1978).
16. B. WOODWARD & S. ARMSTRONG, THE BRETHREN (1979).

of Woodward and Armstrong into the Supreme Court, I do not think we would feel embarrassed but, instead, rather surprised.

For these reasons, I have found it exceedingly difficult to discern something distinctive or doctrinally telegraphic in the civil liberties adjudications of the past decade—with one exception. Finally, yet still by way of introduction, I want to identify that exception.

The "liberties" mentioned in the preceding thumbnail review include most of those individual liberties in vogue in contemporary conversation: freedom of speech, of the press, of religion; freedom of personal life style, freedom from intrusions by government; freedom from arbitrary modes of determining one's fate (whether in civil or in criminal proceedings). These are matters which, in a political context, we might associate with the resolute commitments of organizations like the American Civil Liberties Union with its informal motto that its sole client is the Bill of Rights—liberal political concerns of expression, privacy, fair hearings, and the franchise. They are, as well, of course, the modes of liberty most stressed by the Warren Court.

The difference I see that most nearly distinguishes an entire pattern of decisions and of doctrinal development re-emerging within the past decade from those that immediately preceded it, however, is not revealed in comparing recent decisions with preceding ones in the unidimensionality of this comparison alone. It is, rather, by considering a larger group of cases and by relating them to a different, tighter, more conservative view of liberty: liberty as security of private property; liberty as freedom of entrepreneurial skill; liberty from the impositions of government and of third parties from disposing of "one's own." Liberty, in brief, more in the mode of John Locke[17] and of Adam Smith[18] and somewhat less in the mode of John Mill[19] (or of John Rawls).[20] To that end, I shall speak briefly to what I think *does* represent the basic (albeit still very incomplete) change of direction that marks the "liberty" decisions of the preceding decade: the reemergence of the rights of property.

II
REVITALIZING THE "OLD" CONSTITUTION AND ENTREPRENEURIAL LIBERTY

I mean to touch upon this subject very lightly, but it nonetheless does bear upon our subject and possesses a contextual significance of its own. The preoccupation of recent times almost exclusively with the Bill of Rights and with the fourteenth amendment has tended to suppress the recollection that at

17. J. LOCKE, SECOND TREATISE OF CIVIL GOVERNMENT (1690).
18. A. SMITH, THE WEALTH OF NATIONS (1776).
19. J. MILL, ON LIBERTY (1859).
20. J. RAWLS, A THEORY OF JUSTICE (1971). *Cf.* R. NOZICK, ANARCHY, STATE AND UTOPIA (1974).

least certain kinds of significant "liberty" were shielded by the Constitution of 1789. The ban on state laws impairing the obligation of contracts was one of these,[21] even as reflected in the famous *Dartmouth College* case.[22] The interstate privileges and immunities clause in Article IV[23] derived from the free trade clause of the Articles of Confederation, and expounded in *Corfield v. Coryell*,[24] was another. The exclusionary implications of the commerce clause, construed in *Gibbons v. Ogden*[25] as per se disallowing either discriminatory or unreasonably burdensome state interferences within a nationwide free trade zone, is of course yet another. The subsequent enactment of the "takings" clause, i.e., the eminent domain provision of the fifth amendment,[26] is a fourth.

Each of these, especially in close relation with the others, quite genuinely "nationalized" the protection of certain private rights and the entrepreneurial liberties: principally, the conjunction between John Locke's *Second Treatise of Civil Government* (published in 1690) and Adam Smith's *The Wealth of Nations* (published in 1776). Locke's influential *Treatise* declared that the chief end of civil government is to protect the security of private property virtually as an extension of oneself. The second, Adam Smith's durable volume, stressed the superior efficiency of private exchange and of a relatively untrammeled market in satisfying individual wants.

Fifteen years ago, in an excellent article, William Howard Mann devoted an unhurried 128-page review to the manner in which the Marshall Court protected these important economic freedoms[27] and I will not presume to summarize those developments still again. Rather, I mean but to observe that at least in comparison with recent decades past, the current decade has brought back from relative obscurity some of these clauses and some of this sense of commercial liberty. For instance, after a long eclipse signalled vividly in the Great Depression by the *Blaisdell* case,[28] the provision against laws impairing obligations of contracts has been revived and twice applied against abridging state legislation.[29] Similarly, in at least three instances state laws

---

21. "No State shall . . . pass any . . . Law impairing the Obligation of Contracts . . . ." U.S. CONST. art. I, § 10, cl. 1.

22. Trustees of Dartmouth College v. Woodward, 17 U.S. (4 Wheat.) 518 (1819).

23. "The Citizens of each State shall be entitled to all Privileges and Immunities of Citizens in the several States." U.S. CONST. art. 4, § 2, cl. 1.

24. 6 Fed. Cas. 546, No. 3,230 (C.C.E.D.Pa., 1823).

25. 22 U.S. (9 Wheat.) 1 (1824).

26. "[N]or shall private property be taken for public use without just compensation." U.S. CONST. amend. S.

27. Mann, *The Marshall Court: Nationalization of Private Rights and Personal Liberty from the Authority of the Commerce Clause*, 38 INDIANA L.J. 117 (1963).

28. Home Building & Loan Association v. Blaisdell, 290 U.S. 398 (1934); *see also* El Paso v. Simmons, 379 U.S. 497 (1965).

29. United States Trust Co. v. New Jersey, 431 U.S. 1 (1977); Allied Structural Steel Co. v. Spannaus, 438 U.S. 234 (1978).

rather egregiously favoring local economic interests from fairer competition within a national market have been held invalid pursuant to the interstate privileges and immunities clause.[30] And again, in several instances the Court has not been content to wait for Congress to act against substantial state-imposed burdens on interstate commerce justified by rather marginal local interests, but has itself applied the commerce clause to hold those regulations unconstitutional.[31]

Even the "takings" clause of the fifth amendment has experienced a recent revival in behalf of private property and entrepreneurial freedom. After a very close contest within the Court in which the clause was held not to be offended in the *Penn Central* case,[32] a decision in December 1979, did hold the clause applicable to forbid the government from imposing an-unpaid-for public servitude upon a valuable commercial development in Hawaii.[33]

None of these is a "revolution" in constitutional law and none is the least earth shattering either by itself or in combination with the other cases linked by common themes of private property, competition, a national market, and entrepreneurial freedom. Insofar as they tend to show that some of the "old" liberties have not yet wholly yielded to the social impulse to regulate or to redistribute, however, they are not unimportant. They do, moreover, seem to me to suggest a difference in emphasis from the more personal, more "Millian," liberties best known during the preoccupations of the Warren Court—as they also provide a context for what has become of those less property-bound liberties during the past several years. Indeed, for reasons I now intend to examine at greater length, I think these cases are circumstantially significant, furnishing a renewed emphasis upon entrepreneurial rights as an important civil liberty of the nineteen-seventies.

III

THE ENLARGEMENT OF PRIVATE PROPERTY AND THE ATROPHY OF LIBERTY FOR THOSE WHO LACK IT

On November 13, 1979, the Supreme Court set down, for full briefing and for oral argument, a case with the unprepossessing title of *Pruneyard Shopping Center v. Robins*.[34] Regardless of *Pruneyard*'s eventual disposition on

30. Hicklin v. Orbeck, 437 U.S. 518 (1978); Austin v. New Hampshire, 420 U.S. 656 (1975); Gordon v. Committee on Character & Fitness, 48 N.Y. 2d 266, 397 N.E. 2d 1309, 422 N.Y.S.2d 641 (1979) (New York statute requiring proof of residency of six months prior to admission to the State Bar held unconstitutional as violative of federal interstate privileges and immunities clause. *Cf.* Baldwin v. Fish and Game Comm'n, 436 U.S. 371 (1978).

31. *See, e.g.*, Hughes v. Oklahoma, 441 U.S. 322 (1979); Raymond Motor Transportation, Inc. v. Rice, 434 U.S. 429 (1978); Hunt v. Washington State Apple Advertising Comm'n, 432 U.S. 333 (1977); Allenburg Cotton Co. v. Pittman, 419 U.S. 20 (1974).

32. Penn Central Transportation Co. v. New York, 438 U.S. 104 (1978).

33. Kaiser Aetna v. United States, 100 S. Ct. 383 (1979).

34. 48 U.S.L.W. 3319.

the merits,[35] the fact that the Court regarded the questions pressed by the petitioner in this case as *substantial* constitutional questions is immensely instructive of several judicial changes wrought during this most recent decade. The message they convey is both *Lockeian* and *Lochnerian*. They represent the recrudescence of libertarian thought that identifies liberty with private property, liberty with prerogatives of property—to exclude from it, to contract with reference to it, to identify it as part of oneself. Burrowed within the runways of other decisions of this decade, moreover, is a closely related message: that private property is once again not merely important and often sufficient to assert one's essential liberty; it may also be a *necessary* condition to the practical realization of that liberty.

In the not-distant past, not to have private property was quite frequently fatal to one's abstract freedoms. One may have had an abstract freedom of speech. To exercise it, however, he must stand in some place or speak over some medium. If he had no front porch of his own, he could not, on that account commandeer his neighbor's. Neither could he commandeer the state's. For the prevailing view, very well represented in an early decision by Justice Holmes, was that property under government ownership carried with it exclusionary prerogatives fully equivalent to those possessed by private parties.[36] As long as the state merely cordoned off its own property, reserving public access for certain purposes only, and uniformly barring all persons equally from access for any other purposes, it was no more vulnerable to trespasses than a private owner.

Private property, its acquisition, ownership, and disposition, was thus the pivot of civil liberties. Though Holmes dissented in *Lochner v. New York*, aphoristically observing that "[t]he fourteenth amendment does not enact Mr. Herbert Spencer's *Social Statics*,"[37] as the author of the Supreme Court's opinion in *Pennsylvania Coal Co. v. Mahon* [38] and as the judge who denied that the state as property owner has fewer exclusionary prerogatives than private owners,[39] he did not quite deny that the Constitution may have enacted a system predisposed to a property theory of civil liberties. A great deal of this point of view has now returned. The renewed emphasis upon private property greatly helps, I believe, to fit together a significant number of otherwise disparate "civil liberties" cases.

35. It is possible that the merits will ultimately not be addressed at all; the Court postponed further consideration of the question of jurisdiction until after full hearing on the merits. See 48 U.S.L.W. at 3322 (Nov. 13, 1979).

36. Commonwealth v. Davis, 162 Mass. 510, 511, 39 N.E. 113 (1895), *aff'd*, 167 U.S. 43 (1897): "For the legislature absolutely or conditionally to forbid public speaking in a highway or public park is no more an infringement of the rights of a member of the public than for the owner of a private house to forbid it in his house."

37. Lochner v. New York, 198 U.S. 45, 75 (1905).

38. 260 U.S. 393 (1922).

39. *See* note 37, *supra*.

The Pruneyard Shopping Center,[40] in Santa Clara, California, attracts 25,000 customers daily to its twenty-one acres containing sixty-five shops, ten restaurants, a cinema, walkways, and a plaza. Michael Robins, a Santa Clara County schoolboy, sought to gather signatures from people frequenting the mall. His petition expressed opposition to a recent United Nations Resolution which identified Zionism with racism. Robins intended to send his petition to the President of the United States, evidently as some indication that many persons, himself included, did not agree with the United Nations. His activity was apparently nondisruptive and reasonably well received by Pruneyard patrons. Nonetheless, he was required to leave the shopping center on order of a security guard responsible for the enforcement of a company policy forbidding any expressive activity anywhere within the mall. Robins sought recourse to the California courts, to determine whether he might re-enter the mall to canvass for his petition.

Interestingly, he did not rely upon the first or the fourteenth amendments' guarantees of free speech, peaceable assembly, or rights of petition. He could not do so, because a decision by the Supreme Court issued in 1968[41] (by the Warren Court) had first been severely restricted by a subsequent decision in 1972[42] and then flatly overruled by a more recent decision in 1976.[43] The 1968 decision, a shopping center case, was derived from a prior decision of 1946, *Marsh v. Alabama*,[44] which was derived from a prior decision of 1946, *Thornhill v. Alabama*,[45] where nondisruptive picketing had been held to be constitutionally sheltered although it occurred within the boundary of privately-held land. The 1976 decision restored the exclusivity of private property prerogatives, finding insufficient verisimilitude between large, corporately-held shopping plazas and either public parks or complete company towns, for free speech freedoms to be applicable. The fact that Robins could make no argument based on the fourteenth or first amendments, whereas but two or three years earlier a similarly situated individual could almost surely have made a successful argument, is itself declarative of one significant judicial trend.

Without reliance upon those amendments, Robins did, however, rely upon a provision in the California Constitution, a provision phrased somewhat differently from the first amendment.[46] In a four-to-three decision, the

40. The following factual description of the case is taken from the California Supreme Court opinion, 23 Cal. 3rd 909, 153 Cal. Rptr. 854, 592 P.2d 341 (1979).

41. Amalgamated Food Employees Union v. Logan Valley Plaza, 391 U.S. 308 (1968).

42. Lloyd Corp. v. Tanner, 407 U.S. 551 (1972).

43. Hudgens v. NLRB, 424 U.S. 507 (1976).

44. Marsh v. Alabama, 326 U.S. 501 (1946).

45. Thornhill v. Alabama, 310 U.S. 88 (1940).

46. Calif. Const., Art. I, § 2: "Every person may freely speak, write and publish his or her sentiments on all subjects, being responsible for the abuse of this right. A law may not restrain or

California Supreme Court agreed that the state constitutional provision was applicable to the shopping center, given its quasi-public characteristics, the virtual disappearance of any traditional downtown area as a place of common resort, and the nondisruptive character of Robins's activity. This, too, is not uninstructive respecting developments in civil liberties within the past decade: quite generally, as decisions from the Supreme Court have rebuffed or withdrawn previously-existing "rights," a number of state courts have reinvigorated moribund portions of their respective state constitutions to re-establish the line of protection under *state* law.[47] There was, in this respect as well, nothing newly remarkable in the California Supreme Court's treatment of the case.

What is remarkable, however, is that the case did not end here as one might suppose that it would. The meaning and applicability of the California Constitution being an issue of state law within the exclusive and final determination of that state's own highest court, one would suppose that no federal question would be present and thus there would be no basis for appeal from that court to the Supreme Court of the United States.[48] That reasoning assumes a great deal; it assumes that the liberty of private property is not sufficiently entrenched as to be protected by the fourteenth amendment from limitations imposed by a state constitution enabling third parties to come upon it for purposes of nondisruptive petitioning, at least when the property (as in this case) is otherwise open to public use, corporately-held, commercial in character, and functionally very much like a traditional center-of-town. In agreeing to hear *Pruneyard*, however, the Supreme Court now regards *that* question to be a substantial one. The questions framed for review are precisely those which I have identified .[49]

This change of "questions" within a decade is breathtaking. When I was a

---

abridge liberty of speech or press." (Quoted in Robins v. Pruneyard Shopping Center, 153 Cal. Rptr. 854, 859, 23 Cal. 2d 899, 908 (1979)).

47. *See* Howard, *State Courts and Constitutional Rights in the Day of the Burger Court*, 62 VA. L. REV. 873 (1976). Justice Brennan has personally urged such developments. Brennan, *State Constitutions and the Protection of Individual Rights*, 90 HARV. L. REV. 489 (1977).

48. *See, e.g.*, Herb v. Pitcairn, 324 U.S. 117, 125-26 (1945); Fox Film Corp. v. Muller, 296 U.S. 207 (1935); Murdock v. City of Memphis, 87 U.S. (20 Wall.) 590, 626 (1875).

49. (1) Does owner of private shopping center that has not been dedicated to public use and that is not functional equivalent of municipality have property right under Fifth and Fourteenth Amendments to prohibit non-business-related petitioning on premises of center when persons who wish to engage in such petitioning have other adequate and effective channels of communication in area?

(2) Does owner of private shopping center that has not been dedicated to public use and that is not functional equivalent of municipality have free speech right under First and Fourteenth Amendments to prohibit non-business-related petitioning on premises of center, when persons who wish to engage in such petitioning have other adequate and effective channels of communication in area?

"Questions presented," 48 U.S.L.W. 3319 (Nov. 13, 1979).

Stanford law student in the mid-1950s, the question posed to me by Phil Neal in our course on constitutional law was one raised by the company town case of *Marsh v. Alabama*;[50] namely whether the first and fourteenth amendments would secure some degree of third party free speech in the newly-planned Stanford shopping center. Professor Neal appeared to imply that presumably those amendments would apply and events in the sixties seemed to make him an excellent prophet. The question now posed is dramatically different: whether it unconstitutionally abridges property rights insofar as, by force of state constitutional law, some degree of third party free speech is allowed at all. Regardless of the outcome on the merits in the Supreme Court, the resemblance to *Lochner*[51] (and to cases predating *Euchid v. Ambler*)[52] is not very strained. In the context of the decision of but a few weeks ago, holding that the imposition of a public servitude on a commercially-developed private harbor in Hawaii constituted an uncompensated "taking" of the property in violation of the fifth amendment,[53] the grant of review in the *Pruneyard* case is extremely telegraphic.

The linkage of free speech with private property is made clearer in other cases as well. In *Pruneyard*, the shopping center will argue in the Supreme Court not merely that substantive due process precludes the state from subjecting its property to forum uses by others; it is arguing also that its right to use its property in this (exclusionary) respect is also an aspect of the corporation's *own* freedom of speech—and thus the California Supreme Court is *twice* wrong in what it did.[54] The claim is no longer a frivolous one; an entire line of decisions emergent in the seventies provides excellent ground for the shopping center argument which links "speech uses" of private property, even in a wholly commercial setting, with increasingly-protected first amendment prerogatives of business enterprise. One such line of cases is that which has overruled *Valentine v. Chrestensen*[55] and has brought entrepreneurial commercial advertising prerogatives within the bounds of the first amendment.[56] Closely related is the 1978 decision in *First National Bank v. Belotti*,[57] invalidating a

50. *See* note 43, *supra*.
51. *See* note 36, *supra*.
52. Village of Euclid v. Ambler Realty Co., 272 U.S. 365 (1926).
53. *See* note 34, *supra*.
54. *See* the second question presented in the case, note 49, *supra*.
55. 316 U.S. 52 (1942).
56. *See* Bates v. State Bar, 433 U.S. 350 (1977); Virginia State Board of Pharmacy v. Virginia Citizens Consumer Council, Inc., 425 U.S. 748 (1976); Bigelow v. Virginia, 421 U.S. 809 (1975). For refinements, *see, e.g.*, Ohralik v. Ohio State Bar Assn., 436 U.S. 447 (1978); In re Primus, 436 U.S. 412 (1978); National Society of Professional Engineers v. United States, 435 U.S. 679 (1978); Young v. American Mini Theatres, 427 U.S. 50 (1976); Pittsburgh Press Co. v. Pittsburgh Commission on Human Relations, 413 U.S. 376 (1973); Capital Broadcasting Co. v. Mitchell, 333 F. Supp. 582 (D.D.C. 1971), *aff'd without opinion sub nom.* Capital Broadcasting Co. v. Acting Attorney General Kleindienst, 405 U.S. 1000 (1972).
57. 435 U.S. 765 (1978).

state law forbidding commercial corporations from spending corporate funds to influence ballot issues. Connected as well, surely, is that part of *Buckley v. Valeo*,[58] decided in 1976, invalidating spending restrictions imposed upon one's own money or one's own resources respecting election to office or political issues at large.

It is difficult to avoid the impression simultaneously that "property" made at least part of the difference in the opposite outcomes of the two principal "right of reply" cases of the past decade. In *Red Lion Broadcasting*,[59] a unanimous Court sustained a federal regulation compelling a privately-owned radio station to furnish cost-free reply time to an individual mentioned disparagingly in the course of a brief, fifteen minute program. In 1974, on the other hand, a unanimous Court held unconstitutional a similar state statute compelling a privately-owned newspaper to furnish cost-free reply space to an individual mentioned disparagingly in the course of a brief editorial.[60] One difference (not the only one, to be sure) was this: by statute, some decades earlier, Congress had presumed to assert *national* ownership over the airwaves, further providing that no person, company, or licensee could acquire *any* "property" in those airwaves—that, at most, they could receive a three year conditional license of use.[61] In Florida, there was, of course, no equivalent statute precluding conventional private ownership of the newsprint on which the Miami *Herald* was printed: that ownership was complete, it carried with it full first amendment protections, and the state right-of-reply statute was correspondingly an abridgment of the newspaper's private property rights and freedom-of-speech: to exclude access by third parties.

It seems quite clear, then, that the security of private property as an extension of oneself and the corresponding liberty of free speech with respect to ownership dominion of that private property, is a clear and powerful development of the seventies. As several of these cases display, moreover, the development is very much related to the resurgence of entrepreneurial interests—a recrudescent faith in the superiority of the marketplace, limited not very much any longer by egalitarian themes from the first (or fourteenth) amendment but, rather, by the more restrained limits of the antitrust laws alone.

The importance of owning private property as the necessary-and-sufficient condition for free speech has been underscored in additional ways. As entrepreneurial prerogatives of expression have been reinvigorated, and as the contour of "state action" has been drawn back again to exempt private prop-

58. 424 U.S. 1 (1976).

59. Red Lion Broadcasting Co. v. FCC, 395 U.S. 367 (1969).

60. Miami Herald Publishing Co. v. Tornillo, 418 U.S. 241 (1974). For a comparison with Red Lion, *see* Van Alstyne, *The Möbius Strip of the First Amendment: Perspectives on Red Lion*, 29 So. CAR. L. REV. 539 (1978).

61. *See* 47 U.S.C. § 301 (1970).

erty from third party claims,[62] the dimensions of the public forum itself have also undergone considerable revision: they have shrunk. The result is that the first amendment is geographically less applicable even to state-owned property at the end of the seventies, as it is geographically less applicable (as imposing third party speech servitudes) to privately-held property as well. At least so long as the government does not utilize its proprietary dominion over its own property to "take sides" in public controversy, it may now forbid first amendment uses more substantially than was the case ten years ago. The point is well illustrated by the Court's decision on *Greer v. Spock*,[63] a 1976 decision upholding a flat handbilling ban imposed throughout a military base of enormous size, despite its crisscrossing by public roads, its germaneness as a place for the particular handbills, and the absence of incompatibility of the proposed handbilling with alternatives of more particular (but less inhibiting) regulation of mere time, place, or manner. Similarly, the 1974 decision in *Lehman v. City of Shaker Heights*,[64] utilizing placcard space in public buses for the rental of commercial advertisements, but denying that space for political advertisements, is a decision which I believe would not have been sustained six years earlier.

Equivalently, I am much impressed with Justice Stevens's dissent in *Houchins v. KQED*,[65] the recent jail access case. There, the issue as the majority of the Court attempted to frame it was whether members of the institutional press could assert greater information-seeking first amendment access rights than others. But the issue, as Justice Stevens noted, was also, that, *assuming* an investigative journalist could not claim any *special* access, i.e., a greater right of access than a representative of the NAACP (which was interested in the conditions within the jail as a result of one suicide and several letters of complaint from prisoners), whether the extent of the sheriff's severe restrictions on access were adequately justified as to *either*. The majority did not particularly press for an adequate justification respecting the extent of the sheriff's restrictions, as neither was the matter pressed with any vigor in the courtroom, pretrial closure case of *Gannet Co. v. DePasquale*.[66] While that case

62. The retrenchment of "state action" which frees entrepreneurial prerogatives from constitutional constraints is evident in other areas as well. *See, e.g.*, Flagg Brothers, Inc. v. Brooks, 436 U.S. 149 (1978); Jackson v. Metropolitan Edison Co., 419 U.S. 345 (1974) (fourteenth amendment not binding to require that heavily protected and regulated private utility observe due process). Compare Memphis Light, Gas, and Water Division v. Craft, 436 U.S. 1 (1978). See also Moose Lodge Number 107 v. Irvis, 407 U.S. 163 (1972) (private association holding one of a limited number of state-granted liquor licenses not constrained by the equal protection clause of the fourteenth amendment).

63. 424 U.S. 828 (1976). Compare Flower v. United States, 407 U.S. 197 (1972).

64. 418 U.S. 298 (1974). Compare Police Department v. Mosley, 408 U.S. 92 (1972).

65. 438 U.S. 1, 19 (1978) (Stevens, J., dissenting).

66. 99 S. Ct. 2898 (1979).

is clearly not the last word on courtroom access, the following portion of Justice Rehnquist's concurring opinion (in *Gannet*) is extremely dramatic:

> Despite the Court's seeming reservation of the question whether the First Amendment guarantees the public a right of access to pretrial proceedings, it is clear that . . . there is *no* First Amendment right of access in the public or the press to judicial or other governmental proceedings. [Emphasis added][67]

Greer, with related cases during the seventies, not insignificantly shrank the scope of publicly-owned property available for the exercise of free speech. *Gannet*, *Houchins*, and related cases not insignificantly restricted access to publicly-owned property which access may inform one's speech. There is in respect to each a sense of very heavy retrenchment: neither property "owned" by others nor property "owned" by the state is as widely available as decisions in the preceding decade appeared to imply[68]—as constitutionally accessible for the exercise of first amendment liberties. Simultaneously, the free speech claims of private property, commercial property and entrepreneurial property are more important than before.

IV
THE RE-EMERGENCE OF LOCKE IN THE ALLOCATION OF CIVIL LIBERTIES

Thus far, our examples respecting the importance of private property as the principal fulcrum for the practical exercise of civil liberties have been confined to liberties, such as speech, that we associate with the first amendment. The same theme respecting the importance of property (who owns it, who controls access to it, what conditions may be attached to its enjoyment) is equally evident in two other sets of cases. The first relates to privacy in the strict constitutional sense, i.e., fourth amendment search warrant requirements as a condition of state intrusion. The second relates to due process before personally fateful matters are adjudicated of an individual. Both have been newly treated with distinctions of property clearly in mind: not merely whether one has it, but by what means (and on what conditions) did one acquire it?

When the property one holds is held as a presumed consequence of earnings, exchange, skill, or thrift, it comes closer to the "rightness" of deserving full protection in a distinctly Lockeian sense. Then indeed it is one's *own*, in evident contrast with what one holds unearned and at public sufferance. The latter, not easily defended on the basis of Locke's labor theory of (property) value, is less rightful in its entitlements. At least this point of view is evident in older cases of constitutional law—and now it has emerged once again. It ac-

67. *Id.* at 2918. (Rehnquist, J., concurring).
68. *See, e.g.*, Brown v. Louisiana, 383 U.S. 131 (1966) (anteroom of public library subject to first amendment use for nondisruptive protest of alleged library policy).

counts in part, I believe, for the difference between *Wyman v. James*[69] and *Marshall v. Barlow's Inc.*,[70] both within this decade of the Supreme Court.

Wyman involved a warrantless search of a welfare recipient's apartment under pain of terminating public assistance if access were refused. *Marshall* involved a warrantless search of business premises under pain of civil fine if access were refused. In neither case was there probable cause to believe that evidence of illegal activity was to be found; in each, however, there was some reason for the government official to request access, as he did. In the first instance, it was to determine whether a welfare-assisted child was being maintained under reasonable conditions; in the second, it was to determine whether the conditions of the business premises were in compliance with standards of safety as prescribed by federal law. In the first, a majority of the Court concluded that the warrantless search could be enforced by terminating assistance if consent under duress were refused; in the second, a majority concluded that it could not be enforced under duress if consent were refused—and that a warrant would have to be secured.

A fourth amendment amenity, some kind of warrant, was constitutionally prerequisite for entry onto business premises. An equivalent amenity was not deemed constitutionally prerequisite for entry into the welfare recipient's apartment. The cases certainly cannot be reconciled on the thought that nonpublic areas of a business establishment are more protected by the fourth amendment than an apartment.[71] Neither, I think, can they be reconciled on the ground that the threat of a civil fine for nonconsent was more coercive in *Barlow* than the threat to terminate assistance in *Wyman*; nor in differing degrees of cause, appropriateness, or general "reasonableness" of the time, place, or manner of the proposed search. Rather, I believe the difference relates to distinctions we have already been noting at some length.[72]

The *Barlow* case involved private property, private enterprise, and warrantless administrative intrusions to determine whether regulations are being violated on those premises. *Wyman* involved warrantless administrative intrusions not to determine whether the welfare recipient was operating "her" property in conformity with the law; it was to determine whether the welfare recipient was living up to the conditions the state imposed as conditions of *its* largess. In the former case, there is the unarticulated assumption that the intrusion

69. 400 U.S. 309 (1971).

70. 436 U.S. 307 (1978).

71. The fourth amendment (as well as the third amendment) is explicit in its application to "houses," and applicable merely by way of sensible implication to other places.

72. In what is surely one of his more trenchant dissents, Justice Marshall put the majority's "explanation" of its analysis in Wyman v. James as follows:

> We are told that there is no search involved in this case; that even if there were a search, it would not be unreasonable; and that even if this were an unreasonable search, a welfare recipient waives her right to object by accepting benefits. I emphatically disagree with all three conclusions.

400 U.S. at 338 (Marshall, J., dissenting).

needs greater justification than in the latter case—the greater justifications demanded to interfere with private property acquired by thrift, exchange, labor, or skill. Never mind that the fourth amendment does not, on its face, express that distinction. Never mind, either, that an apartment may be a more intimate precinct of personal sanctuary than the nonpublic portions of business premises. The antecedents of the fourth amendment are subconsciously drawn upon—and they, quite emphatically, are assumed to express that distinction: privacy within property acquired without aid of the state is a basic civil liberty; privacy with respect to incidents of state aid is not.

Something akin to this distinction is evidently also at work in the Supreme Court's jurisprudence of procedural due process as well. Prior to 1972, the extent to which grievous personal loss was buffered by procedural due process depended most of all on the supposed importance of the threatened loss. Since 1972, however, even "grievous loss" is not subject to any due process requirements of one who cannot locate some vested private property in the thing thus threatened. These cases and their doctrines have been thoroughly reviewed elsewhere.[73] Here, it should be sufficient simply to note that they complete the cycle of emphasis most notable of the seventies: the "old" property (private property) has received additional fortification under the Constitution through its liberty clauses as well as through its commercial clauses; the "new" property (access and status interests in the public sector) has all but succumbed.

V
CONCLUSION

In the second quotation that I chose to preface this brief review, the Supreme Court identified a crucial interdependence "between the personal right to liberty and the personal right in property." It declared further that "[t]he right to enjoy property" is "*no less* than the right to speak or the right to travel;" that, indeed, "rights in property are *basic* civil rights. [emphasis added][74] John Locke would certainly have approved, and the Constitution is, in part, the very enactment of John Locke's *Second Treatise on Civil Government*. A great number of the Court's decisions during the past decade have been concerned to restore that connection—and they have.

At the same time, this Court has tended, perhaps inadvertently, to overfulfill the very thoughtful jurisprudence of John Locke. Ironically, its de-

73. *See* cases and references in Van Alstyne, *Cracks in "The Property:" Adjudicative Due Process in the Administrative State*, 62 CORNELL L. REV. 445 (1977). The California Supreme Court has recently rejected the U.S. Supreme Court's "property" distinction, proceeding on the adequate and independent basis of the California Constitution. The California Supreme Court identifies "freedom from arbitrary adjudicative procedures" as "a substantive element of one's liberty," thus putting it beyond the capacity of government to avoid furnishing any due process whatever through the expedient of defining "property." See People v. Ramirez, 158 Cal. Rptr. 316, 321 (1979).

74. Lynch v. Household Finance Corp., 405 U.S. 538, 552 (1972).

cisions have thus made the connection between private property and personal liberty something of a self-fulfilling prophecy. They have done so by contributing to the certainty that those without personal rights in property have only the weakest and most tenuous claim to personal liberties—whether of speech, of privacy, or of due process of law. The Court's decisions now enable the government to be less generous than it was once required to be in respect to public property and liberty, even as they have also restored to private owners exclusionary prerogatives and entitlements of use that leave those without property of their own dramatically unequal in the possession of their more meager liberties.

Simultaneously, as Professor Grey outlines in his paper,[75] this Court also has been overall less tolerant of sheltering personal liberties offensive to majoritarian morality or conventional virtue, and even here its disposition displays a preference for the values of (middle-class) "property."[76] Commercial speech is newly protected; scatological utterances are newly censurable. Reputation has its compensable claims in renewed possibilities for large libel actions; speech must be correspondingly more carefully weighed, considered, and researched.[77] "Liberty" is less lively, less spacious, and a little less shared than in the decade preceding the seventies—the uses of that liberty are bound more tightly than before to the importance of property as an essential condition of its free exercise. The net effect is not that there is necessarily less constitutionally-protected liberty overall than there was a decade ago, but that that liberty has been reapportioned in ways that confirm the value of private property.

75. Grey, *Eros, Civilization and the Burger Court*, 43:3 LAW & CONTEMP. PROB. 83 (1980).
76. *See* notes 3 and 8, *supra*.
77. *See* note 6, *supra*.

Constitutional Law—Was it Intended That the Fourteenth Amendment Incorporate the Bill of Rights?

The Supreme Court in 1833 established the principle that the Bill of Rights did not apply to the states.[1] Following the Civil War the fourteenth amendment, with its "privileges or immunities" and "due process" clauses, cast doubt on this principle and raised the possibility of applying the Bill of Rights to the states by incorporating them into the amendment.[2]

[illegible] 261 N.C. at 35, 134 S.E.2d at 190.

[1] Barron v. Baltimore, 32 U.S. (7 Pet.) 243 (1833).

[2] U.S. CONST. amend. XIV, § 1, provides: "All persons born or naturalized in the United States, and subject to the jurisdiction thereof, are citizens of the United States and of the State wherein they reside. No State shall make or enforce any law which shall abridge the privileges or immunities of

The Court early held in the *Slaughter House Cases*[3] that the "privileges or immunities" clause prevented the states from abridging those privileges or immunities that a person holds due to his United States citizenship, but not those privileges or immunities he might hold due to state citizenship. Thus, the decision in effect nullified the importance of this clause for purposes of incorporation.[4]

The "due process" clause, however, has not been construed so strictly. Instead, it has been utilized many times, particularly recently, to make certain parts of the Bill of Rights applicable to the states.[5] The majority position of the Court has achieved this result by a selective process of incorporating into the fourteenth amendment only those parts of the Bill of Rights the violation of which would also violate "those fundamental principles of liberty and justice which lie at the base of all our civil and political institutions."[6] Under this process, the Court has clearly incorporated freedom of religion,[7] of speech,[8] of press,[9] and of assembly;[10] protection from unreasonable searches and seizures;[11] requirements of just compensation for property;[12] assistance of counsel;[13] protection from cruel and unusual punishments;[14] and the privilege against self-incrimination.[14a]

A minority position, led by Justice Black, contends that any act in violation of the Bill of Rights also violates the fourteenth amendment.[15] Justice Black bases this conclusion on his belief that the framers of the fourteenth amendment intended that the Bill of

---

citizens of the United States; nor shall any State deprive any person of life, liberty, or property, without due process of law; nor deny to any person within its jurisdiction the equal protection of the laws."

[3] 83 U.S. (16 Wall.) 36 (1873).

[4] CORWIN, THE CONSTITUTION AND WHAT IT MEANS TODAY 187 (10th ed. 1948).

[5] *E.g.*, Gideon v. Wainright, 372 U.S. 335 (1963); Mapp v. Ohio, 367 U.S. 643 (1961).

[6] *In re* Kemmler, 136 U.S. 436, 448 (1890). This basic idea was earlier stated in Murray's Lessee v. Hoboken Land & Improvement Co., 59 U.S. (18 How.) 272, 277 (1856).

[7] Everson v. Board of Educ., 330 U.S. 1 (1947).

[8] Gitlow v. New York, 268 U.S. 652 (1925).

[9] Near v. Minnesota, 283 U.S. 697 (1931).

[10] De Jonge v. Oregon, 299 U.S. 353 (1937).

[11] Mapp v. Ohio, 367 U.S. 643 (1961).

[12] Chicago, B. & Q. R.R. v. Chicago, 166 U.S. 226 (1897).

[13] Gideon v. Wainright, 372 U.S. 335 (1963).

[14] Robinson v. California, 370 U.S. 660 (1962).

[14a] Malloy v. Hogan, 32 U.S.L. WEEK 4507 (U.S. June 15, 1964).

[15] Adamson v. California, 332 U.S. 46, 68 (1947) (dissenting opinion). Dissenting with Justice Black were Justices Douglas, Murphy, and Rutledge.

Rights be applicable to the states.[16] Legal scholars differ on this question of intent.[17] The purposes of this note are, first, to study the events pertinent to the passage of the amendment in order to determine the intent behind its passage, and, second, to discuss the influence which this intent should have on present Supreme Court decisions.

When the new Congress convened after the Civil War, the Constitution had been construed so as to give little protection against state action.[18] *Barron v. Baltimore*[19] had limited the effect of the Bill of Rights to the federal government, and the *Dred Scott*[20] decision had eliminated any possibility of the "privileges and immunities" clause of article IV, section 2 being used to protect the Negro. Since these decisions gave the Negro little protection against the "Black Codes"[21] passed by many southern states, the new Con-

---

16 Justice Black states: "My study of the historical events that culminated in the Fourteenth Amendment ... persuades me that one of the chief objects that the provisions of the Amendment's first section, separately, and as a whole, were intended to accomplish was to make the Bill of Rights applicable to the states." *Id.* at 71.

17 Favoring the intent-to-incorporate theory are: FLACK, THE ADOPTION OF THE FOURTEENTH AMENDMENT (1908) [hereinafter cited as FLACK]; GUTHRIE, THE FOURTEENTH AMENDMENT TO THE CONSTITUTION OF THE UNITED STATES (1898). Opposing this theory are: Fairman, *Does the Fourteenth Amendment Incorporate the Bill of Rights?*, 2 STAN. L. REV. 5 (1949) [hereinafter cited as Fairman]; Graham, *Our "Declaratory" Fourteenth Amendment*, 7 STAN. L. REV. 3 (1954).

Many writers contend that the fourteenth amendment was intended to greatly expand the federal power, but they make no mention of a specific intent to incorporate the Bill of Rights. COLLINS, THE FOURTEENTH AMENDMENT AND THE STATES (1912); CORWIN, THE CONSTITUTION AND WHAT IT MEANS TODAY (10th ed. 1948); 2 WARREN, THE SUPREME COURT IN UNITED STATES HISTORY (1926); Royal, *The Fourteenth Amendment: The Slaughter House Cases*, 4 So. L. REV. 558 (1879).

18 Prior to the Civil War three decisions had severly limited federal control over state action. First, in Corfield v. Coryell, 6 Fed. Cas. 546 (No. 3230) (C.C.E.D. Pa. 1823), Justice Washington adopted a limited construction of the original "privileges and immunities" clause in article IV, section 2, so that each state was required to give only the fundamental rights to citizens of other states. Next, in 1833, the Court in the landmark case of Barron v. Baltimore, 32 U.S. (7 Pet.) 243 (1833), held that the Bill of Rights did not apply to the states. Finally, in Scott v. Sanford, 60 U.S. (19 How.) 393 (1857), the Court again limited the scope of the "privileges and immunities" clause of article IV, section 2, so that what coverage remained after *Corfield* did not apply to protect the Negro.

19 *Supra* note 18.

20 Scott v. Sanford, 60 U.S. (19 How.) 393 (1857).

21 For a general comparison of these laws see Message of the President of the United States to the House of Representatives, *Freedmen*, H.R. Doc. No. 118, 39th Cong., 1st Sess. (1886).

gress immediately sought to pass remedial legislation.[22]

The Civil Rights Act of 1866[23] was the first product. Although it finally passed the Act over President Johnson's veto,[24] Congress itself was uncertain of its constitutional power to pass such a measure.[25] Thus, in order to assure constitutionality, the 39th Congress began work on a constitutional amendment.[26] The job of drafting what was to become the fourteenth amendment was given to the Joint Committee on Reconstruction. The first proposal from the Committee was drafted by Representative Bingham;[27] and, like the Civil Rights Act, the apparent purpose was to protect the Negro from discrimination by the southern states.[28] Up to this time there had been no proposals, bills or discussion which could possibly be construed as an attempt or desire to apply the Bill of Rights to the states via the new amendment. Before this first draft was permanently pigeonholed, however, it gave rise to some ambiguous discussion.

On February 26, 1866, Representative Bingham, in an opening speech to the House, outlined his conception of the problem:[29] although every word of the proposed amendment was already in the Constitution, Congress had heretofore lacked the power of enforcement.[30] He further declared that if Congress had previously had this power and had been able to exercise it, there would have been

---

[22] HICKS & MOWRY, A SHORT HISTORY OF AMERICAN DEMOCRACY 339 (2d ed. 1956).

[23] Ch. 31, 14 Stat. 27 (1866). This bill provided that persons born in the United States under United States jurisdiction were citizens of the United States, and without regard to color, were entitled in every state and territory to the same right to contract, sue, give evidence, and take, hold and convey property, and to the equal benefit of all laws for security of person and property, as was enjoyed by white citizens.

In his opening speech to the Senate, Senator Trumbull clearly expressed that the purpose of the Act was to prevent discrimination in civil rights on account of race and to give all persons equal protection of the laws. CONG. GLOBE, 39th Cong., 1st Sess. 474 (1865-1866).

[24] *Id.* at 1809.

[25] *Id.* at 1151.

[26] *Id.* at 2459.

[27] *Id.* at 806.

[28] This proposal provided: "The Congress shall have power to make all laws which shall be necessary and proper to secure to the citizens of each State all privileges and immunities of citizens in the several States; and to all persons in the several States equal protection in the rights of life, liberty, and property." *Ibid.*

[29] *Id.* at 1033.

[30] *Id.* at 1034. The proposed amendment was nothing more than a reiteration of article IV, section 2, and the fifth amendment. See note 28 *supra.*

no rebellion.[31] Bingham then concluded that the purpose of the new amendment was to give Congress power to enforce "this immortal bill of rights" upon the states.[32] Use of this phrase has given rise to conflicting interpretations as to what was intended by "bill of rights."[33]

After Bingham's opening speech to the House, there were no more references to the "bill of rights" until his closing speech, where he stated that the purpose of the proposed amendment was to arm Congress with the power to enforce the Bill of Rights against the states.[34] He then stated:

> Gentlemen, admit the force of the provisions in the bill of rights, that the citizens of the United States shall be entitled to all the privileges and immunities of citizens of the United States in the several States, and that no person shall be deprived of life, liberty, or property without due process of law....[35]

Shortly after Representative Bingham's closing speech, consideration of this draft was permanently pigeonholed.[36] However, the Joint Committee on Reconstruction immediately framed a new draft which was to become, after the Senate's definition of

---

[31] CONG. GLOBE, *op. cit. supra* note 23, at 1034.

[32] In part, Bingham's words were: "And, sir, it is equally clear by every construction of the Constitution,... that these great provisions of the Constitution, this immortal bill of rights embodied in the Constitution, rested for its execution and enforcement hitherto upon the fidelity of the States." *Ibid.*

[33] Fairman contends that "this immortal bill of rights" is to Bingham a "fine literary phrase not referring precisely to the first eight amendments." He argues that Bingham was referring to "the privileges or immunities" of article IV, section 2, and to the right of life, liberty, and property of the fifth amendment. He reasons further that if Bingham had intended to include the first eight amendments, this would have been inconsistent with his statement that had Congress had and exercised this power there would have been no rebellion, for enforcement of the first amendment would not have prevented secession. Fairman 44. On the other hand, Flack interprets Bingham's language more literally, contending that "it meant nothing less than the conferring upon Congress the power to enforce, in every State of the Union, the Bill of Rights, as found in the first eight Amendments." FLACK 57.

[34] CONG. GLOBE, *op. cit. supra* note 23, at 1088.

[35] *Id.* at 1089. Fairman again believes that Bingham did not mean "the first eight amendments" when he used the phrase "bill of rights," contending that, in this statement, Bingham made it clear from the context that he was referring to the fundamental freedoms of the "due process" and "privileges or immunities" clause. Fairman 34. Flack does not analyze the speech in detail but simply says that Bingham stated that the purpose of the amendment was to give Congress power to enforce the Bill of Rights. FLACK 59.

[36] CONG. GLOBE, *op. cit. supra* note 23, at 1095.

a citizen was added,[37] the final version of the fourteenth amendment. Thaddeus Stevens introduced this new draft into the House on May 8, 1866,[38] stating that he felt the purpose of the amendment was to give Congress power to correct the unjust legislation of the states.[39] He further expressed his belief that equal protection, designed to cure the evil of discrimination, was the dominant purpose of section 1.[40] Stevens reasoned that while the Civil Rights Bill secured the same protection, an amendment would prevent repeal of the protection by a simple majority of Congress.[41]

During the last day of the House debate, Representative Bingham added his reasons for giving Congress power to enforce the Constitution against the states,[42] stating: "Contrary to the express letter of your Constitution, cruel and unusual punishments have been inflicted under state laws within the Union upon your citizens . . . ."[43]

After passage of the amendment in the House,[44] Senator Howard introduced the proposal into the Senate.[45] His introductory speech furnishes the strongest evidence that Congress intended to incorporate the Bill of Rights into the fourteenth amendment. In defining the privileges and immunities to be covered by the amendment, Senator Howard quoted from *Corfield v. Coryell*,[46] which had defined them as being those privileges and immunities which are in their nature fundamental.[47] In furtherance of this definition, he stated: "To these privileges and immunities . . . should be added the

[37] *Id.* at 2897.
[38] *Id.* at 2459.
[39] *Ibid.*
[40] *Ibid.*
[41] *Ibid.* Fairman utilizes Representative Stevens' speech to substantiate the position that no incorporation was intended, noting that over and over in the discussion, the correlation between section 1 and the Civil Rights Act is mentioned, and that since no one intended for the Civil Rights Act to incorporate the Bill of Rights, no one intended that the amendment do so. Fairman 44.
[42] *Id.* at 2542.
[43] *Ibid.* Flack relies on Bingham's reference to "cruel and unusual punishments" as further evidence that the Bill of Rights was intended to be incorporated. FLACK 79-80. Fairman answers this by contending that Bingham was only arguing in favor of a selective incorporation process by means of the "due process" clause. Fairman 53.
[44] CONG. GLOBE, *op. cit. supra* note 23, at 2545. This was done only after three days debate, the vote being 128 for and 37 against. *Ibid.*
[45] *Id.* at 2765.
[46] 6 Fed. Cas. 546 (No. 3230) (C.C.E.D. Pa. 1823).
[47] *Id.* at 551-52.

personal rights guaranteed and secured by the first eight amendments to the Constitution . . . ."[48] Senator Howard then proceeded to read each of the first eight amendments,[49] stating that there was no power in the Constitution for Congress to enforce them, and that the purpose of the proposed amendment was to give Congress such power.[50]

After passage by the Senate,[51] the amendment was submitted to the states on June 16, 1866,[52] and was adopted two years later.[53] There was practically no discussion in the state legislatures of the conflict that the first eight amendments might have with their present state laws.[54] To this there was one notable exception. In the Massachusetts House the proposed amendment received an unfavorable report from its Committee on Federal Relations.[55] The Committee considered section 1 of the fourteenth amendment to be surplusage, stating that it did not see where this section differed from article IV,

---

[48] CONG. GLOBE, *op. cit. supra* note 23, at 2765.

[49] *Ibid.*

[50] *Id.* at 2766. Flack points out that Howard's interpretation of the amendment was not questioned by anyone, and that since no member of the Committee gave a different interpretation or questioned his statement, his interpretation must be accepted as that of the Committee. FLACK 87. The opposing view agrees that what is said by a member for a reporting committee is ordinarily entitled to very special consideration, "but others may, without challenging those views, have supported the measure for quite inconsistent reasons." Fairman 66. It should also be noted in this context that the minority opposed the amendment for the very reasons that Howard gave in support of it. FLACK 87.

Fairman points out the repetition in incorporating the "due process" clause of the fifth amendment and also restating it in the fourteenth. Fairman 58. It would appear that this contention is somewhat irrelevant. It is true that Congress would be repeating itself by including two "due process" clauses, but this does not explain away Howard's belief that the fourteenth amendment included the Bill of Rights.

[51] CONG. GLOBE, *op. cit. supra* note 23, at 3042. This was done on June 8, 1866, the vote being 33 for, 11 against, with 5 absent. *Ibid.*

[52] FLACK 140.

[53] FLACK 191 n.117.

[54] Fairman 82. Professor Fairman points to several of the state laws which would conflict with the fourteenth amendment as evidence that the states did not intend to incorporate. He notes further that several states (Connecticut, Kansas, and Michigan) did not require that a person charged with "a capital or otherwise infamous crime" be indicted by a grand jury as is required by the fifth amendment. Yet, says Fairman, there was no suggestion by their legislatures that their state law conflicted with the fifth amendment.

Fairman also noted that New Hampshire's Constitution made provision for the support and maintenance of Protestant ministers, yet no question of the first amendment's provision for freedom of religion was discussed by the legislature.

[55] H.R. Doc. No. 149, 1, 25 (Mass. 1867).

section 2, and amendments I, II, V, and VIII.[56] During the period in which the question of ratification was before the state legislatures, there were no statements in the newspapers as to whether the first eight amendments were to be applicable to the states.[57]

Less than a year after the states had adopted the fourteenth amendment, the Supreme Court in *Twitchell v. Pennsylvania*[58] refused to consider whether the fifth and sixth amendments applied to the states. Citing *Barron*, Chief Justice Case spoke for an unanimous court in refusing to take jurisdiction by writ of error, stating that application of the fifth and sixth amendments to the states was "no longer a subject of discussion."[59]

Two years later, in 1871, the question arose in the House as to whether the "privileges or immunities" clause of the fourteenth amendment was intended to incorporate the Bill of Rights.[60] During this debate Representative Bingham read each of the first eight amendments and stated that the "privileges or immunities" clause

---

[56] *Ibid.* Professor Flack states that this Committee report is valuable because it shows that the legislature, in adopting the report, "accepted the statements made in it that the first section was but a reiteration of the guarantees enumerated in the Amendments." FLACK 188.

Professor Fairman points out that the Committee was completely wrong in believing that the Bill of Rights applied to the states, citing *Barron*. Fairman 120. This explanation appears irrelevant for there is no significance in the fact that the Committee was unaware of this decision. What is important is that the Committee thought that the fourteenth amendment included some of the Bill of Rights.

[57] FLACK 153. Flack states that, "it may be inferred that this was recognized to be the logical result by those who thought that the freedom of speech and of the press as well as due process of law, including jury trial, were secured by it." *Id.* at 153-54.

Professor Fairman points out that it may be equally inferred that these persons suggested a "selective" incorporation of certain freedoms expressed in the Bill of Rights. Fairman 81.

[58] 74 U.S. (7 Wall.) 321 (1869). The petitioner had been sentenced to death for murder. In seeking a writ of error it was contended that he had not been indicted by a grand jury, which was in violation of the fifth amendment, and that he had not been informed of the nature and cause of the accusation, which was in violation of the sixth amendment. The fourteenth amendment now guarantees the protection of the fifth amendment's privilege against self-incrimination. Malloy v. Hogan, 32 U.S.L. WEEK 4507 (U.S. June 15, 1964).

[59] 74 U.S. (7 Wall.) at 325. This case is cited as showing that the fourteenth amendment was not intended to incorporate the Bill of Rights. Fairman 132. Part of what was "no longer a subject of discussion" in *Twitchell* is now. See Malloy v. Hogan, *supra* note 58.

[60] CONG. GLOBE, 42d Cong., 1st Sess. 111-18 (1871). The fact that this question was debated within five years after passage is an indication of the conflicting intentions within Congress.

made them an express prohibition upon every state.[61] It would seem that this speech by Bingham is conclusive evidence that he intended the Bill of Rights to be incorporated.[62]

Reviewing the Congressional debate, the state legislative discussion, and the general public response, it can be seen that the evidence in favor of the intent-to-incorporate theory consists of Representative Bingham's speeches in the House, Senator Howard's introductory speech in the Senate, and the Committee Report in the Massachusetts legislature. On the other hand, the evidence opposed to the intent-to-incorporate theory consists of the total lack of newspaper discussion about incorporation, the lack of discussion in the state legislatures (except Massachusetts), and of the Supreme Court decision in *Twitchell.* Note that the evidence in favor of the intent to incorporate theory is found entirely within the congressional debates, while the evidence opposed is found entirely outside of the debates. Thus, the conclusion follows that Congress intended incorporation, while the states and the general public did not.[63] However, the above conclusion raises the additional problem: how could the states blindly ratify an amendment not knowing its actual intent? The post-Civil War atmosphere, which is difficult for us to comprehend today, supplies the answer. It would appear that the framers desired a strong amendment limiting states' rights and including the Bill of Rights.[64] Yet they saw that sufficient support in Congress did not necessarily mean sufficient support by the states.[65]

---

[61] After reading the Bill of Rights, one by one, Bingham said, "These eight articles . . . never were a limitation upon the power of the State, until made so by the Fourteenth Amendment. The words of that Amendment 'no State shall make or enforce any law which shall abridge the privileges or immunities of citizens of the United States' are an express prohibition upon every State." *Id.* at 115.

[62] Thus, Professor Fairman's contention that Bingham was using the term "bill of rights" as a fine literary phrase becomes more difficult to accept. See note 33 *supra.*

[63] 2 WARREN, THE SUPREME COURT IN UNITED STATES HISTORY 539-41 (1926); Green, *The Bill of Rights, The Fourteenth Amendment and the Supreme Court,* 46 MICH. L. REV. 869, 904 (1948); Note, *Purpose and Scope of the Fourteenth Amendment,* 21 So. CAL. L. REV. 47, 53 (1947); Note, *The Fourteenth Amendment Challenged,* 36 GEO. L.J. 398, 410 (1948).

[64] COLLINS, THE FOURTEENTH AMENDMENT AND THE STATES 10 (1912); FLACK 94; GUTHRIE, THE FOURTEENTH AMENDMENT TO THE CONSTITUTION OF THE UNITED STATES 60-61 (1898); *The Fourteenth Amendment Challenged, supra* note 63, at 405; Note, *The Bill of Rights and the Fourteenth Amendment,* 33 IOWA L. REV. 666, 667 (1948).

[65] COLLINS, *op. cit. supra* note 64, at 10; *The Fourteenth Amendment Challenged, supra* note 63, at 405; *The Bill of Rights and the Fourteenth Amendment, supra* note 64, at 667.

Therefore, the framers resorted to broad language that was accepted by the House after only three days of discussion and by the Senate after five days of discussion and that was ratified during the post-Civil War hate-the-South-and-help-the-Negro period.[66] In addition, the attention of the general population and their representatives was focused on punishing the South and finding some way to protect the newly freed Negro from the "Black Codes."[67] This explains why most of the discussion in Congress centered around the effects the new amendment would have on the Negro. Congress and the states no doubt thought that passing the amendment would give Congress power to carry out a program of reconstruction and that use of this power would focus naturally against the southern states.[68] Moreover, ratification was achieved by requiring the southern states to ratify before being re-admitted to the Union.[69]

The conflicting intentions of Congress and of the states raise the constructional problem of whose intent will be given the greater weight.[70] In *Maxwell v. Dow*[71] the Supreme Court stated that in the case of an ambiguous constitutional amendment the Court should not only evaluate Congress's intention but should also look to the ratifying states' intentions. In the case of an ambiguous amendment it would appear that since an amendment has no effect until ratified by the states, it should be given no broader construction than the states intended.[72] Thus, it follows that the fourteenth amendment was not intended to incorporate the Bill of Rights.

But, assuming that the intent-to-incorporate theory might be correct, an additional problem needs clarifying: which particular clause incorporates the Bill of Rights? Either the "privileges or immuni-

---

[66] COLLINS, *op. cit. supra* note 64, at 10-12; 2 WARREN, *op. cit. supra* note 63, at 539-40; *The Fourteenth Amendment Challenged, supra* note 63, at 405; *The Bill of Rights and the Fourteenth Amendment, supra* note 64, at 667.

[67] COLLINS, *op. cit. supra* note 64, at 9; 2 WARREN, *op. cit. supra* note 63, at 540; Corwin, *The Supreme Court and the Fourteenth Amendment*, 7 MICH. L. REV. 643, 645 (1908).

[68] COLLINS, *op. cit. supra* note 64, at 10; FLACK 94.

[69] COLLINS, *op. cit. supra* note 64, at 142; *The Bill of Rights and the Fourteenth Amendment, supra* note 64, at 667.

[70] This problem assumes that "intent" should be considered in interpreting a law. See tenBroek, *Use by The United States Supreme Court of Extrinsic Aids in Constitutional Construction*, 26 CAL. L. REV. 437 (1938), for reasons for rejecting the "intent" theory.

[71] 176 U.S. 581, 602 (1900).

[72] tenBroek, *supra* note 70, at 453; IV Worthington, Letters and Other Writings of James Madison 211 (1884).

ties" clause or the "due process" clause may be relied upon to support the incorporation theory.[73] Three reasons favor incorporation through the "privileges or immunities" clause.

First, all the evidence (the speeches of Bingham and Howard and the Massachusetts Committee Report) in support of the incorporation theory pointed toward incorporation through the "privileges or immunities" clause, not the "due process" clause. Both Howard in his Senate address[74] and the Massachusetts Committee Report[75] stated that the privileges or immunities were those expressed in the first eight amendments. Also, Bingham said in his explanation to the House in 1871 that he intended the "privileges or immunities" clause to include the first eight amendments.[76] No such statements were made about the "due process" clause.

Second, the "due process" clause of the fifth amendment had been recently (1856) and clearly defined in *Murray's Lessee v. Hoboken Land & Improvement Co.*[77] There the Supreme Court held that an act was not due process if it violated "those settled usages and modes of proceeding existing in the common and statute law of England . . . ."[78] This decision supports the natural law construction of the majority of the Court but not the full incorporation theory advocated by Black.

Third, the natural reading of the "privileges or immunities" clause in conjunction with the "citizenship" clause supports the incorporation theory.[79] Thus, incorporation must take place, if at all, through the "privileges or immunities" clause.[80]

Even if the intent-to-incorporate theory is correct, it does not

[73] Justice Black does not take a position on the question. See note 17 *supra*.

[74] CONG. GLOBE, 39th Cong., 1st Sess. 2765 (1865-1866).

[75] H. R. Doc. No. 149, 1, 25 (Mass. 1867).

[76] CONG. GLOBE, *supra* note 60, at 115.

[77] 59 U.S. (18 How.) 272 (1856).

[78] *Id.* at 277.

[79] Justice Black in Adamson v. California, 332 U.S. 76 (1947), agrees with this natural reading and favorably quotes Professor Royal who stated in *The Fourteenth Amendment: The Slaughter-House Cases*, 4 So. L. REV. 558 (1870), "Ninety-nine out of every one hundred educated men, upon reading this section over, would at first say that it forbade a State to make or enforce a law which abridged any privilege or immunity whatever of one who was a citizen of the United States." *Id.* at 563.

[80] GUTHRIE, THE FOURTEENTH AMENDMENT TO THE CONSTITUTION OF THE UNITED STATES 60-61 (1898); *Purpose and Scope of the Fourteenth Amendment, supra* note 63, at 57; *The Bill of Rights and the Fourteenth Amendment, supra* note 64, at 668.

necessarily follow that the Supreme Court should today incorporate the Bill of Rights. Rather, stare decisis and the social pressures to incorporate should be considered.

The social pressures to incorporate have been held to a minimum by the "due process" clause. In order to insure justice, the Supreme Court has not needed to incorporate the Bill of Rights in its entirety.[81] Instead, the Court, relying on the due process clause, need only find that the state action violates "those fundamental principles of liberty and justice which lie at the base of all our civil and political institutions."[82]

This selective process has the advantage of not requiring that all of the first eight amendments be applied against the states.[83] Some of the amendments are no longer as necessary as they once were. For example, the second amendment guaranteeing the right to bear arms is not as important today as it once was. Also, the seventh amendment's twenty dollar maximum limit on certain trials without a jury is outdated due to inflation.

Thus, even if it be assumed that the fourteenth amendment was intended to incorporate the Bill of Rights, respect for stare decisis, plus lack of pressure to overrule past decisions are sufficient reasons to reject Justice Black's incorporation theory.[84]

FRANK H. WALKER, JR.

---

[81] Green, *supra* note 63, at 906; Comment, *The Adamson Case: A Study in Constitutional Technique*, 58 YALE L.J. 268, 287 (1949); *The Bill of Rights and the Fourteenth Amendment*, *supra* note 64, at 675.

[82] Palko v. Connecticut, 302 U.S. 319, 325 (1937).

[83] Green, *supra* note 89, at 906.

[84] *Purpose and Scope of the Fourteenth Amendment*, *supra* note 89, at 47; *A Study in Constitutional Technique*, *supra* note 106, at 268; *The Bill of Rights and the Fourteenth Amendment*, *supra* note 90.

THE NEW "LIBERTY" UNDER THE FOURTEENTH AMENDMENT

THE recent very general acceptance of the view that the constitutionality of the Tennessee Anti-Evolution-Teaching Law would eventually be tested in the United States Supreme Court is a striking commentary upon the progress we have made away from the principles of government believed in by the framers of the Constitution. Those framers of 1787 believed that they should impose few limitations upon the authority of the State Legislatures, except such as were necessary from a National standpoint. Matters of local interest, the relations between a State and its own citizens, were jealously preserved against National interference, protection, or restriction. Clearly, if anything can be said to be purely a local matter and of no National concern, it must be the relation of the State to subjects to be taught in its schools. Certainly, if anything has no need of National protection, it is the relation between a State and its own pupils. Yet owing to the existence of the Due Process Clause of the Fourteenth Amendment, and to the constantly expanding interpretation which the Court has given to the language of that Clause, the general public has now acquired the habit of assuming that practically every new State statute is to be submitted to final test before that Court.

In 1858, sixty-seven years ago, Samuel Ames, Chief Justice of the Supreme Court of Rhode Island, said in an opinion: "Surely, if any clause in the Constitution has a definite meaning, which should exclude all vagaries which would render Courts the tyrants of the Constitution, this clause [the Due Process Clause], embodying, as it does, with improvements, the precious fruits of our English liberty, can claim to have, both from its history and long received interpretation. It is no vague declaration concerning the rights of property, which can be made to mean anything and everything." [1] The years ensuing since 1858, however, have made it plain that the Due Process Clause has a

[1] State *v.* Keeran, 5 R. I. 497, 505 (1858).

very far from "definite meaning"; and the United States Supreme Court, in its opinion in a recent case, *New York* v. *Gitlow*,[2] decided on June 8, 1925, has expanded the meaning of one word of that Clause, in a manner which is likely to have important consequences, the extent of which has received little attention as yet.

This *Gitlow* case involved the constitutionality of the Criminal Anarchy Law of New York of 1902 and 1909. In its decision sustaining the statute, the Court said, through Judge Sanford: "For present purposes, we may and do assume that freedom of speech and of the press — which are protected by the First Amendment from abridgment by Congress — are among the fundamental personal rights and 'liberties' protected by the due process clause of the Fourteenth Amendment from impairment by the States." This was the first time that the Court had ever assumed that the word "liberty," in "life, liberty or property," included within its meaning the right of free speech. So far from ever having held this doctrine, the Court, in 1907, had expressly declined to rule on the point (although Judge Harlan in a dissenting opinion had specifically held that "liberty" included the right of free speech); and, in 1922, only three years prior to the *Gitlow* case, the Court had, through Judge Pitney, expressly stated that: "Neither the Fourteenth Amendment nor any other provision of the Constitution of the United States imposes upon the States any restriction about 'freedom of speech.'"[3]

This *Gitlow* case, therefore, affords an illuminating example of the manner in which our constitutional law grows; and it is not the only instance in which early dissenting opinions have quietly become, at a later date, the opinion of the Court, without the direct overruling of previous majority decisions. No one who read Judge Sanford's opinion would imagine that, for over fifty years, counsel had, time and again, attempted to get the Court to hold that rights similar to the right of freedom of speech were protected by the Fourteenth Amendment against infringement by State legislation, and that in every instance the Court had

---

[2] 268 U. S. 652 (1925).

[3] See Prudential Ins. Co. *v.* Cheek, 259 U. S. 530, 538, 543 (1922); Patterson *v.* Colorado, 205 U. S. 454 (1907).

declined so to hold. Yet, in this *Gitlow* case, without even mentioning these previous cases, the Court assumes, without argument, that this right of free speech is so protected by the Fourteenth Amendment. Thus, by one short sentence, rights, the protection of which have hitherto been supposed to be within the scope of the State Courts alone, are now brought within the scope of Federal protection and of the United States Supreme Court.

The history of the attempt to secure Federal guarantee and protection of rights arising simply under State Constitutions and State laws has been a long one; and this most recent development in its course may well awaken serious thoughts as to whether there is not danger now that the " liberty " of the States is being unduly sacrificed to this new conception of the " liberty " of the individual.

When the Constitution went before the people for ratification in 1787, the demand at once arose that the people should be protected against violations by Congress of the rights which the peoples of the States had regarded as fundamental, and which, from 1776 to 1787, they had guaranteed by their own State Bills of Rights. In response to this demand, Congress proposed the first Ten Amendments which prohibited Congress and the Federal Government from violating certain defined rights of the people.

The original Constitution, as drafted, was not intended to regulate or restrain the relations of the States to their own peoples, and contained no such restraints, except (as Chief Justice Marshall said, later) " on subjects intrusted to the General Government, or in which the people of all the States feel an interest." [4] And there had been no demand from the States that it should be amended so as to impose further restrictions on the States. Accordingly, the Ten Amendments, as adopted by Congress and submitted to the States, contained no such restrictions. That this preservation of State powers was deliberate and expressly intended is made very clear by the history of the progress of these Amendments through the First Congress.[5]

---

[4] Barron *v.* Baltimore, 7 Pet. (U. S.) 243 (1833).

[5] ANN. CONG., 1st Cong., 1st Sess., in the House, June 8, July 21, 28, Aug. 13, 17, 20, Sept. 10, 24; in the Senate, Sept. 8, 9, 25, 1789; SENATE JOURNAL,

When James Madison, on June 8, 1789, introduced the draft made by him of proposed Amendments, he included the following: "No State shall violate the equal rights of conscience, or the freedom of the press, or the trial by jury in criminal cases." He argued, in its behalf, that: "It is proper that every Government shall be disarmed of powers which trench upon these particular rights. . . . I cannot see any reason against obtaining even a double security on those points . . . because it must be admitted, on all hands, that the State Governments are as liable to attack these invaluable privileges as the General Government is, and therefore ought to be as cautiously guarded against." The Select Committee of one Representative from each State, to which was referred Madison's draft, reported an Amendment providing that: "No State shall infringe the equal rights of conscience, nor the freedom of speech, or of the press, nor of the right of trial by jury in criminal cases," the Committee thus adding to Madison's draft the words "freedom of speech." This Amendment was opposed, in debate in the House, by Thomas Tucker of South Carolina, who said: "It will be much better, I apprehend, to leave the State Governments to themselves, and not interfere with them more than we already do, and that is thought by many to be too much." Madison again supported it, saying that he "conceived this to be the most valuable Amendment in the whole lot. If there were any reason to restrain the Government of the United States from infringing these essential rights, it was equally necessary that they should be secured against the State Governments. He thought that if they provided against the one, it was as necessary to provide against the other."[6] On motion of Livermore of New Hampshire, this Amendment was re-phrased so as to read: "The equal rights of conscience, the freedom of speech or of the press, and the right of trial by jury in criminal cases, shall not be infringed

---

Sept. 2–13, 1789. See also Report of the Select Committee, July 28, 1789, not printed in the *Annals of Congress*, but published in *Gazette of the United States*, Aug. 1, 1789; *New York Daily Advertiser*, July 29, 1789.

[6] That there was some public sentiment for restricting the powers of the State Legislatures as proposed by Madison is seen from articles in the *New York Daily Advertiser*, July 3, 1789, and *Pennsylvania Packet*, Aug. 29, 1789, quoted by Charles Warren, "New Light on the History of the Federal Judiciary Act of 1789," 37 HARV. L. REV. 49, 121.

by any State." In this form, the Amendment was passed by the House. When the seventeen House Amendments went over to the Senate, that body struck out this particular one restricting the powers of the States; and the House later concurred with the Senate's action.

By its express action, therefore, Congress, in 1789, declined to recommend further restraints on State powers in its Ten Constitutional Amendments. Apparently, however, lawyers soon forgot that the people had thus deliberately refused to restrict the States; and attempts soon began to be made by the Bar to challenge the validity of State legislation, on the ground that it violated the provisions of these Ten Amendments. As early as 1833, however, Chief Justice Marshall, in one of his leading opinions, held with conclusive force that: "These Amendments contain no expression indicating an intention to apply them to the State governments. This Court cannot so apply them; " and that they were "intended solely as a limitation on the exercise of power by the Government of the United States" and "not applicable to the legislation of the States." And he sagaciously remarked that:

> "Had Congress engaged in the extraordinary occupation of improving the Constitution of the several States by affording the people additional protection from the exercise of power by their own governments in matters which concerned themselves alone, they would have declared this purpose in plain and intelligible language." [7]

It might have been supposed that this explicit decision would have settled the point; but fourteen years later, in 1847, the Court felt obliged, through Judge Daniel, to reiterate that the first eight Amendments were "exclusively restrictions upon federal power, intended to prevent interference with the rights of the States, and their citizens . . . such indeed is the only rational and intelligible interpretation . . . since it is neither probable nor credible that the States should have anxiously insisted to ingraft upon the federal constitution restrictions upon their own authority." And in 1857, in another masterly opinion by Judge Daniel, the Court again reasserted the point, stating that Marshall's reasoning had been "so full, so unanswerable" that the

[7] Barron *v.* Baltimore, *supra*, note 4.

doctrine could not be shaken and must be "a guide to the future." [8]

Apparently, the Bar was not even then discouraged from attempting to overturn Marshall's decision; for the point was again raised in a Pennsylvania case, in 1869, on which occasion, Chief Justice Chase said that it was "no longer subject of discussion." It was raised again in 1876, when Chief Justice Waite said: "It is now too late to question the correctness of this construction." [9] In spite of this emphatic language, counsel for defendants, whether by reason of ignorance, incorrigible optimism, or desire for delay, continued to urge (chiefly in murder and other criminal cases), that the Federal Bill of Rights applied to State legislation. In at least twenty cases between 1877 and 1907, the Court was required to rule upon this point and to reaffirm Marshall's decision of 1833, in opinions in which it asserted that the doctrine had been "held over and over again," "elementary," "well established," "so frequently held, as not to warrant the citation of many authorities." [10]

Parallel with this attempt to induce the Federal Courts to pass on questions of conflict of State legislation with the first eight Amendments to the Federal Constitution, attempts were made, as early as 1869, to attack State legislation dealing with individual rights, on the ground that such legislation violated the then-recent Fourteenth Amendment. It was contended that rights arising under State Constitutions and State laws were

---

[8] Fox *v.* Ohio, 5 How. (U. S.) 410, 434 (1847); Smith *v.* Maryland, 18 How. (U. S.) 71 (1855); Withers *v.* Buckley, 20 How. (U. S.) 84 (1857). Similar decisions were made by State Courts; see Livingston *v.* New York, 8 Wend. (N. Y.) 85, 100 (1831); Murphy *v.* People, 2 Cow. (N. Y.) 815 (1824); Colt *v.* Eves, 12 Conn. 243 (1837); Reed *v.* Rice, 2 J. J. Marsh. (Ky.) 44 (1829); Lincoln *v.* Smith, 27 Vt. 328 (1855).

[9] Twitchell *v.* Pennsylvania, 7 Wall. (U. S.) 321, 325 (1868); United States *v.* Cruikshank, 92 U. S. 542, 552 (1875). See also Pervear *v.* Massachusetts, 5 Wall. (U. S.) 475 (1867); Edwards *v.* Elliott, 20 Wall. (U. S.) 557 (1874).

[10] Pearson *v.* Yewdall, 95 U. S. 294 (1877); Capital City Dairy Co. *v.* Ohio, 183 U. S. 238 (1902); Ohio *v.* Dollison, 194 U. S. 445 (1904); Jack *v.* Kansas, 199 U. S. 372 (1905); Barrington *v.* Missouri, 205 U. S. 483 (1907). See also Spies *v.* Illinois, 123 U. S. 131 (1887); *In re* Sawyer, 124 U. S. 200 (1888); Eilenbecker *v.* Plymouth County, 134 U. S. 31 (1890); Davis *v.* Texas, 139 U. S. 651 (1891); McElvaine *v.* Brush, 142 U. S. 155 (1891); Thorington *v.* Montgomery, 147 U. S. 490 (1893); Miller *v.* Texas, 153 U. S. 535 (1894); Brown *v.* New Jersey, 175 U. S. 172 (1899).

"privileges and immunities of citizens of the United States," which under Section 1 of the Fourteenth Amendment, the States were forbidden to abridge by any law. This was the contention that was denied by the Court in the famous *Slaughter House Cases*[11] in 1873, when Judge Miller, speaking for the majority of the Court, held that the Fourteenth Amendment did not apply to "privileges and immunities" derived from the States, or to the civil rights "which belong to citizens of the States as such." In opposition to this decision, however, Judges Field, Bradley, and Swayne (with whom Chief Justice Chase concurred) delivered very vigorous dissenting opinions, in which the ground was taken that "the privileges and immunities designated are those which of right belong to the citizens of all free governments" (as Judge Field said); or that they were all rights to life, liberty, property, and pursuit of happiness, all "fundamental rights" (as Judges Bradley and Swayne said).[12] In many later cases, Judges Field, Bradley, and Swayne continued to express their strong dissenting views as to the scope of the term "privileges and immunities of citizens of the United States," and in these views they were later joined by Judge Harlan. And while the Court itself continued unshaken in its adherence to Judge Miller's decision, the strength of the minority opinions evidently encouraged the Bar of the country, on every possible occasion, to urge the Court to sustain its Federal jurisdiction. The Court was asked to hold that all kinds of civil rights, derived from the States alone, were entitled

[11] 16 Wall. (U. S.) 36 (1873).

[12] See especially the explanation of their position by Judges Bradley and Field in their concurring opinions in Bartemeyer *v.* Iowa, 18 Wall. (U. S.) 129 (1873). And see also concurring opinions of Judges Bradley and Field in Butchers' Union etc. Co. *v.* Crescent City etc. Co., 111 U. S. 746 (1884).; Judge Bradley stated that his view was that "privileges and immunities of citizens of the United States" included all "those fundamental privileges and immunities which belong essentially to the citizens of every free government." The definition which Judge Field finally adopted was stated by him in O'Neil *v.* Vermont, 144 U. S. 323 (1892), as follows: "After much reflection I think the definition given at one time before this court by a distinguished advocate — Mr. John Randolph Tucker, of Virginia — is correct, that the privileges and immunities of citizens of the United States are such as have their recognition in or guaranty from the Constitution of the United States." Spies *v.* Illinois, 123 U. S. 131, 150.

Judge Woods, sitting in the Circuit Court in Alabama in 1871, had held that freedom of speech was a privilege and immunity of a citizen of the United States guaranteed by the Fourteenth Amendment. United States *v.* Hall, Fed. Cas. No. 15, 282 (C. C. D. Ala., 1871).

to Federal protection under that Amendment, as being privileges and immunities of United States citizens, — the right of suffrage, the right of peaceful assembly, the right to bear arms, the right of freedom from unreasonable search and seizure, the right of impartial and speedy trial, the right against cruel and unusual punishment, the right against compulsory self-incrimination, the right to hold intoxicating liquors for personal use.[13] In each of these cases, and in many others between 1875 and 1925, the Court refused to construe the Fourteenth Amendment as providing Federal protection to such rights.[14]

Undiscouraged by the failure of these two lines of attack on the constitutionality of State legislation, the Bar attempted a third method of obtaining Federal protection for individual rights. In 1887, in the Chicago Anarchists Case, *Spies* v. *Illinois*,[15] Roger A. Pryor, John Randolph Tucker, and Benjamin R. Butler contended that, although it might be true that such ordinary civil rights as the right to pursue a trade uncontrolled by State legislation granting a monopoly (which was the right involved in the *Slaughter House Cases*) were not "privileges and immunities of citizens of the United States," nevertheless, all those rights which were contained in the first Eight Amendments must, of necessity, be such privileges and immunities, and must, as such, be protected against State legislation by the Fourteenth Amendment. This was a new point; but the Court declined to pass upon it, as it held that it was not set up in the record in the State Court.[16] In 1891, in a case involving the electrocution law of New York, *McElvaine* v. *Brush*,[17] the Court rather summarily

[13] Minor *v.* Happersett, 21 Wall. (U. S.) 162 (1874); United States *v.* Cruikshank, 92 U. S. 542 (1875); Presser *v.* Illinois, 116 U. S. 252 (1886); Spies *v.* Illinois, 123 U. S. 131 (1887); *In re* Kemmler, 136 U. S. 436 (1890); Twining *v.* New Jersey, 211 U. S. 78 (1908); Crane *v.* Campbell, 245 U. S. 304 (1917). See also Duncan *v.* Missouri, 152 U. S. 377 (1894).

[14] Prudential Ins. Co. *v.* Cheek, 259 U. S. 530, 539 (1922), *per* Pitney, J.: "As this court more than once has pointed out, the privileges or immunities of citizens protected by the Fourteenth Amendment against abridgment by state laws are not those fundamental privileges and immunities inherent in *state* citizenship, but only those which owe their existence to the Federal Government, its national character, its constitution, or its laws."

[15] 123 U. S. 131 (1887).

[16] See William H. Dunbar, "The Anarchists' Case before the Supreme Court of the United States," 1 HARV. L. REV. 307.

[17] 142 U. S. 155 (1891).

disposed of the contention that "so far as those Amendments secure the fundamental rights of the individual, they make them his privileges and immunities as a citizen of the United States," by saying that a previous case had been decisive of this point. In 1900, however, in *Maxwell* v. *Dow,*[18] the Court, through Judge Peckham, considered in detail the contention raised by counsel, and specifically held that neither the Fourth, Fifth, nor Sixth Amendment granted rights which were "privileges and immunities of citizens of the United States." [19]

This decision seemed to be a final block to all attempts to secure Federal protection to ordinary civil rights of the individual, through the Privileges and Immunities Clause of the Fourteenth Amendment.

Meanwhile, however, skilful counsel had attempted to find another method of securing Federal protection to such rights, through another clause of the same Amendment — the Due Process Clause. The Bar began to contend that the words "liberty" and "property" which the States were forbidden to deprive a person of, "without due process of law," might be construed so as to include within their scope all civil rights pertaining to the individual. The word "liberty" seemed an especially convenient vehicle into which to pack all kinds of rights.

In determining the meaning of the word "liberty," it should be borne in mind that the Supreme Court has more than once said that the Due Process Clause in the Fourteenth Amendment has the same scope as the similar Clause in the Fifth Amendment.[20] The Court has, moreover, stated that the Fourteenth Amendment "conferred no new and additional rights, but only

---

[18] 176 U. S. 581 (1900).

[19] See also Twining *v.* New Jersey, 211 U. S. 78 (1908), *per* Moody, J.

[20] Slaughter House Cases, 16 Wall. (U. S.) 36 (1873), *per* Miller, J.; French *v.* Barber Asphalt Paving Co., 181 U. S. 324, 329 (1901), *per* Shiras, J.; and Hibben *v.* Smith, 191 U. S. 310, 325 (1903), *per* Peckham, J.: "The Fourteenth Amendment, it has been held, legitimately operates to extend to the citizens and residents of the States the same protection against arbitrary state legislation, affecting life, liberty, and property, as is offered by the Fifth Amendment against similar legislation by Congress." *Cf.*, however, Holmes, J., in Carroll *v.* Greenwich Ins. Co., 199 U. S. 401 (1905), and Shiras, J., in Wight *v.* Davidson, 181 U. S. 371 (1901), for qualifications of the general doctrine. And see, *contra,* E. Parmelee Prentice, "Congress, and the Regulation of Corporations," 19 HARV. L. REV. 168, 179–188.

extended the protection of the Federal Constitution over rights of life, liberty, and property *that previously existed under all state constitutions*." [21] (Italics ours.) If, therefore, the meaning of the word "liberty" in the Fifth Amendment adopted by Congress in 1789, and in the early State Constitution be ascertained, it should follow that that was the "liberty" which the Fourteenth Amendment protected against State encroachment.

The phrase, "life, liberty or property without due process of law" came to us from the English common law; and there seems to be little question that, under the common law, the word "liberty" meant simply "liberty of the person," or, in other words, "the right to have one's person free from physical restraint." It did not include all a person's civil rights. It was not, in any way, the equivalent of "privileges and immunities." [22] When the American States embodied Bills of Rights in their early Constitutions, from 1780 to 1787, substantially every State inserted a provision that no person should be deprived of his life, liberty or property "without due process of law," or except "by the law of the land." There is no intimation in legal or historical documents of those days that this phrase in the Bills of Rights in those early State Constitutions meant anything more than it meant at common law — in other words, the "liberty," so referred to, meant "freedom from physical restraint of the person." [23]

It is unquestionable that when the First Congress adopted the Fifth Amendment and inserted the Due Process Clause, they took it directly from the then existing State Constitutions, and they took it with the meaning it then bore. And there is convincing evidence that "liberty" in the Fifth Amendment was not intended to include civil rights like the right of free speech. For those rights were expressly protected against violation by Con-

---

[21] Mobile & Ohio R. R. *v.* Tennessee, 153 U. S. 486, 506 (1894).

[22] See especially Charles G. Shattuck, "The True Meaning of the Term 'Liberty' in those Clauses in the Federal and State Constitutions which Protect 'Life, Liberty, and Property,'" 4 HARV. L. REV. 365.

[23] See the Pennsylvania *Habeas Corpus* Act of Feb. 18, 1785, c. 621, which contained the following recital: "Whereas personal liberty is a principal blessing derived from free constitutions of government, and certain methods of proceeding should be prescribed so that all wrongful restraints thereof may be easily and speedily redressed."

gress in the First Amendment, which provided that "Congress shall make no laws . . . abridging the freedom of speech." If "liberty" included the right of free speech, then the Due Process Clause of the Fifth Amendment must be construed as if it read: "No person shall be deprived of . . . freedom of speech . . . without due process of law." It is hardly conceivable that the framers of that Amendment, having already provided in the First Amendment an *absolute prohibition* on Congress to take away certain rights, would in the Fifth Amendment, declare or imply that Congress *might* take away the same rights by due process of law. Equally unlikely is it, that the rights of life, liberty or property which might be taken by due process should include rights which prior provisions of the Amendments absolutely forbade Congress or the Federal Government to take away under any circumstances. Hence, the word "liberty" clearly meaning, in 1789, only "freedom from physical restraint of the person," the question then arises: How was it construed by the Courts, between 1789 and 1868 (the date of the Fourteenth Amendment)? As is well known, the Due Process Clause was considered by the United States Supreme Court, during those years, in only two cases, in neither of which was the word "liberty" defined.[24] In the State Courts, during the same years, there were a number of decisions construing this Clause in the State Constitutions; but most of the decisions were concerned with interpreting the words "due process," and more especially with the question whether the methods of enforcement of the statute involved constituted "due process." Gradually, however, a class of cases arose in which the Court was forced to consider the phrases, "due process" and "law of the land," *not* as restrictions upon the power of the Legislature in the enactment of procedure merely, but from their character as restrictions upon the power of legislation in general.[25] And, in connection with this class of statutes involving substantive law rather than procedure, the State Courts found themselves obliged to construe the meaning of the words "deprive," "property," and "liberty," as well as

[24] Bank of Columbia *v.* Okely, 4 Wheat. (U. S.) 235, 244 (1819), *per* Johnson, J.; Murray *v.* Hoboken Land & Improvement Co., 18 How. (U. S.) 272 (1855), *per* Curtis, J.

[25] Edward S. Corwin, "The Doctrine of Due Process of Law before the Civil War," 24 HARV. L. REV. 366.

the meaning of the "due process" by which the Legislature might affect property and liberty.

In the first place, it should be noted that there were some State Courts which regarded the Due Process Clause as having no relation whatever to legislation on substantive matters, and as applicable only to procedure in criminal cases. They pointed out that in all the Bills of Rights, the Due Process Clause was combined solely with clauses relating to criminal prosecutions.[26] Chief Justice Ames said in Rhode Island: "We are pressed by this inference from it, that the constitution . . . must certainly have designed to inhibit the legislature from regulating the vendibility of property in the state, by prohibiting its sale in certain modes and for certain purposes, deemed to be injurious to the health, morals, and general well-being of the community. . . . This article . . . admits of no such vague and general application. With us, it is the constitutional shield of *one accused of crime* against the sovereign many who are prosecuting him, and not a sword to cut down the power of the many, legislatively expressed, to declare what shall constitute a crime, when in future done by any or all." It could not, he said, "be set up in avoidance of every act of the legislature calculated consequentially to impair the value of property."

Even in those State Courts which extended the Due Process Clause to legislation on substantive matters, the words "property" and "liberty" were given a restricted scope. Most of the cases involved rights of property; and with reference to property, the Courts laid the chief stress on determining how far a State Legislature could go without being held to "deprive" a person of his property. Many State laws were upheld on the ground that they did not so "deprive," being merely a valid exercise of the State's police power or power to impose reasonable restraints for the public health and welfare.[27] Thus, laws were upheld regu-

[26] State *v.* Keeran, 5 R. I. 497, 505–507 (1858). Chief Justice Ames complained about the number of cases then in the Courts raising constitutional question: "There is hardly any act of ordinary legislation, passed to meet the new and constantly changing emergencies of society, that is not made to raise a plentiful crop of constitutional questions; so that a class of questions of the gravest and most important character have been thus brought into jest and ridicule." See also Lincoln *v.* Smith, 27 Vt. 328, 341 (1855).

[27] These laws, as stated by Judge Storrs, in 1856, in State *v.* Wheeler, 25

lating sale of anthracite coal by weight; the weight and price of bread; prohibiting open restaurants after ten P.M.; playing music, and entry of females, in saloons after midnight; forbidding store-keeping on Sunday; licensing lawyers; licensing bowling alleys, and similar legislation.[28]

The chief class of cases in which the application of the Due Process Clause to rights of property was considered, were those involving liquor legislation. Between 1840 and 1860, statutes of Massachusetts, New Hampshire, Connecticut, Vermont, Rhode Island, and Michigan, and other States, were held constitutional as not depriving a person of property without due process of law;[29] and only one Court — the Court of Appeals of New York — held a State liquor law invalid under the Due Process Clause.[30] In New York also, there was one case in which a statute fixing the amount which a person drafted in the war might pay for a substitute was held invalid, as depriving him of property without due process.[31]

The term "liberty" in the Due Process Clause was construed by the State Courts in very few cases. Practically in only one case prior to the Fourteenth Amendment is there any trace of a decision that "liberty" meant anything more than freedom from physical restraint; and the Supreme Court of Vermont, in 1855, expressed what was undoubtedly the conception of the meaning of that word held by Courts and lawyers prior to 1868: "The

---

Conn. 290, 298, were "based on the power possessed by every sovereign state, to provide by law, as it shall deem fit, for the health, morals, peace and general welfare of the state." And as said by Judge Baldwin, in *Ex parte* Andrews, 18 Cal. 678, 682 (1861): "Unquestionably, under our system, the Legislature has power to repress whatever is hurtful to the general good. This is a great purpose and end of all government. It is just as true that in our theory the Legislature must generally be the exclusive judge of what is or is not hurtful."

[28] Stokes *v.* New York, 14 Wend. (N. Y.) 87 (1835); Mobile *v.* Yuille, 3 Ala. 137 (1841); State *v.* Freeman, 38 N. H. 426 (1859); *Ex parte* Smith, 38 Cal. 702 (1869); *Ex parte* Andrews, 18 Cal. 678 (1861); Cousins *v.* State, 50 Ala. 113 (1873); State *v.* Noyes, 30 N. H. 279 (1855).

[29] Commonwealth *v.* Blackington, 24 Pick. (Mass.) 352 (1837); Fisher *v.* McGirr, 1 Gray (Mass.) 1 (1854); Commonwealth *v.* Clapp, 5 Gray (Mass.) 97 (1855); State *v.* Clark, 28 N. H. 176 (1854); State *v.* Wheeler, 25 Conn. 290 (1856); Lincoln *v.* Smith, 27 Vt. 328 (1855); State *v.* Keeran, 5 R. I. 492 (1858); State *v.* Paul, 5 R. I. 185 (1858); People *v.* Gallagher, 4 Mich. 244 (1856).

[30] Wynehamer *v.* People, 13 N. Y. 378 (1856).

[31] Powers *v.* Shepard, 45 Barb. (N. Y.) 524 (1865).

liberty, spoken of in our bill of rights, is the liberty of the person of every subject."[32] Statutes involving restraints of the person were upheld as not depriving a person of his liberty without due process of law as follows: a statute providing for committal to an almshouse for abandonment of a minor child; a statute providing for enforced guardianship of habitual drunkards; compulsory military enrollment; a poorhouse law.[33] In a case in Pennsylvania, the Federal Conscription Act of March 3, 1863, was held invalid as depriving a person of his liberty without due process of law.[34]

In only one case does the term "liberty" seem to have been given a wider scope, prior to 1868. Judge Perkins of the Indiana Supreme Court, in a *habeas corpus* proceeding involving a liquor statute, held, in 1855, that the State prohibition law was invalid as an invasion of liberty, saying: [35]

> "We lay down this proposition, then, as applicable to the present case; that the right of liberty and pursuing happiness secured by the constitution, embraces the right, in each *compos mentis* individual, of selecting what he will eat and drink, in short, his beverages, so far as he may be capable of producing them, or they may be within his reach, and that the legislature cannot take away that right by direct enactment. If the constitution does not secure this right to the people, it secures nothing of value. . . . If the people are . . . incompetent to determine anything in relation to their living, and should be placed at

---

[32] Lincoln *v.* Smith, 27 Vt. 328, 361 (1855).

[33] McCarthy *v.* Hinman, 35 Conn. 538 (1869); Devin *v.* Scott, 34 Ind. 67 (1870); Parker *v.* Kaughman, 34 Ga. 136 (1865); Nott's Case, 11 Me. 208 (1834).

[34] Kneedler *v.* Land, 45 Pa. St. 238 (1863).

[35] Herman *v.* State, 8 Ind. 545, 558–563 (1855); reasserted in Beebe *v.* State, 6 Ind. 501 (1855).

In Lunt's Case, 6 Me. 413 (1830), the Court remarked incidentally that the liquor license law there involved was not "an unreasonable restraint upon the liberty of the citizen."

In 1869, after the Fourteenth Amendment, the Supreme Court of California said, as to an ordinance prohibiting music and entrance of females into saloons after midnight, that "in a certain sense it may be said that the ordinance interferes with the enjoyment of life and liberty," but it continued: "This provision of the Constitution is not to be understood as putting life or liberty entirely beyond the reach of the Government, if, from misconduct, the general welfare of the community demands its sacrifice or restraint." *Ex parte* Smith, 38 Cal. 702 (1869).

once in a state of pupilage to a set of government sumptuary officers; eulogies upon the dignity of human nature should cease; and the doctrine of the competency of the people for self-government be declared a deluding rhetorical flourish. . . . This law . . . is based on the principle that a man shall not use at all for enjoyment what his neighbor may abuse, a doctrine that would, if enforced by law in general practice, annihilate society, make eunuchs of all men, or drive them into the cells of the monks, and bring the human race to an end, or continue it under the direction of licensed county agents.

"Such, however, is not the principle upon which the Almighty governs the world."

Such had been the decisions of the State Courts as to due process at the time when the Fourteenth Amendment was ratified, in 1868; and, as before noted, the Supreme Court of the United States has expressly stated that the Amendment "conferred no new and additional rights, but only extended the protection of the Federal Constitution over rights of life, liberty, and property that previously existed under all state constitutions." [36]

For nearly twenty years after 1868, the United States Supreme Court found no occasion to define the term "liberty." In fact, for a number of years, the cases presented for the Court's attention, so far as the Due Process Clause was involved, involved only the determination whether the procedural provisions of the various State statutes concerned did or did not constitute "due process." But in one instance, — in the *Slaughter House Cases,* in 1873 — the meaning of "liberty" under the Fourteenth Amendment was presented for consideration, when the plaintiffs challenged the Louisiana butcher monopoly statute, there involved, as depriving them of liberty and property without due process of law, by its substantive provisions and not by reason of any procedural provisions. Judge Miller, speaking for the Court, did not even notice the contention that the statute involved deprived a person of his "liberty"; and as to "property" he said: "The argument has not been pressed in these cases that the defendant's charter deprives the plaintiffs of their property without due process of law. . . . We are not without judicial interpretation . . . both State and National, of the meaning of this clause. And it is sufficient to say that under no construction of that provision that

[36] Mobile & Ohio R. R. *v.* Tennessee, 153 U. S. 486, 506 (1894).

we have ever seen, . . . can the restraint imposed by the State of Louisiana upon the exercise of their trade by the butchers of New Orleans be held to be a deprivation of property within the meaning of that provision." [37] Two of the dissenting Judges in the *Slaughter House Cases,* however, in their zeal to overthrow the State law, held that it violated not only the Privileges and Immunities Clause of the Fourteenth Amendment, but also the Due Process Clause; and they attempted a definition of "liberty." "In my view," said Judge Bradley, "a law which prohibits a large class of citizens from adopting a lawful employment, or from following a lawful employment previously adopted, does deprive them of liberty as well as property, without due process of law. Their right of choice is a portion of their liberty; their occupation is their property." [38] He thus expanded the definition of "liberty," by adding to mere freedom of restraint of the person, freedom of choice of an occupation. Judge Swayne defined "liberty" as "freedom from all restraints but such as are justly imposed by him;" and this definition has been characterized by William D. Guthrie as "terse and emphatic," although it seems to be a complete reasoning in a circle, the whole question to be decided being: What restraints *are* "justly imposed by law"? [39]

Eleven years later, in 1884, the validity of the Louisiana slaughter house monopoly again arose, in *Butchers' Union, etc. Co.* v. *Crescent City, etc. Co.;* [40] and it was again upheld, this time on the ground that it did not impair the obligation of contract.

---

[37] 16 Wall. (U. S.) at 80.

[38] At p. 122.

[39] GUTHRIE, THE FOURTEENTH ARTICLE OF AMENDMENT TO THE CONSTITUTION, 109 n 1. For adverse comments on Mr. Guthrie's doctrine that "liberty" is equivalent to "freedom in the pursuit of happiness" and includes all a person's civil privileges and immunities, see review in 12 HARV. L. REV. 439.

Three years later, in United States *v.* Cruikshank, 92 U. S. 542, 554 (1875), the Court, through Chief Justice Waite, said that the Due Process Clause of the Fourteenth Amendment "simply furnishes an additional guaranty against any encroachment by the States upon the fundamental rights which belong to every citizen as a member of society." But this did not add anything by way of definition; for the whole question remained for decision: "What are those fundamental rights?"

Chief Justice Waite's statement was repeated by Chief Justice Fuller in *In re* Kemmler, 136 U. S. 436, 448 (1890).

[40] 111 U. S. 746 (1884).

Judges Bradley and Field concurred, but they reiterated their dissenting views expressed in the previous *Slaughter House Cases* (and gained adherents in the new Judges, Harlan and Woods), as to the wide scope of the privileges and immunities protected by the Fourteenth Amendment; and they now took the occasion to expand their definition of "liberty." Judge Bradley said:

> "But if it does not abridge the privileges and immunities of a citizen of the United States to prohibit him from pursuing his chosen calling, and giving to others the exclusive right of pursuing it,—it certainly does deprive him (to a certain extent) of his liberty; for it takes from him the freedom of adopting and following the pursuit which he prefers; which, as already intimated, is a material part of the liberty of the citizen. . . . The right to follow any of the common occupations of life is an inalienable right; it was formulated as such under the phrase 'pursuit of happiness' in the Declaration of Independence. . . . This right is a large ingredient in the civil liberty of the citizens."[41]

And Judge Field agreed again, and spoke of the inalienable right of men to "pursue their happiness, by which is meant the right to pursue any lawful business or vocation, in any manner not inconsistent with the equal rights of others, which may increase their prosperity or develop their faculties, so as to give them their highest enjoyment."[42]

Thus one and the same right, *viz.*, "the right to pursue any lawful business," was termed by these Judges both a "privilege and immunity" of a United States citizen, which under the Fourteenth Amendment, a State was forbidden to abridge at all under any circumstances, and a "liberty" which a State was only forbidden not to deprive a person of, without due process of law.

Four years later, in 1888, Judge Harlan in *Powell* v. *Pennsylvania*,[43] a case involving the constitutionality of the Pennsylvania oleomargarine statute, held that the law was a legitimate exercise of the police power of the State. He then recited the defendant's contention that "enjoyment, upon terms of equality with all others in similar circumstances, of the privilege of pursuing an ordinary calling or trade, and of acquiring, holding and selling property is an essential part of his rights of liberty and property, as guaranteed by the Fourteenth Amendment," and, said Judge

[41] At pp. 765, 762. [42] At p. 757. [43] 127 U. S. 678 (1888).

Harlan: "The Court assents to this general proposition as embodying a sound principle of constitutional law." This statement was a pure dictum. Judge Field, dissenting, stated that the Due Process Clause " has always been supposed to secure every person the essential conditions for the pursuit of happiness and is therefore not to be construed in a narrow or restricted sense." He then proceeded to cite, at length, the two New York cases (*In re Jacobs*,[44] in 1885, involving a statute forbidding cigarmaking in tenement houses, and *People* v. *Marx*,[45] involving an oleomargarine statute) for a broad definition of the term " liberty," which, he said, " meant something more than freedom from physical restraint or imprisonment. It means freedom not merely to go wherever one may choose, but to do such acts as he may judge for his best interests, not inconsistent with the equal rights of others; that is, to follow such pursuits as may be best adapted to his faculties, and which will give him the highest enjoyment." Judge Field failed to notice, however, that these New York decisions were based largely on Judge Bradley's individual opinion in the *Butchers' Co.* case.[46]

It was not until 1897, that the Supreme Court of the United States adopted specifically these dissenting opinions of Judges Bradley and Field, as the opinion of the Court with reference to the meaning of the word "liberty." In *Allgeyer* v. *Louisiana*,[47] Judge Peckham stated that: " The liberty mentioned in that Amendment means, not only the right of the citizen to be free from the mere physical restraint of his person, as by incarceration, but the term is deemed to embrace the right of the citizen to be free in the enjoyment of all his faculties; to be free to use them in all lawful ways; to live and work where he will; to earn his livelihood by any lawful calling; to pursue any livelihood or avocation, and for that purpose to enter into all contracts which may be proper, necessary and essential to his carrying out to a successful conclusion the purposes above mentioned." After citing Judge Bradley's individual opinion in the *Butchers' Co.*

[44] 98 N. Y. 98 (1885).

[45] 99 N. Y. 377, 2 N. E. 29 (1885).

[46] The decision in *In re* Jacobs was also based on a previous New York case, Bertholf *v.* O'Reilly, 74 N. Y. 509 (1878), in which the Court had said the right to liberty includes " the right to exercise his faculties and to follow a lawful avocation for the support of life."

[47] 165 U. S. 578 (1897).

case (together with Judge Harlan's dictum in the *Powell* case), Judge Peckham said: "The foregoing extracts have been made for the purpose of showing that general definitions have been given in regard to the meaning of the word 'liberty' as used in the Amendment." Judge Peckham spoke of Judge Bradley's "concurring opinion" in the *Butchers' Co.* case, but failed to note that Bradley concurred only in the result of the decision, and that his views were at swords' points with those of the majority of the Court. Judge Peckham then continued: "In the privilege of pursuing an ordinary calling or trade and of acquiring, holding and selling property must be embraced the right to make all proper contracts in relation thereto;" and he proceeded to hold the Louisiana statute involved, violative of the Due Process Clause of the Fourteenth Amendment as an infringement of the citizen's liberty of contract. It has been pointed out that the bulk of the language used by Judge Peckham, in defining "liberty," was copied almost *verbatim* from the opinion of the New York Court of Appeals in *In re Jacobs,* twelve years before; and that *In re Jacobs* itself was in turn based chiefly on Judge Bradley's so-called "concurring," but in reality "dissenting," opinion in the *Butchers' Co.* case.[48] Whatever may be pedigree of the *Allgeyer* case definition, it is clear that the Court had departed from the original definition of "liberty" which prevailed in 1789, and which had been the definition adopted by the State Courts prior to 1868. Moreover, it was an unnecessary extension of the word "liberty"; for the right to make all proper contracts might well have been held to be included within the limits of the term "property," as indeed it has been held in many later cases.

Even in this *Allgeyer* case, however, the Court was still far from holding that "liberty" embraced liberty of speech and all the rights contained in the first eight Amendments to the Federal Constitution. Three years went by before the Court again at-

---

[48] See Robert P. Reeder, "The Due Process Clause and 'The Substance of Individual Rights,'" 58 U. of Pa. L. Rev. 191. See also Charles M. Hough, "Due Process of Law Today," 32 Harv. L. Rev. 218; Francis W. Bird, "The Evolution of Due Process of Law," 13 Col. L. Rev. 37.

It is to be noted that *In re* Jacobs was decided in New York in 1885, and Judge Peckham himself became a member of the New York Court of Appeals in 1887.

tempted to define "liberty"; but in 1900, in *Williams* v. *Fears*,[49] through Chief Justice Fuller, it said: "Undoubtedly, the right of locomotion, the right to remove from one place to another, according to inclination is an attribute of personal liberty." This, however, did not add anything; because freedom of locomotion may well be treated as a part of freedom of restraint of the person. In the same year, in *Taylor* v. *Beckham*,[50] the case which involved the Kentucky gubernatorial election, Judge Harlan, in a dissenting opinion, held that the right to hold office was included in the term "liberty"; and he gave the following extraordinarily broad definition, which was not warranted by anything theretofore held by the Court: "In my judgment, the words 'life, liberty or property' in the Fourteenth Amendment should be interpreted as embracing every right that may be brought within judicial cognizance." Such a definition would have included within the rights secured by the Fourteenth Amendment, every single right guaranteed by any Bill of Rights of the Federal or of any State Government.

In 1902, in *Booth* v. *Illinois*,[51] the Court, through Judge Harlan, said that the declarations in the *Allgeyer* case "state in condensed form principles which had been announced in previous cases, and which may be regarded as expressing the deliberate judgment of this Court." Such a statement was erroneous; for the principles of the *Allgeyer* case had not been announced by the Court in previous cases, but only by dissenting Judges and by Judge Harlan himself in a dictum.[52]

In 1905, in *Jacobson* v. *Massachusetts*,[53] a case involving a State compulsory vaccination law, the Court had before it a

---

[49] 179 U. S. 270 (1900). [50] 178 U. S. 548 (1900). [51] 184 U. S. 425 (1902).

[52] In this Booth case, the Court proceeded to dilute very considerably the Allgeyer case doctrine by continuing (at p. 428): "When it is said that the liberty of the citizen includes freedom to use his faculties 'in all lawful ways,' and to earn his living by any 'lawful calling,' the inquiry remains whether the particular calling or the particular way brought in question in a given case is lawful, that is, consistent with such rules of action as have been rightfully prescribed, by the State." This simply amounted to saying that a man is free to pursue a lawful calling, provided the calling is lawful under a law which is lawful — a solemn piece of tautology. In other words, no man could tell whether his calling was lawful until after the Court should have decided whether the statute affecting it was in itself lawful and "rightfully prescribed" rules of action as to it.

[53] 197 U. S. 11 (1905).

statute involving "liberty" in its original sense of restraint of the person. It was claimed by the defendant that the law was "hostile to the inherent right of every free man to care for his own body and health in such way as to him seems best." The Court, through Judge Harlan, held that the "liberty" secured by the Constitution "does not impart an absolute right in each person to be, at all times and in all circumstances, wholly freed from restraint. There are manifold restraints to which every person is necessarily subject for the common good. . . . It is not true, therefore, that the power of the public to guard itself against inimical danger depends in every case involving the control of one's body upon his willingness to submit to reasonable regulations established by the constituted authorities under the sanction of the State, for the purpose of protecting the public collectively against such danger."

In 1908, in *Berea College* v. *Kentucky*,[54] Judge Harlan, in a dissenting opinion, again gave an impetus to an extremely broad definition of "liberty," saying:

> "The capacity to impart instruction to others is given by the Almighty for beneficent purposes and its use may not be forbidden or interfered with by Government — certainly not, unless such instruction is, in its nature, harmful to the public morals or imperils the public safety. The right to impart instruction, harmless in itself or beneficial to those who receive it, is a substantial right of property — especially, where services are rendered for compensation. But even if such right be not strictly a property right, it is, beyond question, part of one's liberty as guaranteed against hostile state action by the Constitution of the United States. . . . If pupils, of whatever race — certainly if they be citizens — choose with the consent of their parents or voluntarily to sit together in a private institution of learning while receiving instruction which is not in its nature harmful or dangerous to the public, no government, whether Federal or state, can legally forbid their coming together, or being together temporarily, for such an innocent purpose. . . . The right to enjoy one's religious belief, unmolested by any human power, is no more sacred nor more fully or distinctly recognized than is the right to impart and receive instruction not harmful to the public. The denial of either right would be an infringement of the liberty inherent in the freedom secured by the fundamental law."[55]

---

[54] 211 U. S. 45 (1908).

[55] At p. 67.

In *Twining* v. *New Jersey*,[56] in 1908, the Court, through Judge Moody, after reaffirming its settled doctrines that the provisions of the Ten Amendments were not rights of citizens of the United States which the Fourteenth Amendment protected against violation by the States, proceeded to say that:

> "It is possible that some of the personal rights safeguarded by the first eight Amendments against National action may also be safeguarded against state action, because a denial of them would be a denial of due process of law. If this is so, it is not because those rights are enumerated in the first eight Amendments, but because they are of such a nature that they are included in the conception of due process of law." [57]

The Court then proceeded to hold that a law removing provisions against a compulsory self-incrimination might be "due process." The Court, however, did not consider the question whether the substantive right not to be compelled to incriminate oneself was not, itself, one of the fundamental rights comprised in the term "liberty," under the Fourteenth Amendment, and in consequence not to be taken away by a State "without due process." Judge Harlan, dissenting, held that the right against self-incrimination was clearly a privilege and immunity of a citizen of the United States, and also that it was "a part of the liberty guaranteed by the Fourteenth Amendment against hostile State action."

In 1911, in *C., B. & Q. R. R.* v. *McGuire*,[58] the Court, through Judge Hughes, emphasized the fact that that portion of "liberty" which consisted in the right of contract was, like the "liberty" to be free from physical restraint, equally subject to restriction by the State, under the police power. "Freedom of contract is a qualified, and not an absolute right. . . . Liberty implies the absence of arbitrary restraint, not immunity from reasonable regulations and prohibitions imposed in the interests of the community." [59]

---

[56] 211 U. S. 78 (1908).

[57] At p. 99.

[58] 219 U. S. 549 (1911).

[59] And see McLean *v.* Arkansas, 211 U. S. 539 (1909); and Middleton *v.* Texas Power & Light Co., 249 U. S. 152, 163 (1919), in which it was held, through Judge Pitney: "What plaintiff has lost, therefore, is only a part of his

In 1915, in *Coppage* v. *Kansas*,[60] the Court said, through Judge Pitney: "Included in the right of personal liberty and the right of private property — partaking of the nature of each — is the right to make contracts for the acquisition of property. . . . If this right be struck down or arbitrarily interfered with, there is a substantial impairment of liberty *in the long-established constitutional sense.*" (Italics ours.) And in *Truax* v. *Raich*,[61] the Court said, through Judge Hughes: "*It requires no argument* to show that the right to work for a living in the common occupation of the community is of the essence of the personal freedom and opportunity that it was the purpose of the [Fourteenth] Amendment to secure." (Italics ours.) Thus, by the year 1915, a definition of "liberty" which was first promulgated by the Court in the year 1897, had become its "long-established constitutional sense" which "requires no argument."[62]

In 1916, in *Butler* v. *Perry*,[63] the Court said, through Judge McReynolds, that: "*That [Fourteenth] Amendment was intended to preserve and protect fundamental rights long recognized under the common law system.*" (Italics ours.) It is difficult to see how this expression can be reconciled with its modern definition of "liberty"; for it is clear that "liberty," as now defined, was never a "fundamental right long recognized under the common law system."[64]

Thus far, however, while the Court had indulged in these general statements about "fundamental rights" guaranteed by

---

liberty to make such a contract as he pleased with a particular employer and to pursue his employment under the rules of law that previously had obtained fixing responsibility upon the employer for any personal injuries the plaintiff might sustain through the negligence of the employer or his agents. But, as has been held so often, the liberty of the citizen does not include among its incidents any vested right to have the rules of law remain unchanged."

[60] 236 U. S. 1 (1915).

[61] 239 U. S. 33 (1915).

[62] See also Smith *v.* Texas, 233 U. S. 630 (1914).

[63] 240 U. S. 328 (1916).

[64] See Crane *v.* Campbell, 245 U. S. 304 (1917), in which the Court, through Judge McReynolds, stated, in upholding an Idaho statute penalizing possession of liquor, that "the right to hold intoxicating liquors for personal use is not one of the fundamental rights of a citizen of the United States which no State may abridge."

In Nicchia *v.* New York, 254 U. S. 228 (1920), a New York dog license statute was held valid, through Judge McReynolds, on the ground that it did not "deprive dog owners of liberty without due process of law."

the Fourteenth Amendment, it had actually only recognized a few rights as comprised in the term "liberty," in addition to freedom from restraint of the person, namely, the following: right of freedom to choose one's occupation, freedom of locomotion from State to State, freedom of contract, and freedom to labor.[65]

In 1923, in *Meyer* v. *Nebraska*,[66] the Court decided that the Nebraska statute forbidding the teaching in school of any language other than English was unconstitutional, and, through Judge McReynolds, it said:

> "While this Court has not attempted to define with exactness the liberty thus guaranteed, the term has received much consideration and some of the included things have been definitely stated. Without doubt, it denotes not merely freedom from bodily restraint but also the right of the individual to contract, to engage in any of the common occupations of life, to acquire useful knowledge, to marry, establish a home and bring up children, to worship God according to the dictates of his own conscience, and generally to enjoy those privileges long recognized at common law as essential to the orderly pursuit of happiness by free men." [67]

But Judge McReynolds went on to hold that: "Plaintiff in error taught this language in school as part of his occupation. His right thus to teach and the right of parents to engage him so to instruct their children, we think, are within the liberty of the Amendment." [68] The actual decision of the case, therefore, apart from the incidental definition of "liberty," went no farther than previous decisions upholding the right of a man to engage in a lawful occupation, without arbitrary or unreasonable restraint by the State.

On June 1, 1925, however, the Court gave a broad interpretation to the meaning of "liberty" in the Due Process Clause.

---

[65] See Wolff Packing Co. *v.* Court of Industrial Relations, 262 U. S. 522, 540 (1923), in which Chief Justice Taft said: "It will be impossible to reconcile such result with the freedom of contract and of labor secured by the Fourteenth Amendment."

[66] 262 U. S. 390 (1923).

[67] At p. 399.

[68] The Court might well have decided all these cases on the ground that they involved "property" rather than "liberty." Freedom to choose an occupation, to contract, and to labor are, in law, rights of property. "Every man has a Property in his own Person," wrote John Locke in his TREATISE ON GOVERNMENT, in 1689.

For in *Pierce* v. *Society of the Sisters of the Holy Names of Jesus and Mary*,[69] involving the Oregon Private-School Law, it said, again through Judge McReynolds:

> " We think it entirely plain that the Act of 1922 unreasonably interferes with the liberty of parents and guardians to direct the upbringing and education of children under their control. . . . The fundamental theory of liberty upon which all governments in this Union repose excludes any general power of the state to standardize its children by forcing them to accept instructions from public teachers only." [70]

Thus, it was held that the word " liberty " included the right of parents to direct the upbringing of their children. But as no parent was involved as a party to the case, and as the only parties were corporations, and as the Court had previously held that a corporation could not claim protection for " liberty " under the Fourteenth Amendment, the Court proceeded to decide the case on the ground that property of the corporations was threatened with restraint and interference " without due process of law."

It was only a week after this *Oregon School Law Case* that the Court decided the *Gitlow* case and again extended the definition of " liberty " by making it include the right of freedom of speech. That this was clearly a new enlargement of " liberty " by purely judicial decision is to be seen from a brief recital of previous attempts to get the Court to decide the point. In 1907, in *Patterson* v. *Colorado*,[71] a judgment of a State Court holding for contempt a newspaper editor on account of publication of articles and cartoons alleged to reflect on the motives and conduct of the State Supreme Court was attacked as a violation of the Due Process Clause of the Federal Constitution, the claim being that the judgment infringed the right of free speech. The Court dismissed the writ of error, and Judge Holmes in his opinion said:

> " We leave undecided the question whether there is to be found in the Fourteenth Amendment a prohibition similar to that in the First. But even if we were to assume that freedom of speech and freedom of the press were protected from abridgment on the part not only of the United States but also of the States, still we should be far from the conclusion that the plaintiff in error would have us reach." [72]

---

[69] 268 U. S. 510 (1925).
[70] At p. 534.
[71] 205 U. S. 454 (1907).
[72] At p. 462.

Judge Harlan, dissenting, stated, however, in adherence to similar views long held by him, that "the First Amendment, although in form prohibitory is to be regarded as having a reflex character and as affirmatively recognizing freedom of speech and freedom of the press as rights belonging to citizens of the United States, that is, those rights as to be deemed attributes of national citizenship of the United States." He reiterated the doctrine which had been absolutely settled to the contrary, seven years before, in *Maxwell* v. *Dow*,[73] that rights granted by the First Amendment were privileges and immunities of citizens of the United States which the Fourteenth Amendment guaranteed against infringement by the States. But Judge Harlan took also a step in advance over any previous decision and opinion of the Court or of any of its Judges; for he continued:

> "I go further and hold that the privileges of free speech and of a free press, belonging to every citizen of the United States constitute essential parts of every man's liberty, and are protected against violation by that clause of the Fourteenth Amendment forbidding a State to deprive any person of his liberty without due process of law. It is, I think, impossible to conceive of liberty, as secured by the Constitution against hostile action, whether by the Nation or by the States, which does not embrace the right to enjoy free speech and the right to have a free press." [74]

Thirteen years passed before anyone attempted to assert that "liberty" included freedom of speech. But in 1920, in *Gilbert* v. *Minnesota*,[75] the statute of Minnesota penalizing interference with a discouragement of enlistment in the military or naval service of the United States was attacked as obnoxious to "the inherent right of free speech." Judge McKenna, in his opinion, passed over the question as to whether the State statute could be attacked on this ground, saying:

> "But without so deciding or considering the freedom asserted as guaranteed or secured either by the Constitution of the United States or by the constitution of the State, we pass immediately to the contention and for the purposes of this case may concede it, that is, concede that the asserted freedom is natural and inherent, but it is not absolute, it is subject to restriction and limitation." [76]

---

[73] 176 U. S. 581 (1900).
[74] 205 U. S. at 464.
[75] 254 U. S. 325 (1920).
[76] At p. 332.

He then proceeded to hold that the State statute was a lawful limitation. Judge Brandeis, dissenting, held that the right in question was one of the privileges and immunities of a citizen of the United States and therefore guaranteed, by the Fourteenth Amendment, against State action, but he continued:

" As the Minnesota statute is in my opinion invalid because it interferes with federal functions and with the right of a citizen of the United States to discuss them, I see no occasion to consider whether it violates also the Fourteenth Amendment. But I have difficulty in believing that the liberty guaranteed by the Constitution, which has been held to protect against state denial the right of an employer to discriminate against a workman because he is a member of a trade union, *Coppage v. Kansas,* 236 U. S. 1, the right of a business man to conduct a private employment agency, *Adams v. Tanner,* 244 U. S. 590, or to contract outside the State for insurance of his property, *Allgeyer v. Louisiana,* 165 U. S. 578, 589, although the legislature deems it inimical to the public welfare, does not include liberty to teach, either in the privacy of the home or publicly, the doctrine of pacificism; so long, at least, as Congress had not declared that the public safety demands its suppression. I cannot believe that the liberty guaranteed by the Fourteenth Amendment includes only liberty to acquire and to enjoy property." [77]

As late as 1922, in *Prudential Ins. Co.* v. *Cheek,*[78] the Court specifically said, through Judge Pitney:

" . . . The Constitution of the United States imposes upon the States no obligation to confer upon those within their jurisdiction either the right of free speech or the right of silence. . . . As we have stated, neither the Fourteenth Amendment nor any other provision of the Constitution of the United States imposes upon the States any restrictions about ' freedom of speech ' or the ' liberty of silence ' ; nor, we may add, does it confer any right of privacy upon either persons or corporations."

Yet only three years after this decision in the *Cheek* case, Judge Sanford, speaking for the Court, in the *Gitlow* case, said:

" For present purposes we *may and do assume* that freedom of speech and of the press — which are protected by the First Amendment from abridgement by Congress — are among the fundamental personal rights

[77] At p. 343.

[78] 259 U. S. 530, 538, 543 (1922).

and 'liberties' protected by the due process clause of the Fourteenth Amendment from impairment by the States. We do not regard the incidental statement in *Prudential Ins. Co. v. Cheek,* 259 U. S. 530, 543, that the Fourteenth Amendment imposes no restrictions on the States concerning freedom of speech, as determinative of this question." [79] (Italics ours.)

Judge Holmes and Judge Brandeis, in dissenting opinions, stated:

"The general principle of free speech, it seems to me, must be taken to be included in the Fourteenth Amendment, in view of the scope that has been given to the word 'liberty' as there used, although it may be accepted with a somewhat larger latitude of interpretation than is allowed to Congress by the sweeping language that governs or ought to govern the laws of the United States." [80]

Thus, we have this situation: in 1907, the Court expressly left the question undecided; in 1920, it stated that it did not consider it or decide it, but simply conceded it for the purposes of the case; in 1922, it stated that the Federal Constitution "imposes upon the States no obligation to confer upon those within their jurisdiction either the right of free speech or the right of silence." Yet, in 1925, it stated that "we may and do assume" that freedom of speech and of the press is one of the "fundamental personal rights and liberties" protected by the Due Process Clause. And hence, in 1925, the Court adopted as the law on this point, the dissenting opinions of Judge Harlan in 1907, and of Judge Brandeis in 1920.

One may well view with some apprehension the field of interference with State legislation to which a logical extension of the *Gitlow* case doctrine must inevitably lead the Court. For, if as now assumed, the right of freedom of speech contained in the First Amendment to the Federal Constitution is a part of a person's "liberty" protected against State legislation by the Fourteenth Amendment, then the right of free exercise of his religion

---

[79] 268 U. S. at 666. It should be noted that Judge Sanford cites no authority for holding the word "liberty" to include the right to free speech and free press. In a note to his opinion, he says "compare *Patterson v. Colorado*" and six other cases; but not one of the cases supports the contention.

[80] At p. 672.

contained in the First Amendment must be also a part of a person's "liberty," similarly protected against State action. And on this ground, the United States Supreme Court may be called upon to pass on State laws as to religion and religious sects — a subject which, of all others, ought to be purely the concern of the State and its own people, and in no wise subject to interference by the National Government.

So, too, if "liberty" includes the right of free speech of the First Amendment, why does it not also include the right "to keep and bear arms" contained in the Second Amendment? Yet so to hold, the Court must overrule *Presser* v. *Illinois;*[81] for, in that case, the Court not only decided that the right to "keep and bear arms" was not one of the "privileges and immunities of a citizen of the United States"; but also that the contention that the said right was part of a person's "liberty," of which he had been deprived by the State statute, "is so clearly untenable as to require no discussion." If the right of freedom of speech contained in the First Amendment is a "liberty" protected by the Fourteenth Amendment, why is not the right "peaceably to assemble," contained in the same First Amendment, also a "liberty" protected by the Fourteenth Amendment? So to hold, the Court would not be obliged to overrule *United States* v. *Cruikshank;*[82] for it simply decided in that case, that the right "peaceably to assemble" was not one of the "privileges and immunities of a citizen of the United States"; it did not decide that it was not a "liberty" of which a person could not be deprived by a State "without due process of law."

So also, why should not the right to be free from infliction of cruel and unusual punishment contained in the Eighth Amendment be held to be as much a part of a person's "liberty," as his right of free speech contained in the First Amendment? The cases of *In re Kemmler,*[83] *McElvaine* v. *Brush,*[84] and *O'Neil* v. *Vermont*[85] need not disturb the Court; for they only held that this right was not a privilege or immunity of a citizen of the United States. Why is not a right to jury trial contained in the Sixth and Seventh Amendments, and appearing in every Bill

[81] 116 U. S. 252 (1886).
[82] 92 U. S. 542 (1875).
[83] 136 U. S. 436 (1890).
[84] 142 U. S. 155 (1891).
[85] 144 U. S. 323 (1892).

of Rights of the States prior to 1787, as much a part of a person's "liberty" as his right of freedom of speech? The Court might so hold, without overruling *Walker* v. *Sauvinet*,[86] *Hurtado* v. *California*,[87] or *Brown* v. *New Jersey*;[88] for those cases only held that jury trial was not a necessary part of "due process;" they did *not* hold that it was not a "liberty" which a State by legislation could not deprive a person of "without due process." Nor need the Court feel itself bound by *Maxwell* v. *Dow*;[89] for that case only held that the right of jury under the Sixth and Seventh Amendments and the right of indictment by a grand jury under the Fifth Amendment were not "privileges and immunities of a citizen of the United States"; it did not hold that such rights were not part of a person's "liberty."

Why is not a right against self-incrimination contained in the Fifth Amendment as much a part of a person's "liberty" as his right of freedom of speech? The Court might so hold, without overruling *Twining* v. *New Jersey*;[90] for that case only considered the question whether a State law removing provisions against compulsory self-incrimination was a failure of "due process"; it did not consider whether the right in question was a "liberty" which the State could not deprive Twining of, "without due process of law." Certainly, the right to be free from unreasonable search and seizure, contained in the Fourth Amendment, is as much a part of a person's "liberty" as his right of freedom of speech.

Thus, if the doctrine of the *Gitlow* case is to be carried to its logical and inevitable conclusion, every one of the rights contained in the Bill of Rights ought to be and must be included within the definition of "liberty," and must be held to be guaranteed by the Fourteenth Amendment against deprivation by a State "without due process of law."

The Court in the *Gitlow* case, speaks of freedom of speech and of the press as "among the fundamental personal rights and 'liberties' protected by the due process clause of the Fourteenth

---

[86] 92 U. S. 90 (1876).

[87] 110 U. S. 516 (1884).

[88] 175 U. S. 172 (1899). See also New York Central R. R. *v.* White, 243 U. S. 188 (1917); Missouri *v.* Lewis, 101 U. S. 22, 31 (1880).

[89] 176 U. S. 581 (1900).

[90] 211 U. S. 78 (1908).

Amendment." It is to be noted, however, that as a matter of fact and history, and as a matter of law, the right of free speech was not in any degree as "fundamental" as most of the other rights recited in the Bill of Rights. For, it is a singular and little known fact that the right of free speech was not included as one of a person's fundamental and inalienable rights in any Bill of Rights adopted by any of the States prior to the Federal Constitution. The only right of free speech specifically guaranteed by any State, prior to 1789, was the right to speak freely on the floor of the Legislature, without being held to account in Court. The right to freedom of speech in general, as a separate guaranty, was *created* for the first time in this country by the First Amendment to the Constitution. There is a very general misunderstanding of this fact by judges, lawyers, and historians.[91] The inhabitants of the various States in 1787 would have been profoundly amazed if they had been told that the provisions in their State Constitutions guaranteeing their life, liberty and property established for them a right to freedom of speech. They well knew that such was neither the fact nor the law.

On the other hand, while no State had in its Bill of Rights a declaration of right to freedom of speech, practically every State had a declaration of right to freedom of religion, of right to keep and bear arms, of right to be free from unreasonable search and seizure, and of right to jury trial. Hence, as above stated, from the standpoint of historical accuracy, the right of freedom of speech, if it is to be considered a part of a person's "liberty," was and is a less fundamental part than many other rights. This historical fact makes it all the more clear, therefore, that if any right contained in the Bill of Rights is to be regarded as a part of the "liberty" protected by the Due Process Clause of the Fourteenth Amendment, on the ground of its being "fundamental," then certainly *all* the rights which were considered by the States prior to 1787 as "fundamental" must be similarly protected.

There is another serious aspect of the logical result of this new interpretation of "liberty" in the *Gitlow* case, — namely, its bearing upon the doctrine laid down by the Court in the

---

[91] Warren, Congress, the Constitution and the Supreme Court, 84–85.

Insular Cases; [92] to the effect that, while the Constitution in its entirety is not applicable to our insular possessions, yet there are certain fundamental parts of it which are applicable and inevitably are in force in those possessions. Now it has been held as late as 1922 by Chief Justice Taft, in *Balzac* v. *Porto Rico,*[93] that "the guarantees of certain fundamental personal rights declared in the Constitution, as for instance that no person could be deprived of life, liberty or property without due process of law, had from the beginning full application in the Philippines and Porto Rico." [94]

If the Due Process Clause of the Fifth Amendment is in force in our insular possessions, and if as the Court has held, the words used in the Fourteenth Amendment have the same meaning as in the Fifth Amendment, then this newly defined "liberty" must be in force in the Philippines. There may be considerable doubt as to whether some of our Philippine legislation could stand this new "liberty" test.

It remains to be seen how far the Court will follow its *Gitlow* case expressions to their inevitable and logical conclusions. If it shall do so, then the doctrines of the *Slaughter House Cases* will be practically reversed, even if not specifically overruled. For the very thing which the dissenting Judges in those cases contended for will be brought about, *viz.*, the civil rights belonging to a person purely as a citizen of State will be given protection by the Fourteenth Amendment, by means of the Due Process Clause, (instead of by the Privileges and Immunities Clause as claimed by the dissenting Judges). And thus the simple word "liberty" will have become a tremendous engine for attack on State legislation — an engine which could not have been conceived possible by the framers of the first Ten Amendments or by the framers of the Fourteenth Amendment itself. And the foreboding of Chief Justice Taney, in 1849, will have been justified, when he said: "If in this court we are at liberty to give old words new meanings when we find them in the Constitution, there is no

[92] De Lima *v.* Bidwell, 182 U. S. 1 (1900); Downes *v.* Bidwell, 182 U. S. 244 (1901); Huus *v.* New York & Porto Rico S. S. Co., 182 U. S. 392 (1901); Goetze *v.* United States, 182 U. S. 221 (1901); Fourteen Diamond Rings *v.* United States, 183 U. S. 176 (1901); Dooley *v.* United States, 182 U. S. 222 (1901).

[93] 258 U. S. 298, 312 (1922).

[94] See also Hawaii *v.* Mankichi, 190 U. S. 197, 217 (1903), *per* Brown, J.

power which may not, by this mode of construction, be conferred on the general government and denied to the States."[95]

There is one distinction, however, which should be noted, between the protection given by the Privileges and Immunities Clause and that given by the Due Process Clause. A state is forbidden absolutely and without limitation, to make or enforce a law abridging a privilege or immunity. It is not forbidden to deprive a person of a right of liberty or property, provided it deprives him by due process of law. In other words, the mere decision that the right of free speech or any other fundamental right is included within the term "liberty," does not protect such right against State legislation, unless the Court goes further and decides that the State legislation involved did not constitute "due process." To illustrate: in the *Gitlow* case, it is somewhat difficult to learn from the Court's language whether the actual decision was to the effect that the right of freedom of speech did not include the right to speak the things denounced by the statute,[96] or whether the decision was to the effect that Gitlow's right (whatever it may have been) was not taken away from him "without due process." But suppose that the Court had clearly found that the New York statute *did* deprive Gitlow of his "liberty" of free speech; such finding would not necessarily have settled the case in Gitlow's favor; for in other cases in which rights of liberty and property have been affected, the Court has said that the provisions of a statute constituted "due process," if they were not arbitrary, and if they had a reasonable relation to some purpose of public welfare designed to be accomplished by the passage of the statute.[97] Hence if the question were presented whether the provisions of the statute depriving a man of

---

[95] Passenger Cases, 7 How. (U. S.) 283, 478 (1849).

[96] Thus the Court says (at p. 630): "It is a fundamental principle, long established that the freedom of speech and of the press which is secured by the Constitution does not confer an absolute right to speak or publish, without responsibility, whatever one may choose, or an unrestricted and unbridled license that gives immunity for every possible use of language, and prevents the punishment of those who abuse this freedom."

[97] As Judge Pitney said in Coppage *v.* Kansas, 236 U. S. 1 (1915): "The Fourteenth Amendment debars the State from striking down personal liberty or property rights or materially restricting their normal exercise, *excepting so far as may be incidentally necessary for the accomplishment of some other and paramount object, and one that concerns the public welfare.*" (Italics ours.)

his " liberty " of free speech constituted " due process," the State might fairly contend that the statute was not arbitrary and that its provisions had a clear and reasonable relation to some other object concerning the public welfare.

If the Court shall, in the future, give a broad interpretation to the words " due process " as affecting " liberty "; if it shall be slow and reluctant to regard a State statute as arbitrary or as bearing no reasonable relation to some object of public welfare, then the Court may, by such action, counteract some of the evils of undue interference with State legislation, which otherwise may flow from the enlarged definition of " liberty " recently adopted by it.

If, on the other hand, the Court shall continue to enlarge " liberty " without, at the same time, viewing with a highly elastic mind " due process," then other fundamental questions may be presented in the near future which will require serious consideration. These will *not* be questions as to the power of the Court to hold State statutes invalid; for if the restrictions placed upon the States and upon the Nation respectively by the Constitution are to have any binding effect, and if the lines between State and Nation are to be preserved, they must be enforceable by the Court of the Nation or otherwise they will not be enforced. But, assuming the necessity of the Court's power to enforce restrictions, the inquiry always remains open as to the necessity for the existence of any particular restriction upon the States or upon the Nation, in the Constitution; and hence it is quite possible that the continuance of the existence of the Due Process Clause of the Fourteenth Amendment may become a question to be agitated.

To what extent is that Clause, as now construed, a desirable feature in our federal form of government? In the change of conditions from the year 1868, is the " liberty " of the citizen to be freed from State restraint, by National interposition, of greater or less importance than the " liberty " of the State to control its own affairs and to regulate its own welfare and good order, under its own State Constitution as construed by its own State Courts? Is it, or is it not, a good thing that the legislation enacted by each State to meet local conditions and to regulate local relations should be standardized, by being forced to comply to a new definition of "liberty" applied to every State by the judicial branch of the National Government?

Does the validity of State legislation affecting local property and local liberty so concern the general welfare of the Nation as to require National judicial interposition? Is it of National importance that persons resident, or possessing property, within a State should have any greater personal, civil, or property rights than the State Constitution, as interpreted by the State Court, guarantees (provided, of course, that the State legislation involved does not infringe any right, privilege, or immunity of a citizen of the United States, or any other provision of the Constitution of the United States, excepting the Due Process Clause)? While these questions may not now be pressing, their future possibility is something to be envisaged.

Charles Warren.

WASHINGTON, D. C.